Tokyo 東京

timeout.com/tokyo

Penguin Books

PENGUIN BOOKS

Published by the Penguin Group
Penguin Books Ltd, 27 Wrights Lane, London W8 5TZ, England
Penguin Books USA Inc., 375 Hudson Street, New York, New York 10014, USA
Penguin Books Australia Ltd, Ringwood, Victoria, Australia
Penguin Books Canada Ltd, 10 Alcorn Avenue, Toronto, Ontario, Canada M4V 3B2
Penguin Books (NZ) Ltd, 182-190 Wairau Road, Auckland 10, New Zealand

Penguin Books Ltd, Registered Offices: Harmondsworth, Middlesex, England

First published 1999
Second edition 2001
10 9 8 7 6 5 4 3 2 1

Colour reprographics by Icon, Crown House, 56-58 Southwark Street, London SE1
and Precise Litho, 34-35 Great Sutton Street, London EC1
Printed and bound by Cayfosa-Quebecor, Ctra. de Caldes, Km 3 08 130 Sta, Perpètua de Mogoda, Barcelona, Spain

Edited and designed by
Time Out Guides Limited
Universal House
251 Tottenham Court Road
London W1T 7AB
Tel + 44 (020) 7813 3000
Fax + 44 (020) 7813 6001
Email guides@timeout.com
www.timeout.com

Editorial

Editor Nigel Kendall
Deputy Editor Nicholas Royle
Researcher Hosoe Masami
Listings Checkers Hosoe Masami, Tomioka Tomoko, Obe Mitsuru, Obe Rie
Proofreader Rosamund Sales
Indexer Anna Raikes

Editorial Director Peter Fiennes
Series Editor Ruth Jarvis
Deputy Series Editor Jonathan Cox
Guides Co-ordinator Jenny Noden

Design

Art Director John Oakey
Art Editor Mandy Martin
Senior Designer Scott Moore
Designers Benjamin de Lotz, Lucy Grant, Kate Vincent-Smith
Scanning/Imaging Dan Conway
Picture Editor Kerri Miles
Deputy Picture Editor Olivia Duncan-Jones
Ad Make-up Glen Impey

Advertising

Group Commercial Director Lesley Gill
Sales Director Mark Phillips
International Sales Co-ordinator Ross Canadé
Advertisement Sales (Tokyo) Alison Jambert
Advertising Assistant Catherine Shepherd

Administration

Publisher Tony Elliott
Managing Director Mike Hardwick
Group Financial Director Kevin Ellis
Marketing Director Christine Cort
Marketing Manager Mandy Martinez
Group General Manager Nichola Coulthard
Production Manager Mark Lamond
Production Controller Samantha Furniss
Accountant Sarah Bostock

Features in this guide were written and researched by:

Introduction Nigel Kendall. **History** Steve Walsh. **Tokyo Today** Clive Victor France. **Architecture** Steve Walsh. **Geography** Steve Walsh. **Cartoon City** Nigel Kendall. **Accommodation** Nigel Kendall. **Sightseeing introduction** Nigel Kendall. **Asakusa** Matthew Green. **Ginza** Jin Fumiko. **Harajuku** Chloe Reuter. **Ikebukuro** Anji Harkness. **Marunouchi** François Trahan. **Roppongi** Tom Boatman. **Shibuya** Bruce Rutledge. **Shinjuku** Matthew Green. **Shitamachi** François Trahan. **Ueno** Bruce Rutledge. **Outside the Yamanote Line: By Chuo Line** Clive Victor France; **By Toyoko Line** Nigel Kendall; **By Odakyu Line** Chloe Reuter. **Sightseeing** Nigel Kendall, Izumi Naho. **Museums** Jennifer Purvis. **Restaurants** Robbie Swinnerton. **Menu Reader** Hosoe Masami. **Coffee Shops** Steve Walsh. **Bars** Alex Vega, Nigel Kendall. **Shops & Services** John Paul Catton. **By Season** Steve Walsh. **Children** Obe Mitsuru, Obe Rie. **Film** Kobayashi Mika. **Galleries** Jennifer Purvis. **Gay & Lesbian** Alex Vega. **Music** Amano Jun, François Trahan. **Nightlife** Igarashi Daisuke (*Drugs* Tin Brown). **Performing Arts** Jean Wilson, Nigel Kendall (*Ohno – it's Butoh* Tani Kazue). **Sport & Fitness** Steve Walsh. **Trips Out of Town: World Cup 2002** Steve Walsh; **Yokohama** Hosoe Masami; **Hakone** Nigel Kendall; **Kamakura** François Trahan; **Mountains** François Trahan; **Beaches** François Trahan; **Nikko** François Trahan. **Directory** Kobayashi Mika, Nigel Kendall, Hosoe Masami, Clive Victor France (*Internet* Alex Vega; *Business* J Michael Owen).

The Editor would like to thank:

Hosoe Masami, Tin Brown, Sonobe Yuka, Aeve Baldwin, Kobayashi Mika, Steve Martin and all the staff at Cornucopia, Daisuke Ito, Sophie Blacksell, Kate Ryan, Nakano Miwako, Christi Daugherty, Selena Cox, Will Fulford-Jones, Lesley McCave, Rosamund Sales.

Maps by MMGraphics and Tin Brown/© Time Out Group Ltd.

Photography by Adam Eastland except: page 6 The Bridgeman Art Library; pages 22 and 26-28 Nigel Kendall; page 61 Anji Harkness; pages 96, 236, 239, 242, 244, 245, 247, 248, 249, 251, 252, 255 and 256 Japan National Tourist Organisation; pages 202, 204, 205, 210, 214 and 217 Beezer; page 226 Associated Press.
The following images were supplied by the featured establishments: pages 32, 34, 35, 36, 37, 196, 221, 223 and 233-235.

Contents

Introduction

Despite its prominence as the capital city of the world's second largest economic force, Tokyo remains a city pretty much unknown to travellers. Deterred perhaps by the city's distance from home and its legendary expense, people 'doing the world' have left Tokyo alone to get on with its life, to remain resolutely, almost defiantly, foreign in the face of the global dominance of the English language and the American way of life. For every Starbucks here, there is something that acts as a counterbalance, a reminder that you really are somewhere different.

For those of us who live in the city and love it, this is, of course, one of its major charms. Whisper it quietly, but this is one of the easiest cities in the world to live in. Tokyo's community of long-term foreign residents is full of people who came for two weeks and never went home.

Why? Well, the trains run on time; violence and crime are all but unknown; licensing laws are virtually non-existent; there's high-quality food all over the world; and the people, by and large, are friendly, helpful and great company.

For the first-time visitor, Tokyo is one of those cities that polarises opinions. People either really love it here, or really hate it. There is no in-between. The reasons for this are manifold. Prominent among them is the feeling of being lost, like a two-year-old child. More than half of the signs are illegible, unless you've taken the time and trouble to learn some Japanese (studying at least *katakana* before you get here is highly recommended, *see p276*), and just about everything seems to work differently to how

it is at home. Whether this is a source of endless stimulation or frustration depends entirely on you.

Given the limitations imposed on the first-time visitor by the language, it is hardly surprising that the most common first reaction when getting off the plane at Narita is one of fear. Otherwise hardened voyagers will find their way to their hotel rooms and then be too scared to move, to take the train, for fear of getting lost. While this book is designed to relieve some of that fear, getting lost in this city is one of the great joys of being here: around every corner lies something new, be it a restaurant, a bar or a building that becomes your own personal discovery. If only you could find it again...

The powers that be in Tokyo make less effort to attract tourists here than just about any other comparable city on the planet. The practical upshot of this is that Tokyo, perhaps more than anywhere else, is what you make of it. If you hanker for peace and tranquillity, there are scores of beautiful historic gardens and temples; if you want to hurl yourself into the late-night action, the city provides more places to eat, drink and make merry than one person can visit in five lifetimes.

In recent years, an entire journalistic sub-genre has sprung up, wherein writers spend thousand of words agonising over Tokyo's myriad contradictions: a city of neon lights, massage parlours and love hotels, where politeness, tradition and formality are still much in evidence. The best way to enjoy this city is not to bother with any of this. Accept the contradictions and revel in them. After all, everybody else does.

ABOUT THE TIME OUT CITY GUIDES

The *Time Out Tokyo Guide* is one of an expanding series of *Time Out* City Guides, now numbering over 30, produced by the people behind London and New York's successful listings magazines. Our guides are all written and updated by resident experts who have striven to provide you with all the most up-to-date information you'll need to explore the city or read up on its background, whether you're a local or a first-time visitor.

THE LOWDOWN ON THE LISTINGS

Above all, we've tried to make this book as useful as possible. Addresses, telephone

numbers, websites, transport information, opening times, admission prices and credit card details have all been included in the listings. And, as far as possible, we've given details of facilities, services and events, all checked and correct as we went to press. However, owners and managers can change their arrangements at any time. Before you go out of your way, we'd advise you to telephone and check opening times, ticket prices and other particulars.

There is an online version of this guide, as well as weekly events listings for over 30 international cities, at www.timeout.com.

While every effort has been made to ensure the accuracy of the information contained in this guide, the publishers cannot accept responsibility for any errors it may contain.

OPENING TIMES

Throughout the guide, we have provided the opening and closing times of all the places we list. Note that restaurants, museums and galleries will generally not admit people less than 30 minutes before they close. Bar opening times tend to be more relaxed. The easy-going licensing laws means that they will generally stay open until empty.

PRICES AND PAYMENT

We have noted where venues such as shops, hotels and restaurants accept the following credit cards: American Express (**AmEx**), Diners Club (**DC**), MasterCard (**MC**) and Visa (**V**). Remember, though, that Japan is still predominantly a cash-based society. Time your visits to the cash machines well and always carry a minimum of ¥20,000 to cope with unexpected expenses. This may be more than you're used to carrying in your home country. Have no fear. You are extremely unlikely to be robbed or mugged.

THE LIE OF THE LAND

The street plan of Tokyo was originally laid out to confuse potential invaders, and the plan is still working a treat today. Thanks to the complicated address system (*see p271* **Making sense of addresses**), even locals get lost here, and most destinations will provide by fax, on request, a map of how to get there. Our schematic maps of the major areas (*see p292-*

316) are designed to help you find the places we list. In addition, all Tokyo railway stations provide a map of the area near the exit. Most destinations are on the JR and Eidan subway lines, but where they are not, throughout the guide, we give the line in brackets after the station name.

TELEPHONE NUMBERS

The area code for central Tokyo is 03. This is always followed by an eight-digit number. All central telephone numbers given in this guide omit the 03 prefix. The outlying areas of the city have different codes. For such places, the full telephone number, including the code, is provided. For more details of phone codes and charges, *see p270*. The international dialling code for Japan is 81.

ESSENTIAL INFORMATION

For all the practical information you might need for visiting Tokyo, including visa and customs information, advice on disabled facilities and access, emergency telephone numbers and local transport, turn to the **Directory** chapter at the back of the guide. It starts on page 257.

MAPS

The maps section at the back of this book breaks the city down into several of the most popular areas around the railway stations, and is designed to help you find your way to the places we recommend. Because Tokyo does not generally have street names, our recommendations are clearly marked on the maps and cross-referenced to where they occur in the text. This also helps you make the most of any given area by showing at a glance what it has to offer. Maps start on p287.

LET US KNOW WHAT YOU THINK

We hope you enjoy the *Time Out Tokyo Guide*, and we'd like to know what you think of it. We welcome tips for places that you consider we should include in future editions and take note of your criticism of our choices. There's a reader's reply card at the back of this book for your feedback, or you can email us at tokyoguide@timeout.com.

timeout.com

The World's Living Guide

In Context

Sumida River at Ommaya Embankment in a woodblock print, c1834, by Utagawa Kuniyoshi.

History

How to get from rope-cord pottery and shell mounds to bullet trains and subway gas attacks in 6,000 years. Start here.

Archaeological evidence suggests today's metropolitan area was inhabited as long ago as the late Paleolithic period, and stone tools belonging to hunter-gatherers of pre-ceramic culture have been discovered at sites such as Nogawa in western Tokyo Prefecture. Pottery featuring rope-cord patterns developed in Japan during the Jomon period (10,000-300 BC). Around 6,000 years ago, Tokyo Bay rose as far as the edge of the high ground that makes up the central *yamanote* area of the modern city; its retreat left behind a marshy shoreline that provided a rich food source. The Late Jomon shell mounds at Omori, identified in 1877 by US zoologist ES Morse as he gazed from a Shinbashi-Yokohama train, were the site of Japan's first modern archaeological dig and forerunner to a long line of similar excavations.

The Yayoi period (300 BC-AD 300) is named after the Yayoi-cho district near Tokyo University in Hongo, where in 1884 the Mukogaoka shell mound yielded the first evidence of a more sophisticated form of pottery. Along with other advances, such as wet-rice cultivation and the use of iron, this seems to have been introduced from the Asian mainland. Only after arriving on Kyushu did new techniques spread through Honshu.

BACKWATER

Kanto remained a distant outpost as the early Japanese state started to take shape around the Yamato court, which emerged in the fourth century as a loose confederation of chieftains in what is now Nara Prefecture, before gradually extending to other parts of the country. Chinese ideographs and Buddhism arrived via the Korean peninsula, while members of Japan's ruling elite were buried in tumuli, similar to tombs found on the nearest part of the continent.

Senso-ji Temple (*see p51*) is said to date back to AD 628, when two fishermen brothers discovered a gold statue of the Bodhisattva Kannon in their nets. Under Taika Reform from 645, the land on which Tokyo now stands became part of Musashi province, governed from Kokufu (modern-day Fuchu City). State administration was centralised in emulation of the Tang imperial model and China's advanced civilisation exerted a strong influence.

After the imperial capital was moved to Heian (Kyoto) in 794, a court culture flourished. Emperors became figureheads, manipulated by a series of powerful regents from the dominant Fujiwara family. The invention of the *kana* syllabary helped the writing of literary classics such as Sei Shonagon's *Pillow Book* and Murasaki Shikibu's *Tale of Genji*, but the political power of the Kyoto court nobles went into slow decline as control of the regions fell into the hands of the local military aristocracy.

BIRTH OF EDO

Tokyo's original name, Edo ('Rivergate'), is thought to have derived from a settlement located near where the Sumida River enters Tokyo Bay. Its first known use goes back to a member of the Taira clan, Edo Shigenaga, who is thought to have adopted it after making his home in the area. In August 1180 Shigenaga attacked the forces of Miura Yoshizumi, an ally of the rival Minamoto clan. He switched sides later, just as *shogun*-to-be Minamoto no Yoritomo entered Musashi province.

KAMAKURA SHOGUNATE

By the late 12th century, the rise of provincial warrior clans had developed into the struggle between the Taira and Minamoto families later chronicled in *The Tale of Heike*. After Minamoto no Yoritomo wiped out the last Taira remnants in 1185, the emperor designated him Seii Tai Shogun ('Barbarian-Subduing Generalissimo'). Yoritomo shunned the imperial capital of Kyoto, setting up his government in Kamakura (*see p246*).

This inaugurated a period of military rule that was to last till the 19th century. *Bushido*, 'the way of the warrior', emphasised martial virtues, while the *samurai* class emerged as a powerful force in feudal society. Nevertheless, attempted invasions of Japan by the Mongols in 1274 and 1281 were only driven back by stormy seas off Kyushu, something attributed to the *kamikaze*, or 'wind of the gods'. Dissatisfaction grew with the Kamakura government, now controlled by a series of regents, and in 1333 Ashikaga Takauji established a new shogunate in the Muromachi district of Kyoto.

OTA DOKAN

The first castle at Edo was erected in 1457 by Ota Dokan, a *waka* poet known as Ota Sekenaga before taking a monk's tonsure in 1478, now celebrated as Tokyo's original founder. Above Hibiya Inlet, he constructed a set of fortifications overlooking the entrance to Kanto plain for northbound travellers along the Pacific sea road. To improve local navigation, he also diverted the Hirakawa east at Kandabashi to form the Nihonbashi River.

In 1486, during a military clash between branches of the locally powerful Uesugi family, Ota was falsely accused of betraying his lord, and met his end at the home of Uesugi Sadamasa in Sagami (modern-day Kanagawa).

WARRING STATES

Central government authority disappeared following the Onin War (1467-77), as regional lords, or *daimyo*, fought for dominance. Only after a century or so of on-off civil strife did the country begin to regain unity under Oda Nobunaga, although his assassination in 1582 meant that final reunification was left to Toyotomi Hideyoshi. In 1590, Hideyoshi established control of the Kanto region after successfully besieging the Odawara Castle stronghold of the powerful Go-Hojo family.

Hideyoshi ordered his ally Tokugawa Ieyasu to exchange his lands in Shizuoka and Aichi for the former Go-Hojo domains in Kanto. Rather than Odawara, which lies in present-day Kanagawa Prefecture, Ieyasu chose Edo as his headquarters. Construction started on a new castle on the site of Ota Dokan's crumbling fortifications. After Hideyoshi's death, Ieyasu was victorious in the struggle for national power at the Battle of Sekigahara in 1600, and three years later was named *shogun*. The emperor remained, as ever, in Kyoto, but Edo became the government capital of Japan.

EDO ERA (1600-1868)

When Ieyasu arrived in 1590, Edo was little more than a few houses at the edge of Hibiya Inlet. This changed quickly with building and land reclamation projects. Divided almost equally between military and townspeople, the population grew dramatically before levelling off in the early 18th century at around 1.2 million. In an age when London still had under one million people, Edo was probably the world's biggest metropolis.

POWER OF THE SHOGUN

Fifteen successive Tokugawa *shogun* ruled Japan, and their domination lasted for more than 250 years. All roads led to Edo: five major highways radiated out from the city, with communications aided by regular post stations, including Shinagawa, Shinjuku, Itabashi and Senju. Feudal lords retained local autonomy, but a system of alternate annual residence forced them to divide their time between their own lands and the capital of the *shogun*, under the watchful eye of the government. *Daimyo* finances were drained by the regular journeys with their retinues along the highways, as well as by the need to maintain large Edo residences. There was little chance to foment trouble in the provinces, and as a further inducement to loyalty, family members were kept in Edo as permanent hostages.

Although Tokugawa Ieyasu's advisors had included Englishman Will Adams (whose story is fictionalised in *Shogun*), a national seclusion policy was introduced in 1639. Contact with western countries was restricted to a Dutch trade mission on the distant island of Dejima.

DIVIDED CITY

The layout of Edo reflected the social order, with the *yamanote* high ground being the preserve of the military classes and the townspeople occupying the *shitamachi*, 'low city', areas outside the castle walls to the east.

Completed in 1638, Edo Castle was the world's largest. Its defences extended 16 kilometres (ten miles). The most important of the four sets of fortifications, the *hon-maru* or principle fortress, contained the residence of the *shogun*, the halls of state and the inner chambers, where the *shogun*'s wife and concubines lived. The castle keep stood on a hill alongside, overlooking the city. Between the castle's double set of moats, regional *daimyo* had their Edo mansions arranged in a strict hierarchy of 'dependent' and 'outside' lords. Outside the castle walls to the east, the low-lying *shitamachi* districts were home to the merchants, craftsmen, labourers and others attracted to the wealth and power of Edo. Less than one-fifth of the land of Edo, much of it having been reclaimed, held around half of its population. Nihonbashi's curving wooden bridge was the hub of the nation's highways and the spot from which all distances to Edo were measured.

Nearby were wealthy merchants' residences and grand shops such as Echigoya, forerunner of today's Mitsukoshi; the city's prison; and the fish market. Behind grand thoroughfares, the crowded backstreet tenements of Nihonbashi and Kanda were a breeding ground for disease and were in constant danger of flooding. Fires were common in the largely wooden city.

LONG SLEEVES FIRE

The original castle buildings were just one victim of the disastrous Long Sleeves Fire of 1657. Over 100,000 people died, around a quarter of Edo's total population, in three days of conflagrations that raged across both military and townspeople areas. The flames began at a temple, Hommyo-ji in Hongo, where monks had been burning two long-sleeved *kimono* belonging to young women who had recently died. By the morning of the fourth day, three-quarters of Edo had been destroyed.

Reconstruction work was soon under way. Roads were widened, fire breaks introduced. Many people had perished because they couldn't escape across the Sumida River, which, for military reasons, had no bridges: opening up Fukagawa and Honjo for development, a bridge was erected at Ryogoku. There was a dispersal of temples and shrines to outlying areas such as Yanaka and newly reclaimed land in Tsukiji. The Yoshiwara pleasure quarters were moved out, too – from Ningyocho to beyond Asakusa and the newly extended city limits.

New secondary residences for *daimyo* were established outside the walls of the castle, leading to a more patchwork mix of noble estates and townspeople districts, although the basic pattern of *shitamachi* areas in the east was retained. *Daimyo* mansions inside the castle were rebuilt in a more restrained style. The innermost section of the reconstructed castle was more subdued, lacking the high tower of its predecessor.

47 RONIN INCIDENT

One by-product of the Tokugawa regime's stability was that the military personnel stationed in Edo found themselves with little to do. A complex bureaucracy developed, and there were ceremonial duties, but members of the top strata of the feudal system found themselves outstripped economically by the city's merchants. In these circumstances, a vendetta attack staged by the band of masterless *samurai* known later as the 47 *ronin* caused a sensation. In 1701, after being provoked by Kira Yoshinaka, the *shogun*'s chief of protocol, Lord Ako had drawn his sword inside Edo Castle, an illegal act for which he was forced to commit ritual suicide. Two years later, 46 of his loyal former retainers (one dropped out at the last moment) attacked the Edo mansion of the man they blamed for his death. Emerging with Kira's head, they marched through the city to offer it to Lord Ako's grave at Sengaku-ji Temple (*see p90*). Despite public acclaim for their righteous actions, the 46 were themselves now sentenced to ritual suicide.

The incident forms the basis of a popular *kabuki* play, *Kanadehon Chushinjura* (*The Treasury of the Loyal Retainers*), written originally for *bunraku* puppet theatre and first staged in 1748. The story was diplomatically relocated to 14th-century Kamakura.

CULTURE CAPITAL

A vibrant new urban culture grew up in Edo's *shitamachi* districts. During the long years of peace and relative prosperity, the pursuit of pleasure provided the populace, particularly the city's wealthy merchants, with welcome relief

Superstitious minds

In a city where pavement fortune-tellers can still be found plying their trade in the plushest parts of town, it's never been advisable to take too many risks with fate.

The first *shogun*, Tokugawa Ieyasu, did his best to conform to Chinese principles of geomancy by having the two temples that would hold the Tokugawa family tombs, Kan'ei-ji and Zojo-ji, in the auspicious north-east and south-west of the city. More problematically, since Mount Fuji lay west rather than north, the traditionally favoured direction for a mountain, Edo Castle's main Ote gate was placed on its east side, instead of the usual south.

Nearby, now surrounded by high buildings, stands the final resting place of Taira no Masakado. After his defeat by central government forces in 940, grisly evidence of Masakado's demise was dispatched to Kyoto.

Legend has it that his severed head took to the skies one night and flew back to be reunited with his other remains at his grave in the fishing village of Shibasaki. The site is now in the central financial district of Otemachi but has remained untouched by successive generations of city builders, fearful of Masakado's vengeful spirit. (Masakado Kubizuka, Otemachi station, exit C5.)

Over in Asakusa, local residents credited a statue of popular *kabuki* star Danjuro with saving the historic temple of Senso-ji from destruction in the aftermath of the 1923 earthquake by turning back the flames that swept through large parts of the city. War-time authorities failed to heed the lesson, however. The figure of the auspicious actor was requisitioned, and many of Senso-ji's older buildings burned down in US bombing raids.

from the feudal system's stifling social confines. Landscape artists such as Hiroshige (1797-1868) depict a city of theatres, temples, scenic bridges, festivals and fairs. There were numerous seasonal celebrations, including big firework displays to celebrate the summer opening of the Sumida River, as well as cherry-blossom viewing along its banks in spring.

Kabuki, an Edo favourite, didn't always meet the approval of the high city. In 1842, a government edict banished theatres up the Sumida River to Asakusa, where they stayed until after the fall of the shogunate. As the district already boasted Senso-ji Temple, with its fairs and festivals, and the Yoshiwara pleasure quarters lay only a short distance away, the act merely cemented Asakusa's position as Edo's favoured relaxation centre.

BLACK SHIPS

Notice that Japan could no longer seal itself off from the outside world arrived in Edo Bay in 1853 in the shape of four US 'black ships' under the command of Commodore Matthew Perry. Local defences were useless, and the treaty signed with Perry the following year proved to be the thin end of the wedge, as western powers forced a series of further concessions. In 1855, Edo suffered a major quake that killed over 7,000 and destroyed large parts of the lower city. In 1859, Townsend Harris, the first US consul-general, arrived to set up a mission at Zenpuku-ji Temple in Azabu.

Voices of discontent had already been raised: there were frequent famines, and proponents of 'National Learning' called for a return to a purer form of Shinto tradition. The foreign threat now polarised opinion. Feelings ran high in Mito and among *samurai* from Choshu and Satsuma. In 1860, the senior councillor of the shogunate government, Ii Naosuke, was assassinated outside Edo Castle. Under the slogan 'expel the barbarian, revere the emperor', a series of incidents took place against foreigners. Power drained from Edo as the government looked to build a unified national policy by securing imperial backing in Kyoto. *Daimyo* residences in Edo were abandoned after the alternate residence requirement was abolished in 1862.

The Tokugawa regime was finally overthrown early in 1868, when a coalition of forces from the south declared an imperial 'restoration' in Kyoto in the name of the 15-year-old Meiji emperor, then won a resounding military victory at Toba-Fushimi. Edo's population fell to around half its former level as remaining residents of the *yamanote* areas departed. A last stand by shogunate loyalists in Ueno was hopeless, and left in ruins large parts of the Kan'ei-ji Temple complex, which housed the tombs of several Tokugawa *shogun*.

MEIJI ERA (1868-1912)

Edo was renamed Tokyo ('Eastern Capital') when the emperor's residence was transferred from Kyoto in 1868. It became the political and imperial capital, with the inner section of Edo Castle serving as the new Imperial Palace. The population had reverted to its earlier level by the mid-1880s, but the *shitamachi* districts lost much of their cultural distinctiveness as wealthier residents moved to smarter locations. Industrialisation continued to bring newcomers from the countryside. By the end of the Meiji era Tokyo housed nearly two million people.

RICH COUNTRY, STRONG ARMY

To the south-west of the palace, Nagatacho and Kasumigaseki became the heart of the nation's new government and bureaucratic establishment. 'Rich country, strong army' was the rallying cry, but learning from abroad was recognised to be essential: government missions were dispatched overseas, foreign experts brought in, and radical reforms initiated in everything from education to land ownership.

Laying the foundations of a modern state meant sweeping away much of the old feudal structure. Government was centralised and the *daimyo* pensioned off. Conscription, in 1873, ended the exclusive role of the warrior class. Disaffected elements, led by Saigo Takamori, rebelled in Satsuma in 1877, but were defeated. The next year, six former *samurai* from Satsuma staged a revenge attack and murdered Meiji government leader Okubo Toshimichi.

Ending social restrictions fuelled economic development. The Bank of Japan was established in 1882, bringing greater stability. Factories sprang up near the Sumida River and overlooking Tokyo Bay. Marunouchi became home to a business district called 'London Town' after its Victorian-style office buildings. In 1889, a constitution declared the emperor 'sacred and inviolable'. Power remained with government leaders but there was a nod to greater popular representation. Elections were held among the top 1.5 per cent of taxpayers, and the first session of the Imperial Diet took place in 1890. By the early 1890s, the government was making progress on ending the hated 'unequal treaties' earlier conceded to the west. Taking a leaf from the imperialists' book, Japan seized Taiwan in 1895 after a war with China. Ten years later its forces defeated Russia, but there were riots in Hibiya Park at the perceived leniency of the peace treaty. In 1910, Japan annexed neighbouring Korea.

EAST MEETS WEST

New goods and ideas from overseas started to pour into Tokyo, especially after Japan's first train line started services between Yokohama and Shinbashi station in 1872. Men abandoned traditional topknots; married women followed the lead of the empress and stopped blackening their teeth. There were gas lights, beer halls, the first public parks and department stores, and even ballroom dancing at Hibiya's glittering Rokumeikan, where the elite gathered in their best foreign finery to display their mastery of the advanced new ways.

The artisan district of Ginza was redeveloped with 900 brick buildings after a major fire in 1872, and newspaper offices flocked to what would become Tokyo's most fashionable area. Asakusa kept in touch with popular tastes through attractions such as the Ryounkaku, which had the city's first elevator, and was Tokyo's tallest building, with 12 storeys. Asakusa was also home to Japan's first permanent cinema, which opened in 1903, and the cinemas, theatres and music halls of Asakusa's Rokku district remained popular throughout the early part of the new century.

TAISHO ERA (1912-26)

The funeral of Emperor Meiji was accompanied by the ritual suicide of General Nogi, a hero of the Russo-Japanese War. The new emperor was in constant poor health and his son, Hirohito, became regent in 1921.

There was a brief flowering of 'Taisho Democracy': in 1918 Hara Takashi became the first prime minister from a political party, an appointment that came after a sudden rise in rice prices prompted national disturbances, including five days of rioting in the capital. Hara was assassinated in 1921 by a right-wing extremist, but universal male suffrage was finally introduced in 1925.

The city was starting to spill over its boundaries and part of Shinjuku was brought inside the city limits for the first time in 1920, a first indication of the capital's tendency to westward drift with the growth of suburban train lines. Ginza was enjoying its heyday as a strolling spot for fashionable youth. In nearby Hibiya, the new Imperial Hotel, designed by Frank Lloyd Wright, opened in 1923.

GREAT KANTO EARTHQUAKE

Shortly before noon on 1 September 1923, the Kanto region was hit by a devastating earthquake of 7.9 magnitude on the Japanese scale. High winds fanned the flames of cooking fires and two days of terrible blazes swept through Tokyo and surrounding areas, including Yokohama, leaving over 140,000 dead and destroying large areas. Around 63 per cent of Tokyo homes were destroyed, with the traditional wooden buildings of the *shitamachi* areas hardest hit. In the confusion, rumours of well-poisoning and other misdeeds led vigilante groups to massacre several thousand Koreans before martial law was imposed. Temporary structures were quickly in place and there was a short building boom. The destruction in eastern areas accelerated the population movement to the west, but plans to remodel the city were largely laid aside because of cost.

SHOWA ERA (1926-89)

The reign of Hirohito, the longest of any Japanese emperor, coincided with a period of extraordinary change and turbulence. Tokyo recovered gradually from the effects of the 1923 quake and continued growing, but the country slid into dark days of militarism and war. In March 1945, Allied bombing brought huge devastation to the capital once more. Defeat was followed by occupation, but Tokyo was to rise again as Japan entered a new era of peace and unprecedented economic prosperity.

CITY EXPANSION

Post-quake reconstruction was declared officially over in 1930. In 1932, Tokyo's boundaries underwent major revision to take account of changing population patterns, with growing western districts such as Shibuya and Ikebukuro, and the remaining parts of Shinjuku, coming within the city limits. The total number of wards jumped from 15 to 35 (later simplified to the 23 of today) and the city's land area increased sevenfold. At a stroke, the population doubled to over five million, making Tokyo the world's second most populous city after New York.

MILITARISM AND WAR

The era of parliamentary government didn't last. Political stability fell victim to the slump that followed a domestic banking collapse in 1927 and the Wall Street crash of 1929. Nationalists saw expansion overseas as the answer. In November 1930, after signing a naval disarmament treaty, prime minister Hamaguchi Osachi was killed by a right-wing extremist in Tokyo station (where Hara had been mortally wounded nine years earlier).

In 1931, dissident officers staged a military takeover of Manchuria, bringing conflict with world opinion. Pre-war party government ended after a brief rebellion of younger officers on 15 May 1932; prime minister Inukai Tsuyoshi and other cabinet members were assassinated and a series of national unity governments took over, dependent on military support. A puppet state, Manchukuo, was declared in Manchuria, and Japan left the League of Nations. On 26 February 1936, the army's First Division mutinied and attempted a coup in the name of 'Showa Restoration'. The rebellion was put down.

In an atmosphere of increasing nationalist fervour at home, Japan became involved in an ever-widening international conflict. Full-scale hostilities with China broke out in July 1937, but Japanese forces were bogged down after early advances. Western powers, led by the US, declared a total embargo of Japan in 1941. Negotiations between the two sides reached an impasse, and on 7 December 1941, Japan attacked the US Pacific fleet at Pearl Harbor.

After successes in the Pacific and south-east Asia, Japanese forces began to be pushed back after the Battle of Midway in June 1942. By late 1944, Tokyo lay within range of American bombers. Incendiary attacks devastated the capital; the one on 10 March 1945 left around 100,000 dead. On 6 August, an atomic bomb was dropped on Hiroshima, followed by another on Nagasaki three days later. Cabinet deadlock left the casting vote to the emperor, whose radio broadcast to the nation on 15 August announced Japan's surrender.

POST-WAR

Much of Tokyo lay in ruins; food and shelter posed immediate problems. As many as one in ten slept in temporary shelters during the first post-war winter. General MacArthur set about demilitarising Japan and promoting democratic reform. The emperor kept his throne, but renounced his divinity. Article nine of the new constitution included strict pacifist provisions and the armed forces were disbanded. In 1948, seven Class A war criminals, including wartime prime minister Tojo Hideki, were executed.

The outbreak of the Korean War in 1950 provided a tremendous boost to the Japanese economy, with large contracts to supply UN forces. Under MacArthur's orders, a limited rearmament took place, leading to the eventual founding of the Self-Defence Forces. Occupation ended in 1952 and there was a new security treaty with the USA.

With national defence left largely in US hands, economic growth was the priority under the long rule of the pro-business Liberal Democratic Party, formed in 1955. Prosperity started to manifest itself in the shape of large new office buildings in central Tokyo. In 1960, prime minister Ikeda Hayato announced a plan to double national income over a decade – a target achieved with ease in the economic miracle years that followed.

The Olympics were held in Tokyo in 1964, the same year *shinkansen* bullet trains started running between the capital and Osaka. Infrastructure improvements were made inside the city. Even after the Olympics, Tokyo's redevelopment continued apace. Frank Lloyd Wright's Imperial Hotel, a survivor of both the 1923 earthquake and the war, was demolished in 1967, the year the city's inner 23 wards achieved their peak population of almost nine million. To the west of Shinjuku station, Tokyo's first concentration of skyscrapers started to take shape during the early '70s.

Despite the economic progress, there was an undercurrent of social discontent. Hundreds of thousands demonstrated against renewal of the security treaty with the United States in 1960, and the end of the decade saw students in violent revolt. In 1970, novelist Mishima Yukio dramatically ended his life after failing to spark a nationalist uprising at Ichigaya barracks. In Chiba, radical groups from the other end of the political spectrum joined local farmers to battle with riot police, delaying completion of Tokyo's new international airport at Narita from 1971 to 1975 and its opening until 1978.

The post-war fixed exchange rate ended in 1971 and growth came to a temporary halt with the oil crisis of 1974, but the Japanese economy continued to outperform its western competitors. Trade friction developed, particularly with the USA. After the Plaza agreement of 1985, the yen jumped to new highs, inflating the value of Japanese financial assets. Shoppers switched to designer labels as a building frenzy gripped Tokyo, the world's most expensive city. Land values soared and wild speculation fuelled a 'bubble economy'.

Ginza, in the 1950s, when postwar prosperity began to manifest itself (*see p11*), and today.

HEISEI ERA (1989-)
The death of Hirohito came at the beginning of the global changes marking the end of the Cold War. As the 1990s wore on, the system that had served Japan so well in the post-war era began to stumble. A collapse in land and stock market prices brought the bubble economy to an end in 1990 and left Japanese banks with a mountain of bad debt. An economy that had been the envy of the world a decade earlier became mired in its deepest recession since the end of the war.

Demands for an end to 'money politics' finally proved irresistible in 1993, when the LDP lost power for the first time in 38 years. A shortlived nine-party coalition under Hosokawa Morihiro of the Japan New Party enacted a programme of political reform, but the LDP clawed its way back to government in 1994 in an unlikely partnership with its erstwhile foe, the rapidly declining Socialists. Voter apathy grew as new coalitions came and went.

Tokyo ushered in a new era in 1991, when the metropolitan government moved to a thrusting new skyscraper in Shinjuku, symbolising the capital's shift away from its traditional centre. In January 1995, however, the Kobe earthquake reminded Tokyo residents of their vulnerability to natural disaster. Soon after, a sarin gas attack on city subways by members of the Aum Shinrikyo doomsday cult provoked more horror and much agonised debate. Discussions about moving the national government to a less quake-prone location continued.

In a new climate of job insecurity and fragile consumer confidence, the 'Heisei recession' proved largely resilient to the traditional stimulus of public works programmes. Big-name bankruptcies, foreign takeovers and the US dominance of the new economy prompted endless debate about the need for far-reaching structural and economic reforms. In April 1999, attracted by the promise of strong leadership, Tokyo voters elected a hawkish former-LDP independent, Ishihara Shintaro, as their new governor.

Mori Yoshiro, who took over as PM from Obuchi Keizo in April 2000, quickly attracted attention by describing Japan as 'a divine country with the emperor at its centre'. A reorganisation of government ministries was carried out at the start of 2001, but leading LDP figures soon found themselves caught up in familiar-sounding corruption scandals. Meanwhile, growth rates started sinking back into negative territory amid fears of a global slowdown. The sinking of a Japanese fishing vessel by an American submarine in February 2001 proved the last straw for Mori, who finished a round of golf before reacting to the news, and subsequently stepped aside.

Key events

c10,000-300 BC Jomon period.
c300 BC-AD 300 Yayoi period; wet-rice growing, bronze/ironware from continental Asia.
1st century AD Japan ('land of Wa') first mentioned in Chinese chronicles.
4th century Yamato court exists in Nara area.
538 or 552 Buddhism introduced from Korea.
710 Nara becomes imperial capital.
794 Capital moves to Heian (Kyoto).
1002-19 Murasaki Shikibu writes *Tale of Genji*.
1180 First recorded use of name Edo.
1185-1333 Kamakura is site of government.
1274, 1281 Attempted Mongol invasions.
1457 Ota Dokan builds first castle at Edo.
1549 St Francis Xavier arrives in Japan.
1590 Edo becomes HQ of Tokugawa Ieyasu. Construction of Edo Castle begins.
1592 Hideyoshi invades Korea.
1598 Withdrawal from Korea.
1603 Ieyasu named *shogun*; Edo becomes seat of government. Bridge built at Nihonbashi.
1616 Tokugawa Ieyasu dies.
1639 National seclusion policy established.
1657 Long Sleeves Fire destroys much of Edo.
1688-1704 Genroku cultural flowering.
1703 47 *ronin* vendetta carried out.
1707 Mount Fuji erupts; ash falls on Edo.
1720 Ban on import of foreign books lifted.
1742 Floods and storms kill 4,000 in Edo.
1787-93 Kansei reforms; rice granaries set up in Edo after famine and riots.
1804-29 Bunka-Bunsei period; peak of Edo merchant culture.
1825 'Order for Repelling of Foreign Ships'.
1841-3 Reforms to strengthen economy.
1853 Arrival of US 'Black Ships' at Uraga.
1854 Treaty of Kanagawa signed with Perry.
1855 Major quake kills over 7,000 in Edo.
1858 Treaties with western powers.
1860 Ii Naosuke assassinated.
1862 End of alternate residence system.
1868 Meiji Restoration. Imperial residence moved from Kyoto; Edo renamed Tokyo.
1869 Yasukuni Shrine built to honour Japan's war dead. Rickshaws appear in Tokyo.
1871-3 Meiji leaders tour US and Europe.
1872 Shinbashi to Yokohama train service.
1874 Tokyo's first gas lights, in Ginza.
1877 Saigo Takamori leads Satsuma rebellion.
1889 Meiji constitution promulgated.
1890 Ryounkaku brick tower built in Asakusa.
1894-5 Sino-Japanese War.
1902 Anglo-Japanese alliance signed.
1904-5 Russo-Japanese war.

1910 Korea incorporated into empire.
1912 Emperor Meiji dies; Taisho era begins.
1923 Great Kanto Earthquake leaves 100,000 dead; fire destroys much of Tokyo.
1925 Universal male suffrage introduced.
1926 Hirohito becomes emperor; Showa era begins.
1927 Asia's first subway line, between Asakusa and Ueno; extended to Ginza and Shibuya by 1939.
1931 Manchurian Incident.
1932 PM Inukai Tsuyoshi assassinated. Major extension of Tokyo boundaries.
1933 Japan leaves League of Nations.
1934 Yomiuri Giants baseball team founded.
1936 Army rebellion in central Tokyo.
1937 Rape of Nanking.
1940 Tripartite Pact with Germany and Italy.
1941 Pearl Harbor attack begins Pacific War.
1945 Incendiary bombing of Tokyo. Atom bombs fall on Hiroshima and Nagasaki. Japan surrenders; occupation begins.
1946 Emperor renounces divinity. New constitution promulgated.
1950-3 Korean War.
1951 Security treaty signed with US.
1952 Occupation ends.
1954 Release of first *Godzilla* film.
1955 Liberal Democratic Party formed, along with Japan Socialist Party.
1958 Tokyo Tower completed.
1960 Demonstrations against renewal of US-Japan security treaty.
1964 Tokyo Olympic Games. First *shinkansen* bullet train runs between Tokyo and Osaka.
1966 Beatles play at Nippon Budokan.
1968-9 Student unrest.
1970 Writer Mishima Yukio commits suicide.
1971 Yen revalued from 360 to 308/US$.
1973 Oil crisis.
1988 *Akira* released. Tokyo Dome completed.
1989 Hirohito dies; Heisei era begins. Recruit scandal forces PM Takeshita Noboru to resign.
1990 End of 'bubble economy'.
1993 LDP loses power to political reform coalition under Hosokawa Morihito.
1994 Japan Socialist Party leader Murayama Tomiichi becomes PM in coalition with LDP.
1995 Kobe earthquake. Sarin gas attack on Tokyo subway. Yen briefly reaches 80/US$.
1998 Economic crisis spreads from Thailand.
1999 Ishihara elected Tokyo governor.
2000 Mori Yoshiro replaces Obuchi Keizo as LDP leader and PM. He lasts just over a year.

Tokyo Today

As comedians and writers cruise the corridors of power, the recession bites and the expense account becomes history.

The big 'Welcome to Tokyo' pronounced on signs throughout New Tokyo International Airport fails to prepare the visitor for Japan's two initial surprises. Firstly, the airport is situated at Narita, 66 kilometres (41 miles) from Tokyo. This distance can be covered by the high-speed Skyliner shuttle, which does Narita to Ueno in 60 minutes. The train, however, nixes the second surprise, of the controversy that has engulfed the airport since its inception.

Catch the Limousine Bus and the airport's formidable fortifications and riot police presence immediately come into view. They represent one of postwar Japan's longest running and most documented disputes. To initiate and subsequently expand the country's busiest air terminal, farming communities have been 'persuaded' to move from land they have

worked for generations. In a country where agricultural land accounts for only 13.4 per cent of its total area, this is no small issue. For two decades local villagers, together with a mixed bag of supporters that included students, communists and anti-war protesters (who believed the facilities would be used for military flights), fought pitched battles with the police outside the airport gates, and legal battles with the authorities in court. The dispute continues to smoulder, as two families who stubbornly refuse to sell up and leave have frustrated attempts to add a second runway to what is one of the world's most congested airports.

Tokyoites today are less prone to outbursts of political passion than they were 30 or 40 years ago. The low turnout on election day is a clear indication of the cynicism many have about the goings-on in the corridors of power. Politics is widely viewed as a self-serving world of faceless ministers jostling for wealth and influence. Since April 1995, however, when the office of governor in both Tokyo and Osaka fell to outsiders, the picture of local government has looked considerably rosier.

Running as independents, 'Knock' Yokoyama, comedian-turned-politician, and Aoshima Yukio, a former scriptwriter, actor and novelist, brought a human face to the seedy world of city politics, and subsequently launched a thousand imitators in local governments throughout the country. Yokoyama initially excelled at his new post of governor of Osaka, and was easily reelected in April 1999, when only the communists dared field a candidate against him. His downfall came a year later, when he repeatedly denied, and then abruptly admitted, molesting a 21-year-old female staffer while seated in the back of a campaign van. The outcome was indicative of a country in change – the plaintiff received a record ¥11 million in damages; and Osaka's governor today is Fusae Ota, the first woman to hold the office anywhere in Japan.

Aoshima's 'human face' was quickly battered, and by the time he stepped down Tokyoites had written him off as a pawn of the bureaucrats, Japan's most powerful political class. In a scramble to fill the vacuum, 19 candidates ran in the gubernatorial elections held in Tokyo in April 1999. The winner, by a good furlong, was Ishihara Shintaro, a maverick writer-politician known for his nationalistic and xenophobic views.

A former member of the ruling Liberal Democratic Party until he quit in 1995, Ishihara's notoriety stems from both his hawkish remarks and his inflammatory book, *The Japan That Can Say No*, co-authored with former Sony chairman Morita Akio. While the book takes aim at the government's spineless acquiescence to anything out of Washington, his outbursts have found targets almost everywhere.

His dislike of the Chinese – 'We must divide China…' – is offset by his phobia of America – 'Japan should do what the US most fears: sell treasury bonds' (it owns an estimated three trillion dollars' worth). His desire to see the Emperor made head of state, his prophecies of regional war and his loathing of fellow politicians are all well documented.

But in April 2000, many people believed he had crossed the line. In a speech to Japan's Self Defence Forces (the de facto military), Ishihara emphasised that 'atrocious crimes have been committed again and again by *sangokujin* [derogatory term for people of Japan's former colonies] who have illegally entered Japan'. He further suggested that troops (and tanks)

be used to quell rioting by foreigners in aftermath of a natural disaster.

Surprisingly, the Japan Communist Party (which goes to great pains to distance itself from its overseas counterparts) repeatedly garners support in Tokyo. Of late, many of its successful candidates have been middle-aged women – the all-pearls-and-lipstick brigade – who rally their housewife cadres with the cry for retail revolution.

This cash register stumping has found an ideal platform in the consumption tax. In 1989, when the new tax was introduced at three per cent, suburbia rang with loudspeakers calling for a united front to oppose it. When, in 1994, the tax was increased to five per cent, the same candidates were back on the streets calling for a return to the good old days of three per cent. The struggle continues.

On the opposing side, the ballot box holds little attraction for the parties of the ultra right. But eschewing democracy does have its rewards, as the nationalists can flaunt their enfant terrible image with pulpit-banging speeches long after the polling booths have closed.

'The notorious *yakuza* have their fingers in most criminal pies.'

From atop their armoured trucks and buses, uniformed lieutenants harangue Tokyo on a near-daily basis with apocalyptic threats against Japan's enemies – Russia, America, China, communism, the incumbent government, the teachers union, foreigners staying illegally in the country – while annually, a convoy of nationalist pride converges on Yasukuni-jinja to pay homage to the 2.5 million war-dead enshrined there, among whom are convicted war criminals and *kamikaze* pilots.

The far right's affiliations with organised crime are no secret. Many an ardent defender of Japan by day is, by night, a petty gangster, and indeed, the same foot soldiers that rail against Tokyo's burgeoning foreign community gladly reap huge rewards from the lucrative trafficking of Thai prostitutes to Japan.

The notorious *yakuza* have their fingers in most criminal pies. The three main gangs, Yamaguchi-gumi, Sumiyoshi-kai and Inagawa-kai, have some 42,000 members nationwide, and their activities, from drug smuggling to gambling, span the underworld's horizon. Their weakness is for extortion, a particularly undemanding task that ensures a regular flow of yen. Many a Tokyo restaurateur, bar owner, company president and even shareholder can look forward to the eventual knock at the door, ar-impossible to refuse. distance, tending to valry turns to warfare. he *yakuza* still carries mas depict him as the ...dering *samurai* driven to crime by his own privation; in contemporary film he is a moralist, torn between gangland duty and a latent yearning to do good. Back in the real world the average hood is neither.

Initiation rights are given young: members may be school drop-outs who have passed into the underworld through motorcycle gangs, part-time work or crime. The swaggering confidence of this rank and file does little to conceal its

affiliations, and the preening that distinguishes Japanese males is nowhere more obsessive than in the testosterone-fuelled world of gangsterism.

Although it's no surprise to find that the *yakuza* don prefers the Godfatherly touch – black Mercedes, coat draped over shoulders, tinted glasses, hair scraped back – it is bizarre that in a profession where facial scars and torso-sized tattoos are de rigueur, the chosen look should be a tightly knit 'punch perm', an in-yer-face-coloured trouser suit, sunglasses, and heeled sandals, usually a few sizes too small.

Since the mid-1970s, crime in Japan has increased dramatically. In 1973 there were fewer than 1,200 offences per 100,000 people;

Confessions of a *pachinko* addict

What is it with these expat experts? Why do they never have anything nice to say about *pachinko*? When it comes to Japan's national pastime, their 'thoroughly researched' guides either condemn it as an aberration or cast it into cultural oblivion by omitting it altogether. Like some boil on their collective behind, it hurts whether they prod it or not.

Pachinko sets little alarm bells ringing in polite society. As with nose-picking, it is something that nobody will admit to. Needless to say, everyone's at it. Or everyone except our Japanapologist friends, who usually offer this somewhat distorted sketch: Sit down at a *pachinko* machine, put your coins in to buy some balls, flick the balls up into the machine, and if, by some twist of fate, you win, you get to take home a heap of worthless prizes.

Firstly, you don't simply plonk yourself down at any machine. No, you reconnoitre, you suss the place out; you observe what's going on, who's winning, which machines haven't paid out. This detective work also draws credibility, very important when gambling.

Gambling? Didn't anyone mention gambling? Surely you don't think that the Japanese, who are drowning in 'worthless prizes', would spend so much precious time and money in pursuit of anything but cold cash? Pachi-pros, as the serial gamblers are known, can reap up to ¥300,000 on a good day. Bad days are bad.

Right, you've chosen your machine. Now throw a pack of cigarettes into the trough to mark your spot. Smoking is compulsory, so if you don't have any fags, get some. On your way back, pick up a ¥2000 card (from the card machine). The days of coin *pachinko* are

fast disappearing. Any coin machines you do find will be infested by old people. Stick to the cards, it's where the action is.

Slide the card into the machine, push the ball-eject button, turn the handle to flick the balls, and you're rolling. Now comes the tricky part. The balls have to land in the centre hole to start the numbers on the screen. This is done by inching the handle back and forth to find the optimum setting. Once you're satisfied they're going in (aim for at least ten hits every ¥500), wedge a coin into the handle to hold it in place and wait.

What for? You wait to win; to match up two numbers and, through a variety of animated cliffhangers, pray the third will come in. If it does, expect a sudden ejaculation of steel balls and an overwhelming sense of relief. Open up the trough hole to let the balls dribble into the box, and, when it's all over, change them up or continue playing.

The last stage is where it all gets a bit hazy. Balls are exchanged for a card or a ticket, which is then exchanged at the counter. What you are usually given are tiny bars of gold, each encased in plastic. There are two varieties, one worth more than the other. These you then carry off to a small window a short walk away (look on the counter for a map) where you finally get to see some money.

If you don't win, however, you may start feeling slightly delirious. As you go to buy yet another card, you may begin to question your actions – When should I stop? How much can I afford to lose? Can I even recoup my losses? – and even of those around you – Why is that fat old bag next to me winning? This is quite normal, and can be easily remedied. Just stop and walk out.

Shibuya: the best and worst of '90s Tokyo.

increased in both number and viciousness, peaking in 1998 when, it seemed, not a week went by without another stabbing, and the news stations falling over themselves to capture the nation's tears on video. Inevitably, knives have given way to more ingenious methods, as the bombing of a Tokyo video store in December 2000 showed. And more random methods: days later a youth went on a rampage, clubbing Shibuya commuters with a metal baseball bat. Both culprits were 17 years old, and neither expressed any remorse over their actions.

For girls, the uproar has been about the euphemistically termed practice of *enjo kosai*, or 'compensated dating'. Since the start of the '90s, a deepening recession has forced drastic changes in consumer habits as workers are left facing an increasingly uncertain future. Born into the boom years of the so-called bubble economy, most Tokyo teenagers know little restraint and, evident in the thriving sub-economy that their materialistic demands fuel, adolescent girls have yet to be gripped by the fears of their elders. Egged on by a media that actively dictates what today's young require, the shopping list of the average Tokyo teenage girl is a far cry from the spartan days of her parents' youth. Mobile phones, Prada handbags, designer clothes, overseas trips – all require a budget that flipping hamburgers simply cannot sustain. Yet *enjo kosai* could not have become so widespread without the salacious appetite of the Japanese 'salaryman' for young girls. This ignominious chemistry has resulted in an almost Faustian pact: many adult men are quite willing to pay for casual sex, and many teenage girls quite happy to deliver.

One survey of junior high school girls in their final year revealed that 17 per cent found nothing distasteful about the concept of 'compensated dating' and 13 per cent felt no reluctance to actually doing it. In 1998, these alarming figures finally moved the government to enact a law that will leave those who encourage minors to sell sex liable to prison terms of up to one year and a fine of ¥500,000. Although there are outward signs that the practice of 'compensated dating' is on the decline, the materialistic pressures of Japanese society and the plenitude of 'love hotels' guarantees its survival.

Surprisingly, the inequality of the sexes still prevalent in Japanese society has left professional women in Tokyo with a remarkable amount of independence. Not having the responsibilities and opportunities in the workplace afforded their male counterparts has allowed women a freedom of choice unprecedented in the country's history.

by 1997 the number had reached 1,900. This figure includes offences committed by foreigners, which have skyrocketed from 1,725 offences in 1985 to a total of 21,670 in 1997, and serious crimes, such as rape and murder, which have risen steadily since the '80s. But these figures can be misleading. Tokyo is still a remarkably safe place to live, work and play: 87.7 per cent of 1997's crimes were theft-related, whereas violence occurred in a mere 2.1 per cent.

Juvenile crime, which, since 1993, has doubled, accounts for much of this rise. Teenage filching and spray-paint graffiti, once the mainstay of kiddie-crime, has been superseded by rape, stabbings, kidnapping, and even the murder of teachers. For boys, the uproar has been about weapons. Fatal stabbings of fellow students, and even a rage knifing to death of a young woman teacher by a pupil, revealed a countrywide fascination for carrying, and using, 'butterfly' knives. Fanned by Japan's sensationalist media, the incidents

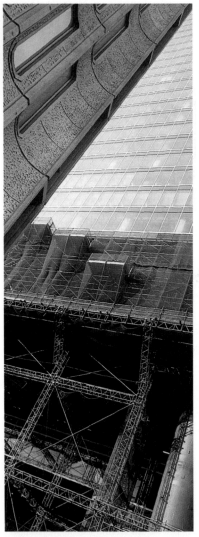

Recession bites, but the building goes on.

after 25 years old (implying that, after the 25th, she would be left on the shelf).

Although Tokyo's fusty academics were quick to coin the now widely used term 'Parasite Singles' to bemoan young working women who live at home, show little interest in marriage, and spend their salaries having fun, this newfound freedom is in no way restricted to the young. Since the postwar baby boom of 1947, the birthrate has plummeted, with the present figure a perilous all-time low.

Older women, free from the shackles that tied an earlier generation of mothers to a legion of offspring, are now reaping the rewards of their husbands' 'employment for life'. Department stores, art galleries, theatres, domestic package holidays and chic 'coffee and cake' shops all cater predominantly to a middle-aged sisterhood that is both affluent and liberated after years of housewife drudgery.

The Tokyo male, on the other hand, has little to celebrate. With a family tucked away in the suburbs, an undemanding mortgage, and a steady job that looked set to last for eternity, the average salaryman's life was, up until ten years ago, a carefree one. His days were spent at a desk that, over his working life, he would come to know inside out. The evenings, after mandatory overtime, he could enjoy on Tokyo's neonlit tiles, secure in the fact that the company would foot the bill, no questions asked.

A decade later he must be wondering what hit him. As the economy nose-dived, the first casualty was the much-abused corporate expense account. No longer would his colleagues turn a blind eye to the horrendous sums spent cavorting in hostess clubs and girly bars. Coinciding with the IT and digital revolution, next up for the chop was the system of promotion based on age and loyal service.

In an ironic twist, the same Tokyo companies that preached the success of 'the Japanese way' to their overseas counterparts in the '80s are now looking to the west for guidance in the unfamiliar climate of meritocracy. This policy shift has left membership in *madogiwa-zoku*, or 'tribe by the window' – workers, with their days of productivity behind them, waiting for retirement – an enviable alternative to outright expulsion. As companies close one after another, the number of unskilled middle-aged men out of work sadly reflects the naïve trust the 'job-for-life' system induced.

Tokyo now looks to the future, perhaps anticipating a period of stability after two decades of boom and bust. But one eye will remain fixed on the past, hoping to find an explanation for the difficulties still to be faced.

Although marriage remains high on the agenda, more and more of Tokyo's new brides are choosing to enjoy the financial privileges of a double income over the restraints of early motherhood. Marriage itself, when it does happen, is happening later in life. No longer do women fear the 'Christmas cake' moniker, a derogatory term used for a woman still single

Rafael Vinoly's stunning **Tokyo International Forum** (1996). *See p21.*

Architecture

Responses to the fires and earthquakes that have ravaged
Tokyo include 'urban tombstones' and 'trophy architecture'.

Since it flung open its doors to the world
in 1868, Tokyo has been a laboratory for
the synthesis of local and western styles
that continues to inform the development
of Japanese architecture today. Lacking the
ancient temples of Kyoto and Nara, Tokyo has
been stripped of much of its own heritage by
fires, earthquakes and bombing, compounded
by post-war economic development and an
unsentimental lack of attachment to the old.

TRADITIONAL STYLES

Japanese architecture has traditionally been
based on the use of wooden materials. Very
few original structures remain from the
city's former incarnation as Edo, capital of
the Tokugawa *shogun*, although parts of the
imposing pre-modern fortifications of Edo
Castle can still be seen when walking around
the moat and gardens of the Imperial Palace,
built on the castle site. The original wooden
houses and shops of Edo-era *shitamachi*
(downtown) have now almost completely
disappeared, although later examples in similar
styles can often be found in older residential

districts. Outside the heart of the city, eaves
and tiled roofs are still widely used on modern
suburban housing, while *tatami* mats and
sliding doors are common inside even more
western-style apartment blocks.

Shrines and temples are overwhelmingly
traditional in form. The **Meiji Shrine**
(*see p89*) is an impressive example of the
austere style and restrained colours typical of
Shinto architecture, which is usually distinct
from that of Buddhist temples, where the
greater influence of Chinese and Korean
styles is usually apparent. Many present-day
buildings of older religious institutions are
reconstructions; the temples of Sensoji and
Zojoji are both examples, although in these
cases some remnants of earlier structures also
survive. The 1605 **Sanmon Gate of Zojoji
Temple** and **Gokokuji Temple**, which dates
from 1681, are rare, unreconstructed survivors.

In contrast, when the wooden building of
the **Honganji Temple** in Tsukiji burned down
for the ninth time in the temple's long history,
after the 1923 earthquake, it was rebuilt in
sturdier stone. The design, by architect Ito

Chuta, earlier responsible for the Meiji Shrine, was also quite different: an eye-catching affair recalling Buddhism's roots in ancient India.

WESTERNISATION AND REACTION

After the Meiji Restoration of 1868, the twin influences of westernisation and modernisation made themselves felt in Tokyo, the new capital. Early attempts to combine western and traditional elements by local architects resulted in hybrids featuring Japanese-style sloping roofs rising above wooden constructions with ornate front façades of a distinctly western style. Kisuke Shimizu's Hoterukan (1868) at the Foreign Settlement in Tsukiji and his First National Bank (1872) in Nihonbashi were two notable examples. Neither survives today.

Tokyo's earliest buildings of purely western design were the work of overseas architects brought to Japan by the new Meiji government. Englishman Thomas Waters oversaw the post-1872 redevelopment of Ginza with around 900 red-brick buildings, thought to be more resilient than wooden Japanese houses. Ironically, none of them made it through the 1923 earthquake. Waters' fellow-countryman Josiah Conder, who taught at Tokyo Imperial University, was the most influential western architect of the early Meiji period, with important projects in the capital including ministry buildings, the original Imperial Museum at Ueno (1881) and Hibiya's Rokumeikan reception hall (1883). His **Furukawa mansion** in Komagome (1917) and **Nikolai Cathedral** in Ochanomizu (1891) still exist, although the latter was badly damaged in the 1923 earthquake.

Later Meiji architecture was often a close reflection of western styles, although it was Japanese architects who increasingly handled the prestige projects. Remaining red-brick structures of the period include the **Ministry of Justice** (1895), built in Kasumigaseki by the German firm of Ende and Bockman, and the Crafts Gallery of the **National Museum of Modern Art** (1910; see p98), which once housed the administrative headquarters of the Imperial Guard. The imposing **Bank of Japan** building (1896) was built by one of Conder's former students, Tatsuno Kingo, who was also responsible for the Marunouchi wing of **Tokyo Station** (1914), modelled on Centraal Station in Amsterdam. A far more grandiose overseas inspiration, that of Versailles, is said to have been used for **Akasaka Detached Palace** (1909), created by Katayama Tokuma, whose other work includes the Hyokeikan building of the **National Museum** in Ueno (also completed in 1909; see p100).

The era after World War I saw the completion of Frank Lloyd Wright's highly

Post-quake innovation: *ikanbanî* style.

distinctive **Imperial Hotel** (1922; see p36), which survived the Tokyo earthquake, but has since been demolished. The period after the earthquake saw the spread of social housing, and a prominent example that still exists, although now used largely for shops, is the **Dojunkai Aoyama** tenement apartment blocks (1926) on Omotesando. Another post-quake innovation was the *ikanbanî* (signboard) style, designed to protect buildings against fire by a cloaking of sheet copper, and often still seen today in the heavily oxidised green mantles of surviving pre-war shops.

The influence of contemporary overseas trends can be discerned in the modernism of Yoshida Tetsuro's **Tokyo Central Post Office** (1931) and the art deco of **Tokyo Metropolitan Teien Art Museum** (1933; see p100), built as a mansion for Prince Asaka and planned mainly by French designer Henri Rapin. The present-day **Diet Building** (1936) also shows a strong art deco influence, but its design became a source of heated debate in the increasingly nationalist climate of the period when it was completed.

A reaction against westernisation had already been apparent in the work of Ito Chuta, who had looked toward Asian models. The **Kabuki-za** (1925) harked back to the medieval Momoyama era. Demands for a distinctive national look led to the 'Imperial Crown' style, usually represented by the main building of the **Tokyo National Museum** (1938; see p105) in Ueno. This was the design of Watanabe Hitoshi, whose other works include the **Hattori Building** (1932) of Wako department store at Ginza 4-chome crossing, and the **Daiichi Insurance Building** (1938).

POST-WAR TOKYO

The priority in the early post-war period was often to provide extra office space for companies trying to cope with the demands of an economy hurtling along at double-digit growth rates, or a rapid answer to the pressing housing needs of the city's growing population. Seismic instability meant that tall buildings were not initially an option, and anonymous, box-like structures proliferated.

Even as confidence grew about new construction techniques, designed to provide greater protection against earthquakes, many of the initial results were undistinguished. The city's first and only real cluster of skyscrapers, built in west Shinjuku from the early 1970s, has been described as resembling a set of urban tombstones. Even so, a later addition, the twin-tower **Tokyo Metropolitan Government complex** (1991) by Tange Kenzo (*see below* **Pritzker Prize winners**), is now among the capital's best-known landmarks.

The dominant figure of post-war Japanese architecture, Tange had a long career connecting different generations of Japanese architects. One collaborator was Maekawa Kunio, a pre-war student of Le Corbusier who became one of Japan's foremost modern architects with works such as **Tokyo Metropolitan Festival Hall** (1961) and the **Tokyo Metropolitan Museum of Art** (1975; *see p100*). Someone who also worked with Tange was Isozaki Arata, now one of Japan's most distinguished post-modernist architects, whose work in Tokyo includes the **Panasonic Globe** in Okubo (1988) and the **Ochanomizu Square** building (1987).

Tokyo ordered itself a post-modernist make-over as the bubble economy took hold in the 1980s, and this splurge of 'trophy architecture' has left the city a string of new, eye-catching

landmarks. One that's difficult to ignore is the **Super Dry Hall** in Asakusa by Philippe Starck, one of the increasing number of foreign architects to have worked in Tokyo in recent years. Others include Rafael Vinoly, responsible for the **Tokyo International Forum** (1996), and Norman Foster, whose **Century Tower** (1991) is located near Ochanomizu.

The reclamation of Tokyo Bay has opened up land for a wide range of projects, such as Tange's **Fuji TV** headquarters (1996) and Sato Sogokeikau's **Tokyo Big Sight** (1994), both on Odaiba. Over in south Shinjuku, **Takashimaya Times Square** (1996) and the nearby **NTT DoCoMo building**, a scaled-down Empire State clone, both suggest a continuing fascination with overseas models. Finally, a municipal project that should be mentioned is Kikutake Kiyonori's **Edo-Tokyo Museum** (1992; *see p103*) in Ryogoku, its alien-spacecraft look comprised of traditional elements recalling the city's past, and its height of 62 metres (203 feet) matching that of Edo Castle.

As for the future, one thing is certain: Tokyo will continue to rebuild itself, as it has for hundreds of years. If the buildings here today aren't to your taste, come back in 20 years and there'll be a whole new set for you to enjoy.

Pritzker Prize winners

Three contemporary Japanese architects have been honoured with their profession's most prestigious international award, the Pritzker Prize.

Tange Kenzo, the 1987 winner, was responsible for the landmark twin-tower **Tokyo Metropolitan Government** skyscraper complex in west Shinjuku (1991), as well as its now-demolished predecessor in Yurakucho (1957). Embracing both modernist and traditional Japanese elements, Tange's astonishing variety of high-profile Tokyo projects includes steel-clad **St Mary's Cathedral** near Edogawabashi (1963), **Yoyogi National Stadium** (1964; *see picture*), **Sogetsu Arts Centre** (1977) and the **UN University** (1992) in Aoyama, the **Hanae Mori** building on Omotesando (1978), and the **Akasaka Prince Hotel** (1983) and **Fuji TV** HQ on Odaiba (1996).

Maki Fumihiko, the Pritzker Prize recipient in 1993, was a student of Tange's at Tokyo University. A co-founder of the Metabolist

group back in 1960, Maki has worked extensively in his native Tokyo. One contribution to the new city look is his landmark **Spiral** building (1985) in Aoyama; another is the strange and low-level **Tokyo Metropolitan Gymnasium** (1990) in Sendagaya. Nearby is his **Tepia** building (1989) in Gaienmae, while out in Chiba a much larger-scale project is the huge **Makuhara Messe** exhibition centre (1989).

Ando Tadao, a Pritzker winner in 1995, was based for many years in his home town of Osaka, but one accessible example of his work in the capital is the **Collezione** building (1989) in Aoyama. Appointed professor at Tokyo University in 1997, Ando is a former boxer who travelled widely before becoming a self-taught architect. Although his lack of formal qualifications would have stopped him from setting up practice in Britain, in 1997 he was awarded the Royal Gold Medal, the UK's top architecture honour.

Geography

Know your *yamanote* from your *shitamachi*.

Tokyo has long since slipped the confines of the city's original boundaries around the present-day Imperial Palace area. Today, it lies at one end of the highly developed Pacific belt that runs west along the coast of Japan's main Honshu island to Osaka and holds around half the national population of 126.92 million. In a country where up to two-thirds of the land is mountainous, the greater Tokyo metropolis sprawls over much of the Kanto plain, Japan's largest and a natural population magnet.

But while distant commuter suburbs and satellite towns spread outward over the hinterland, the balance inside the capital itself is also constantly shifting. Older districts have lost ground to upstart newcomers, as huge development and infrastructure projects continue to remodel the landscape and draw new crowds to different areas of the city.

SHIFTING CENTRE

At the heart of Tokyo lie the city's 23 inner wards, or *ku*, covering 616 square kilometres (238 square miles) and home to 8.13 million people. Perhaps in reaction to recent land price

falls, there seems to be a drift back to the bright lights of the city proper, with the 23 wards registering their first overall population increase for 15 years in the 2000 census. Even so, the current figure still stands below the peak of nearly nine million recorded in the late 1960s.

Visitors to Tokyo are usually advised to orientate themselves by the Yamanote train line that circles the central areas of the city, linking important districts such as Shinjuku, Shibuya and Ikebukuro in the west, and Ueno, Tokyo and Shinagawa in the east. The growth of these huge transport hubs, connected to subways and suburban train lines, means Japan's capital lacks the focus of a single central area but instead possesses a whole series of multi-functional sub-centres, each one boasting its own unique flavour.

The name of the Yamanote line recalls an older division between the smarter *yamanote* areas on the higher ground to the west and south of the city and the lower-lying *shitamachi* downtown districts. The comparison is far from exact, however, since the present-day loop runs through both old *yamanote* and old *shitamachi* districts, as well as through western areas that lay outside the official city limits until as late as 1932. Even so, the broad sweep of the magic Yamanote circle is generally taken to define the central part of the city.

To an extent, this illustrates a westward shift in Tokyo's centre of gravity, particularly in the post-war era. In the early years of Japan's modernisation, areas to the east of the Imperial Palace in the vicinity of Tokyo station, such as Ginza, Marunouchi, Otemachi and Nihonbashi, were the focus of commercial and financial activities. Ueno stood almost directly north of them, while further east lay the old *shitamachi* districts, including the popular entertainment area of Asakusa near Sumida River.

In more recent times, growth has been strongest in what were previously considered outposts for suburban train connections along the west side of the Yamanote line, such as Shibuya, Shinjuku and Ikebukuro. The 1964 Olympics provided a boost for Harajuku and the nearby fashionable districts of Omotesando, Aoyama and Roppongi. In 1991 the Tokyo Metropolitan Government recognised the city's new western axis by relocating from Yurakucho to a gleaming-new Gotham-style skyscraper in Shinjuku.

Outside the central part of the city, but reflecting the same trend, population has continued to grow in suburban wards west of the Yamanote line such as Setagaya-ku. Conversely, many of the less-wealthy industrial wards are still located in the north and east of the city, clustered around the Sumida, Arakawa and Edogawa rivers that empty into Tokyo Bay.

A WORK IN PROGRESS
The Japanese capital remains capable of unexpected twists and changes of direction. In recent years, the huge waterfront development at Odaiba has turned attention back to the Tokyo Bay area in general, continuing a long tradition of land reclamation that goes back to the earliest days of the city.

Indeed, Tokyo has never been averse to improving on its own natural endowments. Furiously remodelled over the centuries, many physical features of the city are often scarcely recognisable in their original form, even allowing for the present-day concrete cladding. Hills and valleys have been evened out; lakes and marshes drained; rivers re-routed. What was once a city of canals and waterways is now joined together by networks of overhead trains and highways, with natural greenery at a premium.

Making the best use of every last inch still remains a priority in the central areas, despite

the post-bubble crash in real-estate prices. Housing conditions throughout the city are still cramped by western standards, while park area per head remains a mere one-tenth of that in New York. In a country that takes pride in its closeness to nature, the capital has scarcely a trickling stream without ugly man-made embankments. The headlong rush to development has also raised continuing concerns about air pollution and the urgent need for more recycling.

OUTWARD BOUND
In common with other large Japanese cities, Tokyo has felt the effects of the rapid population shift from countryside to city since the end of the war. But as the rural population came one way, Tokyo itself was heading in the opposite direction. With the height of its buildings traditionally limited by possible earthquakes (*see p25* **Shaking all over**), the metropolis has tended to grow outward rather than upward, and the paddy fields have been covered over by concrete. Commuters retreating to distant suburbs pay the price for cheaper housing and more spacious living conditions with famously long journeys to work.

One result of the city's headlong march into the surrounding countryside, however, is that defining just where Tokyo's sprawling

Geographical centre, the **Imperial Palace**.

Cartographical centre, **Nihonbashi Bridge**, from which road distances are measured.

metropolis begins and ends sometimes appears to be a matter of arbitrary choice. Official boundaries turn out to be nothing more than lines on a map as the urban landscape stretches endlessly towards the distant hills, as well as around Tokyo Bay in both directions.

Tokyo prefecture, the 2,187 square kilometres (844 square miles) administered from the skyscraper offices of the Metropolitan Government in Shinjuku, provides one wider definition. According to the 2000 census, the prefecture's total population now stands at 12.05 million. As well as the 23 inner wards, this larger area includes what the authorities classify as 27 cities, five towns and eight villages. These mainly consist of commuter belt and semi-rural districts on the Musashino plain in the western part of the prefecture. Also under metropolitan administration, however, are nine sets of scattered Pacific islands (two towns and seven villages), most of them part of the Izu Islands, but also including the semi-tropical Ogasawara Islands, lying some 1,000 kilometres south of the inner wards.

Meanwhile, the UN Department of Economic and Social Affairs Population Division ranks Tokyo as the world's largest urban agglomeration, defined as 'the population contained within the contours of contiguous territory inhabited at urban levels of residential density without regard to administrative boundaries'. By this measure, the 1999 Tokyo population figure was 26.4

million; over 20 per cent of Japan's entire population, all living on less than two per cent of the nation's land. Tokyo remains far ahead of second-place Mexico City, Mumbai (Bombay), Sao Paulo and New York, although some projections have Mumbai taking top spot within the next 20 years.

Finally, probably the widest measure of the greater Tokyo area is the National Capital Region, established for planning purposes in 1954, and taking in all seven Kanto prefectures plus Yamanashi. Together these have a population of over 40 million, mostly in metropolitan Tokyo and neighbouring Kanagawa, Chiba and Saitama. The outlying four prefectures of Tochigi, Gunma, Ibaraki and Yamanashi remain more rural and mountainous, particularly Yamanashi, which contains Mount Fuji on its southern borders.

CLIMATE

The Japanese take great pride in the fact that their country boasts four distinct seasons, something they apparently believe to be unique to Japan. Visitors should be grateful for small mercies: under the old solar calendar in Japan, the year was divided into 24 'mini-seasons', ranging from 'the lesser cold' in January to 'the greater snow' in December.

Implicit in Japanese talk about the seasons is the connection that even hardened city dwellers feel with nature. In this temperate country, which until recently was composed largely of farmers, the concept of being at one with nature is part of daily life, with people's life cycles mirroring the changing seasons. In the city, this celebration of the seasons shows itself most clearly in spring, when first the plum trees, then the cherry trees come into bloom, leading to weeks of partying and celebration. No less important to the Japanese is autumn: when the leaves change colour in Tokyo's finest parks, it takes a brave person to jostle through the massed ranks of amateur photographers to get to a good viewing spot. Broadly speaking, the four seasons in Tokyo can be summarised as follows. *See also p272* **When to go**.

Winter

Sitting on roughly the same latitude as Los Angeles and Teheran, Tokyo escapes the harsh Siberian winter snows blowing east from the Asian mainland courtesy of the rugged protection given by the mountain ranges that run along the central spine of Japan's main island. Snow may fall for a couple of days in January, but rarely sticks.

Spring

The cherry blossoms of late March to early April are the official harbinger of spring, their arrival giving rise to mass celebrations. The general mood becomes more optimistic in the face of the annual rebirth of nature.

Summer

This is a good time to be out of the city, and many Tokyoites escape to the mountains from the city's oppressive heat. The hot air blasting out of air-conditioners all over Tokyo makes the capital a couple of degrees hotter than elsewhere. Late June and early July bring the summer rains, rather like walking around in a lukewarm shower. Always carry an umbrella.

Autumn

September to early October can bring typhoons, and when the trees change colour, parks and gardens are crammed with people admiring the spectacular leaves.

Political centre, **Tokyo Metropolitan Government Building**.

Shaking all over

Ever wondered what it's like to be in a major earthquake? The much-feared Big One could strike seismically vulnerable Tokyo at any time, but a less life-threatening taste of the experience is provided by the earthquake simulation room of the Ikebukuro Life Safety Education Centre. Here, visitors practise emergency procedures while walls sway alarmingly and the floor shakes beneath their feet.

The Kobe earthquake of 1995, which left over 6,000 dead, provided a disturbing reminder to Tokyo residents that their city stands on unstable geological foundations. In 1923, the Great Kanto earthquake destroyed much of the capital and around 100,000 people were killed (*see chapter* **History**). The city hasn't suffered a natural catastrophe since then, but the chances of a future disaster remain high.

While the metropolitan government still holds city-wide exercises every year on 1 September, the anniversary of the 1923 quake, the Life Safety Education Centre attempts to equip individuals with some basic training in what to do if the worst does happen. The earthquake simulation room is only part of this, and comes at the end of a two-hour programme that includes first-aid, fire fighting and finding your way out of a smoke-filled maze.

Preparation will be one of the keys to survival in the event of a disaster, so Tokyo residents are advised to keep a small bag handy at home containing essentials such as a bottle of water, preserved foodstuffs, some cash and a torch. And if you're unlucky enough to experience the real thing, attempt to shut off any stoves and gas mains, secure an exit, and look for a table or similar to protect your body, especially the head.

Ikebukuro Life Safety Education Centre (Ikebukuro Bosai-kan)

2-37-8 Nishi-Ikebukuro, Toshima-ku (3590 6565/www.tfd.metro.tokyo.jp/ bosai/ikeb.htm). Ikebukuro station. **Open** 9am-5pm (last entry 4pm) Mon, Wed-Sun (closed 3rd Wed of month). **Admission** free. Phone ahead to book. Staff speak limited English.

Cartoon City

Tokyo has some very strange authority figures indeed.

Take a look at the giant cartoon mouse that adorns this page, looking like Tom and Jerry's Jerry with a blue condom on its head. Now try and guess what it represents. Is it an advertisement for a new theme park? A logo for one of Tokyo's hottest new designers? No. Quake in your boots, folks. It's the cops.

This sweet little fellow is in fact the public face of the Tokyo police. He's called Pi-Po chan, Pi-Po being the noise police cars make in Japanese, and wherever you see him, he'll be exhorting you to behave, watch your speed, not drink too much, or face the consequences. Welcome to Tokyo, Cartoon City.

It's probably a little unfair to single out Pi-Po chan for special treatment. Wherever

you go in this larger-than-life city, cartoon figures will accompany you. If you try to open a bank account, perhaps you'd like to opt for a cashcard with a picture of your favourite cartoon character on it? Sakura Bank (now part of Mitsui-Sumitomo Bank) has the option on Doraemon, Asahi Bank deals in Miffy cards and passbooks, while Dai-ichi Kangyo Bank offers Kitty-chan (Hello Kitty) financial essentials.

Perhaps you're feeling sick? Take a medicine with instructions written in both Japanese and cartoon form. If the road outside your house is being dug up, expect to find a cartoon mole with a hard hat apologising for the inconvenience; if a road is closed, expect to be diverted by a sign consisting of a workman bowing to apologise.

When Japan Railways computerised its ticket machines, how did it cope with the loss of personal contact? With a cartoon woman who bows thank you at you once you've bought your ticket, of course. It's difficult to imagine a similar approach working in London or New York.

But why does it work so well here? The simplest explanation is, of course, that people are used to it. The Japanese love of comic figures, or *manga*, is well known. Every year, *manga* magazines, many of them 400 or 500 pages thick, sell over 2.1 billion copies. One of the many theories behind their popularity is that because the written Japanese language is based on ideograms, rather than letters, people here are accustomed to thinking in more visual terms than in the west.

The lineage of Japanese comic and cartoon characters can be traced back to the *Ukiyo-e* ('floating world') pictures of the 18th and 19th centuries, but the man most often credited with being the father of modern *manga* is Tezuka Osamu (1928-1989), whose creation of Atom Boy (known variously in the west as Astro Boy and the Mighty Atom) in 1952 set a style for the mainstream that has been followed ever since.

'Not until the 1970s could *manga* come out from under the coffee table.'

Borrowing from Disney, Tezuka gave his characters the big round eyes that have become a hallmark of Japanese *manga* and animation. For the following 20 years, *manga* struggled as an underground art form, hated by the establishment for its debasement of the written word and trivialisation of life. Not until the 1970s could it come out from under the coffee table.

Now its influence is everywhere and, ground-breaking *manga* such as Otomo Katsuhiro's *Akira* notwithstanding, the hand of Tezuka can be detected in nearly all of them. Modern *manga* come in all shapes and sizes, and deal with subjects ranging from superheroes to marital

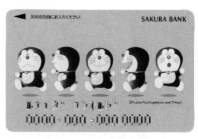

Bank customers can gaze at **Doraemon**.

break-ups, office life, and violent murder and rape. They can be cute, salacious or downright disturbing, and their often graphic depictions of sex are shocking to western eyes. On the street, though, on billboards, hoardings and in train carriages, the dominant image is still cartoon-like.

Even if you don't read Japanese, a visit to a Tokyo bookstore will be an eye-opener. Leading characters such as blue cartoon cat Doraemon not only have their own books for children, but whole series aimed at adults, such as *Doraemon Explains the Workings of the Japanese Economy*.

The other aspect of Japanese life that cartoons tap into is the all-pervading love of the *kawaii*, or cute. This is the land that produced Hello Kitty, after all, a cartoon cat with no mouth. But isn't Kitty-chan *kawaii*? Take a walk round Harajuku or Shibuya, where Tokyo's teenagers try out their latest fads and fashions, and listen out for how many times you hear this word, spoken in a squeaky upper register with the last syllable stretching out into infinity. It's not too much of a leap to say that in these areas in recent years Tokyo's teens have spent vast amounts of time and money turning themselves into cartoon characters.

Sporting fake tans, dyed hair, high-rise platform heels and inches of make-up, the girls in these areas particularly have become caricatures – a group of humans dressed up as two-dimensional characters. The less real they look, the more 'attractive' they become.

Walk this way, folks. Follow the cartoon chickens and avoid the nasty roadworks.

The new Gameboy kicks off its advertising.

ピカチュウ

シール①を
はろう

コイル

でんきタイプ

●でんきを つかう こうげきが とくい。

カイロス

シール⑨を
はろう

キャタピー

むしタイプ

●はちや ちょうなど、むしに にた
すがたを して いる。

Pokemon: Japan's biggest cartoon export.

For all the dominating cuteness of the images, however, there is also a sinister subtext to the Japanese fondness for cartoon figures, particularly where Tokyo is concerned. At the most basic level, such images offer reassurance and comfort in a world that is changing too quickly for comfort. Fifty years ago, Tokyo was a bomb site. The post-war reconstruction has taken place with a rapidity and ruthlessness that left many city dwellers feeling alienated.

'There is a sinister subtext to the Japanese fondness for cartoon figures.'

This is not a planned city. Planning regulations are laughable; plots are randomly redeveloped as towering office blocks seemingly overnight. With all this going on around them, the population needed to be reassured that despite all the changes, this was still a place with the same heart and soul as ever. The chosen medium? Cartoon characters, which have the bonus of appealing to those at both ends of the alienation spectrum: kids who can't yet read the messages and adults worried about their changing surroundings.

The influence of cartoons also spreads into the home. Let's not forget that, conformity being the norm, this is a nation of precision-made stereotypes, from the blue-suited salaryman to the corrupt politician, and as such it lends itself to interpretation as a cartoon. Switch on the TV on a Sunday night and catch long-standing cartoon series such as *Chibi-Maruko-chan* (first broadcast 1990) or *Sazae-san* (first broadcast 1969), which offer a misty-eyed view of growing up or raising a family in a Japan that hasn't truly existed since the 1960s. It's *The Simpsons* on Valium, where dad comes home and slips into a *yukata* while the wife dishes him up a hot meal and a flask of *sake* and asks him about his day. Cartoons over, stick around for the variety shows. Watch as the presenters are regularly morphed into cartoon characters, or how every word that's spoken on screen instantly appears as a giant cartoon subtitle. Exclamations of surprise are a particular favourite.

In the end, how you feel about constantly being bombarded by these images is a matter of personal taste. For some people, they're as essential a part of life in Tokyo as the Yamanote line, for others they're the epitome of everything that's wrong with the city, and by extension with Japan itself. One thing is for sure. Despite all the unbearable violence and cuteness of cartoon images, this is one of the safest, most liveable-in cities in the world. Keep up the good work, Pi-Po chan.

How to use those tricky train ticket gates.

Sorry we're digging up your street again.

Sanrio's strawberry-shaped shop in Denenchofu, purveyor of Kitty-chan to the masses.

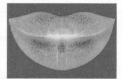

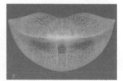
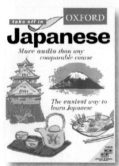

Accommodation

Accommodation   **32**

Feature boxes

Accommodation

Luxury accommodation abounds, leaving budget travellers facing a challenge.

Land prices in Tokyo remain among the world's highest, and the astronomical cost of building and maintenance is invariably passed on to the consumer. The result is that Tokyo suffers from a chronic imbalance in accommodation, with an abundance of modern tower-block hotels but a dearth of reasonably priced hotel rooms. For those on unlimited expense accounts, this may be good news. At the top end of the market, it's hard to go wrong. Rooms are pristine, service is impeccable, and multi-lingual staff make you feel you never left home in the first place.

For regular human beings who balk at spending ¥40,000 per night or more, there are reasonably priced options, but even these will rarely set you back less than ¥10,000 per night. For this sort of money, you're either looking at a soulless business hotel or a *ryokan* (Japanese inn) in one of the less fashionable parts of town.

People staying for longer than a few days may find one of the long-term options given at the end of this chapter to be worthwhile. By opting to stay in a one-room apartment you may forsake room service, but with prices from ¥70,000 per month, you'll also be saving cash.

Whatever your budget, the area you stay in will be crucial to how much you enjoy Tokyo. Before choosing a hotel, have a look at the rest of this book and decide which area best suits. If you're here for business, Shinjuku will do you proud. Historical sightseeing? Ueno. Nightlife? Roppongi. Shopping? Shibuya. And so on…

Types of hotel

Deluxe
Most top hotels offer western-style rooms; some also offer a pricier Japanese-style room. Since these hotels offer every possible convenience, we do not list their services separately.

Business hotels
Designed with commercial travellers in mind. A step down in quality and service, they offer value for money, though rooms are often small.

Ryokan
Staying at a *ryokan*, or Japanese-style inn, is one of the best ways to enhance your enjoyment of Tokyo. The Japanese-style accommodation means there will be *tatami* (woven straw mats)

Swim way above sea level at the **Park Hyatt**. *See p33*.

on the floor, and futons, not beds. Most *ryokan* are happy to accommodate several guests in one room, bringing down the price per head. For more on *ryokan*, *see p44* **Ryokan rules**.

Capsule hotels

Drunk? Lost? Missed the last train and can't raise the mortgage for a taxi? Join the throng at a capsule hotel, where small tubes, complete with TV, provide a suitably *Star Trek* sleeping experience. Most capsule hotels are men only.

Deluxe

Shinjuku

Century Hyatt Tokyo

2-7-2 Nishi-Shinjuku, Shinjuku-ku (3349 0111/fax 3344 5575/www.centuryhyatt.co.jp/en/menu.html). Shinjuku station. **Rooms** 766. **Rates** ¥23,000-¥26,000 single; ¥32,000-¥36,000 double; ¥32,000-¥36,000 Regency Club double; ¥70,000-¥400,000 suite. **Credit** AmEx, DC, JCB, MC, €$£TC, V. **Map** 1a.

This red-brick-effect hotel stands out from the forest of hotels and tower blocks around it because it's so ugly. Still, it is one of the city's most prestigious hotels and the splendid modern interior more than makes up for the aesthetic shortcomings of the exterior. The standards of accommodation and service are both flawless. For those with too much money, there's the Regency Club, a hotel within a hotel, with bigger rooms, individual service, a lounge and more.

Keio Plaza Intercontinental

2-2-1 Nishi-Shinjuku, Shinjuku-ku (3344 0111/fax 3345 8269/www.keioplaza.co.jp). Shinjuku station. **Rooms** 1,450. **Rates** ¥18,500-¥20,000 single; ¥26,000-¥39,000 double; ¥80,000-¥250,000 suite. **Credit** AmEx, DC, JCB, MC, €$£TC, V. **Map** 1a.

One of the first hotels in west Shinjuku, this one is now starting to look its age. Some may find the '70s interior charmingly retro, but whether that charm is strong enough to make up for the shortcomings in the smallish rooms is another matter. Still, service is fabulous, as are the views from the 47th-floor bars. An executive centre offers support for business folk.

Park Hyatt

3-7-1-2 Nishi-Shinjuku, Shinjuku-ku (5322 1234/fax 5322 1288/www.parkhyatttokyo.com). Shinjuku station. **Rooms** 178. **Rates** ¥49,000-¥60,000 double; ¥94,000-¥500,000 suite. **Credit** AmEx, DC, JCB, MC, €$£TC, V. **Map** 1a.

If you're spending this sort of money, you're entitled to something special. The Park Hyatt delivers in spades. Reception, on the 41st floor, towers over the city, and floor-to-ceiling windows ensure you don't miss the view. Every room, too, has its own view, and decor throughout is pleasantly subdued. All rooms have their own laserdisc player, and guests have free use of a film library. It's the most popular hotel in town with those on expenses, so book ahead, and watch the night descend over Tokyo from the 47th-floor gym.

Tokyo Hilton

6-6-2 Nishi-Shinjuku, Shinjuku-ku (3344 5111/fax 3342 6094/www.hilton.co.jp). Shinjuku station. **Rooms** 807. **Rates** ¥29,000 single; ¥35,000 double; ¥35,000 executive floor single; ¥41,000 executive floor double; ¥50,000 or ¥90,000 Japanese-style room; ¥70,000-¥240,000 suite. **Credit** AmEx, DC, JCB, MC, €$£TC, V. **Map** 1a.

The best Hotels

For party animals and rock stars

It's got to be the **Roppongi Prince Hotel** (*see p38*), with its central open-air pool that's just perfect for making a splash with that colour TV.

For chic modern style in a chic modern setting

With its astronomical prices, you may be paying for a stay at the **Park Hyatt** (*see p33*) for the rest of your life, but it's certainly an experience you won't forget.

For unadulterated luxury in a quiet setting

The **Four Seasons at Chinzan-so** (*see p36*) comes with its own ancient garden, littered with equally ancient statues. A byword in urban extravagance with the feel of the countryside.

For those on a budget

Centrally located, with a light, bright atmosphere, the **Sakura Hotel** (*see p45*) takes this category, just ahead of the **Kimi Ryokan** (*see p45*).

To write that masterpiece

Do as the Japanese do, and polish off that novel at the **Hilltop Hotel** (*see p39*). Novelist Mishima Yukio stayed here shortly before killing himself, but countless others have lived to tell the tale and get published.

For the full Japanese experience

Homeikan Daimachibekkan (*see p42*) looks and smells exactly like a Japanese *ryokan* should. A bit out of the way, but well worth the walk.

For history on your doorstep

The **Ryokan Shigetsu** in Asakusa (*see p42*) takes the prize: it's barely five strides away from Tokyo's biggest tourist attraction, the Asakusa temple complex.

Room at the top: the **Tokyo Hilton**. *See p33.*

The Hilton, an architecturally unremarkable building, opened in 1984. Rooms are a good size, although the views, often blocked by other towers, can be disappointing. For business travellers, the hotel offers five executive floors, with separate check-in, a fax machine in each room and their own guest-relations officers. You can even get married here – in either a Christian or Shinto chapel – and have the reception in the 1,100-capacity banqueting suite or one of 17 smaller private function rooms.

Roppongi & Akasaka

Akasaka Prince Hotel

1-2 Kioi-cho, Chiyoda-ku (3234 1111/fax 3262 5163/www.princehotels.co.jp). Akasaka Mitsuke/ Kojimachi/Nagatacho station. **Rooms** 761.
Rates ¥27,000-¥36,000 single; ¥34,000-¥42,000 double; ¥39,000-¥43,000 business suite; ¥100,000-¥120,000 Japanese/western suite. **Credit** AmEx, DC, JCB, MC, €$£TC, V. **Map** 10.
The 40-storey Akasaka Prince main building is designed, by award-winning architect Kenzo Tange, to remind the viewer of a Japanese folding screen. It stands at the centre of a complex that includes a convention centre, a European-style guesthouse and a banqueting building. The main tower is very overstated '80s, all glitter, marble and bright lights. The stepped 'folding screen' design means that every room manages to occupy a corner.

ANA Hotel Tokyo

1-12-33 Akasaka, Minato-ku (3505 1111/fax 3505 1155/www.anahotels.com). Tameike Sanno station. **Rooms** 900. **Rates** ¥24,000-¥26,000 single; ¥32,000-¥37,000 double; ¥60,000-¥280,000 suite. **Credit** AmEx, DC, JCB, MC, €$£TC, V. **Map** 4.

Ten minutes on foot from the nightlife of Roppongi stands this 15-year-old glamourpuss. At the foot of its 29 storeys is the Ark Hills complex, a shopping, restaurant and office building, or series of buildings, that also contains one of Tokyo's premier classical music venues, Suntory Hall. As with many Tokyo hotels from the '80s, the interior dazzles with a vast marble and gold entrance hall and lobby. The price of the spacious, well-equipped rooms rises the higher in the hotel you go: on a clear day, from the open-air pool at the top, you can see Mount Fuji.

Capitol Tokyu

2-10-3 Nagatacho, Chiyoda-ku (3581 4511/fax 3581 5822/www.capitoltokyu.com). Kokkaigijido-mae/Tameike-Sanno stations. **Rooms** 459.
Rates ¥23,000-¥37,500 single; ¥35,500-¥55,000 double; ¥90,000-¥380,000 suite. **Credit** AmEx, DC, JCB, MC, €£$¥TC, V. **Map** 7.
The Capitol Tokyu opened one year ahead of the 1964 Tokyo Olympics, and like other hotels of the era, it blends the best of Japanese design and style with western influences; with wood panelling and dim lighting, it retains an old-fashioned charm. Refurbishment, begun in 2000, is bringing facilities up to date, with an optical fibre network bringing Internet access into every room via the TV. One of the hotel's best features is its location: close enough to the centre to be interesting, yet isolated enough, overlooking the Hie Shrine, for quiet. Rooms are spacious and well equipped, with nice Japanese touches such as paper screens in the windows.

Hotel New Otani

4-1 Kioi-cho, Chiyoda-ku (3265 1111/fax 3221 2619/ www.newotani.co.jp). Akasaka Mitsuke or Nagatacho station. **Rooms** 1,600. **Rates** ¥28,500 single; ¥30,000-¥49,000 double; ¥70,000-¥180,000 suite.
Credit AmEx, DC, JCB, MC, $£TC, V. **Map** 10.
The New Otani and its associated designer-label shopping mall occupy a tract of land in a peaceful area of Akasaka. From the outside, the building bears the unattractive hallmarks of its 1969 construction, but inside the dim lighting and spacious foyers produce the feeling of an ocean liner. To the rear of the hotel there's a lovingly tended Japanese garden, the remnants of an ancient garden that was a bequest to one of his generals by Shogun Ieyasu Tokugawa four centuries ago. In it stand several of the hotel's 34 restaurants. Capacity was increased in 1979 by the addition of a 40-storey tower.

Hotel Okura

2-10-4 Toranomon, Minato-ku (3582 0111/fax 3582 3707/www.okura.com). Roppongi-Itchome station. **Rooms** 858. **Rates** ¥28,500-¥41,000 single; ¥32,000-¥57,000 double; ¥75,000-¥500,000 suite.
Credit AmEx, DC, JCB, MC, €$£TC, V. **Map** 4.
The Okura opened in 1962, and its interior, like that of the Capitol Tokyu (*see p34*), is a reminder of that time, reflecting both classical Japanese traditions and a western influence. In 2000, it underwent refurbishment, ending a near 40-year tradition of offering Japanese rooms, and extending coverage of

faxes, dataports and Internet TV to all rooms. The location, opposite the American Embassy and a ten-minute walk from the business district, has long made the hotel a favourite of politicians and businessmen. Locals come for the restaurants, all nine of which are highly regarded.

Ginza & Imperial Palace

Dai-ichi Hotel Tokyo

1-2-6 Shinbashi, Minato-ku (3501 4411/fax 3595 2634/www.daiichihotel-Tokyo.com). Shinbashi station. **Rooms** 275. **Rates** ¥27,000-¥38,000 single; ¥34,000-¥48,000 double; ¥80,000-¥350,000 suite. **Credit** AmEx, DC, JCB, MC, €$£¥TC, V. **Map 20.**
The group that owns this hotel, built in 1993, went bankrupt in 2000, and the hotel is currently run by administrators, with, they say, no loss of quality. The interior is a mix of styles, the entrance hall an echo of old European luxury, but the rooms are superb, a good size and beautifully decorated, with high ceilings. The selection of Japanese and foreign restaurants is a tribute to the designers' ability to cram many different styles of decor into one building. Another Dai-ichi hotel, the Ginza Dai-ichi, is a little cheaper and a five minute walk away (3542 5311). **Branches**: all over Tokyo.

Hotel Seiyo Ginza

1-11-2 Ginza, Chuo-ku (3535 1111/fax 3535 1110/ www.seiyo-ginza.com). Kyobashi station. **Rooms** 72. **Rates** ¥42,000-¥55,000 double; ¥65,000-¥125,000 one-bedroom suite; ¥110,000-¥175,000 two-bedroom suite; ¥200,000 premier suite. **Credit** AmEx, DC, JCB, MC, €£$TC, V. **Map 6.**

Well located in an area that straddles the finance district and Tokyo's premier shopping district, Ginza, the Seiyo is a boutique-style modern hotel that combines great service with antique drawing room-style decor. The hotel prides itself on its personal services: business travellers, for example, benefit from a personal secretarial service. All rooms come with their own stereo, fax and video-on-demand service. The marble bathroom suites in all rooms are magnificent, while some bathrooms also offer a steam bath. All rooms are spacious.

Imperial Hotel

1-1-1 Uchisawaicho, Chiyoda-ku (3504 1111/fax 3581 9146/www.imperialhotel.co.jp). Hibiya/JR Yurakucho station. **Rooms** 1,059. **Rates** ¥30,000-¥56,000 single; ¥35,000-¥61,000 double; ¥60,000-¥800,000 suite. **Credit** AmEx, DC, JCB, MC, €$£¥TC, V. **Map 6.**
The Imperial makes you aware of its history straight away, with uniformed attendants and an atrium that serves as one of Tokyo's favourite meeting places for businesspeople. In a fit of '60s shortsightedness, Frank Lloyd Wright's 1923 building was demolished, replaced by the current 1970 building, already starting to show its age. The relatively small rooms and cramped feel of the corridors is attributable to the period, although service remains impeccable.

Palace Hotel

1-1-1 Marunouchi, Chiyoda-ku (3211 5211/fax 3211 6987/www.palacehotel.co.jp). Otemachi/Tokyo stations. **Rooms** 391. **Rates** ¥24,000-¥29,000 single; ¥29,000-¥41,000 double; ¥56,000 business suite; ¥100,000-¥380,000 suite. **Credit** AmEx, DC, JCB, MC, €£$TC, V. **Map 8.**

The newly refurbished **Capitol Tokyu**. *See p34.*

Austere yet hip, the 40-year-old **Hotel Okura**. *See p34.*

Another '70s monolith, perched on the edge of the Imperial Palace moat, the Palace has neither the reputation nor the easy opulence of its near neighbour, the Imperial. Some people may find that the views over the moat from some rooms make up for this, but many will be disappointed with the gloomy feeling that emanates from the decor. Non-residents can take in the view from the Crown Bar on the top floor.

Elsewhere

Four Seasons at Chinzan-so

2-10-8 Sekiguchi, Bunkyo-ku (3943 2222/fax 3943 2300/www.fourseasons-tokyo.com). Mejiro station, then 61 bus. **Rooms** 264. **Rates** ¥42,000-¥44,000 single; ¥47,000-¥49,000 double; ¥65,000-¥500,000 suite. **Credit** AmEx, DC, JCB, MC, €$£¥TC, V. **Map** 22.

For many, this hotel, out in the wilds of northern Tokyo, vies with the Park Hyatt (*see p33*) for the right to be called the best in town. What makes this place so great is the attention to detail. Iced tea, for example, is served with ice cubes made of tea, so as

Hidden extras

The more expensive the hotel you stay at in Tokyo, the more unpleasant surprises are likely to be loaded on to your bill. In most top-notch places, a service charge of ten per cent will already be factored into your room rate, although this can vary. All hotels will add the standard five per cent tax to your bill, and if your bill, including service charges, comes to more than ¥15,000 per night, you will be liable to an additional three per cent local tax.

not to dilute the drink. The building is splendid, light and airy, set in a beautiful Japanese garden littered with statues from Nara and Kamakura. Rooms are generously proportioned, and while there's not much to do locally of an evening you might prefer to while the time away in the hotel's own spa and gym, which comes complete with outdoor pool.

Hotel Inter-Continental Tokyo Bay

1-16-2 Kaigan, Minato-ku (5404 2222/fax 5404 2111/www.interconti.co.jp). Takeshiba (Yurikamome line) or Hamamatsucho station. **Rooms** 339. **Rates** ¥35,000-¥38,000 double; ¥100,000-¥300,000 suite. **Credit** AmEx, DC, JCB, MC, V €$¥TC.

The Inter-Continental opened in 1995 in the frankly unattractive area that fronts Tokyo's Sumida River; the luxurious hotel and the adjoining New Pier Takeshiba shopping and dining complex stand out like a diamond in a cow pat. Location is the hotel's main shortcoming, but its main selling point is the view, over the river and the spectacular Rainbow Bridge, to the recently developed area of Odaiba. All rooms, and their bathrooms, have a view of the river, although half face upstream towards unpicturesque wharves. The Inter-Continental offers a four-floor 'hotel within a hotel', Club Inter-Continental, which offers separate check-in and business services.

Le Meridien Grand Pacific

2-6-1 Daiba, Minato-ku (5500 6711/www.htl-pacific.co.jp). Daiba station (Yurikamome line). **Rooms** 884. **Rates** ¥23,000 single; ¥31,000-¥48,000 double; ¥70,000-¥400,000 suite. **Credit** AmEx, DC, JCB, MC, €$£¥TC, V.

Luxury hotels simply do not come much more self-consciously opulent than this. The Meridien opened in 1998 on the new island area of Odaiba and boasts spectacular views over Rainbow Bridge and the Tokyo skyline (rooms with a view are extra). The drawback is that it's in, or on, Odaiba, a great place for a day out but inconvenient as a base. As if aware of the lack of local character, the hotel supplies some of its own, in the form of an art gallery on the third floor and a museum of music boxes on the second. Even if you don't stay here, stop by the Sky Lounge on the 30th floor for one of the best views over Tokyo and the bay. Check out the banquet room on the 29th floor: Victorian railway station meets Versailles palace.

Royal Park Hotel

2-1-1 Nihonbashi-Kakigara-cho, Chuo-ku (3667 1111/fax 3667 1115/www.royalparkhotels.co.jp). Suitengumae station. **Rooms** 450. **Rates** ¥22,000-¥39,000 single; ¥30,000-¥43,000 double; ¥80,000-¥230,000 suite. **Credit** AmEx, DC, JCB, MC, €$£¥TC, V.

A true luxury hotel in a truly unappealing position, the Royal Park does most of its business with travelling businesspeople, for whom the Nihonbashi address, in the middle of Tokyo's business district, is a bonus. The lobby evokes a certain tranquillity by means of its curious waterfall. The hotel will occasionally make an attempt to entice non-business types with special themed months in its restaurants and bars. Air travellers may wish to note that the Royal Park is right next door to T-CAT, the city-centre check-in service (*see p258*). Rooms are spacious and well equipped, and executives can pay a ¥4,000 premium to upgrade their accommodation to executive standard, which includes in-room fax machine, free translation and interpretation, and cocktails.

Hotel inter-Continental Tokyo Bay. *See p36.*

The Westin Tokyo

1-4-1 Mita, Meguro-ku (5423 7000/fax 5423 7600/ www.westin.co.jp). Ebisu station. **Rooms** 444. **Rates** ¥42,000-¥49,000 single; ¥47,000-¥54,000 double; ¥100,000, ¥150,000, ¥400,000 suite. **Credit** AmEx, DC, JCB, MC, €$£¥TC, V. **Map** 3.

The Westin opened in 1994 with a mission to become one of Tokyo's great hotels. Its location, close to Ebisu and Shibuya and with great shopping and museums below, wins half the battle for it. Rooms are palatial and feature soft lighting and antique-style furniture. The hotel towers over most buildings around it, so a view is pretty much guaranteed. For a premium of ¥12,000, the Westin Executive Club offers superior accommodation, free breakfast, cocktails and use of the fitness club.

Expensive

Asakusa

Asakusa View Hotel

3-17-1 Nishi Asakusa, Taito-ku (3847 1111/fax 3842 2117/www.viewhotels.co.jp/asakusa). Tawaramachi station. **Rooms** 333. **Rates** ¥13,000-¥18,000 single; ¥21,000-¥31,000 double; ¥40,000-¥63,000 Japanese style; ¥50,000-¥300,000 suite. **Credit** AmEx, DC, JCB, MC, £$¥TC, V. **Map** 13.

Towering over ancient Asakusa, this 28-storey hotel is smaller and more compact than many of Tokyo's upmarket hotels. For those who want a little luxury with their history, this is the only choice in the area. If you want to make the hotel live up to its name, go as high up as you can: the view over Asakusa and the Sumida River is worth catching. If the hotel is beyond your budget, the Belvedere lounge on the 28th floor offers the chance to take in the view over a drink. The sixth floor is given over to Japanese-style rooms, creating a sort of *ryokan* within a hotel. **Hotel services** *Air-conditioning. Bars (3). Beauty salon. Conference facilities. Fax. Fitness centre. Karaoke room. Laundry. Multilingual staff. No-smoking rooms. Parking (¥1,000). Pharmacy. Restaurants (6). Safe. Shopping arcade. Swimming pool. Wedding chapels (2).* **Room services** *Hairdryer. Ironing facilities (on request). Minibar. Modem line. Radio. Room service (6am-2am). Satellite TV. Tea (Japanese).*

Shinjuku

Shinjuku Prince Hotel

1-30-1 Kabuki-cho, Shinjuku-ku (3205 1111/fax 3205 1952/www.princehotels.co.jp). Shinjuku station. **Rooms** 571. **Rates** ¥16,000 single; ¥18,000 double; ¥28,000, ¥32,000 twin. **Credit** AmEx, JCB, MC, V €£$TC. **Map** 1b.

Japan's Prince chain prides itself on the appearance of its hotels, and Tokyo has some beauties, notably in Akasaka and Roppongi. This is the ugly duckling, a red-brick monstrosity above the Shinjuku terminus of the Seibu-Shinjuku rail line. If you can live with the outside, though, it represents value for money, with fine service and facilities and a great location, especially for night owls, on the doorstep of the Kabuki-cho entertainment area of Shinjuku. Rooms (western style) are smallish and minimally furnished but clean. Great views over the neon forest from the 25th-floor Châtelaine French restaurant.

Branches: all over Tokyo.
Hotel services *Air-conditioning. Bar. Conference rooms (2). Fax. Laundry. Multilingual staff. No-smoking floor. Parking (¥2,000) Restaurants (8). Safe. Shopping centre. Pool.* **Room services** *Cable TV. Hairdryer. Minibar. Safe. Room service (11am-midnight).*

Shinjuku Washington Hotel

3-2-9 Nishi-Shinjuku, Shinjuku-ku (3343 3111/ fax 3342 2575/www.wh-rsv.com). Shinjuku station.
Rooms 1,638. **Rates** ¥11,300-14,500 single; ¥17,000-¥24,000 double; ¥26,500-¥30,000 triple; ¥30,000 deluxe twin. **Credit** AmEx, DC, JCB, MC, $TC, V.
Map 1a.
A step down in price and luxury from many of the hotels surrounding it, the Washington nevertheless offers high standards of accommodation and service. Its main target market is businessmen, so rooms tend to be small and bland, but efficiently furnished. For frequent visitors, there's an automatic check-in and -out service. The new annex contains 337 of the 1,638 rooms, and is slightly pricier.
Branch: Akihabara Washington Hotel, 1-8-3 Sakuma-cho, Kanda, Chiyoda-ku (3255 3311).
Hotel services *Air-conditioning. Bar (2). Beauty salons. Conference facilities. Fax. Laundry. Multilingual staff. No-smoking rooms. Parking. Pharmacy. Restaurants (7). Safe. Travel agent.* **Room services** *Cable TV. Hairdryer. Light meals. Minibar. Radio. Tea (Japanese). Trouser press. Voicemail.*

Roppongi & Akasaka

Akasaka Tokyu Hotel

2-14-3 Nagatacho Chiyoda-ku (3580 2311/fax 3580 6066). Akasaka-mitsuke station. **Rooms** 535. **Rates** ¥15,000-¥22,000 single; ¥28,000 double; ¥80,000-¥150,000 suite. **Credit** AmEx, DC, JCB, MC, $£€TC, V. **Map** 7.
In an area dominated by luxury hotels – ANA Hotel Tokyo, Capitol Tokyu, Akasaka Prince Hotel (for all, *see p34*) – the pink-and-white striped Akasaka Tokyu is a step downmarket. In reality, it's a slightly superior business hotel, with reasonably sized rooms and a great location near the Hie shrine.
Branches: Capitol Tokyu (*see p34*); Tokyo Bay Hotel Tokyu, 1-7 Maihama, Urayasu-shi, Chiba-ken (0473 55 2411); Haneda Tokyu, 2-8-6 Haneda Airport, Ota-ku (3747 0311).
Hotel services *Air-conditioning. Babysitting (by arrangement). Bar. Business services. Conference facilities. Currency exchange. Fax. Laundry. Multilingual staff. No-smoking rooms (20). Parking (¥1,000/day). Restaurant. Safe.* **Room services** *Cable TV. Hairdryer. Minibar. Modem line. Radio. Room service (7am-midnight). Tea (Japanese).*

Roppongi Prince Hotel

3-2-7 Roppongi, Minato-ku (3587 1111/fax 3587 0770/www.princehotels.co.jp). Roppongi station.
Rooms 216. **Rates** ¥19,500 single; ¥24,500-¥26,500 double; ¥50,000-¥60,000 suite. **Credit** AmEx, DC, JCB, MC, £$€TC, V. **Map** 4.
This unusual building was designed around a perspex-sided open-air swimming pool, heated to 30°C. It's reminiscent of something from a Spanish holiday brochure but better situated, five minutes from the nightlife of Roppongi. The rooms are well furnished, with just enough of a hint of the interior designer about them to remind you you're staying somewhere special. A favourite with visiting rock stars.
Hotel services *Air-conditioning. Bar. Business services. Conference facilities. Currency exchange. Fax. Laundry. Multilingual staff. No-smoking floor. Restaurants (4). Safe. Swimming pool (outdoor).* **Room services** *Cable TV. Hairdryer. Modem line. Radio. Room service (7am-midnight).*

Booking from abroad

Hotels and *ryokan* in Tokyo and the rest of Japan can be booked from abroad, or in Japan, via the following organisations:

Hotel Hotline

http://jgl.biglobe.ne.jp/english/
This Internet-led service offers substantial discounts – up to ¥10,000 per night – on standard rates at many top hotels, including the Imperial Hotel (*see p35*) and the Park Hyatt (*see p33*). Reservations can also be made by fax (3433 8388).

Japanese Inn Group

http://members.aol.com/jinngroup
Japanese Inn Group specialises in providing *ryokan* accommodation all over Japan, and produces a leaflet of its inns, available free from Tourist Information Centres (TIC; *see p271*).

Welcome Inns

www.jnto.go.jp
Run by the Japan National Tourist Organisation, this offers both *ryokan* and western-style accommodation for under ¥8,000 per person per night. A free booklet is available from TIC (*see p271*), and reservations can be made in person at a TIC, by fax (3211 9009) or by e-mail via the website. Many Welcome Inns hotels also feature in the Japanese Inn Group pamphlet.

Ginza & Imperial Palace

Ginza Renaissance Tobu Hotel

6-14-10 Ginza, Chuo-ku (3546 0111/fax 3546 8990). Higashi-Ginza station. **Rooms** 206. **Rates** ¥17,000-¥30,000 single; ¥28,000-¥35,000 double; ¥60,000-¥200,000 suite. **Credit** AmEx, DC, JCB, MC, £$¥TC, V. **Map** 6.

Located a stone's throw from Ginza's Kabuki-za, the Renaissance is an unprepossessing building whose main interior motif is shiny and golden. This may explain its popularity as a venue for young couples tieing the knot. The rooms are comfortable in a functional, bland sort of way, and service is good.
Hotel services *Air-conditioning. Babysitting (by arrangement). Bars (2). Beauty salon. Business services. Conference facilities. Currency exchange. Fax. Laundry. Multilingual staff. Parking (¥1,000/day). Restaurants (2). Safe. Wedding chapels (2).* **Room services** *Cable TV. Hairdryer. Minibar. Modem line. Radio. Room service (6.30am-midnight). Tea (Japanese). Voicemail.*

Mitsui Urban Hotel

6-15-8 Ginza, Chuo-ku (3572 4131/fax 3572 4254/www.mitsuikanko.co.jp). Shinbashi station. **Rooms** 265. **Rates** ¥14,000-¥17,000 single; ¥21,000-¥30,000 double. **Credit** AmEx, DC, JCB, MC, £$¥TC, V. **Map** 6.

Opened in 1978, the Mitsui was refurbished in the late 1990s and remains an unassuming, practical choice on the edge of Ginza. Rooms are small and basic, and the relative lack of facilities is reflected in the prices. Reception is on the second floor.
Hotel services *Air-conditioning. Bar. Currency exchange. Fax. Laundry. Multilingual staff. No-smoking floor. Parking (¥1,000/day). Safe.* **Room services** *Cable/satellite TV. Hairdryer. Ironing facilities (on request). Minibar. Modem line. Radio. Room service (night only). Tea (Japanese).*

Elsewhere

Arimax

11-15 Kamiyamacho, Shibuya-ku (5454 1122/fax 3460 6513). Shibuya station. **Rates** ¥18,000-¥27,000 single; ¥23,000-¥28,000 double; ¥28,000-¥30,000 family rooms; ¥30,000-¥46,200 suite. **Credit** AmEx, DC, JCB, MC, V. **Map** 2.

With just 23 rooms, the Arimax is a tiny hotel by Tokyo standards, situated around the corner from the headquarters of Japan's state broadcaster, NHK. Modelled on European boutique hotels, the Arimax offers a choice of English or neo-Classical styles and exudes the atmosphere of a gentlemen's club, with warm, dim lighting and wood panelling the dominant decorative themes. The fourth and fifth floors host the private, members-only Arimax Club. Another favourite with visiting rock stars.
Hotel services *Bar. Conference room. Fax. Laundry. Parking (free). Restaurant. Safe.* **Room services** *Cable TV. Radio. Modem line. Ironing facilities (on request). Hairdryer. Minibar. Tea (Japanese).*

Hilltop Hotel

1-1 Kanda-Surugadai, Chiyoda-ku (3293 2311/fax 3233 4567/www.yamanoue-hotel.co.jp). Ochanomizu station. **Rooms** 75. **Rates** ¥15,000-¥18,000 single; ¥22,000-¥25,000 double; ¥40,000-¥50,000 suite. **Credit** AmEx, DC, JCB, MC, $¥TC, V. **Map** 15.

One of the few hotels to exude old world charm, the Hilltop is a celebrated haunt of Japan's writers and intellectuals. To that end, each room comes complete with a beautiful antique writing desk, and to aid the thought processes, negatively charged air ions are pumped into each and every room. Some rooms have their own miniature garden. The basement wine bar is as celebrated as the hotel, and boasts a cosy atmosphere and a reliable list of wines.
Hotel services *Air-conditioning. Babysitting (by arrangement). Bars (3). Beauty salon. Conference facilities. Currency exchange. Fax. Japanese/western rooms. Laundry. Multilingual staff. Parking (¥1,000/day). Restaurants (7). Safe. Wedding chapel.* **Room services** *Hairdryer. Ironing facilities (on request). Minibar. Modem line. Radio. Room service (7am-2am). Satellite TV. Tea (Japanese) in room.*

Hotel Sofitel Tokyo

2-1-48 Ikenohata, Taito-ku (5685 7111/fax 5685 6171/www.sofiteltokyo.com). Yushima station. **Rooms** 83. **Rates** ¥24,000-¥35,000 single; ¥30,000 double; ¥50,000-¥90,000 suite. **Credit** AmEx, DC, JCB, MC, €£$¥TC, V. **Map** 14.

This extraordinary building overlooking Ueno Park was completed in 1994 and looks like a series of pyramids stacked one on top of the other. In 2000, the hotel reopened after extensive refurbishment under the aegis of French designer Pierre Yves Rochon. The result is a European feel to the place, which carries through from the remodelled lobby to the brand-new restaurant, Provence. Rooms are comfortable and larger than average. The water tanks in the roof of the hotel are programmed to counterbalance the building in the event of an earthquake.
Hotel services *Air-conditioning. Bar. Business services. Conference facilities. Currency exchange. Fax. Laundry. Multilingual staff. No-smoking rooms (12). Parking (¥1,500/day). Restaurants (3). Safe.* **Room services** *Hairdryer. Ironing facilities (on request). Minibar. Modem line. Room service (24hrs). Satellite TV. Tea (Japanese)/coffee in room.*

Le Meridien Pacific Tokyo

3-13-3 Takanawa, Minato-ku (3445 6711/fax 3445 5733). Shinagawa station. **Rooms** 954. **Rates** ¥21,000-¥25,500 single; ¥25,000-¥33,000 double; ¥50,000-¥300,000 suite. **Credit** AmEx, DC, JCB, MC, €£$TC, V. **Map** 21.

This 1971 monolith benefits from a pleasant garden that gives it a sense of space that many Tokyo hotels lack. It looks its age from the outside, but within it is immaculate. Rooms are of a good size and a constant modernisation means facilities are up to date. For those on package deals or long stopovers, the Meridien is one of the hotels most commonly chosen by travel agents. The Sky lounge on the 30th floor offers cabaret and views over the city.

Hotel services *Air-conditioning. Bars (4). Beauty salons. Business services. Conference facilities. Currency exchange. Fax. Laundry. Multilingual staff. No-smoking rooms. Parking (free). Restaurants (6). Safe. Swimming pool (summer only). Wedding chapels (2).* **Room services** *Cable TV. Hairdryer. Ironing facilities (on request). Minibar. Modem line. Radio. Room service (6.30am-1am). Tea/coffee in room.*

New Takanawa Prince Hotel

3-13-1 Takanawa, Minato-ku (3442 1111/fax3444 1234/www.princehotels.co.jp). Shinagawa station. **Rooms** 946 (New Takanawa Prince) + 309 (Sakura Tower) + 414 (Takanawa Prince). **Rates** ¥25,000 single; ¥31,000-¥37,000 double; ¥70,000-¥85,000 suite. **Credit** AmEx, DC, JCB, MC, £¥TC, V. **Map** 21.
The Prince chain is owned by the Seibu corporation, which bought much of the ground on which its hotels are built when Japanese princes were stripped of their lands during the American occupation. Here, there are three Prince hotels – the Takanawa Prince, the Sakura Tower and the New Takanawa Prince – which operate as separate hotels, with separate tariffs, but which are linked by glorious landscaped grounds; guests at one hotel may use the facilities of another. The Takanawa Prince is the oldest and has a reassuring elegance. The New Takanawa Prince is gaudy from the outside, but impressive within, while the Sakura Tower, a pink monster, offers the newest facilities and priciest rooms. The European-style house in which the dispossessed prince originally lived is now the hotels' Kihinkan guesthouse, where foreign dignitaries and businessmen are entertained. Hotel services *Air-conditioning. Babysitting (by arrangement). Bars (6). Beauty salons (3). Bridal salon. Business services. Conference facilities. Convenience stores (2). Currency exchange. Disabled: access; toilets. Fax. Fitness centre. Japanese/western rooms. Laundry. Multilingual staff. No-smoking rooms. Parking (free). Restaurants (13). Safe. Station shuttle bus. Swimming pools (3) (summer only). Wedding chapels (3).* **Room services** *Cable TV. Hairdryer. Ironing facilities (on request). Minibar. Modem line. Radio. Room service (24 hours). Rooms adapted for disabled (2). Tea/coffee. Voicemail.*

Moderate

Shinjuku

New City Hotel

4-31-1 Nishi-Shinjuku, Shinjuku-ku (3375 6511/fax 3375 6535). JR Shinjuku station. **Rooms** 400. **Rates** ¥8,000-¥11,000 single; ¥15,000 double; ¥14,300-¥16,600 twin; ¥18,000 triple. **Credit** AmEx, DC, JCB, MC, V. **Map** 1a.
A poor relation of the skyscraper hotels in west Shinjuku, the New City does offer spectacular views from some rooms. The interior has seen better days, but is clean and comfortable. A plus is the natural hot spring bath and sauna. The hotel is popular with Japanese visitors, less so with foreign tourists, so don't expect much English from the staff.

Hotel services *Air-conditioning. Bar. Conference facilities. Fax. Laundry. Multilingual staff. No-smoking rooms. Parking (¥1,500/24hrs). Restaurant. Safe. Station shuttle bus.* **Room services** *Hairdryer. Ironing facilities. Modem line. Radio. Tea (Japanese). TV.*

Shinjuku Palace Hotel

2-8-12 Kabuki-cho, Shinjuku-ku (3209 1231). Shinjuku station. **Rooms** 34. **Rates** ¥6,700-¥6,800 single; ¥9,800 double; ¥10,500 twin. **No credit cards. Map** 1b.
This business hotel in the heart of Shinjuku's nightlife centre, Kabuki-cho, offers basic accommodation aimed at local businessmen or salarymen who've stayed one drink too long and missed the last train home. Still, it's clean and friendly; just don't expect to be able to make much meaningful communication in English. Rooms are small, but with the bars and clubs around you open all night, how much time are you going to spend here anyway?
Hotel services *Air-conditioning. Fax. Japanese-style rooms on request.* **Room services** *Hairdryer. Tea (Japanese). TV.*

Star Hotel Tokyo

7-10-5 Nishi-Shinjuku, Shinjuku-ku (3361 1111/ fax 3369 4216). Shinjuku station. **Rooms** 214. **Rates** ¥9,000-¥11,500 single; ¥17,000-¥18,000 double. **Credit** AmEx, JCB, MC, V. **Map** 1a.
In terms of position, the Star offers everything its more expensive west Shinjuku rivals do; in fact, it's closer to the station than most. It has the sort of decor you expect from a business hotel coupled with the standard of service and facilities offered by a tourist hotel. The gaudy bars and restaurants aren't the sort of places you'd want to hang around in long, but east Shinjuku is just five minutes' walk away.
Hotel services *Air-conditioning. Bars (2). Conference facilities. Fax. Karaoke room. Laundry. Multilingual staff. No-smoking rooms. Parking (¥1,500/night). Restaurant.* **Room services** *Hairdryer. Room service (5-11pm). Trouser press. TV.*

Shibuya

Excel Hotel Tokyu

1-12-2 Dogenzaka, Shibuya-ku (5457 0109/fax 5457 0309/www.tokyu.co.jp/inn). Shibuya station. **Rooms** 408. **Rates** ¥17,000-¥19,000 single; ¥20,000-¥22,000 double; ¥30,000 triple. **Credit** AmEx, JCB, MC, €£$TC, V. **Map** 2.
A new, middle-ranking hotel that opened in autumn 2000 in the Mark City complex attached to Shibuya station. Pleasant, clean, with good-sized rooms offering good views of the city, this hotel is notable for its location, in an area that has long suffered from a shortage of good-quality accommodation.
Hotel services *Air-conditioning. Bar. Restaurants (3). Conference facilities. Fax. Laundry. Disabled access. Parking (¥1,500). Non-smoking rooms. Safe.* **Room services** *Cable/satellite TV. Disabled room. Hairdryer. Ironing facilities. Modem line. Radio. Room service (7-9pm). Video on request. Voicemail.*

Hotel Excellent

1-9-5 Ebisu-nishi, Shibuya-ku (5458 0087/fax 5458 8787). Ebisu station. **Rooms** 127. **Rates** ¥8,700 single; ¥11,000 double; ¥12,500 twin. **Credit** DC, MC, V. **Map** 3.

A basic but very popular business hotel offering no-frills accommodation in functional, intensely unexciting rooms. The main reason for its popularity is its location, one stop away from Shibuya on the Yamanote line and in the heart of Ebisu, which has enough dining and entertainment options to please even the hardest-to-please customers.
Hotel services *Air-conditioning. Bar. Coffee shop. No-smoking floors. Restaurant. Safe. Vending machines.* **Room services** *Cable/satellite TV. Hairdryer. Ironing facilities (on request). Tea (Japanese).*

Roppongi & Akasaka

Hotel Ibis

7-14-4 Roppongi, Minato-ku (3403 4411/fax 3479 0609). Roppongi station. **Rooms** 182. **Rates** ¥11,500-¥16,000 single; ¥14,100-¥23,000 double; ¥36,000 suite. **Credit** AmEx, DC, JCB, MC, $,£,€TC. **Map** 4.

Looking for a place close to the centre of Tokyo's hottest nightlife action? This is the closest hotel to the centre of Roppongi; it's also the cheapest. Luxurious it isn't: furnished in late airport hotel style, the Ibis does its job and not much more. Room size is adequate. If you want more, there are six 'designer' bedrooms. The Ibis can get busy at weekends, when those who've still got cash to spare after a night on the town stay here before catching the train home.
Hotel services *Air-conditioning. Business services. Conference facilities. Currency exchange. Fax. Laundry. Multilingual staff. No-smoking floor. Parking (¥2,100/night). Restaurants (3). Safe. Wedding chapel.* **Room services** *Cable TV. Hairdryer. Ironing facilities. Minibar. Modem line. Radio. Room service. Tea/coffee free on request.*

Ginza & Imperial Palace

Hotel Alcyone

4-14-3 Ginza, Chuo-ku (3541 3621/fax 3541 3263/ www.yin.or.jp/user/syscargo). Higashi Ginza station. **Rooms** 70. **Rates** ¥10,000 single; ¥17,000-¥23,000 double. **Credit** AmEx, DC, JCB, MC, $¥TC, V. **Map** 6.

One of the cheapest places in Ginza, the Alcyone is a superior business hotel that offers many of the services of its more luxurious rivals. The entrance hall and the rooms are clean but betray their '70s origins, although an effort to inject a bit of class has been made in the reproduction furniture. Room size is adequate, but Japanese style is the same price as western, so opt for the former.
Hotel services *Air-conditioning. Conference facilities. Fax. Japanese/western rooms. Laundry. Multilingual staff. Parking (¥1,000/day). Safe. Wedding chapel.* **Room services** *Hairdryer (on request). Ironing facilities (on request). Room service (7am-9.30pm). Tea (Japanese) in room. TV.*

Hotel Ginza Daiei

3-12-1 Ginza, Chuo-ku (3545 1111/fax 3545 1177). Higashi Ginza station. **Rooms** 100. **Rates** ¥11,400-¥13,300 single; ¥15,600-¥20,800 twin. **Credit** AmEx, DC, JCB, MC, V. **Map** 6.

A modern, well-furnished and well-situated hotel that provides a few more comforts than you might expect for the price. Modern-looking rooms are of a good size, with functional pine furniture and inoffensive decor. If you opt for the top price 'Healthy Twin' room, you'll get the bonus of a jet bath.
Hotel services *Air-conditioning. Business services. Conference facilities. Currency exchange ($ only). Fax. Laundry. Multilingual staff. Parking (¥1,000). Safe.* **Room services** *Cable/satellite TV. Hairdryer. Ironing facilities (on request). Minibar. Modem line. Radio. Room service (6pm-midnight).*

Nihonbashi

Kayabacho Pearl Hotel

1-2-5 Shinkawa, Chuo-ku (3553 8080/fax 3555 1849). Kayabacho station. **Rooms** 268. **Rates** ¥8,500-¥8,900 single; ¥11,200 semi-double. **Credit** AmEx, DC, JCB, MC, V. **Map** 8.

So dedicated is this hotel to its business clientele that its largest rooms are semi-doubles. Still, rooms are of a reasonable size, and the location, in the heart of the business district, is convenient for transport. One plus is the canalside location; it may not be pretty, but it makes a change. Convenient for T-CAT air terminal (*see p258*).
Hotel services *Air-conditioning. Business services. Conference facilities. Currency exchange ($ only). Fax. Laundry. Multilingual staff. Parking (¥1,500). Restaurant. Safe.* **Room services** *Hairdryer. Ironing facilities (on request). Modem line. Satellite TV. Tea (Japanese). Video (on request).*

Hotel Kazusaya

4-7-15 Nihonbashi-Honcho, Chuo-ku (3241 1045/fax 3241 1077/www.h-kazusaya.co.jp). Shin-Nihonbashi station. **Rooms** 71. **Rates** ¥8,800-¥9,500 single; ¥12,000-¥14,000 double; ¥11,000-¥16,000 twin; ¥21,000 Japanese-style room (sleeps three). **Credit** AmEx, DC, JCB, MC, ¥TC, V. **Map** 16.

Although there has been a Hotel Kazusaya in Nihonbashi since 1891, you wouldn't think it to look at the exterior of this modern building, in one of the last *shitamachi* (downtown) areas in the heart of Tokyo's business district. Inside, the Kazusaya offers good-sized, functional rooms decorated in pastel shades. Service is obliging, although only minimal English is spoken. If you're not here on business, you might find the area a little too restful.
Hotel services *Air-conditioning. Bar. Conference facilities. Disabled: access; toilets. Fax. Japanese/western rooms. Laundry. Parking (¥2,000/day). Restaurant. Safe.* **Room services** *Free newspapers (morning and evening). Hairdryer (on request). Ironing facilities. Satellite TV. Tea (Japanese).*

Sumisho Hotel

9-14 Nihonbashi-Kobunacho, Chuo-ku (3661 4603/fax 3661 4639/www.sumisho-hotel.co.jp). Ningyocho station. **Rooms** 63. **Rates** ¥7,000 single; ¥11,000-¥13,500 double; ¥13,500 Japanese-style double (extra people ¥3,000 each). **Credit** AmEx, DC, JCB, MC, V. **Map** 8.

Tricky to find, this charming hotel takes an ugly modern Tokyo building and imbues it with something quintessentially Japanese, in this case a pond with slabs for stepping stones, which you need to cross to get to the foyer. Refurbished in 2001, the hotel has managed to retain its charm, and has good facilities and a high level of service, although non-Japanese speakers may find it difficult to make themselves understood. It's convenient for the T-CAT terminal (*see p258*), but there's little else going on. **Hotel services** *Air-conditioning. Conference facilities. Disabled: access; toilets. Fax. Japanese/western rooms. Laundry. Pets by prior arrangement. Restaurant.* **Room services** *Cable/satellite TV. Hairdryer (on request). Ironing facilities (on request). Modem line (on request). Tea (Japanese) in room.*

Asakusa

Hotel Sunroute Asakusa

1-8-5 Kaminarimon, Taito-ku (3847 1511/fax 3847 1509/www.sunroute-asakusa.co.jp). Tawaramachi station. **Rooms** 120. **Rates** ¥7,800-¥8,600 single; ¥13,000-¥17,000 double. **Credit** AmEx, DC, MC, V. **Map** 13.

Small rooms and lack of facilities notwithstanding, this business hotel offers value for money for those determined to sleep in beds rather than on futons. The building itself is so bland and unremarkable there's a danger of walking straight past it: look out for the Jonathan's restaurant sign on the street. This second-floor American-style eaterie doubles as the hotel's restaurant and is open 24 hours a day. **Hotel services** *Air-conditioning. Disabled: access; toilets. Fax. Laundry. Multilingual staff. Parking (¥1,500/day). Restaurant. Safe.* **Room services** *Disabled: adapted rooms. Hairdryer. Minibar. Modem line. Radio. Satellite TV. Tea (Japanese). Telephone message system.*

Ryokan Shigetsu

1-31-11 Asakusa, Taito-ku (3843 2345/fax 3843 2348). Asakusa station. **Rooms** 24. **Rates** ¥7,300-¥8,000 single; ¥14,000-¥15,000 double. **Credit** AmEx, MC, $¥TC, V. **Map** 13.

For the first-time visitor intent on exploring Tokyo's history, this hotel is perfectly located, a 20-second stroll from Asakusa's market and temple complex. It offers comfortable rooms in Japanese and western styles, the latter slightly cheaper. All have their own bathrooms, although there is a Japanese-style communal bath on the top floor with a view over the area. Due to the hotel's size and popularity, booking ahead is recommended, particularly at national holidays. Bookings can be made with the Japanese Inn Group (*see p38* **Booking from abroad**).

Hotel services *Air-conditioning. Currency exchange ($ only). Fax. Japanese/western rooms. Laundry. Multilingual staff. No-smoking floors (2). Restaurant. Safe.* **Room services** *Hairdryer. Ironing facilities (on request). Minibar. Radio. TV. Tea (Japanese).*

Sukeroku No Yado Sadachiyo

2-20-1 Asakusa, Taito-ku (3842 6431/fax 3842 6433). Asakusa/Tawaramachi stations. **Rooms** 22. **Rates** ¥10,300 single; ¥7,900-¥17,500 double. **Credit** AmEx, DC, JCB, MC, V. **Map** 13.

This modern *ryokan* is situated five minutes' walk from Asakusa's temple and pagoda tourist traps. From outside it looks oddly like a European chalet, but within it's pure Japanese, with receptionists shuffling around the desk in *kimono*. Staff are obliging but speak only minimal English. All rooms are Japanese style and come in a variety of sizes, the smallest being just five mats. The communal Japanese baths help make a stay here a memorable, relaxing experience. Rates vary according to season, and there's a ¥3,000 supplement for Fridays or the day before a national holiday. During high season (30 Dec-5 Jan, 7 May-30 June, 15 Sept-30 Nov) rates rise by an average of ¥1,000. Breakfast costs ¥1,500. **Hotel services** *Air-conditioning. Fax. Japanese rooms. Restaurant. Room service (4-10pm). Safe.* **Room services** *Tea (Japanese). TV.*

Ueno

Homeikan Daimachibekkan

5-10-5 Hongo, Bunkyo ku (3811 1181/fax 3811 1764/www1.odn.ne.jp/homeikan/info_e.html). Hongosanchome station. **Rooms** 57. **Rates** ¥6,400 single; ¥11,200 double (special long-stay rate available). **Credit** AmEx, DC, JCB, MC, ¥TC, UC, V.

Given the scarcity of old buildings in Tokyo, this highly traditional Japanese inn, hidden deep in otherwise anonymous back streets, is a real find. With a small ornamental garden at the front and a reception area redolent of old wood and polish, Homeikan is the genuine article. Even the slightly tatty furniture is part of the charm. The *ryokan* is divided into two buildings that face each other across the street, while the branch is a five-minute walk away. A drawback is its location, 20 minutes' walk from the action around Ueno or Ochanomizu stations. **Branch:** Morikawabekkan, 6-23-5 Hongo, Bunkyo ku (3811 1181/fax 3811 8120).

Hotel services *Air-conditioning. Fax. Japanese rooms. Parking (3 spaces). Safe.* **Room services** *Hairdryer (on request). Ironing facilities (on request). Tea (Japanese).*

Hotel Park Side

2-11-18 Ueno, Taito-ku (3836-5711/fax 3836 3459/www.parkside.co.jp) Ueno station. **Rooms** 128. **Rates** ¥9,200-¥11,500 single; ¥14,000-¥17,500 double. **Credit** AmEx, DC, JCB, MC, ¥TC, V. **Map** 14.

The hotel's name is something of a misnomer, as it's one street away from the Shinobazu pond end of Ueno Park, bang in the middle of Ueno's late-night drinking and entertainment district. Still, if you're

lucky and get a park-facing room on one of the upper floors, you might just about be able to convince yourself you're in the thick of the countryside. Western-style rooms are a bit small, so go Japanese and put the futons away in the morning.
Hotel services *Air-conditioning. Bar. Conference facilities. Fax. Japanese/western rooms. Laundry. Multilingual staff. Parking (¥1,000). Restaurants (4). Safe. Wedding chapel.* **Room services** *Hairdryer (on request). Minibar. Radio. Room service (3-10.30pm). Rooms adapted for disabled. Tea (Japanese). Telephone message system. TV.*

Ueno First City Hotel

1-14-8 Ueno, Taito-ku (3831 8215/fax 3837 8469). Okachimachi station. **Rooms** 77. **Rates** ¥8,000-¥8,500 single; ¥13,000 double. **Credit** AmEx, DC, JCB, MC, V. **Map** 14.
A cut above the normal business hotel, this offers comfortable accommodation in an unprepossessing modern red-brick block not far from Ueno Park. Western-style rooms are pleasantly furnished and decorated in pastel shades, while Japanese rooms have the usual *tatami* and olive colour scheme.
Hotel services *Air-conditioning. Bar. Coffeeshop. Conference facilities. Fax. Laundry. Japanese/western rooms. Restaurant.* **Room services** *Hairdryer. Massage (paid). Satellite TV. Tea/coffee.*

Elsewhere

Hotel Bellegrande

2-19-1 Ryogoku, Sumida-ku (3631 8111/fax 3631 8112). Ryogoku station. **Rooms** 150. **Rates** ¥8,000-¥9,000 single; ¥14,000-¥40,000 double; ¥16,000-¥19,000 twin; ¥80,000 suite. **Credit** AmEx, DC, JCB, V. **Map** 24.
When there's no sumo tournament on at the nearby Ryogoku stadium, this hotel finds itself in one of Tokyo's deadest areas, ten minutes by train from Tokyo and the wrong side of the river from Akihabara's electric town. Such shortcomings are reflected in the prices of the rooms, which are small but comfortable. There's a Sky Lounge cocktail bar, Etoile, from where you can watch the twinkling lights of the big city. Booking is essential if your visit coincides with a sumo tournament.
Hotel services *Air-conditioning. Bar. Conference facilities (2). Fax. Japanese/western rooms. Laundry. Parking (¥1,500). Restaurant (3). Safe.* **Room services** *Hairdryer. Tea (Japanese). TV.*

Keihin Hotel

4-10-20 Takanawa, Minato-ku (3449 5711/fax 3441 7230/http://gnavi.joy.ne.jp/keihin-h). Shinagawa station. **Rooms** 52. **Rates** ¥8,000-¥8,500 single; ¥14,000 double. **Credit** AmEx, DC, JCB, MC, V. **Map** 21.
There has been a Keihin Hotel here since 1871, but this building dates from the 1960s. Overshadowed by its glitzy neighbours, the Prince hotels and the Meridien Pacific, the Keihin has a certain shabby appeal. It's clean and rooms are of a reasonable size. Staff are helpful, but speak only minimal English.

Hotel services *Air-conditioning. Bars (2). Conference facilities. Fax. Japanese/western rooms. Laundry. Restaurants (5). Safe.* **Room services** *Hairdryer (on request). Minibar. Radio. Room service (24hrs). Tea (Japanese). Trouser press. TV.*

River Hotel

2-13-8 Ryogoku, Sumida-ku (3634 1711/fax 3625 2874). Ryogoku station. **Rooms** 97. **Rates** ¥6,600-¥7,200 single; ¥11,000-¥12,000 twin; ¥11,000-¥12,000 double. **Credit** AmEx, DC, JCB, MC, V. **Map** 24.
A neighbour of the Hotel Bellegrande (*see above*), this offers tiny, slightly shabby western-style, or – much better value – Japanese-style rooms. Booking is recommended if there's a sumo tournament on.
Hotel services *Air-conditioning. Bar. Conference room. Fax. Laundry. Restaurant (Japanese).* **Room services** *Hairdryer. Satellite TV. Tea/coffee.*

Ryokan Ryumeikan Honten

3-4 Kanda Surugadai, Chiyoda-ku (3251 1135/fax 3251 0270/www.ryumeikan.co.jp). Ochanomizu station. **Rooms** 12. **Rates** ¥10,000 single; ¥17,000 double. **Credit** AmEx, DC, JCB, MC, V. **Map** 15.
From outside, this traditional Japanese-style *ryokan* is, frankly, a nightmare, situated in an office block five minutes' walk from Ochanomizu's Russian cathedral. Inside, though, it's a testament to the skill of Japanese interior designers that they have made the place so pleasant and comfortable. Rooms are of a good size and service is friendly and professional. The branch, in Nihonbashi, is slightly cheaper.
Branch: Hotel Yaesu Ryumeikan, 1-3-22 Yaesu Chuo-ku (3271 0971/fax 3271 0977).
Hotel Services *Air-conditioning. Conference facilities. Fax. Laundry. Multilingual staff. Parking. Restaurants (2). Safe.* **Room services** *Cable/satellite TV. Hairdryer (rental). Ironing facilities (rental). Room service (7.30am-10pm). Tea (Japanese).*

Budget

Asakusa

Asakusa Ryokan

2-17-4 Asakusa, Taito-ku (3844 5570). Tawaramachi station. **Rooms** 6. **Rates** ¥4,000 single; ¥5,000 double. **No credit cards.** **Map** 13.
A shabby, rundown *ryokan* whose main virtues are its location, near Asakusa's tourist sights, and its bargain-basement prices. If you decide to stay here, be prepared to communicate in Japanese and brush up on your bathing etiquette: the family who own the place expressed concern that foreigners might not know how to use the communal bath properly (no rooms have their own bathroom).
Hotel services *Air-conditioning. Japanese/western style rooms. Japanese bath.* **Room services** *Hairdryer (on request). Tea (Japanese). TV.*

Ueno

Economy Hotel New Koyo

2-26-13 Nihonzutumi, Taito-ku (3873 0343/fax 3873 1358/www.newkoyo.com). Minowa station. **Rooms** 75. **Rates** ¥2,500-¥2,700 single; ¥4,800 double. **Credit** AmEx, MC, V, ¥TC.

Quite possibly the cheapest accommodation option in Tokyo, the New Koyo is geared for travellers on a budget. Single rooms are tiny and come in both Japanese and western styles. If you want a double, book well ahead as the hotel only has two. Still, it's clean, friendly and has facilities that put many more expensive hotels to shame, including a fabulous English website, from where you can book online. **Hotel services** *Air-conditioning. Bicycle hire. Coin laundry. Internet terminal. Japanese/western style rooms. Kitchen. Japanese bath. Showers.* **Room services** *TV.*

Hotel Edoya

3-20-3 Yushima, Bunkyo-ku (3833 8751/fax 3833 8759). Yushima station. **Rooms** 49. **Rates** ¥7,850-¥8,950 (¥5,890-¥6,930 weekends) single; ¥12,930 (¥9,930 weekends) double. **Credit** AmEx, DC, JCB, MC, V. **Map** 17.

This mainly Japanese-style *ryokan* near Ueno Park offers good accommodation at reasonable prices. There's a small Japanese tearoom and garden on the first floor, and the roof has an open-air hot bath open to both men and women. The mahjong room package is popular with local gamblers.

Hotel services *Air-conditioning. Fax. Laundry. Multilingual staff. Japanese restaurant. Parking (free).* **Room services** *Hairdryer. Modem line. Tea (Japanese)/coffee.*

Ryokan Katsutaro

4-16-8 Ikenohata, Taito-ku (3821 9808/fax 3821 4789). Nezu station. **Rooms** 7. **Rates** ¥4,500 single (no bath); ¥8,400-¥9,000 double. **Credit** AmEx, MC, V. **Map** 14.

In a back street on one side of Ueno Park, Katsutaro is a small, friendly *ryokan* with good-sized rooms and the atmosphere of a family home (which it is). As is the case with many *ryokan*, rooms can be occupied by up to four people, at an extra charge of roughly ¥4,000 per person. The owner speaks a little English, but have a phrasebook handy if you want the conversation to progress.

Hotel services *Air-conditioning. Fax. Japanese rooms. Laundry. Safe. Tea/coffee downstairs.* **Room services** *Hairdryer (on request). Ironing facilities (on request). TV.*

Ryokan Sawanoya

2-3-11 Yanaka, Taito-ku (3822 2251/fax 3822 2252). Nezu station. **Rooms** 12. **Rates** ¥4,700-¥5,000 single (no bath); ¥8,800-¥9,400 double. **Credit** AmEx, MC, ¥TC, V. **Map** 25.

A *ryokan* that's reinvented itself as a haven for tourists on a budget, Sawanoya has a small library of English-language guidebooks and novels and the owner is studying to improve her already passable English. Rooms are small but comfortable, and there

Ryokan rules

Staying in a *ryokan*, or Japanese-style inn, is a memorable experience. Although Japanese hosts are always forgiving of westerners' social *faux pas*, there are some simple rules of conduct. On arrival, you are expected to take off your shoes in the entrance hall and wear the slippers provided. The slippers are for walking through the communal areas. Once you arrive at your room, remove your slippers and walk on the *tatami* (straw mat floor) barefoot or in stockinged feet. One thing you may notice is the absence of a bed. Later in the evening (usually around 8pm), staff will come to make your futon up for you on the floor.

Inside the room, Japanese green tea and a flask of hot water are provided, perhaps with Japanese biscuits or sweets. The decor will include a *shoji* (paper sliding screen) and a

tokonoma (alcove), which is for decoration, not luggage storage. Inside the cupboard, you'll find a *yukata* (dressing gown) and a *tanzen* (bed jacket), which you can wear around the *ryokan* and which double as pyjamas. When you don the *yukata*, put the left side over the right.

Many *ryokan* have communal bathing facilities, and the usual rules for bathing in Japan apply (*see p261*). After a bath and a good night's sleep, you will usually be awoken at around 8am with a Japanese-style breakfast, and staff will tidy away your futon.

Please note that because most *ryokan* are small family-run businesses, they tend to lock up early. If you think you may return or arrive late, try to give your hosts fair warning. Some even impose curfews.

are signs in English reminding you how to behave and how to use the bath. It's well situated for exploring the delights of Ueno Park and visiting the old quarters of the Yanaka area. More expensive rooms have their own bath, cheaper ones have access to the communal bath and shower. A small dining area provides space to study the guidebooks.
Hotel services *Air-conditioning. Free tea/coffee in dining area. Safe.* **Room services** *Hairdryer. Ironing facilities (on request). Tea (Japanese). TV.*

Tsukuba Hotel

2-7-8 Moto-Asakusa, Taito-ku (3834 2556/fax 3839 1785). Inaricho or Ueno station. **Rooms** 109. **Rates** ¥4,500-¥5,800 single; ¥7,500 semi-double; ¥8,000 double. **No credit cards. Map** 14.

A basic business hotel in the downtown area of Ueno, the Tsukuba is clean and good value for money. If you have the chance, opt for a Japanese-style room, partly because it's more fun, partly because tidying the futon away in the morning will make the tiny room seem that much bigger. Western-style rooms come with their own bathing facilities, but if you stay in a Japanese room you'll be expected to bathe Japanese-style in the communal bath on the ground floor. The hotel is two minutes' walk from Inaricho station on the Ginza line.
Branch: Iriya Station Hotel, 1-25-1 Iriya, Taito-ku (3872 7111/fax 3872 7111).
Hotel services *Air-conditioning. Japanese/western style rooms. Japanese bath.* **Room services** *Tea (Japanese). TV (coin).*

Nihonbashi

Hotel Nihonbashi Saibo

3-16-3 Nihonbashi-Ningyocho, Chuo-ku (3668 2323/fax 3668 1669/saibo@pop12.odn.ne.jp). Ningyocho station. **Rooms** 126. **Rates** ¥7,800-¥8,400 single; ¥9,000 double; ¥12,000 twin.
Credit AmEx, DC, MC, JCB, V.

This hotel squeezes into the budget category on account of its double-room price. Rooms, however, are quite small and western-style, with beds rather than futons. That said, there are business hotels offering a similar standard of accommodation but charging much more. Don't expect to be able to get across anything but the most basic requests in English. Convenient for T-CAT (see p258).
Hotel services *Air-conditioning. Conference facilities. Fax. Restaurants (2). Safe.* **Room services** *Hairdryer. Ironing facilities (on request). Modem line (third floor only). Radio. Tea (Japanese). TV.*

Elsewhere

Asia Center of Japan

8-10-32 Akasaka, Minato-ku (3402 6111/fax 3402 0738/asiacntl@blue.ocn.ne.jp). Nogizaka station. **Rooms** 167. **Rates** ¥5,100-¥7,500 single; ¥6,800-¥10,500 double. **Credit** JCB, MC, £$TC, V. **Map** 12.

Founded by the Ministry of Foreign Affairs in the 1950s as a cheap place for visiting students, this has long since outgrown its origins and offers comfortable, no-frills accommodation to all visitors on a budget. Tiny rooms – the cheapest of which don't have baths – still bear the hallmarks of their institutional beginnings, but the grateful backpackers constantly trooping out into the fashionable Aoyama area of Tokyo don't seem to mind. Rooms have recently undergone an extensive refurbishment programme.
Hotel services *Air-conditioning. Business services. Coffeeshop. Conference facilities. Currency exchange. Fax. Laundry. Multilingual staff. Parking. Restaurant. Safe.* **Room services** *Disabled: adapted room. Hairdryer (new wing). Ironing facilities (on request). Modem line (on request). Tea (Japanese). TV.*

Juyoh Hotel

2-15-3 Kiyokawa, Taito-ku (3875 5362/fax 5603 5775/http://plaza16.mbn.or.jp/~JUYOH). Minami-Senju station. **Rooms** 80. **Rates** single ¥3,200; double ¥6,000. **No credit cards.**

One of the cheapest accommodation options in town, the Juyoh is clean, pleasant and extremely foreigner-friendly. All rooms are tiny Japanese-style, with tatami flooring. Although no credit cards are accepted, bookings are taken via the Internet, where you can gain an additional ¥500 discount at the click of a mouse. The first floor is set aside for women only, and there's a communal bath on the top floor, as well as private showers on the second.
Hotel services *Laundrette.* **Room services** *Air-conditioning. Fridge. TV.*

Kimi Ryokan

2-36-8 Ikebukuro, Toshima-ku (3971 3766/fax 3987 1326/www2.dango.ne.jp/kimi/). Ikebukuro station. **Rooms** 41. **Rates** ¥4,500 single; ¥6,500-¥7,500 double. **No credit cards. Map** 5.

A backpackers' haven in the lively Ikebukuro area, Kimi has passed into legend among impecunious visitors. Bathing and toilet facilities are communal but immaculately clean; there's even a Japanese bath for use at set times. Downstairs in the communal lounge, travellers exchange gossip, and the noticeboard carries job and long-term accommodation information. Kimi runs an information and accommodation service for foreigners apartment-hunting in Tokyo (3986 1604), and a telephone answering service for businesspeople (3986 1895). It's phenomenally popular with budget travellers, so book ahead.
Hotel services *Air-conditioning. Fax. Multilingual staff. Safe. Tea in lounge. TV in lounge.* **Room services** *Hairdryer (on request). Ironing facilities (on request).*

Sakura Hotel

2-21-4 Kanda-Jinbocho, Chiyoda-ku (3261 3939/fax 3264 2777/www.sakura-hotel.co.jp). Jinbocho station. **Rooms** 42. **Rates** ¥6,800 single; ¥8,000 double.
Credit AmEx, DC, JCB, MC, V. **Map** 15.

Love hotels

As quintessentially Japanese as karaoke or *kimono*, love hotels offer a practical solution to an everyday problem. In a city as cramped as this, where children often live with their parents until well into their twenties, where do you go for a bit of quiet (or not so quiet) nooky?

On entry to most hotels, you will be greeted by a panel of photographs of the rooms the hotel has to offer. Facilities and prices are described next to a button on each photo. If the photo is lit up, the room is available. To choose a room, punch a button and (usually) proceed to a till where a person, whose face is hidden to protect your anonymity, will hand you a key to a room. Some love hotels are totally automatic. If there's no obvious till, take the ticket from the bottom of the machine and proceed to your room. Inside the room, there's another machine where you pay when you've finished. There are usually two rates, a 'rest' rate and a 'stay' rate; the former is usually limited to two hours, the latter is an all-nighter. During the day, rates may be cheaper.

Although it's an appealing idea, love hotels are not well-suited to long-stay budget tourists. For a start, these are not places you check in and out of. Once you're in, you can't leave until you're ready to leave for ever. Furthermore, most love hotels do not accept overnight guests before 10pm. If you're prepared to leave your luggage in a station coin locker every day and change hotels every night, you might just be able to make it.

The main love hotel areas are Ikebukuro, Shibuya and Shinjuku, each of which has around 40 clustered in a very small area. In addition, most suburban areas have at least one, usually a very short walk from the station. Suburban ones tend to be cheaper and more run-down.

Bron Mode

2-29-7 Kabuki-cho, Shinjuku-ku (3208 6061). Shinjuku station. **Rates** *rest* ¥5,700-¥9,800; *stay* ¥9,300-¥19,800. **Credit** AmEx, JCB, MC, V. **Map** 1b.
Very flashy and futuristic looking, the Bron Mode fancies itself as a little bit upmarket. Rooms all have karaoke, jet bath/Jacuzzi and sauna.

Gallery Hotel

21-6 Kami-Meguro, Meguro-ku (3494 1211). Meguro station. **Rates** *rest* ¥8,000-¥13,000; *stay* ¥12,000-¥20,000. **Credit** AmEx, JCB, MC, V. **Map** 18.
A famous love hotel, standing on its own like a fairytale palace in dowdy Meguro. Check in and pay in the foyer via machine. Rooms are huge and well furnished, with free drinks. Karaoke, jet bath and sauna are standard, as are microwaves. Don't ask why.

If

2-20-15 Dogenzaka, Shibuya-ku (3462 1776). Shibuya station. **Rates** *rest* ¥4,300-¥4,500; *stay* ¥7,800-¥8,000. **No credit cards. Map** 2.
A popular choice with young

A haven for backpackers, the Sakura Hotel offers the option of shared rooms sleeping six people for a reasonable ¥3,600 per person per night. All staff speak good English and are on duty 24 hours. The rooms might be tiny but they're also clean, and all are non-smoking. Bibliophiles may care to note that the hotel is located in Tokyo's second-hand book district. A testament to Sakura's popularity is the message board on the first floor, where grateful messages from all over the world are posted by guests past and present. It's advisable to book your stay well in advance. The website, incidentally, is extremely cute.

Hotel services *Air-conditioning. Bar. Coffeeshop. Fax. Laundry. Multilingual staff. No-smoking rooms. Safe.* **Room services** *Hairdryer (on request). Ironing facilities (on request). Modem line (6 rooms). Tea (Japanese). TV.*

couples, this budget passion pit was refurbished in late 1999. There's karaoke and jet baths in some rooms.

J girl

1-1-14 Ikebukuro, Toshima-ku (5951 6833/ www.d2.dion.ne.jp/~rise/). Ikebukuro station. **Rates** *rest* ¥4,900-¥7,000; *stay* ¥8,000-¥13,500. **No credit cards. Map** 5.

One of the few love hotels with its own website. Jet bath and karaoke are standard, although the rather exposed street-corner location might put some off.

J-MEX

2-5-6 Kabuki-cho, Shinjuku-ku (3205 2223). Shinjuku station. **Rates** *rest* ¥4,800-¥8,800; *stay* ¥9,000-¥17,000. **No credit cards. Map** 1b.

Opened in 1999, this hotel offers a variety of rooms, with karaoke, jet bath/Jacuzzi and, in some rooms, a sauna.

Lala Dogenzaka

2-13-1 Dogenzaka, Shibuya-ku (3496 2929). Shibuya station. **Rates** *rest* ¥5,800-¥9,800; *stay* ¥9,800-¥15,800. **No credit cards. Map** 2.

A mid-priced love hotel in the Shibuya love hotel district. Jet bath or Jacuzzi and karaoke are standard in all rooms. The rest period is three hours, rather than the usual two.

P&A Plaza

1-17-9 Dogenzaka, Shibuya-ku (3780 5211). Shibuya station. **Rates** *rest* ¥4,700-¥13,000; *stay* ¥9,100-¥25,000. **Credit** AmEx, JCB, MC, V. **Map** 2.

One of the most famous love hotels in Tokyo, the P&A's top-price suite is supposed to have cost over ¥10 million yen to build, as it contains a pool. Jet bath or Jacuzzi is standard in all rooms.

Sakura Ryokan

2-6-2 Iriya, Taito-ku (3876 8118/fax 3873 9456/ www.sakura-ryokan.com). Iriya station. **Rooms** 18. **Rates** ¥5,300-¥6,300 single; ¥9,600-¥10,600 double. **Credit** AmEx, JCB, MC, ¥TC, V.

Ten minutes' walk from Asakusa's temple complex, in the traditional *shitamachi* area of Iriya, the Sakura is a friendly, traditional family-run *ryokan* that dates back over 70 years. Of the 12 Japanese-style rooms,

only two have their own bathrooms, while seven of the eight western-style rooms have baths. There's a communal bath on each floor. By the reception desk there's a rack of helpful tourist leaflets and information in English.

Hotel services *Air-conditioning. Beer vending machine. Fax. Japanese/western rooms. Laundry.* **Room services** *Hairdryer (on request). Ironing facilities (on request). Satellite TV. Tea/coffee.*

YMCA Asia Youth Center

2-5-5 Sarugaku-cho Chiyoda-ku (3233 0611/fax 3233 0633). Suidobashi station. **Rooms** 55. **Rates** *Non-members* ¥6,300 single (weekdays), ¥5,040 (weekends); ¥11,550 twin (weekdays), ¥9,240 (weekends); ¥14,490 triple (weekdays), ¥11,592 (weekends). *Members* receive a 10 per cent reduction on these prices. **Credit** JCB, MC, ¥TC, V. **Map** 15.

More like a regular hotel than many YMCAs, in terms of both price and appearance, the YMCA Asia Youth Center is also more expensive than you might expect. In terms of location, it shares many advantages with the nearby Hilltop Hotel (*see p39*). The smallish rooms are western-style with their own bathrooms.

Hotel services *Air-conditioning. Conference facilities. Fax. Laundry. Multilingual staff. Restaurant. Safe.* **Room services** *TV.*

Minshuku

A *minshuku* is the Japanese equivalent of bed and breakfast accommodation, offering visitors the chance to stay in a real family environment for around ¥5,000 per night. Reservations should be made at least two days in advance.

Japan Minshuku Association

4-10-15 Takadanobaba, Shinjuku-ku (3364 1855). Takadanobaba station. **Open** 10am-4pm Mon-Fri; 10am-1pm Sat. **Map** 22.

Accommodation slightly out of the centre, in the studenty area of Takadanobaba.

Japan Minshuku Centre

Kotsu Kaikan Bldg B1, 2-10-1 Yurakucho, Chiyoda-ku (3216 6556/fax 3216 6557). Yurakucho station. **Open** *mid June-mid Aug* 9am-9pm Mon-Sat; *mid Aug-mid June* 10am-8pm Mon-Sat. **Map** 6.

Located in the basement of the gigantic shopping and eating complex over on the Ginza side of Yurakucho station. English-speaking assistants will help you find a *minshuku* to suit.

Capsule hotels

Business Inn Shinbashi & Annex

4-12-11 Shinbashi, Minato-ku, 4-12-10 Shinbashi, Minato-ku (3431 1391/annex 3431 1020). Shinbashi station. **Capsules** 88 (56 annex). **Rates** ¥4,300 Mon-Fri; ¥3,950 Sat, Sun and hols. Closed 31 Dec-3 Jan. **Credit** AmEx, DC, JCB, MC, V. **Map** 2.

Men only. Air-conditioned. Alarm. Daytime shower. Radio. Reading lamp. TV.

Capsule Hotel Azuma

3-15-1 Higashi-Ueno, Taito-ku (3831 4047/fax 3831 7103). Ueno station. **Capsules** 144. **Rate** ¥3,500. **No credit cards. Map** 14.
Men only. Alarm. Bath. Fax (paid). Intercom. Japanese restaurant. Sauna. Video (paid). Towel. Toothbrush (free). TV.

Capsule Inn Akasaka

6-14-1 Akasaka, Minato-ku (3588 1811/fax 3505 2377). Akasaka station. **Credit** AmEx, DC, JCB, MC, V. **Map** 7.
Men only. Bath. Sauna. Shower. TV. Video (paid). Free razor, towel, soap and toothbrush.

Shinjuku Kuyakusyo-Mae Capsule Hotel

1-2-5 Kabuki-cho, Shinjuku-ku (3232-1110 /fax 3208 0084). Shinjuku station. **Capsules** 458. **Rates** ¥4,500; ¥2,800 between 5am-4pm. **No credit cards. Map** 1b.
Men only. Japanese restaurant. Massage. Sauna.

Long-term accommodation

If you're thinking of moving to Tokyo for the long term, then you'll need two things in abundance: patience and money. First of all, many landlords here are reluctant to rent to foreigners, and the requirement for a local guarantor can cause immense problems for those without Japanese relatives or a sympathetic company boss.

Then there's the cash. When you find an apartment, you will be required to pay a damage deposit (*shikikin*), usually equivalent to between one and three months' rent, a brokerage fee (*chukairyo*) to the agent, usually another month's rent, and finally and most ridiculously, key money (*reikin*), usually one or two months' rent. This last element often has foreigners (and people from outside Tokyo) chewing the rug in frustration: it's simply a non-refundable way of saying thank you to the landlord for having you. You then have to find a month's rent in advance.

Understandably deterred by the cost of finding somewhere of their own, many foreigners fall back on so-called *gaijin* houses – apartment buildings full of foreigners who share bathrooms, cooking facilities and, in some cases, rooms. All the places listed below are used to dealing with foreigners and offer a range of accommodation, from dormitory style to individual apartments. Deposits are refundable.

If you really do decide to make a go of it in Tokyo, you may find the best way to find an apartment is to take it over from another foreigner. The best source of such 'inheritances' are the small ads in the weekly free sheet *Tokyo Notice Board (see p268).*

Asahi Homes

3-2-19 Roppongi, Minato-ku (3583 7551/fax 3583 7587/apt@asahihomes.co.jp/www.asahihomes.co.jp). *Roppongi station.* **Credit** AmEx, MC, V.
Upmarket agency offering fully serviced apartments in well chosen locations, with a minimum stay of one week. Rent starts from ¥73,500 for a studio, rising to ¥280,000 for a luxurious three-bedroom apartment.

Crystal Village

1-2-10 Arai, Nakano-ku (3388 7625/fax 3388 7627/crystal.iijima@nifty.ne.jp). Nakano station. **Credit** AmEx, MC, V.
This agency offers private rooms with shared bathroom and kitchen for ¥21,500 per week, or ¥75,000 per month. Studio apartments cost ¥44,000 per week or ¥130,000 per month (¥30,000 deposit required).

Fontana

3-31-5 Chuo, Nakano-ku (3382 0151/fax 3382 0018/fontana@gol.com). Shin-Nakano station. **No credit cards.**
A bona fide estate agent with a section devoted to English-speaking clients, Fontana can also find medium-term accommodation. Studio apartments are ¥39,000-¥45,000 a week (¥50,000 deposit), family-sized apartments ¥120,000-¥500,000 a month (¥100,000 deposit; for terms of three months or longer, one month's deposit).

Hoyo Tokyo

Hoyo Daini Bldg, 4-19-7 Kita-Shinjuku, Shinjuku (3362 0658/fax 3362 9438/hoyo-tokyo@md.neweb. ne.jp). Higashi-Nakano station. **No credit cards.**
Studio apartments are ¥39,000-¥65,000 per week (¥50,000 deposit) or ¥120,000-¥230,000 per month, family apartments are ¥300,000-¥500,000 a month (¥100,000 deposit; for terms of three months or longer, one month's deposit).

Sakura House

K-1 Bldg 8F, 7-2-6 Nishi-Shinjuku, Shinjuku-ku (5330 5250/fax 5330 5251/info@sakura-house.com/ www.sakura-house.com). Shinjuku station. **No credit cards.**
Owned by the people who operate the Sakura Hotel *(see p45).* A room in a guest house with shared bathroom and kitchen costs ¥60,000-¥110,000 a month, apartments run from ¥105,000 to ¥190,000 per month. A ¥30,000 deposit is required.

Tokyu Stay

8-14, Shinsen-cho, Shibuya-ku (3477 1091/fax 3477 1092/www.tokyustay.co.jp/english/shibuya/). Shibuya station. **Credit** AmEx, JCB, MC, V.
Apartment-type accommodation in a modern block close to NHK headquarters. Stay length starts at a single night, but the longer you stay the less it costs per night, the single studio rate falling to ¥6,000 from ¥8,000 for stays of 30 nights or more. The dearest apartment-type accommodation starts at ¥19,000 on a single-night basis, falling to ¥14,300 for a stay of 30 nights or more. Other branches in less lively areas, including Shinbashi, Nihonbashi and Yotsuya.

Sightseeing

Introduction

Time to get out and about.

Tokyo is not one of the world's great cities for traditional sightseeing. The fact that the city was destroyed and rebuilt twice in the 20th century has left relatively little of genuine historic value here. Even 'ancient' buildings in the oldest, most traditional parts of the city such as Asakusa (see p51) are usually post-war reconstructions of what was there before.

This does not mean, however, that there is nothing to see here. Just the opposite. The rush to rebuild and renew the city after the devastating firebombing of WWII not only created some remarkable modern buildings but also left the whole city architecturally mismatched, with old wooden buildings sometimes peeking out from in between brutal 50-storey skyscrapers. These incongruities are a major part of what makes Tokyo such an enjoyable city to get lost in. Here you never can tell what's lurking around the next corner, a faceless skyscraper or a little wooden shack, a shrine or temple that looks to have been dropped here through a hole in time.

Rather than seeing Tokyo as one huge city, it's probably helpful to think of it as a collection of mini-cities, each with an identity and feel all of its own. Don't go to these areas expecting them to have the sort of village atmosphere you sometimes find in London or Paris, though: the population of Shibuya alone is twice that of Amsterdam, and twice the population of Brussels passes through Shinjuku station every day of the week. Take the time to get to know any one of these areas and each one of them will yield its own discoveries and rewards. In the end you will, like most of the people who live here, develop an attachment for one particular place, the city within a city that suits you best, and find yourself returning there time and again, to shop, stroll, eat or play.

Over the following pages, we provide short profiles of the most prominent areas of Tokyo, with selections of highlights and recommendations to help you on your way. Each of these areas has enough in it to satisfy even the most demanding of sightseers and each has its own distinct character, from the unscathed pre-war *shitamachi* area of town (p74) to the neon forests and all-night action of Roppongi (see p64).

There's also plenty here for those in search of culture. Tokyo is often under-appreciated as

Tokyo Tower: erected in 1958. *See p91.*

a centre of excellence in the arts, but in Ueno Park (see p76) it has the highest concentration of top-class museums in the world, and the breadth and scope of the modern art and photography shows here are at least the equal of anything any other city has to offer. The music scene, too, is vibrant, in all its forms, from jazz to rock to classical and beyond.

This is a marvellous city to visit, and if you devote enough time to exploring each of the places we've selected, you'll almost certainly find points to fascinate or charm in the most unexpected of places. You may even find your appetite whetted for more, which is why we have ventured out of the traditional Yamanote line loop on pages 78-85, to give you a taste of the different atmospheres and activities that await. While you're reading this, the city is getting on without you. What are waiting for? Get a train ticket, get out there and join in the fun.

Asakusa 浅草

There's more to Tokyo's biggest tourist attraction than just temples.

Map 13

Visitors to Tokyo whose schedules do not include Kamakura or Kyoto may find traces of traditional Japan in Asakusa. Not only is the area home to Tokyo's largest temple complex, but the streets surrounding the sacred site evoke an atmosphere of old Edo reminiscent of Ozu's *Tokyo Story*. Before the Meiji period, Asakusa was Tokyo's hotspot for *kabuki*, music and striptease. Only the striptease remains. Before the red-light district of Yoshiwara was closed down in the late 1950s, Asakusa enjoyed a reputation as Tokyo's sin city.

Meaning 'short grass', Asakusa consisted of little else for much of the Edo period. In spite of its riverside location, Asakusa was a geomancer's worst nightmare in that it lay north-east of Edo Castle. Superstitious *samurai* shunned the area. Were it not for an unusual catch by two brothers fishing on the Sumida River, the area may have remained perpetually pasture-like. In AD 628, the story goes, the two brothers found a statue of Kannon, the goddess of mercy, in their net. The village head rebuilt his house to enshrine the statue. The house stood on the spot were the bustling temple of **Senso-ji** is currently located.

SHRINES AND TEMPLES

Visitors approach Asakusa on the Ginza line, the oldest stretch of the subway, opened in 1927 to link Ueno and Asakusa. It is a two-minute walk from Exit 1 of the station to the Senso-ji complex. **Kaminarimon** (Thunder Gate) is an impressive entrance to the temple grounds. The ten-foot (three-metre) red paper lantern is one of Tokyo's most recognisable sights, as are the statues of the gods protecting Kannon: Raijin, god of thunder, and Fujin, god of wind.

The gate leads to **Nakamise Dori**, a corridor lined with almost 100 stalls selling crafts, toys and foods. Many sell Asakusa's most famous snack, the *Kaminari Okoshi* or thunder crackers. Connoisseurs insist the best examples are to be found at **Tokiwado** (*see p53*) to the west of Kaminarimon. After the row of shops on the left is a series of paintings depicting the founding of the temple.

Nakamise Dori leads to the two-storey **Hozomon** (Treasure House Gate), once called Niomon for the pair of guardian *Nio* figures to frighten evil spirits. The gate's name comes from its upper section, which houses old *sutras*

Bathing in the healing smoke at **Senso-ji**.

and temple treasures. The last stage before Senso-ji is the incense burner, or *okoro*, where the smoke is said to cure the body parts it touches. Crowds of people gather round to 'bathe' in the healing smoke.

Senso-ji, affectionately known as Kannon-sama, was rebuilt after the war, a replica of the structure that stood there for 300 years. This Buddhist temple became the centre of worship to Kannon in the Kamakura period (1188-1333). In 1600, *Shogun* Tokugawa Ieyasu came to pray to Kannon before the Battle of Sekigahara. He was duly granted victory in one of the most important battles in Japanese history. Kannon's reputation flourishes today – *kabuki* actors and *sumo* wrestlers pray to the goddess before plays and bouts, and throngs of worshippers visit the temple, especially at New Year.

Part of the New Year ritual and popular all year round is fortune-telling by lots, or *o-mikuji*. At various points around Senso-ji, depositing ¥100 in a slot entitles you to pull a stick from a container. This will have a number written on it, which corresponds to a drawer in which a piece of paper detailing future happiness or misfortune may be found. If the fortune is bad, disaster may be averted by tying the paper to a nearby tree or stand. Unusually, Senso-ji offers glimpses of the future in English.

On the right of Senso-ji is **Asakusa-jinja**, a Shinto shrine dedicated to the Hinokuma brothers who found the statue, and their master. Also called Sanja-sama, it is the starting point of the Sanja Matsuri, Tokyo's greatest annual festival. Held on the weekend closest to 18 May and lasting three days, around 100 *mikoshi* (portable shrines) are carried through the streets in a frenzied affair. On 17 and 18

December the shrine plays host to the Hagoita Ichi fair, a low-key affair at which decorated wooden paddles are sold. At the back of the building is another shrine, **Hikan-inari**, one of three structures to survive the air raids.

The other two are **Nitenmon**, built in 1618 and all that remains of a temple dedicated to Tokugawa, and the small **hexagonal temple**, dating from the Muromachi period (1336-1573). Around this small temple you'll find a garden and a number of small shrines. The **pagoda** dates from AD 942, but this third incarnation was built in 1973. Behind the pagoda lies **Denbo-in**, a temple that opens its gardens to visitors. To visit them you must get permission from the office (open from 9am-3pm; closed on Sundays, holidays or when in use by the monks), which you'll find through the door on the left of the pagoda. Follow the perimeter and you'll come to a small shrine, **Chingodo**, originally dedicated to *tanuki* (raccoon dogs). Now it is popular for praying for success in business, the arts and entertainment.

The last monuments connected with the temple are back across Nakamise Dori: two **statues of Buddha**, and a little further on **Bentenyama** mound, a temple and a **bell**. The bell inspired a poem by Basho and is rung on New Year's Eve 108 times to cleanse all sins.

RINKY-TINK TOWN

The streets to the west of the Temple complex are known as **Rokku**, or Sixth District, once famous as Tokyo's least salubrious entertainment area. It was named Rokku after the division of the temple compound after the Meiji Restoration, and was specifically for entertainment. Literature of the late 19th and early 20th centuries speaks fondly of Rokku. *Kabuki* was banished to this area by the *shogunate*, and other arts such as *rakugo, kodan* (forms of storytelling) and *bunraku* (puppet theatre) thrived. The tradition continues today with crowds lining up to see *rakugo* performances at the **Engei Hall** (*see p53*), which also attracts comedians – Kitano (Beat) Takeshi trod the boards here before gaining fame as a comedian and film director.

Rokku was also famous for its cinemas and sex shows, Tokyo's first cinema opening in the district in 1903. The north end of Sushiya Dori is still packed with old-fashioned cinemas, showing old-fashioned films. **Shin Gekijo**, **Meiga-za** and **Toho** are the kind of places to catch a monster movie, gangster film or 40 winks.

Nearby is the **Hanayashiki Amusement Park** (*see p53*). Opened in 1853, the park boasts the world's oldest steel track roller coaster and a famous haunted house.

With strip joints and ghost trains making for thirsty work, the parched may find refreshment in Asakusa's famous Denki Bran or Electric Brandy. An invention of **Kamiya Bar** (*see p156*), Tokyo's oldest western-style hostelry, the cocktail of brandy, wine, vermouth, gin and curaçao has been slaking thirsts since 1883 and accounts for the youthful good looks of the nonagenarians who populate the bar. Those seeking harder liquor should head for **Manosu** (*see p53*), Asakusa's only Russian restaurant, located south of the Kaminarimon and frequently packed. If a simple lager is more to your taste, two separate beer halls across the river at the imaginative headquarters of the **Asahi Brewery** can provide the necessaries. With his design, Philippe Starck hoped to evoke a golden flame atop a giant pedestal. Unfortunately for Starck, the edifice has earned itself the nickname of Unku Biru or the 'turd building'. Those not put off by this moniker may enjoy hops-based beverages in the **Flamme d'Or** and **Sky Room** bars (*see p152*).

KITCHENWARE AND CRAFTS

More beers can be had on **Kappabashi-dogu-gai**, a ten-minute walk west of Senso-ji. Just don't expect them to quench your thirst. In spite of its realism, any food or drink to be had in Asakusa's kitchenware town is of the plastic variety used in restaurant display cases. Crockery and cutlery can also be found here. Popular venues include **Union** (*see p53*), a caffeine fiend's dream with every conceivable coffee device save the intravenous drip.

Asakusa is home to artisans and shops supplying traditional goods. The block between Nakamise Dori, Kaminarimon Dori, Kokusai Dori and Denpo-in gardens is home to old food stores and crafts shops, including a comb shop, a *shamisen* (Japanese lute) maker and a restaurant making *soba*. Many shops close on Monday. Examples of crafts can be found at the **Gallery Takumi** (*see p53*).

FESTIVALS

The main form of entertainment in Asakusa today is the festivals. Sanja Matsuri is the biggest and noisiest, though rivalled by a night of fireworks along the river at the end of July. Up to a million people line the banks for an event that has been happening for 250 years. The Brazilian samba festival at the end of August is also popular. Two other traditional festivals worth seeing are the Kinryu no Mai (Golden Dragon Dance) on 18 March and 18 October, and the Shirasagi no Mai (White Heron Dance) on 3 November. On that day there is also the Tokyo Jidai Matsuri, which aims to recreate some of the city's history. To make sure you don't miss out on any festival, check the board on the left just before Hozomon Gate.

While in Asakusa, take in one of Tokyo's oldest funfairs or buy souvenirs in the market.

None of the following accepts credit cards.

Asakusa Tourist Information Centre
2-18-9 Kaminarimon, Taito-ku (3842 5566).
Open 9.30am-8pm daily, with English assistance available 10am-5pm.

Engei Hall
1-43-12 Asakusa, Taito-ku (3841 6545/ www.lifeserver.co.jp/co/asakusaengeihall).
Open 11.30am-9pm daily. **Admission** ¥2,500.

Gallery Takumi
2-22-13 Asakusa, Taito-ku (3842 1990).
Open 10am-8pm daily.

Hanayashiki Amusement Park
2-28-1 Asakusa, Taito-ku (3842 8780/ www.hanayashiki.net). **Open** *Term time* 10am-6pm Mon, Wed-Sun. *School holidays* 10am-6pm daily.
Admission ¥900; ¥400 concessions.

Manosu
2-17-4 Kaminarimon, Taito-ku (3843 8286).
Open 11.30am-3pm, 4.30-10.30pm Mon, Wed-Sun.

Meiga-za
2-9-12 Asakusa, Taito-ku (3841 3028).
Open 10am-8.30pm daily. **Admission** ¥1,200; ¥900 concessions.

Shin Gekijo
2-9-11 Asakusa, Taito-ku (3841 2815).
Open 9.30am-8.30pm daily. **Admission** ¥1,000; ¥800 before 11am.

Toho
2-6-10 Asakusa, Taito-ku (3844 3141).
Open 11.35am-8.30pm daily. **Admission** ¥1,800; ¥1,500 concessions.

Tokiwado
1-3-2 Asakusa, Taito-ku (3841 5656).
Open 9am-9pm daily.

Union
2-22-6 Nishi-Asakusa, Taito-ku (3842 4041).
Open 9am-6pm Mon-Sat; 10am-5pm Sun.

Wins Asakusa
2-10-11 Asakusa, Taito-ku (3844 7091).
Open 9am-5pm Tue-Sun.

Getting there

Asakusa is on the Eidan Ginza and Toei Asakusa lines. You can also take a waterbus along the Sumida River from Hinode Pier to Asakusa pier. Boats depart every 35 mins. Japan's only double-decker bus service departs Ueno's Suzumoto Theatre for Kaminarimon every 30 mins (more frequently at weekends). After 7pm the subway is the only option.

Ginza 銀座

Tokyo's most exclusive shopping area is a great place for a leisurely wander.

Map 6

Sunday, just before noon. A police car appears on Ginza Dori and its loudspeaker crackles into life: 'This avenue will be turned into *hokosha tengoku* [pedestrian heaven] soon. No vehicles will be allowed between Ginza 1-chome and Ginza 8-chome until 7pm. Please remove your parked cars immediately.' As if by magic, the traffic vanishes.

At noon, Ginza Dori (officially Chuo Dori, or Central Avenue) looks wide enough for Godzilla to wander down without touching a building. Nowhere else in centre of the city has the same sense of space and freedom. Tables and chairs are set up on the street, allowing pedestrians to rest, chat, or just watch people pass by. This is the best time to indulge in the Tokyo pastime of *ginbura* (Ginza strolling), first popularised in the early decades of the 20th century by the fashionably modern youth of a bygone era.

The atmosphere is surprisingly peaceful. Busking is frowned upon here, unlike in other areas closed to traffic on Sundays. When Elvis Costello toured Japan in 1984 he came to Ginza during *hokosha tengoku* and attempted to drum up interest for his gigs with a live set from the back of a truck. No one took any notice.

Ginza ('Silver Seat') was originally the Edo-era nickname for the area around the silver mint, built in 1612 near where **Tiffany's** (*see p180*) now stands on Ginza Dori. The mint moved to Nihonbashi in 1800, but the district was officially given the name Ginza by the new Meiji government in 1869. It became the symbol of modern, fashionable Tokyo after the city's first rail hub opened at nearby Shinbashi and Ginza Dori was redeveloped with rows of western-style red-brick buildings.

Rising from the ashes after the devastation of the earthquake, and again after the air raids of World War II, Ginza continued to grow, consolidating its reputation as the city's most exclusive district. Today, shopping and dining in Ginza maintain an air of luxury. Compared to places such as Shinjuku or Shibuya, the age profile is higher and the dress code smarter. Still, this is the only part of Tokyo where older fashions mix easily with the latest trends. There are elegant department stores such as **Mitsukoshi** (*see p163*) and **Matsuya** (*see p162*), wooden shops selling traditional items, brand-name boutiques, small old galleries

exhibiting avant-garde art, showrooms where you can touch and test the latest high-tech products and a huge number of coffee shops and Japanese tea rooms. Foreign retail chains choose to have their first Japanese outlets in prestigious Ginza before opening up elsewhere.

Daytime is the best time for bargains. The special lunch offers of Ginza's up-market restaurants can provide a different meal every day of the year. On weekdays between 11.30am and 2pm, and also at weekends at some establishments, high-quality set meals are offered for around ¥1,000, up to ten times cheaper than the same dishes on evening menus. Explore the back streets and look outside restaurants for signs, together with a list of prices. Alternatively, if you fancy a picnic in nearby Hibiya Park, the food halls of department stores offer top-quality food at reasonable prices to take away. In the run-up to closing times, around 7.30pm, many items go for as little as half the regular price.

At night, Ginza is the favoured haunt of the expense-account set. Karaoke boxes and convenience shops, familiar sights in Tokyo's other entertainment quarters, are scarce. Around seven or eight o'clock, high-class bar hostesses can be seen out in restaurants and coffee shops, often with favoured customers who will later accompany them to work, earning extra commission. Reasonably priced food becomes tougher to find when a simple *tempura* meal for two may set you back ¥20,000. Avoid anywhere that has no menu outside showing prices. Similarly, top-end drinking establishments are accessible only to those willing to splash out. As well as élite businessmen and politicians, these include the shady owners of large and expensive foreign cars that stand parked on both sides of Ginza's narrow side streets during the evening.

GINZA STROLLING

There are many ways to explore Ginza on foot, but setting off from Yurakucho station is best. Take the exit for Ginza and walk down the narrow street with the **Ciné La Sept** cinema (*see p194*) on the corner. Continue straight through the arcade running inside the Mullion complex – home to the **Seibu** and **Hankyu** department stores (*see p163, p162*) and several cinemas – and you come out at the multi-directional zebra crossings of Sukiyabashi

(Sukiya Bridge). Confusingly, there is no bridge. There used to be one going from the present-day Sukiyabashi Hankyu department store towards Hibiya, across the old outer moat of Edo Castle (now the Imperial Palace), but both bridge and waterway were casualties of 1960s road construction. Today, a small monument marks the spot where the bridge stood.

Standing with Sukiyabashi Hankyu department store on your right, you will see a large **Sony** sign on the other side of the crossing. This tall, slim building offers eight floors of entertainment (*see p93*). Technology and games fans can easily spend hours there, but even for non-obsessives it is still an enjoyable place to kill time. Sounds, visuals, computers – all the latest Sony models are on display and can be tried out. The sixth floor is

dedicated to PlayStation and you can requ. games to play. This section is packed with k. at weekends, so try to be there during the week.

If you carry on up Harumi Dori away from Yurakucho, you pass the recently opened Boots, a surprisingly upmarket version of the British high-street chemist, and come to Ginza 4-chome crossing. Walk down Sotobori Dori (Outer Moat Avenue, once part of Edo Castle's waterway defences), towards Ginza 8-chome and Shinbashi. Ginza streets are named and laid out in a grid, so it's difficult to get lost. On your way down to 8-chome, stop off at some of the small galleries, most of which are free to enter. When you reach the boundary of Ginza at Gomon Dori, turn left towards Ginza Dori and the narrower streets of Sony Dori, Namiki Dori, Nishi Gobangai Dori and Suzuran Dori.

Godzilla's statue watches over Ginza's shiny brand-name shops and high-tech showrooms.

Free reads at **World Magazine Gallery**.

Whichever route you take back to Harumi Dori, the atmospheric streets between Ginza Dori and Sotobori Dori are the best pottering area in Ginza. Zigzag towards 4-chome crossing, enjoying the back streets and Ginza-dori window-shopping on on the way. When you reach the 4-chome crossing, you will see **Le Café Doutor Espresso** (*see p144*), of the Doutor coffee shop chain. Next to it is **Kyukyodo** (*see below*), a stationery shop known not only for its quality products but for marking the spot usually quoted as the nation's most expensive piece of real estate. On the other side of the crossing is **Wako** (*see p180*), a watch and jewellery department store famous for its dazzling window displays; its mini clock-tower is the popular symbol of Ginza. In Ozu's *Tokyo Story* (1953), two women are chauffeur-driven past Wako, the store representing the high-class, modern face of Tokyo. 'Outside Wako at 4-chome crossing' is a common meeting spot.

Another meeting place is the **Nissan Gallery** (*see below*), also on the corner of the crossing. Latest models are exhibited on the ground floor. Since admission is free, the ground floor gets busy on rainy days. Take the last right turning before Miharabashi Crossing, where Harumi Dori meets Showa Dori, and on your right you will see the **Okome Gallery** (*see below*). Here, learn all about Japanese sticky rice, and eat cheap set meals with a bowl of delicious rice. *Onigiri* (rice balls) are available to take away.

Further down Harumi Dori is the **Kabuki-za** theatre (*see p220*), home of *kabuki*. Reserved seats cost up to ¥16,800, but a single act of the day-long programme can be enjoyed for around ¥1,000. Although you have to queue for tickets, and good opera glasses are essential, this is a good way to get a taste of traditional performing arts. Another way of seeing Ginza is to begin the day here (performances start at 11am), then head off and sample the delights listed above. Alternatively, visit **World Magazine Gallery** (*see p268*), tucked away behind Kabuki-za, where you can browse 800 titles for free.

Kyukyodo

5-7-4 Ginza, Chuo-ku (3571 4429). **Open** 10am-7.30pm Mon-Sat; 11am-7pm Sun. **Map** 6.

Nissan Gallery

Nissan Motors Bldg 1F, 6-17-1 Ginza, Chuo-ku (5565 2389). **Open** 8.30am-6.30pm Mon-Fri; 8.30am-5.30pm Sat. **Map** 6.

Okome Gallery

Ginza Crest Bldg 1F, 5-11-4 Ginza, Chuo-ku (3248 4131). **Open** 10am-6pm Mon-Sat. **Map** 6.

Getting there

Ginza station is on the Ginza, Hibiya and Marunouchi subway lines. The best way to tour the area is to start at Yurakucho station, on the JR Yamanote line, and walk down.

Taxi!

Tokyo's taxi-drivers know all the best places. Ginza tops the list, especially late in the evening, but you may be disappointed if you try to hail a cab after midnight. That's not to say the area's night-time streets aren't clogged with cabs, all eager to whisk well-behaved and financially flush passengers off home to distant suburbs. Far from it. The city's taxi-drivers naturally gravitate to Ginza as the trains start to close down. The resulting traffic congestion and competition for customers, however, led the local authorities to ban street-side pick-ups in the area between 10pm and 1am. Instead, a more orderly system of taxi-ranks is used. So if you're wandering around Ginza in the middle of the night wondering why nobody wants to stop, make your way to one of the stands on Ginza Dori or Harumi Dori. And join the queue.

Harajuku 原宿

The juxtaposition of the solemn Meiji Shrine and the trendy shops of Takeshita Dori sum up the dichotomy of modern Japan.

Map 11

Harajuku is an area for the young and young at heart. Platform-shod girls walk in pairs, chatting and thumbing their mobile phones. Cries of '*kawaii*' ('cute') reach fever pitch, whether to describe a Hello Kitty wallet, a Mandarin-speaking wristwatch or a pair of funky striped socks. Takeshita Dori, a narrow lane leading from Harajuku station to Meiji Dori, is the place to find the very latest stuff. Prices range from cheap to outrageous, as do the fashions. It's madhouse crowded, but it's your best bet for figuring out what's hot, be it fishnet tights, Burberry scarves or nose rings. That wide-cuffed, dark-jean look? Invented in Harajuku, years before Gap appropriated it. Harajuku put the street into Tokyo street fashion. A number of designers, such as label 20471120, which made its debut here, now appear on Paris catwalks. Underground has gone above ground. Sundays attract the wilder and wackier. Youths parade the streets in S&M gear with whips and leather, now doctor's get-up decorated with fake blood. Make sure you stop by the main entrance of **Meiji Shrine** (*see p88*) where they assemble in packs. Do not be shy about taking pictures, they love to pose.

HARAJUKU ON FOOT

Built in 1924, Harajuku station is one of the few in Tokyo that has retained its original architecture, a European half-timbered look. If you take the Omotesando exit and walk down the north side of the street towards Meiji Dori, you'll pass stores such as Polo Ralph Lauren, Benetton, J Crew, **Mujirushi Ryohin** – known in the UK as Muji (*see p180*) – the no-brand store specialising in casual clothing, basics and home furnishing. There are also a number of conveyor belt 'Kaiten' *sushi* restaurants and other cheap eateries. You'll soon hit Meiji Dori. Next to a three-floor Gap is **Sony Plaza** (*see p59*). Don't be fooled by the name, it is in fact a department store geared towards young women. Above Sony Plaza is **Pizza Express** (*see p59*), the British chain, which opened its first restaurant in Japan in this prime location, and Elephant Café, a large pan-Asian restaurant. Over the street is Condomania, selling both gimmicky and utilitarian prophylactics. The contraceptive pill only became legal in 1999 and condoms are still the most popular method of choice. Japanese condoms enjoy a reputation for variety (though not for generous size).

Meiji Dori towards Shibuya affords a mix of stores including British pharmacy Boots, Kookai, Jigsaw, Vivienne Tam, North Face and **Uniqlo** (*see p168*), the successful Japanese cheap casual clothing chain. If you go left at the adobe building on Meiji you'll hit **Laforet** (*see p167*), a teeming centre for young fashions. Go on past Laforet, take a left at the crêperie and follow the road up the hill to find **Ukiyo-e Ota Memorial Museum of Art** (*see p97*). Its collection of woodblock prints provides a refreshing reminder of old Japan.

Past the intersection between Takeshita and Meiji is the green canopied **Aux Bacchanales** (*see p59*), the most popular of the French-style bakery-cafés that have sprung up over the past few years. If you are lucky enough to get a table outside, it's a good spot for people-watching.

Just further from Aux Bacchanales is the entrance to the Togo Shrine, named after Admiral Togo, the commander who defeated the Russian fleet at the straits of Tsushima in the 1904-04 war. The shrine has a beautiful garden and pond, and is a popular venue for weddings. An eclectic antique market is held in the grounds of the shrine on the first, fourth and fifth Sundays on the month.

Across Meiji Dori is another small alleyway that begins where Takeshita left off; this is Harajuku Dori. Less busy, it, too, is lined with shops worth exploring. Harajuku Dori intersects Kyu Shibuyagawa Promenade. In the curves of the cemented-in promenade, you can feel the flow of its namesake Shibuya River. The **Candy Stripper** clothing shop (*see p59*) stands out with its bright-red front, punctuated with bubble-mirror windows. **Give Life** (*see p59*) is a store that specialises in clothes made entirely from natural products. **Café Vasy** (*see p59*) is on the corner of the promenade and Harajuku Dori and serves latte in giant soup bowls. There are also an astonishing number of hairdressers along this street offering an array of services such as multicoloured hair extensions, perms, makeup lessons and fake eyelashes. Just nearby, **Go Go Café** (*see p59*) is a funky café showing black-and-white films.

The promenade leads back to Omotesando, where on the north side of this stretch between Meiji and Aoyama Dori are the Dojunkai Aoyama Apartments, so named after the company that built them two years after the 1923 Great Kanto earthquake. Housing was badly needed and most people could not afford single homes. Today, these first of Tokyo's apartments look as if they could be in New York, with their ivy-covered concrete walls and slightly rundown appearance. They have become prized real estate and many now accommodate tiny boutiques, galleries, second-hand stores and beauty salons – a uniquely intimate setting for shopping.

Across the street, near the pedestrian bridge over Omotesando, you'll find Italian coffee bar **Perbacco!** (*see p59*). Amidst air kisses and cries of 'Ciao!', expat Italians line up for an extensive selection of coffees as well as *panini* and ice-creams. A table charge makes it more expensive to sit rather than imbibe at the bar – but the people-watching the former affords is second to none. Perbacco! stands where Omotesando hits the river promenade again, leading straight through to Shibuya. To the right of Perbacco! on Omotesando is **Café de Ropé** (*see p144*), one of the original French cafés along this boulevard (and a little the worse for wear).

Further up the street, towards Omotesando station, is the **Oriental Bazaar** (*see p169*), a large three-floor building in green, red and white, filled with traditional Japanese crafts and antiques ranging from affordable to overpriced. It's a good place to find books on Japan and other interesting souvenirs. Further on is the **Tokyo Union Church** (*see p59*), with striking stained-glass art by designer Miura Keiko in its sanctuary. Keeping up with consumer demand – the majority of young Japanese women either have or want a Louis Vuitton bag – the French retailer will open its largest store in the world in spring 2002 next to the Tokyo Union Church.

The enormous glass-covered building down the street, toward Aoyama Dori, is the Hanae Mori building named after one of Japan's best-known designers. Tange Kenzo created the geometrically intricate design; he is also behind numerous other landmarks in the area, amongst them the striking **United Nations University** (*see p59*).

On both sides of Omotesando, on the wide pavement outside shops and cafés, you'll usually find a cluster of potraitists and trinket sellers. The trees – and Omotesando proper – end at Aoyama Dori, though the street itself continues through to Roppongi. The street narrows and becomes Tokyo's Bond Street – home to all sorts of top international and Japanese designers such

as Issey Miyake, Calvin Klein, Versace and Comme des Garçons. At the end of the street (turn left for Roppongi and walk through the Aoyama cemetery) on the right, is the **Nezu Institute of Fine Arts** (*see p96*), which shows Japanese, Chinese and Korean art. Most people visit the museum to admire its stunning Japanese garden, which is free to enter.

At the intersection of Omotesando and Aoyama Dori, on the left corner is a *koban* (police box) and a bright orange store, the **Will V** showroom (*see p59*). Here you can witness futuristic Japanese brand marketing: under the Will V brand name many different companies have grouped together to offer their products, which range from cars to chocolate, from beer to holidays.

On the right is Fuji Bank, a popular meeting place. The street running behind the *koban* has yet another cluster of shops and restaurants, including the cosy and casual French restaurant **Red Pepper** (*see p59*). If you take a right on to Aoyama Dori, you'll be heading towards Shibuya. Take a right at the first alley and look for **News Deli** (*see p59*), which might be the closest thing to a New York deli in this area, albeit with loud music playing. There are bagels, but its honey toast may end up being your new favourite Sunday brunch option. Wandering down towards Shibuya, take a right after Muji. Down the street is **Las Chicas** (*see p136*), a great place for lunch and dinner (outdoors in the summer) or a drink with friends.

ANTIQUES TO HIGH FASHION

Back on Aoyama Dori, the road opposite Kinokuniya is Kotto Dori, or Antique Street. Leading to Nishi-Azabu, this street has some 40 antique shops, mostly high-end, though striking a bargain is not unheard of in the smaller establishments. Back out on Aoyama Dori, heading back towards Omotesando, you'll pass the **Spiral Building** (*see p100*), noted for its unusual curved architecture by Maki Fumihiko. Returning to Omotesando and the Meiji Dori intersection, you'll see the popular **Andersen** bakery (*see p140* **Breakfast**) on your right, on the south-east corner. Nearby is **Gallery 360** (*see p198*), one of many galleries in this area.

Besides giving the name to this swank district, Aoyama is also the name of one of four national cemeteries built during the Meiji era. Like Yanaka Cemetery in Nippori, **Aoyama Cemetery** (Aoyama Bochi; *see p59*) was one of Japan's first public cemeteries. Cherry trees line a central straight road, attracting legions of *hanami* (cherry-blossom viewing) revellers celebrating spring's blooms with the dead. Aoyama, in fact, had once been covered with a different kind of tree: mulberry

It was Harajuku that put the street into Tokyo street fashion.

trees were planted in an ill-conceived plan to earn revenue by exporting silk. The Meiji government realised its error and by 1876 had uprooted them all.

Walking north along Aoyama Dori towards Gaien Nishi Dori ('outer-garden west avenue'), you'll hit Plaza 246 and its **Japan Traditional Crafts Centre** (*see p102*) on the south-west corner. Bell Commons is diagonally across from Plaza 246, and is another common meeting spot. Making a left down Gaien Nishi Dori leads you to Killer Dori, whose name comes either for the steep hill down and the accidents it precipitates or for its 'killer' fashion boutiques and galleries. Either way the unusually named street offers an abundance of distractions. At the bottom of Killer Dori, turn left and you'll eventually loop back in the direction of Harajuku station.

None of the following accepts credit cards.

Aoyama Cemetery
2 Minami-Aoyama, Minato-ku.

Café Vasy
3-20-9 Jingumae, Shibuya-ku (3401 6757). **Open** 11am-10pm Mon-Thur; 11am-10.30pm Fri, Sat; 11am-8pm Sun.

Candy Stripper
4-26-27 Jingumae, Shibuya-ku (5770 2204). **Open** 11am-8pm daily.

Elephant Café
3F, Harajuku T building, 4-30-4 Jingumae, Shibuya-ku (3478 2233). **Open** 5pm-late daily.

Give Life
3-18-21 Jingumae, Shibuya-ku (3404 1348). **Open** 10am-8pm daily.

Go Go Café
3-18-23 Jingumae, Shibuya-ku (3404 1255). **Open** 11.30am-10pm daily.

News Deli
SJ Bldg 1F, 3-6-26 Kita-Aoyama, Minato-ku (3407 1715). **Open** 11am-11pm daily.

Perbacco!
Omotesando Vivre 1F, 5-10-1 Jingumae, Shibuya-ku (5466 4666). **Open** 10am-12.30am Mon-Thur; 10am-11pm Fri, Sat.

Pizza Express
3F, Harajuku T Building, Jingumae 4-30-4, Shibuya-ku (5775 3894). **Open** 11am-11pm Mon-Sat; 11am-10pm Sun.

Red Pepper
Shimizu Bldg 1F, 3-5-25 Kita-Aoyama, Minato-ku (3478 1264). **Open** 5pm-midnight Mon-Fri; 5-11.30pm Sat.

Sony Plaza
4-30-3 Jingumae, Shibuya-ku (5775 3605). **Open** 11am-9pm daily.

Tokyo Union Church
5-7-7 Jingumae, Shibuya-ku (3400 0047).

United Nations University
5-53-70 Jingumae, Shibuya-ku (3499 2811).

Will V's Square Aoyama
3-5-27 Aoyama, Shibuya-ku (5772 6870). **Open** 11am-9pm Tue-Sun.

Getting there
Harajuku station is on the JR Yamanote line. The station is adjacent to Meiji-Jingumae station on the Eidan subway Chiyoda line.

Ikebukuro 池袋

Shop till you drop without breaking the bank.

Map 5

Offering a relaxing atmosphere in which to shop, eat or just hang out, Ikebukuro ranks behind Shinjuku and Shibuya as the third main subcentre of Tokyo. Undeserving of its uncool reputation, Ikebukuro's unfavourable image actually acts in its favour. Because there is less pressure to wear the most fashionable clothes, and the competition to be the coolest is less fierce, Ikebukuro is the least pretentious of the 'cities within a city'. People feel more inclined to be themselves, and are consequently friendlier and more laid back. Recently, Ikebukuro has become more popular, for the simple reason that it's cheaper, while the choice is no less extensive. The area is crammed with shops, bars, restaurants and karaoke rooms.

In the early 1900s, the region was served by the Tobu and Musashino lines (now the Tobu Tojo and Seibu Ikebukuro lines), but as the population grew and sleepy villages became one large town, more train and subway lines were built to pass through Ikebukuro, resulting in a major junction. Yasujiro Tsutsumi and Kaichiro Nezu, arch-rivals responsible for developing the Seibu and Tobu lines respectively, encouraged expansion of the area by each building a department store by the station. Both stores mushroomed. Other stores then wanted in on the action, and discount shops filled in the gaps. Cafés and restaurants materialised, followed by bars and clubs.

Ikebukuro station is renowned – even among locals – for being confusing. There are over 40 exits, and no maps to give you any clue as to which one might be most convenient for you. The main exits are clearly signposted, however, and it is often easiest to get out at the nearest one and navigate by the department stores.

In keeping with Tokyo's tradition of contradictions, the **Seibu** store (*see p163*) – whose name originates from 'west area railway line' – is located at the east side of the station, and **Tobu** (*see p164*) – the 'east area railway line' – has the west side covered, quite literally. The areas around the two are the main starting points for visitors to Ikebukuro. Before leaving the station, check the two stores out. It's advisable to pick up a store map, as there's a real danger of getting lost. If you fancy trying out the local cuisine but find whole platefuls somewhat daunting, or if you just feel like a snack, do what the locals do – trot down to the food hall and help yourself to the free samples.

EAST SIDE

There are two main exits on this side of the station – the East exit and the Seibu exit. Turn left out of either and you will come to **Parco** (*see p171*), part of the Seibu complex. P'Parco is further along, and the clothes on sale here make you wonder if those youngsters who frequent the trendier areas of Tokyo come here in disguise to buy their clothes. Tower Records is on the fifth and sixth floors, and Ishibashi, a musical instrument specialist, is on the seventh.

Turning right out of the station from Seibu will bring you to **Mujirushi Ryohin** (*see p178*), the 'brandless brand' store, and across the street you will find a warren of restaurants and bars. If you're especially hungry, try **MoMoParadise** (*see p61*) – a shabu-shabu restaurant offering a 90-minute all you can eat/drink deal for ¥2,800 per person. **Junkudo** (*see p61*), further along the main street, carries the best selection of foreign books in Ikebukuro.

If you think the areas to the left and right of Seibu are mobbed, try making your way to the main centre of Ikebukuro – **Sunshine 60 Street**. You can tell the busiest parts of Tokyo by the concentration of tissue distributors and karaoke touts. The corner before the entrance to Sunshine 60 Street is so packed with them that by the time you've made it to the crossing, you're in a position to rival a Kleenex factory.

Sunshine 60 Street is packed with shops, restaurants and cinemas. The Sanrio shop is worth a giggle – two floors offering a mind-boggling range of Hello Kitty goods. Half way down the street on the right is the new HMV (*see p181*). Sunshine 60 Street is so called because it ultimately leads to the Sunshine 60 building, part of the Sunshine City complex. Here, in this massive marble mall, you can find all kinds of fashion shops and restaurants and, within the complex, an observatory, an aquarium, a planetarium, a theme park, and the Ancient Orient Museum, among other attractions. Behind Sunshine City you will find a wide selection of love hotels, along with offers of relevant entertainment from scantily clad young ladies who happen

Sunshine 60 Street draws teeming crowds to its myriad shops and restaurants. *See p60.*

to be strolling in the area late at night. There are plenty of clubs and bars on this side of the station. The **Black Sheep** (*see below*) behind Mitsukoshi is a popular spot, with occasional live bands. Next door, in the basement, is reggae/ska lounge **Never Mind** (*see below*). Both stay open late and are within stumbling distance of the taxi rank at the station. Otherwise, when the bars close, you can wait for the first train in the 24-hour Denny's on Sunshine 60 Street. Or go to the other side of the station.

WEST SIDE

This side of the station is quieter than the east. The number of little shops and bars, however, is still mind boggling, and you will wonder how they all stay in business. Aside from Tobu, the only other major department store is **Marui** (*see p171*), which is directly down the street perpendicular to the West exit. The area between the station and Marui is full of small shops, clubs, bars and restaurants. All other main shopping action is towards the south.

Opposite the Metropolitan exit is Tobu Spice, another building packed with restaurants. In the basement of the building behind it is **Dubliners** (*see below*), a bar attracting foreign residents and Japanese regulars. Further along, the **Tokyo Metropolitan Art Space** (*see below*) houses the world's largest pipe organ, which costs ¥5 million a year in upkeep. A rather long escalator takes you to the fifth floor, where an art gallery offers free exhibitions.

If you cross the park from there towards the north side, you'll come across tiny discount clothes stores catering to the reggae/rap/ska/grunge crowd before reaching the seedy entertainment section of the west side. You can find tiny, sweaty clubs in the most unexpected places. The **New Delhi** restaurant (*see below*) is down the first alley you come to, and offers some of the best Indian fare in Tokyo. One floor above is **Bobby's Bar** (*see below*), a very popular place that often has live music. If you

miss the last train and don't want to take a taxi, there's a 24-hour *izakaya* outside the north exit of the station. **Daitokai** (*see below*) is staffed mainly by Malaysians, and offers Japanese cuisine and alcohol round the clock.

None of the following accepts credit cards.

Black Sheep
1-7-12 Higashi-Ikebukuro, Toshima-ku (3987 2289). **Open** 6pm-late Mon-Sat.

Bobby's Bar
1-18-1 Nishi-Ikebukuro, Toshima-ku (3980 8875). **Open** 6pm-late Tue, Thur-Sun.

Daitokai
1-29-1 Nishi-Ikebukuro, Toshima-ku (3986 4564).

Dubliners
B1F San Gurou Bldg, 1-10-8 Nishi-Ikebukuro, Toshima-ku (5951 3614). **Open** 3-11.30pm Mon-Sat; 11.30am-11pm Sun.

Junkudo
2-15-5 Minami-Ikebukuro, Toshima-ku (5956 6111). **Open** 10am-9pm daily.

MoMoParadise
8F, 1-21-2 Minami-Ikebukuro, Toshima-ku (5950 4129). **Open** 11.30am-3pm, 5-11pm Mon-Fri; 11.30am-11pm Sat, Sun.

Never Mind
Higashi-Ikebukuro, Toshima-ku (3984 9736). **Open** 7pm-2am daily.

New Delhi
1-18-10 Nishi-Ikebukuro, Toshima-ku (5391 9449). **Open** 11.30am-midnight daily.

Tokyo Metropolitan Art Space
1-8-1 Nishi-Ikebukuro, Toshima-ku (5391 2215).

Getting there

Ikebukuro is on the JR Yamanote and Saikyo lines, the Eidan Subway Marunouchi and Yurakucho lines, the Seibu Ikebukuro line and the Tobu Tojo line. The Narita Express also stops here on a limited service.

Marunouchi 丸の内

Tokyo's historic centre is a surprisingly quiet place for a contemplative stroll.

Maps 8 & 9

The Marunouchi area, which starts in front of Tokyo station, does not buzz with life, like the brasher new towns of Shinjuku and Shibuya, but it is the historic centre of Tokyo, the centre of the city since the establishment of old Edo.

The main feature in the district is the **Imperial Palace** (see p91), unfortunately inaccessible to visitors, except on the emperor's birthday, 23 December, and on 2 January (9.30am-3pm only). The grounds where the palace now stands are where Dokan Ota built the original Edo castle in 1457. When the military government gave way to imperial rule in 1867, the castle grounds became the Imperial Palace. Three sections of the old castle grounds have become public parkland: Higashi Gyoen, still within the walls and open in the daytime only, Kokyo-mae-hiroba along Hibiya Dori, and Kitanomaru Park to the north, both the latter open at all times.

The palace grounds were once much larger, and most of modern Marunouchi and Hibiya lay within the walls. Marunouchi simply means 'within the moat or castle walls'.

THE GREAT SELL-OFF

After the Meiji Restoration, the land where Marunouchi now stands belonged to the army and was sold to Mitsubishi in 1890. Many derided the purchase, but the area slowly turned into the financial and business centre of Tokyo and Japan. At first Mitsubishi turned the area into Itcho Rondon, or London Town, with Mitsubishi No.1 Hall the first London-style building. Many other brick buildings were to follow, the most admired of which was Tokyo station, modelled after Amsterdam's Centraal Station and completed in 1914. Unlike many of the other brick buildings, it survived the 1923 earthquake and is intact to this day, with the exception of the roof, which was destroyed in the air raids of the last war. It is one of only two buildings surviving from that era, the other being the Banker's Club, on the road leading to the National Diet.

To the west side of the former castle grounds is Hibiya, also the residence of feudal lords in Edo. The site adjacent to the castle first became a military parade ground, but was turned into Japan's first western-style park early this century.

Despite the proximity of Tokyo station to the imperial, political and financial centres of power, the area surrounding it has nothing of the bustle that characterises most of Tokyo's other major stations. Until recently, there was very little in the way of food or drink worth recommending in the area. Now, however, things are starting to perk up, with the recent opening of several casual cafés, notably the **Dragonfly Café** (see p63) and, slightly further afield, the **Marunouchi Café** (see p147), which has free internet terminals and allows you to linger for hours over a single cup of coffee. Diagonally over the road is **Mikuni's Café** (see p140 **Breakfast**), another newcomer to the area, which offers great home-baked bread and serves a mean breakfast.

Back in the station building is one of the area's few concessions to food for the soul: the **Tokyo Station Gallery** (see p63). To the left is **Tokyo Central Post Office** (see p63), the principal mail centre in the city.

Heading to the right leads to the Otemachi district, in reality nothing but an extension of Marunouchi, home to many financial and publishing organisations.

A STROLL THROUGH THE PARK

At the end of Eitai Dori, the street that divides Marunouchi from Otemachi, is Ote-mon, one of three gates to enter **Higashi Gyoen** (see p63), the main park area in the old castle grounds. The garden is almost an island, being surrounded by moats, and the gates are probably the most interesting constructions. There is also the Sanno maru-shozukan, or **Museum of Imperial Collections** (see p63), displaying Japanese arts and crafts from the imperial family's collection. There are no views of the palace from anywhere in the park. The two main paths in Higashi Gyoen lead to Kita-Hanebashi gate. At the exit the foundation stones of the old castle and the moat are at their most dramatic, dropping at a very steep angle.

Across the road is **Kitanomaru Park**. On the right of the main road leading into the park is the **National Museum of Modern Art** (see p98). The park is also home to the **Japan Science Foundation Science Museum** (see p110) and the **Nippon Budokan** (see p207), built for judo competitions in the 1964 Olympics, but now more famous as a music venue.

Sightseeing

Hibiya Park (top) and the **Imperial Palace**.

of the national government ar
Diet (Japanese parliament) bu
display. In the Meiji era the D
wooden buildings nearby, but
down twice, the current granit_ —————— ———
constructed in the 1930s. You can visit the
National Diet (*see below*) but tours are slightly
disorganised. To visit, go to the Information
Office of the House of Representatives, located
at the back of the Diet building, near exit 1 of
Kokkai-gijidomae station.

The road continues on to **Hibiya Park**, a
very popular hangout, particularly with courting
couples. There are a number of good-value
restaurants and cafés, some with seats outside.
It's a pleasant place for an afternoon stroll.

The *pièce de résistance* of the area, the
Tokyo International Forum (*see p207*), is
close by. Designed by Rafael Vinoly and opened
in 1996, it is divided into two buildings, the
glass hall being a genuine architectural wonder.
Take the lift to the seventh floor from the lobby
for a great view of the extraordinary roof. A
path descends three floors along the glass wall.
The adjacent building has convention and
exhibition halls and in the basement you'll find
a number of restaurants, as well as the **Tourist
Information Centre** (*see p271*), which
provides free maps and information in English
on destinations and accommodation.

Dragonfly Café
*Yusen Bldg 1F, 2-3-2 Marunouchi, Chiyoda-ku
(5220 2503).* **Open** 8am-8pm Mon-Fri; 11am-8pm
Sat, Sun. **No credit cards**.

Higashi Gyoen
Open *Mar-Oct* 9am-4.30pm Tue-Thur, Sat, Sun.
Nov-Feb 9am-4pm Tue-Thur, Sat, Sun.

Museum of Imperial Collections
1-1 Chiyoda, Chiyoda-ku (3213 1111).
Open *Mar-Oct* 9.15-4.15pm Tue-Thur, Sat, Sun.
Nov-Feb 9.15-3.45pm Tue-Thur, Sat, Sun.

National Diet
1-7-1 Nagatacho, Chiyoda-ku. **Open** *Museum*
9.30am-4.30pm daily. *Diet building* by guided
tour only.

Tokyo Central Post Office
2-7-2 Marunouchi, Chiyoda-ku (3284 9500).
Open 24hrs (postal services only).

Tokyo Station Gallery
1-9-1 Marunouchi, Chiyoda-ku (3212 2485).
Open 10am-8pm Tue-Thur; 10am-6pm Sat, Sun.

Getting there

Tokyo station is on the JR Chuo and Yamanote
lines, plus many others, and on the Eidan
Marunouchi subway line.

At the exit to the main road, turning left
and left again along Chidorigafuchi moat takes
you down a 500-metre path lined with cherry
trees. It's picturesque and very popular when
the trees are in bloom. Boats can be rented
between 1 March and 15 December (9.30am-
4.30pm daily), ¥300 for 30 minutes.

The path leads to Uchibori Dori, which
follows the moats back towards Tokyo station.
The road passes alongside the **National
Theatre of Japan** (*see p222*). Next door is the
Supreme Court. At the Aoyama Dori crossing,
straying away from the moat in almost a
straight line leads to the **National Diet** library
on the right and the small Parliamentary
Museum on the left. Memorabilia on the history

Roppongi 六本木

Where the night-owls come to get down and dirty until the wee small hours.

Map 4

'High Touch Town' is the phrase chiselled into the concrete on the highway overpass at the epicentre of Roppongi's main crossing (4-chome). Mention of this usually brings a smirk to the face of any foreigner who's lived in Tokyo for more than a few months. Most have their first exposure to Japan's nightlife within the district. It's sometimes called the '*gaijin* ghetto' by snooty locals, even though an astounding number of upmarket drinking, dining and entertainment establishments are packed into Roppongi's six *chome*.

For travellers, Roppongi is a mesmerising glimpse of the energy that makes Tokyo so exciting. A deluge of neon lights and video message boards reminiscent of *Blade Runner*'s LA. A cornucopia of ethnicity, with virtually every nation represented. Narrow streets packed with traffic and bustling until dawn, and just about everything you could imagine to pass the evening in bliss.

Located just outside the south-eastern arc of the JR Yamanote line, Roppongi is not actually a crossroads. In fact, it's a bit out of the way. For decades its only true subway link was the Hibiya line. The Chiyoda line stops in close-by Nogizaka. However, the much-heralded, long-awaited and mega-expensive Oedo line, which opened in December 2000, has linked Roppongi with points north, including Shinjuku and far-flung Nerima Prefecture. In addition, the sparkling new Namboku line makes a stop at Roppongi I-chome, a brisk walk from the action.

Young and middle-aged alike have flocked to Roppongi's hilly, zigzagging streets for fun after dark since the early 1960s. The area's origins are rooted in the military establishment. At one time there was a barracks not far from the main crossing. During the American occupation these were taken over by the US Army and quite a few bars stayed open very late to cater to the soldiers. The Americans moved out in 1959, a year after Tokyo Tower opened.

It's not easy to come up with a working list of hot spots in Roppongi, because there's no telling how long they'll last. Each season brings a slew of new clubs and bars. The key landmarks in this text appear to have gained a foothold on Roppongi's merry-go-round of commerce.

TOWARDS TOKYO TOWER

Perhaps the best way to attack Roppongi is from the main crossing of Gaien-Higashi Dori and Roppongi Dori, also known as 4-chome. You can walk down either main street in either direction and happen upon all kinds of action. Both the Hibiya and Oedo subway lines allow you to exit near the crossing.

At one point of the intersection you will find the café **Almond** (*see p67*). This is *the* Roppongi meeting place. On any evening this corner will be packed with touts and tarts alike, blind dates nervously glancing at their watches, business folk and wide-eyed travellers. If you're male, you'll almost certainly be approached by a man with a handbill for a strip show or hostess bar. These establishments cater to executives on expense accounts. Prices start at around ¥7,000.

If you exit the subway on the Almond side and head up Roppongi Dori towards Gaien-Higashi Dori, you will first pass Almond and then a narrow sloping side street on your right. Don't cross the main intersection, but turn right and head down Gaien-Higashi Dori in the general direction of Tokyo Tower. Now drink in the action. You will pass a Starbuck's on your right before you reach McDonald's.

If you turn right down the side street alongside McDonald's, keep going and follow the bend in the road to the left a little you'll come to the **Hard Rock Café** (*see p67*). You can't fail to notice the life-size King Kong climbing the outer wall. If you need souvenirs, the gift shop is a little booth out in front of the car park. If you're hungry for Californian cuisine, down a one-metre-wide path, you'll find Wolfgang Puck's second-floor **Spago** restaurant (*see p67*).

Across the parking lot in front of the Hard Rock is a well-lit building with several establishments vying for your attention. The most prominent of these will be **Charleston & Son Pizzeria** (*see p67*), one of many 'Charleston' establishments in the area. Besides the fact that it features open-air seating in warm weather, it's an entirely forgettable experience. Forget it, but enter the Reine Building and head for **Bauhaus** (*see p67*) on the second floor.

No tour of Roppongi would be complete without a visit to Bauhaus. One of those 'only

Sightseeing

Tokyo Tower: your main orientation point while in Roppongi.

in Japan' experiences, this is a music venue that has featured the same house band for more than 20 years – the ultimate Japanese garage band. Nowhere else in the world can you jam to flawless covers of the Rolling Stones, Pink Floyd, Rainbow, Guns N Roses and even Madonna, performed by men and women who can't speak three words of English, and then have them serve you food and drinks in between. Bauhaus is on the pricey side: ¥3,500 with one drink. Sets are every hour.

Leave Bauhaus and make a left down the narrow road and you'll come to another Tokyo oddity, the **Cavern Club** (*see p67*). Unlike London Bridge, the Cavern Club was not uprooted and reassembled in an alien land. But the music played here sounds awfully familiar, and the boys playing it might remind you of the Mop Tops themselves (if you squint). Just beyond the Cavern Club is **Quest** (*see p67*), a cosy spot for meeting locals interested in meeting those who are not. The Quest motto is, 'Your search is over'.

If you return to Gaien-Higashi Dori and continue towards Tokyo Tower, you will happen upon one of the weirdest establishments in Roppongi. From the outside it looks like a dilapidated old subway car covered with graffiti. A licence plate over the door reads BB-160. Inside it's no bigger than a subway car, with just enough room for the bar and five or six patrons. It's called **Mistral Blue** (*see p67*).

Mistral Blue is actually connected to the Roi Building, another Roppongi institution, packed from basement to roof with restaurants, bars, meeting facilities and boutiques. Curve around to the right you'll encounter an interesting little bar that's ancient by Tokyo standards. The **Wonder Bar** (*see p67*) was established in 1982. It looks like a train coach from an Agatha Christie novel and features a fine selection of spirits behind an oblong bar. It's a sane alternative to crowded Almond corner for meeting friends.

Past the Wonder Bar, further down Gaien-Higashi Dori, you'll happen upon a slew of sexually oriented establishments with names like Uprise, Climax and Splash. The pictures on the signs will give you a good idea of what's going on inside. They are not for the thin of wallet and most don't welcome foreigners. There are, however, some legitimate massage and *shiatsu* places mixed in that cater to foreigners. Look for signs in English that offer a range of prices for massages ranging from ten minutes to an hour. These places, for the most part, feature competent professional therapists and are usually good value for money when you want to unwind the holistic way.

Half a dozen and **Mistral Blue** is packed.

Across Gaien Higashi Dori from the Wonder Bar and down a side street, you'll arrive at the **Gas Panic** building (*see p67*), an edifice that looks as if it ought to be on the Las Vegas strip. Gas Panic is a Roppongi institution of depravity. There are several Gas Panic installations in the area, three in the Gas Panic Building and one closer to Roppongi Dori, **Gas Panic Club** (*see p67*). If the scene at Gas Panic turns your stomach, there's a public toilet right across the street, and on the other side of the toilet, a spooky little cemetery, Roppongi Sanchen Jidouyen. If you look out across the cemetery, you should be able to spy the **Charleston Club** (*see p67*).

Head back down Gaien Higashi Dori and stop at the first corner directly opposite the Roi Building (across the street). On the second floor of the Yua Roppongi Building you can get a healthy dose of **Propaganda**. If it's happy hour (6-9pm) all drinks are half price. Propaganda gets going early by Roppongi standards and is open till dawn. If you stumble out of Propaganda feeling you haven't had enough, stumble in to the **Hideout Bar** in the basement of the same building. It gets going very late or early, depending on what you consider the 6am to noon time block to be.

AWAY FROM TOKYO TOWER

Directly across Roppongi Dori from Almond is the **Seisido** bookstore (*see p67*), with a large video board above it. Seisido is another good meeting spot and has a small selection of English books and magazines to look at while you're waiting. You will also find a lot of shady, scantily clad characters hanging out at this corner. Directly across Gaien Higashi Dori from the bookstore are a Tokyo-Mitsubishi Bank and a police box.

Cross Roppongi Dori, to the Tokyo-Mitsubishi Bank and police box, and head down away from the intersection. You will pass a beef-rice bowl restaurant, then come to the only cinema in Roppongi, the **Haiyu-za Talkie Night** (*see p195*). This is one of the most unusual spaces in Roppongi, and perhaps all of Tokyo. The cinema is a throwback to the days when going to the movies was a cultural experience. Wide sweeping staircases wind up to an alluring, graceful balcony. It's a dreamy place to watch a movie, and features only the most offbeat and avant-garde films.

If, instead of doing the above, you exit the subway, then go right and head towards Nogizaka station (Chiyoda line), you will pass an area that's being redeveloped. It used to belong to the military. After a stretch with no shops or restaurants you'll come to **George's** (*see below*), a tiny place that has been here since Roppongi's main customers were soldiers. They play Motown and serve expensive drinks. Three customers and it's crowded. George's marks the edge of Roppongi, one of the last symbols of the area's fading history.

Another approach from the Seisido book store on the 4-chome crossing is to head down Roppongi Dori towards Nishi Azabu and Shibuya. On the way, you will pass hordes of touts, either scantily clad women or garishly clad men who may ignore you (they're after Japanese businessmen looking for sex). Almost immediately on the right near the subway exit, look up and find **Geronimo** (*see below*), a place for hard drinking and meeting foreigners and expats. It gets rolling around 1am.

Pass one small street on your right, a bank, and then at the next small street go right. On the left is **Agave** (*see below*), one of the more interesting theme bars in Roppongi. Head down the narrow steps, thrust open the heavy wooden door and you'll enter a spacious cave with great wooden archways and stucco ceilings that might remind you of a hacienda. Agave has 400 different kinds of tequila, but little food. You can also purchase and smoke cigars there.

Continue down Roppongi Dori and you'll pass the imported foods supermarket, **Meidiya** (*see p178*) and come to **Bengawan Solo** (*see p131*), which serves very good Indonesian food. It's been around since 1954, an eternity in Tokyo. There you can wash your satay and gado-gado down with Bintan beer before heading off for yet more Bacchanalian action.

All the bars listed open at around 6pm and close when empty. None takes credit cards.

Agave
Clover Bldg B1F, 7-15-10 Roppongi, Minato-ku (3497 0229).

Almond
6-1-26 Roppongi, Minato-ku (3402 1800). **Open** 9am-5am Mon-Thur; 9am-6am Fri, Sat; 9am-3am Sun.

Bauhaus
Reine Bldg, 5-3-4 Roppongi, Minato-ku (3403 0092).

Cavern Club
Saito Bldg, 5-3-2 Roppongi, Minato-ku (3405 5207).

Charleston Club
3-8-11 Roppongi, Minato-ku (3402-0372).

Charleston & Son Pizzeria
Reine Bldg, 5-3-4 Roppongi, Minato-ku (3479 0595). **Open** 11.30am-4.30am Mon-Thur; 11.30am-5.30am Fri, Sat. **Credit** AmEx, DC, MC, V.

Gas Panic Building
3-15-24 Roppongi, Minato-ku (3405 0633).

Gas Panic Club
Marina Bldg 3F, 3-10-5 Roppongi, Minato-ku (3402 7054).

George's
9-7-55 Akasaka, Minato-ku (3409 9049).

Geronimo
7-14-10 Roppongi, Minato-ku (3478 7449).

Hard Rock Café
5-4-20 Roppongi, Minato-ku (3408 7018). **Open** 11.30am-2am Mon-Thur; 11.30am-4am Fri, Sat; 11.30am-11.30pm Sun. **Credit** AmEx, DC, MC, V.

Hideout Bar
Yua Roppongi Building B1F, 3-14-9 Roppongi, Minato-ku (3497 5219).

Mistral Blue
5-5-1 Roppongi, Minato-ku (3423 0082).

Propaganda
Yua Roppongi Building 2F, Roppongi 3-14-9, Minato-ku (3423 0988).

Quest
Nakano Bldg 2F, 5-8-3 Roppongi, Minato-ku (3409 6077).

Seisido
7-14-10 Roppongi, Minato-ku (3404 8551). **Open** 8.30am-11.30pm Mon-Sat; 10am-9pm Sun. **Credit** AmEx, DC, MC, V.

Spago
5-7-8 Roppongi, Minato-ku (3423 4025). **Open** 11.30am-2pm, 6-10pm daily. **Credit** AmEx, DC, MC, V.

Wonder Bar
5-5-1 Roppongi, Minato-ku (3423 4666).

Getting there
Roppongi station is on the Hibiya line and the Toei Oedo line.

Shibuya 渋谷

Hard-core consumerism and youth culture fuse into an unending romp.

Map 2

Shibuya, a hub at the south-west corner of the city, has become the mecca of all that is trendy in Tokyo. The streets are catwalks for the latest fashions; the stores overflow with CDs, books, magazines, brightly coloured clothes and cell phones practically screaming 'buy me'; the entertainment emporiums seem to expand at will, offering everything from virtual dance partners to virtual fishing; and the whole district is dotted with coffee shops to ensure that everyone remains very, very caffeinated.

Wade through the crowds at Shibuya station – about three million people pass through it on a busy day – and make your way to **Shibuya Crossing**, which offers a sensorial assault setting the tone for the neighbourhood. Screens bombard you with the latest ads and music videos; music is piped through loudspeakers lining the street on the far side. As you face the video screens, you'll see a large Starbuck's, which is beginning to rival the statue of the little dog, Hachiko, as a Shibuya meeting place.

BUSINESS FACE

At Shibuya Crossing, chances are you'll see girls in platform shoes and boots so high they have to step gingerly so as not to topple over; you'll also see waves of dyed blonde hair, dreadlocked boys, miniskirted girls in cowboy hats, as well as lots of frosted makeup, artificial tans, goths and plenty of hip-hop baggy pants and bad-ass attitudes. In fact, despite Shibuya's reputation as a youthful playland, in recent years the district has become a business hub. To the dotcom generation, Shibuya is known as Bit Valley, a phrase taken from one possible translation of Shibuya as 'Bitter Valley'. By shortening 'bitter' to the more technofriendly 'bit,' the dotcommers found a name that could hold its own alongside Silicon Valley and New York's Silicon Alley. There are hundreds of internet startups sprinkled around Shibuya.

From Shibuya Crossing, head west along Dogenzaka. When the road forks, you'll be at Tokyu's **109 Building** (*see p70*), a popular meeting place and shopping paradise for the young. The 109 Building is eight floors of youth fashion (mostly for women) and restaurants. The shops have names like Sneep Dip, Me Jane, Pinky Girls, Shake Shake, Love Girls Market, Rose Fan Fan, Flapper and, of course, Egoist, the ultimate in Shibuya chic.

The Egoist boutique, renovated in February 2001, is on the fourth floor of the 109 Building, just to the left of the escalator. Frosted hair, miniskirts and bright pastel colours rule. Egoist sales staff add to the atmosphere by acting more like models than saleswomen.

Back down on the street, and next to the 109 Building on Bunkamura Dori is a restaurant that would be hard to find just about anywhere else in the world, with the possible exception of Norway: Kujiraya, which literally means 'The Whale Shop', serves whale boiled, grilled, deep-fried, just about any way you could imagine.

For less controversial fare, head further up Dogenzaka past the Prime building and you'll come to one of two **Katsuichi** *tonkatsu* (breaded pork cutlets) restaurants in Shibuya. The other is a block further up on the right. From 11am to 3pm everything is under ¥1,000 and extra helpings of rice, miso soup and shredded cabbage are free. Try the cheese *katsu*, breaded pork stuffed with melted cheese. Just make sure you have a defibrillator handy.

Once you reach the second Katsuichi, turn right and head up the hill, known as Love Hotel Hill. Walk past the sex shops, head shops and love hotels toward the pink sign that says **BYG**, a hole-in-the-wall bar with a good collection of rock albums. Next door is the **Lion** (*see p147*), a musty old coffee shop for classical music lovers. All the chairs, shabbily covered, face a massive stereo system with huge speakers. Only classical music is played and new releases are featured every day at 3pm and 7pm. There is a schedule to tell the real *otaku*, or fanatic, what records will be played each day. People go to listen, not to chat.

Back out on the street, turn left out of the Lion and past an assortment of sex bars, love hotels and shops specialising in erotica. Down the hill, you'll find **Club Asia** (*see p212*), a late-night spot frequented by clubbers coming from **On Air East** and **On Air West** (for both, *see p209*), music venues a little further up the hill.

At the bottom of the hill, you'll be facing **Bunkamura**, or Culture Village, a Tokyu Corporation building with restaurants, shops, cinemas, a theatre, concert hall, gallery and coffee shop. Behind it, in the Shoto district, is some of Tokyo's most expensive real estate. The change from shopping centre to exclusive residential neighbourhood is abrupt. Shoto is

The **109 Building**, for teenage fads. *See p68.*

Shibuya Crossing, for street fashion. *See p68.*

the name of the tea that used to be produced in Shibuya. During the Edo Period (1603-1868), the district was dominated by the Shibuya family, which had a castle in what was then an outpost on the edge of Edo. After the Meiji Restoration, which began in 1868, the district turned to tea cultivation, which continued until the Great Kanto Earthquake of 1923. The quake and the bombing of Tokyo by US warplanes some two decades later pushed people out of the city and into western neighbourhoods such as Shibuya.

PIPING HOT JAVA

Instead of venturing into Shoto, turn right in front of Bunkamura and head back into the fray. On the right is Coffee Row, with offerings from Donatello, Starbuck's and, around the

corner, Segafredo. Across 1st, a five-storey booksh Japanese titles. The stree is lined with restaurants, karaoke boxes and elabo with a wide variety of Pr machines that take your it on a sheet of stickers) and video games.

For Shibuya, futuristic entertainment complexes are old hat. Its station was quite futuristic for its day, with trains emerging at different levels and exits leading into sudden shopping alternatives thanks to the adjacent Tokyu department store. The Ginza line ends here, the train rising up from under ground after leaving Omote Sando station and ending up on the third floor of Shibuya station, giving passengers a brief panorama of Shibuya Crossing.

If you go left in front of Book 1st and take the first possible right, you'll be approaching Inokashira-dori. On your left you'll pass the Nature Trail restaurant in the front part of a big wooden building that also houses a couple of boutiques. The menu at Nature Trail is mostly Italian with a selection of beer and wine. Further up on the left, just before the police box, is **Ryu no Hige**, a good Taiwanese restaurant.

Around this area at night you are likely to see a relatively new development in the Shibuya landscape: the presence of head shops and street stalls selling magic mushrooms. Some of the mushroom dealers operate a few dozen paces from the Udagawacho police box, but because the hallucinogenic fungi are not illegal in Japan, dealers and police coexist peacefully (*see also p218* **Drugs**).

At the police box, if you turn left, you'll see NHK, the giant public broadcaster. On the way, you'll find, on the right, **Tokyu Hands** (*see p178*), a sort of upscale hardware store, or, in its own words, a 'creative life store'. At Tokyu Hands you can find supplies for fixing up your home as well as all manner of baubles and trinkets, such as the tiny alarm you stick in your ear to wake you up at the right moment when you're napping on the train.

Back at the Udagawacho police box, turn right and you'll head back toward the station, past a huge **HMV** store (*see p181*) and a **Seibu** department store (*see p163*). Rock and jazz bands play live in front of Seibu from around 9pm to 11pm on Fridays. They are allowed to play loud, so you'll have no problem finding them – and many are surprisingly good.

On your way towards Seibu and HMV, look for a narrow lane heading upwards on your right. This is Spain Dori. At the top of this hill, you'll find three **Parco** department stores (*see p171*), called Parco Part I, II and III, and a

cinemas. **Cinema Rise** (*see p194*) is
the city's more popular theatres for less
mainstream fare.

Past Parco Part II, you'll find the **Tobacco
& Salt Museum** (*see p105*) on the right, and
NHK, the Olympic Arena and Small Olympic
Arena straight ahead. The arenas, built for
the 1964 Olympics, were designed by Tange
Kenzo. The larger of the two has a sweeping
roof suspended by steel cables. Sports events
and concerts are held inside.

DEPARTMENT STORE WARS

Take a hard right at the intersection in front of
NHK, and you'll head toward an immigration
office and an unemployment office (known as
Hello Work centres). Before you reach these
you'll find a Kate Spade shop on the right and
Cafe Madu (*see below*), a restaurant and bar,
on the left. In the basement below Cafe Madu is
Tete's (*see below*), a spacious Thai and
Vietnam restaurant that serves tasty lunch sets
of Vietnameses noodles and Thai dishes.

Turn right on Fire Dori, which leads all
the way back to Shibuya station. On your
way to the station, you'll pass not one **Marui**
department store, not two, but three (*see p171*).
The name is written OIOI and many a foreigner
has unwittingly pronounced it 'oyoy' to the
amusement of Japanese friends, but *marui*
is Japanese for circular, and the O is supposed
to be read as *maru*, another indication of the
Japanese love of wordplay. The three Marui
stores have different themes. First – and
furthest from the station – is Marui One, which
has athletic and casual wear for men and
women; then, on your right, is Marui City,
which has more upscale offerings as well as
cosmetics and accessories for women; finally,
on your left and just before the station, Marui
Young has a lot of contemporary fashion.

Marui has a strong presence in Shibuya,
but not nearly as strong as Tokyu and Seibu.
Tokyu is still the dominant force, with its
new **Mark City** complex, which opened last
year next to the station, adding a hotel and
more shops to its arsenal. Tokyu owns two
of the most heavily travelled train lines
in Tokyo's western suburbs – the Toyoko
and Shin-Tamagawa lines – and both have
Shibuya as their final stop, although the Shin-
Tamagawa line continues on as the Hanzomon
Line after Shibuya.

On your way back to the station, you'll pass
Tower Records, which has an extensive
collection of English-language magazines,
newspapers and books on the seventh floor.

Back at Shibuya Crossing, the little dog,
Hachiko, waits. Hachiko, an Akita, would
accompany his owner, a university professor,

on his daily walks to Shibuya station during the
1920s. When the professor returned from work,
Hachiko was waiting for him. Then, one day in
1925, the professor died while away from home.
For the next seven years, Hachiko continued to
come to the station every day in search of his
master. When Hachiko died in 1935, all the
major newspapers carried his obituary.

That's how the story goes, but revisionists
suggest that the stationmaster and his staff
were giving Hachiko another reason to turn up:
they were feeding him scraps.

109 Building

2-29-1 Dogenzaka, Shibuya-ku (3477 5111).
Open *Shops* 10am-9pm daily. *Restaurants* 11am-
10.30pm daily. Times may vary. **Credit** varies.

Cafe Madu

1-8-19 Jinnan, Shibuya-ku (5456 7533).
Open 11am-11pm Mon-Sat; 11am-10pm Sun.
No credit cards.

Tete's

1-8-19 Jinnan, Shibuya-ku (5456 7534).
Open 11.30am-11pm Mon-Fri; noon-11pm Sat;
noon-10pm Sun. **No credit cards**.

Getting there

Shibuya station is on the JR Yamanote line, Eidan
Ginza and Hanzomon subway lines, the Keio
Inokashira, Tokyu Toyoko and Shin-Tamagawa lines.

Mark City, Shibuya's latest shopping
complex, opened in April 2000.

Shinjuku 新宿

If you can find your way out of the station, a world of shopping plazas, *yakitori* bars and massage parlours awaits you.

Maps 1a & 1b

If you're looking for one place that captures all the contradictions and contrasts of Tokyo, look no further. While the skyline here boasts seven of Tokyo's ten tallest buildings, the mini-city offers nooks and crannies packed with temples, tea shops and taverns. The neon-lit streets around Shinjuku station are always crowded with shoppers, drinkers and good-time girls.

Shinjuku ('new lodging') was born in the early days of Edo, as a resting place on the road to Kyoto. One of five roads out of Edo, it was less well used than the Tokaido route to the old capital, which went closer to the coast. Nevertheless, Naito Shinjuku, as it was known, was busy enough for tea houses, inns, stores and brothels to prosper. Shinjuku station appeared on the Shinagawa line between Shinagawa and Akabane in 1885. It became a junction four years later when a new line was built to Hachioji.

The earthquake of 1923 largely spared the area, and an influx of people followed. By the early Showa era, the late '20s and early '30s, Shinjuku was one of the most crowded places in Tokyo and its reputation as an entertainment area grew with the theatres, which attracted people from all over. Then came World War II. Shinjuku, almost totally destroyed in the firebombing of Tokyo, became home to black markets operated by gangs near the station's exits. One street on the west side, Piss Alley (*see p73*), is a remnant of those days, as is **Golden Gai** (*see p73 and p159*). Everything else has been rebuilt, but the spirit of consumption and the area's reputation for dodgy dealings remain, the latter especially true in Kabuki-cho.

More than half of Tokyo's four million commuters pass through Shinjuku station each day. Merely, arriving at the station can be stressful. The multiple exits don't make the experience any easier, nor does the labyrinthine system of tunnels and walkways that connects the main JR station with the various subway stations and private railways. JR Shinjuku's three main exits (West, East and South) are clearly signposted in English. Taking the East Exit will land you in the main shopping area, with an option to stroll down to Kabuki-cho; West will take you to the skyscrapers, while South and 'New South' (Shin-Minami) will take you in the direction of **Takashimaya Times Square**, the world's biggest department store building. The west side is also where the

Sightseeing

The neon forest of **Shinjuku**, looking east.

Takashimaya Times Square. *See p71.*

private train lines Odakyu and Keio terminate. Should you exit the station in the wrong place, an underground passage, the Metro Promenade, connects the East to West exits and provides access to the subway stations of Shinjuku San-chome and Shinjuku Nishi-guchi. Look out for confused out-of-towners and minotaurs.

EAST AND SOUTH EXITS: GOLDEN TRIANGLE

The thoroughfares of Yasukuni Dori and Meiji Dori, along with the station itself, form the boundaries of Shinjuku's Golden Triangle of shops, restaurants, amusement centres, sex and gambling establishments. Shopping complexes crowd the South Exit. Directly above the station is **Lumine 2** (*see p162*), which features nine floors of shops and restaurants.

South of the station, bordering the railway lines to the east, is Takashimaya Times Square. The building is home to both the upmarket department store **Takashimaya** (*see p164*) and **Tokyu Hands** (*see p178*) as well as a large Sega amusement theme park and **Joypolis** (*see p73*). The 12th to 14th floors are devoted to cafés and restaurants. Next door to Times Square is one of two branches of **Kinokuniya** (*see p168*) in Shinjuku. The sixth floor of the Times Square Kinokuniya has a large selection of foreign magazines and books.

At the East exit of the station is MyCity, a shopping complex full of fashion boutiques. On the ground floor is a branch of **Japan Railways (JR) View Travel Service Centre** (*see p73*), where staff speak basic English. It's the main counter in the area for tourists and the office validates the JR rail pass

(*see p259*). In the same building is a **Tourist Information Centre** (*see p271*). Outside the JR travel centre, across Shinjuku Dori, is Studio Alta, marked by a huge video screen that is the most popular meeting spot in Shinjuku.

The half-kilometre stretch of Shinjuku Dori from the Studio Alta to Meiji Dori boasts the world's largest Gucci store at its western end as well as branches of Louis Vuitton and **Tiffany's** (*see p180*). On Shinjuku Dori you'll also find two of Shinjuku's *grande dame* department stores, **Isetan** (*see p162*) and **Mitsukoshi** (*see p163*). Much of Isetan's 1933 building is original. West of Isetan is a branch of Kinokuniya bookshop and **Manga Kissa Gera Gera** (*see p73*), a 24-hour comic book coffee shop that also offers Internet access.

WEST EXITS: HIGH AND MIGHTY

The most famous of Nishi-Shinjuku's skyscrapers are Tange Kenzo's three lofty landmarks. His **Tokyo Metropolitan Government Building** (To-cho; *see p93*) opened in 1991 and consists of two structures divided into five towers. Entry to the 45th-floor observatories of the To-cho's main building is free. On a clear day Mount Fuji is visible.

In front of the To-cho is To-min (Citizens') Plaza, a semi-circular open space modelled on the Campo in Siena. Adjacent to the towers is **Shinjuku Central Park**, modelled on New York's Central Park. Some of the people evicted from their cardboard dwellings in the station now live here. Most of the other skyscrapers have viewing areas, too. In the **Sumitomo Building** (*see p73*) across Chuo Dori it's on the 51st floor. Most restaurants on that floor or the two below have lunch specials from ¥1,000. The Shinjuku Centre Building has an observation area on the 53rd floor, and the Nomura Building on Ome Kaido has one on its 50th floor. Also on Ome Kaido, on the 42nd floor of the Yasuda Fire Building, is the **Yasuda Fire Museum of Art** (*see p100*).

Twenty minutes' walk from Shinjuku station's western exits on Koshu-kaido is the **Tokyo Opera City** complex (*see p207*). The complex, which is right by Hatsudai station on the Keio New Line, consists of two main buildings – the **New National Theatre** (*see p222*) and the Tokyo Opera City Building. The confusingly named Tokyo Opera City Building contains no opera house but offers a concert hall and two galleries – the **Tokyo Opera City Gallery** (*see below*) and the **NTT Inter Communication Centre** (*see p98*).

The area from Koshu-kaido towards Shinjuku post office is alive with neon at night and has many restaurants and a few bars.

Close to the station, on the other side of the Odakyu department store towards Kabuki-cho, is a small street called Shonben Yokocho, or Piss Alley, so called because most of its eating places share toilets. It's a narrow 30-metre (98-foot) stretch of *yakitori* bars, *ramen* shops and *izakayas*. Piss Alley and Golden Gai are the only two clusters of old buildings left near the station. They look daunting, but even the strangest or most drunken characters are harmless. Eating in Piss Alley is an experience. Most places serve decent food – choose one that's crowded and you won't go far wrong. The area across Ome Kaido, parallel to the railway lines, is famous for record shops. More than 30 shops specialise in bootleg recordings, or in particular eras or styles.

KABUKI-CHO: DOWN AND DIRTY

The lights in Kabuki-cho are not just red; after dark Tokyo's sin city is ablaze with lights of every colour. A centre of underground culture since the black market thrived here after WWII, the city's pleasure zone offers everything from video arcades, cinemas and restaurants to strip shows, massage parlours and no-panties coffee shops. The Japanese gangster, the Filipino hostess and the Turkish kebab salesman all rub shoulders in the quarter of Tokyo said to have inspired the look of Ridley Scott's *Blade Runner*. Kabuki-cho's main drag starts to the left of Studio Alta and leads to entertainment complexes, cinemas and a plaza. Across the plaza is the Shinjuku Toho Hall entertainment complex, home to the **Code** nightclub (*see p213*), cinemas, bowling alleys and a 24-hour pool hall. On the right of the plaza is the Humax Pavilion containing the **Liquid Room** (*see*

p209 and p214). Nearby bars include **Olé Bar** (*see p157*), **Mon Chéri** (*see p156*) and **Hub** (*see p153*), with **La Scala** coffee shop providing hot drinks in surreal surroundings (*see p148*).

East Kabuki-cho offers a respite from sleaze in the form of Richard Rogers' Kabuki-cho Building. The ten-storey tower is Rogers' only building in Japan. The Kabuki area even has a shrine, **Hanazono** (*see below*), where, on the first, fourth and fifth Sundays of the month, there is a flea market. Behind it lies Golden Gai, which you can walk through in less than five minutes, but there are around 200 bars here. Many cater only to members or regulars, but a few friendly ones will serve anybody as long as there's space. Try Bon's or **Shot Bar Shadow** (*see p157*). The tree-lined Shiki no michi promenade leads from the Golden Gai area back up to Yasukuni Dori. In the other direction are hundreds of busy love hotels. Just follow the neon signs and the smell of cheap perfume.

Transport for the following is Shinjuku station unless otherwise stated.

Hanazono Shrine
5-17-3 Shinjuku, Shinjuku-ku (3200-3093). Shinjuku San-chome station. **Map** 1b.

Joypolis
Takashimaya Times Square 10-11F, 5-24-2 Sendagaya, Shibuya-ku (5361 3040). **Open** 10am-midnight daily. **Admission** from ¥300. **Map** 1b.

JR View Travel Service Centre
Shinjuku station (3354 4826). **Open** 10am-6pm Mon-Sat; 10am-5pm Sun. **Map** 1a.

Manga Kissa Gera Gera
Sashita Bldg B2F, 3-22-7 Shinjuku, Shinjuku-ku (3353 4138/www.geragera.co.jp). **Open** 24hrs daily. **Internet access** 1hr ¥380; additional 10mins ¥50. **Map** 1b.

Sumitomo Building
2-6-1 Nishi-Shinjuku, Shinjuku-ku (3344 6941). **Map** 1a.

Tokyo Opera City Gallery
Tokyo Opera City Tower 3F, 3-20-2 Nishi-Shinjuku, Shinjuku-ku (5353-0756/www.tokyooperacity-cf.or.jp). **Open** noon-8pm Tue-Thur, Sun; noon-9pm Fri, Sat. **Admission** ¥1000. **Map** 1a.

Getting there

Shinjuku station is on the JR Chuo, Saikyo, Sobu and Yamanote lines, on the Eidan subway Marunouchi line, the Toei subway Shinjuku and Oedo lines and the Keio and Odakyu private lines. The Maronouchi and Shinjuku lines also serve Shinjuku 3-chome station. The Oedo line serves Shinjuku Nishi-Guchi. Seibu private line trains terminate at Seibu Shinjuku station, north of the main station complex.

Shitamachi 下町

Leave the high-rise city behind and head for Tokyo's old 'low town' areas.

Map 25

Edo (the name of Tokyo before the Meiji Restoration) was divided into three areas: the castle, *yamanote* and *shitamachi*. The last originally defined the low city, which consisted mainly of the area between the castle and the Sumida River. It was where the common people settled, as opposed to *yamanote*, the higher grounds west of the castle where the feudal lords and rich merchants lived. *Shitamachi* stretched from north of Asakusa to Nihonbashi and beyond, but constant destruction and rebuilding resulted in the disappearance of old areas, and today only small pockets remain. The word has now come to mean traditional commercial districts, but all *shitamachi* areas are still in the low city.

One such area is around the intersection of Shinobazu Dori and Kototoi Dori, near Nezu station on the Chiyoda line. Adjacent is Yanaka, one of the four first cemeteries in Edo. Many temples were relocated here after the Long Sleeves Fire of 1657 (*see p8*). Yanaka became a famous temple town, with **Tenno-ji** one of the busiest temples in Edo. The area is one of the few to have survived the air raids of World War II. It is also celebrated as the home and last resting place of many writers and artists. The last *shogun*, Yoshinobu Tokugawa, was also interred in Yanaka.

The only way to discover the area is on foot. Starting at Nishi-Nippori station on the Yamanote line, take the exit away from Ueno. Once you're outside, turn left. Take the first left, uphill along the tracks, just before the *koban* (police box). The area at the top near the park, Dokanyama, was a popular scenic spot in the Edo period, with its commanding views. Walking away from the park takes you first to **Suwa Jinja**, an unkempt shrine and grounds with old buildings and tombs. It is said to date from 1205. As you exit the *torii* (gate), you're at the gate of Jojoki. A couple of minutes down the road you'll find **Yofuku-ji**. Inside the gate are four old statues: the two in front are Nio figures, sculpted in the Kamakura-era style, and behind are two statues of gods dating from a similar era. The original temple was founded in 1704, but the main building has been rebuilt. There are other stone statues and an old bell in the grounds.

On the left at the intersection at the end of the street is Kio-ji, the gate showing bullet holes

from the 1868 fighting (*see p77*). The temple inside is one of the most interesting in the area, but it's not possible to get a close look.

If you go to the right at the intersection, you'll find **Enmei-in Temple** just off the street, then some stairs leading to a *shotengai* (shopping street) with some traditional shops and a neighbourly feel. Taking the first right after the steps, you'll come across a number of small temples and eventually arrive at a main road.

Just to the right around the corner is **Daien-ji**, an interesting temple in that the left section is Buddhist and the right Shinto. The building is more than 150 years old and has great carvings. The grounds are famous for containing the grave of Kasamori Osen, one of the three beauties of Edo, as well as that of the artist who drew her. Across the road on the corner is Isetatsu, a famous paper shop. If you head uphill on the main road, you'll soon come to **Zenshoan**, with its four-metre (13 feet) golden statue of Buddha. Across the road are the grounds of Tenriu-ji, divided into two sections.

If you continue uphill from Zenshoan and turn right at the first intersection, you'll soon reach Anritsu-ji, with its attractive small hall. At the end of the street an old gate leads to a compound behind the wall. To the right is a *tsuijibei*, a traditional roof mud wall about 200 years old.

At the next intersection turn left and very soon you'll arrive at **Kannon-ji**, a temple connected to the 47 *ronin* (samurai without master; *see p8*) allowed to commit ritual suicide for having avenged the murder of their master. In the grounds there's a notable grave monument and an old well. Further up the street on the right is **Asakura Sculpture Museum**, the house of sculptor Asakura Fumio, with a superb garden (*see p94*).

Turn right at the next road (you're back across Kio-ji, seen earlier) and down the hill. Just before the station, take the steps to the right and follow the long path through the cemetery. It leads to Tenno-ji, another casualty of the 1868 battle, but while the temple itself is recent, the Daibutsu (Buddha statue) was cast in 1690. The small old building in the grounds was built recently, too, out of the leftovers from the old five-storey wooden pagoda that used to stand on the avenue. A landmark in the area, it was burnt down in the late 1950s in a love

Sightseeing

Collection of *jizo* at **Jomyoin Temple**.

suicide. The foundation stones remain next to the *koban*, at which a right-hand turn up to the next crossing brings you to **Choan-ji**. The main attractions here are three *itabi* (stone board stupa) from the Kamakura period.

As you come out, turn right; opposite is an art gallery and shop in a house dating back to 1847. A few antiques and artworks are sold in three small rooms, but it's worth going in just to see the inside of an old building.

Turn right at the next intersection, then take the first left. You'll soon reach **Shiyamo-ji**. A few metres away across the road is **Saiko-ji**, housing a number of statues and stones. It's only a small temple but worth a look. Walk all the way to the end, turn left and you'll see Aizen-do (also known as Jisho-in), where your prayers for marriage partners and household harmony might be answered. At the intersection with the main road is **Scai the Bathhouse**, a former public bath turned art gallery (*see p199*). Turn right; on the left at the main intersection is the Shitamachi Museum Annexe, a traditional late-17th-century shop that's open from 9.30am to 4.30pm Tuesday to Sunday. Admission is free.

As you come out of the annexe turn left and follow Kototoi Dori; in a few minutes you'll arrive at **Jomyoin Temple**, which is famous for its collection of *jizo* (Buddhist saints in search of truth/guardians of children) statues. The grounds are stacked with the small statues, but they still haven't reached their goal of 84,000.

If you turn right coming out of the annexe, at the second street you'll see **Ichio-ji**, a temple resembling a house or inn. Up the side street you'll come across **Daiyo-ji**. At the next corner go left and take the first left again: at the first intersection on the right there's a row of old gates, houses and a small temple. At the end of the street is **Zuirin-ji**, the biggest temple in the area.

Return to the intersection, turn right and you soon come to **Renge-ji**, a small temple with a peaceful atmosphere. If you continue straight ahead and follow the road to the right, you'll arrive at **Ryogen-ji**, a modern concrete temple in the grounds of which tools, pottery and clam shells dating from the Jomon period (3000-1000BC) were found. The area used to be very close to the river and the sea and its current location gives a good idea of how much Tokyo has been subjected to landfill and waterways diversion by successive rulers, town planners and governments.

Across from Renge-ji is **Enjyu-ji**, another small place but definitely worth a look. When you come out, turn right and follow the small street, where a temple a few metres away has a bell tower and statues near its entrance. Continuing along the street you'll pass a small temple, and at the end of a lane to the right you'll see another temple about 20 metres away. Once there, take the path between the walls on your left: at the bottom of some steps you'll see an old hand pump, at which the neighbourhood used to draw its water. You'll soon arrive at the grounds of **Gyokurin-ji**, a leafy and peaceful spot.

Around this area are a number of old-style shops. Taking the main exit from Gyokurin-ji, turn right and then first right. You'll walk past two temples and come to **Rinko-ji**, across the car park. It's untidy but its architecture is quite different from the other temples in the area. As you come out, turn right, then take the first right uphill. At the top there's a modern white temple, on the left a compound with black buildings. Inside this compound is the Daimyo Clock Museum (*see px102*), which has timepieces from the Edo period.

Take the second left after the museum and walk about 200 metres past the main road (Shinobazu Dori) to get to Nezu Shrine, which is fairly old, with well-trodden grounds. On the side are rows of orange *torii* leading to a monument dedicated to Inari, the deity of cereals. It's also popular because of its azaleas, which bloom in early spring. Head back to the main road, cross it again and take the first right, leading to Kototoi Dori. Cross Kototoi Dori at the lights, turn left and take the first right along the main road (Shinobazu Dori). You'll come to two wooden buildings about 50 metres down the street. On the right is **Hantei**, a three-storey restaurant (*see p123*), and right opposite is a two-storey house with flats. The small street just before the wooden block of flats leads to an interesting group of three old buildings.

If you turn left at the corner, you'll be back at Kototoi Dori, and not far away is **Tengen-ji**. The nearest subway station is Nezu, back on Shinobazu Dori.

Getting there

Nishi-Nippori station is on the JR Yamanote line.

Ueno 上野

Ueno has seen it all. Now it's your turn.

Map 14

Ueno Park, home to some of Tokyo's greatest cultural treasures and its most respected museums, is also filled with cherry trees. If you picture couples strolling alongside Shinobazu Pond, pausing on Benten Bridge, breathing in the fresh spring air and gazing at the light pink blossoms, you obviously know nothing about Ueno. Every spring, amid the museums of Ueno Park, thousands of Tokyoites drink, dance, sing, laugh raucously and leave behind mountains of trash as they celebrate the evanescent beauty of cherry blossoms in the moonlight. That, in a nutshell, is Ueno.

Or is it? On the outskirts of Ueno, near Nezu station and Yushima station on the Chiyoda line, Tokyo can be at its most refined. The University of Tokyo is situated between these stations. Nezu Shrine, founded around 2,000 years ago, sits quietly in this area, too. In late April and early May, its azalea bushes explode into colour, but the blossoms don't spark the rowdy parties seen in Ueno Park. Also in Nezu is the **Ryokan Sawanoya** (*see p44*), a traditional Japanese *ryokan* with baths. Soaking in them, it's easy to forget you're in the middle of one of the world's biggest cities.

The neighbourhoods around Ueno seem more confident, less frantic than the area between Ueno and Asakusa stations. That's partly because of a twist of fate. While Ueno was hammered by both the Great Kanto Earthquake of 1923 and the US bombs of World War II, the University of Tokyo and its environs came out of both tragedies relatively unscathed.

BARGAIN CENTRAL

Ueno station has introduced Japan to many things. It was the site of the first subway in Asia, which opened in 1927. The train ran from Ueno to Asakusa. Ueno station is still the gateway to the country's northern prefectures, which has helped form the distinct Ueno vibe. In Japan, the folks from Tohoku to the north of Tokyo are not seen as being particularly sophisticated, so the shopping in Ueno is more geared towards bargains than designer brands. A lot of foreigners who live in Tokyo barely ever bother to come here. But they're missing out. If designer labels and haute cuisine are not your bag, you're likely to enjoy Ueno more than the trendy western districts of Tokyo.

As you leave the station by either the main JR exit or the No.5 exit from the Ginza or Hibiya subway lines, you'll see **Ameyokocho**, a street lined with shops and stalls. To make sure you're in the right place, look to your right and you should see several souvenir stores across the street, a beer hall in the shape of a train, and a cinema. Cross the street and look for Café Solare on the left. Ameyokocho begins in front of Café Solare and hugs the JR tracks for several blocks. The market ends at Kasuga Dori, in front of Okachimachi station on the JR line.

The streets around Ameyokocho are lined with stalls and shops selling a hodgepodge of sneakers, ties, watches, bags, sunglasses, pickled vegetables, fresh fish, tea, coffee, golf clubs and so on. After strolling through for a couple of blocks, you'll hit a fork in the road. Head off to the right and keep a lookout for the **Marutoku Japan Shop** (*see p77*), a block or so up on your left, which is handy for souvenirs. Keep walking toward Kasuga Dori, past the ¥100 shop on the left, and you'll hit **Matsuzakaya**, a slightly tatty department store that has been in Ueno since 1768 (*see p163*). Its star has faded recently, but it still takes up the better part of two blocks. If you didn't find what you wanted in terms of souvenirs at Marutoku, try your luck here.

Doubling back, take a right on the street before the Marutoku Japan Shop, walk one block, and you'll find the ABAB building on your right. **Uniqlo**, the clothing retailer (*see p171*), is on the sixth floor, and **HMV** is on the seventh. Across the street, between Ueno Hirokoji station on the Ginza line and Yushima station on the Chiyoda line, is an assortment of

Marine life at **Ameyokocho** street market.

Pond life at museum-filled **Ueno Park**.

pubs, restaurants and sleazy establishments. Walk past the Dandy sauna and capsule hotel and you'll find the Ueno Foods Museum on your right. This is actually not a museum at all, but a building with four restaurants (a grill, a *soba* noodle shop, a specialist in Hokkaido crab and a Chinese restaurant) and the **500 Bar** (*see below*), where all drinks are ¥500.

Turn right down the next street and you'll see a tank of blowfish, or *fugu*, at eye level on your left. This is Tetsuchiri, specialising in blowfish cuisine. Meals start at ¥1,980, not bad for the usually expensive blowfish. Beware: they can be lethal if not prepared correctly. Down at the end of this alley is Hoppel Poppel, a beer hall that serves stews, *nabe*, in winter.

Turn left in front of Hoppel Poppel and you'll end up on Kasuga Dori again. Further down you'll find Yushima station on the Chiyoda line. Turn right in front of the subway exit and you'll be on your way to **Ueno Park**.

PARK LIFE

This was Tokyo's first public park when it opened in 1873. It's still one of the city's most important parks, with stately museums, temples and Shinobazu Pond, which you will see as you walk down from Yushima station.

Shinobazu is famous for its lotus blossoms, which bloom in summer. The pond itself is very shallow. Follow the path to your right and you'll head to the boathouse, where you can rent rowing boats to go out on the pond. Carry on and you'll reach the **Shitamachi Museum** (*see p105*), which houses a replica of a Tokyo street from before the Great Kanto Earthquake of 1923, complete with shops and houses.

Once you've passed the Shitamachi Museum, head around the pond until you see a large flight of steps across a street on your right. These take you into the heart of Ueno Park, to the **Toshogu Shrine** (*see p90*) and **Ueno Zoo** (*see p191*) as well as other smaller shrines and statues. Behind Ueno Zoo is the Nezu neighbourhood and the Nezu Shrine.

The park is also where you'll find **Kaneiji Temple** (*see p89*), famous as the site where six of Japan's 15 *shogun* were buried. The temple was burned to the ground during the Ueno War of 1868. This 'war', which was more of a short but bloody skirmish, pitted the new Meiji government against Tokugawa loyalists, who lost the battle, but not before much of Ueno Park was destroyed. The temple you see today is a smaller version of the original.

Down from Kaneiji and on the left is an old Japanese restaurant, Ryumatsutei, that serves *kaiseki* cuisine. *Kaiseki* is basically a set meal that is somewhat skimpy by western standards but is a feast for the eyes. Originating in the tea ceremonies of Kyoto, where it started out as a light snack to have with the bitter tea, *kaiseki* now comes in set menus like the ones at Ryumatsutei, offering all sorts of painstakingly prepared dishes that reflect the changes of the seasons. Don't be surprised to find a red maple leaf on your plate in the autumn, or a twig with budding plum blossom in winter. Take a look at the pictures out front to see what's being featured and order by choosing the price of your set. *Kaiseki* is not cheap, however. Sets start at ¥3,500.

Head down the park's main thoroughfare and you'll see a large water fountain in the middle of the park. Behind it is the **Tokyo National Museum** (*see p105*), home to the world's best collection of Japanese art. To your right will be the **National Museum of Western Art** (*see p98*), designed by Le Corbusier, and further back, the **National Science Museum** (*see p110*), which you'll spot by the huge sculpture of a blue whale outside.

From here, you can head out beyond the park towards the Ueno hills, where the *shogun* loyalists hid out during the Ueno War. You'll pass a series of old wooden houses and find a walkway heading towards Uguisudani station on the JR Yamanote line. Or double back and head to Ueno station.

At one time Ueno was at the thriving centre of Tokyo. Those days are long gone, but Ueno still has the power to charm some and alarm others. Here you feel as if you've broken through Japan's modern veneer and obtained a glimpse of a not-so-distant past, when life was a little rougher around the edges.

500 Bar

2-7-12 Ueno, Taito-ku (5816 0533). **Open** 5pm-5am Mon-Sat; 5pm-1am Sun. **No credit cards**.

Marutoku Japan Shop

4-5-11 Ueno, Taito-ku (3836 0019). **Open** 10am-8pm daily. **No credit cards**.

Getting there

JR, the Ginza and Hibiya subway lines and the Keisei line all have stops in Ueno. Bullet and express trains leave for the northern prefectures from the JR station as well. The Keisei line has an express Ueno-Narita Airport service.

Sightseeing

Outside the Yamanote Line

Jump on a train and head outside JR's inner loop, and you'll be rewarded with a different Tokyo, a quirky city where strange bars, restaurants and shops abound.

Sightseeing

By Chuo Line

The orange trains of the Chuo line leave Tokyo station and curve hesitantly into a course west. With somewhat more resolve they cross the rump of the commercial district and pull up in Shinjuku, where a short pause readies them for the long haul into suburbia. The first six stations on this final stretch peg a line that touches city centre at one end and residential heartland at the other. This is the Chuo line's main drag, an architecturally chaotic area of back-to-back housing, covered shopping arcades, neon-lit back alleys, and tiny bars.

Although recognised as an enclave for artists and musicians, the area has little of central Tokyo's dynamism; for much of the time a kind of post-Vietnam '70s mood prevails. Together with the contradictory nature of its inhabitants, what makes this area so intriguing is the air of almost passive disobedience. This quality has kept it relatively untouched by the pseudo-American glaze threatening much of Tokyo.

See relevant maps for places marked in **bold**.

Nakano　中野

Map 26

An evening stroll through 5-chome, the web of alleyways to the north of the station, dispels any image of residential repose. Here, among the red neon of *izakaya* and the provocative purples and pinks of the girly bars, lies the heart of this first stop out of Shinjuku.

Start by the tracks with **Karma**'s curries and cluttered hippy chic, and work your way in. While **Mori Mori-ya** offers garlicky respite for pasta-lovers (be sure to get there before 'lust orders'), **Coconuts**, a doll's-house Thai restaurant, and the Indian, **Bharat**, continue in the ethnic vein. For those who choose to skip supper altogether, there's **Bar 300**, so named for its ¥300 cocktail and beer menu, and the tubular, UV-lit **Rock Bar Side**. What the latter loses in girth it more than makes up for in invisibility.

For some of Tokyo's best Indian dishes, and worst interior decor, one must venture to **Papera** on Nakano's south side. An Indian and Pakistani restaurant renowned for its friendly service and spicy lunch and dinner sets, Papera's kitsch merely adds a ring of authenticity. Après-curry refreshments can be enjoyed at **Zinc**, whose selection of European beers makes it worth the ten-minute walk.

Nakano by day can be uninspiring, although browsing the quirky shops in the **Broadway Centre** shopping mall (*see p166*), sipping a mud-like coffee at **Classic** (*see p144*), a higgledy-piggledy coffee house popular with classical music fans and lowlifes, and leafing through the foreign-language books at the state-of-the-art **Nakano Central Library** may bring some relief while waiting for night to fall.

Koenji　高円寺

Map 27

Next up is Koenji, one of Tokyo's few areas synonymous with sub-culture. The alcohol-shaped hole left by the closure of Geroppa Soul Bar has yet to be filled, but there is more than enough to keep even the most jaded pleasure-seeker preoccupied. **Matahari** is Koenji's best-kept secret. A spacious, dimly lit restaurant specialising in Asian foods, its furnishings have been laid out to suit all occasions, be it a beer out with the boys or a romantic tryst away from prying eyes. Also on the north side of the station is the diminutive **Gu**, run by the diminutive Kuma-san, or 'Mr Bear'. His somewhat disaffected approach and irregular appearances have done little to deter clients, and the place is often full. A Thai restaurant, **Baan-Esan**, is just around the corner, as is the live house **Ina'oiza**, a 20-odd-year-old mainstay of Koenji counterculture. Expect to pay about ¥1,500 for an evening of rhythmic ear-bashing.

Follow the red brick road, Naka Dori, that angles out from the tracks and you will pass a string of bars of varying interest and inclination. **Troubadour** ('60s and '70s rock), **White and Black** (anything), **After Hours** (jazz),

A **Chuo line train** on its way west from Shinjuku, ferrying commuters back to home ground.

Zizitop (more '60s and '70s rock), and **Asyl** (Asian music) are all worth a quick one.

On the south side can be found **Orange**, a rather soulless soul bar, **Mist**, a swanky all-nighter with a whiff of French Caribbean, and **Funky Flames** and **Club Dolphin**, two mini clubs with appropriately mini dance floors.

Unlike Nakano, Koenji does have a semblance of day-life, and simply pottering about can have serendipitous results. Again on the north side is **Glacier Café**, which does a range of bready snacks, and almost opposite stands **Gallery No'usagi** (Wild Rabbit), an exquisite example of how Japanese interior design can, and should, look. Further down is **European Papa**, a browser-friendly used CD store that throws up some astonishing finds. For highbrow second-hand literature, **Tomaru**, under the tracks, deserves a look. No description of Koenji would be complete without noting the Chuo line's very own Godzilla specialist, **Godzilla Ya 2**.

Asagaya 阿佐ヶ谷

Map 28

Whereas Koenji is wanton youth and '60s outcasts, Asagaya is graphic design, goatees and jazz – a district to which the upwardly mobile gravitate. The cream of Asagaya's nightspots is conveniently located on a grid

of back streets to the west of the station. Due to this proximity, many of the establishments practise a whole-hearted catch-all approach, evident on their menus, many of which list spaghetti immediately below *sashimi*, and *sake* after Samuel Smith's.

One such place is **Ifudodo**, whose pizzas are filling and lighting nebulously suited to couples eating incognito. For the Asagaya experience, though, one must move on to **I-No-Ichi-Ban**, a short walk away. With *izakaya* flair, waiters yell for orders, smoke billows out of the open kitchen, and crimson-faced diners converse in inebriated animation. Also in the vicinity is the first-floor **Uneri-tei**, which blends the cuisine of Okinawa with the 'riddims' of Jamaica. The master's offish manner helps remind you you're still in Tokyo. If you'd rather not be, then **150 Ichikoro**'s take on a US bar, along with US rock videos, and American-owned **Gecko's Lounge** just might do the trick.

For those who've not had enough of the stuff, **Sawasdee**, above the Sun Mall arcade north of the station, churns out reasonable Thai dishes and boasts an English menu. Window tables offer views of the tree-lined Nakasugi Dori, which every October hosts **Jazz Streets**, an internationally acclaimed jazz festival.

A saunter up **Pearl Centre**, the covered arcade off Nakasugi Dori, can be a pleasant way to kill an afternoon and pick up a few traditional knick-knacks for the folks back home. **Nejime**, half way up on the right, is well suited to this pursuit. You may then wish to retreat to the serenity of **Shinmeigu Shrine** or drop by the legendary *gyoza* restaurant, **Nakayoshi** (invariably packed in the evening).

Ogikubo 荻窪

Map 29

Equidistant from Kichijoji and Koenji, Ogikubo is strung out along Ome Kaido and, as with much of Tokyo, some hit-and-miss footwork is required. Pedestrian in more ways than one, it can seem dull after the urbanity of Asagaya: a place to entertain your baseball buddies rather than proposition a prospective spouse.

Out of the north exit to the right is an open beer-and-*yakitori* knock-up ideal for anyone with anthropological aspirations. **Haruki-ya**, just around the corner, embodies the Japanese obsession with *ramen*. Don't be surprised if you have to join a lengthy queue for your noodles. Renowned for its high-quality Niigata *sake*, complementing dishes and aesthetically pleasing interiors, **Saru-no-Kura**, nearby, is also worth investigating.

Over-imbibing the national grog can have disastrous results. One reason, perhaps, for the presence of **Yu-topia**, a high-rise all-night bath-house on the south side. For ¥2,000, the numerous takes on the neighbourhood *sento* promise to absolve all guilt, leaving you squeaky-clean and gagging for a drink. This can be in the form of wine, of which the sommelier-owned **Dominus** has a fine selection, or something a little stronger, say at the canine-friendly jazz bar, **Stone Cotton**, further south of the station. Bowls of water are on the house.

Vegetarians, a rare species in Tokyo, get to flip a coin, as Ogikubo boasts two flesh-free restaurants of distinction. On the south-east side, directly below the International Yoga Centre (IYC), **Nataraj** (*see p135*) offers authentic Indian cuisine, and some 50 metres further on from the station is the Japanese **Basho**. Elsewhere on the south side, **Gruppe** claims vegetarianship, but diners, distracted by no smoking signs, may discover they've been slipped a fish or two. Family-run **Tomato**, just around the corner, does a bit of everything: Japanese, curries and no smoking.

For a hands-on experience of what Tokyoites get up to in the kitchen, a morning wade through the food stalls in the basement of **Ogikubo Town Seven** can be fascinating as the market retains the atmosphere of its post-war origins. Alternatively, for an olfactory experience, drop by the **Spice House**.

Nishi-Ogikubo 西荻窪

Map 30

Eclipsed by its neighbours, Nishi-Ogikubo (or Nishi-Ogi to the locals) seems something of an afterthought, and there is little of outstanding interest. What it can claim, however, is a booming second-hand economy. Dotted about are up to 75 junk shops stocking everything from collectable art to tacky Americana.

Many of the better eateries are located on what passes as the main street, which runs parallel to the tracks and is garishly signposted by McDonald's on the corner. Steering well clear of this, continue down, keeping your eyes peeled for **El Quixico**, an untidy but snug Mexican restaurant on the right. The imported beers and Latin beats are upstaged only by the sizeable servings. Further along, on the left, can be found **Mata'uemon**, a jazz bar cum *izakaya*, and **Aikazura**, an Okinawan ceramics gallery cum Italian restaurant. For reasons not fully clarified, members of the media are unwelcome at the former. At the latter, where trade is far from roaring, they are met with open arms.

Those craving musical abuse should retrace their steps to **Watts**, a live house buried safely below *terra firma*. With punky pizzazz, the place allows guests to bring in their own booze,

Vending machines crop up in unlikely places.

Keep **Koenji** tidy, says the banner beneath the sign for the station's south exit. *See p78.*

a service much acclaimed by the fans of Gore Beyond Necropsy, Bonkinn' Craper and the ever-fashionable Side Burns.

Running the gauntlet of *yakitori* lean-tos that corridor the far end of the South Exit will bring you out on to an open street winding alongside the tracks towards Kichijoji. Either take a right, which leads to the compact Turkish restaurant, **Ajichubo**, or go on 50 metres to **Shwedagon**. The name suggests Burmese, but it's a spicy northern Thai with a well-stocked European/Asian bar. Affable owner and chef Nané is happy to help out non-Japanese diners, as too is that siren of the dark, the elusive Mieko.

Finally, in every sense, is **Barl's**, a Tom Waits kind of bar where heartbroken men get to meet heartbroken men. The master does his best to liven things up, but failing miserably will retire to the cellar to check on his reserves of Echigo beer.

Kichijoji 吉祥寺

Map 31

Although included as part of Tokyo proper, Kichijoji is outside the 23 wards (*ku*) that make up the central part of the city and therefore behaves as something of a capital for the outlying towns and surrounding suburbs. This unique position has given rise to a competitive environment in its high streets and entertainment districts. While this is no

doubt good news for the consumer, it does mean that businesses in this area go under as frequently and as rapidly as they come up.

Size isn't everything, as the popular **Inokashira Park** (*see p87*) proves. Though hardly expansive, the park is exceptional in that its carp-infested boating pond, secluded waterfront benches and pocket-sized zoo attract a cross-section of Tokyo rarely seen in any sort of shared activity. Youth dominates, especially when armed with electric guitar, drum kit and a future of oblivion, but young families, not-so-young couples, and the young at heart can all be seen strolling the many wooded paths.

Kichijoji essentially begins on the other side of the station, the north side, where **Sun Road**, the main arcade, swallows up shoppers as fast as the station can disgorge them. To the left of this main drag is a clutch of nightspots that epitomises Tokyo's diverse tastes. With the upcoming World Cup to be co-hosted by Japan, many eyes will be on the wall-sized screen of the **Hub**, a spacious London pub mock-up and favoured hangout of Kichijoji's monolingual English-teaching set.

A world apart, but just around the corner, is **D-ray**, *the* place to bring a date. Personable, but in no way garrulous, the waiters hover in the background, cognisant of your needs for both privacy and provisions. The menu comprises an extensive range of Euro-cuisine with the emphasis on getting smashed. Another nearby option is the also-roomy Turkish restaurant **Pamukkale**, whose costumed staff are enough to make Ataturk turn in his grave, and **Some Time**, a hip jazz joint that has live sets nightly and hip prices to match. For piped jazz and healthy food, **Monk's Food** (Thelonious, not Buddhist), back over by the park, is one of Kichijoji's more original eateries. The dishes are simple – vegetarian, fish and chicken sets; boiled vegetables; subtle oils and aromatic herbs – and the lighting and prices guaranteed not to dazzle.

While in Kichijoji, be sure to visit the Copa family: **Copa Jalibu**, almost directly opposite, **Copa Bros** and, again on the north side, **Copa Café**. All three mush it up, knocking out thumping reggae, good grub and cool drinks. Another café, though only in name, that puts music up front is the two-tiered basement club **Star Pine's Café** (SPC). Primarily a nightclub, it casts its net wide, bravely attempting everything from fringe theatre to 'spiritual rock'. **Suisha**, towards Itsukaichi Dori, doesn't quite make it into the 21st century, but if your needs encompass Credence Clearwater and the Ramones, then it's the place to head for.

By Toyoko Line

The busiest private line in Tokyo, the 26-kilometre (16-mile) Tokyu Toyoko line connects Shibuya station with Yokohama's futuristic mini-city of Sakuragicho, site of the Minato-Mirai development (*see p236*). The line is operated by the giant Tokyu corporation, which owns everything from hotels and construction companies to cable TV companies, department stores and golf courses. It also owns much of the land surrounding the Toyoko line tracks. In Shibuya alone there are three department stores bearing its name, a Tokyu hotel in Mark City and two branches of the trendy fashion store 109 (which can be read as 'Tokyu' in Japanese).

The Shibuya terminus of the railway is above ground, a little to the east of the JR Yamanote line platforms. Because it is a private railway, separate tickets must be purchased. The good news is that it's one of the cheapest railways in town, minimum fare being ¥110.

On its way down to Yokohama, the Toyoko line cuts through some of Tokyo's most exclusive districts, before crossing the Tama River into Kanagawa. There are three types of train: stopping trains, express trains and super express trains. For the purposes of the three stops we are highlighting, the stopping train will do. To visit Yokohama or the terminus, Sakuragi-cho, taking an express will save you around 20 minutes' journey time.

Daikanyama 代官山

Map 32

Daikanyama, one stop out of Shibuya, was one of the few areas to benefit from a planned reconstruction programme after the earthquake of 1923, and the new buildings erected then (now mostly gone) set a refined tone for the area that is still apparent today. Determinedly low-rise, with wide pavements and intriguing back streets, Daikanyama has in recent years emerged as one of the most fashionable places to shop and be seen in Tokyo.

Its rise has taken place in tandem with the boom in cafés and brasseries. If you're looking for somewhere you can sip espresso, chew on a *croque-monsieur* and watch the world go by, then Daikanyama is the place for you. One of the leading exponents in the area is **Café Artifagose**, where tables spill out on to the small paved square around 50 metres down from the central exit of the station. As well as great coffee, it has a range of teas at around ¥700, and a bakery that makes the French bread that is the main component of its

Daikanyama's giant sunflower statue looms.

sandwiches. There's a good wine list, too, the only blot on an otherwise great place being a ridiculously early closing time. It's often packed, but a quick right out of the square back on to the main road offers a plethora of other café choices. Continue down the street for about five minutes on the right-hand side and on a corner you'll find the cheapest and cutest, the **Stand 300 of Joy**, where espresso and cappuccino can be had for ¥300, along with a selection of bagels. In the evening it transforms itself into a bar with similarly bargain prices. For a more laid-back atmosphere, try **Pole Pole**, a 'World Music Café' just back up the road towards the station.

Coffee is all well and good, but the reason Tokyo, particularly the female half of it, comes to Daikanyama is to shop. This area has one of the highest concentrations of international designers in the city. **Jean Paul Gaultier**, **Vivienne Westwood**, **Issey Miyake** and **Tsumori Chisato** all have outlets here, while for younger fashion bunnies into big shoes and bright clothes, there's **Love Girls Market**, a reminder that Shibuya isn't that far away.

This being Tokyo, as soon as developers get a whiff of money to be made, they set about destroying old buildings to throw up a new shopping centre. Daikanyama's is called **La Fuente**, and opened in December 2000. An upmarket four-storey complex containing around 30 lifestyle and fashion stores, and a dozen or so basement restaurants, it does at least provide shelter on a rainy day.

Jiyugaoka　自由が丘

Map 33

If Daikanyama is Tokyo at its hippest, then Jiyugaoka is Tokyo at its hippiest. Perhaps the abundance of natural food stores and ethnic goods shops in the area is connected with its topography. One of the most difficult areas of Tokyo to negotiate, Jiyugaoka is the meeting point of two railway lines that bisect the area and go off in opposite directions, making keeping your bearings challenging to say the least. It's also the meeting point of two Tokyo wards, so some addresses are in Meguro-ku, some in Setagaya-ku. Each side of the station is a maze of shops and alleyways, and although chainstores such as Daimaru/Peacock, Tokyu (naturally) and Next have branches here, it's the small, laid-back shops that dominate.

Leaving the station by the central exit is as good a way to start a walk round this area as any. The square in front of you is dominated by bank buildings, although a small indoor market to the right is worth a browse. Heading straight down the right side of the square, down the

main road and over the lights will bring you within sniffing distance of **O'Carolan's** Irish pub (see p157), but it's the other shops in the area that might hold your attention. Selling a variety of household goods and imported treats, they include **Coh House**, which specialises in importing American furniture from Boston and New England. There's a boom in this style of furniture in Tokyo at present, as the existence of **Country Spice**, down the road to the left, also illustrates.

Those who worry about their food or who have food allergies will find the all-natural stock at **Chikyu-Jin Club** a godsend. Devoted to fair trade, it stocks only organic produce, from fresh fruit and vegetables to French jams and additive-free American breakfast cereals. It also issues a regular healthy food newsletter. Next door is **Rinze**, which stocks hand-made silverware, fashion goods and accessories that might make great gifts.

A stroll around the streets and by-ways will yield more tiny stores, selling clothing and jewellery from all over. If it all gets too much, head for the **Rude Boy Café** and be lulled back into the real world over a curry or a coffee consumed to a ska soundtrack. For those with jazzier tastes, the nearby **Café Mardi Gras** should suit. It has a wide selection of vinyl and occasionally hosts gigs in its tiny basement space. The speciality is gumbo, and the master is kind, friendly and tolerant of drunks.

Denenchofu　田園調布

Map 34

Once you've shopped till you dropped in Daikanyama and Jiyugaoka, you may need a bit of a break. This quiet, upmarket residential area is the place to provide it. Modelled on an English country village and built by Tokyu at the same time as the railway line, in the 1920s and '30s, this is where Tokyo's movers and shakers live. Politicians, pop stars and TV personalities live here in seclusion in massive detached houses. There are few shops (when you're this rich, you have things delivered), but there is a sense of space and easy affluence. If you want to see how Japan's other half lives, this is a great place for a leisurely stroll.

Coming from Shibuya, just get out of the station and cross back over the tracks. You'll find yourself in a 'village square', with a series of roads radiating off it. To the left is **R1**, the only restaurant of any note in the area, which has a pleasant outdoor patio dining area to the rear that's open all year round. A favourite with ladies who lunch, R1 serves good pasta dishes, the lunch-time sets being particularly good value, at around ¥1,400 for three courses.

Sightseeing

The back streets of **Jiyugaoka** are disorientating, but a great place to lose yourself. *See p83.*

Duly refreshed, take the centre road from the village square and roam. As in all similar areas of major cities, the main point of interest is the ostentation of the architecture. The occasional graceful old building appears between modern monolithic monstrosities that provide proof, if it were needed, that money can buy everything but taste. Bearing left will bring you to **Horai Koen**, a hillside park. If you descend through this to the left, you will arrive at Tamagawa-en, the next station on the Toyoko line, which is adjacent to a riverside walkway leading through a series of ancient burial mounds. This is the end of Tokyo, although you might not know it. On the other side of the river is Kanagawa.

By Odakyu Line

The line that ferries stressed Tokyoites out to the mountains and hot springs of Hakone (*see p242*) is, like the Toyoko line, owned by a company that also runs department stores. The Shinjuku terminus of the line is inside the main Odakyu department store in Shinjuku.

As the line works its way out west, it passes through Yoyogi-Uehara, an unremarkable but quaint area of neighbourhood shops. Because it's close to the centre of town, yet has the feel

of the suburbs, it's popular with the expat community, which flocks to **West Park Café** (23-11, Motoyoyogi-cho, Shibuya-ku, 5478 6065, 11.30am-10pm daily) on Sunday, a few minutes' walk from the station's east exit, for brunch.

The jewel of the Odakyu line is undoubtedly Shimo-Kitazawa, a few stops down the line.

Shimo-Kitazawa 下北沢

Map 35

Shimo-Kitazawa is a perfect place for idling away an afternoon or an evening. The area has an air of unpretentious cool – something of a uniquely bohemian atmosphere. Its pedestrian streets are thronged with teenagers and students whose easy-going, funky and casual attitude is reflected in the local fashions, shops and venues. Catering for this energetic clientele is a host of restaurants, coffee shops, *pachinko* parlours, boutiques and shops with unusual selections of goods, from records to home accessories and gadgets. Harley Davidsons glide by and smooth jazz floats through the air.

The neighbourhood is centred on the station – the Odakyu line is at street level and effectively divides Shimo-Kitazawa in two. There are two exits from the station, north and south, the south being the busier at night. The best way to take it all in is simply to wander through the streets and alleys – everything is within a ten-minute walk of the station.

Shimo-Kitazawa has had a reputation as an arty enclave since the '60s, when local theatres were experimenting with unconventional forms. While few of these acquired much of a reputation outside Tokyo, their presence was enough to attract those in search of intellectual stimulation and alternative ideas. With them came their music, notably jazz, a love affair that lingers on in the local coffee shops and shops.

Unsurprisingly, Shimo-Kitazawa is also known for its live houses, of which it has one of the largest concentrations in Tokyo. Every night, several groups of local hopefuls will be plying their trade. There are plenty of bars, too, varied enough to satisfy the most eclectic tastes.

NORTH OF THE ODAKYU LINE

There is no shortage of places for food in Shimo-Kitazawa. In the middle of the area there's **Deli & Baking Co**, a good place to sit down and have a sandwich, bagel or the daily special. It's at street level, so good for watching the crowds wander by. Upstairs is **Sunday Brunch**, a café/restaurant with European-style food. Across the street a little further down, in the basement, is **Café Plants**, which serves tea in the afternoon and does wining and dining at night. Strangely, it's also a plant shop.

If you head into the area after nightfall, there's also a good selection of bars, most of which are along Ichibangai. If you fancy a spot of the local tipple, head for Japanese bar **Kagiya**, which has a good selection of *sake*. Further up is **Delta Blue**, a third-floor blues, R&B, soul, wine and food bar.

If you're neither drinking nor eating, chances are you'll be shopping. Every street is home to clusters of second-hand shops and it is one of the best places to find young street fashion and alternative music. For new clothes and accessories the coolest place is **In Due**, along the Inokashira line tracks. Clothes are from more than 30 young local designers, with plenty of unusual items. Each designer's selection often fits on only one rack.

For music, try **Schooler** on Ichibangai for punk and hardcore. In the same building on the second floor, **Time to Galaxy** concentrates on techno, drum 'n' bass and ambient.

SOUTH OF THE ODAKYU LINE

Starting off with food once more, the south side of the station offers just as many options for the discerning diner. Close to the station is **Tarato**, a Thai restaurant with cheap lunches and sets. The street heading left just before Vietnamese restaurant **Little Saigon** leads to **Shirube**, a

popular *izakaya*. Further down the street is one of the oddest restaurants in town, **Asa**, specialising in dishes prepared with hemp.

For a lighter meal, or just a break, try **Palazzo**, an Italian-style café and bar near the station. Tucked away behind the supermarket is the jazz coffee shop **Masako** (*see p147*), a stalwart of the area, where fans congregate to listen to their favourite music while reading a newspaper or sipping a beer.

The south side comes alive at night, and a host of bars and clubs line the Odakyu railway tracks. On Azuma Dori there's **Bar Duke**, an American south-west joint on two floors. By the tracks you'll find **Idiot Savant**. Its neighbour **Eat a Peach** has gained a reputation for being one of the smallest bars in town. Just nearby are rock café **Stories** and all-night café **Le Grand Ecart**. By Chazawa Dori there's **Shelter**, a live house until 9pm, which then turns into a bar, open until 4am (*see p209*).

On Minamiguchi-Shotengai is a well frequented hangout, **Club Que** (*see p209*). Further down is **Space Shower Brunch**, a funky, modern, minimalist café with music videos and home-made cakes. One of the comfiest venues to relax in here is off Minamiguchi Dori: **Heaven's Door**, a bar run by Englishman Paul Davies, is furnished with deep comfy sofas and boasts a tempting mix of imported beers and chatter. Down the same street in a basement is **Y-uno**, a jazz and hip-hop bar. The outdoor market by the main intersection turns into a music venue and bar late at night. Further down on the main road is a celebrated live house, **Club 251** (*see p208*).

For shopaholics in search of young, trendy clothes, the most interesting goods come from a shop which goes by the unpromising name of **Pile of Trash**. Record stores are also a feature of the area. For Japanese indie punk and rock, try **High Line Records**, a source of information about upcoming gigs. In the same building on the second floor is Jazz Cab, a second-hand jazz specialist. More mainstream tastes are catered for by the branch of Recofan. **Rakstone Records** on Azuma Dori, by the tracks, caters for lovers of ska, roots and R&B. If all this isn't enough, check out the back of the buildings, where dozens of smaller music specialists lurk in the shadows.

No guide to shopping in Shimo-Kitazawa would be complete without **Vilidz Vanguard** (Village Vanguard), easily the weirdest shop in the area (and there's a lot of competition). It stocks a wide range of books and magazines, and aims to sell titles not found in conventional bookstores. It also sells motorbikes, toys and gadgets, household goods, and other items too numerous and varied to mention.

Sightseeing

Genuine history is hard to find, but there's still plenty to see and enjoy.

Unlike many European cities, Tokyo cannot boast of a plethora of ancient buildings and sights. The fact that it was destroyed twice in the 20th century – once by the Great Kanto Earthquake of 1923, once by firebombing in World War II – means that relatively little of genuine historic interest has survived. Even those ancient sites that do exist are often post-WWII reconstructions of what was destroyed.

That said, there are many wonderful places to see and explore. A random walk around any area of this ultra-safe city never fails to produce fascinating curiosities, while the ancient gardens that have survived the uncontrolled redevelopment of the post-war years are true oases of calm; even some of the modern buildings (see p19) are worthy of attention.

None of the attractions listed below accepts credit cards unless otherwise indicated.

Amusement parks

Hanayashiki

2-28-1 Asakusa, Taito-ku (3842 8780).
Asakusa station. **Open** 10am-6pm Mon, Wed-Sun. **Admission** ¥900; ¥400 concessions. **Map** 13.
Japan's oldest amusement park is located right next to Asakusa's Senso-ji (see p51) and has been in business since 1885. It still draws crowds, but while most rides have been upgraded over the years, their scope is limited due to the park's small size. There are about 20 rides, more appealing for nostalgia than for thrills; the roller-coaster is Japan's oldest.

Korakuen

1-3-61 Koraku, Bunkyo-ku (3817 6098).
Suidobashi station. **Open** Jan-June, Sept-Dec 10am-8pm Mon-Fri; 9.30am-9pm Sat, Sun. July, Aug 9.30am-10pm daily. **Admission** All rides ¥4,100 (¥2,500 after 5pm). Five rides ¥3,100 (¥2,000 after 5pm). All rides & attractions ¥4,900. Admission only ¥1,500 (¥1000 after 5pm). Each ride costs ¥200-¥900. **Map** 15.
Right next to Tokyo Dome, Korakuen offers close to 30 rides and attractions. Parachute Land and Tower Hacker are its main attractions, but the park is currently undergoing a major multi-billion-yen refurbishment to bring it bang up to date. Full re-opening is scheduled for late 2002.

MegaWeb

1 Aomi, Koto-ku (3599 0808). Odaiba Kaihin Koen station (Yurikamome line). **Open** Futureworld 11am-11pm daily. Toyota City Showcase 11am-9pm daily. History Garage 11am-10pm daily. **Admission** free.

Part of a huge development that opened on the island of Odaiba in 1999 (see p92 **Waterfront**), MegaWeb certainly lives up to its name, with a giant funfair, Futureworld, whose big wheel is visible for miles, and brightly illuminated at night. Part of the MegaWeb complex is the largest Toyota showroom in Japan, where you can sit in the newest models, take a virtual drive (¥600), or be ferried around in the company's self-driving electric town-car prototypes (¥200). Expect a queue for tickets, especially at weekends. In the basement, there's a small car museum, History Garage.

Toshimaen

3-25-1 Koyama, Nerima-ku (3990 8800).
Toshimaen station (Toei Oedo line/Seibu Toshima line). **Open** July, Aug 9am-7pm daily (precise dates vary). **Admission** ¥4,200; ¥1,200-¥3,800 concessions.
The opening of the Oedo line in 2000 has made this out-of-the-way entertainment complex more accessible to all. Located inside a leafy park, it offers big, thrilling rides. The jewel in its crown is Hydropolis, a waterpark that includes a surf pool and a very elaborate set of waterslides. For the more sedate, there's also a restored turn-of-the-century carousel.

Theme parks

Nikko Edomura

470-2 Karakura, Fujiwara-machi, Shioya-gun, Tochigi-ken (0288 77 1777). Kinugawa Onsen station (Tobu Kinugawa line). **Open** 9am-5pm daily. **Admission** ¥3,500; ¥2,300 concessions.
While you won't find samurai and geisha strutting the streets of Tokyo, you will find fantastic ninja shows, costumed geisha and other exciting attractions to take you back in time at this sprawling theme park that is a fairly accurate reproduction of old Edo. It's a two-hour ride from Asakusa station.

Tokyo Disneyland

1-1 Maihama, Urayasu-shi, Chiba (English-language information 045 683 3333/ www.tokyodisneyland.co.jp). Maihama station. **Open** varies. **Admission** One-day passport ¥5,200; ¥3,570-¥4,590 concessions.
Ticket office: *Tokyo Disneyland Ticket Centre, Hibiya Mitsui Bldg, 1-1-2 Yurakucho, Chiyoda-ku (3595 1777).* **Open** 10am-7pm daily. **Map** 6.
Sitting on 204 acres in Tokyo Bay, Tokyo Disneyland is one of the most popular theme parks in the world. The park, the first Disneyland outside the United States, opened in 1983 and is modelled on that in California. Its seven zones boast 45 attractions.

Tokyo Tower: 333 metres of it. *See p91.*

September 2001 was due to see the opening of Tokyo DisneySea, a theme park within a theme park that contains everything from a reconstruction of a Mediterranean port to a virtual voyage to the bottom of the sea. Whatever you may feel about the Disney machine, it's virtually impossible not to have a great day out here. Go early, and preferably on a weekday, to avoid the queues. To get there, take the Keiyo line from Tokyo station. The journey takes around 15 minutes. Tickets may be purchased in advance from the ticket office.

Parks & gardens

Aoyama Cemetery
2-33 Minami-Aoyama, Minato-ku (no phone). Nogizaka station. **Open** *24hrs daily.* **Map 12.**
This giant necropolis occupies some of the most expensive land in Tokyo. Once part of the local *daimyo*'s estate, it has been a cemetery since 1872. It now contains over 100,000 graves and is a good spot for *hanami* (cherry-blossom viewing; *see p187*) in April, when the whole area turns bright pink.

Hama-rikyu Detached Garden
1-1 Hama-rikyu Teien, Chuo-ku (no phone). Shinbashi station, then 15min walk. **Open** *9am-5pm daily.* **Admission** *¥300; free over-65s.* **Map 20.**
This 62-acre garden was a hunting ground for the Tokugawa shogunate in the 17th century. Eventually, it reverted to the emperor, who donated it to the city after World War II. Its main appeal lies in the abundance of water in and around it and the fact that it feels deceptively large, thanks to its beautiful landscaping. The park itself is on an island, surrounded by an ancient walled moat with only one entrance, over the Nanmon Bridge (it's also possible to reach Hama-rikyu by boat from Asakusa; *see p51*). Its focal point is the huge Shiori Pond, which has two islands of its own, connected to the shore by charming wooden bridges. The surrounding jumble of concrete overpasses and building sites is, unfortunately, hideous.

Hibiya Park
1-6 Hibiya Koen, Chiyoda-ku. Hibiya or Kasumigaseki station. **Open** *24hrs daily.* **Map 6.**
Next to the Imperial Palace and five minutes' walk from Ginza, Hibiya Park was once the parade ground for the Japanese army (*see p63*), but was turned into the nation's first western-style park in 1903, complete with rose gardens, bandstand and open-air theatre. It's very popular with courting couples and, increasingly, with homeless people.

Imperial Palace East Garden (Kokyo Higashi Gyoen)
Chiyoda, Chiyoda-ku. Otemachi station. **Open** *Mar-Oct 9am-4.30pm Tue-Thur, Sat, Sun. Nov-Feb 9am-4pm Tue-Thur, Sat, Sun.* **Admission** *free (token collected at gate to be submitted on leaving).* **Map 9.**
This is the main park of the Imperial Palace, accessible through three old gates: Ote-mon (located near Otemachi station), Hirakawa-mon (close to Takebashi Bridge) and Kita-Hanebashi (near Kitanomaru Park). The park dates from the early days of Tokyo and is mostly landscaped. Inside is the Museum of Imperial Collections (*see p62*), as well as two old watch-houses and the remains of a dungeon dating from the days of Edo Castle (*see p62*).

Inokashira Park
1-18-31 Gotenyama, Musashino-shi (0422 44 3796). Kichijoji station, then a 10min walk. **Open** *Park 24 hrs daily. Zoo & boat rentals 9.30am-4.30pm daily.* **Admission** *Zoo ¥300; free under-12s.* **Map 31.**
Located just 15 minutes from the centre of Tokyo in the trendy area of Kichijoji (*see p81*), this park has more than enough to keep you busy for a full afternoon including a zoo (not the greatest in the world), a pond with rental boats, a petting zoo and playground facilities to keep the little ones happy. At weekends the park comes alive with street musicians and artists.

Kitanomaru Koen
1-1 Kitanomaru Koen, Chiyoda-ku. Kudanshita station. **Open** *24hrs daily.* **Map 9.**
Part of the Imperial Palace grounds till 1969, and now a public park. Home to several museums, including the National Museum of Modern Art (*see p98*) and the Japan Science Foundation Science Museum (*see p110*).

Koishikawa Botanical Garden (Koishikawa Shokubutsuen)
3-7-1 Hakusan, Bunkyo-ku (3814 0138). Myogadani station, then 10min walk. **Open** *9am-4.30pm Sun.* **Admission** *¥330 (tickets from Yoneda Food Shop across the road).*
A seven-hectare (18-acre) botanical garden with a history stretching back over 300 years, Koishikawa was once a herbal garden attached to a paupers' hospital. It is now beautifully landscaped in a mixture of Japanese and Chinese styles, with bridges, stone monuments and ponds teeming with carp.

Sightseeing

Asakusa: historic heart of Tokyo. *See p89.*

Koishikawa Korakuen

1-6-6 Koraku, Bunkyo-ku (3811 3015). Iidabashi station. **Open** 9am-5pm (last admission 4.30pm) daily. **Admission** ¥300.

The oldest garden in Tokyo, first laid out in 1629, Koishikawa once occupied 26 hectares. Redevelopment, earthquake and war damage have reduced this to just six hectares. This is still an astonishingly beautiful park, with a range of walks, bridges, hills and vistas (often the miniatures of more famous originals) that encourage quiet contemplation. The entrance, tucked away down a side street, can be a little difficult to find.

Meiji Shrine Park (Meiji Jingu Gyoen)

Yoyogi-kamizono-cho, Shibuya-ku. Harajuku station. **Open** 5am-6pm daily. **Admission** free. **Map** 11.

A thickly wooded park with a shrine dedicated to Emperor Meiji and Empress Shoken in the centre. The shrine's atmosphere of serenity stretches to encompass the whole park, which has many tranquil paths, as well as dense overhanging foliage that keeps it cool even at the height of summer. The best approach is from the Harajuku end of Omotesando.

Meiji Jingu Inner Garden

Yoyogi-kamizono-cho, Shibuya-ku. Harajuku station. **Open** 8am-5pm daily. **Admission** ¥500. **Map** 11.

There are two entrances to the garden, just off the main path to Meiji Shrine, yet few people take time to go through it. It's neither large nor especially beautiful but it is quiet – except in June when the iris field attracts many admirers. Vegetation is so dense that access is limited to the few trails, all leading towards the pond and teahouse.

Kyu Shiba-Rikyu Garden

1-4-1 Kaigan, Minato-ku (no phone). Hamamatsucho station. **Open** 9am-5pm (last admission 4.30pm) daily. **Admission** ¥150.

Another beautiful landscaped garden, not far from the larger Hama-rikyu Detached Garden (*see p87*). This one is laid out around a central pond, with an island connected by a stone walkway (a miniature of an ancient Chinese original) on one side, and a bridge on the other. There's also an archery range, which costs an additional ¥140 per hour.

Rikugien

6-16-3 Hon-Komagome, Bunkyo-ku (3941 2222). Komagome station. **Open** 9am-5pm (last entrance 4.30pm) daily. **Admission** ¥300.

A relatively small but attractive place that combines landscaped gardens and islands in a large pond with trails in the woods around it. Rikugien was established in 1702 and the water, landscapes and flora create 88 scenes described in famous poems. It's hard to see any of the literary connections but it is surprisingly peaceful.

Shiba Park

4-10-17 Shiba Koen, Minato-ku (3431 4359). Hamamatsucho station. **Open** *garden* 8.30am-5pm daily. **Admission** free. **Map** 4.

Situated near Tokyo Tower (*see p91*), this park is the spot for great memorial photos of your trip, with the Tower and Zojo-ji Temple (*see p90*) framed in a classic Tokyo shot. In the summer several pools open to the public and there are playgrounds, a bowling alley and other attractions all of which are located within walking distance.

Shinjuku Gyoen

Naito-cho, Shinjuku-ku (3350 0151). Shinjuku Gyoenmae station. **Open** *Park* 9am-4.30pm Tue-Sun. *Greenhouse* 11am-3.30pm Tue-Sun. Open seven days during cherry (early Apr) and chrysanthemum (early Nov) flowering. **Admission** ¥200. **Map** 1b.

Shinjuku Gyoen was completed as the imperial garden in 1906, during Japan's great push for westernisation, and was the first place in Japan that many non-indigenous species were planted. The fascination with the west continues into the layout of the garden, which contains both English- and French-style sections, as well as a traditional Japanese garden. The park is spectacular at *hanami* (cherry blossom viewing; *see p187*), when its 1,500 trees paint the whole place pink.

Tetsugakudo Park

1-34-28 Matsugaoka, Nakano-ku (3954 4881). Arai Yakushi-mae station (Seibu Shinjuku line), then 10min walk south. **Open** 9am-5pm daily. **Admission** free.

A small hillside park founded by the philosopher Inoue Enryo, who wanted to enshrine philosophical theory in physical form. The park contains 77 spots that symbolise different doctrines, and on the top of the hill is a cluster of six Meiji-era buildings that are open to the public during *hanami* (cherry blossom viewing; *see p187*) in March/April and on weekends and public holidays in October.

Yoyogi Park

2-1 Yoyogi-Kamizono-cho, Shibuya-ku (3469 6081). Harajuku station. **Open** 24hrs daily. **Map** 11.

A favourite with couples and families, who spend warm afternoons lounging on the grass. Across Inokashira Dori is architect Tange Kenzo's 1964 Yoyogi National Stadium, still one of Tokyo's most famous modern landmarks (*see p21*).

Temples & shrines

Asakusa Kannon Temple (Senso-ji)
2-3-1 Asakusa, Taito-ku (3842 0181). Asakusa station. **Open** *Temple* 6am-5pm daily. *Grounds* 24hrs daily. **Map 13.**

The origins of Tokyo's oldest temple are said to date back to the year 628, when three fishermen found a statue of Kannon in their nets. The temple is now the centrepiece of Tokyo's biggest historic tourist attraction (*see p51*).

Asakusa Shrine (Asakusa Jinja)
2-3-1 Asakusa, Taito-ku (3844 1575). Asakusa station. **Open** 6.30am-5pm daily. **Map 13.**

The Asakusa Shrine was established in 1649 to honour the three fishermen who, 1,000 years before, had found the Kannon statue in their nets that led to the founding of the Asakusa Kannon Temple (*see p51*). Nicknamed 'Sanja-sama' ('the three shrines'), the shrine is host to the annual Sanja matsuri (Sanja festival) in May (*see p188*), where hundreds of *mikoshi* (portable shrines) are carried boisterously through the neighbouring streets.

Hie Jinja
2-10-15 Nagatacho, Chiyoda-ku (3581 2471). Kokkaidogijido-mae station. **Open** *Apr-Sept* 5am-6pm, *Oct-Mar* 6am-5pm daily. **Map 7.**

Nicknamed 'Sanno-sama' ('Mountain god'), the Hie shrine was originally established in the grounds of Edo Castle, to protect it from its enemies. It moved here in 1659, its role as protector of Edo Castle (now the Imperial Palace) unchanged. Every two years, in June, the shrine hosts one of Tokyo's biggest *matsuri* (*see p188*), and participants have the rare privilege of entering the castle gates.

Joren-ji Temple
5-28-3 Akatsuka, Itabashi-ku (3975 3326). Narimasu station (Tobu Tojo line), then 2 bus. **Open** *Apr-Sept* 8am-4.30pm daily. *Oct-Mar* 8am-4pm daily.

A hillside temple way out in northern Tokyo that was once a favourite resting point for travellers. Its main point of interest is a giant Buddha, the third largest in Japan.

Kanda Myojin Shrine
2-16-2 Soto-Kanda, Chiyoda-ku (3254 0753). Ochanomizu station. **Open** *Shrine* 9am-4pm daily. *Grounds* 24hrs daily. **Map 15.**

This shrine is said to have been established in Otemachi in 730, but was moved here in the 17th century. One legend connected with the shrine is that the head of an executed rebel leader flew back to Kanda Myojin in 935 to rejoin his body (*see p9* **Superstitious minds**). The original 17th-century building was destroyed in the Great Kanto Earthquake of 1923, and the building that stands here today, surrounded by a host of smaller shrines, is a concrete replica built in 1924.

Kaneiji Temple
1-14-11 Ueno Sakuragi, Taito-ku (3821 1259). Ueno station. **Open** 24hrs daily. **Map 14.**

Built in 1625 to protect the Imperial Palace from spirits coming from the north-east, Kaneiji was once the centre of a massive temple town (*see p77*), consisting of 36 temples, most of which were destroyed in the 1868 battle of Ueno.

Meiji Jingu Shrine
1-1 Kamizonocho, Yoyogi, Shibuya-ku (3379 5511). Harajuku station. **Open** *Spring, autumn* 5.40am-5.20pm daily. *Summer* 4am-5pm daily. *Winter* 6am-5pm daily. **Admission** *Shrine* free. *Treasure house* ¥200. **Map 11.**

Tsukiji

One of Tokyo's greatest attractions, the **Tsukiji Fish Market** is the largest in the world, selling just about anything with a fin, at the rate of 2.2 million kg (4.8 million pounds) per day. One sixth of the world's fish passes through this place at high speed, and the energy and frantic activity of the early-morning rush have to be seen to be believed.

Subways and trains start running at around 5am every day and should get you to the market in time to catch all the action. The closest station is Tsukiji on the Hibiya line. Take exit 1.

The highlight of the morning is undoubtedly the tuna auction, which starts every day before 6am and is over in under an hour. Achieved without the help of technological wizardry, it is like taking a step back in time. Most of the fish are taken away by market stallholders, to be cut, displayed and sold to *sushi* restaurants and fishmongers. The auction is officially closed to visitors but nobody objects to a background presence.

The main market is adjacent to the site of the auction, and is packed with marine life of every shape and size imaginable – and some that aren't. There's still plenty happening as late as 9am, but remember that you are competing for space with frenzied fish-buyers, so be prepared to be brushed aside.

The market starts to wind down mid-morning and by early afternoon it's all over. There is no market on Sundays and holidays. In 2001, the market announced its intention to move to a new site in Tokyo Bay some time in the next few years. Make the most of Tsukiji while you can.

Surrounded by the shady trees of Meiji Shrine Park (see p88), this important shrine is an impressive example of the austere style and restrained colours typical of Shinto architecture. Originally opened in 1920, it is dedicated to Emperor Meiji, whose long reign (1868-1912) coincided with Japan's modernisation after two centuries of seclusion. The current building dates from 1958: a reconstruction after the original was destroyed during the war. At the entrance on the Harajuku side stands an 11m-high (36-ft) *torii* (gate), the largest in the country, built from 1,600-year-old Japanese Cypress trees imported from Taiwan.

Sengaku-ji Temple

2-11-1 Takanawa, Minato-ku (3441 5560). Sengaku-ji station (Toei Asakusa line). **Open** *Temple 7am-5pm daily. Museum 9am-4pm, daily.*
The most interesting thing about this otherwise unremarkable temple is its connection with one of Japan's most famous stories – that of 47 *samurai* attached to a lord called Lord Ako (see p8). After he drew his sword on a rival, Kira Yoshinaka, in Edo Castle (a serious breach of protocol), Ako was ordered to commit seppuku (death by ritual disembowelment). He was buried here. His 47 loyal followers then became *ronin*, or *samurai* without a master, bent on avenging their master's death. They killed Kira and were then themselves permitted to die in the same manner as their master, and to be buried close to him, here at Sengaku-ji. Their tombs are at the top of a flight of steps. Follow the smoke trails from the incense left by well-wishers.

Toshogu

9-8 Ueno Koen, Taito-ku (3822 3455). Ueno station. **Open** 9am-sunset daily. **Admission** *Main hall* ¥200; otherwise free. **Map 14.**
Built in the early 17th century, the shrine is a designated National Treasure, and the dragons on its gates, sculpted by Hidari Jingoro ('Lefty' Jingoro), are said to be so life-like that they descend to the nearby Shinobazu pond to drink at night (see p77).

Yasukuni Shrine (Yasukuni Jinja)

3-1-1 Kudankita, Chiyoda-ku (3261 8326/ www.yasukuni.or.jp). Kudanshita station. **Open** 9am-4.30pm daily. **Admission** ¥500; ¥100-¥200 concessions. **Map 9.**
Yasukuni, which means 'peaceful country', annually invites controversy when a high-ranking politician visits on 15 August, the anniversary of Japan's World War II defeat (see p104 **Japanese War-Dead Memorial Museum**).

Yushima Seido Shrine

1-4-25 Yushima, Bunkyo-ku (no phone). Ochanomizu station. **Open** *Hall* 10am-5pm Sat, Sun. *Grounds* 10am-5pm daily. **Map 15.**
Founded in Ueno Park in 1631, this shrine, dedicated to Confucius, moved here 60 years later and evolved into an elite academy for the study of the classics. The hall itself was rebuilt in the 1930s. A statue of Confucius stands in the grounds.

Yushima Tenjin Shrine

3-30-1 Yushima, Bunkyo-ku (3836 0753). Yushima station. **Open** 9am-7.30pm daily.
This shrine was founded in the 14th century, in honour of ninth-century poet and statesman Michizane Sugawara, who was given the title *tenjin* ('heavenly god') after his death. At exam time, thousands of students from nearby universities come to pray for success, leaving hopeful messages on *ema*, small wooden tablets hung outside the main hall.

Zenpuku-ji Temple

1-6-21 Moto-Azabu, Minato-ku (3451 7402). Hiroo station. **Open** 9am-5pm daily. **Map 4.**
The Zenpuku-ji temple, founded in 832, has been repeatedly destroyed by fire, most recently in World War II, after which it was rebuilt again. Its main claim to fame is as the site of the first American legation to Japan under the leadership of Townsend Harris, from1859 to 1875.

Zojo-ji Temple

4-7-35 Shiba Koen, Minato-ku (3432 1431). Hamamatsucho station. **Open** *Temple* 5.30am-5.30pm daily. *Grounds* 24hrs daily.
Today, Zojo-ji is something of a disappointment: it's hard to imagine that at one point in the 17th century, there stood 48 temples on this site. The main hall has been destroyed three times by fire in the last century, the current building being a post-WWII reconstruction. The most interesting thing in the temple grounds is the historic Sanmon gate, which in each of its three sections represents three of the stages that are necessary to attain nirvana. The gate, which dates back to 1605, is the oldest wooden structure in Tokyo.

Historic buildings

Akasaka Detached Palace (Geihinkan)

2-1-1 Moto-Asakusa, Minato-ku (3478 1111). Yotsuya station. **Not open to the public. Map 10.**
Tokyo is not famous for the uniformity of its architecture, but even in a city as jumbled as this, this building comes as something of a surprise. Its construction, in the early years of the 20th century, was intended to prove that Japan could do anything the west could, including build royal palaces. On the outside, the building is a copy of Buckingham Palace, while inside it's a replica of Versailles. The late emperor Hirohito lived here when he was crown prince, but the only people who are allowed in these days are visiting state dignitaries. A great pity.

Bank of Japan

2-1-1 Nihonbashi Hongoku-cho, Chuo-ku (English tour reservations 3279 1111/www.boj.or.jp). Mitsukoshi-mae station. **Open** 10am-3pm Mon-Fri. **Admission** free. **Map 8.**
The first western-style building to be built by Japanese people is modelled on the Bank of England in London.

Asakusa, where monks played battledore.

Imperial Palace

Chiyoda, Chiyoda-ku. Tokyo station. **Map 9.**
Tokyo has been home to the Japanese royal family
since 1868 and the Imperial Palace occupies
1.15-sq km of prime real estate slap bang in the
centre of the city. It is located on part of the former
site of Edo Castle, the seat of the Tokugawa *shogun*.
The non-Imperial masses are graciously allowed
into part of the Imperial Palace grounds twice a year
(2 January and the emperor's birthday on 22
December; for details of both occasions, *see chapter*
By Season). Otherwise, it's a matter of walking
around the outside (a popular jogging course; *see
p229*), visiting the Imperial East and Outer Gardens
(*see pp87-8*), and maybe stopping off to admire the
scenic view and take a photgraph or two from
Nijubashi Bridge.

Nikolai Cathedral

*4-1 Kanda-Surugadai, Chiyoda-ku (3295 6879).
Ochanomizu station.* **Open** *Visitors* 1-4pm Tue-Sat.
Service (in Japanese) 10am-12.30pm Sun.
Map 15.
This cruciform Russian Orthodox church, complete
with an onion dome, was designed by the British
architect Josiah Conder (*see p20*) and completed in
1891. The original, larger, dome was destroyed in
the 1923 earthquake. Visits during service hours are
no longer permitted; call for further information.

Nogi Shrine

*8-11-27 Akasaka, Minato-ku (3478 3001). Nogizaka
station.* **Open** *Shrine* 10am-5pm daily. *Grounds* 9am-
4pm daily. *House* 12-13 Sept 9.30am-4.30pm.
Map 12.
The Nogi Shrine is dedicated to the memory of
General Nogi Maresuke whose house and stables are
adjacent to the site where the shrine now stands.
When Meiji Emperor died, on 13 September 1912,
the general and his wife proved their loyaly by joining him in death; he killed himself by *seppuku*, she
by slitting her throat with a knife. The house in
which they did away with themselves is open only
two days a year, on the eve of and the anniversary
of their deaths, but an elevated walkway around it
allows you to take a voyeuristic peer in through the
windows, one of which even affords you a glimpse
of Nogi's bloodstained shirt.

Tokyo Stock Exchange

*2-1 Nihonbashi-Kabuto-cho, Chuo-ku (3665 1881/
www.tse.or.jp) Kayaba-cho station, then a 5min walk.*
Open 9am-4pm Mon-Fri (except public holidays).
English tour 1.30 pm daily. **Admission** free.
Map 8.
If you've seen the pictures on television, where herds
of rampant speculators charge around the trading
floor making vaguely obscene gestures at each
other, then prepare yourself for a disappointment.
The TSE, home to global giants such as Toyota and
Sony, abolished its trading floor in April 1999. The
stock market of the world's second largest economy
is now run almost entirely by sophisticated computers, which means the building is eerily quiet; the
former trading floor taken over by a huge glass
cylinder with the names and real-time stock prices
of listed companies revolving at the top. Apart from
the cylinder, there is very little movement. If you
want to catch what little action there is left, head for
the Stock Exchange on a weekday between 9am and
11am, or 12.30pm and 3pm. The English-language
guided tour lasts approximately 40 minutes and
includes a 20-minute video explaining the history
and function of the TSE. On the way out, don't forget to pause to invest in a souvenir T-shirt, mug or
some golf balls.

Tokyo Tower

*4-2-8 Shiba-Koen, Minato-ku (3433 5111/2/www.tokyo
tower.co.jp). Hamamatsucho station.* **Open** *Tower* mid
Mar-mid July, Sept-mid Nov 9am-8pm daily; Aug 9am-
9pm daily; mid Nov-mid Mar 9am-7pm daily. *Other
attractions* mid Mar-mid July, Sept-mid Nov 10am-8pm
daily; Aug 10am-9pm daily; mid Nov-mid Mar 10am-
7pm daily. **Admission** *Main observatory* ¥820; ¥310-
¥460 concessions. *Special observatory* (additional
charge) ¥600; ¥350-¥400 concessions. *Waxwork
museum* ¥870; ¥460 concessions. *Mysterious Walking
Zone* ¥410; ¥300 concessions. *Trick Art Gallery* ¥400;
¥300 concessions. **No credit cards. Map** 4.
When it was built, in 1958, Tokyo Tower must have
been a monster, its 333m (1093ft) – deliberately 13m
(43ft) more than the Eiffel Tower – looming over
Tokyo's low-rise skyline. Since then, a great deal of
the tower's original magic has been lost, as a
succession of increasingly tall skyscrapers and high
rises has blunted the novelty of high buildings, not
to mention taken the edge off the view from the top.
The tower itself was designed as a television and
radio transmitting tower, and still performs this
function to this day. But it was also intended to echo
the more famous tower in Paris – a comparison that
Tokyo Tower's current owners are still very fond of
making. A more apt comparison, however, might be
with Britain's Blackpool Tower, since the attractions
inside – a waxwork museum (3F), aquarium (1F),
Hollywood Collection (1F; check out Keanu Reeves'
Matrix sunglasses!), Trick Art Gallery (4F);
Mysterious Walking World (3F) and hologram
gallery – mean there's a lot more tat than class about
the tower these days. Still, it looks undeniably
lovely when illuminated at night.

Waterfront

It is sometimes easy to forget that Tokyo stands on the sea, and for years the waterfront area was neglected by both locals and town planners. Despite a shaky start, the area known as Odaiba, or Rainbow Town, is changing all that. Odaiba is a district of Tokyo designed at the height of the '80s bubble economy on an island of reclaimed land in Tokyo Bay. The island is connected to one of the 19th-century gun emplacements, or *daiba*, that were built to protect old Edo from invasion. By the time the magnificent new Rainbow Bridge opened in 1993, connecting Odaiba to the city, the building project was in trouble, and by 1995 Suzuki Shunichi, the Tokyo mayor who had championed Odaiba's development, was booted out of office by disgruntled voters.

Since then, however, this strange island has come into its own, and become a favourite day out for city dwellers looking for a little breathing space. As well as numerous shopping centres, a giant funfair and the world's largest car showroom, Odaiba also has an artificial beach and numerous examples of spectacular modern architecture.

The quickest way there is via the Yurikamome line, from Shinbashi station. This is a fully automatic train line that makes a complete circuit of Odaiba before terminating in Ariake. A single ticket to Daiba station costs ¥380. If you plan to make a day of it, buy a one-day pass for ¥800. The train ride, over Rainbow Bridge, almost justifies the trip in itself. If you're feeling energetic on the way home, you can return on foot along the bridge's pedestrian walkway.

Animals & nature

Kasai Seaside Park

6 Rinkai-cho, Edogawa-ku (5696 1331). Kasai-Rinkai Koen station. **Open** *Park* 24hrs daily. *Birdwatching centre & viewpoint visitors' centre* 9.30am-4.30pm daily. *Beach* 9am-5pm daily. **Admission** free.

Located by the water at the eastern edge of the city limits, most of this park was built to recreate a natural seashore environment. While traces of the city are evident on three sides (the Disney castle is especially incongruous) the park still makes a good escape. Inside are the Tokyo Sea Life Park, a couple of small beaches, a Japanese garden and a lotus pond. The birdwatching area includes two ponds as well as tidal flats.

Shinagawa Aquarium

3-2-1 Katsushima, Shinagawa-ku (3762 3431). Omorikaigan station (Keihin Kyuko line). **Open** 10am-5pm Mon, Wed-Sun. **Admission** ¥900; ¥300-¥500 concessions.

Divided into sea surface and sea floor levels, Shinagawa Aquarium (which is actually some distance from Shinagawa station) covers most aspects of marine life. The main attractions are the dolphin and sea lion shows (four or five times a day) as well as the tunnel water tank, in which you walk through a tank of fish. Other displays include freshwater fish and river life, corals, fish that make sounds, unusual sealife and the sea at Shinagawa. To get there, take the train from Shinagawa.

Sunshine International Aquarium & Planetarium

Sunshine City, World Import Mart Bldg 10F, 3-1-3 Higashi-Ikebukuro, Toshima-ku (3989 3466). Ikebukuro station. **Open** *Aquarium* 10am-5.30pm Mon-Sat; 10-6pm Sun. *Planetarium* 11.45am-6pm Mon-Fri; 10.45am-7pm Sat, Sun. **Admission** *Aquarium* ¥1,600. *Planetarium* ¥800. **Map** 5.

Over 20,000 fish from 400 different species are on show in the aquarium, the first one in the world to be set in a high-rise building. The planetarium is on the same floor.

Messing about on the river

Funasei Yakatabune

1-16-8 Kita-shinagawa, Shinagawa-ku (5479 2731/ http://gnavi.joy.ne.jp/gn/En/G165700h.htm). Shinagawa station. **Open** noon-7pm Mon-Sat; noon-5.30pm Sun (last boat returns 9.30pm). **Average** incl food ¥10,000. **No credit cards. Map** 21.

This is one of the few covered dining boats on the Sumida river that accepts bookings from individuals as well as parties. Choose between traditional Japanese meals of sushi and sashimi or western-style dishes, especially created for visitors. The booking number is operated in Japanese only, so get someone to call for you. Book early for the best view of the Sumida fireworks in July (*see p189*).

Sea Line Tokyo Company Ltd

Suzue Baydium 2F, 1-15-1 Kaigan, Minato-ku (restaurant reservations 3798 8101/whole boat reservations 3435 8105/sealine@symphony-cruise.co.jp/www.symphony-cruise.co.jp/). Hamamatsucho station.

If you want to take in Tokyo Bay in style, Sea Line offers four departures a day from Hinoda Pier, at 11.50am, 3pm, 4.30pm and 7.10pm. At lunch and dinner there's a choice of Italian or French meals in the ship's plush restaurant (bookings required; average ¥13,000), though you're free just to take in the scenery of the Bay, which will include Rainbow

Bridge, Disneyland and a glimpse of the open sea. Cruises last 50, 120 or 150 minutes, depending on the time of day.

Tokyo Cruise Ship Company
Asakusa 3841 9178/Hinoda Pier 3457 7830/ www.suijobus.co.jp.
Five lines of waterbus up and down the Sumida River, stopping at destinations such as Shinagawa Aquarium, Odaiba Seaside Park and Kasai Sealife Park, taking in the old bridges and the new Rainbow Bridge en route. The lines converge at Hinoda Pier, a five-minute walk from Hamamatsucho station, but for many the best point of departure is Asakusa (*see p53*), where the boats leave a pier next to Azuma Bridge before heading off towards the beautiful Hama-rikyu Detached Garden (*see p87*). Boats depart every 40-45 minutes and tickets cost ¥620 (there's an entry fee for Hama-rikyu).

Rooms with a view

Sunshine 60 Building
3-1-1 Higashi-Ikebukuro, Toshima-ku (3989 3331). Ikebukuro station. **Open** 10am-8pm daily. **Admission** ¥620; ¥310 concessions. **No credit cards**. **Map** 5.
One of the fastest lifts in the world will whisk you to the top of one of the tallest buildings in Asia in around 35 seconds. The building is actually the centre of a complex of four buildings that occupy the former site of Sugamo Prison, where General Tojo Hideki and six other class-A war criminals were hanged in December 1948 after the Japanese war trials. Other attractions in the complex (*see p60*) include shopping mall World Import Mart, a planetarium, an aquarium (*see p92*), a theatre, a museum and an amusement park, Namjatown.

Tokyo Metropolitan Government Building Twin Observatories
2-8-1 Nishi-Shinjuku, Shinjuku-ku (5321 1111). Shinjuku station. **Open** 9.30am-5.30pm Tue-Fri; 9.30am-7.30pm Sat, Sun. **Admission** free. **Map** 1a.
One of the best views over Tokyo has the added bonus of being free. Each of the TMG twin towers has an observatory on the 45th floor, affording an uninterrupted view of surroundings that is obscured only by the other tower. Admire the view while sipping a coffee from the cafeteria in the centre of the vast floor. Other buildings in west Shinjuku with free viewing areas include the Sumitomo Building (51F), the Shinjuku Centre Building (53F) and the Nomura Building (49F), all of which are open later than the TMG.

Showrooms

Amlux Toyota Auto Salon
3-3-5 Higashi-Ikebukuro, Toshima-ku (5391 5900). Ikebukuro station. **Open** 11am-8pm Tue-Sat; 10am-7.30pm Sun. **Admission** free. **Map** 5.

Toyota used to claim this was the ... showroom, but just to make sur ... bigger one in MegaWeb (*see p8* ... to this place than cars. As well ... and fiddle with controls in all of ... can watch free 20-minute films in the Amlux Theatre, on chairs that vibrate in time with what's on screen. There's also a virtual driving experience that's so realistic you're not allowed to use it unless you can produce a valid driving licence.

Honda
2-1-1 Minami-Aoyama, Minato-ku (3423 4118). Aoyama-itchome station. **Open** 10am-6pm daily. **Admission** free. **Map** 12.
All of Honda's cars and motorbikes are on display, and most can be touched and petted.

NAIS
Shinjuku Monolith Bldg 3-5F, 2-3-1 Nishi-Shinjuku, Shinjuku-ku (5381 8211). Shinjuku station. **Open** 10am-6pm daily. **Admission** free. **Map** 1a.
The third and fourth floors of this showcase for National Panasonic's household products are, frankly, missable, although the bathroom department is quite entertaining. Head instead for the fifth floor, where a range of massage equipment is there to be played with. Sit in a reclining massage chair and have all your cares kneaded away.

Sake Information Centre
Nihon Syuzo Centre Bldg 1F, 4F, 1-1-21 Nishi-Shinbashi, Minato-ku (3519 2091). Toranomon station. **Open** 10am-6pm Mon-Fri. **Admission** free. **Map** 20.
Free booze! Try ten different types of *sake* without paying a penny. There is, of course, a catch. You have to mark each of the tastings according to preference on a postcard, which is then returned to you to let you know how your palate measures up against the experts'.

Sony Building
5-3-1 Ginza, Chuo-ku (3573 2371). Ginza station. **Open** 11am-7pm daily. **Admission** free. **Map** 6.
Play to your heart's content with seven floors of Sony products at this high-tech mecca. One floor is devoted to PlayStation, where you can request games to play on the giant screens, while another floor shows you the insides of many of Sony's best-selling products (*see p55*).

Toto Super Space
L-Tower Bldg 26-27F, 1-6-1 Nishi-Shinjuku (3345 1010). Shinjuku station. **Open** 10am-6pm daily. Closed 1st Wed of month. **Admission** free. **Map** 1a.
It's hard to spend any time at all in Japan without building up an interest in toilet technology. This showroom, operated by the country's leading maker of bathroom hardware, has something to intrigue even the most jaded toilet user. As well as the now standard bidet toilets, Toto also makes baths that fill themselves to the brim automatically and can be switched on via the internet.

Museums

From top exhibitions to eccentric collections, Tokyo has something for everyone.

As in many things, Tokyo is generally underestimated as a centre of excellence for museums. The fact is that public museums here are the equal of any other city, while Ueno Park is host to the highest concentration of world-class museums in the world. T]he money lavished on such places by the government in recent years would be the envy of many such institutions in the west.

The city also has a thriving private museum scene. It's a characteristic of the way things are done here that many museums are funded or owned by large corporations or department stores, for which they provide both kudos and good PR. As the recession of the 1990s started to bite and costs were cut, some have been forced to close, notably the Seibu and Tobu museums of art in Ikebukuro. It's early yet, but there are encouraging signs that the slack is being taken up by a new wave of smaller private galleries (*see chapter* **Galleries**).

Away from the large institutions, Tokyo also possesses a plethora of tiny museums, some of them the result of one person's obsession. How many other cities boast a museum devoted to drums, kites or buttons? These charming mini-museums, often housed in one room, are an integral part of what gives this city its character. Like so much else here, they are the sort of place you tend to find out about by word of mouth. We've included some of our favourites, but there are literally dozens more, devoted to everything from cigarette lighters to the history of rubber baseballs. Do not leave Tokyo without visiting at least one such museum.

A few ground rules: museum labels are not always in English but many museums have translated at least a simple introduction to their collections; if you're not handed one, ask for it by saying, 'Eigo no gaido ga arimasu ka?' You'll also find that you don't always need a full translation to get the gist. As Japan is still a cash-based society, credit cards are generally not accepted, except at some larger gift shops. You generally need ID to get a student or senior citizen's discount on admission; the very young, the disabled and those over 65 usually get in free. Note that, as with most places in Tokyo, disabled access is the exception.

Museums generally shut their doors half an hour before the closing times listed. Most are closed on Monday; if a public holiday falls on a Monday, they are open then and closed on Tuesday. (Museums that take their day off on Wednesday follow this rule, too.) In addition to closing dates listed, all museums are closed from about 26 December to 4 January. Some also close during Golden Week in May and Obon in August; others make a point of being open then. When in doubt, call first.

Art & artefacts: Asian & local artists

Asakura Sculpture Museum
7-18-10 Yanaka, Taito-ku (3821 4549). Nippori station. **Open** 9.30am-4.30pm Tue-Thur, Sat, Sun. **Admission** ¥400; ¥150 concessions. **No credit cards. Map** 25.
Regarded as the father of modern Japanese sculpture, Asakura Fumio (1883-1964) was crazy about cats and his sculptures of them can be seen at his combination house and studio, now a museum in the graceful Yanaka district. This 1936 three-level building was designed by the artist and is a melding of modernist and traditional Japanese architecture. His studio was the high-ceilinged concrete portion, with his living quarters – in the style of a tea ceremony room – situated behind. The house was built around a beautifully elegant Japanese landscaped water garden – also designed by the artist – and so evocative of another more peaceful era it is worth coming here to contemplate this alone.
Gift shop.

Hatakeyama Memorial Museum
2-20-12 Shirokanedai, Minato-ku (3447 5787). Takanawadai station. **Open** *Apr-Sept* 10am-5pm Tue-Sun. *Oct-Mar* 10am-4.30pm Tue-Sun. **Admission** ¥500; ¥350 concessions. **No credit cards. Map** 18.
The back streets of the Shirokanedai are an apt location for the small but exquisite collection of industrialist Hatakeyama Issei. Changed each season, its exhibitions reflect the Ebara Corporation founder's interest in *Noh* and the tea ceremony.
Gift shop.

Kume Art Museum
Kume Bldg 8F, 2-25-5 Kami-Osaki, Shinagawa-ku (3491 1510). Meguro station. **Open** 10am-5pm Tue, Thur-Sun. **Admission** ¥500; ¥200-¥300 concessions. **No credit cards. Map** 18.
Kume Kuchiro was one of the first Japanese artists to embrace the Impressionist style; the Kume Art

John Lennon Museum

On 9 October 2000, the day that would have marked John Lennon's 60th birthday, the only museum in the world devoted to a single rock musician opened in Saitama, a 40-minute train from central Tokyo. The museum itself is part of a massive redevelopment of previously barren land and shares a building with a newly constructed super arena that also hosts rock concerts. What Lennon would have made of all this fuss is difficult to say, but with the assistance of his widow, Yoko Ono, the curators of the museum have been able to amass a unique collection of personal belongings that would fetch millions on the open market. Exhibits are divided into nine zones, each of them reflecting one stage of Lennon's life, from early childhood to his five-year retirement from music via, of course, the Beatles and the 'Imagine' period. Exhibits are labelled in both Japanese and English, but for the English speaker the greatest joy is to be derived from peering into the glass cases and reading the great man's handwritten words. From his school scrapbooks to the original scrawled lyrics for 'Nowhere Man' and 'Woman', Lennon fans will no doubt be overawed by the sense of his presence. The rest of us are more likely to be overawed by the price of the tickets, a whopping ¥1,500. The inevitable gift shop sells pricey designer goods under its own Imagine label.

John Lennon Museum

Saitama Super Arena (048 601 0009/ www.taisei.co.jp/museum). Kita Yono station (JR Saikyo line) or Saitama Shin-toshin station (JR Keihin Tohoku line). **Open** 11am-6pm Mon, Wed, Thur, Sat, Sun; 11am-8pm Fri. **Admission** ¥1,500; ¥500-¥1,000 concessions.

Takagi Bonsai Museum: started small.

Museum has changing displays of his paintings, with a range of themes taken from his mammoth 1871-2 trek across the globe.
Gift shop.

Matsuoka Museum of Art

Matsuoka Tamura Bldg 9F, 5-22-10 Shinbashi, Minato-ku (3431 8284). Shinbashi station. **Open** 10am-5pm Tue-Sun. **Admission** ¥550; ¥200 concessions. **No credit cards. Map** 20.
Over a lifetime spanning nearly a century, real-estate developer Matsuoka Seiji became a connoisseur of Japanese paintings, oriental ceramics and ancient sculpture and carvings from China, Rome and Egypt. The quality and condition of the antiquities (labelled in English) is remarkable. Centuries-old temple carvings, door jambs and schists from India stand alongside a 12th-century Khmer sculpture of Uma, Shiva's consort. Various Bodhisattvas and Buddha carvings line the perimeter of displays containing a wealth of Chinese ceramics.
Gift shop.

Mukai Junkichi Annexe, Setagaya Art Museum

2-5-1 Tsurumaki, Setagaya-ku (5450 9581). Komazawa Daigaku station (Tokyu Shin-Tamagawa line). **Open** 10am-6pm Tue-Sun. **Admission** ¥200; ¥100-¥150 concessions. **No credit cards.**
Born in 1901, painter Mukai Junkichi made his home and studio in this traditional Japanese house. He donated it along with 500 paintings to the **Setagaya Art Museum** *(see p100)* in July 1993. Mukai's life-long effort to capture in his art Japan's disappearing thatched farmhouses is evident from the oil and watercolour paintings and illustrations, some of which are charred from a 1961 fire. The garden's carefully maintained oaks hark to the Tsurumaki area's past as part of the Musashino forest.
Gift shop.

Nezu Institute of Fine Arts

6-5-1 Minami-Aoyama, Minato-ku (3400 2536/ www.nezu-muse.or.jp). Omotesando station. **Open** 9.30am-4.30pm Tue-Sun. **Admission** ¥1,000; ¥700 concessions. **No credit cards. Map** 4.
Set in more than 20sq km (8sq miles) of prime real estate in swish Aoyama, the Nezu Institute of Fine Arts represents the wide-ranging collection of Nezu Kaichiro, who died in 1940. The founder of the Tobu Railway, he had a penchant for Chinese art, including bronzes from the Shang and Zhou dynasties, lacquerware, metalwork and Buddhist figures, all of which are shown in rotated displays. In 1909 a trip to America inspired an interest in the tea ceremony, which he began to practise, collecting utensils and artwork. The grounds are a wooded oasis in the middle of Tokyo, with a pond of carp swimming among stone trails to seven teahouses.
Café gazebo. Gift shop.

Okamoto Taro Memorial Museum

6-1-19 Minami-Aoyama, Minato-ku (3406 0801/ www.taro-okamoto.or.jp). Omotesando station. **Open** 10am-6pm Mon, Wed-Sun. **Admission** ¥600; ¥300 concessions. **No credit cards. Map** 4.
For a dose of whimsy, check out this two-storey museum, once the studio of artist Okamoto Taro, who died in 1996 at the age of 84. Okamoto's lithographs, silkscreens, oils and sculptures look like something out of *Alice in Wonderland*, with tentacle limbs and wacky, blissed-out visages. Other work includes candy-coloured seats shaped like giant hands and sunburst-inspired abstracts. Sculptures hide among the foliage in the garden.
Gift shop.

Okura Museum

2-10-3 Toranomon, Minato-ku (3583 0781). Roppongi-Itchome station. **Open** 10am-4.30pm Tue-Sun. **Admission** ¥700; ¥600 concessions. **No credit cards. Map** 4.
Just in front of the hilltop **Hotel Okura** *(see p34)* sits an impressive two-storey Chinese-style building, the pagoda decor of which jars somewhat with the hotel's western retro-modern design. Inside is a dark museum containing a small but interesting mix of Asian antiquities. The collection comprises paintings, calligraphy, Buddhist sculpture, textiles, ceramics, swords, unearthed artefacts, lacquerware and metalwork, and is rotated at least five or six times a year.
Gift shop.

Takagi Bonsai Museum

Meiko Shokai Bldg 8-9F, 1-1 Gobancho, Chiyoda-ku (3221 0006). Ichigaya station. **Open** 10am-5pm Tue-Sun. **Admission** ¥800; ¥500 concessions. **No credit cards. Map** 10.
Some decades ago Takagi Reiki started a business repairing nylon stockings but soon expanded into restoration on a much grander scale, with recycling machinery. His company, Meiko Shokai, combines its recycling philosophy with the theme of longevity as exemplified by the art of bonsai. On the ninth floor of the company headquarters is a rooftop garden, a serene spot for meditating upon the 500-year-old pine that is the museum's centrepiece. Takagi has some 300 bonsai in his collection, now cared for by a namesake horticultural foundation.
Tearoom. Gift shop.

Ukiyo-e Ota Memorial Museum of Art

1-10-10 Jingumae, Shibuya-ku (3403 0880).
Harajuku station. **Open** 10.30am-5.30pm Tue-Sun.
Closed from 1st to 4th of each month. **Admission**
¥500; ¥400 concessions. **No credit cards. Map** 11.
Take off your shoes and pad through this *tatami*-floored museum, a dimly lit paean to the evocative expression of *ukiyo-e* woodblock prints. The late Ota Seizo, chairman of Toho Mutual Life Insurance, began collecting the prints after he observed that Japan was losing many examples of its traditional art to western museums and collectors. The 12,000-strong Ota collection includes work by Hiroshige, Hokusai and many others.
Gift shop.

Yayoi & Takehisa Yumeji Museum & Tachihara Michizo Memorial Museum

2-4-3 Yayoi, Bunkyo-ku (3812 0012); 2-4-5 Yayoi, Bunkyo-ku (56848780). Nezu station. **Open** 10am-5pm Tue-Sun. **Admission** ¥900; ¥700 concessions. **No credit cards. Map** 25.
These three small museums face one of Tokyo University's historic entrance gates. The first two are housed under the same roof and are dedicated to Japanese *manga* (cartoons) and illustrations, as featured on magazine covers and other print media. There are no English translations. The third museum is dedicated to Tachihara Michizo, an artist noted for his works in pastels who died aged 25.
Gift shop. Restaurant.

Yokoyama Taikan Memorial Hall

1-4-24 Ikenohata, Taito-ku (3821 1017). Ueno station. **Open** 10am-4pm Thur-Sun. **Admission** ¥500; ¥200 concessions. **No credit cards. Map** 14.
Regarded as one of Japan's great modern painters, Yokoyama Taikan was born in the year of the Meiji Restoration (1868) and saw vast changes in his 89 years. In his traditional Japanese house (rebuilt after damage sustained during World War II fire bombings) just outside Ueno Park, Yokoyama practised *nihonga* (traditional Japanese painting), taking Mount Fuji and other images from nature as his inspiration. An English pamphlet is available.
Gift shop.

Art & artefacts: western & modern

Bunkamura The Museum

Bunkamura B1, 2-24-1 Dogenzaka, Shibuya-ku (3477 9252). Shibuya station. **Open** 10am-7pm Tue-Sun. **Admission** varies. **Credit** AmEx, MC, V. **Map** 2.
This gallery holds great international blockbuster exhibitions that are beautifully staged and always accompanied by very good catalogues. A Giorgio de Chirico exhibition in 2000 displayed many rarely seen paintings and an earlier Salvador Dali show ranged through film, lithographs, photographs, sculpture and paintings.

Gallery Deux

2-10-17 Kakinokizaka Meguro-ku (3717 0020). Meguro station. **Open** 11am-5pm Tue-Sat. **Admission** free. **Map** 18.
Gallery Deux is one of the loveliest private galleries in town. A high spacious room on ground level does great justice to the important artists, Japanese and international, that are always shown here in long running exhibitions. Well worth visiting and a must if you are interested in contemporary art as seen in Tokyo. Informative staff speak good English.

Hara Museum of Contemporary Art

4-7-25 Kita-Shinagawa, Shinagawa-ku (3445 0651/www.haramuseum.or.jp).Shinagawa station. **Open** *Apr-Sept* 11am-8pm Tue-Sun. *Oct-Mar* 11am-5pm Tue-Sun. **Admission** ¥1,000; ¥500-¥700 concessions. **Credit** AmEx, DC, MC, V. **Map** 21.
The 'best of' contemporary art is shown here in a funky art deco house built by art collector Hara Toshio in 1938. The six rooms and long corridors of this fan-shaped building are the perfect size for showing an eclectic and changing display of

Sightseeing

The best Museums

For making the most fundamental topic seem exciting
Tokyo Metropolitan Water Science Museum. *See p113.*

For hi-tech wizardry
NTT Inter Communication Centre. *See p98.*

For special exhibitions
Museum of Contemporary Art (MoT), Tokyo. *See p98.*

For an intimate slice of old Tokyo
Zoshigaya Missionary Museum. *See p105.*

For children
Fire Museum. *See p103.*

For the unsqueamish
Parasite Museum. *See p112.*

For interactive fun
Museum of Maritime Science. *See p110.*

For chilling out
Asakura Sculpture Museum. *See p94.*

internationally important work by artists such as Andy Warhol, Nam June Paik, Tadanori Yokoo, Yanagi Miwa, Robert Mapplethorpe, Sophie Calle and Yayoi Kusama. Generally considered a forum for artists who have made it.
Café. Gift shop.

Isetan Gallery

Isetan Shinjuku store 8F, 3-14-1 Shinjuku, Shinjuku-ku (3352 1111). Shinjuku San-chome station. **Open** 10am-7.30pm daily. **Admission** varies. **Credit** AmEx, DC, JCB, MC, V. **Map** 1b.
One of the few surviving department store galleries, following the closure of Seibu and Tobu's galleries in Ikebukuro. There are signs that this place, too, may be feeling the strain, as recent shows have gone unashamedly for popular appeal.

Laforet Museum

Laforet 6F, 1-11-6 Jingumae, Shibuya-ku (3475 0411). Harajuku station. **Open** 11am-8pm daily **Admission** varies. **Credit** AmEx, JCB, MC, V. **Map** 11.
This gallery is on top of the seminal trend-spotting fashion nexus of Tokyo, where international design-ers target when they want to get street fashion ideas. The gallery hosts many different events, recently the Res digital film festival, and British graphic design collective Tomato's new venture into prod-uct design. Current and cool.

Machida City Museum of Graphic Arts

4-23-1 Haramachida, Machida City (0427 260860/ http://art.by.arena.ne.jp). Machida station (Odakyu line). **Open** 10am-5pm Tue-Sun. **Admission** varies. **No credit cards**.
At one hour by train from Shinjuku, Machida is a little out of the way, but it has great shopping (much cheaper than central Tokyo) and this institution set in airy grounds. Devoted to graphic design, it dis-plays 16,000 works. The museum also organises Internet graphic design competitions based on con-ceptual themes, judged by an international panel and backed by major corporations.

Museum of Contemporary Art (MoT), Tokyo

4-1-1 Miyoshi, Koto-ku (5245 4111). Kiba station. **Open** 10am-6pm Tue-Thur, Sat, Sun; 10am-9pm Fri. **Admission** ¥500; ¥250 concessions. **Credit** *shop* JCB, MC, V.
Opened in March 1995, somewhat controversially in the slightly far-flung Kiba district, this shrine to modernity is located on reclaimed swampland in one of the older, quainter districts of Tokyo. Supplemented by a searchable database and an extensive video library (both available in English), it has a changing roster of artwork, foreign and Japanese, taken from its 3,500-strong permanent col-lection. Exhibitions are always well presented and the big money spent to realise them is well utilised. A must-see for art lovers.
Café. Cloakroom. Gift shop. Lockers. Restaurant.

Museum of Contemporary Sculpture

4-12-18 Naka-Meguro (3792 5858). Meguro or Naka-Meguro stations. **Open** 10am-5pm Tue-Sun. **Admission** free. **No credit cards**. **Map** 18.
Three adjacent tiled-over outdoor areas filled with larger and mostly conceptual works complement the two storeys of figurative studies inside the museum, built in 1982. All are part of the Watanabe Collection, which comprises more than 200 pieces by 56 con-temporary Japanese artists. The monolithic marble tombstones in the graveyard next door provide an interesting counterpoint.
Coffee shop.

National Museum of Modern Art

3 Kitanomaru Koen, Chiyoda-ku (3272 8600/ www.momat.go.jp). Takebashi station. **Open** July, Aug 10am-5pm Tue-Sun. Sept-June 10am-5pm Tue-Sun. **Admission** ¥420; ¥70-¥130 concessions. **No credit cards**. **Map** 9.
One of Tokyo's oldest national art museums, this comprises Japanese and foreign paintings, water-colours, sculptures, illustrations, photographs and other genres, from the first decade of the 20th cen-tury on. The first and second floors are devoted to temporary exhibitions, usually headlining acts bor-rowed from top-flight institutions abroad. At the time of writing, the main building is undergoing refurbishment, to reopen in January 2002.
Gift shop. Lockers. Tea room.

National Museum of Western Art

7-7 Ueno Koen, Taito-ku (3828 5131). Ueno station. **Open** 9.30am-5pm Tue-Thur, Sat, Sun; 9.30am-8pm Fri. **Admission** ¥490; ¥250-¥450 concessions. **No credit cards**. **Map** 14.
In 1959 Le Corbusier designed the main building that houses the Masataka Collection, named after a pres-ident of the Kawasaki Shipping Company. The bulk of this collection consists of French Impressionists. A second building built by Kunio Maekawa in 1979 augments the collection with other giants of western art from the museum's permanent collection along with usually great travelling exhibitions.

NTT Inter Communication Centre

Tokyo Opera City Tower 5F, 6F, 3-20-2 Nishi-Shinjuku, Shinjuku-ku (0120 144199/ www.ntticc.or.jp). Hatsudai station. **Open** 10am-6pm Tue-Thur, Sat, Sun; 10am-9pm Fri. Closed second Sun in Feb, 1st Sun in Aug. **Admission** ¥800; ¥400-¥600 concessions. **Credit** *shop* AmEx, DC, JCB, MC, V. **Map** 1a.
The museum of the future, set in the 54-storey Tokyo Opera City tower complex, opened in 1996. ICC's focus is on multimedia art that combines tech-nology with creativity. Featuring noted Japanese and overseas artists, shows explore how machines can be used to create art and can become art them-selves. Renovated in 2001, the ICC gallery moved to

Laforet Museum:
current and cool.
See p98.

occupy the fifth and sixth floors, while phone company NTT East opened its own exhibition space in the ICC's former fourth-floor premises.
Gift shop. Internet café. Lockers.

Parco Gallery
Shibuya Parco Space part 1 8f, 15-1 Udagawa-cho, Shibuya-ku (3477 5873). Shibuya station.
Open 10am-8pm daily. **Admission** ¥500; ¥400 concessions. **Credit** AmEx, DC, JCB, MC, V. **Map 2**.
This gallery shows a lot of great work by young artists from the world around such as Kim Gordon (from Sonic Youth), whose first curatorial foray, 'My Bedroom', was shown here.

Setagaya Art Museum
1-2 Kinuta Koen, Setagaya-ku (3272 8600/ www.setagayaartmuseum.or.jp). Yoga station (Shin-Tamagawa line). **Open** 10am-5.30pm Mon-Fri; 10am-7.30pm Sat. Closed 2nd, 4th Mon of month.
Admission ¥400; ¥200-¥300 concessions.
No credit cards.
Unlike other ward art museums, this one, in a beautifully kept park, compares favourably to better private museums in Tokyo, with the well-proportioned galleries complementing a previously edgy selection of international temporary exhibitions. Recently, however, the shows have become more conservative since innovative curator Yuko Hasegawa left. But, no matter what the show, the lovely building and grounds are reason enough to pay a visit here.
Gift shop. Lockers. Restaurant.

Spiral Garden
Spiral Bldg 1F, 5-6-23 Minami-Aoyama, Minato-ku (3498 1171). Omotesando station. **Open** 11am-8pm daily. **Admission** free. **Map 11**.
This gallery gains its name from the spiral ramp around an open central space, designed by Maki Fumihiko. Exhibitions are often site specific and there is one permanent involuntary acquisition – a micro sculpture installed by Jack McClean on the wall at the top of the ramp, which is fun to hunt down. It's not easy to find, but it's there.

Tokyo Metropolitan Museum of Art
8-6 Ueno Koen, Taito-ku (3823 6921). Ueno station.
Open 9am-5pm daily. Closed 3rd Mon of month.
Admission free. **Credit** *shop, purchases over ¥3,000* JCB, MC, V. **Map 14**.
Largely constructed underground to remain unobtrusive in the park, this modern museum, built by Kunio Maekawa, features contemporary Japanese art, exhibiting over 3,000 examples ranging from *ikebana* (flower arranging) to sculpture and oils.

Tokyo Metropolitan Teien Art Museum
5-21-9 Shirokanedai, Minato-ku (3443 0201). Meguro station. **Open** 10am-6pm daily. Closed 2nd, 4th Mon of month. **Admission** varies. *Garden* ¥100; ¥50 concessions. **No credit cards**. **Map 18**.
Next to a lovely landscaped garden and teahouse,

this 1933 art deco mansion was once the home of Prince Asaka Yasuhiko, the uncle of Emperor Hirohito, and his wife Princess Nobuko, the eighth daughter of Emperor Meiji. The prince returned from a three-year stint in 1920s Paris enamoured of art deco and decided to build his house in the modern style. Henri Rapin designed most of the interior, while René Lalique added his touch in the crystal chandeliers and glass doors. The house was completed by architects of the Imperial Household Department, foremost among them Yokichi Gondo. The exhibitions held throughout the galleries are all excellent; recent examples have featured the Russian avant-garde and the work of Caravaggio.
Gift shop. Lockers. Lounge.

Tokyo National Museum, Hyokeikan
13-9 Ueno, Ueno Park, Taito-ku (3822 1111). Ueno station. **Open** 9.30am-5pm Tue-Sun.
Admission ¥450; ¥70 concessions.
No credit cards. **Map 14**.
This wonderful old museum opened in 1909 and was the first in Japan devoted to modern art after the Meiji period. Designed by the Imperial Architect Katayama Tokuma, who incorporated an ornate dome, Roman arches and mosaic tiles into the structure, it survived the great earthquake of 1923.

Yamatane Museum of Art
Sanbancho KS Bldg 1F, 2 Sanbancho, Chiyoda-ku (3239 5911). Kudanshita station. **Open** 10am-5pm Tue-Sun. **Admission** ¥500; ¥400 concessions.
Credit *shop* DC. **Map 9**.
Yamatane, which takes its name from Yamatane Securities, opened in 1966. It once resided on the top floors of the company's downtown headquarters but will make a move to Roppongi in 2002. Meanwhile, those interested in modern Japanese art – from *nihonga* to western-style art– can visit the collection's temporary home.
Gift shop.

Yasuda Fire Museum of Art
Yasuda Fire Bldg 42F, 1-26-1 Nishi-Shinjuku, Shinjuku-ku (3349 3081). Shinjuku station. **Open** 9.30am-5pm Tue-Sun. Closed 4th Sun of month.
Admission ¥500; ¥300 concessions. **No credit cards**. **Map 1a**.
The views from the Yasuda Fire Building's 42nd floor are truly spectacular. So breathtaking a setting obviously deserves art that can hold its own – perhaps that explains why Yasuda purchased, at the record-breaking expense of over ¥5 billion (£24 million), Van Gogh's 1889 *Sunflowers* in October 1987. This symbol of Japan's bubble years hangs alongside other gems of western art, including Cézanne's *Pommes et Serviette* (bought in January 1990), although the museum's core work is by Japanese artists, specifically Togo Seiji (1897-1978), who donated 200 of his own pieces and 250 items from his art collection to the museum.
Gift shop.

Fashion

Ace World Bags & Luggage Museum

Ace Bldg 8F, 1-8-10 Komagata, Taito-ku (3847 5515). Asakusa station. **Open** 10am-4.30pm Mon-Fri. **Admission** free. **Map** 13.

Inspired by a leather museum he saw in Germany, Ace Luggage owner Shinkawa Ryusaku opened this museum on the eighth floor of his company's HQ in 1975. The subject may sound dull, but this three-room museum is a fascinating look at materials and fashion through the decades and around the world. Thailand is represented by a 1974 purse made from a patchwork of frog skins and a 1977 handbag graced with the fan-like arcs of anteater leather. If that isn't squirm-inducing enough, take a look at the Japanese bag made from the skin of an unborn calf – now illegal.

Bunka Gakuen Costume Museum

Endo Memorial Hall 3F, Bunka Gakuen, 3-22-1 Yoyogi, Shibuya-ku (3299 2387). Shinjuku station. **Open** 10am-4.30pm Mon-Fri; 10am-3pm Sat. **Admission** ¥300; ¥100-¥200 concessions. **No credit cards**. **Map** 1a.

Women's fashion college Bunka Gakuen founded this museum on its 60th anniversary in 1979. The small collection includes historical Japanese clothing, such as an Edo-era fire fighting coat and a brightly coloured, 12-layer *karaginumo* outfit, seemingly unchanged from centuries earlier. Kamakura-period scrolls include illustrations of dress among different classes of people. The collection rotates four or five times a year.
Gift shop.

Button Museum

Iris Bldg 4F, 1-11-8 Nihonbashi-Hamacho, Chuo-ku (3864 6537/www.iris.co.jp) Higashi-Nihonbashi station. **Open** 10am-5pm Mon-Fri. **Admission** ¥300. **No credit cards**. Visit by prior reservation preferred.

Iris has been manufacturing buttons for more than half a century. Its vast company museum is worthy of the sweeping fourth-floor view of the Sumida River. A short video introduces the glass-encased objects in the next room. (A sketchy English translation is available.) The first button was discovered in Egypt and dates from 4000 BC; Japan first used buttons, which were imported from Portugal, during the Edo period. Animal horn, embroidery, enamel, porcelain, glass mosaic, gold-plating, ceramic and glass are just some of the materials represented. Look for the Halley's Comet, lion's head Chanel and Betty Boop buttons.
Gift shop.

Sugino Costume Museum

4-6-19 Kami-Osaki, Shinagawa-ku (3491 8151). Meguro station. **Open** 10am-4pm Mon-Sat. Closed mid Aug-mid Sept. **Admission** ¥200; ¥100-¥160 concessions. **No credit cards**. **Map** 18.

Sugino College's four-floor costume museum presents a small collection of old western and Japanese fashions, along with some ethnic costumes from around the world, but it's a dingy affair, with old linoleum floors, fluorescent lighting, chipped mannequins and dusty display cases. (Also, the address on the gate reads 4-6-13 but the museum insists its address ends in 19.) Still, those interested in historical clothing won't be disappointed. A flapper dress from the 1920s greets visitors on the first floor, along with other 19th- and 20th-century western clothing. The fourth floor's Japanese clothing is the most interesting, with Edo-period textile swatches, hair accessories, Ainu tribal wear and a reproduction of a woman's Heian-period outfit.
Gift shop.

Handicrafts

Commodity Museum of Meiji University

University Hall 3F, 1-1 Kanda-Surugadai, Chiyoda-ku (3296 4431). Ochanomizu station. **Open** 10am-7pm Mon,Tue; 10am-5pm Wed-Fri; 10am-1pm Sat. **Admission** free. **Map** 15.

Down the hall from the **Criminology Museum of Meiji University** (*see p102*) is this small exhibition room dedicated to Japanese handicrafts. With models and photos, the museum depicts the step-by-step process involved in making lacquer-ware, from carving the wood to applying the layers of lacquer and polish.

Crafts Gallery, National Museum of Modern Art

1-1 Kitanomaru Koen, Chiyoda-ku (3272 8600/ www.momat.go.jp). Takebashi station. **Open** 10am-5pm Tue-Sun. **Admission** ¥420; ¥70-¥130 concessions. **No credit cards**. **Map** 9.

This 1910 Gothic-style red-brick building was once the base for guards overseeing the Imperial Palace. Now it houses the Crafts Gallery, which exhibits Japanese and foreign handicrafts from the Meiji era to the present. Along with artist demonstration videos and regular talks, it has more than 2,000 pieces on rotating display.
Gift shop. Lockers.

Japan Folk Crafts Museum

4-3-33 Komaba, Meguro-ku (3467 4527). Komaba-Todaimae station (Inokashira line). **Open** 10am-5pm Tue-Sun. **Admission** ¥1,000; ¥200-¥500 concessions. **No credit cards**.

The Japan Folk Crafts Museum is a wonderful antidote to the bustling city. As befits its contents – pre-industrial Japanese handicrafts — the museum is housed in a 150-year-old traditional residential building awash with dark wood, *shoji*-screen doors and other Japanese features. Kyoto University professor Yanagi Soetsu created it in 1936 to spotlight *mingei*, 'arts of the people': the criteria for these were that they should be made anonymously, by hand and in large quantities and be inexpensive,

)resentative of the region in which
Vanagi collected ceramics, metal-
textiles, paintings and other
..cins from Japan, China, Korea, Taiwan
and Okinawa at a time when their beauty wasn't always recognised. Handwritten labels (all in Japanese) beautifully complement their rustic feel, as do the simple wooden display cases.
Gift shop.

Japan Traditional Crafts Centre

Plaza 246 Bldg 2F, 3-1-1 Minami-Aoyama.
Minato-ku (3403 2460). Gaienmae station.
Open 10am-6pm Mon-Wed, Fri-Sun.
Admission free. **Credit** AmEx, MC, V. **Map** 12.
This crafts centre offers a good introduction to traditional handicrafts. Buy examples of what you've seen in museums: lacquerware, ceramics, porcelain, paper, textiles, *kimono*, chopsticks and knives.

Sword Museum

4-25-10 Yoyogi, Shibuya-ku (3379 1386).
Sangubashi station (Odakyu line).
Open 10am-4pm Tue-Sun. **Admission** ¥525;
¥310 concessions. **No credit cards**.
The confiscation of swords as offensive weapons during the American occupation meant that a traditional Japanese craft was in danger of disappearing. To safeguard it, the Society for the Preservation of Japanese Art Swords was set up in 1948, opening this museum two decades later to display its collection of centuries-old swords and fittings, which even non-enthusiasts will find mesmerising. Temper patterns, which are used to date the swords, appear as mysterious, wave-like shadows on the blade.
Gift shop.

Toguri Museum of Art

1-11-3 Shoto, Shibuya-ku (3465 0070).
Shibuya station. **Open** 9.30am-5pm Tue-Sun.
Admission ¥1,030; ¥420-¥730 concessions.
Credit AmEx, DC, JCB, MC, V. **Map** 2.
The exquisite art of porcelain is the focus of this quiet museum in the shadow of crowded Shibuya. Its 3,000 pieces of antique Chinese and Japanese porcelain are rotated in four annual shows. Mirrors show the detailed undersides of some pieces; all are accompanied by captions in Japanese and English.
Gift shop. Lounge.

History

Archaeological Museum of Meiji University

University Hall 4F, 1-1 Kanda Surugadai, Chiyoda-ku (3296 4432). Ochanomizu station. **Open** 10am-7pm Mon,Tue; 10am-5pm Wed-Fri; 10am-1pm Sat.
Admission free. **Map** 15.
This is an excellent museum replete with objects found on digs around Japan. Detailed English translations describe the results of the excavation and restoration work Meiji University's Archaeological Institute has undertaken over the past four decades.

Represented is every age and region in Japan, including stone tools found in Iwajuku, Gunma Prefecture, which are the earliest proof of human habitation in Japan, dating from the Pleistocene Age.

Banknote & Postage Stamp Museum

9-5 Ichigaya-Honmuracho, Shinjuku-ku (3268 3271).
Ichigaya station. **Open** 9.30am-4.30pm Tue-Sun.
Admission free. **Map** 9.
Run by the Finance Ministry, this gives a historical overview of the role of the Printing Bureau, founded in 1871 as the Paper Money Office. First, try to lift the stack of ¥100 million near the entranceway (it's encased in glass, and stamped *mihon* – 'sample' – in case people get ideas). Japanese currency owes a debt to Edoardo Chiossone, an Italian *intaglio* plate engraver who did much to improve the look of Japan's money in the late 19th century, including making the empress's visage on a banknote look more Japanese. There are also dozens of examples of money and stamps from around the world.

Criminology Museum of Meiji University

University Hall 3F, 1-1 Kanda Surugadai, Chiyoda-ku (3296 4431). Ochanomizu station. **Open** 10am-7pm Mon,Tue; 10am-5pm Wed-Fri; 10am-1pm Sat.
Admission free. **No credit cards**. **Map** 15.
Housed in one building on Meiji University's campus in bustling Jinbocho are three interesting (and free) museums. The university was originally the Meiji Judicial School, founded back in 1881, so its Criminology Museum is a logical sideshow. It showcases a small selection culled from the school's 250,000 Edo period and Meiji era crime-related objects. A series of enlarged woodblock prints vividly depicts the various punishments – rock throwing, whipping, decapitation – meted out to criminals.
Gift shop.

Currency Museum

1-3-1 Nihonbashi Hongokucho, Chuo-ku (3277 3037/ www.imes.boj.go.jp/cum). Mitsukoshimae station. **Open** 9.30am-4.30pm Tue-Sun.
Admission free. **Map** 8.
The Bank of Japan has put together a sterling museum about Japanese money in its annexe. It traces the long history of money in Japan, from the use of imported Chinese coins in the late Heian period (12th century) to the creation of the yen and the central bank in the second half of the 19th century. A very good English pamphlet translates most of the exhibition descriptions.

Daimyo Clock Museum

2-1-27 Yanaka, Taito-ku (3821 6913). Nezu station. **Open** 10am-4pm Tue-Sun. Closed Aug, Sept. **Admission** ¥300; ¥100-¥200 concessions.
No credit cards. **Map** 25.
An unassuming room filled with several dozen clocks, from 200 to 700 years old. *Daimyo* were princely lords during the time of the *shogun*; since only they could afford these clocks, which required

readjusting twice a day, they became known as *daimyo* clocks. They used a unique way of keeping time, tied to the rising and setting of the sun; the length of an hour changed with the season, becoming longer in the summer and shorter in winter.

Edo-Tokyo Museum

1-4-1 Yokoami, Sumida-ku (3626 9974). Ryogoku station. **Open** 10am-6pmTue, Wed, Sat, Sun; 10am-8pm Thur, Fri. **Admission** ¥600; ¥300 concessions. **No credit cards**. **Map** 24.

A futuristic eight-storey building belying the history within, the Edo-Tokyo Museum integrates life-size reconstructions of historical buildings, scale models, photographs, audio-visual and high-definition TV presentations, along with an impressive collection of actual artefacts, to trace all aspects of everyday life in Edo, renamed Tokyo with the Meiji Restoration in 1868. Everything is covered, from a *samurai*'s everyday life to Tokyo's growing role as the centre of culture and commerce. The museum shows how disasters, both natural (floods, the 1657 Meiriki fire, the 1923 earthquake), and manmade (World War II), altered the city's landscape. Free English and other foreign-language guides.
Coffeeshop. Giftshop. Lockers. Restaurant.

Edo-Tokyo Open Air Architectural Museum

3-7-1 Sakura-cho, Koganei City (042 388 3300). Musashi Koganei station north exit, then bus 12, 13, 14, 15 or 21 to Koganei Koen Nishi Guchi. **Open** *Apr-Sept* 9.30am-5.30pm Tue-Sun. *Oct-Mar* 9.30am-4.30pm Tue-Sun. **Admission** ¥400; ¥200 concessions. **No credit cards**.

A branch of the **Edo-Tokyo Museum** (*see above*) that illustrates the capital's architectural heritage with an unexpectedly rich hoard of preserved buildings. As well as upmarket private residences and downtown shops, there's a host of fascinating one-offs that include an ornate bathhouse and a mausoleum built in memory of a *shogun*'s wife. Even the visitors' centre once served as a ceremonial pavilion in front of the Imperial Palace. Be prepared for lots of slipping in and out of shoes if you want to check out the interiors.
Gift shop. Free umbrella loans in rain.

Fire Museum

3-10 Yotsuya, Shinjuku-ku (3353 9119). Yotsuya-Sanchome station. **Open** 9.30am-5pm Tue-Sun. **Admission** free. **No credit cards**. **Map** 10.

Between 1603 and 1868, Edo experienced 97 major conflagrations, and large swathes of the city had to be renewed each time. The Tokyo Fire Department draws from a great wealth of material for its museum, and traces the cultural history of fire-fighting. Highly detailed scale models and slick audio-visual displays, one of which uses traditional Japanese puppets, re-enact Edo-period blazes. Others use hologram videos to explain how to avoid fire hazards. Kids can guide a fire engine towards a blaze in one of several computer simulations.
Gift shop.

Fukagawa Edo Museum

1-3-28 Shirakawa, Koto-ku (3630 8625). Monzen-Nakacho station. **Open** 9.30am-5pm daily. Closed 2nd & 4th Mon of month. **Admission** ¥300; ¥50 concessions. **No credit cards**.

Sightseeing

Shitamachi Museum: faithful re-creations of Edo-period downtown life. *See p105.*

Tokyo has three museums that re-create Edo period *shitamachi* (downtown) existence in life-size reproductions; this one is perhaps better realised than Ueno Park's somewhat cramped **Shitamachi Museum** (*see p105*) but pales beside the sheer grandiosity and scale of the **Edo-Tokyo Museum** (*see p103*). Still, it's definitely worth seeking out. Everything about its carefully reproduced corner of a typical 1840 Edo town is accurate: you can walk along the street and duck into the vegetable store, rice storehouse, boathouse tavern and tenement house. You can even peek into the rubbish bin, next to the outdoor loo.

Japan Open-Air Folk House Museum

7-1-1 Masugata, Tama-ku, Kawasaki City (044 922 2181). Mukogaoka Yuen station (Odakyu line). **Open** 9.30am-4pm Tue-Sun. **Admission** ¥300; ¥100 concessions. **No credit cards**.

The Japan Open-Air Folk House Museum, 20 minutes by express train from Shinjuku, showcases 23 fine examples of traditional buildings up to 300 years old, brought together from all over the country and preserved in a peaceful hillside setting. The focus is on different styles of rural residences, with highlights including snow country dwellings featuring steeply sloping thatched roofs. Among the numerous other attractions are a still-revolving water wheel, a warehouse on stilts, and a ferryman's hut of minuscule dimensions.

Japanese War-Dead Memorial Museum

Yasukuni Shrine 3-1-1 Kudankita, Chiyoda-ku (3261 8326/www.yasukuni.or.jp). Kudanshita station. **Open** *Nov-Feb* 9am-4.30pm daily. *Mar-Oct* 9am-5pm daily. **Admission** ¥500; ¥100-¥200 concessions. **No credit cards**. **Map 9**.

Yasukuni ('peaceful country') invites controversy every 15 August, the anniversary of Japan's WWII defeat, when one high-ranking politician or another visits. The Shinto religion honours the spirits of Japan's war dead, from those who died during the Meiji Restoration (1868) on, and the name, date and place of death and address of each of the 2.5 million dead men and women is recorded here. That this list includes convicted war criminals – such as General Tojo – makes the glorification unsettling. Over two floors is a fascinating array of soldiers' personal effects from conflicts such as the Sino-Japanese War (1894-95), the Russo-Japanese War (1904-05) and World War II, with its *kamikaze* suicide pilots. The US army is thanked for letting the museum borrow one of Japan's human torpedoes, found in Hawaii.

Map Museum

2-1-36 Kudan-Minami, Chiyoda-ku (3261 0075). Kudanshita station. **Open** 10am-4pm Mon-Sat. **Admission** ¥300; ¥150-¥200 concessions. **No credit cards**. **Map 9**.

The illustrious Satakes, a powerful *daimyo* family living in Hitachi, were punished for remaining neutral in the 1600 Battle of Sekigahara and moved to

Tobacco and Salt Museum: both were, until recently, held as state monopolies. *See p105*.

Akita, with their fiefdom reduced by half. They thrived, building a castle and ruling for 12 generations, until the Meiji Restoration in 1868 placed the land and people in the emperor's hands. Satake Yoshiharu (34th generation) bequeathed the maps, ancient documents, paintings, personal seals, monograms and stamps used by his family for hundreds of years to form this museum on the site of Lord Satake's Edo residence. Edo period maps detail the *shogun*'s holdings; with their fine detail they appear more like paintings. Included for comparison are maps of present-day Tokyo. You can see how crowded 1960s Tokyo was able to build highways for the 1964 Olympics – by filling in most of its canals. *Gift shop.*

Shitamachi Museum

2-1 Ueno Koen, Taito-ku (3823 7451). Ueno station. **Open** 9.30am-4.30pm Tue-Sun. **Admission** ¥200; ¥100 concessions. **No credit cards. Map** 14.
Shitamachi is the Japanese term for the downtown life of the old Edo period and this museum does a great job of recapturing it, with life-size displays of a merchant's shop, a coppersmith's workshop, a sweetshop and a merchant's home with an outdoor toilet. Partake in the spirit, open doors and drawers, take off your shoes to experience the *tatami* lifestyle that many still enjoy today. Upstairs, rotating exhibitions feature aspects of *shitamachi* life rendered on video and in artefacts.

Tobacco & Salt Museum

1-16-8 Jinnan, Shibuya-ku (3476 2041). Shibuya station. **Open** 10am-6pm Tue-Sun. **Admission** ¥100; ¥50 concessions. **No credit cards. Map** 2.
This quirky museum provides an introduction to two items that, until recently, were held as monopolies by the Japanese government. There's a globe tracing the worldwide tobacco business, cigarette packets from around the world, interactive displays, historical artefacts such as Chinese snuff boxes, a re-creation of Edo period tobacco production and salt harvesting models. At the gift shop purchase some unusual Japanese cigarettes, including Golden Bat, launched in 1906 and recently reintroduced. *Coffee shop. Gift shop.*

Tokyo Metropolitan Memorial & Tokyo Reconstruction Memorial Museum

2-3-25 Yokoami, Sumida-ku (3623 1200). Ryogoku station. **Open** 9am-4.30pm Tue-Sun. **Admission** free. **No credit cards. Map** 24.
Yokoami Park was the site of an enormous number of deaths following the Great Kanto earthquake, which took place on 1 September 1923. After the 7.9 Richter scale quake struck, at one minute, 16 seconds before noon, firestorms broke out across the city, and thousands of panicking citizens gathered at a former military clothing factory here, the only open space in the area. Approximately 40,000 perished at this spot as sparks set clothing and bedding alight, and the fiery aftermath raged for nearly a day

and a half. In the end, three-quarters of the city was destroyed and about 140,000 people died. Seven years after the devastation, a three-storey pagoda-topped building was built in memory of the dead. Designed by architect Ito Chuta, it blends Christian pews and a Buddhist incense-filled altar (Shinto is represented by the exterior stairs). Following World War II, the memorial's name was changed to include the 100,000 people who died in air raids on Tokyo. *Gift shop.*

Tokyo National Museum

13-9 Ueno Koen, Taito-ku (3822 1111/ www.tnm.go.jp). Ueno station. **Open** Apr-Sept 9.30am-8pm Tue-Sun. Oct-Mar 9.30am-5pm Tue-Thur, Sat, Sun; 9.30am-8pm Fri. **Admission** ¥420; ¥70-¥130 concessions; free every 2nd Sat. **No credit cards. Map** 14.
Housing a collection of more than 89,000 items, this museum is Japan's oldest and largest. If you have just one day to devote to museum-going in Tokyo and are interested in Japanese art and artefacts, this is a good bet. Its ornate gateway and guardhouses, taken from the Ikeda Mansion in Marunouchi, open into a wide courtyard and fountain surrounded by three main buildings. The 1937 Chinese-roofed building directly in front is the Honkan, the main gallery, housing Japanese arts and antiquities. The contents of the Honkan's 25 exhibition rooms – paintings, ceramics, metalwork, calligraphy, textiles, lacquerware and sculpture – are organised by genre. To the entrance's right, in a Japanese log cabin-style building built in 1968, is the Toyokan, featuring three floors of antiquities from other Asian countries. For a review of the museum's other building, the Hyokeikan, *see p100.*
Café. Gift shop. Lockers.

Zoshigaya Missionary Museum

1-25-5 Zoshigaya, Toshima-ku (3985 4081). Higashi Ikebukuro station. **Open** 9am-4.30pm Tue-Sun. Closed 3rd Sun of month. **Admission** free. **Map** 5.
In Tokyo, very few of the homes of early foreign residents have escaped the ravages of time and development. This one, built in 1907, belonged to an American missionary, JM McCaleb, and was saved from demolition by a campaign led by local residents a few years back. Now restored and open to visitors, the two-storey building stands strangely displaced in time and location, time-warped to contemporary Tokyo from the small-town streets of a bygone American era.

Literature

Basho Memorial Museum

1-6-3 Tokiwa, Koto-ku (3631 1448). Morishita station. **Open** 9.30am-5pm Tue-Sun. **Admission** ¥100; ¥50 concessions. **No credit cards.**
The 17th-century poet Basho Matsuo, most famous for his *haiku*, made this spot on the Sumida River his home, in a corner of timber tycoon Sugiyama

Sanpu's villa estate. Trails near the museum lead to a shrine marking the cottage's location. Plantains (*basho*) grew there; the poet came to like the plain banana's symbolism – its easily torn leaves reminded him of a poet's sensitivity – and he took it as his name. The museum holds three floors of Basho's poetry, his personal items such as travel clothes and maps of his routes; you can see *haiku* in his own handwriting, along with paintings and poems by his disciples. The lack of English translations makes this museum for diehard Basho buffs only.

Tokyo Metropolitan Museum of Modern Japanese Literature

4-3-55 Komaba, Meguro-ku (3466 5150). Komaba-Todaimae station (Inokashira line). **Open** 9am-4.30pm daily. Closed 1st & 3rd Mon of month. **Admission** free.

Once owned by the royal Maeda family, the large two-storey brick mansion housing this museum was designed as an exemplar of English Tudor architecture in 1929. Wide stairwells, lofty ceilings and dark-wood accents provide the university-library setting for the collection of original manuscripts, first editions, photographs and other memorabilia from modern Japanese writers. None of the descriptions is in English. Next door is the Japan Museum of Modern Literature (3486 4181; 9.30am-4.30pm Tue-Sat), with more manuscripts by well-known Japanese authors. Everything here, too, is in Japanese only, and the setting's far less spectacular. *Lockers. Lounge.*

Offbeat

Beer Museum Yebisu

4-20-1 Ebisu Garden Place, Shibuya-ku (5423 7255/www.sapporobeer.co.jp). Ebisu station. **Open** 10am-6pm Tue-Sun. **Admission** free; beer ¥200. **No credit cards**. **Map** 3.

Part of the outdoor mall-like Ebisu Garden Place (built in 1994), this spacious museum was established by Sapporo where one of its breweries once stood. Displays recount the history of beer around the world and the science of brewing. Amid the historical photographs, beer labels and ads are video displays and touch-screen computers, and there's also a virtual-reality brewery tour. After learning how beer is made, you can taste the real thing in the bar-like lounge. *Gift shop. Tasting lounge.*

Drum Museum

Nishi-Asakusa Bldg 4F, 2-1-1 Nishi-Asakusa, Taito-ku (3842 5622). Asakusa station. **Open** 10am-5pm Wed-Sun. **Admission** ¥300; ¥150 concessions. **No credit cards**. **Map** 13.

Interactive museum-going at its best. Bang away on hundreds of drums from all over the world in this well-organised museum above a family-run drum and Buddhist festival shop. Not all can be played, however. Look for the blue dot; red means no. *Gift shop.*

Eyeglass Museum

Iris Optical 6-7F, 2-29-18 Dogenzaka, Shibuya-ku (3496 3315). Shibuya station. **Open** 11am-5pm Tue-Sun. **Admission** free. **No credit cards**. **Map** 2.

The first spectacles appeared in Italy in 1280 but Japan had to endure blurry vision till the 16th century, when Jesuit priest Francis de Xavier brought a pair over. There's a large statue of him in the corner, a pair of glasses dangling from his hand. The 6,000-strong collection is periodically changed. On the sixth floor the museum has rebuilt an 1800 French eyeglass workshop, shipped over in its entirety from the French Alps.

Japan Stationery Museum

1-1-15 Yanagibashi, Taito-ku (3861 4905). Asakusabashi station. **Open** 10am-4pm Mon-Fri; 10am-noon Sat. **Admission** free. **No credit cards**. **Map** 24.

One floor dedicated to the history of writing and calculating implements, with exhibits ranging from Egyptian papyrus and abacuses – still widely used all over Asia – to manual typewriters with interchangeable *kanji* keys. In the back is a 14kg (31lb) brush made from the hair of more than 50 horses; some examples of calligraphy using smaller brushes hang on the wall. As you walk out, an elderly gentleman hands you a free Pilot pen.

Kite Museum

Taimeiken 5F, 1-12-10 Nihonbashi, Chuo-ku (3271 2465). Nihonbashi station. **Open** 11am-5pm Mon, Tue, Thur-Sat. **Admission** ¥200; ¥100 concessions. **No credit cards**. **Map** 8.

Located in drab Nihonbashi, this museum is a cornucopia of colourful kites. Layered on the walls, packed in display cases and crowding the ceiling, the 2,000 kites represent the lifelong collecting efforts of the former owner of the first-floor restaurant (one of Tokyo's earliest forays into western-style dining). The global collection ranges from dried flat leaves from Indonesia to giant woodblock-print *samurai* kites. *Gift shop.*

Photography & film

JCII Camera Museum

JCII Ichibancho Bldg B1, 25 Ichibancho, Chiyoda-ku (3263 7110). Hanzomon station. **Open** 10am-5pm Tue-Sun. **Admission** ¥300; ¥100 concessions. **No credit cards**. **Map** 9.

Operated by the organisation that tests and inspects Japanese cameras, the JCII Camera Museum displays 500 cameras from around the world. The first camera ever made, the 1839 Giroux Daguerrotype, is here; it's a surprisingly compact wooden box. Newer models are represented by pocket-size cameras that use the Advanced Photo System jointly devised (in a rare moment of co-operation) by Fuji Film and Kodak. *Gift shop.*

This reconstruction of an 1800 French workshop is one of the highlights of the **Eyeglass Museum**. *See p106.*

National Film Centre, National Museum of Modern Art
3-7-6 Kyobashi, Chuo-ku (3561 0823).
Kyobashi station. **Open** 10.30am-5.30pm
Tue-Fri. **Admission** ¥210; ¥90-¥120 concessions.
No credit cards. **Map** 8.

Japan's only national facility devoted to the preservation and study of films fills its two cinemas for screenings of archival films in themed festivals throughout the year. It has a strong collection of about 19,000 Japanese and foreign films. Film fanatics, meanwhile, can indulge in the film-book library

Little museums of Sumida-ku

The Little Museums of Sumida are spread out between the Sumida River to the west and Arakawa to the east. In the main they are operational craft shops with historical displays that have been awarded the well-deserved title of 'meister' by the Sumida ward.

The age-old traditions, many extant since the Edo period, will have you awestruck. Most of these museums are not easily accessible, however, and they appear, if anything, to be getting harder for non-Japanese speakers to visit, as the Sumida City Office has stopped publishing information about them in English. Very few of the craftspeople who own these workshops and galleries speak English, and as you need to make an appointment before going, it is almost impossible to do so unless you speak Japanese.

Because most of these places are small businesses, opening times are erratic. Do not be put off, though, the Sumida City Office is very helpful despite their fiscal retraction, and if you are organised and plan your visit ahead they will give you all the advice you will need (*see below*). There is an incredible range of crafts on offer, unique to Japan, and maybe only to be seen here for another generation or so, as four have closed since last year. Once you have made your arrangements to visit the museums, you then have to find them: the best way is not to hurry and take the time to enjoy trailing down the twisted old back streets following the detailed map that you can obtain at the Sumida City Office.

Sumida City Office

Cultural Affairs Department, Sumida City, 1-23-20 Azumabashi, Sumida City (5608 6186). Narihirabashi Station (Tobu Isezaki line). **Open** 10am-5pm Mon-Fri.
The Sumida City Office has an international section to assist non-Japanese speakers. If you need help making reservations call 5608 6212 and ask for Ashida-san ('Ashida-san, onegaishimasu').

Aizome Museum

Kyonjima 1-29-1, Sumida -ku (3611 6761). Hikifune station (Keisei line). **Open** 1-5pm Mon-Sat.
Everything you could want to know about dyeing *yukata* is made known to you here.

Alloy Casting Museum

Lions Mansion Oshige 403, 3-4-13 Harihira (3642 2494). Narihirabashi station (Tobu Isezaki line). **Open** 10am-5pm Mon-Sat.
Learn how the Giant Buddha in Kamakura was made.

Battledore Museum

5-43-25 Mukojima (3623 1305). Hikifune station (Tobu Isezaki/Kameido lines). **Open** 10am-5pm Thur-Sat. Closed 15 June-15 July, 1 Nov-20 Jan.
Pre-war battledore bats.

Cigarette Lighter Museum

Ivy Antiques Gallery 3F, 1-27-6 Mukojima (3622 1649). Narihirabashi station (Tobu Isezaki line). **Open** 10am-6.30pm daily.
More than 800 lighters to spark your interest.

Construction Tools & Wooden Frame Museum

1-5-33 Kikukawa (3633 0328). Morishita station. **Open** 10am-4pm Sat, 4th Sun of month.
Find out how they built wooden houses without the use of nails.

Fabric Dying Museum (Some-Komon Museum)

Oomatu Dye Factory, 2-24-9 Yahiro (3611 5019). Hikifune station (Keisei line). **Open** 11am-5pm Mon-Fri.
Komon are the intricate graphic patterns you see on *kimono*. View patterns here.

Fortune Seal Museum

2-10-9 Kyojima (3612 1691). Hikifune station (Tobu Isezaki/Kameido lines). **Open** 1-5pm Wed.
Fortune seals were stuck on temples and shrine poles.

on the fourth floor or take in the changing exhibitions in the seventh-floor gallery, which presents shows of film-related items and photographs, as well as graphic design, often drawn from its own considerable store of posters, screenplays and stills. *Café.*

Tokyo Metropolitan Museum of Photography
1-13-3 Mita, Meguro-ku (3280 0031/www.tokyo-photo-museum.or.jp). Ebisu station. **Open** 10am-6pm Tue, Wed, Sat, Sun; 10am-8pm Thur, Fri. **Admission** ¥500; ¥250 concessions. **No credit cards**. **Map** 3.

Kawashima Knit Works Museum
3-9-8 Mukojima (3622 6350). Narihirabashi station (Tobu Isezaki line). **Open** 10am-5pm Mon-Fri.
Knit one, pearl one, knit one, pearl one.

Kobayashi Doll Museum
6-31-2 Yahiro (3612 1644). Yahiro station (Keisei Oshiage line). **Open** 10.30am-5pm Fri-Sun.
Watch dolls being made in the workshop. See *kamikaze* pilots' 'honour dolls', too.

Ko-imari Porcelain Museum
A-S Motors 2F, 5-23-9 Yahiro (3619 3867). Yahira station (Keisei Oshiage line). **Open** 11am-6pm Sat.
Domestic ware from the Edo period.

Noh Mask Museum
5-10-5 Narihira (3623 3055). Nariharabashi station (Tobu Isezaki line). **Open** 9am-5pm Tue, Sat, 4th Sun of month.
See how *Noh* masks are made.

Paulownia Wood Furniture Museum
4-1-8 Ryogoku (3632 0341). Ryogoku station. **Open** 10am-6pm Tue, Thur-Sun.
Musical instruments, furniture and sculpture.

Portable Folding Screen Museum
1-31-6 Mukojima (3622 4470). Narihirabashi station (Tobu Isezaki line). **Open** 9am-5pm Mon-Sat. Closed 2nd & 4th Sat of month May-Sept.
Screens and tools from Nara to Edo periods.

Rubber Baseball Museum
2-36-190 Sumida (3614 3501) Kanagafuchi station (Tobu Isezaki line). **Open** 9am-5pm Mon-Fri, 1st & 3rd Sat of month.
The history of balls, bats and gloves.

Safe & Key Museum
3-4-1 Chitose (3633 9151). Morishita station (Toei Shinjuku line). **Open** 10am-5pm 1st & 3rd Sat & Sun of month. Closed Aug.
Where *did* the Japanese Army store those secret codes during the war? Find out here.

Sumo Photograph Museum
3-13-2 Ryogoku (3631 2150). Ryogoku station. **Open** 10am-5pm Tue; open daily during the Jan, May and Sept tournaments.
Photographs and other memorabilia donated by the Japan Sumo Association.

Suzuki Woodwork Museum
6-38-15 Higashi-Mukojima (3616 5008). Higashi-Mukojima station (Tobu Isezaki line). **Open** 10am-4pm Mon-Fri.
Here you will see examples of embossing and lashing and handmade woodwork.

Tabi Museum
1-9-3 Midori (3631 0092). Ryogoku station. **Open** 9am-6pm Mon-Sat.
See traditional split-toe socks here.

Takinami Glassware Museum
1-18-19 Taihei (3622 4141). Kinshicho station. **Open** 10am-6.30pm daily. Closed 2nd Mon of month. Factory closes at 5pm, classes 10am-4pm.
Displays and how-to. Classes available.

Tortoiseshell Work Museum
2-5-5 Yokoami (3625 5875). Ryogoku station. **Open** 10am-5.30pm daily.
Tools and ornamental hairpins.

Traditional Wood Sculpture Museum
4-7-8 Higashi-Komagata (3623 0273). Narihirabashi station (Tobu Isezaki line). **Open** noon-5pm 1st, 2nd & 3rd Fri & Sat of month.
Sculptures that decorated temples and shrines.

Wooden House Museum
1-7-16 Tsumi (3612 7724). Higashi Mukojima station (Tobu Isezaki line). **Open** 10am-4pm Sat, 4th Sun of month.
Ingeniously simple woodworking tools.

Woodwork Museum
2-9-11 Kinshi (3625 2401). Kinshicho station. **Open** 10am-5pm daily.
Toys, handcrafts and 'dry wood' furniture.

Sightseeing

Tokyo has dozens of interesting little photography galleries, but this museum, filling four shiny floors in a corner of the Ebisu Garden Place complex, outdoes them in terms of sheer scale and technology and benefits from curators who do an excellent job of framing the changing displays of its permanent collection. Photography's natural segue into the moving picture has not been neglected, either: in the basement, the Images and Technology Gallery presents a multimedia history of film as well as temporary exhibitions featuring numerous mixed-media and video artists.
Café. Gift shop. Lockers.

Zeit Foto Salon
Yagicho Building, 5F, 1-7-2 Nihonbashi, Muromachi, Chuo-ku (3246 1370/ www.zeit-foto.com). Mitsukoshi-mae station. **Open** 10.30am-6.30pm Tue-Fri; 10.30am-5.30pm Sat. **Admission** varies. **No credit cards.** **Map 8.**
Zeit Foto Salon is one of the leading photography galleries in Tokyo, whose exhibitions are always well chosen and evocative. It's easy to find and not to be overlooked.

Science & technology

Communications Museum
2-3-1 Otemachi, Chiyoda-ku (3244 6811). Otemachi station. **Open** 9am-4.30pm Tue-Thur, Sat, Sun; 9am-6.30pm Fri. **Admission** ¥110; ¥50 concessions. **No credit cards.** **Map 8.**
This massive museum tells the stories of several of Japan's enormous communications entities, including national broadcaster NHK, telecommunications companies NTT and KDD, and the Post and Telecommunications Ministry. Histories of each institution, conveyed by artefacts, such as early cable wiring and transmitters, combine with state-of-the-art multimedia displays. A company or ministry sponsors each portion of the museum, so the up-with-technology propaganda can be overbearing (there's no talk of harmful monopolies or environmental concerns). Among the most popular items is a bank of TVs with video games and NHK shows. NHK's Hi-Vision theatre is also popular – seats in front of the large, high-definition screen are filled with adults taking a nap.
Gift shop. Lounge.

Japan Science Foundation Science Museum
2-1 Kitanomaru Koen, Chiyoda-ku (3212 8544/ www.jsf.or.jp/index). Kudanshita station. **Open** 9.30am-4pm daily. **Admission** ¥600; ¥250-¥400 concessions. **No credit cards.** **Map 9.**
The Japan Science Foundation Science Museum takes the maxim 'learning by doing' to the extreme. Located in a corner of Kitanomaru Park, the unique five-spoke building comprises five floors of interactive exhibits. Don't let its drab, dated entranceway put you off, because the displays are great. Kids

can learn about science as they stand inside a huge soap bubble, lift a small car using pulleys or generate electricity by jumping or shouting. Naturally, there are plenty of computers, high-definition television sets and other audio-visual aids. There's not a lot of English to be found, though much of the interaction needs no translation.
Gift shop.

Museum of Maritime Science
3-1 Higashi-Yashio, Shinagawa-ku (5500 1111). Tokyo Teleport station (Rinka-Fukutoshin line)/ferry from Hinode Sambashi to Fune-no-kagakukan. **Open** 10am-5pm Mon-Fri; 10am-6pm Sat, Sun. **Admission** varies. **No credit cards.**
A ship-shaped building housing all manner of nautical delights, this museum offers everything from historical replicas to up-to-the-minute displays and interactive games and a special effects theatre. The restaurant is decked out like a cruise liner.
Restaurant.

National Science Museum
7-20 Ueno Koen, Taito-ku (3822 1111/ www.kahaku.go.jp). Ueno station. **Open** *Apr-Sept* 9.30am-8pm Tue-Sun. *Oct-Mar* 9am-4.30pm Tue-Sun. **Admission** ¥420; ¥70 concessions; free 2nd Sat of month. **No credit cards.** **Map 14.**
The whole wide world of science is on show here, from dinosaurs to mummies, spiders and snakes. The English guidebook, which you can purchase at the front desk, is helpful because the exhibits are all labelled in Japanese.

Nature Study Institute & Park
5-21-5 Shiroganedai, Minato-ku (3441 7176). Meguro station. **Open** *Sept-Apr* 9am-4pm Tue-Sun. *May-Aug* 9am-5pm Tue-Sun. **Admission** ¥210; ¥60 concessions. **No credit cards.** **Map 18.**
The Nature Study Institute and Park, which fill 20 hectares (49 acres), retain the original wildlife characteristics of the historic Musashino (Musashi Plain), which, after six centuries of existence, was turned into a space for the study of nature in 1949. About 750 plants, 100 birds and 1,300 types of insect make their homes here. The one-room museum at the entrance shows how the amount of greenery in Tokyo has decreased since 1677, largely as a result of dwindling temple grounds. Push-buttons allow you to hear the calls of the various stuffed birds in the central display.
Gift shop.

NHK Broadcast Museum
2-1-1 Atago, Minato-ku (5400 6900/ www.nhk.or.jp/bunken/museum-en). Kamiyacho station. **Open** 9.30am-4.30pm Tue-Sun. **Admission** free. **Map 4.**
Tracing the history of radio and television, this museum is run by Japan's national broadcaster and is located at the birthplace of Japan's first broadcasting station, which began transmitting radio waves in July 1925. (NHK itself has since moved to bigger digs in Shibuya.) There are two floors of

**TEPCO Electric Energy
Museum**: seven floors
of electrifying displays
See p112.

early equipment along with actual examples of radios and television sets, such as a refrigerator-sized television set whose images were watched via a mirror. Among the historical microphones, television cameras and transmitters, vintage television shows and news broadcasts play (some are available for viewing at the video library). See the vinyl disk containing the recording of Emperor Showa's announcement of Japan's surrender, ending World War II; it was the first time the public had heard the emperor's voice.
Gift shop.

Parasite Museum

4-1-1 Shimo-Meguro, Meguro-ku (3716 1264). Meguro station. **Open** 10am-5pm Tue-Sun. **Admission** free. **Map** 18.

Medical doctor Kamegai Satoru opened this museum in 1953 after he noticed that his post-war practice increasingly dealt with parasites because of widespread unsanitary conditions. The museum now displays some 300 samples of 45,000 parasites he has collected, among them 20 that are his foundation's new discoveries. The second floor has a display of an 8.8m (29ft) tapeworm taken from the body of a 40-year-old man. Parasites preserved in plastic keyrings are available at the gift shop.
Gift shop.

Sony Science Museum

Sony Headquarters Bldg, 6-7-35 Kita Shinagawa-ku (5448 4455). Gotanda or Osaki station. **Open** 10am-5pm Mon-Fri. **Admission** free. **Map** 19.

Sony products from the early days to the present are on display here, but the most interesting part of this museum is the interactive Environmental Exhibition Room. You can find out all you want to know about the recycling of electronic equipment, and, best of all, how Sony has recently developed a process using an ingredient from oranges to re-assimilate Styrofoam harmlessly back into the environment. Sounds boring, but it's not.

TEPCO Electric Energy Museum

1-12-10 Jinnan, Shibuya-ku (3477 1191). Shibuya station. **Open** 10am-6pm Tue, Thur-Sun. **Admission** free. **Map** 2.

TEPCO (Tokyo Electric Company) has put together seven punchy floors of displays about electricity, including computer games and toys related to energy usage, touch-screen computer quizzes hosted by Enomon (Energy Monster), virtual-reality tours of Shibuya by bike and walk-in models of different power generators. Most displays are in Japanese, but there's enough intuitive interactivity to light up any kid's eyes. There's always a queue, so get here early.
Café. Gift shop.

Ueno Park

In the afternoon sun Ueno Park has a feeling far removed from the tightly packed streets of Tokyo as thousands of people mooch around among the trees lining the broad avenues that lead from one huge cultural institution to another, or just flop on the ground. Founded in 1873, it is the oldest city park in Japan and was built on the grounds of the former Kaneiji temple, an enormous complex that was also the *shogun* burial ground. Some of these temples still remain, but it is temples of another kind that dominate the park now – the national shrines to art and culture.

The park hosts the world's largest concentration of top-class museums. At the main entrance is the **Tokyo Festival Hall** with its great music library, while close by is the **Japan Art Academy**. Next along is the **Royal Ueno Museum**, which is free when not showing special exhibitions. Taking a stroll across the park you will see the **Tokyo Metropolitan Museum of Art** (*see p100*), past the grand central fountain and the statue of Dr Bauduin. Designed by Kunio Maekawa, it is built largely underground so as not to intrude on the scenery. Behind this

is the **Tokyo National University of Fine Arts and Music** that has a big yearly exhibition of students' work. Cross the street to the main entrance of another cluster of museums and galleries with the **Tokyo National Museum** (*see p105*) taking central position. This is one of Japan's oldest museums and houses some 89,000 historical objects. To the left is the majestic **Hyokeikan** (*see p100*). Opened in 1909, it displayed traditional archaeological exhibits until 1999 and now holds temporary exhibitions. The **Horyu-ji Treasure House** beside it was recently built by architect Yoshio Taniguchi and is home to priceless treasures from the Horyu-ji temple.

The **National Science Museum** (*see p110*) is back across the street. Finally, back full circle is the **National Museum of Western Art** (*see p98*). The main building was designed by Le Corbusier and houses the Masataka Collection, given back to Japan by France after WWII, with the new annexe exhibiting temporary shows.

Ueno Koen

Taito-ku (information centre 5685 1181/park office 3828 5644). Ueno station.

Railway enthusiasts of all ages will be delighted by the **Transportation Museum**.

Tokyo Metropolitan Water Science Museum

2-4-1 Ariake 2-chome, Koto-ku (3528 2366). Kokusai Tenji-Jyo Seimonmae station (Yurikamome line). **Open** 9.30am-5pm Tue-Sun. **Admission** free.
It is impossible to have a museum dedicated to something more fundamental than water, and this one really goes to town on displays and interactive games to teach you all about how wonderful and exciting it is. If big machines give you a thrill, the enormous underground pump will be right up your street. The cutting power of water under pressure is demonstrated and you can enjoy a virtual ride down a river: sound effects, movement and all. All scientific facts about water are here to be discovered and after your brain is drenched with information you can chill out for eight minutes watching big water bubbles pass through enormous tubes in a dimly lit room. Manager Sosei Morita couldn't be keener to help out. Drinks are available on the first floor.

Transportation Museum

1-25 Kanda-Sudacho, Chiyoda-ku (3251 8481). Akihabara station. **Open** 9.30am-5pm Tue-Sun. **Admission** ¥310; ¥150 concessions. **No credit cards. Map** 17.
At the crossroads of four subway lines, two train lines and a river, the Transportation Museum could not be better located. After starting out as a railway museum in 1921, it has grown to include an exhaustive compendium of transportation over land, sea, air and space, from rockets to rickshaws. Train buffs will have a field day with the oldest train used in Tokyo, an 1872 steam locomotive made in England that travelled between Shinbashi and Yokohama. A must-try among the range of interactive displays is steering a Yamanote line train through Tokyo in a real conductor car, complete with knobs and levers. *Café. Gift shop. Lockers.*

Toys

Japan Toys Museum

Tsukuda Group Bldg 9F, 1-36-10 Hashiba, Taito-ku (3874 5133). Asakusa station. **Open** 9.30am-5pm Wed-Sun. Closed 3rd Wed of month. **Admission** ¥200; ¥100 concessions. **No credit cards.**
Cartoon icon Hello Kitty greets visitors outside this nondescript building. For collectors, the trek may be worth it, but the 8,000 toys categorised by year sit tantalisingly out of reach, in glass cases. Everything from Meiji-era wooden toys and a plastic Astro Boy (c1964) to a remote-controlled Godzilla is here. In one corner sits a stack of toys that can be handled. *Gift shop.*

Toy Museum

2-12-10 Arai, Nakano-ku (3387 5461). Nakano station. **Open** 10.30am-4.30pm Mon-Thur, Sat. **Admission** ¥500. **No credit cards. Map** 26.
More hands-on than the Japan Toys Museum (*see above*), the arts-and-crafts oriented Toy Museum has no shortage of local kids to enjoy its toys. *Gift shop.*

Wise men follow the star.
www.heineken.co.jp

Eat, Drink, Shop

Restaurants

There are probably more places to eat here than any other city in the world, and the good news is that you don't have to break the bank to eat out.

Eat, Drink, Shop

Tokyo is one of the world's great cities for eating out. It is home to more than 100,000 restaurants, taverns, mom-and-pop noodle joints and assorted hole-in-the-wall eateries, offering a staggering variety of foods, not just Japanese but from all corners of the globe. And to eat out in Tokyo is simultaneously to explore a vital aspect of Japanese social culture.

There is nowhere better for sampling the remarkable depth and range of Japanese food. This can range from rarified multi-course banquets of Kyoto-style *kaiseki* costing over ¥50,000 per head to street corner vendors selling savory *mochi* rice cakes at ¥100 a time. *Sushi, tempura* and *sukiyaki* have penetrated most areas of the world. But there is much more to eat than this. Every prefecture of the country, from Hokkaido down to Okinawa, has its own regional food and drink specialities, and all are available in the nation's capital.

Japanese cuisine focuses on seasonal ingredients to a much higher degree than anwhere in the west. This inevitably means that fresh ingredients (especially seafood and vegetables) will vary throughout the year. Even at the humblest eateries and street stalls, food quality is invariably high and hygiene standards impeccable.

Tokyo can be terrifyingly expensive, especially at the high end – although not vastly more so than London and other European capitals. But it is not hard to find good, satisfying fare at reasonable prices, if you know where and how to look. One strategy is to have your main meal in the middle of the day. Many restaurants offer special lunch discounts and set meals. Noodle shops offer filling fare that is never expensive. Follow the example of housewives and young people: in areas with student populations there will be plenty of low-priced eateries. If all else fails, there are many family restaurants and fast food chains, both Japanese and western. Or drop into one of the ubiquitous convenience stores and pick up a lunch box, *sushi* roll or *onigiri* rice ball.

Unlike most Japanese restaurants in the west, most eateries in Japan specialise in one cuisine, be it grilled chicken, broiled eel, blowfish or the *sumo* stews. However, restaurants serving a range of different styles are often found on the top floors of department stores or in the basements of large office buildings.

And then there are *izakaya*. Literally, 'a place where there is *sake*', the word covers a wide spectrum from cheap and cheerful taverns to discreet drinking holes serving premium *sake* in reverential (and pricey) ambience. What they all have in common is that they are places to eat, drink, talk and unwind after the day is over. Some serve food of memorable quality; others are raucous, crowded and smoky *yakitori* joints. Those with lanterns outside (red usually, or white) are likely to be less expensive. Push aside the *noren* curtain, step inside: it is likely to be a memorable experience.

Unless otherwise noted, prices given are for one person with moderate amounts of alcohol.

Rice

Japanese rice is short-grained, moist and usually eaten plain. It is most often served at the end of a meal, along with a bowl of *miso* soup, some crunchy pickled vegetables and a cup of green tea. Since rice and *sake* are never consumed together, ordering rice at the end of the meal signifies that you have finished drinking. Rice bowl (*donburi*) restaurants offer rice in large portions with a variety of toppings (*sashimi, tempura, tonkatsu*, eel), but there are other ways of serving it. It may be formed into round or triangular patties (*onigiri*) – either plain, wrapped in *nori* seaweed (*nori-maki*) or basted with soy and then grilled (*yaki-onigiri*); cooked in the remaining broth – as at *nabe* restaurants – to form a thick porridge (*ojiya*); or drenched in green tea (*ochazuke*) in the bowl, usually with a simple topping, and then half eaten, half drunk.

Haute cuisine

KAISEKI RYORI
Kaiseki ryori is Japan's beautiful, formal haute cuisine and originated over four centuries ago as a light accompaniment to the tea ceremony. A *kaiseki* meal is a sequence

of small dishes, apparently simple but always immaculately prepared and presented to reflect the seasons. Courses follow one another, but slowly; a one-hour parade would be considered hurried. The formal order of the meal is a first course; then *sashimi*; a clear soup; then a series of dishes that are grilled; steamed; served with a dressing; deep-fried; and with a vinegar dressing. The main ingredients are fish and vegetables, including mountain herbs (*sansai*) and mushrooms, plus small amounts of beef or chicken. Rice is served at the end of the meal.

Roppongi

Kisso
Axis Bldg B1, 5-17-1 Roppongi, Minato-ku (3582 4191). Roppongi station. **Open** 11.30am-2pm, 5.30-10pm (last orders 9pm) Mon-Sat. **Average** ¥1,200-¥5,000 lunch; ¥10,000 dinner. **Credit** AmEx, DC, JCB, MC, V. **No English menu. Map 4.**
Kisso is *kaiseki* in a contemporary setting – the main dining area is decked out in stylish black, with deep chairs surrounded by artfully arranged flowers, track lighting and a subtle jazz soundtrack. The meals are a sequence of small dishes ordered as a set; most will include *sashimi* and cooked fish with grated *daikon*, *miso* soup with tofu, *wakame* (seaweed) and *mitsuba* (Japanese parsley), seasonal and often unusual vegetables and a small amount of meat, with pungent hot mustard.

SHOJIN RYORI
The vegetarian precepts of Zen Buddhism spread through Japan from the 14th century, along with the tea ceremony. *Shojin ryori* follows the same lines as mainstream *kaiseki*, except that no fish is used, and cooking stocks are prepared with shiitake mushrooms and kombu seaweed. *Tofu* and *yuba* feature prominently in *shojin* meals. A variation known as *fucha ryori* was introduced from China later, and incorporates subtle preparations of wheat gluten to simulate meat dishes.

Kamiyacho

Daigo
2-4-2 Atago, Minato-ku (3431 0811). Kamiyacho station. **Open** noon-2pm, 5-9pm daily. **Average** from ¥12,000 lunch; from ¥14,000 dinner. **Credit** AmEx, DC, JCB. **No English menu. Map 4.**
Daigo started out as a branch of a *ryotei* in Hida-Takayama. It now serves expensive Buddhist temple *kaiseki* meals in private *tatami* rooms overlooking peaceful gardens. A ten- to 15-course meal revolving around seasonal offerings is lovingly and artfully presented. An elegant slice of Japanese traditional cuisine. Reservations absolutely required.

The best Restaurants

For upmarket *sushi*
Fukuzushi is elegant and foreigner-friendly. *See p119.*

For a superior sky-high dining experience
Take in the skyscrapers with your meal at the **New York Bar & Grill**. *See p141.*

For sky-high dining at down-to-earth prices
Head for Korean *yakiniku* at **Shinjuku Jojoen**. *See p135.*

For interior design to make you go 'woo!'
It has to be Ginza's **Daidaiya**. *See p127.*

For people with kids
Crayon House Hiroba is child-friendly and serves natural food. *See p130.*

For traditional Japanese vegetarian food
Bon offers seasonal delicacies in a tranquil setting. *See below.*

For non-Japanese veggie food
Take a short trip out to **Nataraj**. *See p135.*

For east-meets-west fusion food
Book early to get a table at **Rojak**. *See p136.*

For drinking by the water
Confident cuisine and fresh-brewed beer make **TY Harbor Brewery** a must-visit. *See p141.*

For name dropping
Darling! Didn't I see you in **Nobu Tokyo** last night? *See p136.*

Ueno area

Bon
1-2-11 Ryusen, Taito-ku (3872 0234). Iriya station. **Open** noon-1.30pm, 5-9pm (last orders 7pm) Mon, Wed-Fri; noon-8pm (last orders 6pm) Sat, Sun. **Average** ¥3,800 lunch; ¥8,000 dinner. **No credit cards. Menu in English. Map 14.**
Exquisitely prepared *fucha ryori* in a tranquil setting. One course is served, the details of which change with the seasons. Enjoy the succession of morsels as a living expression of Japanese culture.

TOFU RYORI

The humble beancurd is celebrated both for its protein content and its remarkable versatility, and features strongly in Japanese cooking. It is one of the delicacies of Kyoto, where there are numerous restaurants serving it up in a remarkable variety of shapes and forms. Because *tofu* restaurants tend to use fish or chicken (often in soup stocks), they are classified separately from the strict *shojin* tradition.

Ueno area

Goemon
1-1-26 Hon-Komagome, Bunkyo-ku (3811 2015). Hon-Komagome station. **Open** noon-2pm, 5-10pm Mon-Sat. **Average** ¥2,700 lunch; ¥5,500 dinner. **No credit cards. No English menu. Map** 25.
With its bamboo-lined entrance and garden with waterfalls, carp ponds and bowers, Goemon is almost a substitute for a trip to Kyoto. In winter the speciality is *yudofu* (piping hot *tofu* in broth); in summer order the chilled *hiya yakko*. One of the city's best-kept secrets.

Sasanoyuki
2-15-10 Negishi, Taito-ku (3873 1145). Nippori station. **Open** 11am-9pm Tue-Sun. **Average** ¥1,600 lunch (11am-2pm Tue-Fri); ¥3,500 dinner. **Credit** AmEx, DC, MC, V. **Menu in English. Map** 25.
Tokyo's most famous *tofu* restaurant has an imperial legacy: it was founded by a *tofu*-maker lured from Kyoto by the Kanei-ji Temple's imperial abbot. But Sasanoyuki is as down-home as the Nippori neighbourhood in which it sits, and also very reasonably priced. Order the top-of-the-line course and you'll have enough *tofu* to last you for your entire stay in Japan.

Regional cuisine

Ginza

Little Okinawa
8-7-10 Ginza, Chuo-ku (3572 2930). Ginza or Shinbashi station. **Open** 5pm-3am Mon-Sat; 5pm-midnight Sun. **Average** ¥3,500. **Credit** AmEx, DC, MC, V. **No English menu. Map** 6.
The foods of Japan's southernmost islands incorporate many influences from China, especially in their predilection for noodles and pork – incorporating almost every part of the pig from ears to trotters. The 'national' dish is *goya champuru*, a stir-fry of *tofu* and bitter gourd, and the drink of choice is *awamori*, a rice-based rocket-fuel liquor with a highly distinctive taste. Cheerful and always busy, Little Okinawa is the best place in the city to start your exploration.

Tradition holds strong at **Botan**. *See p119.*

Ohmatsuya
Ail d'Or Bldg 2F, 6-5-8 Ginza, Chuo-ku (3571 7053). Ginza Station. **Open** 5-10.30pm (last orders 9.30pm) Mon-Sat. **Average** ¥7,500. **Credit** AmEx, DC, MC, V. **Menu in English. Map** 6.
Ascending from the swish streets of Ginza, you emerge into a remarkable *faux*-rustic inn with wooden beams and folksy decor. Ohmatsuya specialises in the cuisine of rural Yamagata Prefecture, which means farmhouse foods, but prepared with style: plenty of mountain herbs and fresh seafood from the Japan Sea coast, not to mention some of the best *sake* in the country. Every table and side room has its own individual charcoal fireplace on which duck and meat dishes are grilled in front of your eyes. End your meal with buckwheat noodles and *hojicha* tea.

Nakano area

Rera Chise
1-37-12 Arai, Nakano-ku (3387 2252). Arai-Yakushi station (Seibu-Shinjuku line). **Open** 5-11pm (last orders 10pm) Mon-Sat. **Average** ¥3,000. **No credit cards. No English menu. Map** 26.
This is Tokyo's first Ainu restaurant, and doubles as an unofficial Ainu cultural centre. It's also a casual hangout for local students who come for inexpensive Hokkaido food and atmosphere. The

menu is heavy on salmon, potatoes and spiced with liberal amounts of garlic and ginger. There's also a good *ishikari nabe* (salmon casserole) in winter.

Sushi

Arranging raw fish and other delicacies on patties of vinegared rice dates back to the 18th century, when it became a popular street food in Edo (present-day Tokyo). Since it used seafood from the bay, it became known as *Edo-mae sushi*. In Osaka and western Japan, *chirashi sushi* is more popular, in which colourful ingredients (raw fish, shredded omelette, seaweed and vegetables) are scattered on top of large bowls of vinegared rice. Top *sushi* shops can be daunting, as they don't post their prices and customers are expected to know their *uni* from their *ikura*. The best (and cheapest) way to learn your way around the etiquette and vocabulary is to explore the many *kaiten* (conveyor belt) *sushi* shops (*see below **Kaiten zushi***), where prices are fixed and you can take what you want without having to order. When you're up to speed, try one of the following.

Ginza area

Tsukiji Edogin Honten
4-5-1 Tsukiji, Chuo-ku (3543 4401). Tsukiji station. **Open** 11am-9.30pm Mon-Sat; 11.30am-9pm Sun. **Average** ¥1,000 per dish. **Credit** AmEx, DC, MC. **Sushi list in English**. **Map** 20.
The portion sizes at Edogin are legendary, and you're just round the corner from the central fish market, so the ingredients couldn't be fresher. That's why it's always popular, despite the almost production-line service and lack of character. Choose your fish from the tank in the cavernous dining room and it will be served at your table still quivering.

Roppongi

Fukuzushi
5-7-8 Roppongi, Minato-ku (3402 4116). Roppongi station. **Open** 11.30am-2pm, 5.30-10pm Mon-Sat. **Average** ¥3,000 lunch; ¥14,000 dinner. **Credit** AmEx, DC, JCB, MC, V. **Menu in English**. **Map** 4.
Fukuzushi is not necessarily the best *sushi* in Tokyo, but it is certainly as good as you will ever need to try – especially if you're not dining on an expense account. It's a stylish place, worth getting dressed up for. Best of all, the staff are absolutely used to foreigners. Like the clientele, the *sushi* is elegant, generous and perfectly formed.

Sukiyaki & shabu-shabu

Sukiyaki is a dish of tender, thinly sliced meat (usually beef, but sometimes pork, horse or chicken), vegetables, *tofu* and other ingredients, such as *shirataki* noodles), cooked in a soy sauce been slightly sweetened with (sweet cooking *sake*).
As the ingredients cook, fi... dip them into a dip of beaten raw egg. *Shabu-shabu* refers to the sound made as paper-thin beef is swished back and forth in a steaming, bubbling broth, cooked at the table, usually in a special copper pot.

Kanda

Botan
1-15 Kanda Sudacho, Chiyoda-ku (3251 0577). Kanda station. **Open** 11.30am-9pm Mon-Sat. **Average** ¥7,000. **No credit cards**. **No English menu**. **Map** 16.
No need to order: there's only one thing on the menu here, chicken *sukiyaki*, and it's done very well. *Botan*, meaning both button and peony, was founded more than one hundred years ago by a button-maker and still stands in one of the few neighbourhoods to have escaped earthquakes, bombing and major development. Leave your shoes in the hallway, and be led to your minuscule table. A *kimono*-clad waitress will light the charcoal in

Kaiten zushi

Even in Japan, *sushi* is expensive. A night out at a decent place, with *sake* or beer, will run to at least ¥6,000 per person. One alternative is *kaiten zushi*. Located everywhere, especially in arcades near train stations, *kaiten zushi* (revolving *sushi*) is *sushi* served on moving conveyor belts. *Sushi* chefs stand in the middle of the island replenishing the quickly disappearing plates and taking special orders. While the quality isn't as good as at a *sushi* restaurant, it's usually fairly consistent, and the price is right. Most plates cost about ¥120 to ¥240 and are colour-coded for price; there should be a sign indicating the price per plate.

Grab a seat at the counter. Serve yourself to green tea from the push-button tap on the counter, and wait for something you fancy to appear on the conveyor belt. (If you don't see what you want, ask for it.) Help yourself to soy sauce and ginger, and tuck in. When you finish your plate, stack it in a pile; your bill will be tallied up from your stack of plates, and you pay at the register. The average *kaiten* bill, excluding beer, is approximately ¥1,000.

...azier, set a small iron dish on top, then start ...king: chicken, onion, *tofu* and other vegetables ...mmering in the house sauce.

Roppongi

Hassan Hinazushi
6-1-20 Roppongi, Minato-ku (3403 8333).
Roppongi station. **Open** 11.30am-11pm Mon-Sat;
noon-10pm Sun. **Average** ¥1,000 lunch; ¥5,000
dinner. **Credit** AmEx, MC, V. **Menu in English.**
Map 4.
Hassan serves elaborate all-you-can-eat *shabu-shabu*
meals, featuring beautifully marbled, paper-thin
slices of premium Japanese *wagyu* (often known as
Kobe beef but actually from Matsuzaka). The interior incorporates classic Japanese motifs – *washi*
paper screens and lamps, wooden beams and even
a miniature bamboo garden.

Tempura

The Portuguese are credited with introducing
the technique of deep-frying fish, seafood and
vegetables – and also the name itself. But in
Japan the dish has been elevated to a fine art.
Good *tempura* should have a batter covering
that is thin and crisp, and never too oily; it
should also be eaten as hot as possible, so
try to get a seat at the counter.

Ginza

Ten-Ichi
6-6-5 Ginza, Chuo-ku (3571 1949). Ginza station.
Open 11.30am-9.30pm daily. **Average** ¥7,500
lunch; ¥10,000 dinner. **Credit** AmEx, DC, MC, V.
Menu in English. Map 6.
Tokyo's best-known *tempura* house displays a
photograph at the entrance of the latest dignitary
to visit (most recently, France's President Chirac).
The atmosphere is tranquil and pampering. You
sit at the counter and receive a constant flow of
perfectly cooked morsels straight from the wok.
The *tempura* is light and aromatic, using the finest
ingredients. Dinner courses start at ¥8,500, and
include rice, tea and dessert. The Ginza flagship
shop is the most refined, but any branch guarantees
top-quality *tempura*.
Branches: Imperial Hotel, 1-1 Uchisaiwaicho,
Chiyoda-ku (3503 1001); Sony Bldg B1, 5-3-1
Ginza, Chuo-ku (3571 3837); CI Plaza B1,
2-3-1 Kita-Aoyama, Minato-ku (3497 8465);
Mitsui Bldg, B1, 2-1-1 Nishi-Shinjuku,
Shinjuku-ku (3344 4706).

Ten-ichi Deux
Nishi Ginza Depato 1F, 4-1 Ginza (3566
4188). Yurakucho station. **Open** 11.30am-10pm
daily. **Average** ¥1,500 lunch; ¥3,000-¥4,000
dinner. **Credit** AmEx, DC, MC, V.
No English menu. Map 6.
Casual, lower-priced offshoot of the highly reputable
Ten-ichi chain. Ten-ichi Deux specialises in light
dishes such as *ten-don* (*tempura* prawns on a rice
bowl) with simple side dishes. A popular lunch and
early evening spot.

Shinjuku

Tsunahachi
3-31-8 Shinjuku, Shinjuku-ku (3352-1012).
Shinjuku station. **Open** 11.30am-3pm, 5-9.30pm
daily. **Average** ¥5,000. **Credit** AmEx, DC, MC, V.
Menu in English. Map 1b.
Surviving amid the gleaming modern buildings of
Shinjuku, Tsunahachi's battered wooden premises
are something of a throwback to the early days of
the post-WWII era. So are the prices: this is the best
bargain in town. So what if the whole place is filled
with the whiff of oil? For a more rarefied version,
easily a match for Ten-Ichi, try the upmarket branch
around the corner.
Branch: 3-28-4 Shinjuku, Shinjuku-ku
(3358 2788).

Nabemono & one-pot cooking

Nabemono is a winter cuisine – one-pot stews
cooked at the table, in a casserole (*nabe*) of
iron or heavy earthenware over a gas flame.
Everyone is served from the one pot: pluck
out choice, seasonal titbits with special long
chopsticks, drop them into the small bowl
provided or dip in sauce before enjoying.
Favourite *nabe* styles include chicken; oyster;
mixed (*yose-nabe*); *tofu* (*yu-dofu*); *fugu* (*fuguchiri*); and *chanko nabe* – the sumo wrestlers'
stew of meat, fish and vegetables.

Kanda

Isegen
1-11 Kanda Suda-cho, Chiyoda-ku (3251 1229).
Kanda station. **Open** 11.30am-2pm, 4-10pm
Mon-Fri. **Average** ¥5,000 lunch; ¥7,000 dinner.
No credit cards. No English menu. Map 16.
In the same bomb-spared neighbourhood as Botan
(*see p119*), Isegen has been serving its legendary
anko (monkfish) *nabe* for over 150 years. The present sprawling wooden premises date back to the
1930s. *Anko* are only in season from October to
March. In the off-season Isegen serves river fish –
specifically *ayu* (sweetfish), carp and loach.

Elsewhere

Yoshiba
2-14-5 Yokoami, Sumida-ku (3623 4480). Ryogoku
station. **Open** 5-10pm Mon-Sat. **Average** ¥6,000.
Credit JCB, V. **No English menu. Map** 24.

Chanko nabe is the food of sumo wrestlers, reputed to help them put on those layers of bulk – but only if eaten in huge volumes late at night. For the rest of us, it's an enjoyable mixed casserole. Nowhere is more atmospheric to sample it than here, a converted sumo stable where you sit around the ring where wrestlers used to practise.

Grills & counter foods

YAKITORI AND *KUSHIYAKI*
Yakitori are skewered pieces of chicken cooked over a crackling charcoal grill, served with salt or a slightly sweet soy-based glaze. Usually served in small, smoke-filled *izakaya*, *yakitori* is a tasty accompaniment to beer, *sake* or *shochu*. Though *yakitori* is literally grilled chicken, most *yakitori-ya* also do wonderful things with skewered vegetables, grilled until tender with a crust of salt, often served with lemon juice.

Ginza

Shichirinya
7-108 Saki-Ginza, Chuo-ku (3289 0020). Ginza or Shinbashi station. **Open** 5.30pm-4am Mon-Fri; 5.30-11pm Sat, Sun. **Credit** AmEx, DC, MC, V. **No English menu. Map** 20.
The *shichirin* charcoal brazier used in a type of grilled cuisine called *aburiyaki* was once synonymous with post-war deprivation and austerity. Now it's the chic way to prepare your food. Smokeless grills, quality ingredients and sophisticated service: this is the way it's done in Ginza, and it's very satisfying, especially in the colder months.

Yurakucho Under the Tracks
2-1 Yurakucho, Chiyoda-ku (no phones).
Yurakucho station. **Open** early evening-midnight daily. **Average** ¥2,500. **No credit cards.**
No English menu. Map 6.
For a cheap night's entertainment and a quintessential Japanese experience, don't miss the *yakitori* roadshow that takes place nightly beneath the tracks of the Yamanote line. Open-air eateries are wedged into tiny spaces, and the master dishes out *yakitori* and other titbits from behind the counter.

Roppongi

Bincho
Marina Bldg 2F, 3-10-5 Roppongi, Minato-ku (5474 0755). Roppongi station. **Open** 6pm-midnight daily. **Average** ¥5,000. **Credit** AmEx, DC, MC, V. **Menu in English. Map** 4.
Dark, romantic Japanese-style interior complemented by the smoky aroma of charcoal-grilled *yakitori* and an array of *sake*. Grilled chicken or vegetables may be ordered by the stick or as part of a course. **Branch:** 2-40-14 Hongo, Bunkyo-ku (3812 4163).

Shibuya

Vingt2
ICI Bldg 1F, 1-6-7 Shibuya, Shibuya-ku (3407 9494). Shibuya station. **Open** 11.30am-2pm, 5-11pm Mon-Sat. **Average** ¥900 lunch; ¥3,500 dinner. **Credit** AmEx, DC, JCB, V. **Menu in English. Map** 2.
An extensive selection of charcoal-grilled fish, meat and vegetable *kushi-yaki* (skewered foods) located near Children's Castle (*see p192*).

Elsewhere

Birdland
3-37-9 Asagaya-Minami, Suginami-ku (3392 8941) Asagaya Station. **Open** 6-10pm Tue-Fri, Sun; 5.30-11pm Sat. **Credit** AmEx, DC, MC, V. **Average** ¥7,000. **No English menu. Map** 28.
Birdland was one of the first places to produce gourmet *yakitori*, served with imported beers and a selection of fine wines. Top-quality free-range bantam chickens are used; they're so tasty you can enjoy their meat raw as *sashimi*. It's a small place, and very popular. Some evenings a time limit is imposed, so keep a flow of orders going, including chicken liver pâté, *yakitori*, and the superb *sansai-yaki* (breast meat grilled with Japanese pepper).

Vin Chou
2-2-13 Nishi-Asakusa, Taito-ku (3845 4430). Tawaramachi Station. **Open** 5-11pm Mon, Tue, Thur-Sun. **Credit** V. **Average** ¥4,000. **No English menu. Map** 13.
This five-star charcoal-grilled *yakitori* shop is an offshoot of the nearby French bistro, La Chèvre. That explains why it offers Bresse chicken, quail, and a range of good wines and cheese. The style is casual, and the look is simple, but this is some of the best food in the neighbourhood.

UNAGI
Unagi, or eel, is another of Japan's great delicacies. Eels are split open, filleted, basted with an aromatic brown glaze of soy sauce and *mirin* and very slowly broiled (often over charcoal). *Unagi* is thought to be a restorative, and is consumed fanatically during the hot months of July and August for stamina, to improve eyesight and even virility.

Asakusa

Hatsuogawa
2-8-4 Kaminarimon, Taito-ku (3844 2723). Asakusa station. **Open** noon-2pm, 5-8pm Mon-Sat; 5-8pm Sun. **Average** ¥3,000. **No credit cards. No English menu. Map** 13.
A tradition-steeped restaurant in historic Asakusa. The tiny entrance is graced with stones, plants, bamboo latticework and a white *noren* emblazoned with the word *unagi*. Step into this tiny world of wooden

Eat, Drink, Shop

beams and traditional Japanese decor and enjoy the taste of succulent broiled eel, prepared by a third-generation family member. The *unaju* box set is delicious, or try *kabayaki: unagi* on a stick. This place is so popular during festivals and firework displays that the queue winds down the street.

Kanda

Myojin-shita Kandagawa Honten
2-5-11 Soto-Kanda, Chiyoda-ku (3251 5031).
Ochanomizu station. **Open** 11.30am-2pm,
5-7.30pm Mon-Sat. Closed every 2nd Sat.
Average ¥6,000. **Credit** DC, MC, V.
No English menu. Map 16.
Another of Tokyo's most famous *unagi* restaurants, where *kimono*-clad waitresses serve exquisite *unagi* cooked over charcoal and basted with a sweet sauce. The result is succulent and tender, and the setting magnificent: an antique Japanese house overlooking a traditional garden. Reservations recommended.

Roppongi area

Nodaiwa
1-5-4 Higashi-Azabu, Minato-ku (3583 7852).
Kamiyacho station. **Open** 11am-1.30pm, 5-8pm
Mon-Sat. **Average** ¥4,000. **No credit cards.**
Menu in English. Map 4.
Housed in an old storehouse transported from the mountains, Nodaiwa is arguably the best *unagi* shop in town (and there are hundreds of them). Only eels that have been caught in the wild are used, rather than the cheaper, flabbier fish cultivated in artificial conditions. You really can taste the difference in the texture, especially if you try the *shiraya-ki*, which is broiled without any added sauce, and eaten with a dip of *shoyu* and *wasabi*. This is true gourmet fare.

TEPPANYAKI, OKONOMIYAKI, MONJA
Beef is a luxury item in Japan, but Japanese beef (especially Kobe beef) is exceptionally good. Grilled on the *teppan* ('metal surface'), this is a wonderful way to experience Japanese-style steak. Tender, thin slices of beef, seafood and vegetables will be grilled to sizzling perfection in front of you.

Okonomiyaki ('grilled whatever you like') is often described as a Japanese pancake, though you can also think of it as a well-stuffed omelette. An egg-based batter is cooked on a grill, in some shops by the customer, and filled with seafood, meat and/or vegetables. Choose whatever ingredients you want. Many places also do *yaki-soba* (fried Chinese-style noodles). Originally from western Japan (Hiroshima and Osaka both lay claim to it), *okonomiyaki* is cheap, robust and satisfying – and usually very hot if you're sitting near the grill. The Tokyo version is known as *monja*.

Asakusa area

Sometaro
2-2-2 Nishi-Asakusa, Taito-ku (3844 9502).
Tawaramachi Station. **Open** noon-10.30pm
Tue-Sun. **Average** ¥1,000. **No credit cards.**
Menu in English. Map 13.
Comfort food in a funky wooden shack, within easy walking distance of the tourist sights of Asakusa. It can get incredibly sweaty in summer, but sitting round the *okonomiyaki* pan, the intimate atmosphere has a wonderfully authentic feel.

Ebisu & area

Chibo
Yebisu Garden Place Tower 38F,
4-20-3 Ebisu, Shibuya-ku (5424 1011).
Ebisu station. **Open** 11am-3pm, 5-11pm
Mon-Sat; 11am-11pm Sun. **Average** ¥1,500
lunch; ¥2,500 dinner. **Credit** AmEx, DC, JCB,
MC, V. **Menu in English. Map** 3.
This branch of an Osaka *okonomiyaki* restaurant uses the original Osaka-style recipe. In addition to all the usual meats and seafood, stuffings include asparagus, *mochi* or cheese and, of course, mayonnaise. Friendly staff, reasonable prices, an extensive menu, plus a gorgeous view, make Chibo a very popular place.

Jinroku
6-23-2 Shirogane, Minato-ku (3441 1436).
Hiroo station. **Open** 6pm-3am Tue-Sat; 6-11pm
Sun. **Average** ¥4,500. **Credit** AmEx, MC, V.
Menu in English. Map 3.
Jinroku is all about *okonomiyaki* raised to new heights, in gleaming, modern, upmarket surroundings. Besides the standard pancakes, Jinroku also serves up excellent *gyoza* dumplings, *teppanyaki* seafood, *tofu* steak and fried *yaki-soba*. Give the *negi-yaki* a try; it substitutes chopped green leek for the more usual Chinese cabbage. Wash it all down with Chilean wine.

Elsewhere

Monja Maruyama
1-4-10 Tsukishima, Chuo-ku (3533 3504).
Tsukishima station. **Open** 5-10.30pm
Tue-Sun. **Average** ¥2,000. **No credit
cards. No English menu.**
Monja, the crêpe-like concoction of batter, vegetables, seafood and meat cooked on a griddle, is perhaps not for everyone. But for those who do want to give it a try, Tsukishima, with its dozens of little restaurants, is *monja* heaven. Mr Maruyama, a Tsukishima native, founded his place ten years ago to experiment with variations on the theme. Thus you'll find rarities such as pitch-black *monja* with squid's ink, or *mochi mochi* crêpe, with *mochi*, the sticky pounded rice used in many Japanese dishes around New Year.

ODEN

Oden is a simple seasonal dish of fish cakes, *tofu*, vegetables and *konyaku* (devil's tongue) simmered in a light, kelp-based broth, served with a dash of *karashi* (hot mustard) for flavouring and usually accompanied by *sake*. It is often served at outdoor *yatai* (covered street stalls). Although the cheap *oden* of outdoor stands and convenience stores has a smell that can be chokingly pungent, the subtle flavours in the finest restaurants are a revelation.

Akasaka

Densan

Getsusekai Bldg B1F, 3-10-4 Akasaka, Minato-ku (3585 7550). Akasaka-Mitsuke station. **Open** 4.30pm-5am Mon-Sat; 4.30-11.30pm Sun. **Average** ¥4,000. **Credit** AmEx, DC, MC, V. **Menu in English. Map 7.**
Densan marries two Japanese 'traditions': *oden* and *karaoke*. Oden is prepared Kyoto-style and is much lighter than the Tokyo version. The broth is delicate and subtle, with only a hint of soy sauce, allowing the flavours of the ingredients to shine. Other specialities are *yakitori* from free-range chickens, and *sake*, with an emphasis on Niigata Prefecture, whose high-quality rice produces some of Japan's best. When your vocal cords are well lubricated, stumble into the private *karaoke* rooms, which are equipped with the latest hi-tech system.

Ueno area

Otafuku

1-6-2 Sento, Taito-ku (3871 2521). Iriya station. **Open** 5-11pm Tue-Sat; 3-10pm Sun. **Average** ¥100-¥500 per piece. **Credit** AmEx, DC, MC, V. **Menu in English. Map 14.**
This place has been serving *oden* since the Meiji era. It specialises in Kansai-style *oden*; the broth is much lighter on soy flavour than the Tokyo version, and the chef takes great pride in it. Otafuku also offers quality *sake*, which goes well with the delicate flavour of vegetables and fish cakes.

TONKATSU AND KUSHI-AGE

The '*katsu*' in '*tonkatsu*' means cutlet, a very popular dish first introduced during the Meiji period when eating meat began to catch on. The *katsu* is now almost always pork, usually very lean cuts of sirloin, dredged in flour, dipped in egg, rolled in breadcrumbs and deep-fried.

In *kushi-age*, pieces of meat, seafood and vegetables are skewered and deep fried to a golden brown in a coating of fine breadcrumbs, usually eaten with a sweetened soy-based sauce, salt or even a dab of curry powder. Wash it down with beer, and round off the meal with rice and miso soup.

Ueno & area

Hantei

2-12-15 Nezu, Bunkyo-ku (3828 1440). Nezu station. **Open** 5-10.30pm Mon-Sat. **Average** ¥6,000. **Menu in English. No credit cards. Map 14.**
Kushi-age is not gourmet fare, but Hantei elevates this proletarian food to new levels of appreciation. Partly this is due to the care that goes into the ingredients and preparation, but mostly because of the beautiful old wooden building in which it is housed. There's no need to order (just your drinks): the staff will just bring course after course, stopping after every six to ask if you want to continue.

Honke Ponta

3-23-3 Ueno, Taito-ku (3831 2351). Ueno station. **Open** 11am-2pm, 4.30-8pm Tue-Sun. **Average** ¥4,000. **No credit cards. No English menu. Map 17.**
Honke Ponta was the first place in the city to serve *tonkatsu* pork cutlet, but it prefers to think of itself as a western-style restaurant and so also serves meltingly tender steak. Try the tender *katsuretsu* (cutlet), *ika* (squid) or *kisu* (whiting). Order rice and soup separately and you'll get a dark and viscous *akadashi* soup (red *miso*, *nameko* mushrooms and scallions). There are no prices on the menu, but it doesn't seem to bother the housewives with time on their hands who frequent the place.

Omotesando

Maisen

4-8-5 Jingumae, Shibuya-ku (3470 0071). Omotesando station. **Open** 11am-10pm daily. **Average** ¥600 lunch; ¥1,000 dinner. **Credit** DC, JCB, MC, V. **Menu in English. Map 11.**
This branch of this chain *tonkatsu* shop is a converted bath-house. If you're able to get a seat in the huge, airy dining room in the back, you'll notice several tell-tale signs: 30-foot ceilings and a small garden pond. You can't miss with any of the *teishoku* (set meals): standard *rosu katsu* or lean *hire katsu* are both good choices, each coming with rice, soup and pickled *daikon*.
Branch: Mitsui Bldg B1F, 1-1-2 Yurakucho, Chiyoda-ku (3503 1886).

NOODLES

Noodles are hugely popular, especially at lunchtime. There are two main indigenous varieties: *soba* (thin grey-coloured noodles made form buckwheat and wheat); and *udon* (chunkier wheat noodles, usually white). These can be eaten either chilled, served on a bamboo 'plate' with a soy-based dipping sauce; or hot, usually in soy-flavoured broth topped with chopped spring onions, *tempura* or other ingredients. Even more popular than these are the crinkly, yellowish Chinese-style noodles known as *ramen*, which are served

Eat, Drink, Shop

Kanda Yabu Soba: a living museum, in historic premises, dedicated to the art of the noodle.

in a rich, meat-based stock, flavoured with *miso*, soy sauce or salt, and topped with vegetables or *cha-shu* – sliced barbecued pork.

Ebisu

Jigoku Ramen Hyottoko

Okumiya Bldg 1F, 1-8-4 Ebisu-Minami, Shibuya-ku (3791 7376). Ebisu station. **Open** 11.30am-10.30pm Mon-Sat. **Average** ¥800. **No credit cards. No English menu. Map** 3.

The house speciality is *ramen* in a bright red soup. Each dish has an equally colourful name, expressive of its relative heat and spiciness: *aka-oni* (red *ogre*, *shoyu* broth), *ao-oni* (green *ogre*, salt broth), *enma* (king of hell, spicy *miso*), *jigoku* (hell, spicy *miso*) and the *jigoku ramen* special (spicy *miso*). A sign on the wall warns that if you order the special and can't finish it, you'll have to wash the dishes.

Kanda & area

Izumo Soba Honke

1-51 Kanda-Jinbocho, Chiyoda-ku (3291 3005) Jinbocho station. **Open** 11am-8.30pm Mon-Fri; 11am-3.30pm Sat. **Average** ¥2,000. **No credit cards. No English menu. Map** 15.

If you sit downstairs you can watch your noodles being chopped before your eyes. They make the *soba* in the dark, country style popular in Izumo, western Japan, and serve it chilled in stacks of five small trays along with a variety of condiments. A good range of hot noodles in broth is also available.

Kanda Yabu Soba

2-10 Kanda-Awajicho, Chiyoda-ku (3251 0287). Awajicho station. **Open** 11.30am-8pm daily. **Average** ¥2,000. **No credit cards. Menu in English. Map** 17.

Indisputably Tokyo's most famous *soba* shop, Yabu is almost a living museum dedicated to the art of the noodle. The premises, officially listed as historic in early 2001, are a beautiful old Japanese house with a small garden, decked with *shoji* screens, *tatami* and woodblock prints. The noodles are more refined than at other shops.

Omotesando

Daruma-ya

5-9-5 Minami-Aoyama, Minato-ku (3499 6295). Omotesando station. **Open** 11.30am-9.30pm Mon-Sat. **Average** ¥1,000. **No credit cards. Menu in English. Map** 4.

Daruma-ya takes its name from *daruma*, roly-poly legless caricatures of the fifth-century Indian priest Bodhidharma that are a Japanese good luck charm. Famous for its handmade Chinese noodles (*ramen*) executed with a Japanese twist, the most popular are *takana soba* – *ramen* topped with a leafy domestic vegetable that defies translation.

Hokuto

Haruki Bldg B1, 3-5-17 Kita-Aoyama, Minato-ku (3403 0078). Omotesando station. **Open** 11am-midnight Mon-Fri; 11am-10pm Sat, Sun. **Average** ¥1,500. **Credit** AmEx, DC, MC, V. **No English menu. Map** 11.

Daidaiya: probably the most remarkable interior in Tokyo. The food's good, too. *See p127.*

Hokuto is really a Chinese restaurant, but its *ramen* are so good it deserves to be in a class all by itself. The atmosphere, too, is a step above what you find in the average *ramen* joint: large tables allow more space than usual. The *goma ramen* (sesame noodles) have been known to send people into raptures.
Branches: Ponte Bldg 1F, 1-17-1 Jingumae, Shibuya-ku (3405 9015); Fuso Bldg B1, 7-8-8 Ginza, Chuo-ku (3289 8683).

Kyushu Jangara Ramen

Shanzeru Harajuku Ni-go-kan 1-2F, 1-13-21 Jingumae, Shibuya-ku (3404 5572). Harajuku station. **Open** 11am-midnight Mon-Thur; 11am-3.30am Fri, Sat; 11am-11.30pm Sun. **Average** ¥650. **No credit cards. No English menu. Map** 11.
Popular with the young set that congregates around the Meiji-Jingu end of Omotesando, this whimsically decorated *ramen* restaurant always has queues snaking down the stairs. Don't worry: 73 seats mean you won't be waiting long. Kyushu *ramen* from Fukuoka City is the speciality here, but you get to choose whether you want the broth light or heavy, the noodles thin, thick or somewhere in between, and whether you want a large or small portion.
Branches: 3-11-6 Soto-Kanda, Chiyoda-ku (3251 4059); 7-11-10 Ginza, Chuo-ku (3289 2307); 2-12-8 Nagata-cho, Chiyoda-ku (3595 2130); 1-7-7 Nihonbashi, Chuo-ku, (3281 0701).

Senda

4-4-7 Jingumae, Shibuya-ku (5474 5977). Harajuku station. **Open** 11am-10.30pm daily. **Average** ¥1,500. **Credit** DC, MC, V. **No English menu. Map** 11.

Senda specialises in *soba, udon* and *kishimen.* The star of the line-up is *kurumi soba,* a choice of noodles served with a creamy walnut dipping sauce. A nice way to sample a number of dips is the *makunouchi:* three to five pretty little bowls served in a (fake) wooden box. You can try *oroshi* (grated *daikon* with mushrooms), *tororo* (grated mountain yam), *tempura,* walnut and *sansai* (wild mountain vegetables).
Branches: 4-1-13 Nihonbashi-Honcho, Chuo-ku (3270 7100); 11-1 Kanda Matsunagacho, Chiyoda-ku (3251 8645); 1-4-1 Yurakucho, Chiyoda-ku (3591 7384); Onuki Bldg, 2-9-7 Kanda-Kajicho, Chiyoda-ku (3251 8007).

Shibuya

Myoko

Shinto Bldg 1F, 1-17-2 Shibuya, Shibuya-ku (3499 3450). Shibuya station. **Open** 11.30am-11pm Mon-Sat; 11.30am-2.30pm Sun. **Average** ¥1,200. **Credit** AmEx, DC, MC, V. **No English menu. Map** 2.
The speciality at Myoko is *hoto,* a hearty mountain-style stew made with flat wide *udon* noodles. Other ingredients include oysters, *kimchee* (spicy Korean pickled cabbage), mushroom, pork, or *sansai* (wild mountain vegetables) cooked in a *miso*-based broth with lots of vegetables served bubbling hot in an iron kettle. There are also numerous cold dishes, such as 'salad *udon*', chilled noodles and vegetables, plus good-value lunch set meals. A large picture menu makes ordering simple despite the lack of English menu. Don't be afraid of acting dumb and just pointing.

Ueno area

Ikenohata Yabu Soba

3-44-7 Yushima, Bunkyo-ku (3831 8977).
Yushima station. **Open** 11.30am-2pm,
4.30-8pm, Mon, Tue, Thur-Sat; 11.30am-8pm Sun.
Average ¥2,000 lunch; ¥3,500 dinner. **No credit**
cards. **No English menu**. **Map 14**.
Kanda Yabu Soba has spawned numerous shops
run by former chefs. This one does excellent *soba* at
reasonable prices in a modern setting. Ikenohata
may lacks the charm of the original, but the *soba* is
still some of the most delectable in Tokyo.

Elsewhere

Torijaya

4-2 Kagurazaka, Shinjuku-ku (3260 6661).
Kagurazaka station. **Open** 11.30am-2.30pm,
5-10.30pm Mon-Sat; 11.30am-3.30pm, 4-10pm Sun.
Average ¥2,000 lunch; ¥7,000 dinner. **Credit**
(dinner only) AmEx, MC, V. **No English menu**.
This traditional restaurant specialises in Kyoto-style
udon cuisine. It calls itself *udon kaiseki*, but things
never get too formal. The centrepiece of any meal is
udon-suki, and hearty *nabe* of chicken and vegetables with thick-cut wheat noodles. Dinner courses
start from ¥5,500 and include side dishes.

General Japanese

Akasaka

Jidaiya

Naritaya Bldg 1F, 3-14-3 Akasaka, Minato-ku
(3588 0489/fax 3589 6276). Akasaka-Mitsuke
station. **Open** 11.30am-2pm, 5pm-4am Mon-Fri;
5-11pm Sat. **Average** ¥6,000. **Credit** AmEx, DC,
MC, V. **No English menu**. **Map 7**.

Fugu

No aspect of Japanese food has a greater
mystique than *fugu* (blowfish). All *fugu*
chefs have to pass special tests for a
licence to prepare it, since the blowfish
contains a powerful and fast-moving
neurotoxin, which if not carefully removed
will result in numbness and even death.
Most commonly eaten as *sashimi* or *nabe*,
fugu has a white meat that is so subtle it's
virtually tasteless. Even so, it is one of the
foods most eagerly awaited by enthusiasts
– perhaps because the season only lasts
from October and March, and perhaps
because of the thrill of knowing your meal
is potentially a culinary Russian roulette.

Jidaiya enthusiastically recreates the interior of a
rustic Japanese farmhouse complete with *tatami*
mats, dried ears of corn, fish-shaped hanging fireplace fixtures and heaps of old-looking wooden
furniture. The atmosphere is a bit contrived, but
fun nevertheless, helped by large shared tables. The
food is all Japanese, with an emphasis on seafood,
meat and vegetables cooked at the table. The à la
carte selections make occasional forays into the
world of western food: Camembert *monja* once
showed up on the menu.
Branches: Isomura Bldg B1F, 5-1-4 Akasaka,
Minato-ku (3224 1505). Uni Roppongi Bldg B1F,
7-15-17 Roppongi (3403 3563).

Zakuro

TBS Kaikan Bldg B1, 5-3-3 Akasaka, Minato-ku
(3582 6841). Akasaka-Mitsuke station. **Open** 11am-
11pm daily. **Average** ¥9,000. **Credit** AmEx, DC,
MC, V. **Menu in English**. **Map 7**.
Zakuro established its reputation on the strength of
its *shabu-shabu*. But it also serves a range of traditional cuisine – *sukiyaki*, *tempura* and other dishes
featuring fine seasonal ingredients. Smart, but not
as formal as a full-blown *kaiseki* restaurant, it offers
a choice of dining options: either *tatami* or western-
style, allowing you to sit at the counter of an open
kitchen or to book a private *tatami* room for parties
of four or more.
Branches: 4-6-1 Ginza, Chuo-ku (3535 4421);
Nihon Jitensha Kaikan, 1-9-15 Akasaka,
Minato-ku (3582 2661); Shin Nihonbashi Bldg B1F,
3-8-2 Nihonbashi, Chuo-ku (3271 3791); Shin Yaesu
Bldg B1F, 1-7-1 Kyobashi, Chuo-ku (3563 5031);
Chiba Bin Bldg B1F, 1-5-3 Nihonbashi-Muromachi,
Chuo-ku (3241 4841).

Ebisu area

Wasabiya

ITO Bldg B1F, 2-17-8 Ebisu-Nishi, Shibuya-ku
(3770 2604). Ebisu station. **Open** 6pm-1am
Mon-Sat. **Average** ¥4,500. **Credit** AmEx, MC, V.
Menu in English. **Map 32**.
This is how the stylish people of Daikanyama like
to graze these days: the owner sports a ponytail and
the decor is in the best modern-Japanese vein. Sit at
the counter or install yourself at low tables on the
floor. There's a good variety of dishes from *sashimi*
through grills to *tempura* – much of it served with
a dap of trademark pungent *wasabi*.

Ginza

Daidaiya

8-5 Ginza-Nine No.1 2F, Ginza-Nishi, Chuo-ku
(5537-3566). Shinbashi station. **Open** 5pm-1am
daily. **Average** ¥7,000. **Credit** V. **Menu in**
English. **Map 20**.
With its quite spectacular lighting and intricate
dining arrangements, Daidaiya boasts probably the
most remarkable interior in Tokyo. The food is
good, too, based around a confident, hybrid take

Eat, Drink, Shop

nouvelle cuisine **japonaise**

dai**dai**ya

on the traditional staples of Japanese cuisine. More a place to experience than to eat in, Daidaiya has to be seen to be believed.

Oshima
Ginza Core Bldg 9F, 5-8-20 Ginza, Chuo-ku (3574 8080). Ginza station. **Open** 11am-10pm (last orders 9pm) daily. **Average** ¥2,500 lunch; ¥6,000 dinner. **Credit** AmEx, DC, MC, V. **No English menu. Map 6.**
Traditional Japanese food served up in a tasteful, modern, comfortable setting. Not all of the courses are stellar, but the food is always well prepared and beautifully presented, and the timing of the waitresses is exquisite.
Branches: Odakyu Halc 8F, 1-5-1 Nishi Shinjuku, Shinjuku-ku (3348 8080); Hotel Pacific Tokyo, 3-13-3 Takanawa, Minato-ku (3445 6711).

Shin-Hinamoto
2-4-4 Yurakucho, Chiyoda-ku (3214 8021). Yurakucho station. **Open** 6pm-midnight Mon-Sat. **Average** ¥3,500. **No credit cards. No English menu. Map 6.**
Built right into the brickwork that supports the Yamanote line trains as they trundle around central Tokyo, Shin-Hinamoto is cramped but cosy, friendly, noisy and excellent value. In short, it's the quintessential Tokyo after-work drinking hole in every respect but one – the master of the house is a Brit who married into the family business and has been serving out the *sashimi* seafood, grilled fish and flagons of *sake* ever since.

Omotesando

Denpachi
5-9-9 Minami-Aoyama, Minato-ku (3406 8240). Omotesando station. **Open** 5pm-midnight daily. **Average** ¥3,000. **No credit cards. No English menu. Map 11.**
An *izakaya* known among its many regulars as 'the sardine place', Denpachi also serves up a mean array of beef tongue dishes. But mostly it does wicked things to the humble sardine (*iwashi*). Small strips of very tender fish appear as *iwashi sashimi*, while *iwashi tataki* is a tender rendering of sardines into small, carpaccio-like pieces. Don't miss the *iwashi wonton* soup, a delicately flavoured broth in which swim two wonton stuffed with – you guessed it – ground sardine.
Branches: 4-8-7 Ginza, Chuo-ku (3562 3957); 1-5 Kabuki-cho, Shinjuku-ku (3200 8003).

Shinjuku & area

Yui-An
Shinjuku Sumitomo Bldg 52F, 2-6-1 Nishi-Shinjuku, Shinjuku-ku (3342 5671). Shinjuku station. **Open** 5-11.30pm Mon-Sat; 4-10.30pm Sun. **Average** ¥4,500. **Credit** AmEx, MC, V. **No English menu. Map 1a.**
The waiters all act like automata and the modern

izakaya food is quite average. But the view over the night sky of Shinjuku is nothing short of spectacular, so call ahead and ask for one of the tables by the 52nd-floor window. Prices are reasonable, which has made Yui-an very popular with dating couples and groups of young people.

Yukun-tei
3-26 Arakicho, Shinjuku-ku (3356 3351). Yotsuya-Sanchome station. **Open** 11.30am-11pm Mon-Fri; 5-9pm Sat. **Average** ¥1,000 lunch; ¥6,500 dinner. **Credit** AmEx, DC, MC, V. **No English menu. Map 10.**
A friendly Kyushu *izakaya* with cheerful Kyushu waitresses and delightful Kyushu cuisine. Many of the names on the menu sound foreign even to Japanese ears and, indeed, there's something undeniably exotic – and southern – about the food on offer. The lunch sets are fantastic: *onigiri teishoku* has two enormous *onigiri* (rice balls), while *inaka udon teishoku* will net you a very generous bowl of *udon* with rice and mysterious little side dishes. (All dishes come with a little snake's-eye sampler of the smooth house *sake*, which is available nowhere else.) In the evening take your pick from the extensive selection of *sashimi*, grilled and simmered goodies.

Elsewhere

Aguri
Kojima Bldg 1F, 1-6-7 Kami-Meguro, Meguro-ku (3792 3792). Naka-Meguro station. **Open** 5.30-11pm daily. **Average** ¥4,000. **Credit** AmEx, MC, V. **No English menu. Map 32.**
This big, friendly, casual eaterie has just enough style to raise it above the average. Platters of pre-pared foods line the counter tapas-style, while short-order cooks stand ready to cook up grilled fish and *teppanyaki* meat and vegetables. Just point to whatever you fancy, including a good choice of *sake*.

Komahachi
5-12-4 Shiba, Minato-ku (3456 1271). Tamachi or Mita station (Toei Mita/Asakusa lines). **Open** 5-11pm Mon-Sat. **Average** ¥3,500. **No credit cards. Menu in English.**
Even though there are now a dozen spin-offs around this end of the city, for many people, Komahachi sums up the experience of the neighbourhood *izakaya*: it's cosy and friendly; there's a variety of interesting dishes and *sake*; the waiters take care of you; and it's all reasonably priced.
Branches: all over Tokyo.

Shirube
Pine Crest Kitazawa Bldg 1F, 2-18-2 Kitazawa, Setagaya-ku (3413 3784). Shimo-Kitazawa station (Inokashira/Odakyu lines). **Open** 5.30-11.30pm daily. **Average** ¥3,000. **No credit cards. No English menu. Map 35.**
Anyone who goes to Shirube adopts it as one of their favourite restaurants. A riotous cacophony of

mostly young people can be observed having the time of their lives here, ordering dish after dish of *izakaya* food cooked with flair. Don't let the lack of an English-language menu discourage you from eating here; the offerings change so often that they would not be able to keep up. Just ask for a seat at the counter and point at whatever takes your fancy.

Natural foods/vegetarian

Because so much of the diet is based on fish (with fish stock used in most soups), even noodles that contain no meat are rarely strictly vegetarian. *Shojin-ryori* (*see p117*) uses no meat or fish, but is invariably pricey. Most Indian restaurants offer vegetarian options.

Harajuku/Omotesando/Shibuya

Crayon House Hiroba
3-8-15 Kita-Aoyama, Minato-ku (3406-6409).
Omotesando station. **Open** 11am-10pm daily.
Average ¥1,200 lunch; ¥2,000 dinner.
No credit cards. No English menu. Map 11.
Set up alongside a natural-foods store, Crayon House is not exclusively vegetarian, but offers a good selection of well-prepared wholesome dishes, many of them featuring organic ingredients.

Down to Earth
2-5 Sarugaku-cho, Shibuya-ku (3461 5872).
Shibuya station. **Open** noon-3pm, 5-11pm Mon-Fri; 2-11pm Sat, Sun. **Average** ¥1,000 lunch; ¥3,000 dinner. **Credit** AmEx, DC, MC, V.
Menu in English. Map 2.
Down to Earth attracts a mostly young clientele (and even the occasional celebrity) with its casual atmosphere and wholesome food. While it's not completely vegetarian, hefty garden burgers with all the trimmings and a mixed bag of ethnic offerings will satisfy even the vegans.

Natural Harmony Angolo
3-38-12 Jingumae, Shibuya-ku (3405 8393).
Harajuku station. **Open** 11.30am-2.30pm, 5.30-9.30pm daily. **Average** ¥1,300 lunch; ¥3,500 dinner.
No credit cards. Menu in English. Map 11.
Currently Tokyo's best natural-foods restaurant, this boasts a simple interior that's no-smoking and additive-free. The food is very tasty, and although some fish is served, the ethos is strongly supportive of vegetarians. The baked aubergine is great; the wholewheat pizzas less so. There's a good range of organic beer, *sake* and wine.

Elsewhere

Gruppe
5-27-5 Ogikubo, Suginami-ku (3393 1224).
Ogikubo station. **Open** 11.30am-2pm, 5.30-10pm Mon-Sat. **Average** ¥1,000 lunch; ¥2,500 dinner.
No credit cards. No English menu. Map 29.

Located above a natural food shop, this caters to both locals and regulars. If you speak Japanese, staff will do their best to gear your choices towards whatever ails or concerns you. That's not to say that the food is medicinal – just healthy Japanese stuff of the brown rice variety. There's a white board on which the menu changes frequently. Smoking is not allowed, but you can imbibe from a selection of organic beers and even brown rice *sake*.

Alcohol

Japan's traditional tipple is **sake** (also known as *nihonshu*), which has a history stretching back more than one thousand years. *Sake* is fermented (not distilled) from rice; it is usually colourless and typically boasts an alcohol content of 15 to 19 per cent. The cheapest brews can induce wicked hangovers, but the top-quality grades can be as flavourful and rewarding as a fine wine. Most restaurants only serve a couple of varieties, but specialist *izakaya* may stock dozens of different brands, sourced from the more than 1,000 breweries around the country. *Sake* comes in a bewildering variety of styles and classifications: the basic product (*honjozo*) is blended with brewer's alcohol, which makes for a smoother product; *junmaishu* (made with no additives) is usually better quality, while the most distinctive *sake* is *ginjoshu*, which is made from more refined rice and with greater care.

Premium *sake* is usually served chilled (ask for *reishu*) in a glass or cup; others are best served heated up (*atsukan*) – but never so hot that they lose their flavour – in small carafes (*tokkuri*). In the end the one you choose is a matter of individual preference.

Shochu is a potent liquor akin to vodka, made from grains such as rice, barley or potato. The top brands can be drunk on the rocks, but the cheap stuff is usually mixed (either hot or cold) with lemon or *oolong* tea.

Japanese **beer** is invariably of the lager type. There is little to distinguish between the standard output of the three big breweries, Asahi, Kirin and Sapporo, although the latter's premium Yebisu is often considered the cream of the crop. There are also a growing number of regional microbreweries, whose products can sometimes be found in Tokyo.

Asian

Akasaka & area

Shisen Hanten

Zenkoku Ryokan Kaikan 5-6F, 2-5-5 Hirakawa-cho, Chiyoda-ku (3263 9371). Nagata-cho station. **Open** 11.30am-2pm, 5-10pm daily. **Average** ¥8,000. **Credit** AmEx, DC, MC, V. **No English menu. Map 9.**

A popular summer dish is *hiyashi chuka*: cold Chinese-style noodles and vegetables topped with either a sesame or vinegar sauce. It makes a refreshing summer treat in servings just right for lunch.

Kusa no Ya

Mita Bldg 3F, 2-14-33 Akasaka, Minato-ku (3589 0779). Akasaka station. **Open** 11.30am-12.30am Mon-Sat. **Average** ¥7,000. **Credit** AmEx, DC, MC, V. **Menu in English. Map 7.**

This popular, famous Korean restaurant started out in Azabu Juban. People come for the *yakiniku*: thinly sliced marinated beef cooked at the table and devoured family-style with side dishes of pickled *kimchee* and copious amounts of beer.
Branches: A&K Bldg 8F, 4-6-8 Azabu Juban, Minato-ku (3455 8356); 2-10-1 Shinbashi, Minato-ku (3591 4569).

Shinmasan-ya

Iito Bldg 1F, 3-12-5 Akasaka, Minato-ku (3583 6120). Akasaka-Mitsuke station. **Open** 11.30am-3am Mon-Sat; 4.30-11.30pm Sun. **Average** ¥3,500. **Credit** AmEx, JCB, MC, V. **Menu in English. Map 7.**

There may be better Korean restaurants in Akasaka, but Shinmasan-ya is a Korean-run place that attracts a loyal following. It offers home-style cooking, specialising in dishes other than the ubiquitous *yakiniku*, and also serves the best *bibimbap* in Tokyo. Ask to be seated on the floor: your legs can dangle under the table, while the heated floor warms the parts of you that the food can't reach.

Ebisu

Ninniku-ya

1-26-12 Ebisu, Shibuya-ku (5488 5540). Ebisu station. **Open** 6-11pm Tue-Sun. **Average** ¥4,000. **No credit cards. Menu in English. Map 3.**

Ninniku is the Japanese word for garlic, and everything on the menu, with the possible exception of the drinks, is laced with copious amounts of the stuff. The odours of towering garlic bread, vicious Thai curries, mouthwatering pasta and rice dishes with Chinese, Thai, Indian and other ethnic twists waft out on the streets, luring the uncommitted.

Ginza & area

Kihachi China

3-7-1 Ginza, Chuo-ku (5524 0761). Ginza station. **Open** 11.30am-3pm (*dim sum* only), 5.30-9.30pm daily. **Average** ¥3,000 lunch; ¥6,000 dinner. **Credit** AmEx, DC, MC, V. **No English menu. Map 6.**

If it's Chinese with style you're looking for, this understated, tasteful restaurant is the place to go. The *dim sum* lunch set (¥2,500) is great. An afternoon's repast of these little stuffed dumplings nestled in bamboo steamers is guaranteed to touch your heart. Reservations recommended.
Branch: 2-11-1 Sendagaya, Shibuya-ku (5770 1555).

Harajuku/Omotesando

Fumin

Aoyama Ohara Bldg B1, 5-7-17 Minami-Aoyama, Minato-ku (3498 4466). Omotesando station. **Open** noon-3pm, 5.30-10.30pm Mon-Fri; noon-3pm, 5-10pm Sat. **Average** ¥1,000 lunch; ¥2,500 dinner. **No credit cards. Menu in English. Map 4.**

Most people in Tokyo haven't actually eaten at Fumin; sure, they've tried, but been forced to give up because of a long wait made torturous by the heady smells of garlic and Chinese seasonings. But oh, how the wait is worth it to sample the extensive menu of funky home-style Chinese characterised by large, liberally seasoned servings. Don't miss the (scallion) *wonton* or the greasy, garlicky aubergine.

Jap Cho Ok

Alteka Belte Plaza B1F, 4-1-15 Minami-Aoyama, Minato-ku (5410-3408). Harajuku or Meiji-Jingumae station. **Open** 11.30am-2pm, 5.30pm-3am Mon-Sat; 5.30-11pm Sun. **Average** ¥6,000. **Credit** AmEx, MC, V. **Menu in English. Map 11.**

Demonstrating that there's more to Korean food than *yakiniku* and *kimchee*, the 'House of Weeds' is a cross between a Buddhist temple refectory and an oriental apothecary. Medicinal herbs hang from the walls, while the paper screens and lamps evoke the spare grandeur of a Korean mountain monastery. The menu includes a raft of vegetarian options, as well as meat and fish. A stylish crowd gather here, as much for the ambience as the cuisine.

Roppongi & area

Bangkok

Woo Bldg 2F, 3-8-8 Roppongi, Minato-ku (3408 7353). Roppongi station. **Open** 11.30am-3pm, 5-11pm Mon-Sat; noon-9pm Sun. Closed every 3rd Sun. **Average** ¥3,000. **No credit cards. Menu in English. Map 4.**

The menu is huge, the food is good and service is fast – just the ticket to set you back out into Roppongi playland. *Tom kha kai* soup arrives in a clay pot, turned a beautiful orange colour from the liberal dose of peppers. Try it with the minced meat *larbs*, well flavoured with lemon grass, cooling here and tangy onion. There's plenty of veggie fare, too.

Bengawan Solo

Kaneko Bldg 1F, 7-18-13 Roppongi, Minato-ku (3408 5698). Roppongi station. **Open** 11.30am-2.30pm, 5-11pm daily. **Average** ¥1,000 lunch; ¥4,000 dinner. **Credit** AmEx, DC, MC, V. **Menu in English. Map 4.**

Eat, Drink, Shop

Indonesian fare in Tokyo has long been synonymous with Bengawan Solo. It's been around since 1954, and as one of the first 'ethnic' joints to open, is often credited with single-handedly launching Tokyo's spicy food awakening. While the menu never changes, it remains consistently yummy: great *gado gado* (a salad smothered in a rich, spicy peanut sauce), shrimp in coconut cream, plus lots of curries and noodles.

Cyclo

Piramide Bldg 1F, 6-6-9 Roppongi, Minato-ku (3478 4964). Roppongi Station. **Open** 11.30am-3pm, 6pm-2am Mon-Fri; 6pm-2am Sat; 5-11.30pm Sun. **Average** ¥1,200 lunch; ¥4,500 dinner. **Credit** AmEx, MC, V. **Menu in English. Map** 4.
Cyclo offers a sleek version of Saigon staple foods, including good *goi cuon* spring rolls. Despite the cyclo trishaw parked at the entrance, it's not a particularly authentic experience; the food is toned down for Japanese tastes (or perhaps coriander leaf is too expensive). Nevertheless, Cyclo is a stylish space, and it serves 333 beer.

Erawan

Roi Bldg 13F, 5-5-1 Roppongi, Minato-ku (3404 5741). Roppongi station. **Open** 5-11.30pm daily. **Average** ¥5,000. **Credit** AmEx, DC, MC, V. **Menu in English. Map** 4.
While the quality of food at Erawan can be a little erratic, its place on the 13th floor of Roppongi's Roi Building (notorious for the hanky-panky that goes on on some other floors) offers one of the best dining views in town. Also in its favour is its teak decor, understated Thai decorations, and enviable elbow room – if only the staff would get over the habit of seating all the customers right next to each other.

Hong Kong Garden

4-5-2 Nishi-Azabu, Minato-ku (3486 8611). Hiroo station. **Open** 11.30am-3pm, 5.30-10.30pm Mon-Fri; 11.30am-4pm, 5.30-10.30pm Sat; 5.30-10pm Sun. **Average** ¥3,000 lunch; ¥4,000 dinner. **Credit** AmEx, MC, V. **Menu in English. Map** 4.
Huge gastrodome (seating 800-plus) devoted to the pleasures of Hong Kong-style cooking. The main dishes are Cantonese-lite, but very pleasant, especially the stir-fried organic beef with subtle hints of star anise. The trolley-borne *dim sum* are not totally authentic, but as good as you can expect in Tokyo.

Kaikatei

Odakyu Minami-Aoyama Bldg B1F, 7-8-1 Minami-Aoyama, Minato-ku (3499 5872). Omotesando station. **Open** 11.30am-2pm, 6-10.30pm Mon-Sat. **Average** ¥1,000 lunch; ¥5,000 dinner. **No credit cards. Menu in English. Map** 4.
Take a step back in time to 1930s Shanghai: old beer posters, wooden clocks, dated LPs and odd murals of barbarian foreigners lend an air of wartime mystery to this Chinese restaurant. Shrimp in crab sauce is delicately flavoured with ginger, spring onion and shrimp and goes well with mildly spicy Peking-style chicken with cashew nuts and rich black bean sauce. Avoid the *gyoza* and flat Heartland beer.

Monsoon Café

2-10-1 Nishi-Azabu, Minato-ku (5467 5221). Roppongi station. **Open** 11.30am-5am daily. **Average** ¥2,500. **Credit** AmEx, DC, JCB, MC, V. **Menu in English. Map** 4.
The *faux*-Indonesian jungle decor might be a little contrived, but the bar is good, the food varied, and the mixed foreign/Japanese crowd tends to be a slightly more sophisticated (read older) than the twentysomething crowd that haunts much of Shibuya. The menu will please all-comers: curries, salads, soups and satay use free-range chicken, organically grown rice and no MSG, while spice is adjusted to suit your heat tolerance.
Branches: 15-4 Hachiyama-cho, Shibuya-ku (5489 3789); 1-6-8 Jinnan, Shibuya-ku (5489 1611); Minami-Aoyama Kougyo Bldg 1-2F; 7-3-1 Minami-Aoyama, Minato-ku (3400 7200); Mediage Bldg 4F, 1-7-1, Daiba Minato-ku (3599 4805).

Szechwan (Shisen Honten)

Uni Roppongi Bldg 4F, 7-15-17 Roppongi, Minato-ku (3402 3465). Roppongi station.
Open 11.30am-3pm; 5-10pm daily. **Average** ¥1,500 lunch; ¥3,500 dinner. **Credit** AmEx, MC, V. **Menu in English. Map** 4.
Good, solid, dependable Szechwan cuisine from Chinese-born chef Ching Ken-ichi, who has risen to fame on the back of the *Iron Chef* TV cooking contests. The spices are suitably authentic – not just fiery chilli but also plenty of brown pepper and star anise. Good braised *tofu* and spicy *tanmen* noodles.

Shibuya

Jembatan Merah

Jembatan Mela 109 Bldg 8F, 2-29-1 Dogenzaka, Shibuya-ku (3476 6424). Shibuya station.
Open 11am-11pm Mon-Sat; 5.30-11pm Sun. **Average** ¥2,500. **Credit** (bills over ¥3,000) AmEx, DC, MC, V. **No English menu. Map** 2.
The Indonesian fare at Jembatan Merah is perhaps not quite as good as at Bengawan Solo (*see p131*) and quality does vary from location to location. But with branches dotted conveniently around the JR Yamanote line, it does greatly broaden Tokyo's Indonesian horizon with the added attraction of good vegetarian offerings. There are seven dishes, starring *tempeh* (a fermented soybean patty with a slightly nutty flavour), middling *gado gado* salad, and an extravagant 12-course 'special menu' for those who can't be bothered to navigate the many pages of the standard listings.
Branches: I-Land Tower B1, 6-5-1 Nishi-Shinjuku, Shinjuku-ku (5323 4214); 3-20-6 Akasaka, Minato-ku (3588 0794); Sunshine City Alpa B1, 3-1 Higashi-Ikebukuro, Toshima-ku (3987 2290).

Raj Mahal/Raj Palace

Jow Bldg 5F, 30-5 Udagawa-cho, Shibuya-ku (3770 7677). Shibuya station. **Open** 11.30am-11pm daily. **Average** ¥2,000. **Credit** AmEx, DC, MC, V. **Menu in English. Map** 2.

Despite its chain status, the Raj Mahal/Palace restaurants have good service and above-average Moghul-style food. Menus are extensive. **Branches**: Urban Bldg 4F, 7-13-2 Roppongi, Minato-ku (5411 2525); Peace Bldg 5F, 3-34-11 Shinjuku, Shinjuku-ku (5379 2525); Hakuba Bldg 4F, 26-11 Udagawa-cho, Shibuya-ku (3780 6531); Taiyo Bldg 4F, 8-8-5 Ginza Chuo Dori, Chuo-ku (5568 8080).

Shinjuku & area

Angkor Wat

1-38-13 Yoyogi, Shibuya-ku (3370 3019). Yoyogi station. **Open** 11am-2pm, 5-10pm daily. **Average** ¥1,000 lunch; ¥2,000 dinner. **No credit cards. No English menu. Map 23.**

What this Cambodian rest it makes up for in food. and indeed the food com but that may only be bec: up to get in. Cheerful Can ters of the proprietor) w menu; be sure to order chicken salad and

Ban Thai

Dai-ichi Metro Bldg 3F, 1-23-14 Kabuki-cho, Shinjuku-ku (3207 0068). Shinjuku station. **Open** 5pm-midnight Mon-Fri; 11.30am-midnight Sat, Sun. **Average** ¥2,500. **Credit** AmEx, DC, MC, V. **Menu in English. Map 1b.**
Conveniently situated at one end of raunchy Kabuki-cho, this is the longest-standing Thai institution in town, and no wonder: while no longer the best (try

Eating etiquette

When you enter a restaurant you'll be greeted with a shouted chorus of '*Irasshaimase!*' ('Welcome!'). The waiter will ask you how many people there are in your party – '*Nanmei sama?*', to which you should answer by holding up the appropriate number of fingers.

After you have been seated you will be given an *oshibori* (hot towel) to wipe your hands. You'll also be given a menu and asked if you would like anything to drink ('*O-nomimono wa*?').

Hands cleaned and drinks on the way, it's now time to order. If you're in a speciality restaurant, a good deal of the guesswork has already been done for you. You know you'll be eating *tempura*, for instance; the only decision is what kind. After you've ordered a small selection, say '*Toriaezu*' ('For now' or 'For starters'). If all else fails and you're feeling trusting, say '*Omakaseshimasu*' ('I leave it up to you').

Just like anywhere else, Japan has its own dining etiquette. As a foreigner, you will usually be forgiven minor gaffs. However, paying heed to the following guidelines will ensure that you don't unintentionally insult your hosts.

Slurping, talking with your mouth full and consuming your food at grand prix speed are all quite acceptable, but it is considered the height of rudeness to blow one's nose at the table.

It is perfectly acceptable to lift a bowl towards your mouth. Soups, like *miso*, are drunk straight from the bowl. Drinking *miso* with a spoon is like enjoying a fine wine with a straw.

Much of Japanese food, especially food eaten in *izakaya*, is intended to be shared with your fellow diners. Even in western restaurants, particularly Italian ones, groups of Japanese people will order dishes to be shared, and kitchens will provide small dishes so that each person can help themselves.

There is almost nothing a foreigner can do wrong with chopsticks. Even the most ham-fisted user will be rewarded with a hearty (and quite sincere) '*O-hashi jozu desu ne!*' ('My, you're so good at using chopsticks!'). However, there are two things one should never do, as they are related to funeral rituals and will genuinely shock fellow diners. First, never plant your chopsticks upright in a bowl of rice. Second, never pass food from one pair of chopsticks to another, as this mimics the act of conveying the bones of a recently departed from cremation tray to urn.

In most places you pay as you leave, at the cash register by the door. The bill will often be at the table – either a slip of paper or an itemised list attached to a small clipboard; if there is no bill, it is being held at the cash register. In some upscale joints (mostly western) the bill is paid at the table. You can signal for it by making an 'X' sign with two index fingers crossed one over the other, or say '*O-kanjo kudasai*' ('The bill, please'). On the way out, it's polite to nod your head and say '*Gochisosama deshita*' ('I enjoyed the meal').

There is no tipping in Japanese eateries. Many restaurants and hotel bills include a ten per cent service charge.

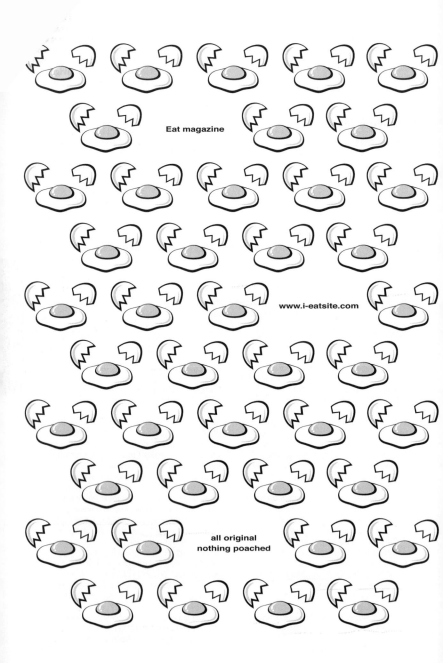

Eat magazine

www.i-eatsite.com

all original
nothing poached

Bangkok in Roppongi instead, *see p131*), there's nothing on the extensive menu here that will disappoint. The curries are especially good.

China Grill – Xenlon
Odakyu Hotel Century Southern Tower 19F, 2-2-1 Yoyogi, Shibuya-ku (3374 2080). Shinjuku station. Open 11.30am-4.30pm, 5-11pm daily. **Average** ¥3,000 lunch; ¥8,000 dinner. **Credit** AmEx, DC, MC, V. **No English menu. Map** 1a.
Impeccable service and great views of the neon skyline make this Chinese restaurant worth the splurge. Cantonese fare, with a nod towards western influences, includes over 36 choices of *dim sum* at lunch, and multi-dish courses or à la carte at dinner.

Hyakunincho Yataimura
2-20-25 Hyakunincho, Shinjuku-ku (5386 3320). Shin-Okubo station. Open 5pm-4am Mon-Sat; 5pm-2am Sun. **Average** ¥2,500. **No credit cards. No English menu. Map** 22.
Just the place if you find yourself out all night or looking for a break from polite Japanese service. It's a low-rent place where the 'waiters' might dish out your rice while puffing on a cigarette in true Asian style. Yataimura (Foodstall Village) is a collection of small cooking stands around a central eating area. The various proprietors vie aggressively for your custom, so sit down and quickly order some beer and snacks or you will be swarmed by as many as five people brandishing menus. There are choices from places as diverse as Thailand, Indonesia, Taiwan and Fukien; servings are huge.

Shinjuku Jojoen
Tokyo Opera City Tower 53F, 3-20-2 Nishi-Shinjuku, Shinjuku-ku (5353 0089). Hatsudai station (Keio line). Open 11.30am-11.30pm daily. **Average** ¥6,000. **Credit** AmEx, DC, JCB, MC, V. **Menu in English. Map** 1a.
This is not honest, down-home Korean cooking; it's *yakiniku* with a view. And what a view! From the 53rd floor, the Shinjuku skyline at night is breathtaking. If there are only two of you, make a reservation (Mon-Sat only) for one of the 'pair seats' – two comfortable chairs facing the window.

Tokaien
1-6-3 Kabuki-cho, Shinjuku-ku (3200 2924). Shinjuku station. Open 11am-4am daily. **Average** All-you-can eat ¥2,250 for 90 mins; à la carte prices vary. **Credit** AmEx, DC, MC, V. **No English menu. Map** 1b.
If *yakiniku* is a religion, then Tokaien is its temple: nine floors dedicated to *yakiniku* and home-style Korean cooking. The sixth floor features all-you-can-eat ('tabe-hodai' in Japanese) *yakiniku*.

Elsewhere

Jiang's
Kurokawa Bldg 3F, 3-5-7 Tamagawa, Setagaya-ku (3700 2475). Futako-Tamagawa station (Tokyu Denentoshi line). Open 5-10pm Tue-Thur; 11.30am-2pm, 5-10pm Fri-Sun. **Average** ¥3,000. **Credit** AmEx, MC, V. **Menu in English.**

Nguyen Thi Giang was born in Hanoi but raised in south Vietnam, and the menu in her spotless little restaurant reflects both influences. The hearty *cha gio* are cooked in northern Vietnamese style, full of flavourful pork, while the delicate *banh xeo* pancakes are as sweet and satisfying as any you'd find in Hue. The best home-style Vietnamese food in Tokyo.

Namaste Kathmandu
85 Tokyo Bldg B1, 1-8-10 Kichijoji-Honcho, Kichijoji, Musashino-shi (042 221 0057). Kichijoji station. Open 11am-10.30pm daily, **Average** ¥1,500. **Credit** AmEx, DC, MC, V. **Menu in English. Map** 31.
One of the friendliest places in Tokyo, this cosy little Nepalese den makes you feel as if you've walked into someone's home: the proprietors treat customers like family, passing around snapshots from Nepal and urging you to visit. There's only one chef, six tiny tables and a counter. Stay away from the *alu tama* and you'll do just fine.

Nataraj
Fukumura Sangyo Bldg B1F, 5-30-6 Ogikubo, Suginami-ku (3398 5108). Ogikubo station. Open 11.30am-10.30pm daily. **Average** ¥2,000. **Credit** AmEx, DC, MC, V. **Menu in English. Map** 29.
Vegetarian fare is hard to come by in Tokyo, but at Nataraj (God of Dance) the Indian food is sure to satisfy both vegetarians and carnivores. Servings are moderate, so choose an assortment from the extensive curry menu or select from one of five special sets with rice, *naan*, salad, chutney, popadom, *dal wara* and a choice of curries.

Peppermint Café
Grand Maison Kichijoji B1F, 1-15-14 Kichijoji Minami-cho, Kichijoji, Musashino-shi (0422 79 3930). Kichijoji station. Open 5.30pm-1am daily. **Average** ¥2,500. **No credit cards. Menu in English. Map** 31.
Horikotatsu tables, lovely reclining cushions from Thailand, and lights and bamboo latticework from Bali and Hong Kong decorate the interior of this 'Thai, Asian Foods Paradise Restaurant Bar,' just a stone's throw from Inokashira Park. An open kitchen dishes up Thai mainstays such as *tom yom koong* soup, *pad Thai* and green curry, plus Korean *bibimbap*, chicken salad Kampuchea-style and Vietnamese vegetable rolls.

East meets west

Harajuku/Omotesando

Fujimamas
6-3-2 Jingumae, Shibuya-ku (5485 2262). Meiji-Jingumae or Harajuku station. Open 11am-11pm daily. **Average** ¥3,500. **Credit** AmEx, DC, MC, V. **Menu in English. Map** 11.
Fujimamas offers confident east-west fusion cuisine

Eat, Drink, Shop

Enjoy some 'Things That Make You Go UMMMMMMMMM' at **Fujimamas**. *See p135.*

in a casual setting. Servings are large and the prices are good, given the swanky address and sunny decor. A jokey seasonal menu lets you know that this place doesn't take itself too seriously. Entrées, under the title 'Let's Go For a Wok' or 'Things that Make You Go UMMMMMMMMM' won't disappoint.

Nobu Tokyo

6-10-17 Minami-Aoyama, Minato-ku (5467 0022). Omotesando station then a 10min walk. **Open** *Restaurant* 11.30am-3.30pm (last entry 2pm), 6-11.30pm (last entry 10pm) Mon-Fri; 6-11.30pm (last entry 10pm) Sat, Sun. *Bar* 5.30pm-4am (last orders 3.30am) Mon-Sat; 5.30-11pm (last entry 10pm) Sun. **Average** ¥6,000 lunch; ¥10,000 dinner. **Credit** AmEx, DC, MC, V. **Menu in English**. **Map** 4.
Nobu Matsuhisa started as a *sushi* chef in Tokyo before striking out for Peru, Argentina and the US. His restaurant Nobu electrified jaded New York palates and set the standard for nouvelle Japanese cuisine. In addition to restaurants in New York, London, Beverly Hills and Aspen, Nobu comes home to Japan in an elegant, sophisticated setting serving world-class fusion cuisine. Black cod with *miso* is purportedly actor Robert De Niro's favourite, though Nobu Matsuhisa is most renowned for his *sushi* rolls.

Rojak

B1-B2F, 6-3-14 Minami-Aoyama, Minato-ku (3409 6764). Omotesando station. **Open** 11.30am-2.30pm, 5-11pm Mon-Thur; 11.30am-2.30pm, 5pm-midnight Fri; 5pm-midnight Sat; 5-11pm Sun. **Average** ¥1,000 lunch; ¥4,500 dinner. **Credit** AmEx, DC, JCB, MC, V. **Menu in English**. **Map** 4.
Western-influenced Asian food in a lovely basement with candlelit nooks, high ceilings and jungle-motif wall coverings. Next to the dining room is a comfy

bar area with soft sofas and a cigar humidor. Stellar salads with a unique house dressing are served in large, dark wood bowls that match the tables. Noodles, curries and seafood, especially *sashimi*, get reinvented at Rojak in sublime ways. There's a fair selection of wines (mostly Australian), plus German and Belgian beers and the locally brewed Tokyo Ale.

Vision Network/Las Chicas

5-47-6 Jingumae, Shibuya-ku (3407 6865). Omotesando station. **Open** 11am-11pm daily. **Average** ¥1,000 lunch; ¥4,000 dinner. **Credit** AmEx, DC, JCB, MC, V. **Menu in English**. **Map** 2.
The most creative, foreigner-friendly space in town, Vision Network is a gorgeous complex encompassing several restaurants and bars (Las Chicas, Tokyo Salon, Nude and Crome) that host revolving exhibitions of local talent. The bilingual staff (mostly Australian) are friendly and helpful, and are clearly so close to the cutting edge of fashion as to constitute an exhibition in themselves. Potato wedges with sour cream and Thai chilli sauce, cheesy polenta chips or homemade bread with real butter are perfect mates for earthy, sensuous Australian wines.

Roppongi & area

Ken's Dining

1-15-4 Nishi-Azabu, Minato-ku (5771-5788). Hiroo or Roppongi station. **Open** 6pm-1am daily. **Average** ¥5,000. **Credit** AmEx, MC, V. **Menu in English**. **Map** 4.
One of the most stylish openings of the past few years, Ken's is the flagship operation of the Chanto Dining group, an Osaka-based company that's now

making inroads into the Tokyo region. There's substance to back up the chic good looks, though. Ken Okada has produced an intriguing menu that fuses Japanese with Korean (plenty of *kimchee*), Chinese and even a touch of Italian. Not only does it work most of the time, it's also quite affordable for this neck of the Nishi-Azabu woods.

Noodles

2-21-7 Azabu-Juban, Minato-ku (3452 3112). Azabu-Juban station. **Open** 11.30am-2.30pm, 6pm-4am Mon-Sat; 11.30am-2.30pm, 6-11pm Sun. **Average** ¥4,500. **Credit** MC, V. **Menu in English. Map** 4.
You can tell all you need to know from the name, the trendy orange exterior and the eye-catching arrangement of jars of *soba, bifun* and pasta in the front window. Noodles serves its pan-Asian fare with style and verve, with plenty of New World wines, a jazzy sound track and waiters who wear their jeans rolled up to the knee. Things are so relaxed here that the local trendies treat it like a family restaurant.

Phothai Down Under

Five Plaza Bldg 2F, 5-18-21 Roppongi, Minato-ku (3505 1504). Roppongi station. **Open** noon-2.30pm, 5pm-5am daily. **Average** ¥3,000. **Credit** AmEx, DC, JCB, MC, V. **Menu in English. Map** 4.
A Thai-Australian restaurant that serves a fairly extensive menu of middling-quality Thai food and enormous Aussie steaks. Think of the Thai dishes as starters, choose a cut of meat from the tray brought to your table, and wash it all down with Australian wine or Thai beer. Better yet, try mixing it all together – somehow it works.

French

Harajuku/Omotesando/Aoyama

Aux Bacchanales

Palais France 1F, 1-6 Jingumae, Shibuya-ku (5474 0076). Meiji-Jingumae or Harajuku station. **Open** *Brasserie/café* 9am-midnight daily. *Restaurant* 6pm-midnight daily. **Average** ¥6,000. **Credit** (restaurant only) AmEx, DC, JCB, MC, V. **Menu in French. Map** 11.
One of the rare Tokyo places where the action spills out on the streets and people go to watch and be watched – and drink themselves silly on relatively inexpensive red wine. French cooking is served in a casual bistro setting on 'authentic' French café furniture, and all things considered it's pretty good. The less atmospheric branch is in an office block in the business district.
Branch: Ark Mori Bldg 2F, 1-12-32 Akasaka, Minato-ku (3582 2225).

Chez Pierre

1-23-10 Minami-Aoyama, Minato-ku (3475 1400). Aoyama-Itchome station. **Open** 11.30am-2.30pm, 6-10pm Tue-Sun. **Average** ¥2,000 lunch; ¥10,000 dinner. **Credit** AmEx, DC, JCB, MC, V. **Menu in French. Map** 12.

Charming, unpretentious n[...] that serves French provinc[...] is especially popular. Insid[...] inviting, while the floor-to[...] café terrace make it a perf[...] tea and pastries. The care[...] changes regularly.

Shinjuku & area

La Dinette

2-6-10 Takadanobaba, Shinjuku-ku (3200 6571). Takadanobaba station. **Open** 11.30am-1.30pm, 6-9pm Mon-Sat. **Average** ¥1,500 lunch; ¥4,000 dinner. **Credit** AmEx, DC, JCB, MC, V. **Menu in French. Map** 22.
Reservations are definitely advised for this pleasingly authentic bistro in the low-rent student district of Takadanobaba. La Dinette has been around for ages because it serves simple French cuisine at affordable prices in student-friendly portions. Almost always crowded, it's not designed for romantic evenings, but to sate prodigious appetites and send you out to play.

Italian

Marunouchi

Elio Locanda Italiana

2-5-2 Kojimachi, Chiyoda-ku (3239 6771). Hanzomon station. **Open** 11.45am-2.15pm, 5.45-10.15pm daily. **Average** ¥2,500 lunch; ¥7,000 dinner. **Credit** AmEx, DC, JCB, MC, V. **Menu in English. Map** 9.
Elio Orsara hails from Calabria, and honed his considerable culinary skills in Florence and Milan. His kitchen (with his brother at the helm) melds these influences into one of the most satisfying Italian restaurants in the city. Excellent southern-style bean soups and some hearty Tuscan fare make this eaterie a consistent favourite with Tokyo's various expat communities, while Elio's florid, expansive character invariably ensures an all-round enjoyable dining experience.

MSG warning

The taste-enhancer known best by its proprietary Japanese name 'Aji-no-moto' is used liberally in all but the highest-quality restaurants. It was originally synthesised from the active ingredients found in *kombu* seaweed and *katsuobushi* (preserved bonito). The white crystall is now a chemical derived from a variety of sources, including corn starch and animal biproducts.

...armine Edochiano

9-13 Arakicho, Shinjuku-ku (3225 6767). Yotsuya-Sanchome station. **Open** noon-2pm, 6-10pm daily. **Average** ¥2,500 lunch; ¥8,000 dinner. **Credit** AmEx, DC, JCB, MC, V. **Menu in Italian. Map** 10.
Carmine Cozzolini was one of the pioneers of good, cheap trattoria and pizzerias in Tokyo, but Edochiano (Italian for 'Edo style') is unlike any other. Converted from a Japanese *ryotei*, this quite remarkable-looking *ristorante* fuses traditional architecture with a stylish northern Italian sensibility. The Tuscan fare is adequate rather than brilliant, but the surroundings are not to be missed.

Omotesando

Giliola

Aoyama Obara Kaikan B1, 5-7-17 Minami-Aoyama, Minato-ku (5485 3516). Omotesando station. **Open** 11.30am-3pm, 5.30-11pm Mon-Sat. **Average** ¥1,000 lunch; ¥5,000 dinner. **Credit** (evenings only) AmEx, DC, JCB, MC, V. **Menu in Italian. Map** 4.
This tiny underground trattoria serves up fantastically executed homestyle Italian cooking. There's a small list of Italian wines to accompany it, and a larger selection of *grappa* to round off the meal. The grand menu changes three times a year, and seasonal specials are marked up on a chalkboard.

La' Grotta Celeste

Aoyama Centre Bldg 1F, 3-8-40 Minami-Aoyama, Minato-ku (3401 1261). Omotesando station. **Open** 11.30am-3pm, 5.30-11pm daily. **Average** ¥1,600 lunch; ¥5,000 dinner. **Credit** AmEx, DC, JCB, MC, V. **Menu in Italian. Map** 12.
This is the place for a special-occasion splurge, offering excellent service and exquisite Italian food in a lovely pink-hued setting. It's hard to decide which is better: the grotto room with its brick lattice walls and Italianate ceiling fresco or the centre room with a view of the kitchen and its wood-burning stove.

Tokyo Salon

5-47-6 Jingumae, Shibuya-ku (3407 6865). Omotesando station. **Open** 11am-11pm daily (members only after 5pm). **Average** ¥3,000. **Credit** AmEx, DC, JCB, MC, V. **Menu in English. Map** 2.
Tokyo Salon is officially a Mediterranean restaurant, but Chef Dante Fazzina will happily adapt his cooking to whatever culinary trip you're on. At night it's a member's club; the yearly fee of ¥10,000 allows you into one of the most creative spaces in Tokyo, where large wooden chairs, a *tatami* room, exquisite flower arrangements, live music and dozens of candles make it one of the un-stuffiest clubs on earth. The intimately prepared food includes sublime baked aubergine, lively vegetable soup and a mixed antipasto platter. The Salon is open to non-members until 5pm, and for special events.

Elsewhere

La Befana

5-31-3 Daita, Setagaya-ku (3411 9500) Shimo-Kitazawa station (Inokashira/Odakyu lines). **Open** noon-2pm, 5.30-10.30pm daily. **Average** ¥4,000. **Credit** AmEx, JCB, MC, V. **Menu in Italian. Map** 35.
Angelo Cozzolini, brother of Carmine, has created one of Tokyo's best pizzerias with a real wood-fired oven and plenty of style. He also serves solid, dependable oven-roasted fish and tasty side dishes.

Primi Baci

Inokashira Parkside Bldg 2F, 1-21-1 Kichijoji Minami-cho, Musashino-shi (0422 72 8202). Kichijoji station. **Open** 11.30am-2.30pm, 2.30-10pm Mon-Fri; 11.30am-10pm Sat, Sun. **Average** ¥4,000. **Credit** AmEx, DC, JCB, MC, V. **Menu in English. Map** 31.
In a splendid setting overlooking Inokashira Park, Primi Baci (which translates as 'First Kiss') has both exquisite service and well-executed Tuscan cuisine. The waiters are charming, unpretentious and eager to test their English, while the open and airy interior boasts well-spaced tables set with fresh flowers. For starters don't miss the *tartara di tonno*, a column of tender tuna tartare garnished with marche salad and slivered fried leeks, or the *torretta di melanzane*, an aubergine, mozzarella and tomato tower bathed in swirls of basil sauce.

Mexican

Daikanyama

La Casita

Selsa Daikanyama 2F, 13-4 Daikanyama-cho, Shibuya-ku (3496 1850). Daikanyama station (Tokyu Toyoko line). **Open** 11am-10pm daily. **Average** ¥3,500. **Credit** AmEx, DC, JCB, MC, V. **Menu in Spanish. Map** 32.
Like most of Tokyo's Mexican restaurants, La Casita isn't very authentic. But once the heady aroma of corn tortillas grabs you it won't let go until you've sampled the near-perfect *camarones al mojo de ajo* (grilled shrimp with garlic Acapulco style) or the *enchiladas rojos* bathed in spicy tomato sauce.

Middle Eastern

Shibuya

Ankara

Social Dogenzaka B1, 1-14-9 Dogenzaka, Shibuya-ku (3780 1366). Shibuya station. **Open** 11.30am-3pm, 5-11.30pm daily. **Average** ¥3,000. **Credit** MC, V. **Menu in English. Map** 2.
Tucked away in the backstreets of Shibuya, this snug little restaurant serves up an array of healthy, delicious *meze* and other Turkish delights.

Eat, Drink, Shop

Good Honest Grub: does what it says on the tin.

have a pizza with two kinds of olives, or an [...]ian one, or a Santa Fe, with chicken, onions [...] camole, washed down with beer and a Caesar [...] on the side – well, that's what Brendan's is here [...]

Ebisu & area

Fummy's Grill

2-1-5 Ebisu, Shibuya-ku (3473 9629). Ebisu station. **Open** 11.30am-2am daily. **Average** ¥4,500. **Credit** AmEx, MC, V. **Menu in English**. **Map** 3.
Fumihiro Nakamura opened his original Californian bistro back in 1996, and in many people's books it's still the best. That's because it's casual, friendly and cheap, and the food still has a good creative spark. BYO wine, or explore his mostly New World offerings in the company of a mixed crowd of arty types and business suits, locals and expats.

Good Honest Grub

1-11-11 Ebisu-Minami, Shibuya-ku (3710 0400). Ebisu station. **Open** 11am-midnight daily. **Average** ¥1,000 lunch; ¥3,000 dinner. **Credit** AmEx, MC, V. **Menu in English**. **Map** 3.
No-nonsense food in a sidewalk café setting. Portions are generous, and there's plenty for vegetarians. Awesome shakes and good desserts, too.

Ricos Kitchen

4-23-7 Ebisu, Shibuya-ku (5791 4649). Ebisu station. **Open** 11.30am-2pm, 5.30-10pm daily. **Average** ¥1,000 lunch; ¥4,500 dinner. **Credit** AmEx, MC, V. **Menu in English**. **Map** 3.
Up-and-coming chef Haurki Natsume produces a suave and never-less-than-satisfying new American cuisine, which is the main reason why Ricos has been full virtually every day of the week since it opened in September '98. Also contributing to its popularity is the chic and airy interior, and the cellar of Californian wines. Brunch is served from 11.30am to 2pm at the weekend.

Stellato

Shiroganedai 4-19-17, Minato-ku (3442 5588). Shiroganedai station. **Open** 5.30pm-2am (last orders for food 11pm) daily. **Average** ¥10,000. **Credit** AmEx, MC, V. **Menu in English**. **Map** 18.
Like its sister restaurant, **Tableaux** (*see p141*), Stellato combines a flair for the dramatic (here huge chandeliers, a blazing log fire and an immodest *faux*-Moorish façade) with food that is always interesting, and frequently exceptional. The best touch is the rooftop lounge with its view of Tokyo Tower.

Shinjuku area

Hannibal

Urban Bldg B1F, 1-11-1 Hyakunincho, Shinjuku-ku (5389 7313). Shin-Okubo station. **Open** 5pm-12.30am Mon-Sat. **Average** ¥3,500. **Credit** AmEx, MC, V. **Menu in English**.
Currently Hannibal is Tokyo's only source of Tunisian food – and it's very good. Chef Mondher Gheribi cooks a confident Mediterranean cuisine with plenty of highlights from his home country – including *mechoui* salad, great roast chicken, home-made *khobz* bread and spicy home-made *harissa*.

North American

Roppongi

Brendan's Pizzakaya

Daiichi Koyama Bldg 203, 3-1-19 Nishi-Azabu, Minato-ku (3479 8383). Roppongi station. **Open** 6-11pm Tue-Thur; 6pm-2am Fri; 6pm-midnight Sat; 4-10pm Sun. **Average** ¥2,500 for two. **Credit** JCB, MC, V. **Menu in English**. **Map** 4.
You didn't come all the way to Tokyo for pizza. But if you've been here a while, and absolutely have to

Omotesando

Roy's

Riviera Minami-Aoyama Bldg 1F, 3-3-3 Minami-Aoyama, Minato-ku (5474 8181). Omotesando station. **Open** 11.30am-3.30pm, 5.45-11pm Mon-Fri; 11am-3.30pm Sat, Sun. **Average** ¥1,400-¥3,500 lunch; ¥8,000 dinner. **Credit** AmEx, DC, JCB, MC, V. **Menu in English**. **Map** 12.

Eat, Drink, Shop

imple but exciting Euro-
nbined with intimate ser-
panese flavours – *shoyu*,
in exquisitely arranged
shrimp with spicy *miso*
seafood *fritatta* accom-
...u ginger and spicy sprouts. The
...u brunch that's served here is excellent. Tuck
into home-made muffins, *dim sum*-style appetisers,
devastating entrées and some scrumptious desserts,
washed down with all-you-can-drink wine.

Branches: 1-1-40 Hiroo, Shibuya-ku (3406 2277);
5-25-11 Nakamachi, Setagaya-ku (5706 6555).

Shibuya & area

Bar & Grill Lunchan
*1-2-5 Shibuya, Shibuya-ku (5466 1398). Shibuya
station.* **Open** 11.30am-2.30pm, 2.30-11pm Mon-Sat;
11am-10pm Sun. **Average** ¥2,500 Sunday brunch;
¥1,000 lunch; ¥4,000 dinner. **Credit** AmEx, DC, JCB,
MC, V. **Menu in English**. **Map 2**.

Breakfast

Breakfast is not a meal that features
prominently in modern urban Japan. The
average commuting salaryman has little
time for much more than a slurp of coffee
or a *genki* drink (caffeine-laden vitamin
drinks sold on station platforms) on his
way to work. As for the traditional Japanese
breakfast, few people other than farmers
who have been up since daybreak are ready
to sit down to a table groaning with rice,
miso soup, grilled fish, raw egg, fermented
natto beans, pickles and tea.

Most of the large hotels offer a choice
of breakfast fare – Japanese, cooked
western or Continental. But if you're
looking for early-morning sustenance
out on the street the choices are more
limited. Most coffee shops are likely to offer
something in the way of toast and a hard-
boiled egg, along with complimentary
second-hand cigarette smoke.

Here are a few places that have a more
enterprising and appetising approach to
the first meal of the day.

Andersen
*Ark Mori Bldg 2F, 1-12-32 Akasaka, Minato-ku
(3585 0879). Tameike-sanno station.*
Open *Bakery* 8am-10pm Mon-Fri; 8am-7pm
Sat, Sun. *Restaurant* 1am-10pm daily.
Average ¥1,000. **No credit cards**. **Map 4**.
A choice of Continental breakfast or eggs,
bacon, toast and coffee will set you back
about ¥1,000. Great bread and pastries
and good sandwiches may be purchased
from the on-site bakery all day long.

Chef's Table
*3-20-6 Toranomon, Minato-ku (5405 4473).
Toranomon station.* **Open** 7am-9pm Mon-Fri.
Average ¥500. **No credit cards**. **Map 4**.
Freshly baked croissants and *pains au
chocolat*, plus teas and coffees, soups,
salads and other deli items to takeaway.

Denis Allemand
*Sanno Park Tower Annexe, 2-11-1 Nagata-
cho, Chiyoda-ku (3519 7051). Tameike-sanno
station.* **Open** 8am-11pm Mon-Sat; 10.30am-
11pm Sun. **Average** ¥1,500. **Credit** AmEx,
DC, MC, V. **Map 7**.
This striking modern restaurant at the foot of
the Hie Shrine in Akasaka is the jewel in the
crown of the Royal Group, best known for its
airport delis. A stylish Continental breakfast
costs ¥1,300; American breakfast is ¥1,800
and there's a brunch menu on Sunday.

⚡ Dragonfly Cafe - *by hotel*
*2-3-2 Marunouchi, Chiyoda-ku (5220
2503). Tokyo station.* **Open** 8am-8pm
Mon-Fri. **Average** ¥1,000. **Credit** AmEx,
DC, MC, V. **Map 8**.
There's a cool, modernist feel to this
contemporary deli-style café, which is
especially popular with the expats who
populate this office district. Breakfast here is
an expanded Continental-style set menu, with
juice, muffin and toast to go with your coffee.

Good Honest Grub
*1-11-11 Ebisu-Minami, Shibuya-ku (3710
0400). Ebisu station.* **Open** 8.30am-11pm
Mon, Tue, Thur-Sun. **Average** ¥1,000.
No credit cards. **Map 3**.
This casual café-style diner is owned
and operated by a native of Newfoundland,
where they know a thing or two about
hearty, warming breakfasts. Good coffee,
friendly service.

Mikuni's Marunouchi Café
*Furukawa Sogo Bldg, 2-6-1 Marunouchi,
Chiyoda-ku (5220 3921). Tokyo station.*
Open *Breakfast* 7-11am Mon-Fri.
Average ¥1,000. **No credit cards**. **Map 8**.
The cooked breakfast buffet is good
value at ¥900, and there are also takeaway
sandwiches, pastries and deli items.

No one can quite figure out the name – is it a misspelling? – or why the interior is so ugly, but it is very easy indeed to forget such piffling trivialities once you start tucking into the ample and reasonably priced Sunday brunch, served with complimentary champagne or Mimosa. Lunchan also does a good array of California-meets-Asia curries, and pizza and pasta dishes, well complemented by a friendly little wine list.

Tableaux

Sarugakucho 11-6, Shibuya-ku (5489 2201). Daikanyama station. **Open** 5.30pm-1am (last orders for food 11pm) daily. **Average** ¥10,000. **Credit** AmEx, MC, V. **Menu in English. Map** 32.

There is more than a touch of kitsch to the decor here, but the eclectic Pacific Rim fusion food is entirely serious. Tableaux has become a favourite port of call with the well-heeled Daikanyama set, many of whom drop by just for a Havana and cognac in the adjoining cigar bar.

Shinjuku

New York Bar & Grill

Park Hyatt Tokyo 52F, 3-7-1-2 Nishi-Shinjuku, Shinjuku-ku (5323-3458). Shinjuku station. **Open** *Restaurant* 11.30am-2.30pm, 5.30-10.30pm Mon-Sat; 11.30am-2.30pm, 5.30-10pm Sun. *Bar* 5pm-midnight Mon-Sat; 4-11pm Sun. **Average** ¥6,000 brunch; ¥2,800 lunch; ¥13,000 dinner. **Credit** AmEx, DC, JCB, MC, V. **Menu in English. Map** 1a.

The New York Grill offers a sky-high view food to match, and it really is worth every yen l. the fantastic skyline panorama from this ultra-chic pinnacle at the apex of the **Park Hyatt** hotel (*see p33*). There's an extensive menu of seafood and meat dishes, highlights of which include baked black mussels, lobster ceviche with ginger, tomato and coriander, and home-grown Maezawa tenderloins and sirloins. Sunday brunch has, in fact, become something of an institution among expats in Tokyo, as are evening cocktails in the adjoining bar (admission ¥1,700).

Elsewhere

TY Harbor Brewery

2-1-3 Higashi-Shinagawa, Bond Street, Shinagawa-ku (5479 4555). Tennozu Isle station (Tokyo monorail). **Open** 5.30-11pm Mon-Fri; 11.30am-4pm, 5.30pm-11pm Sat; 11.30am-4pm, 5.30-10pm Sun. **Average** ¥4,000. **Credit** AmEx, DC, JCB, V. **Menu in English.**

TY Harbor Brewery's main disadvantage – its inconvenient location – is also its prime virtue. It's one of the few places in the city where you can sit outside by the waterfront and it is also Tokyo's best brew pub, with a range of pale and amber ales, porter and Weizen beer. The attached restaurant serves straightforward Californian diner fare that's consistent if uninspired – watching the sun go down over the post-industrial canal-side cityscape on a balmy September evening is good enough inspiration for most.

TY Harbor Brewery: waterfront setting and Tokyo's best brew pub. What more could you want?

MAIN TYPES OF RESTAURANT

寿司屋　*sushi-ya*
sushi restaurants

イクラ	*ikura*	salmon roe
タコ	*tako*	octopus
マグロ	*maguro*	tuna
こはだ	*kohada*	punctatus
トロ	*toro*	belly of tuna
ホタテ	*hotate*	scallop
ウニ	*uni*	sea urchin roe
エビ	*ebi*	prawn
ヒラメ	*hirame*	flounder
アナゴ	*anago*	ark shell
イカ	*ika*	squid
玉子焼き	*tamago-yaki*	sweet egg omelette
かっぱ巻き	*kappa maki*	rolled cucumber
鉄火巻き	*tekka maki*	rolled tuna
お新香巻き	*oshinko maki*	rolled pickles

蕎麦屋（そば屋）*soba-ya*
Japanese noodle restaurants

天ぷらそば うどん　*tempura soba, udon*
noodles topped with shrimp tempura

ざるそば うどん　*zaru soba, udon*
noodles served on a bamboo rack in a lacquer box

きつねそば うどん　*kitsune soba, udon*
noodles in hot broth topped with spring onion and fried tofu

たぬきそば うどん　*tanuki soba, udon*
noodles in hot broth with fried tempura batter

月見そば うどん　*tsukimi soba, udon*
raw egg broken over noodles in their hot broth

あんかけうどん　*ankake udon*
wheat noodles in a thick fish bouillon/soy sauce soup with fishcake slices and vegetables

鍋焼きうどん　*nabeyaki udon*
noodles boiled in an earthenware pot with other ingredients and stock. Mainly eaten in winter.

居酒屋　*izakaya*
Japanese-style bars

日本酒	*nihon-shu*	Japanese sake
冷酒	*rei-shu*	cold sake
焼酎	*shoochuu*	grain wine

チュウハイ　*chuuhai*
grain wine with soda pop

生ビール	*nama-biiru*	draft beer
黒ビール	*kuro-biiru*	dark beer
梅酒	*ume-shu*	plum wine

ひれ酒　*hirezake*
sake with toasted blowfish fins

焼き魚　*yaki zakana*　grilled fish

煮魚　*ni zakana*
fish cooked in various sauces

刺し身　*sashimi*
raw fish in bite-sized pieces, served with soy sauce and horseradish

揚げ出し豆腐　*agedasi doofu*
lightly fried plain tofu

枝豆　*edamame*
boiled young soybeans in the pod

おにぎり　*onigiri*
rice parcel with savoury filling

焼きおにぎり　*yaki onigiri*
grilled rice balls

フグ刺し　*fugusashi*
thinly sliced sashimi, usually spectacularly arranged and served with ponzu sauce

フグちり　*fuguchiri*
chunks of fugu in a vegetable stew

雑炊　*zosui*
cooked rice and egg added to the above

Eat, Drink, Shop

焼き鳥屋　*yakitori-ya*
yakitori restaurants

焼き鳥　*yakitori*
barbecued chicken pieces marinated in sweet soy sauce

つくね　*tsukune*　minced chicken balls

タン　*tan*　tongue

ハツ　*hatsu*　heart

シロ　*shiro*　tripe

レバー　*reba*　liver

ガツ　*gatsu*　intestines

鳥皮　*tori-kawa*　skin

ネギ間　*negima*　chicken with spring onions

おでん屋　*oden-ya*
oden restaurants or street stalls

さつま揚げ　*satsuma-age*　fish cake

昆布　*konbu*　kelp rolls

大根　*daikon*　radish

厚揚げ　*atsu-age*　fried tofu

OTHER TYPES OF RESTAURANT

料亭　*ryotei*
high-class, traditional restaurants

ラーメン屋　*ramen-ya*
Japanese-style ramen or Chinese noodle restaurants

天ぷら屋　*tempura-ya*　tempura restaurants

すき焼き屋　*sukiyaki-ya*
sukiyaki restaurants

トンカツ屋　*tonkatsu-ya*
tonkatsu restaurants

お好み焼き屋　*okonomi yaki-ya*
okonomiyaki restaurants

ESSENTIAL VOCABULARY

A table for..., please　*...onegai shimasu*

one/two/three/four
hitori/futari/san-nin/yo-nin

Is this seat free?　*kono seki aite masu ka*

Could we sit...?　*...ni suware masu ka*

over there　*soko*

outside　*soto*

in a non-smoking area　*kin-en-seki*

by the window　*madogiwa*

Excuse me
sumimasen/onegai shimasu

May I see the menu, please
menyuu o onegai shimasu

Do you have a set menu?
setto menyuu/teishoku wa arimasu ka

I'd like...　*...o kudasai*

I'll have...　*...ni shimasu*

a bottle/glass...
...o ippon/ippai kudasai

I can't eat food containing...
...ga haitte iru mono wa taberare masen

Do you have vegetarian meals?
bejitarian no shokuji wa arimasu ka

Do you have a children's menu?
kodomo-yoo no menyuu wa arimasu ka

The bill, please
o-kanjyoo onegai shimasu

That was delicious, thank you
gochisou sama deshita

We'd like to pay separately
betsubetsu ni onegai shimasu

It's all together, please
issho ni onegai shimasu

Is service included?
saabisu-ryoo komi desu ka

Can I pay with a credit card?
kurejitto caado o tsukae masu ka

Could I have a receipt, please?
reshiito onegai shimasu

Coffee Shops

Tokyo's long-established coffee shops are facing up to their flashy new rivals.

If you're looking for a coffee shop in a particular area, refer to the maps on pages 292 to 316.

Angelus
1-17-6 Asakusa, Taito-ku (3841 2208).
Asakusa station. **Open** 10am-9.30pm Tue-Sun.
No credit cards. Map 13.
Perhaps, at some point in the distant past, this was the way local upmarket operations got to grips with handling new-fangled foreign delicacies. Out front is a smart counter selling a fancy selection of western-style cakes; further inside, the coffee shop section is a more Spartan affair of plain walls and dark-wood trimmings.

Ben's Café
1-29-21 Takadanobaba, Shinjuku-ku (3202 2445/ www.benscafe.com). Takadanobaba station. **Open** 11.30am-midnight daily.
No credit cards. Map 22.
A New York-style café, famed locally for its cakes, bagels and easygoing ambience. Also hosts occasional art shows, comedy evenings and poetry readings. Friendly staff speak English and serve great coffee.

Bon
Toriichi Bldg B1, 3-23-1 Shinjuku, Shinjuku-ku (3341 0179). Shinjuku station. **Open** 12.30-11.50pm daily. **No credit cards. Map 1b.**
The search for true coffee excellence is pursued with vigour at this pricey but popular Shinjuku basement location. The cheapest choice from the menu sets you back a cool ¥1,000, but coffee cups are selected from an enormous bone china collection. Special tasting events are held periodically for connoisseurs.

Le Café Doutor Espresso
1F San'ai Bldg, Ginza 5-7-2, Chuo-ku (5537 8959).
Ginza station. **Open** 7.30am-11pm Mon-Fri; 8pm-11pm Sat; 8pm-10pm Sun. **No credit cards. Map 6.**
A one-off upmarket branch of the cheap and cheerful chain that proliferated across the city during the recession-hit '90s. Located on a prime piece of real estate at Ginza 4-chome crossing, its drinks and sandwiches move beyond the standard Doutor fare. Outside tables provide places for watching the bustling crowds and checking out the famous Wako clock tower across the street.

Café de Flore
5-1-2 Jingumae, Shibuya-ku (3406 8605).
Omotesando station. **Open** 9.30am-11pm daily **No credit cards. Map 11.**
The Parisian original was a great favourite of Sartre and the Existentialist crowd, but the busy Tokyo branch remains free of too many intellectual pre-

tensions. The street-level terrace is the fashionable people-watching option. At least the coffee is good, and the separate jugs of espresso and milk provide more than one cup of *café crème* for ¥850.

Café Fontana
Abe Building B1, 5-5-9 Ginza, Chuo-ku (3572 7320).
Ginza station. **Open** noon-midnight Mon-Fri; 2-11pm Sat, Sun. **No credit cards. Map 6.**
A typically genteel Ginza basement establishment, but one where the individually served apple pies come in distinctly non-dainty proportions. Each steaming specimen contains a whole fruit, thinly covered in pastry, then doused thoroughly in cream.

Café Paulista
Nagasaki Centre 1F, 8-9-16 Ginza, Chuo-ku (3572 6160). Ginza station. **Open** 8.30am-10.30pm Mon-Sat; noon-8pm Sun. **No credit cards. Map 6.**
Brazilian flags hang proudly both outside and within this veteran Ginza establishment, founded back in 1914. All-natural beans are directly imported, keeping blend coffee prices down to ¥480, a bargain for the area. Low leather seats, plants and wall engravings feature in a brown-and-green motif, while soft samba keeps things nice and relaxed.

Café de Ropé
6-1-8 Jingumae, Shibuya-ku (3406 6845).
Omotesando station. **Open** noon-10pm Mon-Fri, Sun; noon-10.30pm Sat. **No credit cards. Map 11.**
A Tokyo institution, a short walk down Omotesando from **Café de Flore** (*see above*). Pleasantly light and airy, and a great place for watching the fashion parade up Omotesando. *Café au lait* so thick you can rest your sugar lump on it.

Cantina
Aso Bldg 1F 1-28-6 Shoto, Shibuya-ku (5728 2515/ www.cantina.co.jp). Shibuya station.
Open 1-11pm Tue-Sun. **No credit cards. Map 2.**
Bills itself as a 'Toys & Café Bar', but there's more than a hint of *Star Wars* obsession in this cramped tribute to the classic SF merchandising empire. Stacks of *Star Wars* goods still in their boxes reach the ceiling, plus there's a themed pinball machine, cabinets full of figures from the movie series, a large-screen TV for continuous DVD playback, and much else besides. Serves alcohol, as well as coffee at a bargain ¥300, with a small table charge after 6pm. May the force be with you.

Classic
5-66-8 Nakano, Nakano-ku (3387 0571).
Nakano station. **Open** noon-9.25pm Tue-Sun.
No credit cards. Map 26.

Coffee 3.4 Sunsea: sitar, tabla, cushions, sofas, carvings, fish… and coffee.

This ramshackle relic of eccentricity is a creaky one-off that's survived the winds of change since 1930. Classical music drifts eerily over the sound system as the Gothic gloom reveals sloping floors, ancient leather chairs, long-deceased and undusted clocks. The paintings that adorn the walls are all by the shop's original, now dead, owner. Tickets for coffee, tea or juice are ¥400 and purchased at the entrance; cream has been known to arrive in bottle caps.

Coffee 3.4 Sunsea

Takano Bldg 1F, 10-2 Udagawacho, Shibuya-ku (3496 2295). Shibuya station. **Open** 1-11pm daily. **No credit cards. Map** 2.
Kathmandu hippy chic and postmodern Shibuya cool meet in this laid-back retreat, with classical Indian sitar and tabla on soundtrack. Cushion-strewn sofas, ethnic wooden carvings and a large tank of hypnotic tropical fish all add to the dreamy effect. Self-indulgent sensory overload guaranteed from the sensational coffee float. It's somehow in keeping with the mood of the place that the owners don't have fixed days off; they close whenever they feel like it, so call ahead to confirm.

Daibo

2F, 3-13-20 Minami-Aoyama, Minato-ku (3403 7155). Omotesando station. **Open** 9am-10pm Mon-Sat; noon-8pm Sun. **No credit cards. Map** 11.
The biggest treat at this cosy wood-bedecked outpost is the excellent milk coffee, which comes lovingly hand-dripped into large pottery bowls. Even

the regular blend coffee reveals a true craftsman's pride, and comes in four varieties. Just one long wooden counter, in addition to a couple of tables, but the restrained decoration and low-volume jazz on the stereo combine to soothing and restful effect.

Danwashitsu Takizawa

Sugichu Bldg B1, 3-36-12 Shinjuku, Shinjuku-ku (3356 5661). Shinjuku station. **Open** 9am-9.50pm Mon-Sat; 9am-9.30pm Sun. **No credit cards. Map** 1b.

Just in case you ever want to experience the perverse pleasure of blowing ¥1,000 on a single cup of coffee, this is where to do it. Artfully simple yet completely comfortable, it's the kind of place you could stay all day: water trickles over rocks for a vaguely Zen-like sense of tranquillity and staff bow with quite extraordinary politeness. Discount tickets for future visits after you pay the bill.

ef

2-19-18 Kaminarimon, Taito-ku (3841 0114/gallery 3841 0442/www.tctv.ne.jp/get2-ef). Asakusa station. **Open** *Café & gallery* 11am-7pm daily. *Bar* 6pm-midnight Mon, Wed, Thur, Sat; 6pm-2am Fri; 6-10pm Sun. **No credit cards. Map** 13.

This retrofitted hangout is a welcome attempt to inject a little Harajuku cool into musty Asakusa, but among its own more surprising attractions is a small art gallery converted from a 130-year-old warehouse. Duck through the low entrance at the back

Logo wars

Lawsuits are a relative rarity in litigation-averse Japan. Imagine, then, the surprise of Doutor, the nation's biggest coffee-shop chain, when in summer 2000 it found itself slapped with a court injunction by Starbucks. The brand-conscious multinational, currently opening new branches in Japan at the rate of 100 a year, claimed it was losing customers because of the particular shade of green employed in the logo of Excelsior Café, an espresso-dispensing competitor owned by its local rival.

Doutor protested in vain that it had chosen the colour for its revamped upmarket chain in homage to the flag of Italy. Not wishing to get involved in a lengthy dispute, however, it soon backed down and switched the colour of the disputed logo to blue. And, just to show it really meant to make amends, the same colour was also used in the Excelsior Café name at the entrance to each outlet. Only the first letter, though. The rest remained a stylish, vaguely Italian, green.

and suddenly you're out of the '50s Americana and into *tatami* territory, admittance to the main exhibits being up a steep set of traditional wooden steps. A place to try when you're tired of the local temples.

Jazz Coffee Masako

2-20-2 Kitazawa, Setagaya-ku (3410 7994). Shimo-Kitazawa station (Odakyu/Inokashira lines). **Open** 11.30am-11pm daily. **No credit cards. Map** 35.

A real homely feel, as well as all the jazz coffee shop essentials that are present and correct: excellent sound system, enormous stack of records and CDs behind the counter, walls and low ceiling painted black and all plastered in posters and pictures. The noticeboard at the flower-filled entrance proudly announces any recently obtained recordings; inside, there are bookcases and sofas among the lived-in furnishings.

Ki No Hana

4-13-1 Ginza, Chuo-ku (3543 5280). Higashi-Ginza station. **Open** 10.30am-8pm Mon-Fri; noon-6pm 1st and 2nd Sat of month. **No credit cards. Map** 6.

The pair of signed John Lennon cartoons on the walls is the legacy of a chance visit by the former Beatle one afternoon in 1978. With its peaceful atmosphere, tasteful floral decorations, herbal teas and lunchtime vegetarian curries, it isn't too difficult to understand Lennon's appreciation of the place. Apparently, the overawed son of the former owner also preserved the great man's full ashtray, including butts. Alas, he kept this as a personal memento, so it isn't on display.

Kissa Hibiya

1-2-5 Yurakucho, Chiyoda-ku (3580 0203). Hibiya station. **Open** 9.30am-10.30pm Mon-Sat; 9.30am-8.40pm Sun. **No credit cards. Map** 6.

A classic old-school operation, inviting you to shut out the rest of the world and snuggle down for a long stay. Comfortable and spacious with three floors to spread out on, but it's the top one of these that offers the best place to admire the distinctively retro use of coloured glass for interior decoration. Blend coffee only ¥500.

Lion

2-19-13 Dogenzaka, Shibuya-ku (3461 6858). Shibuya station. **Open** 11am-10.30pm daily. **No credit cards. Map** 2.

There's a church-like air of reverence at this sleepy shrine to classical music. A pamphlet listing stereophonic offerings is laid out helpfully before the customer, seating is arranged in pew-style rows facing an enormous pair of speakers, and conversations are discouraged. If you must talk, whisper. The imposing grey building is an unexpected period piece set amid the gaudy love hotels of Dogenzaka.

Marunouchi Café

1F Fuji Bldg, 3-2-3 Marunouchi, Chiyoda-ku (3212 5025/www.marunouchicafe.com). Tokyo station. **Open** 8am-8pm Mon-Fri; 10am-6pm Sat. **No credit cards. Map** 8.

If the Japanese coffee shop is essentially a place to hang out, this popular innovator could be a glimpse of a new low-cost future. Connoisseurs may not care for canned coffee dispensed from vending machines, but it's difficult to argue with the price. Surroundings are comfortably spacious and Asian generic, with internet access and magazines available.

Miró

2-4-6 Kanda-Surugadai, Chiyoda-ku (3291 3088).
Ochanomizu station. **Open** 9am-11pm Mon-Sat.
No credit cards. Map 15.
Named after Catalan Surrealist Joan Miró (1893-1983), several of whose works adorn the walls. Ambience and decor appear untouched by the passing decades. The location is pretty well hidden, down a tiny alley opposite Ochanomizu station.

Mironga

1-3 Kanda-Jinbocho, Chiyoda-ku (3295 1716).
Jinbocho station. **Open** 10.30am-11pm Mon-Fri;
11.30am-7pm Sat, Sun. **No credit cards. Map** 15.
Probably the only place in the metropolis where non-stop tango provides seductive old-style dance music accompaniment to the liquid refreshments. Argentina's finest exponents feature in the impressive array of fading monochromes up on the walls, and there's also a useful selection of printed works on related subjects lining the bookshelves. Of the two rooms, the larger and darker gets the nod for atmosphere. A good selection of imported beers and reasonable food, as well as a wide range of coffees.

New Dug

B1, 3-15-12 Shinjuku, Shinjuku-ku (3341 9339/
www.dug.co.jp). Shinjuku station. **Open** noon-2am
Mon-Sat; noon-midnight Sun. **No credit cards.**
Map 1b.
Way back in the 1960s and early '70s, Shinjuku was sprinkled with jazz coffee shops. Celebrated names of that bygone era include Dug, an establishment whose present-day incarnation is a cramped brick-lined basement on Yasukuni Dori. Everything about the place speaks serious jazz credentials, with carefully crafted authenticity and assorted memorabilia. A basement bar annexe below the nearby KFC is used for live performances.

Pow Wow

2-7 Kagurazaka, Shinjuku-ku (3267 8324).
Iidabashi station. **Open** 10.30am-10.30pm Mon-Sat;
12.30-7pm Sun. **No credit cards.**
Heavy on the old-fashioned virtues of dark wood and tasteful pottery, this spacious traditionalist features an extraordinary coffee-brewing performance in its narrow counter section, where glass flasks bubble away over tiny glass candles in the manner of some mysterious chemistry experiment. Blend coffee is ¥650. There's an upstairs gallery space.

Rihaku

2-24 Kanda-Jinbocho, Chiyoda-ku (3264 6292).
Jinbocho station. **Open** 11am-7pm Mon-Sat.
No credit cards. Map 15.

Named after Sung dynasty Chinese poet Li Po (AD 701-62), whose works include the celebrated lament 'Drinking Alone', this is a place more attuned to eastern tradition than most. The high ceiling and wooden layout of the interior are reminiscent of some old Japanese farmhouse, but resist the temptation to slip off the shoes as you enter.

Saboru

1-11 Kanda-Jinbocho, Chiyoda-ku (3291 8404).
Jinbocho station. **Open** 9am-11pm Mon-Sat.
No credit cards. Map 15.
Wooden masks on the walls, tree pillars rising to the ceiling and a menu that features banana juice all lend a strangely South Sea island air to this cosy triple-level establishment squeezed into a brick building reverting to jungle on a Jinbocho back street. It's cheap, too, with blend coffee a snip at ¥400. Next door is the less extravagantly furnished sequel, Saboru 2.

La Scala

1-14-1 Kabuki-cho, Shinjuku-ku (3200 3320).
Shinjuku station. **Open** 10am-11pm Mon-Thur, Sun;
10am-11.30pm Fri-Sat. **No credit cards. Map** 1b.
Step inside this impeccably maintained ivy-covered building and it's another century altogether. Graced by a glittering chandelier, antique furniture, enormous mirrors and plush seating, this proud purveyor of 'coffee and classical mood music' keeps up an old-world grandeur at odds with its neon-clad neighbours on the back streets of Kabuki-cho. Window tables are best for appreciating the contrast. *Café au lait* is ¥700.

Tajimaya

1-2-6 Nishi-Shinjuku, Shinjuku-ku (3342 0881).
Shinjuku station. **Open** 10am-11pm daily. **No credit
cards. Map** 1a.
Caught between the early post-war grunge of its immediate neighbours and the skyscraper bustle of the rest of west Shinjuku, Tajimaya responds with abundant bone china, coffees from all over the world, non-fetishist use of classical music, and milk in the best copperware. Scones on the menu and the unusual selection of ornaments provide further evidence of advanced sensibilities, but the deeply yellowed walls and battered wood suggest a struggle to keep up appearances.

Yomu-yomu

Kawase Bldg B2, 3-17-5 Shinjuku, Shinjuku-ku
(3352 6065). Shinjuku station. **Open** 8am-9.50pm
Mon-Sat; 9am-9.50pm Sun. **No credit cards.**
Map 1b.
Usually credited as being the first of the capital's many *manga* coffee shops, Yomu-yomu ('Read-read') opened in 1994 and sparked an amazing boom in copycat places offering the same winning combination of coffee and Japanese comic books. Non-*otaku* interlopers might find the serried rows of heads poring over vintage volumes a bit intimidating, but internet access and PlayStation consoles provide alternative diversions.

Conversation is discouraged at **Lion**, where classical music is king. *See p147.*

Bars

From early evening to morning or beyond, the drinking stops when you fall over.

Bernd's Bar: German *Gemütlichkeit* in Tokyo. *See p151.*

Drinking is a major activity in Japan and also a major lubricant. Most business deals are sealed over a glass or ten of *sake* or beer, and many friendships have been forged or, indeed, destroyed by the demon drink.

Drinking here is almost always accompanied by eating. Even in western-style bars, a plate of snacks will appear unbidden if you do not order any food to go with your drink. In fact, until the recent spate of Irish/British pub openings, the idea of simply sitting somewhere to have a few drinks hardly existed at all.

The practical upshot of this is that the dividing line between bars and restaurants is difficult to draw. Most serious drinking is still done in *izakaya*, a word which is often misleadingly translated as 'Japanese pub'. These places offer extensive menus of Japanese foods at reasonable prices, and because people rarely entertain at home, this is where most socialising goes on. Some have special 'all you can drink' deals. Look out for the sign outside.

Most other, smaller bars serve some food to keep customers happy, and many of these demand a table charge (usually ¥500, but it can be more) to cover the cost of snacks. Most of the bars listed here make no charge unless otherwise indicated. Normally, a no-charge bar will say so clearly outside. A good general rule is, if you can't see a price list, don't go in.

Despite the rules of drinking etiquette, public drunkenness is treated very kindly; no one will frown at you for staggering around trying to find that last train home, and public vomiting is an all too frequent occurrence, especially on the Friday night Chuo line. To locate a bar near you, refer to the maps on pages 292-316.

AIP

B1, 6-1-4 Jingumae, Shibuya-ku (5468 5100). Meiji-Jingumae station. **Open** noon-7am daily. **No credit cards**. **Map** 11.

Conveniently located, stylish bar for the designer set just off Omotesando on the pedestrian thoroughfare known as Cat Street. The metal-meets-matt-black and leather decor sometimes feels slightly cooler-than-thou, and everyone – staff and customers – looks far too beautiful. Still, this is New Japan at its hippest and AIP has customer-friendly hours, serves good drinks, plays funky music and its eye candy doesn't come much better. The service is sometimes unnaturally slow (the prerogative of the beautiful?), but the food menu (last orders midnight) isn't bad if you pick carefully. Admission ¥700 after 10pm.

A-Sign Bar

Agawa Bldg 3F, 5-32-7 Daizawa, Setagaya-ku (3413 6489). Shimokitazawa station. **Open** 8pm-4am daily. **No credit cards. Map** 35.

The name of this Okinawan bar refers to the 'Approved for US Military' signs that once appeared outside select drinking holes on the southern Japanese island during its American occupation. The interior includes pictures and TV programmes from the era, an old jukebox and antique pinball machine. An even more interesting drinks policy means that the per-glass price for spirits gets cheaper if you bulk order. As well as the island's own Orion beer, on offer are 47 types of Okinawan *sake*, or *awamori,* notorious for its strength. Food from the Okinawan restaurant below can be ordered at the bar.

Bar Kitsune

Chatolet Shibuya B1F, 2-20-13 Higashi, Shibuya-ku (5766 5911). Ebisu station. **Open** 6pm-5am Mon-Fri; 6pm-8am Sat; 6pm-midnight Sun. **No credit cards. Map** 3.

This hot new bar on Meiji Dori between Ebisu and Shibuya pushes the boundaries between restaurant, DJ bar and club right to the limit but stops short of

How to drink

If you're out drinking with Japanese business partners or friends over a meal, you will not generally be expected to refill your own drink. Someone at your table will keep a close eye on the level in your glass and top it up accordingly. 'No' is generally not taken as an answer, so drinking slowly is the surest way to minimise your consumption. Be sure to return the favour by refilling companions' glasses. Even if they pour your drink, they will not refill their own at the same time.

providing a dance floor. That doesn't stop the ever-changing DJs from getting the punters grooving in the aisles, or the acrobatic waiters from serving food late into the night. It's rare to see a foreign face here, as Kitsune hasn't been colonised by those bar and club hoppers who vilify the lack of dancing space. The most striking aspect of the slick interior is the phenomenal, ever-changing light radiating from all four walls. There's a charge (¥2,000 with two drinks) at weekends, but once inside, drinks at the bar are ¥500 a throw, and the Saturday-night party continues till 8am so you get your money's worth.

Bernd's Bar

Pure 2F, 5-18-1 Roppongi, Minato-ku (5563 9232). Roppongi station. **Open** 5-late Mon-Sat. **Credit** AmEx, MC. **Map** 4.

If you're German, you'll feel right at home in this friendly second-floor bar, which doesn't close until it's empty. Fresh pretzels are stacked on the tables; Bitburger and Erdinger, among other beers, are ready on tap for washing down your Wiener schnitzel. Even if you're not German, you'll like it. Try and get a table by the window, for the view over the nightlife area of Roppongi. The owner, Bernd Haag, can chat to his customers in English, German or Spanish, as well as Japanese.

Brussels

3-16-1 Kanda-Ogawa-cho, Chiyoda-ku (3233 4247). Jinbocho station. **Open** 5.30pm-2am Mon-Fri; 5.30-11pm Sat. **No credit cards. Map** 15.

One of a small chain of Belgian bars with a dazzling array of over 30 beers imported from the old country and served in their proper glasses. The Jinbocho branch, which spreads over three wood-panelled floors of a very narrow building, is a favourite with local students and journalists from the many magazines based in the area. Should the urge take you, there's great Belgian food on offer (around ¥1,000), but there's no obligation to eat, and no cover charge. **Branches**: 1-10-23 Jingumae, Shibuya-ku (3403 3972); 1-3-4 Nihonbashi-Kayabacho, Chuo-ku (5641 1929); 75 Yarai-cho, Shinjuku-ku (3235 1890).

Karaoke

One of Japan's major cultural exports of the late 20th century, karaoke ('empty orchestra') is believed to have been started up in the 1970s by a hard-pressed bar owner who was looking for a fresh way to pull in the punters.

Since then, the process has been refined, and made more discreet. Although traditional karaoke bars do still exist, most karaoke these days is sung in small rooms, or boxes, inside purpose-built complexes. Rooms are rented by the hour, usually at a cost of ¥500 per hour or so, although during the daytime rates usually fall considerably.

All karaoke boxes serve alcohol, and a quick call to the front desk will bring a member of staff running with a tray of beer or cocktails to keep those vocal cords lubricated. At some places, all the booze you can drink is included in the price.

Eat, Drink, Shop

Clubhouse

Marunaka Bldg 3F, 3-7-3 Shinjuku, Shinjuku-ku (3359 7785/www.clubhouse-tokyo.com). Shinjuku-Sanchome station. **Open** 5pm-midnight Tue-Thur; 5pm-late Fri; noon-late Sat; 3pm-midnight Sun. **No credit cards. Map** 1b.

Owned and run by a Japanese man who spent rather too long teaching Japanese in Wales and returned home addicted to rugby, the Clubhouse is a cut above run-of-the-mill sports bars, with ample seating and an adventurous menu of well-prepared Japanese and Korean dishes. Not surprisingly, it tends to get packed with large-gutted gentlemen during rugby tournaments.

Dubliners

Shinjuku Lion Hall 2F, 3-28-9 Shinjuku, Shinjuku-ku (3352 6606). Shinjuku station. **Open** 11.30am-11.30pm Mon-Sat; 11.30am-10pm Sun. **Credit** AmEx, MC, V. **Map** 1b.

Owned and operated by Japanese brewing giant Sapporo, this popular Irish pub serves reasonable pub food. The only inauthentic touch is the very welcome addition of waiter service. Downstairs is a branch of Sapporo's Lion Hall, a near-ubiquitous chain of *izakaya* serving passable Japanese food and lots of Sapporo beer. In 2000 a new branch was added in Akasaka, and more are rumoured to be following in the pipeline.

Branches: Sun Grow Bldg B1, 1-10-8 Nishi-Ikebukuro, Toshima-ku (5951 3614); Sanno Park Tower B1F, 2-11-1 Nagata-cho, Chiyoda-ku (3539 3615).

The Fiddler

2-1-2 Takadanobaba B1, Shinjuku-ku (3204 2698). Takadanobaba station. **Open** 6pm-3am Mon-Thur, Sun; 6pm-5am Fri, Sat. **No credit cards. Map** 22.

This place run by two UK expats smells like pubs back home, only it's open every night until the wee hours. There are live music or comedy acts almost every night for no extra charge, and although most of them are local *gaijin* groups, the occasional up-and-coming Japanese band plays the Fiddler as well. The food is fairly acceptable and the kitchen stays open till midnight.

Flamme d'Or

Asahi Super Dry Building 1F, 2F, 1-25 Azumabashi, Taito-ku (5608 5381). Asakusa station. **Open** 11.30am-11pm daily. **Credit** AmEx, MC, V. **Map** 13.

One of Tokyo's quirkier landmarks, the enormous gold-coloured object lying atop French architect Philippe Starck's ultra-modern building (across the river from the temples of Asakusa) is most often compared with some as-yet-undiscovered form of giant root vegetable. The dark tetrahedral Super Dry Building itself is said to be modelled on the shape of a cut-off beer glass, and it was named after a brand of beer. The Flamme d'Or beer hall inside is also quite distinctive: oddly shaped pillars, tiny porthole windows high overhead and sweeping curved walls covered in soft grey cushioning. English menus are available, plus a choice of German bar snacks and Asahi draught beers. On the 22nd floor is another bar, the Asahi Sky Room, which serves beer and coffee from 10am to 9pm daily.

Footnik

Marujo Building B1, 3-12-8 Takadanobaba, Shinjuku-ku (5330 5301). Takadanobaba station. **Open** 5pm-1am daily. **No credit cards. Map** 22.

In the days before that nice Mr Murdoch brought Sky to Japan, the opening of Footnik in summer 1996 came as manna from heaven for sad souls deprived of their regular Premiership football fix. Since then, others have followed, but only Footnik retains the dingy appeal of a genuine British pub. It boasts a 56-inch TV screen, walls plastered with banners, and it screens live matches on Saturday and Sunday nights, with highlights and taped *Match of the Day* later in the week. Another branch is scheduled to open in Ebisu in late 2001.

Gas Panic

3-15-24 Roppongi, Minato-ku (3405 0633). Roppongi station. **Open** 6pm-5am daily. **No credit cards. Map** 4.

Gas Panic is a Roppongi institution of depravity. More like an American frat party than a bar, it's primarily for the young and immature, or those who wish to reclaim their salad days. If you can talk the talk, this is an excellent place for men to meet young Japanese women looking for foreigners (who can pay, if they choose, in American dollars). The drinks are among the cheapest in town, particularly on Thursdays, when everything is ¥300 all day. There are several Gas Panic installations around Tokyo: three in the Gas Panic Building, one closer to Roppongi Dori, Gas Panic Club (3402 7054), and one on Shibuya's Centre Gai.

gmartini's

Five Plaza Bldg 4F, 5-18-21 Roppongi, Minato-ku (3588 6147). Roppongi station. **Open** 7pm-6am daily. **No credit cards. Map** 4.

Bars to avoid

As you wander the streets of Tokyo, you will (particularly if you read *katakana*) spot hundreds of places that call themselves 'Pub', 'Snack' or 'Snack bar'. Most of these are dimly lit premises with windows, where there are any, deliberately obscured to keep out prying eyes. Don't be misled by the name. These bars cater to a regular clientele and strangers are unwelcome. If you do go in, you may be landed with a whopping cover charge or forced to hand over a fortune for a drink. Unless you're in the company of a regular, it's safest not to venture into one of these places at all.

Be shaken, not stirred at **gmartini's**. *See p152*.

This is where Austin Powers drinks when he's in town. A zebra-striped sofa dominates the bar area, while the adjacent room is covered wall to wall in thick carpet and is called, wait for it, the 'shag room'. Upstairs, there's another small area to take your drinks, which are mostly variations on the martini theme. The James Bond is particularly lethal, baby.

Go-Go Lounge
Le Ponte Bldg 3F, 1-14-12 Jingumae, Shibuya-ku (3401 5155). Harajuku station. **Open** 7pm-4am Mon-Fri; 7pm-midnight Sun. **No credit cards.** **Map** 11.

This young, clubby bar opposite the Takeshita exit of Harajuku station is something of a stalwart among local youth as a place where wannabe DJs can hone their spinning skills and budding artists can show off their work. On the one hand the place could do with a paint job to restore what was once a smart minimalist decor, but as it is the Go-Go Lounge retains a semi-bohemian atmosphere for the new century in a slick, clean, packaged, Japanese kind of way. Be prepared to pay a cover charge (usually ¥1,000 with one drink) for some events.

Hanezawa Beer Garden
3-12-15 Hiroo, Shibuya-ku (3400 6500). Hiroo station. **Open** 5-9pm daily in summer. **Credit** AmEx, MC, V. **Map** 3.

Hanezawa is a real garden (most beer 'gardens' are concrete monstrosities) that was established in the Meiji era. The property was once owned by a feudal lord but was converted into a public beer garden without losing its special touches: a carp pond, hanging lanterns and attentive, if slightly surly, service.

It's now a Tokyo institution in the hot, sticky summer months. The food is unremarkable but the beer is cold and comes in enormous mugs (*dai jokki*). Feel free to traipse around among the lanterns, dodging cats underfoot and mosquitoes overhead. One complaint – it closes way too early.

Hub
Poan Shibuya Bldg B1, 3-10 Udagawa-cho, Shibuya-ku (3496 0765). Shibuya station. **Open** noon-midnight Mon-Thur, Sun; noon-2am Fri, Sat. **No credit cards.** **Map** 2.

One of a medium-sized chain of British-style pubs which boasts one of the finest happy hours in Tokyo, with cocktails just ¥180 5-7pmdaily. This branch also has the added attraction of real table football. **Branches:** all over Tokyo.

Hungry Humphrey
1-1-10 Kabuki-cho, Shinjuku-ku (3200 6156). Shinjuku station. **Open** 6.30pm-1.30am Mon-Sat. **No credit cards.** **Map** 1b.

Another foreigner-friendly bar in the Golden Gai area of Shinjuku.

Ieyasu Hon-jin
1-30 Jinbocho, Kanda, Chiyoda-ku (3291 6228). Jinbocho station. **Open** 5-10pm Mon-Fri. **No credit cards.** **Map** 15.

Genial host Taisho bangs the drum behind the bar to greet each new customer to this cosy, top-class *yakitori* bar named after the first of the Tokugawa *shogun*. There are only a dozen seats, so everyone crowds around the counter, where a wide choice of foodstuffs (including mushrooms and beef as well

Sooty and Sweep's Japanese cousins? No, it's just another average evening at **Kaga-ya**.

as the usual chicken) lies in glass cases, already on sticks, ready to be popped on the coals and grilled. All the food is excellent, as is the beer (Kirin Brau Meister) and *sake*, which Taisho dispenses with natural flair, pouring into small cups from a great height. Not cheap (expect around ¥4,000-¥7,000 for a couple of hours' eating and drinking), but still good value. Try to avoid the 6-8pm after-work rush and don't go in a group of more than two or three.

In Blue

1F, 4-3-13 Jingumae, Shibuya-ku (no phone). Omotesando station. **Open** 6pm-5am daily. **No credit cards. Map** 11.

Lilliputian bar behind Benetton on Omotesando Dori. Anyone over five feet tall will have to duck to get through the tiny silver door. Inside is all silver and blue, giving the place the feel of a rather smart, concrete igloo. The barman Hiroshi and his partner realised a childhood dream when they opened In Blue a couple of years back. Both work incredibly hard keeping up with Aoyama's all-night crowd, and the place is always busier at 3am than at 10pm.

Inishmore

1-24-3 Ebisu-Minami, Shibuya-ku (5722 5431). Ebisu station. **Open** 5.30pm-2am Mon-Thur, Sun; 5.30pm-5am Fri, Sat. **No credit cards. Map** 3.

A very pleasant, independently owned bar that serves a mean pint of Guinness and decent food. Can get crowded at weekends, when it's often standing room only. Free internet access, too.

La Jetée

1-1-8 Kabukicho, Shinjuku-ku (3208 9645). Shinjuku station. **Open** 7pm till empty daily. **No credit cards. Map** 1b.

Among the Golden Gai bars that accept foreigners, this is possibly the friendliest. Run by film buff and Jean-Luc Godard fanatic Kawai Tomoyo, this is where Quentin Tarantino and his ilk stop off for a quick one when in town.

Kaga-ya

B1, 2-15-12 Shinbashi, Minato-ku (3591 2347). Shinbashi station. **Open** 5.30-11.30pm Mon-Sat. **No credit cards. Map** 20.

When the awards for the strangest place in Tokyo are handed out, the master of this bar, who goes by the very un-Japanese name of Mark, will be somewhere near the front of the queue. On arrival, you will be handed a cocktail list which is nothing more than a list of countries. Once you've placed your order, the master will disappear into a cupboard and reappear dressed in a costume reflecting the country you've chosen. The drink itself may be in a

Eat, Drink, Shop

vibrating glass, a glass that moos when picked up, or a soup bowl. Once the drinks round is over, you will be encouraged to play games and dress up. Small portions of delicious food are provided as part of the ¥500 cover charge, cooked by the master's tolerant mother. Go in a party of at least six (call to book, it's a small place) and you'll have the time of your life. The billing system is mysterious; no matter how much you eat and drink here, it always seems to come to ¥2,500 a head.

Kamiya Bar

1-1-1 Asakusa, Taito-ku (3841 5400). Asakusa station. **Open** 11.30am-10pm daily. **No credit cards. Map** 13.

Established in the late 1800s, Kamiya is the oldest western-style bar in Tokyo and is quintessential Asakusa. The crowds aren't there for decor or even drink: the interior is Formica-table coffee shop and too-bright lighting. But the atmosphere – loud, smoky, sometimes raucous – is, in a word, *shitamachi*. Try the house *Denki Bran* (Electric Brandy) – not so much for its taste, but for the experience of having tried the domestic stuff. Makes a dubious gift to take home as well.

Lion Beer Hall

7-9-20 Ginza, Chuo-ku (3571 2590). Ginza station. **Open** 11.30am-11pm Mon-Sat; 11.30am-10.30pm Sun. **Credit** AmEx, MC, V. **Map** 6.

This 1930s beer hall, part of the Sapporo Lion chain, is a tourist attraction. The tiled, wood-panelled interior looks as if it's been transplanted from Bavaria.

The menu, with its plethora of sausage choices, adds to the effect. For those who want to eat more than drink, there is a restaurant upstairs.

Mother

5-36-14 Kitazawa, Setagaya-ku (3412 5318). Shimokitazawa station (Odakyu/Inokashira lines). **Open** 6pm-2am daily. **No credit cards. Map** 35.

The extreme kitsch of this only-in-Japan bar, which resembles a mix between a gingerbread house, a tree house and a sub-aquatic pub, betrays what is in fact a classy establishment. The no-hard-edges interior is a combination of ceramic mosaic walls dotted with glowing blue 'stone' lights and *faux* wood seating. The drinks are generous and there is wide range of bottled beers, as well as a high-quality menu of mainly Okinawan and Thai dishes, always freshly made. You can bring your own CDs and they'll play them for you, although their own playlist, mostly comprising legends such as Sly and the Family Stone, the Rolling Stones, Bob Dylan and the like, is pretty flawless.

Mon Chéri

B1, 2-37-2 Kabuki-cho, Shinjuku-ku (3209 9718). Shinjuku station. **Open** 6pm-5am daily. **No credit cards. Map** 1b.

A small basement cocktail bar with friendly, uniformed staff and no cover charge. Cocktails cost around ¥700, and on a good night the bearded master will run through his repertoire of magic tricks behind the bar. Head here later in the evening and you're almost guaranteed to become embroiled

Pool, movies, restaurant – **Oh God!** *See p157.*

'No food, all drink' and plenty of chit-chat at the friendly **Olé Bar**.

in conversation with one of the regulars as they teeter precariously on their bar stools. Come alone, and the bar staff will keep you talking.

O'Carolan's

3F, 2-15-22 Jiyugaoka, Meguro-ku (3723 5533).
Jiyugaoka station (Tokyu Toyoko line). **Open** 11am-midnight daily. **No credit cards. Map** 33.
An unusually spacious Irish bar in the former premises of an Italian restaurant, which explains the bizarre mural of angels and cherubs on the far wall. Guinness and Kilkenny are on tap, and during happy hour (5-7pm Mon-Thur) all drinks are ¥500. Away from the cherubs at the other end of the room there's a pleasant greenhouse area where you can sip your drinks on wicker sofas.

Oh God!

B1, 6-7-18 Jingumae, Shibuya-ku (3406 3206).
Harajuku station. **No credit cards. Map** 11.
Open 6pm-6am daily.
Oh God! is the nearest Tokyo has to the bars on Bangkok's Khao-san Road. Films are shown nightly on a giant screen to an audience more interested in knocking back the ¥700 beer. Also has pool and pinball tables. A schedule for the week's films is posted outside.

Olé Bar

Metro Building 1F, 2-38-22 Kabuki-cho, Shinjuku-ku (3200 2249). Shinjuku station. **Open** 8pm till empty, daily. **No credit cards. Map** 1b.
Miguel, the original owner of this popular foreigners' hangout, died in tragic circumstances in 2000, but the mantle has been taken up by long-time collaborator Esteban, who soldiers on with Miguel's laudable 'no food, all drink' policy. Eccentric bar games and lively conversation with whoever you end up sitting next to you are virtually guaranteed. Prices, for Tokyo, are rock bottom, and Esteban mixes a mean cocktail, too.

Paddy Foley's Irish Pub

B1, 5-5-1 Roppongi, Minato-ku (3423 2250).
Roppongi station. **Open** 5pm-2.30am Mon-Sat; 4.30pm-12.30am Sun. **Credit** AmEx, MC, V. **Map** 4.
Just about every bar owner worth his salt is opening an Irish pub in Tokyo these days, but it's this place that takes the credit for getting the ball rolling. Step in and you find yourself transported halfway round the world. Guinness, naturally, is the house speciality and the food is good. Paddy Foley's can get as crowded as a London pub at weekends, something the locals (who always sit down to drink) regard with mild bemusement.

Paranoia Café

Victory Bldg 3F, 4-12-5 Roppongi, Minato-ku (5411 8018). Roppongi station. **Open** 7pm-midnight Mon-Thur; 7pm-5am Fri, Sat. **No credit cards. Map** 4.
One of the partners of Paranoia is Crazy George, who was a make-up artist for the cult zombie thriller *Dawn of the Dead*. Being here is like being an extra in that film. The walls and ceiling are liberally 'decorated' with screaming heads, and slasher movies run endlessly on monitors as Goth-rock and heavy metal blares from the sound system. If that isn't enough, you can look through a catalogue of cuts, contusions and full-scale weirdnesses to decide how you want to get made up. For free. One of the assistants will create a strikingly realistic gash on your forehead. A lot of laughs on the train ride home.

Pierrôt

2-1-8 Kitazawa, Setagaya-ku (no phone).
Shimokitazawa station. **Open** 8pm-late daily.
No credit cards. Map 35.
By day a used clothes shop, at 8pm the racks are wheeled away and this shack at the very bottom of Shimo's main shopping street turns into an open-air bar. The Tokyo climate is not well suited to open-air bars, and while in summer the city needs far more al fresco watering holes like this, in winter

Pierrôt is left out in the cold, so to speak. Nevertheless, it's worth stopping by at any time of the year for the free live music, which is almost always excellent. In winter there is a variety of warm cocktails on offer as well as the usual range of beers and mixers. The coffee is best avoided.

Pink Cow

1-10-1 Jingumae, Shibuya-ku (5411 6777). Meiji-Jingumae station. **Open** 5pm till empty, Tue-Sun. **No credit cards.** **Map** 11.
A short walk from exit 3 of the subway station, the Pink Cow is a comfortable, relaxed new bar that has quickly become a home to Tokyo's artistically inclined expat community. Good home-cooked food (catch the ¥2,500 buffet dinner on Friday and Saturdays from 7 to 10pm) is complemented by the occasional art exhibition.

Radio Bar

2-31-7 Jingumae, Shibuya-ku (3405 5490). Harajuku station. **Open** 7pm-2am Mon-Sat. **No credit cards.** **Map** 11.
Dazzlingly designed, in a 19th-meets-21st-century style, and dazzlingly expensive, Radio Bar is a wonderful place to enjoy superior cocktails or to sample a wide range of Scotch whiskies. For the money (around ¥1,500 per cocktail, plus ¥1,500 cover charge), you get attentive service by tuxedo-clad barmen. There are nine tall bar stools at the long wood counter, and in a corner, under a dim light, sits the star of the show – an antique short-wave radio. The cover charge entitles you to nibble on a beautifully presented arrangement of fruits, vegetables and cheese.

radio:on:studio

Black Aoyama Bldg 7F, 3-2-7 Minami Aoyama, Minato-ku (5785 3046). Gaienmae station. **Open** 6pm-late daily. **No credit cards.** **Map** 12.
Home of the cable radio station of the same name, this place is notable for its friendly, bilingual staff, night view, reliable hours, lack of cover charge, impressive drink prices (draft beer is ¥500 a glass) and excellent soundtrack. DJs play most kinds of music nightly, but cool, cutting-edge electronica dominates. From time to time there's big-name local talent spinning. Also worth visiting for its fine selection of Australian wines.

The Shamrock

B1, 1-13-3 Nishi-Shinjuku, Shinjuku-ku (3348 4609). Shinjuku station. **Open** noon-11pm Mon-Thur; noon-12.30am Fri, Sat; noon-10.30pm Sun. **No credit cards.** **Map** 1a.
A strangely shaped basement bar with genuine Irish fittings that opened for business in 1998. You'll find all the usual beers, good food and great Irish coffee, although the happy hour (5-7pm daily) only applies to the selection of cocktails.

Shot Bar Shadow

1-1-8 Kabuki-cho, Shinjuku-ku (3209 9530). Shinjuku station. **Open** 5pm-midnight Mon-Fri; 6pm-midnight Sat (members only after midnight). **No credit cards.** **Map** 1b.
Run by an eccentric master who speaks Spanish, German, Arabic and Russian in addition to his native Japanese, this tiny bar in Golden Gai has daunting membership requirements for those wishing to stay after midnight: to qualify, the master must remember your name.

Milk the chance to chew the cud at the **Pink Cow.**

Golden Gai

Not one hundred metres from the high rises and neon lights of Shinjuku is this tiny block of ramshackle bars that has defied the post-war winds of change by simply staying put.

A walk around Golden Gai is a trip back in time to the Tokyo of the 1950s, when much of the city was in ruins and black marketeers set up shop around major stations. In this tiny area are crammed around 200 *nomiya*, or small bars, each one seating around eight people in comfort. Many do not welcome foreigners, particularly those who do not speak Japanese. If you're not in the company of someone who knows a particular bar, then stick to the ones we recommend in the listings and all will be fine.

The best time to head for Golden Gai is around 11pm, when the bars are starting to get going and some are actively touting for custom. Even if you don't go in, you should be able to catch a glimpse of some intriguing interiors through the open doors.

Shunju

Sanno Park Tower 27F, 2-11-1 Nagatacho, Chiyoda-ku (3592 5288). Tameike-sanno/Kokkaigijidomae stations. **Open** 11.30am-2.30pm, 5-11pm daily. **No credit cards. Map** 7.

From this up-market whisky and cigar bar high in the Stalinesque Sanno Park Tower you get a good view of the jumbled cityscape looking out towards Shibuya. The illuminated glass wine cellar and shelf after shelf of Scotch (prices from ¥1,000 to ¥10,000 a glass) stand out strikingly amidst the bar's dark elegance, and ensure that you truly feel a world apart from the chaos buzzing away 27 floors below. As for drinks, the seasonal cocktails are recommended and staff serve a mean martini. The bar menu dishes from the adjoining restaurant are minuscule, but tasty and beautifully presented. A very welcome feature is a separate, glass-walled cigar room with extractor fans.

Soft

B1F, 3-1-9 Shibuya, Shibuya-ku (5467 5817). Shibuya station. **Open** 6pm-4am Mon-Sat. **No credit cards. Map** 2.

Bizarre Alice in Wonderland kind of space with one of the city's most impressive selections of imported bottled beer. Lights flicker on automatically as you descend the curved stairs into the surprisingly small bar decked out in orange and white with little tables suspended from the ceiling. Don't forgo a visit to the bathroom, entered through a tiny waist-high door, where the loo paper hangs from high above your head; check out the taps, too. Soft is on the underground DJ circuit most weekends. (Expect a cover charge of ¥1,000-¥2,500, including one or two drinks.)

Space Punch

Sato Bldg 1F, 1-13-5 Ebisu-Nishi, Shibuya-ku (3496 2484). Ebisu station. **Open** 7pm-dawn daily. **No credit cards. Map** 3.

This small watering hole on Ebisu's west side resembles a bar in a big nuclear cooling tube. The warm glow of the illuminated orange bar bounces off the rounded metal walls punctuated with little mini TVs to create a very futuristic vibe. Space Punch also has a selection of less space-age but cool pop-up toys and games to keep the punters amused, and a visit to the red toilet is a must. It may be too clean to be *Blade Runner*, but it's certainly a small taste of the futuristic Tokyo that many come to the city to find.

Tantra

Ichimainoe Bldg B1, 3-5-5 Shibuya, Shibuya-ku (5485 8414). Shibuya station. **Open** 8pm-5am daily. **No credit cards. Map** 2.

The purpose of many Tokyo bars seems to be to take the tired punter as far away from the rigours of the city as possible, for one night at least. Tantra is one such place. Blink and you'll miss the entrance, the only sign of which is a small, dimly lit 'T' above a nondescript stairwell on the corner of a nondescript office building on the south side of Roppongi Dori near Shibuya. Heave open the imposing metal door and you'll find yourself in what resembles a secret, subterranean drinking club, with stone pillars, veiled alcoves, flickering candles and statues depicting scenes from the *Karma Sutra*. On your first visit you'll feel like you've gatecrashed a very private party, but have courage and don't be put off by the ice-cool staff. Tantra its best enjoyed when its light 'Arabic' techno soundtrack is in full swing. The ¥1,000 cover charge is a warning not to enter without a substantial wad in your wallet.

Tokyo Sports Café

7-15-31 Roppongi, Minato-ku (3404 3675). Roppongi station. **Open** 6pm-late daily. **Credit** AmEx, MC, V. **Map** 4.

This large, friendly bar, run by genial Yorkshireman Paul Wagstaff, has widescreen TVs showing live sporting events from all over the world, including Premiership soccer and NFL American football. The happy hour (6-9pm) is notable for being one of the few in Tokyo to include Guinness. There's also a pool table, electronic darts and a craps table.

Warrior Celt

3F, 6-9-22 Ueno, Taito-ku (3836 8588/ www.warriorcelt.com). Ueno station. **Open** 5pm-5am daily. **No credit cards. Map** 14.

A tiny, incredibly friendly British/Irish bar with a host of loyal locals, the Celt also sells hard-to-come-by imported bitter and cider. Live music on Saturday nights cuts down on floor space and can restrict access to the (single) toilet.

What the Dickens

Roob 6 Bldg 4F, 1-13-3 Ebisu-nishi, Shibuya-ku (3780 2099). Ebisu station. **Open** 5pm-1am Tue, Wed; 5pm-2am Thur-Sat; 3pm-midnight Sun. **No credit cards. Map** 3.

On the top two floors of the building that houses nightclub Milk (*see p215*) is this giant and wildly popular British-style pub. The walls are decorated with illustrated Dickens manuscripts, which have been liberally re-captioned in the gents' toilets. Food is, unfortunately, of genuine British pub standard – cottage pie and boiled veg kept warm on a hot-plate under glass. Local bands play live nightly.

Bitter, cider and dodgy guitars pack 'em in at **Warrior Celt**.

Shops & Services

If you can't find what you're looking for in Tokyo, it probably doesn't exist.

Tokyo may well have more shops than any other city on the planet. For the large chains, one branch is never enough and the biggest ones have outlets in all of the major shopping centres of Ikebukuro, Shibuya and Shinjuku. Yet there is far more to Tokyo than just vast outlets in impersonal shopping centres. Areas such as Aoyama are home to a host of upmarket designer and antique shops. Here and in, say, Harajuku, global brand names exist alongside those still pushing for their big break. During your shopping spree around Tokyo, you'll see a number of familiar faces – and thanks to the economy, the 'foreign invaders' are gaining ground. Some of the most high-profile include Benetton, Gap, and even Boots the Chemist.

On a local level, a small stores law designed to protect small shopkeepers from rapacious supermarkets has ensured that the local shopping street has survived in a way it hasn't in the UK. Walk down any given street and you'll find traditional businesses selling rice crackers next door to a bank or supermarket.

To locate a particular shop or service, refer to the maps on pages 292-316.

One-stop shopping

Department stores

Japanese 'depato' share certain basic similarities. Food halls are always in the basement, along with restaurants and cafés. The first two floors are women's clothing and accessories, with menswear beginning on the third or maybe the fourth. The higher levels include restaurants that stay open at night after the main store has closed, and the rooftops are used as beer gardens in the summer. Almost all stores offer tax-exemption services for purchases (mainly clothing) over ¥10,000, if you bring your passport with your purchase to the customer service counter. Most of them have sections where Japanese craft products can be bought as souvenirs, and some have delivery services to anywhere in the world. Store guides in English are available at the information desk. 'Depatos' are closed approximately one day every two months, so it's worth calling before you go. Also, please remember that for every store, the closing times differ from branch to branch.

Shop till you drop in Ginza's upmarket stores.

Eat, Drink, Shop

H2 Sukiyabashi Hankyu

2-5-1 Ginza Chuo-ku (3575 2231/www.hankyu-dept.co.jp). Ginza station. **Open** 10.30am-9pm daily. **Credit** AmEx, DC, JCB, MC, V. **Map** 6.

There are two main stores, this branch and Yurakucho Hankyu nearby. H2 houses numerous household goods and accessories, the giants HMV and Gap, and a customer service counter on the third floor. Yurakucho Hankyu, meanwhile, sells mainly clothes and cosmetics.

Isetan

3-14-1 Shinjuku, Shinjuku-ku (3352 1111/www.isetan.co.jp). Shinjuku station. **Open** 10am-7.30pm daily. **Credit** AmEx, DC, JCB, MC, V. **Map** 1b.

Contains the I-Club, a special service for foreign customers (*see p181* **Bargain hunting**). Membership enquiries can be made at the Customer Services desk on the seventh floor. The monthly newsletter contains comprehensive news of forthcoming sales, discounts and special promotions. It also contains details of the clothing ranges available in sizes larger than the usual Japanese ones. Isetan is split into seven buildings very close to each other – the Main Building, the Annex building, Isetan Kaikan (for restaurants). In the main building, the overseas shipping service is in the basement, and the tax exemption counter is on the seventh floor. The basement second floor contains BPQC – an eclectic selection of stores selling cosmetics, household goods, perfume, and a branch of the Bonjour CD shop. **Branch**: 1-11-5 Kichijoji Honcho, Musashino-shi, Kichijoji (0422 211 111).

Keio

1-1-4 Nishi-Shinjuku, Shinjuku (3342 2111/www.keonet.com). Shinjuku station. **Open** 10am-8pm daily. **Credit** AmEx, DC, JCB, MC, V. **Map** 1a.

Situated between Odakyu, My Lord and Lumine, with exits leading directly from Shinjuku station, Keio offers ladies accessories on the first four floors, menswear on the fifth, *kimono*, jewellery and furniture on the sixth, children's clothes and sporting goods on the seventh and office supplies on the eighth. There is a recycle shop called 'With You' on the third floor – in Japan, 'recycle' means second-hand. The tax exemption and currency exchange counters are on the sixth floor. **Branch**: Keio Seiseki-Sakuragaoka, 1-10-1 Sekido, Tama-shi (042 337 2111).

Lumine 1 & 2

1-1-5 Nishi-Shinjuku, Shinjuku (3348 5211/www.lumine.co.jp). Shinjuku station. **Open** 11am-9pm daily. **Credit** AmEx, DC, JCB, MC, V. **Map** 1a.

This very confusingly laid-out store takes up two sides of Shinjuku station South Exit. Lumine 1 contains clothes and jewellery for ladies, with the food hall on the basement second floor. Lumine 2 sells menswear, accessories and sporting goods. There is no duty-free service available.

Matsuya

3-6-1 Ginza, Chuo-ku (3567 1211/www.matsuya.com). Ginza station. **Open** 10am-8pm daily. **Credit** AmEx, DC, JCB, MC, V. **Map** 6.

Matsuya reopened in March 2000 after an extensive refurbishing, which added, among other things, 'Soho's Room', a designer furniture store. There's a

The fake sky over the Greco-Roman **Venus Fort** mall even changes colour. *See p165.*

section for men's and women's clothing designed by Issey Miyake on the third floor. Traditional Japanese souvenirs and the Matsuya Art Gallery are on the seventh floor. The tax exemption and overseas shipping services are on the third floor. Watch out for the confusing English-language store guide.

Matsuzakaya

6-10-1 Ginza, Chuo-ku, (3572 1111/
www.matsuzakaya-dept.co.jp). Ginza station. **Open** 10.30am-7.30pm Mon-Sat; 10.30am-8pm Sun and national holidays. **Credit** AmEx, DC, JCB, MC, V. **Map** 6.

The main branch of Matsuzakaya is actually in Ueno, but foreign visitors are usually more familiar with this branch in Ginza. In the more-frequented Ginza branch, tax exemption and currency exchange counters are in the basement second floor, traditional Japanese souvenirs are on the sixth. The Annex building contains a beauty salon, art gallery, exhibition hall, and even a ladies' deportment school. **Branch**: 3-29-5 Ueno, Taito-ku, (3832-1111).

Mitsukoshi

1-4-1 Nihonbashi Muromachi, Chuo-ku (3241 3311/
www.mitsukoshi.co.jp). Mitsukoshimae station. **Open** 10am-7pm. **Credit** AmEx, DC, JCB, MC, V. **Map** 8.

The oldest surviving department store in Japan, and visitors to the main store are greeted by a huge statue of Tennyo Magokoro, the Buddhist goddess of sincerity. Mitsukoshi owns the Tokyo franchise to the jewellery giant Tiffany's. The Ginza store has a tax exemption counter in the basement third floor, currency exchange counter and Japanese souvenirs (the store is called 'Japanesque') on the seventh. **Branches**: 4-6-16 Ginza, Chuo-ku (3562 1111); 3-29-1 Shinjuku, Shinjuku-ku (3354 1111); 1-5-7 Higashi-Ikebukuro, Toshima-ku, (3987 1111).

My Lord

1-1-3 Shinjuku, Shinjuku-ku. (3349 5611). Shinjuku station. **Open** 11am-9pm. **Credit** Most major cards. **Map** 1a.

My Lord (pronounced mih-lord-oh) has a number of clothing stores, but what's worth looking at is the sloping street between Keio and Odakyu department stores. Here are many shops devoted to kitsch, retro, and cute cartoon characters from around the world. There's also an entire shop devoted to the Sony Post Pet e-mail phenomenon.

Odakyu

1-1-3 Nishi-Shinjuku, Shinjuku. (3342 1111/
www.odakyu-dept.co.jp). Shinjuku station. **Open** 10am-8pm daily. **Credit** AmEx, DC, JCB, MC, V. **Map** 1a.

The store is split into two buildings, the main building and the Annex (Halc) building, which are connected by an elevated walkway and underground passageways. The main building sells ladieswear with *kimono* on the seventh floor and haberdashery on the eighth, while the Halc building has menswear, sportswear and Japanese furniture on the sixth, and an outlet of Troisgros delicatessen in the basement

food hall. The tenth to the fourteenth floors of the main buildings are called Manhattan Hills, and contain a dental clinic, a barber for men, restaurants, and the Odakyu Museum. The currency exchange counter is on the first floor of the main building, and the tax exemption counters are on the main building sixth floor and the Halc fifth floor.

Seibu

21-1 Udagawa-cho, Shibuya-ku (3462 0111/
www.seibu.co.jp). **Open** 10am-8pm daily. **Credit** AmEx, DC, JCB, MC, V. **Map** 2.

Opening times

Just about every store in Tokyo has been trying to beat the recession, so the opening hours of shops in general and department stores in particular have been extended. Opening at 10am, or sometimes 11am, most retail outlets stay open until 8pm, with some exceptions; popular boutiques close at 9pm, and very busy stores, such as the chemist Matsumoto Kiyoshi, close at 10pm.

Sunday is a normal shopping day in Japan, as it has no religious significance. That does mean, however, that large stores are usually very crowded, becoming almost unbearable during the summer sales and the New Year holiday. There is plenty of seasonal tack on display during the Christmas holiday season, although 25 December is a normal working day, with ordinary office hours. What's more, the Christmas decorations come down at the stroke of midnight, to make space for more traditional New Year celebrations, a practice that can be bewildering for foreign visitors.

As far as the national holidays (*see* p184) are concerned, most large stores will be open, but if you have a specific place in mind, it's worth calling before you go, to make sure. In more prosperous times, department stores would close once a week, which later went down to one day a month. Now, with a change in the laws governing the retail sector, even that requirement has gone. Look for large notices inside the stores announcing if they have a holiday that month, and if they do, what day that will be. Almost all places are closed on both 1 and 2 January, with the department store sales beginning on 3 January and lasting for about five days.

The Shibuya main store is split into two buildings, A and B, which face each other across the street. A Building sells mainly ladieswear, with B building selling menswear, children's clothes and accessories. The tax exemption counter is on the M2 (Mezzanine) floor of A building. Seibu also runs Loft, Seed and Movida, all of which are within easy walking distance of the Shibuya store. Loft is for the 18 to 35 age range, selling household goods and beauty care products, with novelty goods on the fifth floor and a Wave record store on the 6th. Seed and Movida have boutiques for Japanese in their teens and 20s.
Branch: 1-28-1, Minami-Ikebukuro, Toshima-ku (3981 0111).

Takashimaya

2-4-1 Nihonbashi, Chuo-ku. (3211 4111/ www.takashimaya.co.jp). **Open** 10am-7pm daily. **Credit** AmEx, DC, JCB, MC, V. **Map 8**.
This store shares much of the opulence and grandeur of its neighbour Mitsukoshi, and based a lot of its interior style on Harrods of London. Menswear is on the first and second floor, ladieswear is on the third and fourth, children's on the fifth, furniture on the sixth and *kimono* on the seventh. The tax exemption

counter is on the first floor and the overseas shipping service is on the basement first floor. The Shinjuku branch (Takashimaya Times Square) is now the largest single department store building in Japan, and contains a large number of boutiques, a branch of the hardware store Tokyu Hands, the Kinokuniya International Bookshop in the Annex building, and a IMAX digitally enhanced 3-D cinema.
Branch: Takashimaya Times Square, 5-24-2 Sendagaya, Shibuya-ku (5361 1111).

Tobu

1-1-25 Nishi-Ikebukuro, Toshima-ku (3981 2211/www.tobu.co.jp). **Open** 10am-8pm daily. **Credit** AmEx, DC, JCB, MC, V. **Map 5.**
This sprawling complex, comprising three connected buildings, was until recently the largest department store in the world. The Main Building houses clothing for all occasions (including *kimono* on the ninth floor) and restaurants from the 11th to the 17th floors. The Central Building sells clothing in larger sizes, interior goods and office supplies. The Plaza Building contains the designer collection. The currency exchange and tax exemption counters are in the Basement first floor of the Central Building.

Depato

Eat, Drink, Shop

The last day of trading at Sogo department store, Yurakucho, was a highly emotional affair. Before a throng of long-time customers and respectfully silent staff, the white-gloved company president gave a stirring speech thanking the public for their custom, after which the steel shutters were lowered for the last time.

It was yet another sign of how things that were taken for granted in Bubble-era Japan are now collapsing or mutating. The *depato*, the flagships of Japan's retail economy, are in big trouble. Overall sales in central Tokyo have dropped consistently through the last decade. The demise of Sogo, leaving liabilities of trillions of yen, has been the most dramatic example of the problem, changing the landscape of the Japanese retail sector for ever.

The problem is exacerbated by aggressive competition from without and within. Foreign retail giants such as **Benetton** (*see p172*) and **Sephora** (*see p175*) are opening more stores across Tokyo. The joint-venture company American Malls International is planning to open a series of Walmart-style supermalls across Japan (the first one, X-site, opened in Kanagawa prefecture, while Carrefour and Costco have opened stores in

Kaihin-Makuhari, just outside Tokyo. As if that wasn't enough, the tremendous success of the homegrown **Uniqlo** (*see p171*) has sent shockwaves through the entire industry.

However, it's fair to say that the *depato* are starting to fight back.One avenue of progression is through alliances with potential competitors. Other alliances have been forged with internationally famous names, such as Fauchon and L'Occitaine, which then open branches within the department stores themselves.

One aspect that has actually boomed during the recession is the basement food halls (or *depa-chikka*). Each store has sought to consolidate its gains by expanding these floors, and bringing in delicatessens such as Seijo Ishii or Troisgros, selling imported luxury foods.

Another technique, which has worked in the past, is to simply invent a new reason for buying. The Japanese have a long tradition of giving and accepting presents, and stores have been exploiting this since 1958, when Isetan began selling chocolates as Valentine's Day gifts. The latest addition to the long list of honorary present-giving days is Grandchildren's Day, on the third Sunday in October.

Tokyu Honten

2-24-1 Dogenzaka, Shibuya-ku (3477 3111/
www.tokyu-depart.co.jp). Shibuya station.
Open 10am-8pm; Tokyu Food Show 10am-9pm.
daily. **Credit** AmEx, DC, JCB, MC, V. **Map** 2.
The main store (above) sells designer fashions for
men and women and interior goods for the home.
The Tokyu Toyoko store is situated directly above
Shibuya JR station, consisting of a South wing, a
West wing and East wing. Goods on sale include
clothes, electrical appliances and porcelain. The
recently revamped food hall in the basement (Tokyu
Food Show) holds a branch of the extremely popular delicatessen Seijo Ishii. The Tokyu Plaza store,
behind Shibuya station, sells ladies fashion, cosmetics and accessories, and has a CD shop and a
branch of the Kinokuniya bookshop on the fifth floor
(however, it does not sell books in English).

Shopping malls

These are the latest addition to the Japanese
retail sector; massive buildings housing the
trendiest branches of Japanese and foreign
stores. Located within easy reach of the city
centre, these are not to be confused with what
the Japanese call '*ao-to-re-to*' ('outlets') – cut-
price stores usually located out of the city, in
suburban areas.

Alpa

3-2-2 Higashi-Ikebukuro, Toshima-ku (3989 3331).
Ikebukuro station. **Open** 10am-8pm daily. **Credit**
AmEx, DC, JCB, MC, V. **Map** 5.

Alpa is one of the buildings that form the Sunshine
City complex (*see chapter* **Ikebukuro**). It contains
a large number of boutiques and restaurants, including the 'foreign invaders' Body Shop and Benetton,
and the intriguing Franc Franc (*see p178*).

Atre

1-5-5 Ebisu-Minami, Shibuya-ku, Shibuya-ku (5475
8500). Ebisu station. **Open** 10am -9pm Mon-Sat;
10am-8pm Sun. **Credit** AmEx, DC, JCB, MC, V.
Map 3.
Atre, and the nearby Ebisu Garden Place, was the
prototype of Tokyo's major urban malls. The JR station exit is on the second floor, and food and pharmaceuticals are in the basement. Restaurants are on
the sixth, clothing on the fourth and fifth, and a
small but extremely well-stocked branch of the delicatessen Seijo Ishii is on the second.

Mark City

1-12-1 Dogenzaka, Shibuya-ku (3780 6503). Shibuya
station. **Open** 10am-9pm.daily. **Credit** varies.
Map 2.
This is a major addition to the Shibuya shopping
scene, presenting a number of boutiques and
'lifestyle' stores in one building, connected via a
walkway to JR Shibuya station. Restaurants are on
the fourth floor, accessories and cosmetics are on the
first, and more boutiques and imported food and
novelties are in the basement.

Venus Fort

Palette Town, 1 Aomi, Koto-ku (3599 0700). Ome
station (Yurikamome line). **Open** 11am-10pm daily.
Credit varies.

Join the hip young ladies of Tokyo at eye-catching **Candy Stripper**. *See p170.*

Widely touted as the 'first theme park exclusively for women', this unusual mall is decorated in a faux-classic Greco-Roman style designed to evoke feelings of strolling through Florence or Milan (it even has an artificial sky which periodically changes colour). Venus Fort contains mainly boutiques and is part of the O-Daiba bayfront complex.

YM Square

4-31-10 Jingumae, Shibuya-ku (various telephone numbers). Harajuku station. **Open** 11am-11.30pm Mon-Fri; 10am-11.30pm Sat; 10am-10.30pm Sun. 10am-8pm Sun-Thur; 10am-9pm Fri, Sat. **Credit** AmEx, DC, JCB, MC, V. **Map** 11.

Another huge building, in one of the trendiest areas of Tokyo, that shows the prevailing trend in shops and malls; a glass-fronted exterior and an interior that unashamedly targets female consumers. It contains what is said to be the largest branch of the Sephora cosmetics chain in the world, plus designer clothes and household goods, and the inevitable restaurants on the top floor.

✄ Shotengai

Although Japanese shoppers are always hunting for new and trendy places to see and be seen, the *shotengai* are the local neighbourhood places to which they will always return. The *shotengai*, or shopping streets, are the long roads near railway stations that are home to long-established shopkeepers and marketeers. Their architecture and inhabitants are both direct and unpretentious. Below are several which are notable for their history or unusual shops.

Ameyoko Plaza Food & Clothes Market

6-10-7 Ueno, Taito-ku, Ueno station. **Open** 9am-7pm daily. **No credit cards. Map** 14.

This maze of streets is actually two markets, Ueno Centre Mall and Ameyoko itself. The centre mall sells souvenirs and clothes, while the other market specialises in fresh food, especially fish. If you're bargain-hunting, go at the end of the day, when the vendors knock down the prices.

Kappa Bashi

Taito-ku. A five-minute walk from Tawaramachi station, along Asakusa Dori. **Open** varies. **Credit** varies, but cash usually preferred. **Map** 13.

One feature of Tokyo that never fails to impress visitors is the ubiquitous displays of plastic fake food outside restaurants. Kappa Bashi Dogu-gai is the area where the samples of the realistic-looking fake food are sold. There are about 200 wholesale stores of professional cooking utensils and tableware, used in making *sushi* etc.

Nakamise Dori

Asakusa, Taito-ku. **Open** 8am-8pm daily. **No credit cards. Map** 13.

This maze of stalls and tiny shops leading up to the entrance to Sensoji Temple in Asakusa sells Japanese souvenirs, some expensive, some tacky. It also sells the kind of food associated with festivals and brand-name watches.

Nakano Broadway

Opposite north exit of JR Nakano station. **Open** varies. **Credit** varies. **Map** 26.

Walk down this cathedral-like shopping street and you will come to the covered 'Broadway' section. On the second and third floors can be found several branches of Mandarake, a store selling new and secondhand *manga* and comics-related memorabilia. The second floor also has cult TV-related rarities from abroad. Broadway houses several branches of Fujiya Avic, a CD/DVD/Anime store where rarities and bootlegs can invariably be found.

Nishi-Ogikubo

Nishi-Ogikubo station, Suginami-ku. **Open** varies. **Credit** cash preferred. **Map** 30.

The area where four main roads cross at the Zenpukuji river is home to around 75 antique, secondhand and 'recycle' shops. They sell everything from Japanese ceramics to 1950s American memorabilia. To ensure you can find your way around, go out the station's north exit, stop at the *koban* (police box) and ask for a copy of the 'an-tik-ku map-pu'.

✄ Takeshita Dori

Open varies. **Credit** varies. **Map** 11.

The centre of teenybopper culture in Tokyo (*see* chapter **Harajuku**). Down this packed street can be found secondhand clothes and CD stores with wacky Jap-lish names like Nudy Boy and Octopus Army, stores that specialise in body piercing and the flamboyant costumes of the 'Visual Kei' fans, tacky memorabilia of Japanese idols past and present. Take it all in while you're munching a crêpe at one of the many corner stands.

Antique fairs & flea markets

To find a real slice of history among bewildering kitsch, check out a flea market. And don't follow normal Japanese attitudes towards haggling; here, it's expected.

Aoyama Oval Plaza Antiques Market

Aoyama Oval Plaza, 5-52-2 Jingumae, Shibuya-ku (info 3917 5962). Omotesando station. **Open** 6am-8pm. **No credit cards. Map** 11.

Attracts 45 dealers every third Saturday of the month. Open if it rains.

Arai Yakushi Antique Fair

Arai Yakushi shrine, 5-3-5 Arai, Nakano-ku (info 3319 6033). Arai Yakushi station (Seibu Shinjuku line). **Open** sunrise to sunset. **No credit cards. Map** 26.

This market features around 50 dealers every first Sunday of the month. Cancelled if it rains.

Japanese fashion

Fashion commentator Alan Bilzerian once said, 'Every single fashion designer has copied their skirts, shapes, wraps… they [the Japanese] have inspired the entire world.' A little dramatically put perhaps, but Tokyo is one of the top five cities in the fashion world, and the names of Issey Miyake, Hanae Mori, Yohji Yamamoto and Comme des Garçons will be familiar to the fashion-conscious everywhere. But what are the Japanese themselves buying – and wearing?

The 1980s saw the Japanese rightfully proud of their economic strength, but paradoxically paranoid about their own appearance. The fashions coveted most were the top luxury brands of Europe, spawning a new stereotype, the 'Office Lady' burdened down with bags of Vuitton, Gucci, Hermès, Chanel. While sales of these brands have continued to do well, despite the recession, the 'lost decade' of the 1990s saw Japanese youths struggling to find a new identity for themselves, and one way they expressed that new identity was through what they wore.

Japanese schools have traditionally strict rules concerning uniform, but the new breed of teenagers found ways to rebel. Girls' skirts hemlines went up and their socks got white and very, very baggy. Artificially tanned skin was in, along with silver eye-shadow and lipstick, a trend started by pop singer Namie Amuro. For boys, hair went from short and spiky to towering neo-Afros.

For late teens and twentysomethings, the last five years have seen fashion go to extremes that are not just ridiculous, but aesthetically disastrous. Platform soles returned with a vengeance, with 12-centimetre boots leading to many cases of broken ankles and (in some well-publicised incidents) crashed cars. Hair colours seen most often are *kinpatsu* (blonde), or *chapatsu* reddy-brown, and in the late 1990s, the hottest hair colour was, unaccountably, ash-grey. Accompanying orangey-tanned skin with white eye shadow and lipstick, this look, originating in the trendy Shibuya district, became known as the *ganguro* look. Innovative to some, sexy to the Shibuya kids, older Japanese had a different word for it: nauseating.

With the *ganguro* look thankfully consigned to history, young Japanese continue to experiment, still searching for that elusive look that can define what it means to be right here, right now. The streets have generated a new breed of Japanese designers who are bringing their visions to a receptive audience. The Japanese labels Hysteric Glamour, Super Lovers and Betty's Blue are now familiar the world over, and new creators such as A Bathing Ape, FNC and Gomme are set to follow them into the mainstream. For the first time in their history, the Japanese are free to choose who they want to be.

Iidabashi Ramura Antique Market
Central Plaza Ramura, 2-1 Kagurazaka, Shinjuku-ku (info 3917 5426). Iidabashi station. **Open** 6am-sunset. **No credit cards.**
This market attracts around 50 dealers on the first Saturday of every month. Open if it rains.

Nogi Shrine Antique Market
Nogi Shrine, 8-11-27 Akasaka, Minato-ku (info 0426 91 3572). Nogizaka station. **Open** 8am-3pm 7am-3pm. **No credit cards. Map** 12.
This market features around 35 dealers and takes place on the second Sunday of every month. Cancelled if it rains.

Roppongi Antique Market
Roppongi Roi Bldg, 5-5-1 Roppongi, Minato-ku (no phone). Roppongi station. **Open** varies. **No credit cards. Map** 4.
You'll find around 25 dealers at the Roppongi Antique Market on the fourth Thursday and Friday of every month. Open if it rains.

Yasukuni Antique Market
Yasukuni Shrine, 3-1-1 Kudan-Kita, Chiyoda-ku (info 3791 0006). Kudanshita station. **Open** sunrise to sunset. **No credit cards. Map** 9.
This market includes about 100 dealers on the third Sunday of every month. Open if it rains.

Books

Below we have listed some of the best bookstores for books in English and other languages. If you're looking for curiosities and bargains, and have a day to spare, head for the Kanda-Jinbocho area (Jinbocho station) and browse in some of the second-hand bookshops that line Yasukuni-Dori.

Aoyama Book Centre
Cosmos Bldg, 5-53-67 Jingumae, Shibuya-ku (5485 5511/www.aoyamabc.co.jp). Omotesando station. **Open** 10am-10pm 7.30pm. **Credit** AmEx, DC, JCB, MC, V. **Map** 2.

Eat, Drink, Shop

...he head store is in Aoyama behind the United Nations University Building, but of special interest to book-loving clubbers is the Roppongi branch, open at weekends until 5pm. Have a bleary-eyed browse while you're waiting for the first train home.
Branches: all over Tokyo.

Good Day Books

3F, 1-11-2 Ebisu, Shibuya-ku (5421 0957). Ebisu station. **Open** 11am-8pm Wed-Sat; 11am-6pm Sun; Closed Tue. **Credit** AmEx, DC, JCB, MC, V for purchases over ¥5,000. **Map** 3.

Stocks 30,000 used books and 7,000 new, mostly in English. An extensive selection of second-hand books on Japan and Japanese language texts.

Kinokuniya Bookstore

3-17-7 Shinjuku, Shinjuku-ku (3354 0131/www. kinokuniya.co.jp). Shinjuku station. **Open** 10am-8pm daily. **Credit** AmEx, DC, JCB, MC, V. **Map** 1b.

Kinokuniya has perhaps the largest selection of new books in Tokyo – but this does come at a price, with a recent paperback costing about ¥1,500. The owners claim to have about 1 million books in stock in English and other languages, and can order more from the UK and USA if you're looking for something really obscure.
Branch: Takashimaya Times Square Annex Bldg, 5-24-2 Sendagaya, Shibuya-ku (5361 3301).

Kitazawa

2-5 Kanda-Jinbocho, Chiyoda-ku (3263 0011). Jinbocho station. **Open** 10am-6pm Mon-Sat. **Credit** AmEx, DC, JCB, MC, V. **Map** 15.

This bookshop stands out thanks to its massive granite exterior and its brass spiral staircase leading to the second floor. A small patio outside the entrance holds a number of paperbacks for knocked-down prices. Inside it has a very scholarly atmosphere, with new works of reference and non-fiction on the first floor, and a selection of extremely rare antique books on the second.

Electronics

For the visitor, the place of interest is Akihabara (*see p179*), but there are other stores almost matching its prices along the main urban thoroughfares. The most notable are Bic Camera, Yodabashi Camera and Sakuraya, although they are geared towards domestic customers. If you are interested in photography, take a stroll around the back streets of Shinjuku near Studio Alta and you will find plenty to interest you.

Bic Camera

1-41-5 Higashi-Ikebukuro, Toshima-ku (5396 1111/www.biccamera.co.jp). Ikebukuro station. **Open** 10am-8pm.daily. **Credit** AmEx, DC, JCB, MC, V. **Map** 5.

Like the other large electronics retailers, Sakuraya and Yodabashi Camera, the 'main branch' is in fact split into a number of different buildings, all fairly close to each other. Bic sells every kind of modern

electronic appliance, as well as a limited amount of household furniture. Some knowledge of Japanese is required for making enquiries.
Branches: all over Tokyo.

IT Net

B1F, 1-15-12 Soto-Kanda, Chiyoda-ku (5298 8201). Akihabara station. **Open** 10am-8pm. **No credit cards. Map** 17.

This small basement shop has English-language catalogues for J-Phone mobile phone products – as well as user's manuals in English.

Laox

1-2-9 Soto-Kanda, Chiyoda-ku (3253 7111/ www.laox.co.jp). Akihabara station. **Open** 10am-8pm Mon-Sat. **Credit** AmEx, DC, JCB, MC, V. **Map** 17.

In the main store, the duty-free section is located on the fourth to seventh floors. A worldwide delivery service is available, and most of the staff speak good English. They have English-language catalogues for all kinds of products.
Branches: all over Tokyo, but not duty-free.

Minami Musen Denki

4-3-3 Soto-Kanda, Chiyoda-ku (3526 7711/ www.tzone.com). Akihabara station. **Open** 10.30am-8pm Mon-Sat; 10am-7.30pm Sun. **Credit** AmEx, DC, JCB, MC, V. **Map** 17.

Look for the sign that says 'T-Zone', a few doors up from Yamagiwa (*see p169*) on the Chuo-dori. Minami Musen Denki is on the first two floors of the T-Zone building.

NTT DoCoMo

1-15-13 Soto-Kanda, Chiyoda-ku (5256 4646/www. nttdocomo.co.jp). Akihabara station. **Open** 10am-6.30pm. **Credit** AmEx, DC, JCB, MC, V. **Map** 17.

NTT DoCoMo is the giant behind the hugely successful 'i-mode' wireless Internet-access system, which is now making inroads into the global market. This store, close to Akihabara station, contains a catalogue of their products in English.
Branches: all over Tokyo.

Sakuraya

1-1-1 Nishi-Shinjuku, Shinjuku-ku (5324 3636/ www.sakuraya.co.jp). Shinjuku station. **Open** 9.30am-9.30pm daily. **Credit** AmEx, DC, JCB, MC, V. **Map** 1a.

Sakuraya has recently opened its flagship store in Shinjuku, next to Odakyu department store (*see p163*). Sells every kind of modern electric appliance. Some knowledge of Japanese is required for making enquiries.
Branches: throughout Shinjuku.

Takarada

1-14-7 Soto-Kanda, Chiyoda-ku (3253 0101). Akihabara station. **Open** 11am-8pm daily. **Credit** AmEx, DC, JCB, MC, V. **Map** 17.

This small but very busy shop is close to the station, and has several bilingual staff members to help you find what you want. Their top floor also sells a range of Japanese souvenirs, ceramics etc.

Tsukumo Robocon Magazine Kan

1-9-7 Soto-Kanda, Chiyoda-ku (3253 5599). Akihabara station. **Open** 10.45am-8.30pm Mon-Sat; 10.15am-7pm Sun. **Credit** AmEx, DC, JCB, MC, V. **Map** 17.

This fascinating store specialises in robots – the cute, intelligent kind that the Japanese have been so good at in recent years. Cats, dogs, birds that charm their owners, the insect-like WonderBorg that is capable of remembering and learning, and some that defy description. Unfortunately the only robot kit that comes with English explanations is the imported Lego 'Mindstorms', but the lower-price range robots are fairly easy to understand and operate. There are many Tsukumo branches scattered around Akihabara; ask in one and they'll give you a map showing where this shop is.

Virtual Computer Networks

8F Isuzu Bldg, 4-6-2 Soto-Kanda, Chiyoda-ku (3251 1114). Akihabara station. **Open** 12noon-8pm Wed-Mon. **No credit cards. Map** 17.

Imagine this situation: you're in Japan for a while, you haven't got a lot of money but you'd like a cheap second-hand computer for email and Internet. If this sounds familiar, then this is the shop for you. The shop is difficult to find (the entrance is in a tiny back street behind Citibank) but once you're there, you'll find English-speaking staff to help you. There aren't any English manuals, and no technical support – but at these prices, with PCs starting at ¥25,000 and notebooks at ¥35,000, that's to be expected.

Wako stocks serious jewellery. *See p180.*

Yamagiwa

4-1-1 Soto-Kanda, Chiyoda-ku Akihabara station. **Open** 10.30 10am-7.30pm Sat and Sun. **Cre** MC, V. **Map** 17.

The duty-free store is on a co about ten minutes' walk from Akihabara station. Their English-language catalogues are mainly for Sony products.

Yodobashi Camera

1-11-1 Nishi-Shinjuku, Shinjuku-ku (3346 1010/ www.yodobashi.co.jp). Shinjuku station. **Open** 9.30am-9pm. **Credit** AmEx, DC, JCB, MC, V. **Map** 1a.

Like its rivals Bic and Sakuraya, this store's main office is to be found in six branches scattered around Shinjuku. It sells every kind of electrical appliance, but some knowledge of Japanese is required if you want to make enquiries.
Branches: 3-14-5 Koto-bashi Sumida-ku (3632-1010); 4-9-8 Ueno, Taito-ku (3837-1010).

Fashion

Looking good is still an obsession with Tokyoites, and the city streets are an immense melting pot of styles. Imported luxury brands such as Louis Vuitton, Prada and Hermes are posting increased sales despite the recession, while Japanese designers are receiving adulation at catwalks the world over. Younger, less famous designers are also arising from the underground and gaining a firmer grip upon the popular imagination, the latest hive of bohemian creativity being the tiny streets of Harajuku, behind the Gap megastore. What's more, there are always the tasteless crazes of teenage Japanese girls, which can be seen on a stroll anytime around Shibuya or Harajuku. It's a fashion jungle out there.

109

2-29-1 Dogenzaka, Shibuya-ku (3477 5111/ www.welcome-shibuya.co.jp). Shibuya station. **Open** 10am-9pm daily. **Credit** AmEx, DC, JCB, MC, V. **Map** 2.

This mall is the mecca of the *Joshikosei* – the fashionably minded teenage girl. It's worth a visit to experience the flashy, tacky, sometimes downright bizarre trends that appear and disappear with lightning speed on the Tokyo high streets.

5351

28-2 Sarugaku-cho Shibuya-ku (5459 6391). Daikanyama station (Tokyu Toyoko line). **Open** 11am-8pm daily. **Credit** AmEx, DC, JCB, MC, V. **Map** 32.

Daikanyama has, for several years, been regarded as the home of the stylish. Inside this steel and glass store for designer apparel and jewellery, you can see why. An impressive range of fabrics and styles for both men and women.

Eat, Drink, Shop

Bright colours and tempting bargains at **Ameyoko Plaza Food & Clothes Market**. *See p166.*

Candy Stripper

4-26-27 Jingumae, Shibuya-ku (5770 2200). Harajuku station. **Open** 11am-8pm daily. **Credit** AmEx, DC, JCB, MC, V. **Map 11.**

This store has a jaw-dropping exterior and a stylish minimalist interior. It stocks clothes, accessories and jewellery for forward-thinking young ladies. In fact, while you're in the area, any shop on this tiny, dark street is worth visiting.

Comme Ça Store

3-26-6 Shinjuku, Shinjuku-ku (5367 5551). Shinjuku station. **Open** 11am-9pm Mon-Sat; 11am-8pm Sun. **Credit** AmEx, DC, JCB, MC, V. **Map 1b.**

This rather confusing chain is also known as 'Comme Ça Store' and 'FIVE FOXes' (sic), and is no relation to Comme des Garçons (below). As well as affordable fashions in warm colours and fabrics, they also produce tableware, stationery and household goods.

Branches: all over Tokyo.

Comme des Garçons

5-2-1 Minami-Aoyama, Minato-ku (3406 3951). Omotesando station. **Open** 11am-8pm daily. **Credit** AmEx, DC, JCB, MC, V. **Map 4.**

After a strong showing at the 2000 Paris collection, this range of fashions designed by Rei Kawakubo has gone from strength to strength. The extraordinary front of this store beckons the shopper into a tempting maze of psychedelic prints, classically-themed suits and smart formal wear. A tax exemption service is available.

Branches: outlets at many department stores.

Final Home

Parco Part 1, 15-1 Udagawa-cho, Shibuya-ku (3477 5922/www.finalhome.com). Shibuya station. **Open** 10am-8.30pm daily. **Credit** AmEx, DC, JCB, MC, V. **Map 2.**

Final Home is the brainchild of Kosuke Tsumura, a designer who previously worked for Issey Miyake. Tsumura's range of odd and sometimes controversial clothing is designed as what he calls 'clothing solutions' for outdoor urban life. The emphasis is on practicality as well as style, and uses a variety of tough, hi-tech fabrics.

The Ginza

7-8-10 Ginza, Chuo-ku (3571 7731). Ginza station. **Open** 11am- 8pm 10am-8pm Mon-Sat; 11pm-7pm 10am-7pm Sun. **Credit** AmEx, DC, JCB, MC, V. **Map 6.**

Located in the central shopping nexus of Ginza, this impressive store sells its own designer brand of casual and formal wear for men and women.

Hanae Mori

3-6-1 Kita-Aoyama, Minato-ku (3400 3301/www.hanaemori.com). Omotesando station. **Open** 10.30am-7pm daily. **Credit** AmEx, DC, JCB, MC, V. **Map 11.**

Hanae Mori is globally renowned for combining classical European flair with traditional Oriental touches, such as evening gowns decorated with the brush-strokes of Japanese calligraphy, and dresses combining features of the *kimono*. A tax exemption service is available.

Branches: outlets in many department stores.

Eat, Drink, Shop

Issey Miyake

3-18-11 Minami-Aoyama, Minato-ku (3423 1407/1408/www.pleatsplease.com). Omotesando station. **Open** 11am-9pm daily. **Credit** AmEx, DC, JCB, MC, V. **Map** 4.

If Hanae Mori represents Japan's traditional past, then Issey Miyake represents its mixed-up present and chaotic future. His range of pleated hemp material and polyester jersey fabric, 'Pleats Please', which he developed in the early 1990s, is perhaps his best-known line internationally. Note that the Miyake website (www.pleatsplease.com) needs Flash plug-in to access. A tax exemption service is available.

Branches: outlets in many department stores.

Laforet Harajuku/Foret Harajuku

1-11-6 Jingumae, Shibuya-ku. (3475 0411/ www.laforet.ne.jp/harajuku). Harajuku station. **Open** Laforet Harajuku 11am-8pm daily; Foret Harajuku 11am-9pm daily. **Credit** AmEx, DC, JCB, MC, V. **Map** 11.

Laforet contains about 100 small boutiques aimed at young wearers of garish, eccentric fashion. After a major renovation during the first three months of 2001, during which it acquired a new name (formerly it was plain old Laforet 1 and 2), the store is now giving Shibuya teen-fashion rival 109 a serious run for its money.

Marui

3-30-16 Shinjuku, Shinjuku-ku (3354 0101/ www.0101.co.jp). Shinjuku station. **Open** 11am-8pm daily. **Credit** AmEx, DC, JCB, MC, V. **Map** 1b.

There are five large stores in Shinjuku alone, very close to each other. They sell a mixture of contemporary men's and ladieswear, accessories, imported designers and sportswear. The rather confusing logo looks like 'zero-one zero-one'; the idea behind is that 'maru' means 'circle' or 'zero' in Japanese.

Branches: all over Tokyo.

Parco

15-1 Udagawa-cho, Shibuya-ku (3464 5111/ www.parco.co.jp). Shibuya station. **Open** 10am-8.30pm daily. **Credit** AmEx, DC, JCB, MC, V. **Map** 2.

This mid-range clothing store is spilt into three buildings. Part 1 houses a theatre and an art bookshop, while part 3 contains an exhibition hall hosting innovative young artists. The Shibuya branch is the home of the concert hall Club Quattro.

Branches: 1-28-2 Minami-Ikebukuro, Toshima-ku (5391 8000); 1-5-1 Honcho, Kichijoji, Musashino-shi (0422 21 8111).

Uniqlo

6-10-8 Jingumae, Shibuya-ku (5468 7313/ www.uniqlo.co.jp). Harajuku station. **Open** 11am-9pm daily. **Credit** AmEx, DC, JCB, MC, V. **Map** 11.

Residents of London may already be familiar with the name. This store is following in the footsteps of Gap in providing cut-price, high-quality clothing.

Branches: all over Tokyo.

Yohji Yamamoto

5-3-6 Minami-Aoyama, Minato-ku (3409 6006/ www.yohjiyamamoto.co.jp). Omotesando station. **Open** 11am-8pm daily. **Credit** AmEx, DC, JCB, MC, V. **Map** 4.

.ole for designing the costumes for the Beat akeshi-directed film *Brother*. His latest collection shows the gangster influence of the film in his heavy coats, boxy suits and flat caps. Tax exemption service available.
Branches: at many Tokyo department stores.

International stores

Benetton
4-3-10 Jingumae, Shibuya-ku (5474 7155/ www.benetton.co.jp). Omotesando station. **Open** 11am-8pm daily. **Credit** AmEx, DC, JCB, MC, V. **Map** 11.
December 2000 saw the opening of the Benetton Megastore on Omotesando, with their unusual range of clothes, accessories and interior goods.
Branches: all over Tokyo.

Diesel
1-23-25 Shibuya, Shibuya-ku (5468 1461/ www.diesel.co.jp). Shibuya station. **Open** 11am-8pm daily. **Credit** AmEx, DC, JCB, MC, V. **Map** 2.
The home of the prankster King Frank, and a range of casual clothes for men and women.

Gap
4-30-3 Jingumae, Shibuya-ku (5414 2441). Harajuku station. **Open** 10am-9pm daily. **Credit** AmEx, MC, V, JCB. **Map** 11.
A familiar name to millions. Very popular in Japan.
Branches: all over Tokyo.

Next
2-10-18 Jiyugaoka, Meguro-ku (5731 2227/ www.nextfromuk.co.jp). Jiyugaoka station (Tokyu Toyoko line). **Open** 11am-8pm daily. **Credit** AmEx, DC, JCB, MC, V. **Map** 33.
At the moment only present in three central Tokyo stores, but planning to expand.
Branches: Ebisu Mitsukoshi B1F, 4-20-7 Ebisu, Shibuya-ku (3280 1851); Aqua City Odaiba 3F, 1-7-1 Daiba, Minato-ku (3599 5560).

Food

Confectionery

It may be correct to say that the Japanese have a sweet tooth, but their sense of 'sweet' is definitely different from European or American sensibilities. The taste of Japanese confectionery is based upon *anko* – a red paste made from *azuki* beans. For the more refined, there is *wagashi*, a colourful candy made from sugar and sometimes used in tea ceremonies.

Akebono
5-7-19 Ginza, Chuo-ku (3571 0483) Ginza station. **Open** 9am-9pm Mon-Sat; 9am-8pm Sun. **Credit** AmEx, DC, JCB, MC, V. **Map** 6.
This shop's variety of mouth-watering Japanese sweets is also available in major Tokyo department

stores, on sale in the basement food halls. While your visiting, make sure you also try the shop's delicious *senbei* (rice-crackers).
Branches: all over Tokyo.

Kimuraya
4-5-7 Ginza, Chuo-ku (3561 0368/www.kimuraya-sohonten.co.jp). Ginza station. **Open** 10am-9pm. **Credit** cash preferred. **Map** 6.
This venerable shop, next door to Wako jewellery store (*see p180*), is historically significant for being the first Tokyo shop to sell 'anpan' – bread rolls filled with anko.

Toraya
4-9-22 Akasaka, Minato-ku (3408 4121/www.toraya-group.co.jp). Akasaka-Mitsuke station. **Open** 8.30am-8pm Mon-Fri; 8.30am-6pm Sat and Sun. **Credit** AmEx, DC, JCB, MC, V. **Map** 7.
This store is highly unusual in that it has an excellent English pamphlet explaining the history and composition of wagashi and anko. Some of their confectionery is meant to be eaten on the day it's bought – ask about the 'best-by' dates.
Branch: 7-8-6 Ginza. Chuo-ku. (3571-3679).

Shichijo Kansyudo
B2F, Odakyu Halc department store, 1-1-3 Nishi-Shinjuku (3342 1111). Shinjuku station. **Open** 10am-8pm daily. **Credit** AmEx, DC, JCB, MC, V. **Map** 1a.
Here's an interesting idea; performing the tea ceremony, drinking from a beautiful, well-made cup – and then eating it. The cups sold in this branch, in the basement of the Odakyu Halc building, are actually very large *wagashi*.
Branches: in department stores around Tokyo. Most sell ordinary *wagashi*.

Imported foods

If your stay in Japan is longer than a few weeks, then you'll get a hankering for some of the comforts of home. Listed below are the stores that cater to expatriates, and to Japanese people looking for something a bit different.

Kinokuniya International
3-11-7 Kita-Aoyama, Minato-ku (3409 1231/www.e-kinokuniya.com). Omotesando station. **Open** 9.30am-8pm daily. **Credit** AmEx, DC, JCB, MC, V. **Map** 2.
A wide range of international foods is on offer, as well as English-language newspapers, magazines, and a number of customer services.

Meidiya
2-6-7 Ginza, Chuo-ku, Tokyo (3563 0221/www.meidi-ya.co.jp). Ginza station. **Open** 10am-9pm daily. **Credit** AmEx, DC, JCB, MC, V. **Map** 6.
An attractive array of imported foods, and a good wine cellar. The Hiroo store has free parking.
Branches: 5-6-6 Hiroo, Shibuya-ku (3444 6221); 7-15-14 Roppongi, Minato-ku (3401 8511).

Miuraya

*1-9-10 Honcho, Musashino-shi (0422 21 1020/
www.miuraya.co.jp). Kichijoji station.* **Open** 10am-
9pm daily. Closed 3rd Mon of month. **Credit** AmEx,
DC, JCB, MC, V. **Map** 31.
This is a fairly new Japanese supermarket with a
large section of specialist imported foods. Worth
keeping an eye out for.
Branches: all over Tokyo.

National Azabu

*4-5-2 Minami-Azabu, Minato-ku (3442
3181/st5.yahoo.co.jp/national). Hiroo station.* **Open**
9.30am-7pm. **Credit** AmEx, DC, JCB, MC, V.
National Azabu has a long history of serving the
international community.

Sanmi Discount Store

4-8-12 Ginza, Chuo-ku (3561 9891). Ginza station.
Open 9am-8pm Mon-Sat. **No credit cards. Map** 6.
This store may be small, but it's extremely well-
stocked, and it's also handily close to the heart of the
Ginza shopping area.

Gift & craft shops

Aoi Art

*4-22-11 Yoyogi, Shibuya-ku (3375 5553/www.aoi-
art.ab.psiweb.com). Yoyogi station.* **Open** 11am-7pm
Tue-Sun. **Credit** AmEx, DC, JCB, MC, V. **Map** 23.
The sword is an enduring image of Japan and its
samurai warriors. Aoi Art is one of Tokyo's oldest

buyers and sellers of antique and modern swords.
A certificate of authenticity is presented with the
purchase, with the signature of the swordsmith.

Ayahata

*2-21-2 Akasaka, Minato-ku (3582 9969). Akasaka
station.* **Open** 11am-7pm Mon-Sat. **Credit** AmEx,
DC, JCB, MC, V. **Map** 7.
Contains a selection of secondhand and antique
kimono. Antique *kimono* are usually 'one-off' designs
by professional artists, and prices tend to reflect this.

Bingo-ya

*10-6 Wakamatsucho, Shinjuku-ku (3202 8778).
Wakamatsu-Kawada station (Toei Oedo line).* **Open**
10am-7pm Tue-Sun. **Credit** AmEx, DC, JCB, MC, V.
Although a little off the beaten track, this is definte-
ly worth a visit. Bingo-ya sells folk crafts from all over
Japan and has a wide selection of traditional toys.

Fuji Torii

*6-1-10 Jingumae, Shibuya-ku (3400 2777). Harajuku
station.* **Open** 11am-6pm Wed-Mon. Closed 3rd Mon
of month. **Credit** AmEx, DC, JCB, MC, V. **Map** 11.
This store is just a few doors up from Oriental
Bazaar, heading in the direction of Harajuku station.
It is particularly good on paper goods, greetings
cards and *kakejiku* (hanging scrolls).

Gift Center Japan

*Daiko-Asahi Bldg. 5F, 3-8-12 Ginza, Chuo-ku (3564
0302). Ginza station.* **Open** 9am-6pm Mon-Sat.
No credit cards. Map 6.

Sweets and other delicacies tickle the tastebuds at **Akebono**. *See p172.*

Vending machines

One thing that never fails to amaze, after finally setting foot outside Narita airport, is the number of vending machines in Tokyo. The product of the Japanese dual obsessions with technology and convenience, these machines can be seen on just about every street corner, whether it be in the city centre or out in a suburb.

Although most of them sell beverages or cigarettes, the rest contain a vast and sometimes bewildering range of products – newspapers, fresh flowers, hot noodles, phone cards, rice and even *onsen* (spa) water. The machine that's alleged to sell sealed packs of schoolgirl's used knickers has acquired the status of an urban legend, but you will certainly see – in the more dubious areas – machines stocking videos,

magazines, sex toys and the batteries to power them with.

The year 2000, however, saw a drastic reduction in the number of beer machines. Due to widespread concern over underage drinking, 70 per cent of the machines across the country were removed; those left now require buyers to insert their driving licence as well as the money, so their date of birth can be verified.

One final word of advice; don't try kicking one. Attacks on vending machines have been on the rise, prompting manufacturers to come up with a high-tech alarm system. If vandalised, a shock sensor will trip an alarm transmitting a signal to the nearest police station – and an inbuilt digital camera will photograph the attackers in the act.

Formerly a shop, Gift Center Japan now runs a mail order service, with next-day delivery for catalogue orders received in the morning. The catalogues are free and fully detailed.

Hanato
2-25-6 Asakusa, Taito-ku (3841 6411). Asakusa station. **Open** 10am-8.30pm Wed-Mon. **No credit cards. Map** 13.
Specialises in the decorative paper lanterns that can be seen outside stalls, shops and temples everywhere in Japan.

Hara Shobo
2-3 Kanda-Jinbocho, Chiyoda-ku (5212 7801/www.harashobo.com). Jinbocho Station. **Open** 10am-6pm Tue-Sat. **Credit** AmEx, DC, JCB, MC, V. **Map** 15.
Sells every kind of woodblock print, old and new. They issue their catalogue, 'Edo Geijitsu', twice a year. The staff speak good English. Some samples can be seen on their website.

Hasebe-ya
1-5-24 Azabu-Juban, Minato-ku (3401 9998). Azabu-Juban station. **Open** 10am-7pm daily. **Credit** AmEx, DC, JCB, MC, V. **Map** 4.
Specialises in pottery (*yakimono*) and furniture (*kagu*). The furniture is not all antique – there are some bargains to be found.

Hayashi Kimono
2-1-1 Yurakucho, Chiyoda-ku (3501 4012). Yurakucho station. **Open** 9.45am-6.45pm Mon-Sat; 10am-6pm Sun. **Credit** AmEx, DC, JCB, MC, V. **Map** 6.
Hayashi Kimono has the largest stock of second-hand *kimono* in Tokyo, and offers tax-free shopping and a mail order service. International Arcade is located opposite the Imperial Hotel, actually under

the train tracks which stretch between Yurakucho and Ginza. The arcade also contains a number of shops that sell high-quality Japanese souvenirs.

Japan Sword
3-8-1 Toranomon, Minato-ku (3434 4321). Toranomon station. **Open** 9.30am-6pm Mon-Fri; 9.30am-5pm Sat. **Credit** AmEx, DC, JCB, MC, V. **Map** 4.
The oldest and possibly the most famous purveyor of *samurai* swords in Tokyo.

Lynn Matsuoka Studio
2-9-10 Moto-Azabu, Minato-ku (3443 1443/ www.lynnmatsuoka.com). Hiroo station. **Open** by appointment. **Credit** MC, V.
The Tokyo studio represents the drawings, paintings and prints of New York artist Lynn Matsuoka, who has been living and working in the esoteric worlds of sumo and kabuki for 28 years. Her work is a unique document of living Japanese traditions. The studio offers posters, postcards and portrait commissions, and also represents the work of furniture designer Keith Barker.

Ohya Shobo
1-1 Kanda-Jinbocho, Chiyoda-ku (3291 0062). Jinbocho station. **Open** 10am-6pm Mon-Sat. **No credit cards. Map** 15.
Boasts the world's largest stock of old illustrated books (some dating back 300 years, to the Edo period), also *ukiyo-e* and other prints, old maps, early manga: basically any kind of Japanese graphic art.

Oriental Bazaar
5-9-13 Jingumae, Shibuya-ku (3400 3933). Meiji-Jingumae station. **Open** 9.30am-6.30pm Fri-Wed. **Credit** AmEx, DC, JCB, MC, V for purchases of ¥2,000 or more. **Map** 11.

Eat, Drink, Shop

Probably the most well-known gift shop in Tokyo. *Kimono, yukata* and chinaware are in the basement, books, stationery and furniture are on the first floor, and antiques, screens and vases are on the second. The staff speak extremely good English
Branch: Narita airport, No.1 Terminal Building 4F, 1-1 Goryo Bukujo, Sanrizuka, Narita-shi, Chiba-ken (0476 32 9333).

Sagemonoya
Yotsuya 4-chome, 28-20-703 Shinjuku-ku (3352 6286/www.netsuke.com). Yotsuya station. **Open** 1-6pm Tue-Sat, or by appointment. **Credit** AmEx, DC, JCB, MC, V. **Map** 10.
In the Edo era, it was forbidden for lower-ranking *samurai* to overdo the decorations on their *kimono*, so instead they decorated the tiny accessories they used to hold their tobacco or medicine. These became known as *netsuke* and *sagemono*. This shop's staff hold hundreds of collectibles, and can answer enquiries in English, French and German.

Tolman Collection
2-2-18 Shiba-Daimon, Minato-ku (3434 1300). Hamamatsucho station. **Open** 11am-7pm Wed-Mon. **Credit** AmEx, DC, JCB, MC, V.
Specialises in high-quality prints, including the world-famous *ukiyo-e*, which are often reproduced in publications on the subject of Japan. During their frequent special sales, only cash is accepted.

Tachikichi
5-6-13 Ginza, Chuo-ku (3573 1986). Ginza station. **Open** 11am-7pm Mon-Sat. **Credit** AmEx, DC, JCB, MC, V. **Map** 6.
Specialises in pottery and ceramics. The range is drawn from regions all over Japan, showing a wide variety of styles and techniques.

Washikobo
1-8-11 Nishi-Azabu, Minato-ku (3405 1841). Roppongi station. **Open** 10am-6pm Mon-Sat. **Credit** AmEx, DC, JCB, MC, V. **Map** 4.
Specialises in all things made of Japanese *washi* paper – chests of drawers, jewellery boxes, dolls and (of course) stationery.

Health & beauty

Beauty services

Boudoir
2-25-3 Jingumae, Shibuya-ku (3478 5898). Jingumae station. **Open** 10am-8pm daily. **Credit** AmEx, DC, JCB, MC, V. **Map** 11.
Mostly non-Japanese beauticians offer a full range of beauty and body treatments, in a salon located in one of the most stylish areas of Tokyo. Services from facials and waxing to yoga and meditation.

Maiko Make Over Studio
7F Su Bldg, 3-1 Uguisudani, Shibuya-ku (5459 1230/www.maiko-henshin.com). Shibuya station. **Open** 10am-6.30pm daily. **No credit cards**. **Map** 2.

Have you ever wondered what it would feel like to wear the traditional clothes and makeup of a *geisha* or *maiko*? This studio can realise that dream, transform you with *kimono, obi,* wig and sandals, and present you with a souvenir photo. Prices from ¥9,500.

Chiropractors

Tokyo Chiropractic Centre
3-5-9 Kita-Aoyama, Minato-ku (3478 2713). Omotesando station. **Open** 9am-6pm, Mon-Wed, Fri-Sat. **No credit cards**. **Map** 11.
All forms of back ailments and injuries treated. Appointments necessary. Insurance accepted. Bring all your documents to appointment.

Cosmetics

Kanebo
Kanebo Bldg, 3-20-20 Kaigan, Minato-ku (5446 3111/www.kanebo.co.jp). Hinode station (Yurikamome line). **Open** varies. **Credit** varies according to branch.
An extremely popular store with a range of products to suit every complexion and occasion.
Branches: all over Tokyo.

Opaque
3-5-8 Ginza, Chuo-ku (5250 1305). Ginza station. **Open** 11am-9pm Mon-Sat; 11am-8pm Sun. **Credit** AmEx, DC, JCB, MC, V. **Map** 6.
A compact but fascinating cosmetics store, featuring the creations of make-up artist Chiaki Shimada. Staff speak competent English.

Sephora
YM Square, 4-31-10 Jingumae, Shibuya-ku (5775 7481). Harajuku station. **Open** 10am-8pm. **Credit** AmEx, DC, JCB, MC, V. **Map** 11.
Apparently the world's biggest branch of this store. A vast range of cosmetics, going down very well with the local ladies.
Branches: all over Tokyo.

Shiseido
7-5-5 Ginza, Chuo-ku (3572 5111/ www.shiseido.co.jp). Ginza station. **Open** varies. **Credit** AmEx, DC, JCB, MC, V. **Map** 6.
The first western-style pharmacy established in Japan, with a history dating back to 1872. Their new 'bio-performance' range of products takes a holistic and multi-action approach to skincare.
Branches: all over Tokyo.

Hairdressers

Peekaboo
4-2-15 Jingumae, Shibuya-ku (5411 5422). Omotesando station. **Open** 10am-7pm, Tue-Sun. **Credit** AmEx, DC, JCB, MC, V. **Map** 11.
Famous throughout the whole of Japan, Peekaboo features internationally trained hair stylists, many of whom speak English. All forms of hair treatment

Eat, Drink, Shop

Pokemon Centre: join hordes of kids at the home of Pikachu and friends. *See p182.*

Craft work

When thinking of Japanese crafts, in particular what would make stylish and affordable gifts to take back home, the first things that probably come to mind are the *ukiyo-e* woodblock prints painted by artists such as Hiroshige and Hokusai. Internationally, the best known examples of the art form are perhaps Hiroshige's *Hundred views of Mount Fuji*, but there is a multitude of artists and styles to be explored, and antiques stores such as those in the Kanda/Jinbocho area are ideal places to start. Other distinctively Japanese items that make ideal gifts are lacquerware, ceramics, the carved miniatures known as *netsuke*, and *kimono* with their accessories (such as hairpieces and sashes). There is also the incredibly resilient Japanese paper called *washi*, which is used in making toys, lanterns, Edo-style waxed umbrellas, and even doors (the famous sliding *shoji*).

Arts and crafts fall into two broad categories. *Dento kogei* are the fine traditional crafts, where what matters is the quality of technique and refinement of finish. *Mingei* are the folk crafts intended for everyday use, which have a more robust, 'unfinished' look, although frequently they end up as objects of decoration and veneration. That means that a plain, ordinary-looking cup may have a heritage going back centuries, and may have enjoyed the patronage of *shogun* and emperors. In addition, every prefecture in Japan has its own variations on *dento kogei* and *mingei*, such as the pottery racoon-dogs of Shigaraki.

Japanese crafts also have a strong affinity with the seasons, a thread that runs through the Japanese aesthetic. For centuries, the Japanese have closely observed the passing of the seasons, recording the minute changes in nature and transforming them into works of art. In terms of the *kimono*, to take just one example, this means a wide range of fabrics and designs, designed to be worn at set times of the year.

Although there are many high street stores selling reasonably well-made craft items as souvenirs, one highly enjoyable way of finding a lasting souvenir of Japan is by checking out the open-air antique and flea markets (*see p166*). The first one opened at Nogi Shrine in the 1970s, and since then, they have proved immensely popular with both casual shoppers and seasoned collectors. If you're thinking of going, don't forget to get there early, and to take your time browsing before making a purchase. There will be a bewildering variety of styles and prices on offer, so don't be afraid to try asking the stallholder – antiques markets are social and cultural experiences, much more than business transactions. Which, really, can be said about the whole of the Japanese crafts industry.

---

are available. Peekaboo's popularity is clearly demonstrated by the fact that there are six branches in the Omote-Sando area alone.

Sinden
3-4-12 Jingumae, Shibuya-ku (3405 4409/ www.sinden.com). Omotesando station. **Open** 10am-7.30pm daily. **Credit** AmEx, DC, JCB, MC, V. **Map** 11.
Sinden has mostly non-Japanese staff with a wide range of expertise. All hair services are offered, including colouring, perming and styling, for both men and women.

Opthalmologists & opticians

Fuji Optical Service International
Otemachi Bldg 1F, 1-6-1 Otemachi, Chiyoda-ku (3214 4751). Otemachi station. **Open** 10am-6pm Mon-Fri; 10am-6pm Sat. **No credit cards. Map** 9.
Call to make an appointment, as only one optician speaks English.

International Vision Centre
3F Kyowa Gotankan Bldg, 3-3-13 Kita-Aoyama, Minato-ku (3497 1491). Omotesando station. **Open** Mon-Sat 10am-6pm. **No credit cards. Map** 11.
The practice of Dr Iida. Prescriptions can be checked, and eye-tests for new glasses or contacts can be given. If you have your previous prescription, even if it's written in English, please bring it with you to the Centre when you have a check-up, along with your insurance documents.

Nozaki Eye Clinic
Kasuya Bldg, 2-9 Sakuragaoka-machi, Shibuya-ku (3461 1671). Shibuya station. **Open** 1-6pm Mon, Tue; 10am-6pm Wed, Fri, Sat, 10am-6pm. **No credit cards. Map** 2.
This clinic is the practice of Dr. Nichio Nozaki, gradute of Keio University and an eye specialist for several years at Wills Eye Hospital, Philadelphia. Appointments are required. Bring your insurance documents with you.

Pharmacies

The following all have English-speaking staff. A late-night service (until 2am daily) is offered by **Roppongi Pharmacy**.

American Pharmacy

Hibiya Park Bldg, 1-8-1 Yurakucho, Chiyoda-ku (3271 4034). Yurakucho station. **Open** 9.30am-8pm Mon-Sat; 10am-6.30pm Sun. **Credit** AmEx, DC, JCB, MC, V. **Map** 6.

If you get sick during your stay, then the address of the American Pharmacy is worth remembering. It doesn't sell medicine from abroad – Japanese law is extremely confusing on this point – but it does have bilingual staff who will explain the products and make prescriptions for you. Directions for use are available in English.

Boots the Chemist

6-5-3 Jingumae, Shibuya-ku (3708 6011/ www.boots.co.jp). Meiji-Jingumae station. **Open** 11am-8.30pm Mon-Fri; 11am-9pm Sat, Sun. **Credit** MC, V. **Map** 11.

Many eyes were opened when the UK's most popular chemist threw open its doors in Tokyo's trendiest areas. So far, it's been a smash hit, but only Japanese pharmaceuticals are sold here.

Kaken International Pharmacy

Kaken Tsukiji Bldg, 11-16 Akashicho, Chuo-ku (3248 6631). Tsukiji station. **Open** 8.30am-5.45pm Mon-Fri. **No credit cards.**

Koyasu Drug Store Hotel Okura

Hotel Okura Main Bldg 1F, 2-10-4 Toranomon, Minato-ku (3583 7958). Roppongi-Itchome station. **Open** 8.30am-9pm Mon-Sat; 10am-9pm Sun & public holidays. **Credit** AmEx, DC, MC, V. **Map** 4.

National Azabu Supermarket Pharmacy

4-5-2 Minami Azabu, Minato-ku (3442 3495). Hiroo station. **Open** 9.30am-7pm daily. Closed 1-3 Jan. **Credit** AmEx, DC, MC, V.

Roppongi Pharmacy

6-8-8 Roppongi, Minato-ku (3403 8879). Roppongi station. **Open** 10.30am-2am daily. **No credit cards.** **Map** 4.

Home & lifestyle shops

Afternoon Tearoom

Shinjuku Flags Bldg, 3-37-1 Shinjuku, Shinjuku-ku (5366 5427/www.afternoon-tea.net). Shinjuku station. **Open** 11am-9pm daily. **Credit** AmEx, DC, JCB, MC, V. **Map** 1b.

The Afternoon Tearoom offers a charming and very reasonably-priced range of household goods, tableware, interior accessories, ornaments and stationery. As an added bonus, the shops are invariably attached to a pleasant café.
Branches: all over Tokyo.

Franc Franc

Shinjuku Southern Terrace, 2-2-1 Yoyogi, Shibuya-ku (5333 7701/www.francfranc.com). Shinjuku station. **Open** 11am-9pm daily. **Credit** AmEx, DC, JCB, MC, V. **Map** 23.

Although the address is Shibuya-ku, the main branch is actually on Shinjuku's Southern Terrace, opposite Takashimaya Times Square. This is a very stylish 'lifestyle' shop, with goods for the bath, the kitchen, the bedroom and rather intriguingly, their own line of compilation CDs.
Branches: all over Tokyo.

It's Demo

1-9-18 Jingumae, Shibuya-ku (5414 0738). Harajuku station. **Open** 11am-10pm daily. **Credit** AmEx, DC, JCB, MC, V. **Map** 11.

This rather strange name is the romajii pronunciation of the Japanese *itsudemo*, meaning 'whenever'. A recent addition to the popular lifestyle stores, following in the footsteps of Muji and Franc Franc. Household goods, menswear and ladies wear, and a small selection of imported CDs.
Branch: 2-27-5 Kitazawa, Setagaya-ku (5790 2323).

Mujirushi Ryohin

1-8-21 Ginza, Chuo-ku (3535 2061/www.muji.co.jp). Ginza station. **Open** 11am-8.30 Mon-Sat; 11am-8pm Sun. **Credit** AmEx, DC, JCB, MC, V. **Map** 6.

The original no-brand designer brand. This is where the all-purpose one-stop store got started, before it went on to conquer London, where it's known and loved as Muji.
Branches: 2-12-28 Kita-Aoyama, Minato-ku (3478 5800); B2F Marui City Ueno, 6-15-1 Ueno Taito-ku (3836 1414).

People Tree (Global Village)

3-7-2 Jiyugaoka, Meguro-ku (5701 3361/www.globalvillage.or.jp). Jiyugaoka station (Tokyu Toyoko line). **Open** 11am-8pm daily. **Credit** AmEx, DC, JCB, MC, V. **Map** 33.

Global Village is a fair-trade company selling goods from 70 producers in over 20 countries. The range of organic foods, accessories and household goods are all aimed at sustaining and improving Third World trade.

Tokyu Hands

12-18 Udagawa-cho, Shibuya-ku (5489 5111/ www.tokyu-hands.co.jp). Shibuya station. **Open** 10am-8pm daily. **Credit** AmEx, DC, JCB, MC, V. **Map** 2.

This is the largest hardware store in Tokyo – and in it you'll find things that you never realised you wanted. Amongst other things, the basement contains novelty goods, fancy dress costumes and games, and is a perfect introduction to the Japanese sense of humour. Be warned, however, the Shibuya main store can be a very confusing place to try and find your way around.
Branches: Takashimaya Times Square, 5-24-2 Sendagaya, Shibuya-ku (5361 3111); 1-28-10 Higashi-Ikebukuro, Toshima-ku (3980 6111).

Akihabara

Each district of Tokyo has a distinct atmosphere: Nishi-Shinjuku has its powerhouse skyscrapers, and Ueno its downtown graininess, but the best place in town to remind you that you're still in Asia is Akihabara. Buildings encrusted with indecipherable neon signs, vendors shouting the price of software from the pavements, delivery-cyclists precariously balancing bowls of noodles as they peddle down the narrow streets, grey-suited salarymen rubbing shoulders with DIY *otaku* fanatics. This is Electric Town, several city blocks filled with cheap electronics retailers all squeezed suffocatingly close together. Welcome to *Blade Runner* country.

Before WWII, Akihabara was well known as a district of ramshackle radio shops. As Japan rebuilt itself, the range of products increased to include things like washing machines, refrigerators, televisions until the area was firmly established as Electric Town.

For foreign visitors, the main reason for coming to Akihabara is that they have goods available for export, and so exempted from tax. The duty free shops are clearly signposted outside, and the staff within generally speak good English. The main places are listed in the electronics and cameras section. The requirements are that you must be in Japan for less than six months, bring a copy of your passport

with you, and buy something costing more than ¥10,000. The mains voltage, TV and video systems in Japan are not compatible with the UK, but as these are multi-systems here for export, running them and recharging them back home presents no problem. If you buy Japanese kit, you'll need a mains converter to go with it.

What products are worth looking out for? Japan, being the master of miniaturisation, is particularly hot on mini-audio products. Having led the world a few years back in the development of MiniDisc players and recorders, the country has now embraced the MP3 phenomenon, with a range of products from the big boys, including Panasonic, Aiwa and Sony. PDAs and tiny cameras are also plentiful, but unfortunately, hot items like Sony's Aibo or PlayStation 2 are not currently available for export.

Mobile phones are another matter. In Japan, sales have gone through the roof, with social commentators describing them as either essential for urban life or a sign of the destruction of human society. Buy a mobile phone in Akihabara,and you have the choice of brands such as Nikko or Motorola, which you can use back home. If you want to use a mobile phone in Japan during your stay, you are faced with J-Phone, KDD, or NTT DoCoMo. You can also explore the wildly popular Internet browsing capabilities, such as NTT's i-mode or KDD's AU (AU includes 50 English websites and a foreign-language support service). Not to mention the much-touted, long-awaited 3G technology. The J-Phone products have the Skywalker text messaging system and, more conveniently, English-language instructions in the back of the Japanese user's manual.

Eat, Drink, Shop

...oria Sports

*...i Kanda-Ogawamachi, Chiyoda-ku (3295 2955/
.www.victoria.co.jp). Ochanomizu station.* **Open**
11am-8pm Mon-Sat; 10.30am-7.30pm Sun. **Credit**
AmEx, DC, JCB, MC, V. **Map** 15.

The area leading from the Jinbocho bookstores to
Ochanomizu station contains a number of discount
sportwear stores and musical instrument stores,
whose main customers tend to be students from the
nearby university. Victoria Sports is probably the
cheapest on the whole strip – and every change in
seasons brings a sale.
Branches: all over Tokyo.

Head shops

Booty

*Golden Bldg 2F, 4-10 Udagawa-cho, Shibuya-ku
(5459 2613/www2.neweb.ne.jp/wd/mushrom).
Shibuya station.* **Open** 1-10pm daily. **No credit
cards**. **Map** 2.

Booty is one of a growing number of 'head shops'
that has sprung up in Tokyo in recent years,
exploiting a loophole in the law that allows the sale
(but not consumption) of magic mushrooms. At this
particular outlet mushrooms start at ¥1,000 for a
one-gramme bag.

Psychedelic Garden

*Fukuya Bldg B1F, 7-8-2 Nishi-Shinjuku, Shinjuku-ku
(5925 2588). Shinjuku station.* **Open** noon-9pm
daily. **No credit cards**. **Map** 1a.

Another 'head shop' where you can stock up on
magic mushrooms from around ¥2,000 for a two-
gramme bag.

Jewellery

Mikimoto

4-5-5, Ginza, Chuo-ku (3535 4611). Ginza station.
Open 10.30am-6.30pm daily. **Credit** AmEx, DC,
JCB, MC, V. **Map** 6.

The fascinating story of how the world's first
cultured pearls came from Japan is the story of
Kokichi Mikimoto, the founder of this world-famous
store. There is a magnificent range of pearl jewellery
on display here, and a museum upstairs.
Branch: Imperial Hotel Arcade, 1-1-1 Uchisaiwaicho,
Chiyoda-ku (3591-5001).

Tasaki Shinju

5-7-5 Ginza, Chuo-ku (3289 1111). Ginza station.
Open 10.30am-7.30pm daily. **Credit** AmEx, DC,
JCB, MC, V. **Map** 6.

AKA the Jewellery Tower, this building is fairly
close to Mikimoto (*see above*) and also has jewellery
using pearls to beautiful effect. The third floor displays a range of south sea pearls, diamonds and
other precious stones; the fourth floor focuses on
engagement and wedding gifts, while the fifth is
a jewellery museum featuring some intriguing
multimedia displays.
Branch: 8-9-15 Ginza, Chuo-ku (3575 4180)

Tiffany's

*Inside Mitsukoshi department store, 3-29-1 Shinjuku,
Shinjuku-ku (5368 8911). Shinjuku station.* **Open**
10am-8pm daily. **Credit** AmEx, DC, JCB, MC, V.
Map 1b.

Tiffany's is still an obsession with young Japanese
ladies, along with the Audrey Hepburn movie that
eulogises it. The most in-demand item is the open-
heart necklace.
Branch: 2-7-17 Ginza, Chuo-ku, (5250 2900).

Wako

4-5-11 Ginza, Chuo-ku (3562 2111). Ginza station.
Open 10.30am-6pm Mon-Sat. **Credit** AmEx, DC,
JCB, MC, V. **Map** 6.

Based on the architecture found in Kensington and
Chelsea, the grandeur of the exterior at Wako is
matched only by the hushed ambience of the shop's
interior. Once you've bought your jewellery, the
shop also sells designer apparel and accessories to
go with it.

Music

The Japanese are well-known for taking their
obsessions very seriously. When the younger
generation get into it, they do so with a
dedication and tenacity that puts most train-
spotters to shame. Consequently, the range of
rarities, re-releases and bootlegs on the shelves
in Tokyo's second-hand record shops is
astonishing. Included here are a handful of
second-hand shops, along with some of the
multi-national big boys.

Bonjour Records

*24-1 Sarugaku-cho, Shibuya-ku (5458 6020/
www.bonjour.co.jp). Daikanyama station.* **Open**
11am-8pm daily. **Credit** AmEx, DC, JCB, MC, V.
Map 32.

For several years, trendy young Japanese have been
taking an interest in French and Italian pop. Bonjour
is the flagship of this movement, but its got other
genres in store, too. Also on its eclectic racks are
world music, leftfield techno, jazz, drum 'n' bass,
loungecore and more.
Branch: BPQC, Isetan B2F, 3-14-1 Shinjuku
Shinjuku, Shinjuku-ku (5458 6020).

Cisco

*11-11 Udagawa-cho, Shibuya-ku (3462 0366).
Shibuya station.* **Open** 11am-9pm daily. **Credit**
AmEx, DC, JCB, MC, V for purchases over ¥5,000.
Map 2.

Cisco is at the cutting-edge of dance-music, and its
Shibuya branch is actually five buildings close to
each other, divided according to various sub-genres
of techno. Here's where you will find well-known DJs
holding earnest discussions with the shop owners
across the turntables.
Branches: Studio Alta 6F, 3-24-3 Shinjuku,
Shinjuku-ku (3341 7495); 6-8-4 Ueno-ku, Taito-ku
(3837 0404).

Eat, Drink, Shop

Disc Union

3-31-4 Shinjuku Shinjuku-ku (3352 2691/ www.discunion.co.jp). Shinjuku station. **Open** 11am-8pm daily. **Credit** AmEx, DC, JCB, MC, V. **Map** 1b.
The Shinjuku main store is a tall narrow building with entire floors devoted to different genres of music. Features thousands of used CDs.
Branches: all over Tokyo.

Fujiya Avic

5-52-15 Nakano, Nakano-ku. (3386 5554). Nakano station. **Open** 10.30am-8pm. **Credit** AmEx, DC, JCB, MC, V. **Map** 26.
One store is mainly second-hand Japanese bands, the rest of the world is in the shop right next door. Thousands of used CDs, all at reasonable prices – on the third floor of the Nakano Broadway arcade.

HMV

24-1 Udagawa-cho, Shibuya-ku (5458 3411/ www.hmv.co.jp). Shibuya station. **Open** 10am-11pm daily. **Credit** AmEx, DC, JCB, MC, V. **Map** 2.
HMV is pretty much what you'd expect anywhere – an eclectic and detailed range of music in all formats.

Of special interest is the preview a floor, where viewers can chill out latest video and DVD releases.
Branches: all over Tokyo.

Rare Records

5-66-4 Nakano, Nakano-ku (3389 5110). Nakano station. **Open** 11am-9pm daily. **Credit** MC, V, JCB. **Map** 26.
Rare Records is close to Fujiya Avic (*see above*), and has a small but unfailingly interesting stock.

Tower Records

1-22-14 Jinnan, Shibuya-ku (3496 3661). Shibuya station. **Open** 10am-11pm daily. **Credit** AmEx, DC, JCB, MC, V. **Map** 2.
'No music no life', or so they say – this is still the favourite record shop of many a Tokyo music lover. It's not just the six floors devoted to all genres of music and video; there's also one of Tokyo's best bookstores on the seventh floor, with a wide range of books, magazines and newspapers in English.
Branches: Flags Bldg, 7-10F, 3-37-1 Shinjuku, Shinjuku (5360 7811); Ikebukuro Parco 5-6F, 1-50-35 Higashi-Ikebukuro, Toshima-ku (3983 2010).

Bargain hunting

Despite their reputation for profligacy, the Japanese, like everyone else, love a bargain. The hunt for value often starts with department stores, which have a series of set sale seasons. The New Year sales start on 3 January and continue for about a week. One gimmick that the different stores all share is the *fukubukuro*, or Lucky Bag. They sell at various prices, and contain a lucky dip of designer accessories, their combined worth being far more than the sale price. The summer sales start in either July or August, and there are also sometimes special one-off sales, for example if a baseball team sponsored by the store wins the Japan series.

Discount shops and stores exist in most neighbourhoods. There are the ubiquitous ¥100 shops, selling cutlery, toys and assorted knick-knacks. Secondhand shops have been springing up like mushrooms – just look for the word 'recycle' in Japanese. There are also the *kinken* shops, that sell discounted tickets for *shinkansen*, cinemas and department stores. Two well known *kinken* shops are **Ticket Showa** (Shinbashi station, 3580 7175) and **Go Go Ticket** (near Tokyu Hands, Shibuya, 3463 3000).

For foreign residents who are missing the comforts of home, and find the department stores and international supermarkets too

expensive, there are some great cheap finds to be had. The **Foreign Buyers Club** (www.fbcusa.com), operating from an island off the shores of Kobe, imports food and many other goods at discount prices. For cheap reads, you can spend a day browsing among the secondhand bookshops of the Yasukuni-Dori near Jinbocho station. Elsewhere, the I-Club of **Isetan** in Shinjuku (*see p162*) offers free membership to foreign residents. Benefits of joining the club include five per cent off all non-food purchases and free admission to all exhibitions at the **Isetan Gallery** (*see p98*).

However, if low-priced traditional Japanese memorabilia is what you're after, take a wander down one of the streets lined with antiques shops, such as Nishi-Ogikubo, Koto-dori, or the stalls around Sensoji Temple in Asakusa. There's a lot of junk, but you may find some surprises. There are also regular flea-markets held at various places once or twice a month (*see p166*).

Last but not least, the expat community in Tokyo is in a constant state of flux. There are city-wide information networks which allow you to find something you really need through the '*sayonara* sales', the best of places to look are the free magazines such as *Tokyo Noticeboard,* and the excellent *Tokyo Classified.*

Eat, Drink, Shop

inyl

Shop One; 7-4-7 Nishi-Shinjuku, Shinjuku-ku (3365 0910/www.vinyljapan.com). Shinjuku station. **Open** 12pm-9pm daily. **Credit** AmEx, DC, JCB, MC, V for purchases over ¥5,000. **Map** 1a.

The sheer range of this shop boggles the mind. Rare '60s, '70s, progressive rock, punk, mod, hip-hop, Japanese indies – it's all here on CD and, of course, vinyl. Take a stroll around this part of Shinjuku and you'll find a number of other shops selling rarities in bygone genres, from psychobilly to grunge.
Branches: Shop Two, 7-5-5 Nishi-Shinjuku, Shinjuku (5330-9141); Shop Three, 7-4-9 Nishi-Shinjuku, Shinjuku (3371-5961).

☆Virgin Megastore

3-30-16 Shinjuku, Shinjuku-ku (3353 0056/ www.virginmegastore.co.jp). Shinjuku San-chome station. **Open** 11am-10pm Thus-Tues.
Credit AmEx, DC, JCB, MC, V. **Map** 1b.

This arm of the Branson global empire can be found in the basement of the Marui City building. Although pretty much what you'd expect, the store does have an annoying habit of frequently rear-ranging its shelves, making things difficult to find on return visits.
Branch: Marui City Ikebukuro, B1, 3-28-13 Nishi-Ikebukuro, Toshima-ku (5952 5600).

Novelties & toys

The Japanese are renowned for making those peculiar, idiosyncratic, cute novelty items that are now such an integral part of the world's pop-culture. The shops below present a selection where you can buy some daffy souvenirs to take back with you.

Atom

1-16-4 Jingumae, Shibuya-ku (3403 9848). Harajuku station. **Open** 10.30am-7.30pm daily. **Credit** V.
Map 11.

This store, located on Takeshita-Dori, sells memo-rabilia of immortal anime character, Tetsuwan Atom, known as 'Astro-Boy' in the west. The other half of the shop sells cute and scatty accessories to cute and scatty teenagers.

Dept

B1, 6-25-8, Jingumae, Shibuya-ku (3499 2225). Harajuku station. **Open** 11am-8pm daily. **Credit** AmEx, DC, JCB, MC, V. **Map** 11.

Not purely Japanese tack, but an impressive display of indescribable subculture tack, nevertheless. Also sells second-hand clothes and jewellery.
Branches: 3-20-13, Jingumae, Shibuya-ku (3408-0561); 30-3 Sarugaku-cho Shibuya-ku (3464-4087).

Don Quixote

1-16-5 Kabuki-cho, Shinjuku (5291 9211/ www.donki.com). Shinjuku station. **Open** varies.
Credit cash preferred. **Map** 1b.

Roughly the same concept as Japan's ¥100 stores, but the interior and products could have been designed by Salvador Dali with a hangover. Some of the vast range of products on sale are Chinese Santa Claus costumes, cut-price robot insects, imported toffee with real (but dead) Mexican scor-pions in the middle. Or you could buy something sensible at prices much cheaper than a department store. The Shinjuku store is open 24 hours.
Branches: all over Tokyo.

Kiddyland

6-1-9 Jingumae, Shibuya-ku (3409 3431/ www.kiddyland.co.jp). Harajuku station. **Open** 10am-8pm daily. Closed third Tue of month. **Credit** AmEx, DC, JCB, MC, V. **Map** 11.

Contains everything from cuddly toys for babies to ultra-violent *anime* figures for... whoever. Although ostensibly a children's shop, its main clientele seems to be Japanese women in their twenties. A great place to shop for offbeat souvenirs and that Pikachu pencil-sharpener you've always wanted.

Lilliput

1F Softown Aoyama, 3-1-24 Jingumae, Shibuya-ku (3470 2020). Gaienmae station. **Open** 12noon-7pm daily. **Credit** AmEx, DC, JCB, MC, V. **Map** 12.

You thought Japanese mobile phones were small? Wait till you see this shop and its stock of miniature literature. Goods range from palm-sized cookery-books to a 13 millimetre by 9 millimetre copy of The Ten Commandments.

Manga no Mori

12-10 Udagawa-cho, Shibuya-ku (5489 0257/ www.manganomori.net). Shibuya station. **Open** 11am-9pm daily. **Credit** AmEx, DC, JCB, MC, V.
Map 2.

It's not really fair to describe *manga* (Japanese comics) as a novelty, seeing the part they have played in shaping post-war Japanese culture. Manga no Mori has one of the most comprehensive selec-tions in Tokyo – and for the sake of comparison, the Shibuya store has the latest imported titles from Marvel, DC and others.
Branches: 3-35-1 Shinjuku, Shinjuku-ku (3341 0921); 1-28-1 Higashi-Ikebukuro, (5396 1245).

Pokemon Centre

3-2-5 Nihonbashi, Chuo-ku (5200 0707). Nihonbashi station. **Open** 11am-8pm Thur-Tue. **Credit** AmEx, DC, JCB, MC, V. **Map** 8.

You've played the game, watched the films, bought the irritatingly cute merchandise, now visit the home of Pikachu and friends.

Village Vanguard

2-10-15 Kitazawa, Setagaya-ku, (3460 6145/ www.vvvnet.com). Shimo-Kitazawa station (Odakyu line). **Open** 10am-12midnight daily. **Credit** AmEx, DC, JCB, MC, V. **Map** 35.

At Village Vanguard you'll find movie posters, action figures, art books and a heap of nostalgic toys and products that will take you back to the child-hood age of discovery. They're all piled around the store in various forms of organised chaos.
Branches: all over Tokyo.

Arts &
Entertainment

By Season

A feast of festivals and special days keeps the city buzzing all year round.

Public holidays

Japan has 14 public holidays: New Year's Day (*Ganjitsu*) 1 January; Coming of Age Day (*Seijin no Hi*) second Monday in January; National Foundation Day (*Kenkoku Kinen no Hi*) 11 February; Vernal Equinox Day (*Shumbun no Hi*) around 21 March; Greenery Day (*Midori no Hi*) 29 April; Constitution Day (*Kempo Kinenbi*) 3 May; Children's Day (*Kodomo no Hi*) 5 May; Marine Day (*Umi no Hi*) 20 July; Respect for the Aged Day (*Keiro no Hi*) 15 September; Autumnal Equinox Day (*Shubun no Hi*) around 23 September; Sports Day (*Taiiku no Hi*) second Monday in October; Culture Day (*Bunka no Hi*) 3 November; Labour Thanksgiving Day (*Kinro Kansha no Hi*) 23 November; Emperor's Birthday (*Tenno Tanjobi*) 23 December.

Saturday is an official workday, but holidays falling on a Sunday shift to Monday. If both 3 May and 5 May fall on weekdays, 4 May also becomes a holiday.

Winter

Toyota Cup
National Stadium (Ticket Pia 5237 9999). Sendagaya station. **Date** late Nov.
Once the unofficial world club championship, the status and future of the Toyota Cup now seem less certain since FIFA has an alternative tournament featuring the top teams from every continent.

47 Ronin Memorial Service (Ako Gishi-sai)
Sengakuji Temple (information 3441 5560). Sengakuji station. **Date** various times 13-14 Dec.
The famous vendetta attack took place in the early hours of 31 January 1703, or 15 December by the old calendar. Two days of events, including dances, a parade in period costume and a Buddhist memorial ceremony, take place at the temple where the warriors are buried alongside their former master. There's also a parade in Ginza.

Battledore Market (Hagoita Ichi)
Sensoji Temple (information 3842 0181). Asakusa station.
Hagoita are paddle-shaped bats used to hit the shuttlecock in the traditional New Year game of *hanetsuki*. Ornamental versions come festooned with colourful pictures and many temples hold markets selling them in December. Sensoji is Tokyo's largest.

Emperor's Birthday (Tenno Tanjobi)
Date 23 Dec.
The only day apart from 2 January when the public is allowed to enter the inner palace grounds.

Christmas
Date 24-25 Dec.
The most romantic day of the year is Christmas Eve: couples celebrate with extravagant dates, involving fancy restaurants and love hotels. Not many locals do anything special to mark the following day, despite the battery of fairy lights, decorated trees and piped carols deployed by department stores.

Year End

Date 28-31 Dec.

The last official day of work is 28 December; people then begin a frantic round of last-minute house cleaning, decoration-hanging and food preparation. Many stay at home on the last night of the year to catch NHK's eternally popular *Red and White Singing Contest*, although huge crowds make it to shrines and temples for midnight, when bells are rung 108 times to welcome in the New Year.

New Year's Day (Ganjitsu)

Many locations, including Meiji Shrine & Sensoji Temple (tourist information 3201 3331). **Date** 1 Jan.

The most important holiday of the year sees large crowds fill temples and shrines to bursting point for that all-important first visit of the New Year. Otherwise, New Year's Day is a quiet family affair, except for postmen staggering under enormous sacks of New Year cards, which are traditionally sent to just about anyone you've ever met. Only the first day of the year is an official holiday but most shops and businesses close until 4 January.

Emperor's Cup Final

Information 5237 9955/Ticket Pia 5237 9999. **Date** 1 Jan.

The showpiece event of Japan's domestic soccer season at the National Stadium (*see p230*) is the climax of the main cup competition. It kicks off at 1.30pm.

New Year Congratulatory Visit (Ippan Sanga)

Date 2 Jan.

The public is allowed into the inner grounds of the Imperial Palace (*see p62*) on two days a year; this is one of them (the emperor's birthday is the other). Seven times during the day, between 9.30am and 3pm, the symbol of the state appears on a balcony of the palace with other members of the royal family to wave to the crowds from behind bullet-proof glass.

St Patrick's Day Parade gives locals the chance to dress up and demonstrate their skills in Gaelic dancing and music. *See p186.*

Tokyo Metropolitan Fire Brigade Parade (Dezome-shiki)

Plaza in front of Tokyo Big Site, 3-21-2 Ariake, Koto-ku (tourist information 3201 3331). **Date** morning of 6 Jan.

The highlight is a display by members of the Preservation Association of the old Edo Fire Brigade, who dress in traditional *hikeshi* firefighters' garb and perform acrobatic stunts at the top of long ladders. Modern equipment is also featured.

New Year Grand Sumo Tournament (Ozumo Hatsu Basho)

Kokugikan, Ryogoku station. **Date** 10am-6pm mid-Jan.

First of the year's three full 15-day sumo tournaments in Tokyo. These are held from the second to the fourth Sunday of January, May and September.

Coming of Age Day (Seijin no Hi)

Meiji Shrine & others (tourist information 3201 3331). **Date** 2nd Mon of Jan.

Those reaching the age of 20 in the 12 months to April make their way to shrines in their best *kimono* and suits for blessings and photos. The traditional date of 15 January generally coincides with New Year's Day under the old lunar calendar.

Chinese New Year

Yokohama Chinatown, East Gate (Yokohama tourist information 045 641 4759). Ishikawacho station (JR Keihin Tohoku line). **Date** Jan/Feb.

Cymbals crash and dragon dancers weave their way along the restaurant-lined streets of Yokohama Chinatown as the local community celebrates its big party of the year.

Setsubun

Various locations, including Sensoji Temple & Zojoji Temple (tourist information 3201 3331). **Date** 3 Feb.

Much hurling of soybeans to cries of '*oni wa soto, fuki wa uchi*' ('demons out, good luck in') as the last day of winter by the lunar calendar is celebrated in homes, shrines and temples. The tradition is to eat one bean for every year of one's age. Sumo wrestlers and other celebrities are among those doing the casting out in ceremonies at well-known Tokyo shrines.

National Foundation Day (Kenkoku Kinen no Hi)

Date 11 Feb.

A public holiday commemorating the supposed beginnings of Japan's imperial line in 660 BC, the date when mythical first emperor Jimmu, a descendent of sun goddess Amaterasu Omikami, is said to have ascended to the throne. After World War II, the public holiday on 11 February was abolished; this one was inaugurated, amid controversy, in 1966.

Valentine's Day

Date 14 Feb.

Introduced into Japan by confectionery company innovators as the day when women give chocolates to men: there's a large heart-shaped treat for that special someone, plus *giri choko* (obligation chocolates) to a wider circle of male associates. In theory, favours get returned in kind by the boys one month later, on White Day.

Plum Blossoms

Yushima Tenjin Shrine (information 3836 0753). **Date** mid-Feb to mid-Mar

The delicate white blooms arrive a little earlier than the better known cherry blossoms, and are generally celebrated in a more restrained fashion. Yushima Tenjin Shrine, a prime viewing spot, also holds a month-long festival featuring traditional arts such as *ikebana* (flower-arranging) and tea ceremony.

Dolls Festival (Hina Matsuri)

Date 3-4 Mar.

A special festival for girls. *Kimono*-clad dolls representing traditional court figures are displayed on a multi-tiered red stand, and the arrangement takes pride of place in the home on the big day.

Daruma Fair

Jindaiji Shrine (information 0424 86 5511). **Date** 3-4 Mar.

After meditating in a cave for nine years, Bodhidharma, a Zen monk from ancient India, is reputed to have lost the use of all four limbs. The cuddly red figure of the Daruma doll, which is modelled after him, also lacks eyes; the first gets painted in for good luck when a difficult task is undertaken, the second on its successful completion. Jindaiji was first established in AD 733, making it among the oldest temples in Tokyo. Its Daruma fair is one of the biggest.

Spring

Fire-Walking Ceremony (Hi-watari)

Kotsu Anzen Kitosho (information 0426 61 1115). Takaosan-guchi station (Keio line). **Date** mid-Mar.

At the foot of Mount Takao, hardy *yamabushi* mountain monks from Yakuoin Temple walk barefoot across burning coals while chanting incantations. Members of the public are then invited to test their own hardiness of soul and sole by following suit.

White Day

Date 14 Mar.

Male recipients of Valentine's Day confectionery are supposed to show their appreciation with a return gift of white chocolates.

St Patrick's Day Parade

Omotesando Dori. Harajuku station. **Date** from around noon on 17 Mar or nearest Sun.

Local devotees of traditional Gaelic culture demonstrate their baton-twirling, drumming, pipe-playing and dancing skills at this popular parade, which is led by Ireland's ambassador and celebrated its tenth anniversary in 2001. Along the route, friendly representatives of the city's Irish hosteleries hand out discount vouchers for liquid refreshment.

The end of March brings cherry blossom, an excuse for the week of excess that is *Hanami*.

Tokyo Game Show

Makuhari Messe Convention Centre (information 3591 1421/www.cesa.or.jp/tgs/english.html). Kaihin Makuhari station (Keiyo line). **Date** late Mar & late Sept. **Admission** ¥1,200.

The biggest computer and video game show on the planet pulls in crowds of up to 200,000 for two weekends, one in spring and one in autumn.

Vernal Equinox Day (Shumbun no Hi)

Date around 21 Mar.

Many people visit family graves on this day, since it falls in the middle of *higan*, a week-long, twice-yearly Buddhist memorial service.

Cherry-Blossom Viewing (Hanami)

Popular spots include Ueno Park, Sumida Park, Yasukuni Shrine, Shinjuku-Gyoen, Aoyama Cemetery (information 3201 3331). **Date** late Mar-early Apr.

The great outdoor event of the year sees popular viewing spots invaded by hordes of nature-loving locals. Some prefer quiet contemplation of the explosion of pink petals up on the trees, while others use the occasion for some serious partying. Cases of alcohol poisoning are not unknown and ambulance crews remain on alert.

New Fiscal Year

Date 1 Apr.

April Fool's Day marks the start of Japan's financial and academic calendars. Big companies hold speech-filled ceremonies to welcome the year's graduate intake to the rigours of corporate life.

Start of Baseball Season

Tokyo Dome or Jingu Baseball Stadium (information 3811 2111/Ticket Pia 5237 9999). **Date** early Apr.

The long and winding road to the October play-offs usually gets underway with a three-game Central League series featuring the Giants, the city's perennial favourites. There's extra spice if the opposition is the Swallows, the capital's other big team, or the Giants' deadliest rivals, the Hanshin Tigers.

Horseback Archery (Yabusame)

Sumida Park (information 5246 1111). Asakusa station. **Date** mid-Apr.

Mounted riders in medieval warrior gear shoot arrows at stationary targets while galloping along at full tilt. There's also a big *yabusame* festival at Tsurugaoka Hachimangu Shrine in Kamakura in mid-September; the practice can also be seen during the autumn festival at Meiji Shrine on 3 November.

Meiji Jingu Shrine Spring Festival (Haru no Taisai)

Meiji Jingu Shrine, 1-1 Kamizonocho, Yoyogi, Shibuya-ku. (information 3379 5511). Harajuku station. **Date** 29 Apr, 2-3 May. **Admission** free.

Daily free performances of traditional entertainment, including *gagaku* and *bugaku* imperial court music and dance, plus *noh* and *kyogen* drama.

Golden Week

Date 29 Apr-5 May.

Put three public holidays (Greenery Day, Constitution Day and Children's Day) in close proximity on the calendar and there's the serious vacation opportunity known as Golden Week. Planes, trains

Arts & Entertainment

and automobiles hit double gridlock as people flee the big city *en masse*, then all head home again together. Tokyo remains relatively quiet, with many smaller shops and restaurants closed for the duration of the week.

Greenery Day (Midori no Hi)
Date 29 Apr.
A nature appreciation day to begin Golden Week. Previously celebrated as the birthday of Emperor Showa (Hirohito).

International Labour Day
Date 1 May.
Despite falling in the middle of Golden Week, the day when workers of the world unite in celebration is not an official holiday in Japan. Many vacationing trade unionists meet for a rally in Yoyogi Park.

Constitution Day (Kempo Kinenbi)
Date 3 May.
Commemorates the day in 1947 when the US-imposed pacifist constitution came into operation.

Children's Day (Kodomo no Hi)
Date 5 May.
A traditional festival for boys; the corresponding one for girls is the dolls' festival on 3-4 March (which isn't a public holiday). Celebrations include the hanging of paper streamers in the shape of carp.

Kanda Festival
Organised from Kanda Myojin Shrine (information 3254 0753). Date mid-May.
One of the city's traditional 'Big Three' festivals, this is held in odd-numbered years, alternating with the Sanno festival. In Edo days, it was a particular favourite of the local townspeople, due to Kanda Myojin's links with the popular tenth-century rebel Taira no Masakado. Events include *shinkosai* rites with participants parading in Heian costume, plus a gala procession that crisscrosses the Kanda area and features a number of festival floats and *mikoshi* portable shrines.

Sanja Festival
Organised from Asakusa Shrine (information 3844 1575). Date mid-May.
The biggest of the city's annual festivals, Sanja attracts huge crowds to Asakusa and honours the three seventh-century founders of Sensoji Temple. It climaxes after several days of events with three huge *mikoshi* portable shrines (*sanja*) that carry the spirits of the three men being paraded around local streets. Each needs dozens of people to carry it.

Tokyo Lesbian & Gay Parade
Yoyogi Park (information 3380 0363/www.tlgp.org/index.html). Harajuku station. Date late May.
A recent addition to the Tokyo scene, which organisers are hoping to make a regular annual event.

Summer

Sanno Festival
Organised from Hie Shrine (information 3581 2471). Date 10-16 June.
Another of the 'Big Three' festivals, Sanno alternates with the Kanda festival and is held in its full splendour on even-numbered years. Hie Shrine, which had close links with the Tokugawa *shogun*, is near today's central government district. The main procession skirts the edge of the Imperial Palace, with participants in Heian-period costumes and priests on horses, plus all the usual festival floats and *mikoshi*. Participants are historically allowed to penetrate the inner sanctum of the Imperial Palace.

Iris Viewing
Various locations, including Meiji Shrine Inner Garden & Horikiri Iris Garden (information 3201 3331). Date mid-June.
The annual blooming of the purple and white flowers falls during the grey humid days of the rainy season, but is no less popular for that.

Mount Fuji Climbing Season
Date 1 July-31 Aug.
It's claimed that everyone should climb Mount Fuji once in their life, though more than that is said to be excessive. The perfectly formed cone of Japan's favourite dormant volcano is all but lost in the summer haze from most Tokyo vantage points, but many enthusiastic walkers head out for that one-off push to the summit, often at night in order to catch the sunrise.

Ground-Cherry Market (Hozuchi-ichi)
Sensoji Temple, 2-3-1 Asakusa, Taito-ku (information 3842 0181). Asakusa station. Date 9-10 July.
On these two days in July, prayers at Sensoji are said to be the spiritual equivalent of 46,000 days' worth at other times. Big crowds are attracted by this spiritual bargain. A ground-cherry market takes place at the temple over the same period.

International Lesbian & Gay Film Festival
Spiral Bldg, 5-6-23 Minami-Aoyama, Minato-ku. (information 5380 5760/http://l-gff.gender.ne.jp/). Omotesando station. Date mid-July.
Celebrating its tenth anniversary in 2001, the LGFF lasts around five days and offers a rare chance for locals to catch up on the best of gay cinema from around the world. In past years the venues have switched regularly, so keep an eye on the website.

Marine Day (Umi no Hi)
Date 20 July.
Introduced in 1996, this is a public holiday celebrating the benefits and bounty of the sea.

Sumida River Fireworks

Asakusa station area (information 5246 1111).
Date 7pm on last Sat in July.
First held in 1733, this is the daddy of Tokyo's many summer firework events: the oldest, biggest and most crowded. Up to 20,000 *hanabi* ('flower-fires') light up the night skies, and as many as a million people pack streets, bridges and rooftops, eyes trained upward. Waterfront locations also tend to be favoured for other big displays. Get there early to be sure of a decent view, as the event regularly attracts crowds of close to one million people.

Fuji Rock Festival

Naeba Ski Resort, Niigata (information 3444 6751/ http://smash-jpn.com). **Date** late July/early Aug.
This annual outdoor music mega-festival pulls together major rock and dance acts from Japan and overseas, with a 2000 line-up that featured Foo Fighters, Primal Scream and Moby, among many others. Despite the name, the festival has not been held near Japan's most famous mountain since the inaugural event back in 1997 was hit by a typhoon.

Obon

Date 13-15 Aug.
The souls of the departed are supposed to return briefly to the world of the living during this Buddhist festival honouring the spirits of ancestors. Observances include welcoming fires, *Bon* dances and night-time floating of lanterns on open water. Although there's no public holiday, many companies give workers time off to visit the folks back home, leaving the capital unusually, and refreshingly, quiet for a few days.

War-End Anniversary

Yasukuni Shrine. Ichigaya station. **Date** 15 Aug.
The annual anniversary of Japan's surrender to the allied forces is still a source of diplomatic friction with neighbouring countries. Many leading politicians mark the day by visiting Yasukuni Shrine, where the souls of Japan's war-dead, including those executed as war criminals, are honoured.

Asakusa Samba Carnival

Asakusa station area (information 3847 0038).
Date late Aug.
Thousands of gorgeously costumed samba dancers, some Brazilian but most Japanese, shake their stuff in the heart of old downtown Tokyo. It's a startling spectacle, with plenty of competition among teams for the cash prize that goes to the parade's top troupe, along with the honour of closing the festival.

Awa Odori

Koenji station area (information 3312 2111). **Date** late Aug.
Street carnival Japanese-style. This annual shindig features a form of traditional Tokushima folk dance known as the Fool's Dance. As the raucous refrain of the accompanying light-hearted song puts it, 'You're a fool whether you dance or not, so you may as well dance'.

Tokyo's parks in autumn can be spectacular.

Autumn

Tokyo Earthquake Anniversary

Date 1 Sept.
The day when the city authorities test emergency relief preparations and hold practice drills across the city, on the anniversary of the 1923 disaster.

International Super Track & Field

Yokohama International Stadium (information 045 477 5000/Ticket Pia 5237 9999). Shin-Yokohama station. **Date** mid-Sept.
Usually the last big outdoor meeting of the international athletics calendar, so there tends to be a relaxed atmosphere among the assembled galaxy of record-setters, medal-winners and other track stars.

Respect for the Aged Day (Keiro no Hi)

Date 15 Sept.
Respect for the Aged Day is held to mark the 1966 enactment of the Law on Welfare for the Aged. Japan has the world's highest life expectancy and a population that is ageing rapidly: in 1997 people aged 65 or over exceeded those aged 14 or under.

Autumnal Equinox Day (Shubun no Hi)

Date on or around 23 Sept.
Like the spring equinox, the autumn equinox coincides with the mid-point of *higan*, the seven-day Buddhist memorial service.

Arts & Entertainment

γ the harvest moon have been ...y ever since the Edo era, but the search for clear night-skies means that somewhat less urban venues are favoured nowadays. Some non-traditionalists find solace in the annual 'Tsukimi Burger' promotion, recognising a distinctly lunar quality to the fried egg that comes as an added seasonal ingredient. Traditionalists may head out for *tsukimi soba*, which comes complete with raw egg.

Takigi Noh

Various venues. **Date** various times in Sept/Oct.
Atmospheric outdoor performances of medieval *noh* drama are staged at a number of shrines, temples and parks, illuminated by flickering flames from bonfires and torches.

CEATEC Japan

Makuhari Messe Convention Centre (information 5402 7603). Kaihin Makuhari station (Keiyo line). **Date** early Oct. **Admission** ¥1,000
Bringing together the Japan Electronics Show and COM JAPAN, this was held for the first time in 2000. The new format means it's not only the place to check out all the latest gadgets before they hit the shops, but also where to see cutting-edge communications and information technology in action.

Japan Tennis Open

Ariake Coliseum (information 5474 5944/Ticket Pia 5237 9999). Ariake station (Yurikamome line). **Date** early Oct.
The international tennis circus hits town for the nation's premier event. Local interest tends to focus on the women's tournament.

Sports Day (Taiiku no Hi)

Date 2nd Mon in Oct.
The traditional date of 10 October commemorates the opening day of the 1964 Tokyo Olympics.

Tokyo Motor Show

Makuhari Messe Convention Centre (information 3211 8829/www.motorshow.or.jp). Kaihin Makuhari station (Keiyo line). **Date** late Oct-early Nov. **Admission** ¥1,000.
The Tokyo Motor Show is an important showcase for the gleaming new high-tech products of car manufacturers both domestic and foreign. Passenger cars and motorbikes are featured in odd-numbered years; commercial vehicles in even ones.

Chrysanthemum Festival

Meiji Shrine Inner Garden (information 3379 5511). **Date** late Oct-late Nov.
The start of autumn was traditionally marked in Japan by the Chrysanthemum festival on the ninth day of the ninth month of the old lunar calendar. The delicate pale blooms are also represented on the crest of Japan's Imperial family.

Culture Day (Bunka no Hi)

Date 3 Nov.
A host of Japanese artists and writers, plus other luminaries, pick up Order of Culture government awards on a day set aside for cultural activities to celebrate the peace-loving democratic ideals of the constitution, promulgated on this day in 1946.

Meiji Jingu Shrine Grand Autumn Festival (Reisai)

Meiji Jingu Shrine (information 3379 5511). Harajuku station. **Date** 3 Nov. **Admission** free.
In former times, Culture Day celebrated the birthday of the Meiji Emperor (1852-1912), and the biggest annual festival of the Meiji Shrine still takes place on the same date. There are performances of traditional music and theatre, along with *yabusame* horseback archery.

Tokyo International Film Festival

Bunkamura & other venues in Shibuya (information 3563 6407/www.tokyo-filmfest.or.jp). **Date** early Nov.
The largest film festival in Japan attracts a glittering influx of international movie talent for the serious business of the various competitions and special promotional screenings of upcoming Hollywood blockbusters. There are also Japanese cinema classics, an Asian film award, as well as an International Fantastic Film Festival, Women's Film Week and other related events.

Seven-Five-Three Festival (Shichi-go-san)

Various locations, including Meiji Jingu Shrine (information 3201 3331). **Date** 15 Nov.
Tradition has it that children of certain ages (three, five and seven) are strangely susceptible to misfortune. One way out of this problem is to get any family member with the wrong number of birthday cake candles down to a Shinto shrine on 15 November to pray for divine protection, so important shrines are besieged by hordes of kids in their best *kimono*.

Autumn Leaves (Koyo)

Many locations, including Shinjuku Gyoen, Ueno Park & Meiji Jingu Gaien Park (information 3201 3331). **Date** 2nd half of Nov.
The spectacular autumnal colours of maple and ginko trees transform many of Tokyo's parks and gardens into a blaze of reds and yellows.

Labour Thanksgiving Day (Kinro Kansha no Hi)

Date 23 Nov.
A public holiday when people are supposed to thank one another for all their hard work through the year.

Japan Cup

Tokyo Racetrack (information 042 363 3141/Ticket Pia 5237 9999). Fuchu-honmachi station (JR Musashino line). **Date** late Nov.
Top horses and jockeys from round the world race Japan's elite over 2,400m.

Children

Bright lights, big city, little horrors.

The deep-rooted idea that Tokyo is a concrete jungle dies hard. The truth is, Tokyo's economic power has made possible the preservation of many natural areas and playgrounds, while the large concentration of population has made the operation of many children's facilities economically viable. In short, Tokyo is actually a better place for raising kids than many other Japanese cities. As with many Tokyo sights and buildings, facilities often close on Monday, except when Monday is a national holiday, in which case they close on Tuesday instead. None of the venues listed accepts credit cards.

Meeting other families

Gaien Higashi Jido Yuen
1-7-5 Kita-Aoyama, Minato-ku (3478 0550). Aoyama-Itchome station. **Open** *Mar-Oct* 9.30am-5pm daily. *Nov-Feb* 9.30am-4.30pm daily. **Admission** ¥200; ¥50 2-12s. **Map** 12.
This is a good place to find playmates for your children. The park is set in the pleasant surroundings of the Jingu Gaien, the outer gardens of the Meiji Jingu shrine, which also contain baseball and rugby stadiums, an athletics track and other sporting facilities. The admission fee is unusual for such a small park, but is justified by its excellent playing equipment. The park is divided into sections for toddlers, pre-schoolers and school-age children, but an ambitious child can tackle the equipment for older kids under parental supervision. Vending machines sell ice-cream, hamburgers and cup noodles. **Yoyogi Park** and **Shinjuku Gyoen** (*see p88 for both*) are other popular weekend destinations for families.

Furry friends

Inokashira Nature & Culture Park
1-17-6 Gotenyama, Musashino-shi (0422 461100). Kichijoji station. **Open** 9.30am-4.30pm Tue-Sun. **Admission** ¥400; ¥150 middle school children. **Map** 31.
This park, adjacent to Inokashira Park, never gets overcrowded, and features a zoo, greenhouse and small amusement park. Near the entrance is a guinea-pig petting section, but most kids gravitate towards Hanako the elephant. Another popular attraction is the caged squirrels; visitors are free to enter the cage and feed them. At the far end of the park, there is a range of 100-yen rides, including a minitrain and a merry-go-round. A ride on the mini bullet train is particularly exciting.

Ueno Zoo
9-83 Ueno-Koen, Taito-ku (3828 5171). Ueno station. **Open** 9.30am-5pm Tue-Sun. **Admission** ¥500; ¥200 middle school children living or studying outside Tokyo. **Map** 14.
This is the oldest and best-known zoo in Japan, though sensitive parents may balk at the conditions some animals are kept in. The star attraction for kids is the lone panda that has survived the death of its two playmates. At weekends, expect to see more of the heads of other visitors than of animals. Pushchairs are available to parents with small children at a cost of ¥300. Zoo staff in the petting section take great pains to teach children how to feed and interact with cattle.

Aquariums

Itabashi Ward Aquarium
3-50-1 Itabashi, Itabashi-ku (aquarium 3962 8419/ zoo 3963 8003). Itabashi Kuyakusho-Mae station (Toei Mita line). **Open** *Mar-Nov* 10am-4.30pm Tue-Sun. *Dec-Feb* 10am-4pm Tue-Sun. **Admission** free.
This freshwater aquarium is inside Itabashi Higashi Park, where you'll also find the Itabashi Ward Children's Zoo. The zoo and aquarium, although small, are among the least-explored such facilities in Tokyo, and offer a real opportunity to mingle with animals. The aquarium keeps most of the creatures, including turtles and shrimps, in open tanks, so you can see and smell them (not always the most pleasant experience) close up. The Children's Zoo offers free pony rides twice a day at 10.30am and 3.30pm, with riding tickets handed out 30 minutes ahead of each riding time. The zoo has two petting sections, one for guinea pigs and another for sheep and goats. Zoo staff keep the petting sections clean and tidy, and washing facilities are provided to make sure your kids go home the same way.

Tokyo Sea Life Park
6-2-3 Rinkai-cho, Edogawa-ku (3869 5152). Kasai Rinkai Koen station. **Open** 9.30am-5pm Tue-Sun (ticket sales end at 4pm). **Admission** ¥800; ¥300 middle school children.
Located within Kasai Seaside Park, this is Tokyo's most popular aquarium with young city dwellers, situated as it is right next door to Disneyland. It's also a popular spot for dating couples. The park and aquarium are best described as modern, perhaps too modern. The aquarium keeps fish from around the world, including tuna and sharks, in beautifully lit tanks, but they can only be observed through thick glass windows. The concrete seashore detracts somewhat from the park's already limited charm.

Making a splash

Hyogoshima Park

3-2-1 Tamagawa, Setagaya-ku (3704 4972).
Futako-Tamagawa station (Tokyu Shintamagawa/
Ooimachi lines).

For those who want to dip their toes in a less crowded, more natural setting, this is the place to go. Located conveniently near the Futako Tamagawa station, the park is basically a dry riverbed formed between the Tama and No rivers. The park offers several shallow streams where kids can dip their legs and splash, all in view of the Tama riverbank. The park is adjacent to fields. Further upstream there is a cycling course.

Toshimaen Hydropolis

3-25-1 Koyama, Nerima-ku (3990 8800). Toshimaen
station (Toei Oedo line/Seibu Toshima line). **Open**
July, Aug 9am-7pm daily (precise dates vary each year). **Admission** ¥4,200; ¥3,800 elementary school children; ¥1,200 pre-school children over 3.

Toshimaen, one of the oldest amusement parks in Tokyo, has swimming facilities including a wave pool, a flowing pool and waterfalls, with the highlight being 31 water slides, which come in a variety of shapes and sizes. Long queues usually form at these slides during the school summer holidays from late July through August. Access has improved dramatically since the completion of the Oedo line in December 2000.

Cycling with kids

Recreational cycling courses, away from Tokyo's crowded pavements and roads.

Futako Tamagawa Ryokuchi Undojo

1-3-5 Kamata, Setagaya-ku (3709 3104). Futako-
Tamagawa station (Tokyu Shintamagawa/Ooimachi
lines), then bus to Kinuta Honmura.

The athletics fields by the Tama River offer two cycling paths; a 2.2km (1.4-mile) course within the fields and a 2.4km (1.5-mile) trip along the riverbank toward the Tomei Expressway. Seventy rental bikes, including 20 for kids, are available free of charge for an hour, but only on Sundays and holidays.

Koganei Park

1-13-1 Sekino-machi, Koganei-shi (042 385 5611).
Musashi-Koganei station.

A cycling track here lets you explore the central part of this large park in western Tokyo. About 120 bikes are available for pre-schoolers and their parents. If your child tires of pedalling, they can try sledging down an artificial turf-covered slope built into one of the park's grassy knolls. The 17-degree slope is wide enough for at least a dozen sledges to race down at the same time. Many visitors to the park bring their own sledges, but you can buy one at a nearby concession stand or borrow one of the park's by queueing at the bottom of the slope. With plenty of grass to sit on, Koganei Park is one of

Animal antics at **Ueno Zoo**. *See p191.*

Tokyo's pleasantest, for both parents and children. It also houses the outdoor branch of the **Edo-Tokyo Museum**, a fascinating collection of buildings saved from the bulldozer (*see p103*).

Indoor amusements

National Children's Castle

5-53-1 Jingumae, Shibuya-ku (3797 5666/
www.kodomo-shiro.or.jp). Shibuya or
Omotesando station. **Open** 12.30-5.30pm
Tue-Fri; 10am-5.30pm Sat, Sun. **Admission** ¥500;
¥400 3-17s. **Map** 2.

Another fabulous play hall near the Metropolitan Children's Hall (*see below*), with similar services on a fee-paying basis. Facilities include indoor climbing equipment and a playhouse on the third floor, and a music lobby on the fourth floor. The playport in the roof garden on the fifth floor is the castle's biggest attraction, combining a jungle gym with large ball pools. Access to the playport is restricted to children over the age of three, and it closes on rainy days. A 25m x 10m swimming pool on the second basement floor reopened in April 2001, but requires an additional fee.

Tokyo Metropolitan Children's Hall

1-18-24 Shibuya, Shibuya-ku (3409 6361/
www.jidokaikan.metro.tokyo.jp). Shibuya station.
Open *July, Aug* 9am-6pm daily. *Sept-June* 9am-5pm daily. Closed 2nd, 4th Mon of month, 29 Dec-3 Jan. **Admission** free. **Map** 2.

Located conveniently near Shibuya, the Tokyo Metropolitan Children's Hall, a public facility, is a real gem, its six-storey building packed with recreational and educational facilities. It is also the largest of 600 public children's halls in Tokyo. (For information about children's halls near your place of stay, contact the **Tokyo Metropolitan Government Foreign Residents' Advisory Service**; *see p271.*) The second floor here is reserved for pre-schoolers, offering large wooden climbing frames and wooden toys. The third floor features a handicraft section, the 'human body maze' and a ball pool, the simplest and virtually always the most popular play area. Books can be borrowed from a library on the fifth floor, while up on the roof, kids can have a go at rollerskating and unicycling. Each floor has plenty of lockers, so you can stash your belongings here while playing with your kids. On your way out, be sure to pick up a copy of the monthly events schedule at the information centre.

Transportation Museum
1-25 Kanda-Sudacho, Chiyoda-ku (3251 8481/ www.kouhaku.or.jp). Akihabara or Kanda station.
Open 9.30am-5pm Tue-Sun. Closed 29 Dec-2 Jan.
Admission ¥310; ¥150 4-15s. **Map** 17.
Young railway enthusiasts and public service vehicle fans of all ages congregate here to clamber over a variety of steam engines, train carriages and drivers' cabs. A simulator offers the chance to drive a train for yourself.

Shopping

Akachan Honpo
7-18 Yokoyama-cho, Nihonbashi, Chuo-ku (3662 7651/www.akachan.co.jp). Bakuracho or Bakura Yokoyama station (Toei Shinjuku line).
Open 10am-6pm daily.
This speciality shop offers children's equipment at budget prices. A membership fee of ¥1,000 entitles you to shop at Akachan Honpo's four outlets in Tokyo and receive information about special sales. Akachan Honpo's main outlet in Nihonbashi sells children's and maternity goods, while toys and holiday supplies are provided at two separate outlets nearby. The main store's seven-storey building, with its small toilets, is not popular with parents. The outlets in Nihonbashi and Gotanda have no car park, but limited parking space is available at outlets in Adachi and Itabashi.

BorneLund
Hara Bldg 1F, 6-10-9 Jingumae, Shibuya-ku (5485 3430/www.bornelund.co.jp). Meiji Jingumae or Harajuku station. **Open** 11am-7.30pm daily. Closed 30 Dec-2 Jan. **Map** 11.
This small shop near Omotesando has a great selection of wooden toys, mostly imports from Europe and North America. Unless you are more likely to find better Christmas presents here than in other local rivals, such as **Kiddyland** (*see p182*).

Toys R' Us
1-1-1 Kasuga-cho, Nerima-ku (3998 0114/ www.toysrus.co.jp). Toshimaen station (Toei Oedo/Seibu Toshima lines).
Open 10am-8pm daily.
Set up in November 2000, this massive warehouse is the US toy maker's first independent outlet in inner Tokyo. It is conveniently located next to the station and Toshimaen amusement park. Spacious toilets, breastfeeding rooms and hot water for mixing formula are a boon to mothers. Toys R' Us allows shoppers to touch and play with most toys before purchasing, so both parents and kids are sure to have great time here. The store sells computer games and early learning equipment, too. Toys R' Us has smaller outlets in Kameido, Ikebukuro, Odaiba and Itabashi.

Babysitting

The following babysitter services are reputable and each one comes highly recommended by Tokyo parents. Your hotel may be able to arrange babysitting, but the following agencies all have qualified, well-trained and caring staff.

Rates vary but expect to pay between ¥1,500 and ¥2,200 per hour. Some agencies demand a minimum of three hours at a set rate before they agree to send out a sitter, then you pay for each additional hour, with different rates for late-night and early-morning services.

As a rule do not expect the agencies to speak a wide variety of languages, though from time to time some do have babysitters who speak a little English or French.

Japan Baby-Sitter Service
(3423 1251). **Open** 9am-6pm Mon-Fri.
One of the oldest services in Tokyo, specialising in grandmotherly types. Reserve 24 hours in advance.

Little Mate
Keio Plaza Hotel (3345 1439). **Open** 24hrs daily.
Okura Hotel (3582 0111 ext 3838). **Open** 10am-8pm daily.
Little Mate is a day nursery where you can drop your children off for an hour or longer. Reservations are required by 7pm the previous day. For hotel addresses, *see p33.*

Poppins Service
(3447 2100). **Open** 9.30 am-5.30pm Mon-Sat.
Expect either a young lady trained in early childhood education or a retired veteran teacher when you request a sitter from Poppins. One of the best, one of the most expensive.

Tom Sawyer Agency
(3770 9530). **Open** 9am-10.30pm Mon-Fri; 12.30-9.30pm Sat, Sun. 24hr reservation system.
This very reputable Shibuya agency has branches all over Japan. Reserve by 8pm the night before you plan to go out.

Arts & Entertainment

Film

Art houses and indies offer the best chance of a good night at the flicks.

Going to a film in Tokyo can be a chaotic, dispiriting experience. Advance tickets are sold at convenience stores, not just the cinema, so for any given screening, any number of people can turn up with a valid ticket. If you want to book a seat in advance, you will have to pay a premium of ¥200-¥1,200 on top of the already inflated price of around ¥1,800. At popular cinemas, queues often start one hour early, and once the previous show is over, the next wave of viewers rushes in to grab the best seats.

The highlight of the cinematic year is the Tokyo Film Festival, which takes place in the cinemas of Shibuya every October and occasionally screens major world premières. The blockbuster multiplex is a recent arrival here, and most are sited out in the sticks. On the plus side, art-house cinemas, so-called 'Mini Theatres' are becoming increasingly common, offering idiosyncratic programming, cheaper seats, and sometimes bizarre pricing policies (*see p195* **It costs *how* much?**). None of the cinemas listed accepts credit cards.

Ciné La Sept for international charmers.

Cinemas

Athénée Français Cultural Centre

4F, 2-11 Kanda Surugadai, Chiyoda-ku (3291 4339). Suidobashi station. **Tickets** ¥600-¥1,000 members; ¥1,000-¥1,500 non-members. **Map 15.**
Hall accompanying a language school. Main themes are the re-evaluation of classics and the discovery of new film-makers.

Box Higashi Nakano

Polepoleza Bldg B1/2F, 4-4-1 Higashi Nakano, Nakano-ku (5389 6780). Higashi-Nakano station. **Tickets** ¥1,700.
Small, subterranean cinema showing everything from Japanese classics to cult movies such as *The Rocky Horror Picture Show.*

Ciné Amuse

ÇSF, 2-23-12 Dogenzaka, Shibuya-ku (3496 2888). Shibuya station. **Tickets** ¥1,800. **Map 2.**
Divided into two screens, East and West, Ciné Amuse shows a mixture of classics and new films from around world.

Ciné La Sept

2-8-6 Yurakucho, Chiyoda-ku (3212 3761). Yurakucho station. **Tickets** ¥1,800. **Map 6.**
An interesting mixture of home-grown films and less-well-known international charmers in this authentic-looking art house.

Ciné Pathos

4-8-7 Ginza, Chuo-ku (3561 4660). Ginza station. **Tickets** ¥1,800. **Map 6.**
Three screens showing recent independent films.

Cinema Qualité

Shinjuku Musashino Bldg 3F, 3-27-10 Shinjuku-ku (3354 5670). Shinjuku station. **Tickets** ¥1,800. **Map 1b.**
Three-screen cinema that mixes new films with revivals. Great for black-and-white classics.

Ciné Quinto

Parco Part3 8F, 14-5 Udagawa-cho, Shibuya-ku (3477 5905). Shibuya station. **Tickets** ¥1,800. **Map 2.**
New British films are shown here frequently. Good sound and comfortable seats.

Cinema Rise

13-17 Udagawa-cho, Shibuya-ku (3464 0051). Shibuya station. **Tickets** ¥1,800. **Map 2.**
A champion of independent cinema, this is the place where *Trainspotting* first hit Tokyo. Two screens.

Cinema Shimokitazawa

1-45-15 Kitazawa, Setagaya-ku (5452 1400). Shimokitazawa station (Odakyu line). **Tickets** ¥1,500. **Map 35.**
A little wooden hut built by film studio staff. Independent films from around the world are shown.

Cinema Square Tokyu

Tokyu Milano Bldg 3F, 1-29-1 Kabukicho, Shinjuku-ku (3202 1189). Shinjuku station. **Tickets** ¥1,800. **Map 1b.**
The pioneer of art-house cinemas in Tokyo.

It costs *how* much?

Tokyo cinema tickets are the most expensive in the world. Yet film buffs still manage to keep their eyes on the screen without breaking the bank, thanks to a series of often bizarre discount packages. Here are our magnificent seven ways of saving moolah on the movies.

1. Lady's Day An outrageously sexist and well-established system that allows women to get into the following cinemas (at certain times) for between ¥900 and ¥1,000: Shibuya Cinema Society (Monday); Shimo-takaido Cinema (Tuesday); Cinema Mediage, Mediage (*see p196* **Love Seats**), Ciné Pathos, Cinema Square Tokyu, Cinema Qualité, Kichijoji Baus Theatre (Wednesday); Ciné Switch (Friday).

2. Nice Guy Day Only ¥1,300 for nice men on Mondays at Kichijoji Baus Theatre. Nasty guys, fear not. We believe no one has ever been turned down.

3. Service Day Both sexes get in for ¥1,000 on Wednesdays at Ginza Théâtre Cinema, Ciné Saison Shibuya and Kineca Omori.

4. Foreigner discounts Positive racial discrimination in action gets non-Japanese a year-round ¥300 discount at Ciné Amuse. Overseas students pay only ¥1,000 at Cinema Rise, but must show valid ID or a passport.

5. Themed Dress discount Weirder still, this discount at Ciné Quinto is based on the content of the film. For example, when British film *The Acid House* was on, a person with a mohawk or a pregnant woman got an ¥800 discount. If the two were a couple, they got in free. Rules are stipulated for each film.

6. Membership Pay just ¥10,000 for membership of the repertory Cinema Club at Iidabashi Ginrei Hall and you can go as much as you like for a whole year without paying another yen.

7. Dirt cheap The Charity Show at TEPCO Electric Energy Museum (*see p112*) costs ¥100 for the first 100 arrivals. The hall shows second-run films every Monday at 10.20am, 12.55pm and 3.30pm, and there is always a queue, so get there early.

Ciné Saison Shibuya
The Prime 6F, 2-29-5 Dogenzaka, Shibuya-ku (3770 1721). Shibuya station. Tickets ¥1,800. Map 2.
Revivals, mini-festivals and independent productions are the lifeblood of this comfortable cinema.

Ciné Switch Ginza
Ginza-Hata Bldg 4-4-5 Ginza, Chuo-ku (3561 0707). Ginza station. Tickets ¥1,800. Map 6.
Two screens show recent European films.

Ebisu Garden Cinema
4-20-2 Ebisu Garden Place, Ebisu, Shibuya-ku (5420 6161). Ebisu station. Tickets ¥1,800. Map 3.
Two comfortable screens in Garden Place show a mixture of blockbusters and limited-release films from around the world.

Euro Space
Tobu-Fuji Bldg 2F, 24-4 Sakuragaoka-cho, Shibuya-ku (3461 0211). Shibuya station. Tickets ¥1,700. Map 2.
Independent films from Europe and Asia are regularly introduced here. The annual Art Documentary Film Festival is held here in November. There are two screens.

Ginza Théâtre Cinema
Ginza Théâtre Bldg 5F, 1-11-2 Ginza, Chuo-ku (3535 6000). Ginza-itchome station. Tickets ¥1,800. Map 6.
Late-night shows with interesting programming.

Haiyu-za Talkie Night
4-9-2 Roppongi, Minato-ku (3401 4073). Roppongi station. Tickets ¥1,700. Map 4.
Weird and avant-garde films from all over the world are the speciality at Haiyu-za Talkie Night.

Hibiya Chanter Ciné
1-2-2 Yurakucho, Chiyoda-ku (3591 1511). Hibiya station. Tickets ¥1,800. Map 6.
Three screens showing mainly European and American films.

Iidabashi Ginrei Hall
2-19 Kagurazaka, Shinjuku-ku (3269 3852). Iidabashi station. Tickets ¥1,500.
Special double-feature screenings offer interesting combinations of second-run films.

Iwanami Hall
2-1 Kanda-Jimbo-cho, Chiyoda-ku (3262 5252). Jimbo-cho station (Toei Shinjuku line). Tickets ¥1,800. Map 15.
A specialist in social realism since the 1970s.

Kichijoji Baus Theatre
1-11-23 Kichijoji-honmachi, Musashino-shi (0422 22 3555). Kichijoji station. Tickets ¥1,800. Map 31.
Three screens showing everything from Hollywood blockbusters to Japanese independent films.

Kineca Omori
Seiyu 5F, 6-27-25 Minami Oi, Shinagawa-ku (3762 6000). Omori station. Tickets ¥1,800.

Arts & Entertainment

Three screens, with one showing only Asian films. Late-night show with interesting programming such as 'The Films of John Cassavetes'.

Le Cinéma
Bunkamura 6F, 2-24-1 Dogenzaka, Shibuya-ku (3477 9264). Shibuya station. **Tickets** ¥1,800. **Map** 2.
Two screens in the giant Bunkamura arts complex, often offering French films.

Sanbyakunin Gekijo
2-29-10, Honkomagome, Bunkyo-ku (3944 5451). Sengoku station (Toei Mita line). **Tickets** ¥1,800.
Art-house cinema specialising in classics; Fritz Lang was featured in 1999.

Sangenjaya Chuo Gekijo
2-14-5 Sangenjaya, Setagaya-ku (3421 4610). Sangenjaya station (Denentoshi line). **Tickets** ¥1,300.
Good second-run cinema with interesting double-bills. A recent example was *Buena Vista Social Club* and *Stop Making Sense*.

Shibuya Cinema Society
Fuji-Bldg37 B1F, 1-18 Dogenzaka, Shibuya-ku (3496 3203). Shibuya station. **Tickets** ¥1,800. **Map** 2.
Shows classics in the morning, independent films in the afternoon and a special programme at night. A special 'One Day Through Pass' lasting 24 hours is also available for ¥3,500.

Kitano Takeshi – director, writer, comedian...

Shibuya Hermitage
Shibuya Toei Plaza 9F, 1-24-12 Shibuya, Shibuya-ku (5467 5774) Shibuya station. **Tickets** ¥1,800. **Map** 2.
Recent American and European films.

Shimo-takaido Cinema
3-27-26 Matsubara, Setagaya-ku (3328 1008). Shimo-Takaido station (Keio line). **Tickets** ¥1,600.
Repertory cinema with interesting programming.

Shin-Bungeiza
Maruhan-Ikebukuro Bldg 3F, 1-43-5 Higashi-Ikebukuro, Toshima-ku (3971 9422) Ikebukuro station. **Tickets** ¥1,300. **Map** 5.
Near-legendary repertory cinema that reopened in December 2000. Shows a wide range of films, from outstanding Japanese masterpieces to standard Hollywood no-brainers.

Theatre Image Forum
2-10-10 Shibuya, Shibuya-ku (5766 0114). Shibuya station. **Tickets** ¥1,800. **Map** 2.
Opened in September 2000. New art films, classics, and avant-garde features.

Tollywood
2F, 5-32-5 Daisawa, Setagaya-ku (3414 0433). Shimokitazawa station (Odakyu line). **Tickets** ¥600-¥1,500. **Map** 35.
Art-house cinema specialising in short films. Big-name directors' early works and new indie films.

Uplink Factory
Yokoyama Bldg 5F, 1-8-17 Jinnan, Shibuya-ku (5489 0750). Shibuya station. **Tickets** varies. **Map** 2.
Fascinating programme ranging from features such as those by Derek Jarman to the latest in Japanese animation. Film workshops and live performances are held regularly.

Waseda Shochiku
1-5-16 Takadanobaba, Shinjuku-ku (3200 8968). Takadanobaba station. **Tickets** ¥1,300; ¥900 concessions. **Map** 22.
Arty fleapit in the student area of Takadanobaba.

Love Seats

With the arrival of the multiplex in Tokyo has come the Love Seat, a double cinema chair apparently designed as much for fondling as for film-viewing. Due to high land costs, most multiplexes are situated way out of the centre of Tokyo, but the one on Odaiba is both the closest to the centre and has supposedly the best Love Seats in town. Our extensive testing of the so-called 'Super Premium Seat', however, revealed a few shortcomings. The 165cm-wide seat is actually quite hard, making snuggling up to your date less of a pleasure than a feat of endurance. Still, it makes for an interesting film-going experience. Reservations are required and, at the time of going to press, tickets cost a whopping ¥6,000 per couple, for which you also get the use of an exclusive lounge area.

Cinema Mediage, Mediage
1/2F, 1-7-1 Daiba, Minato-ku (5531 7878). Daiba station (Yurikamome line).

Galleries

Scarce public funding means artists fend for themselves, with intriguing results.

The most prominent area for small private galleries is Ginza, whose grid layout and flagship department stores may remind you of the area around New York's Fifth Avenue. If so, then the 400 or so galleries in Ginza and Kyobashi to the north are akin to the brand-name galleries in Manhattan's Midtown area.

Concentrated east of the Yamanote line, in Ginza's 8-chome area and moving up towards Tokyo station to Ginza 1-chome, the galleries come in all shapes and sizes and show everything from contemporary photography and traditional Japanese paintings to ceramic ware and Asian antiques. Chic Ginza can be edgy too, but for cutting-edge art, the best places are trendy Omotesando, Aoyama, Shibuya or Daikanyama. A stroll around their back streets guarantees a gallery discovery or three among the myriad shops and restaurants.

Gallery space is often funded through shops selling eclectic art-related merchandise (postcards and coffee-table books) and other adjunct businesses (graphic design studios, restaurants), and many of the smaller galleries charge the artists a rental fee to show their work for a week. A selective sample of galleries in these districts follows, along with a few notables in other areas, such as Shinjuku and its photography galleries. For current listings in English, see Saturday's *Japan Times*, *Daily Yomiuri* on Thursday or *Tokyo Classified*.

Whether credit cards are accepted at any of the galleries listed below varies according to the artist(s) exhibiting.

Ginza

The majority of these galleries are easily reached via the Ginza, Marunouchi and Hibiya subways to Ginza; the Toei Asakusa subway to Higashi-Ginza; Yurakucho subway to Ginza-Itchome, or the JR Yamanote line to Yurakucho (exceptions noted). All are in Chuo Ward (Chuo-ku), and on Map 6, unless otherwise marked.

Fuji Photo Salon
Sukibayashi Center 2F, 5-1 Ginza (3571 9411).
Open 10am-8pm daily.
Exhibitions feature professionals and amateurs.

Gallery Asuka
Daisan Taiyo Bldg 3F, 1-5-16 Ginza (5250 0845).
Open 11am-7pm Mon-Sat.
Handicrafts, including exquisite ceramic ware.

Gallery Q
Tosei Bldg B2, 8-10-7 Ginza (3535 2524).
Open 11am-7pm Mon-Sat.
Two basement galleries showing great contemporary Asian art.

Ginza Nikon Salon
Ginza Crest Bldg 2F, 5-11-4 Ginza (3248 3783).
Open 10am-7pm Mon-Sat.
Gonza Nikon Salon moved here in July 2000, and takes applications for exhibitions by upcoming photographers. If accepted, space is given free.

INAX Gallery
INAX 2F, 3-6-18 Kyobashi, Chuo-ku (5250 6530). Kyobashi station. **Open** 10am-6pm Mon-Sat. **Map 8.**
This maker of ceramic kitchen fixtures sponsors two galleries in Ginza showing architecture-related and contemporary artworks. INAX also has gallery/showrooms in Nishi-Shinjuku (3340 1700).

Kobayashi Gallery
Yamato Bldg B1, 3-8-12 Ginza (3561 0515).
Open 11.30am-7pm Mon-Sat.
Work in various media by young Japanese artists.

Kyocera Contax Salon
Tokyo Kyukyodo Bldg 5F, 6F, 5-7-4 Ginza (3572 1921). **Open** *5F* 10.30am-6.30pm Mon, Tue, Thur-Sun. *6F* 10.30am-6.30pm Mon, Tue, Thur-Sun.
International and Japanese photographers are shown.

Leica Gallery Tokyo
Matsushima Gankyo Bldg 3F, 3-5-6 Ginza (3567 6706). **Open** 10.30am-5.30pm Tue-Sat.
The former premises of Ginza's Nikon Salon were taken over by Leica in July 2000.

Picture this: **Leica Gallery Tokyo.**

Moris Gallery
Taiyo No.5 Bldg 1F, 7-10-8 Ginza (3573 5328).
Open 11.30am-7pm daily.
Moris occasionally hosts cutting-edge shows.

Pepper's Gallery
Ginza Pine Bldg B1, 7-13-2 Ginza (3544 3240).
Open 11am-7pm Mon-Sat.
One show's theme was 'botany' – an installation with plants.

Shirota Gallery
Taiyo No.5 Bldg B1, 7-10-8 Ginza (3572 7972).
Open 11am-7pm Mon-Sat.
Oils, sculptures and prints, including those by contemporary Japanese printmakers.

Shiseido Gallery
Ginza Shiseido Bldg B1, 8-8-3 Ginza (3572 2121).
Open 11am-6.30pm Mon-Sat.
This new gallery replaces the old Ginza Art Space, but as the same people are running it we can expect similar eye-popping shows by leading world and Japanese artists.

Wacoal Ginza Art Space
Miyuki No.1 Bldg B1, 5-1-15 Ginza (3573 3798).
Open 11am-7pm Mon-Sat.
Wacoal Ginza Art Space offers interesting shows of contemporary art in any media.

Aoyama/Shibuya

(F) denotes a gallery's involvement in the Favourite! movement; for more on the movement, *see p201* **Favourite! galleries**.

Aki-Ex Gallery
Minami Aoyama City House, 5-4-44 Minami Aoyama, Minato-ku (3499 4254). Omotesando station. **Open** *Gallery* 1-6pm Mon-Sat. *Restaurant* 11am-10pm Mon-Sat. **Map** 4.
This great little upstairs gallery invariably has interesting shows in many media.

Art Shop NADiff
4-9-8 Jingumae, Shibuya-ku (3403 8814) Omotesando station. **Open** 11am-8pm daily. **Map** 11.
A small one-room gallery smack in the middle of an art bookshop. **(F)**

Canadian Embassy Gallery
Canadian Embassy B1F, 7-3-38 Akasaka, Minato-ku (5412 6200). Aoyama-Itchome station. **Open** 9am-5.30pm Mon-Fri. **Map** 12.
This space shows the Canadian cutting edge in a high wall- spaced gallery in the bowls of the Goliath concrete embassy building.

Gallery 360°
5-1-27 Minami-Aoyama, Minato-ku (3406 5823). Omotesando station. **Open** noon-7pm Mon-Sat. **Map** 4.
Contemporary art focusing on printed matter and design, both Japanese and foreign, and a gift shop strong in art postcards and books. **(F)**

Gallery Le Déco
Towa Bldg, 3, 5, 6F, 3-16-3 Shibuya, Shibuya-ku (5485 5188). Shibuya station. **Open** 11am-7pm daily. **Map** 2.
This space used to look like an office building until Kei Tominaga completed the interior design for the new café on the ground floor in cool white, metal and silver. Each of its six floors showcases a variety of art and the gallery also has a policy of holding new exhibitions by unknown artists.

Gallery Koyanagi
1-7-5 Chuo-ku (3561 1896). Ginza station. **Open** 11am-7pm Mon-Sat. **Map** 6.
The best established gallery of them all, with an icy cool green-glass façade. **(F)**

Gallery Saatchi & Saatchi
Infini Akasaka 1F, 8-7-15 Akasaka, Minato-ku (5775 1888). Aoyama-Itchome station. **Open** 10am-6pm Mon-Fri. **Map** 12.
Newly opened in 2000, this high, light gallery exhibits a wide range of new art, primarily from emerging Japanese artists.

Gallery Side 2
Shima-crest Bldg B1, 1-29-4 Sendagaya, Shibuya-ku (5771 5263). Sendagaya station. **Open** 11am-7pm Tue-Sat. **Map** 23.
Opened in 1999, this small basement space took off right away, showing art from both home and abroad. **(F)**

Kenji Taki Gallery
3-18-2 Nishi-Shinjuku, Shinjuku-ku (3378 6051). Hatsudai station (Keio line). **Open** noon-7pm Mon-Sat. **Map** 1a.
There are frequently edgy, interesting shows to be seen here. **(F)**

Masataka Hayakawa Gallery
1-16-1 Ebisu-Nishi, Shibuya-ku (5457 7991). Ebisu station. **Open** 11am-7pm Tue-Sat. **Map** 3.
Teresita Fenandez exhibits here regularly. **(F)**

Mizuma Art Gallery
5-46-13 Jingumae, Shibuya-ku (3499 0226). Omotesando station. **Open** 11am-7pm Tue-Sat. **Map** 4.
Mizuma goes for the wilder side of contemporary Japanese art in a big-for-Tokyo street-level gallery. **(F)**

Ota Fine Arts
2-8-1 Ebisu-Nishi, Shibuya-ku (3780 0911). Ebisu station. **Open** 11am-7pm Mon-Sat. **Map** 3.
Where the Favourite! movement began; it's definitely worth checking out this catalyst. **(F)**

Rontgen Kunstraum
3-14-13 Minami-Aoyama, Minato-ku (3401 1466). Omotesando station. **Open** 1-7pm Mon-Sat. **Map** 11.
Rontgen Kunstraum hosts very cool shows in what used to be a traditional four-*tatami*-mat-sized gallery, but which has since been extended into a two-room space. A lot of great work from Germany is shown here. **(F)**

Scai the Bathhouse.

Scai the Bathhouse

6-1-23 Yanaka, Taito-ku (3821 1144). Nippori or Nezu station. **Open** noon-7pm Tue-Sat. **Map** 25
A converted bathhouse that has high ceilings and a timeless ambience. Anish Kapoor and Julian Opie show here. (**F**)

Skydoor Art Place Aoyama

Galerie Bldg, 5-51-4 Jingumae Shibuya-ku (5485 9573). Omotesando station. **Open** 11am-7pm Mon-Sat. **Map** 4.
A variety of shows are offered in this interesting and quite large downstairs space.

Taka Ishii Gallery

3-27-6 Kita-Otsuka, Toshima-ku (3915 7784). Otsuka station. **Open** 11am-7pm Tue-Sat.
A lovely space with an international reputation. (**F**)

Taro Nasu Gallery

1-8-13 Saga, Koto-ku (no phone). Monzennakacho station. **Open** 11am-7pm Tue-Sat.
A cutting-edge gallery in an amazing former rice warehouse near the Sumida river. The schedule leans towards photographic exhibitions. (**F**)

Tokyo Opera City Art Gallery

3-20-2 Nishi Shinjuku, Shinjuku-ku (5353 0756) Hatsudai station (Keio line). **Open** noon-8pm Tue-Sun. **Map** 1a.
A massive space in the centre of Tokyo that makes a good job of blockbuster shows. (**F**)

Tomio Koyama Gallery

1-8-13 Saga, Koto-ku (3630 2205). Monzennakacho station. **Open** 11am-7pm Tue-Sat.

Another gallery housed in the old rice warehouse on the Sumida river. (**F**)

Wako Works of Art

3-18-2 Nishi-Shinjuku, Shinjuku-ku (3373 2860) Hatsudai station (Keio line). **Open** 11am-7pm Tue-Sat. **Map** 1a.
A brightly lit gallery near Tokyo Opera City, usually hosting big-name shows. (**F**)

Watari-um

3-7-6 Jingumae, Shibuya-ku (3402 3001) Gaienmae station. **Open** 11am-7pm Tue, Thur-Sun; 11am-9pm Wed. **Map** 12.
One of the most important private museums in Tokyo, Watari-um is not afraid to show 'difficult' art. It's an efficient space that includes a gift shop, café and bookshop. (**F**)

Rental galleries

A rental gallery is typically a small space that charges the artist to exhibit, usually only for a week, with prices starting at ¥30,000. The rental galleries, for their part, are expected to provide a good mailing list of clients who may be interested in buying the work. This pragmatic system developed because of a serious lack of government funding for the contemporary arts. Rental galleries give unknown artists a chance for exposure and the galleries don't have to rely on making a sale to stay afloat. The problem with this system is that anyone can get an exhibition, and short

Arts & Entertainment

runs mean media exposure is limited. This is beginning to change, however, with the recent wave of dealer galleries opening up (*see p201* **Favourite! galleries**). Anyone with an interest in what emerging artists are doing should scout out these places. Credit cards are not accepted at any of the galleries listed.

Bun Po Do Gallery

Bun Po Do Bldg 4F, 1-21-1 Kanda-Jinbocho, Chiyoda-ku (3294 7200). Jinbocho station. **Open** 10am-6.30pm Mon-Sat. **Map 15.**

G Art Gallery

Ginza Shirai Bldg BF1, 2-5-18 Ginza, Chuo-ku (3562 5858). Ginza-Itchome station. **Open** 11am-6.30pm Mon-Sat. **Map 6.**

Gallery Aoyama

Pal Aoyama 2F, 2-12-27 Kita Aoyama, Minato-ku (3404 9543). Gaienmae station. **Open** 11am-7pm Tue-Sun. **Map 12.**

Gallery Gen

Ginza-Daiichi Bldg. 3F, 1-10-19 Ginza, Chuo-ku (3561 6869). Ginza station. **Open** 11.30am-7pm Tue-Sat. **Map 6.**

Gallery Hinoki

Takagi Bldg 1F, 3-11-2 Ginza, Chuo-ku (3545 3240). Ginza station. **Open** 11.30am-7pm Mon-Sat. **Map 6.**

Gallery Idea

Kyodo Bldg Shin Aoyama 2F, 5-9-15 Minami Aoyama, Minato-ku (3406 3721). Omotesando station. **Open** 11am-7pm Mon-Sat. **Map 12.**

Gallery Iseyoshi

Iseyu Bldg 2F, 8-8-19 Ginza, Chuo-ku (3571 8388) Ginza station. **Open** 11am-7pm Mon-Sat. **Map 6.**

Gallery K

Daini-Ginryoku Bldg 3F, 1-9-6 Ginza, Chuo-ku (3563 4578). Ginza station. **Open** 11am-7pm Tue-Sat. **Map 6.**

Galeria Rasen

Nogi Bldg 5F, 1-9-44 Naka, Kunitachi-shi (042 571 2558). Kunitachi station. **Open** noon-8pm Mon-Sat. This great little space needs a special mention because it is so far flung. It's where art students from nearby Musashino University get their initial break.

Galerie SOL

Mitsururi Bldg 1F, 74 Waseda-machi, Shinjuku-ku (3203 8646). Waseda station. **Open** 11am-8pm Mon-Sat.

Key Gallery

New Ginza Dai-Ichi Building, 7-11-10 Ginza, Chuo-Ku (3571 3633). Ginza station. **Open** noon-7.30pm Mon-Sat. **Map 6.**

Saison Art Program (SAP) Gallery

Cosmos Aoyama 1F, 5-53-67 Jingumae, Shibuya-ku (5464 0197). Omotesando station. **Open** 11am-6pm Tue-Sat. **Map 4.**

SAP is not a rental gallery, but the organiser of an annual local art showcase called 'Art-ing', and the host of interesting month-long exhibitions. A definite must-see in the area, it also has a great collection of art magazines, books and artists' portfolios.

Spica Museum

4-6-5 Minami-Aoyama, Minato-ku (5414 2264). Omotesando station. **Open** noon-7pm Mon-Sat. **Map 12.**

Toki Art Space

Saion Bldg, 3-42-5 Jingumae, Shibuya-ku (3479 0332). Gaienmae station. **Open** 11.30am-7pm Mon, Tue, Thur-Sun. **Map 12.**

Design galleries

Over the last few years, Tokyo has seen a burst of activity in the area of design, with many new free exhibition spaces opening up for designers and artists in unusual places – bars, shops and showrooms. Last year saw furniture company Cassina moving into the art market – it's since begun to exhibit art in its showroom – while design agent HA Deux has gone one step further by opening a gallery.

Design producers act in much the same way as dealer galleries by producing work from a stable of designers – some of whom reach superstar status, such as Mark Newson who was 'discovered' here. Tokyo Designers' Week, which marks its fifth birthday in 2002, is beginning to draw a great international pool of renowned designers and is becoming an important showcase for emerging Japanese design. Held every October, it's a week-long bonanza of events and exhibitions in galleries and shops. Below are the major players in the Tokyo design scene.

Abode

3-12-16 Kita-Aoyama, Minato-ku (3486 0100). Omotesando station. **Open** 11am-8pm Mon, Tue, Thur-Sun. **Map 11.**
This two-level furniture shop and exhibition space is a great supporter of new designers and leans towards 'conceptual design' exhibitions with work from a new breed of Japanese artist-designers.

Cassina

2-9-6 Higashi, Shibuya-ku (3498 2448). Shibuya station. **Open** 11am-7pm daily. Closed 1st Wed of mth. **Map 2.**
Cassina's spacious white showroom is a great place for checking out furniture reading design and architecture books. It also sells inexpensive art to complement the designer gadgets and furniture.

E & Y

4-2-5 Shibuya, Shibuya-ku (5485 8461). Shibuya or Omotesando station. **Open** 11am-7pm Mon, Tue, Thur-Sun. **Map 2.**

Favourite! galleries

For years, the art scene in Tokyo lacked the vibrancy of that in, say, London or New York. Given Japan's wealth, contemporary art here is under-funded and it has been left to the private sector to develop and nurture the scene. Big corporations, such as department stores, put on blockbuster international contemporary art shows in the centre of Tokyo and small rental galleries (*see p199*) took care of the smaller fry.

The problem with this system was that no sense of competition was able to develop. Japanese artists who did become famous, such as Yayoi Kusama or Araki, generally made their reputations overseas. But the Japanese recession of the 1990s has forced changes. The private sector that traditionally propped up the contemporary arts in Japan began to clamp down on cultural spending. Corporations either scaled down considerably, or closed altogether, as happened with the Seizon and Tobu museums of art in Ikebukuro. The ones that remained needed to pull in the crowds. The Isetan Gallery (*see p98*), for instance, once hosted cutting-edge shows, but in 2001 followed an exhibition of watches with a show of Marilyn Monroe photographs.

The ripple effects of this change are now starting to be felt, as many disillusioned young curators who worked in these institutions have left to start their own small dealer galleries, to promote young Japanese artists and stimulate the local market with big-name international artists.

In 1997, these new spaces organised a small art fair at Spiral Hall. It was a great success, resulting in a monthly paper entitled *Favourite!* (in English and Japanese) to keep the public abreast of what exhibitions were being shown where and – very important in Tokyo – how to find the spaces. Most importantly, though, the Favourite! list has helped foster a sense of community.

Two museums have now become involved in the Favourite! movement – the Watari-um and Tokyo Opera City Gallery (for both, *see p199*). International artists showing in these larger spaces have also started holding adjunct exhibitions in one of the smaller dealer galleries: Luc Tymans, for instance, was simultaneously exhibiting at Tokyo Opera City Gallery and Wako Works of Art (*see p199*). *Favourite! galleries are denoted in the listings by (F).*

Always on the look-out for new designers, this shop and tiny gallery space is worth digging around the back streets off Koto Dori to find.

HA Deux
1-28-9 Higashi, Shibuya-ku (5774 1775). Shibuya station. **Open** 10am-7pm Mon-Fri. **Map 2.**
Design agent Shegitoshi Haraki moved to this converted plastics factory in 2000 and opened a gallery in the process. There's great furniture by French designers and new art by upcoming artists.

hhstyle.com
6-14-2 Jingumae, Shibuya-ku (3400 3434). Harajuku station. **Open** noon-8pm daily. **Map 11.**
With a spanking new glass wonderwall building designed by Kazuyo Sejima, hhstyle.com has taken design out of four walls and into the street, at least visually. Try and check it out during the week, as it's always packed over the weekend.

Idee
6-1-16 Minami-Aoyama, Minato-ku (3409 6581). Omotesando station. **Open** 11am-7pm daily. **Map 4.**
Teruo Kurosaki, a well-established mover and shaker in Tokyo, owns this large enterprise, packed with the best of current international and national product and furniture design. There are exhibitions in the upstairs gallery showcase innovative design.

Ozone Living Design Centre
Shinjuku Park Tower, 3-7-1 Nishi-Shinjuku, Shinjuku-ku (5322 6500). Hatsudai station. **Open** 10.30am-6.30pm Mon, Tue, Thur-Sun. **Map 1a.**
This up-to-the-minute design centre is serious about providing you with design that is 'going to help you match your values so you can live in comfort'.

Tricot Open
Tricot B1F, 6-9-1 Jingumae, Shibuya-ku (3486 1790). Harajuku station. **Open** 11am-8pm Mon, Tue, Thur-Sun. **Map 11.**
Tricot has been important in opening up the design scene in Tokyo, outing emerging Japanese designers while also finding the time to bring over and represent many international designers. This three-storey building houses a café and exhibition space, plus a product design shop selling an assortment of curious designer objects.
Branch: 2-27-4 Jingumae, Shibuya-ku (5775 5321).

Yamagiwa
12-5 Gobancho, Chiyoda-ku (3253 5111). Yotsuya station. **Open** 10am-6pm Mon-Fri. **Map 10.**
This enormous building, which houses exhibition spaces, showrooms and even a conference centre, holds several big theme- or designer-based shows every year.

Arts & Entertainment

Gay & Lesbian

The scene may be small, but size doesn't matter. Right?

For hundreds of years, homosexuality had a dominant role in Japanese society, and love between two men (or often between a man and a boy) was considered among the noble *samurai* classes to be purer than love between a man and a woman. Times change, and as western influences flowed into the country, homosexuality came to be seen less as one of many styles of love and sex, and more as an identifiable characteristic. These days, the state of gay and lesbian life in Japan is a case of 'don't bother us and we won't bother you'.

Nevertheless, Japan remains a nation founded on Buddhist rather than Christian values and as such there is less intrinsic social homophobia compared to many other countries, beyond the view that homosexuality is an abnormality in a society that craves conformity. There is a huge gay culture in Japan, and even if you can't read Japanese it's probably worth picking up a copy of the brick-sized *Badi* magazine just to see for yourself the true scope of the scene. Shinjuku Ni-chome, the country's homosexual heartland, contains over 300 gay and lesbian bars and clubs of various genres. Of those, only a handful regularly welcome

foreign customers and to get into the others you'll need to be taken by a Japanese friend.

One point to remember: although the rate of HIV infection in Japan remains way below that in most other Asian nations, it is increasing, and visitors should take all the precautions they would take at home.

For more information on the scene get online (*see p274*), or pick up a copy of *Metropolis*, which has a gay and lesbian section of classified ads and publicises gay parties and other irregular events. For the club scene, pick up the CIA (Club Information Agency) booklet, which advertises most of the monthly gay parties and is available at most of the places listed below.

Bars & clubs

Ace

Daini Hayakawaya Bldg B1F, 2-14-6 Shinjuku, Shinjuku-ku (3352 6297). Shinjuku San-chome station. **Open** 8pm-5am Wed-Sun. **Admission** varies. **Map** 1b.

This venue for many smaller gay dance parties has events most weekends. Check CIA for details.

Advocates

7th Tenka Bldg 1F, 2-18-1 Shinjuku, Shinjuku-ku (3358 3988). Shinjuku San-chome station. **Open** 6pm-5am Mon-Sat; 6pm-1am Sun. **Map** 1b.
Small mixed bar on Naka Dori with almost no space inside. Punters generally hang out on the street (a welcome novelty in Ni-chome). Great in summer; wrap up warm in winter. Happy hour 6-9pm Mon-Fri. Also has a 'Beer Blast' from 6-9pm on Sun.

Arty Farty

Lily Mansion 1F, 2-17-4 Shinjuku, Shinjuku-ku (3356 5388). Shinjuku San-chome station. **Open** 5pm-5am Mon-Fri; 3pm-5am Sat, Sun. **Map** 1b.
Extremely popular foreigner-friendly bar with a primarily young crowd. The Sunday afternoon 'Beer Blast' (all the beer you can drink, 3-7pm, for ¥1,000) and Wednesday's all-night happy hour are both popular. Women allowed 'with gay friends' on Sundays.

Blue Oyster Lounge

7th Tenka Bldg B1F, 2-18-1 Shinjuku, Shinjuku-ku (3358 8638). Shinjuku San-chome station. **Open** 8pm-4am Mon-Sat. **Map** 1b.
Newest bar/club in Ni-chome, undoubtedly the most glamorous and possibly the best. Famous for its drag shows most nights after 10pm and for the beautiful staff. Can get ridiculously crowded at weekends. Men-only on Saturday night.

Club Zip

Futami Bldg 1F, 2-14-11 Shinjuku, Shinjuku-ku (3356 5029). Shinjuku San-chome station. **Open** 3pm-5am daily. **Map** 1b.
Made famous when it appeared in Japan's first gay TV drama series, Zip is a pleasant bar affiliated with Arty Farty (*see above*) but much less crowded and with an older feel to it. Also on offer is a pasta and pizza menu, and cheap drinks before 7pm.

Dragon

Accord Bldg B1F, 2-12-4 Shinjuku, Shinjuku-ku (3341 0606). Shinjuku San-chome station. **Open** 8pm-5am Tue-Thur, Sun; 9pm-5am Fri, Sat. **Admission** *Men* ¥1,000 Fri, Sat. *Women* ¥2,000 Fri, Sat. *Both* free Tue-Thur, Sun. **Map** 1b.
Dark, basement meet-market mostly for the after-GB crowd, with a small dancefloor, almost-naked staff and video entertainment. Can get very crowded and sweaty. Ranges from fabulously fun to dire.

Fuji

B104, Cent Four Bldg, 2-12-16 Shinjuku, Shinjuku-ku (3354 2707). Shinjuku San-chome station. **Open** 8pm-2am Mon-Fri; 8pm-5am Sat, Sun. **Map** 1b.
Basement karaoke bar that's been around for years and caters mostly to an older crowd. Don't be put off by the dingy decor; this is a fun place with plenty of English karaoke songs, friendly staff and customers. Women always welcome.

Gamos

2-Chome Center Bldg B1F, 2-11-10 Shinjuku, Shinjuku-ku (3354 5519). Shinjuku San-chome station. **Open** 9pm-5am daily. **Admission** varies. **Map** 1b.

Club events

Most of Tokyo's major gay or gay-mix club events happen outside Ni-chome. Tokyo's longest-running gay-mix party, **The Ring**, takes place on the last Saturday of the month – at Luners in Azabu-Juban (*see p215*), at the time of going to press – and is still as popular as ever. **Passion**, a large progressive house night held every second Friday at Code in Shinjuku (*see p213*), has a mixed crowd and a 'glamour room' playing mostly gay house. Another perennially popular party held less regularly is **Red** (also at Luners), famous for attracting the most beautiful boys in Tokyo. **Deep**, at Shinjuku Liquid Room (*see p215*) on the first Saturday of the month, has also been running for many years and has a large muscle contingent. **Friends** at Code on the last Sunday of the month is a *neruton* numbers match-making event. There are usually another couple of large events per month advertised in the CIA club guide booklet.

The main monthly women-only event, **Goldfinger**, happens every last Friday, currently at Pasha Club in Nishi Azabu. Other women-only events include **Diamond Cutter** on the first Friday at Ace (*see p202*), **Bravissima** on the second Friday at Gamos (*see p215*) and **Duralmin Bitch** at Maniac Love in Aoyama (*see p215*) on the third Wednesday. The fetish scene's monthly shindig happens at On Air West in Shibuya (*see p209*) and is called **Department H** (H for *echi*, a Japanese word for sex), although it's more of a congress of the extraordinary rather than a party per se. This being Tokyo, things change rapidly. Parties come and go, venues change, new clubs open and old ones close. For the latest information on all these parties check CIA or *Metropolis*.

The pleasantest of all the Ni-chome clubs, Gamos attracts a mixed gay/straight clientele and a variety of gay-oriented events, often playing host to some of Tokyo's top DJs.

GB

Business Hotel T Bldg B1F, 2-12-3 Shinjuku, Shinjuku-ku (3352 8972). Shinjuku San-chome station. **Open** 8pm-2am daily. **Map** 1b.
The most infamous foreigner-friendly meet-market in Tokyo, GB is conveniently attached to a 'business hotel'. It's men only, except on Halloween (and no, we're not kidding).

Lesbian & Gay Parade

The date was 27 August 2000. The event was Tokyo's first Lesbian and Gay Parade, a symbolic turning point for gay and lesbian rights in a country where, even if there is little aggressive homophobia, sexual minorities suffer an oppression of silent injustice and a level of psychological pressure that non-Japanese will find hard to understand.

It was certainly a learning experience for Tokyoites when 6,000 gays, lesbians and transsexuals from all over Japan marched through the centre of the Harajuku and Shibuya districts in an ordered but joyful display of solidarity and liberation, warmly supported by thousands of delighted, if slightly bemused, onlookers. If it lacked the debauched party atmosphere of more famous parades around the world, this pioneering event was no less inspiring

Hug

2-15-8 Shinjuku, Shinjuku-ku (5379 5085). Shinjuku San-chome station. **Open** *9pm-6am daily.* **Map** *1b.*
Women-only karaoke bar attracting over-30s.

Karaoke Rafu

B1, 2-16-8 Shinjuku, Shinjuku-ku (3353 0290). Shinjuku San-chome station. **Open** *3pm-5am daily.* **Admission** ¥300 for 1hr with 1 drink before 5pm; ¥650 for 1hr with limited free drinks after 5pm. Prices go up by ¥100 on Sat, Sun and nights before public holidays. **Map** *1b.*
This basement karaoke box venue, always packed with gay customers murdering Madonna hits, is old, worn and dirty enough to be grungy and hip. Thin walls make listening to other Whitney wannabes an inevitable, if not always pleasurable, experience.

Kinsmen

2F, 2-18-5 Shinjuku, Shinjuku-ku (3354-4949). Shinjuku San-chome station. **Open** *9pm-5am Mon, Wed-Sun.* **Map** *1b.*
Once one of the most popular foreigner-friendly bars in Ni-chome. These days it's the place to go to get away from everyone else. Famous for its *ikebana* flower arrangements.

Kinswomyn

Daiichi Tenka Bldg 3F, 2-15-10 Shinjuku, Shinjuku-ku (3354 8720). Shinjuku San-chome station. **Open** *8pm-4am Mon-Sat.* **Map** *1b.*
Kinswomyn (sibling of the men's bar, Kinsmen, *see above*) is Tokyo's most popular women-only bar. Old guard butch-femme types occasionally drop by, but for the most part it's a hip, relaxed crowd.

Monsoon

Shimazaki Bldg 6F, 2-14-9 Shinjuku, Shinjuku-ku (3354 0470). Shinjuku San-chome station. **Open** *3pm-6am daily.* **Map** *1b.*
Small, friendly, men-only bar with conveniently long opening hours catering to a young crowd. Become a member of the 'Mas Club' (it's free) and have your photo taken and put in a match-making book where you can also leave messages for any of the 3,500 or so other guys whose photos you like.

Rainbow Café

2-13-10 Shinjuku, Shinjuku-ku (3356 6687). Shinjuku San-chome station. **Open** *2pm-5am daily.* **Map** *1b.*
Tiny coffee shop on Ni-chome's central Naka Dori street with tasty cakes and a mixed clientele.

considering the different state of play of homosexual politics in Japan. The parade was followed by the first Ni-chome Rainbow Matsuri festival, with shows, floats, stalls and crowds filling the district's main Naka Dori street. What difference the day really made, bar invigorating the self-esteem of the community, is as yet unclear. However, the inclusion of clauses protecting the rights of sexual minorities by the Tokyo Metropolitan Government in its human rights guidelines several months later – after it had earlier threatened to exclude them from the document – is an encouraging sign that indifference may at last be giving way to acceptance.

Tamago Bar
Yamahara Heights 1F, 2-12-15 Shinjuku, Shinjuku-ku (3351 4838). Shinjuku San-chome station. **Open** 9pm-5am daily. **Map** 1b.
Pricey women-only bar, where customers are served by *onabe* hosts (women dressed as men).

Sex clubs

Dock
Daini Seiko Bldg B1, 2-18-5 Shinjuku, Shinjuku-ku (3226 4006). Shinjuku San-chome station.
Open 9pm-4am daily. **Admission** ¥1,200 including 1 drink. **Map** 1b.
Cruising bar with different theme nights, handily located two doors down from Arty Farty (*see p203*).

HX
UI Bldg 1F, 5-9-6 Shinjuku, Shinjuku-ku (3226 4448). Shinjuku San-chome station. **Open** 3pm-10am Mon-Thur; 24hrs Fri-Sun. **Admission** ¥1,500; ¥1,000 7-11am. **Map** 1b.
Very small club catering mostly to a leather crowd with the occasional foreign customer. On the other side of Yasukuni Dori from Ni-chome, down the alley next to MosBurger on the right.

King of College
2-14-5 Shinjuku, Shinjuku-ku (3352 3930). Shinjuku San-chome station. **Open** 6pm-10am daily. **Map** 1b.
Friendly, English-speaking staff make this place ideal. You can rent 'hosts' by the hour in a private room at the club or at your home or hotel room.

Slamdunk
Room 107, 2-4-12 Shinjuku, Shinjuku-ku (3355 7178). Shinjuku San-chome station. **Open** 24hrs daily. **Admission** ¥1,500; ¥1,000 4-11am. **Map** 1b.
Small club that welcomes foreign customers with different theme nights every day of the week (although the basic theme is the same). Go down the alley next to am/pm on the other side of Shinjuku Dori from Ni-chome. Slamdunk is behind the small brown door at the end.

Treffpunkt
Maeda Bldg 4F, 5-4-17, Akasaka, Minato-ku (5563 0523). Akasaka station. **Open** noon-midnight Mon-Thur, Sat, Sun; noon-5am Fri. **Admission** ¥1,700; ¥1,000 noon-3pm Mon-Thur, after midnight Fri. **Map** 7.
Small club, closer to the business areas of the city, that accepts foreign customers. Underwear optional during the week, forbidden at weekends.

Bathhouses & saunas

Jinya
2-30-19 Ikebukuro, Toshima-ku (5951 0995). Ikebukuro station. **Open** 2pm-11am Mon-Fri; 24hrs Sat, Sun. **Admission** ¥2,200. **Map** 5.
Respectable-looking establishment servicing an older clientele than most. Facilities include a TV room, private rooms and a porno viewing area.

Paragon
1F, 2-17-4 Shinjuku, Shinjuku-ku (3353 3306). Shinjuku San-chome station. **Open** 3pm-noon Mon-Sat; 24hrs Sun. **Admission** ¥1,800; ¥1,300 students; ¥1,200 5am-noon; ¥1,000 5am-noon students. **Map** 1b.
Small, convenient, well-equipped sauna, with a bizarre pricing policy and a seemingly discretionary admissions policy. When you arrive, a voice will ask if you speak Japanese. Say '*hai*'. If staff don't feel like letting you in, they won't. Fridays are naked days.

24 Kaikan Asakusa
2-29-16 Asakusa, Taito-ku (3844 7715). Asakusa station. **Open** 24hrs daily. **Admission** ¥2,400. **Map** 13.
Most cruising for non-Japanese at this busy sauna goes on in the bath/shower area. Condoms available at the front desk.

24 Kaikan Ueno
1-8-7 Kita-Ueno, Taito-ku (3847 2424). Ueno station. **Open** 24hrs daily. **Admission** ¥2,400. **Map** 14.
Huge six-floor foreigner-friendly sauna with a rooftop sun deck, gym, restaurant and karaoke bar, and other places to enjoy yourself in public and private.

Music

Tokyo has top pops, great classical and a thriving underground scene.

Classical Music

Classical music has enjoyed huge popularity in Japan ever since the country opened itself up to the outside world in the nineteenth century. In recent years, Japan has produced its own classical music stars, from conductor Seiji Ozawa to pianist Mitsuko Uchida.

As befits one of the world's great cities, Tokyo has a host of high-quality venues catering for the needs of classical music buffs. Many of them are run by private companies, such as Suntory, in a typically Japanese partnership between industry and the arts. Tickets are best purchased well in advance, especially for a performance by one of the many foreign orchestras that stop by.

Frustratingly, performances of classical Japanese music are rather harder to come by, although Bunkamura occasionally hosts concerts by well-known players.

Major venues

Casals Hall
1-6 Kanda-Surugadai, Chiyoda-ku (3294 1229). Ochanomizu station. **Capacity** 511. **Map** 15.
A beautiful hall with marvellous acoustics in the heart of Tokyo's university/bookshop district. For a truly historic experience, treat yourself to a meal at Sarafan, a nearby Russian restaurant where the staff don't seem to have heard of the tsar's abdication, and then head over to Casals Hall for a relaxing dose of baroque sounds.

Kan'i Hoken Hall
8-4-13 Nishi-Gotanda, Shinagawa-ku (3490 5111). Gotanda station. **Capacity** 1,826. **Map** 19.
About five minutes' walk from JR Gotanda station, this venue is famous with Tokyo's classical cognoscenti for its fine acoustics. Occasionally hosts rock and jazz concerts, too.

Orchard Hall
2-24-1 Dogenzaka, Shibuya-ku (3477 9111). Shibuya station. **Capacity** 2,150. **Map** 2.
One of the first 'shoe box' concert/opera halls, characterised by high ceilings, vertical walls, shallow balconies and rectangular design. Perfect for opera and classics and occasionally used for pop and rock. The venue is in the Bunkamura ('culture village') complex. Avoid seats near the front, as the high stage makes neck ache a near inevitability.

Tokyo International Forum. *See p207.*

Sogetsu Hall
7-2-21 Akasaka, Minato-ku.3408 1129. Aoyama-Itchome station. **Capacity** 530. **Map** 7.
An intimate venue belonging to the *sogetsu-ryu* school of *ikebana* (flower arranging). As well as classical music, also hosts poetry readings, Japanese music recitals and film previews.

Sumida Triphony
1-2-3 Kinshi, Sumida-ku (5608 1212). Kinshicho station. **Capacity** *Big hall* 1,800. *Small hall* 250.
New venue with a warm, welcoming atmosphere. Features regular concerts by the New Japan Philharmonic and visiting international artistes. A bit out of the way, but worth the trip.

Suntory Hall
1-13-1 Akasaka, Minato-ku (3505 1001). Akasaka or Tameike-sanno station. **Capacity** *Big hall* 2,006. *Small hall* 400. **Map** 7.
A fine concert hall, operated by local brewer Suntory and used mostly for western and Japanese classical music. Has one of the largest pipe organs in Japan.

Tokyo Bunka Kaikan
5-45 Ueno Koen, Taito-ku (3828 2111). Ueno station.
Capacity *Big hall* 2,303. *Small hall* 650. **Map** 14.
Pleasantly located amid Ueno Park's greenery, this nondescript concert facility underwent refurbishment in 1999, having fallen behind Casals Hall (*see p206*) and Tokyo Opera City (*see below*) as one of Tokyo's premier classical music venues.

Tokyo International Forum
3-5-1 Marunouchi, Chiyoda-ku (5221 9000). Yurakucho or Ginza station. **Capacity** *Hall A* 5,012. *Hall C* 1,500. **Map** 6.
A vast complex of concert halls, exhibition halls and convention rooms, located in the middle of Tokyo's Marunouchi business district. Hall C was designed exclusively for classical concerts and musicals, and other halls are put to a variety of uses, from pop concerts to film previews. The building itself, an orgy of sculpted glass, is definitely worth a look.

Tokyo Metropolitan Art Space
1-8-1 Nishi-Ikebukuro, Toshima-ku (5391 2111). Ikebukuro station. **Capacity** *Big hall* 1,999. *Middle hall* 841. *Small hall 1* 300. *Small hall 2* 300. **Map** 5.
The main feature of this arts complex in the northern area of Ikebukuro is its escalator, which hoists audiences from the ground to the fifth floor. The venue comprises four halls and an exhibition space, which are used for everything from jazz to rock as well as classical music.

Tokyo Opera City
3-20-2 Nishi-Shinjuku, Shinjuku-ku (5353 0770). Hatsudai station (Keio line). **Capacity** 1,632. **Map** 1a.
New concert hall just outside sprawling and rapidly changing west Shinjuku. Good acoustics, according to those with well-trained ears, but what really makes this an exciting venue is the innovative and varied concert programme.

Rock, Roots & Jazz

As anyone who has ever trawled through the racks at the hundreds of CD shops in west Shinjuku can testify, Tokyo is a great city for rock music, and the fact that local acts such as Cornelius, Pizzicato Five and Boom Boom Satellites are starting to make an international impression has produced a new wave of guitar- and turntable-toting kids keen to emulate them.

The range of venues is mind-boggling, from 50,000-capacity stadiums to subterranean holes so small that just turning around requires a Herculean effort. Although foreign bands make regular stops here on international tours, it's often worth taking the risk and stepping into a small live house to see what's on. At these smaller venues, entrance is cheap, crowds friendly and opening hours more flexible.

Booking tickets

Advance tickets for plays, events and gigs are rarely purchased from the venues themselves. If you want to buy a ticket, your first stop should be your local convenience store, many of which act as ticket agencies. Lawson Ticket (3569 9900), owned by the *combini* of the same name, is a big one. Other prominent agencies include Pia (5237 9999, can handle enquiries in English) and CN Playguide (3257 9999, Japanese only). Credit cards are not accepted.

The way bigger venues operate here is often something of a shock to the visitor. Firstly, concerts in Japan start and finish incredibly early, usually running from 7pm to 9pm so people can make their train home. Secondly, live music is incredibly expensive. Expect to pay a minimum of ¥7,000 to see an established act, with the really big ones sometimes costing much more.

Stadiums & large venues

Akasaka Blitz
TBS Square 5-3-6 Akasaka, Minato-ku (3224 0567/ www.tbs.co.jp/blitz). Akasaka station. **Capacity** *Standing* 1,944. *Seated* 910. **Map** 7.
Since opening back in 1996, Blitz has hosted 800-odd Japanese acts, such as Hikaru Utada, the Yellow Monkey and Misia, as well as touring foreign acts. More recently, the venue has become popular with the techno/trance party crowd, which has moved here from Shinjuku's Liquid Room (*see p209*).

Budokan
2-3 Kitanomaru-Koen, Chiyoda-ku (3216 5100/ www.nipponbudokan.or.jp). Kudanshita station. **Capacity** 13,721. **Map** 9.
Built for the martial arts competition in the 1964 Olympics, the Budokan is an unlikely venue for rock concerts. Indeed, when the Beatles became the first rock band to play here in the mid '60s, it sparked protest demos outside. Acoustically, Budokan is terrible, and it's famous for being one of the few places in Tokyo where alcohol is not sold. If you can't get a ticket the regular way, the street leading to the venue from Kudanshita station fills up with touts.

Ebisu Garden Hall
Ebisu Garden Place, 1-13-2 Mita, Meguro-ku. (5423 7111/5424 0111/www.gardenplace.co.jp). Ebisu station. **Capacity** 775. **Map** 3.
Located in the heart of shopping complex Ebisu Garden Place, this pristine hall opened in 1994. It's more upmarket than its main rival, Akasaka

Blitz (*see p207*), although locker provision for bags is woefully inadequate. You're best advised to use the cloakroom if you can.

Hibiya Kokaido

1-3 Hibiya Koen, Chiyoda-ku (3591 6388).
Kasumigaseki, Hibiya or Uchisaiwaicho station.
Capacity 2,075. **Map** 6.
One of the oldest concert halls in Tokyo, built in 1929. Used for concerts, political rallies and dance parties. The scene of the 1960 assassination of Japan's then Socialist Party leader.

Hibiya Yagai Ongaku-do

1-3 Hibiya Koen, Chiyoda-ku (3591 6388).
Kasumigaseki, Hibiya or Uchisaiwaicho station.
Capacity 3,114. **Map** 6.
A medium-sized outdoor venue in the south-east of Hibiya Park. As with all outdoor venues, the elements play a big part in its success, and an afternoon on the concrete bench seating can seem like an eternity in a rainstorm.

Koseinenkin Kaikan

5-3-1 Shinjuku, Shinjuku-ku (3356 1111). Shinjuku San-chome station. **Capacity** 2,062. **Map** 1b.
One of the busiest venues in Tokyo, hosting concerts by local and international artistes.

Nakano Sun Plaza Hall

4-1-1 Nakano, Nakano-ku. (3388 1151). Nakano station. **Capacity** 2,222. **Map** 26.
Medium-sized venue on the Chuo line which sometimes plays host to top acts, who have included Sonny Rollins and the Clash. Famed for the list of prohibitions ('no photographs, no standing, no dancing, no lighting of matches or cigarette lighters') recited before the start of every show.

National Yoyogi Stadium

2-1-1 Jinnan, Shibuya-ku. (3468 1171).
Harajuku, Meiji-Jingumae or Shibuya station.
Capacity 10,000. **Map** 11.
Another former 1964 Olympic venue that's occasionally pressed into service for local and international chart-topping acts. There are two stadiums, although the second is rarely used for anything other than gymnastic events.

NHK Hall

2-2-1 Jinnan, Shibuya-ku. (3465 1751). Shibuya station. **Capacity** 3,443. **Map** 2.
Operated by state broadcaster NHK, this is one of the better halls in Shibuya, with good acoustics and a pleasant atmosphere. Watch out for the dodgy air-conditioning, though.

Shibuya AX

2-1-1 Jinnan, Shibuya-ku (5738 2020/
www.shibuya-ax.com). Harajuku station.
Capacity 1,500. **Map** 2.
A new live house that opened at the end of 2000, almost next door to the Yoyogi stadium complex. Concentrates mainly on local big names such as Penicillin, Love Psychedelico and Dragon Ash.

Shibuya Kokaido

1-1 Udagawacho, Shibuya-ku (3463 5001). Shibuya station. **Capacity** 2,318. **Map** 2.
Yet another music venue that started life as a location for the 1964 Olympics. Now a favourite first-night venue for bands about to embark on a national or international tour, thanks to its fine acoustics and relatively intimate atmosphere.

Tokyo Bay NK Hall

1-8 Maihama, Urayasu-shi, Chiba (047 355 7007).
Maihama station (JR Keiyo line). **Capacity** 6,000.
A giant of a concert hall, out in the middle of nowhere near Tokyo Disneyland. Only worth the trip if you simply *must* see the band that's on.

Tokyo Dome (aka 'Big Egg')

1-3 Koraku, Bunkyo-ku (5800 9999). Suidobashi or Korakuen station. **Capacity** 55,000. **Map** 15.
The home of the Giants baseball team also hosts those bands just too darned big to play elsewhere. Since the venue is covered to protect it from the unpredictable elements, seats can get uncomfortably sticky on Tokyo's too-hot summer nights. Food and drink are overpriced. Bring your own.

Zepp Tokyo

Palette Town 1F, Odaiba, Koto-ku (3529 1015/
www.zepp.co.jp). Daiba Kaihin Koen station
(Yurikamome line). **Capacity** 2,700.
Charmless venue that opened in out-of-the-way Odaiba in 1999. Started out with a flurry of foreign acts but has since started hosting DJ nights on the rare nights it's open.

Clubs & live houses

Astro Hall

B1F, New Wave Harajuku Bldg, 4-32-12 Jingumae, Shibuya-ku (3401-5352/www.astro-hall.com).
Harajuku station. **Capacity** 400. **Map** 11.
Once the venue of choice for local indie bands, Astro Hall has had some of its limelight stolen by Shibuya AX (*see above*), just down the road. Whether it can adapt and survive remains to be seen.

Blue Note Tokyo

Raika Bldg B1, 6-3-16 Minami-Aoyama, Minato-ku.
(5485 0088/www.bluenote.co.jp). Omotesando station. **Capacity** 300. **Map** 12.
Premier jazz and blues venue that opened in 1988 and moved to its current venue in '98. Attracts acts of genuine international quality, who usually play two sets a night in a week-long residency. Audiences dine as they tap their feet, and tickets are expensive, costing anything up to ¥10,000.

Club 251

Mikami Bldg B1 5-29-15 Daizawa, Setagaya-ku (5481 4141). Shimokitazawa station. **Capacity** 400.
Map 35.
Another hard-to-find small live house in Shimokitazawa. Mainly hosts local rock, hardcore, rap, punk and other alternative acts.

Arts & Entertainment

Club Asia
1-8, Maruyama-cho, Shibuya-ku (5458 7176).
Shibuya station. **Capacity** 700. **Map** 2.
The biggest event space/club in the Shibuya area
also serves as an Asian restaurant during the hours
of daylight. Live appearances tend to be restricted
to DJs and techno acts.

Club Eggsite Shibuya
1-6-8 Jinnan, Shibuya-ku. (3496 1561). Shibuya
station. **Capacity** 400. **Map** 2.
One of the best places in town to check out up-and-
coming acts before they're grabbed by a record
company. Occasionally the venue of choice for secret
gigs by visiting foreign acts.

Club Que
Big Ben Bldg B2, 2-5-2 Kitazawa, Setagaya-ku
(3412 9979). Shimokitazawa station. **Capacity** 250.
Map 35.
One of the biggest live houses in the resolutely alternative Shimokitazawa area. During the week hosts
rock, punk and hardcore acts, but weekends, after
the gig, reinvents itself as a turntable club.

Club Quattro Shibuya
4F Quattro by Parco, 32-13 Udagawa-cho,
Shibuya-ku (3477 8750). Shibuya station.
Capacity 700. **Map** 2.
One of the pleasantest venues in Shibuya, located,
improbably, inside a department store. Has the feel
of a TV studio, with the band only slightly raised
from the mostly standing crowd.

Crocodile Shibuya
New Sekiguchi Bldg. B1, 6-18-8 Jingumae, Shibuya-
ku (3499 5205). Shibuya, Harajuku or Meiji-
Jingumae station. **Capacity** 250. **Map** 11.
One of the first places in Tokyo to mix live music
with food. Hosts everything from rock to country
and western, and salsa.

Heaven's Door
B1 Keio Hallo Bldg, 1-33-19 Sangenjaya, Setagaya-
ku (3410 9581). Sangenjaya station. **Capacity** 300.
One of the most raucous nights out in town is
guaranteed at this rough and ready venue that
specialises in punk and hardcore.

La.mama Shibuya
B1F Premier Dogenzaka, 1-15-3 Dogenzaka,
Shibuya-ku (3464 0801). Shibuya station.
Capacity 300. **Map** 2.
Another spot to see talented amateurs and indies
before they get signed by a major label. Intriguingly,
the venue also has its own record label, Engine.

Liquid Room
7F Humax Pavilion, 1-20-1 Kabuki-cho, Shinjuku-ku
(3200 6831/www.liquidroom.net). Shinjuku.station.
Capacity 700. **Map** 1b.
One of the most famous live spaces and clubs in
town, Shinjuku's Liquid Room is a long climb up
six flights of stairs, leaving you in need of refreshment from the moment of arrival. It often hosts

big-name acts from around the world who have
yet to break in Japan, as well as lots of DJ nights.
Definitely a venue worth watching.

Mandala Minami-Aoyama
B1F MR Bldg, 3-2-2 Minami-Aoyama, Minato-ku.
(5474 0411). Gaienmae station. **Capacity** 120.
Map 12.
A stylish venue that's more like a restaurant with
live music added as an appetising afterthought.

Mandala2 Kichijoji
2-8-6 Kichijoji Minami-cho, Musashino-shi (0422 42
1579). Kichijoji station. **Capacity** 80. **Map** 31.
Sister venue of Mandala Minami-Aoyama (*see*
above). Specialises in the esoteric side of musical life,
such as Mongolian throat singing.

Milk
Roob6 B1F-B2F, 1-13-2 Ebisu-nishi, Shibuya-ku
(5458 2826). Ebisu station. **Capacity** 100. **Map** 2.
Crowded, cramped and sweaty, Milk opened in 1995
with a mission to seek out the best in upcoming
Japanese rock. It remains as fresh as ever, something
due in no small part to the subterranean layout.

On Air East
2-14-9 Dogenzaka, Shibuya-ku (3476 8787). Shibuya
station. **Capacity** 800-1,000. **Map** 2.
Nestling in the heart of Shibuya's love hotel district,
On Air East is a functional box of a venue with
standing room only. Another popular venue for
foreign bands trying to break Japan.

On Air West
2-3 Maruyama-cho, Shibuya-ku (5458 4646).
Shibuya station. **Capacity** 500. **Map** 2.
Don't let the totally different address fool you. This
venue is right across the street from On Air East
(*see above*). Smaller than its sibling, it hosts indie
music or cult sounds and, occasionally, shows films.

Shelter Shimokitazawa
Senda Bldg B1F, 2-6-10 Kitazawa, Setagaya-ku
(3466 7430). Shimokitazawa station. **Capacity** 300.
Map 35.
Hardcore and ska bands dominate at this Shimo-
kitazawa sister venue to Shinjuku Loft (*see below*).
Audience and artiste are virtually nose to nose here,
so a good vibe is guaranteed.

Shinjuku Loft
Tatehana Bldg B2F, 1-12-9 Kabuki-cho, Shinjuku-ku
(5287 3766). Shinjuku station. **Capacity** live stage
550; sub-stage 100. **Map** 1b.
A venerable name on the Tokyo live scene has survived a 1999 move across the Shinjuku tracks with
its reputation intact. For most of its 24-year history,
Loft has focused on rock, alternative, punk and hardcore; many Japanese acts took their first steps here.

Shinjuku Loft Plus One
Hayashi Bldg B2F, 1-14-7 Kabuki-cho,
Shinjuku-ku (3205 6864). Shinjuku station.
Capacity 100. **Map** 1b.

Arts & Entertainment

Standing room only at **On Air East**, tucked away among Shibuya's love hotels. *See p209.*

If you don't count the cover charge of ¥600 for sitting at a table, music at this sister venue of Loft (*see p209*) is free. Its speciality is a genre called 'Talk-live', incorporating hi-tech beats and poetic ranting.

Shibuya Nest

On Air West 5F and 6F, 2-3 Maruyama-cho, Shibuya-ku (3462 4420). Shibuya station. **Capacity** 100-250. **Map** 2.

Shibuya's On Air couple (*see p209*) have spawned this charming little baby, which spreads over two floors of On Air West. Interesting atmosphere.

Star Pine's Cafe

1-20-16 Kichijoji-Honcho, Musashino-shi (0422 232251). Kichijoji station. **Capacity** 100. **Map** 31.

Another sister venue of Mandala Minami-Aoyama (*see p209*), located beside Kintetsu department store in Kichijoji. It's a cosy rock and DJ venue with a unique feature, a grand piano on the stage. Can appear daunting to the uninitiated, but there's really nothing to be afraid of.

STB139

6-7-11 Roppongi, Minato-ku (5474 1395/ http://stb139.co.jp). Roppongi station. **Capacity** *Standing* 500. *Seated* 270. **Map** 4.

Wine and dine while listening to some of the world's most celebrated crooners at this stylish Roppongi venue. Music ranges from pops, rock and soul to Latin, R&B, jazz and classics. The only serious rival to Blue Note Tokyo (*see p208*).

Vuenos Bar Tokyo

2-21-7 Dogenzaka, Shibuya-ku (5458 5963). Shibuya station. **Capacity** 500. **Map** 2.

Sister venue of Club Asia (*see p209*) and located just across the road. Vuenos, as its name implies, relies heavily on salsa and other Latin music to pull in the punters. Has recently begun branching out into other musical areas, too, such as hip-hop, rock and hardcore.

Womb

Studio Arias, 2-16 Maruyama-ho, Shibuya-ku (5459 0039). Shibuya station. **Capacity** 500. **Map** 2.

A brand new space, Womb boasts one of the best sound systems in Tokyo. The lavish interior is a throwback to the days before the country's economy started to go down the toilet. Its weakest point is its location, buried in Shibuya's Maruyama-cho love hotel area. Pressure from love hotel owners has led to it closing by 1am.

Nightlife

Catch the latest craze, if you can, on Tokyo's fast-changing club scene.

Kabuki-cho, Shinjuku's very own sin city, is one of the main centres of Tokyo nightlife.

Arts & Entertainment

With the new millennium, Tokyo's nightlife scene has accelerated its already bewildering pace of change and further diversified. Many venues have been forced out of business by the prolonged economic recession, while others are busy refurbishing their interiors and new ones continue to pop up overnight. All have one thing in common, though: the emphasis here is increasingly on quality of sound rather than glitzy decor to pull in the punters.

Tokyo venues can technically be divided into two categories: discos and clubs. Discos charge higher entrance fees of around ¥4,000, including one or two drinks. They sometimes have giant dance floors, lighting and sound systems, and bar lounges, crowded with men and women on the look-out for a one-night stand. Stricter dress codes are usually applied.

Clubs, on the other hand, usually have smaller dance floors and bars, are more dimly lit and cosy. They are also often in a basement. They usually charge around ¥2,000 to get in, which also includes one or two drinks. Their customers tend to be more music-oriented

(as are the clubs themselves) and regularly visit one venue, where many of them become friends.

As Japanese DJs have recently started to conquer the world, so the club scene has developed a new confidence, though not all of the crazes here would find favour in the west.

At the time of writing, the latest club craze is *parapara*, a sort of hands-only Japanese line dance based on synchronisation and uniformity that appeals to the heavily tanned girls with big boots who hang around Shibuya, perhaps because their feet are too heavy to move. With their no-less-tanned boyfriends, they happily hand-jive the night away.

Alcohol is sold till 5am in most clubs. Although it's technically illegal for most clubs to open after midnight (this is connected with a ridiculous law about dancing after the witching hour), most clubs ignore the rules and some even reopen at 5am for after-hours parties, which last until noon. Maniac Love (*see p215*), which starts at 5am on Sunday morning, is one of the most famous in Tokyo, and it's not unusual to see the place full at 6am.

As in most cities, the best source of club information in Tokyo is flyers, many of which are in English as well as Japanese. A good source is HMV in Shibuya (see p181). They often double as discount vouchers, so keep them. Bigger clubs usually post schedules near the entrance. Weekly free magazine *Tokyo Classified* also keeps you up to date in its 'After Dark' section, along with monthly magazine *Tokyo Journal*'s 'Night Life' pages (see p268 for both). For club information on the internet, see p275. None of the venues listed below takes credit cards.

Venues

328 (San Ni Hachi)

B1F, 3-24-20 Nishi-Azabu, Minato-ku (3401 4968). Roppongi station. **Open** 8pm-midnight daily. **Admission** ¥2,000 Mon-Thur (incl 2 drinks); ¥2,500 Fri-Sun (incl 2 drinks). **Dress code** none. **Map** 4.
328 opened in 1979, undergoing total refurbishment. in 1998. From the street, you'll spot its large neon sign from Nishi-Azabu crossing. Music is a mixture of genres, ranging from soul to dance classics, and there are live performances of drums and blues harp at weekends, when this small venue gets packed.

Ball

Kuretake Bldg 4F, 4-9 Udagawa-cho, Shibuya-ku (3476 6533). Shibuya station. **Open** 9pm-5am Mon-Sat; varies with events on Sun. **Admission** ¥2,000 Mon-Fri (incl 2 drinks); varies with events Sat. **Dress code** none. **Map** 2.
There's a great night view of Shibuya to be had from this small venue, but sadly that is its best feature, despite the reasonably priced bar (drinks from ¥600). The PA isn't up to scratch – given that the choice of music is house, this is a very serious shortcoming indeed. What's more, the dance floor is tiny.

Bar Drop

Ichibe Bldg 2F, 1-29-6 Kichijoji-Honcho, Musashino-shi (0422 20 0737). Kichijoji station. **Open** 9pm-midnight daily. **Admission** ¥1,500 Mon-Thur (incl 1 drink); usually ¥2,000 Fri-Sun (incl 1 drink) but can vary. **Dress code** none. **Map** 31.
On its two dance floors (2F and B1F), Bar Drop features a variety of '90s US and UK pop, with the downstairs floor offering a slightly more eclectic choice of sounds. Unusually for Tokyo, there's a lounge space, with tables and chairs to cool off at.

Bed

Fukuri Bldg B1F, 3-29-9 Nishi-Ikebukuro, Toshima-ku (3981 5300). Ikebukuro station. **Open** 10pm-5am daily. **Admission** ¥2,000 Mon-Thur, Sun (incl 2 drinks); ¥2,500 Fri, Sat (incl 2 drinks). **Dress code** none. **Map** 5.
As you descend to Bed, you're greeted by photo montages of previous, apparently well-satisfied, customers. The clientele here is on the young side, and the music played is mainly hip hop, plus some occasional techno and warp house.

Café & Club Fura

3-26-25 Shibuya, Shibuya-ku (5485 4011). Shibuya station. **Open** 9pm-5am daily. **Admission** ¥1,000 (incl 1 drink for men); ¥1,000 (incl 2 drinks for women) before 11 pm Mon-Thur; ¥3,000 (incl 2 drinks) Fri-Sun. **Dress code** no beachwear. **Map** 2.
Café & Club Fura is a four-storey complex with an Italian restaurant on the first floor, a relatively roomy dance floor on the second and a bar-cum-lounge space on the floor above. The venue has relaxed its dress code and now allows denim pants-clad kids to get in, seeing off its once-snobby image. The place is heaving, even on weekdays, with Saturday nights the busiest.

Club Acid Tokyo

Kowa Bldg B1F, 2-3-12 Shinjuku, Shinjuku-ku (3352 3338). Shinjuku-Gyoenmae station. **Open** 8pm-midnight daily. **Admission** ¥2,000 (incl 2 drinks). **Dress code** none. **Map** 1b.
Finding the entrance to Club Acid is something of a challenge in itself. Only a small sign on Shinjuku Dori gives any hint of its existence. The best way of finding it is to pay close attention to the stairways of neighbouring buildings and follow your ears: on different nights you can hear anything booming out of here, from ska to rock, hip hop to Latin, R&B to techno to drum 'n' bass. Check the schedule to see what's on when.

Club Asia

1-8 Maruyama-cho, Shibuya-ku (5458 1996). Shibuya station. **Open** 11pm-5am daily. **Admission** varies with events. **Dress code** none. **Map** 2.
Club Asia is a favourite space with private-party organisers, so for individual events you should be sure to check out the schedule by the entrance. There is a bar and cloakroom on the first floor, a small dance floor and bar on the second, and by the stairway that leads from the second floor there's a moderately roomy dance floor and bar. The stairway to the main hall is an unusual feature, but it can get crowded, particularly on Friday nights. The main hall's high ceiling looks great but can make the sound a bit uneven.

Club Bar Family

Shimizu Bldg B1F, 1-10-2 Shibuya, Shibuya-ku (3400 9182). Shibuya station. **Open** 10pm-midnight daily. **Admission** varies with events. **Dress code** none. **Map** 2.
A small venue with a bar and dance floor where you can dance the night away to soul and dance classics, R&B and hip hop. The interior is not outstanding, and the clientele is relatively young, including herds of young girls with fake tans and platform boots. Drinks are around ¥600.

Club Chu

Oba B-Bldg B1F, 28-4 Maruyama-cho, Shibuya-ku (3770 3786). Shibuya station. **Open** 10pm-5am Mon-Sat; 6-11pm Sun. **Admission** ¥2,000 (incl 2 drinks). **Dress code** none. **Map** 2.

Arts & Entertainment

Private parties are a big deal at **Club Asia**, so check the schedule first. *See p212.*

Chu means sky or space, and the decor at this club is designed to give the feeling of floating in space. The cool ambience is intended to attract a more adult clientele than many other clubs – people seeking a lounge space with good music and drink, rather than serious dance nuts or date-hunters. The small lounge opens irregularly, and only on Sundays.

Club Complex Code

Shinjuku Toho Kaikan 4F, 1-19-2 Kabuki-cho, Shinjuku-ku (3209 0702/www.so-net.ne.jp/ CYBERJAPAN/contents/clubzone/code). Shinjuku station. **Open** 7pm-3am Mon-Thur, Sun; 7pm-5am Fri, Sat. **Admission** ¥2,500 Mon-Thur, Sun (incl 2 drinks); ¥3,500 Fri (incl two drinks); ¥3,000 Sat (incl 2 drinks). **Dress code** no sandals. **Map** 1b.

With three dance floors (two small, one gigantic), Club Complex Code is a monster nightclub that can host a variety of different events and special nights (sometimes at the same time). Its location, on the fourth floor of a Kabuki-cho building, means that from the outside you get no real impression of its vast size: with a capacity of 2,000 people, Code is one of the biggest clubs in Japan. The biggest of the three dance floors is called En-Code, and is sometimes used as a live stage. En-Code itself has a capacity of 1,000, plus four gigantic screens where you can watch the VJs doing their stuff. Sub-floor De-Code holds 120. There is also a main bar room and lounge, Ba-Code, and a snack bar beside the main floor, where a ¥500 token buys you anything from a bottle of mineral water to a small buffet. *See also p203* **Club events.**

Club Hachi

Aoyama Bldg 2-4F, 4-5-9 Shibuya, Shibuya-ku (5469 1676). Omotesando station. **Open** 10pm-5am daily. **Admission** varies with events. **Dress code** none. **Map** 2.

Club Hachi occupies the whole of a run-down three-storey building on Roppongi Dori. The first-floor café bar has recently been converted into a western-style *yakitori* bar. The venue was once the home of globally fêted DJs Ken Ishii and Kensei, who used to play here regularly. Check out the drum 'n' bass event every third Saturday.

Club Jamaica

Nishi-Azabu Ishibashi Bldg B1F, 4-16-14 Nishi-Azabu, Minato-ku (3407 8844). Roppongi station. **Open** 10pm-5am Thur-Sat. **Admission** ¥2,500 (incl 2 drinks). **Dress code** none. **Map** 4.

Opened by a reggae fanatic in 1989, Club Jamaica is still blasting out the booming sounds of Jamaica's finest. It's a small venue with an entrance that can be difficult to find, but it's definitely worth persevering because the atmosphere is friendly and the sound system excellent.

Club Kuaile

Square Bldg 10F, 3-10-3 Roppongi, Minato-ku (3470 7421). Roppongi station. **Open** 10pm-midnight daily. **Admission** ¥2,500 (incl 2 drinks), can vary with events. **Dress code** no sandals or shorts. **Map** 4.

The main bill of fare is speed garage, pumped out at high volume through a superior sound system. A roomy venue with great views over Roppongi from its tenth-floor vantage point.

Core takes some finding, a sub-basement venue with no sign outside. It's worth the effort.

Club Que Shimo-Kitazawa

Big Ben Bldg B2F, 2-5-2 Kitazawa, Setagaya-ku (3412 9979). Shimo-Kitazawa station (Inokashira/ Odakyu lines). **Open** 6.30pm-4am Mon-Thur, Sun; 11pm-4pm Fri, Sat. **Admission** varies with events. **Dress code** none. **Map** 35.

Club Que's main *raison d'être* is as a live house for rock bands, but once the weekend gigs are over it transforms itself into a club. Music tends to be rock-oriented, with healthy doses of alternative rock, guitar pop and vintage rock thrown in. Worth a trip.

Club Salem Byblos

Jule A Bldg B1F, 1-10-10 Azabu-Juban, Minato-ku (3568 2380/www.byblos-group.com). Azabu-Juban station. **Open** 7pm-midnight daily. **Admission** *Men* ¥3,500 Fri, Sat (incl 2 drinks); ¥3,000 Mon-Thur, Sun (incl 2 drinks). *Women* ¥2,500 (incl 2 drinks). **Dress code** not casual.

A giant venue festooned with Salem cigarette signs. Tunes range from hip hop to house and techno. Miniskirt-clad Salem girls walk around giving away free sample cigarettes and even climb up on stage for a 15-minute dance every Friday. Saturday's regular event with DJs Minoru Ujita and Hi-G is also worth checking out. Because of its location, you may find yourself grappling with hordes of besuited salarymen to get in.

Club The Earth

1-13-3 Kaigan, Minato-ku (3436 6330). Takeshiba Sanbashi station (Yurikamome line). **Open** 7pm-midnight Tue-Sun. **Admission** *Men* ¥3,000 (incl 2 drinks). *Women* ¥2,500 (incl 2 drinks). *Both* free before 9pm. **Dress code** not casual.

Club The Earth is a mammoth venue located near Takeshiba Pier, launched in 1999 by the company that produced **Café & Club Fura** in Shibuya (*see p212*). Earth is one of the largest clubs in Tokyo, populated by neatly dressed punters in their mid-twenties. The main dance floor features four mirror balls and three bars, where drinks start at ¥700. Those who get tired with the parade of hits on offer can go to the smaller dance floor upstairs and cool off to cosy house and R&B tunes.

Core

MT Bldg B2F, 3-8-18 Roppongi, Minato-ku (3470 5944). Roppongi station. **Open** 10pm-midnight daily. **Admission** varies with events. **Dress code** none. **Map** 4.

Discretion is taken to new heights at Core, whose owner claims he didn't put a sign outside because he didn't want everyone to know it was there. The dance floor is surprisingly roomy given its sub-basement location. The bar snacks are impressive; there's even steak. Drinks start at ¥600. Core features house and techno, and it has proved popular with TV and sports personalities on their nights off. Every second Friday, it hosts a house and R&B event, 'Scene', where DJ Funakoshi and Yo-Gin spin the tracks.

Fai

Hachihonkan Bldg B2F, 5-10-1 Minami-Aoyama, Minato-ku (3486 4910). Omotesando station. **Open** 9pm-5am daily. **Admission** varies with events. **Dress code** none. **Map** 4.

Only punk and techno are left off the musical menu at Fai, whose speciality is music from the '70s and '80s. Drinks start at ¥700.

Gamos

2-chome Center Bldg B1F, 2-11-10 Shinjuku, Shinjuku-ku (3354 5519/www.interq.or.jp/ japan/gamos). Shinjuku-Sanchome station. **Open** 10pm-5am daily. **Admission** varies with events. **Dress code** none. **Map** 1b.

This area of Shinjuku is famous for its gay and lesbian bars and clubs, but Gamos is no longer exclusively gay. The club features mainly basic house. Check out their house event 'Source' on Fridays.

Ism Shibuya

Social Dogenzaka Bldg 2F, 1-14-9 Dogenzaka, Shibuya-ku (3780 6320). Shibuya station. **Open** 10pm-midnight daily. **Admission** varies. **Dress code** none. **Map** 2.

Sister venue of Rockwest Shibuya (*see p216*), located in the area near the Mark City complex. Its brother venue, Rockwest, has now abandoned its original small-club purpose to attract the crowds by hosting a variety of events. Ism takes the old Rockwest ethos and hosts a number of small techno, house, trance and happy hardcore parties.

Liquid Room

Humax Pavilion 7F, 1-20-1 Kabuki-cho, Shinjuku-ku (3200 6831). Shinjuku station. **Open** varies with events. **Admission** varies with events. **Dress code** none. **Map** 1b.

Liquid Room is a large club and live house located in the middle of frantic Kabuki-cho. Although it does host its own events two or three times a month, most of the time the space is rented out, so you never know what might be happening: it could be a live house one night, featuring big-name acts from around the world (*see p209*) and a hip hop club the next. It has two bars and, thankfully, plenty of toilets. Liquid Room's monthly schedule is available free from big record stores such as **Tower** or **HMV** (*see p181 for both*).

Loop

Nihon Fudo Bldg B1F, 2-1-13 Shibuya, Shibuya-ku (3797 9933/www.baseplanning.co.jp). Shibuya station. **Open** 10pm-5am daily. **Admission** ¥2,000 Mon-Thur (incl 1 drink); ¥2,500 Fri-Sun (incl 1 drink), ¥2,000 with flyer (incl 1 drink). **Dress code** none. **Map** 2.

Loop is located between Shibuya and Omotesando stations. A warmly lit lounge space with stylish bare-concrete interiors serves as an ideal hide-out for die-hard techno buffs seeking to keep their distance from wannabe club-goers. The dance floor has a friendly vibe, moody lighting and an excellent sound system. DJ Mochizuki hosts the Saturday event 'In the Mix', featuring techno, broken beats and future jazz, occasionally with invited, mainly British, foreign performers.

Luners

Fukao Bldg B1F, 1-4-5 Azabu-Juban, Minato-ku (3586 6383). Azabu-Juban station. **Open** daily, times vary. **Admission** varies with events. **Dress code** none.

A relatively large venue with a huge mirror ball hanging above the main floor. You can admire the whole crowd from its lounge in the loft. If the main stage and its giant screen leave you cold, you can make your own stage out of the terrace between the down- and upstairs. A first-floor restaurant offers internet access and a quiet environment for more intimate tête-à-têtes.

Maniac Love

Tera-Asiosu Omotesando Bldg B1F, 5-10-6 Minami-Aoyama, Minato-ku (3406 1166). Omotesando station. **Open** 10pm-midnight Mon-Sat. **Admission** ¥2,000 Mon-Thur (incl 1 drink); ¥2,500 Fri, Sat (incl 1 drink); ¥1,000 Sun from 5am (incl free coffee). **Dress code** none. **Map** 4.

With its immense sound system and cool lighting effects, Maniac Love was designed to be the mecca for dance music in Tokyo. The venue, like many others in Tokyo, is a little tricky to find, located in the basement of a plain-looking building. It attracts serious dance music lovers, so don't come here looking for a date. Drinks start at ¥700. The after-hours party on Sunday mornings has built up a loyal following, and it's not unusual to see the place full to bursting at 7am. Check out the techno/break beats event, 'Machine Gun', with DJ Captain Funk every first Friday of the month.

Milk

Roob 6 Bldg B1F/B2F, 1-13-3 Ebisu-Nishi, Shibuya-ku (5458 2826). Ebisu station. **Open** 9pm-midnight daily. **Admission** ¥1,000 (no drinks); ¥2,000 for events (no drinks). **Dress code** none. **Map** 3.

Milk's mission when it opened in 1995 was to bring the best of rock, punk and hardcore to Tokyo. These days, however, even Milk has succumbed to the techno and house sound that has swept Tokyo clubland, although on Saturday nights it goes back to its roots and occasionally hosts live rock acts. The venue itself is maze-like, occupying three floors below ground of the same building as a pub, What The Dickens (*see p160*). At the bottom of the club is a lounge area with a mysteriously lit morgue-like kitchen, where you can have a quiet conversation while up above the dancing continues on the cramped dance floor.

Organ Bar

Kuretake Bldg 3F, 4-9 Udagawa-cho, Shibuya-ku (5489 5460). Shibuya station. **Open** 9pm-5am daily. **Admission** varies with events. **Dress code** none. **Map** 2.

Another small joint in the same building as Ball (*see p212*). It features soul and jazz, and Yasuharu Konishi, of world-famous Japanese band Pizzicato Five, plays here every second Friday of the month. Drinks are all ¥800.

Oto

Wadakyu Bldg 2F, 1-17-5 Kabuki-cho, Shinjuku-ku (5273 8264). Shinjuku station. **Open** 10pm-midnight daily. **Admission** varies with events. **Dress code** none. **Map** 1b.

Oto (meaning 'sound' in Japanese) lives up to its name, with a sound system that would do a much larger place credit. Music runs from hip hop to techno, and drinks are all ¥700.

Pylon
TSK Bldg B1F/B2F, 7-15-30 Roppongi,
Minato-ku (3497 1818). Roppongi station.
Open 9pm-5am Fri-Sun. **Admission** *Men* ¥3,500 (incl 2 drinks). *Women* ¥3,000 (incl 2 drinks). **Dress code** none. **Map** 4.
Pylon moved here from Shibuya in 2000. The entry charge system is somewhat bizarre. The first time you go, you'll be given a membership card, which costs ¥3,500 (men) or ¥3,000 (women). From your second visit, the card gives you a ¥1,000 discount off the price of admission. Pylon attracts a young crowd, mainly 16- to 22-year-olds out for a wild night on the town.

Ring
Kohama Bldg 1F/2F, 1-8-8 Nishi-Azabu,
Minato-ku (5411 4300). Roppongi station.
Open 10pm-5am Tue-Sun. **Admission** ¥2,500 Tue-Thur (incl 2 drinks). *Men* ¥3,000 Fri, Sat, before holiday (incl 2 drinks; free Sun. *Women* ¥2,500 Fri, Sat (incl 2 drinks; free Sun. **Dress code** not too casual. **Map** 4.
Look out for a small sign on Roppongi Dori and you've found this place, which plays soul and dance classics to a very appreciative crowd. After its low-key exterior, the size of the dance floor and bar areas comes as a pleasant surprise. Expect crowds on Fridays and Saturdays.

Rockwest Shibuya
Tosen Udagawa-cho Bldg 7F, 4-7 Udagawa-cho,
Shibuya-ku (5459 7988). Shibuya station.
Open 10pm-5am daily. **Admission** ¥2,500 (incl 2 drinks); ¥2,000 (with flyer or advance ticket, incl 1 drink). **Dress code** none. **Map** 2.
Rockwest is one of the best places in town for a happy hardcore night out. There's a good sound system, air-conditioning and a relatively roomy dance floor, and re-entry is allowed.

The Room
Daihachi Tohto Bldg B1F, 15-19 Sakuraga-oka,
Shibuya-ku (3461 7167). Shibuya station.
Open 10pm-midnight Mon-Sat. **Admission** ¥1,000 Mon; ¥2,000 Tue-Thur (incl 1 drink); ¥1,000 Fri, Sat before 11pm (incl 1 drink); ¥2,500 Fri, Sat after 11pm (incl 2 drinks). **Dress code** none. **Map** 2.
A small, wood-panelled venue, famous for its cocktails. Sometimes plays host to top DJs who come here to practise new routines on their nights off.

Simoon
3-26-16 Shibuya, Shibuya-ku (5774 1669). Shibuya station. **Open** 10pm-midnight daily, but varies with events. **Admission** approx ¥2,500 (incl 1 or 2 drinks). **Dress code** no shorts, sandals. **Map** 2.
Cosy, decent-sized space that opened in December 2000. The entrance may look a little like a bicycle parking lot, but inside a warmly lit lounge awaits

you with comfortable couches. The basement dance floor boasts a good-quality sound system for its size. Selected hard-house and techno tunes.

Soul Kiss
Ienek Roppongi Bldg B1F, B2 7-12-3 Roppongi,
Minato-ku (5785 2745). Roppongi station.
Open 8pm-5am daily. **Admission** free.
Dress code none. **Map** 4.
A cosy venue that opened in January 2001. Black-and-white portraits decorating the wall accentuate its chic atmosphere, while extremely comfortable couches in the corridor-like lounge heal your body. The best thing here is free admission, which is very rare among Tokyo clubs. At the entrance, it may take a while to figure out how to get in when you see a thick, black steel door without any buttons or handles. Drinks start from ¥800.

Space Lab Yellow
Cesaurus Nishi-Azabu Bldg, 1-10-11 Nishi-Azabu,
Minato-ku (3479 0690/www.space-lab-yellow.com).
Roppongi station. **Open** varies with events.
Admission varies with events. **Dress code** none.
Map 4.
This relatively big space is a popular venue for events and parties, and the dance floor is big enough to accommodate the occasional live act. There's also a snack bar and roomy lounge. On Saturday, guest appearances by visiting foreign DJs fill the place.

Sugar High DJ Bar & Club
Yubun Bldg 3F, 2-16-3 Dogenzaka, Shibuya-ku
(3780 3022). Shibuya station. **Open** 7pm-2am Mon-Thur, Sun; 7pm-5am Fri, Sat. **Admission** varies with events. **Dress code** none. **Map** 2.
From Shibuya station, head left at the intersection of 109, climb up the Dogenzaka slope for about 200m, and you'll see the Sugar High sign on your left. Admission charge varies with events, from nothing to ¥2,500. Cocktails are all ¥500.

Sugar Hill
Azabudai Mansion 101, 3-4-14 Azabudai, Minato-ku
(3583 6223). Roppongi station. **Open** 8pm-5am daily. **Admission** ¥700. **Dress code** none. **Map** 4.
A lounge-style hideout in Roppongi. One apartment room is stuffed with thousands of classic records from the late '70s and early '80s. As well as finding your favourite dance track, you can also indulge in Italian and your favourite Japanese food: *tempura* and *udon* are brought in from neighbouring restaurants and sold at reasonable prices.

Twin Star
2-11 Kagurazaka, Shinjuku-ku (3269 0005),
Iidabashi station. **Open** 6.30pm-midnight Tue-Fri. **Admission** *Men* ¥4,000 (incl 5 drinks). *Women* ¥3,000 (incl 5 drinks). **Dress code** not too casual.
Twin Star has become the mecca of Japanese *para-para* dance (see p211). This giant disco, opened in late 1991, has a somewhat garish interior and a spacious dance floor, reviving memories of Japan's bubble economy. But this *parapara* sanctuary is

Stairway to Heaven?

now slowly trying to evolve in a new direction, as evidenced by Friday's 3-D event. Tuesday's *para-para* party is definitely worth checking out.

Velfarre

Velfarre Bldg, 7-14-22 Roppongi, Minato-ku (3402 8000/velfarre.avex.co.jp). Roppongi station. **Open** 6pm-1am Fri, Sat; 6pm-midnight Thur, Sun. **Admission** *Men* ¥3,000 (incl 2 drinks) Thur, Sat, Sun; ¥3,500 (incl 2 drinks) Fri. *Women* ¥2,000 (incl 2 drinks) Thur, Sat; ¥2,500 (incl 2 drinks) Fri; free Sun. **Dress code** not too casual. **Map** 4.

The largest disco in Asia, Velfarre reopened for business in March 1998. This gigantic disco and live house space, with a capacity of over 2,000, is a real throwback to the mirror ball days of the '80s, with marble staircases and other extravagances. It has a vast dance floor with an automated movable stage and giant mirror ball at the bottom, and more bars, restrooms and snack bars than you can count. If you're feeling brave, try to blag your way into one of the VIP lounges, from where you can watch the action without actually having to dance.

Vuenos Bar Tokyo

1F/B1F, 2-21-7 Dogenzaka, Shibuya-ku (5458 5963/ www.clubasia.co.jp). Shibuya station. **Open** *Club* 11pm-5am daily. *Bar* 7pm-5am daily. **Admission** varies. **Dress code** none. **Map** 2.

A Latin music club across from Club Asia (*see p212*), owned and operated by the same company as its neighbour. Vuenos opened in October 1998 with a mission to spread the word about Latin, soul and dance music, in contrast with Club Asia's mainly techno and house events. Clubbers who come here tend be older than average for Tokyo, mostly around 25 or above, and a ¥1,000 ticket buys two drinks. The admission charge varies with events but is usually around ¥2,500.

Web

B1F, 3-30-10 Ikejiri, Setagaya-ku (3422 1405). Ikejiri-Ohashi station (Shin-Tamagawa line). **Open** 10pm-midnight Thur-Sat. **Admission** ¥2,000 Thur (incl 2 drinks); ¥2,500 Fri, Sat (incl 2 drinks). **Dress code** none.

A small joint that squeezes in nearly 100 people. Web serves a variety of cocktails, and the menu changes monthly. DJs spin music of all genres.

Womb

2-16 Maruyama-cho, Shibuya-ku (5459 0039). Shibuya station. **Open** varies with events. **Admission** ¥2,500 (incl 1 drink). **Dress code** no sandals. **Map** 2.

In the middle of one of the biggest 'love hotel' districts in Tokyo, this gymnasium-like disco sits in a bare concrete building. The main floor, whose ceiling is almost 9m (30ft) high, is enormous and its huge mirror ball, almost 2m (7ft) in diameter, is amazing when lit up. The venue also boasts upstairs lounge areas and a super-bass sound system shipped all the way from New York. Check out Friday's party with DJ Ko Kimura.

Drugs

The use of recreational drugs is (mostly) illegal in Japan, and those caught importing or using them face heavy fines, prison sentences or deportation.

That said, there are, of course, drugs to be had on the streets and in the clubs of Tokyo, just as there are in every other major city. Drug use, though, is by no means as widespread as in, say, London. At the height of the water-drinking ecstasy craze, for example, Tokyo clubbers were seen to wave the requisite bottles of Evian, without having consumed the E to go with it.

Street prices for what drugs there are are higher than you might be used to, if you indulge in that sort of thing. The most popular drug of choice, unsurprisingly, is cannabis, but its price of ¥2,000-¥3,000 per gramme leads many regular users to grow it for themselves. The police rarely go out of their way to hunt down growers, but getting caught with rolling papers will provoke suspicion.

Another widely used drug is speed, (amphetamines) or *shabu*. A typical 30mg dose sells for around ¥2,000 and its use permeates society, from 80-hour-a-week execs to late-night taxi drivers and their teenage sons and daughters.

In contrast, cocaine and heroin are virtually impossible to come by. Rumour has it that this is because of a deal struck by *yakuza* to keep hard stuff out of the country in return for a certain amount of tolerance.

Intriguingly, there is one massive loophole in Japan's drug laws: magic mushrooms. For some inexplicable reason, mushrooms have escaped the eagle eye of the legislators and can be legally sold. Numerous shops have sprung up to cater for mushroom fiends (*see p180*), and one reliable dealer is to be found nightly diagonally across from the *koban* (police box) at Shibuya's Hachiko crossing. He provides a rundown of his products' provenance and likely effects. Cheapest mushrooms are ¥3,000 for a small bag of around 30. This legal loophole is sure to close if there's a high-profile mushroom-related incident.

Performing Arts

The traditions of Japanese drama are a world apart from the western norm.

Japanese theatre is a feast of colour and texture: the exquisite costumes, the make-up, the colourful backdrops, even the embroidered fire curtains. To the colour and texture add sound and smell – the exotic tones of various instruments that accompany the actors' intriguing speech patterns and impassioned exchanges, and in some plays the perfume or incense wafting over the audience. Japanese theatre is to be felt, too – in the tingling of your scalp, the stirred emotions, the held breath and the collective tension of the audience.

In common with the performing arts throughout Asia, Japanese traditional theatre genres integrate dance, music and lyrical narrative. The emphasis is on aesthetic beauty, symbolism and imagery as opposed to western theatre's realism and logic. Another important element distinguishing Japanese theatre from that of the west is *ma*, perhaps best translated as a 'pregnant pause'. It is not considered silence; rather it is the space between musical notes or words and is used to heighten the intensity of the dramatic moment.

The various genres of Japanese drama tend to share certain popular themes, the most common of which are clan squabbles; family, group or servant-master loyalty; commitment to or longing for one's home town or homeland; conflicts between duty and feelings; revenge; corruption and justice; and the supernatural.

Types of theatre

Noh and *kyogen*

Noh plays are ritualistic and formulaic. They are grouped into categories, which can be likened to a formal meal of five courses, each with a different flavour. Invigorating celebratory dances about gods are followed by battle plays of warrior-ghosts; next are lyrical pieces about women, then themes of insanity and finally demons. Presentation is mostly sombre, slow and deliberate. Plays explore the transience of this world, the sin of killing and the spiritual comfort to be found in Buddhism.

There are no group rehearsals: there is a pre-performance meeting, but the actors and

Tips for theatre-going

Buy tickets as early as possible. Most tickets go on sale one month or more before the day of the performance. Most theatres reserve a small number of tickets to be sold on the day of the performance, but they go quickly.

Do souvenir buying at the theatre. Almost every theatre has stalls selling a variety of goods such as jewellery, handbags, fans and food. Biscuits or sweet bean-filled cakes featuring the star's face are common, as well as sweatshirts, ties, towels, handkerchiefs, lighters, keyrings and other items, some bearing the star's autograph, name or face. Theatre doors usually open 20 to 30 minutes before curtain-up to allow for shopping.

Take your own food and drink to save money. Theatres have their own restaurants and sell boxed meals, but eating this way can be costly. There is no bar in Japanese theatres, although some do sell Japanese *sake* and cans of beer. Soft drinks and beverages are available from service

counters or vending machines at all theatres. If you do want to eat in the restaurant, make a reservation as soon as you arrive at the theatre.

Be prepared for using the Japanese squat-type toilets (*see p269*), as many theatres still have only one or two western-style ones.

Lastly, do not expect to sit and watch a performance in total silence. Theatre-going is considered a social outing, and Japanese people go armed with packed meals, flasks and rustling vinyl bags full of goodies. Eating in the theatre seat during or between acts, and commenting on the players and their performances during the show, is all part of the enjoyment in many theatres. While audiences are much quieter now than they were, say, 20 years ago, they can still be noisy by western standards. Be warned – shushing will have little effect, so instead of getting irritated, sit back and absorb it all as part of the experience.

lay together until the
spontaneity is one of
kind of theatre.
t, humorous interludes that
ss of human nature through
understated portrayal. They are interspersed for
comic relief with *noh* pieces, but are intended to
produce refined laughter, not boisterous humour.

Bunraku

The puppets used in *bunraku* are a half to two-
thirds human size and require great skill and
strength to operate. Each puppet is operated
by two assistants and one chief puppeteer.
Becoming a master puppeteer is a lengthy
process, beginning with ten years' operating
the legs, followed by another ten on the left arm
before being permitted to manipulate the right
arm, head and eyebrows. Four main elements
comprise a *bunraku* performance: the puppets
themselves; the movements they make; the
vocal delivery of the *tayu*, who chants the
narrative and speaks the lines for every
character, changing his voice to suit the
role; and the solo *shamisen* accompaniment.

Kabuki

Of all the traditional performing arts in Japan,
probably the most exciting is *kabuki*. The actor
is the most important element in *kabuki*, and
everything that happens on stage is a vehicle
for displaying his prowess.

Because the actor is central, the props
are used only as long as they show him
to his best advantage. *Koken*, stage hands
dressed in black, symbolising their supposed
invisibility, hand the actor props, make
adjustments to his heavy costume and wig,
and bring him a stool to perch on during
long speeches or periods of inactivity.

The *onnagata* female role specialists portray
a stylised feminine beauty. There is no pretence
at realism, so the actor's real age is irrelevant,
and there is no incongruity in a 75-year-old
actor portraying an 18-year-old maiden.

Most *kabuki* programmes feature one
shosagoto dance piece, one *jidaimono*, and one
sewamono. *Jidaimono* are dramas set in pre-Edo
Japan. They feature gorgeous costumes and
colourful make-up called *kumadori*, which is
painted along the lines of the actor's face. The
actor uses melodramatic elocution, but because
jidaimono originated in the puppet theatre,
the plays also feature accompaniment from a
chanter who relates the storyline and emotions
of the character while the actor expresses
them in movement, facial expressions or
poses. *Sewamono* are stories of everyday life
during the Edo period (1603-1867) and are
closer to western drama.

Every *kabuki* theatre features a *hanamichi*,
an elevated pathway for the performers that
runs through the audience from the back of
the theatre to the main stage. This is used
for entrances and exits and contains a traplift
through which supernatural characters emerge.

Samurai and historical dramas

Samurai dramas set in the Edo period, called
jidai geki, are the most frequently portrayed
type of historical drama on stage. Unlike in
kabuki, female roles are played by women.

No matter how tragic, *jidai geki* must end
with a satisfactory resolution, whether it is the
successful revenge of a murder or the ascent
into heaven of the dead heroine aloft a podium.
However, influenced by western drama, plays
with happy endings are on the increase.

Modern dramas and musicals

The major source for other domestic modern
theatre productions are famous western plays
and musicals translated into Japanese. In
particular, the **New National Theatre** (*see
p222*) in the Opera City complex provides a
forum for the most respected Japanese directors,
who take a contemporary approach to western
classics and other productions.

Musicals are popular and are often staged
annually. Favourites include *Fiddler on the
Roof* and *The Wizard of Oz*. There is also
a thriving underground avant-garde theatre
subculture in the suburb of Shimo-Kitazawa
(*see p84*), with dozens of small venues. For
a city as cosmopolitan as Tokyo, it may come
as a surprise to learn that only a handful of
productions in English are available each year,
and some of those are possible only because of
touring troupes from Britain or America.

Theatres to visit

Kabuki-za

*4-12-15 Ginza, Chuo-ku (info 3541 3131/box office
5565 6000). Higashi-Ginza station.* **Box office**
10am-6pm daily. **Tickets** ¥2,520-¥16,800. **Credit**
AmEx, DC, JCB, MC, V. **Map** 6.
The best place to see *kabuki*. An English-language
programme (¥1,000) and earphone guide (¥650 plus
a refundable deposit of ¥1,000) are invaluable.
Performances last up to five hours, including intervals. Tickets to watch one act from the fourth floor
can be bought from one hour beforehand. The earphone guide cannot be used on the fourth floor.

Koma Gekijo

*1-19-1 Kabuki-cho, Shinjuku-ku (3200 2213).
Shinjuku station.* **Box office** 9.30am-7pm daily.
Tickets ¥3,000-¥8,500. **Credit** MC, JCB, V. **Map** 1b.
A famous theatre with a revolving stage. Most per-
formers are famous singers who appear in a period
drama, then give a concert. No English.

Girls will be boys

Not so much an art form as an experiment in gender manipulation, *takarazuka* bridges the gap between traditional and modern theatre in a way that can seem bizarre. *Takarazuka* is often called the female equivalent of *kabuki*, but it's more than that. Not only are all the roles are taken by females, but 99 per cent of the audience is female, too, and top performers receive the sort of adulation normally reserved for male pop stars, complete with screaming and waiting for autographs. In order to keep the magic of the stage alive, *takarazuka* players are discouraged from making details of their private lives public. The disappointment caused by one of the company's leading 'men' being 'outed' as a married woman, for instance, would have a shattering impact on their careers.

Takarazuka is camp, fun and, unbelievably to western eyes, totally devoid of any sexual connotations. A typical revue consists of a glamorously staged, specially written historical or modern musical drama, sometimes set in Japan, plus a show. Adaptations of major western musicals, such as *Gone With the Wind*, *West Side Story* and *Elizabeth* are also periodically presented.

The first *takarazuka* theatre was built in the spa town of Takarazuka in 1924, and replaced in 1992. This is still in use, having survived substantial damage in the 1995 Hanshin earthquake. A sister theatre in Tokyo, completed in 1934, was razed in 1997, and in its place is the 2,069-seat **Tokyo Takarazuka Gekijo** (*see p222*), which opened on 1 January 2001. However, whether the upmarket theatre with its increased ticket prices and year-round programme will prove successful is a moot point. Many of the best, most popular stars of recent years have moved on, and diehard fans miss the market atmosphere of the old lobby, with walls and stalls plastered with stars' photos, and the excitement of waiting for their favourite hero(in)es to visit Tokyo.

Meiji-za

2-31-1 Nihonbashi-Hamacho, Chuo-ku (3660 3939).
Hamacho station. **Box office** 10am-5pm daily.
Tickets ¥5,000-¥12,000. **Credit** DC, V.
Usually stages *samurai* dramas, often starring
actors who play similar roles on TV. No English.

National Theatre Large Hall

4-1 Hayabusa-cho, Chiyoda-ku (3230 3000)
Hanzomon station. **Box office** 10am-6pm daily.
Tickets ¥1,500-¥9,200. **No credit cards. Map** 9.
Kabuki is staged approximately nine months a year
in the Large Hall. The programme (¥800) includes
the story in English; an earphone guide is available.

National Theatre Small Hall

4-1 Hayabusa-cho, Chiyoda-ku (3230 3000).
Hanzomon station. **Box office** 10am-6pm daily.
Tickets ¥3,500-¥5,800. **No credit cards. Map** 9.
Bunraku for about four months a year. Programme
with story in English and earphone guide.

National Noh Theatre

4-18-1 Sendagaya, Shibuya-ku (3423 1331).
Sendagaya station. **Box office** 10am-6pm daily.
Tickets ¥2,300-¥6,000; ¥1,700 concessions.
No credit cards. Map 23.
Noh performances four or five times a month. A one-
page explanation of the story in English is available.

Shinbashi Embujo

6-18-2 Ginza, Chuo-ku (3541 2600). Higashi-Ginza
station. **Box office** 10am-6pm daily. **Tickets** ¥2,100-
¥15,750. **Credit** AmEx, DC, JCB, MC, V. **Map** 20.
Programme features English explanation of the
story when Ichikawa Ennosuke stages his 'Super-
Kabuki' (April-May). *Samurai* dramas other months.

Tokyo Takarazuka Gekijo

1-1-3 Yurakucho, Chiyoda-ku (5251 2001/
www.hankyu.co.jp/kageki). Yurakucho station.
Box office 10am-6pm Mon, Tue, Thur-Sun.
Tickets ¥3,500-¥10,000. **Credit** JCB, MC, V. **Map** 6.
Musicals by glam female revue troupes. Programme
includes the story in English. *See p221* **Girls will
be boys.**

Western theatres

Panasonic Globe-za

3-1-2 Hyakunincho, Shinjuku-ku (info in English 3360
3540/box office in Japanese 3360 3240). Shin-Okubo
station. **Box office** 10am-6pm Mon-Fri. **Tickets**
¥3,000-¥9,500. **No credit cards. Map** 22.
Performances in English for ten days each in June
and October by visiting UK Shakespearean actors.

Tokyo International Players

c/o The Asia Foundation, 32 Kowa Building 2F,
5-2 Minami Azabu, Minato-ku (3447 1981/
www2.gol.com/users/tip). Hiroo station.
No credit cards.
Keen amateurs. Season runs late September to late
May. Productions are in English and usually take
place at the Tokyo American Club (*see map 4*).

Dance

Aoyama Round Theatre

5-53-1 Jingumae, Shibuya-ku (3797 5678).
Omotesando station. **Box office** 10am-6pm daily
(3797 1400). **Tickets** prices vary. **No credit cards.**
Map 2.
As its name suggests, this is a theatre that can be
used in the round, one of very few in Tokyo, and
attracts leading contemporary artistes keen to make
the most of the space.

Art Sphere

2-3-16 Higashi-Shinagawa, Shinagawa-ku (5460
9999). Tennozu Isle station (Tokyo Monorail).
Box office 10am-6pm daily. **Tickets** prices vary.
No credit cards.
This theatre caters to the whims of well-off young
fans of contemporary modern dance and is sure to
book things that are considered 'in', but not too
avant-garde or risqué. The larger of Art Sphere's
two theatres seats 746, while Sphere Mex seats from
100 to 300.

Bunkamura Theatre Cocoon

2-24-1 Dogenzaka, Shibuya-ku (3477 3244).
Shibuya station. **Box office** 10am-7pm daily; *phone*
bookings 10am-5.30pm daily. **Tickets** prices vary.
Credit AmEx, DC, JCB, MC, V. **Map** 2.
The giant arts centre's mid-sized venue, with 750
seats, is used mainly for musicals, but stages the
occasional dance performance.

Hibiya Outdoor Theatre
(Hibiya Yagai Ongaku-do)

1-5 Hibiya Koen, Chuo-ku (3591 6388).
Hibiya station. **Map** 6.
This large open-air arena, used mainly for music
concerts and open only during the summer months,
plays host to Yoko Komatsubara and her flamenco
group for one night every summer.

National Theatre

4-1 Hayabusa-cho, Chiyoda-ku (3265 7411/
ticketing 3230 3000). Hanzomon station.
Box office 10am-6pm daily. **Tickets** ¥1,500-
¥9,500. **No credit cards. Map** 9.
It's old, it's established, but it's still the best place to
see traditional and contemporary Japanese dance.
The National has three stages, of which one is devoted to puppet theatre. What you see here will usually
be of a high standard.

New National Theatre

1-1-1 Honmachi, Shibuya-ku (5351 3011).
Hatsudai station (Keio line). **Box office** 10am-7pm
daily. **Tickets** prices vary. **Credit** AmEx, MC, V.
Map 1a.
While the National Theatre was and is for traditional dance and theatre, the New National Theatre
caters to the modern generation. It has called its
spaces the Opera House, the Playhouse and the Pit
rather than follow the normal tradition of calling
them Dai Gekijo (big theatre), Chu Gekijo (medium

The highly impressive **New National Theatre** hosts everything from Verdi's *Nabucco* (top) to Tennessee Williams' *A Streetcar Named Desire. See p222.*

Arts & Entertainment

Ohno – it's *Butoh*

Butoh refers to Ankoku Butoh, or dance of the darkness, initiated in Japan by Hijikata Tatsumi in the 1960s. The avant garde art form, which dealt with taboo subjects, was a completely new language of dance that broke with the established rules. The 94-year-old *Butoh* dancer Kazuo Ohno says that defining *Butoh* is just as difficult as defining what humans are. But what you will often see are bodies smeared with white makeup, slow, minute movements and contorted postures. Compared to traditional Japanese dance, *Butoh* represents a more personal way of communicating through movement,

and it's true to say that it has as many different styles as performers.

In western dance in general, the dancer tries to reach up towards heaven, or God. *Butoh* is more earthbound. Its expressions may be absurd, grotesque or mystical, evoking images of decay, fear, desperation, eroticism, stillness.

Among the numerous *Butoh* groups are Sankaijuku, the best-known abroad, Dai Raku Da Kan, led by Maro Akaji and Tokason. Performers include Ohno Kazuo and his son Ohno Yoshito, Kasai Akira, Tanaka Min and Motofuji Akiko, wife of Hijikata Tatsumi.

theatre) and Sho Gekijo (small theatre). The latter two spaces cater to dance, mostly modern, although the Opera House does at times stage classical ballet. The Pit, holding over 500 people, is a leading venue on the contemporary dance circuit. The complex that houses the spaces is worth a visit in its own right.

Session House

158 Yaraicho, Shinjuku-ku (3266 0461).
Kagurazaka station. **Box office** 10am-11pm daily.
Tickets ¥2,000-¥2,500. **No credit cards**.
This is a pure contemporary dance venue, a small, intimate and well-run studio-style theatre owned and run by Naoko Itoh, herself a modern dancer with her own company. She started Session House in order to give solo dancers the opportunity to experiment and express themselves freely. She presents not only local contemporary dancers, but also those from Europe and America. The aim is to showcase pure dance without extensive use of theatrical props and high-tech lighting.

Setagaya Public Theatre

4-1-1 Taishido, Setagaya-ku (5432 1526).
Sangenjaya station (Shin-Tamagawa line).
Box office 10am-7pm daily. **Tickets** prices vary. **No credit cards.**
Like the **New National Theatre** (*see p222*), this venue is a great favourite with fans and performers. Although modelled on a Greek open-air theatre, the space can be changed to proscenium-style. The theatre contains two auditoria, the smaller of which, Theatre Tram, is a popular venue for dance and physical theatre.

Space Zero

2-12-10 Yoyogi, Shibuya-ku (3375 8741). Shinjuku station. **Box office** 10am-6pm Mon-Fri. **Tickets** prices vary. **No credit cards. Map** 1a.
A mid-sized venue (capacity around 550) that specialises in modern jazz dance; performers include the Alok Dance Company.

Comedy

Although Japan has a long tradition of humorous story-telling, called *rakugoh*, there is nowhere in Tokyo that offers translation of such events for the English-speaking visitor. Occasional performances are also held at the Edo-Tokyo Museum (*see p103*).

Suehiro-tei

3-6-12 Shinjuku, Shinjuku-ku (3351 2974). Shinjuku San-chome station. **Box office** noon-8.15pm daily.
Tickets ¥2,200-¥2,700. **No credit cards. Map** 1b.
A charming old theatre that looks alarmingly like a bath-house. It seats 325 and hosts regular performances of *rakugoh*. No English translation.

Tokyo Comedy Store

Bar, Isn't It, MT Bldg 3F, 3-8-18 Roppongi, Minato-ku (3746 1598/www.tokyocomedy.com/english/index.html). Roppongi station. **Performances** Thur.
Tickets ¥1,500 (incl one drink). Enquiries by e-mail to: tokyoc@tokyocomedy.com. **Map** 4.
Tokyo's best-organised English-language comedy group may have the same name as the London venue, but there the similarity ends. Performers are keen amateurs ranging from the hilarious to the dire. New material is always sought, from both Japanese and foreign performers or would-be performers. Performance times can change, so check the website for details before heading out. Also holds improv classes and workshops in Japanese and English.

Tokyo Cynics

The Fiddler, Tajima Bldg B1F, 2-1-2 Takadanobaba, Shinjuku-ku (3204 2698). Takadanobaba station.
Performances 2nd Tue of month. **Admission** free.
Map 22.
A ramshackle bunch of English-speaking amateur comics and outright eccentrics who regularly enliven evenings at one of Tokyo's longest-established and most popular British-style pubs.

Arts & Entertainment

Sport & Fitness

With international events and native specialities such as sumo stable visits and indoor skiing, Tokyo will tickle every sports fan's fancy.

Sport may not be the first thing visitors associate with Japan's crowded capital, but Tokyo can boast a unique range of top-level attractions across the whole of the sporting spectrum. For starters, the metropolis hosts three professional baseball teams, two top-flight JLeague sides, and three full sumo tournaments a year. In terms of infrastructure, the 1964 Olympics left Tokyo with a string of custom-built venues in the Yoyogi area, including the **National Stadium** in Sendagaya (*see p230* **Football**), and the **Nippon Budokan** in Kudanshita (*see p227*).

Tokyo also offers a full range of facilities to those more interested in participating themselves, although sports requiring more space can sometimes be a problem. Finding a *dojo* (gym) for instruction in martial arts usually poses few difficulties. There is also no shortage of fitness clubs or local-authority sports facilities. For team sports, fellow enthusiasts can usually be unearthed via the weekly ads in *Tokyo Classified* (*see p268*).

Spectator sports

Athletics

The only IAAF-permit meeting held locally, the **International Super Track & Field** in September, now takes place at Yokohama International Stadium (*see p189 and p234*). Japan's real athletics favourite, however, is the marathon. Even before Naoko Takahashi swept to the women's gold at the 2000 Sydney Olympics, the 26-mile endurance event had long been something of a national obsession. Tokyo's two marathons have strict entrance requirements and attract some of the world's best runners: the **Tokyo International Marathon** is held in mid-February, starting and finishing at the National Stadium; the **Tokyo International Women's Marathon** follows the same route in November and was the first women-only marathon in the world.

Horse racing

Horse racing in Japan is run under the auspices of the **Japan Racing Association (JRA)**, which manages the ten national tracks, and the **National Association of Racing (NAR)**, which oversees local courses. Race tracks are one of the few places where gambling is legal. For schedules and details in English, log on to the homepage of the **Japan Association for International Horseracing** (www.jair.jrao.ne.jp/).

Oi Racecourse

2-1-2 Katsushima, Shinagawa-ku (3763 2151). Oi Keibajomae station (Tokyo monorail).
Run under the auspices of the NAR, with around 120 days' racing a year. 'Twinkle Races' are evening events that Oi pioneered in the 1990s, and have proved popular with office workers. Other NAR courses around Tokyo include Funabashi in Chiba.

Tokyo Racecourse

1-1 Hiyoshi-cho, Fuchu City (042 363 3141). Fuchu-honmachi station (JR Musashino line).
One of the ten national tracks run by the JRA. There are 40 days' racing a year, all at weekends. Many of the country's most famous races are held here, including the Japan Cup in November. The latter is an international invitational race that attracts top riders and horses from around the world. Major JRA races are graded GI (the highest), GII or GIII.

Hydroplane racing (*kyotei*)

Next to horse racing, this is the most popular focus of betting in Japan. The race itself is between six motor-driven boats in what is essentially a very large swimming pool; boats go round the 600-metre course three times, regularly reaching speeds of over 80 kilometres per hour (50 miles per hour). **Edogawa Kyotei** is the big favourite among Tokyo fans; the race schedule is published in Japanese sports newspapers and on the website www.edogawa-kyotei.co.jp. Betting starts at just ¥100.

Edogawa Kyotei

3-1-1 Higashi-Komatsugawa, Edogawa-ku (3656 0641). Shin-koiwa station, then 21 bus.
Admission ¥50.

Ice hockey

The **Japan Ice Hockey League** started back in 1966 and features six teams: Seibu Tetsudo, Kokudo, Nikko Ice Bucks, Oji Seishi, Snow Brand and Nippon Paper Cranes. Only the first

Sumo

With a history dating back 2,000 years, Japan's national sport uniquely blends tradition, athleticism and religion. Its rules are simple: each combatant must try to force the other out of the ring (*dohyo*) or make him touch the floor with a part of his anatomy other than his feet. Tournaments take place over 15 days, with wrestlers fighting once a day. Those who achieve regular majorities (winning more than they lose) progress up through the rankings, the highest of which is *yokozuna* (grand champion). Wrestlers failing to achieve a majority are demoted. *Yokozuna* must achieve a majority in every tournament or are expected to retire.

Tournaments take place in Tokyo three times a year, in January, May and September, at the **Kokugikan** (*see below*), which opened in 1985. This also hosts one-day tournaments and retirement ceremonies. For ticket information, results and interviews, see the websites of *Sumo World* magazine (www.sumoworld.com) and the Sumo Association (www.sumo.or.jp/index_e.html).

To learn more about sumo, and to witness the rigorous training wrestlers undergo, it is also possible to visit a sumo stable, or *heya*. Most allow visitors, on condition that they remain quiet. Call ahead to ask permission, in Japanese if possible. It's a good idea to take along a small gift, such as a bottle of *sake*, to the stablemaster, to show your appreciation.

Be warned: the day tends to start early. Junior wrestlers are up and about at 4am, and gruelling practice sessions start at around 5am. The higher-ranked wrestlers start to appear at around 8am. There are more than 40 stables in Tokyo, most situated close to the Kokugikan. There's an up-to-date list of addresses online at www.accesscom.com/~abe/heya.html.

Kokugikan

1-3-28 Yokoami, Sumida-ku (3623 5111). Ryogoku station. **Tickets** *Balcony* ¥2,100-¥8,200. **Map** 24.

Advance tickets go on sale at the box office and regular ticket outlets about a month before the start of each tournament. Tickets are now not as difficult to get, but weekends generally sell out and the most expensive box seats are nearly impossible to obtain without corporate connections at any time. A number of unreserved back-row balcony seats are always held back for sale from 8am on the day of the tournament at ¥2,100 (one per person). Many people watch bouts between younger fighters from downstairs box seats until the ticket-holders arrive mid-afternoon.

two of these are based near Tokyo. At the time of going to press, Snow Brand (also known as Yukijirushi) was due to disband at the end of the 2001 season. The official **Japan Ice Hockey Federation** website (www.jihf.or.jp/jihl/index-e.htm) contains schedules, team details and results. The season runs from October to March.

Higashi-Fushimi Ice Arena

3-1-25 Higashi-Fushimi, Hoya-shi (0424 67 7171). Higashi-Fushimi station (Seibu Shinjuku line). Home of Seibu Tetsudo.

National Yoyogi Coliseum 1st Gymnasium

2-1-1, Jinnan, Shibuya-ku (3468 1171). Harajuku station. **Map** 11.

Hosts occasional international games and exhibition matches.

Shin-Yokohama Prince Hotel Skate Centre

2-11 Shin-Yokohama, Kohoku-ku, Yokohama, Kanagawa (045 474 1112). Shin-Yokohama station. Home of Kokudo.

Martial arts

For details of Japan's national sport, *see p226* **Sumo**. For information on how to contact individual *dojo*, *see below* **Nippon Budokan** *and p228* **Martial arts**.

Nippon Budokan
2-3 Kitanomaru Koen, Chiyoda-ku (3216 5100). Kudanshita station. **Map 9.**
The Olympic Nippon Budokan stages the All-Japan championships or equivalent-level demonstration events in all the martial arts with the exception of sumo. Advance tickets are not required, and in most cases admission is free. Dates vary slightly from year to year. In the same complex, martial arts classes may be viewed at Budokan Gakuen school; telephone for details (3216 5143). In addition, the Budokan can provide information about getting in touch with a *dojo*.

Motor sports

Motor sports have a devoted following in Japan. The **Suzuka circuit** (in Mie prefecture towards Nagoya; 0593 78 1111) is the venue of the annual Formula 1 Japan Grand Prix. Large numbers of fans from Tokyo make the return-trip in a day. Closer to the capital, **Twin Ring Motegi** boasts two types of circuit, including an oval course suitable for US-style motor sports. This is used for a CART championship series race in May. The permanent circuit hosts local Formula 3 and Formula Nippon races.

Twin Ring Motegi
120-1 Hiyama, Motegi-machi, Haga-gun, Tochigi-ken (0285 64 0001/ www.twinring.co.jp/english/index.htm). Motegi station (Mooka line).

Rugby union

Japanese rugby union is divided between corporate- and university-level teams. The **National Stadium** in Sendagaya (*see p230* **Football**) stages the annual Waseda-Meiji match, the big university fixture that has traditionally been the season's most popular game. Corporate sides often feature imported talent, some of whom now appear in the Japanese national side. The Japan championship, held in January/February, features the top four sides from the corporate and university worlds, with results in recent years showing that the standard of university rugby is now far below that of the corporate game. Ticket information in English is available at the official site of the **Japan Rugby Football Union** (www.rugby-japan.or.jp).

Prince Chichibu Memorial Stadi
2-8-35 Kita Aoyama, Minato-ku (3401 3881). Sendagaya station. **Map 23.**
Internationals and other big rugby matches that are not held at the National Stadium take place at this venue, next door to the Jingu baseball stadium.

Tennis

Attention to professional tennis in Japan is focused on the women's game. The biggest event is the **Japan Open** every October (*see p190 and below*). The indoor **Toray Pan Pacific Open** in January/February and **Princess Cup** in November are both held at the Tokyo Municipal Gymnasium in Sendagaya (*see below* **Volleyball**). Municipal courts exist for those who want a game themselves.

Metropolitan Ariake Tennis Woods Park
2-2-22 Ariake, Koto-ku (3529 3301). Ariake station (Yurikamome line). **Open** 9am-9pm daily. **Admission** ¥1,500 per hour.
Big, new – home to the Japan Open tournament.

Volleyball

Doffing its cap to soccer's JLeague, in name at least, volleyball's VLeague has been rather less successful, with financial problems leading two teams to announce their closure in 2000. There are two leagues of ten teams: one for women; one for men. Many games are televised live.

Tokyo Municipal Gymnasium
1-17-1 Sendagaya, Shibuya-ku (5474 2111). Sendagaya station. **Map 23.**
The only place within Tokyo that regularly hosts VLeague volleyball matches.

Active sports/fitness

Golf

With time and expense posing big obstacles to the capital's legion of would-be golfers, driving ranges dot the city. The cost of membership at private clubs can easily run to millions of yen, but only three of Tokyo's 19 courses are public facilities. Golf packages with a hotel chain such as **Prince Hotels** (www.princehotels.co.jp) start as low as ¥17,000 yen per person, including room, but can be treble that on August weekends. Those interested in gaining access to the large number of private and public courses within day-trip range of the capital should consult the privately published and annually updated *Tokyo Golf Course Guide*, which costs $39.95 (for ordering details, see www.JapanGolfCourses.com/home.htm).

...ato-ku (5470 1111).
...en 6am-11pm daily.
...0; varies according to

...driving range in central location.

Tokyo Metropolitan Golf Course

1-15-11 Shinden, Adachi-ku (3919 0111).
Oji-kamiya station. **Open** dawn to dusk daily.
Admission from ¥5,000 (¥7,500 after 8am)
Mon-Fri; from ¥9,500 Sat, Sun.
The cheapest of Tokyo's public courses has 18 holes
at par 63. Weekday bookings are taken from 3pm
on the first of the previous month; Saturday book-
ings from 3pm on the 20th of every month; and
Sunday bookings from 3pm on the 15th.

Gyms

Membership of private gyms can be rather
expensive. Large hotels may have swimming
pools or gyms, but if you are in need of some
muscle-pumping action, head for one of these.
A cheaper alternative is to visit one of Tokyo's
public sports centres (*see p230*).

Nautilus Club

Enquiries 3982 4640. **Rates** *Members* ¥15,000 per
month. *Visitors* ¥5,000 per day.
Seven branches. Facilities typically include shower,
aerobics, sauna, weight machines, tanning machine.
Akasaka, Shibuya and Suidobashi branches have
swimming pools.

People Xax

Enquiries 3475 4471. **Open** 7am-11pm Mon-Fri;
10am-8pm Sat, Sun. **Rates** *Members* ¥4,800-¥10,000
per month.
People Xax has ten branches in Tokyo, most with
swimming pool, sauna and weight gyms. Guests are
not usually admitted.

Tipness

Enquiries 3464 3532. **Open** 7am/9.30am-11pm
Mon-Fri; 9.30am-8pm Sat, Sun. **Rates** *Members*
from ¥11,000 per month. *Guests* ¥2,100 accompanied
by a member.
Eleven branches in Tokyo, at Shibuya, Gotanda,
Ikebukuro, Shinjuku, Akasaka, Roppongi, Nakano,
Kichijoji, Machida, Shimo-Kitazawa and Kasai.
(Note that the first five open at 7am Monday to
Friday.) Most have a swimming pool, as well as
aerobics classes and weight gyms.

Horse riding

Tokyo Horse Riding Club

4-8 Kamizono-cho, Yoyogi, Shibuya-ku (3370 0984/
fax 3370 2714). *Sangubashi station (Odakyu line).*
Open *Mar-Nov* 9am-5.45pm Tue-Sun. *Dec-Feb*
9am-4.45pm Tue-Sun. **Admission** *Visitors* ¥6,500
Tue-Fri; ¥7,500 Sat, Sun. **Map 23.**

The oldest riding club in Japan boasts 45 horses and
six instructors. Members have to pay an annual
membership fee of ¥96,000, plus a joining fee of ¥2
million, and need to be recommended by two existing members. Book a day in advance.

Ice-skating

Championship events are held at the **National
Yoyogi Coliseum** (*see p226*). In winter, Tokyo
also has its very own temporary outdoor rink in
front of a smart uptown building.

Hibiya City Skating Rink

Hibiya Kokusai Bldg, 2-2-3 Uchisaiwaicho, Chiyoda-
ku (3595 02573). Uchisaiwaicho station (Mita line).
Open *early Dec-early Mar* 3pm-8pm Mon-Fri; 11am-
7pm Sat-Sun. **Admission** ¥1,500. **Map 6.**
Open-air rink outside a central shopping centre.
Imagine you're in New York.

Martial arts

There are nine recognised modern martial
arts – aikido, judo, jukendo, karate, kendo,
kyudo, naginata, shorinji kempo and sumo –
and a series of older and more traditional
forms, known collectively as *kobudo*. The
number of people practising them in Japan
is put at almost five million. The national
associations of the different disciplines may
have training facilities where spectators can
view practice sessions, and will also be able
to point you in the direction of individual *dojo*
that welcome visitors or potential students.

Aikido

Aikikai Federation, 17-18 Wakamatsu-cho,
Shinjuku-ku (3203 9236).

Judo

All-Japan Judo Federation, 1-16-30 Kasuga,
Bunkyo-ku (3818 4199).

Jukendo

All-Japan Jukendo Federation, 2-3 Kitanomaru
Koen, Chiyoda-ku (3201 1020).

Karate

Japan Karate Federation, No. 2 Senpaku Shinko
Bldg, 1-11-2 Toranomon, Minato-ku (3503 6637).

Kendo

All-Japan Kendo Federation, Yasukuni Kyudan
Minami Bldg 2F, 2-3-14 Kudan Minami, Chiyoda-ku
(3234 6271).

Kobudo

Nippon Kobudo Association, 2-3 Kitanomaru Koen,
Chiyoda-ku (3216 5114).

Kyudo

All-Japan Kyudo Association, Kishi Kinen
Taiikukaikan, 1-1-1 Jinnan, Shibuya-ku (3481 2387).

Baseball

Most games are held in the evening, with an unceasing cacophony of noise from the stands providing the backdrop to the action on the field. Armed with strangely coloured plastic megaphones, fans chug back beers between organised outbreaks of singing and chanting, while makeshift bands featuring ear-splitting trumpets and drums are also on hand to pump up the players. So much have Japanese made baseball their own that some claim local *yakyu* has evolved its own unique Japanese characteristics. This, though, hasn't stopped US Major League teams from importing an ever-increasing amount of Japanese talent in recent years.

Introduced to Japan by Horace Wilson in 1873, baseball has long held a grip on local hearts and minds. The first pro side, the Yomiuri Giants, was founded in 1934, and by 1950 a professional competition had been set up, comprising 12 teams in two leagues. Each side plays 140 games a season (April to October), with the winners of the Central and Pacific Leagues meeting each other in the Japan Series to decide the championship. Tokyo has three teams: the **Yomiuri Giants**, the **Nippon Ham Fighters** and the **Yakult**

Swallows. In 2000, the Giants claimed their 19th title, and first since 1994, by beating defending champions Fukuoka Daiei Hawks four games to two. Interest is high at amateur level, too. The national high-school baseball tournament is televised live and brings the country to a virtual standstill.

Jingu Baseball Stadium

Kasumigaoka, Shinjuku-ku (3404 8999). *Sendagaya station.* **Capacity** 46,000. **Tickets** ¥1,500-¥3,900. **Map** 23. This stadium, part of the complex that includes the National Stadium, was built for the 1964 Olympics, and is now home to the Yakult Swallows (Central League). Perhaps the best place to go if you're just looking for a taste of baseball Japan-style.

Tokyo Dome

1-3 Koraku, Bunkyo-ku (3811 2111). *Suidobashi station.* **Capacity** 55,000. **Tickets** ¥1,200-¥5,900. **Map** 15. The Dome, or Big Egg, is home to the Yomiuri Giants (Central League) and the Nippon Ham Fighters (Pacific League). Tickets for Giants games, in particular, can be difficult to acquire.

Naginata

All-Japan Naginata Federation (Tokyo office), Kishi Kinen Taiikukaikan, 1-1-1 Jinnan, Shibuya-ku (3481 2411).

Shorinji Kempo

Shorinji Kempo Federation (Tokyo Office), 1-3-5 Uehara, Shibuya-ku (3481 5191).

Sumo (Amateur)

Japan Sumo Federation, Kishi Kinen Taiikukaikan, 1-1-1 Jinnan, Shibuya-ku (3481 2377).

Running

The big events for hobby runners, held on the same day as the **Tokyo Marathon** (*see p225*), are the ten-kilometre and 30-kilometre road races in Ome, north-west Tokyo (information 0428 24 6311). Joggers might want to check out the five-kilometre route marked out at 100-metre intervals around the Imperial Palace.

Skiing & snowboarding

In winter, a 90-minute train ride from Shinjuku will take you to a wide range of snowy slopes. Between December and March, JR ticket

windows in the metropolis have all-in-one deals covering ski-pass and day-return transport for the destination of your choice, with weekday prices starting under ¥10,000. Closer at hand, there's an indoor ski slope in Chiba where people walk around in puffa jackets and gloves when the temperature's 30°C outside. Time on the slope is divided between snowboarding and skiing. The timetable is complex; study it well before you go.

Ski Dome SSAWS

2-3-1 Hama-cho, Funabashi-shi, Chiba (047 432 7000). Minami-Funabashi station (JR Keiyo line). **Open** *Skiing* 1-9.30pm Mon, Tue, Sun; 11am-9.30pm Wed; 11am-4pm Thur; 8am-3pm Sat. *Snowboarding* 8am-1pm Mon, Tue, Sun; 4-10pm Thur; 11am-10pm Fri; 3-10pm Sat. **Admission** *One-day pass* ¥5,400; ¥4,100-¥4,800 concessions. At half a kilometre long, this giant steel structure is impossible to miss. Never fear if you come without gear: everything, except socks, can be rented for about ¥1,500 per item (evening discount after 6.30pm). Note that there's skiing only on Wednesday and snowboarding only on Friday. SSAWS, just in case you were wondering, stands for Spring, Summer, Autumn, Winter Snow.

Arts & Entertainment

Football

With women and children making up a good proportion of spectators, JLeague football sometimes seem to hark back to a more innocent era. Crowd violence is virtually unknown, and flag-bearing fans happily sing and dance the game away in the 'free seats' behind the goals with nobody telling them to sit down.

Not everything is perfect, of course. Playing standards have risen since the start of the JLeague in 1993, but the initial boom has long since ended. The league has expanded from the original ten teams to two divisions. But expansion has taken place in the middle of a recession, with many clubs struggling financially. While baseball remains the nation's favourite sport, the Japan football team picks up strong support in international tournaments. A successful 2002 World Cup would provide a big boost to the game locally (*see chapter* **World Cup 2002**).

For a long time Tokyo was left on the sidelines when it came to JLeague action, but the start of the 2001 season saw the capital with two top-flight teams. **FC Tokyo** (previously Tokyo Gas) won promotion from the second division at the end of the 1999 season, while former champions Kawasaki Verdy relocated to the metropolis and renamed themselves **Tokyo Verdy 1969** in time to kick-off the 2001 campaign. The two sides now share a brand-new 50,000-capacity ground out in the west of the city. The JLeague official website (www.j-league.or.jp) features English-language information on clubs, players and fixtures.

National Stadium

Kasumigaoka-machi, Shinjuku-ku (3403 1151). Sendagaya station. **Capacity** 57,363. **Map** 23.
The 1964 Olympic stadium still hosts international matches, the Emperor's Cup Final (*see p185*) and the Toyota Cup (*see p184*), as well as occasional 'home' matches of Kanto area JLeague teams Urawa Reds and 2000 treble-winners Kashima Antlers.

Tokyo Stadium

376-3 Nishimachi, Chofu (0424 40 0555/ www.tokyostadium.com/). Tobitakyu station (Keio line). **Capacity** 50,000. **Tickets** ¥1,000-¥6,000.
The shiny new home of FC Tokyo and Tokyo Verdy 1969.

Sports centres

Each of the 23 wards has sports facilities, with bargain prices for residents and commuters. Except for those in Shibuya-ku, they're also open to visitors, for higher fees, as listed below.

Chiyoda Kuritsu Sogo Taiikukan Pool

2-1-8 Uchi-Kanda, Chiyoda-ku (3256 8444). Kanda station. **Open** *Pool* noon-8.30pm Mon, Tue, Thur, Sat; 5.30-8.30pm Wed, Fri; 9am-5pm Sun. *Gym* 9am-noon, 1-5pm, 6-9pm daily. Closed every 3rd Mon & Sun. **Admission** pool ¥500; gym ¥250. **Map** 16.
Swimming pool and gym within a weight's throw of Tokyo's business district.

Chuo-ku Sogo Sports Centre

Hama-cho Koen Nai, 2-59-1 Nihonbashi-Hama-cho, Chuo-ku (3666 1501). Hama-cho station. **Open** *Pool* 9.40am-9.10pm daily. *Gym* 8.30am-9.30pm daily. Closed every 3rd Thur. **Admission** pool ¥500; gym ¥400.
With a swimming pool, studio and weight gym.

Minato-ku Sports Centre

3-1-19 Shibaura, Minato-ku (3578 2111). Tamachi station. **Open** 9am-9pm Tue-Sun. **Admission** ¥600.

Sauna, studio, weight gym, aerobics studio and in-line skating yard. Swimming pool is being rebuilt, with reopening scheduled for 2003.

Shinagawa Sogo Taiikukan Pool

5-6-11 Kita-Shinagawa, Shinagawa-ku (3449 4400). Osaki station. **Open** schedule changes monthly. **Admission** *Pool* ¥350 (2hrs). **Map** 19.
No-frills swimming pool. Other sports on offer here include tennis and badminton.

Shinjuku-ku Sports Centre

3-5-1 Okubo, Shinjuku-ku (3232 0171). Takadanobaba station. **Open** 9am-9pm daily. Closed every 4th Mon. **Admission** *Pool* ¥400 (2hrs). *Gym* ¥400 (3hrs). **Map** 22.
Swimming pool and gym.

Tokyo Metropolitan Gymnasium Pool

1-17-1 Sendagaya, Shibuya-ku (5474 2111). Sendagaya station. **Open** *Pool* 9.30am-8.45pm daily. Closed every 3rd Mon, plus competition days. **Admission** *Pool* ¥450. **Map** 23.
Administered by Tokyo Metropolitan Government, this complex has both 25- and 50-metre pools, a weights gym (¥380 extra), arena and athletics field. The 25-metre pool is not open to the public every day and rarely before 1.30pm.

Trips Out of Town

World Cup 2002

Japan is co-hosting the world's biggest sporting event. But where are the venues?

In early summer 2002, Japan and neighbouring South Korea co-host Asia's first-ever World Cup. By the time the winning captain finally lifts the trophy at Yokohama International Stadium on 30 June, 32 countries will have played a total of 64 matches at 20 different venues.

There were many sceptics when FIFA first decreed that the tournament would be jointly staged by the two east Asian nations. A last-minute compromise deal cobbled together for political reasons, the plan seemed to raise a host of logistical and organisational difficulties. Not only were the two countries separated geographically by sea, but also by a long history of mutual hostility and a highly acrimonious World Cup bidding campaign.

Even so, preparations have probably proceeded more smoothly than many initially feared, apart from an unseemly spat over which country's name would go first in the Japanese-language version of the official tournament title. Construction work on a string of shiny new stadiums has gone ahead, despite financial problems in South Korea after the Asian economic collapse of 1997. Japan alone is spending ¥63 billion on preparations, excluding stadium construction costs.

Looking ahead to the tournament itself, anticipation seems to be mixed with some trepidation for many Japanese. Half the 1.35 million tickets for World Cup matches in Japan will be distributed abroad, but visiting football fans from overseas have previously been an extreme rarity. On top of language problems, some misunderstandings look likely due to the local lack of familiarity with football culture from other continents.

Security promises to be tight. As well as a heavy police presence, Japanese organisers say they plan to clamp down on black-market ticket sales by checking the ID of ticket-holders against the original purchaser's name printed on each stub.

The government also seems determined to prevent potential troublemakers from entering the country. Japan's distance from soccer's heartlands may simplify these efforts, with most fans likely to arrive by air. At the time of going to press, there is also a possibility that alcohol sales will be banned inside the grounds, a first in Japan for any sporting event.

SCHEDULE

The local rainy season may put a dampener on proceedings, but the tournament's traditional early summer slot couldn't be changed because of the European league season. Only two of Japan's stadiums have retractable roofs, so organisers will be crossing their fingers and hoping to avoid a rescheduling nightmare.

The 64 games of the tournament have been divided down the middle between the two co-hosts, with each staging 32 matches and four first-stage groups. The prestige matches have also been split: Korea gets the opening match and third-place play-off; each country stages one semi-final; and Japan has the final.

Both players and fans have to be ready to travel. Each first-stage group will have six games, but these will all be at different venues. Co-hosts Japan, for example, play their Group H matches in Saitama, Yokohama and Osaka. At the end of the first stage, half the 16 qualifiers from the groups will swap host countries.

The vast majority of matches will start at 3.30pm, 6pm or 8.30pm, making live games a little tricky for armchair fans on other continents. One game has also been scheduled for 4.30pm, while the third-place play-off and final both kick-off at 8pm.

Group matches	31 May-14 June
Last 16	15-18 June
Quarter-finals	21-22 June
Semi-finals	25-26 June
Third-place	29 June
Final	30 June

BASECAMP TOKYO

Unlike France 98, tickets won't be sold as part of all-inclusive tours. Overseas fans are free to book transport and accommodation through travel agents or to make their own arrangements, either in advance or on the spot. Trains and hotels are expected to be busy during the tournament, although congestion may be eased if other international tourists postpone visits.

Tokyo could prove to be the best base for non-Japanese fans. Many will enter Japan at Narita airport anyway, given its position as the nation's main international gateway. The Japanese government is also planning to start flights from Tokyo's other airport at Haneda to South Korean cities in time for the start of the tournament.

While Tokyo doesn't appear on the list of venues because the metropolitan government didn't apply to be a host, Japan's two largest World Cup stadiums both stand within commuting distance of the city centre, in Yokohama and Saitama. Both will stage three group matches; Saitama also hosts a semi-final and Yokohama the final.

With venues spread right across the country, the capital's central position at the hub of the nation's *shinkansen* (bullet train) and air networks gives it an unbeatable head start as a base for trips out to other venues. If you're a non-resident planning to see at least a couple of games, the bargain-price **Japan Rail Pass** (*see p259*) lets you use high-speed bullet trains and should quickly pay for itself.

At the time of writing, the government was also considering the possibility of introducing a special travel pass aimed at World Cup visitors. Brave souls thinking of hiring a vehicle (*see p260*) to get around might consider the likelihood of bad weather, as well as the certainties of long distances between venues and steep highway tolls.

For accommodation, Tokyo offers Japan's widest variety of choices (*see chapter* **Accommodation**), while those planning to stay in other Japanese cities might want to start their searches at the JNTO website (www.jnto.go.jp). Those attending evening games might note that the last *shinkansen* trains arrive back in Tokyo around midnight and make plans accordingly.

At the time of going to press, local cities had not announced their plans for special events and facilities for visiting fans, but hotel accommodation is expected to be the norm. The likelihood of heavy rains is likely to make camping an uncomfortable option for all but the hardiest.

STADIUMS

All Japan's World Cup stadiums, with the exception of that in Shizuoka, will be regularly used after the tournament by local J League teams, although some second division clubs may find it difficult to fill their magnificent new facilities. Only Saitama and Kashima are soccer-only stadiums, with other grounds featuring running tracks and other features to promote a variety of uses. Sapporo and Oita both have retractable roofs.

Part of Japan's original World Cup bid envisaged the creation of hi-tech 'virtual stadiums' but this idea was abandoned once the decision to co-host the 2002 event had been made. That change also led to the 16 proposed venues in both countries' original bids being cut to ten apiece.

With the North Korean capital of Pyongyang looking increasingly unlikely to host any World Cup matches, the ten Korean venues will be at Seoul, Incheon, Suwon, Daejeon, Jeonju, Gwangju, Daegu, Ulsan, Busan and Seogwipo.

For further details, go to the home page of the Korean World Cup organising committee at www.2002worldcupkorea.org/eng/index.htm. The Japanese equivalent is at www.jawoc.or.jp.

Miyagi

Niigata

MIYAGI

Stadium location 10km (6 miles) from Sendai city centre
Stadium name Miyagi Stadium
Capacity 49,133
Completion March 2000
Local team Vegalta Sendai (J2)
Getting there by rail Tokyo station to Sendai by Tohoku *shinkansen*
How long does it take? 1hr 36mins to 2hr 32mins
Stadium access JR Tohoku main line to Rifu 15mins, then 10mins by taxi
Website www.worldcup-miyagi.com

NIIGATA

Stadium location 4km (2.5 miles) from Niigata city centre
Stadium name Niigata Stadium
Capacity 42,700
Completion March 2001
Local team Albirex Niigata (J2)
Getting there by rail Tokyo station to Niigata by Joetsu *shinkansen*
How long does it take? around 2hrs
Stadium access 10mins by taxi
Website www.pref.niigata.jp/worldcup/

Trips Out of Town

SAPPORO

Stadium location 7.5km (4.8 miles) from Sapporo city centre
Stadium name Sapporo Dome
Capacity 42,122
Completion May 2001
Local team Consadole Sapporo (J2 champions, 2000 season)
Getting there by rail Tokyo Ueno station to Sapporo by express sleeper service called Cassiopeia or Hokuto-sei
How long does it take? around 7hrs
Stadium access Toho subway line to Fukuzumi takes 11 min, then a 10min walk
Getting there by air Tokyo Haneda-Chitose takes 1hr 30mins. Over 40 flights/day. Train or shuttle bus to city centre
Website www.worldcup-sapporo.com/

IBARAKI

Stadium location 3km (2 miles) from Kashima city centre
Stadium name Ibaraki Prefectural Kashima Soccer Stadium
Capacity 41,800
Completion May 2001
Local team Kashima Antlers (Japan treble winners, 2000 season)
Getting there by rail Tokyo station to Chiba by JR Sobu line express, Narita line to Sahara and Kashima line to Kashima-jingu.
How long does it take? approx 2hrs 15mins
Stadium access Oarai Kashima line to Kashima Soccer Stadium station, then 5min walk
Getting there by express bus from Tokyo station Yaesu south exit (match days only), takes 2hrs
Website www.pref.ibaraki.jp/prog/wldcup/wcup.wel.htm

SAITAMA

Stadium location 9km (5.5 miles) from Urawa city centre.
Stadium name Saitama Stadium 2002
Capacity 63,700 seats (Japan's largest football-only stadium)
Completion July 2001
Local team Urawa Red Diamonds
Getting there by subway Namboku line to Oji station, then change to go to Urawa-Misono
How long does it take? from Oji station, 30min
Stadium access 15min walk from Urawa-Misono station
Website www.2002saitama.com/index.html

YOKOHAMA

Stadium location 6km (3.5 miles) from Yokohama city centre
Stadium name International Stadium Yokohama
Capacity 70,564 (Japan's largest stadium)
Completion October 1997
Local team Yokohama F Marinos (J.League first-stage title, 2000)
Getting there by rail Tokyo station to Higashi Kanagawa by Keihin-Tohoku line, then Yokohama line to Shin Yokohama
How long does it take? approx 45mins
Stadium access 10min walk
Getting there by bullet train Tokyo station to Shin Yokohama, 15 mins
Website www.city.yokohama.jp/me/w-cup/index.html

KOBE
Stadium location 5km (3 miles) from Kobe
city centre
Stadium name Kobe Wing Stadium.
Capacity 42,000
Completion October 2001
Local team Vissel Kobe (J1)
Getting there by rail Tokyo station to Shin-Kobe
by Tokaido-Sanyo *shinkansen*
How long does it take? 3hrs 20mins
Stadium access Subway to Sannomiya station,
(2mins), then Kaigan line from Sannomiya-
Hanadokei station to Misaki-koen (10mins).
Website www.city.kobe.jp/cityoffice/
57/080/index.html

OITA
Stadium location 7km (4.5 miles) from Oita
city centre
Stadium name Oita Stadium Big Eye
Capacity 43,254
Completion March 2001
Local team Oita Trinita (J2)
Getting there by rail Tokyo station to Kokura
(Kita Kyushu) by Tokaido-Sanyo *shinkansen*, then
Nippo Honsen line to Oita
How long does it take? approx 6hrs 25mins
Stadium access taxi, 20mins
Getting there by slow train Tokyo to Oita direct
sleeper express, 16hrs 40mins
Getting there by air Tokyo Haneda to Oita, 1hr
30mins. Bus or hovercraft to city centre
Website www2.pref.oita.jp/10200/

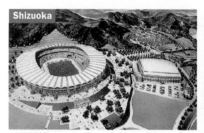

SHIZUOKA
Stadium location Fukuroi, 52km (32 miles) from
Shizuoka city centre
Stadium name Shizuoka Stadium Ecopa
Capacity 51,349
Completion March 2001
Local team none
Getting there by rail Tokyo-Kakegawa by
Tokaido *shinkansen*
How long does it take? 1hr 46mins
Stadium access JR Tokaido line to Aino station,
then 10min walk
Website www2.shizuokanet.ne.jp/worldcup/

OSAKA
Stadium location 10km (6 miles) from Osaka
city centre
Stadium name Nagai Stadium
Capacity 45,409
Completion 1996
Local team Cerezo Osaka (J1)
Getting there by rail Tokyo station to Shin-Osaka
by Tokaido *shinkansen*
How long does it take? about 2hrs 30mins
Stadium access Midosuji subway line to Nagai
station, 28mins
Website www.osakacity.or.jp/index.htm

Trips Out of Town

Yokohama 横浜

With its glorious waterfront location, Japan's second largest city has a totally
different feel to Tokyo, and it's just 30 minutes away by train.

Despite its population of over 3.25 million,
Yokohama exudes a sense of space that Tokyo
lacks, largely thanks to its glorious waterfront
position. Like Liverpool or San Francisco,
Yokohama is also home to a large immigrant
community, and it boasts the largest Chinatown
in Japan. The newly developed Minato Mirai
waterfront area also has some of the most
striking modern architecture in the country.

HISTORY

Yokohama was little more than a fishing
village when US envoy Commodore Perry
arrived in his black ships in 1853 and
demanded that Japan open itself up to
international trade, ending 300 years of self-
imposed national isolation. Under threat of
force, the Japanese government signed the
US-Japan Treaty of Amity in 1858, opening
the port of Yokohama the following year.
A tax office was set up to deal with trade and
to serve as a boundary, dividing the village up

into two areas: a southern, foreign quarter for
traders and their families (now the Motomachi
and Yamate areas) and a northern, Japanese
area. A period of mutual distrust followed,
glamorised in the James Clavell book *Gaijin*.
In 1868 the Edo shogunate was overthrown
and replaced by the Meiji government, which
believed that to compete with foreigners the
Japanese had to learn their secrets instead of
trying to ignore them.

Yokohama subsequently underwent a
wave of modernisation, developing into a major
trading port. Japan's first railway was built
between Shinbashi in Tokyo and Yokohama,
as Yokohama rapidly became Japan's window
on the outside world. Development seemed,
then as now, to be the buzzword. It became
a city in 1889, when its population exceeded
120,000, and despite two major calamities
during the 20th century, it has developed into
a port that more foreign vessels enter and more
domestic exports leave than any other in Japan.

Yokohama, developed as a major port, became Japan's window on the outside world.

Trips Out of Town

YOKOHAMA TODAY

Modern Yokohama has a dream, the 'Yumehama 2010 Plan' (literally, 'Dream Yokohama 2010 Programme'). This vision of a bright tomorrow, aimed at 'fulfilling… residents' dreams' and creating a 'lovely resonance', has culminated in a programme of aggressive urban development. Centred in and around the bay area near Sakuragi-cho station, the new buildings offer a mix of stunning modern architecture, vanity skyscrapers, and the inventive use of old dock buildings. If modernism isn't your thing, head for the sanctuary of the Chinatown (Kannai station) and Motomachi (Ishikawa-cho station) communities, or for the historic hillside district of Yamate (Ishikawa-cho station; *see p240*).

Elevator ride at **Hakkeijima Sea Paradise**.

Sightseeing

Foreign Cemetery

126 Yamate-cho, Naka-ku (045 622 1311). Ishikawa-cho station, then 15min walk. **Open** *Museum* 10am-5pm Tue-Sun. **Admission** free.
Originally established in 1854 for the burial of US sailors from the fleet that accompanied Commodore Perry, the foreign cemetery is now the last resting place of some 4,500 souls from more than 40 countries, dating from the founding of the trading settlement. A rather austere and sombre place, but still interesting in a creepy kind of way. Disappointingly, visitors are not allowed to wander among the tombs.

Hakkeijima Sea Paradise

Hakkeijima, Kanazawa-ku (045 788 8888). Hakkeijima station (Kanazawa Seaside line). **Open** 10am-10pm Mon-Fri; 9am-10pm Sat, Sun (winter times subject to change; call for details). **Admission** *Aqua Museum* ¥2,400; ¥300-¥1,400 concessions. **No credit cards**.
An artificial island with an array of attractions, including a 'white-knuckle' Jet Coaster and the 107m (350ft) 'Blue Fall' freefall ride. The impressive Aqua Museum is in the pyramid at the corner of the island; as well as having a jaw-dropping escalator ride up through one of the biggest indoor aquariums in the world, it also puts on free shows featuring killer whales and dolphins.

Landmark Tower & Sky Garden

2-2-1-1 Minato-Mirai, Nishi-ku (045 222 5030). Sakuragi-cho station. **Open** *Sky Garden* Oct-June 10am-9pm Mon-Fri, Sun; 10am-10pm Sat. July-Sept 10am-10pm daily. **Admission** ¥1,000; ¥500-¥800 concessions. **No credit cards**.
At 296m (970ft) and 70 storeys in height, Japan's tallest building is visible for miles. In the years since its completion in 1993 it has become the symbol of the new Yokohama. The earpopping lift ride to the 69th floor takes just 35 seconds. Vertigo sufferers should check out the highest observatory in Japan, the confusingly named Sky Garden (there is no garden).

Marine Tower

15 Yamashita-cho, Naka-ku (045 641 7838). Ishikawa-cho station, then 15min walk. **Open** 10am-9pm Mon-Fri, Sun; 10am-10pm Sat. **Admission** ¥700; ¥350 concessions. **No credit cards**.
Opposite Yamashita Park, this decagonal inland lighthouse was built to commemorate the centenary of the Port of Yokohama and offers an unexciting view of the area, taller buildings having been built around it.

Mitsubishi Minato-Mirai Industrial Museum

Mitsubishi Jyuko Yokohama Bldg, 3-3-1 Minato-Mirai, Nishi-Ku (045 224 9031). Sakuragi-cho station. **Open** 10am-5.30pm Tue-Sun. **Admission** ¥500; ¥300 concessions. **No credit cards**.
An intriguing corporate showcase for the latest advances in matters connected with space, the ocean, energy and the environment.

Negishi Memorial Racetrack Park & Equine Museum

1-3, Negishidai, Naka-ku (045 662 7581). Negishi station. **Open** 10am-4pm Tue-Sun. **Admission** ¥100; ¥30 concessions. **No credit cards**.
The site of Japan's first western-style horse-racing course, dating from 1857, is now a wonderful park with this museum inside it. Check out the derelict grandstand that still stands on a nearby hillside.

Nippon-Maru Memorial Park & Yokohama Maritime Museum

2-1-1 Minato-Mirai, Nishi-Ku (045 221 0280). Sakuragi-cho station. **Open** *Mar-Jun, Sept, Oct* 10am-5pm Tue-Sun. *Jul, Aug* 10am-6.30pm Tue-Sun. *Nov-Feb* 10am-4.30pm Tue-Sun. **Admission** ¥600; ¥300 concessions. **No credit cards**.
Known as the 'Swan of the Pacific', the Nippon-Maru sailed 1.83 million km between 1930 and 1984, and is moored in this park, adjacent to the Yokohama Maritime Museum. Historical materials in the museum span the period from the arrival of Commodore Perry's black ships up to the present day.

Sankeien Garden

58-1 Honmoku-Sannotani, Naka-ku (045 621 0635). Bus 8 or 125 from Sakuragi-cho station, alight at Honmoku Sankeien-mae; bus 8 or 25 from

Trips Out of Town

Yokohama station (platform 2 station east exit).
Open *Outer garden* 9am-5pm daily. *Inner garden*
9am-4.30pm daily. **Admission** *Outer garden* ¥300;
¥60 concessions. *Inner garden* ¥300;¥120
concessions. **No credit cards**.
A beautiful, traditional Japanese garden that was
constructed by a wealthy silk merchant in 1906. The
extensive grounds contain the famous Rinshun-
kaku, which was built by *shogun* Tokugawa Yoshinobu, a three-storey pagoda and a number of other
historical buildings from Kyoto and Nara designated as national cultural properties.

Silk Centre & Museum
1 Yamashita-cho, Naka-ku (045 641 0841).
Sakuragi-cho station. **Open** 9am-4.30pm
Tue-Sun. **Admission** ¥300; ¥100 concessions.
No credit cards.
The building that houses one of the tourist information centres also has this silk showcase on the
second and third floors, where visitors can learn
about the silk-making process. Silk products are also
on sale here.

Yamashita Park
Yamashita Koen, Yamashita-cho, Naka-ku.
Open *Park* 24hrs daily. *Hikawa-Maru* 9.30am-9pm
Mon-Fri; 9.30am-9.30pm Sat, Sun.
Recently spruced-up bayside park that, in the
evening, becomes a mecca for amorous couples too
young to have their own apartment and too poor to
afford a love hotel. The cruise ship *Hikawa-Maru,*
anchored in front of the park, once ruled the waves
between Japan and America: its luxurious interior,
much still in its original condition, is open to the public, including the guestroom once used by Charlie
Chaplin. This may be the closest you'll come to seeing how life was aboard the *Titanic,* whose most
famous pose tourists are constantly imitating on the
prow. Take a stroll on deck, and peek in through the
windows of the old captain's cabin.

Yamate Museum
247 Yamate-cho, Naka-ku (045 622 1188). Ishikawa-
cho station, then 15min walk. **Open** 11am-4pm daily.
Admission ¥200. **No credit cards**.
Located in the garden of the Yamate Jubankan Café,
this western-style house was built in the Meiji era.
In the two-storey museum, there are artefacts recalling this turbulent period in Japan's history.

Yokohama Bay
Bridge & Sky Walk
1 Daikoku-Futo, Tsurumi-ku (045 506 0500).
Bus 109 from No.6 bus terminal at east exit of
Sakuragi-cho station. **Open** Sky Walk *Apr-Oct*
9am-9pm daily. *Nov-Mar* 10am-6pm daily.
Closed 3rd Mon of month. **Admission** ¥500;
¥300 concessions. **No credit cards**.
This 860m (2,823ft) monster is the gateway to the
Port of Yokohama. The 360m (1,080ft) Sky Walk
promenade leading to the observatory slung under
the bridge is, like the **Landmark Tower** (*see
p237*), an absolute must for height junkies.

Yokohama Doll Museum
18 Yamashita-cho, Naka-ku (045 671 9361).
Ishikawa-cho station, then 13min walk. **Open** *Sept-*
mid July 10am-5pm Tue-Sun. *Mid July-Aug* 10am-
7pm Tue-Sun. **Admission** ¥300; ¥150 concessions.
No credit cards.
The biggest dolls' house in the world, with more
than 9,000 dolls from 135 countries. The puppet
show, for which there is an extra fee, is worth a look.

Yokohama Historical Archives
3 Nihon-Odori, Naka-ku (045 201 2100). Sakuragi-
cho station, then 20min walk. **Open** 9.30am-5pm
Tue-Sun. **Admission** ¥200; ¥100 concessions.
No credit cards.
The Japan-US treaty of 1854 was concluded in the
courtyard of this building, formerly the British consulate. It now hosts a display of artefacts associated with the period.

Yokohama Museum of Art
3-4-1 Minato-Mirai, Nishi-Ku (045 221 0300).
Sakuragi-cho station. **Open** 10am-5.30pm Mon-Wed,
Fri-Sun. **Admission** Adults ¥500; concessions ¥300.
No credit cards.
Celebrated architect Tange Kenzo designed this
splendid museum, which hosts works by the likes
of Cézanne, Magritte and Dali.

Yokohama by boat

Several companies offer tours of the city by
boat, some with dining thrown in.

Marine Rouge
Boats leave from Yamashita pier (information 045
661 0347). Lunch cruise 11am (90mins); afternoon
cruise 1.30pm (90mins); sunset cruise 4pm (90mins);
dinner cruise 7pm (2hrs). **Admission** from ¥2,500;
¥1,250 concessions. **No credit cards**.

Marine Shuttle
Boats leave from Yamashita pier (info 045 661
0347). Departures 10.20am (1hr), 12.20pm (1hr),
2.10pm (1hr), 3.40pm (40mins), 4.50pm (1hr),
6.30pm (90mins) Mon-Fri; 10.20am (1hr), 11.40am
(1hr), 1pm (1hr), 2.20pm (1hr), 3.40pm (40mins),
4.40pm (40mins), 5.30pm (40mins), 6.30pm
(90mins) Sat, Sun. **Admission** *40min course*
¥750; ¥380 concessions. *1hr course* ¥1,200;
¥600 concessions. *90min course* ¥2,000; ¥1,000
concessions. **No credit cards**.

Royal Wing
Leaves Yamashita pier at noon (90min lunch cruise)
and 6.30pm (2hr dinner cruise). (Information 045
662 6125.) **Admission** Lunch ¥5,500; ¥3,450
concessions. Dinner ¥8,500; ¥5,450 concessions.
No credit cards.

Sea Bass
Leaves Yokohama station east exit for Yamashita
pier every 15-20mins until 8.10pm daily
(information 045 661 0347). **Admission** ¥500;
¥250 concessions. **No credit cards**.

Anyone expecting a ride on a giant fish will be disappointed. Sea Bass is the Japanese re-transliteration, back into English, of 'Sea Bus'.

Restaurants & bars

In & around Yokohama station

Bar Star Dust

2-1 Senjyaku-cho, Kanagawa-ku (045 441 1017). Higashi-Kanagawa or Nakakido station. **Open** 5pm-2am daily. **No credit cards.**
A little out of the way, but a little special, Bar Star Dust opened in 1954 and has hardly changed since. Situated in the Mizuho wharf, once a major port of embarkation for the occupying US forces, Star Dust evokes a bygone era with the aid of a jukebox.

Laffits

YT16 Bldg 5F, 2-16-2 Tsuruya-cho, Kanagawa-ku (045 322 3232). Yokohama station. **Open** 7pm-4am daily. *Happy hour* 5-7pm Mon, Tue, Sun. **Average** ¥2,500. **Credit** DC, JCB, MC, V. **No English menu.**
From the full-size, wooden-legged Blackbeard at the door to the skull and crossbones flag on the wall and Death cigarettes on sale at the bar, this is Pirate World. Service can be slow, but the food is good.

The Living Bar

Miyamoto Bldg 2F, 1-10-3 Minami-saiwai, Nishi-ku (045 311 5125). Yokohama station. **Open** 5.30-11.30pm Mon-Thur; 5.30pm-2am Fri, Sat; 5-11.30pm Sun. **Average** ¥2,500. **Credit** AmEx, DC, JCB, MC, V. **Menu in English.**

The Living Bar is a classy joint with such a whiff of European elegance it's hard to believe it's part of a chain. Excellent service from the alert staff. Killer fondue for two at only ¥1,800 and some of the best cocktails in the city.

Sakabune

1-5-6 Sengen-cho, Nishi-ku (045 411 0810). Yokohama station. **Open** 5pm-1am Tue, Thur-Sun. **Average** ¥3,500. **No credit cards.**
A cosy Japanese restaurant with a reputation for fresh fish. The owner buys from fishermen in Yamaguchi Prefecture on Kyushu, a two-hour flight away. The menu ranges from *tempura* to seasonal vegetables and Korean-style *yakitori*.

Samadhi

1-10-8 Minami-saiwai, Nishi-ku (045 311 4422). **Open** 5.30pm-midnight daily. **Average** ¥3,000. **Credit** AmEx, JCB, MC, V. **No English menu.**
It defies belief seeing how many people can fit into a space the size of the average European front room. Samadhi does it and does it well, with a tree-house theme, seating upwards of 40 people as deep reggae, house and hip hop, plus subtle lighting, take you to somewhere altogether more relaxing.

Stoves

2-1-13 Minami-saiwai, Nishi-ku (045 312 2203). Yokohama station. **Open** 4pm-2am Mon-Fri; noon-2am Sat, Sun. **Average** ¥3,000. **No credit cards.**
A laid-back hippy groove with a staff of Japanese deadheads and a background of '60s and '70s music.

Traditional **Sankeien Garden** was created by a wealthy silk merchant in 1906. *See p237.*

Wild Pepper
Ginzaya Bldg 5F, 2-7-8 Minami-saiwai, Nishi-ku (045 314 4444). Yokohama station. **Open** 5pm-3am daily. *Happy hour* 5-7pm daily. **Average** ¥2,500. **No credit cards. Menu in English.**
An indoor jungle. As the name suggests, every dish is hot, with garlic, chilli or spicy sauce. Basic Chinese and Korean dishes are the speciality.

Chinatown

Dohatsu Honkan
1-48 Ishikawa-cho, Naka-ku (045 681 7273). Kannai station. **Open** 11.30am-9.30pm daily. **Average** ¥5,000. **Credit** DC, V. **No English menu.**
Delicious Cantonese fare in a cosy atmosphere. Popular for its Hong Kong-style seafood dishes.

Peking Hanten
79 Yamashita-cho, Naka-ku (045 681 3535). Kannai station. **Open** 11.30am-2am daily. **Average** ¥3,000. **Credit** AmEx, DC, JCB, V. **Menu in English.**
This charming restaurant claims to be the first in Japan to serve Peking duck, the house speciality. A whole duck costs about ¥13,000; smaller portions are ¥2,000.

Suro Saikan Honkan
190 Yamashita-cho, Naka-ku (045 681 3456). Kannai station. **Open** 11.30am-midnight daily. **Average** ¥4,000. **Credit** AmEx, DC, JCB, MC, V. **Menu in English.**
A little hard to find but worth the effort for its quality Shanghai cuisine at reasonable prices. The huge fried carp for ¥3,300 is probably the best deal. The

Chinese chef, Son Kanri, was a long-running winner on Japanese TV show *Ryoori no Tetsujin* (*Cooking Championship*). Expect to wait at lunch.

Minato Mirai 21

Chandler's Crabhouse
202 Queen's Square, 2-3-8 Minato Mirai, Nishi-ku (045 682 2805). Sakuragi-cho station. **Open** 11am-10pm daily. **Average** *Lunch* ¥1,200. *Dinner* ¥3,500. **Credit** AmEx, DC, JCB, MC, V. **Menu in English.**
Yokohama incarnation of the famous Seattle-based seafood restaurant, serving up some of the freshest seafood on the planet. The smoked seafood sampler (¥3,680, serves four), the most popular dish in the house, contains five kinds of sea fare.

Matsuba Sushi
Landmark Tower 1F, 2-2 Minato Mirai, Nishi-ku (045 222 526). Sakuragi-cho station. **Open** 11.30am-10pm daily. **Average** *Lunch* ¥1,000. *Dinner* ¥3,000. **Credit** DC, JCB, MC, V. **No English menu.**
A favourite of girls who lunch, Matsuba serves up its top-quality *sushi* in unusually decorative ways.

Motomachi

Aussie
1-12 Ishikawa-cho, Naka-ku (045 681 3671). Ishikawa-cho station. **Open** 5pm-midnight daily. *Happy hour* 5-7pm daily. **Average** ¥3,500. **Credit** AmEx, JCB, MC, V. **Menu in English.**
This restaurant has gained a big reputation, receiving several visits from the Australian ambassador. It serves anything Australian, the most popular dish

Yamate

This is one of the most historic and picturesque areas of Yokohama. When the Japanese government, in the 19th century, reluctantly decided to allow foreigners into the country, it was determined to do so on its own terms. In 1867, this area of the town was sectioned off and allocated to non-Japanese. Now, the view is obscured by skyscrapers, but back then, it was spectacular. Just how spectacular you can see for yourself in the vintage photographs on display at the **Yamate Museum** (*see p238*), which is located in one of the area's oldest houses, a wooden structure dating from 1909.

The house itself is representative of the curious fusion of western and eastern architectural styles that typifies this area. Because many of the early settlers were wealthy merchants and reluctant to 'go

native', they brought with them from their various countries stylistic features of the buildings they were used to, including lawns, surrounding gardens and sloping roofs. But because the houses themselves were built by Japanese craftsmen unfamiliar with western homes, or unable to get hold of western materials, the end result often manages to be both out of place and utterly Japanese at the same time.

Many of the historic houses are open to the public during the hours of daylight, and an English-language pamphlet is available at each one. The most spectacular house on the bluff belonged to a Japanese diplomat, Uchida Sadatsuchi, who returned from his foreign travels in 1910 to build a Gothic-style mansion in wood. It now stands in the garden that once surrounded the Italian Consulate, on top of a hill overlooking the harbour.

being barbecued kangaroo and crocodile. It's often packed by 7.30pm: get here early for half-price wine, then sit back and soak up the atmosphere.

Mutekiro
2-96 Motomachi, Naka-ku (045 681 2926).
Ishikawa-cho station. **Open** noon-3pm; 5-10pm daily.
Average *Lunch* ¥4,000. *Dinner* ¥14,000-¥30,000.
Credit AmEx, DC, JCB, MC, V.
This upmarket restaurant in an upmarket area boasts its cooking is '*Mode française, coeur japonais*', and judging by the crowds it attracts, it has hit the right balance. Black-suited waiters will cater for your every whim, serving dishes such as *flan de daurade accentué pousse de bambou et combinaison d'algue* (fish with bamboo shoots and seaweed).

Wakana
5-20 Minato-cho, Naka-ku (045 681 1404).
Kannai station. **Open** 11am-9pm Tue, Thur-Sun.
Average ¥2,700. **No credit cards.**
If you visit Japan during the hot, sticky summer months, you might like to try the Japanese remedy: eel, or *unagi*, the speciality of this small restaurant. Japanese people believe the vitamins contained in eel help combat the sapping effects of the heat and humidity. Here you can sample its restorative effects in over 120 different sauces.

Elsewhere

Kirin Yokohama Beer Village
Kirin Beer Yokohama Factory, 1-17-1 Namamugi,
Tsurumi-ku (brewery 045 506 3017/restaurant 045
506 3013/tour bookings 045 503 825). Namamugi
station (Keihin Kyuko line). **Open** *Brewery* 10am-
5pm Tue-Sun. *Restaurant* 11am-9.30pm Tue-Sun.
Credit AmEx, DC, JCB, MC, V.
Get to see how Kirin beer is made, then sample some of the wares at the beer hall and restaurant. Tours of the brewery take 75 minutes, and must be booked in advance.

Shin-Yokohama Ramen Museum
2-14-21 Shin-Yokohama, Kohoku-ku (045 471
0503). Shin-Yokohama station. **Open** 11am-11pm
Mon, Wed-Sun. **Admission** ¥300; ¥100 concessions.
No credit cards.
Fans of *ramen*, the film *Tampopo* or 1950s Japanalia should make a pilgrimage to the world's only museum dedicated to the humble noodle. Between exhibits, collections and a painstaking replica of a *shitamachi* neighbourhood of 1958 are eight *ramen* shops from the four major *ramen* centres, Sapporo, Hakata, Kumamoto and Kyoto, plus four Tokyo/ Yokohama shops.

Shopping

Landmark Plaza
2-2-1 Minato-Mirai, Nishi-ku (045 222 5015).
Sakuragi-cho station. **Open** 11am-8pm daily.
Restaurants/cafés hours vary. **Credit** varies.

Babbling brooks and soothing grand piano recitals provide entertainment and distraction from the hard slog of trawling five floors of shops ranging from Michel Klein to Octopus Army. Relief comes at every turn, with restaurants, cafés and coffee shops.

Queen's Square/AT
2-3 Minato Mirai, Nishi-ku (045 682 1000).
Sakuragi-cho station. **Open** 11am-8pm daily.
Restaurants/cafés times vary. **Credit** varies.
At the heart of this huge complex is a cavernous atrium stretching from basement level three to the fifth floor, lined with all kinds of cuisine. Upmarket shopping, a concert hall and an abundance of decorative indoor greenery make this an altogether relaxing experience.

Yokohama World Porters
2-1-1 Shin-Minato, Naka-ku (045 222 2000)
Sakuragi-cho station. **Open** *Shops* 10am-9pm.
Restaurants 10am-11pm. *Ccinema* 10am-midnight.
Credit varies.
A massive commerical centre just over the water from **Landmark Tower** (*see p237*), World Porters, which opened in 2000, has enough shops, restaurants and entertainment facilities to make it a day out in itself. On the sixth floor, it has a 1,500sq-m Korean fashion market called Tongdaemun. Here, 85 shops sell goods directly imported from South Korea, which means bargain prices. You can even barter, as you would in Seoul.

Getting there

Shin-Yokohama station is only one stop and 17mins on the main Tokyo-Osaka *shinkansen* (bullet train) line, or 25mins from Tokyo station to Yokohama station on the JR Tokaido line. The JR Keihin Tohoku and JR Yokosuka lines also go to Yokohama station. Another option is the Tokyu Toyoko line, which goes from Shibuya to Yokohama (25mins) and Sakuragi-cho (30mins). For Kannai and Ishikawa-cho stations, change to JR Negishi line at Yokohama station.

Tourist information

Kanagawa Prefectural Tourist Information
Silk Centre Bldg 1F, 1 Yamashita-cho, Naka-ku (045
681 0007). **Open** 9am-5.30pm Mon-Fri.

Yokohama Convention & Visitors' Bureau Sakuragi-cho Centre
1-53 Sakuragi-cho, Naka-ku (045 211 0111).
Open 9am-6pm Mon-Thur, Sun; 9am-8pm Fri, Sat.
Next to Sakuragi-cho station, YCVB has free maps of Yokohama and some English-speaking staff.

Yokohama Convention & Visitors' Bureau Sanbo Centre
Sangyo Boeki Centre Bldg 1F, 2 Yamashita-cho,
Naka-ku (045 473 2895). **Open** 10am-6pm Mon-Sat.

Trips Out of Town

Hakone 箱根

Take a trip to the mountains, followed by a bath in steaming hot spring water.

Hakone is where Tokyo comes to relax and get a taste of the countryside. Around one-and-a-half hours from Shinjuku station by train, this mountainous area offers convenient transportation, beautiful scenery, a host of attractions and, best of all, a natural hot spring bath, or *onsen*, around virtually every bend of the roads that twist through the mountains.

The best way to see Hakone is to buy the **Hakone Free Pass** (*see p245*), available at all Odakyu stations. The pass covers all public transportation in Hakone. And what public transportation it has! As well as a picturesque railway and a bus service, the Hakone area also has a funicular railway, a cable car and a boat that crosses Lake Ashi at its centre. All of these means of transport are interlinked, making it possible to 'do' the whole of the Hakone area in a day from Tokyo.

For those in a hurry, this is the Hakone circuit. Get off the train at either Odawara or Hakone Yumoto. From there, transfer to the Tozan mountain railway for the 50-minute ride to its terminus at Gora. At Gora, transfer on to the funicular railway up to the end of the line at

Sounzan. Here, transfer to the cable car, which takes you down to the banks of Lake Ashi at Togendai station. To get across the lake, board one of the pleasure boats and stay on until Hakone-Machi or Moto-Hakone, from where you can take a bus back to where you started, at Hakone-Yumoto or Odawara. The round-trip should take about three hours, although in the busy summer months it may take longer.

While this method will give you your fill of glorious scenery, you'll be missing out on a lot of what Hakone has to offer. If you decide to start your journey at Odawara, it's worth making a detour out of the east exit of the station to take the ten-minute walk to **Odawara Castle** (*see p245*), perched on a hill overlooking the town. First built in 1416, and rebuilt in 1960, this picturesque castle was for centuries an important strategic stronghold. For some reason, the city elders have taken it into their heads to open a miniature zoo in the grounds.

Back on the train, the next major stop, or the starting point for some, is Hakone-Yumoto station. 'Yumoto' means 'source of hot water',

Volcanic activity makes the slopes of **Owakudani** (big boiling valley) steam. *See p244.*

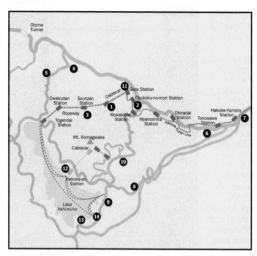

which should give you some clue as to what this small town is about. First mentioned in eighth-century poetry as a place to bathe, the small town became a great favourite in the time of the Tokugawa shogunate (1600-1854), with bathers travelling two or three days on foot from Tokyo (then Edo) in order to reach the springs along the Tokaido way, portions of which can still be seen over the other side of the river from the modern railway station. The station houses a small tourist office, but the main office is up the hill on the left-hand side. Here, there are English-speaking assistants, happy to hand out maps and pamphlets.

For dedicated modern bathers, the day may end in Hakone-Yumoto. Although the modern town is unremarkable, it is dotted with hot spring baths: just about every building of any size is a hotel or *ryokan*, and many allow non-guests to use their facilities. One of the locals' favourites is located on the hillside on the other side of the tracks from the station. **Kappa Tengoku** (*see p245*) has segregated open-air baths surrounded by dense woodland, and a steady army of bathers can be seen trooping up the steep steps to the baths well into the night. Bring your own towel and wash cloth if you want to save money.

Up the hill from the bath is the intriguing **Hakone Toy Museum** (*see p245*). The souvenir shop sells charmingly retro goods imported from China and elsewhere.

Back on the train from Hakone-Yumoto, take some time to enjoy the train itself. This is the world's steepest train line and so sharp are the bends that at three points the train enters a switchback, forwarding and then reversing out of a siding in order to continue its climb.

As you climb the mountain you will see water pouring out of the hillside and cascading under the tracks, some of it still hot.

The next station of any note is Miyanoshita. This is home to one of the highest concentrations of *onsen* baths in the area, and is where the first foreigners in Japan would come and bathe in the 19th century. To cater for them, the **Fujiya Hotel** (*see p245*) was built in 1878. Miraculously, it's still standing today, a wooden mix of Japanese and western styles that's worth a visit in its own right. Non-residents are free to stop here for a coffee, a bite to eat or something stronger in the bar.

Two stops up the line, at Chokoku no Mori station, is one of the great glories of Hakone. The **Hakone Open-Air Museum** (*see p244*) must be one of the most spectacular in the world. Set on a mountainside overlooking a series of valleys leading to the sea, the museum is dedicated to modern sculpture from all over the globe. This being Japan, the curators haven't skimped on the collection. Exposed to the elements are works by Moore, Rodin, Antony Gormley and Taro Okamoto, while there's a world-beating collection of ceramics by Picasso, donated by the artist's daughter, Maya, in a separate pavilion.

From here, it's a ten-minute walk to the next station, Gora, the terminus of the Tozan railway and the start of the funicular railway that climbs the steep mountainside. If you're changing from the train, there will be a carriage waiting for you. The first stop on the funicular, Koen Shita, provides a pleasant diversion in the shape of **Gora Park** (*see p244*), a beautifully landscaped hillside garden that makes great use of the natural hot water in its hot houses and is

Trips Out of Town

particularly beautiful in summer. A walk uphill through the park will bring you to the next stop on the funicular.

The funicular terminates at Sounzan station, and it's here that many people's favourite part of the Hakone experience begins: the cable car, or Hakone Ropeway, as it's called. Riding over the peaks and valleys of Hakone, this 4.3-kilometre (2.7-mile) ride is Japan's longest cable car route. Around halfway along its length is **Owakudani** ('big boiling valley'), one of the most breath-taking sights in Hakone. The car passes over, at a height of around 60 metres (200 feet), a smoking hillside streaked with traces of sulphur from the volcanic activity below. The air simply reeks with the smell of rotten eggs. On top of a mountain peak sits Owakudani station, the centre of a large tourist complex comprising restaurants, gift shops and the **Owakudani Natural History Museum** (see p245). On a clear day you can see the peak of Mount Fuji looming over the mountain range in the distance. There's also a walk to the source of some of the steam that rises out of the mountain, the ancient crater of Mount Kamiyama, the pathway passing over hot streams of water bubbling up. The air is thick with hydrogen sulphide, and signs in Japanese warn of the dangers of standing in one place for too long for fear of being overcome by fumes. If you feel like a snack, the best bet here is a hard-boiled egg. Sold by the half-dozen for ¥500, these eggs have been cooked in the hot spring water, the sulphur turning their shells black. Still warm and washed down with canned tea from a vending machine, they're the perfect pick-me-up for the weary traveller.

From Owakudani, the Hakone Ropeway passes over several more valleys before descending to terminate at Togendai on the banks of Lake Ashi. The lake is believed to be in the crater of a volcano that blew its top 400,000 years ago. The volcanic activity that goes on beneath the waters to this day ensures that it never freezes over. From here, a pair of incredibly tacky pleasure boats, one done out as a Spanish galleon, one as a Mississippi steamer, cross the lake to Hakone-Machi and Moto-Hakone. Only 500 metres or so separate the two destinations, but for ease of walking, get off at Hakone-Machi and turn left with the lake behind you, to head for Moto-Hakone.

On the way is the site of the **Old Hakone Checkpoint** (see p245), where travellers to and from Tokyo (then Edo) were stopped and often interrogated by border guards. Ruins of the original checkpoint still stand, while many of the buildings have been reconstructed and opened to the public as a museum (although on the other side of the road from the original

The **Tozan railway** is an attraction in itself.

ruins; see p245). Set back a little from the modern road is what's left of a cedar avenue, planted along the Tokaido Way in the early 17th century. Paved sections of the Tokaido Way are still extant, and keen walkers can take a short hike from here along one such section, away from the lake towards Hatajuku.

On a promontory into the lake between the two boat stops is the **Hakone Detached Palace Garden** (see below). The garden of an 1887 villa that once belonged to the imperial family but was destroyed in an earthquake, it has been open to the public since 1946. Further along, past Moto-Hakone and down the side of the lake, is Hakone Shrine, its history going back 1,200 years. The site is clearly marked by a red gate, or torii, that stands in the lake.

Once you've walked your fill of the area, head back to Moto-Hakone and take a bus back to Odawara. All buses to Odawara stop in Hakone-Yumoto, too.

Gora Park

1300 Gora, Hakone-Machi, Shimogun (0460 22825/ www.hakone-tozan.co.jp). **Open** 9am-5pm daily. **Admission** ¥900; ¥400 concessions.

Hakone Detached Palace Garden

171 Moto-Hakone, Hakone-Machi, Ashigara-Shimogun (0460 37484). **Open** *July, Aug* 9am-5pm daily. *Sept-June* 9am-5pm Wed-Mon. **Admission** free.

Hakone Open-Air Museum

Ninotaira, Hakone-Machi (0460 21161/ www.HAKONE-OAM.or.jp). **Open** *Mar-Nov* 9am-5pm daily. *Dec-Feb* 9am-4.30pm daily. **Admission** ¥1,600; ¥800 concessions.

Trips Out of Town

Hakone Toy Museum

740 Yumoto, Hakone-Machi, Ashigara-Shimogun (0460 64700/www.hakonetoys.com). **Open** 9am-5pm daily. **Admission** ¥800; ¥400 concessions.

Kappa Tengoku

777 Yumoto, Hakone-Machi, Ashigara-Shimogun (0460 56121). **Admission** ¥700. *Towel* ¥900 (to buy). 10% discount with Hakone Free Pass.

Odawara Castle

(0465 231373). **Open** 10am-4pm Tue-Sun. **Admission** *Park* free. *Castle* ¥400; ¥150 concessions.

Old Hakone Checkpoint

Hakone-Machi (0460 36635). **Open** 9am-4pm daily. **Admission** ¥300; ¥150 concessions.

Owakudani Natural History Museum

1251 Sengokuhara, Hakone (0460 49149). **Open** 9am-4.30pm daily. **Admission** ¥400; ¥250 concessions.

Where to eat & drink

Given that most of the activity in the area is centred around hotels, it's hardly surprising that there are remarkably few places worth seeking out. For the truly hungry, there are snack bars serving curry, noodles and the like at Owakudani and Togendai stations, and on the lake at Hakone-Machi. **The Bella Foresta** restaurant in the Open-Air Museum (*see p244*) serves a decent buffet lunch for around ¥1,500, while all of the large hotels have at least four restaurants that are open to non-residents.

Where to stay

There are hundreds of places to stay in Hakone, ranging from cheap *ryokan* to top-class hotels. All have their own hot springs. Many have separate rates for weekdays and weekends, the former being cheaper. Expect top prices at peak periods such as New Year and Golden Week in May. If you intend to use Hakone-Yumoto as a base, cheap options include **Kappa Tengoku** (777 Yumoto, Hakone-Machi, Ashigara-Shimogun, 0460 56121), where a double room costs ¥6,200 per night on weekdays (¥1,000 more at weekends), although its proximity to the railway tracks might mean an earlier awakening than you'd bargained for. A plusher option is the **Kajikasou** (777 Yumoto, Hakone-Machi, Ashigara-Shimogun, 0460 55561/ www.kajikaso.co.jp), which has a plethora of different baths, including private ones. Rates start at ¥22,000 on weekdays (¥25,000 weekends). Up in the mountains, the **Fujiya Hotel** (359 Miyanoshita, Ashigara-Shimogun, 0460 22211/www.fujiyahotel.co.jp) is peerless, with double rooms starting at ¥16,000 on weekdays (¥25,000 weekends). Overlooking Lake Ashi is a branch of the **Palace Hotel** chain (1245 Sengokuhara, Hakone-Machi, Ashigara-Shimogun, 0460 48501/ hakone.palacehotel.co.jp), where doubles start at ¥24,000. This luxury hotel often advertises special-stay plans in the Tokyo press, which bring the price down to ¥15,000.

Getting there

By train

There are two types of Hakone Free Pass, available at all Odakyu stations and many travel agents. The weekday pass gives you unlimited transport for two days and costs ¥4,700 from Shinjuku station. The weekend pass gives three days' unlimited transport and costs ¥5,500 from Shinjuku station. The ticket price also covers the basic fare on an Odakyu train from Shinjuku to Hakone. If you want to travel in comfort on the super express Romance Car, you will need to pay an express supplement of ¥870. If you hold a JR Pass (*see p259*), the most cost-effective way of reaching the area is to take a JR Tokaido *shinkansen* to Odawara station, then buy your Hakone Free Pass there. Because this pass does not include transport to Tokyo, it costs ¥3,410 (weekdays) or ¥4,130 (weekends). The Free Pass also gives discounts at many local attractions. Look out for the Hakone Free Pass sticker.

Tourist information

Hakone-Yumoto Tourist Information

Kankou Bussankan, 698 Yumoto, Hakone-Machi, Ashigara-Shimogun (0460 58911). **Open** 9am-5pm daily.

Odakyu Railway Information

Odakyu Shinjuku station (5321 7877). **Open** 9am-5pm daily.

Odawara Tourist Information

East exit, Odawara station (0465 331521). **Open** 9am-5pm daily.

Tacky boating on **Lake Ashi**. *See p244.*

Trips Out of Town

Kamakura 鎌倉

Travel 800 years back in time to feudal Japan, 51 minutes from Tokyo station.

For almost 150 years Kamakura was the military and administrative centre of Japan, generating great religious and artistic fervour. What made it a strategic location for the first military government – the fact that it has hills on three sides and Sagami Bay on the other – has also kept the city from creeping in. The feeling in Kamakura is very much that of the country, despite being less than one hour from Tokyo station.

TEMPLE TOWN

The enduring appeal of Kamakura is religious; it has more than 70 temples and shrines, from the large and flamboyant to the small and secluded. They represent different Buddhist sects, among them Rinzai, Pure Land and Nichiren, and many are within walking distance of Kamakura or Kita-Kamakura stations. The grounds of most temples have been lost through fires and earthquakes, or, in the case of Engaku-ji in Kita Kamakura, to make way for the railway line. But many buildings have, in fact, survived since the Kamakura period (1185-1333), when the city was the capital of Japan, giving visitors a rare opportunity to view authentically historic remnants of old Japan.

Kamakura is now a major tourist destination, and the temples and grounds are well looked after. Most temples require a small fee (¥100-¥300), which you should see as a contribution towards upkeep rather than an admission charge. The directions and distances to temples in each vicinity are marked in English at regular intervals all around town. For a detailed map ask the Tourist Information Service right of the station gates at the east exit (*see p249*). Most temples are open daily, but museums and some shops close on Mondays. The town and the main attractions should be avoided at weekends unless you like crowds.

Festival days are also extremely busy. The main ones are the Grand Festival (14-16 September) and the Kamakura festival (from the second to the third Sunday in April). Both take place at Tsurugaoka Hachiman (*see below*). On the last day of the Grand Festival is *yabusame* (mounted archery) in Kamakura-era hunting attire, but viewpoints are scarce. The fireworks on the beach on 10 August attract big crowds, too. As well as these, each temple and shrine holds its own festival.

The area is also well known for its flowers and blossoms, and many people come to see plums, cherries, irises, azaleas and many others throughout the year.

Kamakura's main attractions are scattered around and take a day to see in themselves; you may do better to pick an area and check out the temples and sights there.

Walking to temples in any area will take you through small streets in quiet residential areas, with well-tended gardens, old wooden houses and traditional shops. There's often a smell of incense in the air. Many temples are built on the sides of mountains, so be prepared to climb a few stairs. There are also some hiking courses on ridges leading to temples. Most are fairly easy. The starting points are indicated on the road, as are destinations and estimated durations.

You can also rent bicycles to increase the number of sights you can get around. The rental office is behind the police box on the right at the east exit of the station. It's open daily from 9am to 5pm (¥500 one hour, ¥1,000 three hours; bring ID).

What follows is a list of highlights of the Kamakura area. For information on more sights, check with the Tourist Information Service (*see p249*).

Tsurugaoka Hachiman

The main and most popular shrine in Kamakura, **Tsurugaoka Hachiman** is 15 minutes' walk from the station. The guardian shrine of the Minamoto family, the warring clan that took control of the area in the 12th century, it's always busy and contains many attractions. Hachiman is seen today as the god of war, but in the past was recognised as the guardian of the Japanese nation.

To get to the shrine, follow Komachi Dori, through the *torii* (gate) on the left. It's a pedestrian mall, full of souvenirs and craft shops, boutiques, food stalls and shops, as well as restaurants. At the end, turn right.

The shrine and grounds were built to very strict specifications, the most striking example of which is found near the entrance. On the right (the east, the rising sun) is a large pond with three islands (a propitious number), symbolising the Minamoto family. On the left

Great Budda at Kotokuin Temple.

(the west, the setting sun) is a smaller pond with four islands (an unlucky number) symbolising the Taira clan, the group the Minamoto defeated to gain control of the area. Going straight, you'll come to a dancing stage, then to the steps to the main hall. The two guardian figures in the gate are Yadaijin and Sadaijin, but the ginkgo tree on the left of the steps dwarfs them in majesty. It's purported to be at least as old as the shrine, which was here even before the arrival of the Minamoto. The tree is also famous for having concealed the murderer of the third Minamoto *shogun*, taken by surprise and beheaded on the spot.

Kita-Kamakura

This area is home to many Rinzai sect temples, the HQ of which is the famous **Engaku-ji**, the largest Zen establishment in Kamakura, a few metres from Kita-Kamakura station. The temple was founded in 1282, but the main gate, housing statues of Kannon and Rakan, was reconstructed in 1780. Engaku-ji is also famous for having the largest bell in Kamakura.

On the road along the tracks is the **Kamakura Old Pottery Museum** (10am-5.30pm Tue-Sun) and across the tracks is **Tokei-ji**, for a long time a nunnery offering asylum to women wanting a divorce. It's worth a visit for its beautiful garden and grounds as well as the Treasure House, which keeps old sutras and scrolls.

Nearby is **Jochi-ji**, interesting for its old bridge and steps at the entrance, its bell tower, the burial caves at the back and a tunnel between cemeteries. On the other side of the road is **Meigetsuin**, approached by a pleasant street. The temple has the biggest *yagura* (burial cave) in the area, a small stone garden and statues carved out of the rock in the caves.

On the road towards Kamakura you'll find **Kencho-ji**, the first great Zen temple of Kamakura. It's an imposing place with large buildings and grounds, though only ten of the original 49 sub-temples survive. The oldest Zen temple in Japan, its arrangement has not changed for over 700 years. On the second floor of the main gate are the statues of 500 *rakan* (Buddha's disciples). Behind the last building there's a garden, and, further along, the path leads to steps climbing to **Hanso-bo**, the shrine protecting the temple. Up the stairs near the tunnel on the road is Eno-ji, a very small temple housing statues representing the judges of hell.

West of Tsurugaoka Hachiman

Eisho-ji, the only active Buddhist nunnery in the area, is closed to the public. At nearby **Jufuku-ji**, the temple grounds are closed, too, but you can wander in the old cemetery behind by following the path to the left of the gate. It's a quiet place with many burial caves, some reputed to date from Kamakura's heyday as the capital of Japan.

About 30 minutes away on foot is **Zeniarai Benten** ('Money-washing Shrine'), a must-see. Go through a tunnel under a mountain and enter another world, with small shrines carved in the cliffs, as well as ponds and eerie music. In the cave straight ahead of the entrance you'll find containers to put your money in, notes and all. The more you wash the more you'll get. Use the incense burner if you need to dry the notes.

Back towards the town at a nearby crossing is a lane leading to **Sasuke Inari Shrine**, up steps through more than 100 *torii*. There's not all that much to see up here, but it is very peaceful at the end of the valley.

Another 30 minutes' walk will take you to **Kotokuin Temple**, home of the Daibutsu or Great Buddha. The temple dates from AD 741 and the statue of Buddha from 1252. Nobody really knows how the statue was cast and put together. It was once in a hall that suffered fires and earthquakes and was finally demolished by a tidal wave in 1495. The statue was unscathed and has been in the open ever since. You can go inside and have a look for ¥20.

Trips Out of Town

Kamakura is dotted with beautiful gardens that are ideal for a spot of peaceful meditation.

A few minutes away is **Hase Kannon** or Hase Dera, which boasts many interesting sights. Entry costs ¥300. The main feature is a nine-metre (30-foot), 11-faced statue of Kannon (goddess of mercy and compassion), reputedly the tallest in Japan. It was carved in AD 721 out of a single camphor tree. The temple is especially well known for its thousands of small *jizo* figures offered in memory of deceased children and babies. There's also a revolving *sutra* library containing Buddhist scriptures – worshippers rotating the library receive merit equivalent to reading the entire Buddhist canon – and a small network of caves with statues carved out of the rock. The **Treasure House** (open 9am-4pm daily) contains possessions and artefacts excavated from the temple during rebuilding. Entry is included in the fee for the temple. From Hase Kannon there's a panoramic view of the town, the beach and Sagami Bay.

East of Tsurugaoka Hachiman

This least grandiose of the sightseeing areas is quieter, with many smaller temples. The first shrine as you come from Tsurugaoka Hachiman is **Egara Tenjin**, founded in 1104. Tenjin is the patron deity of scholarship and literature,

so every 25 January there is a burning of writing brushes here. Nearby is **Kamakura shrine**, founded by the Meiji Emperor in 1869.

Turn left up the small road leading to **Kakuon-ji**. This looks a small temple but a 40-minute tour given by a priest (on the hour from 10am to 3pm daily, though not on rainy days) gives the chance to see the extent of the grounds and other buildings. The tour is in Japanese only, but the thatched buildings and old wooden statues speak for themselves.

A 15-minute walk from Kamakura shrine is **Zuisen-ji**, famous for its flowers, especially the plum blossoms in February. It's a small temple, with an old Zen garden created in the 14th century by famous priest and landscape gardener Muso-Kokushi.

From the intersection near Kamakura shrine you can reach **Sugimotodera**, the oldest temple in Kamakura. The gate and temple have thatched roofs and were built in AD 734. Further up across the road is **Hokoku-ji**, known as the bamboo temple because of its large bamboo grove. From here it's a short walk to **Shakado Tunnel**. It is closed to traffic, but pedestrians still use it to cross the ridge.

Back towards the city on the road parallel to Wakamiya Dori, you'll see signs for the **Harakiri Cave**, where the last Hojo regent and more than 800 of his retainers killed themselves after Kamakura fell to the imperial forces.

The traditional sights of old Japan seem a million miles from the neon and bustle of Tokyo.

Down the road (15 minutes from the station) is **Hongaku-ji**, a small temple with a very old gate. Shortly after is **Myohon-ji**, founded in 1260. Between this temple and the beach are many Nichiren sect temples; this is the oldest and largest. There are only a few buildings in the grounds.

Another 15 minutes or so away is **Myoho-ji**, also known as Moss Temple. You can visit the small grounds but the gate leading to the back and top of the hill is generally closed. The priest Nichiren is said to have resided here and the top of the hill was reputedly one of his favourite spots.

Towards the beach along the main road you'll come to **Choso-ji**, a recently renovated structure (though there's been a temple here since 1345). There's a statue of Nichiren between the statues of four celestial kings to protect the place against evil. Very close to the beach is **Komyo-ji**, a large temple established in 1243. There is a path on the right between the temple and the playground leading back up to the road above. You can see the beach, ocean, Enoshima Island and Mount Fuji, although there's nowhere to sit to enjoy the sight.

Down by the beach to the east are the remains of **Wakaejima**, the first artificial port in Japan, built in 1232. It went into terminal decline when Kyoto was restored to being the Japanese capital.

Where to eat & stay

As Kamakura is less than one hour from Tokyo by train, it is easy to do the trip in one day. You might like to try a traditional Japanese *kaiseki* meal at **Kaiko-tei** (3-7 Sakanoshita Kamakura-shi Kanagawa-ken, 0467 25 4494, ¥5,500 lunch, ¥7,000-¥13,000 dinner), an atmospheric 180-year-old restaurant that also serves *soba* and *udon* noodles at lunch time. Reservations are required in the evening. A more eccentric choice might be **Amish Cooking Kamakura** (2-4-23 Yukinoshita, Kamakura-shi, Kanagawa-ken, 0467 25 2533), specialising in traditional Amish cuisine. Go for the sour-cream-based country cake, but be warned, it's only open till 5pm.

Getting there

It's possible to start sightseeing from either Kita-Kamakura or Kamakura stations. Both are on the JR Yokosuka line from Tokyo station. Fares are ¥780 and ¥890 respectively.

Tourist information

Kamakura City Tourist Information Service

1-1-1 Komachi, Kamakura City, Kanagawa-ken (0467 22 3350). **Open** *Apr-Sept* 9am-6pm daily. *Oct-Mar* 9am-5pm daily.

Trips Out of Town

Mountains

To the Japanese, mountains are not just big rocks, they're where the gods live.

Mount Fuji

Once a pilgrimage, the climb to the summit of Mount Fuji is now an experience that anyone can enjoy. Japan's highest mountain, Fuji is renowned for its beauty and spiritual significance. Pilgrimages used to start at Hongu Fuji Sengen Shrine. Established in AD 788, the shrine is dedicated to Konohanasakuya-hime, the patron of Fuji and goddess of the volcano. Mount Fuji is dormant and these days only a wisp of smoke emanates from the crater. The last eruption in 1707 covered Edo (now Tokyo), 100 kilometres (62 miles) away, with ash.

The pilgrimage was restricted to men only until a few years after the Meiji Restoration. The shrines on the way up doubled as inns; pilgrims would pray and rest at each stage before reaching the summit in time for *goraiko*, the sunrise. People still go up the mountain to see the sunrise, but may use transport to the fifth stage, where the road stops. Since Fuji is covered in snow most of the year, the climbing season is restricted to July and August (out of season the trails are open but facilities are closed; in theory, people should enjoy the views from the fifth stage). The best time is the middle four weeks of that period. There is a saying that there are two kinds of fools: those who never climb Fuji and those who climb it twice.

The climb typically starts from the fifth stage in the afternoon, and includes a sleep in the huts along the way before an early rise to reach the summit in time for *goraiko*. Try to get a weather forecast from the tourist information office (*see below*) before you set out, as the view from the peak may be obscured by cloud.

The temperature at the summit can be 20°C lower than at the base. The average in July is 4.9°C and in August 2.7°C. It's often below zero before sunrise. Essential items include a raincoat, torch, water and food (available at huts, but not cheap). Don't forget to bring some toilet paper and some bags for your rubbish.

However you decide to approach Fuji, the only way up from the fifth stage is to walk. On the Kawaguchiko side the 7.5-kilometre (4.7-mile) climb takes five hours, the descent about three. From Gotemba it's six and a half hours up and three down. From the western fifth stage it's a five-hour ascent and three and a half hours to come down.

Some people start the climb quite late from the fifth stages to avoid staying at huts. The latter often cost over ¥7,000 for the few hours, and are rather basic and noisy. Don't expect a good night's sleep. Camping on the mountain is prohibited.

It's still possible to do the climb from the base through the nine stages. You start at Hongu Fuji Sengen Shrine and follow the old pilgrim route, the Yoshidaguchi trail. The shrine is in Fujiyoshida (20 minutes' walk from the station, two stops from Kawaguchiko) and takes up to five hours to the fifth stage. The trail is quiet, passing numerous historical buildings and monuments.

There's not much to do on the summit but enjoy the views and walk around the 220-metre-deep (722 feet) crater, contemplating your own insignificance in the galactic scheme of things.

Getting there

By bus

The fastest and cheapest way to Kawaguchiko, the starting point for a Fuji trip, is by bus from Nishi Shinjuku's Keio Shinjuku Expressway Bus Terminal. The fare is ¥1,700 each way. Buses leave regularly from the Yasuda Seimei Building No.2, just in front of the Yodobashi Camera store. During the climbing season there are also buses daily direct to the fifth stage: reserve with Fuji Kyuko (3374 2221). It costs ¥2,600 from Shinjuku. One or two buses a day also leave from JR Hamamatsucho station (¥1,900): for information, schedules and bookings call Keio Teito reservation centre (5376 2222).

By train

The train to Kawaguchiko is more expensive and takes longer. *Kaisoku* rapid trains (¥2,390) leave Shinjuku in the early evening and take two hours. There's an extra service in the morning on weekends and holidays. From Kawaguchiko station, getting to the fifth stage by bus takes close to another hour. In season there are up to five buses a day (none Dec-Mar). Timetables can be checked with Fuji Kyuko Line Office in Shibuya (3374 2221) or Kawaguchiko (0555 72 2911).

You can also climb Fuji from the south side, starting from one of two new fifth stages. One is near Gotemba, the other further west. There are four daily direct trains on the Odakyu line (express Asagiri) to Gotemba from Shinjuku, taking two hours and costing ¥2,650. From Gotemba there are four buses a day to the new fifth stage (only in season); they take 45 minutes and cost ¥1,080.

Trips Out of Town

Mount Fuji, a dormant volcano, last erupted in 1707. So you never know... *See p250.*

Tourist information

Kawaguchiko Tourist Information
In front of Kawaguchiko station, 3621-5 Funatsu, Kawaguchiko-Machi (0555 72 6700). **Open** 9am-5pm daily.

Yamanashi Prefectural Fuji Visitors' Centre
6663-1 Kenmarubi, Funatsu, Kawaguchiko-Machi (0555 72 0259). **Open** *Mar-Jun, Oct-Nov* 9am-5pm Tue-Sun. *July-Sept* 9am-6pm Tue-Sun. *Dec-Feb* 9am-4pm Tue-Sun.

Mount Takao

Most of Tokyo lies in the Kanto Plain and is surrounded by mountains, which, with the exception of the main valleys, have remained in their natural state. Mount Takao, an hour west of Shinjuku, is a favourite getaway. A sacred mountain, it has retained some tranquillity despite attracting many visitors. The main route to the 600m (1,969ft) summit is often busy and has been turned into a tourist attraction, but other paths leading to the top and circling the mountain are more peaceful. Even so, Takao is not too crowded, and it's the sort of place where passers-by will say '*konnichiwa*' (hello). On a clear day you can see the sprawl of the city on one side and on the other a mountain range with Fuji towering in the background.

From the station a brick-lined path leads to the base of the mountain. Restaurants and shops sell food and souvenirs. This is also the boarding area for the cable car and chairlifts to the observatory (¥470). The main path (hiking course No.1) to the observatory is steep, so you may find handing over the cash worthwhile.

The principal attraction along the main path, Yakuoin Temple, was founded in 744 and has large grounds. It's one of few temples around

Tokyo dedicated to Tengu, the long-nosed goblin. The other path leading to the top (hiking course No.6) starts to the left of the cable car and is a slow steady climb, except for the last stretch. It's a popular but quiet path that runs alongside a stream, and there are religious artefacts in the woods along the way, plus a temple by a waterfall. Information boards describe the local flora and fauna. The course can be done in about an hour.

Where to eat

The approach to the mountain is dotted with run-of-the-mill cafés, but for a special Japanese dining experience, **Ukai Toriyama** (3426 Minami Asakawa-cho, Hachioji-shi, 0426 61 0739, 11am-8pm daily) is the place to go. Nestled in a valley a few minutes from town, it consists of several buildings, seating two to 25 people, in a large manicured garden with ponds. Free buses run from the station. It serves seasonal food from the area for around ¥7,000 a head. Menus are in English and reservations are recommended.

Getting there

Getting to Takao is simple. The easiest way is to catch the Keio line from Shinjuku station to the end of the line at Takao-san Guchi. It takes less than an hour and costs only ¥370. Another option is to take the JR Chuo line to the terminal at Mount Takao: a special rapid from Tokyo will take a little over an hour and cost ¥890. You then transfer to the Keio line for Takao-san Guchi (a further ¥120).

Tourist information

Hachioji City Office
Takao-machi, Hachioji-shi (0426 26 3111/fax 0426-27-5951). **Open** 9am-5pm Mon-Fri.

Beaches

The nearest beaches are an hour away, and almost as crowded as Shinjuku.

Like just about everything else in Japan, beaches have their own official season, which falls in July and August. Outside this period, beaches are almost deserted, though surfers and other sporty types congregate even in winter. The infrastructure and facilities are well organised and dependable, every popular beach having plenty of shops where you can buy and hire equipment for sports and activities, and swarms of restaurants and cafés. Tokyo's nearest beaches are just over an hour away; as a rule, the further away the beach the more attractive it is, though it won't necessarily be any less crowded.

Kamakura & Katase Enoshima

Closest to Tokyo, Kamakura's beaches are also some of the busiest. In summer it's hard to find a spot to lie in, and, in part due to their popularity, the beaches are a bit dirty.

The east exit of the station leads to Wakamiya-dori, Kamakura's main street, from which a right turn and a 15-minute walk leads

to the shore. On the right is Yuigahama beach and on the other side of the Nameri River on the left is Zaimokuza beach.

From Inamuragasaki Point, at the western end of Yuigahama beach, is a long sandy stretch to Koyurugi Point, just before Enoshima, a picturesque island connected to the mainland by a bridge.

The beach on the other side of Enoshima island is nicknamed the Oriental Miami Beach but, despite its tourist attractions and facilities, this is a misnomer. It's as busy as Kamakura, with similar sands, and you should arrive early to get a good spot. Popular activities are yachting, surfing and fishing. The town itself has little to offer.

The five-kilometre (three-mile) beach has been popular since the Meiji era. In the town the main attraction is **Ryuko-ji** (Dragon's Mouth Temple), where the priest Nichiren escaped execution as lightning broke the sword that was about to behead him. The temple was founded in 1337 in his memory and its many old wooden buildings include a five-storey pagoda.

Another very popular attraction is Enoshima island itself, a religious site with a history going

The venerable Enoden train trundles between Kamakura and Enoshima.

back 1,000 years. The main approach across the bridge turns into a shopping street that climbs over the mountainous island to reach the western side. The island has three shrines: Hetsunomiya, rebuilt just over 20 years ago; Nakatsunomiya, founded in AD 853 and rebuilt in 1689; and Okutsunomiya. The main path up and across the island leads through the three shrines. There are escalators, each costing ¥100 to ¥200, but they only go a short distance. From the restaurants on the left of the path, pause to take in the views of Mount Fuji. From the rocks by the sea at the end of the path, another path leads to caves hollowed out by waves; they can be visited in about 20 minutes for ¥500.

Ryuko-ji

*3-13-37 Katase, Fujisawa-shi, Kanagawa-ken (0466 25 7357). **Open** 10am-4pm daily.*

Getting there

Kamakura: trains go directly to Kamakura from Tokyo station (¥890; Yokosuka line) in 55 minutes. **Katase Enoshima**: the Odakyu line goes directly from Shinjuku to Katase Enoshima. The local train takes around 85mins and costs ¥610. Express trains run regularly, cost ¥1,100 and take about 15 minutes less. The other option is to go via Kamakura, then take the historic Enoden line (23mins; five times an hour; ¥250). The JR 'Kamakura-Enoshima Free Kippu' ticket, valid for two days, gives unlimited free access to JR trains, Enoden railway and Shonan monorail between Ofuna, Fujisawa, Enoshima and Kamakura. It costs ¥1,970 and allows only one return trip to Tokyo.

Izu Peninsula & islands

This popular resort area is one of the most seismically active regions in Japan, though most of the quakes that occur are too small to be felt. As a result of this activity the region is dotted with *onsen* (natural hot spring baths), the most accessible in towns along the east coast, which the train line follows. The terminus is at Shimoda, where special US envoy Commodore Perry arrived with his Black Ships in 1853 (*see p9*). A ship's replica sails the waters in the bay. Other attractions in Shimoda include a small castle, a floating aquarium and a cable car up Mount Nesugata, from where the peninsula and the Izu Islands are visible.

The main beach around Shimoda is Shira-hama, three kilometres (two miles) north-east of the town and accessible by bus from the railway station. It stretches over 700 metres and is divided in the middle by a rocky outcrop topped by a *torii* (Japanese gate). The side nearest town has restaurants and shops along the road and is the closest thing to a 'beach town' near Tokyo. It's packed with swimmers

and surfers, even outside the beach season. Closer to Shimoda in a small bay is Sotoura Beach, with quiet waters that are especially good for swimming.

These are officially called the Seven Izu Islands, but in reality they are more numerous. Geologically part of the Izu Peninsula, they're administered by the Tokyo Metropolitan Government. The main island is Oshima, famous for its volcano (an eruption forced the island's evacuation in 1986), beaches, camping and *onsen*. The main surfing beaches are Kobohama, Sanohama and Fudeshima. Nearby lie the smaller Niijima and Shikinejima islands, the former with many beautiful clean beaches with good waves for surfing and the latter with small beaches for swimming. These three islands are easier to access than ones further south.

Getting there

Shimoda: take the Odoriko train from Tokyo or Shinagawa stations. It takes about two and a half hours and costs ¥6,160 each way. **Izu islands**: ferry leaves Takeshiba Pier near Hamamatsucho station at 10pm every night, arriving in Oshima at 6am (¥3,810-¥11,430), Niijima at 8am (an extra ¥1,030) and Shikinejima at 8.40am (an extra ¥1,130). The return boat leaves in the late morning or early afternoon and arrives in Tokyo at around 8pm.

Boso Peninsula

East of Tokyo on the other side of the bay lies the Boso Peninsula, a favourite destination of daytrippers because of its mountains and beaches. The beaches are concentrated near the towns of Tateyama, Chikura, Katsura and Onjuku, but the most famous beach is Kujukurihama, a 60-kilometre (38-mile) stretch of sand facing the Pacific on the east coast. Kujukurihama stretches from Cape Taito and Cape Gyobu and can get rough (good news for surfers). Every morning except Wednesday, Katsura has a fair dating back 400 years. South on the Uchibo line, there is surfing around Chikura, Setohama and Maebara. On the other side of the peninsula, Tateyama has bathing beaches, Kagamigaura being the busiest. Between Tateyama and Chikura at the tip of the peninsula are beaches accessible only by road.

Getting there

It's possible to do a circular trip of the peninsula on the JR Uchibo and Sotobo lines, which meet at Awa-Kamogawa (¥4,090 either way) on the east coast. Both lines leave from Tokyo station; the Uchibo goes along Tokyo Bay while the Sotobo cuts across to follow the Pacific shore south of Kujukurihama.

Trips Out of Town

Nikko 日光

One of Japan's greatest treasures, and home to the three wise monkeys.

Nikko has been famous for its natural beauty since it became a centre of mountain worship more than 1,200 years ago. Centuries later, the first *shogun*, Tokugawa Ieyasu, was so impressed by the place that he chose to be enshrined and buried here. Today, **Toshogu Shrine** and **Shinkyo Bridge**, the sacred river crossing, are among Japan's biggest attractions, with over seven million visitors a year.

Nikko, which means 'sunlight', derives from Futarasan, now called Mount Nantai, where the goddess Kannon lived. A priest, Shodo Shonin, established a centre for Buddhist asceticism on the mountain, and temples flourished over the years, drawing many religious, military and government figures to the area.

Other sights not to be missed in Nikko include **Taiyuin Shrine**, **Lake Chuzenji** and **Kegon Falls**. Around town are also **Rinno-ji** and **Futarasan** temples, **Cryptomeria Avenue**, **Ganmangafuchi Abyss**, several museums and the botanical gardens. Further out is a vast national park, a popular place for sightseeing, *onsen* (natural hot springs), hiking, camping, boating, skiing and skating.

Nikko is two hours from Tokyo, right at the edge of the Kanto Plain, where the mountains start to rise.

From the stations it's a 25-minute walk or five-minute bus ride (¥190; from either platform at Tobu station) to Shinkyo. Antiques shops and restaurants line the main road, many with signs in English. The local delicacy, *yuba* (soy milk skin), features prominently on menus and in souvenir shops.

The road to the left at Shinkyo leads to Lake Chuzenji via the newer part of Nikko, which is filled with souvenir shops. Toshogu is in the national park across the road, ten minutes away.

Shinkyo Bridge

According to legend, the first bridge across the Daiyagawa River was made by two snakes to allow priest Shodo Shonin through on his pilgrimage to Futarasan. In reality, the bridge was built at the same time as Toshogu and is its main approach.

Destroyed by floods in 1902 and rebuilt five years later, Shinkyo Bridge has proved so popular with tourists that it's being reconstructed again and is due to reopen sometime in 2005. The structure is currently completely hidden, but there's a large picture of Shinkyo on a panel.

Rinno-ji, Toshogu, Futarasan & Taiyuin

The cluster of religious buildings on the far side of the bridge includes **Sanbutsudo**, **Toshogu**, **Futarasan** and **Taiyuin**. Entrance fees are ¥400, ¥1,250, ¥200 and ¥500 respectively, but discount tickets for ¥1,000 are available in front of **Rinno-ji**. The ticket also allows entry to Yakushido (inside Toshogu Shrine), though not to the Sleeping Cat, Tokugawa Ieyasu's mausoleum, or Shin'en in the grounds of Futarasan.

Rinno-ji's main hall is called **Sanbutsudo** (Three Buddhas). Founded in AD 766, it's the largest temple in the area. Inside are a few artefacts and statues, including the large golden-wood statues of the Three Buddhas. They stand over five metres (16 feet) high, and depict the Thousand-armed Kannon, Amida Buddha and the Horse-headed Kannon. The exit leads to Sorinto, a tall pillar to repel evil, built in 1643, as well as another hall.

Located in front of Sanbutsudo is **Rinno-ji Treasure House**, where more artefacts from the temple are displayed. It's open from 8am to 4pm daily. Next door is the Edo-style Shoyo-en Garden (also ¥300), where a revered 200-year-old cherry tree has been declared a national monument. On the left of Sanbutsudo stands a black gate, Kuremon, and the path leading to Toshogu.

Toshogu is the main attraction, but its flamboyance gets mixed reviews. It was built during the reign of the third *shogun*, Iemitsu, according to instructions left by Tokugawa Ieyasu himself, who died in 1616. It's not clear when work began, but Toshogu was completed in 1636. The finest craftspeople were brought in and it's said that as many as 15,000 people took part in the construction.

The buildings include both Shinto and Buddhist elements, and some are more Chinese than Japanese in design. Nearly

Nikko's shrines and *torii* boast intricate carvings.

all are brightly painted with extremely ornate and intricate carvings. The grounds are often packed, but do tend to quieten down a bit towards the end of the afternoon. It's open daily from 8am to 5pm in summer and to 4pm in winter (last entrance 30 minutes before closing time).

After the first *torii* (gate) is a five-storey pagoda built in 1818. Up the stairs is Otemon, also called the Deva gate after its statues, said to scare away evil spirits. The building on the left after the gate is Shinkyusha (Sacred Stable), where the sacred horse lives. It's the only unpainted building in the grounds, famous for its set of eight carvings of the Sanzaru (three monkeys) representing the ideal way of life ('hear no evil, see no evil, speak no evil'). The three buildings from the right of Otemon are repositories for costumes and other items used in festivals.

To the left at the top of the stairs is **Yakushido**, famous for the dragon painted on the ceiling and for the roaring echo, which is regularly demonstrated by the priest. There are also a dozen old statues inside.

The next gate is **Yomeimon**, meaning 'twilight gate'. Its 400 carvings reputedly make it the most elaborate in Japan. Following is **Karamon**, leading to the oratory and the main hall. These two gates are decorated in the Chinese style with a dragon, phoenix and other imaginary creatures. The oratory's entrance has more dragon carvings, and inside another 100 more.

To the right of Karamon is the entrance to the *shogun*'s mausoleum (an extra ¥500 if you hold the discount ticket). At the top of the first door is the carving of the Nemurineko (Sleeping Cat), famed for depicting the Buddhist question and answer: 'What about a sleeping kitten under peonies in bloom? I would have nothing to do with it.' The stairs lead up the mountain to a quiet and secluded area with two small

buildings simply painted in blue and gold, and behind is the mausoleum.

Toshogu's festivals take place on 17 and 18 May as well as on 17 October. On 17 May there's horseback archery in hunting attire of the Middle Ages, held in front of the shrine, while on 18 May the Sennin Gyoretsu procession recreates the bringing of the remains of Ieyasu. The 1,000 people taking part are dressed as *samurai*, priests and others in the style of the days of the *shogun*. The 17 October festival is similar but on a smaller scale.

The path leading to the left before the entrance *torii* goes to the **Toshogu Treasure Museum**, where only a small selection of the treasures are exhibited at any one time. It's open daily from 8am to 5pm in the April-November period, and from 8am to 4pm daily, December-March (last entrance 30 minutes before closing). Entrance costs ¥500.

The path to the left between the pagoda and Otemon leads to **Futarasan Temple**, which includes another three shrines: on the summit of Mount Nantai, the shore of Lake Chuzenji and the bank of the Daiyagawa River. Exhibits and access inside this temple are quite limited.

Next is **Taiyuin Shrine**, where the third *shogun*, Iemitsu, is buried. It was built in 1652, in the Buddhist style only, and while similar in tone to Toshogu, it's not as extravagant and extensive. The first gate has Nio guardian figures; soon after comes Nitenmon Gate, with statues of Komokuten and Jikokuten, two Buddhist deities. The next gate is Yashamon, with four statues of Yashan, and the last is Karamon, before the hall of worship. A few artefacts and old treasures are displayed inside. A walk around the main hall leads to Kokamon Gate and towards the mausoleum, though it's locked at all times. Taiyuin is open 8am-5pm daily, April-November, and 8am-4pm daily, December-March.

Trips Out of Town

Relax in a natural hot spring or *onsen*.

Lake Chuzenji & Kegon Falls

Lake Chuzenji is the prime example of Nikko's famed natural beauty. The lake itself is popular for swimming, fishing and boating, with many campsites and hiking trails nearby. At **Kegon Falls**, the lake's waters plunge 100 metres (328 feet) to the Daiyagawa River. An elevator descends to the base of the gorge. The falls, which include 12 minor cascades, are among Japan's finest. Frozen in winter, they look magical. Nearby is the Chanokidaira ropeway, and from the top are views of the lake, Kegon Falls and Mount Nantai. There's also a botanical garden with alpine plants.

North of the lake, Mount Nantai rises almost 2,400 metres (7,877 feet). There's a crater at the top, but most climbers making the five-hour ascent (between May and October only) do so for religious reasons, to visit Okumiya Shrine. The side of the mountain is crowded with worshippers during its festival (31 July-8 August).

There are buses from both train stations to Chuzenji Spa. The Tobu buses cost ¥1,100 each way and depart from either platform. Irohazaka Drive, a series of hairpin bends in the road, is a well-known feature of the area.

Where to stay & eat

Although a day-trip is possible, those wishing to take their time may wish to try the following atmospheric hotels. One of the oldest hotels in Japan, the **Nikko Kanaya Hotel** (1300 Kamihachiisi-machi, Nikko-shi, Tochigi-ken, 0288 54 0001/www.kanayahotel.co.jp, rates ¥8,000-¥35,000) opened for business in 1873. It's a five-minute ride from both stations on a Tobu bus (¥190) heading for Nishisando, Kiyotaki, Okuhosoo, Chuzenji or Yumoto *onsen*. Get off at the Shinkyo stop. Another option is the **Nikko Tamozawa Hotel** (2010 Hanaishi-machi, Nikko-Shi, Tochigi-ken, 0288 54 1152, rates ¥8,000-¥15,000), a 12-minute ride on the same buses. Alight at Rengeseki Tamozawa.

It would be a shame to leave Nikko without trying the local speciality, *yuba*, which is the skin of soya bean milk. **Gyoushin-Tei** (2339-1 Yamauchi, Nikko, Tochigi-ken, 0288 53 3751, 11am-7pm, closed Thur) is set in a 12th-century garden, where it serves *yuba* in *shojin ryori* (¥3,500) or *kaiseki ryori* (¥5,000) courses. **Enya** (443 Ishiya-Machi, Nikko, 0288 53 5605, 11am-2pm, 5-11pm, closed Mon) offers a selection of Japanese and western meat dishes with over 80 different beers from around the world.

Getting there

Two rail lines, Tobu and Japan Railways (JR) go to Nikko and terminate at separate but near-neighbouring stations in the centre of town. Tobu trains are faster and cheaper, their bus service to the sights more regular. The Tobu terminal in Tokyo is at Asakusa. Limited Express trains go directly to Tobu Nikko station, leaving about every hour from 7.30am. They cost ¥2,740 each way and take around 1hr 45mins. The express trains to Shimo-Imaichi, followed by a local train to Tobu Nikko (a few minutes away), cost only ¥200 less. Local trains from Asakusa are the cheapest, at ¥1,320, and take 30mins more, stopping at most stations and requiring a change at Shimo-Imaichi. Tickets for local trains are always available before departure, but Limited Express trains can be full, so you should book, especially on weekends and holidays. JR trains leave from Tokyo or Ueno stations and require a transfer at Utsunomiya. From there it's 45mins on a local train. Each Nikko station has a bus terminal with services to Lake Chuzenji and beyond.

Tourist information

Nikko Information Centre
591 Goko-Machi, Nikko, Tochigi-ken (0288 53 3795). **Open** 9am-5pm daily.

Tobu Nikko Station Information Centre
Tobu Nikko station, 4-3 Matsubara-cho, Nikko, Tochigi-ken (0288 53 4511). **Open** 8.30am-5pm daily.

Directory

Getting Around

Arriving & leaving

From the airport

Almost certainly the airport you'll arrive at, **Tokyo International Airport at Narita** is nearly 70km (43 miles) from Tokyo and is well served by rail and bus links to the city.

JR's **Narita Express** (information 3423 0111) is a convenient way to get to Tokyo but also the most expensive. Seats must be reserved and there's no standing room, so at busy times you may have to wait. All trains go to Tokyo station (¥2,940), with many serving Shinjuku (¥3,110), and some also going to Ikebukuro (¥3,110), Omiya (¥3,740) and Yokohama (¥4,180). Trains depart every 30-40 minutes. JR also operates a rapid train to Tokyo station (¥1,280) leaving about every hour but taking much longer.

The **Keisei Skyliner** (information 0476 32 8505/ 3831 0131 no English service), operated by a private rail company, is cheaper and faster. Trains take you into Ueno station (¥1,920) in around one hour. Cheaper still is a Keisei Limited Express (Tokkyu), a regular train that makes a few stops on its 75-minute route to Ueno station (¥1,000).

Limousine buses (information 3665 7220) run regularly from the airport to the city, costing around ¥3,000. Airport shuttle buses (toll-free information 0120 48 1057) cost about the same and drop off at many of Tokyo's top hotels.

Taxis from Narita are recommended only for those with bottomless wallets: the journey will cost at least ¥30,000 and may take longer than the train.

It's just possible, but highly unlikely, that you'll arrive at **Haneda International Airport**, which handles internal flights and a very limited number of international charter flights.

The Keikyu line links Haneda airport to Shinagawa station (¥400) where it's possible to transfer to many JR lines. Direct trains run every five to ten minutes (or change at Keikyu Kamata to the Kuko line) and take 20 minutes. The monorail also leaves every five to ten minutes and connects with Hamamatsucho station on the JR Yamanote line in 20 minutes (¥470).

Limousine buses (from 5.15am) from Haneda cost about ¥1,200, depending on which part of the city you want to go to. A taxi will cost a minimum of ¥5,000.

Tokyo International Airport at Narita
(flight information & English-language enquiries 0476 34 5000).

Haneda International Airport
(flight information 5757 8111).

To the airport

If you can't face lugging your luggage to Narita or Haneda, **T-CAT**, in Tokyo's business district, offers a check-in and passport-control service, with buses to Narita airport (5am-midnight) leaving every ten minutes (one-way is ¥2,900). Call to check that your airline is served there.

Tokyo City Air Terminal (T-CAT)
42-1 Nihonbashi-Hakozaki-cho, Chuo-ku (3665 7111). Suitengumae station.

Leaving town

By train

One of the fastest but most expensive ways to travel Japan's elongated countryside is by bullet train. Tickets can be purchased at JR reservation 'Green Window' areas or travel agents. Trains depart from different stations depending on destination; most leave from Tokyo or Ueno station. Slower, cheaper trains, some run by private companies, go to many destinations. Train platforms show where the numbered carriages will stop.

A *shinkansen* ticket is essentially two tickets. One is the fare for the standard journey, the second is the actual *shinkansen* reservation ticket and supplement. Both tickets must be inserted into the automatic ticket gates in order to gain access to the platform.

A typical long-distance train ticket gives the starting point and destination across the middle of the ticket. Below this to the right, in Japanese, will be the carriage number, followed by seat row number and postion (usually from A-D).

By coach

One of the cheapest ways to travel, though anyone of above average height may find the seating cramped. Most long-distance buses leave at midnight and arrive early the next morning.

All are air conditioned and have ample space for luggage. Seats can be reserved through a travel agent or a bus company such as **Seibu Bus** (1-28-1 Minami-Ikebukuro, Toshima-ku, 3989 2525, open 9.30am-6pm Mon-Fri, closed holidays). Tickets work in the same way as train tickets, with all passengers having allocated seats.

Public transport

Trains

Tokyo has one of the world's most efficient train systems: in the rare event of delays in the morning rush, staff give out apology slips to office workers to show to their bosses. Trains and subways are fast, clean, safe and reliable. Most stations have signs in English as well as Japanese, and signs telling you which exit to take. Subways and train lines are colour-coded.

Subways and trains operate from 5am to around midnight (central JR lines till around 1am). Rush hours are 7.30-9.30am and 5-7pm. The last train can be a nightmare.

Tokyo's rail network is run by a variety of companies, and changing trains between competing systems can mean paying for two tickets. When travelling in Tokyo, try to stay on one network.

Tickets & passes

Japan Rail Pass

This provides for virtually unlimited travel on the national JR network, including bullet trains (except the new 'Nozomi' super-express), and all JR lines in Tokyo. It's available only to visitors from abroad travelling under the entry status of 'temporary

visitor', and must be purchased before coming to Japan. You have to show your passport when changing the Exchange Order to a ticket. It costs from ¥28,300 for a week, about the same price as a middle-distance *shinkansen* return ticket. JR East, which runs trains in and around Tokyo, has its own version of the pass, which costs from ¥20,000 for five days. The same conditions apply.

Exchange Orders for the pass can be purchased at overseas offices of the Japan Travel Bureau International, Nippon Travel Agency, Kinki Nippon Tourist, Tokyu Tourist Corporation and other associated local travel agents, or at an overseas Japan Airlines office if you're travelling by Japan Airlines.

Passnet

The first (nearly) all-encompassing travel pass in Tokyo is good for 18 different train and subway lines in and around the city, but not for JR lines. Pre-purchase in values of ¥1,000, ¥3,000 and ¥5,000 from subway ticket offices. There is no discount for travel, but it saves you the hassle of queueing for tickets.

Discount tickets

There's a huge number of discount tickets available for the JR and Eidan networks, from pre-paid cards to 11-for-the-price-of-ten tickets. There are also combination tickets and one-day passes for one, two or three networks, though these are unlikely to be worth buying. For more details, call the JR East Infoline (3423 0111).

Regular tickets

Regular tickets for travelling in Tokyo can be purchased from station vending machines, many of which have symbols saying which notes they accept; otherwise, the ticket collector can change

your notes. At JR stations, the touch-screen vending machines can display information in English, but if you're unsure of your destination (or unable to read it from the Japanese map), buy a ticket for the minimum fare (¥130) and settle up in a fare adjustment machine at the other end. All stations have them. Tokyo does not have punitive fines for travellers with incorrect tickets. Children under six travel free, under-12s pay half price.

Transferring from one line to another, provided it is run by the same operator, will be covered in the price of your ticket. If your journey involves transferring from one network to another, you will have to buy a transfer ticket, if available. Or buy another ticket when you arrive at your transfer point.

Subways

Most subways are run by the Teito Rapid Transit Authority, which is often referred to as Eidan. Its eight lines are: Chiyoda (dark green), Ginza (orange), Hanzomon (purple), Hibiya (grey), Marunouchi (red), Namboku (light green), Tozai (turquoise) and Yurakucho (yellow).

Four subway lines are run by the metropolitan government. These 'Toei' lines are slightly more expensive. They are: Toei Asakusa line (pale pink), Toei Mita line (blue), Toei Oedo line (bright pink) and Toei Shinjuku line (green). If transferring from Eidan to Toei trains, buying a transfer ticket is ¥70 cheaper than buying separate tickets. For subway map, *see p290*.

JR trains

Overland trains in Tokyo are operated by Japan Railways East (JR). It's impossible to stay in Tokyo for more than a

Directory

few hours without using JR's Yamanote line: its loop defines the city centre. All Tokyo's subway and rail lines connect at some point with the Yamanote. JR's major lines in Tokyo are: Yamanote (green), Chuo (orange), Sobu (yellow) and Keihin Tohoku (blue).

JR also operates the long-distance trains and *shinkansen* (bullet trains), which run from Tokyo or Ueno stations.

Private lines

These mainly ferry commuters to the city's outlying districts. Because most were founded by companies that also run department stores, they usually terminate inside, or next to, one of their branches. The major private lines are run by Keio, Odakyu, Seibu, Tobu and Tokyu. You can pick up a full map showing all lines and subways from the Airport Information counter on arrival.

Buses

Like the trains, buses here are run by several companies. Travelling by bus can be confusing if you're new to Japan, as signs are rarely in English. Toei bus fares cost ¥200 (¥100 for kids), no matter what the distance. Get on the bus at the front, and off at the back. Drop the exact fare into the slot in front of the driver. If you don't have it, use the change machine, normally to the right, which will deduct your fare from the change. Machines accept ¥50, ¥100 and ¥500 coins, and ¥1,000 notes. Stops are usually announced by a pre-recorded voice. A Toei bus route guide in English is available at Toei subway stations and hotels.

Cycling

The bicycle remains the most common form of local transport in Tokyo, and theft is rare, although unattended bikes should always be locked. Areas in and around stations are usually no-parking zones for bikes, a rule that locals gleefully ignore, but which can result in bikes being impounded.

Eight Rent

Sumitomo-seimei Bldg 1F, 31-16 Sakuragaoka-cho, Shibuya-ku (3462 2383). Shibuya station. **Open** 9am-6pm Mon-Fri. **No credit cards.** ¥1,920 a day. Call to make an appointment. Bring your passport.

Jingu-Gaien Cycling Centre

10 Kasumigaoka-machi, Shinjuku-ku (3405 8753). Kokuritsu-Kyogijo station (Toei Oedo line). **Open** 9.30am-3.30pm Sun.
Free of charge, but cycling restricted to the Jingu-gaien area.

Victoria Sports

3-4 KandaOgawamachi, Chiyoda-ku (3295 2955). Jinbocho station. **Open** 11am-8pm Mon-Sat; 10.30am-7.30pm Sun.
Some staff can speak English. Call to make an appointment. Prices vary.

Driving

Tokyo drivers are notorious lane-weavers, making driving here stressful. Add to this the problem of reading street signs and the super-efficiency of the public transport system, and renting a car becomes a waste of time and money. Outside the city, toll charges on highways often compare unfavourably to the price of a rail ticket. If you rent a car, you'll be obliged to pay astronomical parking fees (usually around ¥300 for 30 minutes, more in the centre).

If you do wish to rent a car, you'll need an international driving licence and at least six months' driving experience.

Japan Automobile Federation publishes a 'Rules of the Road' guide in English. Phone JAF (5395 0111) and ask for the International Affairs Department. A Metropolitan Expressway map, in English, is available from the **Metropolitan Expressway Public Corporation** (3580

1881). English-speaking rental assistance is available at many large hotels and at the airport.

Hertz/Toyota Rent-a-car

Narita International Airport Terminal 1 & 2 (0476 32 1020). **Open** 7am-10pm daily.
If you want to drive outside Tokyo (much safer), JR offers rail and car rental packages. Call the JR East Infoline (3423 0111) for details.

Walking

Tokyo is a great city for walking. There are no no-go areas, and the whole place is 99.9 per cent safe 24 hours a day. Walking is the best way to discover the hidden nooks and crannies that exist in just about every neighbourhood. The **TIC** (*see p271*) offers information on free walking tours of parts of Tokyo.

The worst thing about walking in Tokyo is the crowds. Because it's so safe here, Japanese people have no sense of personal space, and are often unaware of what's going on behind them. This results in colossal 'people jams'. People here also tend to walk at speeds associated with village fêtes, rather than capital cities, so be prepared to experience some frustration.

When crossing the road, always do so at marked crossings and always wait for the green man. If you cross on red, you may be responsible for the death of those behind you, who will blindly follow you into the traffic.

Taxis

The flagfall starts at ¥660 for the first 2km and keeps on climbing. The drivers often do not know how to find specific addresses. Prices rise between 11pm and 5am. Ranks are near stations, department stores, most hotels and main junctions. Don't stand too close to the rear doors. They open automatically.

Resources A-Z

Age restrictions

There is no age of consent in Japan, and the legal age for smoking and drinking is 20, although the ubiquity of vending machines makes the law impossible to enforce. The minimum voting age is also 20.

Attitude & etiquette

Japanese people are generally forgiving of visitors' clumsy attempts at correct behaviour, but there are certain rules that must be followed to avoid offending your hosts.

Shoes: when entering a house, temple or Japanese-style hotel, remove your shoes. Wear shoes that are easy to pull off and on, and make sure your socks are in good condition.

Bathing: bathing is one of the great delights of Japanese life, and every area has a public bath or *sento*, identified by a sign that looks like flames coming out of a handleless frying pan. When bathing, wash and rinse before getting in: the bath is for soaking in, not washing in. Never put your head under water or immerse your washcloth.

Blowing your nose: while it's common to hear old men hawking up great gobs of phlegm, for some reason it's considered impolite to blow one's nose in public. If you must do it, go to the toilet.

Banks & money

The yen is not divided into smaller units, and comes in denominations of ¥1, ¥5, ¥10, ¥50, ¥100 and ¥500 (coins) and ¥1,000, ¥2,000, ¥5,000 and ¥10,000 (notes). Prices on display do not usually include the five per cent purchase tax.

Banks

Opening a bank account is relatively easy if you have an Alien Registration card. With savings accounts you will be issued a book and card. Getting a card can take up to two weeks. It's generally delivered to your address, so you have to be home to sign for it; alternatively, get the bank to inform you when it arrives and pick it up.

You can also open an account at a post office and withdraw money from any other post office branch.

Banks are open 9am-3pm Monday-Friday and closed on public holidays. Queues can be long, especially on Fridays, and the procedure involves taking a number and waiting around.

Foreign exchange

You can cash travellers' cheques or change foreign currency at any Authorised Foreign Exchange Bank (look for the signs).

If you want to exchange money outside regular banking hours, most large hotels exchange travellers' cheques and currency, as do large department stores, which are open until about 8pm. Narita Airport has several *bureaux de change*, staffed by English speakers, which are open daily from 7am to 10pm.

Credit cards & ATMs

Japan is a cash-based society, and restaurants and bars may refuse cards. Larger shops, restaurants and hotels accept major cards, but you should always keep some cash on you. ATMs are rarely open after 7pm and often close at 5pm on Saturdays. Many

banks also cha[...] withdrawals n[...] and on Sundays and public holidays. Still, there is a growing number of 24-hour ATMs in Tokyo, mostly around major train stations. All ATMs have stickers or logos showing which cards are accepted. Some will not accept foreign-issued cards; **Citibank** is your best bet, with 24-hour ATMs all over Tokyo (information 0120 50 4189). Bear in mind that if your home bank network is down (morning in Tokyo is often the middle of the night at home), you will not be able to withdraw cash.

To report lost or stolen credit cards, dial one of the following 24-hour numbers. **American Express** 3220 6100/0120 020 120 (toll free) **Diners' Club** 3570 1555/0120 074 024 (toll free) **Mastercard** 00531 11 3886 (toll free) **Visa** 0120 133 1603 (toll free)

Money transfers

When you're having money sent to a Japanese bank account, you will need to give your bank account number, bank, branch and location. Mail transfers are cheaper than telex/telegraphic but may take longer.

Bathing

One of the great pleasures of Japanese life, bathing can be enjoyed without heading out of town to the *onsen* of Hakone (*see p242*). Sign-posted by their towering chimneys, Japan's public bathhouses, or *sento*, are perhaps the last urban bastions of 'Japanese-ness'. Though rapidly disappearing from the city centre, nostalgia and necessity have kept

Directory

...thhouse culture alive in residential Tokyo, and there is a singular pleasure to be had from an hour of simply scrubbing and dipping on a cold, hungover afternoon.

Few overseas visitors to Tokyo ever get as far as the *sento*. This may be due mostly to unfamiliarity – but certainly, inhibitions about public nudity and *sento*'s strictly adhered-to rules can also dampen enthusiasm. There's little to add to the topic of communal nakedness, but *sento* rules are relatively straightforward.

Upon entering, pay the *bandai* (usually an aged *mama-san*) before going through to your changing room, where you fully undress. No towels or any items of clothing are allowed in the bath area. Stow away all belongings in a locker and enter the bathing area. Close the door firmly behind you. Pick up a stool and bucket from a stack near the door and select a 'scrubbing station'. Here, wash yourself thoroughly (using this opportunity to become acclimatised to the scalding water) before entering one of an array of tubs, some of which can, for the initiate, be extremely hot. Make sure that no soap, either on your body or in your hand, follows you in.

At the time of going to press, admission to all *sento* is pegged at ¥400, thanks to government subsidies.

Aqua

4-9-22, Higashi-Nakano, Nakano-ku (5330 1126). Higashi-Nakano station.
Open 3pm-midnight Tue-Sun.
A modern sento with a variety of baths, including a *rotemburo* (outside bath) and sauna. Stocks cold beers.

Shimizu-yu

3-12-3, Minami-Aoyama, Minato-ku (3401 4404). Omotesando station.
Open 4pm-midnight Tue-Sun.
Nothing particularly outstanding about Shimizu-yu, except its location, in the heart of chic Omotesando.

Tamano-yu

1-13-7, Asagaya Kita, Suginami-ku (3338 7860). Asagaya Station.
Open 3.30pm-1am Tue-Sun.
Tamano-yu is a recently renovated, traditional *sento* with a number of novelty tubs, including a *denkiburo* (electric bath).

Daikoku-yu

32-6 Senju Kotobuki-cho, Adachi-ku (3881 3001). Kita-Senju Station, then 15min walk. **Open** 3pm-12.30am Mon-Wed, Fri-Sun.
A beautifully structured bathhouse of classic Japanese design. It is serenely spacious, and houses its own *rotemburo*. Stocks cold beers.

Hakusan-yu

2-28-11 Narita-Higashi, Suginami-ku (3311 2396). Minami-Asagaya or Shin-Koenji station then 15min walk.
Open 4-11.30pm Mon-Wed, Fri-Sun.
Hakusan-yu offers much of what makes the ideal *sento* experience by retaining the essential charm of the neighbourhood bathhouse. No beers, but a *denkiburo*.

Business services

Doing business in Japan is a very different proposition to doing it in the west. Japanese place great emphasis on personal relationships between business partners, and socialising before and after the deal is done is *de rigueur*.

Biz tips

● Carry plenty of business cards. You will be spraying them around like confetti.
● When out eating with a group, wait for your comrades to indicate your seat.
● Do not write on another person's business card. During a meeting, keep the cards you have just received face up on the table.
● If you need an interpreter, hire one of your own and ask them to interpret body language for you.
● Never offer to split a restaurant bill. Just say thank you if someone else is paying.
● If you receive a gift from your host, do not open it in front of them. If you give a gift, make sure it is professionally wrapped.
● Be prepared to give details of your personal life in a way that would be inappropriate elsewhere.

All of the companies and organisations listed below have the ability to communicate in English unless otherwise noted.

Chambers of commerce

American Chamber of Commerce

(3433 5381/fax 3433 8454/ www.accj.or.jp)

Australian & New Zealand Chamber of Commerce

(5214 0710/fax 5214 0712/www2.gol.com/users/anzccj/)

British Chamber of Commerce

(3267 1901/fax 3267 1903/ www.uknow.or.jp/bccj)

Canadian Chamber of Commerce

(3556 9566/fax 3556 9567/ www.cccj.or.jp)

General information

JETRO (Japan External Trade Organisation)

(3582 5511/fax 3587 0219/www.jetro.go.jp)

Graphic design

Akiko Tanaka

3-17-4, Hiroo, Shibuya-ku (5766 8286/5766 8287/www.akikito.com). Hiroo station.

Kinko's

(0120 001 966 toll-free)
A complete range of print services.
See p266 Internet.

Office space

Servcorp

(5288 5100/offices@servcorp.net).
Has several locations in Tokyo with executive service starting from ¥250,000 yen per month plus deposit.

Public relations

IRI

Hatchobori Building 7F, 2-19-8, Hatchobori, Chuo-ku (5543 1221/ fax 5543 1250/miyashiro@iri-japan.co.jp). Hatchobori station.

Kyodo PR

7-2-22 Ginza, Chuo-ku (3571 5171/ fax 3574 1005/t-kimura@kyodo-pr.co.jp). Ginza station.

Telephone answering service

Bell24 System

(3590 4646/www.tas.bell24.co.jp).
Services start from ¥15,000 yen,
but bilingual service is provided
at a slightly higher cost.

Translation

Communication Professionals

*1-21-7 Hagiyama-cho, Higashi
Murayama (0423 47 5097/fax 0423
47 8109/gerrard@gol.com).*

Simul International

*Shinjuku Green Tower Bldg 9F, 6-
14-1 Nishi-Shinjuku, Shinjuku-ku
(5324 3100/fax 5323 7020/
www.simul.co.jp). Shinjuku station.*

Transpacific Enterprises

*Orizuru Bldg. 201,3-11-12
Shibasaki, Tachikawa (042
528 8282/fax 042 529 3350/
transpac@gol.com).
Tachikawa station.*

Customs

The following limits are
imposed on travellers
coming into Japan: 200
cigarettes or 250g of tobacco;
three 750ml bottles of spirits;
57g of perfume; gifts or
souvenirs up to ¥200,000.
  Penalties for drug
importation are severe:
deportation is the lenient
penalty. Pornography laws
are very strict, too; anything
showing pubic hair may
be confiscated.
  There's no limit on bringing
Japanese or foreign currency
into the country.

Disabled travellers

Tokyo is not easy for those
with disabilities, particularly
when it comes to public
transport, though some
stations have wheelchair-
moving facilities (when lifts
aren't available) and raised
dots on the ground guide the
visually impaired.

Train workers will assist
those in need. There are often
special 'Silver Seats' near train
exits for those requiring them.
  The best resource in
English for travellers
with disabilities is an online
service, **Accessible Tokyo:**
www.ibm.co.jp/japantravel/
index.html.

Kinki Nippon Tourist Company Barrier-free Travel Centre

*Shinjuku Island Wing 10F, 6-3-1,
Nishi-Shinjuku, Shinjuku-ku
(5323 6915). Shinjuku station.*
Open 9.30am-5.30pm Mon-Fri.
Arranges special tours for the
disabled. An English-speaking
service is available.

Drinking

There's a lot of it in Tokyo,
and the legal age to start at
is 20, as it is for smoking.

Drugs

Although drugs can be found
in Tokyo (*see p218* **Drugs**),
the penalties for being
caught in possession are
severe. Expect deportation
or imprisonment.

Electricity & gas

Electric current in Japan
runs, like the USA, at 100v
AC, rather than the 220-240v
European standard. If
bringing electrical appliances
from Europe, you need to
purchase an adapter.
  Electricity in Tokyo is
provided by **Tokyo Electric
Power Company** (TEPCO;
information 3501 8111); gas
by **Tokyo Gas** (information
3433 2111).

Embassies & consulates

Embassies and consulates
usually open from 9am
to 5pm Monday to Friday;
opening hours for visa
sections may vary.

Australia

*2-1-14 Mita, M̶
Azabu-Juban sta̶*

Britain

*1 Ichibancho, Ch̶
1100). Hanzomo̶*

Canada

*7-3-38 Akasaka, Minato-ku (5412
6200). Aoyama-itchome station.*

Ireland

*2-10-7 Kojimachi, Chiyoda-ku (3263
0695). Hanzomon station.*

New Zealand

*20-40 Kamiyamacho, Shibuya-ku
(3467 2271). Yoyogikoen station.*

South Africa

*2-7-9 Hirakawacho, Chiyoda-ku
(3265 3366). Nagatacho station.*

United States

*1-10-5 Akasaka, Minato-ku (3224
5000). Toranomon station.*

Emergencies

Police 110.
Ambulance and fire 119.

The following organisations
have an English-speaking
service:
Tokyo police (3501 0110).
TELL (Tokyo English Life
Line) (3968 4099).
US Air Force Hospital
at Yokota (Poison Control)
(0425 52 2511).
**Tokyo Fire
Department** can be
contacted in Japanese
(3212 2323 in the 23 wards
of central Tokyo; 042 521
2323 in the outlying cities),
and helps callers find
medical centres and provides
consultations on emergencies.

Emergency Translation Service

(5285 8185). **Open** 5-8pm Mon-Fri;
9am-8pm Sat, Sun.
Telephone interpretation
for communication problems
that threaten to stop
foreign nationals from
getting emergency care.
Service available in
English, Chinese, Korean,
Thai and Spanish.

Directory

**tropolitan
ealth & Medical
Information Centre**
(5285 8181). **Open** 9am-8pm
Mon-Fri.
The so-called *himawari* service
provides medical and health
information in English, Spanish,
Chinese, Korean and Thai.

Contraception

Condoms reign supreme in
terms of contraception in
Japan, largely because until
1999 the pill was available
only to women with
menstrual problems. Condom
vending machines can be
found on many street corners,
often near pharmacies.

Health insurance

Japanese are covered by
medical insurance, provided
by their employers or the state,
covering 70-90 per cent of the
cost of treatment. People over
70 pay a token amount
towards healthcare. Travellers
are expected to pay the full
amount, and should take
out medical insurance before
leaving their own countries.

All calls to numbers
below (except Tokyo Medical
Clinic) are answered in
Japanese. Say *'Eigo de ii
desu-ka?'* to be transferred
to an English-speaker.

Dentists

All those listed have English-
speaking staff.

BIS Dental Clinic
*8F, 1-32-14 Ebisu-Nishi,
Shibuya-ku (5458 4618).
Ebisu station.* **Open** 10am-1.30pm,
3pm-6.30pm Mon-Fri.

Sakakibara
Dental Clinic
*Entopia Court Azabu 1F, 2-5-15
Minami-Azabu, Minato-ku (3456
2507). Azabu-Juban station.*
Open 9am-6.30pm Mon-Fri.

Uni Roppongi
Dental Office
*5F, Uni Roppongi Bldg, 7-15-17
Roppongi, Minato-ku (3479 4841).
Roppongi station.* **Open** 10am-
1.30pm, 2.30-6pm Mon-Fri;
10am-1.30pm most Sats.

Hospitals

All those listed have English-
speaking staff.

Tokyo Sanitarium
Hospital
*3-17-3 Amanuma, Suginami-ku
(3392 6151).Ogikubo station.*
Open 8.30-11am Mon-Fri.
No emergencies.

International
Catholic Hospital
*2-5-1 Naka-Ochiai, Shinjuku-ku
(3951 1111). Shimo-Ochiai
station (Seibu Shinjuku line).*
Open 8-11am Mon-Sat for
consultations. Closed 3rd Sat
of month. 24hr emergency service.

Japan Red Cross
Medical Centre
*4-1-22 Hiroo, Shibuya-ku (3400
1311). Hiroo station.* **Open** 8.30-
11am Mon-Fri for consultations.
24hr emergency service.

St Luke's
International Hospital
*9-1 Akashicho, Chuo-ku (3541
5151). Tsukiji station.* **Open** 8.30-
11am Mon-Fri for consultations.
24hr emergency service.

Tokyo Medical
& Surgical Clinic
*32 Mori Bldg, 3-4-30 Shiba Koen,
Minato-ku (3436 3028).
Kamiyacho station.*
Open 9am-5pm Mon-Fri; 9am-1pm
Sat. 24hr emergency service.
All doctors are from Europe,
America or Japan; all of them
speak English. There's a
pharmacy on the first floor.
Also has dentists.

Opticians

See p182.

Pharmacies

All those listed have English-
speaking staff.

American Pharmacy
*Hibiya Park Bldg, 1-8-1 Yurakucho,
Chiyoda-ku (3271 4034).*

Hibiya station. **Open** 9.30am-8pm
Mon-Sat; 10am-6.30pm Sun.

Kaken International
Pharmacy
*Kaken Tsukiji Bldg, 11-16
Akashicho, Chuo-ku (3248 6631).
Tsukiji station.* **Open** 8.30am-5.45pm
Mon-Fri.

National Azabu
Pharmacy
*4-5-2 Minami Azabu, Minato-ku
(3442 3495). Hiroo station.* **Open**
9.30am-7pm daily (closed 1-3 Jan).
Located inside the supermarket of
the same name.

Roppongi Pharmacy
*6-8-8 Roppongi, Minato-ku
(3403 8879). Roppongi station.*
Open 10.30am-2am daily.

Koyasu Drug
Store Hotel Okura
*Hotel Okura Main Bldg 1F, 2-10-4
Toranomon, Minato-ku (3583 7958).
Toranomon station.* **Open** 8.30am-
9pm Mon-Sat; 10am-9pm Sun.

Pharmacies
(late-night)

Some pharmacies in
major centres or near busy
stations are open till
midnight. Some branches
of the 24-hour convenience
store chain AM-PM have
in-store pharmacies. Basic
items, such as sanitary
towels, condoms or sticking
plasters, can be purchased
at any convenience store,
but these are forbidden by law
from selling pharmaceuticals.
Most convenience stores are
open 24 hours daily.

Veterinarian

Hiroo Central
Hospital
*5-24-1 Hiroo, Shibuya-ku (5420
0012). Hiroo station.* **Open** 10am-
1pm, 2-7pm Mon, Tue, Thur-Sun.
24hr emergency service.
English spoken. Call to make
an appointment.

The following companies
offer guided tours of Tokyo
in English, unless otherwise

The meaning of i-mode

While European phone companies would have you believe the internet as accessed via mobiles is useful for booking air tickets, checking stock quotes and clinching last-minute, billion-dollar deals before emailing the wife and daughter to say you'll be late for dinner, on the Tokyo streets things are a little different. According to the i-mode experience, although it might not be long until air tickets and business deals are a reality, for the moment the money and the technology are firmly focused on Japan's tech-savvy, mobile-crazy teen and twentysomething generations.

It helps that the Japanese embrace technology like no other race on earth. It also helps that there are 30 million of those rich technophiles packed into metropolitan Tokyo. But perhaps most importantly, the mobile companies haven't promised the impossible. Instead, they've given this young generation of cyber surfers what they want, cool, hip, fun sites that deliver what they promise: find a date, download a cool ringing tone, search for last-minute bargains, play on-line games, look up what movies are showing, find the nearest public toilet, get tips on how to please your boyfriend, learn a bit of English. It's not very glamorous, but it's pretty clever, and very, very cool. To access i-mode, you need a Japanese mobile phone.

---

stated. Detailed leaflets are on display at **TIC** (*see p271*) and most big hotels.

By bus

Hato Bus Tokyo Sightseeing Tour Company

World Trade Centre Bldg, 2-4-1 Hamamatsucho, Minato-ku (3435 6081/fax 3433 1972/www.hatobus.co.jp/english/index.html). Hamamatsucho station. **Bookings** 9am-7pm daily. **Credit** AmEx, DC, MC, V. One of Tokyo's main sightseeing tour operators. Offers a variety of tours, including half-day, full-day and night tours with English-speaking guides. One snag is that all bookings must be made by fax 14 days before the tour date, to avoid incurring a booking fee. Prices for tours start at around ¥3,500; the Amazing Night Tour is the most expensive, at ¥13,000.

Japan Gray Line Company

3-3-3 Nishi-Shinbashi, Minato-ku (3433 5745/fax 3433 8388/easy5@tky3.3web.ne.jp). Shinbashi station. **Bookings** 24hrs. **Credit** AmEx, DC, MC, V. Morning, afternoon and full-day tours of Tokyo's sights, in English. From ¥3,300 to ¥10,500. Buses pick up at many of Tokyo's top hotels.

Sunrise Tours

5-5-2 Kiba, Koto-ku (5620 9500). Kiba station. **Bookings** 9am-8pm daily. **Credit** AmEx, DC, MC, V. Run by Japan Travel Bureau. Offers the widest range of English-language tours, including trips out of town to Mount Fuji, Disneyland and the hot springs of Hakone, plus full-day, half-day or night tours of Tokyo.

By taxi

Hinomaru Limousine Inc

Ark Hills Mori Bldg, 1-12-32 Akasaka, Minato-ku (3505 1717). If you fancy a self-guided tour in style, then try Tokyo's longest-established limousine operator. Hinomaru offers a selection of luxury automobiles, ranging from a Rolls-Royce to a Lincoln Limousine or a stretch Mercedes-Benz. Minimum rental period is three hours, with prices starting at ¥10,000 per hour for a Mercedes and climbing to ¥15,000 per hour for the Rolls or Lincoln. If you require one, Hinomaru can also provide an English-speaking driver.

Tokyo Jumbo Hire

7-16-23 Iriya, Adachi-ku (3896 0818/fax 3896 8181). **Bookings** 9am-6pm Mon-Fri; 9am-3pm Sat. **No credit cards**. If you feel like seeing the city in style, splash out on a taxi tour. Three-hour courses start at ¥12,000; an eight-hour ride will set you back ¥31,300. English-speaking drivers can be provided.

Hitch-hiking

Illegal in Japan, but anecdotal evidence suggests the law is rarely enforced and drivers are happy to pick people up.

Internet & email

Staggering under monopoly NTT's phone charges, Japan has been slow to embrace home internet access. Recent statistics claimed just 20 per cent of Japanese homes were internet-enabled, compared to over 40 per cent in the US.

Instead of big bulky PCs, the Japanese have so far preferred the mobile phone as the device of choice through which to access the net. NTT, of course, has its finger well inside this pie, too. In fact, it pretty much controls the pie. Its DoCoMo subsidiary is by far the leading mobile phone company in Japan and its mobile internet service, **i-mode** (*see above*), gets a whopping 50,000 new subscribers every day. It is now the world's largest internet service provider. But this is Japan, and 2G phones are almost out of fashion.

In May 2001, DoCoMo became the first company in the world to launch third-generation mobile services, although it may be some time before your average Tanaka in the street is using it.

Directory

Even so, stand and take a look around at any busy station or meeting point in the city and it's hard to believe that Tokyo man ever lived without *keitai*, the Japanese for mobile phone. But people aren't really using the 'phone' in the true sense of the word. They are equally as likely to be sending an email or surfing the net as they are talking like in the 'old days'.

Internet cafés

Largely because of mobile phones, cyber cafés never really took off in Tokyo. Nevertheless there are more than a few places to get online, although the few true cyber cafés serving half-decent food and drinks have mostly closed down now. In their place, comic book cafés – or *manga kissa*, shops where you pay to go and read comic books over a cup of iced tea – have taken up the internet slack.

Avex Base

Sunisei Bldg 1F, 3-1-30 Minami Aoyama, Minato-ku (5413 8555). Gaienmae station. **Open** 10am-8pm daily.
Free internet access provided courtesy of vast Japanese music glomerate Avex. There are only three computers, so be prepared to wait.

@room

B1F BEAM Bldg, 2-31 Udagawa-cho, Shibuya-ku (5457-3765). Shibuya station. **Open** 24hrs. **Internet access** ¥380 for the 1st hour, ¥60 per 10mins after that; all-night 11pm-8am for ¥980. **No credit cards.**
Mid-sized surf spot in the basement of the INTI entertainment centre in the landmark BEAM building. Notable for being non-smoking and for its comfortable leather seats. Discounted rate for two people together who get mini sofas to sit in. Free soft drinks.

Gaiax Café

Kagaya Bldg 2F, 7-10-7 Nishi Shinjuku, Shinjuku-ku (5332 9201). Shinjuku station. **Open** 10am-midnight daily.

Internet access ¥390 per 30 mins (non-members); ¥240 (members). **No credit cards.**
Membership is free at this large, very bright internet café with drinks available from vending machines.
Branch: Kagoya Bldg 2F, 7-10-7 Jinnan, Shibuya-ku (5332 9201).

Gera Gera

Lemina Bldg B1/B2F, 3-17-4 Shinjuku, Shinjuku-ku (3350 5691). Shinjuku station.
Open 24hrs daily. **Internet access** ¥380 for the first hour, ¥50 per 10mins following. **No credit cards.**
This centrally located (next to Citibank on Shinjuku Dori) branch of a huge chain of *manga* cafés is crowded at almost any time of the day or night, although the internet connection is often slow. Video games and consoles can also be rented by the hour. ¥180 buys you unlimited soft drinks.
Branches: Kokeshi Bldg 5F, 28-1 Udagawa-cho, Shibuya-ku (3780 0192); Daichi Nakano Bldg 4F, 1-20-9 Minami Ikebukuro, Toshima-ku (3980 4041).

Ikoi No Mori

Fujigawa Bldg 1F, 2-7-1 Shinjuku, Shinjuku-ku (3226 7121). Shinjuku San-chome station.
Open 11am-11pm. **Internet access** ¥250 for 30mins. **No credit cards.**
Comic book café on Shinjuku Dori near the gay Ni-chome area also has several PCs.
Branch: Palais Ginza Bldg 9F, 6-10-16 Ginza, Chuo-ku (5568 0269).

Kinko's

Tokyu Bldg West 2nd Wing 1F, 3-28-1 Nishi Ikebukuro, Toshima-ku (5979 5171). Ikebukuro station. **Internet access** prices vary. **Open** 24hrs daily. **Credit** AmEx, MC, V.
This chain of 24hr business service shops has both PCs and Macs as well as fax, print and photocopy services. There are about 30 stores in Tokyo and an English-language location guide is available in store.
Branches: all over Tokyo.

Metallic

Shinjuku Yusu Bldg 1F, 4-1-9 Shinjuku, Shinjuku-ku (5827 3910). Shinjuku station. **Internet access** free. **Open** 12.30pm-7pm.
Hyper-slick venue with hyper-fast DSL connections lets you surf the web for free, although emailing is not officially allowed.

Necca

Chitose Kaikan 3F, 13-8 Udagawa-cho, Shibuya-ku (5728 2561). Shibuya station. **Internet access** ¥250 for 30 mins (members only). **Open** 24hrs daily. **No credit cards.**
You must pay ¥200 to become a member of Necca before getting on to the internet. You can also make free international phone calls while online.

Net Diner Wan

Sharumu Bldg 1F, 2-9 Shinsen, Shibuya-ku (5459 2303). Shinsen station (Inokashira line). **Open** 11am-11pm daily. **Internet access** ¥300 per hour. **No credit cards.**
Small, cheap café with two Macs, two PCs and a lunch menu of staple Japanese and Korean dishes. Leave Shinsen station via the north exit, turn left down the lower road and Net Diner Wan is 20 matres down on the left.

Senju Internet

Okubo Watanuma Bldg 402, 2-34 Senju, Adachi-ku (3870 9210). Kita-senju station. **Internet access** ¥400 for 30 mins, ¥100 for 10 mins thereafter. **Open** noon-7pm daily. **No credit cards.**
This place is only really convenient for people staying way out in north-east Tokyo.

TnT

Liberty Ikebukuro Bldg B1, 2-18-1 Ikebukuro, Toshima-ku (3950 9983). Ikebukuro station. **Internet access** ¥1,000 per hour. **Open** noon-10pm daily. **No credit cards.**
No drinks served.

Vision Network

5-47-6 Jingumae, Shibuya-ku (3407 6865). Omotesando station. **Internet access** free. **Open** 11am-11pm. **No credit cards.**
This hip bar/restaurant complex in Aoyama usually has a couple of iMacs available free to customers. At present, one is located downstairs at the bar in Las Chicas, and another is located upstairs in Nude Lounge.

Language

For information on Japanese language and pronunciation, and a list of useful words and phrases, *see p276*.

Hundreds of schools in Tokyo run courses in Japanese. Most offer intensive studies for those who want to learn Japanese as quickly as possible or need Japanese for work or school. They may offer longer courses, too. Private schools tend to be expensive, so check out lessons run by your ward office. Ward lessons cost from ¥100 a month to ¥500 every two months – a bargain compared to ¥3,000 an hour for group lessons.

Arc Academy
(3409 0157/www.arc.ac.jp).
The Arc Academy offers a wide variety of courses.

Temple University
(0120 861 026/www.tuj.ac.jp).
Temple University offers fairly cheap evening classes, as part of their continuing education programme.

Meguro Language Centre
(3493 3727/www.mlcjapanese.co.jp).
A wide range of courses is available, from private lessons to group sessions.

Legal advice

Legal Counselling Centre
Bar Association Bldg, 1-1-3 Kasumigaseki, Chiyoda-ku (3581 2302). Kasumigaseki station. **Open** 1-3pm Mon-Fri (appointment only).
Consultations in English for ¥5,150/half-hour, free for the impoverished on Thursday afternoons. A range of issues, including crime, immigration matters and labour problems, are covered. Appointments on a first-come, first-served basis.

Tokyo Human Rights Counselling Centre
Otemachi Joint Government Building No.3 6F, 1-3-3 Otemachi, Chiyoda-ku (3214 6697). Otemachi station. **Open** 1.30-3.30pm Tue.
Free counselling in English.

Libraries

Each ward has a central lending library with a limited number of English-language books. You need an Alien Registration Card to borrow books. The following

reference libraries have a healthy number of books in English. All libraries close for Japanese national holidays (*see p184*).

British Council Library & Information Centre
Kenkyusha Eigo Centre Bldg 1F, 1-2 Kagurazaka, Shinjuku-ku (3235 8031). Iidabashi station. **Open** 11am-9pm Mon-Fri; 10am-5.30pm Sat.
Info is limited to the UK, but there's internet access and BBC World is always on TV. For ¥500 a day you can use all the facilities. Loans for members only. Closes for UK bank holidays as well as Japanese holidays. Call ahead to confirm it's open. People under 18 not admitted.

Japan Foundation Library
Ark Mori Bldg West Wing 20F, 1-12-32 Akasaka, Minato-ku (5562 3527). Tameike-sanno station. **Open** 10am-5pm Mon-Fri. Closed last Mon of month.
Books, mags, reference material and doctoral works on all aspects of Japan. Specialises in humanities and social sciences, and has translations of Japanese novels. Houses about 25,000 books and 300 magazine titles. Lending as well as reference. People under 18 not admitted.

JETRO Library
Kyodo Tsushin Bldg 6F, 2-2-5 Toranomon, Minato-ku (3582 1775). Toranomon station. **Open** 9am-4.30pm Mon-Fri. Closed 3rd Tue of month.
The Japan External Trade Organisation (JETRO) library houses information about trade, the economy and investment for just about every country in the world. Lots of statistics as well as basic business directories. People under 18 not admitted.

National Diet Library
1-10-1 Nagatacho, Chiyoda-ku (3581 2331/www.ndl.go.jp). Nagatacho station. **Open** 9.30am-5pm Mon-Fri. Closed 3rd & 4th Mon of month.
Japan's main library, with the largest number of foreign-language books and materials. To get a book you fill in a form to gain admittance, go through the catalogues and submit forms to have the book brought to you. Over two million books, 50,000 mags and 1,500 newspapers and periodicals. People under 20 not admitted.

Tokyo Metropolitan Central Library
5-7-13 Minami-Azabu, Minato-ku (3442 8451). Hiroo station. **Open** 1-8pm Mon; 9.30am-8pm Tue-Fri; 9.30am-5pm Sat, Sun. Closed 1st Thur & 3rd Sun of month.
Main library for the Tokyo government, with the largest collection of books about Tokyo. Over 150,000 titles in foreign languages. People under 16 not admitted.

Lost property

If you happen to leave a bag or package somewhere, just go back: it will probably still be there.

If you left it in a train station or any other public area, go either to the stationmaster's office or to the nearest *koban* (police box) and ask for English-speaking assistance. Items handed in at a station are logged in a book. You will have to sign in order to receive your item.

If you leave something in a taxi on the way to or from a hotel, try the hotel reception – taxi drivers often bring the lost item straight back to your hotel.

Lost property offices

JR (3423 0111).
English-speaking service.
Metropolitan Police (3501 0110)
English-speaking service.

The following numbers will all be answered in Japanese, so be sure to ask a Japanese person to call for you.
Eidan subway (3834 5577).
Toei subway (5322 0400).
Taxi (3648 0300).
Toei Bus (3431 1515).
Narita Airport (*Terminal 1* 0476 32 2105. *Terminal 2* 0476 34 5220).
Some staff speak English. Say '*Eigo de ii desu-ka?*' to be transferred to an English-speaker.

Directory

Media

Newspapers

The Japanese are among the world's keenest newspaper readers, with daily sales of over 70 million copies, and *Yomiuri Shinbun* is the world's largest-circulation newspaper, selling 14.5 million copies a day. For those who don't read Japanese, the choice of papers is small.

Daily Yomiuri
www.yomiuri.co.jp/daily
The liveliest of the English-language dailies, thanks to its supplements produced in collaboration with other newspapers around the world, including the *Independent* (Sundays) and the *Washington Post* (Fridays). There's a what's-on supplement published on Thursdays.

IHT/Asahi
iij.asahi.com/english/english.html
Launched in April 2001 as a joint venture between the *International Herald Tribune* and the *Asahi Shinbun*. The first true foreign paper in Tokyo, it already has the others running scared.

Japan Times
www.japantimes.co.jp/
The longest-established English-language newspaper in Japan. Consists mainly of agency reports. Heavy on business. Motto 'All the news without fear or favor', could read 'All the news without fear or flavor'.

Nikkei Weekly
www.nni.nikkei.co.jp
The Japanese equivalent of the *Financial Times* produces this weekly digest from the world of finance.

Free reads

Tokyo Classified
www.tokyoclassified.com
Published on Fridays and distributed via certain subway kiosks and foreigner-friendly bars, this is the foreigner's bible in Tokyo. Although it has a tendency to kowtow too much to its advertisers, it also provides valuable information on events, concerts, clubbing and more. Its 20 pages of classified advertisements every week act as a bulletin board for clubs and societies.

Tokyo Notice Board
www.tokyonoticeboard.co.jp
The most visible rival to *Tokyo Classified*. Smaller and more amateurish.

World Magazine Gallery
3-13-10 Ginza, Chuo-ku (3545 7227). Ginza station.
Open 11am-7pm Mon-Fri. **Map** 6.
A reference-only magazine library, with over 800 titles from all over the world; read them at a table or take them to the coffee shop on the second floor. Also a distribution point for Tokyo's free publications, some of which apear only sporadically.

Magazines

If you read Japanese, there's a wealth of publications to help you find your way around the city; the best known are *Pia* and *Tokyo Walker* (¥320, weekly).

Tokyo Journal
www.tokyo.to
Long-established monthly English-language listings magazine.

Radio

InterFM
www.interfm.co.jp
Broadcasting on 76.1MHz, this is Tokyo's main bilingual station. Plays rock and pop.

Television

Japanese state broadcaster NHK runs two commercial-free terrestrial channels – NHK General (channel 1) and NHK Educational (channel 3) – and two satellite channels, BS1 and BS2. The five remaining terrestrial channels in Tokyo – Nihon TV (channel 4), Tokyo Broadcasting (channel 6), Fuji Television (channel 8), Television Asahi (channel 10) and TV Tokyo (channel 12) – have commercials and show pap, illuminated only occasionally by a good drama or documentary.

NHK 1 news at 7pm and 9pm daily is broadcast in English and Japanese: to access the English sound channel, push a button on the remote to a bilingual TV set (most rooms in big hotels have them). Many non-Japanese films and TV series are also broadcast bilingually.

Digital broadcasting arrived in Japan in early 2001, although early take-up seems disappointing. Rupert Murdoch's Japanese presence is SkyPerfect TV, which offers a multitude of familiar channels, including BBC World and Sky Sports. Most top hotels provide satellite channels.

Opening hours

Larger stores in Tokyo are open daily from 9.30am or 10am to around 8pm. Smaller shops are open the same hours six days a week. Monday and Wednesday are the commonest closing days.

Most restaurants open around 11am and close around 11pm, though some *izakaya* and bars are open till 5am. Some remain open till they're empty.

Office hours are 9am to 5pm. On national holidays, most places keep Sunday holidays, but on 1 and 2 January most are closed. The ubiquitous convenience stores offer 24-hour shopping at slightly higher prices than supermarkets. The major chains are 7-Eleven, AM-PM, Family Mart and Lawson's

Police & security

Japan is one of the safest places to visit, though crime does occur and normal precautions should be taken. *Koban* (police boxes) are everywhere, though officers don't usually speak English (and may not be overly friendly).

In areas such as Roppongi, or Shinjuku's Kabuki-cho, be

Toilet tips

Tokyo is an incontinent's dream: every station has a public loo, and department stores and restaurants have no objection to people popping in for a quick one if taken short.

Many restaurants, homes and hotels have electrically warmed seats with built-in bidet facilities controlled by a panel either to the right of the toilet bowl, or affixed to the wall. The buttons and knobs control everything from the position and strength of the jet of water, to its temperature.

Public toilets are often distinctly unluxurious, particularly those for women. Many older-style toilets, basically glorified squat holes, still survive. To use them, face towards the wall, rather than the door, so the opposite way to the one you are used to. Also, be aware that many public toilets do not provide paper. Hang on to tissues distributed for free outside stations, or buy some from the vending machine that's usually inside the entrance door.

Religion

According to the Religion Yearbook issued by the Agency for Cultural Affairs, 208 million Japanese are members of religious organisations – almost twice the population of Japan. It's not unusual for a family to celebrate birth with Shinto rites, have a Christian marriage, and pay last respects at a Buddhist ceremony. Freedom of worship is a constitutional right.

Rubbish

After the subway sarin gas attack in March 1995, most bins were removed from subway stations. All JR stations, however, have rubbish bins near the exits. They are divided into three sections: cans, newspapers and magazines, and other rubbish. If you can't find a bin, carry your rubbish home with you.

All domestic rubbish should be divided into four categories: burnable, unburnable, recyclable and large items. For more information, contact the relevant section of your local ward office.

Smoking

An estimated 60 per cent of the population of Japan smoke, and cigarettes are relatively cheap at ¥260 per packet. They are available from vending machines, convenience stores and specialist shops.

The legal age for smoking is 20, the same as drinking. Smoking in public is perfectly acceptable, and non-smoking restaurants are few and far between. Even non-smoking areas are a rarity.

cautious. Theft is still amazingly uncommon in Japan, so it's not unusual to walk around with the equivalent of hundreds of pounds in your wallet without giving it a second thought.

Places in which you should exercise some care are airports and packed trains, where pickpockets may indeed be at work.

Postal services

A red-and-white sign like a letter 'T' with a line over it marks a post office. Most big streets have one. Postcards overseas cost ¥70; aerograms cost ¥90; letters under 25g cost ¥110 (North America, Europe, Oceania) or ¥130 (Africa, South America).

Sending parcels by surface mail is cheaper than by air, but items take longer to arrive. Larger department stores can arrange postage if you purchase major items.

Local post offices are open from 9am to 5pm on weekdays, and are closed on public holidays. In the last few years, main district post offices have introduced a 24-hour service.

For *poste restante*, contact the **Central Tokyo Post Office** (3284 9539). You can also receive mail at the main **International Post Office** (3241 4891), near exit A4 of the Otemachi subway. Mail is held for up to 30 days; the post office is open from 9am to 7pm Monday to Friday; 9am-5pm Saturday; 9am-noon Sunday and public holidays. A 24-hour service is available at a counter to the rear of the main building.

When writing addresses, English script is acceptable, as long as it's clearly written. You can get more information in English on the Japanese postal system from the **Postal Services Information** line (5472 5852). It's open 9.30am to 4.30pm Monday to Friday.

Express delivery services

Federal Express
(0120 003200/www.fedex.com/)

Hubnet Ltd
(0120 881084/www.hub-net.co.jp)

Takuhai-bin
Several companies operate cheap domestic parcel delivery services through convenience stores. Small packages cost from ¥1,500.

Directory

Telephones

The area code for central Tokyo is 03. If you are calling from outside Japan, dial 00 81 3, Followed by the number. For domestic calls from outside central Tokyo, dial 03 followed by the number.

Throughout this guide, we have omitted the 03 from the beginning of Tokyo telephone numbers.

The virtual monopoly enjoyed by NTT on domestic telephone services was dismantled in April 2001 with the introduction of the Myline system, which allows customers to choose their domestic providers for local and long-distance calls. If you have your own phone line in Tokyo, call the **Myline Information Centre** (0120 000 406) to register your choice of phone service provider (English-speaking operators available).

NTT still controls nearly all telephone boxes in Tokyo. Calls from call boxes cost ¥10 for the first three minutes, then ¥10 for every minute after that.

There are two types of NTT telephone boxes. One, the older type, contains a grey phone that accepts flexible phonecards. The other, the IC Card phone, has a brownish phone with an open slot for the card. This is an integrated circuit card whose corner must be snapped off before it can be used.

Both types of public phone have sockets for PCs, but international calls from old-style phoneboxes can only be made with cash, and only from those boxes with 'ISDN' or 'International' written on the side. Both types of phone display instructions in English as well as Japanese.

Several companies offer international call services, at roughly the same rates. To make an international call, dial 001 (KDD), 0041 (Japan Telecom), 0033 (NTT Communications) or 0061 (IDC), followed by your country's access code and the telephone number.

NTT phonecards cannot be used to make international calls, so you need to buy a prepaid card or have a lot of change handy. Rates between the three companies differ, but only slightly. The cheapest time to call is between 11pm and 8am, when a 40 per cent off-peak discount applies.

The 'home country direct' service conveniently allows you to charge the call to your home telephone bill, provided you have set up the service in your home country in the first place.

See also p271 **Useful numbers**.

NTT East Information

(0120 364463). English-speaking operators available.

Toll-free numbers

Numbers starting with 0120 are receiver-paid calls under NTT's 'Free Dial 0120' service.

Mobile phones

Since US/UK mobile phones do not work in Japan, you may need to get a mobile. Go either to an outlet operated by one of the mobile phone companies or to an electronics store. You need to show your Foreign Registration Card and passport. Applications will not be accepted if your visa is due to expire within 90 days.

If you're here on a tourist visa or if you're about to renew your visa, you should get a pre-paid mobile phone.

You can purchase a mobile phone for between ¥5,000 and ¥10,000, and a prepaid card for between ¥3,000 and ¥5,000. Some form of ID is required when purchasing pre-paid cards.

For shops that sell mobile phones with English-language manuals, *see p173* **IT Net**, **Laox** *and* **NTT DoCoMo**.

NTT DoCoMo

(0120 005 250/www.nttdocomo.com) NTT Docomo is Japan's biggest mobile phone operator.

Telephone cards

Three kinds of telephone card are available in Tokyo. KDD produces a 'Super World' prepaid card for international phone calls, which is sold at most major convenience stores.

Valued at ¥1,000, ¥3,000, ¥5,000 and ¥7,000, these cards can be used with any push-button telephone.

NTT DoCoMo produces two cards, one primarily for the domestic market, the other – an IC card – can be used for both national and international calls. Both cards sell for ¥1,000 and contain 105 ¥10 units. They are available from most convenience stores as well as from vending machines situated inside some phoneboxes.

Telephone directories

Unless you're fluent, using a Japanese phonebook is out of the question. NTT DoCoMo publishes an English-language phonebook, Town Page. You can get it free from English Townpage Centre (0120 460815). It's also available on the internet at http://english.itp.ne.jp.

Telephone helplines

The following helplines offer information, advice or counselling in English.

Making sense of addresses

The Japanese system of writing addresses is based on numbers rather than street names. Central Tokyo is divided into 23 wards, called *ku*. Within each *ku*, there are many smaller districts, or *cho*, which also have their own names. Most *cho* are further subdivided into numbered areas, or *chome*, then into blocks, and finally into individual buildings, which sometimes have names of their own. Japan uses the Continental system of floor numbering. The abbreviation 1F is the ground floor, English style; 2F means second floor, or first floor English style.

Thus, the address of the Café Fontana – Abe Bldg B1F, 5-5-9 Ginza, Chuo-ku – means it's in the basement of the Abe building, which is the ninth building of the fifth block of the fifth area of Ginza, in Chuo ward.

To help keep track of where you are, look out for the (usually bilingual) metal plaques affixed to lamp-posts. Individual buildings usually have small metal numbers that designate their address.

Confused? Don't worry. Few Tokyoites know the city well enough to navigate by address alone, and providing directions is one of the main functions of the local policeman in his *koban* (police box). Few policemen speak English, but all *koban* are equipped with detailed maps of the immediate area. Maps of areas with individual district and block numbers can also be found at or near the entrances to stations.

If you're serious about finding your way around by address, it's a good idea to buy a bilingual atlas, such as Shobunsha's *Tokyo Metropolitan Atlas* (see p273), that shows all the *cho*, *chome* and numbered blocks within each *ku*.

If you have access to a fax machine, it's common practice in Tokyo to call up your destination and ask them to fax you a map of how to get there. If you're staying at a hotel, they should be happy to let you receive a fax on their machine.

AIDS Hotline
0120 461995 (24hrs daily)

Alcoholics Anonymous
3971 1471 (taped message)

Immigration Information Centre
3213 8523 (9am-4pm Mon-Fri)

Tokyo Foreign Residents' Advisory Centre
5320 7744 (9.30am-noon, 1-4pm Mon-Fri)

HELP Asian Women's Shelter
3368 8855 (10am-5pm Mon-Sat in Japanese and English).

Japan Help Line
0990 53 8127 (24hrs daily).
Jhelp.com is a non-profit worldwide assistance service. Among other services, it produces the Japan Help Line Card, which contains useful telephone numbers and essential information for non-Japanese speakers, as well as a numbered phrase list in English and Japanese for use in emergencies. You can get it free on the web at www.jhelp.com/en/index_e.html.

Useful numbers

Repair Service 113
Moving & Relocating 116
Directory Assistance 104
KDDI Information service 0057
Japan Telecom 0088 41
NTT Communications 0120 540033
Domestic Telegrams 115 (in Japanese)
International Telegrams 005 3519

Time

All of Japan is in the same time zone, nine hours ahead of Greenwich Mean Time (GMT). Daylight Saving Time is not practised, but is a constant topic of debate.

Tipping

Tipping is not expected in Japan and people will generally be embarrassed if you try to tip them. If you leave money on a restaurant table, for example, you will probably be pursued down the street by a member of staff trying to return it. At upmarket establishments, a service charge is often factored into the bill.

Tourist information

Tourist Information Centres (TIC) are affiliated with **Japan National Tourist Organisation (JNTO)**. The TIC in Tokyo is a must-see on any traveller's list as it's located in Rafael Vinoly's brilliant Tokyo International Forum building, which opened in 1996. The office also has a Welcome Inn Reservation Centre, open from 9.15am to noon and from 1pm to 5.15pm (last booking half an hour before closing). TIC has friendly multilingual

Directory

...and a wealth of ...ormation: maps, event ...ooklets, and books on Japanese customs, even NTT English phonebooks.

TIC Narita Office 1
Arrival floor, Terminal 2, New Tokyo International Airport (0476 34 6251). **Open** 9am-8pm daily.

TIC Narita Office 2
Arrival floor, Terminal 1, New Tokyo International Airport (0476 30 3383). **Open** 9am-8pm daily.

TIC Shinjuku
My City 1F, Shinjuku station concourse (no phone). Shinjuku station. **Open** 10am-6.30pm daily. Handles on-the-spot enquiries about Tokyo and Kanto only.

TIC Tokyo Office
Tokyo International Forum B1, 3-5-1 Marunouchi, Chiyoda-ku (3201 3331). Yurakucho station. **Open** 9am-5pm Mon-Fri; 9am-noon Sat.

Yes! Tokyo
www.tcvb.or.jp/ This well-organised web page is packed with useful travel information.

Japan Railways East Infoline
3423 0111 (10am-6pm Mon-Fri).

Japan Travel Phone
0088 22 4800 (9am-5pm daily). A nationwide service for those in need of English-language assistance and travel information on places outside Tokyo and Kyoto. It's free.

Teletourist Service
3201 2911 (24 hours). Recorded information on current and upcoming events.

Visas

By August 1998, Japan had concluded general visa-exemption arrangements with the USA, Canada, the UK and the Republic of Ireland. Citizens of these countries may stay in Japan for up to 90 days.

Japan also has working holiday visa arrangements with Australia, New Zealand and Canada for people aged from 18 to 30. At the time of going to press, a similar agreement was due to be concluded between Japan and the UK.

The following types of visa are available (for more information, contact **Tokyo Immigration Bureau** (1-3-1 Otemachi, Chiyoda-ku; 3286 5241) or the **Immigration Information Centre** (3213 8523).

Tourist Visa
A 'short-term stay' visa, good for anyone not intending to work in Japan.

Working Visa
It's illegal to work here without a visa. If you arrive as a tourist and work, your company has to sponsor you for a work visa. You generally must then go abroad to make the application (South Korea is the cheapest option). If you plan to stay in Japan for more than 90 days, you need an alien registration card. For this, you need to provide two passport-sized photographs, a passport, an address and a signature.

When to go

In Tokyo, winter is marked by clear skies, cold days and the occasional snowstorm. Spring begins with winds and cherry-blossom viewing. The rainy season for Honshu (the main island) begins in June. This is followed by summer with its hot and humid days. Finally, autumn is marked by the changing of the leaves.

Temperatures range from around 3°C in January to 32°C in July/August. The summer months can be unbearable for those not used to humidity. It's advisable to travel during summer with a small hand-held fan, a bottle of water and a wet cotton cloth or small washcloth. Fans are often handed out in the street as part of ad campaigns.

Women travellers

The crime rate in Japan is very low compared to that in many countries. Women should exercise standard precautions, but the risk of rape or assault is not high, and women can ride the subways at night or wander the streets with little concern. A woman alone might be harassed by drunken, staggering salarymen, but they are rarely serious; ignoring them generally does the trick.

This said, Tokyo is not immune from urban dangers, and boys will be boys even in Japan. The low incidence of rape is often attributed by some to under-reporting rather than respect for women. Don't let fear spoil your vacation, but do exercise a little caution at night, particularly in areas such as Roppongi and Shinjuku's Kabuki-cho.

A less serious type of assault occurs every day on packed rush-hour trains, where women are sometimes groped (or worse). Many Japanese women ignore the offence, hesitant to draw attention to themselves. It's pointless to vocalise anyway, as rarely will anyone step in to assist. This doesn't mean you have to stand there and take it: the best recourse is quiet retaliation; dig your nails into the offending hand or, if you're certain of the perpetrator, a swift kick to the shins or a jab in the gut should do the trick. But before taking action, be sure that something really is going on. What might feel like a hand between your legs often turns out to be just a briefcase – or a handbag. Avoiding rush hour is the best strategy.

Some public toilets are not segregated. This may not pose any danger, but some women (and men) find it disconcerting to do their business in mixed company. If this is a concern, look for toilets marked with 'male' and 'female' symbols.

Further Reference

Non-fiction

Birchall, Jonathan *Ultra Nippon*
British journo follows Japanese soccer team, and fans, for a year.

Bird, Isabella *Unbeaten Tracks in Japan*
Amazing memoirs of intrepid Victorian explorer.

Bornoff, Nicholas *Pink Samurai: Love, Marriage and Sex in Contemporary Japan*
All you ever wanted to know about the subjects.

Galbraith, Stuart *Giant Monsters Are Attacking Tokyo: Incredible World of Japanese Fantasy Films*
The ultimate guide to the weird and wacky world of the city-stomping giants of Japanese cinema.

Harper, Philip *The Insider's Guide to Sake*
Readable introduction to Japan's national libation.

Kaplan, David & Marshall, Andrew *The Cult At The End of The World*
Terrifying story of Aum and the subway gas attacks.

Kawakami, Kenji & Don Papia *101 Unuseless Japanese Inventions: The Art of Chindogu*
Everything you never knew you needed.

Kennedy, Rick *Little Adventures in Tokyo*
Entertaining trips through the off-beat side of the city.

Martin, John H & Phyllis G *Tokyo: A Cultural Guide to Japan's Capital City*
Enjoyable ramble through Tokyo.

Okakura, Kazuko *The Book of Tea*
Tea as the answer to life, the universe and everything.

Ototake, Hirotada *No One's Perfect*
True story of a boy who overcome handicaps and prejudice. A record-breaking best-seller.

Pompian, Susan *Tokyo For Free*
Immaculate guide for skinflints. In need of an update, though.

Richie, Donald *Public People, Private People and Tokyo: A View of the City*
Acclaimed writer on the Japanese and their capital.

Richie, Donald *Tokyo*
That man again, with a beautifully produced work from Reaktion Books.

Satterwhite, Robb *What's What in Japanese Restaurants*
An invaluable guide to navigating the menu maze.

Schilling, Mark *Encyclopedia of Japanese Pop Culture*
From karaoke to Hello Kitty, *ramen* to Doraemon.

Schlesinger, Jacob M *Shadow Shoguns: The Rise and Fall of Japan's Postwar Political Machine*
Pretty good non-academic read.

Schodt, Fredrick L *Dreamland Japan: Writings on Modern Manga*
Leading western authority on publishing phenomenon.

Seidensticker, Edward *Tokyo Rising & Low City, High City*
Eminently readable histories of the city.

Sharnoff, Lora *Grand Sumo*
Exhaustive account, if a little on the dry side.

Tajima, Noriyuki *Tokyo: Guide to Recent Architecture*
Pocket-sized guide with outstanding pictures.

Tajima, Noriyuki & Powell, Catherine *Tokyo: Labyrinth City*
LP-sized guide to more recent projects.

Walters, Gary DA *Day Walks Near Tokyo & More Day Walks Near Tokyo*
Detailed routes for escaping the city's crowds.

Whitting, Robert *You Gotta Have Wa*
US baseball stars + Japan = culture clash.

Whitting, Robert *Tokyo Underworld: The Fast Life and Times of an American Gangster in Japan*
Enthralling story of underworld life.

Fiction

Abe Kobe *The Woman in the Dunes*
Weird classic about a lost village of sand.

Birnbaum, Alfred (ed) *Monkey Brain Sushi*
Decent selection of 'younger' Japanese writers.

Erickson, Steve *The Sea Came in at Midnight*
American novel set partly in a Tokyo 'memory hotel'.

Howell, Brian *Head of a Girl & others*
Elegantly weird short story by expat English writer based close to Tokyo.

Kawabata Yasuwari *Snow Country*
Japan's first Nobel prize winner for literature.

Mishima Yukio *Confessions of Mask & others*
Japan's most famous novelist, 20 years after his suicide.

Mitchell, David *Ghostwritten & Number9dream*
Ambitious novels by expat UK writer teaching English in Hiroshima.

Murakami Haruki *Norwegian Wood & others*
Most of Murakami's books are set in Tokyo.

Murakami, Ryu *Coin Locker Babies & others*
Hip modern novelist, unrelated to Haruki.

Oe Kenzoburo *A Personal Matter & others*
Japan's second winner of the Nobel prize.

Yoshimoto, Banana *Kitchen & others*
Modern writer who's made a splash in the west.

Language

Three A Network/Minna no Nihongo Shokyuu
Book 1 for beginners, 2 for pre-intermediate.

Integrated Approach to Intermediate Japanese
Well balanced in grammar, reading and conversation.

A Dictionary of Basic Japanese Grammar
Standard reference book from the *Japan Times*.

The Modern Reader's Japanese-English Dictionary
Known affectionately as Nelson, this is the definitive tool for students of the written language.

Maps & guides

Shobunsha Tokyo Metropolitan Atlas
Negotiate those tricky addresses with confidence.

Japan As It Is
Eccentric explanations of all things Japanese.

Asahi Shinbun's Japan Almanac
The ultimate book of lists, published annually.

Akira
(Otomo Katsuhiro, 1988)
The film that started the *anime* craze in the west – the story of freewheeling youth gangs trying to stay alive in Neo-Tokyo.

...ter.

...at a bizarre tale of love
...aftermath of murder.

Gamera 3
(Shusuke Kaneko, 1999)
Countless Tokyo dwellers' dreams
are realised when the turbo-powered
turtle demolishes Shibuya.

Ghost in the Shell (Kokaku Kidotai)
(Mamoru Oshii, 1995)
A complex and thought-provoking
animated look at a future society
where computers are the home of
human minds – and vice versa.

Godzilla, King of the Monsters
(Honda Inoshiro, 1954)
The big green guy makes his debut,
and promptly smashes up Ginza.

Hana-Bi
(Kitano Takeshi, 1997)
Kitano's best film got him a Venice
prize, but he's still better known in
his native country as a TV comedian.

House of Bamboo
(Samuel Fuller, 1955)
A gang led by an American pulls off
raids in Tokyo and Yokohama.

Mononoke Hime (Princess Mononoke)
(Miyazaki Hiyao, 1997)
Record-breaking animated fable
of humanity's butchery of the
environment, and the spirits
that dwell within it.

Ring
(Nakata Hideo, 1998)
Chilling urban ghost story, which
has spawned a seemingly endless
boom of Psycho-Horror movies.

Tampopo
(Itami Juzo, 1986)
The idiosyncratic and sadly missed
director's trawl through the Japanese
obsession for food, with particular
reference to *ramen* noodles.

Rashomon
(Kurosawa Akira, 1951)
Influential tale of robbery from
Japan's most famous film-maker.

Tokyo Pop
(Fran Rubel Kazui, 1988)
Aspiring artiste can't make it in New
York, so heads off to Tokyo.

Tokyo Story
(Ozu Yasujiro, 1953)
Life in the metropolis and the
generation gap it produces are
explored in Ozu's masterpiece.

Until the End of the World
(Wim Wenders, 1991)
William Hurt and Sam Neill lurk
briefly around Shinjuku in Wenders'
worthy but dull SF epic.

The Yakuza
(Sydney Pollack, 1974)
Robert Mitchum stars in writer Paul
Schrader's tribute to the Japanese
gangster movie.

You Only Live Twice
(Lewis Gilbert, 1967)
Connery's 007 comes to Tokyo.
Look out for the New Otani hotel
doubling as the HQ of the
malevolent Osato Corporation.

Music

Amuro Namie *181920*
The reason so many Japanese girls
died their hair orange.

Cipher *No Ordinary Man*
Jazz saxophonist Theo Travis in lush
ambient project with former Japan
keyboardist Richard Barbieri.

Frank, Lee *Ikebukuro Suite*
A sinister Tokyo soundscape.

Hamasaki Ayumi *Far Away*
Played *ad nauseam* on radio and TV
throughout 2000, this is easily the
teeny-bopper superstar's best song.

Hirai Ken *The Changing Same*
Third album from evergreen Ken.

Karn, Mick *Each Eye a Path*
Latest release from former Japan
member and Zen master of the
fretless bass.

Malm, William P *Traditional
Japanese Music and Musical
Instruments*
Recognised as the single most
authoritative text on traditional
Japanese music, includes a CD.

Puffy *Greatest Hits*
Winsome twosome combine being
infuriatingly cute with being just
infuriating.

Ryokyu Endo *Solar Harmony,
Lunar Spirits and others*
New Age music by *shiatsu* and *aikido*
master, Buddhist priest, author and
maker of the war-game 'Strategem'.

Smap *Smap Vest*
Singing popstars with their own
cookery show.

TM Revolution *DISCORdanza Try
My Remix*
INXS meets U2: singles collection.

Utada Hikaru *Distance*
Japan's answer to Sade.

Websites

Gay

Cruising
*www.cruisingforsex.com/
elsewherelistings.html*
Long list of recommendations plus
good information on saunas.

Gay Net Japan
www.gnj.or.jp
English and Japanese forums,
classifieds and support groups.
Especially good for making short-
term friendships.

Gay Walker
www.gaywalker.com
Professionally produced gay and
lesbian portal has a decent English-
language section with community
information as well as chat rooms.

Lesbian & Gay Film Festival
l-gff.gender.ne.jp/2001/e/index.html
Homepage of the queer film festival
staged annually in July.

Utopia
www.utopia-asia.com/tipsjapn.htm
Useful, fun and informative page of
listings, links and more from this
Asian gay portal site.

Getting around

Japan Travel Updates
www.jnto.go.jp
Site of the Japan National
Tourist Organisation (JNTO),
with travel information, tips, an
online booking service and loose-
reference city maps.

Japanese Guest Houses
www.japaneseguesthouses.com
Guide to traditional *ryokan*
accommodation in Tokyo, Kyoto
and other cities, with online
booking facility.

Mix Pizza
www.mixpizza.co.jp
Portal site with hit-and-miss
searchable maps (the maps are in
Japanese but are sometimes useful).

NTT Townpage
english.itp.ne.jp
NTT's English-language phone
book online.

Shauwecker's Japan Guide
www.japan-guide.com

Shauwecker's guide to Japan online. Practical information covering the whole of the country.

Subway Navigator
www.subwaynavigator.com/bin/select/ english/japan/tokyo
Interactive subway route planner. Enter your departure and destination stations and it'll provide the route as well as how much time to allow for your journey.

Tokyo Life Navigator
www.ima-chan.co.jp/guide/index.htm
The place to start if you know nothing about what to expect in Tokyo and want to swot up before you get here.

Tokyo Subway Maps
www.tokyometro.go.jp/metnet/ 3600e.html
Up-to-date maps of the sometimes baffling subway system.

Media

Daily Yomiuri
www.yomiuri.co.jp/index-e.htm
Tokyo's second English-language newspaper's site (after the *Japan Times*) is smaller but prettier.

Debito's Home Page
www.debito.org
Amusing and informative home page of one Arudou Debito, a former US citizen once called David Aldwinkle (Debito is David in Japanese) now a Japanese national and crusader for foreigners' rights and chronicler of many of the curiosities of life in Japan for non-Japanese.

i-mode Links
www.imodelinks.com
Guide to all that is i-mode and the English-language sites available on this phenomenally successful Japanese mobile internet system.

Japan Inc
www.japaninc.com
Online version of the monthly magazine tracking Japan's progress in the so-called 'New Economy'.

Japan Times
www.japantimes.co.jp
The most comprehensive news about Japan available on the web. Events section only sporadically updated.

Japan Today
www.japantoday.com
New news portal with aspirations.

J-Port
www.j-port.com
Brand-new online free classifieds with zero editorial.

Radio On
www.radioonactive.com
One of Tokyo's best alternative radio stations, on the net.

Sumo World Magazine
www.sumoworld.com
The complete resource for the sumo fiend. Has a full list of stables and major wrestlers.

Weekly Post
www.weeklypost.com
The home page of one of the country's biggest-selling magazines contains English-language news and the occasional bit of gossip.

Music & clubs

CIA (Club Information Agency)
www.ciajapan.com
Online version of this monthly guide to club events in Tokyo has listings and party pictures.

CyberJapan
www.so-net.ne.jp/CYBERJAPAN
Stylish youth-culture site has fashion reports, news and streaming videos from Tokyo clubland.

Smash
www.smash-jpn.com
Hopepage in Japanese and English of one of Tokyo's biggest concert promoters.

Tokyo Record Stores
www.bento.com/rekodoya.html
Where to get your hands on the vinyl you've been hunting for, be it techno, bebop, hip-hop, ambient house, Latin jazz, rockabilly, easy listening, jungle or any other genre you'd care to name. The larger Tokyo Meltdown site is also worth checking.

Portal sites

Insite
www.insite-tokyo.com
An upper-end portal with lots of interesting articles on controversial topics.

Neo Tokyo
www.neo-tokyo.com
Stylishly designed, refreshingly simple and uncomplicated site with an interesting 'weird' section.

Tokyodoko
www.tokyodoko.com
Portal with easy-to-use and relatively in-depth reference search facility.

Tokyo Pop
www.tokyopop.com
Cute site covering Japanese pop culture from every angle.

Zigzag Asia
www.zigzagasia.com
Some original sections, an especially good cars feature and an impressive directory of Japan-related sites make this site worth a visit.

What's on

Cool Girls Japan
www.coolgirlsjapan
Fun page revealing the finer details of fashion and fads among Tokyo's hippest chicks.

Mout Fuji Climbing Info
www.city.fujiyoshida.yamanashi.jp/ english/root.html
All you need to know about climbing Japan's favorite mountain, including daily weather forecasts.

Quirky Japan
www3.tky.3web.ne.jp/~edjacob/ index.html
Off-beat home page 'dedicated to digression, kitsch, eccentricity and originality' with alternative things to do in Tokyo when you're 'tired of shrines and temples'.

Ski Japan
www.skijapanguide.com
In winter, it's more than possible to head off to the mountains for a day's skiing and be back by nightfall. This page tells you exactly how to go about it.

Superfuture
www.superfuture.com
Hyper stylish site mapping all the coolest shops, bars, restaurants and so on, plus trend reporting on what's hot in Tokyo this hour.

Tokyo Classified
www.tokyoclassified.com
The most reliably updated English-language what's-on listings for clubs, concerts and art galleries as well as feature articles and classified ads.

Tokyo Food Page
www.bento.com
An awe-inspiring restaurant guide to the city searchable by cuisine, location or both. Also has recipes, beer news and so much more.

Tokyo Q
www.tokyoq.com
Tokyo's best known online mag, with details on restaurants, hotels, clubs, culture-related features and more.

Directory

Getting By in Japanese

JAPANESE LANGUAGE

Pronunciation

Japanese pronunciation presents few problems for native English speakers, the most difficult trick to master being the doubling of vowels or consonants (see below).

Vowels

a as in bad
e as in bed
i as in feet
o as in long
u as in look

Long vowels

aa as in father
ee as in fair
ii as in feet, but longer
oo as in fought
uu as in chute

Consonants

Consonants in Japanese are pronounced the same as in English, but are always hard ('g' as in 'girl', rather than 'gyrate', for example). The only exceptions are the 'l/r' sound, which is one sound in Japanese, and falls halfway between the English pronunciation of the two letters, and 'v', which is pronounced as a 'b'. When consonants are doubled, they are pronounced as such: a 'tt' as in 'matte' (wait) is pronounced more like the 't' sound in 'get to' than in 'getting'.

Reading the phrases

When reading the phrases given below, remember to separate the syllables. Despite the amusing way it looks in English, the common name Takeshita is pronounced Ta-ke-shi-ta. Similarly, made (until) is 'ma-de', not the English word 'made', and shite (doing) is 'shi-te', rather than anything else. When a 'u' falls at the end of the word, it is barely pronounced: 'desu' is closer to 'dess' than to 'de-su'.

Reading & writing

The Japanese writing system is fiendishly complicated and is the main deterrent to learning the language. Japanese uses two syllabaries (not alphabets, because the letters represent complete sounds), hiragana and katakana, in conjunction with kanji, characters imported from China many centuries ago. The average Japanese person will be able to read over 6,000 kanji. For all but the most determined visitor, learning to read before you go is out of the question. However, learning katakana is relatively simple and will yield quick results, since it is used mainly to spell out foreign words (many imported from English). For books on learning Japanese, *see* **Further Reading**, page 258.

Days

Monday **getsu-yoobi**
Tuesday **ka-yoobi**
Wednesday **sui-yoobi**
Thursday **moku-yoobi**
Friday **kin-yoobi**
Saturday **do-yoobi**
Sunday **nichi-yoobi**

Time

It's at ...o'clock.   **...ji desu**

Excuse me, do you have the time?
sumimasen, ima nan-ji desu ka

Months

January **ichi-gatsu**
July **shichi-gatsu**
February **ni-gatsu**
August **hachi-gatsu**
March **san-gatsu**
September **ku-gatsu**
April **shi-gatsu**
October **juu-gatsu**
May **go-gatsu**
November **juu-ichi-gatsu**
June **roku-gatsu**
December **juu-ni-gatsu**

Dates

yesterday/today/tomorrow
kinoo/kyoo/ashita

last week/this week/next week
sen-shuu/kon-shuu/rai-shuu

the weekend   **shuumatsu**

Numbers

1	**ichi**	2	**ni**	3	**san**
4	**yon**	5	**go**	6	**roku**
7	**nana**	8	**hachi**	9	**kyuu**
10	**juu**	11	**juu-ichi**	12	**juu-ni**
100	**hyaku**	1,000	**sen**	10,000	**man**

Basic expressions

Yes/no *hai/iie*

Okay ***ookee***

Please (asking for a favour) ***onegai shimasu***

Please (offering a favour) ***doozo***

Thank you (very much) ***(doomo) arigatoo***

Hello/hi ***kon nichiwa***

Good morning ***ohayoo gozaimasu***

Good afternoon ***kon nichi wa***

Good evening ***kon ban wa***

Goodnight ***oyasumi nasai***

Goodbye ***sayonara***

Excuse me (getting attention) ***sumimasen***

Excuse me (may I get past?) ***shitsurei shimasu***

Excuse me/sorry ***gomen nasai***

Don't mention it/never mind
ki ni shinai de kudasai

It's okay ***daijyoobu desu***

Communication

Do you speak English?
Eigo o hanashi masu ka

I don't speak (much) Japanese
Nihongo o (amari) hanashi masen

Could you speak more slowly?
yukkuri itte kudasai

Could you repeat that? ***moo ichido itte kudasai***

I understand ***wakari mashita***

I don't understand ***wakari masen***

Do you understand? ***wakari masu ka?***

Where is it? ***doko desu ka***

When is it? ***itsu desu ka***

What is it? ***nan desu ka***

SIGNS

General

左 *hidari* left

右 *migi* right

入口 *iriguchi* entrance

出口 *deguchi* exit

トイレ/お手洗い *toire/o-tearai* toilets

男/男性 *otoko/dansei* men

女/女性 *onna/jyosei* women

禁煙 *kin-en* no smoking

危険 *kiken* danger

立ち入り禁止 *tachiiri kinshi* n

引く/押す *hiku/osu* pull/push

遺失物取扱所 *ishitsu butsu toriatsukai jo*
lost property

水泳禁止 *suiei kinshi* no swimming

飲料水 *inryoosui* drinking water

関係者以外立ち入り禁止
kankeisha igai tachiiri kinshi private

地下道 *chikadoo* underpass (subway)

足元注意 *ashimoto chuui* mind the step

ペンキ塗り立て *penki nuritate* wet paint

頭上注意 *zujoo chuui* mind your head

Road signs

止まれ *tomare* stop

徐行 *jokoo* slow

一方通行 *ippoo tsuukoo* one way

駐車禁止 *chuusha kinshi* no parking

高速道路 *koosoku dooro* motorway

料金 *ryookin* toll

信号 *shingoo* traffic lights

交差点 *koosaten* junction

Airport/station

案内 *an-nai* information

免税 *menzee* duty free

入国管理 *nyuukoku kanri* immigration

到着 *touchaku* arrivals

出発 *shuppatsu* departures

コインロッカー *koin rokkaa* luggage lockers

荷物引き渡し所 *nimotsu hikiwatashi jo*
luggage reclaim

手荷物カート *tenimotsu kaato* trolleys

バス/鉄道 *basu/tetsudoo* bus/train

レンタカー *rentakaa* car rental

地下鉄 *chikatetsu* underground

Hotels/restaurants

フロント *furonto* reception

予約 *yoyaku* reservation

非常口 *hijyooguchi* emergency/fire exit

湯 *yu* hot (water)

令 *ree* cold (water)
バー *baa* bar

Shops

営業中 *eegyoo chuu* open
閉店 *heeten* closed
階 *kai* floor
地下 *chika* basement
エレベーター *erebeetaa* lift
エスカレーター *esukareetaa* escalator
会計 *kaikee* cashier

Sightseeing

入場無料 *nyuujoo muryoo* free admission
大人/子供 小人 *otona/kodomo* adults/children
割引 (学生/高齢者) *waribiki (gakusei/koureisha)*
reduction (students/senior citizens)
お土産 *o-miyage* souvenirs
手を触れないでください
te o furenai de kudasai do not touch
撮影禁止 *satsuei kinshi* no photography

Public buildings

病院 *byooin* hospital
交番 *kouban* police box
銀行 *ginkoo* bank
郵便局 *yuubin kyoku* post office
プール *puuru* swimming pool
博物館 *hakubutsu-kan* museum

ESSENTIAL WORDS & PHRASES

Hotels

Do you have a room?
heya wa arimasu ka

I'd like a single/double room
shinguru/daburu no heya o onegai shimasu

I'd like a room with...
...tsuki no heya o onegai shimasu

a bath/shower **furo/shawa**

Reception

I have a reservation
yoyaku shite arimasu

My name is...
(watashi no namae wa)...desu

Is there...in the room?
heya ni...wa arimasu ka

air-conditioning **eakon**

TV/telephone **terebi/denwa**

We'll be staying... **...tomari masu**

one night only **ippaku dake**

a week **isshuu-kan**

I don't know yet **mada wakari masen**

I'd like to stay an extra night
moo ippaku sasete kudasai

How much is it...? **...ikura desu ka**

including/excluding breakfast
chooshoku komi/nuki de

Does the price include...?
kono nedan wa...komi desu ka

sales tax (VAT) **shoohi zee**

breakfast/meal **chooshoku/shokuji**

Is there a reduction for children?
kodomo no waribiki wa arimasu ka

What time is breakfast served?
chooshoku wa nan-ji desu ka

Is there room service?
ruumu saabisu wa arimasu ka

The key to room..., please.
...goo-shitsu no kagi o kudasai

I've lost my key **kagi o nakushi mashita**

Could you wake me up at...?
...ji ni okoshite kudasai

bath towel/blanket/pillow
basu taoru/moofu/makura

Are there any messages for me?
messeeji wa arimasu ka

What time do we have to checkout by?
chekkuauto wa nan-ji made desu ka

Could I have my bill, please?
kaikei o onegai shimasu

Could I have a receipt please?
reshiito o onegai shimasu

Could you order me a taxi, please?
takushii o yonde kudasai

Shops & services

pharmacy **yakkyoku/doraggu sutoaa**

off-licence/liquor store **saka-ya**

newsstand **kiosuku**

department store **depaato**

Directory

bookshop   *hon-ya*

supermarket   *supaa*

camera store   *kamera-ya*

I'd like...   *...o kudasai*

Do you have...?   *...wa arimasu ka*

How much is that?   *ikura desu ka*

Could you help me?   *onegai shimasu*

I'm looking for...   *...o sagashite imasu*

larger/smaller   *motto ookii/motto chiisai*

I'll take it   *sore ni shimasu*

That's all, thank you   *sore de zenbu desu*

Bank/currency exchange

dollars   *doru*

pounds   *pondo*

yen   *en*

currency exchange   *ryoogae-jo*

I'd like to change some pounds into yen
pondo o en ni kaetain desu ga

Could I have some small change, please?
kozeni o kudasai

Health

Where can I find a hospital/dental surgery?
byooin/hai-sha wa doko desu ka

Is there a doctor/dentist who speaks English?
eego ga dekiru isha/ha-isha wa imasu ka

What are the surgery hours?
shinryoo jikan wa nan-zi desu ka

Could the doctor come to see me here?
ooshin shite kuremasu ka

Could I make an appointment for...?
...yoyaku shitain desu ga

as soon as possible   *dekirudake hayaku*

It's urgent   *shikyuu onegai shimasu*

Symptoms

I feel faint   *memai ga shimasu*

I have a fever   *netsu ga arimasu*

I've been vomiting   *modoshi mashita*

I've got diarrhoea   *geri shitemasu*

It hurts here   *koko ga itai desu*

I have a headache   *zutsu ga shimasu*

I have a sore throat   *nodo ga itai desu*

I have a stomach ache   *onaka ga itai*

I have toothache   *ha ga itai desu*

I've lost a filling/tooth
tsumemono/ha ga toremashita

I don't want it extracted   *nukanaide kudasai*

Sightseeing

Where's the tourist office?
kankoo annai-jo wa doko desu ka

Do you have any information on...?
...no annai wa arimasu ka

sightseeing tour   *kankoo tsuaa*

Are there any trips to...?
...e no tsuaa wa arimasu ka

On tour

We'd like to have a look at the...
...o mitain desu ga

to take photographs   *shasin o toritain desu ga*

to buy souvenirs   *omiyage o kaitain desu ga*

to use the toilets   *toire ni ikitain desu ga*

Can we stop here?   *koko de tomare masu ka*

Could you take a photo of us, please?
shasin o totte kudasai

Travel

To..., please.   *...made onegai shimasu*

Single/return tickets   *katamichi/oofuku kippu*

How much...?   *...wa ikura desu ka?*

I'm here on holiday/business
kankoo/shigoto de kimashita

I'm going to...   *...ni ikimasu*

on my own   *hitori*

with my family   *kazoku to issho*

I'm with a group   *guruupu de kimashita*

ticket office   *kippu-uriba*

ticket gate   *kaisatsu-guchi*

ticket vending machines   *kenbai-ki*

shinkansen   *bullet train*

Where's the nearest underground station?
chikatetsu no eki wa doko desu ka

Where can I buy a ticket?
kippu wa doko de kaemasu ka

Could I have a map of the underground?
chikatetsu no rosenzu o kudasai

Directory

Index

Advertisers' Index

Please refer to the relevant pages for
addresses and telephone numbers.

Maps

Tokyo Overview

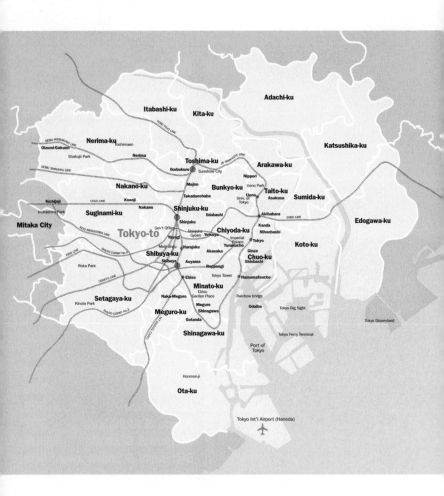

Adachi-ku

Itabashi-ku   Kita-ku

Nerima-ku   Toshimaen   Katsushika-ku
Oizumi-Gakuen
SEIBU IKEBUKURO LINE   Nerima
Shakujii Park   Toshima-ku   Arakawa-ku
SEIBU SHINJUKU LINE   Ikebukuro   Sunshine City
                                                                Nippori
Kichijoji   Nakano-ku   Koenji   Mejiro   Bunkyo-ku   Ueno   Taito-ku
Inokashira Park   CHUO LINE   Takadanobaba   Univ. of   Ueno Park   Sumida-ku
                                      Nakano   Tokyo   Asakusa
Mitaka City   Suginami-ku   Shinjuku-ku   Iidabashi   Akihabara   Edogawa-ku
                        KEIO INOKASHIRA LINE   SOBU LINE
                        Tokyo-to   Shinjuku   Kanda
                              Gov't Office   Shinjuku   Chiyoda-ku Nihonbashi   Koto-ku
                              Tokyo   Gyoen Yotsuya   Imperial   Tokyo
                        KEIO LINE   Meiji-jingu   Harajuku   Palace Ginza
Roka Park   Shibuya-ku   Aoyama   Akasaka Yurakucho   Chuo-ku
                      Shibuya   Roppongi Shinbashi
                          Ebisu   Tokyo Tower Hamamatsucho
                                      Ebisu   Minato-ku
                    Setagaya-ku   Naka-Meguro Garden Place   Rainbow bridge
Kinuta Park   Meguro   Odaiba   Tokyo Big Sight
                    Meguro-ku   Gotanda Shinagawa   Tokyo Disneyland
                                                Tokyo Ferry Terminal
                        Shinagawa-ku
                                        Port of
                                        Tokyo
            Honmon-ji
                    Ota-ku

                    Tokyo Int'l Airport (Haneda)

Yamanote Connections

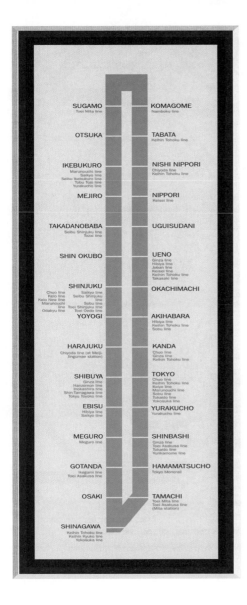

SUGAMO
Toei Mita line

KOMAGOME
Namboku line

OTSUKA

TABATA
Keihin Tohoku line

IKEBUKURO
Marunouchi line
Saikyo line
Seibu Ikebukuro line
Tobu Tojo line
Yurakucho line

NISHI NIPPORI
Chiyoda line
Keihin Tohoku line

MEJIRO

NIPPORI
Keisei line

TAKADANOBABA
Seibu Shinjuku line
Tozai line

UGUISUDANI

SHIN OKUBO

UENO
Ginza line
Hibiya line
Joban line
Keisei line
Keihin Tohoku line
Takasaki line

SHINJUKU
Chuo line   Saikyo line
Keio line   Seibu Shinjuku
Keio New line   line
Marunouchi   Sobu line
       line   Toei Shinjuku line
Odakyu line   Toei Oedo line

OKACHIMACHI

YOYOGI

AKIHABARA
Hibiya line
Keihin Tohoku line
Sobu line

HARAJUKU
Chiyoda line (at Meiji-
Jingumae station)

KANDA
Chuo line
Ginza line
Keihin Tohoku line

SHIBUYA
Ginza line
Hanzomon line
Inokashira line
Shin-Tamagawa line
Tokyu Toyoko line

TOKYO
Chuo line
Keihin Tohoku line
Keiyo line
Marunouchi line
Sobu line
Tokaido line
Yokosuka line

EBISU
Hibiya line
Saikyo line

YURAKUCHO
Yurakucho line

MEGURO
Meguro line

SHINBASHI
Ginza line
Toei Asakusa line
Tokaido line
Yurikamome line

GOTANDA
Ikegami line
Toei Asakusa line

HAMAMATSUCHO
Tokyo Monorail

OSAKI

TAMACHI
Toei Mita line
Toei Asakusa line
(Mita station)

SHINAGAWA
Keihin Tohoku line
Keihin Kyuko line
Yokosuka line

Map Key
Maps start overleaf

〒　Post Office

卍　Temple

Ħ　Shrine

Ｓ　Subway station
(Eidan or Toei systems)

　Building of interest

　Overground station

　Urban expressway

27　Address marker
(Accurate to within one block)

•　Place of interest

—　Japanese gateway

Subway Map

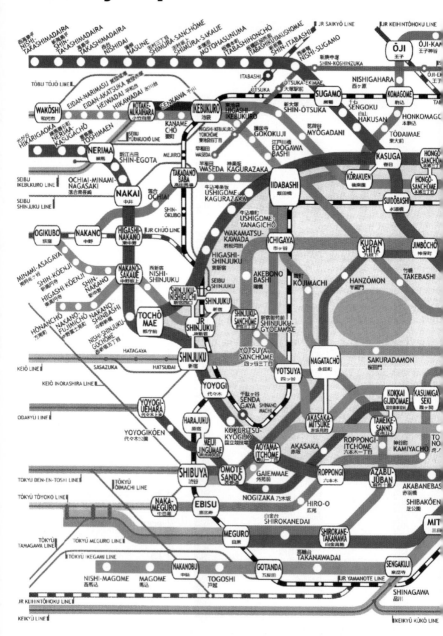

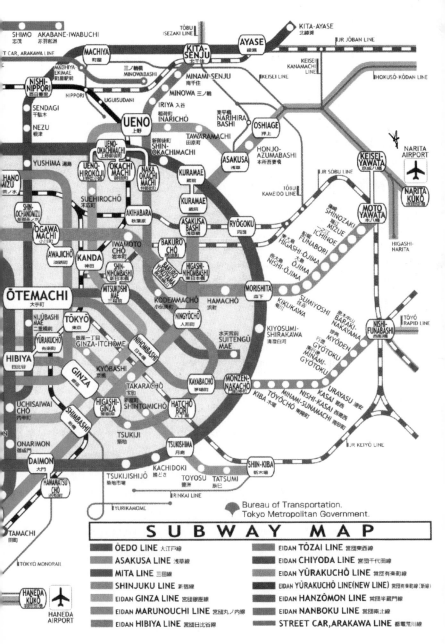

Map 1a: West Shinjuku

Kumano Shrine

Shinjuku Central Park

Jofu-ji Temple

JUNISO DORI

KOEN DORI

Tokyo Metropolitan Govt Twin Towers

No.1

No.2

TOCHO DORI

Sumitomo Bldg

MINAMI DORI

KITA DORI

Nishi Shinjuku Station

GIJIDO DORI

Mitsui Bldg

OME KAIDO

FUREAI DORI

CHUO DORI

HIGASHI DORI

Shinjuku Centre Bldg

Nomura Bldg

Bunka Womens' University

NTT

Yasuda Kasai Bldg

KOSHU KAIDO

PLAZA DORI

Toei Shinjuku Line

Keio Shinjuku Station

Odakyu Shinjuku Station

Seibu Shinjuku Station

JR Shinjuku Station

Marunouchi Line

Toei Shinjuku Station

Takashimaya Times Square

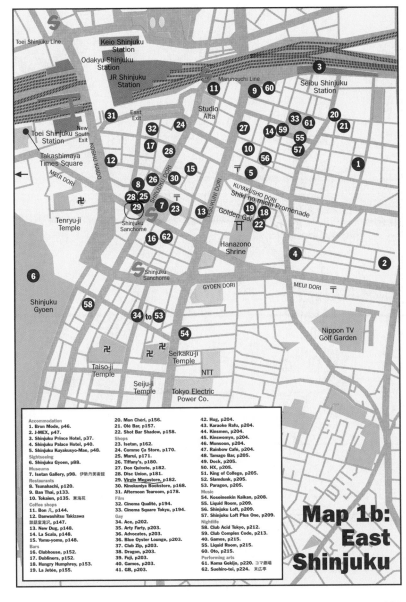

**Map 1b:
East
Shinjuku**

Toei Shinjuku Line

Keio Shinjuku
Station

Odakyu Shinjuku
Station

JR Shinjuku
Station

Marunouchi Line

Seibu Shinjuku
Station

East
Exit

Studio
Alta

New
Toei Shinjuku South
Station Exit

Takashimaya
Times Square

KOSHU KAIDO

MEIJI DORI

SHINJUKU DORI

YASUKUNI DORI

Tenryu-ji
Temple

Shinjuku
Sanchome

KUYAKUSHO DORI

Shiki no michi Promenade

Golden Gai

Hanazono
Shrine

Shinjuku
Sanchome

GYOEN DORI

MEIJI DORI

Shinjuku
Gyoen

Nippon TV
Golf Garden

Seikaku-ji
Temple

Taiso-ji
Temple

NTT

Seiju-ji
Temple

Tokyo Electric
Power Co.

Accommodation
1. Bron Mode, p46.
2. J-MEX, p47.
3. Shinjuku Prince Hotel, p37.
4. Shinjuku Palace Hotel, p40.
5. Shinjuku Kuyakusyo-Mae, p48.
Sightseeing
6. Shinjuku Gyoen, p88.
Museums
7. Isetan Gallery, p98. 伊勢丹美術館
Restaurants
8. Tsunahachi, p120.
9. Ban Thai, p133.
10. Tokaien, p135. 東海苑
Coffee shops
11. Bon 凡, p144.
12. Danwashitsu Takizawa
談話室滝沢, p147.
13. New Dug, p148.
14. La Scala, p148.
15. Yomu-yomu, p148.
Bars
16. Clubhouse, p152.
17. Dubliners, p152.
18. Hungry Humphrey, p153.
19. La Jetée, p155.

20. Mon Chéri, p156.
21. Olé Bar, p157.
22. Shot Bar Shadow, p158.
Shops
23. Isetan, p162.
24. Comme Ça Store, p170.
25. Marui, p171.
26. Tiffany's, p180.
27. Don Quixote, p182.
28. Disc Union, p181.
29. Virgin Megastore, p182.
30. Kinokuniya Bookstore, p168.
31. Afternoon Tearoom, p178.
Film
32. Cinema Qualité, p194.
33. Cinema Square Tokyu, p194.
Gay
34. Ace, p202.
35. Arty Farty, p203.
36. Advocates, p203.
37. Blue Oyster Lounge, p203.
37. Club Zip, p203.
38. Dragon, p203.
39. Fuji, p203.
40. Gamos, p203.
41. GB, p203.

42. Hug, p204.
43. Karaoke Rafu, p204.
44. Kinsmen, p204.
45. Kinswomyn, p204.
46. Monsoon, p204.
47. Rainbow Café, p204.
48. Tamago Bar, p205.
49. Dock, p205.
50. HX, p205.
51. King of College, p205.
52. Slamdunk, p205.
53. Paragon, p205.
Music
54. Koseinenkin Kaikan, p208.
55. Liquid Room, p209.
56. Shinjuku Loft, p209.
57. Shinjuku Loft Plus One, p209.
Nightlife
58. Club Acid Tokyo, p212.
59. Club Complex Code, p213.
40. Gamos, p215.
55. Liquid Room, p215.
60. Oto, p215.
Performing arts
61. Koma Gekijo, p220. コマ劇場
62. Suehiro-tei, p224. 末広亭

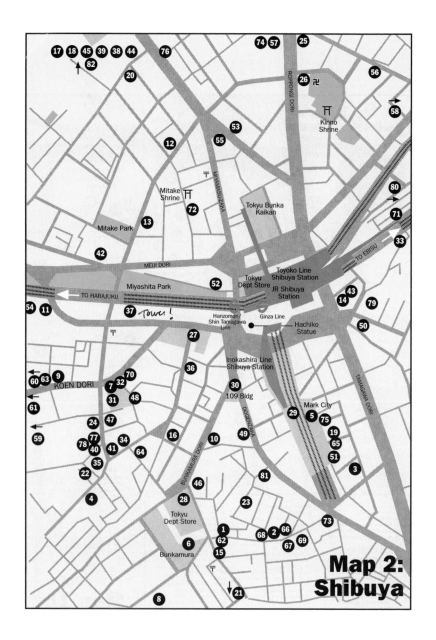

Map 2:
Shibuya

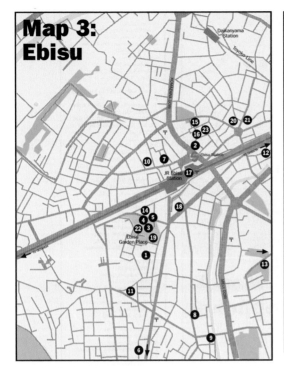

Map 3:
Ebisu

Accommodation
1. The Westin Tokyo, p37.
2. Hotel Excellent, p41.
Museums
3. Beer Museum Yebisu, 恵比寿麦酒記念館, p106.
4. Tokyo Metropolitan Museum of Photography 東京都写真美術館, p109.
Restaurants
5. Chibo 千房, p122.
6. Jinroku 甚六, p122.
7. Jigoku Ramen Hyottoko 地獄ラーメンひょっとこ, p125.
8. Ninniku-ya, p131.
9. Fummy's Grill, p139.
10. Good Honest Grub, p139.
11. Ricos Kitchen, p139.
Bars
12. Bar Kitsune, p151.
13. Hanezawa Beer Garden, p153.
14. Inishmore, p155.
15. Space Punch, p159.
16. What the Dickens, p160.
Shops
17. Atre, p165.
18. Good Day Books, p168.
Film
19. Ebisu Garden Cinema, p195.
Galleries
20. Masataka Hayakawa Gallery, p198.
21. Ota Fine Arts, p198.
Music
22. Ebisu Garden Hall, p207.
23. Milk, p209.
Nightlife
23. Milk, p215.

Shibuya Key

Accommodation
1. If, p46.
2. Lala Dogenzaka, p47.
3. P&A Plaza, p47.
4. Arimax, p39.
5. Excel Hotel Tokyu, p40.
Museums
6. Bunkamura The Museum, p97.
7. Parco Gallery, p100.
8. Toguri Museum of Art 戸栗美術館, p102.
9. Tobacco & Salt Museum　たばこと塩の博物館, p105.
10. Eyeglass Museum　アイリス眼鏡博物館, p106.
11. TEPCO Electric Energy Museum　電力館, p112.
Restaurants
12. Vingt2, p121.
13. Myoko, p126.
14. Down to Earth, p130.
15. Jembatan Merah, p132.
16. Raj Mahal/Raj Palace, p132.
17. Vision Network/Las Chicas, p136.
18. Tokyo Salon, p138.
19. Ankara, p138.
20. Bar & Grill Lunchan, p140.
Coffee shops
21. Cantina, p144.
22. Coffee 3.4 Sunsea, p145.
23. Lion, p147.
Bars
24. Hub, p153.
25. Soft, p159.
26. Tantra, p160.
Shops
27. Seibu, p163.
28. Tokyu Honten, p165.

29. Mark City, p165.
30. 109, p169.
31. Final Home, p170.
32. Parco, p171.
33. Maiko Make Over Studio, p175.
34. Manga no Mori, p182.
35. Cisco, p180.
36. HMV, p181.
37. Tower Records, p181.
38. Kinokuniya International, p168.
39. Aoyama Book Centre, p167.
40. Booty, p180.
41. Tokyu Hands, p178.
42. Diesel, p172.
43. Nozaki Eye Clinic, p177.
Children
44. National Children's Castle　こどもの城, p192.
45. Tokyo Metropolitan Children's Hall　東京都児童会館, p192.
Film
46. Ciné Amuse, p194.
47. Ciné Quinto, p194.
48. Cinema Rise, p194.
49. Ciné Saison Shibuya, p195.
50. Euro Space, p195.
6. Le Cinéma, p196.
51. Shibuya Cinema Society, p196.
52. Shibuya Hermitage, p196.
53. Theatre Image Forum, p196.
54. Uplink Factory, p196.
Galleries
55. Gallery Le Déco, p198.
56. Cassina, p200.
57. E & Y, p200.
58. HA Deux, p201.

Music
6. Orchard Hall, p206.
59. NHK Hall, p208.
60. Shibuya AX, p208.
61. Shibuya Kokaido, p208.
62. Club Asia, p209.
63. Club Eggsite Shibuya, p209.
64. Club Quattro Shibuya, p209.
65. La.mama Shibuya, p209.
66. On Air East, p209.
67. On Air West, p209.
68. Shibuya Nest, p210.
69. Vuenos Bar Tokyo, p210.
69. Womb, p210.
Nightlife
70. Ball, p212.
71. Cafe & Club Fura, p212.
62. Club Asia, p212.
72. Club Bar Family, p212.
73. Club Chu, p212.
74. Club Hachi, p213.
75. Ism Shibuya, p215.
76. Loop, p215.
77. Organ Bar, p215.
79. Rockwest, p216.
79. The Room, p216.
80. Simoon, p216.
81. Sugar High DJ Bar & Club, p216.
68. Vuenos Bar Tokyo, p218.
69. Womb, p218.
Performing arts
82. Aoyama Round Theatre, p222.
6. Bunkamura Theatre Cocoon, p222.

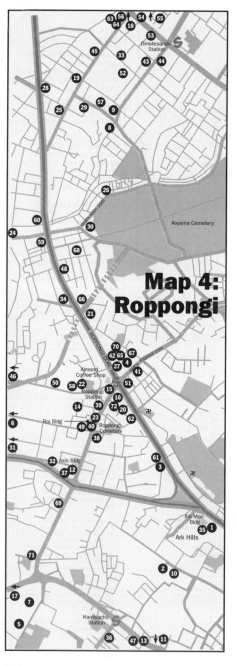

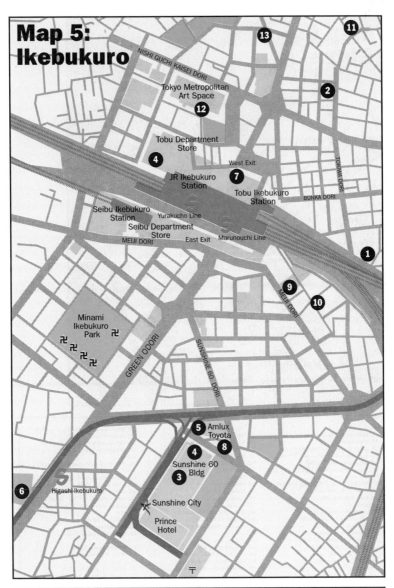

Map 5:
Ikebukuro

NISHI GUCHI KAISEI DORI

Tokyo Metropolitan
Art Space

12

Tobu Department
Store

4

West Exit

JR Ikebukuro
Station

7

Tobu Ikebukuro
Station

Seibu Ikebukuro
Station   Yurakucho Line

Seibu Department
Store

MEIJI DORI   East Exit   Marunouchi Line

BUNKA DORI

TOKIWA DORI

13

11

2

1

Minami
Ikebukuro
Park 卍

卍 卍 卍
卍 卍

GREEN O'DORI

SUNSHINE 60 DORI

MEIJI DORI

9

10

5 Amlux
Toyota

4

8

Sunshine 60
3 Bldg

6   Higashi-Ikebukuro

〒 Sunshine City

Prince
Hotel

〒

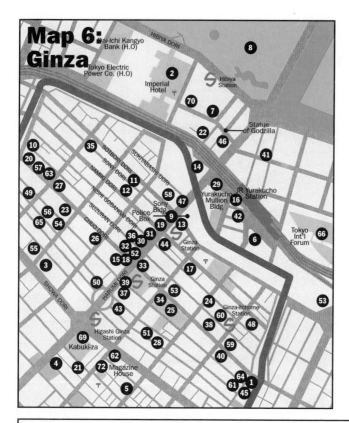

Map 6: Ginza

Dai-Ichi Kangyo Bank (H.O)

HIBIYA DORI

Tokyo Electric Power Co. (H.O)

Imperial Hotel **2**

Hibiya Station

Statue of Godzilla

8

70

7

22

46

41

10

35

SOTOBORI DORI

SUKIYABASHI DORI

SONY DORI

20

57

63

27

NAMIKI DORI

11

14

29

JR Yurakucho Station

49

NISHI GOBANGAI DORI

12

58

47

Yurakucho Mullion Bldg

16

56

23

SUZURAN DORI

Sony Bldg

9

42

65

54

CHUO DORI

Police Box

19

13

Tokyo Int'l Forum

66

55

26

36

31

44

6

Ginza Station

32

30

52

3

15

18

33

17

Ginza Station

50

HARUMI DORI

39

37

53

SHOWA DORI

43

34

25

24

Ginza-itchome Station

60

53

38

48

69

Higashi Ginza Station

51

28

59

Kabuki-za

62

40

4

21

72

Magazine House

5

64

61

1

45

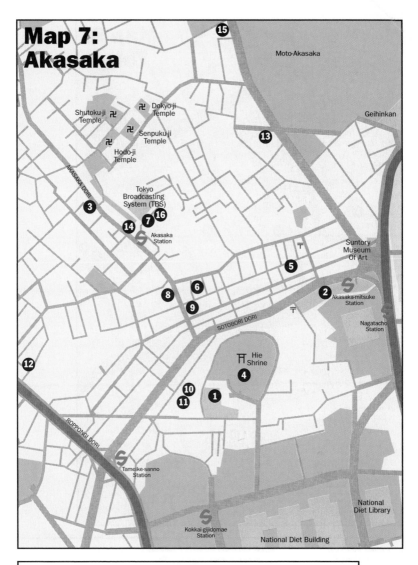

Map 7:
Akasaka

Moto-Akasaka

Geihinkan

Shutoku-ji 卍 卍 Dokyo-ji
Temple 卍 Temple
卍 Senpuku-ji
卍 Temple
Hodo-ji
Temple

Tokyo
Broadcasting
System (TBS)

❸

⓮ ❼ ⓰

Akasaka
Station

Suntory
Museum
Of Art

〒

❺

❷
Akasaka-mitsuke
Station

❽

❻

SOTOBORI DORI

〒

Nagatacho
Station

❾

卍 Hie
Shrine

❹

⓬

❿
⓫

❶

ROPPONGI DORI

Tameike-sanno
Station

National
Diet Library

Kokkai-gijidomae
Station

National Diet Building

❶❺

⓭

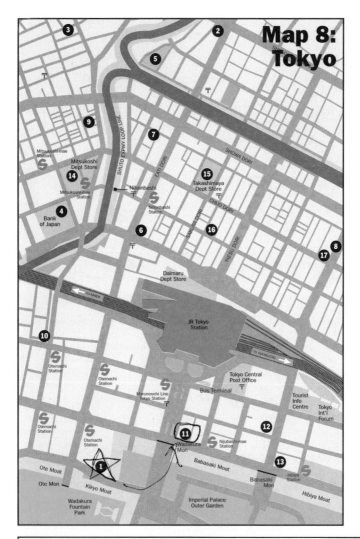

Map 8:
Tokyo

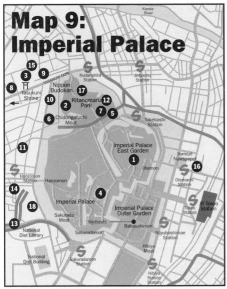

Map 9: Imperial Palace

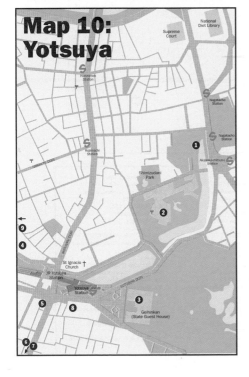

Map 10: Yotsuya

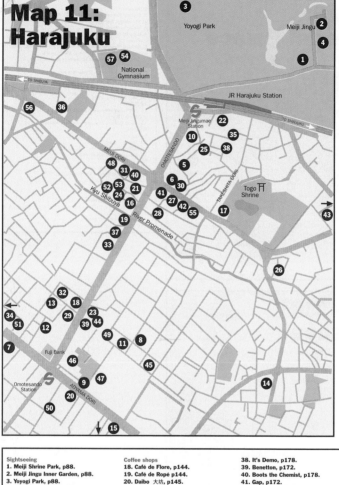

Map 11:
Harajuku

Yoyogi Park

Meiji Jingu ②
④
①

③

⑤⑦ ⑤④
National
Gymnasium

TO SHIBUYA

JR Harajuku Station

⑤⑥   ③⑥

TO SHINJUKU

Meiji Jingumae
Station

㉒
⑩   ③⑤
㉕   ③⑧
⑤

MEIJI DORI
④⑧
③① ④⓪
⑤②⑤③㉔ ②①
Kyu Shibuya   ⑥
    ①⑥ ④①㉗④②⑤⑤
        ②⑧
River Promenade ①⑨
    ③⑦
③③

OMOTESANDO

Togo 卄
Shrine

TAKESHITA DORI
①⑦

④③

㉖

③②
①③ ①⑧
㉙ ㉓④④
①② ③⑨
    ④⑨ ①① ⑧
③④
⑤①
⑦

Fuji Bank

④⑥

④⑦   ④⑤
⑨   ①④
Omotesando
Station   ②⓪

AOYAMA DORI

⑤⓪

①⑤

Sightseeing
1. Meiji Shrine Park, p88.
2. Meiji Jingu Inner Garden, p88.
3. Yoyogi Park, p88.
4. Meiji Jingu Shrine, p89.
Museums
5. Ukiyo-e Ota Memorial Museum of Art, p97.
浮世絵太田記念美術館
6. Laforet Museum, p98.
7. Spiral Garden, p100.
Restaurants
8. Maisen まい泉, p123.
9. Hokuto 北斗, p125.
10. Kyushu Jangara Ramen 九州じゃんが ららぁめん, p126.
11. Senda 仙田, p126.
12. Denpachi でん八, p129.
13. Crayon House Hiroba クレヨンハウス 広場, p130.
14. Natural Harmony Angolo, p130.
15. Jap Cho Ok, p131.
16. Fujimamas, p135.
17. Aux Bacchanales, p137.

Coffee shops
18. Café de Flore, p144.
19. Café de Ropé p144.
20. Daibo 大坊, p145.
Bars
21. AIP, p150.
22. Go-Go Lounge, p153.
23. In Blue, p155.
24. Oh God!, p157.
25. Pink Cow, p158.
26. Radio Bar, p158.
Shops
27. YM Square, p166.
28. Candy Stripper, p170.
29. Hanae Mori, p170.
30. Laforet Harajuku/Foret Harajuku, p171.
31. Uniqlo, p171.
32. Fuji Torii, p173.
33. Oriental Bazaar, p174.
34. Aoyama Oval Plaza, p166.
35. Atom, p182.
36. Dept, p182.
37. Kiddyland, p182.

38. It's Demo, p178.
39. Benetton, p172.
40. Boots the Chemist, p178.
41. Gap, p172.
42. Sephora, p175.
43. Boudoir, p175.
44. Peekaboo, p175.
45. Sinden, p177.
46. Tokyo Chiropractic Centre, p175.
47. International Vision Centre, p177.
48. BorneLund
Galleries
49. Art Shop NADiff, p198.
50. Rontgen Kunstraum, p198.
51. Abode, p200.
52. hhstyle.com, p201.
53. Tricot Open, p201.
Music
54. National Yoyogi Stadium, p208.
55. Astro Hall, p208.
56. Crocodile Shibuya, p209.
Sport
57. National Yoyogi Coliseum, p226.

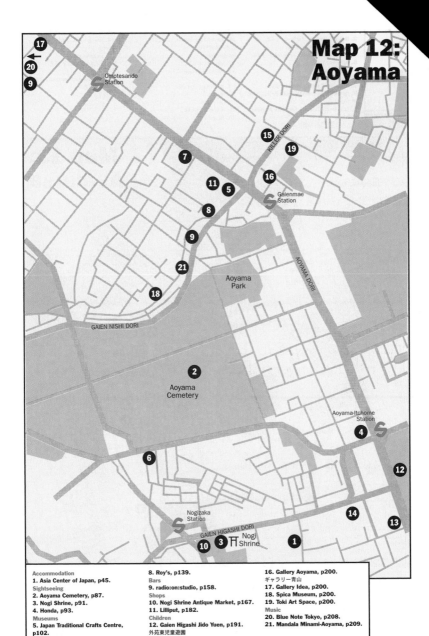

Map 12:
Aoyama

Omotesando
Station

KILLER DORI

Gaienmae
Station

AOYAMA DORI

Aoyama
Park

GAIEN NISHI DORI

Aoyama
Cemetery

Aoyama-Itchome
Station

Nogizaka
Station

GAIEN HIGASHI DORI

Nogi
Shrine

Accommodation
Asakusa View Hotel, p37.
Hotel Sunroute Asakusa, p42.
Ryokan Shigetsu, p42.
Sukeroku No Yado Sadachiyo, p42.
Asakusa Ryokan, p43.
Sightseeing
6. Hanayashiki , p86.
7. Asakusa Kannon Temple, p89.
8. Asakusa Shrine (Asakusa Jinja), p89.
Museums
9. Ace World Bags & Luggage Museum,
p101.
エース世界のかばん館

10. Drum Museum, p106.
太鼓博物館
11. Japan Toys Museum, p113.
日本玩具博物館
Restaurants
12. Vin Chou, p121.
13. Hatsuogawa, p121.
初小川
14. Sometaro, p122.
染太郎
Coffee shops
15. Angelus, p144.
16. ef, p147.

Bars
17. Flamme d'Or, p152.
18. Kamiya Bar, p156.
Shops
19. Hanato, p174.
20. Kappa Bashi, p166.
Gay
21. 24 Kaikan Asakusa, p205.
２４会館「浅草」

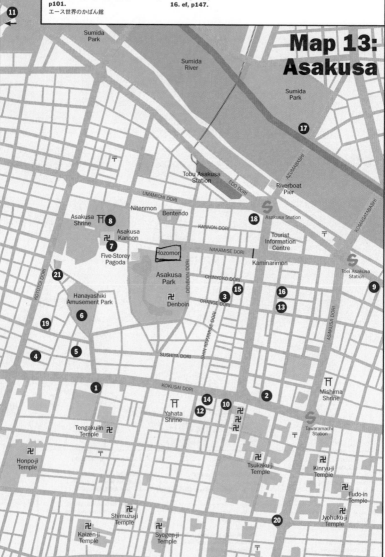

Map 13: Asakusa

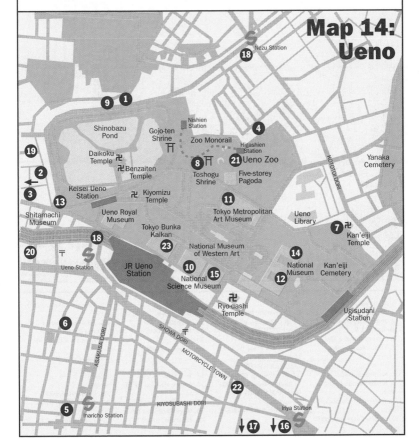

Map 14: Ueno

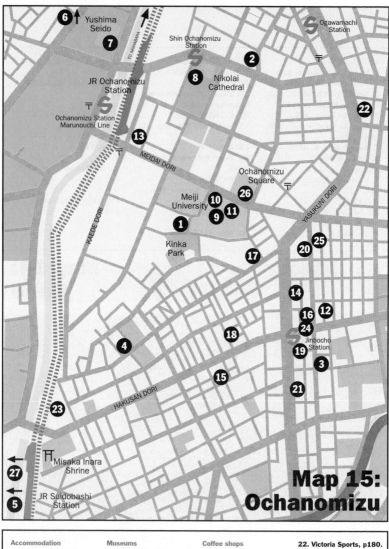

Map 15:
Ochanomizu

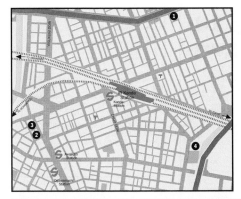

Map 16

Accommodation
1. Hotel Kazusaya, p41.
Restaurants
2. Botan, p119.
ぼたん
3. Isegen, p120.
いせ源
Sport
4. Chiyoda Kuritsu Sogo Taiikukan Pool, p230.

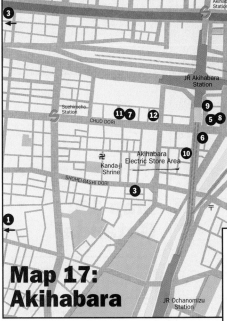

Map 17: Akihabara

Accommodation
1. Hotel Edoya, p44.
Museums
2. Transportation Museum, p113.
交通博物館
Restaurants
3. Honke Ponta, p123.
4. Kanda Yabu Soba, p119.
神田藪そば
Shops
5. IT Net, p168.
6. Laox, p168.
7. Minami Musen Denki, p168.
8. NTT DoCoMo, p168.
9. Takarada, p168.
10. Tsukumo Robocon Magazine Kan, p169.
11. Virtual Computer Networks, p169.
12. Yamagiwa, p169.
Children
2. Transportation Museum, p113.

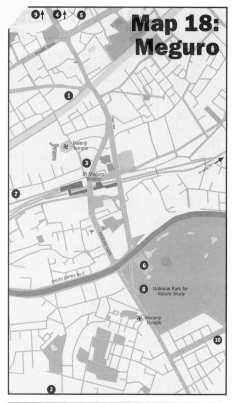

Map 18: Meguro

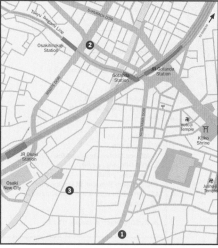

Map 19: Gotanda

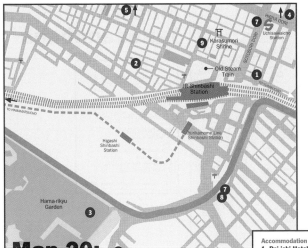

Map 20:
Shinbashi

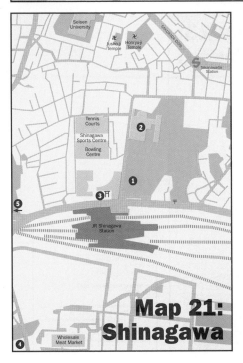

Map 21:
Shinagawa

Accommodation
1. Dai-ichi Hotel Tokyo, p35.
2. Business Inn Shinbashi & Annex, p47.
Sightseeing
3. Hama-rikyu Detached Garden, p87.
4. Sake Information Centre, p93.
Museums
5. Matsuoka Museum of Art, p96.
松岡美術館
Restaurants
6. Tsukiji Edogin Honten, p119.
7. Shichirinya, p121.
七輪や
8. Daidaiya, p127.
橙家
Bars
9. Kaga-ya, p155.
かがや
Performing arts
10. Shinbashi Embujo, p222.
新橋演舞場

Accommodation
1. Le Meridien Pacific Tokyo, p39.
2. New Takanawa Prince Hotel, p40.
3. Keihin Hotel, p43.
Sightseeing
4. Funasei Yakatabune, p92.
Museums
5. Hara Museum of Contemporary Art, p97.
原美術館

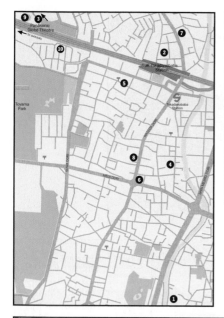

Map 22:
Takadanobaba

Accommodation
1. Four Seasons at Chinzan-so, p36.
2. Japan Minshuku Association, p47.
Restaurants
3. Hyakunincho Yataimura, p135.
4. La Dinette, p137.
Coffee shops
5. Ben's Café, p144.
Bars
6. The Fiddler, p152.
7. Footnik, p152.
Film
8. Waseda Shochiku, p196.
Performing arts
9. Panasonic Globe-za, p222.
6. Tokyo Cynics, p224.
Sport
10. Shinjuku-ku Sports Centre, p230.

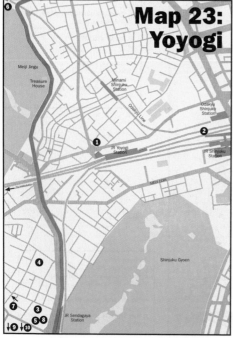

Map 23:
Yoyogi

Restaurants
1. Angkor Wat, p133.
Shops
2. Franc Franc, p178.
Galleries
3. Gallery Side 2, p198.
Performing arts
4. National Noh Theatre, p222.
国立能劇場
Sport
5. Tokyo Metropolitan Gymnasium Pool, p230.
6. Tokyo Horse Riding Club, p228.
7. Prince Chichibu Memorial Stadium, p227.
8. Tokyo Gymnasium, p227.
9. Jingu Baseball Stadium, p229.
10. National Stadium, p230.

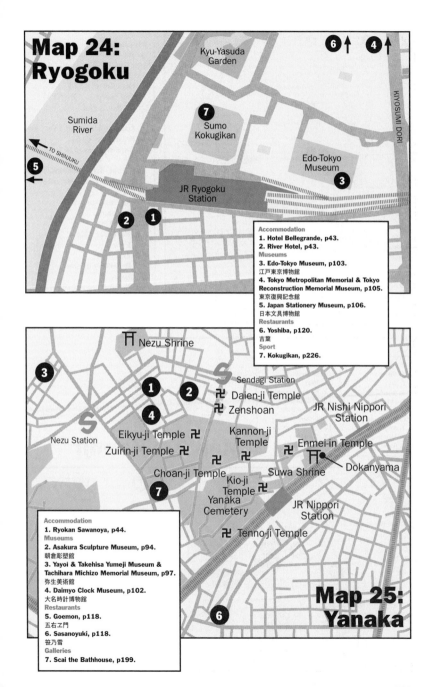

Map 24:
Ryogoku

Kyu-Yasuda
Garden

6 ↑   4 ↑

KIYOSUMI DORI

Sumida
River

Sumo
Kokugikan   7

TO SHINJUKU

Edo-Tokyo
Museum   3

5

JR Ryogoku
Station

2   1

Accommodation
1. Hotel Bellegrande, p43.
2. River Hotel, p43.
Museums
3. Edo-Tokyo Museum, p103.
江戸東京博物館
4. Tokyo Metropolitan Memorial & Tokyo
Reconstruction Memorial Museum, p105.
東京復興記念館
5. Japan Stationery Museum, p106.
日本文具博物館
Restaurants
6. Yoshiba, p120.
吉葉
Sport
7. Kokugikan, p226.

卍 Nezu Shrine

3

1   2   卍 Daien-ji Temple
4   卍 Zenshoan

Sendagi Station

JR Nishi Nippori
Station

Nezu Station

Eikyu-ji Temple 卍
Zuirin-ji Temple 卍

Kannon-ji
Temple
卍   卍

Enmei-in Temple

卍   鳥居   Dokanyama

Choan-ji Temple
7
Kio-ji
Temple 卍
Yanaka
Cemetery

Suwa Shrine

JR Nippori
Station

卍 Tenno-ji Temple

Accommodation
1. Ryokan Sawanoya, p44.
Museums
2. Asakura Sculpture Museum, p94.
朝倉彫塑館
3. Yayoi & Takehisa Yumeji Museum &
Tachihara Michizo Memorial Museum, p97.
弥生美術館
4. Daimyo Clock Museum, p102.
大名時計博物館
Restaurants
5. Goemon, p118.
五右ヱ門
6. Sasanoyuki, p118.
笹乃雪
Galleries
7. Scai the Bathhouse, p199.

6

Map 25:
Yanaka

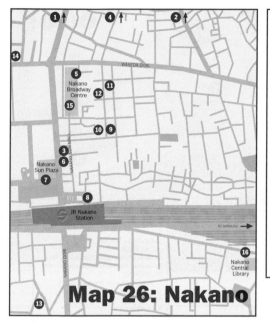

Map 26: Nakano

Map 27: Koenji

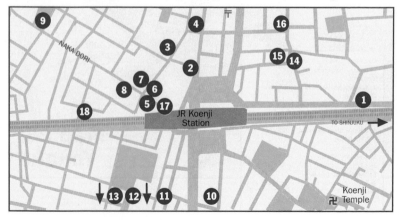

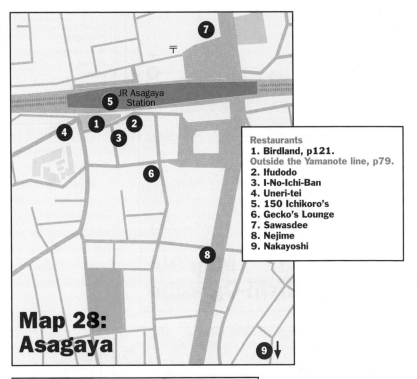

Map 28: Asagaya

JR Asagaya Station

Restaurants
1. Birdland, p121.
Outside the Yamanote line, p79.
2. Ifudodo
3. I-No-Ichi-Ban
4. Uneri-tei
5. 150 Ichikoro's
6. Gecko's Lounge
7. Sawasdee
8. Nejime
9. Nakayoshi

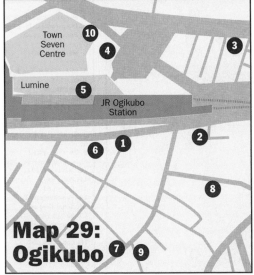

Map 29: Ogikubo

Town Seven Centre

Lumine

JR Ogikubo Station

Restaurants
1. Gruppe, p130.
2. Nataraj, p135.
Outside the Yamanote line, p80.
3. Haruki-ya
4. Saru-no-Kura
5. Yu-topia
6. Dominus
7. Stone Cotton
2. Nataraj
8. Basho
1. Gruppe
9. Tomato
10. Spice House

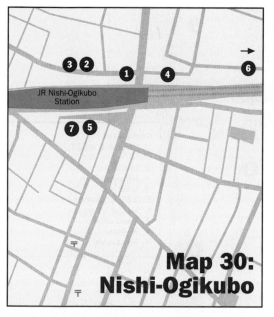

JR Nishi-Ogikubo
Station

Map 30:
Nishi-Ogikubo

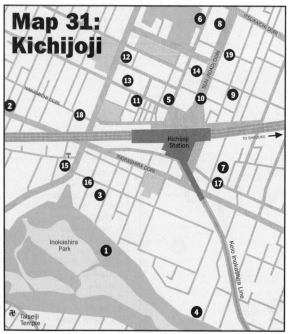

Map 31:
Kichijoji

ITSUKAICHI DORI

SUU (ROAD) DORI

NAKAMICHI DORI

INOKASHIRA DORI

Kichijoji
Station

TO SHINJUKU →

Keio Inokashira Line

Inokashira
Park

卍 Taiseiji
Temple

**Map 32:
Daikanyama**

Daikanyama Station

Restaurants
1. Wasabiya, p127.
わさび家
2. Aguri, p129.
庵グリ
3. La Casita, p138.
4. Tableaux, p141.
Shops
5. 5351, p169.
6. Bonjour Records, p180.
Outside the Yamanote line, p82.
7. Café Artifagose
8. Stand 300 of Joy
9. Pole Pole
10. Jean Paul Gaultier
11. Vivienne Westwood
12. Issey Miyake
13. Tsumori Chisato
14. Love Girls Market
15. La Fuente

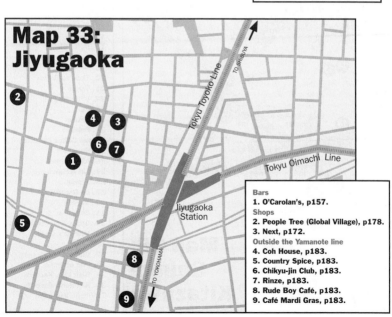

**Map 33:
Jiyugaoka**

Tokyu Toyoko Line

TO SHIBUYA

Tokyu Oimachi Line

Jiyugaoka
Station

TO YOKOHAMA

Bars
1. O'Carolan's, p157.
Shops
2. People Tree (Global Village), p178.
3. Next, p172.
Outside the Yamanote line
4. Coh House, p183.
5. Country Spice, p183.
6. Chikyu-jin Club, p183.
7. Rinze, p183.
8. Rude Boy Café, p183.
9. Café Mardi Gras, p183.

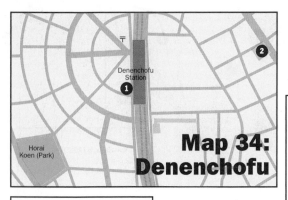

Map 34: Denenchofu

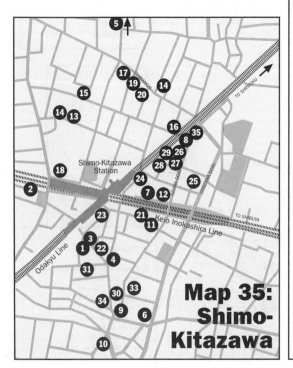

Map 35: Shimo-Kitazawa

Biocatalyst Design
for
Stability and Specificity

ACS SYMPOSIUM SERIES **516**

Biocatalyst Design
for
Stability and Specificity

Michael E. Himmel, EDITOR
National Renewable Energy Laboratory

George Georgiou, EDITOR
The University of Texas

Developed from a symposium sponsored
by the Division of Biochemical Technology
of the American Chemical Society
at the Fourth Chemical Congress of North America
(202nd National Meeting of the American Chemical Society),
New York, New York
August 25–30, 1991

American Chemical Society, Washington, DC 1993

Library of Congress Cataloging-in-Publication Data

Chemical Congress of North America (4th: 1991: New York, N.Y.)
  Biocatalyst design for stability and specificity /   [edited by] Michael
E. Himmel, George Georgiou.

     p.   cm.—(ACS Symposium Series, 0097–6156; 516).

  "Developed from a symposium sponsored by the Division of
Biochemical Technology of the American Chemical Society at the
Fourth Chemical Congress of North America (202nd National Meeting
of the American Chemical Society) New York, New York, August
25–30, 1991."

  Includes bibliographical references and index.

  ISBN 0–8412–2518–4

  1. Enzymes—Biotechnology—Congresses. 2. Protein engineering—
Congresses. 3. Protein folding—Congresses. I. Himmel, Michael E.,
1952–   . II. Georgiou, George, 1959–   . III. American Chemical
Society. Division of Biochemical Technology. IV. American Chemical
Society. Meeting (202nd: 1991: New York, N. Y.). V. Title
VI. Series.

TP248.65.E59C5   1993
660′.634—dc20   92–38473
                                                CIP

The paper used in this publication meets the minimum requirements of American National
Standard for Information Sciences—Permanence of Paper for Printed Library Materials, ANSI
Z39.48–1984.   ∞

TP248
.65
E59 C5
1991
CHEM

Foreword

THE ACS SYMPOSIUM SERIES was first published in 1974 to provide a mechanism for publishing symposia quickly in book form. The purpose of this series is to publish comprehensive books developed from symposia, which are usually "snapshots in time" of the current research being done on a topic, plus some review material on the topic. For this reason, it is necessary that the papers be published as quickly as possible.

Before a symposium-based book is put under contract, the proposed table of contents is reviewed for appropriateness to the topic and for comprehensiveness of the collection. Some papers are excluded at this point, and others are added to round out the scope of the volume. In addition, a draft of each paper is peer-reviewed prior to final acceptance or rejection. This anonymous review process is supervised by the organizer(s) of the symposium, who become the editor(s) of the book. The authors then revise their papers according to the recommendations of both the reviewers and the editors, prepare camera-ready copy, and submit the final papers to the editors, who check that all necessary revisions have been made.

As a rule, only original research papers and original review papers are included in the volumes. Verbatim reproductions of previously published papers are not accepted.

M. Joan Comstock
Series Editor

Contents

MULTIFUNCTIONAL PROTEINS

Preface

Enzyme-based processes are currently recognized as crucial to many industrial interests, including pharmaceuticals, specialty chemicals, and the production of commodity chemicals and fuels. Enzymes are often the catalysts of choice when issues of specificity, mild operating conditions, and adaptability are considered. However, they are less robust under many industrial process conditions than are their chemical equivalents, especially where heat cycling, pumping shear, protease exposure, and general aging conspire to denature proteins. Also, enzymes in nature often have limited activity as a result of adaptation pressure imposed by requirements for survival. The successful use of enzymes as tools, therefore, may require an amalgam of properties not important in nature, such as the combination of catalytic and polymer binding domains to suit individual requirements.

Biocatalyst Design for Stability and Specificity features 25 chapters written by many of the leading international authorities in the fields of protein biochemistry and molecular biology. These chapters not only highlight the diversity of approaches used in understanding the function of proteins; they illustrate how this understanding is applied to improving protein design for biotechnology applications. We believe the authors collectively bring a unique perspective to enzyme biochemistry and engineering in their presentations on studies of protein structure, folding (refolding), and stability, and in their examinations of the methods (both chemical and recombinant) currently used to improve the usefulness of these enzymes.

The book is grouped into 5 major areas of interest and concern. The first section, "Protein Stability", describes ongoing research into the interactions that underly protein stability and discusses the effects of mutations on the thermodynamic properties of proteins, the relative contributions of the hydrophobic effect and hydrogen bonding on protein stability, the assessment of protein structure by circular dichroism, studies of *Trichoderma reesei* cellobiohydrolase I stability, the stabilization of proteins via metal binding, and the factors that affect the function of proteins in organic solvents. The effect of protein structure on the stability of proteins from thermophilic and psychrophilic microorganisms is discussed in Chapters 4 and 5.

"Protein Folding" emphasizes the renaturation of functional proteins from the aggregated state. Topics covered include: mutational analysis of protein aggregation in vivo, characterization of inclusion bodies, function of the GroE chaperonins, and finally the effects of detergents and cosolvents on the efficiency of protein folding.

An area of considerable interest in enzyme engineering is the relationship between the structure and function of multifunctional proteins and the design of artificial multifunctional enzymes by genetic engineering. "Multifunctional Proteins" is comprised of 4 excellent chapters on the function of natural multifunctional proteins, the genetic engineering of bifunctional enzymes, and the use of fusion to a cellulose binding domain for protein purification and immobilization.

"Design of Cellulases by Recombinant Methods" contains 4 chapters on recent advances in improving the design of cellulases through recombinant technology. Chapter 18 describes important properties of *T. reesei* cellobiohydrolase II, following carefully designed site directed mutagenesis studies, and Chapter 19 reports a successful recombinant project with another *T. reesei* enzyme, β-D-glucosidase. Chapter 20 reviews progress in the field of *Thermomonospora fusca* and bacterial cellulase cloning, and Chapter 21 describes a new model for the mechanism of cellulose hydrolysis exhibited by the *Clostridium thermocellum* cellulosome.

The last section, "Improving Natural Enzymes by Chemical Cross-Linking" is dedicated to the use of chemical modification to improve enzymes. These 4 chapters include an overview of the subject, a review of glutaraldehyde modification chemistry, and examples of successful applications of the technology.

Acknowledgments

We are grateful to the Division of Biochemical Technology of the ACS for supplying the forum for this work and for their support, along with that of Genencor International, Inc., and Merck and Company in partially funding the symposium or its functions. The program coordinators for the Division of Biochemical Technology to the ACS meeting, Jonathan Woodward and Douglas C. Cameron, deserve special commendation. We also wish to thank the organizers and moderators of the four sessions around which the symposium and book were constructed: Anne Lee, Session I; John O. Baker, Session II; Michael E. Himmel, Session III; and Sharon P. Shoemaker, Session IV. Their contribution was essential to the success of the symposium and the book. The editors wish to bring special attention to participation in the symposium by Rainier Jaenicke and Minishwar Gupta; their expense and sacrifice incurred in order to participate was greater than our own, and we respect this dedication to the field. Our Acquisitions Editor at ACS Books was Barbara C. Tansill. Her efficient processing of the manuscripts and her guidance were key to the timely publication of the book.

Last, and probably most important, we appreciate the timely and thoughtful reports of research progress or reviews of research contributed by the authors. We wish them continued good fortune in their research and in their lives.

MICHAEL E. HIMMEL
Applied Biological Sciences Branch
National Renewable Energy Laboratory
Golden, CO 80401

GEORGE GEORGIOU
Department of Chemical Engineering
The University of Texas
Austin, TX 78712

August 20, 1992

PROTEIN STABILITY

Chapter 1

Effects of Mutations on Thermodynamic Properties of Proteins

Julian M. Sturtevant

Departments of Chemistry, Molecular Biophysics, and Biochemistry, Yale University, New Haven, CT 06511

Differential scanning (DSC) and isothermal titration (ITC) microcalorimetry are employed in studying the effects of amino acid replacements on the thermodynamic properties of proteins. The proteins studied by DSC include the lysozyme of phage T4 (17 mutations), staphylococcal nuclease (9 mutations) and the lambda repressor of *E. coli* (15 mutations). ITC is used in the study of the effects of replacements in S-peptide on the binding of S-peptide to S-protein to form ribonuclease-S. Although partial explanations, based on crystallographic structures, of some of the results are presented, it seems evident that we are very far from being able to rationalize the results in any really satisfactory manner. One outstanding feature of the results is the lack of correlation between the free energy changes and the enthalpy changes produced by the replacements. The enthalpy changes are generally much larger than the free energy changes, and frequently of opposite sign.

A central problem in biophysics is to achieve a quantitative understanding of the intra- and intermolecular forces which cause biopolymers to fold into their specific native structures, and to retain these structures through various more or less severe perturbations. It seems evident that a useful way of attacking at least the second part of this problem with respect to proteins would be to make small known changes, such as single amino acid replacements, in a protein and to measure the energetic consequences thereof (1). Our present state of ignorance concerning the quantitative aspects of intermolecular forces does not permit fully satisfactory interpretations of the thermodynamic results of such experiments (2). Even a small protein of only 100 amino acid residues will probably have hundreds of energetically significant intramolecular interactions. Nevertheless, I am convinced that it is worthwhile to obtain such experimental results, if for no other

0097–6156/93/0516–0002$06.00/0

reason than to supply data with which theoretical calculations can be compared.

One of the most interesting features of many proteins is that they have perfectly cooperative structures. As nearly as we can tell, when such a structure is thermally unfolded, only two states, the initial folded state and the final unfolded state, are significantly populated. This is illustrated in Figure 1 where differential scanning calorimetric (DSC) curves of the apparent excess specific heat as a function of temperature are shown for wild type (WT) staphylococcal nuclease (SNase) at two different values of the pH. In each case the experimental data (solid curves) are very well reproduced by data (dashed curves) calculated for the transition on the basis that it obeys the van't Hoff equation

$$\frac{d \ln K}{dT} = \frac{\Delta H_{vH}}{RT^2} \qquad (1)$$

where K is the equilibrium constant for the reaction folded $\rightleftharpoons$ unfolded, T is the absolute temperature and ΔH_{vH} is the van't Hoff enthalpy, which in the case of a truly two state process will equal the calorimetric, or true, enthalpy, ΔH_{cal}. For SNase, the all-or-none model was extended to include dimerization of the unfolded protein. It is evident that at each pH there is a substantial permanent change in specific heat, which means that ΔH_{cal} is a strong function of the temperature, and it is assumed that ΔH_{vH} shows the same variation with temperature. Of course, this variation must be included in the curve fitting calculation. In the present case, at pH 3.84, ΔH_{cal} is near zero at 20°C and equal to 60 kcal mol^{-1} at 47°C.

Two important methods for obtaining biothermodynamic data for which excellent instruments are commercially available involve differential scanning calorimetry (DSC) and isothermal titration calorimetry (ITC). We employ for DSC studies the MC-2 microcalorimeter (Microcal, Inc., Northampon, MA) and the DASM-4 microcalorimeter (Biopribor, Puschchino, Moscow Region, Russia), and for ITC studies the Omega microcalorimeter (also Microcal, Inc.).

Differential Scanning Calorimetry

I will first review some of our recent DSC methods and results, some published and some unpublished. We generally evaluate the thermodynamic parameters for the unfolding transition by the curve fitting procedure indicated in Figure 1, generalized to permit ΔH_{vH} to be different from ΔH_{cal}, and to accommodate transitions made up of several two-state steps (3).

A convenient summary of the evaluated thermodynamic parameters for a mutant protein is in terms of $\Delta\Delta G_d^o$, $\Delta\Delta S_d^o$ and $\Delta\Delta H_d$ where ΔG_d^o is a standard free energy of unfolding, ΔS_d^o is the standard unfolding entropy, and ΔH_d is the enthalpy of unfolding, and the significance of $\Delta\Delta$ is as shown in equation 2,

$$\Delta\Delta J_d = \Delta J_d(\text{mutant}) - \Delta J(\text{WT}) \qquad (2)$$

with the thermodynamic parameters evaluated at the temperature of

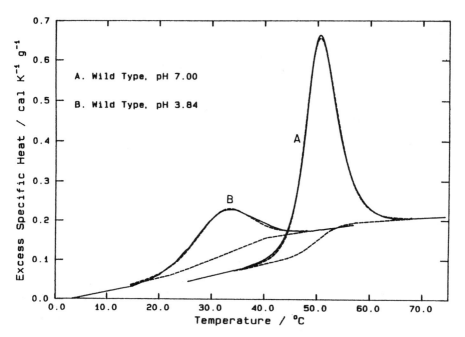

Figure 1. Differential scanning calorimetric scans showing the variation with temperature of the apparent excess specific heat of staphylococcal nuclease at pH 7.00 (curve A) and pH 3.84 (curve B). In each case the solid curve represents the observed data after subtraction of the instrumental baseline, and the dashed curves show the calculated chemical baseline and data calculated for an all-or-none model modified to include dimerization of the unfolded protein.

half-denaturation, $t_{1/2}$, of the WT protein by means of the equations

$$\Delta H_d(\text{at } T_1) = \Delta H_d(\text{at } T_2) - \Delta Cp(T_2 - T_1) \tag{3}$$

$$\Delta G_d^o(\text{at } T_1) = \Delta H_d(\text{at } T_2) \frac{T_2 - T_1}{T_2} - \Delta Cp \left[T_2 - T_1 + T_1 \ln \frac{T_1}{T_2}\right] \tag{4}$$

$$\Delta S_d^o = (\Delta H_d - \Delta G^o{}_d)/T \tag{5}$$

Here T_1 and T_2 are equal to $t_{1/2} + 273.15$ for the WT and mutant proteins respectively and ΔCp is the change in molar heat capacity accompanying the transition of the mutant protein. As mentioned above, since ΔCp is frequently as large as 2 to 3 kcal $K^{-1} mol^{-1}$, it is important that it be included in calculating $\Delta\Delta J_d$. According to the definition in equation 2, a negative value for $\Delta\Delta G^{o}_{d}$ indicates apparent destabilization (destabliization of the folded form or stabilization of the unfolded form or both) by the mutation. (To conform with the current usage in the literature, the definition of $\Delta\Delta J_{d}$ given in equation (2) is reversed from the form used in papers from this laboratory published prior to March, 1992, so that care must be used in reading the earlier papers to avoid confusion.)

DSC of T4 Lysozyme. As mentioned earlier, we have studied a total of 17 mutant forms of the lysozyme of phage T4, kindly supplied to us by Brian Matthews and Joan Wozniak of the University of Oregon. The results for the WT protein and 8 of the mutants have been published (4,5,6). In all cases, the thermal unfolding, which is reversible, occurs at a temperature which is strongly dependent on pH, and with a large change in heat capacity. These features are qualitatively similar to those illustrated in Figure 1 for SNase. For each form of T4 lysozyme the values for $t_{1/2}$ can be expressed as

$$t_{1/2} = A + B \text{ pH} \tag{6}$$

and those for ΔH_{cal} as

$$\Delta H_{cal} = \Delta H_{o} + \Delta Cp \text{ } t \tag{7}$$

the four constants being evaluated by linear least squaring. These constants are employed in the calculation of $\Delta\Delta J_{d}$ by equations 3, 4 and 5.

The results calculated for WT and the mutant T4 lysozymes at pH 2.5, where $t_{1/2}$ for the WT protein is 46.2°C, are summarized in Table I. Similar results were calculated at pH 2.0 and 3.0. The largest change in stability is an apparent destabilization of 4 kcal mol^{-1} caused by the R96H mutation, which also causes a substantial change in the entropy of denaturation. An important feature of the data in Table I is the lack of correlation with respect to either sign or size between the free energy changes and the changes in the other thermodynamic quantities. This is illustrated in Figure 2 for the seven replacements of Thr 157 which we have studied. The largest compensating entropy changes, those for I3F and I3E, amount to 49 cal $K^{-1}mol^{-1}$. It would seem that any fully satisfactory theoretical interpretation of the effects of these mutations should include an elucidation of the origins of such significant entropy and enthalpy effects.

In a recent paper Tidor and Karplus (7) undertook a simulation analysis of the effects of the R96H replacement. The complexity of such an analysis is illustrated by the fact that 44 contributions to the free energy change of converting Arg to His in the folded protein and 30 to the conversion in the unfolded form were included, giving a result in fair agreement with our experimental value. No indication of the enthalpy and entropy make-up of these free energy values was given.

Table I. Changes in Thermodynamic Parameters at pH 2.5 Produced
by Various Mutations of T4 Lysozyme

$(t_{1/2} = 46.2\,^{\circ}C,\ \Delta H_{cal} = 108\ \text{kcal mol}^{-1}$, for WT Protein at pH 2.5)

Protein	$\Delta\Delta G^{o}_{d}$	$\Delta\Delta H_{d}$	$\Delta\Delta S^{o}_{d}$	$\Delta\Delta Cp$
A82P	0.5	5	15	-110
A93P	0.5	6	18	-530
R96H	-4.0	6	32	90
G113A	0.5	5	15	310
I3F	-1.5	14	49	-470
I3E	-1.8	13	49	-60
I3L	0.85	9	25	-290
I3P	-3.0	3	19	390
I3T	-2.5	11	42	220
T157A	-0.9	3	13	170
T157E	-1.3	-12	-33	-300
T157I	-1.9	1	9	-150
T157L	-1.7	-9	-23	-260
T157N	-1.1	6	21	280
T157R	-0.6	2	7	-230
T157V	-1.6	-1	2	60
C54T:C79A	-0.8	-2	-4	-630

$\Delta\Delta G^{o}_{d}$, $\Delta\Delta H_{d}$, kcal mol^{-1}; $\Delta\Delta S^{o}_{d}$, $\Delta\Delta Cp$, cal K^{-1}mol^{-1}.
Estimated uncertainties: $\Delta\Delta G^{o}_{d}$, ± 0.4 kcal mol^{-1}; $\Delta\Delta H_{d}$, ± 4 kcal
mol^{-1} (average value); $\Delta\Delta S^{o}_{d}$, ± 10 cal K^{-1}mol^{-1}; $\Delta\Delta Cp$, ± 200 cal
K^{-1}mol^{-1}.

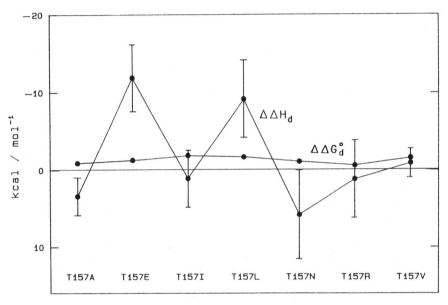

Figure 2. Values of $\Delta\Delta G_d^o$ and $\Delta\Delta H_d$ as determined by DSC at pH 2.5 for seven different replacements of T157 in T4 lysozyme, illustrating the lack of correlation frequently observed between changes in the standard free energy and enthalpy of unfolding resulting from amino acid replacements. (Adapted from ref. 5. Copyright 1991 American Chemical Society.)

Weaver and Matthews (8) determined by x-ray crystallography the structure of R96H to a resolution of 1.7Å. The authors concluded on the basis of comparisons with the structure of the WT protein, that the two most important sources of the apparent destabilization of the mutant were the loss of a helix-dipole interaction involving the C-terminus of helix 82-90, and significant strain caused by the introduction of the imidazole ring of histidine. Tidor and Karplus, on the other hand, state that the helix-dipole model is inappropriate for this case.

In the Thr 157 series, it is interesting that T157I and T157L have nearly equal values of $\Delta\Delta G_d^o$ but values of $\Delta\Delta H_d$ and $\Delta\Delta S_d^o$ differing by 10 kcal mol^{-1} and 32 cal K^{-1}mol^{-1} respectively. The x-ray data of Alber et al. (9) show that the introduction of Ile at position 157 forces the side chain of Asp 159 to move 1.1Å from its position in the WT protein, a much larger motion than caused by any of the other T157 substitutions studied. It is accordingly difficult to understand why the substitution of Leu at position 157 causes a much larger change in enthalpy than the introduction of either Ile or Val.

Because of the large values of $\Delta\Delta Cp$ in some cases, the thermodynamic parameters will vary significantly with temperature and also with pH. In the case of T157R, for example, $\Delta\Delta G_d^o$ changes from an apparent destabilization at pH 2.0 and 38.8 °C ($\Delta\Delta G_d^o$ = -1.1 kcal mol^{-1}) to a small apparent stabilization at pH 3.0 and 53.6°C ($\Delta\Delta G_d^o$ = +0.3 kcal mol^{-1}). Alber et al. (9) observed on the basis of CD melting curves that the apparent destabilization of the T157R mutant was less at pH 6.5 than at pH 2.0, probably because of the ionization of Asp 159 and the resulting formation of the Arg-Asp hydrogen-bonded ion pair indicated by the crystallographic data. The DSC result suggests that significant ionization of Asp 159 has already taken place by pH 3.0.

Dang et al. (10) have applied molecular dynamics/free energy perturbation calculations to the T157V mutation to obtain the value $\Delta\Delta G_d^o$ = -1.9±1.1 kcal mol^{-1}, in reasonable agreement with the DSC result, $\Delta\Delta G_d^o$ = -1.6±0.4 at pH 2.0. It happens that in this case the enthalpy and free energy changes are of similar magnitude.

DSC of Staphylococcal Nuclease. We have studied by means of DSC (Engelman et al., manuscript in preparation) several mutants of SNase, namely L25A, V66L, G79S, G88V, A90S and H124L, the multiple mutants V66L:G88V and V66L:G79S:G88V (11) and an unusual mutant, ΔNase, (12) formed by removing a six-residue segment from the Ω-loop of the WT protein. It was found with all these proteins that $t_{1/2}$ decreases significantly as the concentration is increased, indicating that the unfolded form of the protein is more aggregated than the folded form. In fact, good curve fits were obtained in most cases on the assumption that the folded form is monomeric while the unfolded form is nearly completely dimerized. We have arbitrarily selected 500 μM as a standard concentration at which quantities such as $\Delta\Delta G_d^o$ are calculated and compared, interpolation being based on least squared van't Hoff plots of ln concentration vs $(t_{1/2} + 273.15)^{-1}$ for $t_{1/2}$ and on least squared linear plots of ΔH_{cal} vs $t_{1/2}$ for ΔH_{cal}.

The changes in thermodynamic quantities resulting from the various mutations are listed in Table II. The first point which may be made here is that the data for the double and triple mutations indicate approximate additivity of $\Delta\Delta G_d^o$ and $\Delta\Delta H_d$. For the double mutant the calculated and observed values for $\Delta\Delta G_d^o$ are respectively +1.3 and +1.0 for the $\Delta\Delta H_d$ -31 and -24 (all in kcal mol^{-1}); similarly for the triple mutant the figures are 0 and +0.4 and -45 and -52. Approximate additivity in the effects of mutations has been observed in other cases as well, as will be discussed below.

Table II. Changes in Thermodynamic Parameters at pH 5.0 and 7.0 Produced by Various Mutations of Staphylococcal Nuclease ($t_{1/2}$ = 47.0°C, ΔH_{cal} = 64 kcal mol^{-1}, at pH 5.0, and 51.4°C, 73 kcal mol^{-1} at pH 7.0 for the WT Protein)

	pH 7.0			pH 5.0			
Protein	$\Delta\Delta G_d^o$	$\Delta\Delta H_d$	$\Delta\Delta S_d^o$	$\Delta\Delta G_d^o$	$\Delta\Delta H_d$	$\Delta\Delta S_d^o$	$\Delta\Delta Cp$
L25A	-2.6	11	-40	-2.8	10	40	300
V66L	0.8	-14	-45	0.6	-13	-45	-130
G79S	-1.3	-14	-40	-1.2	-13	-40	-250
G88V	0.5	-17	-55	0.6	-18	-60	270
A90S	-2.5	13	50	-2.6	12	45	220
H124L	1.2	2	3	1.9	3	4	-210
V66L:G88V	1.0	-24	75	1.4	-28	-90	(-1110)*
V66L:G79S:G88V	0.4	-52	-160	0.7	-41	-130	(10)*
ΔNase	1.8	7	16	2.1	4	6	-280

$\Delta\Delta G_d^o$, $\Delta\Delta H_d$, kcal mol^{-1}; $\Delta\Delta S_d^o$, $\Delta\Delta Cp$, cal K^{-1}mol^{-1}. Estimated uncertainties:$\Delta\Delta G_d^o$, ±0.4 kcal mol^{-1}; $\Delta\Delta H_d$, ±4 kcal mol^{-1} (average value); $\Delta\Delta S_d^o$ ± 10 cal K^{-1}mol^{-1}; $\Delta\Delta Cp$, ± 200 cal K^{-1}mol^{-1}.
*Based on the values observed in individual experiments at pH 5 and pH 7.

As is the case with the mutants of T4 lysozyme, there is no discernible correlation between the values for $\Delta\Delta G_d^o$ and those for $\Delta\Delta H_d$. An extreme example of this is shown by the triple mutant, for which the entropy of unfolding at pH 7.0 is reduced from 228 to 68 cal K^{-1}mol^{-1}. What might appear to be a very minor disturbance of the energetics of the molecule, as judged by the value of $\Delta\Delta G_d^o$ = 0.4 kcal mol^{-1}, obviously involves profound changes in enthalpy and entropy which are probably distributed throughout the molecule. In fact, it seems safe to assume that this huge entropy effect is mainly an increase in the entropy of the folded state due to a severe loosening of its three dimensional structure, certainly an effect which could not be predicted to result from the replacement of three amino acid residues in a protein which contains 149 residues. These considerations lead us again to emphasize the importance of including such significant thermodynamic changes in any theoretical analysis of the effects of mutations on protein energetics.

David Shortle (11), who originally prepared most of the mutants used in our study and supplied us with plasmids, investigated the thermal stability of some of these mutants and certain other ones by means of fluorescence melting curves. There are significant differences between the results obtained by Shortle et al. and our results, due at least in part to the facts that the fluorescence method can determine only van't Hoff enthalpies, and that DSC experiments require much higher protein concentrations. Shortle et al. argue, largely on the basis of the apparent enthalpy-entropy compensation exhibited by these mutants, that the mutations cause alterations in the hydration of the denatured state, and that these alterations in hydration are the primary cause of the mutational change in stability. If this argument is valid, then it would appear to follow that for other proteins the primary effects of mutations are on the unfolded rather than the folded state, since it appears to be a general rule that largely compensating enthalpy and entropy effects are characteristic of protein thermal unfolding. The apparently random distribution of $\Delta\Delta H_d$ between positive and negative values makes this seem quite unlikely, as do also the many instances of significant mutational changes observed by x-ray crystallography in the structure of the folded form. It seems evident, as discussed above, that the massive enthalpy and entropy effects shown by V66L:G79S:G88V must be almost entirely due to changes in the folded protein.

DSC of λ Repressor. In collaboration with Robert Sauer and his colleagues at M.I.T. we have looked at 14 single replacements and 1 double replacement in the N-terminal domain of the λ repressor of *E. coli* (13, 14, 15). The results observed with 6 of these mutants are shown in Figure 3 and the complete results are summarized in Table III. It is evident in the figure that the unfolded N-terminal domain has no significant effect on the unfolding of the C-terminal domain, as would be expected on the basis of Brandts' model for domain interactions (16). The one apparent exception, A66T, was found after the DSC result became available to have a previously undetected mutation, Y210H, in the C-terminal domain. The mutations causing the largest stabilizations are at buried sites. All the N-terminal peaks, except that for A66T, and all the C-terminal peaks are hypersharp and unsymmetrical for unknown reasons; only the A66T peak satisfies the two-state criterion of $\Delta H_{vH} = \Delta H_{cal}$.

Table III lists the data for 8 mutants causing apparent stabilization and 7 destabilizing mutants. Two of the latter cause unusually large drops in $t_{1/2}$. It is interesting that replacing His by Phe in the second of these causes a weak stabilization. Although any correlation between $\Delta t_{1/2}$ and ΔH_{cal} is very weak, it may be noted that all the mutants which lower $t_{1/2}$ also lower ΔH_{cal} by as much as 37 kcal mol^{-1}. This suggests that part of the mutational effect on ΔH_{cal} may in fact be a ΔCp effect. It is not possible to estimate values of ΔCp for individual mutants from complex traces such as those in Figure 3. Linear least squaring of the values of ΔH_{cal} vs $t_{1/2}$ gives $\Delta Cp = 1.13$ kcal K^{-1}mol^{-1}, with a standard deviation in ΔH_{cal} of ±7.2 kcal mol^{-1} and a coefficient of determination of only 0.7. Values of $\Delta\Delta G_d^o$, $\Delta\Delta H_d$ and $\Delta\Delta S_d^o$ are given

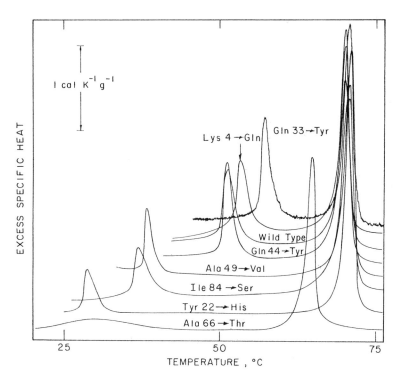

Figure 3. The DSC traces for wild type and seven mutant forms of the λ repressor of *E. coli*. This protein at pH 8.0 shows two clearly separated peaks, the low temperature one resulting from the unfolding of the N-terminal domain and the high temperature one from the unfolding of the C-terminal domain. All the amino acid replacements were located in the N-terminal domain of the protein except for an accidental one, Y210H, in the C-terminal domain. It is shown in Table III that the replacements caused a wide range of changes in the denaturational thermodynamics. (Reproduced from ref. 13. Copyright 1984 J. M. Sturtevant.)

Table III. Changes in Thermodynamic Parameters at pH 8.0 Produced by Various Mutations in the N-terminal Domain of λ Repressor ($t_{1/2}$ = 53.4°C, ΔH_{cal} = 66 kcal mol^{-1} for WT Protein at pH 8.0)

Protein	$\Delta t_{1/2}$, °C	ΔH_{cal}, kcal mol^{-1}	$\Delta\Delta G_d^o$, kcal mol^{-1}		$\Delta\Delta H_d$, kcal mol^{-1}		$\Delta\Delta S_d^o$, cal K^{-1} mol^{-1}	
			A	B	A	B	A	B
Stabilizing Mutations								
Y22F	1.9	56	0.3	0.3	-10	-12	-32	-38
K4Q	2.0	70	0.4	0.4	4	2	11	4
G46A	3.1	70	0.7	0.6	4	1	10	0
G48S	4.0	55	0.7	0.6	-11	-16	-36	-50
G48N	4.1	62	0.8	0.7	-4	-9	-15	-29
G48A	4.7	62	0.9	0.8	-4	-9	-15	-31
Q33Y	5.9	74	1.3	1.3	8	1	20	0
G46A·G48A	6.2	59	1.1	1.0	-7	-14	-25	-46
Destabilizing Mutations								
Q44Y	-0.1	60	-0	-0	-6	-6	-18	-18
E34K	-1.9	51	-0.3	-0.3	-15	-13	-45	-38
E83K	-3.6	59	-0.7	-0.7	-7	-3	-19	-7
A49V	-13.0	29	-1.2	-1.5	-37	-22	-110	-64
I84S	-14.3	49	-2.2	-2.6	-17	-1	-43	6
A66T	-22.5	40	-2.8	-3.9	-26	-1	-71	10
Y22H	-22.7	30	-2.2	-3.2	-36	-10	-103	-22

A: Calculated assuming ΔCp = 0; B: calculated assuming ΔCp = 1.13 k cal K^{-1} mol^{-1}.
Estimated uncertainties: $\Delta\Delta G_d^o$ ± 0.4 kcal mol^{-1}, $\Delta\Delta H_d$, $\Delta\Delta S_d^o$, see discussion in text.

in Table III based on $\Delta Cp = 0$ and $\Delta Cp = 1.13$ kcal $K^{-1}mol^{-1}$ as indicated. Introducing ΔCp has a negligible effect on $\Delta\Delta G_d^o$ except in the last two mutants in the table, but rather large effects on $\Delta\Delta H_d$ and $\Delta\Delta S_d^o$. In view of the large uncertainty in ΔCp, the values obtained taking $\Delta Cp = 0$ are probably to be preferred.

The largest apparent stabilization observed in this series of experiments is that of Q33Y. It was suggested to us by Gregory Petsko that this stabilization is due at least in part to the fact that the aromatic ring of Tyr 33 is oriented perpendicularly to that of Tyr 22, in the minimal energy orientation seen in crystalline benzene.

Replacement of Gly 46 by Ala in the third α-helix in the N-terminal domain led to an apparent stabilization of 0.7 kcal mol^{-1}, and of Gly 48 by Ala, Asn or Ser to stabilization of 0.9, 0.8 or 0.7 kcal mol^{-1}, respectively (15). The double mutant, with both of these Gly's replaced by Ala, showed stabilization of 1.1 kcal mol^{-1}, with rough additivity. These results are consistent with the usual view (17) that the Gly residue is a poor helix former while the Ala residue is one of the best, and Asn and Ser residues are intermediate.

Prediction of Mutational Effects; Protein Engineering.

In the above discussion we have emphasized the difficulty in accounting for the thermodynamic effects of mutations in terms of molecular energetics. However, there are many known cases where, at least in qualitative terms, changes in the thermal stability of a protein can be understood and where predicted changes in stability have been realized (18). Several examples of apparently successful explanations or predictions will be given here.

Stearman et al. (19), working with the separated dimeric N-terminal domain of λ-repressor, introduced the G46A and G48A mutations mentioned earlier, which in the holoprotein produced a total increase of $6.2°C$ in $t_{1/2}$ (15), and in addition a Y88C mutation which permitted formation of an intersubunit disulfide bond. It had previously been shown (20) that this mutation caused an increase in $t_{1/2}$ of $8°C$. The protein containing all three mutations showed $\Delta t_{1/2} = 16°C$, a very substantial apparent stabilization, probably including a contribution from decreased entropy of the unfolded state. A similar engineered disulfide bond introduced into T4 lysozyme (21) was found to enhance the stability of the protein.

Presumably there would be pharmacological or other importance in engineering an increase in thermostability for certain proteins. In this connection it should not be overlooked that nature has already designed some very stable proteins. An outstanding example of this is given by the tryptophan aporepressor of *E. coli*, hardly a thermophilic bacterium (22). This protein is a dimer of molecular weight 24.7 kDa, containing no metal or other non-amino acid component, and of ordinary appearing amino acid sequence. Yet when it is heated at pH 7.5 in 10 mM phosphate buffer containing 100 mM KCl, it undergoes unfolding and dissociation into monomeric units in a transition centered at $93°C$. If the heating is interrupted at $100°C$ and the solution cooled to $50°C$ during 30 min, the unfolding-

dissociation transition is found to be quantitatively repeated on reheating.
A striking case of additivity of mutational effects on stability as measured by thermal changes in the degree of helicity was reported by Merutka and Stellwagen (23) for the model peptide $CH_3COAEAAAKEAAAKEAAAKCONH_2$. Replacing the central Ala in an Ala_3 group by Ser lowered $t_{1/2}$, the temperature at which the content of α-helix was half the maximal value for the original peptide, by 11°C regardless of which Ala_3 group was changed. Making simultaneous replacements in two groups lowered $t_{1/2}$ by 22°C regardless of which two groups were affected, and changing all three groups caused a 31°C lowering. Replacements of the central Ala by Met were also additive, with effects approximately two-thirds as large as those produced by Ser.
Andersen et al. (24) have presented a convincing picture of an important stabilizing salt bridge in T4 lysozyme (see also 25). The x-ray structure for the C54T:C97A mutant, designated WT*, shows that His 31 and Asp 70 are well placed to form a salt bridge. Andersen et al. determined by NMR that the pK_a of His 31 is 9.05 in the folded form and 6.8 in the unfolded form, and that of Asp 70 is 0.5 in the folded and 3.5 - 4.0 in the unfolded protein. The pK_a of His 31 is 6.9 in the mutant D70N, showing that the change in this pK_a in WT* is due to the presence of Asp 70. When WT* unfolds the change in the free energy of ionization of His 31 is approximately 3 kcal mol^{-1} and that of Asp 70 is approximately 3.9 kcal mol^{-1}. Thus the salt bridge contributes at least 4-5 kcal mol^{-1} to the stabilization free energy of the protein. Correspondingly, $t_{1/2}$ for D70N is about 12°C lower than that of WT*.

Isothermal Titration Calorimetry

ITC is a very useful method for the determination of the thermodynamics of reactions, having as its main advantage over other isothermal methods that enthalpies are directly determined. Titration calorimeters have been developed to the point that a total enthalpy change of as little as a hundred microcalories is adequate for obtaining 20 points on a titration curve in a time duration of 60-90 min, provided the reaction being studied has a half time of less than a minute, and the equilibrium constant for the reaction lies in the range $10^3 M^{-1}$ to $10^8 M^{-1}$. Reaction half times greater than a minute can be handled with longer periods between injections of titrant, but a value greater than 10 min would probably lead to a serious loss of accuracy.
A curve fitting analysis of the titration data leads to a value for the equilibrium constant, K, and therefore the standard free energy change

$$\Delta G^o = -RT \ln K \qquad (8)$$

the enthalpy change, ΔH_{cal}, and therefore also the standard entropy change, ΔS^o, and a value for the number of interaction sites, N, per molecule of substrate. Titrations over a temperature range permit evaluation of the heat capacity change in the reaction, ΔCp, and the van't Hoff enthalpy, ΔH_{vH}.

In 1959, Richards and Vithayathil (*26*) observed that mild proteolysis of ribonuclease A (RNaseA) severed one peptide bond between residues 20 and 21 near the N-terminus. The product, RNase S, had full enzymic activity and unchanged x-ray structure. At low pH the peptide and protein can be separated, and at neutral pH they recombine to form RNaseS' which is indistinguishable from RNase S. We have used the Omega microcalorimeter (*27*) to study in detail the binding of modified S-peptides to S-protein to form modified RNaseS'. In our work (*28, 29*) we have used abbreviated peptides lacking the residues 16 to 20, which do not appear to have much effect on the binding, with Met 13 replaced by various other residues.

It may be noted here that the effects of mutations on this type of reaction might well be more susceptible to quantitative analysis than has been possible for protein thermal denaturations. Here one is starting with the same protein in each case and is adding 15-residue peptides none of which has significant specific structure in solution. Thus all variations in thermodynamic properties resulting from changes at position 13 can with some confidence be attributed to differences in the products formed. The crystal structures of these products are currently being determined to high resolution.

The results of our study are summarized in Table IV. The large decreases in entropy accompanying these reactions can be

Table IV. Changes in the Thermodynamic Parameters for the Modified S-peptide S-protein Interaction at pH 6.0, 5° - 25°C, Produced by Replacing M13 in the Peptide by the Indicated Residues

(WT at pH 6.0, 25°C: ΔG^{o} = -9.4 kcal mol^{-1}; ΔH = 41.3 kcal mol^{-1}; ΔS^{o} = 108.1 cal K^{-1}mol^{-1}; ΔC_p = 910 cal K^{-1}mol^{-1}

Peptide	$\Delta\Delta G^{o}(25°C)$ kcal mol^{-1}	$\Delta\Delta H(25°C)$ kcal mol^{-1}	$\Delta\Delta S^{o}(25°C)$ cal K^{-1}mol^{-1}	$\Delta\Delta C_p$ cal K^{-1}mol^{-1}
M13A	4.0	5.0	3	-50
M13ANB[a]	1.3	9.5	28	200
M13V	-0.4	4.8	17	270
M13I	-0.3	5.8	21	250
M13L	0.1	5.8	19	100
M13F	2.7	4.4	6	20

[a]α-Amino-n-butyrate residue.

largely attributed to a general tightening of the structure of the protein on addition of the peptide, as is also indicated by the observation of Rosa and Richards (*30*) that the rate of proton exchange in S-protein is 1000 times that in RNase S.

It has been argued that the heat capacity increment on protein unfolding is associated primarily with the ordering of water molecules around newly exposed non-polar groups (*31, 32, 33*). However, the differences in heat capacity shown in Table IV cannot be accounted for on that basis. With the exception of M13A and M13F, the observed values for $\Delta\Delta C_p$ are at least an order of magnitude larger than those calculated on the basis of the treatment proposed by Spolar et al.(*32*), assuming that the only differences in the non-polar surface areas that become buried are those between Met13 and the groups which replace it. It seems likely that the different peptides cause differing degrees of tightening of the S-protein, which could also be detected by measurements of proton exchange rates. This sort of effect may not be detectable by x-ray crystallography. It should be added that an additional significant contribution to ΔCp, which can become very large at temperatures above 25°C, arises from the difference between the thermal unfolding behavior of S-protein and that of RNase S' as demonstrated by DSC (*29,34*). This contribution would also probably vary between the various RNase S' products.

It is evident that, as seen for the thermal denaturation of mutant proteins, there is no correlation between the values for $\Delta\Delta G^o$ and $\Delta\Delta H$. Actually in this system the values for $\Delta\Delta G^o$ cover a much wider fractional range, -0.3 kcal mol^{-1} for M13I to 4.0 kcal mol^{-1} for M13A, than do the values for $\Delta\Delta H$. It will probably be very difficult to account quantitatively for a 4.3 kcal mol^{-1} difference between the binding free energies for these two peptides. It seems likely that the changes, and the differences in the changes, in the S-protein caused by the binding of the various S-peptides are distributed widely in the protein molecule.

Acknowledgements

The individuals from whom we have received generous supplies of proteins have been mentioned above. The author is greatly indebted to Drs. John Brandts (University of Massachusetts), Brian Matthews (University of Oregon), and Frederic Richards (Yale University) for very useful discussions and other aids. Most of the actual experimentation was carried out by my colleagues S.-J. Bae, P. Connolly, L. Ghosaini, C.-Q. Hu, N. Kishore, S. Kitamura, J. Ladbury, A. Tanaka, J. Thomson and R. Varadarajan.

Literature Cited

1. Matthews, B. W. *Biochemistry* **1987**, *26*, 6885-6888.
2. Avbelj, F.; Moult, J.; Kitson, D.H.; James, M.N.G.; Hagler, A.T. *Biochemistry* **1990**, *29*, 8658-8676.
3. Sturtevant, J.M. *Ann. Rev. Phys. Chem.* **1987**, *38*, 463-488.
4. Kitamura, S.; Sturtevant, J.M. *Biochemistry* **1989**, *28*, 3788-3792.
5. Connolly, P. R.; Ghosaini, L.; Hu, C.-Q.; Kitamura, S.; Tanaka, A.; Sturtevant, J.M. *Biochemistry* **1991**, *30*, 1887-1892.
6. Hu, C.-Q.; Kitamura, S.; Tanaka, A.; Sturtevant, J.M. *Biochemistry* **1992** *31*, 1643-1647.
7. Tidor, B.; Karplus, M. *Biochemistry* **1991**, *30*, 3217-3228.
8. Weaver, L.H.; Matthews, B.W. *J. Mol. Biol.* **1977**, *193*, 189- 199.
9. Alber, T.; Dao-pin, S.; Wilson, K.; Wozniak, J.A.; Cook, S.P.; Matthews, B.W. *Nature* **1987**, *330*, 41-46.
10. Dang, L.X.; Merz, K.M.; Kollman, P.A. *J. Am. Chem. Soc.* **1989**, *111*, 8505-8508.
11. Shortle, D.; Meeker, A.K.; Freire, E. *Biochemistry* **1988**, *27*, 4761-4768.

12. Poole, L.B.; Loveys, D.A.; Hale, S.P.; Gerlt, J.A.; Stanczyk, S.M.; Bolton, P.H. *Biochemistry* **1991**, *30*, 3621-3627.
13. Hecht, M.H.; Sturtevant, J.M.; Sauer, R.T. *Proc. Natl. Acad. Sci. USA* **1984**, *81*, 5685-5689.
14. Hecht, M.; Hehir, K.; Nelson, H.; Sturtevant, J.; Sauer, R. *J. Cellular Biochem.* **1985**, *29*, 217-224.
15. Hecht, M.H.; Sturtevant, J.M.; Sauer, R.T. *Proteins: Struct., Funct., Genet.* **1986**, *1*, 43-46.
16. Brandts, J.F.; Hu, C.-Q.; Lin, L.N. *Biochemistry* **1989** *28*, 8588-8596.
17. Chou, P.Y.; Fasman, G.D. *Advanced Enzymol.* **1978**, *47*, 45-148.
18. Matthews, B.W.; Nicholson, H.; Becktel, W.J. *Proc. Natl. Acad. Sci. USA* **1987**, *84*, 6663-6667.
19. Stearman, R.S.; Frankel, A.D.; Freire, E.; Lui, B.; Pabo, C.O. *Biochemistry* **1988**, *27*, 7571-7574.
20. Sauer, R.T.; Hehir, K.; Stearman, R.S.; Weiss, M.A.; Jeitler-Nikson, A.; Suchanek, E.G.; Pabo, C.O. *Biochemistry* **1986** *25*, 5992-5998.
21. Matsumara, M.; Matthews, B.W. *Science* **1989** *243*, 792-794.
22. Bae, S.-J.; Chou, W.-Y.; Matthews, K.S.; Sturtevant, J.M. *Proc. Natl. Acad. Sci. USA* **1988**, *85*, 6731-6732.
23. Merutka, G.; Stellwagen, E. *Biochemistry* **1990**, *29*, 894-898.
24. Andersen, D.E.; Becktel, W.J.; Dahlquist, F.W. *Biochemistry* **1990**, *29*, 2403-2408.
25. Dao-pin, S.; Sauer, U.; Nicholson, H.; Matthews, B.W. *Biochemistry* **1991**, *30*, 7142-7153.
26. Richards, F.M.; Vithayathil, P.J. *J. Biol. Chem.* **1959** *234*, 1459-1465.
27. Wiseman, T.; Williston, S.; Brandts, J.; Lin, L. *Anal. Biochem.* **1989**, *179*, 131-137.
28. Connelly, P.R.; Varadarajan, R.; Sturtevant, J.M.; Richards, F.M. *Biochemistry* **1990**, *29*, 6108-6114.
29. Varadarajan, R.; Connelly, P.R.; Sturtevant, J.M.; Richards, F.M. *Biochemistry*, in press.
30. Rosa, J.J.; Richards, F.M. *J. Mol. Biol.* **1981**, *145*, 834-851.
31. Baldwin, R.L. *Proc. Natl. Acad. Sci. USA* **1986**, *83*, 8069-8072.
32. Spolar, R.S.; Ha, J.; Record, T.M. *Proc. Natl. Acad. Sci. USA* **1989**, *86*, 8382-8385.
33. Murphy, K.P.; Privalov, P.L.; Gill, S.J. *Science* **1990**, *247*, 559-561.
34. Hearn, R.P.; Richards, F.M.; Sturtevant, J.M.; Watt, G.D. *Biochemistry* **1971**, *10*, 806-817.

RECEIVED March 31, 1992

Chapter 2

Contribution of Hydrogen Bonding and the Hydrophobic Effect to Conformational Stability of Ribonuclease T1

C. Nick Pace, Ketan Gajiwala, and Bret A. Shirley

Departments of Medical Biochemistry and Genetics, Biochemistry and Biophysics, Center for Macromolecular Design, Texas A&M University, College Station, TX 77843

When RNase T1 folds, 86 intramolecular hydrogen bonds are formed and 82% of the nonpolar side chains are buried. Twelve mutants of RNase T1 (Tyr --> Phe (5), Ser --> Ala (3), and Asn --> Ala (4)) have been prepared that remove 17 of the hydrogen bonds. Based on urea and thermal unfolding studies of these mutants, the average decrease in conformational stability due to hydrogen bonding is 1.3 kcal/mole per hydrogen bond. This estimate is in good agreement with results from several related systems. Thus, we estimate that hydrogen bonding contributes about 112 kcal/mole to the conformational stability of RNase T1, and that hydrophobic interactions make a comparable contribution to the stability. Accepting the idea that intramolecular hydrogen bonds contribute 1.3 ± 0.6 kcal/mole to the stability of systems in an aqueous environment makes it easier to understand the stability of the "molten globule" states of proteins, and the α-helical conformations of small peptides.

Most of the important tasks in living cells are carried out by proteins in which the polypeptide chain is tightly folded into a globular conformation that is essential for their biological activity. Consequently, there is great interest in the forces that stabilize globular proteins. In early discussions of protein structure, hydrogen bonding was thought to be the most important force contributing to the conformational stability. The main proponent of this view was Linus Pauling, who wrote with Mirsky in 1936 (1): "The importance of the hydrogen bond in protein structure can hardly be overemphasized". However, by the 1950s the emphasis had shifted and the importance of hydrophobic interactions was stressed first by Kauzmann (2) and later by Tanford (3), who used model compound data and calculations based on a simple model to conclude: " ⋯ the stability of the native conformation in water can be

0097–6156/93/0516–0018$06.00/0

explained ··· entirely on the basis of the hydrophobic interactions of the non-polar parts of the molecule". The view that hydrophobic interactions make a more important contribution than hydrogen bonding to globular protein stability is still widely held today. As examples from 1990, Kim and Baldwin state (*4*): "Stripping H_2O from nonpolar side chains to form a hydrophobic core provides the main source of free energy stabilizing a folded protein"; Creighton states (*5*): "Nevertheless, the hydrophobic interaction is probably the major stabilizing factor"; and, in a recent review that gives an excellent overview of the forces contributing to globular protein stability, Dill states (*6*): "More than 30 years after Kauzmann's insightful hypothesis, there is now strong accumulated evidence that hydrophobicity is the dominant force of protein folding, provided that "hydrophobic" is operationally defined in terms of the transfer of nonpolar amino acids from water into a medium that is nonpolar and preferably capable of hydrogen bonding". This is the definition for "hydrophobic" used here.

In this article, we suggest that hydrogen bonding and hydrophobic interactions make comparable contributions to the conformational stability of ribonuclease T1 and other small globular proteins. This is based on studies reported here of mutants of RNase T1 designed to improve our understanding of hydrogen bonding, and on results from a number of other laboratories published in the last five years (*7-14*).

Hydrogen Bonding in RNase T1

RNase T1 contains 293 nitrogen and oxygen atoms capable of donating or accepting hydrogen bonds, 205 are in the backbone and are in the side chains. These atoms can form a total of 503 hydrogen bonds, 312 by the backbone and 191 by the side chains, based on the hydrogen bonding capabilities given by Baker and Hubbard (*15*). Using the geometrical criteria suggested by these authors, folded RNase T1 contains 86 intramolecular hydrogen bonds with an average length of 2.95 Å. (See Table I for references and information on the hydrogen bonding analysis of RNase T1). Fifty two of these hydrogen bonds are between peptide groups in the polypeptide backbone, mostly in the secondary structure, 22 are between peptide groups and side chains, and 12 are between side chains. Another 168 hydrogen bonds to water molecules have been identified.

Our main interest is to estimate how much the intramolecular hydrogen bonds contribute to the conformational stability of RNase T1. As one approach, we have selected 12 side chains that participate in intramolecular hydrogen bonds and used site-directed mutagenesis to substitute an amino acid that removes the hydrogen bonding capability. To disrupt the folded structure as little as possible, the substitutions made were: 5 (Tyr → Phe), 3 (Ser → Ala), and 4 (Asn → Ala) substitutions. These groups are capable of participating in 2, 3, and 4 hydrogen bonds, and can serve as either hydrogen bond donors or acceptors. Table I lists the side chains selected, and relevant information about the hydrogen bonds of each in wild type RNase T1. Note that nine of the groups form one hydrogen bond, one forms two hydrogen bonds, and two form three hydrogen bonds. The average donor-acceptor distance for these 17 hydrogen bonds is 2.93 Å.

Table I. RNase T1 Hydrogen Bonds Removed by Amino Acid Substitutions[a]

Residue	H-Bond & partner		Length(Å)	Angle(°)	%Buried	
Tyr 11	OH ••• OD2	Asp 76	2.69	132	99	99
Tyr 42	OH ••• OD1	Asn 44	2.97	133	98	99
Tyr 56	OH ••• O	Val 52	2.83	157	90	73
Tyr 57	OH ••• OE2	Glu 82	2.56	124	85	70
Tyr 68	OH ••• O	Gly 71	2.68	139	99	98
Ser 12	OH ••• OH	Ser 14	2.71	131	54	88
	OH ••• N	Asp 15	3.24	134		88
Ser 17	OH ••• O	Ser 13	3.19	136	26	24
Ser 64	OH ••• N	Asp 66	3.17	115	53	91
Asn 9	ND2 ••• OD1	Asp 76	2.89	137	66	57
Asn 36	OD1 ••• OH	Ser 35	3.01	115	28	30
Asn 44	ND2 ••• O	Phe 48	2.90	137	81	76
	OD1 ••• N	Phe 48	3.16	102		100
	OD1 ••• OH	Tyr 42	2.97	133		100
Asn 81	OD1 ••• N	Asn 83	2.97	114	100	100
	OD1 ••• N	Gln 85	2.91	143		100
	ND2 ••• OE1	Gln 85	2.94	126		99

[a]The analysis of the hydrogen bonding was done with a program written by Presta and Rose (62) and is based on the 1.5 Å crystal structure determined by Martinez-Oyanedel et al. (51). Only hydrogen bonds with lengths greater than 3.5 Å and angles greater than 90° were included. Groups that form three center hydrogen bonds, such as some of the amide NH groups in the α-helix, were counted only once.
[b]The accessibility (% buried) of the side chain (e.g., for Ser, $-CH_2-OH$), and of the individual group that actually forms the hydrogen bond (e.g., for Ser, -OH) are given in the last two columns. The accessibilities were estimated using the Lee and Richards Program (25).

Measured Changes in Stability

The unfolding of RNase T1 has been shown to closely approach a two-state folding mechanism (*16, 17*), and the conformational stability has been carefully measured under a variety of conditions (*17, 18*). For our previous studies, wild type RNase T1 had Gln at position 25, Gln 25-RNase T1. This is the RNase T1 first isolated in 1957 by Sato and Egami (*19*) and used for most of the subsequent studies in countries other than Germany. However, all of the crystal structures determined by Saenger's group (*20*) have been determined with a RNase T1 variant with Lys at position 25, Lys 25-RNase T1. For this reason and also because the solubility and conformational stability of Lys 25-RNase T1 are greater than for Gln 25-RNase T1 (*21*), we plan to denote Lys 25-RNase T1 as wild type in the future. Thus, all of the RNase T1 mutants discussed here have Lys at position 25.

The differences in conformational stability between wild type RNase T1 and the hydrogen bonding mutants were determined using both urea and thermal unfolding experiments. As explained elsewhere (*22*), an analysis of urea unfolding experiments yields ΔG as a function of urea concentration, and an analysis of thermal unfolding experiments yields ΔG as a function of temperature. From plots of these data, the midpoints of the transitions (where $\Delta G = 0$), $(\text{urea})_{1/2}$ or T_m, and measures of the steepness of the transitions, m or ΔS_m (the slopes of plots of ΔG versus urea, m, or temperature, ΔS_m), can be determined. These parameters are listed in Table II along with estimates of the difference in stability, $\Delta(\Delta G)$, from both the urea and thermal unfolding experiments. It can be seen that the estimates from the two different experiments are in excellent agreement. This need not have been the case because the results apply to different sets of conditions: 25°C in the presence of 2.9 to 6.3 M urea for the results from urea unfolding, and 42 to 55°C in the absence of urea for the results from thermal unfolding. The close agreement between the two sets of data gives us considerable confidence that the measured differences in stability are quite reliable.

Contribution of Hydrogen Bonding

A difficult problem in interpreting results from stability studies of mutant proteins is how to correct for the contribution of conformational entropy to the observed differences in stability. Conformational entropy can effect the $\Delta(\Delta G)$ values in several ways. First, the amino acid side chain can effect rotation around the N-C_α, ϕ, and $\text{C}_\alpha\text{-C}_{\text{carbonyl}}$, ψ, bonds in the unfolded protein (*23*). This is especially important for substitutions involving Pro residues where rotation around ϕ is largely eliminated, and for substitutions involving Gly residues where rotation around both ϕ and ψ is much less restricted. This effect has been investigated experimentally with mutants of T4 lysozyme (*24*). This effect should make an insignificant contribution for the three types of mutants studied here. Second, conformational entropy can contribute to $\Delta(\Delta G)$ for any amino acid substitution that changes the number of bonds in the side chain since rotation around these bonds will generally be more restricted in the folded

Table II. Parameters Characterizing the Urea and Thermal Unfolding of Wild Type RNase T1 (Lys 25-Rnase T1) and Twelve Hydrogen Bonding Mutants in 30 mM MOPS Buffer, pH 7 [a]

Protein	Urea Unfolding			Thermal Unfolding			
	m	$(urea)_{1/2}$	$\Delta(\Delta G)$	ΔH_m	ΔS_m	T_m	$\Delta(\Delta G)$
	cal/M	M	kcal	kcal	cal/°C	°C	kcal
RNase T1	1210	5.30		110	339	50.9	
Tyr 11 Phe	1270	3.56	-2.11	101	317	44.9	-2.03
Tyr 42 Phe	1170	6.24	1.14	106	325	54.3	1.15
Tyr 56 Phe	1260	4.65	-0.78	99	306	48.8	-0.71
Tyr 57 Phe	1285	4.88	-0.50	107	332	49.6	-0.44
Tyr 68 Phe	1320	4.17	-1.36	89	279	46.9	-1.35
Ser 12 Ala	1275	4.29	-1.23	99	309	47.7	-1.08
Ser 17 Ala	1215	5.85	0.67	109	334	52.6	0.57
Ser 64 Ala	1375	4.11	-1.44	104	324	46.3	-1.56
Asn 9 Ala	1275	4.56	-0.90	101	313	48.8	-0.71
Asn 36 Ala	1310	5.31	0.03	111	344	50.9	0.00
Asn 44 Ala	1300	3.59	-2.08	91	287	45.4	-1.86
Asn 81 Ala	1435	2.92	-2.87	91	287	42.3	-2.91

[a] m and ΔS_m are the slopes of plots of ΔG versus urea and T, respectively; and $(urea)_{1/2}$ and T_m are the midpoints ($\Delta G = 0$) of urea and thermal denaturation curves (22). For the urea data, $\Delta(\Delta G) = \Delta[(urea)_{1/2}] \times m$ (wild type). For the thermal data, $\Delta(\Delta G) = \Delta T_m \times \Delta S_m$ (wild type). Based on many independent experiments, the uncertainties are estimated to be ±50 in m, ±0.05 in $(urea)_{1/2}$, ±15 in ΔS_m, and ±0.5 in T_m. These give rise to an uncertainty of about ±0.25 kcal/mole in the $\Delta(\Delta G)$ values.

protein than in the unfolded protein. Finally, conformational entropy can contribute to $\Delta(\Delta G)$ for any mutation that fills or creates a hole in the folded protein. Little is known about these latter two effects. Richards (25) has shown that Tyr and Phe residues occupy almost the same volume in folded proteins, that Ser residues are $\approx$ 8 Å^3 larger than Ala residues, and that Asn residues are $\approx$ 44 Å^3 larger than Ala residues. For comparison, adding a -CH$_2$- or CH$_3$ group increases the volume of the residue by $\approx$ 26 Å^3. On reflection, it seems likely that conformational entropy will make a smaller contribution to the measured $\Delta(\Delta G)$ values for Tyr --> Phe and Ser --> Ala mutants than for any other of the mutations that can be used to study hydrogen bonding or hydrophobic interactions, and may well be less than the experimental error for our $\Delta(\Delta G)$ values. For the Asn --> Ala mutants, the contribution of conformational entropy should be larger, but the magnitude is unknown and there is presently no way to make corrections.

For each of the three types of amino acid substitutions reported here, the amino acid side chain in wild type RNase T1 is less hydrophobic than the side chain in the mutant. This effect by itself is expected to increase the stability of the mutants relative to wild type RNase T1, and will surely contribute to the measured $\Delta(\Delta G)$ listed in Table II. We will be able to get a more accurate assessment of the contribution of hydrogen bonding to the differences in stability if we can correct, at least approximately, for this effect. Measurements in several different solvent systems have been used to assess the magnitude of hydrophobic interactions for the amino acid side chains (26-30). In Table III (A), we give estimates of the free energy of transfer, ΔG_{tr}, of a -CH$_2$- group from several different solvent systems to water. The question is which of these solvents is the best model for the interior of a protein? Hexane and cyclohexane are surely too nonpolar, and formamide and methanol are surely too polar. All of the other solvents give comparable ΔG_{tr} values and, consequently, we have chosen to use the complete set of data available for n-octanol (28) to make the corrections described in Table IV, and for the calculations presented below in Table V. Note that the octanol data are consistent with the definition suggested by Dill (6) (see the Introduction). The octanol phase in the partitioning experiments used to determine the ΔG_{tr} values is capable of hydrogen bonding since it contains 2.5 M H$_2$O in addition to the octanol. Thus, the ΔG_{tr} values should reflect only changes in hydrophobicity and not hydrogen bonding.

In support of this choice, studies of hydrophobic interactions based on experimental results from mutant proteins generally show reasonable correlations with either the octanol data (31-33) or the ethanol data (34, 35), although the magnitude of the effect may be larger than predicted (32, 34, 36, 37). The best results to consider are for Ile --> Val mutants since they differ by only a -CH$_2$- group and this will minimize the size of the hole in the mutant, and possible conformational entropy effects. (Leu --> Val mutants are more likely to have unfavorable steric effects). Results for nine Ile --> Val mutants from four different proteins are given in Table III (B). The average $\Delta(\Delta G)$ is 1.1 ± 0.3 kcal/mole. This is 50% higher than the ΔG_{tr} value for a -CH$_2$- group based on the octanol data. Thus, these results point out the possibility that the ΔG_{tr} values from the octanol data might underestimate the contribution of hydrophobic interactions. Some possible explanations for this have been discussed (5, 32, 38).

Table III. ΔG_{tr} (solvent ---> water) Values for a -CH$_2$- Group Based on Studies with Model Compounds (A), and $\Delta(\Delta G)$ Values for Ile ---> Val Mutants (B) (kcal/mole)

A		B		
Solvent	ΔG_{tr}	Protein	Residue	$\Delta(\Delta G)$
Formamide[26]	0.32	S. Nuclease[36]	15	0.8
N-methylacetamide[a,27]	0.74		18	1.1
Acetone[26]	0.67		72	1.8
Methanol[26]	0.60		92	0.5
Ethanol[26]	0.67		139	1.5
Butanol[26]	0.73	Barnase[32]	88	1.3
Heptanol[26]	0.73		96	1.2
Octanol[a,28]	0.73	Gene 5 protein[37]	47	1.2
Cyclohexane[a,29]	0.88	T4 lysozyme[31]	3	<u>0.5</u>
Hexane[a,30]	1.00	Average = 1.1 ± 0.3 kcal/mole		

[a]The average of the difference between the ΔG_{tr} values for Leu & Val and for Ile is used for these solvents.

Table IV. Estimate of the Contribution of Hydrogen Bonding to the Measured Differences in Stability

Protein	H-bonds[a]	$\Delta(\Delta G)$[b]	$\Delta(\Delta G)$[c]	$\Delta(\Delta G)$/H-bond
	number	kcal/mol	kcal/mol	kcal/mol
Tyr 11 Phe	1	-2.07	-3.2	-3.2
Tyr 42 Phe	1	1.15	0	0
Tyr 56 Phe	1	-0.75	-1.8	-1.8
Tyr 57 Phe	1	-0.47	-1.4	-1.4
Tyr 68 Phe	1	-1.36	-1.5	-2.5
Ser 12 Ala	2	-1.16	-1.4	-0.7
Ser 17 Ala	1	0.62	0	0
Ser 64 Ala	1	-1.50	-1.7	-1.7
Asn 9 Ala	1	-0.81	-1.6	-1.6
Asn 36 Ala	1	0.02	-0.6	-0.6
Asn 44 Ala	3	-1.97	-3.0	-1.0
Asn 81 Ala	3	-2.89	-4.1	-1.4

[a]The number of intramolecular hydrogen bonds in wild type RNase T1 (see Table I).
[b]This is the average of the $\Delta(\Delta G)$ values in Table III from urea and thermal unfolding experiments.
[c]The $\Delta(\Delta G)$ values in the preceding column have been corrected for the effect of differences in hydrophobicity between the amino acid in wild type RNase T1 and the mutants by multiplying the following $\Delta(\Delta G_{tr})$ values: -1.1 (Tyr ---> Phe), -0.4 (Ser ---> Ala), and -1.2 (Asn ---> Ala) (in kcal/mole) by the accessibility of the side chain in the wild type protein given in Table I, as described in the text. In addition, for the Ser 17 Ala mutant a -0.5 kcal/mole correction was applied to correct for the differential effect that the two residues have on the stability of the α-helix, as described in the text.

Table V. Contribution of Hydrophobic Interactions to the Conformational Stability
of RNase T1

Side Chain	#Present	#Buried[a]	ΔG_{tr}[b]	#Buried x ΔG_{tr}
Trp	1	1.0	3.1	3.1
Phe	4	3.8	2.4	9.2
Ile + Leu	5	4.3	2.4	10.3
Val	8	6.7	1.7	11.4
Tyr	9	7.7	1.3	10.0
Cys	4	3.2	1.3	4.2
Pro	4	3.2	1.0	3.2
Thr	6	3.3	0.4	1.3
Ala	7	4.7	0.4	1.9
His	3	2.2	0.2	0.4
Ser	15	3.9	0.0	0.0
Gln	2	1.3	-0.3	-0.4
Asn	9	5.0	-0.8	-4.0
-CH_2-[c]	29	19.4	0.7	13.6
				64.3 kcal/mol

[a]Calculated with the Lee & Richards accessibility program (25).
[b]Fauchere and Pliska (28) (ΔG_{tr}: n-octanol ---> water).
[c]-CH_2- groups from the Lys, Arg, Glu, and Asp side chains.

The corrections made in Table IV take into account the difference between the ΔG_{tr} values for the pairs: Tyr-Phe (1.1 kcal/mol), Asn-Ala (1.2 kcal/mol), and Ser-Ala (0.4 kcal/mol); and the accessibility of the side chain in the wild type protein estimated using the Lee and Richards procedure (*25*). (The accessibility of each of the side chains in wild type RNase T1 is given in Table I). One further correction was made for the Ser 17 Ala mutant because it occurs at a largely exposed site in the α-helix of RNase T1. Recent studies of peptides have provided quantitative estimates of the helix-forming tendencies of the amino acids (*39-42*). The Ser 17 Ala substitution is expected to stabilize the mutant because Ala has a greater helix-forming tendency than Ser. The predicted stabilization is 0.51 kcal/mole based on the data of Lyu et al. (*40*), 0.46 kcal/mole based on the data of Merutka and Stellwagen (*41*), and 0.42 kcal/mole based on the data of O'Neil and DeGrado (*42*). A value of 0.5 kcal/mole was used for the correction of the Ser 17 Ala data in Table IV.

Before the corrections, three of the $\Delta(\Delta G)$ values were positive, i.e., the mutants were more stable than wild type RNase T1. After the corrections, two of the $\Delta(\Delta G)$ values are zero and the rest are negative, ranging as high as -4.1 kcal/mole for the Asn 81 Ala mutant that potentially removes three hydrogen bonds. On a per hydrogen bond basis, the values range from 0 to -3.2 kcal/mole with an average value of -1.3 kcal/mole. Thus, we think the $\Delta(\Delta G)$ values given in the last two columns in Table IV are due mainly to changes in the hydrogen bonding in the mutants.

The results in Table IV cannot be interpreted with any certainty until three-dimensional structures are available for the mutant proteins. (All of the mutants have enzyme activity suggesting that their conformations do not differ too much from wild type RNase T1). A key question is what happens to the hydrogen bonding partner in the mutants: does it form a new intramolecular hydrogen bond, does it form a hydrogen bond to a water molecule, or does it fail to form any hydrogen bonds? In the first case, the $\Delta(\Delta G)$ value should be close to zero if the new hydrogen bond is approximately equivalent to the hydrogen bond in wild type RNase T1. This may be the case for the two mutants for which $\Delta(\Delta G) \approx 0$. In the second case, the $\Delta(\Delta G)$ value would give the estimate that we are most interested in, namely, what the formation of a single intramolecular hydrogen bond contributes to the conformational stability of the protein. We argue below that this is the case for most of the mutants studied here. In the final case, the $\Delta(\Delta G)$ values should be considerably more negative because now both the loss of the intramolecular hydrogen bond, and the formation of hydrogen bonds to water in the unfolded protein by the unpaired partner will contribute to the decrease in conformational stability. This may be the reason that the $\Delta(\Delta G)$ value for Tyr 11 Phe is considerably more negative than any of the other values.

For the Tyr 11 hydrogen bond, neither the hydrogen bond donor nor acceptor forms a hydrogen bond with water in wild type RNase T1. Furthermore, the side chains of Tyr 11 and Asp 76 are almost completely buried (99%). Thus, it is certainly possible that the carboxyl group of Asp 76 may not be able to form a hydrogen bond in the Tyr 11 Phe mutant, and that this contributes to the very negative $\Delta(\Delta G)$ value that is observed. In addition, the hydrogen bond lost is a good hydrogen bond and it is probably to a charged acceptor since Asp 76 is likely to be ionized at pH 7. There is no evidence from the titration curve for RNase T1 (*43*) or from the pH dependence of the stability (*44*) for the presence of a carboxyl group with a pK of 7 or higher. Note that the hydrogen bonds of Tyr 57 and Asn 9 are also probably to charged acceptors.

For all of the other hydrogen bonds considered here, either the hydrogen bond donor or acceptor forms a hydrogen bond with a water molecule in addition to the intramolecular hydrogen bonds described in Table I. For this reason and because more room is available for hydrogen bonding to water molecules in the mutants, we think that the hydrogen bonding partner will most often form a hydrogen bond to a water molecule in the mutant. Since the same group should also hydrogen bond to water molecules in the unfolded protein, they should no longer contribute significantly to the conformational stability through hydrogen bonding. On this basis, we assume that the eight $\Delta(\Delta G)$ values between -0.6 and -1.8 kcal/mole in the last column of Table IV give the contribution of single hydrogen bonds to the conformational stability of RNase T1. The average of these eight values is -1.3 kcal/mole which does not differ significantly from the average of -1.3 kcal/mole for all twelve of the $\Delta(\Delta G)$ values. We will see below that this estimate is in good agreement with estimates from completely different systems.

Related Studies of Hydrogen Bonding

The longstanding question is whether the formation of intramolecular hydrogen bonds in folded proteins makes a net favorable contribution to protein stability, i.e., is ΔG favorable for the reaction:

$$(>C=O\cdots(H_2O)_2 + H_2O\cdots H\text{-}N<)_{water} \longleftrightarrow (>C=O\cdots H\text{-}N<)_{protein}$$

Pauling and Corey (45) thought so: "With proteins in an aqueous environment the effective energy of hydrogen bonds is not so great, inasmuch as the difference between the energy of the system with the N-H$\cdots$O hydrogen bonds surrounded by water and a system with the N-H group and the O atom forming hydrogen bonds with water molecules may be no more than around 2 kcal/mole". However, a variety of model compound studies failed to give an unequivocal answer, and some even suggested that the hydrogen bonds with water would be favored (See Dill (6) for a review of this literature). These studies strengthened the idea that hydrophobic interactions are the dominant force in protein folding.

With the advent of site-directed mutagenesis, it has been possible to estimate ΔG for the hydrogen bonding reaction shown above more directly. Fersht (7) summarized these studies and concluded "$\cdots$an individual uncharged hydrogen bond contributes some 0.5 to 1.8 kcal/mole to binding energy$\cdots$." Similar estimates had been obtained much earlier in studies with nucleic acids. In 1964 Crothers and Zimm (46) suggested that each hydrogen bond between the bases in double-helical nucleic acids contributes 1 kcal/mole to the stabilizing free energy. This estimate has since been substantiated by extensive studies by Turner's group (8). More recent studies of enzyme-substrate (13), protein-sulfate (14), and protein-base (9) hydrogen bonds give comparable estimates. Why the intramolecular hydrogen bonds are more favorable than the hydrogen bonds to water is not clear. It could be due to stronger electrostatic interactions in the more nonpolar, solid-like environment of the intramolecular hydrogen bonds, or differences in entropy effects (*5, 6*). In any event, the estimates of the contribution of individual hydrogen bonds to the conformational stability of RNase T1 given in Table IV are in good agreement with other studies of hydrogen bonding in an aqueous environment.

The Conformational Stability of RNase T1

The major force favoring the unfolding of proteins is conformational entropy. In the folded protein, rotation around the bonds in the backbone and side chains will generally be more limited than in the unfolded protein. Kauzmann (*47*) made a rough guess that this would favor unfolding by about 1.2 kcal/mole per residue, and Privalov (*48*) has pointed out that this is consistent with one interpretation of experimental results on the thermodynamics of unfolding of small, monomeric globular proteins. (See Dill et al. (*49*) for a method of estimating the conformational entropy based on a different approach that gives a considerably lower estimate). Using this estimate, conformational entropy would favor unfolding by 125 kcal/mole for RNase T1. Experimental studies (*50*) have shown that this would be lowered by about 7 kcal/mole due to the restraints imposed by the two disulfide bonds in RNase T1. Thus, this admittedly crude estimate suggests that conformational entropy favors unfolding by ≈ 118 kcal/mole. How is this overcome?

The approach used to estimate the contribution of hydrophobic interactions to the conformational stability of RNase T1 is given in Table 5. We assume that all of the side chains are fully exposed in the unfolded protein and estimate the number of side chains buried in the folded protein using the Lee and Richards algorithm (*25*) and the 1.5 Å resolution crystal structure of RNase T1 (*51*). The ΔG_{tr} values are based on the octanol data. This analysis suggests that hydrophobic interactions contribute 64 kcal/mole favoring folded RNase T1. Based on the experimental studies of Ile --> Val mutants (Table 3 (B)), these ΔG_{tr} values may be too low. If the ΔG_{tr} values are increased by 50%, the contribution of hydrophobic interactions becomes 96 kcal/mole. Spolar et al. (*52*) have used a related approach based on a different set of model compound data (ΔC_p measurements of a series of hydrocarbons) to conclude that the contribution of hydrophobic interactions can be estimated using: ΔG (hydrophobic interactions) = $(80 \pm 10) \times \Delta C_p$. Values of $\Delta C_p = 1220$ (*53*), 1240 (*54*), 1590 (*54*), and 1650 (*55*) cal/mole/K have been determined for RNase T1 unfolding using different approaches. These ΔC_p values lead to estimates of the contribution of hydrophobic interactions to the stability of 98 to 132 kcal/mole, which is larger than the estimate based on the octanol data (Table III (A)), but comparable to the estimate based on the larger ΔG_{tr} values (Table III (B)). These should be regarded as upper estimates of the contribution of hydrophobic interactions to the stability because they assume that the nonpolar side chains are completely accessible to solvent in the unfolded protein. There is mounting evidence that RNase T1 (*44, 56*) and other proteins (*57*) do not unfold completely after urea or thermal denaturation.

The 17 intramolecular hydrogen bonds described in Table I are typical of the 86 intramolecular hydrogen bonds observed in folded RNase T1. Based on the results in Table IV, we suggest that the average hydrogen bond in RNase T1 contributes 1.3 kcal/mole to the conformational stability. This leads to the conclusion that hydrogen bonding contributes 112 kcal/mole to the conformational stability of RNase T1.

So, we suggest that hydrogen bonding and hydrophobic interactions make comparable contributions to the conformational stability of RNase T1. Note that the sum of these stabilizing interactions is considerably greater than our estimate of the destabilizing contribution from conformational entropy. There are, of course, a number of other forces that will contribute to the conformational stability that we have not considered. We will mention two that will favor unfolding.

As noted above, unfilled hydrogen bonds in the folded protein should decrease the conformational stability because hydrogen bonding to water molecules will occur when the protein unfolds. In terms of groups, 41 of the 293 groups capable of hydrogen bonding do not form intramolecular hydrogen bonds and do not appear to form hydrogen bonds to water molecules in the crystal structure. (In terms of hydrogen bonds, 165 of the 503 possible hydrogen bonds are not formed). However, the extent of hydrogen bonding with water molecules in solution is sure to be greater because only those water molecules that are largely immobilized will be observed in the crystal structure. Out of the 41 groups that are not hydrogen bonded, only one (the N-H group of Val 52) is completely buried, and seven are actually hyperexposed compared to the model tripeptide used to estimate the accessibility (25). Thus, it seems likely that most of these 41 groups will be at least partially hydrogen bonded to water molecules in the folded protein. Nevertheless, unfilled hydrogen bonds in the folded protein will surely contribute unfavorably to the conformational stability, but it is not possible to estimate the magnitude of this contribution at present.

Another factor that will favor unfolding is the transfer of peptide groups from a more nonpolar environment to water on unfolding. For RNase T1, about 70% of the peptide groups are buried in the folded protein. Based on model compound data, the ΔG_{tr} of a hydrogen bonded peptide group from octanol to water is about -1.1 kcal/mole (58). Thus, this is potentially a large contribution favoring unfolding that is generally not considered.

Concluding Remarks

On folding, RNase A forms 129 (59) and α-chymotrypsin 217 (60) intramolecular hydrogen bonds. Using 1.3 kcal/mole per hydrogen bond as above, suggests that hydrogen bonding contributes 168 and 282 kcal/mole to the stability of these two proteins. Using the approach outlined in Table V, we estimate that hydrophobic interactions will contribute 111 kcal/mole to the conformational stability of RNase A, and 205 kcal/mole to the conformational stability of α-chymotrypsin. Thus, RNase T1 is not unique, and we do not agree that " ⋯ hydrophobicity is the dominant force of protein folding" (6). We suggest instead that hydrogen bonding and hydrophobic interactions make comparable contributions to the conformational stability of small, monomeric globular proteins.

The evidence is strong that most intramolecular hydrogen bonds contribute 1.3 ± 0.6 kcal/mole to the stability of structures such as globular proteins and double-helical nucleic acids in an aqueous environment. Accepting this makes it easier to understand the stability of "molten globules" (*4, 5, 61*) and of the α-helical conformations observed with some small peptides (*4*).

Acknowledgments

This research was supported by grants from NIH (GM 37039), the Robert A. Welch Foundation (A-1060), the Tom & Jean McMullin Professorship, and the Bill & Wanda Pace Trust. We thank Udo Heinemann & Wolfram Saenger for providing us with the 1.5 Å crystal structure of RNase T1, and Leonard Presta and George Rose for providing us with their program for analyzing hydrogen bonding.

Literature Cited

1. A. E. Mirsky; L. Pauling, *Proc. Nat. Acad. Sci. U.S.A.* **22**, *439* (1936).
2. W. Kauzmann, *Adv. Prot. Chem.* **14**, *1* (1959).
3. C. Tanford, *J. Am. Chem. Soc.* **84**, *4240* (1962).
4. P. S. Kim and R. L. Baldwin, *Annu. Rev. Biochem.* **59**, *631* (1990).
5. T. E. Creighton, *Biochem. J.* **270**, *1* (1990).
6. K. A. Dill, *Biochemistry* **29**, *7133* (1990).
7. A. R. Fersht, *Trends Biochem. Sci.* **12**, *310* (1987).
8. S. M. Freier et al., *Biochemistry* **25**, *3214* (1986).
9. D. R. Lesser, M. R. Kurpiewski, L. Jen-Jacobson, *Science* **250**, *776* (1990).
10. B. L. Bass and T. R. Cech, *Nature* **308**, *820* (1984).
11. N. K. Tanner and T. R. Cech, *Biochemistry* **26**, *3330* (1987).
12. I. P. Street, C. R. Armstrong, S. G. Withers, *Biochemistry* **25**, *6021* (1986).
13. J. Steyaert, C. Opsomer, L. Wyns, P. Stanssens, *Biochemistry* **30**, *494* (1991).
14. J. J. He and F. A. Quiocho, *Science* **251**, *1479* (1991).
15. E. N. Baker and R. E. Hubbard, *Prog. Biophys. Molec. Biol.* **44**, *97* (1984).
16. J. A. Thomson, B. A, Shirley, G. R. Grimsley, C. N. Pace, *J. Biol. Chem.* **264**, *11614* (1989).
17. T. Kiefhaber et al., *Biochemistry* **29**, *8250* (1990).
18. C. N. Pace, *Trends Biochem. Sci.* **15**, *14* (1990).
19. K. Sato and F. Egami, *J. Biochem. (Tokyo)* **44**, *753* (1957).
20. C. N. Pace, U. Heinemann, U. Hahn, W. Saenger, *Angew. Chem. Int. Ed.* **30**, *343* (1991).
21. B. A. Shirley, P. Stanssens, J. Steyaert, C. N. Pace, *J. Biol. Chem.* **264**, *11621* (1989).
22. C. N. Pace, B. A. Shirley, J. A. Thomson, in Protein Structure: a practical approach, T. E. Creighton, Ed. (IRL Press, Oxford, 1989), p.311.
23. G. Nemethy, S. J. Leach, H. A. Scheraga, *J. Phys. Chem.* **70**, *998* (1966).
24. B. W. Matthews, H. Nicholson, W. J. Becktel, *Proc. Nat. Acad. Sci. U.S.A.* **84**, *6663* (1987).

25. F. M. Richards, *Ann. Rev. Biophys. Bioeng.* **6**, *151* (1977).
26. E. J. Cohn and J. T. Edsall, Proteins, Amino Acids, and Peptides (Hafner Publishing, New York, 1965) p. 212.
27. S. Damodaran and K. B. Song, *J. Biol. Chem.* **261**, *7220* (1986).
28. J. -L. Fauchere and V. E. Pliska, *Eur. J. Med. Chem.- Chem. Therm.* **18**, *369* (1983).
29. A. Radzicka and R. Wolfenden, *Biochemistry* **27**, *1644* (1988).
30. J. H. Fendler, F. Nome, J. Nagyvary, *J. Mol. Evol.* **6**, *215* (1975).
31. M. Matsumura, W. J. Becktel, B. W. Matthews, *Nature* **334**, *406* (1988).
32. J. T. Kellis, K. Nyberg, A. R. Fersht, *Biochemistry* **28**, *4914* (1989).
33. A. A. Pakula and R. T. Sauer, *Nature* **344**, *363* (1990).
34. K. Yutani, K. Ogasahara, T. Tsujita, Y. Sugino, *Proc. Nat. Acad. Sci. U.S.A.* **84**, *4441* (1987).
35. M. Matsumura et al., *Eur. J. Biochem.* **171**, *715* (1988).
36. D. Shortle, W. E. Stites, A. K. Meeker, *Biochemistry* **29**, *8033* (1990).
37. W. S. Sandberg and T. C. Terwilliger, *Science* **245**, *54* (1989).
38. J. Bello, *J. Theor. Biol.* **67**, *335* (1977).
39. S. Padmanabhan et al., *Nature* **344**, *268* (1990).
40. P. C. Lyu, M. I. Liff, L. A. Marky, N. R. Kallenbach, *Science* **250**, *669* (1990).
41. G. Merutka and E. Stellwagen, *Biochemistry* **29**, *894* (1990).
42. K. T. O'Neil and W. F. Degrado, *Science* **250**, *646* (1990).
43. S. Iida and T. Ooi, *Biochemistry* **8**, *3897* (1969).
44. C. N. Pace, D. L. Laurents, J. A. Thomson, *Biochemistry* **29**, *2564* (1990).
45. L. Pauling and R. B. Corey, *Proc. Nat. Acad. Sci. U.S.A.* **37**, *729* (1954).
46. D. M. Crothers and B. H. Zimm, *J. Mol. Biol.* **9**, *1* (1964).
47. W. Kauzmann, in The Mechanism of Enzyme Action, W. D. McElroy and B. Glass, Eds., The Johns Hopkins Press: Baltimore, MD, 1954.
48. P. L. Privalov, *Adv. Prot. Chem.* **33**, *167* (1979).
49. K. A. Dill, D. O. V. Alonso, K. Hutchinson, *Biochemistry* **28**, *5439* (1989).
50. C. N. Pace, G. R. Grimsley, J. A. Thomson, B. J. Barnett, *J. Biol. Chem.* **263**, *11820* (1988).
51. J. Martinez-Oyanedel, U. Heinemann, W. Saenger, *J. Mol. Biol.* **222**, *335* (1991).
52. R. S. Spolar, J. -H. Ha, M. T. Record, Jr., *Proc. Nat. Acad. Sci. U.S.A.* **86**, *8382* (1989).
53. T. Kiefhaber et al., *Biochemistry* **29**, *8250* (1990).
54. C. Q. Hu and J. M. Sturtevant, unpublished observations.
55. C. N. Pace and D. V. Laurents, *Biochemistry* **28**, *2520* (1989).
56. C. N. Pace, R. Erickson, and D. V. Laurents, unpublished observations.
57. K. A. Dill and D. Shortle, *Ann. Rev. Biochem.* **60**, *795* (1991).
58. C. N. Pace, unpublished observations.
59. G. W. Harris et al., *Biochim. Biophys. Acta* **912**, *348* (1987).
60. J. J. Birktoft and D. M. Blow, *J. Mol. Biol.* **68**, *187* (1972).
61. K. Kuwajima, *Proteins: Struc. Func. Gen.* **6**, *87* (1989).
62. L. G. Presta and G. D. Rose, *Science* **240**, *1632* (1988).
63. B. A. Shirley and D. V. Laurents, *J. Biochem. Biophys. Methods* **20**, *181* (1990).

RECEIVED May 5, 1992

Chapter 3

Protein Structure and Stability Assessment by Circular Dichroism Spectroscopy

Mark C. Manning

School of Pharmacy, Campus Box 297, University of Colorado, Boulder, CO 80309

With the advent of biotechnology and recombinant DNA methodology, there has been a renewed interest in protein folding and protein stability. One of the most powerful techniques available for the study of changes in protein structure is circular dichroism (CD) spectroscopy. Various applications of CD spectroscopy to the study of proteins are described, including analysis of denaturation curves, calculation of secondary structure composition, observation of changes in both secondary and tertiary structure, characterization of folding intermediates, and evaluation of the effects of site-directed mutagenesis. Finally, a case study on fibrolase, a metalloprotease from snake venom, is presented.

Advances in recombinant DNA technology have lead to an increased interest in the structure, function, and stability of proteins. Coupled with a growing understanding of protein folding processes, there has been a renaissance in the use of spectroscopic methods in the study of protein structure. One of the most powerful techniques for investigating the overall secondary and tertiary structure of proteins is circular dichroism (CD) spectroscopy. While CD spectroscopy has some limitations in that it can be used only for proteins in dilute solution and and cannot provide site-specific information (1), it is highly sensitive to changes in both the secondary and tertiary structure of proteins (2,3). In addition, semiquantitative estimates of the secondary structure composition of a protein can be obtained as well (4-6). While a number of reviews on the CD of proteins and other macromolecules are available (1-12), little has been published regarding the use of CD spectroscopy to assess protein stability. This article summarizes some of the more common current applications of CD to the study of protein stability and folding problems. Considering the number of examples reported on the use of CD to assess changes in stability and structure, this article will not seek to be exhaustive. However, the work cited herein should provide an adequate description of the current state of the use of CD spectroscopy in the study of proteins. Finally, the article will conclude with a detailed examination of the stability of fibrolase, a metalloprotease isolated from snake venom, in order to more completely demonstrate the capabilities of CD spectroscopy.

0097–6156/93/0516–0033$06.00/0
© 1993 American Chemical Society

Denaturation Curves as an Indicator of Protein Stability

One of the primary mechanisms of protein degradation is the loss of globular structure (13,14). This process, termed denaturation, leads to a partially or completely unfolded species which usually lacks any of the biological activity of the native protein. A variety of methods have been employed to monitor the denaturation of proteins, including fluorescence, infrared, nuclear magnetic resonance (NMR), and CD spectroscopy. As CD is very sensitive to changes in both secondary and tertiary structure, its application to the study of protein folding and unfolding has been widespread.

Denaturation of a protein can be induced by a number of conditions, including subjecting the protein to extremes in pH, increasing or decreasing the temperature, or by the addition of salts, organic solvents, chelating agents, or denaturants (such as guanidinium hydrochloride, GnHCl, or urea). One advantage of CD spectroscopy is that these changes in solvent composition are essentially transparent to the CD experiment (provided the concentrations are relatively low), allowing examination of most denaturation processes. The primary exceptions are in the case of urea and GnHCl, where concentrations usually exceed 1 M in order to denature most proteins, limiting CD measurements in the far UV region.

Thermal denaturation of proteins is one of the most common determinations of protein stability. By monitoring the change in CD intensity at a particular wavelength, one can determine the degree of unfolding as a function of temperature. For example, it has been shown that there exists a correlation between α helix content of a protein and its molar ellipticity at 222 nm (15). A plot of the CD signal as a function of temperature provides the raw data for construction of a denaturation curve. In the vicinity of the melting temperature, T_m, defined as the temperature where half of the protein is unfolded, there is a rapid, cooperative transition from a relatively rigid, folded structure to a flexible, unfolded conformation. This transition may involve denaturation of the entire protein, unfolding of a single domain, or even denaturation of just a small, independent portion. An increase in the T_m value is then taken to indicate an increase in protein stability (14,16-26).

Analysis of a thermal melting curve can provide thermodynamic information regarding the unfolding process (14,19-26). From the relative fractions of folded and unfolded protein at a given temperature near T_m, one can determine an equilibrium constant and, thus, a free energy of unfolding (ΔG_u) at that temperature. A plot of ΔG_u versus temperature provides an estimate (from the slope) of the entropy of denaturation. The enthalpy of unfolding can then be calculated from the Gibbs-Helmholz equation.

Lowering the temperature can also cause a protein to unfold in a process termed 'cold' denaturation (27-30). This arises primarily from the thermodynamics of hydrophobic interactions which lead to globular protein structures (14,24). A number of examples of this phenomenon have been described (27-29) and have been detected using CD spectroscopy. Frequently, because many proteins only cold denature below the freezing point of water, nonaqueous solvents and solvent mixtures must be employed to maintain fluidity of the solution (27,28). In the case of staphylococcal nuclease (27), the unfolding was measured in an aqueous solution containing 2 M urea. Spectra taken at -7° C indicated a greater degree of unfolding than for heat-denatured material at 55° C.

Another common indication of protein stability is the concentration of either urea or GnHCl required to unfold half of the protein available. This concentration, given the symbol $[D]_{1/2}$, is analogous to the T_m value from thermal denaturation curves. Increase or decrease in $[D]_{1/2}$ is presumed to indicate a corresponding increase or decrease in protein stability, respectively. Analysis of these curves can also provide thermodynamic information (20,21,26,31). As these experiments can be done at any temperature, they are more useful in that they can provide information regarding stability at or near room temperature.

Denaturation resulting from either heating the sample or the addition of a denaturant can be followed observing changes in either the near or far UV region of the spectrum. In the near UV, the signals arise from aromatic groups and, to a lesser extent, disulfides. Typically, changes in this region are thought to reflect an alteration of the tertiary structure (8,9). Conversely, changes in the far UV represent changes in secondary structure, although contributions from side chains and prosthetic groups may not be negligible at these wavelengths (1). Not only do these two regions possess information on different aspects of the globular structure of a protein, they also differ in the intensities of the signals. Typically, the signals in the near UV are one to three orders of magnitude weaker than those in the far UV. As a result, the pathlengths and concentrations used for work in the near UV must be significantly greater. Usually, pathlengths of 5 to 10 mm must be used with protein concentrations in the range of 1 to 5 mg/ml. The sample volumes are between 600 μl and 3000 μl. In order to obtain reasonable far UV CD spectra, the demands are more modest, with pathlengths ranging from 0.1 mm to 1 mm and concentrations typically between 0.05 and 0.50 mg/ml with sample volumes of 100 μl to 1.5 μl. It should be noted that at very low protein concentrations, adsorption to the cell may cause diminished CD intensity (32). Still, coupled with its high sensitivity and its nondestructive nature, its minimal sample requirements have been among the primary reasons for CD spectroscopy being the method of choice in the study of protein structure and stability.

Protein Stability as Determined by Changes in Secondary Structure Composition

Often, it is necessary to analyze the entire spectrum rather than just monitor changes at a single wavelength. This is particularly true if changes in secondary structure composition occur. Certainly, CD spectra can be qualitatively assessed for differences upon changes in conditions. However, numerous algorithms exist to deconvolute far UV CD spectra in order to determine quantitatively the relative amounts of α helix, β sheet, β turns, and other structures (4-6,33). While early methods only used CD data down to 200 nm, newer approaches (4,5,33) have shown that improved accuracy can be obtained if data is available to wavelengths as short as 176 nm, near the limit of commercial instrumentation. While these methods make numerous assumptions (1), they have been shown to be reasonably accurate for a wide range of proteins. Therefore, whether qualitative or quantitative analysis of the changes in secondary structure is performed, CD is an extremely sensitive tool for monitoring alterations in globular structure.

Secondary structure has been found to affected not only by changes in solution conditions (i.e, pH, salt concentrations, temperature, etc.), but also by mutagenesis of specific amino acid residues, the concentration of the protein, and by the introduction of nonaqueous solvents, reducing agents, and chelators. Examples of the use of CD to examine each of these effects can be found in the literature.

Interaction with lipids, surfactants, or membranes can induce the formation of secondary structure (34-38), particularly in peptides, where they may exist as highly flexible species in solution (39). Provided that the lipids form micelles which are relatively small and uniform, CD can be used to measure secondary structure in the presence and absence of lipids. Glucagon is a peptide hormone found in the gastrointestinal tract. In dilute solution, glucagon possesses only a small amount of ordered structure. However, in the presence of phospholipids, there is a significant increase in α helix content from 15% to 30-35% (40). Similar increases have been observed for calcitonin gene-related peptide. Both CGRP (41,42) and CGRP[8-37] (42, M.C. Manning, unpublished results) display marked increases in α helix content upon addition of anionic detergents such as sodium dodecyl sulfate. Fluorinated alcohols, such as trifluoroethanol (TFE) and hexafluoroisopropanol (HFIP), also stabilize α helices (41-48). Stabilization by these solvents and by lipids and detergents (34-38,40) appears to be a general phenomenon for peptides and can be used to assess secondary structure stability (44,46), although there may be some difficulties in obtaining reliable estimates of secondary structure composition for small peptides in nonaqueous solvents such as TFE and HFIP (45).

Protein Stability as Determined by Changes in Tertiary Structure

It is possible to assess protein stability by observing changes in the near UV CD spectrum as well. As stated above, these signals arise from aromatic residues and disulfides (8,9). Decrease in CD intensity in the near UV is usually associated with a loss of tertiary structure or a localized unfolding of the protein in the vicinity of a particular aromatic group. Also, through the use of site-directed mutagenesis, it is possible to systematically replace individual aromatic groups in order to assess their contributions to the near UV CD spectrum. Examples of each of these types of studies are given below.

Acid treatment of ovalbumin does not change the far UV CD, but it does alter the near UV CD dramatically (49). This indicates that the mobility of the aromatic groups (and most likely, the mobility of all of the side chains) is increased. At lower pH values, the protein displays an increased rate of unfolding in urea and behaves like a 'molten globule' type of species (50,51).

The denaturation of insulin and proinsulin have been examined in detail by Brems et al. (52). They have shown that GnHCl-induced denaturation is a reversible, cooperative process for insulin, whether detected by either far or near UV CD spectroscopy. The ΔG_u for the unfolding of insulin was determined to be 4.5 ± 0.5 kcal/mole. The unfolding of proinsulin, on the other hand, appears to be multiphasic as monitored by far UV CD. However, when the contributions of the C-terminal connecting peptide are considered, the denaturation of proinsulin is nearly identical to that of insulin itself. Apparently, the connecting peptide acts as an individual folding unit, complicating the analysis of the denaturation of proinsulin.

Characterization of Folding Intermediates by CD Spectroscopy

A major focus in biophysics and biochemistry is to understand the protein folding process, that is, the mechanism by which a newly synthesized protein adopts its native conformation. The kinetics of protein folding have been measured using a number of techniques, including CD. As proteins are usually completely folded within seconds, this requires either fast detection techniques, such as stopped flow methodology or means to trap folding intermediates. Stopped flow CD has been used although it is limited to single wavelength detection (53). One promising new approach is the development of ultrafast CD equipment (54,55). With such an apparatus, CD signals can be measured in the microsecond time frame, fast enough to observe all but the fastest steps of protein folding. It should be noted that the major problem with measuring protein folding kinetics is not instrumental, but resides in the difficulty of initiating the folding process. Mixing solutions in order to change solute concentrations, a common method of beginning the folding process, cannot be done faster than the millisecond time scale. Only if protein folding (or unfolding) can be initiated by changing some other condition, such as temperature or pressure, could microsecond CD measurements provide information on folding kinetics.

Refolding of acid- and base-denatured proteins has lead to the observation of compact, non-native structures termed 'molten globules' (49-51,56,57). These structures possess a significant amount of secondary structure, but little, if any, tertiary structure. As CD can detect the presence of both types of higher order structure in proteins, it is ideal for characterization of 'molten globule' structures.

Acid-treated β-lactamase is known to lose both secondary and tertiary structure as determined by CD measurements (56). However, upon addition of 0.5 M KCl, it refolds into a compact structure (termed A-type) which possesses some secondary structure, but still lacks any near UV CD signals (see Table I). Similar types of structures (B-type) can be obtained following base treatment. Lack of a near UV spectrum along with a native-like far UV CD indicates that the new conformation has some globular structure, but does not have any organized tertiary structure, as in the native state. This represents a utilization of CD spectroscopy to characterize globular, non-native states of proteins. These states are proposed to be similar to early folding intermediates. Similar behavior has been seen for ovalbumin. Lowering the pH produces little change in the far UV CD spectrum, but the near UV displays loss of intensity, suggesting increased flexibility in the side chains (49).

Table I. Circular Dichroism of Various Conformations of
β-Lactamase (adapted from reference 56)

Conformation	pH	Ionic Strength[a]	FUV CD[b]	NUV CD[c]	α Helix %
Native	7	I = 0.05	+	+	26
	7	0.5 M KCl	+	+	26
Unfolded	2	I = 0.05	-	-	4
A-Form	2	0.5 M KCl	+	-	25
Unfolded	12	I = 0.05	-	-	6
B-Form	12	0.5 M KCl	+	-	20

a- Ionic strength of buffer or of added KCl
b- Observation (+) or lack (-) of significant CD intensity in the far UV
c- Observation (+) or lack (-) of significant CD intensity in the near UV

The kinetics of protein folding have been measured using conventional CD instrumentation. For example, upon dilution of bovine growth hormone (bGH) from 6.0 M GnHCl to 2.2 M, the protein spontaneously refolds (58). Following the molar ellipticity at 222 nm (indicating changes in secondary structure) and the absorbance at 290 nm (indicating changes in tertiary structure), it has been shown that the formation of secondary structure is more rapid than formation of tertiary structure, consistent with the framework model of protein folding (59). Both recombinant and pituitary-derived bGH folded at the same rate, suggesting that differences in the N-terminal sequence do not affect folding of bGH.

Effects of Amino Acid Replacements on Protein Stability and Structure

Site-directed mutagenesis is a powerful tool for altering the primary structure of a protein in a controlled fashion. The effect of such changes on protein stability has been widely studied (60,61). However, it is also of interest to determine the effects of these point mutations on the folding of the protein.

Bovine growth hormone (bGH) is a 191 amino acid residue protein which adopts a four-helix bundle motif. Changes in the sequence within this bundle can greatly affect the conformational stability of the protein, as well as its propensity to aggregate. Replacement of lysine-112 with leucine (Leu) produces a species which is much more prone to aggregate than the wild type (62). The aggregate of the mutant displays reduced CD intensity in the far UV.

In our laboratory, we are investigating the effects of replacement of both Tyr and Phe in bovine pancreatic trypsin inhibitor (BPTI) (D.P. Goldenberg, M.C. Manning, unpublished results). Replacement of phenylalanine (Phe) residues, which are not expected to contribute strongly to the near UV CD (relative to tyrosine), can have a dramatic effect. Figure 1 shows the near UV CD spectra of wild type BPTI and the nutant where Phe-22 has been replaced by leucine. The result is a CD signal which has been significantly attenuated. Theoretical studies suggest that this may be a result of modifying the interactions of other aromatic groups (such as tyrosine) in close proximity to that particular group.

Effects of Aggregation on Protein Stability and Structure

While certain proteins are only active after the correct assembly of the various subunits, other proteins exhibit aggregation phenomena which may diminish their biological function. In fact, aggregation may proceed precipitation of the protein from solution (*13, 63*).

Insulin is well known to exist in a number of different aggregation states, ranging from monomeric to hexameric. Recently, a study of the far UV CD of various insulin forms was reported using an instrument which was capable of obtaining CD spectra into the vacuum UV (*64*). Comparison of the CD spectra of zinc free preparations, the 2-Zn form, and two engineered monomeric insulin showed striking differences in the far UV. The structure of the C-terminal portion of the B-chain undergoes conformational change upon association, especially in the formation of hexameric insulin. In the insulin which is engineered to remain monomeric, this section has been modified or deleted. Secondary structure analysis indicated that monomeric insulins possess 10-15 % more β sheet than hexameric insulin.

Interferon-γ (IFN-γ) is a pharmaceutically important protein whose stability is particularly sensitive to pH (*65*). Both rapid denaturation and aggregation have been observed at both acidic and basic pH values. Using light scattering methods, Mulkerrin and Wetzel were able to monitor the rate of aggregation at different temperatures. Onset of aggregation was always delayed by a period of seconds to minutes. Using CD spectroscopy, they were able to demonstrate that the lag time corresponded to an initial unfolding of IFN-γ. This unfolded species then went on the associate and form soluble aggregates.

Unfolded intermediates have been observed for bovine antithrombin (*66*). Biphasic unfolding was observed in the presence of GnHCl, with $D_{1/2}$ values of 0.8 M and 2.8 M determined by monitoring the signal at 220 nm. The second $D_{1/2}$ value is typical for complete unfolding of a protein. Renaturation experiments demonstrated that this process was reversible. However, the first step was not reversible. It appears to arise from exposure of certain hydrophobic groups, as both the near UV and far UV CD spectra are affected. This partial unfolding leads to rapid aggregation which cannot be reversed by removal of the GnHCl.

During unfolding of bGH, a self-associated, partially unfolded intermediate is formed (*67,68*). Characterization of this intermeidate has been accomplished using hydrodymanic measurements, gel permeation chromatography, as well as CD spectroscopy. The intermediate displays increased CD intensity in the near UV relative to the native state. A significant concentration dependence of the near UV CD is observed, consistent with it associating to form soluble aggregates, particularly dimers.

Effects of Metal Binding on Protein Stability and Structure

Interactions with metal ions, whether intrinsic or extrinsic, can alter the stability of a protein. Loss of an intrinsic metal atom often leads to localized unfolding of the protein and significant, if not total, loss of biological activity. Removal of intrinsic metals can be accomplished by the addition of chelating agents, by increase in the temperature, or by lowering the pH. These effects have been studied in detail for fibrolase (see below), a zinc-containing metalloenzyme (69,70).

Calcium binding is an important aspect of the physiological function of many proteins. Loss of calcium may lead to a structure which cannot function properly (71,72). For example, apo-actin, which has been depleted of calcium, adopts a structure which is nearly indistinguishable from that of heat-denatured actin as determined by CD (71). Upon removal of calcium, the α helix content drops from 33 % to 19 %. Further loss of structure was not observed, even upon heating to 95° C. Similar behavior has been noted for fibrolase (see below).

Conversely, the native structure of a protein can be induced upon addition of calcium. Bayley and co-workers have shown that calmodulin adopts its native conformation only in the presence of calcium (72). Lack of calcium produces a species which appears to be partially unfolded as determined by far UV CD spectroscopy.

Replacement of intrinsic metals with other metals which can be used as spectroscopic probes is a technique which has been widely employed in biophysical investigations, especially for fluorescence and NMR studies. Cobalt, because it possesses absorption bands in the visble region of the spectrum and is known to exhibit CD sgnals when placed in chiral environments (73), has been used to probe structural changes in insulin (74,75). The T -> R transition in zinc-containing hexameric insulin is difficult to detect spectroscopically. However, replacement of zinc with cobalt provides an additional spectroscopic probe. Induced CD from the cobalt occupying a discrete chiral environment produces visible CD bands which correlate to the T and R states of insulin (74).

Stability Study of Fibrolase, a Metalloprotease from Snake Venom

Effects of pH. From the discussion above, it is clear that CD can be employed in a variety of ways to assess protein stability and structure. However, it might be instructive to provide a detailed example of the use of CD in a comprehensive stability study. The stability of fibrolase, a small (203 amino acids) proteolytic enzyme isolated from snake venom, was examined. Fibrolase contains one intrinsic zinc atom per molecule of fibrolase (76) and is a direct fibrinolytic agent (77,78).

The total protein concentration in solution was determined over the pH range of 1 to 10 (Figure 2). Protein concentrations were nearly unchanged in the neutral to alkaline pH range (6.5 to 10.0). However, as the pH became acidic, the total amount of fibrolase in solution decreased with an apparent minimum at pH 5.0. At even lower pH values, the overall concentration increased to substantial levels (30 to 90% of initial protein at pH 1 to 4).

The effect of pH on specific proteolytic activity of fibrolase was evaluated over the pH range 1 to 10 using azocasein and insulin B-chain substrates (Figure 3). At neutral to alkaline pH values (6.5 to 9.0), no significant change in proteolytic activity of fibrolase was observed. At pH 10.0, the data suggested a slight loss of activity. This decrease was greater for the azocasein substrate relative to the insulin B-chain substrate. As the pH was lowered, the activity of fibrolase decreased. At pH 5.0, approximately 85% of the initial activity remained. However, at pH 4.0, only 20% of the initial activity was detected. At pH 1.0 and 2.5, azocaseinolytic activity was less than 10%. Activity versus insulin B-chain was also low at these pH values, but showed high variability in the assay results.

Gel electrophoresis results (data not shown) correlated well with activity and concentration results. SDS-PAGE gels of reduced and non-reduced samples showed no change in the location of the fibrolase band over the entire pH range 1 to 10. Band intensity corresponded qualitatively to protein concentration results, as expected. Native gels of samples at pH 5 to 10 showed no variation in migration of the fibrolase

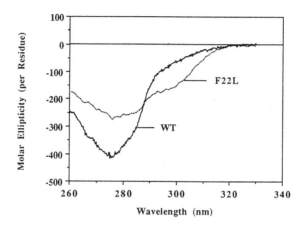

Figure 1.   Near UV CD spectrum of wild type bovine pancreatic trypsin
               inhibitor (WT) and its Phe-22 -> Leu (F22L) mutant.

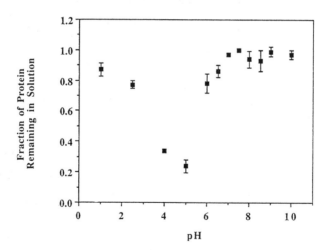

Figure 2.   Protein concentration (as percentage of initial concentration) as a
               function of pH. The error bars represent ± one standard deviation.

band. However, at more acidic pH values, no fibrolase band was seen. Instead, staining was observed as a streak or as multiple bands with increased mobility compared to fibrolase. These results were consistent with the lack of proteolytic activity at acidic pH.

Consideration of specific activity data together with the protein concentration data over the pH range 1 to 10 indicates several interesting effects as a result of changing pH. In the neutral to alkaline pH range, both activity and total protein in solution were not significantly changed. As the pH was lowered, protein concentration decreased to an apparent minimum at pH 5.0, yet the protein remaining in solution had a specific activity of about 0.85. As the pH was lowered even further, most of the proteolytic activity of the protein was lost, yet substantial amounts of protein remained in solution.

The apparent minimum solubility of fibrolase at pH 5.0 does not correspond to the isoelectric point of 6.7 (*69,70*). Minimum protein solubility would be predicted to occur near the isoelectric pH, if the native state of the protein underwent aggregation (*13*). This solubility behavior suggests the formation of an unfolded state which is more prone to aggregate than the native conformation. It should be noted that these studies were not designed as solubility measurements per se (i.e., an excess of protein was not present, thus equilibrium might not have been attained), therefore, the maximum solubility can not be deduced from the data.

Far UV CD spectra of fibrolase displayed essentially no change in band shape or position over the pH range 5 to 9 (Figure 4). However, some variations in intensity were observed. While some differences in intensity were observed in the far UV CD spectra of fibrolase with change in pH (from 5 to 9), the band positions and shapes were invariant. Assuming a 10% error in determination of the protein concentrations, most of the variations in intensity fall within experimental error. Otherwise, these differences could be accounted for by small increases (one or two turns) in the α helix content of the protein. Together, it appears that small variation or error in protein concentration and/or CD measurements is sufficient to account for any intensity variations of the far UV CD spectra within the pH 5 to 9 range. At pH 2 and 3, significant differences were found compared to the pH range 5 to 9 (Figure 5). The spectral changes at pH 2 and 3 were consistent with loss of α-helical structure and were similar to changes observed upon thermal denaturation (see below).

Effects of Temperature. At 37° C, rapid loss of proteolytic activity was observed. Greater than 10% of the activity was lost in less than one day, and essentially no activity against either substrate remained after 10 days. SDS-PAGE gels of non-reduced samples showed loss in intensity of the fibrolase band and lower molecular weight bands. Similar results were observed for reduced samples. In contrast to the activity and gel results, total protein remained unchanged in solution over 16 days.

The observed changes could be due to chemical or physical degradation mechanisms (*13*). Fibrolase contains potential sites for deamidation, oxidation, and hydrolysis, although in order to account for the observed loss, the rates of these reactions would have to be greater than predicted for the experimental conditions (*13*). One other mechanism specific to proteases which could account for the observed instability of fibrolase at 37° C would be autoproteolysis. Activity results were not inconsistent with an autoproteolytic mechanism assuming that degradation products would be inactive. Electrophoresis did not detect smaller protein species, however, autoproteolysis at multiple cleavage sites might produce low molecular weight fragments which would not be visible on the gels.

Physical instability such as adsorption, aggregation, denaturation, etc., could account for the observed loss of activity at 37° C. Significant physical changes commonly result in precipitation of protein, which was not observed. In addition, significant conformational changes at 37° C were not detected by CD, although the CD

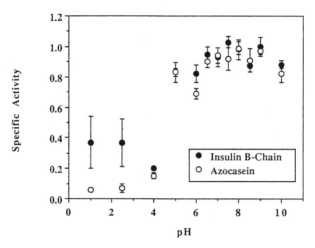

Figure 3.   Specific proteolytic activity of fibrolase (expressed as fraction of initial activity) as a function of pH for both azocasein and insulin B-chain as substrates. The error bars represent ± one standard deviation.

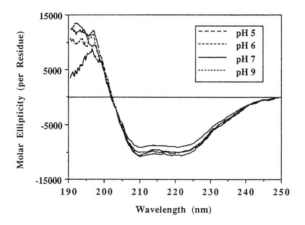

Figure 4.   Far UV CD spectra of fibrolase at pH 5, pH 7, pH 8, and pH 9. The solutions contained 10 mM phosphate buffer and fibrolase concentrations ranged from 100 to 400 μg/ml.

samples were maintained at 37° C for a maximum time of only about 10 minutes. Visible absorbance did increase somewhat upon heating to 37° C, indicating the formation of soluble aggregates of fibrolase.

The far UV CD spectrum of fibrolase at pH 8 is typical of a protein possessing a significant amount of α-helical structure (Figure 4). Secondary structure analysis indicates that approximately 25% of the residues in fibrolase are in an α-helical conformation (Figure 6). The globular structure appears to be stable over the temperature range of 15° to 40° C. Above 40° C, some of the secondary structure of fibrolase is rapidly lost in a highly cooperative, irreversible transition with a T_m of ~50° C (Figures 6, 7, and 8). At 70° C, only 8-10 % of the α-helix content remains. Little variation between lots was observed in the T_m (Figure 8). Changes in the CD spectrum were consistent with loss of only α-helical structure, as shown by the loss of intensity at 222 nm and the appearance of a negative band near 200 nm (Figure 7). Presence of an isodichroic point at 207 nm suggested that the thermal denaturation of fibrolase could be well approximated by a two-state model, meaning no evidence for partially unfolded intermediates was found. However, it is important to note that even at 70° C, a significant portion of fibrolase remains folded (as indicated by the residual ellipticity at 222 nm) and fibrolase can only be completely denatured by 6 M GnHCl (results not shown).

Varying pH also affected the thermal stability of fibrolase. At pH 5, the T_m dropped to 43° C, compared to 50° C at pH 8 (Figure 9). In addition, at pH 5, the cooperativity of the transition was less. Some destabilization of fibrolase with decreasing pH is indicated by the lower T_m observed at pH 5 compared to pH 8 (Figure 9). Destabilization resulting in the lower T_m value would not necessarily be apparent in CD spectra taken at room temperature. The destabilization could be a result of unfavorable changes in the electrostatic network of the protein (*65*).

Spectral changes induced by elevated temperatures are similar to those resulting from acid treatment (Figure 10). At 48° C, where the protein is 30-40 % unfolded, the far UV CD spectrum of fibrolase at pH 8 greatly resembles that of fibrolase at pH 2 and 27° C.

Effects of Zinc Removal. The presence of an essential zinc ion (*64*) is a crucial consideration in evaluating the stability of fibrolase. Loss of structure and activity upon exposure to extremes of pH and temperature can be rationalized on the basis of removal of the zinc atom. Denaturation of fibrolase under these conditions leads to a marked tendency to aggregate and precipitate (see below). Various studies were performed in order to examine the strength of zinc binding, the effect of zinc on the structure and activity and secondary structure, and to determine the metal binding site.

The effect of EDTA on the activity and conformation of fibrolase was of interest due to the classification of fibrolase as a zinc metalloprotein (*69,75*). Other investigators had previously observed inhibition of azocaseinolytic activity of fibrolase by EDTA, and, in fact, these studies contributed to the characterization of fibrolase as a metalloprotein (*76,77*). It was of interest to investigate what concentrations of EDTA affected fibrolase activity, and what other changes (e.g., structural) were caused by EDTA.

The effect of EDTA on proteolytic activity of fibrolase was dependent on the EDTA concentration added (see Table II). Partial inhibition was observed for EDTA concentrations as low as 0.1 mM. Complete inhibition occurred at 0.9 mM EDTA for activity versus the insulin B-chain. Further increases in EDTA concentration had no effect. Activity for the insulin B-chain was inhibited to a greater extent than was the azocaseinolytic activity. About half of the azocaseinolytic activity remained in the presence of 1 mM EDTA. A higher EDTA concentration of 5 mM was required for essentially complete (98%) inhibition of azocaseinolytic activity.

The reason for the difference in effective inhibitory concentrations of EDTA might be related to the difference in molecular size of the two substrates. The

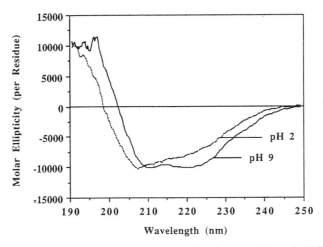

Figure 5.   Far UV CD spectra of fibrolase at pH 2 and pH 9.

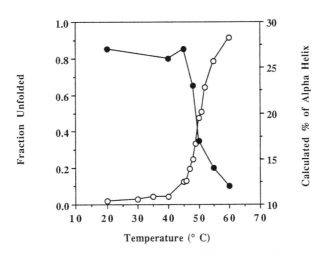

Figure 6.   Plot of α helix content (●) and degree of unfolding (○) as a function of temperature.

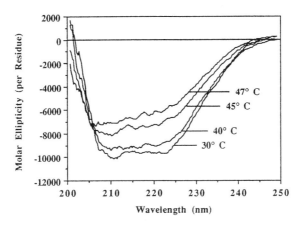

Figure 7.   Effects of temperature on the far UV CD spectrum of fibrolase (pH 8). The pathlength was 1.0 mm.

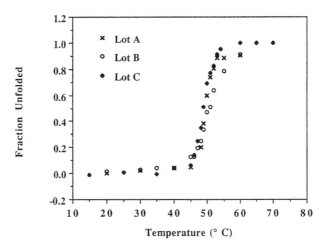

Figure 8.   Variation in T_m for three lots of fibrolase as monitored by CD spectroscopy at 222 nm.

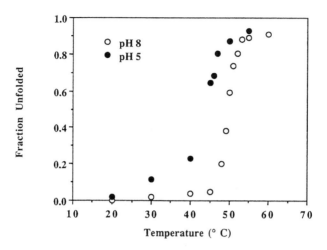

Figure 9.   Thermal denaturation curves for fibrolase at pH 5 and pH 8, as
             determined by molar ellipticity at 222 nm.

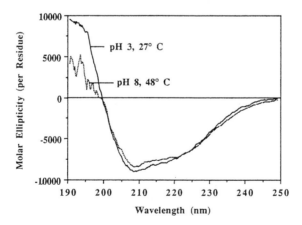

Figure 10.   Far UV CD spectra of fibrolase at pH 3 and 27° C and at pH 8 and
             48° C.

molecular weight of insulin B-chain is about 3800, while that of azocasein is about 25,000. Because of the size difference, the substrates might be subject to different constraints around the active site of fibrolase. The data indicated that the active site constraints, or importance of metal binding, might be greater for the insulin B-chain, since this activity was inhibited at lower EDTA concentrations. It is interesting to note that these observations are in contrast to activity results for previous studies which suggested that azocaseinolytic activity was lost more readily than was activity for the insulin B-chain at pH extremes and after extended storage at room temperature. These results suggested that different effects might occur in the protein upon EDTA addition. The time course of EDTA inhibition was rapid (see Table III). Inhibition was complete at the first measurable time point for 6 and 20 mM EDTA, and remained complete over one hour. The time course of inhibition was not followed for other EDTA concentrations.

Table II. Proteolytic Activity of Fibrolase in the Presence of EDTA

[EDTA] (mM)	% Activity Remaining Relative to Control[a]	
	vs. Insulin B-Chain	vs. Azocasein
0.1	51.4 (9.3)	55.2 (12.0)
0.2	51.8 (15.8)	50.1 (12.5)
0.5	32.7 (6.9)	49.6 (14.5)
0.9	0	nd
1.0	nd	42.1 (12.5)
2.0	nd	22.6 (3.8)
5.0	nd	2.3 (0.1)
6.0	0	nd
20.0	0	nd

a- No EDTA was added to the control samples. Initial fibrolase concentration was ~100 mg/ml. Numbers reported are the mean of at least three determinations, with standard deviations given in parentheses.
nd- Not determined.

While submillimolar concentrations of EDTA (< 1 mM) resulted in partial loss of activity versus insulin B-chain and azocasein, changes in CD spectra were also noted at these EDTA concentrations (Figure 11). These amounts of EDTA represent only a small molar excess of EDTA compared to fibrolase. At 0.1 mM EDTA, the molar excess of EDTA over fibrolase was only about 25 for studies examining the effect on activity and 10-15 in the case of the CD work. The low concentration and molar excess of EDTA effective in inducing activity and structural changes in fibrolase indicated that the zinc ion might be bound quite loosely to the protein.

CD results (ellipticity at 222 nm) were correlated with the observed activity changes. At submillimolar EDTA concentrations, structural changes were evident by CD as indicated by decreasing elliptical intensity at 222 nm (Figure 11), and partial inhibition of activity was also observed (Table II). At EDTA concentrations greater than or equal to 0.9 mM, structural changes observed by CD appeared to be complete, and correlated well with inhibition of activity for the insulin B-chain. Changes similar to those observed upon addition of EDTA were noted upon addition of DTT (Figure 12). While it is a well known reducing agent, it is also a good chelating agent (79), and it removed the zinc from fibrolase rapidly and easily. The resulting structure is similar to that found upon EDTA addition.

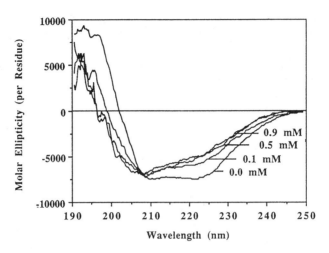

Figure 11.   Far UV CD spectra of fibrolase in 10 mM phosphate buffer containing 0.0 mM, 0.1mM, 0.5mM, and 0.9mM.

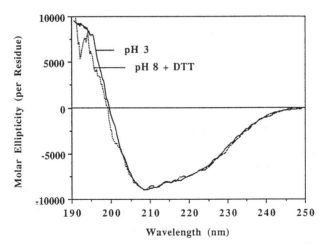

Figure 12.   Far UV CD spectrum of fibrolase at pH 3 and of fibrolase at pH 8 with 10 mM DTT added.

Table III. Time Course of EDTA Inhibition of Fibrolase Proteolytic Activity[a]

Time (min) EDTA	PEAK AREA (x 10^{-2})[b]		
	0.0 mM EDTA	6 mM EDTA	20 mM
0	8.16	8.48	8.69
5	4.78	-----	8.84
10	4.07	-----	8.73
15	-----	8.13	-----
20	2.89	-----	8.52
30	2.48	9.16	8.55
45	2.06	-----	7.82
60	1.49	8.00	8.63

a- Proteolytic activity measured vs. insulin B-chain.
b- Peak area of insulin B-chain substrate. Decreasing peak area indicates proteolysis by fibrolase. Peak areas are reported for one determination. Typical assay variability was ~5%.

The structural changes observed by CD upon EDTA addition to fibrolase were corroborated by native gel electrophoresis. Fibrolase samples containing EDTA (> 1 mM) consistently migrated further on native gels relative to fibrolase without EDTA present. These observed changes in the activity and conformation of fibrolase with EDTA supported involvement of zinc in the active site of the protein. The data showed that not only is the presence of the metal ion critical for proteolytic activity, it is also important to the structure of the protein. The metal ion may bind to several remote sites of the protein, and when the ion is removed by EDTA treatment, these residues might not retain the driving force for association, resulting in extensive structural perturbation.

Overall, EDTA treatment, acidic pH, and elevated temperatures produce species which are similar in secondary structure. In each of these, a significant portion of the secondary structure remains intact, but most of the helical structure is lost. In addition, the loss of secondary structure seems to correlate with the loss of zinc and enzymatic activity. It is believed that each of these conditions (elevated temperature, acidic pH, addition of chelators) leads to loss of zinc with concomittant unfolding of the metal binding site. The remainder of the fibrolase molecule appears to remain folded, as there is still signficant intenisty at 222 nm and the near UV CD spectrum does not change. Therefore, any efforts aimed at ensuring the stability of fibrolase with respect to denaturation should focus on avoiding conditions which would lead to loss of the intrinsic zinc atom.

Conclusions

The ability to accurately evaluate the stability of proteins is an important aspect of protein engineering. Certainly, specific descriptions of protein stability need to be defined, as proteins can decompose via a number of mechanisms. However, if the resistance of a protein to denaturation is taken to indicate stability, then CD spectroscopy should be the primary tool for the evaluation of protein stability. Changes in both overall and local structure can be detected and characterized. In addition, the effects of atering the sequence and aggregation state of a protein can be investigated with this technique.

Acknowledgements

The support of the University of Kansas General Research Fund and Marion Merrell Dow is gratefully acknowledged. The work on fibrolase was done in collaboration with James Mitchell and Brenda Schiulteis (Marion Merrell Dow Research Institute), David Vander Velde and Chris Smith (University of Kansas) and Denise Pretzer (Merck Sharp and Dohme). Mutants of BPTI were provided by David Goldenberg (University of Utah).

Literature Cited

1. Manning, M.C. *J. Pharm. Biomed. Anal.* **1989**, *7*, 1103-1119.
2. Woody, R.W. *J. Polymer Sci.: Macromol. Rev.* **1977**, *12*, 181-321.
3. Woody, R.W. in *The Peptides: Analysis, Synthesis, Biology*; Hruby, V.J., Ed.; Academic Press: Orlando, Florida, 1985, Volume 7; pp. 16-114.
4. Johnson, W.C., Jr. *Ann. Rev. Biophys. Biophys. Chem.* **1988**, *17*, 145-166.
5. Johnson, W.C. Jr. *Proteins: Structure, Function, Genetics* **1990**, *7*, 205-214.
6. Yang, J.T.; Wu, C.-S. C.; Martinez, H. *Meth. Enzymol.* **1986**, *130*, 208-269.
7. Bayley, P.M. *Prog. Biophys. Mol. Biol.* **1973**, *27*, 3-76.
8. Strickland, E.H. *CRC Crit. Rev. Biochem.* **1974**, *2*, 113-174.
9. Kahn, P.C. *Methods Enzymol.* **1978**, *61*, 339-378.
10. Schellman, J.A. *Chem. Rev.* **1975**, *75*, 323-331.
11. Sears, D.W.; Beychok, S. in *Physical Principles and Techniques of Protein Chemistry, Part C*; Leach, S.J., Ed., 1973, pp. 445-593.
12. Bannister, W.H.; Bannister, J.V. *Int. J. Biochem.* **1974**, *5*, 673-677.
13. Manning, M.C.; Patel, K.; Borchardt, R.T. *Pharmaceutical Research* **1989**, *6*, 903-918.
14. Tanford, C. *Adv. Protein Chem.* **1968**, *23*, 121-282.
15. Chen, Y.-H.; Yang, J.T.; Martinez, H.M. *Biochemistry* **1972**, *11*, 4120-4131.
16. Hecht, M.H.; Sturtevant, J.M.; Sauer, R.T. *Proteins: Structure, Function, Genetics* **1986**, *1*, 43-46.
17. Hecht, M.H.; Hehir, K.M.; Nelson, H.C.M.; Sturtevant, J.M.; Sauer, R.T. *J. Cell. Biochem.* **1985**, *29*, 217-224.
18. Nicholson, H.; Becktel, W.J.; Matthews, B.W. *Nature* **1988**, *336*, 651-656.
19. Schellman, J.A. *Ann. Rev. Biophys. Biophys. Chem.* **1987**, *16*, 115-137.
20. Becktel, W.J.; Schellman, J.A. *Biopolymers* **1987**, *26*, 1859-1877.
21. Goodenough, P.W.; Jenkins, J.A. *Biochem. Soc. Trans.* **1991**, *19*, 655-662.
22. Privalov, P.L. *Ann. Rev. Biophys. Biophys. Chem.* **1978**, *18*, 47-69.
23. Privalov, P.L. *Curr. Trends Life Sci.* **1984**, *12*, 17-21.
24. Privalov, P.L. and Gill, S.J. *Adv. Protein Chem.* **1988**, *39*, 191-238.
25. Tombs, M.P. *J. Appl. Biochem.* **1985**, *7*, 3-24.
26. Shirley, B.A. in *Pharmaceutical Biotechnology*; Volume 2, Ahern, T.J., Manning, M.C., Ed.; Plenum Press, New York, 1992, pp. 000-000.
27. Griko, Y.V.; Privalov, P.L.; Sturtevant, J.M.; Venyaminov, S.Y. *Proc. Natl. Acad. Sci. USA* **1988**, *85*, 3343-3347.
28. Fink, A.L.; Anderson, W.D.; Antonio, L. *FEBS Lett.* **1988**, *229*, 123-126.
29. Hatley, R.H.M.; Franks, F. *Cryo-Letters* **1986**, *7*, 226-233.
30. Brandts, J.F. *J. Am. Chem. Soc.* **1964**, *86*, 4291-4301.
31. Pace, C.N. *Methods Enzymol.* **1986**, *131*, 266-280.
32. Wu, C.-S.C.; Chen, G.C. *Anal. Biochem.* **1989**, *177*, 178-182.
33. van Stokkum, I.H.M.; Spoelder, H.J.W.; Bloemendal, M.; van Grondelle, R.; Groen, F.C.A. *Anal. Biochem.* **1990**, *191*, 110-118.

34. Schwyzer, R. *EMBO J.* **1987**, *6*, 2255-2259.
35. Kaiser, E.T.; Kézdy, F.J. *Ann. Rev. Biophys. Biophys. Chem.* **1987**, *16*, 561-581.
36. Wu, C.-S. C.; Yang, J.T. *Mol. Cell. Biochem.* **1981**, *40*, 109-122.
37. Schwyzer, R. *Biochemistry* **1986**, *25*, 6335-6342.
38. Schwyzer, R. *Biopolymers* **1991**, *31*, 785-792.
39. Wright, P.E.; Dyson, H.J.; Lerner, R.A. *Biochemistry* **1988**, *27*, 7167-7175.
40. Pasta, P.; Vecchio, G.; Carrea, G. *Biochim. Biophys. Acta* **1988**, *953*, 314-320.
41. Manning, M.C. *Biochem. Biophys. Res. Commun.* **1989**, *160*, 388-392.
42. Hubbard, J.A.; Martin, S.R.; Chaplin, L.C.; Bose, C.; Kelly, S.M.; Price, N.C. *Biochem. J.* **1991**, *275*, 785-788.
43. Mammi, S.; Mammi, N.J.; Peggion, E. *Biochemistry* **1988**, *27*, 1374-1379.
44. Lehrman, S.R.; Tuls, J.L.; Lund, M. *Biochemistry* **1990**, *29*, 5590-5596.
45. Holladay, L.A. *Biophys. Chem.* **1977**, *7*, 41-49.
46. Nelson, J.W.; Kallenbach, N.R. *Proteins: Structure, Function, Genetics* **1986**, *1*, 211-217.
47. Bayley, P.; Martin, S.; Jones, G. *FEBS Lett.* **1988**, *238*, 61-66.
48. Honda, S.; Ohashi, S.; Morii, H.; Uedira, H. *Biopolymers* **1991**, *31*, 869-876.
49. Koseki, T.; Kitabatake, N.; Doi, E. *J. Biochem.* **1988**, *103*, 425-430.
50. Ohgushi, M.; Waada, A. *FEBS Lett.* **1983**, *164*, 21-24.
51. Ptitsyn, O.B. *J. Protein Chem.* **1987**, *6*, 273-293.
52. Brems, D.N.; Brown, P.L.; Heckenlaible, L.A.; Frank, B.H. *Biochemistry* **1990**, *29*, 9289-9293.
53. Bayley, P.M. *Prog. Biophys. Mol. Biol.* **1981**, *37*, 149-180.
54. Einterz, C.M.; Lewis, J.W.; Milder, S.J.; Kliger, D.S. *J. Phys. Chem.* **1985**, *89*, 3845-3853.
55. Lewis, J.W.; Tilton, R.F.; Einterz, C.M.; Milder, S.J.; Kuntz, I.D.; Kliger, D.S. *J. Phys. Chem.* **1985**, 89, 289-294.
56. Goto, Y.; Fink, A.L. *Biochemistry* **1989**, *28*, 945-952.
57. Brems, D.N.; Havel, H.A. *Proteins: Structure, Function, Genetics* **1989**, *5*, 93-95.
58. Brems, D.N.; Plaisted, S.M.; Dougherty, J.J., Jr.; Holzmann, T.F. *J. Biol. Chem.* **1987**, *262*, 2590-2596.
59. Kim, P.S.; Baldwin, R.L. *Ann. Rev. Biochem.* **1982**, *51*, 459-489.
60. Shortle, D. *J. Biol. Chem.* **1989**, *264*, 5315-5318.
61. Alber, T. *Ann. Rev. Biochem.* **1989**, *58*, 765-798.
62. Brems, D.N.; Plaisted, S.M.; Havel, H.A.; Tomich, C.-S.C. *Proc. Natl. Acad. Sci. USA* **1988**, *85*, 3367-3371.
63. Glatz, C.E. in *Pharmaceutical Biotechnology* ; Volume 2, Ahern, T.J., Manning, M.C., Ed.; Plenum Press, New York, 1992, pp. 000-000.
64. Melberg, S.G.; Johnson, W.C., Jr. *Proteins: Structure, Function, Genetics* **1990**, *8*, 280-286.
65. Mulkerrin, M.G.; Wetzel, R. *Biochemistry* **1989**, *28*, 6556-6561.
66. Fish, W.W.; Danielsson, A.; Nordling, K.; Miller, S.H.; Lam, C.F.; Björk, I. *Biochemistry* **1985**, *24*, 1510-1517.
67. Havel, H.A.; Kauffman, E.W.; Plaisted, S.M.; Brems, D.N. *Biochemistry* **1986**, *25*, 6533-6538.
68. Brems, D.N.; Plaisted, S.M.; Kauffman, E.W.; Havel, H.A. *Biochemistry* **1986**, *25*, 6539-6543.
69. Pretzer, D.; Schulteis, B.; Vander Velde, D.G.; Smith, C.D.; Mitchell, J.W.; Manning, M.C. *Pharmaceutical Research* **1991**, *8*, 1103-1112.

70. Pretzer, D.; Schulteis, B.; Vander Velde, D.G.; Smith, C.D.; Mitchell, J.W.; Manning, M.C. in *Pharmaceutical Biotechnology* ; Wang, Y.J.; Pearlman, R., Eds.; Plenum Press, New York, 1992; Volume 5, pp. 000-000.
71. Bertazzon, A.; Tian, G.H.; Lamblin, A.; Tsong, T.Y. *Biochemistry* **1990**, *29*, 291-298.
72. Martin, S.R.; Bayley, P.M. *Biochem. J.* **1986**, *238*, 485-490.
73. DeW. Horrocks, W., Jr.; Ishley, J.N.; Holmquist, B.; Thompson, J.S. *J. Inorg. Biochem.* **1980**, *12*, 131-141.
74. Thomas, B.; Wollmer, A. *Biol. Chem. Hoppe-Seyler* **1989**, *370*, 1235-1244.
75. Mirmira, R.G.; Tager, H.S. *Biochemistry* **1991**, *30*, 8222-8229.
76. Markland, F.S.; Reddy, K.N.N.; Guan, L. in: *Hemostasis and Animal Venoms*, Pirkle, H. and Markland, F.S., Ed., Marcel Dekker, New York, 1988, pp. 173-189.
77. Ahmed, N.K.; Tennant, K.D.; Markland, F.S.; Lacz, J.P. *Haemostasis* **1990**, *20*, 147-154.
78. Bajwa, S.S., Kirakossian, H., Reddy, K.N.N., and Marklan, F.S. *Toxicon* **1982**, *20*, 427-432.
79. Miller, J.; McLachlan, A.D.; Klug, A. *EMBO J.* **1985**, *4*, 1609-1614.

RECEIVED March 31, 1992

Chapter 4

Structure–Function Relationship of Hyperthermophilic Enzymes

Rainer Jaenicke

Institut für Biophysik und Physikalische Biochemie, Universität Regensburg, Universitätstrasse 31, Regensburg D–8400, Federal Republic of Germany

The upper limit of thermal adaptation in the biosphere ($\approx 110°C$) coincides with the temperature where hydrophobic hydration vanishes and biomolecules start undergoing hydrothermal decomposition. Regarding T_{max}, hyperthermophilic microorganisms come close to this limit. *Thermotoga maritima* ($T_{opt} \leq 90°C$) has adapted its cellular inventory to $T \geq 100°C$. Enzymes purified to homogeneity show intrinsic stability up to $\approx 110°C$. Their overall properties at physiological temperature resemble those of their mesophilic counterparts: Mutative adaptation tends to maintain "corresponding states" regarding structure, flexibility and ligand binding. Physical, enzymatic and folding properties of glyceraldehyde-3-phosphate dehydrogenase, lactate dehydrogenase and amylase are discussed. Enhanced stability may be ascribed to improved packing and enhanced ligand and/or subunit interactions. Due to the minute adaptive changes in ΔG no general strategy of thermophilism can be given.

There is life on the entire globe. The limits of viability for the biologically relevant variables are: for temperature $\leq 110°C$, for hydrostatic pressure ≤ 120 MPa, for water activity ≥ 0.6 (corresponding to salinities up to 6 M), and for pH, values below 2 and beyond 10. Organisms exposed to extreme conditions may respond either by "avoidance", or they have to adapt their cellular components. In the first case, the stress parameter is excluded or compensated, for example, by neutralizing the anomalous external pH, or by levelling a salt gradient through isosmotic concentrations of "compatible" cytoplasmic components; in the second, mutations have resulted in the increased stability requirements, so that all the cell's constituents are intrinsically resistant against the specific variable. Evidently, external structural elements facing the outside world cannot avoid stress parameters. Similarly, because of the isothermal and isobaric conditions in a given habitat, the entire cell inventory of organisms adapted to extremes of

0097–6156/93/0516–0053$06.00/0

temperature and pressure is expected to show enhanced intrinsic stability. However, there are extrinsic effects and effectors which may assist cellular components to overcome stress (1).

Organisms which have evolved such that they *require* extreme conditions for their whole life cycle are called "extremophiles", or, more specific for extremes of temperature, pressure, salinity and pH: *thermo-* or *psychrophiles, barophiles, halophiles* and *acido-* or *alkalophiles*. In the present paper we are dealing with high temperature, focusing our attention to the upper limit. "Hyperthermophilic" organisms require temperatures close to the boiling point of water for full metabolic activity and reproduction. Correspondingly, their protein inventory is expected to exhibit anomalous thermal stability. In the following, we address the question how this is brought about, and whether general mechanisms of heat stabilization can be deduced from physicochemical studies on the most extreme examples of thermophilic proteins that are presently known. It is obvious that the answer to the question has technological, as well as biological implications: *technological*, because the molecular mechanism of thermal adaptation might be applicable to produce engineered thermostable proteins in connection with bioreactors or biosensors; *biological*, because of the evolutionary aspect of adaptive response reactions to physiological stress.

Organisms and Representative Proteins

Proteins discussed in this article were isolated (i) from *Thermotoga maritima*, an early descendant of the eubacterial evolutionary "tree" which can be grown to high cell mass under strictly anaerobic conditions, and (ii) from *Pyrodictium occultum*, one of the most extreme representatives among the thermophilic archaea known today (2).

Classical chromatographic methods, including (metal-)affinity chromatography and immuno-adsorption chromatography, were applied for purification (3-5, A. Tomschy, H. Schurig, R. Glockshuber, R. Jaenicke, unpublished results). After establishing (partial) sequences, homology modelling and energy minimization were applied for structure predictions (6). In the case of D-glyceraldehyde-3-phosphate dehydrogenase (GAPDH) from *Thermotoga maritima*, where the full amino acid sequence has been determined both at the protein and the DNA level (7; A. Tomschy, unpublished results), cloning and expression of the gene in *Escherichia coli* clearly indicates that the hyperthermophilic enzyme is expressed in active form under non-thermophilic conditions. Obviously, the acquisition of the native structure in the heterologous host does not require the physiological temperature conditions of the guest. This is not trivial since the weak intermolecular interactions stabilizing the native structure of proteins show characteristic temperature dependences which, far below the optimum temperature, may cause cold denaturation (8,9; see below). In the present case, the temperature difference amounts to ca. 60°C. Less dramatic examples have been reported in (1).

Limits of Growth - Limits of Stability of the Covalent Structure

As indicated, hyperthermophilic GAPDH from *Thermotoga maritima* still forms its native three-dimensional structure when it is expressed about 60 degrees below its optimum temperature. As will be shown, upon reconstitution at 0°C, or in the presence of low concentrations of chaotropic agents, the enzyme does show a certain degree of low-temperature destabilization, probably due to the involvement of hydrophobic interactions upon forming the native tertiary and quaternary structure (*10-12*).

Apart from temperature-induced perturbations of the native three-dimensional structure, common Arrhenius behavior leads to a more or less complete loss of catalytic function at low temperature. In the case of *Thermotoga maritima* or *Pyrodictium occultum*, significant cell growth requires temperatures beyond 50°C (*2,13*). Considering the temperature effect on the metabolic network, it is obvious that temperature adaptation not only requires directed alterations of the intrinsic stability of cell constituents, but also tuning of the kinetics. Depending on the activation energies of the reactions involved, shifts in the optimum temperature from mesophiles to thermophiles may cause dramatic kinetic dislocations (Table I).

Table I. Alterations of Relative Reaction Rates Normalized to 20°C

T (°C)	Activation Energy (kJ/mol)		
	16	32	64
20	1	1	1
60	3	10	90
100	14	186	30 000

On the high-temperature extreme, one may ask why there seems to be a definite limit of growth and reproduction at temperatures around 120°C. Considering this limit and the reversible deactivation of enzymes at water contents below the normal degree of hydration of proteins (≤ 0.25 g H_2O/g protein), the ultimate requirement for life seems to be the presence of liquid water. In testing this hypothesis, stabilization of the liquid state of water at high hydrostatic pressure proves that the temperature limit of viability (T_{max}) cannot be shifted significantly (*14*). Life under "Black Smoker" conditions (26 MPa and 250°C) must be science fiction: the susceptibility of the covalent structure of the polypeptide chain toward hydrolysis, and the hydrothermal degradation of essential biomolecules (*15,16*) would require compensatory "anaplerotic reactions" which are incompatible with the relatively low metabolic activity of most extremophilic organisms.

It is worth mentioning that the hydrophobic hydration also seems to vanish close to the above temperature limit (*17-19*) so that one may assume that both the stability of the covalent structure of the polypeptide chain and its sidechains and their weak interactions determine the upper limit of protein stability. In this context it is important to note that the building blocks of proteins from extremophiles (including hyperthermophiles) are exclusively the canonical 20 natural amino acids. Thus, molecular adaptation to altered environmental conditions can merely depend on the mutative change in the local and global distribution of the amino acids along the polypeptide chain[1]. From studies on synthetic polypeptides it became clear that the natural amino acids basically allow to build protein molecules with stabilities beyond those commonly observed for natural proteins (20). The conclusion we may draw from this observation is that molecular adaptation obviously results in optimum protein flexibility rather than maximum stability.

Conformational stability of proteins

The central issue in the adaptation of biomolecules to extreme conditions is the conservation of their functional state which is characterized by a well-balanced compromise of stability and flexibility. There exist proteins with exceedingly high intrinsic thermal stability and, as has been mentioned, the given repertoire of natural amino acids would have allowed evolution to develop even more stable proteins if they were advantageous (11,20).

Basic mechanisms of molecular adaptation are changes in packing density, charge distribution, hydrophobic surface area, and in the ratio of polar/nonpolar or acidic/basic residues. Evidently, dramatic changes in stabilization energy do not occur, even under the most extreme conditions. In general, the overall free energy of stabilization of globular proteins in their natural solvent environment is only marginal. The requirement for flexibility is fulfilled by the subtle compensation of attractive and repulsive interactions. Their individual contributions to the free energy are exceedingly large; however, their superposition yields a small difference between big numbers. Considering the energy contributions of the relevant weak intermolecular forces involved in protein stabilization, on balance, stability is attributable to the equivalent of a few hydrogen bonds, ion pairs or hydrophobic interactions. Taking a known three-dimensional structure such as ribonuclease T1 as an example, its native secondary structure and the packing of its hydrophobic inner core is stabilized by 2 disulfide bridges, 87 intramolecular hydrogen bonds and hydrophobic interactions involving $\approx$ 85% of its non-polar residues; nevertheless, the free energy of stabilization, ΔG_{stab}, at pH 7 and 25°C is no more than 24 kJ/mol, corresponding to the equivalent of just one ion pair or 2-3 hydrogen bonds. The question whether H-bonds do contribute to protein stability, i.e., whether there is a difference in bond strength between water-water and water-protein hydrogen bonds, has been a long-standing controversy (11,12,18,21). Obviously, the answer turns out to be positive: Using again ribonuclease T1 as an example, elimination of single hydrogen bonds by site-directed mutagenesis has shown that the stability increment per H-bond is of the order of 5 kJ/mol, which would clearly indicate that H-bonding in ribonuclease T1 contributes equally, or even to a higher extent, to the conformational stability than hydrophobic interactions (C.N.Pace, personal communication).

The above ΔG_{stab} value observed for ribonuclease T1 can be generalized: the free energies of stabilization for a wide variety of globular proteins with totally

---

[1] In contrast, membrane lipids of extremophiles have been shown to contain a whole spectrum of unusual components (2).

unrelated structures have been shown to cluster in a narrow range between 25 and 65 kJ/mol, independent of both the size of the protein and the mode of denaturation (*1,22*). Determining the stability increment per residue, the resulting figure is one order of magnitude below the thermal energy (kT). This proves clearly, that the overall stability of a polypeptide chain must involve cooperativity because the addition of stability increments per amino-acid residue in the process of structure formation would not allow to overcome the thermal energy. In cases where the molecular mass of a protein is too small to provide the necessary size of a cooperative unit, the structure may be stabilized by covalent cross-linking or ligand binding. Both improve the stability of the entire molecule by decreasing the entropy of unfolding. For a discussion of the stability of local structures in proteins, see (*11,23-26*).

Extremophilic proteins do not exhibit properties qualitatively different from non-extremophilic ones. The essential adaptive alteration tends to shift the normal characteristics to the respective extreme in the sense that under the mutual physiological conditions the molecular properties are comparable; with other words, adaptation to extremes of physical conditions tends to maintain "corresponding states" regarding overall topology, flexibility and solvation. Considering the parabolic profile of the temperature dependence of the free energy of stabilization (*18,19,22*), it is evident that enhanced thermal stability may be accomplished by a variety of possible mechanisms. As depicted schematically in Fig. 1A, the profile of the mesophilic wild-type could either be shifted to higher temperature, or it could be lowered, or flattened; in all three cases, the "melting temperature" of the protein would be shifted to a (hyper-)thermophilic higher value. Experimental evidence seems to indicate that the third alternative holds true (Fig. 1B). Thus, the temperature dependence of ΔG_{stab} of thermophilic proteins is less pronounced than the one of the corresponding wild-type protein. A similar independence of temperature has been found for the free energy of ligand binding to enzymes; in this case, entropy-enthalpy compensation renders thermal adaptation unnecessary (Fig. 1C).

In summarizing the thermodynamics of thermophilic adaptation in quantitative terms, even for *hyper*thermophiles, the changes in free energy, $\Delta\Delta G_{stab}$, generally do not exceed the equivalent of a few additional weak interactions. At present, no comparative X-ray analysis of any protein from a mesophile, thermophile and hyperthermophile has been put forward at sufficiently high resolution to pin down specific residues responsible for the gradual increase in protein stability. The most thorough studies in this context refer to X-ray crystallographic and thermodynamic studies on pointmutants of bacteriophage T4 lysozyme (*1,27*). The results illustrate how subtle the different weak interactions are balanced in native globular proteins, and how much, even marginal local strain in the three-dimensional structure may affect protein stability. From the point of view of protein engineering and the attempt to provide deeper insight into the mechanisms of thermophilic adaptation, the results are a test case to prove that presently no unambiguous predictions or general strategies of protein stabilization can be given. One problem in this context is the fact that high-resolution X-ray structures may not be adequate to detect the real structural changes accompanying "isomorphous single point mutations", because the lattice forces in protein crystals may freeze or shift positions of the polypeptide backbone which are not representative for the relevant *local* solution structure.

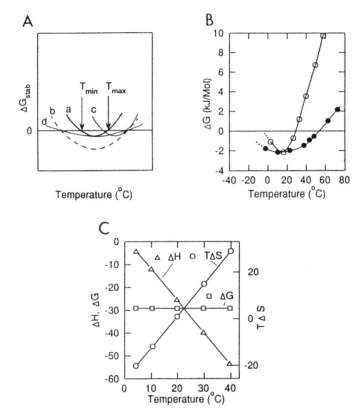

Figure 1. Temperature dependence of the free energy of stabilization and ligand binding. (A) Hypothetical ΔG_{stab} profiles for mesophilic (a) and thermophilic (b-d) proteins. (B) ΔG_{stab} for phosphoglycerate kinase from yeast (o) and *Thermus thermophilus* (•), in the presence of 0.5 M (o) and 2.3 M GdmCl (•). (C) Entropy/enthalpy compensation upon binding of NADH to porcine muscle LDH-M_4.

Selected Examples : Enzymes from *Thermotoga maritima*

Thermophilic adaptation of proteins occurs at the DNA level leading to specific local alterations in structural genes and, subsequently, amino-acid sequences. For almost a decade, such changes have been assumed to be manifested in certain well-defined shifts in the amino-acid composition. The significance of the proposed "rules" for the "gross traffic" in the case of thermal stabilization cannot be considered unambiguous (*1,3,4,28*). The reason is obvious: The previously mentioned low values of the extrafree energy of stabilization ($\Delta\Delta G_{stab}$) required for the increase in stability can be provided by an astronomically large number of subtle changes in local weak interactions. Evidently, summarizing these changes in terms of preferred amino-acid exchanges, minimization of crevices, or enhanced ion-pair formation etc. is an oversimplification. What seems to be well-established are the following observations:
1. Proteins from thermophilic sources commonly exhibit high *intrinsic* stability which becomes marginal at their respective physiological temperatures. At optimum temperature, homologous enzymes show similar conformational flexibility. The increase in rigidity of thermophilic proteins at room-temperature is evident from decreased exchange rates of amide protons, as well as increased resistance against proteolysis and denaturation using mesophilic homologs as references. 2. Available structural data prove that thermophilic proteins are closely similar to their mesophilic counterparts as far as their basic topology, activity and enzyme mechanism are concerned. Correspondingly, virtually all the amino acids constituting the active sites are conserved. 3. The correlation of sequence alterations with changes in thermal stability is expected to be highly complex. It is closely related to the protein folding problem, as increased stability is equivalent to the difference in minimum energy of the thermophilic *vs.* the mesophilic polypeptide chains. So far, no general strategy of thermal stabilization is available.

In the following, specific characteristics regarding compartmentation, enzymatic and solution properties, as well as self-organization of amylases, glyceraldehyde-3-phosphate dehydrogenase and lactate dehydrogenase from *Thermotoga maritima*, will be discussed.

Amylases. *Thermotoga maritima* can be grown on minimal medium with starch as carbon source. The uptake of glucose is not accomplished by secreting amylases into the outside medium: less than 1% of the total amylase activity is detected in the supernatant of the cells. Similarly, there is no release of activity from the periplasm after lysozyme treatment of the cells. Thus, starch as a nutrient must be degraded on the cell surface in order to be able to pass the outer sheath and the periplasm. As shown by Percoll gradient centrifugation, in fact, more than 85% of the total α-, ß- and glucoamylase activity are found to be associated with the "toga". The expression of the three isoenzymes is too low to isolate the pure proteins in mg quantities which would be required for a detailed characterization. Compared with α-amylase from *Bacillus licheniformis* (T_{max} = 75°C), the amylases from *Thermotoga* show high intrinsic stability with upper temperature limits at ≥ 95°C (Table II). Significant turnover of the enzyme occurs only beyond 70°C, i.e., under optimal growth conditions.

Table II. Amylases from *Thermotoga maritima* and *Bacillus licheniformis*

| | *Thermotoga maritima* | | *Bacillus licheniformis* |
	Fraction I	Fraction II	
Compartmentation	associated with toga		secreted
Number of active bands	2	1	1
Molecular mass (kDa)	≈ 60	≈ 60	60
Specificity	ß	α and gluco	α
Optimum temperature (°C)	95	90	70-75
Activation energy (kJ/mol)	98	60	14
K_M in % starch at (°C)	0.23 (80)	0.22 (80)	0.15 (45)
pH optimum	5.0	6.0	6.8
Cross-reactivity with H-α*	-	-	+

* Cross-reaction with human salivary α-amylase monoclonal antibody
Adapted from ref.5. Copyright 1991.

D-Glyceraldehyde-3-phosphate Dehydrogenase. Among the cytosolic enzymes which have been screened, GAPDH shows the highest expression level. Since a series of GAPDH's from various sources has been investigated in great detail, this enzyme was chosen to compare homologs with widely differing thermal stabilities. The enzyme has been purified to homogeneity (*3*); its amino-acid sequence has been determined at the protein (*7*) and DNA level (A. Tomschy, unpublished), and its physicochemical and enzymological properties have been compared with the enzyme from mesophiles and other thermophiles (*3,6*). Considering the amino-acid compositions (Table III), it is obvious that only the exchanges Lys → Arg, Ser → Thr and Val → Ile agree with the results of previous statistical analyses (*28*). The primary structure is highly homologous with the enzyme from other thermophilic bacteria: comparing the sequences of the enzyme from *Thermotoga, Bacillus stearothermophilus* and *Thermus aquaticus*, 63 and 59% identity are observed, only 8% of the exchanges are non-conservative; taking all known structures together, about 33% of the residues are identical.

Homology modelling yields equal topologies (*6*), in accordance with the observation that the quaternary and secondary structure are closely similar and that the essential residues in the active site are conserved in all species. Marked differences regarding the physical properties of hyperthermophilic GAPDH and its non-thermophilic counterparts are (cf. Table IV and Fig. 2): (a) enhanced intrinsic stability; (b) decreased exchange rates in H-D exchange experiments (*3*); (c) a smaller difference in the change in hydrodynamic volume upon coenzyme binding (Rehaber, V.; Jaenicke, R. *J. Biol. Chem.* 1992, in press); (d) low-temperature intermediate(s) on the pathway of reconstitution with a shift of the tetramer-monomer equilibrium at 0°C (*29*); (e) activation of the enzyme at low denaturant concentrations (Rehaber, V; Jaenicke, R. *J. Biol. Chem.* 1992, in press). The characteristics confirm the tight packing of the *Thermotoga* enzyme and the inhibitory effect of the decreased flexibility on the catalytic function at low temperature; in addition they suggest a significant contribution of hydrophobic interactions to the tertiary and quaternary structure of the enzyme.

Table III. Amino-acid Composition of GAPDH's from *Thermotoga maritima* and Other Sources (given in numbers of residues per polypeptide chain)

Amino acid	*Thermotoga*	Yeast	Thermophiles	Mesophiles
G	24	27	25-26	26-35
A	25	32	38-44	32-34
V	36	37	28-42	33-38
L	26	20	26-31	18-20
I	30	19	19-22	18-21
M	4	6	5-7	6-10
F	8	10	5-6	10-15
W	2	3	2-3	2-3
P	14	12	11-12	11-13
S	15	29	13-18	18-29
T	27	23	18-22	18-23
B	35	36	34-40	29-39
Z	26	19	24-28	18-24
C	3	2	1-3	2-5
Y	9	11	8-10	9-11
K	27	26	23-24	24-28
R	14	11	14-16	9-11
H	7	8	9-10	5-11
Sum	332	331	333-335	332-336

Lactate Dehydrogenase. In contrast to GAPDH, LDH shows an extremely low expression level. Due to its structural similarity and its anomalous sequence homology with GAPDH this causes extreme difficulties in the purification and cloning of the enzyme (*4,30,31*). Therefore, the sequence of the enzyme has yet to be elucidated. Table V summarizes the amino-acid composition. At the present stage, again, it is not possible to detect significant trends.

As in the case of GAPDH, the structural properties of the hyperthermophilic enzyme and its mesophilic homologs are closely similar (Table IV). The enzyme exhibits undiminished activity up to the boiling point of water; in the Arrhenius plot neither cold-denaturation nor any significant curvature at maximum temperature can be detected (*4*) (Fig. 2). NAD^+ has a strong stabilizing effect: deactivation of the *apo*enzyme becomes significant at temperatures below 85°C. Fructose-1.6-bisphosphate (in the absence of divalent ions) also serves as an extrinsic stabilizing factor; both ligands bind with high affinity, their effect is additive (*4,32*). In this connection, two points deserve mentioning: 1. Considering the various ligands involved in catalysis and activation, it is obvious that enzymes under physiological conditions do not necessarily operate with maximum efficiency: K_M for NADH and pyruvate show a dramatic *increase* with increasing temperature (*32*). The reason may be that proteins have multiple

Table IV. Properties of homologous mesophilic and thermophilic GAPDHs and LDHs

Property	GAPDH		LDH	
	Thermotoga	Yeast	*Thermotoga*	Pig (H_4)
Molecular mass (M_4) (kDa)	145	144	144	140
Subunit mass (M_1) (kDa)	37	36	36	35
Change in $s_{20,w}$ (holo minus apo)	3.5%	5.3%	n.d.	7.0%
Thermal denaturation (T_m holo °C)	109	40	91	42
Denaturation in GdmCl ($c_{1/2}$ 20°C)	2.1M	0.5M	1.8M	0.5M
Activation at 0.5 M GdmCl (70°C)	300%	0%	n.d.	n.d.
Half-time of thermal denaturation at 100°C (h)	>2	$< 10^{-2}$	≈1	$< 10^{-2}$
Rel. H-D exchange rate (β_{rel} 25°C)	64	100	n.d.	n.d.
Specific activity U/mg at (°C)	200 (85)	70 (20)	≈1000 (55)	400 (25)
Michaelis constant K_M (μM)				
μM substrate (°C)	400 (60)	160 (25)	60 (55)	76 (25)
μM NAD^+/$NADH$ (°C)	79 (60)	44 (25)	27 (55)	10 (25)
Activation energy of enzyme reaction limiting values (kJ/mol)	33-79	25-80	57-104	38-63
Opt. reactivation at 0°C/≥30°C	0%/85%	35%/85%	n.d.	50%/95%

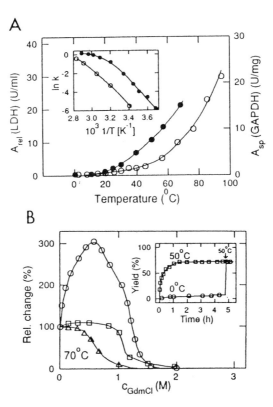

Figure 2.   Temperature dependence and denaturation/renaturation of LDH and GAPDH from *Thermotoga maritima*. (A) T-dependence of the enzymatic activity of LDH (o) and GAPDH (●) under standard conditions (*3,4*, Rehaber, V; Jaenicke, R. *J. Biol. Chem.* **1992**, in press). Insert: Arrhenius plot: LDH in the presence of 3 mM F-1.6-BP; in the case of GAPDH, the assay at T>60°C is perturbed by the instability of NADH and the substrates. (B) GdmCl-dependent denaturation of GAPDH monitored by activity (o), fluorescence (□) and circular dichroism (Δ) (Rehaber, V.; Jaenicke, R. *J. Biol. Chem.* **1992**, in press). Insert: Reactivation after denaturation in 6 M GdmCl at 50°C (□) and 0°C (o); after final state was reached, T was shifted to 50°C (*29*).

Table V. Amino-acid Composition of LDHs from *Thermotoga maritima* and Other Sources (given in mol%)

Aminoacid	*Thermotoga maritima*	*Thermus aquaticus*	*Bac. stearo-thermophilus*	*Bac. sacch-arolyticus*	*Pig heart*
G	9.6	10.2	8.8	8.5	7.2
A	8.6	13.9	10.7	8.2	6.0
V	9.5	12.4	9.5	6.3	11.7
L	10.2	11.3	7.3	8.5	10.8
I	7.5	3.8	8.8	9.7	6.9
M	2.0	0.4	1.9	2.2	2.7
F	4.0	3.4	4.4	4.1	1.5
W	n.d.	1.1	1.0	0.9	1.8
P	3.5	3.0	2.8	3.1	3.3
S	4.1	4.2	3.8	4.1	7.8
T	4.9	4.5	3.8	6.0	4.2
B	10.0	5.3	11.7	12.3	10.8
Z	10.7	11.3	8.2	10.1	9.9
C	n.d.	0	0.6	0.9	1.5
Y	2.8	1.9	3.8	3.8	2.1
K	6.5	2.6	4.4	5.7	7.2
R	4.3	8.7	5.7	4.1	2.4
H	2.0	1.9	2.8	1.6	2.1

functions which cannot be simultaneously optimized, especially under extreme physical conditions. 2. The fact that *in vitro* studies commonly do not include extrinsic factors may be misleading: Ions, metabolites, coenzymes or specific protectants, such as polyphosphates or chaperons may affect the stability properties of cellular components in a significant way.

Concluding remarks

As has been mentioned, the excess free energy of stabilization for a highly stable protein does not involve more than a few percent of the total number of weak interactions involved in the secondary, tertiary and quaternary contacts within the molecule. Considering the three forms of GAPDH from the thermophilic bacteria *Thermotoga maritima, Methanothermus fervidus* and *Bacillus stearothermophilus*, with their respective T_m-values 110, 80 and 68°C, about 100 of the 330 amino acids per subunit differ between the three enzymes; obviously, the answer to the question of which of these is responsible for the increment in thermal stability is not trivial. One way out of this dilemma would be to investigate point mutations yielding proteins of known structures with differing thermal stabilities (cf. *23-27*). For example, single, double and triple mutants of creatinase (a homodimer of 110 kDa molecular mass) exhibit additive increments of stabilization caused by a decrease in hydrophobic surface area and improved packing density; obviously, in this case, subunit interactions do not play a significant role (J. Schumann, unpublished results). In contrast, thermostable point mutations of pyruvate oxidase cause improved coenzyme binding and subunit association, this way promoting the native tetrameric quaternary structure (B. Risse, unpublished results). These investigations try to extend previous studies on the monomeric phage T4 lysozyme (*1,27*) at the next higher level by including ligands and subunit association into the consideration.

Ligands as "extrinsic effectors" have briefly been mentioned. One example is cyclic 2.3 diphosphoglycerate which has been shown to enable non-thermostable proteins to gain thermal stability (*33,34*). Because of their functional analogy to "compatible solutes" and anti-freeze compounds, it should be remembered that similar cellular components allow halotolerant organisms, as well as plants and fish, to survive salt and low-temperature stress without halophilic or psychrophilic adaptation. Further stabilizing factors involving the nascent or folding-competent rather than the native protein, refer to components or parameters "assisting" in structure formation or counteracting misfolding and misassembly (*11,35*). How this "assistance" works, and what is the intermediate state of the nascent or refolding polypeptide chain is not understood. The phenomenon was originally detected as *heat-shock response*, devised to counteract misaggregation as the major consequence of protein heat denaturation. The occurrence of heat-shock proteins in all cells, and their high degree of conservation during evolution led to the view that they must have a fundamental function as "chaperons" for the nascent or infant polypeptide chain (*36,37*). The idea that binding of early folding intermediates to hydrophobic surfaces competes with misfolding, and that additional heat-shock components and/or ATP-hydrolysis lead to conformational changes and subsequent release of the polypeptide chain is a reasonable working hypothesis for future experiments. That such two-step mechanisms may be meaningful has been observed in a number of cases, where reconstitution of thermophilic proteins was arrested at low temperature; after switching to high temperature folding proceeds to high yields at greatly enhanced rate (29). Since aggregation and association are endothermic, low temperature allows the folding polypeptide chain to make the correct tertiary contacts, thus transforming the "molten globule" (11,38) into the native three-dimensional structure.

Acknowledgments

I should like to thank the John E. Fogarty International Center for Advanced Study at the NIH, Bethesda, for generous support and hospitality. Fruitful discussions with Drs. G. Böhm, P.L. Privalov, V. Rehaber, B. Risse, R. Rudolph, F.X. Schmid, J. Schumann, H. Schurig, R. Seckler, A. Wrba and P. Závodszky are gratefully acknowledged. Work performed in the author's laboratory was generously supported by grants of the Deutsche Forschungsgemeinschaft, the Fonds der Chemischen Industrie and the BAP Program of the European Community.

Literature Cited

1. Jaenicke, R. *Eur.J.Biochem.* **1991.** *202*, 715-728.
2. *Thermophiles*; Brock, T. D., Ed.; Wiley: New York, **1986.**
3. Wrba, A.; Schweiger, A.; Schultes, V.; Jaenicke, R.; Závodszky, P. *Biochemistry* **1990**, *29*, 7585-7592.
4. Wrba, A; Jaenicke, R.; Huber, R.; Stetter, K. O. *Eur. J. Biochem.* **1990**, *188*, 195-201.
5. Schumann, J.; Wrba, A.; Jaenicke, R.; Stetter, K. O. *FEBS Lett.* **1991**, *282*, 122-126.
6. Böhm, G. *Strukturmodellierung extremophiler Proteine*: Dissertation, Universität Regensburg,**1992.**
7. Schultes, V.; Deutzmann, R.; Jaenicke, R. *Eur. J. Biochem.* **1990**, *192*, 25-31.
8. Jaenicke, R. *Phil. Trans. R. Soc.* **1990**, *B326*, 535-553.
9. Privalov, P. L. *CRC Crit. Rev. Biochem. Mol. Biol.* **1990**, *25*, 281-305.
10. Jaenicke, R. *Progr. Biophys. Mol. Biol.* **1987**, *49*, 117-237.
11. Jaenicke, R. *Biochemistry* **1990**, *30*, 3147-3161.
12. Dill, K. A. *Biochemistry* **1990**, *29*, 7133-7155.
13. Huber, R.; Langworthy, T. A.; König, H.; Thomm, M.; Woese, C. R.; Sleytr, U. B.; Stetter, K. O. *Arch. Microbiol.* **1986**, *144*, 324-333.
14. Bernhardt, G.; Jaenicke, R.; Lüdemann, H.-D.; König, H.; Stetter, K. O. *Appl. Environ. Microbiol.* **1988**, *54*, 2375-2380.
15. Bernhardt, G.; Lüdemann, H.-D.; Jaenicke, R.; König, H.; Stetter, K. O. *Naturwissenschaften* **1984**, *71*, 583-586.
16. White, R. H. *Nature (London)* **1984**, *310*, 430-432.
17. Baldwin, R. L. *Proc. Natl Acad. Sci. U.S.A.* **1986**, *83*, 8069-8072.
18. Privalov, P. L.; Gill, S. J. *Adv.Prot.Chem.* **1988**, *39*, 193-231.
19. Privalov, P. L.; Gill, S. J. *Pure Appl.Chem.* **1989**, *61*, 1197-1104.
20. De Grado, W. F. *Adv. Prot. Chem.* **1988**, *39*, 51-124.
21. Tanford, C. *Adv. Prot. Chem.* **1968**, *23*, 122-282; **1970**, *24*, 1-95.
22. Privalov, P. L. *Adv. Prot. Chem.* **1979**, *33*, 167-241.

23. Pace, C. N. *Trends Biotechnol.* **1990**, *8*, 93-98.
24. Kim, P. S.; Baldwin, R. L. *Annu. Rev. Biochem.* **1990**, *59*, 631-660.
25. Dobson, C. M. *Curr. Opin. Struct. Biol.* **1991**, *1*, 22-27.
26. Matthews, C. R. *Curr. Opin. Struct. Biol.* **1991**, *1*, 28-35.
27. Matthews, B. W. *Curr. Opin. Struct. Biol.* **1991**, *1*, 17-21.
28. Argos. P.; Rossmann, M. G.; Grau, U. M.; Zuber, H.; Frank, G.; Tratschin, J. D. *Biochemistry* **1979**, *18*, 5698-5703.
29. Schultes, V.; Jaenicke, R. *FEBS Lett.* **1991**, *290*, 235-238.
30. Wrba, A. *Enzyme aus dem extrem thermophilen Eubakterium Thermotoga maritima: Reinigung und Charakterisierung der LDH und GAPDH*: Dissertation, Universität Regensburg, **1989**.
31. Tomschy, A. *Versuch zur Klonierung extrem thermophiler Enzyme aus Thermotoga maritima*: Diplomarbeit, Universität Regensburg, **1990**.
32. Hecht, K.; Wrba, A.; Jaenicke, R. *Eur. J. Biochem.* **1989**, *183*, 69-74.
33. Hensel, R.; König, H. *FEMS Microbiol. Lett.* **1988**, *49*, 75-79.
34. Huber, R.; Kurr, M.; Jannasch, H. W.; Stetter, K. O. *Nature (London)* **1989**, *342*, 833-834.
35. Fischer, G.; Schmid, F. X. *Biochemistry* **1990**, *29*, 2205-2212.
36. Ellis, R. J. *Semin. Cell Biol.* **1990**, *1*, 1-9.
37. Ellis, R. J.; van der Vies, S. *Annu. Rev. Biochem.* **1991**, *60*, 321-347.
38. Christensen, H.; Pain, R. *Eur. Biophys. J.* **1991**, *19*, 221-229.

RECEIVED March 31, 1992

Chapter 5

Psychrophilic Proteinases from Atlantic Cod

J. B. Bjarnason[1], B. Asgeirsson[1], and J. W. Fox[2]

[1]Science Institute, University of Iceland, 107 Reykjavik, Iceland
[2]Department of Microbiology, University of Virginia Medical School,
Charlottesville, VA 22908

One mechanism of cold adaptation in ectothermic organisms
involves alterations of the efficiency of enzyme catalyzed
reactions at lower temperatures. Adaptation of ectothermic
organisms is required so that the normal
physiological/metabolic pathways operate at a flux level
necessary to sustain life at the ambient temperature of the
organism's environment. To meet these physiological
requirements organisms may simply increase the levels of the
enzymes. A more long-term adaptation is the structural
evolution of the enzymes such that their catalytic properties
are optimized for function at low ambient temperatures. The
Atlantic cod, *Gadus morhua*, is a cold-water poikilothermic
fish living in waters with temperatures ranging from 0 to 8°C.
We have isolated and characterized the trypsins,
chymotrypsins and elastases from the digestive tract of this
fish and we have demonstrated that these enzymes have
altered biophysical and functional properties compared with
analogous enzymes from endotherms. Essentially, the cod
enzymes have an increased catalytic efficiency accompanied
by a decrease in thermal stability. This observation leads one
to the hypothesis that the enhanced catalytic characteristics of
the fish enzymes is structurally interfaced with the decreased
thermal stability. Both of these characteristics, increased
catalytic efficiency and decreased thermal stability have some
practical value in industrial applications and the structural
principles underlying these properties may in the future be
exploited by protein engineering of enzyme systems other than
the proteases.

Biochemical attributes of organisms that have adapted to low temperatures
must include the preservation of structural integrity of the macromolecules
as well as the macromolecular assemblies for function in a particular
environment (1). In the case of the adaptation of ectothermic organisms to
low temperature conditions, the evolutionary pattern is such that there is
often observed a compensation of catalytic rates either by varying enzyme

0097–6156/93/0516–0068$06.00/0
© 1993 American Chemical Society

concentrations or increasing the catalytic capacity of enzymes (*1*). Changes in enzyme concentrations are often seen in response to seasonal variations in temperature (*1,2*), however, alteration in catalytic ability is typically more common as an evolutionary mechanism of enzymatic adaptation to low temperature. This adaptation can take the form of changes in the interaction of the enzyme with its substrate as measured by K_m values but in the case of intracellular enzymes the K_m's tend to be conserved in relation to the physiological levels of the substrates.

Alteration of the catalytic efficiency of enzymes of ectothermic, cold adapted organisms is generally the result of enzyme's ability to lower the free energy of activation for the particular reaction. Low and Somero (*3*) have proposed that this can be achieved structurally by an increase in the weak interactions between a substrate and the enzyme which results in further stabilization of the transition state of the reaction. Complimentary to this would be a reduction of weak intramolecular interactions which normally serve to stabilize the protein structure with the result of a generally less-stable but more flexible structure (*1*). On an evolutionary time scale these changes must occur at the level of the primary structure of the enzymes.

We have chosen to study the digestive enzymes of the Atlantic cod, *Gadus morhua*, a poikilothermic teleost fish which inhabits waters with temperatures ranging from 0 to 8°C. These serine proteinases well serve our requirements in trying to unravel the structural basis of the cold-activity of these enzymes since there is abundant literature on the kinetic and biophysical properties of serine proteinases from warm-blooded animals. This allows for ready comparison with the analogous enzymes from low temperature adapted species. It is our recent work on these fish enzymes which we will review in this chapter.

Cod Trypsins

Isolation and biochemical characterization. Three isozymes of trypsin were isolated from the pyloric caeca of the Atlantic cod using a combination of affinity and gel filtration chromatography and chromatofocusing (*4*). All three trypsins had a similar molecular mass of 24.2 kDa. The three isozymes had isoelectric points of 6.6, 6.2 and 5.5. The 6.6 pI species was the most abundant of the three species. The amino acid composition of the primary trypsin is shown in Table I. The composition is similar to the other trypsin compositions shown. The average residue hydrophobicity of the cod trypsin is 3.68 kJ compared to 3.60 kJ/residue for the Greenland cod trypsin, both of which are considerably lower than the 4.35 kJ/residue calculated for bovine trypsin (*4*). The N-terminal amino acid sequence of the major cod trypsin is compared with that of several other trypsins in Table II. Over the 37 residues determined the cod trypsin had 30 identical residues with rat and porcine trypsin, 29 with bovine trypsin, 26 with dogfish trypsin and 6 with crayfish trypsin.

Activity characteristics. The esterolytic and amidolytic kinetic properties of the three cod trypsins were determined with the respective substrates TosArgOMe and BzArg-NH-Np[1]. Table III shows the results of these studies. As can be observed, some differences in the catalytic efficiency (k_{cat}/K_m) between the three cod species as well as bovine trypsin are apparent. Two critical points can be taken from these results. Firstly, all of

Table I. The amino acid composition of Atlantic cod trypsin (enzyme 1) compared with trypsins from other species

	Atlantic cod (enzyme I)	Greenland cod	Bovine	Porcine	Human	Shrimp	Sardine	Catfish
Aspartic acid	19	23	22	18	21	30	31	25
Glutamic acid	27	19	14	17	21	24	16	22
Serine	23	32	33	24	24	24	17	23
Glycine	28	28	25	26	20	28	27	24
Histidine	6	7	3	4	3	5	3	7
Arginine	6	5	2	4	6	3	6	5
Threonine	10	10	10	11	10	10	19	9
Alanine	16	16	14	16	13	16	15	13
Proline	6	10	9	10	9	11	10	13
Tyrosine	10	7	10	8	7	10	13	9
Valine	18	16	17	16	16	18	18	18
Methiomine	6	3	2	2	1	2	1	6
Cysteine	12	8	12	12	8	8	8	12
Isoleucine	8	8	15	15	12	14	11	13
Leucine	16	14	14	16	12	10	10	13
Phenylalanine	3	4	3	4	4	6	4	6
Lysine	8	6	14	10	11	5	17	11
Tryptophan	3	2	4	6	3	3	4	7
Total	225	218	223	219	201	237	230	236

Table II. The N-terminal amino acid sequence of Atlantic cod trypsin (enzyme I) compared to trypsins from other species

	1				5					10					15					20					25					30					35					40
1)	I	V	G	G	Y	Q	C	E	A	H	S	Q	A	H	Q	V	S	L	N	S	G	Y	H	Y	C	G	G	S	L	I	N	-	-	W	V	V	S	A	A
2)	I	V	G	G	Y	T	C	G	A	N	T	V	P	Y	Q	V	S	L	N	S	G	Y	H	P	C	G	G	S	L	I	N	S	Q	W	V	V	S	A	A
3)	I	V	G	G	Y	T	C	A	A	N	S	V	P	Y	Q	V	S	L	N	S	G	Y	H	F	C	G	G	S	L	I	N	S	Q	W	V	V	S	A	A
4)	I	V	G	G	Y	T	C	P	E	H	S	V	P	Y	Q	V	S	L	N	S	G	Y	H	F	C	G	G	S	L	I	N	D	Q	W	V	V	S	A	A
5)	I	V	G	G	Y	E	C	P	K	H	A	A	P	W	T	V	S	L	N	V	G	Y	H	F	C	G	G	S	L	I	A	P	G	W	V	V	S	A	A
6)	I	V	G	G	T	D	A	V	L	G	E	F	P	Y	Q	L	S	F	Q	E	H	F	L	G	F	S	F	H	F	C	G	A	S	I	Y	N	E	N	Y

Table III. Kinetic parameters of trypsins purified from Atlantic cod (enzymes I, II and III) compared to those measured for bovine trypsin. TosArgOMe esterolytic activity and BzArg-NH-Np amidolytic activity were measured at 25°C and pH 8.1.

Substrate	$K_m(mM)$	$k_{cat}(s^{-1})$	$k_{cat}/K_m(s^{-1}mM^{-1})$
TosArgOMe			
Enzyme I	0.029	136.7	4713
Enzyme II	0.021	57.6	2781
Enzyme III	0.049	62.8	1281
Bovine	0.046	86.1	1870
BzArg-NH-Np			
Enzyme I	0.077	4.0	51.9
Enzyme II	0.094	1.9	20.2
Enzyme III	0.102	0.7	6.8
Bovine	0.650	2.0	3.1

the trypsins examined were significantly better esterases than amidases. Secondly, the cod trypsin, at 25°C, has a 17 fold greater amidase and 2.5 fold greater esterase catalytic efficiency than bovine trypsin (4). This is clearly demonstrated in Figure 1, where a comparison is made of the kinetic parameters of bovine trypsin and cod trypsin I at various temperature. The cod enzyme had maximal amidase activity at a pH of approximately 8 which is similar for most serine proteinases. The temperature dependence of the esterolyic activity for the cod trypsin as compared to bovine trypsin is seen in Figure 2. Assay of enzymatic activity of the bovine and cod trypsins at temperatures up to 55°C resulted in an increase in enzymatic activity with increasing temperatures. At temperatures approaching 65°C the bovine trypsin begins to decline in activity. The cod trypsin began to lose activity at a significantly lower temperature (55°C), thus suggesting a greater thermal stability for bovine trypsin as compared to the cod enzyme (Figure 2).

Stability characteristics. The effect of pH on the stability of the cod enzyme was measured by incubating the enzyme for either 30 min or 18 h at 5°C in buffers with increasing pH followed by assay of esterase activity at 25°C, pH 8.1 (4). As seen in Figure 3, the cod trypsin was stable at alkaline pH but becomes rather unstable at pH values less than 5. Although this is contrary to similar studies on bovine trypsin which is very stable at low pH values (5), the results are in accordance with those of trypsins from other fishes (6,7). The effect of temperature on the stability of the cod trypsin was not directly determined, however, certain trends can be inferred from the temperature/activity studies described in the above section. Obviously, the cod enzyme is more sensitive to temperature denaturation than bovine trypsin in that a decline in activity with increasing temperature is observed at a much lower temperature compared to the bovine enzyme (Figure 2) suggesting an enhanced temperature dependent denaturation for the cod trypsin. Our recent studies have indicated that the loss of activity of the cod enzyme with increasing temperature is due to both denaturation and increased autolysis.

Summary. These studies comparing the structural and functional properties of the endothermic bovine trypsin and the ectothermic cod trypsins have brought forth several interesting observations. The cod enzyme is a trypsin analog based upon its substrate specificity. From a structural aspect the cod enzyme is a trypsin homolog, to a degree, as seen from its amino acid composition and N-terminal amino acid sequence, however certain critical structural differences must exist which give rise to the different activity and stability characteristics of the cod trypsin compared to the bovine trypsin. Essentially, the cod trypsin is 2 to 20 fold more active than the bovine enzyme at any temperature in terms of the kinetic parameters. The temperature for the maximal activity for the cod enzyme is approximately 10°C lower than the maximal activity temperature for bovine trypsin.

Some indications for the structural basis of the increase catalytic efficiency of cod trypsin are suggested from the data. Firstly, the amino acid composition of the cod enzyme gives a decreased per residue hydrophobicity compared to the bovine composition which could indicate decreased intramolecular interactions at increasing temperatures. This would translate into a decreased relative stability for the cod molecule. The lower stability is reflected in the temperature/activity study where the cod enzyme is seen to lose activity at a lower temperature compared to the bovine enzyme. To

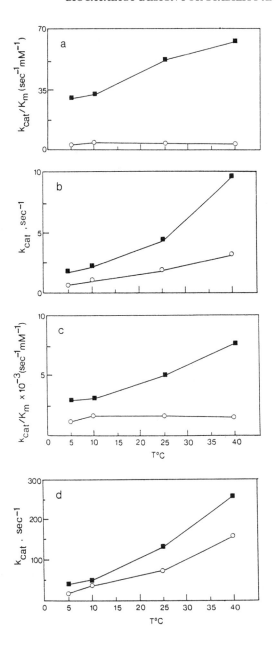

Figure 1. Comparison of catalytic efficiency and turnover number between cod (dark squares) and bovine (circles) trypsins at different temperatures. Amidolysis was determined with the substrate benzoyl-L-arginine p-nitroanilide (a and b) and esterolysis with p-toluenesulfonyl-L-arginine methyl ester (c and d) at pH 8.1.

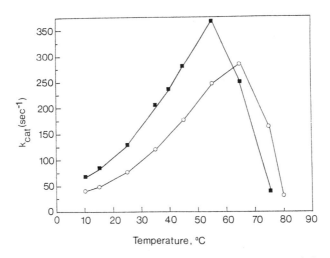

Figure 2. Effect of temperature on the activity of trypsin from Atlantic cod (dark squares) and bovine (circles). The enzymes were added to a preheated thermostatted cuvette, and the average rate of TosArgOMe hydrolysis subsequently determined during a 3 minute period.

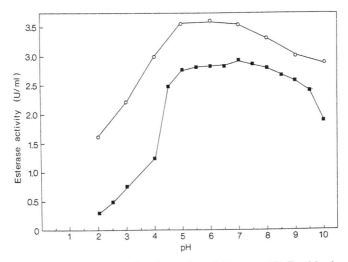

Figure 3. The dependence of cod trypsin stability on pH. Residual activity was determined with TosArgOMe as substrate at pH 8.1 and 25^0C after incubation at 5^0C for 30 min (circles) or 18 h (dark squares).

relate these observations to an increase in the flexibility of the cod enzyme as compared to the bovine we are currently pursuing studies on the structural dynamics of the two enzymes.

Cod Chymotrypsins.

Isolation and biochemical characterization.   Two chymotrypsins were isolated from the pyloric caeca of the Atlantic cod using similar chromatography techniques as exploited in the isolation of the cod trypsins, including affinity, hydrophobic interaction and chromatofocusing chromatography (*8*).   These steps yielded two chymotrypsins, A and B, having isoelectric points of 6.2 and 5.8 respectively.   The estimated molecular mass of the chymotrypsins was 26 kDa. The N-terminal amino acid sequence of chymotrypsin A is seen in Table IV. The cod sequence is obviously homologous to the bovine chymotrypsin sequence. Furthermore, sequence studies on the non-reduced "native" chymotrypsin B gave an indication that as in the case of bovine chymotrypsin an internal cleavage occurs in the region of amino acid position 15.   These data taken in conjunction with SDS-PAGE studies under both reducing and nonreducing conditions suggests that the cod chymotrypsins exist in both a "one chain" and "two chain" form. A similar, although not identical situation is found in the case of bovine chymotrypsin which is often found in either the "two chain" or the ultimate "three-chain" form (*9*).

Activity characteristics. The effect of temperature on the activity of the cod chymotrypsins as compared to bovine chymotrypsin using both ester and amide substrates is shown in Table V. As typically observed for chymotrypsins, the amide substrate gave much lower k_{cat} values, however the K_m values were similar to those found with the ester derivative substrate. It is important to note that the catalytic efficiency (k_{cat}/K_m) of the cod enzymes with the amide derivative substrate at $25^{o}C$ is approximately two to three fold higher than the bovine enzyme. In fact, all across the temperature range assayed ($5-30^{o}C$) the cod enzymes were demonstrated to have greater catalytic efficiencies than the bovine enzyme (*8*).

The pH activity profile (not shown) of the cod chymotrypsins shows a typical bell shaped distribution with the optimal pH at 7.8 which is essentially identical to the pH optimum for bovine chymotrypsin (*8,10*).However, the cod chymotrypsins were irreversibly inactivated at pH values less than 5 which is in contrast to the bovine enzyme which is very stable in acidic solutions of pH 3 (*8,10*).

Stability characteristics. As in the case of the cod trypsins, we have investigated the effect of pH and temperature on the stability of cod chymotrypsins as compared to the bovine enzyme. When the cod enzyme was incubated for 60 min at $5^{o}C$ at various pH values followed by assay for esterase activity at pH 8 the enzyme was seen to be stable over the alkaline pH range but increasingly unstable at pH values less than 5 (Figure 4). When considered together with the pH/activity study mentioned above it appears that the cod enzyme in fact becomes denatured at pH values less than 5 with a concomitant loss of activity, whereas, at pH values greater than 8 there is not an irreversible loss of activity suggesting that the enzyme remains stable at these alkaline pH values.

Table IV. N-terminal sequence of Atlantic cod chymotrypsin compared with bovine α-chymotrypsin where residues 14 and 15 have been removed as the result of autolysis. Underlined residues have not been determined with absolute certainty. The filled circles indicate differences in the two sequences.

	1				5					10				15					20					25					30		
Cod	C	G	S	P	A	I	Q	P	V	I	S	G		I	V	N	G	E	E	A	V	P	H	T	W	Y	W	Q	V
Bovine	C	G	V	P	A	I	Q	P	V	L	S	G	L	I	V	N	G	E	E	A	V	P	G	S	W	P	W	Q	V

Table V. Comparison of the effect of temperature on kinetic constants for ester or amide hydrolysis catalysed by chymotrypsin from Atlantic cod or cattle. The BzTyrOEt activity was determined in 10%(v/v) methanol and BzTyr-NH-Np activity in 10%(v/v) Me_2SO

BzTyrOEt	°C	K_m(mM)	k_{cat}(sec^{-1})	k_{cat}/K_m(sec^{-1}mM^{-1})
Cod-A	35	0.17	329	1935
Cod-B	35	0.10	276	2760
Bovine	35	0.24	142	591
Cod-A	25	0.14	207	1479
Cod-B	25	0.20	214	1070
Bovine	25	0.27	100	370
Cod-A	10	0.12	117	975
Cod-B	10	0.20	120	600
Bovine	10	0.27	43	159

BzTyr-NH-Np	°C	K_m(mM)	k_{cat}(sec^{-1})	k_{cat}/K_m(sec^{-1}mM^{-1})
Cod-A	35	0.14	0.82	5.9
Cod-B	35	0.11	0.72	7.2
Bovine	35	0.21	0.41	1.9
Cod-A	25	0.08	0.41	5.1
Cod-B	25	0.08	0.42	5.3
Bovine	25	0.14	0.30	2.2
Cod-A	10	0.09	0.10	1.1
Cod-B	10	0.11	0.10	0.9
Bovine	10	0.11	0.05	0.4

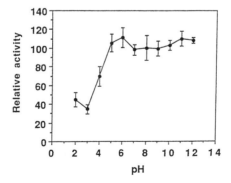

Figure 4. The effect of pH on the stability of Atlantic cod chymotrypsin. The effect of pH on the stability of cod chymotrypsin was estimated by measuring the residual BzTyrOEt activity in 10% (v/v) methanol at 25^0C after incubation at 5^0C for 60 minutes. The following buffers were used at a final concentration of 0.1M; acetate (pH 2-5); Hepes (pH 6-8) and glycinate (pH 9-12). The calcium concentration was 25mM. Each point is the mean of six determinations from three experiments.

To examine the effect of temperature on the stability of the cod chymotrypsin compared to bovine chymotrypsin the enzymes were incubated for 5 min at increasing temperatures, cooled and then assayed at 25°C for esterase activity. From Figure 5 it can be concluded that the cod enzyme is rather more sensitive to increasing temperature than the bovine enzyme. The loss of half maximal activity occurred at 52°C for the cod enzyme compared to 57°C for the bovine chymotrypsin.

Summary. These studies on the two cod chymotrypsins have corroborated our work with the cod trypsins on certain activity and stability properties of this class of enzymes. The cod chymotrypsins are homologous to the bovine chymotrypsin but not identical. These structural differences are reflected by their differing functional characteristics. The cod chymotrypsins have a similar pH/activity profile as the bovine enzyme but the activity is irreversibly lost at low pH values in the case of the cod enzyme whereas the bovine enzyme remains stable. On amidase substrates the cod enzymes were demonstrated to have a significant increase in catalytic efficiency compared to the bovine enzyme and although maximum rate of catalysis for the cod chymotrypsin is greater than that observed for the bovine enzyme the optimal temperature for catalysis by the cod enzyme is lower. With regard to thermal stability the cod chymotrypsin is less stable than compared to the bovine enzyme

Cod Elastase.

Isolations and biochemical characterization. We have purified an elastase from cod pyloric caeca using phenyl Separose hydrophobic chromatography followed by gel filtration and ion exchange chromatorgraphy (*11*). The enzyme has an apparent molecular mass of 25 kDa based upon SDS-PAGE. The isoelectric point of the protein was estimated to be approximately 9.5. These values are similar, although not identical to another elastase isolated from the Atlantic cod which was characterized to have a molecular weight of 28,000 and an isoelectric point greater than 9.3 (*12*). Whether these two enzymes are actually identical remains to be determined.

Activity characteristics. The effect of pH and temperature on the cod elastase was assayed. In the case of pH and activity the porcine and cod elastases have essentially the same pH optimum, pH 8.2 (results not shown). The comparative effect of temperature on the elastase activity of the two species was quite different both in terms of the position and level of maximal activity. The temperature of maximum activity for the cod elastase was observed at approximately 40°C compared to 50°C as observed for the porcine enzyme (Figure 6).

Stability characteristics. The relative stability of the cod elastase to temperature and pH denaturation has also been examined. In Figure 7 the effect of pH on the stability of the cod elastase at two different incubation at two different incubation temperatures is observed. The results of this experiment were similar to the those of the other cod proteinases. Incubation at either 5°C or 25°C did not significantly affect the pH value below which a loss of activity began (approximately pH 5). The cod elastase, similar to the other cod proteinases, was stable at alkaline pH values.

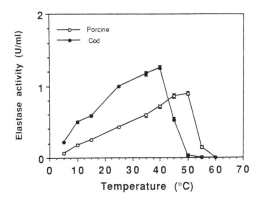

Figure 5. The effect of temperature on the catalytic activity of elastase from Atlantic cod and porcine. The enzyme was in each case added to a preheated medium (0.1 Tris, pH 8.0, containing 1 mM Suc-Ala-Ala-Ala-p-nitroanilide as substrate) and the average enzyme activity determined for the following one minute period.

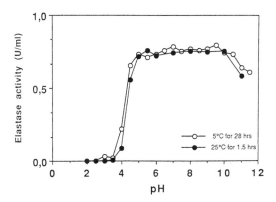

Figure 6. The effect of pH on the stability of elastase from Atlantic cod. The enzyme was incubated in 25 mM sodium phosphate in the pH range of 5.0 to 8.6, and in 25 mM sodium glycine in the pH range of 8.2 to 11.2. After incubation, either at 25^0 C for 1.5 h or at 4^0 C for 28 h, the residual activity was measured at 25^0C with Suc-Ala-Ala-Ala-p-nitroanilide as substrate in 0.1 M Tris at pH 8.0.

In the temperature denaturation experiments the enzymes were incubated for varying lengths of time after which they were cooled and then assayed for elastase activity at 25°C. At 45°C the cod elastase does not maintain full activity longer than 15 seconds whereas the porcine elastase retains full activity for extended periods (data not shown). Comparable to the cod elastase inactivation at 45°C is the inactivation of the porcine enzyme at 55°C; a 10 degree difference.

Summary. As has been demonstrated for the other cod digestive proteinases, the cod elastase also has an overall greater enzymatic activity than the analogous enzyme from a warm-blooded organism however, the temperature of maximal activity is significantly lower than that observed for the porcine elastase. The cod enzyme has a similar stability to pH relationship as that found for the other cod proteinases with these enzymes being relatively stable at alkaline pH values but rapidly and irreversibly losing activity under acidic conditions. Yet with regards to temperature stability, the enzymes from the two species are quite different with the cod elastase being much more sensitive to temperature denaturation.

Biotechnological Applications of Cold Active Proteinases.

As we and others have demonstrated, the cod digestive proteinases all have higher catalytic activities at all temperatures at which they are active, thus permitting the use of less amounts of enzymatic additives necessary for various processes. Associated with the use of enzymes for most industrial processes, particularly in the food industry is the necessity to eliminate the enzymatic activity once the desired results have been attained. Typically this is accomplished by either heat or acid denaturation. For the cod enzymes heat denaturation could be readily performed at lower temperatures than is necessary with many of the enzymes currently in use. This could result in lower energy costs and perhaps higher quality product. Also these cod enzymes appear to be more sensitive to denaturation at acid conditions under which most bovine proteinases remain stable. Mixtures of the digestive enzymes from cod, such as Cryotin contains a different profile of enzymatic activities compared to Pancreatin from bovine pancreas. In the case of Cryotin, the mixture lacks lipase activity which is present in Pancreatin, however, Cryotin has collagenolytic activity, which is not found in Pancreatin. Thus with certain applications the Cryotin may more readily produce the desired result.

Cold-active proteinases, purified or in mixture have many potential uses in industry, medicine and research. The applications in the food processing industrial appear to be especially promising since the ability to inactivate the enzyme adjunct with mild conditions which do not adversely affect the product is critical. The use of these enzymes have proven useful in various fish processing applications such as the skinning of fish, removal of membranes and ripening of herring. These proteinases also have shown potential as digestive aids, both for humans and animals. They are currently undergoing testing as adjuncts in microdiets for fish larvae. In Japan, the pepsin from cod is now in use as an enzyme adjunct in fish feed. Additional food processing applications where use may be found for cold-active enzymes from fish include chill-proofing of beer, biscuit manufacturing, tenderization of meats, hydrolysis of whey, casein and fish proteins, hydrolysis of gelatins and vegetable protein as well as many other proteins, particularly the collagens.

Future Developments.

Our laboratories are currently near completing the cDNA sequence analysis of the cod proteinases discussed in the proceeding sections. Our next step will be to carefully analyze the amino acid sequence differences between the cod and bovine enzymes with the aim of potentially identifying residues which may play a role in the "destabilization" of the cod enzymes relative to the bovine enzyme giving rise to an overall increase in the catalytic efficiency of the cod enzymes compared to their bovine counterparts. We will use this information in the alteration of the bovine enzyme structure by site specific mutagenesis coupled with appropriate assays to determine whether we have been successful in identifying the important residues in psychrophilic cod enzymes. Ultimately, we hope that these studies will contribute to the general knowledge of protein structure and function and that this information will be of potential use in the engineering of other enzymes which could best be utilized under cold temperature applications.

Acknowledgments

We would like to recognize support for this research from the Nordisk Industrifond (JBB), The Icelandic Science Foundation (JBB) and the National Science Foundation (JWF and JBB).

Literature Cited

1.   Hochachka, P.W. ; Somero, G.N. *Biochemical Adaptation*; Princeton University Press: Princeton, MA, 1984, 3-15.
2.   Owen, T.G.; Wiggs, A.J. *Comp. Biochem.Physiol.* **1971**, *40B*, 465-473.
3.   Low, P.S.; Somero, G.N. *Comp. Biochem. Physiol.* **1974**, *49B*, 307-312.
4.   Asgeirsson, B.; Fox, J.W.; Bjarnason, J.B. *Eur. J. Biochem.* **1989**, *180*, 85.
5.   Lazdunski, M.; Delaage, M. *Biochim. Biophys. Acta*, **1967**, *140*, 417-434.
6.   Hjelmeland, K.; Raa, J. *Comp. Biochem. Physiol.* **1982**, *71B*, 557-562.
7.   Simpson, B.K.; Haard, N.F. *Can. J. Biochem. Cell Biol.* **1984**, *62*, 894-900.
8.   Asgeirsson, B.; Bjarnason, J.B. *Comp. Biochem. Physiol.* **1991**, *99B*, 327.
9.   Bender, M.L.; Killheffer, J.V. *CRC Critical Reviews in Biochemistry*, April 1973.
10.   Wilcox, P.E . In *Methods in Enzymology*; Colowick, S.P. and Kaplan, N.O., Eds. 1970, *19*, 64.
11.   Bjarnason, J.B.; Mantyla, E.O.; Asgeirsson, B . *Sarsia*, **1992**, in press.
12.   Gildberg, A.; Overbo, K. *Comp. Biochem. Physiol.*, **1990**, *97B*, 775.

RECEIVED September 10, 1992

Chapter 6

Thermal and pH Stress in Thermal Denaturation of *Trichoderma reesei* Cellobiohydrolase I

Supporting Evidence for a Two-Transition Model

John O. Baker and Michael E. Himmel

Applied Biological Sciences Branch, Alternative Fuels Division, National Renewable Energy Laboratory, 1617 Cole Boulevard, Golden, CO 80401

The structure and thermal denaturation of *Trichoderma reesei* cellobiohydrolase I (CBH I) have been investigated using fluorescence, chemical modification, and differential scanning calorimetry (DSC) techniques. The results of both fluorescence-quenching with cesium ion and chemical modification with N-bromosuccinimide indicate that at least seven, and possibly eight, of the nine tryptophan residues in the CBH I catalytic core region are in "exposed" positions at or near the surface of the native molecule. A biphasic perturbation of the CBH I intrinsic fluorescence reveals that the CBH I core region is capable of binding more than one molecule of cellobiose and suggests that this additional bound molecule may be important for the stabilization of the core region against thermal denaturation. When the temperature of a solution of CBH I (pH 7.5 in 50 mM phosphate) is ramped through its denaturation zone (approximately 28°C - 48°C at this pH), a sharp, sigmoidal change, centered at approximately 36°C, is observed in the polarization of the tryptophan fluorescence of the protein. This polarization change precedes both the endothermic peak maximum (40.15°C) observed in DSC under the same conditions and the second (40.3°C) and larger of two component peaks invoked to explain the asymmetrical shape of the DSC peak. The midpoint of the fluorescence polarization change is much more closely correlated with the first (37.2°C) and smaller of the deconvoluted component peaks. The fluorescence-polarization data thus provide supporting evidence for the component transitions, the existence of which has heretofore rested only on mathematical inference, and thereby for the two-transition model proposed earlier for the denaturation.

0097–6156/93/0516–0083$06.00/0

Cellulose-depolymerizing enzymes have been of considerable industrial interest for years because of their utility in the conversion of cellulosic materials (agricultural residues, paper waste, or crops specifically grown for the purpose) into sugars fermentable into fuel ethanol (*1,2*). In recent years major advances have been made in determining the structures of cellulolytic enzymes and then relating these structures to the observed activities. What might be described as the first benchmark in this process of discovery was drawn from comparisons between the primary sequence of representative enzymes (*3*) and then from small-angle X-ray scattering (SAXS) studies of the overall shape of the enzymes (*4,5*). This benchmark consisted of the realization that cellulolytic enzymes in general, whether exo- or endo-acting, and whether from fungal or bacterial sources, tend to have a bilobed, two-domain structure, with one domain capable of binding tightly to crystalline cellulose, and the other containing the hydrolytic active site (*6-9*).

The second level of understanding followed upon the determination of the three-dimensional structure of a synthetic cellulose-binding domain (CBD) by solution nuclear magnetic resonance (NMR) (*10*) and the crystallization of the proteolytically separated catalytic domain of *T. reesei* cellobiohydrolase II (CBH II) (*11*), which made possible the determination of the tertiary structure of the catalytic domain and the modeling of the interactions between the catalytic domain and substrates and inhibitors (*12*). The most striking revelation provided by these studies of three-dimensional structure is that the actual bond-cleaving site of *T. reesei* CBH II is located in a closed tunnel through the catalytic domain (*12*). This has led to the suggestion that the "exo"-type cellulose depolymerases attack crystalline cellulose by a mechanism in which the cellulose-binding domain of the enzyme molecule pries the end of a cellulose chain away from the crystalline surface, and the chain is then fed across the CBD into the tunnel in the catalytic domain, where successive cellobiosyl fragments are cleaved from the chain (*8*) (and presumably ejected through the far end of the tunnel). In this model for substrate hydrolysis, the enzyme may be considered to hitch its way along the polyglucosyl chain, removing successive cellobiosyl fragments without diffusing away from the chain between hydrolytic events.

Despite the dramatic nature and extremely high value of the three-dimensional protein structures obtained by X-ray crystallography and the molecular-modeling studies they make possible, the existence of such information does not remove the rationale for other approaches, such as circular dichroism (CD), DSC, and fluorescence studies, that are also aimed at revealing the relationship between the structure of enzymes on the one hand and their activities and stabilities on the other. In the most trivially obvious case that could be cited, such alternate methods of structural analysis are indisputably of value for proteins for which detailed three-dimensional structures are not yet available (which happens to be the case, at this writing, for *T. reesei* CBH I, the enzyme with which the present paper is concerned). Even in the case of proteins for which high-resolution X-ray diffraction structures are available, the alternate methods of structural analysis differ from X-ray crystallography in that instead of providing an essentially static picture of the conformation in which the protein happens to crystallize, CD, DSC, and fluorescence are capable of analyzing other forms that may exist in solution, and of monitoring the transitions between forms; i.e., they are capable of providing a dynamic rather than static picture. The types of information provided by the different methods of structural analysis are therefore complementary, rather than redundant.

In an earlier study using DSC to analyze the thermal denaturation process for *Trichoderma* CBH I, we found indications (based on the asymmetry of the overall endothermic peaks) that the unfolding proceeded through a mechanism involving at least two distinct structural transitions (*13*). We proposed that the two transitions are tightly linked, one occurring closely upon the heels of the other, even when the temperature at which the overall denaturation occurs is varied over the range from approximately 64°C down to approximately 33°C, by varying the pH from 4.8 to 8.3 (Figure 1). The overall denaturation process was strongly affected by the presence of the competitive product inhibitor, cellobiose. Cellobiose at 100 mM, a saturating concentration some 5000 times the binding constant for the inhibitor as measured by inhibition of the enzyme activity, increased the denaturation temperature of CBH I by some 8°C at pH 4.8, at which pH the enzyme is at near-maximal stability in the absence of cellobiose, and by almost 19°C under conditions of pH stress at pH 8.34. It appeared that cellobiose should be a useful probe for the analysis of protein structural changes affecting the integrity of the active site.

In the present report, we describe results of a study in which the polarization of the fluorescence emission of the tryptophan residues of the catalytic core region of CBH I was used to monitor changes in the mobility of these residues, and therefore in the state of folding of the core region. These most recent results are complementary to the previous DSC results and appear to provide support for the two-transition model proposed for the thermal unfolding of CBH I core region on the basis of the DSC results.

Materials and Methods

CBH I Purification.   The purification procedure used in this study was that developed earlier (*13*) following the general size exclusion chromatography/anion exchange chromatography protocol described by Shoemaker for the purification of CBH I (*14*).

Differential Scanning Microcalorimetry.   Denaturation thermograms were obtained using a Microcal MC-2 Scanning Calorimeter (Microcal, Northampton, MA), interfaced though a DT 2801 A/D converter to an IBM PC-XT microcomputer. Instrument control and data acquisition were by means of the DA-2 software package (Microcal). The sample cell capacity is 1.130 mL, and runs were made with an overpressure of 30 psig (N_2), at scan rates of 0.5 deg/min and 0.21 deg/min. Protein samples for DSC typically contained 1.0 mg/mL protein in 50 mM sodium phosphate buffer, pH 7.5. The protein samples, along with reference

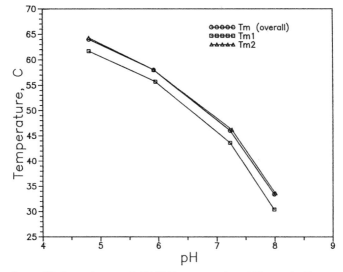

Figure 1.   pH-dependence of CBH I structural stability. Ordinate values plotted are from deconvolution analysis of DSC thermograms (ref. *13*). $T_{m(overall)}$ represents the temperature of maximum differential power input for the overall process as observed; T_{m1} and T_{m2} represent the temperatures of the two deconvoluted component transitions invoked to explain the shape of the overall peak. The pH values as plotted have been corrected, at the corresponding temperatures, for the temperature-dependence of the pK_a values of the buffers employed.

samples consisting of the same buffer system without protein, were equilibrated for 1 h at room temperature and atmospheric pressure, with gentle stirring, before loading into the sample and reference cells, respectively. After filling of the calorimeter cells, the protein concentration of the sample as loaded was determined spectrophotometrically, using the remainder of the solution used to load the sample cell. The extinction coefficient used for CBH I was 1.42 $(g/L)^{-1}$ at 280 nm (*15*).

Deconvolution Analysis of DSC. Data analysis was carried out using the DECONV section of the DA-2 software package. This software, which is based on the deconvolution procedure of Biltonen and Freire (*16*), allows deconvolution of differential heat-capacity peaks either as the result of simple addition of multiple independent transitions or as the result of more complex mathematical processes representing the combination of transitions that interact in such a way that an obligatory reaction sequence is imposed (sequential transitions).

Each thermogram was normalized on scan rate, the corresponding (scan-rate-normalized) buffer-buffer baseline was subtracted, and the differential heat capacity values were divided by the number of moles of protein in the sample, to yield ordinate values in terms of calories $mol^{-1}deg^{-1}$. The resulting files were then analyzed using the deconvolution software.

DSC Nomenclature. The term T_m as used here is not a "melting temperature," but is instead standard DSC usage for the temperature at which the maximum differential heat capacity is observed during the denaturation of a protein sample. ("T_{max}" would be a more extended expression of this term.) For a two-state (single-transition) process, T_m approximates, but is not identical to, the value of T_d or $T_{1/2}$, the temperature at which the transition is half-complete. Detailed discussions of these terms can be found in references (*17-21*).

Fluorescence Measurements. Fluorescence measurements were made with a FLUOROLOG 2 spectrofluorometer (Spex Industries, Inc., Edison, NJ) fitted, when appropriate, with Glan-Thompson excitation and emission polarizers (Spex Model 1935B manual L-format polarization kit). Temperature control of the sample was by water-jacketed cuvette holder with an external circulating water bath; sample temperature was monitored by means of a thermocouple immersed in the stirred sample. Data collection and analysis were carried out with a Spex DM1B Spectroscopy Laboratory Coordinator interfaced to the spectrofluorometer.

Enzyme Kinetic Measurements. The glycohydrolytic activity of CBH I was measured using the fluorogenic substrate 4-methylumbelliferyl-β-D-cellobioside (Sigma Chemical Company, St. Louis, MO). Enzyme and substrate were incubated at pH 7.5 and the temperature of interest in a stirred cuvette in the sample compartment of the spectrofluorometer, and the generation of the aglycone product, 4-methylumbelliferone, was continuously monitored by the change in the intensity of the fluorescence of its anionic form. The excitation wavelength used was 380 nm (bandpass 4.5 nm) and the emission was measured at 455 nm (bandpass 4.5 nm). The extent of hydrolysis was quantitated by means of a standard fluorescence curve for 4-methylumbelliferone, run at the same session, with the same temperature, buffer, and instrumental settings as those used for the enzyme activity measurements. The enzyme concentration was chosen for each set of experiments so that less than 2% (and usually less than 1%) of the substrate was hydrolyzed in a 10-minute assay.

Results and Discussion

T. reesei CBH I contains nine tryptophan residues (*22,23*), all of which are located in the ellipsoidal (*4,5*) catalytic core region of the molecule — none in the cellulose-binding and linker regions. The tryptophan fluorescence of the molecule may therefore be taken as a useful index of changes in the physico-chemical state of the core region alone. (The "tail" of the tadpole-shaped molecule is known from SAXS studies to be in a relatively extended average position in solution (*4,5*), and therefore should not significantly affect the fluorescence of even the surface residues in the core region.)

In the interpretation of changes in the tryptophan fluorescence of the core in terms of changes in the structure of that region, it is advantageous to have as much information as possible about the locations of the tryptophan residues in the native conformation of the protein molecule. To this end, the present study was opened with fluorescence-quenching and chemical-modification experiments designed to estimate the degree of exposure of the tryptophan residues to the external (aqueous) environment at 25°C and pH 4.8, under which conditions the stability of the native form is near-maximal. In a previous study, changes in the wavelength of the maximum emission intensity were used as a measure of changes in the average polarity of the microenvironments of the tryptophan residues, and presumably, therefore, of changes in their exposure to the aqueous external environment during thermal denaturation at pH 4.8 (thermal-scanning fluorescence studies) (*24*). The low-temperature portion of the scans in this previous study revealed a wavelength of maximum emission of approximately 355 nm, indicating a relatively polar (and presumably exposed) average microenvironment for the tryptophan residues in the native molecule (*25*).

Results obtained in the present study bear out this earlier inference, in addition to providing additional information about the distribution of environments among the nine tryptophan residues contributing to the overall fluorescence. Figure 2 illustrates the quenching of the intrinsic fluorescence of CBH I by cesium ion, which, as a charged quencher, is expected to quench exposed residues, but is not expected to penetrate readily into the hydrophobic interior of proteins (*25*). This Stern-Volmer plot (*25*) indicates that a substantial portion (probably well over half) of the tryptophan fluorescence of the core region is quenchable by cesium ion. A comparison of the slopes of the curves in Figure 2 indicates that the tryptophan residues being quenched are less accessible to the quencher than is the small model compound N-acetyl-L-tryptophanamide, as would be expected if the indole side-chains were partly imbedded in the surface of the protein, but by no means

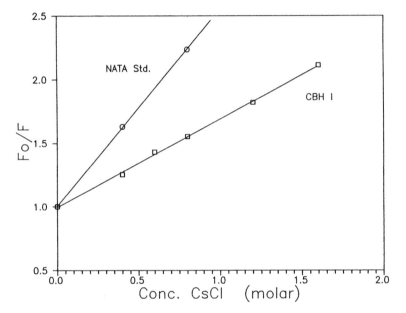

Figure 2.   Quenching by cesium ion of the intrinsic fluorescence of native-conformation CBH I at pH 4.8 (50 mM acetate) and 25°C. Excitation at 305 nm (0.9-nm bandpass); emission measured at 353 nm for CBH I and at 367 nm for N-acetyl-L-tryptophanamide (NATA), with an emission bandpass of 9.0 nm in both cases. Quenching of the model compound NATA is presented to allow comparison of slopes.

completely "buried." From the reasonable linearity of the plot for CBH I, we can also infer that the residues being quenched over this range of quencher concentration do not differ drastically from each other in degree of exposure.

The reciprocal of the ordinate intercept in the "modified Stern-Volmer plot" (25) of the same data (Figure 3) is an estimator of the fraction of the total protein fluorescence that is susceptible to quenching by cesium ion. The least-squares-fit value for the intercept might seem to indicate that all of the residues are accessible, but in view of the fact that there is some noise in the data, it is more appropriate to conclude from these results only that no more than 10% of the total fluorescence, if that much, is inaccessible to the quencher. Quantitative translation of the fraction of total fluorescence that is accessible to quencher into the fraction of tryptophan residues exposed to solvent is rendered approximate at best by the recognition that different tryptophan residues may have different quantum yields. If we assume, however, that the differences in quantum yield are not large, it seems reasonable to adopt the tentative conclusion that of the nine tryptophan residues, probably no more than one, and certainly no more than two, are "completely buried."

Figures 4 and 5 present a chemical modification approach to the estimation of the exposure of CBH I tryptophan residues to the solution. Both figures describe the titration of CBH I tryptophan side-chains with the reagent NBS, which oxidizes the indole ring to the non-fluorescent oxyindole derivative (26). The successive emission spectra recorded during the titration (Figure 4) show that from the beginning, the removal of the contributions from the residues more accessible to NBS results in a blue-shift of the emission spectrum away from the original maximum at 354-355 nm, indicating that the surviving fluorescent residues have an average microenvironment less polar (i.e., less exposed to solvent) than the original average of the microenvironments. The blue-shift is relatively small, however, until more than 60% of the fluorescence has been destroyed. After that the wavelength of maximum fluorescence shifts more rapidly, until it finally slows again near 337 nm, at which point the intensity of the fluorescence (at 337 nm) is approximately 12 % of the intensity originally measured at 354-355 nm.

The peak intensities measured after successive additions of NBS are plotted in Figure 5, as a function of the cumulative molar ratio of added NBS to CBH I. It should be noted that because of competing reactions (notably hydrolysis) that consume reagent, the stoichiometry of NBS added, to tryptophan residues oxidized, is not expected to be exactly 1:1. Under the conditions of our CBH I titration, we have determined that the stoichiometry for the "completely exposed" model compound NATA is approximately 1.2 mol NBS per mol NATA. For somewhat protected (and therefore slower-reacting) tryptophan residues partially buried in proteins, the partitioning of reagent toward solvent rather than tryptophan residues can be expected to occur to greater extents. For this reason, the important quantities to be considered in Figure 7 are the relative values of the slope of the curve at different levels of remaining fluorescence. The shape of the curve can accordingly be rationalized as representing the fairly rapid titration of residues contributing almost 90% of the original intensity, and not differing drastically from each other in accessibility to the reagent, followed by the much slower attack on the residue(s) responsible for the remaining 10%-11% of the intensity. Translation of this

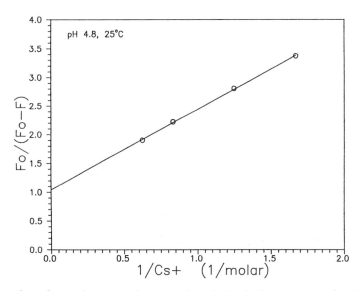

Figure 3.   Quenching by cesium ion of the intrinsic fluorescence of native-conformation CBH I. "Modified Stern-Volmer plot" (ref. *25*) of data from Figure 2, in which the ordinate intercept represents the reciprocal of the fraction of total fluorescence accessible to the quencher.

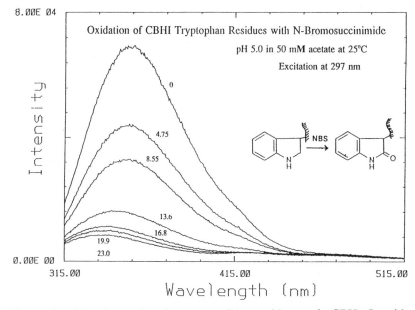

Figure 4.   Titration of solvent-accessible residues of CBH I with N-bromosuccinimide. Numbers adjacent to the spectra denote the cumulative molar ratios of NBS to CBH I applied prior to each spectral scan.

description into the average number of residues oxidized per protein molecule at different points of the titration can be only semi-quantitative at best, because (1) for a given excitation intensity, the quantum efficiency of tryptophan residues can vary with the microenvironment (25), and (2) the arbitrary selection of the (changing) wavelength of maximum intensity for measurement of the emission will underestimate the contribution of those residues with emission maxima significantly removed from the wavelength of maximum intensity for the overall envelope. These disclaimers notwithstanding, we feel that the data shown in Figures 4 and 5 strongly suggest, at least, that of the nine tryptophan residues of the catalytic core region of CBH I, seven, or perhaps eight, are "surface" residues, relatively exposed to the solution, and one residue is "buried."

Binding of Cellobiose to CBH I Monitored by Perturbation of the Protein Fluorescence. Cellobiose is a potent competitive product inhibitor of the hydrolysis of glycosidic substrates by CBH I, with a K_i value of approximately 20 micromolar at pH 5.0, 25°C (27). In the presence of 10 - 100 millimolar cellobiose, CBH I has been shown to be significantly stabilized against thermal denaturation, particularly at pH values at which the enzyme stability, in the absence of cellobiose, is substantially decreased with respect to its maximum stability (13). Although the stabilization by cellobiose develops over a range of cellobiose concentrations far higher than the K_i values for inhibition by cellobiose of the hydrolysis of the small substrate 4-methylumbelliferyl-β-D-cellobioside (K_i is 18-22 micromolar at pH 4.8, 25°C, 35-40 micromolar at pH 7.5, 35°C), it is possible to rationalize the stabilization in terms of the micromolar-level interaction that is reflected in the inhibition of the enzyme activity. The stabilization was so rationalized in our previous publication on the subject (13).

Recent fluorescence data, however, suggest the possibility that additional interactions may occur between cellobiose and the enzyme at higher cellobiose concentrations, and that these additional interactions may play an important role in the observed stabilization. Figure 6(a-c) illustrates the effect of increasing concentrations of cellobiose on the fluorescence emission spectrum of CBH I at pH 7.5 and 35°C. Increasing the cellobiose concentration from 0 to 40 mM (Figure 6a) brings about a biphasic series of changes in the emission spectrum, the biphasic nature of which may be seen more clearly in Figures 6b and 6c, in which the spectra corresponding to individual cellobiose concentrations have been separated out into low-concentration and high-concentration ranges. In Figure 6b, increasing the concentration of cellobiose from 0 to 5 mM produces primarily an increase in the height of the emission peak, with very little shift in the wavelength of maximum emission as marked by the arrows (although we do begin to see some blue-shifting by the time the cellobiose concentration has increased to 5 mM). In Figure 6c, which covers the range from 5 mM to 40 mM cellobiose, the effect seen is almost entirely a blue-shift, as indicated by the short vertical lines marking the peak positions, with no measurable change in peak height. The short vertical lines represent peak wavelengths for cellobiose concentrations increasing from right to left, with the "zero cellobiose" peak position shown on the right for reference. In Figure 6c the spectral curves are in the same order (concentration increasing from

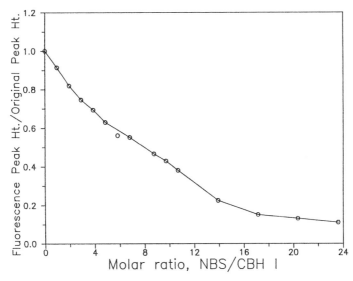

Figure 5.   Titration of CBH I tryptophan residues with N-bromosuccinimide. Fluorescence emission peak height as a function of NBS/CBH I ratio for the titration shown in Figure 4. (See text).

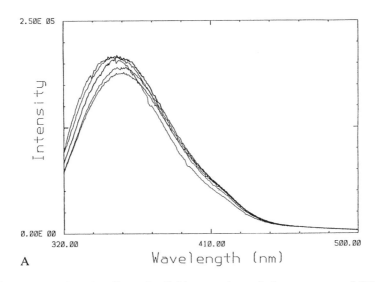

Figure 6.   Biphasic effect of cellobiose on the emission spectrum of CBH I at pH 7.5 (50 mM phosphate), 35°C. A: Wide-range composite plot of spectra in the presence of cellobiose concentrations from 0 to 40 mM.

Continued on next page.

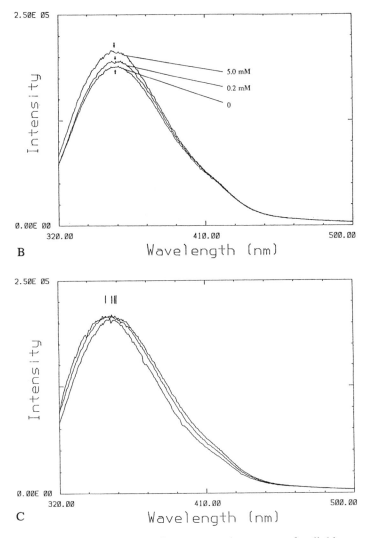

Figure 6. Continued. B: Spectra at a low range of cellobiose concentrations, showing primarily an amplitude effect. (Emission maxima represented by arrows.) C: Spectra at higher cellobiose concentrations, showing a blue-shift of the wavelength of maximum emission with increasing cellobiose concentrations. Peak maxima are indicated by the short vertical line segments above the spectra and represent (from right to left) wavelengths of emission maxima in the presence of 0, 5, 10, and 40 mM celliobose.

right to left) on both sides of the peak maxima (i.e., what is observed here is primarily the result of a simple wavelength shift, not a significant narrowing or broadening of the peak). Similar biphasic fluorescence-perturbation patterns have been obtained at pH 7.5, 25°C and at pH 4.8, 25°C; the data set at pH 7.5, 35°C was chosen for illustration because these conditions fall within the range over which the calorimetrically monitored (DSC) and fluorescence-monitored structural changes to be shown below, and the protection by cellobiose against these changes, are shown to occur. It is significant to point out that under the sets of conditions referred to above, the presence of sucrose in concentrations as high as 40 mM has no detectable effect whatsoever on the emission spectrum of CBH I (data not shown).

The above indications that more than one cellobiose molecule may bind to the CBH I molecule are not particularly surprising in view of the fact that this enzyme binds to and hydrolyzes a homopolymeric substrate and may therefore be expected to have extended binding sites both in the catalytic and the cellulose-binding domains. Rouvinen et al. (*12*), on the basis of X-ray crystallographic and molecular-modeling studies, have identified four clear binding sites for glucosyl residues along the catalytic tunnel through the CBH II core region. If a tunnel of this sort is a general feature of exo-cellulases, as suggested by Rouvinen et al. (*12*), it is not difficult to imagine two cellobiose molecules fitting snugly into a catalytic tunnel in this molecule, occupying the same glucosyl binding sites that would be filled by a cellotetraosyl moiety of a cellulose substrate chain (albeit, perhaps, with some strain between the glucosyl residues in the second and third binding sites). The result may be a substantial bracing of the core region, which would now be effectively a solid molecule.

Actual determination of the specific nature of the different protein/cellobiose interactions indicated here would require data of a more definitive type than that presented here. The conclusions important for the present study are (1) that there are at least two different interactions between cellobiose and CBH I, as indicated by the qualitatively different perturbations of the protein fluorescence in different ranges of cellobiose concentration; and (2) that at least one of these interactions develops over the same range of cellobiose concentrations over which increasing cellobiose concentrations have been shown by DSC (*13*) to stabilize CBH I progressively against major, thermally induced structural changes.

Thermal Denaturation of CBH I as Monitored by the Polarization of Tryptophan Fluorescence Emission. If the locations of most of the tryptophan residues in the core region are as suggested above on the basis of quenching and chemical modification data (i.e., imbedded in the protein surface but with at least one edge of the indole ring effectively exposed to the solution) then one of the most common approaches to using fluorescence to monitor conformational changes, the interpretation of shifts in the wavelength of maximum emission in terms of changing polarity of fluorophore microenvironments upon transfer from hydrophobic protein interior to aqueous solution (*25*), would be expected to be relatively insensitive to the conformational change in this case. The relatively polar environments of the tryptophan side-chains in the native protein simply would not leave much room for large increases in microenvironmental polarity upon unfolding. Indeed, this is what

was found in our earlier study of the thermal unfolding of CBH I at pH 4.8; over
the temperature range from 55°C to 70°C, where it had been found by DSC that
major calorimetrically detectable structural changes occurred, changes in the
wavelength of maximum emission did not rise significantly above the noise level
(*24*).

Given these circumstances, it appeared that fluorescence polarization
measurements, using the depolarization of the tryptophan fluorescence emission as
a measure of the mobility of individual tryptophan residues, might provide a more
effective means of monitoring thermally-induced conformational changes in the
CBH I core region. The results in Figure 7 show that this proved to be the case.
In this wide-range scan, the distinctive feature of the data taken at pH 7.5 is the
sigmoid portion of the curve between approximately 25°C and 43°C. The sigmoid
portion is overlaid on a broader pattern of general decrease of fluorescence
polarization with increasing temperature.   Included in Figure 7 for reference
purposes is a plot of fluorescence polarization as a function of temperature at pH
5.0, at which pH the enzyme is much more thermally stable than at pH 7.5, DSC
studies having shown that it remains essentially native in conformation up to at least
54°-55°C (Figure 1 and reference *13*). The pH 5.0 curve therefore serves, at least
up to 55°C, as a measure of that portion of the total polarization decrease (in both
curves) that may be ascribed to the net effect of increasingly rapid tumbling of a
relatively intact protein molecule with increasing temperature and the temperature-
dependence of fluorescence lifetimes for tryptophans in the basically intact protein
molecule. The additional (sigmoid) decrease in polarization observed at pH 7.5 over
the range 25°-43°C can be ascribed to physical changes associated with unfolding,
such as the more rapid rotations of individual tryptophan side-chains once they are
freed from the protein structure, effects on lifetimes resulting from exposure of
residues to solvent, and possible altered rotational rates for the entire molecule
reflecting size changes upon unfolding. (The data point that is off the pH 5.0 curve
at 61°C is not the result of experimental noise. By this temperature the unfolding
has proceeded to a significant extent, and at this pH at least one unfolded form of
the enzyme has a strong tendency to aggregate into larger particles (*13*), resulting
in a net decrease in tryptophan mobility relative to the trend shown at lower
temperatures. Because of these two changes — unfolding and aggregation — the
pH 5.0 curve therefore serves as a reference curve for an intact molecule only up
to approximately 55°-56°C.)

In the same type of pattern observed when the unfolding of CBH I is monitored
calorimetrically (*13*), increasing concentrations of cellobiose are found to result in
progressively greater thermal stabilization of CBH I, shifting the midpoint of the
polarization-detected sigmoid transition to higher temperatures, as shown in
Figure 8.

**Correlations Between DSC-monitored and Fluorescence-polarization-monitored
Thermal Unfolding.** In Figure 9, the results of a fluorescence-polarization thermal
scan of CBH I are co-plotted with a DSC thermogram of the enzyme under exactly
the same solution conditions. For this plot, the values for the fluorescence
polarization at pH 7.5 have been taken relative to the values interpolated at the same

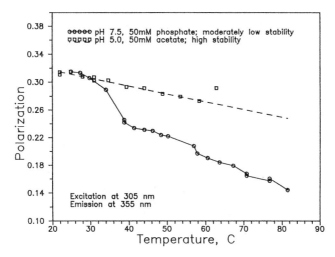

Figure 7. Temperature-dependence of CBH I fluorescence polarization.

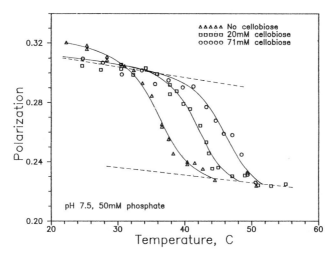

Figure 8. Effect of increasing concentrations of a competitive product inhibitor (cellobiose) on the thermally-induced change in fluorescence polarization.

temperatures from the straight-line approximation to the pH 5.0 data (Figure 7). The temperature-dependent polarization changes shown should therefore be related directly to the unfolding process itself, as explained in the preceding section

The solid line through the data points of the DSC thermogram is the computer-generated two-transition, sequential-model best fit to the data. The peaks shown as dashed lines represent the two mathematically inferred component peaks used to fit the computer model to the observed asymmetrical overall calorimetric envelope. The overall DSC envelope is dominated by the larger of the two deconvoluted component peaks, as shown by the near-coincidence of the maxima for the larger component and the overall envelope (T_{m2} = 40.30°C and $T_{m,overall}$ = 40.15°C). The midpoint of the sigmoid fluorescence-polarization transition at 36.1°C, however, is much more closely correlated with the first (smaller and lower-temperature) of the deconvoluted DSC component transitions (T_{m1} = 37.2°C). An even more telling observation is that by the time the temperature increases to 40°C, the temperature at which both the larger component peak and the overall envelope are nearing their peak differential power inputs (maximum rate of thermally detected structure-breakage), the fluorescence-detected transition is virtually complete.

The temperature-offset between the fluorescence-detected transition and the major calorimetrically detected transition is not the result of a scan-rate effect. The unfolding process is more than 70% reversible under these conditions, and DSC runs at both 0.5°C/min (Figure 8) and at 0.21°C/min (which latter rate is the slowest of which the calorimeter is capable, and is comparable to the "scan rate" used in the fluorescence-polarization studies) showed virtually identical unfolding temperatures.

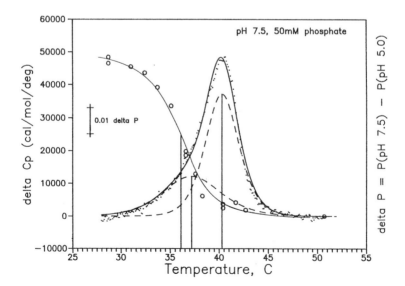

Figure 9.   Co-plot of the calorimetrically monitored and fluorescence-polarization-monitored conformational changes as the temperature of a CBH I solution is ramped through the region of denaturation.

Until the present study, the existence of the two component transitions proposed for the thermal denaturation of CBH I, although indicated consistently by deconvolution procedures applied to DSC thermograms obtained under a wide variety of experimental conditions (*13*), has depended solely upon mathematical inference. For the first time, the present results suggest a method of monitoring one transition independently of the other, by dissecting the overall envelope into one transition that can be monitored by fluorescence polarization techniques, and another transition that is silent in terms of these techniques. Given (Figure 10) the known distribution of the nine tryptophan residues of the CBH I core region along the sequence (fairly evenly distributed along the sequence, not bunched at one end) (*22,23*) and the proposed disulfide-bonding pattern (two disulfide-bonded regions, one including four tryptophan residues, the other including the remaining five) (*28*), the construction of a three-dimensional picture to explain the existence of the "silent" transition promises to provide challenging points of application for this and other fluorescence and calorimetric techniques.

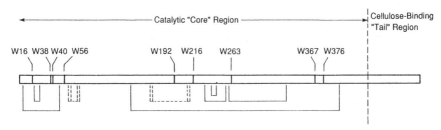

Figure 10.   Schematic representation of the distribution of tryptophan residues and disulfide-linked regions along the sequence of the CBH I catalytic core region. The positions of the tryptophan residues (references *22* and *23*) are represented by heavy vertical lines across the horizontal bar representing the peptide chain. The rectangular loops below the peptide chain represent disulfide cross-links as described by Bhikhabhai and Pettersson (ref. *28*), with solid loops representing disulfide bridges determined experimentally, and the dashed loops representing bridges deduced in ref. *28*.

Acknowledgments

This work was funded by the Ethanol from Biomass Program of the Biofuels Systems Division of the U.S. Department of Energy.

Literature Cited

1. Lynd, L.R.; Cushman, J.H.; Nichols, R.J.; Wyman, C.E. *Science* **1991**, *251*, 1318-1323.
2. Grohmann, K.; Wyman, C.E.; Himmel, M.E. In *Emerging Technologies for Materials and Chemicals from Biomass*; Rowell, R.M.; Schultz, T.P.; Narayan, R., Eds.; ACS Symposium Series No. 476; American Chemical Society: Washington, DC, 1992, pp.354-392.
3. Teeri, T.T.; Lehtovaara, P.; Kauppinen, S.; Salovuori, I.; Knowles, J. *Gene* **1987**, *51*, 43-52.
4. Abuja, P.M.; Schmuck, M.; Pilz, I.; Claeyssens, M.; Esterbauer, H. *Eur. Biophys. J.* **1988**, *15*, 339-342.
5. Esterbauer, H.; Hayn, M.; Abuja, P.M.; Claeyssens, M. In *Enzymes in Biomass Conversion*; Leatham, G.F.; Himmel, M.E., Eds., ACS Symposium Series No. 460; American Chemical Society: Washington, DC, 1991, pp. 301-312.
6. Tomme, P.; van Tilbeurgh, H.; Pettersson, G.; van Damme, J.; Vandekerckhove, J.; Knowles, J.; Teeri, T.; Claeyssens, M. *Eur. J. Biochem.* **1988**, *170*, 575-581.
7. Knowles, J.; Lehtovara, P.; Teeri, T. *Trends Biotechnol.* **1987**, *5*, 255-261.
8. Knowles, J.; Teeri, T.T.; Lehtovaara, P.; Penntila, M.; Saloheimo, M. In *Biochemistry and Genetics of Cellulose Degradation*; Aubert, J.-P.; Beguin, P.; Millet, J., Eds.; Academic Press: London, 1988; pp 153-169.
9. Coughlan, M.P. *Animal Feed Science and Technology* **1991**, *32*, 77-100.
10. Kraulis, P.J.; Clore, M.; Nilges, M.; Jones, T.A.; Pettersson, G.; Knowles, J.; Gronenborn, A.M., *Biochem.* **1989**, *28*, 7241-7257.
11. Bergfors, T.; Rouvinen, J.; Lehtovaara, P.; Caldentey, X.; Tomme, P.; Claeyssens, M.; Pettersson, G.; Teeri, T.; Knowles, J.; Jones, T.A. *J. Mol. Biol.* **1989**, *209*, 167-169.
12. Rouvinen, J.; Bergfors, T.; Teeri, T.; Knowles, J.K.C.; Jones, T.A. *Science* **1990**, *249*, 380-386.
13. Baker, J.O.; Himmel, M.E. In *Enzymes in Biomass Conversion*; Leatham, G.F.; Himmel, M.E., Eds., ACS Symposium Series No. 460; American Chemical Society: Washington, DC, 1991, pp. 313-330.
14. Shoemaker, S.; Watt, K.; Tsitovsky, G.; Cox, R. *Bio/Technology* **1983**, *1*, 687-690.
15. Gum, E.K.; Brown, R.D. *Biochim. Biophys. Acta* **1976**, *446*, 371-386.
16. Biltonen, R.L.; Freire, E. *CRC Crit. Rev. Biochem.* **1978**, *5*, 85-124.
17. Privalov, P.L.; Khechinashvili, N.N. *J. Mol. Biol.* **1974**, *86*, 665-684.
18. Pfeil, W.; Privalov, P.L. *Biophys. Chem.* **1976**, *4*, 23-32.
19. Sturtevant, J.M. *Ann. Rev. Phys. Chem.* **1987**, *38*, 463-88.
20. Privalov, P.L.; Potekhin, S.A. *Methods Enzymol.* **1986**, *131*, 4-51.
21. Privalov, P.L.; Gill, S.J. *Advan. Protein Chem.* **1988**, *39*, 191-234.
22. Shoemaker, S.; Schweickart, V.; Ladner, M.; Gelfand, D.; Kwok, S.; Myambo, K.; Innis, M. *Bio/Technology* **1983**, *1*, 691-696.

23.   Fagerstam, L.G.; Pettersson, L.G.; Engstrom, J.A. *FEBS Lett.* **1984**, 309-315.
24.   Baker, J.O.; Tatsumoto, K.; Grohmann, K.; Woodward, J.; Wichert, J.M.; Shoemaker, S.P.; Himmel, M.E. *Appl. Biochem. Biotechnol.* **1992**, In Press.
25.   Lakowicz, J.R. *Principles of Fluorescence Spectroscopy*; Plenum Press: New York, NY; 1983.
26.   Cooper, A. *Methods Enzymol.* **1982**, *81*, 285-288.
27.   Claeyssens, M.; van Tilbeurgh, H.; Tomme, P.; Wood, T.M.; McCrae, S.I. *Biochem. J.* **1989**, *261*, 819-825.
28.   Bhikhabhai, R.; Pettersson, G. *Biochem. J.* **1984**, *222*, 729-736.

RECEIVED April 29, 1992

Chapter 7

Recombinant Protein Stabilization through Engineered Metal-Chelating Sites

Pablo Umaña, James T. Kellis, Jr., and Frances H. Arnold

Division of Chemistry and Chemical Engineering 210–41,
California Institute of Technology, Pasadena, CA 91125

Simple metal-chelating sites incorporated into common elements of secondary structure located on a protein surface offer a powerful and general strategy for stabilizing recombinant proteins. By binding with higher affinity to the native state of the protein, a metal ion can shift the folding/unfolding equilibrium toward the native state. To demonstrate this approach, we have engineered metal-chelating sites consisting of pairs of histidine residues into *Saccharomyces cerevisiae* iso-1-cytochrome *c*. 1 mM Cu(II) complexed to iminodiacetate stabilizes the cytochrome c variants by 1-2 kcal/mol, as determined by guanidinium chloride-induced unfolding. The increase in the free energy for unfolding is equal to that calculated from the preferential binding of the metal ion to the native protein. The Cu(II) affinities of di-histidine sites introduced in α-helices of bovine somatotropin indicate a potential for increasing stability by as much as 3.5 kcal/mol with a single di-histidine site. Chelating sites are easily introduced into surface α-helices and ß-sheets while introducing minimal or no disruption of the native structure or biological function.

Improving protein stability is an important goal of protein design and engineering, affecting a wide spectrum of biotechnology operations from large-scale purification to the efficacy of protein therapeutics. More flexible purification schemes could be designed for proteins capable of withstanding room temperatures for long periods of time. Robust proteins that retain their native structures at high temperatures or tolerate organic solvents could be isolated economically by selective heat denaturation and precipitation or extraction of undesirable substances. High stability would also dramatically reduce the costs involved in protein storage and shipping. Effective bioconversion processes can be designed for enzymes that are stable at high temperatures or in organic solvents, with advantages that include higher reaction rates, favorable thermodynamic equilibria for synthetic reactions which require low water concentrations (e.g. peptide synthesis by proteases), new synthetic applications for substrates insoluble in aqueous media, and reduced microbial contamination (*1*).

Stabilizing proteins, however, is a delicate process. A protein's stability, or the free energy by which the folded protein is more stable than its unfolded form, is usually quite small--on the order of 5 to 15 kcal/mol. Furthermore, this relatively

0097–6156/93/0516–0102$06.00/0

small free energy difference is the result of two large, opposing driving forces: attractive intramolecular forces plus the entropy of desolvation, which tend to stabilize the folded state, and the destabilizing decrease in chain entropy upon folding. From all the possible sequences of amino acids, nature has selected those consistent with this delicate balance (*2*). The marginal stabilities of natural proteins fulfill the requirements of the organism; proteins can be turned over and replaced on a regular basis, and this continual turnover gives the organism control over cellular processes. However, marginally-stable proteins are far from optimal for industrial purposes.

   One strategy for enhancing protein stability is the substitution of specific amino acid side chains involved in stabilizing the folded state or destabilizing the unfolded state. This is a not a simple task, given our current limited ability to predict the effects on these large and opposing forces of altering the amino acid sequence. Predicting stabilizing mutations in the interior of a protein is particularly difficult, since the interactions arising between groups that become buried during folding are specific to each protein and can involve multiple favorable or unfavorable interactions. We have endeavored to develop general strategies for protein stabilization that are applicable to a wide variety of proteins and rely mainly on the substitution of surface amino acids. Engineering metal-chelating sites is such a strategy (*3,4*). By binding with high affinity to sites that optimally satisfy the bonding requirements of the metal ion when the protein is in its folded state, the metal ion shifts the folding/unfolding equilibrium to provide significant stability to the folded state. As illustrated by the thermodynamic cycle of Figure 1, the increase in the free energy of protein unfolding ($\Delta\Delta G_{unf}$) introduced by metal binding is equal to the difference in free energy of binding of the metal to the unfolded and native states ($\Delta\Delta G_{bind}$) (*3*). The preferential binding to the native state relies on structural "scaffolding" provided by elements of secondary structure common to nearly all proteins. This treatment of the effects of ligand binding on protein stability assumes that folding follows a simple two-state transition. If the denaturing conditions lead to formation of an inactive intermediate which retains the ability to bind the ligand (i.e. the intermediate retains the surface element of secondary structure containing the chelating site), then metal ion chelation may not result in any significant stabilization. In this sense, metal ion binding provides a useful probe of the process of protein folding as well as structure. Ghadiri and coworkers (*5*) have demonstrated the utility of metal ion binding in the stabilization of helical peptides. DeGrado and coworkers (*6*) have observed stabilization of <u>de novo</u> synthetic metal-binding proteins in the presence of various metal ions.

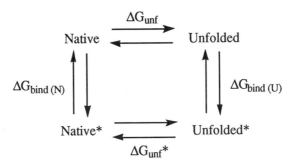

Figure 1. Thermodynamic cycle describing the stabilization of the native state of a protein by preferential binding of a ligand (e.g., a metal ion or metal complex) to the native state. The asterisks denote protein in the ligand-bound state. $\Delta\Delta G_{unf}$ is defined as $\Delta G_{unf}* - \Delta G_{unf}$, and $\Delta\Delta G_{bind}$ is defined as $\Delta G_{bind(U)} - \Delta G_{bind(N)}$.

Basic Principles of Metal Chelation

Metal complexes with vacant coordination sites bind ligating atoms exposed on protein surfaces. Histidine and cysteine are the most important metal-coordinating ligands at neutral pH. Transition metal binding to protein surface residues has been exploited in protein purification by metal-affinity chromatography, extraction, and precipitation (7). Proteins that differ in their content of surface histidines, for example, are easily separated by chromatography on supports containing Cu(II)iminodiacetate (Cu(II)IDA) (8). We have studied the binding of histidine-containing proteins to Cu(II)IDA-PEG by protein partitioning in a PEG/dextran two-phase system and found an average association constant for the complex formed between a single surface histidine and Cu(II)IDA-PEG in a PEG-rich medium (top phase) to be 2.2 x 10^3 M^{-1} (9).

When two histidines are positioned so that they can form coordinate-covalent bonds simultaneously with a single metal ion, the strength of the association can be dramatically enhanced. A di-histidine metal-binding site engineered into the N-terminal α-helix of yeast cytochrome c binds Cu(II)IDA-PEG with 24 times higher affinity than does a single surface histidine. This metal-binding variant, which has only 3 exposed histidines, partitions in Cu(II)IDA-PEG/dextran as if it had 9 or 10 exposed histidines (10). Since few natural proteins have such a large affinity for Cu(II)IDA, these metal-binding sites are extremely useful in purification (4).

The fact that there is a large difference between the free energy for the dissociation of a metal complex formed with a polydentate ligand (e.g. the di-histidine binding site) and the free energy of dissociation of a complex formed with two or more monodentate ligands (independent histidines) can be attributed to a greater translational entropy loss for the binding of two monodentate ligands (11). Thus, a chelate formed with a polydentate ligand is more stable than the analogous complex with the monodentate ligands because the chelate dissociates into a smaller number of molecules. Metal chelates vary in stability, owing to differences in the size of the chelate rings, the number of rings, and other factors such as resonance and steric effects (11). Five-membered rings usually show the greatest chelate effect; increasing the number of atoms in the ring diminishes the chelate stability. This reflects the higher entropic cost of immobilizing a longer, more flexible ligand. A protein with di-histidine chelating site constitutes a bidentate ligand that forms a chelate ring with a large number of atoms. The chelate is stable, however, because the forces that stabilize secondary structure (i.e., hydrogen bonds) provide rigidity to the ring. Therefore, once the protein is folded, bidentate binding occurs at a low entropic cost. The protein's structural rigidity and ability to position the donor atoms to satisfy the stereochemical requirements of the metal constitute the positive contribution of the protein "scaffolding," quantified in the value of $\Delta\Delta G_{bind}$ in Figure 1.

Three variants of bovine somatotropin containing His-X_3-His sites in surface α-helices, His$_{(169),173}$, His$_{15,(19)}$, and His$_{26,30}$, have affinities for Cu(II)IDA that correspond to $\Delta\Delta G_{bind}$ values of 0.9, 2.2, and 3.5 kcal/mol, respectively (12). The lower copper affinity of the His-X_3-His site in His$_{(169),173}$ bovine somatotropin may be related to steric hindrance by neighboring arginine-176 and by the C-terminal loop (12). The higher Cu(II) affinities of the His$_{15,(19)}$ and His$_{26,30}$ bovine somatotropins, as compared to His$_{4,8}$ cytochrome c, may reflect the rigidity of the helices where these sites are located. Formation of the protein-metal chelate complex is favored by a high, negative enthalpy change and by the lowest possible loss of entropy. If the chelating site is introduced into a very flexible region of the protein, then the entropic cost of forming the complex will be high. However, if the helix backbone or nearby amino acid side chains are distorted upon forming the chelate, the enthalpy of the final complex will be higher. To provide the optimal conditions for metal chelation, the chelating site should be positioned in a region of low flexibility that also minimizes strain.

Engineered Metal-Chelating Proteins

Several di-histidine metal-chelating motifs in common elements of protein secondary structure have been identified, including His-X-His in a β-strand, His-X$_2$-His in a reverse β-turn, His-X$_3$-His in an α-helix, and juxtaposed histidines on adjacent strands of a β-sheet (His-X$_n$-His) (*4*). Here we will describe two particular di-histidine sites engineered into an α-helix and a β-sheet structure. We have replaced lysine-4 and threonine-8 (numbering system based on alignment of tuna and rice cytochromes c) in the N-terminal α-helix of yeast iso-1-cytochrome c with histidines to create the His$_{4,8}$ variant depicted in Figure 2A. The 1.23 Å resolution crystal structure of yeast iso-1-cytochrome c shows a very small antiparallel β-sheet, consisting of residues 37-40 and 57-59 (*13*). Because residue 39 is a histidine in the wild-type protein, we mutated the leucine residue at position 58 on the adjacent strand to histidine to create variant His$_{(39),58}$ with a metal-binding site crosslinking the β-strands (Figure 2B). Both variants also have the wild-type cysteine-102 mutated to serine to eliminate the reactive sulfhydryl group. The incorporation of these surface metal-binding sites has not interfered with the cytochrome c biological activity: both His$_{4,8}$ and His$_{(39),58}$ cytochromes c are functionally expressed in *S. cerevisiae*. Paramagnetic proton NMR spectroscopy of the two variants indicates that Cu(II)IDA binding is significantly enhanced at the putative chelating sites (data not shown).

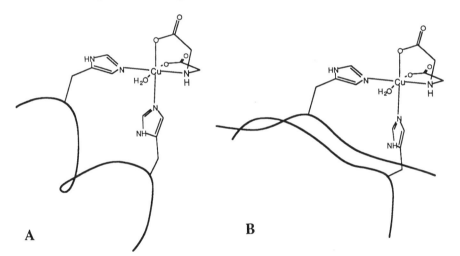

Figure 2. Models of di-histidine metal-binding sites in A) His$_{4,8}$ and B) His$_{(39),58}$ cytochrome c variants forming complexes with Cu(II)IDA. Thick solid lines depict the protein backbone.

Stabilization Studies

Protein stabilities can be determined through equilibrium studies of the reversible unfolding process. Figure 3 shows the guanidinium chloride (Gdm.Cl)-induced unfolding of the His$_{4,8}$ and His$_{(39),58}$ variants of cytochrome c in the absence and presence of Cu(II)IDA. The two variants (and wild-type enzyme) all exhibit essentially equal stability in the absence of the metal complex. Adding 1 mM Cu(II)IDA increases the amount of Gdm.Cl required to unfold the synthetic metal-binding proteins. This effect can be quantitated in terms of free energy of stabilization provided by the metal complex. The change in free energy for the unfolding process

(ΔG_{unf}) at a given Cu(II)IDA concentration is calculated from the relation ΔG_{unf} = - RT ln K_{unf}, where K_{unf} = (fraction unfolded / fraction folded). At Gdm.Cl concentrations where the folded and unfolded forms are present at levels that allow reliable calculation of the equilibrium constants in the presence and absence of the metal ion, the stabilization induced by the metal ion ($\Delta\Delta G_{unf}$) can be readily measured: it is 1.0 kcal/mol for His$_{4,8}$ and 1.7 kcal/mol for His$_{(39),58}$ in 1.0 mM Cu(II)IDA. The mutations have a negligible effect on the stability of the protein in the absence of Cu(II)IDA, compared to the protein lacking the engineered histidines.

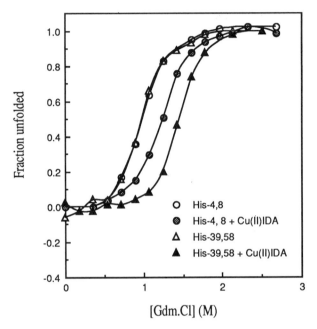

[Gdm.Cl] (M)

Figure 3.   Stabilization of His$_{4,8}$ and His$_{(39),58}$ cytochrome c by 1 mM Cu(II)IDA.

The relation between $\Delta\Delta G_{unf}$ and metal complex concentration can be extrapolated to higher metal concentrations in order to determine the maximal stabilization provided by metal ion chelation. The data for His$_{4,8}$ display saturation behavior, with $\Delta\Delta G_{unf(max)}$ = 1.2 kcal/mol (3). The site cross-linking the β-sheet in His$_{(39),58}$ is slightly more effective, with a maximum stabilization of 1.8 kcal/mol.
The value of $\Delta\Delta G_{unf(max)}$ for the His-X$_3$-His site is equal to that calculated from Cu(II)IDA binding constants, $\Delta\Delta G_{bind}$, as predicted by the thermodynamic cycle in Figure 1. The binding constant K_a for the His-X$_3$-His chelating site is 5.3 x 10^4 M^{-1} in the folded protein (8). The unfolded protein has three histidines available to coordinate Cu(II)IDA, since His-26 becomes exposed upon unfolding. Thus, its binding constant is three times that for a single histidine, or 6.6 x 10^3 M^{-1}. The increase in the change in free energy of binding is calculated using the relation $\Delta\Delta G_{bind}$ = - RTln ($K_{a(unf)}$ / $K_{a(nat)}$), which yields 1.2 kcal/mol.
Metal-affinity partitioning studies carried out on synthetic metal-binding bovine somatotropins have shown that the preferential binding to the folded protein can be as high as 3.5 kcal/mol at a surface His-X$_3$-His site (12). The excellent agreement between $\Delta\Delta G_{unf}$ and $\Delta\Delta G_{bind}$ that we have observed for the His$_{4,8}$ cytochrome c

variant indicates that one can achieve up to 3.5 kcal/mol of stabilization using a single di-histidine chelating site and Cu(II)IDA.

Another practically important measure of protein stability is melting temperature, the temperature required to unfold half the protein molecules. Thermal unfolding studies on the metal-chelating cytochrome c variants indicate that 1 mM Cu(II)IDA increases the melting temperature of the His$_{4,8}$ variant by 6°C and the His$_{(39),58}$ variant by a full 10°C in 1.2 M Gdm.Cl, a remarkable degree of thermal stabilization for a single amino acid substitution (data not shown).

Future Perspectives

In order to develop a comprehensive strategy for applying this method of protein stabilization, additional aspects of the approach must be studied. The stabilization provided by other simple metal-chelating motifs, His-X-His in a ß-strand and His-X$_2$-His in a reverse ß-turn, remain to be studied.   In addition, the effects of using different metal ions or metal complexes, general rules for positioning chelating sites in proteins, the stability afforded by metal chelation and sensitivity to environmental conditions have to be determined. One important question is whether stability is further enhanced when multiple chelating sites are introduced: can one engineer two or more chelating sites into a protein and obtain additive contributions to the free energy of stabilization?   It is also interesting to investigate whether these metal-chelating proteins are stabilized to denaturation in organic solvents. The association between the metal ion and a ligating histidine should be stronger in organic solvents, since the solvent may not compete for ligation to the metal ion to the same extent as water does. However, this enhanced binding would be present in both the native structure and the unfolded form, and the net effect on binding and stability is difficult to predict.

Metal chelating sites can be applied not only to prevent unfolding, but also perhaps to guide refolding during the recovery of aggregated proteins in industrial operations. Still another application can be found in fundamental studies of protein folding pathways. Substitutions of specific residues have revealed their individual contributions to the folding process (*14*). A metal-chelating site would facilitate the study of the formation of elements of secondary structure through kinetic measurements of folding. The influence of the metal ion on the rate of folding would reveal the point at which the ligands in these elements attain their native structure.

Conclusions

Engineered metal chelation is an excellent tool for protein stabilization; even simple di-histidine chelating sites on a protein surface can provide significant stability enhancements. We have demonstrated that histidine pairs inserted into an α-helix or β-sheet can add 1-2 kcal/mol to the free energy of unfolding in cytochrome c. Previous metal-binding studies on variants of bovine somatotropin indicate that a single α-helical His-X$_3$-His site should be able to afford as much as 3.5 kcal/mol of stabilization. The method is generally applicable since the structural "scaffolding" needed to coordinate the metal ion at a low entropic cost is provided by common elements of secondary structure. This also allows introduction of a chelating site with minimal or no disruption of native structure or biological function.

Acknowledgments

This work is supported by the National Science Foundation (P.Y.I. award to F.H.A.) and the Office of Naval Research. F.H.A. gratefully acknowledges a fellowship from the David and Lucile Packard Foundation.

Literature Cited

1. Dordick, J. S. *Enz. Microb. Technol.* **1989**, *11*, 194.
2. Jaenicke, R. *Biochemistry* **1991**, *30*, 3147.
3. Kellis, J. T., Jr.; Todd, R. J.; Arnold, F. H. *Bio/Technology* **1991**, *6*, 994.
4. Arnold, F. H.; Haymore, B. L. *Science* **1991**, *252*, 1796.
5. Ghadiri, M. R.; Choi, C. *J. Am. Chem. Soc.* **1990**, *112*, 1630.
6. Handel, T.; DeGrado, W. F. *J. Am. Chem. Soc.* **1990**, *112*, 6710.
7. Arnold, F. H., *Bio/Technology* **1991**, *9*, 151.
8. Hemdan, E. S.; Zhao, Y.; Sulkowski, E.; Porath, J. *Proc. Natl. Acad. Sci., USA* **1989**, *86*, 1811.
9. Suh, S.; Arnold, F. H. *Biotechnol. Bioeng.* **1990**, *35*, 682.
10. Todd, R. J.; Van Dam, M.; Casimiro, D.; Haymore, B. L.; Arnold, F. H. *Proteins: Struct., Funct., Genet.* **1991**, *10*, 156.
11. Martell, A., "The Relationship of Chemical Structure to Metal-Binding Action." In *Metal Binding in Medicine.* Seven, M. J., Ed; J. B. Lippincott Co., Philadelphia, PA, 1959; pp 1-18.
12. Suh, S.-S.; Haymore, B. L.; Arnold, F. H. *Protein Engineering* **1991**, *4*, 301.
13. Louie, G. V.; Brayer, G. D. *J. Mol Biol.* **1990**, *214*, 527.
14. Matouschek, A.; Kellis, J. T., Jr.; Serrano, L.; Bycroft, M; Fersht, A. R. *Nature* **1990**, *346*, 440.

RECEIVED March 31, 1992

Chapter 8

Engineering Nonaqueous Solvent-Compatible Enzymes

Frances H. Arnold, Keqin Chen, Chara Economou, Wayne Chen, Pascal Martinez, Kyung Pyo Yoon, and Mariana Van Dam

Division of Chemistry and Chemical Engineering 210–41, California Institute of Technology, Pasadena, CA 91125

Given current powerful tools for protein molecular engineering and a continually improving understanding of protein folding and stability, it is possible to construct vastly improved industrial enzyme catalysts. Enzymes are better suited to industrial syntheses if they can be made stable and active in high concentrations of polar organic solvents. Site-directed mutagenesis has been used to test two "design rules" for stabilizing enzymes in organic media. We have shown that surface charge substitution and the introduction of metal-chelating sites provide simple and generally-applicable mechanisms for enzyme stabilization. A variant of α-lytic protease containing two surface charge substitutions is 27 times more stable than wild-type enzyme in 84% DMF. Random mutagenesis and rapid screening techniques have been used to isolate enzyme variants with enhanced catalytic activity in polar organic solvents. Our first experiments resulted in a variant of subtilisin E that is 38 times more active in 85% DMF than the wild-type enzyme. Subsequent rounds of random mutagenesis and screening have yielded a variant 256 times more active in 60% DMF.

Although polar organic solvents provide an excellent medium for many chemical transformations, these solvents often severely compromise enzyme catalysts. Transferring an enzyme from an aqueous environment to a polar organic solvent can drastically reduce both stability and activity (Figure 1). An enzyme in an organic solvent is operating far from the potential it achieved after billions of years of evolutionary optimization. Because the enzyme is "damaged," however, there is considerable room for improvement; the noncovalent forces that contribute to enzyme stability as well as to the stabilization the enzyme imparts to the reaction transition state can be redistributed by making selected substitutions in the amino acid sequence. An evolutionary approach of combining mutations generated by site-directed or random mutagenesis can lead to enzyme variants that exhibit greater stability or activity in the new environment. Because one is starting with a far-from-optimal catalyst, engineering enzymes for use in organic solvents is a particularly promising application of protein engineering (1,2).

0097–6156/93/0516–0109$06.00/0

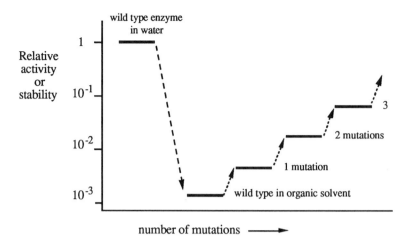

Figure 1. Evolutionary approach to creating enzymes that are optimized for use in nonaqueous solvents. Selected mutations can recover the stability and catalytic activity lost by transfer to the organic solvent.

Our protein engineering studies have been carried out on two proteolytic enzymes, subtilisin E and α-lytic protease. Both are serine proteases that will catalyse specific peptide syntheses and transesterification reactions in organic solvents. α-lytic protease (198 amino acids) is somewhat smaller than subtilisin E (275 amino acids) and contains three disulfide bridges, while subtilisin contains none. Both enzymes are expressed with pre-pro sequences that are eventually cleaved to yield the mature enzymes. Since the pro sequence is required for proper folding, both enzymes unfold irreversibly. As a result, any process that leads to denaturation results in a permanent loss of catalytic activity. If other mechanisms of deactivation (e.g. autolysis, for subtilisin) are excluded by carefully choosing the conditions, the time course of catalytic activity (assayed in any medium) can be interpreted in terms of unfolding events that are related to the protein's thermodynamic stability (3).

Enhancing Enzyme Stability in Organic Solvents

Useful approaches to stabilizing enzymes in polar organic solvents should be generally applicable to a wide variety of enzymes. Because the effects of amino acid substitutions on details of interior packing and hydrogen bonding are unique to each enzyme and are difficult to predict, stabilization approaches based on improving these internal interactions are difficult to implement successfully. We have concentrated instead on stabilization mechanisms that depend on the modification of surface amino acids. These mechanisms are: 1) substitution of charged surface residues (1,3) and 2) introduction of simple metal-chelating sites such as His-X_3-His in an α-helix (4). Because the second mechanism is treated in detail elsewhere in this volume, this paper will discuss only the first.

Desolvation of charged surface residues in organic solvents can contribute to enzyme destabilization. Charged side chains form multiple hydrogen bonds with solvent water molecules; removing water leaves these hydrogen bonding sites unsatisfied. Thus, dehydration could favor conformational changes that allow solvation of charged residues by polar groups elsewhere in the protein. We have proposed that replacing charged side chains renders the surface of the folded protein more compatible with an organic solvent environment and may remove a driving force for formation of alternate (inactive) structures. The substitution of selected charged residues can effectively stabilize the active enzyme in organic solvents.

This hypothesis was tested by replacing charged surface residues that do not participate in catalysis or favorable noncovalent interactions (salt bridges and hydrogen bonds) in both α-lytic protease and subtilisin E. In α-lytic protease, the targeted residues were substituted with as many of the remaining 19 amino acids as possible (5). Seven primarily hydrophobic substitutions at two positions significantly increased enzyme stability in dimethylformamide: replacement of Arg 45 by Glu, Ser, Leu and Ile and Arg 78 by Phe, Leu, and Tyr all stabilize α-lytic protease in 84% DMF. Although Glu is negatively charged, its hydration potential is significantly less than that of Arg (6). As shown in Figure 2, single mutations could be combined to yield a double mutant more stable in 84% DMF than either single mutant. The rate at which this double mutant deactivates in 84% DMF is 27 times less than that of wild-type α-lytic protease. These stabilizing effects were only observed in the organic solvent; no substitution significantly improved the stability of α-lytic protease in aqueous buffer.

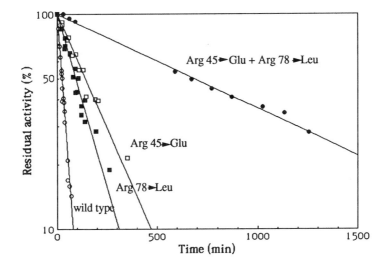

Figure 2. Stabilities of α-lytic protease surface charge variants in 84% (v/v) DMF/16% buffer, pH 8.75, 30 C. o, wild-type; ■, Leu 78; □, Glu 45; ●, Glu 45+Leu 78.

In subtilisin E, Asp 248 was substituted by three amino acids of increasing hydrophobicity, Asn, Ala and Leu, and all three variants were found to be slightly more stable in the presence of high concentrations of the organic solvent (3). These studies provide strong evidence that substitution of surface charged residues is a generally useful mechanism for stabilizing enzymes in high concentrations of polar organic solvents. Our current studies are directed towards determining to what extent this mechanism can be applied: how many surface substitutions will be tolerated, and what is the maximum stabilization that can be achieved?

Enhancing Enzyme Activity in Organic Solvents

The loss of catalytic activity that an enzyme experiences upon transfer to an organic solvent often cannot be attributed solely to the solvent's effect on stability and denaturation--enzymes that are quite stable in organic media also exhibit poor catalytic activity. Because little is known of the exact mechanisms by which polar organic solvents reduce the activity of soluble enzymes, we have relied on a random mutagenesis approach to improve enzyme catalytic performance. Random mutagenesis was carried out on subtilisin E by polymerase chain reaction (PCR) techniques and combined with screening for enhanced activity in the presence of DMF (7). Two amino acid substitutions which increase the activity of subtilisin E in the presence of the organic solvent, Q103R and D60N, were identified by screening the randomly mutated bacterial colonies on agar plates containing DMF and casein.   In this screening process, a colony secreting a subtilisin variant that is more active than wild-type in the presence of DMF produces a visibly larger halo on the casein plate. The effective substitutions identified in this and subsequent studies are located near the substrate binding pocket or in the active site. The effects of one of the substitutions, D60N, were apparent only in the presence of DMF, a result which highlights the importance of screening in the organic solvent.   As with the surface charge substitutions, this mutation improved the enzyme's performance only in organic solvents.

Engineering an enzyme that is truly optimized to function in a polar organic solvent will probably require the accumulation of multiple mutations. If the effects of individual mutations are additive, they can be identified in separate mutagenesis and screening experiments and subsequently combined. A triple mutant was constructed by combining the double random variant D60N+Q103R with N218S, a mutation discovered by random mutagenesis of subtilisin BPN' (8). In water, the triple variant is 7 times more efficient towards the hydrolysis of suc-Ala-Ala-Pro-Met-p-nitroanilide than wild-type subtilisin E; it is 38 times more active in 85% DMF (Figure 3). The triple variant also exhibits significantly higher esterase activity than the wild-type in high DMF concentrations (data not shown). Preliminary experiments show that this

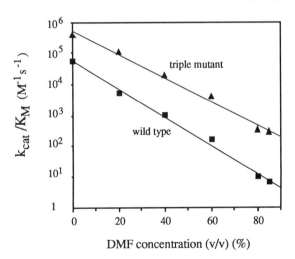

Figure 3. Catalytic efficiencies for hydrolysis of suc-Ala-Ala-Pro-Met-pna by wild-type subtilisin E (■) and triple mutant Q103R+D60N+N218S (▲) in the presence of DMF (7). (Reproduced with permission from Chen, K.; Arnold F. H. *BiolTechnology*, **9**, 1073-1077 (1991). Copyright 1991 Nature Publishing Company).

triple mutant is much more effective in kinetically-controlled peptide synthesis than wild-type subtilisin E (Chen, K; Arnold, F. H., unpublished results). Due to the stabilizing effect of the N218S mutation, the triple variant is also slightly more stable than wild-type subtilisin E (7).

The combined mutations Q103R+D60N+N218S stabilize the reaction transition state by an incremental free energy that is essentially the sum of all the contributions from each of the single mutants (7). These substitutions apparently do not cause more than very localized perturbations in the enzyme's structure. Even if multiple mutations begin to interact in the confined space of the active site, however, effective amino acid substitutions can be accumulated by the "evolutionary" process of sequential mutagenesis in which variant DNA is used as template for generating the next mutation. After three subsequent rounds of mutagenesis and screening in higher organic solvent concentrations, this evolutionary approach has yielded a variant of subtilisin E that is 256 times more active in 60% DMF than the wild-type enzyme. This engineered enzyme represents a dramatic improvement over natural catalysts for applications in peptide and polymer synthesis in organic solvents.

Conclusions

Mechanisms for enhancing both enzyme stability and catalytic activity in organic solvents have been illustrated by site-directed and random mutagenesis techniques. Substitution of selected charged surface residues can stabilize enzymes in high concentrations of organic solvents. Successful implementation of this stabilization strategy requires that the substituted amino acid side chain not be involved in catalysis or important stabilizing interactions. Incorporation of simple metal-chelating sites provides a second general and easy-to-implement strategy for protein stabilization. To improve catalytic activity in organic media, random mutagenesis combined with rapid screening techniques can be very effective. As beneficial mutations accumulate, the screening for enhancements in catalytic activity can be carried out in higher and higher concentrations of the organic solvent. There is clearly great potential for engineering enzymes that are well-suited to synthesis applications in polar organic solvents.

Acknowledgments

This research is supported by the Catalysis and Biocatalysis Program of the Advanced Industrial Concepts Division of the U. S. Department of Energy and by the Office of Naval Research. F.H.A. gratefully acknowledges an NSF PYI award and a fellowship from the David and Lucile Packard Foundation.

Literature Cited

1. Arnold, F. H. *Protein Engineering* **1988**, *2*, 21.
2. Arnold, F. H. *Trends Biotechnol.* **1990**, *8*, 244.
3. Martinez, P.; Van Dam, M. E.; Robinson, A. C.; Chen, K.; Arnold, F. H. *Biotechnol. Bioeng.* **1991**, *39*, 141.
4. Kellis, Jr., J.; Todd, R. J.; Arnold, F. H. *Bio/Technology* **1991**, *9*, 994.
5. Martinez, P.; Arnold, F. H. *J. Am. Chem. Soc.* **1991**, *113*, 6336.
6. Wolfenden, R.; Andersson, L.; Cullis, P. M.; Southgate, C. C. B. *Biochemistry* **1981**, *20*, 849.
7. Chen, K.; Arnold, F. H. *Bio/Technology* **1991**, *9*, 1073.
8. Bryan, P. N.; Rollence, M. L; Pantoliano, M. W.; Wood, J. F.; Finzel, B. C.; Gilliland, G. L.; Howard, A. J; Poulos, T. L. *Proteins: Struct. Funct. Gen.* **1986**, *1*, 326.

RECEIVED March 31, 1992

PROTEIN FOLDING

Chapter 9

Mutational Effects on Inclusion Body Formation

Ronald Wetzel and Boris A. Chrunyk

Macromolecular Sciences Department, SmithKline Beecham
Pharmaceuticals, 709 Swedeland Road, King of Prussia, PA 19406

Specific mutations in the cloned cDNAs for two small, human proteins, interferon-γ and interleukin-1β, lead to dramatic alterations in the partitioning of the gene product into inclusion bodies in *E. coli* expression. Examination of the reported three-dimensional structures of these proteins shows that the mutations generating these effects can be found in elements of α-helix, β-sheet, loops, or disordered sequence, in proteins that are either predominantly helical or β-sheet in structure. In both proteins, other mutations are described which lead to loss of stable accumulation of the gene product in any form in the cell. The results are discussed in terms of the possible roles of folding stability and kinetics in IB formation. Practical applications of mutants exhibiting altered inclusion body levels are also discussed.

Bacteria sequester a wide variety of molecules into inclusion bodies (IBs) *(1)*. Inclusion bodies composed of protein were first observed in bacteria grown on amino acid analogues which were misincorporated into protein during ribosomal synthesis *(2)*. These particles can also be formed as a consequence of the synthesis of unnaturally high levels of normal proteins *(3)*. However, IBs became a familiar phenomenon only with the advent of recombinant DNA techniques for the bacterial synthesis of heterologous gene products *(4, 5)*. Despite the observation of IBs in many cases of heterologous gene expression, and despite the practical and fundamental importance of the phenomenon, the process remains little understood *(6-11)*.

An understanding of the mechanisms by which IBs form would be valuable for a number of reasons. First, it should lead to improved control over their formation. In some cases it may be desirable to suppress IB formation, if recovery of active, native protein by refolding *in vitro* proves difficult (see, for example, reference *(12)*). In other cases it may be desirable to encourage IB formation, for instance to stabilize proteins which might otherwise be degraded by cellular proteases *(13)*, or to provide an initial purification step which would remove most *E. coli* proteins *(6)*. Inclusion bodies also are of interest because of their resemblance to a class of human disease called amyloidosis, which is characterized by the formation of insoluble fibrils of selectively aggregated proteins *(14-18)*. The comparative properties of inclusion bodies and amyloid have been discussed *(11)*. Both particles are highly resistant to dissolution in

0097–6156/93/0516–0116$06.00/0

native buffers, normally requiring high levels of denaturing solutes. Both particles are also highly selectively enriched in a particular protein, in spite of the fact that they are formed in milieux which are rich mixtures of proteins. Another aspect of the selectivity with which proteins are aggregated in these processes is the observation of mutational effects on their formation; that is, in both phenomena, the replacement of as little as a single amino acid can dramatically alter the extent to which insoluble aggregate is formed *(11)*. The selectivity of aggregate formation *in vivo* is one of the main reasons for suspecting that these processes are related somehow to protein folding. Although the aggregation of mixtures of proteins is often an amorphous process which, once begun, tends to include many different components of the mixture, aggregation during *in vitro* refolding experiments can be rather selective. This has led to the idea that the aggregation interface in folding-related aggregation resembles one of the protein's normal inter- or intramolecular packing interfaces, giving the aggregation process the same high specificity found in the protein folding process *(2, 19)*. To the extent that IB formation is, in fact, a reflection of inherent folding or stability properties of the protein being expressed, IB formation might be used as a phenotypic marker for folding/stability mutants in a genetic analysis.

The research described here is directed toward understanding the basis for the sequence specificity of the IB formation process. Simple methods for the identification of IB mutations in a collection of mutants have led to the identification of dramatic IB mutations in two simple globular proteins of known three-dimensional structure expressed by recombinant DNA techniques in *E. coli*: human interferon-γ (IFN-γ) and human interleukin-1β (IL-1β). Work is in progress to identify *in vitro* properties which correlate with the ability of various mutants to form IBs. Evidence is accumulating that supports the idea *(20)* that aspects of the folding pathway can influence inclusion body formation.

Solubility, Stability and Folding in Inclusion Body Formation

Figure 1 is a general mechanism for protein folding which can be used to examine possible mechanisms for IB formation and for mutational effects on IB formation. Some abnormal proteins expressed by recombinant DNA techniques might be expected to be poorly soluble in native buffer both *in vivo* and *in vitro*, either because they cannot fold into a native-like structure, or because, once folded, they are still poorly soluble. Possible examples of this type of protein are some integral membrane proteins and some fusion proteins incorporating extensive unnatural sequences. That such proteins might form IBs during expression is not surprising. A second theoretical mechanism for IB formation postulates a higher tendency to aggregate of unfolded states populated at equilibrium due to a diminished thermodynamic stability of the protein under growth conditions of the cell. For example, the inability of a protein to form disulfide bonds in the cytoplasm will correspondingly diminish its ΔG_{stab} and require it to spend most of its time in an unfolded state - potentially of limited solubility. Similarly, mutations which diminish non-covalent interactions required for folding stability will tend to populate such states if the T_m is reduced to or below the growth temperature. In the third theoretical mechanism, transiently populated, kinetic folding intermediates are responsible for IB formation when they become of sufficiently poor solubility or of sufficiently long kinetic lifetimes. It is not known whether all of these possible mechanisms are responsible for IB formation in *E. coli*, nor how widespread any of them might be.

In addition to these mechanisms, it is also possible that mutations may influence IB formation by altering the interaction surface of the protein with a molecular chaperone responsible for facilitating its folding into a soluble, native molecule. Chaperonins have been shown to reduce losses due to aggregation during protein folding *in vivo* and *in vitro* with several proteins *(21)*.

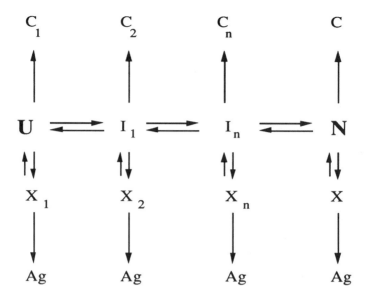

Figure 1. A general mechanism for protein folding accounting for proteolysis and aggregate formation . N = native state, U = unfolded state, I = intermediate, C = covalently modified form, X = associated form, Ag = aggregated form. Reproduced with permission from reference (11). Copyright 1992 Plenum.

Only a few examples of mutational effects on IB formation have been reported. In the work of the King lab, a series of temperature sensitive folding (*tsf*) mutations identified over a decade ago in the tailspike protein of *Salmonella* phage P22 have now been characterized as leading to increased levels of IBs (20). These mutations shift the temperature-dependence of IB formation found for the wild type protein to lower temperature, and also make the temperature-dependence curve more cooperative. The result is that, at the non-permissive temperature of 39° C, where a large percentage of WT tailspike chains fold productively and associate into trimer, *tsf* mutant tailspike chains are exclusively deposited into IBs, and are thus irreversibly lost. Because the *tsf* mutants can be grown at a lower, permissive, temperature to produce folded tailspikes capable of assembling viable phage, these mutations clearly do not simply affect protein solubility. Furthermore, because the T_m values of the folded *tsf* mutants are similar to WT, and much higher than the non-permissive growth temperature, it is clear that they do not influence IB formation *via* large effects on ΔG_{stab}. These mutants are thus presumably defective in folding and/or assembly. Many of the mutations are located in sequences resembling motifs favoring β-turns, consistent with a mechanism involving changes in key folding steps or intermediates related to turn formation.

The characterization of the P22 tailspike *tsf* mutants provided the first example of mutational effects on IB formation (20), and the continuing analysis of these mutants (22-24) is establishing a framework of ideas on how to think about mutational effects on IB formation observed in other systems. Several more anecdotal reports of mutational effects have also been reported (25-28). How widespread will the observation of such mutational effects be? The tailspike protein is large and oligomeric (a trimer of 666 amino acid subunits), β-rich, and of unknown three-dimensional structure. Will it be possible to identify and characterize similar mutations in small, globular proteins of known structure? Are monomeric proteins capable of IB formation and mutational effects on IB formation? Will the locations of IB mutations in the 3D structure, and the *in vitro* measured folding kinetics and stabilities of proteins bearing them, yield clues to the mechanism of formation of IBs and to *in vivo* protein folding in general?

The original observation of the P22 tailspike mutants was possible in spite of their low frequencies of appearance among the classically generated mutagenesis pool because of the availability of a genetic screen for the *tsf* phenotype *(29)*. Modern methods of mutagenesis, built on recombinant DNA techniques, can provide frequencies of one or more mutations per gene segment *(30, 31)*. Such high frequencies of mutation, with correspondingly lower levels of wild type background, allow the use of much less efficient screens for identifying interesting mutants, such as IB mutants, in the pool. This in turn has made possible the introduction of screening methods which do not rely on a functional role of the gene product in the producing organism, thus opening up the possibility of mutational analyses of many heterologous genes. In turn, this makes possible an efficient search for IB mutations in a gene encoding a protein which has been chosen based upon desirable characteristics as a model folding system.

Interferon-γ

Human interferon-γ is a homodimer made up of highly α-helical subunits, each 144 amino acids long when made in *E. coli* (where the initiator Met is not processed off). The X-ray crystal structure shows an extended subunit interface delineated by the intertwining of the subunits *(32)*. This structure does not show the C-terminus beyond residue 120, which is consistent with the disordered structure suggested by the susceptibility of the C-terminus to limited proteolysis both *in vitro* and *in vivo (33)*. The molecule contains no cysteine residues, and exhibits a Tm of 54° C at pH 7 *(34)*. When the wild type sequence is produced in *E. coli* grown at 37° C (17° C lower than its Tm) under control of the *trp* promoter, over 25% of the Coomassie blue staining protein is IFN-γ, and over 95% of this material is found in the insoluble fraction of a native lysate *(35)*. The material is insoluble because it is incorporated into inclusion bodies *(35)*.

In a mutational analysis of the cloned gene directed at elucidating structure/activity relationships *(36, 37)*, mutations were isolated which exhibited significantly higher levels of IFN-γ in soluble cytoplasmic extracts. This phenotype proved to be due, not to an increase in overall expression levels, but rather to an increase in the amount of IFN-γ which partitioned into the soluble fraction *(35)*. Such mutations were conveniently detected by growing and lysing cells in microtiter plate wells, and assaying the soluble fractions by an ELISA using anti-IFN-γ antibodies; very high responses compared to wild type prove to be due to a higher ratio of soluble to insoluble forms of IFN-γ *(35)*. A partial list of sequences which exhibit the phenotype of lower IB formation than WT is listed in Table I. It was of interest to know if mutants similar to the P22 tailspike mutants, yielding higher IB formation than WT, could also be isolated; however, with IB formation already very high in the WT this did not appear feasible. Fortunately, it was possible to overcome this dilemma by adjusting cell culture temperature.

With growth temperature lowered to 30° C, a larger percentage of the wild type protein was found in the soluble fraction *(35)*; this beneficial effect of lower growth temperature on IB formation has been noted with other proteins as well, but is by no means a general rule *(10)*. With a larger amount of wild type protein partitioning into the soluble fraction, it was now possible to screen for mutations, similar to those described for P22 tailspike protein, which directed even more protein into IBs. However, such mutants cannot be unequivocally identified by using an immunoassay

Table I. Levels of Soluble Expression of IFN-γ Variants

```
Mut. #    Sequence Change from Wild Type            ELISA,µg/mlª  Rel.Act.ᵇ
Cassette 1
          120        130          140
WT    EL SPAAKTGKRK RSQMLFRGRR ASQ                      2.8         100

71        S                                            1.6          55
50                  R                                   2.2         174
58                  QP                                  7.5          28
30        S I     E  G                                  6.5           6
36        P       E W                                   1.6         124
47                N      YC ---- ---                    4.8         109
23        LSRR------ ---------- ---                    11.0          ND
1               ------ ---------- ---                   8.0        0.06
25        ---------- ---------- ---                     3.2           3
88                           VDE HPSRS                 10.0         204
55                           EVRCCVEVDE HASRS           8.6          90
56                  Q SE     GVRCCLEVDE HPSRS           8.6        0.17
28        L       Q SE     GVRCC EVDE HPSRS            0.5           8
13        C RLTE SE     GVRSCLGADE HPSRLN               5.3         1.1
74        A                    I         LDLNAVVY HS    0.3           3
68                           RCCS WTS IPVDLNAVVY HS     23.0         150
7         A       SE   E GSVS STS IPVDLNAVVY HS          5.3        0.13
87          RL REAK    E DAV-                          11.8         180
27        AT    P  Q   GVRCC EVDE HPSRS                 2.1          95

Cassette 3
           70        80           90
WT    -SIQKSV ETIKEDMNVK FFNSNKKKRD DFEKL-              0.9         100

66        A       G        K                            0.4         <<1
7                                   Q                     7         250
5                        A                                8         200
56        K             M                               11         <<1
11              S Y                                     13          50
75              H T                                     38          70
```

ªELISA on crude lysis supernatants as described *(35)*. ᵇAntiviral activity assessed on partially purified material as described *(35)*. Adapted from reference *(35)*.

as described above - which can detect only at the amount of soluble protein in the cell - since an observed reduction in cellular levels might be due to loss of protein due to proteolysis rather than IB formation. To distinguish between these two possible fates of the polypeptide, an assay was devised which is capable of detecting levels of gene product accessible only to denaturant. In this assay, an array of cultures producing different mutant IFNs is lysed in parallel by two methods - one native lysis and one denaturant-based - and the replicate lysates assayed by a variation of the ELISA. This produces values which can be manipulated to give ratios indicating greater-than-wild-type or less-than-wild-type levels of IBs. If no appreciable IFN is made available even from cells lysed by denaturant, then it is clear that no IFN accumulated in the cell, presumably due to loss by proteolysis. SDS PAGE analysis confirmed, in most cases tested, the characteristics predicted by the differential lysis assay. Table II shows the results of a survey of randomly generated mutations in IFN-γ. Four classes of mutant were thus identified: wild-type-like, no stable accumulation, greater-than-wild-type levels of IBs, and less-than-wild-type levels of IBs.

Table I also shows that there is no correlation between the partitioning of IFN-γ between soluble and insoluble fractions and the antiviral specific activity of the soluble material. Not only are there some highly inactive mutants which are, like wild type, found almost exclusively in IBs, but there are also highly active mutants which are found almost exclusively in the soluble fraction!

One practical implication of the IFN data is that, in an expression system in which a particular wild type gene product is produced in undesirable IBs, it may be possible to identify mutants which retain good biological activity while at the same time gaining improved expression characteristics such as reduced IB levels. It remains to be seen whether mutations giving improved soluble expression will be a general phenomenon. King and co-workers have recently described the characterization of global suppressor mutations of the *tsf* phenotype in the P22 tailspike system which have the same effect of improving soluble levels of product at the expense of IB formation *(24)*.

It is interesting that the wild type C-terminus, although disordered and relatively hydrophilic in character, nonetheless plays a major role in influencing IB formation. One possible explanation, for which there is no other supportive data, is that the C-terminus is important at some point during the folding of the protein, even if its structural role in the native state is not evident.

Another feature IFN-γ has in common with the P22 tailspike is that both are oligomeric proteins. Since many of the proteins known to give severe aggregation on attempts to refold *in vitro* are oligomeric *(7)*, the possibility exists that folding-related IB formation may be a phenomenon limited mostly to expression of oligomeric proteins. For this reason we sought a monomeric protein of known structure exhibiting mutational effects on IB formation during expression in *E. coli*. Human interleukin-1β proved to be such a protein.

TABLE II. Fate of IFN-γ Variants in *Escherichia Coli* by Mutagenesis Region

Sequence Positions:	(1-26)	(26-56)	(51-65)	(65-95)	(95-123)	(119-143)
Phenotype						
No detectable expression, Soluble or insoluble	55	21	18	38	35	0
Detectable expression:						
Very high in inclusion bodies (+ in Gdn-HCl only)	5	64	14	14	37	0
Wild type levels of expression by native lysis	37	14	57	47	28	89
Low in inclusion bodies (high native lysis expression)	3	1	11	1	0	11

Results are listed as % of all mutants tested from each collection, normally a sample of 500-1000 isolates. Reproduced with permission from reference *(35)*. Copyright 1992 Nature Publishing Co.

Interleukin-1β

IL-1β is a monomeric protein of 153 amino acids long containing two unpaired Cys residues and no disulfide bonds. Its three-dimensional structure has been determined both by Xray crystallography *(38, 39)* and by nmr *(40)*. It exists in a β-barrel structure, folding in a motif first observed for soybean trypsin inhibitor. Its Tm at pH 7 was determined by scanning microcalorimetry to be 62° C (C. Brouilette, unpublished). Conditions for its reversible unfolding induced by solute denaturants have been reported *(41)*. Expressed in *E. coli*, the wild type sequence accumulates to about 10% of the Coomassie staining protein, almost all of which is found in the supernatant after centrifugation of crude lysates. The small percentage of IL-1β in the insoluble fraction is presumably localized in inclusion bodies, since characteristic refractile particles are observed in IL-1β producing cells in phase contrast microscopy (unpublished observations).

Using SDS-PAGE, we surveyed a collection of site-directed (ie., not randomly generated) mutants, prepared over the past several years to explore structure - activity relationships *(42)*, for their stability and solubility when expressed in *E. coli*. As was found for IFN-γ mutants, we observed mutants which gave predominantly soluble expression - like the wild type, mutants which did not accumulate stably in any form in the cell, and mutants which, while produced in approximately the same amount as wild type, distributed greater percentages of the accumulated IL-1β into the insoluble fraction. Table III lists representative mutants from the collection of approximately 70 site-directed mutants surveyed *(43)*.

The table shows that residue positions associated with high levels of inclusion bodies are found both in β sheet and in turns. The table also shows that, in some cases, different mutations at the same residue position can give different phenotypes, depending on the nature of the new amino acid. Relatively subtle effects are apparent, as for example the difference between L10S and L10T, where the presence or absence of a single methyl group appears to determine which of the two major off-pathway reactions, proteolysis or inclusion body formation, dominates IL-1β expression. High IB content does not correlate with the degree of exposure of the residue in the native structure: at three of the positions at which mutations can lead to high levels of IBs, position 10 is essentially fully buried, position 9 is partially buried, and position 97 is essentially fully exposed.

The table also shows that several of the mutants have been purified and their stabilities to reversible unfolding determined. Preliminary results suggest a correlation of extent of IB formation in most of the mutants tested with their *in vitro* stabilities to both reversible unfolding and irreversible thermal aggregation *in vitro*. However, there are some problems with taking this trend as being indicative of a mechanism of IB formation dependant on ΔG_{stab}. First, the temperatures at which mutants aggregate *in vitro* are 5-20° C higher than the growth temperature of 42° C at which IL-1β is synthesized *in vivo*. Second, at least one mutant, K97V, is an extreme outlier to the correlated points, in that it is much more prone to IB formation than WT but is at least as stable as WT to Gdn-HCl unfolding (Table III). The K97V mutant on further examination appears to form IBs through a defect in its folding pathway. Recent data shows a temperature dependence to the aggregation of this molecule *in vitro* during its refolding from Gdn-HCl solution (BC and RW, unpublished data). In contrast, the wild type's refolding *in vitro* is relatively insensitive to temperature. These preliminary results suggest that aggregation during refolding *in vitro* may be a valuable model for IB formation, at least for the K97V mutant, allowing further *in vitro* characterization of the aggregation mechanism. In the future we hope to expand the data set now available by conducting a full mutational analysis using screening methods such as those described above for interferon-γ.

TABLE III. Properties of selected IL-1β mutants

Mutation	Total Expression[a]	% IL-1β as IBs	$\Delta\Delta G_{unfold}$[b], kcal/mole	2° Structure
WT	100	8	0	-
T9A	111	8	0	β-sheet
T9Q	66	24	-1.7	β-sheet
T9G	82	18	nd	β-sheet
T9E	33	47	nd	β-sheet
L10T	78	92	nd	β-sheet
L10F	<10	nd	nd	β-sheet
L10S	<10	nd	nd	β-sheet
L80V	<10	nd	nd	β-sheet
K88L	<10	nd	nd	loop
Y90L	<10	nd	nd	loop
Y90S	<10	nd	nd	loop
E96G	49	6	nd	loop
K97R	117	1	-0.1	loop
K97G	96	24	-1.1	loop
K97V	109	68	1.0	loop
IL-1α	116	68	nd	

[a]From densitometry of SDS gels, normalized to a standard *E. coli* protein; WT=100.
[b]From reversible Gdn-HCl unfolding monitored by tryptophan fluorescence, with ΔG values extrapolated to the Cm of the WT for comparison. Adapted from reference *(43)*. nd= not determined.

Conclusions

The combined IFN-γ and IL-1β results suggest that mutations which affect IB formation can be found in all sorts of secondary structures, and the variation in predicted surface exposure in the native structure of the IL-1β IB mutants shows there is no clear correlation with this parameter either. From this small sampling of two globular proteins it is also clear that specific mutational effects on IB formation can be observed both in proteins rich in α helix and proteins rich in β sheet. The IL-1β results show that IB formation, and mutational effects on IB formation, are not restricted exclusively to oligomeric proteins. Although this does not rule out the possibility that assembly intermediates may not sometimes be key players in IB formation, it is clear that simple monomeric proteins are also capable of mutational effects on IB formation.

It is worth noting that in both systems described here, two types of stability mutations are observed: those which lead to loss of material *via* proteolysis, and those which lead to altered levels of inclusion bodies. *In vivo* proteolysis of proteins can be regarded as depending on the impact of a mutation on the interplay between thermodynamic stability *(44)* and the sequence specificities of proteases and/or other factors which mediate degradation pathways *(45-47)*. It will be of great interest to see whether IL-1β stability mutations such as those described here will support these ideas.

The dramatic influences of seemingly subtle mutations on the cellular fate of IL-1β underscores the importance of off-pathway reactions as guiding forces in protein evolution. It is clear that protein sequence changes are tested by natural selection not only for their contributions to the stability and function of the folded molecule, but also for their influences on the efficiency of the folding process, including the degree to which the folding process can escape off-pathway traps such as proteolysis and aggregation.

That the sequence requirements for a protein's activity can be different from the requirements for stability to proteolysis and inclusion body formation represents an opportunity for biotechnologists, especially in the field of industrial enzymes and other areas where stability and activity are emphasized and immunogenicity is not. One of the principle routes by which proteins become thermally inactivated *in vitro* is *via* aggregation-mediated pathways *(11)*. It is possible that folding intermediates often mediate this aggregation-dependent inactivation. To the extent that such key *in vitro* unfolding intermediates resemble folding intermediates involved in IB formation *in vivo*, mutants which escape IB formation in their cellular production may also prove to have improved *in vitro* stability properties *(9)*. Preliminary data for the IL-1β mutants suggests just such a relationship (BC and RW, unpublished data). Thus, isolation (by serendipity, design, or random mutagenesis and screening) of intragenic mutations associated with altered levels of IB formation may prove to be a useful tool for improving not only the expression characteristics of a desired protein, but also its *in vitro* stability characteristics.

Literature Cited

1. Shively, J.M. *Ann. Rev. Microbiol.* **1974**, 28, 167-187.
2. Prouty, W.F., Karnovsky, M.J. & Goldberg, A.L. *J. Biol. Chem.* **1975**, 250, 1112-1122.
3. Gribskov, M. & Burgess, R.R. *Gene.* **1983**, 26, 109-118.
4. Williams, D.C., Van Frank, R.M., Muth, W.L. & Burnett, J.P. *Science.* **1982**, 215, 687-689.
5. Wetzel, R. & Goeddel, D.V. in *The Peptides: Analysis, Synthesis, Biology;* Meienhofer, J. & Gross, E., Ed.; Academic Press: New York, **1983**; 5; 1-64.
6. Marston, R.A.O. *Biochem. J.* **1986**, 240, 1-12.
7. Mitraki, A. & King, J. *Biotech.* **1989**, 7, 690-697.
8. Schein, C.H. *Biotechnology.* **1989**, 7, 1141-1149.
9. Wetzel, R., Perry, L.J., Mulkerrin, M.G. & Randall, M. in *Protein Design and the Development of New Therapeutics and Vaccines; Proceedings of the Sixth Annual Smith, Kline and French Research Symposium;* Poste, G. & Hook, J.B., Ed.; Plenum: New York, **1990**; 79-115.
10. Wetzel, R. in *Protein Engineering - A Practical Approach;* Rees, A.R., Sternberg, M.J.E. & Wetzel, R., Ed.; IRL Press at Oxford University Press: Oxford, **1992**; In Press.
11. Wetzel, R. in *Stability of Protein Pharmaceuticals: In Vivo Pathways of Degradation and Strategies for Protein Stabilization;* Ahern, T.J. & Manning, M.C., Ed.; Plenum Press: New York, **1992**; In Press.
12. Browner, M.F., Rasor, P., Tugendreich, S. & Fletterick, R.J. *Protein Eng.* **1992**, 4, 351-357.
13. Shortle, D. & Meeker, A.K. *Biochem.* **1989**, 28, 936-944.
14. Glenner, G.G. *New England J. of Med.* **1980**, 302, 1283-1292; 1333-1343.
15. Cohen, A.S. & Connors, L.H. *J. Pathology.* **1987**, 151, 1-10.
16. Benson, M.D. & Wallace, M.R. in *The Metabolic Basis of Inherited Disease;* Scriver, C.R., Beaudet, A.L., Sly, W.S. & Valle, D., Ed.; McGraw-Hill: New York, **1989**; I; 2439-2460.
17. Pepys, M.B. in *Immunological Diseases;* Samter, M.D., Ed.; Little, Brown and Co.: Boston, **1988**; I; 631-674.
18. Stone, M.J. *Blood.* **1990**, 75, 531-45.

19. Buchner, J. & Rudolph, R. in *Current Opinion in Biotechnology;* Freedman, R. & Wetzel, R., Ed.; Current Biology,Ltd.: London, **1991**; 2:4; 532-538.
20. Haase-Pettingell, C.A. & King, J. *J. Biol. Chem.* **1988**, 263, 4977-4983.
21. Gething, M.-J. & Sambrook, J. *Nature.* **1992**, 355, 33-45.
22. King, J., Fane, B., Haase-Pettingell, C., Mitraki, A., Villafane, R. & Yu, M.-H. in *Protein Folding: Deciphering the Second Half of the Genetic Code;* Gierasch, L.M. & King, J., Ed.; American Association for the Advancement of Science: Washington, D.C., **1990**; 225-240.
23. Fane, B., Villafane, R., Mitraki, A. & King, J. *J. Biol. Chem.* **1991**, 261, In press.
24. Mitraki, A., Fane, B., Haase-Pettingell, C., Sturtevant, J. & King, J. *Science.* **1991**, 253, 54-58.
25. Krueger, J.K., Stock, A.M., Schutt, C.E. & Stock, J.B. in *Protein Folding: Deciphering the Second Half of the Genetic Code;* Gierasch, L.M. & King, J., Ed.; American Association for the Advancement of Science: Washington, D.C., **1990**; 136-142.
26. Truong, H.-T.N., Pratt, E.A., Rule, G.S., Hsue, P.Y. & Ho, C. *Biochem.* **1991**, 30, 10722-10729.
27. Fierke, C.A., Calderone, T.L. & Krebs, J.F. *Biochemistry.* **1991**, 30, 11054-11063.
28. Strandberg, L. & Enfors, S.-O. *Appl. Environ. Micro.* **1991**, 57, 1669-1674.
29. Goldenberg, D.P., Smith, D.H. & King, J. *Proc. Natl. Acad. Sci. USA.* **1983**, 80, 7060-7064.
30. Matteucci, M.D. & Heyneker, H.L. *Nucleic Acids Res.* **1983**, 11, 3113-3122.
31. Reidhaar-Olson, J.F. & Sauer, R.T. *Science.* **1988**, 241, 53-57.
32. Ealick, S.E., Cook, W.J., Vijay-Kumar, S., Carson, M., Nagabhushan, T.L., Trotta, P.P. & Bugg, C.E. *Science.* **1991**, 252, 698-702.
33. Rinderknecht, E. & Burton, L.E. in *The Biology of the Interferon System, 1984;* Kirschner, H. & Schellekens, H., Ed.; Elsevier: Amsterdam, **1985**; 397-402.
34. Mulkerrin, M.G. & Wetzel, R. *Biochem.* **1989**, 28, 6556-6561.
35. Wetzel, R., Perry, L.J. & Veilleux, C. *Biotech.* **1991**, 9, 731-737.
36. Wetzel, R., Perry, L.J., Veilleux, C. & Chang, G. *Protein Engineering.* **1990**, 3, 611-623.
37. Wetzel, R., Perry, L.J., Mulkerrin, M.G., Veilleux, C. & Chang, G. in *Protein Engineering '89: The Proceedings of the Second International Conference on Protein Engineering;* Ikehara, M., Oshima, T. & Titani, K., Ed.; Japan Scientific Societies Press: Tokyo, **1990**.
38. Priestle, J.P., Schar, H.-P. & Grutter, M.G. *Proc. Natl. Acad. Sci. USA.* **1989**, 86, 9667-9671.
39. Finzel, B.C., Clancy, L.L., Holland, D.R., Muchmore, S.W., Watenpaugh, K.D. & Einspahr, H.M. *J. Mol. Biol.* **1989**, 209, 779-791.
40. Clore, G.M., Wingfield, P.T. & Gronenborn, A.M. *Biochem.* **1991**, 30, 2315-2323.
41. Craig, S., Schmeissner, U., Wingfield, P. & Pain, R.H. *Biochemistry.* **1987**, 26, 3570-3576.
42. Young, P.R., Lillquist, J.S., Einstein, R., Lee, J., Fenderson, W., Porter, T., Kasyan, K., Green, D., Kumar, V., Sathe, G. & Simon, P.L. *Submitted.*
43. Chrunyk, B.A., Evans, J., Lillquist, J., Young, P. & Wetzel, R. *Ms. in preparation.*
44. Parsell, D.A. & Sauer, R.T. *J. Biol. Chem.* **1989**, 264, 7590-7595.
45. Bachmair, A., Finley, D. & Varshavsky, A. *Science.* **1986**, 234, 179-186.
46. Rogers, S., Wells, R. & Rechsteiner, M. *Science.* **1986**, 234, 364-368.
47. Bowie, J.U. & Sauer, R.T. *J. Biol. Chem.* **1989**, 264, 7596-7602.

RECEIVED May 5, 1992

Chapter 10

Characterization and Refolding of β-Lactamase Inclusion Bodies in *Escherichia coli*

Pascal Valax and George Georgiou

Department of Chemical Engineering, University of Texas, Austin, TX 78712

R_{TEM} β-lactamase was overexpressed in *E. coli* from three different plasmids resulting in the formation of cytoplasmic (plasmid pGB1) and periplasmic (plasmids pKN and pJG108) inclusion bodies. Previous work demonstrated that the inclusion bodies differ in structure and composition according to the cellular compartment in which aggregation occurred (*17*). In this study, we used inclusion bodies purified by sucrose density gradient centrifugation to investigate the effect of the *in vivo* aggregation environment on the properties of the protein within the inclusion bodies. Guanidine hydrochloride and pH solubilization experiments revealed important differences in the interactions involved in the stabilization of the aggregates. In addition, trypsin digestion results suggested a less ordered protein conformation in periplasmic inclusion bodies. The influence of the inclusion body origin on the renaturation of active protein was investigated in detail. The highest recovery was achieved with periplasmic inclusion bodies from RB791(pJG108). The yield of active β-lactamase upon refolding the material obtained from solubilized inclusion bodies was between 20% and 40% of that obtained from the renaturation of the purified protein under identical conditions. Our results suggest that the presence of certain contaminants in the inclusion bodies enhance the reaggregation of the protein during the removal of the denaturant.

High levels of expression of a cloned gene often results in the accumulation of misfolded recombinant protein into large, amorphous aggregates called inclusion bodies. Because of the complexity of intracellular events, very little is known about the mechanism of formation of inclusion bodies, but many growth parameters have been shown to affect *in vivo* aggregation. A high level of expression, and therefore high intracellular protein concentration, enhances aggregation (*1, 2*), whereas low growth temperature favors the production of recombinant proteins in a soluble form (*2-4*). The addition of non-metabolizable sugars, such as sucrose, to the growth medium has been shown to inhibit the formation of β-lactamase periplasmic inclusion bodies in *E. coli* (*1, 17*). Analogous effects of temperature, protein concentration and cosolvents have been

0097–6156/93/0516–0126$06.00/0

observed during the *in vitro* renaturation of purified protein from denaturant solutions (*5-8*). *In vitro* aggregation has been shown to result from the intermolecular interaction of exposed hydrophobic surfaces of a folding intermediate (*9, 10*). Based on analogies with *in vitro* results and recent direct *in vivo* experimental evidence, Mitraki and King suggested that the formation of inclusion bodies follows an similar mechanism (*11, 12*).

Very little information about the conformation of the peptide chains within the aggregates is available. Recent evidence suggests that the protein can be in either a completely misfolded or an active conformation (*13*). In most cases, the recovery of active, correctly folded protein from inclusion bodies involves the complete solubilization of the aggregates under strong denaturing conditions followed by refolding of the protein by dilution or dialysis (*14, 15*). Inhibition of reaggregation during the renaturation step requires careful optimization of the refolding conditions. The properties of the inclusion bodies themselves, such as density, structure and composition, must be taken into consideration for the design of an efficient recovery procedure.

The *E. coli* β-lactamase is a good model protein for the study of both *in vivo* and *in vitro* folding and aggregation (*18*). Overexpression of this protein in *E. coli* from different plasmids has been shown to result in the formation of periplasmic (*1, 16, 17*) or cytoplasmic (*18*) inclusion bodies. The structure and protein composition of β-lactamase inclusion bodies have been shown to depend on the intracellular compartment in which aggregation occurs (*18*). The influence of several growth conditions, such as temperature (*4*), expression level and presence of non-metabolizable sugars in the medium (*1, 17*) on the formation of the periplasmic inclusion bodies have been investigated. Furthermore, the effects of protein concentration, sucrose concentration and temperature on the *in vitro* refolding of pure β-lactamase from denaturant solutions have been shown to be in good agreement with *in vivo* observations (*8*). In this study, experiments were designed to assess differences in aggregated protein conformation among the various types of inclusion bodies. The effect of the origin of the aggregated material on the efficiency of functional protein recovery upon refolding was also investigated.

Materials and Methods.

Materials.   Guanidine hydrochloride (GuHCl) was purchased from International Biotechnologies Inc. (New Haven, CT). Dithiothreitol (DTT) and sucrose were purchased from Sigma.

Cell Growth and Inclusion Body Purification. R_{TEM} β-lactamase was produced in *E. coli* RB791 (*22*) harboring the plasmids pGB1(*18*), pJG108 and pKN (*23-24*). pGB1 expresses the protein from a *tac* promoter and contains a deletion of the region encoding the -20 to -1 amino acids of the signal sequence. In pJG108, the native signal sequence of β-lactamase was replaced by the signal sequence of the outer membrane protein A (Omp A). pKN expresses native β-lactamase from a *tac* promoter and contains a kanamycin resistance gene.

Cultures were grown at 37°C in M9 medium supplemented with 0.2% glucose and 0.2% casein. The cultures were induced with isopropylthiolgalactoside (10^{-4} M final concentration) at an optical density (O.D.$_{600}$) between 0.35 and 0.4. After overnight growth, the cells were harvested by centrifugation (8,000xg for 10 min). For all experiments, the inclusion bodies were isolated from cell lysates by isopycnic sucrose gradient centrifugation as follows: cells from 50 ml of culture were resuspended in 1 ml of 10 mM Tris-HCl, pH 8.0 containing 0.75 M sucrose and 0.2 mg/ml lysozyme. After 10 min incubation at room temperature, 2 ml of ice cold 3 mM

EDTA solution were added. The cells were then lysed in a French press at 20,000 psia. The lysates were subsequently centrifuged at 12,000xg for 30 min and the pellets, which contained the inclusion bodies, were resuspended in 1.25ml of 10 mM Tris-HCl buffer, pH 8.0, containing 0.25 M sucrose 1 mM EDTA and 0.1% sodium azide. The resuspended pellet material was layered on the top of a sucrose step gradient (40%, 53% and 67% w/w) in 1 mM Tris-HCl buffer, pH 8.0, containing 0.1% sodium azide and 1mM EDTA and centrifuged at 108,000xg for 90 min. The inclusion bodies focussed in a band at the interface between the 53% and 67% sucrose layers which was recovered and resuspended in water. The suspension was subsequently centrifuged at 12,000xg for 30 min. The pelleted material was resuspended in 0.25 M sucrose solution and applied to a second sucrose gradient as above. After recovery from the second gradient, the inclusion bodies were washed with water, resuspended in 50 mM potassium phosphate, pH 7.0 containing 0.1% sodium azide and stored at 4°C.

Solubilization Experiments. The effect of GuHCl concentration on the solubilization properties of the inclusion bodies was determined as follows. A known amount of β-lactamase aggregates was dissolved in 50 mM potassium phosphate buffer, pH 7.0 containing 5 mM DTT and various concentrations of GuHCl. The samples were incubated for three hours at room temperature and centrifuged at 8,000xg for 20 min to precipitate any remaining aggregated material. The protein concentration in the supernatant was determined using the Bio Rad assay.

To determine the effect of buffer pH on solubilization, the inclusion bodies were equilibrated with 0.45 M GuHCl and 5 mM EDTA in the following buffers (25): for adjusting the pH between 2.0 and 6.0, buffers were obtained by mixing 0.1 M citric acid solution with a 0.2 M dibasic sodium phosphate solution to specific ratios; buffers with pH values between 6.0 and 7.5 were obtained by mixing a 0.2 M monobasic sodium phosphate solution with a 0.2 M dibasic sodium phosphate solution; 0.2 M Tris buffers were adjusted to pH values between 7.5 and 8.5 and 0.2 M glycine buffers to pH values above 8.5 by addition of concentrated sodium hydroxide. After three hours of incubation at room temperature, the samples were centrifuged at 8,000xg for 20 min and the concentration of solubilized protein in the supernatant was determined as above.

Trypsin Accessibility Experiments. Identical quantities of inclusion bodies were placed in eppendorf centrifuge tubes and dissolved in 50 mM potassium phosphate buffer, pH 7.0. Trypsin was then added to a final concentration of 0.1 mg/ml in all the tubes except the control. The samples were incubated at room temperature for various times. The digestion was then stopped by adding soybean trypsin inhibitor to a final concentration of 0.2 mg/ml. The remaining aggregated material was precipitated by centrifugation at 8,000xg for 20 min. The pellets were resuspended in 50 mM potassium phosphate buffer, pH 7.0, containing 3 M GuHCl and 5 mM DTT and incubated for three hours at room temperature to completely solubilize the aggregated polypeptides (Figure 2). The amount of soluble protein, which corresponds to the remaining undigested material, was measured using the Bio-Rad assay. The tube in which no trypsin was added was used as a reference (100% intact protein).

Refolding of Inclusion Body Protein. β-lactamase inclusion bodies were incubated for three hours at room temperature in 50 mM potassium phosphate buffer, pH 7.0 containing 5 mM DTT and various concentrations of GuHCl. The total protein concentration was either 5 mg/ml or 1 mg/ml as described in the text. The samples were subsequently dialysed against 50 mM potassium phosphate buffer, pH 6.0 for three hours at room temperature in a PIERCE Inc. model 500 microdialyzer apparatus. For all experiments, the final GuHCl concentration was 0.015 M. The remaining aggregated material was precipitated by centrifugation at 8,000xg for 20 min. The total protein concentration and the β-lactamase activity in the supernatant were measured.

Finally, the purified inclusion bodies, the reaggregated protein and the soluble/refolded protein were loaded on a SDS polyacrylamide gel (15% acrylamide).

General Methods. Protein concentrations were measured using the Bio-Rad binding dye assay with bovine serum albumin as the standard. β-lactamase activities were determined spectrophotometrically using 0.5 g/l of penicillin G as the substrate (*19*). The dialysis tubing used in the microdialyzer apparatus was prepared by boiling in 2% sodium bicarbonate, 1 mM EDTA for 10 min, then boiling in 1 mM EDTA for another 10 min (*20*). The membrane was washed with distilled deionized water before and after each boiling. SDS-PAGE (15% acrylamide) was performed according to the method described by Laemmli (*21*). Prior to electrophoresis, the protein was denatured by boiling for 10 min in SDS electrophoresis buffer containing β-mercaptoethanol and bromophenol blue. The gels were stained with Coomassie brilliant blue.

Results and Discussion.

Inclusion Body Purification.   Unlike the highly regulated cytoplasm, the periplasmic space of gram-negative bacteria is affected by the composition of the growth medium. Low molecular weight compounds (such as sucrose) can diffuse freely through the outer membrane and affect the folding and aggregation of secreted proteins (*1, 17*). To investigate the influence of the cellular environment on the formation and properties of inclusion bodies, β-lactamase was overexpressed from three different plasmids. In the plasmid pGB1, the signal sequence of β-lactamase has been deleted resulting in the expression of the mature protein preceded by the sequence Met-Arg-Ile. The absence of leader peptide prevents the translocation of the protein across the inner membrane and leads to the formation of cytoplasmic inclusion bodies consisting of the mature β-lactamase. Cells containing the plasmid pKN express β-lactamase with its native signal sequence from the *tac* promoter. Induction of the *tac* promoter results in the aggregation of mature β-lactamase in the periplasmic space. At high expression levels, a fraction of the precursor protein is unable to interact with the secretory apparatus fast enough and remains in the cytoplasm where it forms pre-β-lactamase inclusion bodies. In the plasmid pJG108, the native signal sequence of β-lactamase has been replaced by the leader peptide of outer membrane protein A. The pre-OmpA-β-lactamase gene is transcribed from the inducible lpp-lac promoter. Induction of protein synthesis leads to the formation of periplasmic inclusion bodies consisting of the mature β-lactamase

  After overnight growth, the cells were harvested, converted to spheroplasts by treatment with lysozyme and EDTA and then lysed. The insoluble material from the lysates was then precipitated by low speed centrifugation. The pellets contain the protein aggregates along with other contaminants such as membrane debris, nucleic acids, etc.   Removal of these contaminants is typically achieved by a series of extraction steps (*26, 18*). DNase I and lysozyme were used to degrade DNA and membrane fragments respectively. Membrane material and proteins adsorbed non-specifically on the surface of the inclusion bodies can be extracted by treatment with detergents such as deoxycholate and Triton X-100.   This purification procedure, however, presents some major disadvantages. The detergents can also solubilize part of the inclusion body itself and therefore affect its properties and structure. The use of detergents can be circumvented by using sucrose density gradient centrifugation to separate the inclusion bodies from the cell debris (*18*). This method exploits the density difference between the protein particles and the other cellular components present in the lysates. The protein aggregates and the membrane debris form two distinct visible bands in the gradient. Silver stained polyacrylamide gels of the inclusion bodies did not reveal the presence of any of the major outer membrane proteins in the inclusion body fraction (*18*). Scanning electron micrographs of cytoplasmic inclusion bodies from RB791(pGB1) purified by both methods are shown in Figure 1. Inclusion bodies purified by sucrose gradient centrifugation were morphologically different from those purified by detergent extraction. The former were more homogeneous and regular in shape. Therefore all inclusion bodies used in this study were purified by sucrose density gradient centrifugation.

Solubilization and Trypsin Accessibility Experiments. The inclusion bodies purified from the three plasmids exhibit different morphologies (*18*). Cytoplasmic inclusion bodies from RB791(pGB1) are highly regular, cylindrical aggregates with a homogeneous surface. Their size can exceed 1.5 µm. Periplasmic inclusion bodies from RB791(pJG108) and RB791(pKN) are small (0.5-1 µm), semi-spherical particles having smooth and rough surfaces. Considering such disparity in structure and surface characteristics, it is tempting to suggest that the conformation of the polypeptide chains within the aggregates and the strength of interchain associations depend on the cellular environment in which the inclusion bodies are formed.

The conformation of proteins in aqueous solvents is dictated by two types of interactions: hydrophobic interactions and electrostatic interactions which include ion pairing, hydrogen bonds and Van der Waals interactions (*27*). The strength of these interactions determines the overall stability of the protein tertiary structure. The intensity of these interactions depends in turn on the environment. The addition of denaturants such as GuHCl or urea to the solvent induces unfolding by weakening the hydrophobic interactions. Changes in pH, on the other hand, affect electrostatic interactions. The extent of inclusion body solubilization in the presence of GuHCl and at different pH values was studied in order to examine the strength of association between the protein molecules within the aggregates. The GuHCl solubilization profiles of the different types of inclusion bodies are shown in Figure 2. Cytoplasmic inclusion bodies from RB791(pGB1) could not be solubilized in the presence of up to 0.75 M GuHCl. At this denaturant concentration, inclusion bodies from RB791(pKN) and RB791(pJG108) experience substantial solubilization (25% and 50% respectively). Complete solubilization occurred at 2.5 M GuHCl, regardless of the origin of the inclusion bodies. These results suggest that the hydrophobic interactions stabilizing the associated protein chains within the cytoplasmic inclusion bodies are stronger than those found in inclusion bodies from RB791(pKN) and RB791(pJG108).

Figure 3 shows the solubilization profiles of the three types of inclusion bodies as a function of the buffer pH. The inclusion bodies were resuspended in buffers of different pH values containing 0.45 M GuHCl and 5 mM DTT. The experiment was conducted in the presence of a moderate concentration of GuHCl to amplify the effect of pH on the stability of the protein aggregates. While the aggregates from RB791(pGB1) show little solubilization over a wide pH range, the inclusion bodies from RB791(pJG108) and to a lesser extent from RB791(pKN) exhibit pH-dependent solubilization. The ionic strength of the buffer also appears to affect the extent of solubilization of the periplasmic inclusion bodies. At pH 7.0, in 50 mM potassium phosphate buffer, the extent of solubilization in 0.45 M GuHCl, 5 mM DTT was 10% for RB791(pKN) inclusion bodies and 30% for RB791(pJG108) aggregates (Figure 2). Under the same conditions but in 0.2 M sodium phosphate buffer, the extent of solubilization was 20% and 50% respectively (Figure 3). The sensitivity of the periplasmic inclusion bodies from RB791(pKN) and especially RB791(pJG108) to pH and ionic strength suggest that electrostatic interactions are involved in stabilizing the aggregate structure. On the other hand, the cytoplasmic inclusion bodies from RB791(pGB1) were not affected by the pH and ionic strength. Therefore it appears that hydrophobic interactions play a dominant role in protein association in the cytoplasm.

The susceptibility of proteins to proteolytic degradation depends on two factors: the presence of the sequences recognized by the protease and the steric accessibility of

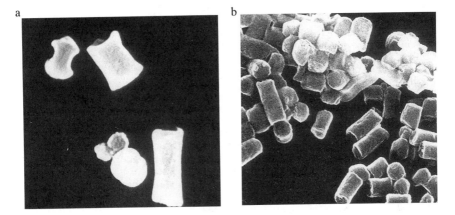

Figure 1. Scanning Electron Microscopy of cytoplasmic inclusion bodies from RB791(pGB1). a. Purified by detergent extraction. b. Purified by sucrose density gradient centrifugation.

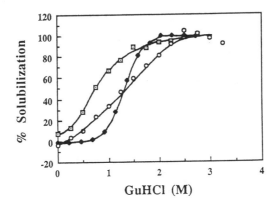

Figure 2. Extent of solubilization of sucrose density gradient centrifugation purified inclusion bodies by incubation with different concentrations of GuHCl. Inclusion bodies from RB791(pGB1) (♦), RB791(pKN) (○), RB791(pJG108) (▣) were resuspended in 50 mM potassium phosphate, pH 7.0 containing 5 mM DTT and various concentrations of GuHCl. After three hours of incubation at 23°C the remaining aggregates were precipitated by centrifugation and the concentration of soluble protein was determined.

these sequences. Consequently, proteolytic degradation is highly dependent on the protein conformation. The mature β-lactamase has been shown to be extremely resistant to digestion by trypsin whereas the β-lactamase precursor and mutants exhibiting altered stability are readily degraded (28-30). Purified inclusion bodies were incubated in a 0.1 mg/ml trypsin solution for various times. The digestion was stopped by adding soybean trypsin inhibitor to a concentration of 0.2 mg/ml. The remaining aggregated material was precipitated by centrifugation, resuspended in potassium phosphate buffer containing 3 M GuHCl and 5 mM DTT and the concentration of solubilized protein was measured by the Bradford assay. Figure 4 shows that inclusion bodies from cells containing the plasmid pGB1 were the most resistant to degradation. The periplasmic inclusion bodies from RB791(pJG108), on the other hand, were digested extremely rapidly. After 20 min of incubation in presence of trypsin, 50% of the initial amount of protein present in the cytoplasmic inclusion bodies (from plasmid pGB1) was digested, compared to more than 70% for RB791(pKN) and about 95% for RB791(pJG108). SDS-PAGE of the aggregated protein remaining after trypsin digestion of the RB791(pKN) inclusion bodies revealed that the precursor was resistant to degradation. On the other hand, the degradation of the mature protein present in periplasmic inclusion bodies was extensive (18). These results suggest that the conformation of the polypeptide chains within the periplasmic aggregates is more accessible to trypsin compared to cytoplasmic inclusion bodies.

Raman spectroscopy can provide information on the conformation of insoluble proteins in membranes in the precipitated state (31). Preliminary studies showed that the protein in cytoplasmic inclusion bodies from RB791(pGB1) exhibits a high degree of α-helicity similar to the native soluble protein. The periplasmic inclusion bodies, on the other hand, contain a mixture of α-helical, β-sheet and random conformations (T. Przybycien, preliminary results). The higher level of organization of the cytoplasmic inclusion bodies is consistent with their greater resistance to GuHCl solubilization and trypsin digestion.

London et al. (9) demonstrated that in vitro aggregation of E. coli tryptophanase results from the specific intermolecular interactions between exposed hydrophobic surfaces of a folding intermediate. If, as proposed by Mitraki and King (11, 12), in vivo aggregation proceeds along a similar pathway, then the conformation of the polypeptide chains inside the inclusion bodies should reflect the conformation of the intermediates responsible for aggregation. Our studies show that the conformation of β-lactamase within the inclusion bodies depends on the cellular compartment in which aggregation occurs. This suggest that different association pathways may be responsible for the formation of different inclusion bodies. In vitro, β-lactamase aggregation from denaturant solutions has been shown to depend on the redox potential, the pH and the cosolvent composition of the renaturation buffer. Large variations of these three parameters occur across the membranes separating the different compartments of a cell. The cytoplasm is a highly regulated reducing environment of nearly constant pH and composition. On the other hand, the pH and the concentration of low molecular weight solutes in the periplasmic space are very sensitive to external conditions. Small molecular weight compounds can diffuse freely through the outer membrane and directly affect the formation of inclusion bodies (1). Differences in the protein composition within cellular compartments might also play an important role. The interaction of folding intermediates with cytoplasmic cellular components such as chaperonins (32-38) and other folding catalysts (10) could dictate the protein association pathway that leads to inclusion body formation. Other proteins could enhance aggregation by interacting non-specifically with the nascent polypeptide. In addition, cellular components such as nucleic acids and phospholipids could also affect the formation of inclusion bodies.

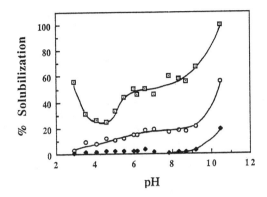

Figure 3. Solubilization of inclusion bodies from RB791(pGB1) (◆), RB791(pKN) (O), RB791(pJG108) (□) in buffers of various pH containing 0.45 M GuHCl and 5 mM DTT.

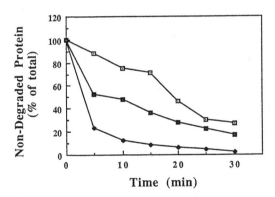

Figure 4. Digestion of inclusion bodies from RB791(pGB1) (□), RB791(pKN) (■), RB791(pJG108) (◆) by trypsin. The aggregates were incubated for various times in 0.1 mg/ml trypsin. The degradation was stopped with 0.2 mg/ml of soybean trypsin inhibitor.

Denaturation-Renaturation Experiments. The expression of recombinant protein into inclusion bodies is sometimes considered to be advantageous for several reasons. The aggregates can be easily precipitated from crude cell lysates by centrifugation. They contain the protein of interest at relatively high purity levels (40% or higher). Also aggregated protein is often more resistant to proteases within the cell. The limiting factor in deciding whether a protein should be expressed in an soluble form or as inclusion bodies resides in the difficulty to recover the native functional protein. The efficiency of the refolding process depends on the properties of the inclusion bodies such as density, solubilization characteristics and composition. SDS polyacrylamide gel electrophoresis shows that the protein composition of purified inclusion bodies varies according to their origin (Figure 7). We have showed that the solubilization characteristics of these inclusion bodies is also plasmid dependent. We therefore investigated in some detail the effect of the origin of the inclusion bodies on the efficiency of β-lactamase recovery upon renaturation. In this study, β-lactamase inclusion bodies were incubated for three hours at room temperature in 50 mM potassium phosphate buffer, pH 7.0, containing 3 M GuHCl and 5 mM DTT. The samples were subsequently dialyzed for three hours at room temperature against 50 mM potassium phosphate buffer, pH 6.0. This denaturation-renaturation procedure was completely reversible when purified β-lactamase was used at a concentration lower than 5 mg/ml. The protein recovery profiles for inclusion bodies from all three plasmids are shown in Figures 5 and 6. In all cases, the highest recoveries, both in term of activities and total soluble protein, were obtained with periplasmic inclusion bodies from RB791(pJG108). The activity recovered from RB791(pGB1) inclusion bodies was roughly half those obtained from RB791(pJG108). The lowest activity recoveries were obtained from RB791(pKN). Figures 5a and 6a also reveal that activities recovered at a total protein concentration of 1 mg/ml were about one fifth the activities obtained at 5 mg/ml. Also, the percent recovery of soluble protein obtained after renaturation at a total protein concentration of 1 mg/ml were practically identical to those obtained with 5 mg/ml (between 15% and 45% recovery depending on the plasmid). Our previous work on the refolding of purified β-lactamase clearly showed that the extent of aggregation depends on the protein concentration (8). When refolding of denatured β-lactamase was performed at concentrations greater than 5 mg/ml, the activity recovery decreased linearly decreasing as the protein concentration was increased. This type of behavior has been observed with numerous other proteins (5-7). The fact that the percent yields obtained from renaturation of inclusion body polypeptide at total protein concentrations of 5 mg/ml and 1 mg/ml were identical therefore seem to indicate that the recoveries achieved at both concentrations are the highest achievable in the conditions of the experiment. The low maximum recovery yield resulting from the solubilization-renaturation of inclusion body protein suggests that some of the contaminants integrated in the inclusion bodies enhance reaggregation of the protein during the refolding step.

To examine the effect of protein contaminants on the renaturation process, the reaggregated and the soluble fractions obtained from the refolding of 5 mg/ml of inclusion body protein from 5 M GuHCl were run on a SDS polyacrylamide gel (Figure 7). The soluble protein fraction obtained by refolding all three types of inclusion bodies was almost exclusively composed of mature β-lactamase. Essentially all the contaminating proteins initially present in the inclusion bodies were sequestered in the aggregates which were formed after the removal of the denaturant. This seems to indicate that the contaminating proteins tend to promote aggregation. Previous work on the refolding of tryptophanase (9) clearly showed that the interactions leading to aggregation of this protein are highly specific. Addition of other proteins or even crude cell lysate did not affect the recovery yields. On the other hand, the interactions leading to the aggregation of egg white lysozyme have been shown to be highly non-specific (10). The effect of protein contaminants on the refolding yield cannot be assessed at this point. Other types of contaminants such as phospholipids may also influence the

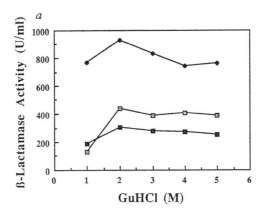

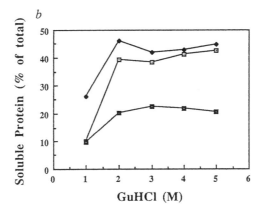

Figure 5. β-lactamase activity (a) and percent of soluble protein (b) obtained upon refolding of inclusion body proteins from RB791(pGB1) (□), RB791(pKN) (■) and RB791(pJG108) (◆). The inclusion bodies were first solubilized in 50 mM potassium phosphate buffer, pH 7.0 containing 5 mM DTT and various concentrations of GuHCl. The samples were then dialyzed against 50 mM potassium phosphate buffer, pH 6.0 for three hours at 23°C. The protein concentration was 1 mg/ml. The final GuHCl concentration was 0.015 M.

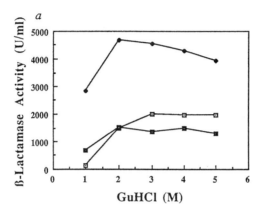

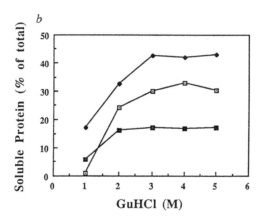

Figure 6. Same as Figure 5 except that the concentration of inclusion bodies was 5 mg/ml.

a

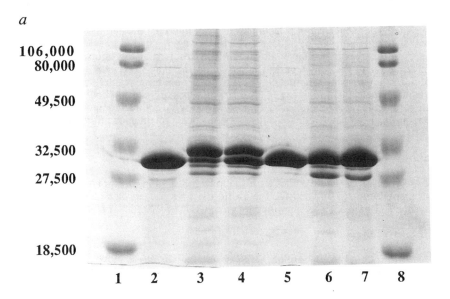

b

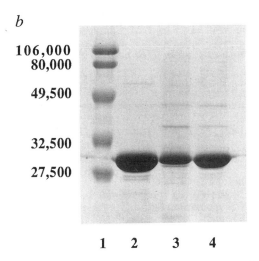

Figure 7. SDS-PAGE analysis of the renaturation of inclusion body protein. The samples correspond to the renaturation of 5 mg/ml of protein from potassium phosphate buffer pH 7.0 containing 5 M GuHCl, 5 mM DTT into the same buffer, pH 6.0. a. Lanes 2-4: RB791(pKN); Lanes 5-7: RB791(pGB1); Lanes 1 and 8 are molecular weight standards.   b. Lanes 2-4: RB791(pJG108); Lane 1 is the molecular weight standard. Lanes 2a, 5 and 2b correspond to the soluble protein obtained after renaturation. Lanes 3a, 6 and 3b correspond to the reaggregated protein. Lanes 4a, 7 and 4b show the composition of the purified inclusion bodies.

recovery of active protein. The fact that the β-lactamase precursor of the RB791(pKN) inclusion bodies was found exclusively in the aggregated fraction is not surprising since the leader sequence of β-lactamase is very hydrophobic and has been shown to slow the folding kinetics *(39)*, factors which favor aggregation.

In this report, we have shown that the structure of inclusion bodies and the conformation of the polypeptide chains within the inclusion bodies depend on the cellular compartment where aggregation occurs. These results suggest that the association mechanisms leading to the different types of inclusion bodies are different. Furthermore, the renaturation studies indicate that some cellular components present in the inclusion bodies may affect the recovery of active protein upon refolding.

Acknowledgements.

We are grateful to Angel Paredes for his help with Scanning Electron Microscopy. We also thank Gregory Bowden for the useful discussions and Daniel Thomas for his assistance. This work was supported by grant CBT 86-57971.

Literature cited.

1.   Bowden, G. A.; Georgiou, G. *Biotechnology progress* **1988**, *4(2)*, 97-101
2.   Takagi, H.; Morinaga, Y.; Tsuchiya, M.; Ikemura, H.; Inouye, M. *Bio/technology* **1988**, *6*, 948-950
3.   Schein, C. H.; Noteborn, M. H. M. *Bio/Technology* **1988**, *6*, 291-294
4.   Chalmers, J. J.; Kim, E.; Telford, J. N.; Wong, E. Y.; Tacon, W. C.; Shuler, M. L.; Wilson B. D. *Applied and Environmental Microbiology* **1990**, *56(1)*, 104-111
5.   Mitraki, A.; Betton, J. M.; Desmadril, M.; Yon, J. M. *Eur. J. Biochem.* **1987**, *163*, 29-34
6.   Burton, S. J.; Quirk, A. V.; Wood, C. P.; *Eur. J. Biochem.* **1989**, *179*, 379-387
7.   Cleland, J. L.; Wang, D. I. C. *Bio/technology* **1990**, *8*, 1274-1278
8.   Valax, P.; Georgiou, G. in *Protein Refolding*; Georgiou, G.; De Bernardez-Clark, E., Ed.; ACS Symposium Series 470; American Chemical Society, 1991, 97-109
9.   London, J.; Skrzynia, C.; Goldberg, M. E. *Eur. J. Biochem.* **1974**, *47*, 409-415
10. Goldberg, M. E.; Rudolph, R.; Jaenicke, R. *Biochemistry* **1991**, *30*, 2790-2797
11. Mitraki, A.; King, J. *Bio/Technology* **1989**, *7*, 690-697
12. Mitraki, A.; Haase Pettingell, C.; King, J. in *Protein Refolding*; Georgiou, G.; De Bernardez-Clark, E., Ed.; ACS Symposium Series 470; American Chemical Society, 1991, 35-49
13. Tokatlidis, K.; Dhurjati, P.; Millet, J.; Béguin, P.; Aubert, J. P. *FEBS* **1991**, *282(1)*, 205-208
14. Lim, W. K.; Smith Somerville, H. E.; Hardman, J. K. *Applied and Environmental Microbiology* **1989**, *55(5)*, 1106-1111
15. Buchner, J.; Rudolph, R. *Bio/Technology* **1991**, *9*, 157-162
16. Georgiou, G.; Telford, J. N.; Shuler, M. L.; Wilson, D. B. *Applied and environmental microbiology* **1986**, *52(5)*, 1157-1161
17. Bowden, G. A.; Georgiou, G. *J. Biol. Chem.* **1990**, *265(28)*, 16760-16766
18. Bowden, G. A.; Paredes, A. M.; Georgiou, G. *Bio/Technology* **1991**,
19. Sigal, I. S.; DeGrado, W. F.; Thomas, B.J.; Petteway, Jr. S. R. *The Journal of Biological Chemistry* **1984**, *259(8)*, 5327-5332

20. Maniatis, T.; Fritsch, E. F.; Sambrook, J. *Molecular Cloning, A Laboratory Manual*; Cold Spring Harbor Laboratory: Cold Spring Harbor, NY, 1982; 456

21. Laemmli, U. K. *Nature* **1970**, *227*, 680-685

22. Brent, R.; Ptashne, M. *Proc. Natl. Acad. Sci. U.S.A.* **1981**, *78*, 4204-4208

23. Ghrayeb, J.; Kimura, H.; Takahara, M.; Hsiung, H.; Masui, Y; Inouye, M. *EMBO J.* **1984**, *3*, 2437-2442

24. Georgiou, G.; Shuler, M. L.; Wilson, D. B. *Biotechnol. Bioeng.* **1988**, *32*, 741-748

25. Gomori, G. In *Methods in Enzymology* ; Academic Press, N.Y., vol. 1, 138-146

26. Marston, F. A. O. In *DNA Cloning: A Practical Approach*; Glover D. M. Ed.; IRL Press, Oxford, 1987; Vol. 3, 59-89

27. Dill, K. A. *Biochemistry* **1990**, *29(31)*, 7133-7155

28. Minsky, A.; Summers, R. G.; knowles, J. R. *Proc. Natl. Acad. Sci. U.S.A.* **1986**, *83*, 4180-4184

29. Dalbadie-McFarland, G.; Neitzel, J. J.; Richards, J. H. *Biochemistry* **1986**, *25*, 332-338

30. Georgiou, G.; Baneyx, F. In *Biochemical Engineering IV*; Goldstein, W. E.; DiBiasio, D.; Petersen, H., Eds.; Annals of the New York Academy of Sciences; New York Academy of Science, New York, 1990; Vol. 589,139-147

31. Przybycien, T. M.; Bailey, J. E. *Biochemica et Biophysica acta* **1989**, *995*, 231-245

32. Rothman, J. E. *Cell* **1989**, *59*, 591-601

33. Ellis, R. J.; Hemmingsen, S. M. *TIBS* **1989**, *14(8)*, 339-342

34. Lubben, T. H.; Donaldson, G. K.; Vitanen, P. V.; Gatenby, A. A. *The plant cell* **1989**, *1*, 1223-1230

35. Goulobinoff, P.; Christeller, J. T.; Gatenby, A. A.; Lorimer, G. H. *Nature* **1989**, *342*, 884-889

36. Kusukawa, N.; Yura, T.; Ueguchi, C.; Akiyama, Y.; Ito, K. *The EMBO Journal* **1989**, *8(11)*, 3517-3521

37. Van Dyk, T. K.; Gatenby, A. A.; LaRossa, R. A. *Nature* **1989**, *342*, 451-453

38. Phillips, G. J.; Silhavy, T. J. *Nature* **1990**, *344*, 882-884

39. Laminet, A. A.; Plückthun, A. *The EMBO Journal* **1989**, *8(5)*, 1469-1477

RECEIVED March 31, 1992

Chapter 11

Participation of GroE Heat Shock Proteins in Polypeptide Folding

Anthony A. Gatenby, Gail K. Donaldson, François Baneyx,
George H. Lorimer, Paul V. Viitanen, and Saskia M. van der Vies

Central Research and Development, E. I. du Pont de Nemours
and Company, Experimental Station, Wilmington, DE 19880–0402

The *in vivo* folding and assembly of numerous proteins, previously
considered to be a spontaneous process, appears to be significantly
influenced by a class of proteins termed molecular chaperones. The
GroE proteins of *Escherichia coli* are the best characterized molecular
chaperones, at both the genetical and biochemical level, and have been
used extensively to investigate interactions between this class of
proteins and a number of target polypeptides. It now appears that
molecular chaperones exert their influence by stabilizing protein
folding intermediates, thus partitioning them towards a pathway
leading to the native state rather than forming inactive aggregated
structures. GroE proteins are active during the early steps in folding
when aggregation-prone intermediates are abundant.

Chaperonins are a highly conserved family of proteins that are present in most, and
probably all, living organisms. They are abundant proteins, and in many
microorganisms the levels of synthesis can be dramatically enhanced in response to
stress. Thus, they are frequently referred to as heat shock or stress proteins, and one
of their cellular functions is probably to provide protection under stress conditions.
The chaperonins themselves are members of a larger class of proteins called molecular
chaperones that are broadly defined as proteins that influence the folding of other
proteins, and yet are not components of the final functional structure (*1*). This
expansive definition has resulted in many proteins now being reconsidered as
molecular chaperones, for example nucleoplasmin, hsp70, signal recognition particle,
SecB and several others (see *2-6* for recent reviews).

Current advances using a number of different experimental systems has led to
the realization that protein folding within cells is more complex than was initially
thought. It was assumed that since a number of chemically denatured proteins can
successfully fold into their functional native structures *in vitro* using information
contained in the primary amino acid sequence (reviewed in *7*), then protein folding *in
vivo* should also be a spontaneous event. The reality, at least for some proteins in the
cell, may be quite different. This is due, in part, to a temporal element, since
polypeptide chains emerging from ribosomes in a linear fashion may initiate folding
before translation of the mRNA is completed. Therefore, the information in the
primary sequence required for successful folding may not be simultaneously available.
Similar constraints would also apply to polypeptides during translocation through

0097–6156/93/0516–0140$06.00/0

membranes prior to correct folding. In addition, the high concentrations of proteins in the cell at various stages of folding, and with potentially interactive surfaces, must coexist without mutual impairment of folding pathways (reviewed in *8, 9*). Molecular chaperones appear to have evolved to interact with the non-native states of proteins in cells and to partition polypeptides towards productive folding pathways. In this chapter the role in protein folding of the most structurally complex of the molecular chaperones, the chaperonins, will be described. We shall concentrate on studies that have involved the bacterial GroES and GroEL chaperonins. Several reviews and papers describing chaperonins from other organisms have been published (*1, 2, 4, 10-20*).

Chaperonin Molecules

There are two basic types of chaperonins of quite distinct sizes (Table I). The larger type contains subunits with an approximate molecular mass of 60 kDa that are arranged in a complex structure comprising two rings of seven subunits stacked on each other (*21, 22*). This type of molecule is known as GroEL (in bacteria), hsp60 (in yeast), rubisco subunit binding protein (in plants), P1 protein (in mammalian mitochondria), or collectively as chaperonin 60 (cpn60) on account of its subunit size. The second type of chaperonin (or co-chaperonin) is significantly smaller and contains subunits of about 10 kDa and, at least in bacteria, these are thought to form a single ring of seven subunits (*23*). This smaller heptameric protein isolated from *E. coli* is called GroES and a related protein in mammalian mitochondria is known as cpn10 (*19*), again reflecting its subunit size. GroEL possesses a weak ATPase activity that requires magnesium and potassium ions for maximal activity (*23, 24*). The ATPase is effectively suppressed when GroES binds to GroEL, an event that itself requires the presence of MgATP (*23, 24*). Self-assembly of the oligomeric form of GroEL from monomers also requires MgATP (*25*). Although the quaternary structure of bacterial GroEL oligomers has been observed by electron microscopy (*21, 22*), the tertiary structure is unknown.

The GroES and GroEL chaperonins from *E. coli* were the first to be studied in detail. The GroE proteins were originally identified because mutations in their genes prevented the growth of several bacteriophages (reviewed in *26*). Subsequent studies revealed that the *groES* and *groEL* genes are essential for bacterial survival (*27*), and that they constitute an operon whose expression is enhanced during heat shock. During a stress response the cellular level of GroEL can be increased from about 2% to 10% of cell protein (*28*). The GroES and GroEL proteins functionally interact (*23, 24*) and influence bacteriophage growth at the level of capsid assembly (*26*). Proteins related to either GroES or GroEL have now been identified in numerous prokaryotic organisms, and display a high degree of amino acid sequence homology (*26*).

GroE Chaperonins Influence Protein Folding and Assembly *in vivo*

Early studies with various bacteriophages and *groE* defective strains demonstrated that chaperonins influenced assembly of head or tail structures (depending on the particular phage), and the sites of these interactions were genetically defined (*26*). It was also established that the *E. coli* GroEL protein was related by amino acid sequence homology to the chloroplast cpn60 (*1*), a protein implicated in the assembly of the photosynthetic enzyme ribulose bisphosphate carboxylase/oxygenase (rubisco) (*16-18*). The rubisco holoenzyme has a rather complex structure of eight large (L, 52 kDa) and eight small (S, 12 kDa) subunits. An expression system which directs synthesis and assembly of the L_8S_8 rubisco holoenzyme from the cyanobacterium *Anacystis nidulans* was developed in *E. coli* (*29*). It therefore became possible to test whether folding and assembly of the photosynthetic enzyme in *E. coli* was influenced by the GroE proteins.

Table I. Molecular Properties of *E. coli* **GroE Chaperonins**

GroEL (cpn60, hsp60)

ubiquitous (bacteria, fungi, plants and animals)

a stress induced protein in some organisms

essential for bacterial cell growth - no deletion mutants described

subunit molecular mass - 60 kDa

native molecular mass - 840 kDa

tetradecamer - two layers of seven subunits

weak K^+-dependent ATPase, k_{cat} 0.1 s^{-1} (based on protomer)

interacts with GroES in the presence of MgATP

requires GroES to be functional *in vivo*

stabilizes folding intermediates of several proteins in binary complexes

groE operon contains *groES* and *groEL* genes

GroES (cpn10)

believed to be ubiquitous (bacteria, chloroplasts, mitochondria)

a stress induced protein in some organisms

essential for bacterial cell growth - no deletion mutants described

subunit molecular mass - 10 kDa

native molecular mass - 70 kDa

heptamer - single ring of subunits

inhibits ATPase activity of GroEL

aids in release of proteins bound to GroEL

To demonstrate that GroE proteins influence the assembly of *A. nidulans* rubisco in *E. coli*, the level of cellular GroE proteins was increased by cloning the *groE* genes on a multicopy plasmid. The *groE* operon was transferred to a chloramphenicol-resistant plasmid (pGroESL) that is compatible with an ampicillin-resistant plasmid (pANK1) that directs the synthesis of rubisco subunits. The presence of the *groE* plasmid increases the levels of GroE proteins in the cell to about 20-30% of total protein (*30*). This high concentration of chaperonins in the cell resulted in a concomitant increase in the level of active L_8S_8 rubisco holoenzyme.

Although chaperonin overexpression resulted in nearly a ten-fold increase in assembled rubisco, there was little change in the amount of rubisco polypeptides. Therefore, the GroE proteins influenced one or more steps in the assembly of the rubisco holoenzyme and not the synthesis or stability of the subunit polypeptides. Additional experiments revealed that overexpression of both *groES* and *groEL* was required for enhanced rubisco assembly, and that *groE* defective strains that prevent bacteriophage morphogenesis also inhibited hexadecameric rubisco assembly (*30*). A structurally simpler dimeric form of rubisco with two large subunits has also been characterized. Assembly of this dimeric form of the rubisco enzyme was similarly influenced by the chaperonin concentration in the cell. Since dimers of L subunits are the basic structural motifs in the more complex L_8S_8 enzyme, assembly of L dimers may be an essential intermediary stage in the formation of the L_8 core, and therefore the influence of GroE proteins on the basic common step of dimer formation can control the subsequent assembly of the more complex form of rubisco. Recent studies have also demonstrated an involvement of GroEL in *nif* gene regulation and nitrogenase assembly (*31*).

GroE Proteins Interact with Many Bacterial Polypeptides

Although a clear involvement of GroE proteins in bacteriophage and rubisco assembly can be demonstrated, these are of course protein targets that are not usually present in *E. coli* cells. In attempts to define the normal role of chaperonins in bacterial cells, the dual techniques of genetic suppression and direct identification of GroEL complexed with target polypeptides have been of value.

Suppression of Heat-Sensitive Mutations. Because successful polypeptide folding can be significantly influenced by temperature, it was suspected that some heat-sensitive mutations in bacteria could be folding mutants. In these types of mutants incubation at non-permissive temperatures might lead to destabilization of folding intermediates, with subsequent aggregation or proteolysis, resulting in the observed growth defects. Increased expression of the GroE chaperonins in a range of heat-sensitive mutants grown at non-permissive temperatures would therefore allow the identification of chaperonin-suppressible mutations.

Initially, heat-sensitive mutations in the *ilv* operon in *Salmonella typhimurium* encoding enzymes of branched chain amino acid biosynthesis were examined. The auxotrophic requirements of one mutation in *ilvGM* and two mutations in *ilvE*, encoding the multimeric enzymes acetolactate synthase II and transaminase B respectively, are suppressed by a multicopy plasmid encoding the *groE* operon from *E. coli* (*32*). These observations were extended by examining the response of numerous mutations to GroES and GroEL overexpression (Table II). Many, but not all, heat-sensitive *hisD*, *hisC* and *hisB* alleles are suppressed by multicopy *groE* plasmids. These genes encode histidinol dehydrogenase, histidinol-phosphate aminotransferase and the bifunctional protein imidazoleglycerol phosphate dehydratase:histidinol phosphate phosphatase, respectively. Suppression of cold-sensitive and temperature-independent alleles was not observed in the *his* system. The presence of the *groE* plasmid also suppresses heat-sensitive growth and secretion defects caused by the *secA51* and *secY24* alleles of *E. coli* (*32*). Thus, mutations causing alterations in enzymes and the protein translocation apparatus are subject to multicopy suppression by *groE*. It should be noted that this suppression requires overexpression of both *groES* and *groEL*. In addition, the levels of GroE proteins required are high, and represent about 20-30% of total cell protein. This is significantly greater than the increased levels of GroE proteins that would be synthesized in cells containing only the chromosomal *groE* operon when plated at the higher non-permissive temperatures.

Table II. Multicopy *groE* Suppression of *Salmonella typhimurium* Heat Sensitive Mutations

Gene	Enzyme	Suppression[a]
hisB	imidazoleglycerol phosphate dehydratase:histidinol phosphatase	1 of 3
hisC	histidinol-phosphate aminotransferase	2 of 7
hisD	histidinol dehydrogenase	7 of 7
ilvE	transaminase B	2 of 2
ilvGM	acetolactate synthase	1 of 11

[a]Suppression expressed as numbers of strains growing at non-permissive temperatures out of the number of mutations tested. Adapted from (*32*).

Overexpression of the *groE* operon in *E. coli* is also known to suppress the heat-sensitive phenotype of several *dnaA* alleles (*33, 34*), suggesting an interaction between the *groE* products and the dnaA protein at the origin of replication. These results, taken together with our observations on general *groE* multicopy suppression, suggest a widespread interaction of GroE proteins with other cellular proteins. Although high concentrations of GroE proteins are required to suppress these heat-sensitive mutations, possibly by trapping unstable mutant proteins to allow partitioning towards correct folding, it is possible that normal levels of chaperonins in cells could help correct errors in protein folding and thus alleviate some weak genetic folding defects.

Direct Interaction of GroEL with Many Bacterial Proteins. Evidence to support the genetic indications that many *E. coli* proteins interact with chaperonins has been obtained by forming stable complexes between GroEL and a random assortment of bacterial proteins (*35*). As described later, it is now well established that stable binary complexes can be formed between GroEL and the non-native states of several purified proteins. These complexes are often sufficiently stable to be isolated by gel filtration or non-denaturing gel electrophoresis. Rather than examining the interactions between GroEL and a large range of purified proteins on an individual basis, we chose to directly examine the interactions of proteins from a total *E. coli* cell extract with the purified chaperonin.

E. coli cells were grown for several generations on minimal medium containing [^{35}S]methionine and a soluble protein extract was prepared. When the native mixture of proteins was incubated with GroEL, and then fractionated on a gel filtration column, very little material was associated with the GroEL peak. This indicated that the native states of proteins in a complex mixture were unable to bind to GroEL in a stable fashion. The failure of native states to interact with GroEL has been observed for a number of purified proteins. In contrast, if the total radiolabelled mixture of proteins is denatured with guanidine-HCl followed by dilution of the chaotrope in the presence of GroEL, stable binary complexes are formed with the chaperonin that can be resolved by gel filtration. It appears that about half of the labelled proteins in their unfolded or partially folded states can interact with GroEL, and are efficiently discharged following the addition of MgATP. This may be an underestimate of the number of cellular proteins that can interact with chaperonins, since some proteins may fold so rapidly that they do not have an opportunity to interact with GroEL, and others may not bind with a sufficiently high affinity to withstand gel filtration. Binary complex formation is reduced when the transient species that interact with GroEL are allowed enough time to progress to more stable states. This suggests that the structural elements that are recognized by GroEL, and that allow complex formation, are only present or accessible in the unfolded or partially folded states of many proteins.

The combined observations of high-affinity binding of many cellular proteins, and the natural abundance of GroEL, taken together with genetic suppression studies, lead us to suspect that the folding of most proteins in *E. coli* does not occur spontaneously while they are in solution, but probably takes place while they are associated with chaperonins. The common interaction between chaperonins and numerous unrelated target proteins has also been observed in eukaryotic organelles when these proteins are either synthesized within chloroplasts (*16-18*) and mitochondria (*36*), or following translocation through the membranes (*13, 20, 37*).

Refolding of Purified Proteins *in vitro* is Influenced by Chaperonins

Protein Folding and Aggregation. In general, the isomerization of proteins from the unfolded (U) state to the native (N) state involves the transient formation of folding intermediates (I). Although initially considered as a highly cooperative single step process, an increasing number of multistep folding pathways have been identified (*38, 39*) that can be populated by distinct partially folded states (*40*). The folding of many proteins analyzed *in vitro* can be considered in its simplest form as a two step process (*39, 41*).

$$U \rightarrow I \rightarrow N$$

The initial fast step involves the conversion of the unfolded (U) polypeptide to the intermediate (I) or molten globule state. The U state will not be highly populated at any one time because of this rapid conversion to the thermodynamically more stable I state. The I or molten globule state is a collapsed yet mobile structure that results from the rapid formation of specific secondary structural elements on a millisecond time-scale. Although the I state is almost as compact as N, it lacks the close packing of the secondary structural elements typical of the N state, and so the amino acid side chains exhibit greater fluctuation and the core residues are accessible to solvent molecules. However, in the second rate-determining step these elements become organized into the specific tertiary structures associated with the N state. In contrast to the rapid and uncooperative transitions between the U and I states, those between the I and N states are both slow and cooperative. The I, or molten globule, state probably has a greater number of hydrophobic residues exposed on its surface than in the N state because the I to N transition is associated with a large change in both enthalpy (ΔH) and in heat capacity (ΔC_p). The I states of proteins are characteristically less soluble than N and have a propensity to aggregate. This predilection for aggregation by the I state most likely results from the interaction of the exposed hydrophobic surfaces with each other. The kinetic partitioning of the I state between the N state or an aggregated state (I_{agg}) is therefore of considerable significance for the efficient folding of a protein under a given set of conditions.

Fortunately, it is possible to control some of the factors that favor aggregation *in vitro* to obtain successful refolding of denatured polypeptides. The simplest ways to suppress aggregation during *in vitro* refolding are to reduce either the concentration of the protein, the temperature of the refolding reaction, or perhaps both. Although the I to N transition is an isomerization reaction, and is therefore independent of the concentration of I, aggregation is highly dependent on [I] since it is a second or higher order process (42). Aggregation can, therefore, occur much faster than first-order folding, and can exceed successful folding as protein concentration increases. Consequently, folding of the maximum number of molecules occurs in very dilute solutions where intermolecular interactions can be reduced (43). Interactions between hydrophobic surfaces, such as those found on molten globules, can be minimized by the simple expedient of reducing the temperature. By suppressing these hydrophobic interactions at low temperatures, conditions that would lead to aggregation can be avoided and partitioning to the native state favored (24)

In the complex and dynamic cellular milieu it is obviously not feasible to reduce protein concentrations to the levels that would prevent intermolecular aggregation events occurring between unfolded or partially folded molecules. Similarly, a reduction in temperature to reduce hydrophobic interactions is not an approach that has found favor in complex biological systems. Because aggregation reactions are both temperature and concentration dependent, conditions within cells thus appear to be particularly unsuitable for protein folding reactions in the normal physiological range of temperatures and protein concentrations. To resolve this dilemma, cells have apparently evolved molecular chaperones to aid in protein folding reactions *in vivo*.

Interactions Between Chaperonins and Other Proteins. The folding and interactions of several different purified proteins in the presence of GroE chaperonins has now been studied in some detail. Current examples include rubisco (24, 35, 44, 45), pre-ß-lactamase (46), rhodanese (47-49), dihydrofolate reductase (49, 50), citrate synthase (51), α-glucosidase (52), lactate dehydrogenase (53) and several thermophilic enzymes (54). In addition, the binding and release of proteins to GroEL in cell extracts has been examined (55, 56). Some common themes have emerged. The first, and perhaps most striking observation, is that the folding of many different proteins is influenced by chaperonins. These proteins bear little resemblance to each other with regard to size, shape, function or cellular location. The interaction of GroE chaperonins with target proteins during folding is therefore a very general mechanism that enables cells to exert some control over the isomerization of a broad range of molecules.

The Association Step. Clearly, the question of the specificity of the interactions between chaperonins and these target proteins becomes paramount. Evidence obtained to date indicates that once proteins have folded to their N states they do not appear to interact with chaperonins, and by implication the structural motifs that impart recognition are either inaccessible or no longer present. These motifs must consequently be exposed on the non-native I states of proteins. Since exposed hydrophobic residues are a characteristic feature of folding intermediates, perhaps these allow the chaperonin·I state recognition event. Based on the observation that chaperonins can substitute for nondenaturing detergents to obtain successful folding of rhodanese, it was proposed that the interactions of hydrophobic surfaces that lead to aggregation can be prevented by the binding of GroEL to partly folded intermediates (47). The presence of hydrophobic surfaces on GroEL itself is suggested by binding of the hydrophobic fluorescent reporter bisANS (47). Studies on the chaperonin-dependent folding of the monomeric enzymes dihydrofolate reductase and rhodanese indicate that GroEL stabilizes these proteins in a structure that resembles the molten globule state (49). The fluorescence properties of α-glucosidase bound to GroEL also suggests a molten globule state for the target protein (52). In contrast, from measurements on the interaction of lactate dehydrogenase with chaperonins it was concluded that GroEL binds to the unfolded and the first transient intermediate in the folding pathway, and not to other later structures such as the molten globule state (53).

It has also been suggested that improperly folded proteins are recognized by excessive stretches of solvent-exposed main-chain polar groups rather than binding to hydrophobic patches (57). To settle these issues, only the use of high-resolution techniques such as NMR spectroscopy will permit the precise structural analysis of material bound to chaperonins. Experimental evidence obtained thus far with such methods supports a proposal that GroEL interacts with sequences in a non-native polypeptide that have the potential to adopt an amphipathic α-helix, and that the chaperonin binding site promotes formation of a helix (58).

The initial partial reaction of chaperonins in the protein folding pathway is the recognition and binding of unstable folding intermediates to form a binary complex. The binding of proteins in non-native states to GroEL does not require the presence of MgATP or the co-chaperonin GroES. These binary complexes are very stable, and in some instances they have been physically isolated by gel filtration (35, 50). An apparent exception to the view that only proteins in non-native states will bind to GroEL are the observations that native mouse dihydrofolate reductase and bacterial pre-ß-lactamase are subject to a net unfolding when incubated with GroEL (46, 50). It is now known that the native states of these two proteins exist in slow conformational equilibria with species that are recognized by GroEL. As a result, most of the native enzyme can eventually be sequestered on the chaperonin in an inactive form. The stoichiometry of binding to chaperonins appears to be one or two target polypeptides bound to each GroEL tetradecamer, with most studies favoring the lower number. In several documented examples the formation of these binary complexes between GroEL and the non-native states of proteins inhibits the development of aggregates. Under appropriate conditions, rhodanese (47), rubisco (24), citrate synthase (51), and α-glucosidase (52) will aggregate following dilution from a solution containing a chaotrope. If GroEL is present during dilution, aggregates are not formed because the partially folded states of these enzymes are trapped by the chaperonin. This stabilizes the I state in a form which not only prevents it from aggregation, but also prevents it from proceeding to the native state.

$$U \rightarrow I + GroEL \rightarrow GroEL\cdot I$$

An interesting study on the aggregation of yeast α-glucosidase demonstrated the reconstitution of a heat shock effect *in vitro* (52). The yeast enzyme is rapidly inactivated at temperatures above 42°C and will aggregate unless GroEL is present. If the bound enzyme is discharged from GroEL with GroES and MgATP at 42°C it will again aggregate, but if discharge occurs at a lower temperature the released polypeptide will fold into an active structure.

The formation of aggregates during refolding depends on the concentration of the protein solution at a particular temperature. Above a threshhold concentration, defined as the critical aggregation concentration (45), aggregation will occur until the concentration is reduced to a value at which the I state can continue to isomerize to the N state. The four enzymes described earlier which aggregate unless GroEL is present, can also refold in the absence of chaperonins at lower temperatures or protein concentrations. However, if GroEL is also present during these spontaneous folding reactions the folding is inhibited (24, 47, 51, 52). This inhibition of successful folding is also observed for pre-ß-lactamase (46), dihydrofolate reductase (49, 50), isocitrate dehydrogenase (54) and lactate dehydrogenase (53, 54). The chaperonins, therefore, not only suppress aggregation, but also inhibit refolding. The common step in these two apparently distinct mechanisms is the interaction of GroEL with unstable folding intermediates. When unfolded proteins rapidly collapse to the I state, and the critical aggregation concentration is exceeded, they will aggregate. At lower concentrations they may refold. If GroEL is present before the concentration dependent partitioning between the alternative productive or non-productive pathways is followed, then the I state is physically trapped by the chaperonin and neither pathway can be pursued.

The Dissociation Step. The release, or discharge, of polypeptides bound to GroEL is effected by adenine nucleotides and the co-chaperonin GroES in the presence of potassium ions. Proteins bound to GroEL behave differently in their requirements for nucleotides and GroES in the dissociation reaction. Many proteins, such as dihydrofolate reductase (49, 50), pre-ß-lactamase (46), citrate synthase (51), lactate dehydrogenase (53) and α-glucosidase (52) can be released and fold to an active form by the addition of MgATP alone. However, it should be appreciated, that in most cases the presence of the co-chaperonin GroES potentiated this ATP-dependent discharge. GroES is therefore not necessarily required for the release process *in vitro*, but instead acts to increase its efficiency, as previously noted (46). These GroES-enhanced rates of release, while not essential to obtain the desired product *in vitro*, may be significant to the physiology of cells and account for the simultaneous requirement of both GroEL and GroES for cell viability (27). There is also some question on whether ATP hydrolysis is necessary for release. Both lactate dehydrogenase (53) and dihydrofolate reductase (50) can be dissociated from GroEL in an active form by the addition of the nonhydrolyzable analogue 5'-adenylyl imidodiphosphate (AMP-PNP). It is noteworthy that adenosine 5'-O-(3-thiotriphosphate) (ATPγS), which competitively inhibits but cannot support the chaperonin-mediated refolding of rubisco (44), is as effective as ATP in releasing bound dihydrofolate reductase from GroEL (50). These observations suggest that *in vitro*, discharge of some proteins complexed to the chaperonin is mediated in part through the binding of ATP to GroEL. In the presence of ATP, or a nonhydrolyzable anologue capable of producing a similar conformational change, there is a significant reduction in the affinity between GroEL and some target proteins. This shifts the equilibrium towards free enzyme, and spontaneous folding resumes. The ATPγS and AMP-PNP analogues were also partially effective in the ATP-dependent self assembly of the GroEL tetradecamer itself (25). The role of ATP in the discharge process appears to be coupled with a requirement for rapid dissociation of the binary complex. The non-specific affinity of chaperonins for many different target proteins would probably require a dissociation mechanism that leads to a gross conformational rearrangement of GroEL when MgATP is present. Such rearrangements of GroEL have recently been detected by measuring changes in protease sensitivity upon adenine nucleotide addition (59).

There are examples in which GroES is essential during the dissociation step for successful recovery of a biologically active proteins. During the chaperonin-dependent refolding of rhodanese (47-49) and rubisco (24, 35, 44, 45) the complete folding reaction must contain GroEL, GroES, MgATP and potassium ions. It is important to distinguish between a requirement for GroES for efficient release of the polypeptide from GroEL, from one for efficient recovery of the active protein. For example, if a binary complex is prepared between GroEL and radioactive folding intermediates of rubisco, the complex is stable and can be resolved by gel filtration (35, 59). The addition of GroES and MgATP results in a substantial dissociation (85-90%) of the complex, and the appearance on the column of two new peaks corresponding to the active rubisco dimer and a small amount of inactive folded monomer. In contrast, when only MgATP is added, a significant proportion (50-75%) of rubisco is discharged from the complex, but it is not resolved on the column and is not catalytically active (35, 59). Thus, MgATP alone causes a conformational change in GroEL that weakens its affinity for the bound rubisco, but the species released does not successfully progress to the native state. This indicates that the degree of foldedness of the discharged rubisco differs depending on whether GroES is present or absent. In the presence of GroES, the bound rubisco is able to progress to a state where it is not susceptible to aggregation on release. A similar conclusion was reached for the chaperonin-dependent folding of rhodanese (49). In the absence of GroES, the rhodanese that was dissociated from GroEL by MgATP was not active and formed aggregates. These latter studies on rhodanese suggested that in the absence of GroES there are repeated cycles of release and binding which does not lead to a progression to the N state (*49*). Presumably, for proteins that can fold into active structures following release from GroEL by MgATP alone, there is competition between re-binding to GroEL and progression to the N state, with partitioning to N being favored. This partitioning to the N state would then be further enhanced for most target proteins when GroES is also present to disrupt the energetically wasteful re-binding reaction.

Literature Cited.

1. Hemmingsen, S. M.; Woolford, C.; van der Vies, S. M.; Tilly, K.; Dennis, D.T.; Georgopoulos, C.P.; Hendrix, R. W.; Ellis, R. J. *Nature* **1988**, *333*, 330.
2. Ellis, R. J. *Plant J.* **1991**, *1*, 9.
3. Ang, D.; Liberek, K.; Skowyra, D.; Zylicz, M.; Georgopoulos, C. *J. Biol. Chem.* **1991**, *266*, 24233.
4. Ellis, R. J.; van der Vies, S. M. *Annu. Rev. Biochem.* **1991**, *60*, 321.
5. Gething, M.-J.; Sambrook. J. *Nature* **1992**, *355*: 33.
6. Rothman, J. E. *Cell* **1989**, *59*, 591.
7. Jaenicke, R. *Prog.Biophys. Mol. Biol.* **1987**, *49*, 117.
8. Fischer, G.; Schmid, F. X. *Biochemistry* **1990**, *29*, 2205.
9. Jaenicke, R. *Biochemistry* **1991**, *30*, 3147.
10. McMullin, T. W.; Hallberg, R. L. *Mol. Cell. Biol.* **1988**, *8*, 371.
11. Reading, D. S.; Hallberg, R. L.; Myers, A. M. *Nature* **1989**, *337*, 655.
12. Jindals, S.; Dudani, A. K.; Singh, B.; Harley, C. B.; Gupta, R. S. *Mol. Cell. Biol.* **1989**, *9*, 2279.
13. Cheng, M. Y.; Hartl, F-U.; Martin, J.; Pollock, R. A.; Kalousek, F.; Neupert, W.; Hallberg, E. M.; Hallberg, R. L.; Horwich, A. L. *Nature* **1989**, *337*, 620.
14. Hutchinson, E. G.; Tichelaar, W.; Hofhaus, G.; Weiss, H.; Leonard, K. R. *EMBO J.* **1989**, *8*, 1500.
15. Ostermann, J.; Horwich, A. L.; Neupert, W.; Hartl, F-U. *Nature* **1989**, *341*, 125.
16. Barraclough, R.; Ellis, R. J. *Biochim. Biophys. Acta* **1980**, *608*, 19.
17. Roy, H.; Bloom, M.; Milos, P.; Monroe, M. *J. Cell Biol.* **1982**, *94*, 20.
18. Bloom, M. V.; Milos, P.; Roy, H. *Proc. Natl. Acad. Sci. USA* **1983**, *80*, 1013.
19. Lubben, T. H.; Gatenby, A. A.; Donaldson, G. K.; Lorimer, G. H.; Viitanen, P. V. *Proc. Natl. Acad. Sci. USA* **1990**, *87*, 7683.
20. Lubben, T. H.; Donaldson, G. K.; Viitanen, P. V.; Gatenby, A. A. *Plant Cell* **1989**, *1*, 1223.
21. Hendrix, R. W. *J. Mol. Biol.* **1979**, *129*, 375.
22. Hohn, T.; Hohn, B.; Engel, A.; Wurtz, M.; Smith, P. R. *J. Mol. Biol.* **1979**, *129*, 359.
23. Chandrasekhar, G. N.; Tilley, K.; Woolford, C.; Hendrix, R.; Georgopoulos, C. *J. Biol. Chem.* **1986**, *261*, 12414.
24. Viitanen, P. V.; Lubben, T. H.; Reed, J.; Goloubinoff, P.; O'Keefe, D. P.; G. H. Lorimer. *Biochemistry* **1990**, *29*, 5665.
25. Lissin, N. M.; Venyaminov, S. Yu.; Girshovich, A. S. *Nature* **1990**, *348*, 339.
26. Zeilstra-Ryalls. J.; Fayet. O.; Georgopoulos. C. *Annu. Rev. Microbiol.* **1991**, *45*: 301.
27. Fayet, O.; Ziegelhoffer, T.; Georgopoulos, C. *J. Bacteriol.* **1989**, *171*, 1379.
28. Neidhardt, F. C.; Phillips, T. A.; van Bogelen, R. A.; Smith, M. W.; Georgalis, Y.; Subramanian, A. R. *J. Bacteriol.* **1981**, *145*, 513.
29. Gatenby, A. A.; van der Vies, S. M.; Bradley, D. *Nature* **1985**, *314*, 617.

30.   Goloubinoff, P.; Gatenby, A. A.; Lorimer, G. H. *Nature* **1989**, *337*, 44.
31.   Govezensky, D.; Greener, T.; Segal, G.; Zamir, A. *J. Bacteriol.* **1991**, *173*, 6339.
32.   Van Dyk, T. K.; Gatenby, A. A.; LaRossa, R. A. *Nature* **1989**, *342*, 451.
33.   Fayet, O.; Louarn, J.-M.; Georgopoulos, C. *Mol. Gen. Genetic.* **1986**, *202*, 435.
34.   Jenkins, A. J.; Marsh, J. B.; Oliver, I. R.; Masters, M. *Mol. Gen. Genetic.* **1986**, *202*, 446.
35.   Viitanen, P. V.; Gatenby, A. A.; Lorimer, G. H. *Protein Sci.* **1992**, (in press).
36.   Prasad, T. K.; Hack, E.; Hallberg, R. L. *Mol. Cell. Biol.* **1990**, *10*, 3979.
37.   Gatenby, A. A.; Lubben, T. H.; Ahlquist, P.; Keegstra, K. *EMBO J.* **1988**, 7, 1307.
38.   Ptitsyn, O. B. *J. Protein Chem.* **1987**, *6*, 273.
39.   Kuwajima, K. *Proteins* **1989**, *6*, 87.
40.   Smith, C. J.; Clarke, A. R.; Chia, W. N.; Irons, L. I.; Atkinson, T.; Holbrook, J. J. *Biochemistry* **1991**, *30*, 1028.
41.   Ptitsyn, O. B.; Pain, R. H.; Semisotnov, G. V.; Zerovnik, E.; Razgulyaev, O. I. *FEBS Lett.* **1990**, *262*, 20.
42.   Zettlmeissl, G.; Rudolph, R.; Jaenicke, R. *Biochemistry* **1979**, *18*, 5567.
43.   Zettlmeissl, G.; Rudolph, R.; Jaenicke, R. *Biochemistry* **1979**, *18*, 5572.
44.   Goloubinoff, P.; Christeller, J. T.; Gatenby, A. A.; Lorimer, G. H. *Nature* **1989**, *342*, 884.
45.   van der Vies, S. M.; Viitanen, P. V.; Gatenby, A. A.; Lorimer, G. H., Jaenicke, R. *Biochemistry* **1992** (in press).
46.   Laminet, A. A.; Ziegelhoffer, T.; Georgopoulos, C.; Pluckthun, A. *EMBO J.* **1990**, *9*, 2315.
47.   Mendoza, J. A.; Rogers, E.; Lorimer, G. H.; Horowitz, P. M. *J. Biol. Chem.* **1991**, *266*, 13044.
48.   Mendoza, J. A.; Lorimer, G. H.; Horowitz, P. M. *J. Biol. Chem.* **1991**, *266*, 16973.
49.   Martin, J.; Langer, T.; Boteva, R.; Schramel, A.; Horwich, A. L.; Hartl, F.-U. *Nature* **1991**, *352*, 36.
50.   Viitanen, P. V.; Donaldson, G. K.; Lorimer, G. H.; Lubben, T. H.; Gatenby, A. A. *Biochemistry* **1991**, *30*, 9716.
51.   Buchner, J.; Schmidt, M.; Fuchs, M.; Jaenicke, R.; Rudolph, R.; Schmid, F. X.; Kiefhaber, T. *Biochemistry* **1991**, *30*, 1586.
52.   Holl-Neugebauer, B.; Rudolph, R.; Schmidt, M.; Buchner, J. *Biochemistry* **1991**, *30*, 11609.
53.   Badcoe, I. G.; Smith, C. J.; Wood, S.; Halsall, D. J.; Holbrook, J. J.; Lund, P.; Clarke, A. R. *Biochemistry* **1991**, *30*, 9195.
54.   Taguchi, H.; Konishi, J.; Ishii, N.; Yoshida, M. *J. Biol. Chem.* **1991**, *266*, 22411.
55.   Bochkareva, E. S.; Lissin, N. M.; Girshovich, A. S. *Nature* **1988**, *336*, 254.
56.   Landry, S. J.; Bartlett, S. G. *J. Biol. Chem.* **1989**, *264*, 9090.
57.   Hubbard, T. J. P.; Sander, C. *Protein Engineering* **1991**, *4*, 711.
58.   Landry, S. J.; Gierasch, L. M. *Biochemistry* **1991**, *30*, 7359.
59.   Baneyx, F.; Gatenby, A. A. *J. Biol. Chem.* (in press)

RECEIVED April 9, 1992

Chapter 12

Cosolvent Effects on Refolding and Aggregation

Jeffrey L. Cleland[1] and Daniel I. C. Wang[2]

[1]Pharmaceutical Research and Development, Genentech, Inc.,
South San Francisco, CA 94080
[2]Biotechnology Process Engineering Center, Department of Chemical
Engineering, Massachusetts Institute of Technology,
Cambridge, MA 02139

During refolding of many proteins, the off-pathway reaction of
aggregation often occurs resulting in a reduced recovery of active
protein. To improve the recovery of active protein during refolding,
cosolvents have been used to prevent aggregation and enhance
refolding. Previous studies on polyethylene glycol (PEG) enhanced
refolding of bovine carbonic anhydrase (CAB) have shown that
complete recovery of active protein can be achieved under aggregating
conditions [Cleland, J. L.; Wang, D. I.C. *Biotechnology* **1990**, *8*, pp.
1274-1278]. The physico-chemical basis for this enhancement in
refolding was examined by using cosolvents with different chemical
properties. Sugars, polyamino acids, PEG, and PEG derivatives were
assessed for their effects on the recovery of active protein during the
refolding of CAB at aggregating conditions. The mode of operation
of these cosolvents appeared to dictate their ability to improve
refolding. Cosolvents, such as sugars, which cause hydration of the
protein inhibited aggregation but did not improve the recovery of
active CAB. Hydrophobic PEG derivatives which bound tightly to a
folding intermediate inhibited the refolding of CAB. On the other
hand, both polyamino acids and PEG enhanced the recovery of active
CAB and prevented aggregation. These cosolvents probably operated
by preventing the aggregation of the molten globule first intermediate
in the refolding pathway of CAB. Cosolvents that enhance protein
refolding should therefore interact with folding intermediates to
prevent association, but they should not inhibit the refolding of these
intermediates. The thermodynamics of cosolvent and native protein
interactions also provided insight into additional cosolvents which may
improve the recovery of active protein during refolding.

The refolding of recombinant proteins has become an essential part of the
recovery operations in the biotechnology industry. Many recombinant proteins

0097–6156/93/0516–0151$06.00/0
© 1993 American Chemical Society

are produced by *Escherichia coli* in the form of intracellular aggregates or inclusion bodies. These insoluble protein aggregates are usually separated from the host cell and solubilized in a denaturant such as urea or guanidine hydrochloride (GuHCl). During the solubilization process, the protein often becomes completely or partially denatured. The protein is then refolded to its native state by removal of the denaturant. Denaturant removal allows the protein to regain its native state, but it is often accompanied by substantial protein aggregation. The aggregation which occurs during refolding dramatically reduces the recovery of the desired native protein. To increase the yield of active protein from the refolding process, the formation of off-pathway intermediates such as partially folded or aggregated species must be reduced.

Several different approaches have been applied in attempts to avoid the problem of aggregation during refolding (*1-9*). Practical approaches to solving this problem usually involve the addition of a refolding aide or aggregation inhibitor (*1-5*). The addition of sugars has been successfully applied to prevent *in vivo* aggregation and allow recovery of native protein without a refolding step (*3*). Other studies have focussed on enhancing the recovery of native proteins during *in vitro* processing. Several polymeric cosolvents have been used to reduce aggregation during refolding (*1,2,4*). By using a surfactant, lauryl maltoside, in the refolding buffer, the recovery of active rhodanese has been significantly improved (*4*). More recent work has indicated that polyethylene glycol (PEG) significantly enhances the refolding of several proteins (*1,2*). In addition, PEG has been shown to prevent aggregation by binding to the first intermediate molten globule of bovine carbonic anhydrase B (CAB) (*10*). PEG therefore has a very desirable cosolvent characteristic. It can bind to a hydrophobic intermediate, but does not inhibit refolding (*1,10*). Other cosolvents may have similar characteristics. Clearly, the best cosolvent is a molecule which prevents aggregation, but does not alter the rate of refolding. The cosolvent must also be easily recovered and not remain bound to the native protein.

To assess the ability of different cosolvents to enhance refolding, a well-characterized protein, CAB, has been used (*11,12*). Previous research on the refolding and aggregation of CAB has revealed that the molten globule first intermediate aggregates to form dimers and larger aggregates (*13-15*). In addition, this intermediate reversibly associates to form a dimer during refolding at conditions which result in complete recovery of active protein (*15*). To enhance refolding of CAB, a cosolvent must therefore prevent the association of the hydrophobic first intermediate. A variety of different cosolvents were examined in an attempt to determine the physicochemical properties of cosolvents that enhance refolding. The ability of each solvent to enhance refolding was measured by refolding at conditions which previously have resulted in reversible association of the first intermediate or irreversible aggregation with a concomitant reduction in final recovery of native protein (*13,15*).

Experimental Procedures

Materials. Bovine serum albumin (BSA), guanidine hydrochloride (GuHCl), Tris-sulfate, ethylenediaminetetraacetic acid (EDTA), sucrose, glucose, and p-nitrophenol acetate (pNPA) were molecular biology grade and purchased from Sigma Chemical Co. (St.Louis, MO). Polyethylene glycol (PEG) and all polyamino acids were also purchased from Sigma Chemical Co. (St. Louis, MO) and used as supplied. JEFFAMINE polymers were donated by Texaco Chemical Company (Houston, TX). HPLC grade acetonitrile was obtained from J.T. Baker Co. (Phillipsburg, NJ). Decahydranapthalene (Decalin) was a racemic mixture obtained from Aldrich (Milwaukee, WI). The SDS-PAGE materials were obtained from Pharmacia LKB Biotechnology (Uppsala, Sweden). All buffers and samples were prepared with distilled water passed through a MilliQ water purification system (Millipore Corp., Bedford, MA).

Bovine Carbonic Anhydrase B (CAB): Lyophilized bovine carbonic anhydrase B (pI = 5.9) was purchased from Sigma Chemical Co. (St. Louis, MO). The purity of each lot was checked by size exclusion high performance liquid chromatography (HPLC) and gel electrophoresis with silver staining. In addition, the native protein in 50 mM Tris-sulfate and 5 mM EDTA at pH 7.5 was measured for activity to ascertain the formation of native protein structure (see Esterase Activity section). For all refolding experiments, the lyophilized protein was solubilized in 5 M GuHCl for at least 6 hours (*11*). Prior to experimental use, the denatured protein was filtered with 0.22 μm syringe filters (Gelman Sciences, Ann Arbor, MI) to remove any remaining insoluble protein.

Protein Concentration. The protein concentration of native CAB in 50 mM Tris-sulfate, 5 mM EDTA, at pH 7.5 was determined by absorbance at 280 ηm using an extinction coefficient of 1.83 (mg/ml protein)$^{-1}$ cm^{-1} and a molecular weight of 30,000 (*16*). Denatured CAB in 5 M GuHCl was assayed for protein concentration by using a colorimetric dye binding assay, Bio-Rad reagent (Bio-Rad Laboratories, Richmond, CA) or BCA reagent (Pierce Chemical Company, Rockford, IL), with bovine serum albumin (BSA) denatured in 5 M GuHCl as the standard.

Esterase Activity (CAB). The enzymatic activity of CAB was measured by analysis of the esterase reaction as described previously (*17*). The unfolded CAB in 5 M GuHCl was rapidly diluted with buffer containing cosolvent to a desired final protein and GuHCl concentration. An aliquot of the refolded sample was analyzed for its enzymatic activity at various times after dilution as detailed previously (*13*). Recovery of activity was determined using the ester hydrolysis rate constant of the native protein at the same concentration in the dilution buffer (50 mM tris sulfate, 5 mM EDTA, pH 7.5) with cosolvents. The initial rate of refolding, R_{Ref}, was defined as the initial slope of the active protein concentration as function of time as reported previously (*1*).

Quasi-Elastic Light Scattering (QLS) Measurements. Quasi-elastic light scattering analysis was performed using two different systems. Initial QLS measurements were performed by using Model N4 submicron particle analyzer (Coulter Electronics, Hialeah, FL) instrumented as described previously (18). Sample analysis and materials preparation were detailed in previous studies (13). Additional QLS measurements were performed using a Brookhaven light scattering system (Brookhaven Instruments, Holtsville, NY). The Brookhaven QLS system consisted of a BI200SM goniometer with a photomultiplier positioned at 90° to the incident laser, 2 W argon ion at 488 ηm (Lexel, Fremont, CA). The goniometer assembly was temperature controlled at 20°C with an external water bath. To reduce flaring from incident laser light, the sample was placed in the goniometer with index matching fluid, cis,trans - decahydronapthalene, surrounding the sample. The photon data was collected using a BI2030 autocorrelator with 136 channels and a personal computer collected the data and controlled the system. Prefiltered samples ($\geq$ 1 ml) were placed in disposable glass culture tubes (12 x 75mm, VWR Scientific, San Francisco, CA) which were checked for imperfections and precleaned by using appropriate glassware procedures (13).

The particle size distributions from QLS autocorrelation function data were calculated by the method of constrained regularization or CONTIN (19). The concentration of each species was then determined by using the previously developed model for CAB aggregation (13). Refolding of denatured CAB in 5 M GuHCl was carried out by rapid dilution with buffer (50 mM Tris-sulfate, 5 mM EDTA, pH 7.5) with or without the cosolvent to the desired final protein and GuHCl concentrations. For kinetic studies, the sample was analyzed by QLS immediately after dilution as detailed previously (13). Each experiment was repeated several times to provide a significant number of time points for kinetic analysis. The rate of dimer formation, R_D, for each experiment was calculated from the initial slope of the dimer concentration as a function of time as described previously (13).

Results

Sugars: Sucrose and Glucose. Significant reductions in *in vivo* aggregation of ß-lactamase have been previously reported using sugars (3). In addition, sugars have been used to improve recovery of active ß-lactamase during *in vitro* refolding (20). To further assess sugars, refolding of CAB was performed with either sucrose or glucose in the dilution buffer. Previous studies indicated that a sugar concentration of 239 g/l (22% wt/vol) was required to observe significant improvements in the refolding of CAB at aggregating conditions (data not shown). Therefore, denatured CAB in 5 M GuHCl was refolded by rapid dilution to 0.24 mg/ml protein and 0.30 M GuHCl (aggregation conditions, 13) with 22% wt/vol sugar in the dilution buffer. Under these conditions, formation of large aggregates was not observed by QLS whereas large aggregates had been previously observed during refolding at these conditions without sugars (1,13). However, the formation of multimers was detected by QLS for refolding with and without the sugars at these conditions. For each case, the initial rate of dimer formation, R_D, was calculated from the initial slope of the dimer concentration as a function of time (13). To measure the competing refolding reaction, the recovery of active protein was measured as a function of time after dilution to the refolding conditions. The initial rate of refolding, R_{Ref}, was defined as the initial slope of the active protein concentration as a function of time (*1*). For each case, the active protein concentration reached a constant value after twenty minutes and the final active protein concentration was defined as the concentration of active protein after refolding for one hour.

As shown in Table 1, the initial rate of dimer formation, R_D, was reduced in the presence of both sugars. The dimer formation rate was similar for both glucose (MW 180) and sucrose (MW 360). However, the initial rate of refolding, R_{Ref}, with sucrose was two-fold greater than the refolding rate with glucose. Both sugars significantly increased the initial rate of refolding. Unfortunately, the recovery of activity after 1 hour was not substantially improved for refolding in either sugar solution (Table 1). For both sugars, the refolded solution contained approximately 30% monomer as determined by QLS after incubation for 1 hour. Control experiments with native CAB and sugars indicated that sugars did not alter the specific activity. Therefore, some of the monomeric species were not able to assume the active CAB conform-ation since only 20% active protein was observed (Table 1). Additional refolding studies were performed by dilution to aggregating conditions, 1.0 - 1.2 mg/ml CAB and 0.5 M GuHCl, in the presence of the sugars. These studies yielded similar refolding rates and little improvement in the final recovery of activity was observed (data not shown).

The observed increase in the initial refolding rate, R_{Ref}, in the presence of sugars was probably caused by an increase in the hydration of the protein. Previous studies involving sugars and native protein stability have revealed that sugars cause preferential hydration of proteins independent of the chemical properties of their surface (*21*). This preferential hydration of the protein resulted in the formation of compact structural states with hydrophillic surface characteristics analogous to the native protein. The thermodynamic forces which caused the rapid formation of compact native structures also resulted in increased stability of other compact structures such as dimers and trimers. Multimers were the most thermodynamically favorable species since these structures have lower accessible surface area that reduces the overall surface tension of the solution. Therefore, the sugars prevented precipitation of the protein by stabilizing both the compact folded structures and the multimers. The observed reductions in the rate of dimer formation using the two sugars probably resulted from both the reduced rate of large aggregate formation and the increased viscosity. The viscous sugar solutions (22% wt/vol, 2 centipoise) may have also decreased dimerization by introducing diffusional limitations for monomer-monomer collisions.

Other refolding studies with sugars also provided insight into the interaction between sugars and partially folded proteins. For example, sucrose did not alter the refolding of porphyrin c (*22*). On the other hand, the rate of ribonuclease refolding was reduced in the presence of sugars (*23*). Glycerol and glucose have also been observed to decrease the rate of refolding of octopine dehydrogenase, a large multimeric protein (*24*). Other studies have shown that sugars reduced the rate of refolding (*25*). For CAB refolding, only two thirds of the monomers in solution were active indicating that the sugars interfered with the refolding process. Although these studies contradict the results of ß-lactamase refolding with sugars (3, 20), they have revealed that the mechanism of sugar-protein interactions, preferential hydration of the protein, may not be desirable for protein refolding. In general, a cosolvent which only causes preferential hydration of the protein will probably not be effective in increasing the recovery of active protein, but it may prevent the formation of large precipitates.

Polymeric Cosolvents: Polyamino acids. Previous research on interactions between amino acids and native proteins indicate that amino acids may either bind to the protein or cause preferential hydration of the protein (26). In addition, protein refolding in the presence of amino acids was previously performed with some success (27). Since amino acids could become incorporated into the protein during refolding, polyamino acids were used in these experiments. Several polyamino acids ranging in molecular weight from 2500 to 3500 Daltons were utilized to determine the cosolvent characteristics that enhance refolding of CAB. The refolding of CAB at aggregating conditions (1.0 mg/ml CAB, 0.50 M GuHCl) was previously enhanced by using 3 g/l PEG (3350 MW) in the refolding buffer (1). Therefore, the polyamino acid solutions (polyalanine, 2500 MW; polylysine, 3000 MW) were prepared at a concentration of 3 g/l. Polyglycine (3500 MW) was not soluble at 3 g/l and was dissolved to its apparent maximum solubility of 1 g/l. These polyamino acid solutions were then used to dilute CAB in 5 M GuHCl to final concentrations of 1.0 mg/ml protein and 0.50 M GuHCl (aggregation conditions, 13). The recovery of active protein for each case was then measured as a function of time after dilution as shown in Figure 1. For comparison, refolding was also performed with a dilution buffer containing 3 g/l PEG (3350 MW). The use of polyglycine and polyalanine resulted in a rate of refolding which was similar to the results for 3 g/l PEG. As shown in Figure 1, the initial rate of refolding was much greater when polylysine was used in the refolding buffer. However, refolding with each polymer resulted in complete recovery of active protein after 1 hour. In contrast, when refolding was performed without the cosolvents, only 30% of the active protein was recovered and the protein formed insoluble aggregates within this 1 hour period. Precipitation was not observed for refolding with the polyamino acids or PEG.

For each polyamino acid, the protein rapidly refolded to a high level of activity and continued to recover activity at a slower rate. This phenomenon was previously observed for refolding in the absence of association of the first intermediate (15). The first intermediate rapidly folded to form the second intermediate which slowly regained the fully active native conformation (15). Therefore, the polyamino acids may have prevented the aggregation of the hydrophobic first intermediate. Previous research indicates that PEG prevented the self association of this intermediate during refolding (28). PEG was also observed to bind to this molten globule first intermediate (10). In addition to inhibiting aggregation, the more hydrophobic polyamino acids, polyalanine and polylysine, may also have increased the rate of refolding through specific interactions with the hydrophobic first intermediate. These

Table 1. Effect of sugars on aggregation and refolding of CAB. Denatured CAB in 5 M GuHCl was rapidly diluted with buffer to 0.24 mg/ml protein and 0.30 M GuHCl. The solution was then analyzed as described in Experimental Procedures.

Buffer	R_D (μM/min)	R_{Ref} (1/min)	Final % Active Protein
No Sugar	100[a]	0.30	19.0
22% wt/vol Glucose	1.4	1.1	20.4
22% wt/vol Sucrose	1.2	2.0	19.9

[a] Theoretical value calculated from dimer rate equation in Ref. 13.

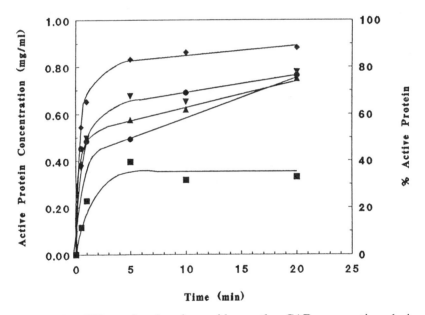

Time (min)

FIGURE 1: Effect of polyamino acids on the CAB aggregation during refolding. The protein in 5 M GuHCl was diluted to 1.0 mg/ml CAB and 0.50 M GuHCl (aggregation conditions) with different polyamino acid solutions. Polyalanine (3000 MW; ▼) and polylysine (2500 MW; ◆) were used at final concentration of 3 g/l. In addition, polyglycine (3500 MW; ●) was used at its solubility limit which was approximately 1 g/l. For comparison, the recovery of activity is displayed for refolding in 3 g/l PEG (3350 MW; ▲) and in the standard dilution buffer (■).

polyamino acids can also form secondary structures which may specifically interact with similar structures on the protein surface. Polylysine will form a beta sheet structure in solution and this structure may interact with hydrophobic beta sheet structures on the surface of an intermediate. In contrast, polyalanine forms a helical structure and polyglycine has a random coil structure. Therefore, the interactions between these amino acid polymers and the folding intermediates may not be structurally related. Further analysis of these cosolvents should be performed to determine if the polyamino acids inhibit aggregation by interacting with specific protein surface structures.

Polyethylene glycol (PEG). As shown in Figure 1, the rate of refolding in the presence of PEG was similar to that obtained with the polyamino acids. In addition, the use of PEG resulted in complete recovery of active protein at these conditions (3 g/l PEG (3350 MW), 1.0 mg/ml CAB, 0.50 M GuHCl). The PEG molecular weight was previously shown to affect the rate of refolding under the same aggregating conditions (1). High molecular weight PEG (8000 MW, 3 g/l) resulted in a slightly more rapid rate of refolding than lower molecular weight PEG (1000 or 3350 MW, 3 g/l) as shown in Figure 2 (1). When denatured CAB in 5 M GuHCl was rapidly diluted to 1.0 mg/ml protein and 0.50 M GuHCl with buffer containing 3 g/l PEG (8000 MW), complete recovery of active protein was achieved in twenty minutes. If PEG increased the rate of refolding by a catalytic mechanism, higher concentrations of PEG should further increase the rate of refolding. To test this hypothesis, CAB was refolded with both concentrated (30 g/l) and dilute (3 g/l) PEG solutions. CAB in 5 M GuHCl was rapidly diluted to 0.50 mg/ml CAB and 1.0 M GuHCl where transient association of the first intermediate was previously observed (15). The rate of refolding with 3 g/l PEG (3350 MW) was slightly greater than 30 g/l PEG (Figure 3). These results suggest that PEG enhanced the rate of refolding in both cases by inhibiting the self association of the first intermediate molten globule (1,10,28). Additional research also indicates that PEG did not increase the rate of refolding (28). These studies also showed that PEG reversibly bound to the first intermediate during refolding (10, 28). In addition, the molecular weight and concentration of PEG have been shown to directly correlate with the extent of recovery (28). For each PEG molecular weight, an optimum range of concentrations was observed and, thus, the difference in refolding rates shown in Figure 2 are likely the result of this stoichiometric relationship (28). Overall, PEG enhanced the refolding of CAB by preventing the aggregation of the hydrophobic first intermediate (28).

The unique physicochemical properties of PEG were probably responsible for the inhibition of aggregation without a reduction in the refolding rate. Unlike the polyamino acids, PEG did not form a rigid structure in solution. Thus, it should be able to interact with the protein by more general chemical mechanisms (ie. hydrophobic interactions). Previous studies of PEG and native proteins have revealed that PEG will cause preferential hydration of the protein when used at high concentrations (>3% wt/vol) and will bind to proteins at dilute concentrations (29). Therefore, PEG can interact with proteins by two different mechanisms. PEG has unique physicochemical properties which include both hydrophobic methylene groups and oxygen (ether bonds) which can weakly interact through hydrogen bonding. Since PEG has

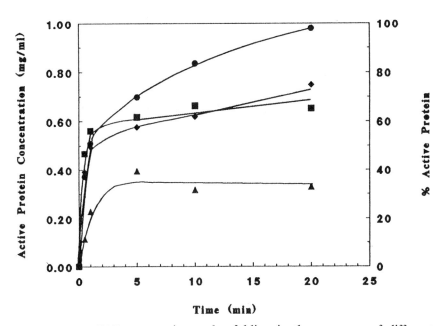

FIGURE 2: CAB aggregation and refolding in the presence of different molecular PEG solutions. CAB in 5 M GuHCl was diluted with 3 g/l PEG to 1.0 mg/ml protein and 0.50 M GuHCl (aggregation conditions). The recovery of activity as a function of time is plotted for the three different molecular weight PEG solutions, 8000 MW (●), 3350 MW (♦), and 1000 MW (■), along with the results for refolding in the absence of PEG in the dilution buffer (▲).

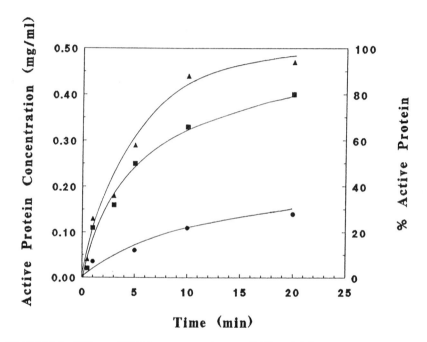

FIGURE 3: Effect of PEG concentration on CAB refolding. Denatured CAB in 5 M GuHCl was diluted to 0.50 mg/ml protein and 1.0 M GuHCl with buffer containing PEG. The recovery of activity is displayed as a function of time for PEG (MW 3350) at 3 (▲) and 30 g/l (■). For comparison, refolding without PEG in the dilution buffer was also measured as a function of time (●).

these unique chemical properties as well as the ability to reversibly bind to a folding intermediate, it should be a useful generic cosolvent for protein refolding. The recovery of active protein for the refolding of two recombinant proteins, deoxyribonuclease and tissue plasminogen activator, was also significantly improved through the use of PEG as a cosolvent (*2*). Further research into the specific interaction between PEG and these proteins should provide insight into the design of cosolvents that inhibit aggregation and enhance refolding of proteins.

Polyethylene Glycol Derivatives. PEG was a successful cosolvent for the inhibition of aggregation during CAB refolding, but it did not catalyze the refolding. Previous research showed that refolding in the presence of PEG proceeds at the same rate as refolding at nonaggregating conditions (*28*). In addition, only a stoichiometric concentration of PEG was required for inhibition of aggregation (*2, 28*). For CAB refolding, a PEG to protein molar ratio ($[CAB]_t/[PEG]_t$) of 3 to 1 was sufficient to completely inhibit aggregation (1.0 mg/ml CAB, 0.50 M GuHCl, 0.34 g/l PEG (3350 MW); *28*). The stoichio-metric concentrations of PEG required for enhanced refolding (*28*) and the previous PEG binding studies (*10*) indicated that the chemical properties of PEG were responsible for its action. To further study these chemical properties, block copolymers of ethylene oxide and propylene oxide were used in refolding experiments. These copolymers are similar to PEG, which is also referred to as poly(ethylene oxide) as shown in Figure 4. These hydrophobic copolymers possessed primary amines at both termini. However, previous refolding studies with bis(amine)polyethylene glycol yielded the same results as unmodified PEG (data not shown). The M series polymers were random co-polymers with the more hydrophobic propylene group distributed throughout the molecule. In constrast, the ED series polymer (ED-6000, 6000 MW) was a block copolymer with hydrophobic propylene termini and a polyethylene oxide center (Figure 4). Each of these polymers was used at a molar ratio of 3 to 1 ($[Polymer]_t/[CAB]_t$) in the refolding of CAB. Denatured CAB in 5 M GuHCl was rapidly diluted with the polymer solution to 0.50 mg/ml and 1.0 M GuHCl (refolding conditions). These conditions should result in complete refolding of the protein after 1 hour or less as previously demonstrated (Figure 3, *1, 13, 15, 28*). The recovery of active protein was dramatically reduced in the presence of these polymers. Refolding with the least hydrophobic polymer (M-1000) yielded the greatest recovery of active protein (20%) after 1 hour. In the case of the other more hydrophobic polymers, only 10% of active protein was recovered after 1 hour (Figure 4). Therefore, these polymers inhibited the refolding of CAB. Since each of these polymers was more hydrophobic than PEG, it is possible that these molecules are able to bind to the first intermediate molten globule more tightly. The first intermediate could thus be prevented from refolding. Clearly, a more hydrophobic cosolvent than PEG had a detrimental effect on the refolding of CAB. Hydrophobic polymers have been successfully used to refold a membrane protein, rhodanese, but it was suggested that less hydrophobic polymers such as PEG would be more effective (*30*).

a   Poly(ethylene oxide) (PEO) = Polyethylene glycol (PEG)

$HO-(CH_2CH_2O)_n-H$

MW (Da)	n
1000	22
3350	76
8000	181

JEFFAMINE - M Series

$R-(CH_2CHO)_n-CH_2CHNH_2$
        | |
        R' CH_3

Trade Name	MW (Da)	PO/EO Ratio
M-1000	1000	3/19
M-2070	2000	10/32

R' = H, EO (ethylene oxide)

R' = CH_3, PO (propylene oxide)

R = $HOCH_2CH_2O$ or $HOCH_2CHO$
                                    |
                                   CH_3

JEFFAMINE- ED Series

$H_2NCHCH_2[OCHCH_2]_{a+1}[OCH_2CH_2]_b[OCH_2CH]_cNH_2$
       | | |
      CH_3 CH_3 CH_3

Trade Name	MW (Da)	b(EO)	a+c (PO)	Overall PO/EO Ratio
ED-6000	6000	132	2.5	3.5/132

b

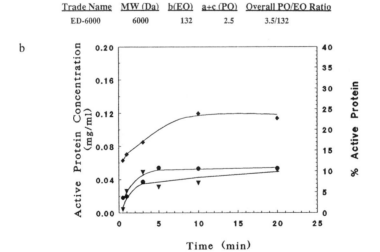

Time (min)

FIGURE 4: (a) Chemical structure of hydrophobic polymers. The hydrophobic block copolymers were provided by Texaco Chemical Company (Houston, TX). These polymers are referred to as the JEFFAMINE polymers by Texaco. The structure and relative ratio of ethylene oxide (EO) and propylene oxide (PO) in each polymer are shown. For comparison, polyethylene glycol (PEG) is also known as polyoxyethylene (PEO). (b) CAB refolding in the presence of hydrophobic polymers. CAB in 5 M GuHCl was refolded by rapid dilution to 0.50 mg/ml (16.7 μm) protein and 1.0 M GuHCl with a final molar ratio of polymer to CAB ($[Polymer]_t/[CAB]_t$) of 3 for three different polymers: M-1000 (♦), M-2000 (●) and ED-6000 (▼).

Discussion

To improve recovery of active protein during refolding, several cosolvents were assessed and preliminary relationships between their effect on refolding and their mode of action were developed. The two primary modes of action of cosolvents are preferential hydration, which is analogous to cosolvent exclusion from the protein surface, and cosolvent binding (*31*). Addition of cosolvents which may act by preferential hydration will stabilize compact protein structures such as the native and multimeric states. This phenomenon can be described by analyzing the thermodynamics of the system. The change in chemical potential of the protein that occurs from cosolvent addition $(\partial\mu_p/\partial m_s)$ has been defined as the product of the change in chemical potential of the cosolvent $(\partial\mu_s/\partial m_s)$ and the preferential interaction of the cosolvent with the protein $(\partial m_s/\partial m_p)$:

$$\left[\frac{\partial\mu_p}{\partial m_s}\right]_{T,P,m_p} = -\left[\frac{\partial m_s}{\partial m_p}\right]_{T,\mu_w,\mu_s}\left[\frac{\partial\mu_s}{\partial m_s}\right]_{T,P,m_p}$$

where μ is the chemical potential, m is the molality, T is the system temperature, P is the system pressure, and the subscripts denote protein (p), cosolvent (s), and water (w). The preferential interaction term $(\partial m_s/\partial m_p)$ can then be used to explain the effect of cosolvents on protein refolding.

For sugars such as sucrose and glycerol used in these studies, the preferential interaction term would be positive since sugars cause hydration of the protein (*32*). The sugars did not significantly enhance the recovery of active CAB during refolding at conditions which result in protein aggregation. Both a native-like monomer and multimers were probably stabilized as the result of the preferential hydration. In addition, the sugars could have interfered with the formation of the active native protein. These results indicated that molecules which cause preferential hydration may not be good cosolvents for protein refolding. However, amino acids have also been reported to cause preferential hydration (*26*) and polyamino acids provided complete recovery of active CAB at aggregation conditions (1.0 mg/ml CAB, 0.50 M GuHCl; *13*). Further analysis of the polyamino acids and CAB refolding should be performed to determine the mode of action of these cosolvents. A cosolvent such as PEG which can act through both mechanisms, hydration and binding, was also tested in the refolding of CAB. PEG can bind to the protein at low concentrations (< 10% w/v) and will become excluded from the protein surface at high concentrations (*21,29*). PEG provided complete recovery of active CAB for refolding at aggregation conditions (1.0 mg/ml CAB, 0.50 M GuHCl; *13*). Previous research with PEG and CAB refolding has shown that PEG reversibly bound to the molten globule first intermediate and prevented its aggregation (*10,28*). The refolding of CAB was not inhibited by PEG (*28*). More hydrophobic derivatives of PEG were also tested for their effect on CAB refolding. All of these polymers inhibited the refolding of CAB. These polymers could have been bound to the hydrophobic first intermediate and prevented further refolding. Thus, cosolvents which have a preferential interaction between hydration and binding ($\partial m_s/\partial m_p \approx 0$) should provide the best results for protein refolding. As shown in Figure 5, many different molecules have been studied for their preferential interaction with native proteins. These molecules should also be assessed for their effect on protein refolding. The results of these studies should provide further insight into the desired cosolvent characteristics for protein refolding and inhibition of aggregation.

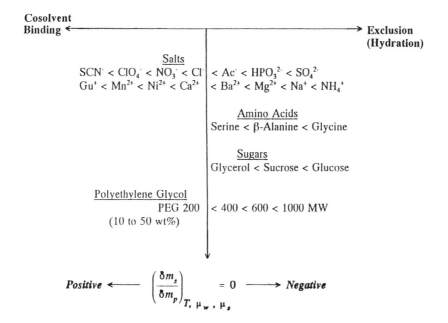

FIGURE 5: Cosolvent interactions with native proteins (*26,29,31-33*). The cosolvents left of the midpoint have been shown to bind nonspecifically to proteins (positive preferential cosolvent interactions). In contrast, the cosolvents to the right of the midpoint have been shown to act by preferential hydration of the protein which involves an increase in the concentration of water at the protein surface (negative preferential cosolvent interaction). The mechanism of interaction for polyethylene glycol (PEG) has been observed to be dependent upon the PEG concentration where high concentrations (10-50 wt%) result in exclusion and low concentrations ($<$ 10 wt%) can result in PEG binding to the protein (*26*).

Acknowledgements

This work was supported by National Science Foundation Grant #CDR-88-03014.

Literature Cited

1. Cleland, J. L.; Wang, D. I. C. *Biotechnology* **1990**, *8*, pp. 1274-1278.

2. Cleland, J. L.; Wang, D. I. C. *Biotechnology* **1992**, *submitted for publication*.

3. Bowden, G. A.; Georgiou, G. *Biotech. Prog.* **1988**, *4*, pp. 97-101.

4. Tandon, S.; Horwitz, P. M. *J. Biol. Chem.* **1987**, *262*, pp. 4486-4491.

5. Brems, D. N.; Stellwagen, E. *J. Biol. Chem.* **1983**, *258*, pp. 3655-3661.

6. Brems, D. N.; Plaisted, S. M.; Havel, H. A.; Tomich, C.-S. C. *P.N.A.S.* **1988**, *85*, pp. 3367-3371.

7. Hagen, A.; Hatton, T. A.; Wang, D. I. C. *Biotech. Bioeng.* **1990**, *35*, pp. 966-975.

8. Creighton, T. E. In *Protein Structure Folding and Design*; Oxender, D. L., Ed.; Alan R. Liss, Inc.: New York, NY, 1985; pp. 249-251.

9. Morris, G. E.; Frost, L. C.; Newport, P. A.; Hudson, N. *Biochem. J.* **1987**, *248*, pp. 53-57.

10. Cleland, J. L.; Randolph, T. W. *J. Biol. Chem.* **1992**, *in press*.

11. Semisotnov, G. V.; Uversky, V. N.; Sokolovsky, I. V.; Gutin, A. M.; Razgulyaev, O. I.; Rodionova, N. A. *J. Mol. Biol.* **1990**, *213*, pp. 561-568.

12. Rodionova, N. A.; Semisotnov, G. V.; Kutyshenko, V. P.; Uverskii, V. N.; Bolotina, I. A.; Bychkova, V. E.; Ptitsyn, O.B. *Mol. Biol.* **1989**, *23*, pp. 683-692.

13. Cleland, J. L.; Wang, D.I.C. *Biochemistry* **1990**, *29*, pp. 11072-11078.

14. Cleland, J. L.; Wang, D. I. C. In *Protein Refolding*; Georgiou, G.; DeBernardez-Clark, E., Eds.; ACS Symposium Series, Vol. 470; American Chemical Society, Washington, D.C., 1991; pp. 169-179.

15. Cleland, J. L.; Wang, D. I. C. *Biotech. Progress* **1992**, *in press*.

16. Wong, K.-P.; Tanford, C. *J. Biol. Chem.* **1973**, *248*, pp. 8518-8523.

17. Pocker, Y.; Stone, J. T. *Biochemistry* **1967**, *6*, pp. 668-678.

18. Yarmush, D. M.; Murphy, R. M.; Colton, C. K.; Fisch, M.; Yarmush, M. L. *Mol. Immun.* **1988**, *25*, pp. 17-32.

19. Provencher, S. W. In *Photon Correlation Techniques*; Schulz-Dubois, E. O., Ed.; Springer-Verlag: New York, NY, 1983; pp. 322-328.

20. Valax, P.; Georgiou, G. In *Protein Refolding*; Georgiou, G.; DeBernardez-Clark, E., Eds.; ACS Symposium Series, Vol. 470; American Chemical Society, Washington, D.C., 1991; pp. 97-109.

21. Arakawa, T.; Bhat, R.; Timasheff, S. N. *Biochemistry* **1990**, *29*, pp. 1924-1930.

22. Brems, D. N.; Lin, Y. C.; Stellwagen, E. *J. Biol. Chem.* **1982**, *257*, pp. 3864-3869.

23. Tsong, T. Y. *Biochemistry* **1982**, *21*, pp. 1493-1497.

24. Teschner, W.; Rudolph, R.; Garel, J.-R. *Biochemistry* **1987**, *26*, pp. 2791-2796.

25. Vaucheret, H.; Signon, L.; Le Bras, G.; Garel, J.-R. *Biochemistry* **1987**, *26*, pp. 2785-2789.

26. Arakawa, T.; Timasheff, S. N. *Biophys. J.* **1985**, *47*, pp. 411-414.

27. Schaffer, S. W.; Ahmed, A.; Wetlaufer, D. B. *J. Biol. Chem.* **1975**, *250*, pp. 8483-8486.

28. Cleland, J. L.; Hedgepeth, C.; Wang, D. I. C. *J. Biol. Chem.* **1992**, *in press*.

29. Arawaka, T.; Timasheff, S. N. *Biochemistry* **1985**, *24*, pp. 6756-6762.

30. Tandon, S.; Horwitz, P. M. *J. Biol. Chemistry* **1986**, *261*, pp. 15615-15618.

31. Timasheff, S. N.; Arakawa, T. *J. Crystal Growth* **1988**, *90*, pp. 39-46.

32. Arakawa, T.; Timasheff, S. N. *Biochemistry* **1982**, *21*, pp. 6536-6544.

33. Arakawa, T.; Timasheff, S. N. *Biochemistry* **1984**, *23*, pp. 5912-5923.

RECEIVED March 31, 1992

Chapter 13

Facilitation of Protein Folding and the Reversibility of Denaturation

P. M. Horowitz

Department of Biochemistry, University of Texas Health Science Center,
San Antonio, TX 78284-7760

The enzyme rhodanese that is isolated from tissue sources cannot easily be refolded after denaturation, even though it is monomeric, and contains virtually all of the folding information present in the amino acid sequence at synthesis. Studies indicate that folding difficulties are due to the facts that: 1) rhodanese is very sensitive to oxidation that can occur even in the presence of common reductants; and 2) aggregation kinetically competes with folding to the active enzyme. This aggregation is due to the appearance of exposed, interactive hydrophobic surfaces on folding intermediates. Thus, successful refolding requires appropriate reducing conditions, and procedures that limit protein association. Procedures have been developed that permit high levels of refolding. These approaches include the use of: a) refolding at high dilution; b) enzyme immobilization; c) non-denaturing detergents; or d) heat shock or chaperonin proteins, groES and groEL from *E. coli*. The chaperonin assisted refolding is of particular interest since it is related to the mechanism and control of *in vivo* protein folding and transport, and it makes protein folding dependent on ATP hydrolysis.

Many proteins do not refold efficiently after being unfolded, even though it is accepted that the amino acid sequence contains the information that determines protein structure (1,2). This raises the questions: What information is in the code for the sequence and what information is in the mechanism or environment in which the code is expressed? i.e. how does the biological machinery affect folding? Among reasons for the apparent discrepancy between expected and observed protein folding is that competing processes kinetically limit renaturation. Thus, though the native state is most stable, it is not accessible in a biologically reasonable time. Aggregation is one of the major kinetic traps that competes with the folding of many proteins. For example, inappropriate association of partially folded proteins has been suggested as leading to the inclusion bodies that limit the production of correctly folded recombinant proteins in *E. coli* (3,3a). My laboratory is interested in the practical control of protein folding and the recovery of active proteins from unfolded, modified or recombinant polypeptides.

0097–6156/93/0516–0167$06.00/0
© 1993 American Chemical Society

Every isolated protein has an *in vivo* history. The protein must be synthesized, folded, processed, transported and compartmentalized. The protein rhodanese, whose folding properties will be described, is synthesized in the cytoplasm of eucaryotic cells and it is then transported into the matrix of the mitochondrion. These diverse processes presumably have different conformational requirements, and it is suggested that the protein may have been subjected to different folding pressures at different times of its life. Interactions within the cell can modulate the folding potentials of the sequence. Translation of the genetic information yields a polypeptide chain that sequentially appears from the ribosome. The folding itself is influenced by processing that may include covalent changes such as proteolysis, side chain modification or cofactor interactions. Protein folding may occur in the presence of extensive interactive surfaces, and there may be influences from non-covalent protein association due to the high protein concentration (4). Interactions with accessory components such as chaperonins or heat shock proteins may modulate the protein folding and/or assist the transport of the protein to its proper compartment (4-6). Further processing and conformational adjustments may then be required to generate the active structure. Finally, every protein is subjected to degradation and turnover which involve further processing steps or conformational changes. Because of the different life histories of isolated proteins, we expect a range of behavior in vitro, from proteins that would readily refold to those that have been extensively processed and will not refold at useful rates under arbitrarily chosen *in vitro* conditions.

The enzyme rhodanese has become an interesting model for studying issues related to protein folding and the recovery of recombinant proteins in their active states. Rhodanese is synthesized in the cytoplasm and then it is transported into the mitochondrial matrix (7). Rhodanese is isolated from tissue sources as a soluble, globular protein, and its high resolution X-ray structure is available (8).

The protein is folded into two independent, equal-sized domains, and the active site of this enzyme, whose job is to transfer sulfur atoms, is at a cysteine residue that is in the vicinity of the interdomain region. The domains are tightly associated, and the interdomain surfaces are strongly hydrophobic. These surfaces can be made accessible with very little change in the structure of the individual domains.

We expect this protein to refold easily for several reasons. First, there is no significant processing of this single chain protein, and essentially all the amino acids in rhodanese at synthesis are present in the mature protein with the exception of the initiating methionine (9). Second, no cofactors, metal ions or side chain modifications are required for the observed structure (8). Third, active rhodanese has all four of its sulfhydryl groups reduced, and therefore, there is no requirement for the correct formation of disulfides. However, both intra- and inter-chain disulfide bonds can form under some circumstances, but this requires a conformational change from the X-ray structure (10,11). In the mitochondrial matrix, rhodanese can partition into soluble and membrane associated forms, another observation that is not compatible with its observed structure in the crystal (12).

Clearly, rhodanese has different folding and conformational requirements at different times of its life, even though all folding information with which the protein was born is present in the mature, isolated enzyme.

Until recently, we were not able to renature unfolded rhodanese. Detailed studies of why refolding failed led to ability to refold this enzyme. To begin, rhodanese is very sensitive to oxidation which can be induced by addition of stoichiometric amounts of hydrogen peroxide (13). This oxidation leads to a loss of activity and exposure of hydrophobic surfaces as assessed by the increased fluorescence of the hydrophobic probe, 8-anilino-1-naphthalene sulfonate (ANS) (10). There is only a short lag in the appearance of hydrophobic surfaces, and the hydrophobic exposure continues after complete inactivation. Reducing agents such as dithiothreitol (DTT) can form hydrogen peroxide as they autooxidize (*14*). Therefore, it is the partial reduction of oxygen that gives rise to many of the irreversible effects. Oxidized rhodanese can be reactivated if reductants are added soon after inactivation, but it is necessary to choose the correct reducing agents in the correct amounts (*13*). The oxidation becomes increasingly irreversible on further incubation, so that there is a temporal window during which reduction is effective. These oxidized states have some conformational properties that are similar to those measured for intermediates in rhodanese folding. e.g. new antigenic determinants appear that are not present on the native state and have been mapped to the interdomain region (*15*).

Even without oxidation, structural perturbations expose hydrophobic surfaces and lead to aggregation. For example, guanidinium hydrochloride (GdmHCl) at sub-denaturing concentrations can induce rhodanese aggregation (*16*). The precipitation, which occurs maximally at a sharply defined critical concentration of GdmHCl, removes almost all of the protein from solution. The structural perturbation increases the hydrophobic exposure and increases the oxidative susceptibility. The precipitation produces discrete species that are built from a dimer that is initially formed (*10*). The presence of the non-denaturing detergent, lauryl maltoside completely prevents precipitation under conditions where the detergent has no effect on the activity of the native enzyme.

It has become clear that there are at least three experimental requirements for successful refolding of rhodanese. First, oxidation has to be prevented by including an appropriate reductant at concentrations that avoid effects of reactive oxygen species formed during autooxidation. Second, conditions are needed to reduce aggregation that follows exposure of extensive hydrophobic surfaces during unfolding/refolding. Third, it is important to stabilize the protein after refolding. Rhodanese is particularly sensitive, and efficient renaturation has been hampered in the past, because even under conditions favorable for folding, the protein could be inactivated at specific side chains (especially sulfhydryl groups) whose reactivities are enhanced in the folded structure.

Folding is first order, while precipitation is higher order so that aggregation can be reduced by lowering the protein concentration. Unassisted folding of rhodanese is possible if, in addition to lowering the protein concentration, the substrate, thiosulfate, and the reductant, mercaptoethanol are present (*17*). Activity measurements show that there is an optimum protein concentration that maximizes refolding. In general, lower protein concentrations give more recovery, but when the protein concentration is too low there is inactivation from adventitious solution components and surface adsorption (*18*). At a given protein concentration, there is higher recovery at higher urea concentration as long as the urea concentration is below the unfolding transition. These results are consistent with the hypothesis that urea concentrations producing "weakly native" folding conditions are capable of solubilizing "sticky" intermediates that would rapidly aggregate if the urea concentration were reduced too far or too quickly (*17*). Studies of the denaturation transition at fixed protein concentrations show partial reversibility, and the results are consistent with the hypothesis that during the unfolding/folding transition part of the enzyme reversibly unfolds and part is kinetically trapped. As expected, the fraction of the refolding rhodanese that is kinetically trapped increases with increased protein concentration.

There are alternative ways to achieve the essential conditions of preventing association of protein molecules that possess interactive surfaces on folding intermediates. For example, immobilization of rhodanese on Sepharose permits reversible thermal denaturation, but this procedure tends not to be a facile approach to general protein folding (19). Detergent assisted refolding was developed as an alternative way of preventing aggregation (20,21). The same detergents are used to facilitate folding as those mild detergents that would be appropriate to solubilize membrane proteins. This approach produces a clear indication that there are folding intermediates that can be kinetically trapped and studied (20,22). After denaturation of rhodanese in 6M GdmHCL, there was no reactivation when denatured enzyme was diluted to concentrations higher than 50 ug/ml in buffer supplemented, singly, with substrate, reductant, or detergent alone. The presence of the pairs of reagents: detergent and thiosulfate; or mercaptoethanol and thiosulfate were not very effective. The combination of detergent and reductant was somewhat effective, and the best results under these conditions led to the recovery of about 30% of the activity when the most effective reductant, thioglycolate, was used. The combined effects of the three components was much greater than the sums of their individual effects, and GdmHCl denatured rhodanese regained more than 90% of its activity when allowed to refold and reactivate in the simultaneous presence of detergent, mercaptoethanol and thiosulfate (23).

Refolding can also be made reversible in urea by the combined use of lauryl maltoside, thiosulfate and mercaptoethanol (22). The observed reversible unfolding/folding transition is asymmetric and can be described as the sum of two individual two-state transitions which indicates that there are intermediate(s) in the folding process. Significant concentrations of the intermediate(s) could be formed under conditions suitable for study by a number of methods. These species were shown to have properties expected for a so-called "molten globule" state described for folding intermediates (24). e.g., they have high secondary structure, are compact, have tryptophan residues with increased accessibility to fluorescence quenchers, and they have increased exposure of hydrophobic surfaces.

Aggregation can be prevented, and folding can be enhanced, by association of the partially folded polypeptide with proteins called chaperonins or heat shock proteins (4-6). This association provides a controllable, energy-dependent folding mechanism. Chaperonins have been suggested to play a general role in folding and mitochondrial import. They have been proposed to function by forming complexes with nascent or imported chain thereby maintaining import competent conformation(s). This complexation by chaperonin keeps folding proteins from aggregating, and prevents interactive intermediates from getting kinetically "stuck". Further, by introducing an energy requirement, the biological system gains an element of control. We have been using proteins from E. coli which consist of the heat shock proteins, cpn60 and cpn10 (also called groEL and groES) to assist refolding of rhodanese. Cpn60 is related to mammalian hsp60 found in the mitochondrial matrix. This protein is an oligomer of 14 60kD subunits arranged as a double doughnut of two stacked 7-mers. Each doughnut appears to contain a relatively small central hole having restricted access to the solvent. These chaperonins are quite effective in refolding rhodanese (25,26). The suggested mode of action of these proteins in folding is that cpn60 sequesters interactive intermediates that are in a state approximating a molten globule. This interaction prevents aggregation. Also, the interaction with cpn60 can maintain a non-native, partially folded conformation in a state that is competent to interact with the other elements of the biological machinery responsible for import or intracellular transport. Subsequent interactions with the second protein, cpn10, and ATP lead to completion of folding and release of the bound protein.

The time course of rhodanese refolding in the presence or absence of chaperonins shows the essential features suggested in the above model (26). There is some spontaneous folding (approximately 30%; $t_{1/2}$=4 min), and the rate of this folding is faster than seen with the chaperonins ($t_{1/2}$=10 min). This spontaneous folding is suppressed with cpn60 since it binds and stabilizes an inactive intermediate. Folding can be resumed on addition of the missing components, cpn10 and ATP. Detergent assisted folding is even slower than the chaperonin assisted case ($t_{1/2}$=35 min) but both reach the same level of refolding which is considerably higher than the unassisted case. This may highlight the fact that the goal of the biological system is not to speed up folding but to control it.

Studies with the fluorescent probe BisANS show that there are a small number of hydrophobic sites on cpn60, and these sites can be modulated by conditions that give the refolding cycle. Conditions that would lead to the release of the bound polypeptide reduce the number of accessible hydrophobic sites on cpn60. This may indicate that hydrophobic interactions between the chaperonins and the partially folded polypeptide chain may be an important component of the mode of folding facilitation.

Low temperature inhibits chaperonin assisted refolding, and this observation can be used to determine the stoichiometry of chaperonin interactions (27). Using inhibition of spontaneous folding which can be made efficient at low temperature, it appears that only 1-2 molecules of rhodanese are bound per cpn60 oligomer. This may indicate that a small region of rhodanese may be involved, e.g. its N-terminus which has the characteristics described for the import signal peptides that are at the N-terminus of mitochondrial protein precursors.

A working hypothesis can be formulated for folding of rhodanese which incorporates what is known so far about this system, and it can serve as a basis for further experiments. On dilution from high concentrations of denaturants, unfolded rhodanese rapidly collapses to a relatively compact state, driven to a large extent by hydrophobic interactions with formation of a large amount of secondary structure. This could correspond to nucleation of the individual domains. This state has the characteristics associated with the so-called molten globule state in that it is compact, has increased flexibility compared with the native state, is relatively open to access by solute components, has exposed hydrophobic surfaces, and contains sulfhydryl groups in a state in which they can be easily oxidized. This structure is enzymatically inactive. This state will aggregate or associate with surfaces if it is formed in sufficient concentrations and not stabilized. A second step that is rate limiting would allow the enzyme to regain its final global structure to give a native-like conformer that is still enzymatically inactive. The addition of thiosulfate would then permit final local readjustments at the active site and lead to reactivation. In this way, aggregation is in kinetic competition with the acquisition of the active monomeric state. One way to optimize folding rates to the stable monomer state is by preventing aggregation while still permitting sufficient flexibility for the protein to search accessible conformations i.e. there is a need for controlled flexibility. This can be achieved by using accessory substances such as detergents or chaperonin proteins or by otherwise arranging conditions so that aggregation is limited.

References

1. Kane,J.F. and Hartly,D.L., *Trends Biotechnol.* **6**, *95* (1988).

2. Marston,F.A.O., *Biochem. J.* **1** 240 (1986).

3. Jaenicke,R., *Prog. Biophys. Mol. Biol.* **49**, *117* (1987).

3a. Mitraki,A. and King,J., *Bio/Technology* **7**, *690* (1989).

4. Rothman,J., *Cell*, **59**, *591* (1989).

5. Randall,L.L., Hardy,S.J.S., and Thom,J.R., *Ann. Rev. Microbiol.* **41**, *507* (1987).

6. Goloubinoff,P., Gatenby,A.A. and Lorimer,G.H., *Nature (London)* **342**, *884* (1989).

7. Horowitz,P.M. and Douglas,M.G., *Fed. Proc. Abstr. 1836, 1859* (1981).

8. Ploegman,J.H., Drent,G., Kalk,K.H., Hol,W.G.J., Heinrikson,R.L., Keim,P., Weng,L., and Russell,J., *Nature* **273**, *124* (1978).

9. Miller,D.M., Delgado,R., Chirgwin,J.M., Hardies,S.J., and Horowitz,P.M., *J. Biol. Chem.* **266**, *4686* (1991).

10. Horowitz,P.M. and Bowman,S., *J. Biol. Chem.* **262**, *8728* (1987).

11. Heinrikson,R.L., Weng,L., and Westley,J., *J. Biol. Chem.* **253**, *8109* (1978).

12. Ogata,K. and Volini,M., *J. Biol. Chem.* **265**, *8087* (1990).

13. Horowitz,P.M. and Bowman,S., *J. Biol. Chem.* **264**, *3311* (1989).

14. Misra,H.P., *J. Biol. Chem.*, **249**, *2151* (1974).

15. Merrill,G.A., Horowitz,P.M., Bowman,S., Bentley,K. and Klebe,R., *J. Biol. Chem.* **263**, *19324* (1988).

16. Horowitz,P.M. and Criscimagna,N. L., *J. Biol. Chem.* **261**, *15652* (1986).

17. Mendoza,J.A., Rogers,E., Lorimer,G.H., and Horowitz,P.M., *J. Biol. Chem.* **266**, *13587* (1991).

18. Aird,B.A. and Horowitz,P.M., *Biochim. Biophys. Acta* **956**, *30* (1988).

19. Horowitz,P. and Bowman,S., *J. Biol. Chem.* **262**, *5587* (1987).

20. Tandon,S. and Horowitz,P.M., *J. Biol. Chem.* **265**, *5967* (1990).

21. Tandon,S. and Horowitz,P.M., *J. Biol. Chem.* **264**, *3311* (1989).

22. Horowitz,P.M. and Criscimagna,N. L., *J. Biol. Chem.* **265**, *2576* (1990).

23. Tandon,S. and Horowitz,P.M., *J. Biol. Chem.* **264**, *9859* (1989)

24. Ptitsyn,O.B.J., *Protein Chem.* **6**, *272* (1987).

25. Martin,J., Langer,T., Boteva,R., Schramel,A., HorwichA.L. and Hartl,F.-U., *Nature* **352**, *36* (1991).

26. Mendoza,J.A., Rogers,E., Lorimer,G.H. and Horowitz,P.M., *J. Biol. Chem.* **266**, *13044* (1991).

27. Mendoza,J.A., Lorimer,G.H. and Horowitz,P.M., *J. Biol. Chem.* **266**, *16973* (1991).

RECEIVED May 5, 1992

MULTIFUNCTIONAL PROTEINS

Chapter 14

Artificial Bifunctional Enzymes
A Tool To Improve Consecutive Enzyme Reactions and Cell Metabolism

Leif Bülow

Department of Pure and Applied Biochemistry, Chemical Center,
P.O. Box 124, Lund S–221 00, Sweden

Two artificial bifunctional enzymes, β-galactosidase/galactokinase
and β-galactosidase/galactose dehydrogenase, have been prepared
by gene fusion and expressed in *E. coli*. The hybrid proteins are
able to catalyze the hydolysis of lactose followed by either
phosphorylation or oxidation of the galactose formed. Both hybrid
enzymes exhibit favorable proximity effects when the coupled
enzyme reactions are analyzed. The effect of the connecting
segment on the function and stability of the bifunctional enzyme
has been studied *in vivo* and *in vitro*. Artificial bifunctional
enzymes are not only used in an isolated form but are also valuable
tools in studies of cell metabolism to evaluate the aspects of
proximity in metabolic maintenance and cell regulation.

SPATIAL ENZYME ORGANIZATION *IN VIVO*

A living cell is a complex entity containing thousands of enzymes involved in the
reactions necessary to maintain the cell status. Most biochemical reactions are
organized into multistep pathways in which several enzymes can be involved (*1*).
Physical arrangements among enzymes in such pathways are less pronounced in
lower organisms but in eucaryotic cells many of the different metabolic pathways
are frequently compartmentalized in organelles, for instance, the replication of
DNA in the nucleus and the tricarboxylic acid cycle in the mitochondrion.
Furthermore, it is believed that the enzymes of a specific reaction pathway within
a single compartment are complexed in ordered or at least nonrandom
arrangements (*2*). Highly organized enzyme systems in processive pathways such

0097–6156/93/0516–0174$06.00/0

as fatty acid synthesis and oxidation as well as nucleotide metabolism have been demonstrated. The enzyme interactions in these pathways are strong and thus have been easy to demonstrate. Such associations between enzymes are usually confirmed when the enzyme activities copurify and the ratio between the activities remains constant during the purification steps.

Multienzymes capable of catalyzing several separate catalytic reactions have been characterized as either multienzyme complexes or multifunctional enzymes. A multifunctional protein is composed of a polypeptide chain(s) carrying two or more active sites. A multienzyme complex also has several active sites, however each on distinct polypeptide chains. These complexes often have a very low dissociation constant (*3*). Expressions like protein machines, enzyme clusters, supramolecular complexes, aggregates and metabolons are all referring to multienzymes. Recommendations for the nomenclature of these multienzymes have now been established and generally accepted (*4,5*).

Multienzymes are often consecutive enzymes in a reaction path or part of a metabolic pathway, i.e. the product of the first enzyme will serve as a substrate for the second enzyme whose product will serve as the substrate for the subsequent enzyme and so forth:

Substrate ──Enzyme 1──▸ Product 1 ──Enzyme 2──▸ Product 2 ──Enzyme 3──▸ ...

Most obviously, by aggregation of polypeptide chains into multienzyme complexes like the pyruvate dehydrogenase complex or multifunctional proteins like fatty acid synthase, the enzyme activities are gathered efficiently in a "microcompartment" . There is even evidence for specific interactions between many of the so called "soluble" consecutive enzymes in a pathway. Most attention has been focused on the two major metabolic pathways, the glycolytic pathway occurring in the cytosol and the tricarboxylic acid cycle in the mitochondrial matrix. The complexation between the enzymes in glycolysis tends to be weak and thus difficult to demonstrate; the enzymes are associated but the organization is loose and only transient (*6-8*). For instance, direct transfer of NAD(H) between glycerol-3-phosphate dehydrogenase and lactic dehydrogenase has been shown *in vitro* (*9, 10*) but the interpretation of the data has been debated (*11, 12*). Other enzymes in glycolysis have also been investigated (*13, 14*). It has been claimed that the dynamic assembly and disassembly of the transiently existing complexes provide a regulatory mechanism for catalytic activity of the enzymes involved (*15, 16*). It has further been suggested that the association of glycolytic enzymes to the cytoskeletal proteins and actin containing structural elements of the cell is responsible for some compartmentalization in the cytoplasm (*17, 18*).

The protein concentration in the mitochondrial matrix is over 50% and it has been proposed that the enzymes in the Krebs cycle probably also exist and behave as a multienzyme entity rather than as free enzymes in solution (*19*). Several publications have presented results indicating physical interactions between the enzymes in the cycle and metabolically related enzymes (summarized in (*20*)). It has also been possible to detect the existence of the Krebs cycle enzymes as a sequential complex (*21*). Moreover, organization of a reaction cycle is not restricted to only one compartment. The urea cycle has been shown to be structured in a sequential association that spans two cellular compartments, the cytoplasm and the mitochondria (*22*).

Importance of proximity

The arrangement of sequentially operating enzymes into multienzyme complexes and multifunctional enzymes involves several advantages for the reactions catalyzed. Different functional consequences of the organization of the enzymes into multienzyme systems have been proposed. Particularly features gained in cellular metabolism have been emphasized (2, 20, 23-26).

Coordination effects. An entire sequence of enzymes can be coordinately activated or inhibited. An example of this phenomenon has been found for the arom conjugate, a multifunctional protein with five distinct consecutive enzymes residing on a dimer of a single polypeptide chain. Four out of the five enzyme activities are activated by the first substrate. In addition, all five activities appear to be coordinately protected from proteolysis when the first substrate is present (27).

Compartmentation. A multienzyme system has the potential of compartmentalizing or containing the substrate of a pathway, which implies that the system prevents interference from an enzyme activity outside the metabolic sequence. This efficient transport of molecules from one enzyme to the next without complete equilibration with the surrounding fluid is also known as substrate channeling. Furthermore, labile intermediates can be protected.

Elimination of lag phases. The intermediate substrate formed does not or only partially diffuses out into the surrounding medium, thereby a high local concentration of substrate for the second enzyme can be obtained. The transient time or the lag phase, defined as the time required to attain a steady-state rate in a series of reactions, is thereby also diminished.

Reduction of diffusion times. The transient time, the time required for the product of one enzymatic reaction to diffuse to the active site of the next enzyme is decreased, particularly if the surrounding medium is viscous (cf. the high protein concentration of the mitochondria).

Biosynthesis is more efficient. The most effective coordination of the biosynthesis of enzyme molecules needed for a reaction path can be achieved if the genetic loci are combined into a single unit encoding a single polypeptide chain.

MODEL SYSTEM MIMICING MULTIENZYMES

As previously indicated, the spatial organization of enzymes appears to be the rule rather than the exception in reflecting enzyme sequences *in vivo*. Therefore, it is important to further delineate the potential advantages gained by reconstruction of proximity between enzymes using different model systems. Three main different approaches have been utilized to mimic naturally occuring enzyme systems; co-immobilization of the enzymes to a solid matrix, chemical cross-linking of the enzymes in a random or an oriented fashion, and preparation of artificial multifunctional enzymes by gene fusion.

Co-immobilization

Mosbach and Mattiasson (27) co-immobilized a two-enzyme system, hexokinase (HK) and glucose-6-phosphate dehydrogenase (G-6-PDH) which catalyze the sequential reactions:

glucose $\xrightarrow[\text{ATP}]{\text{HK}}$ glucose-6-phosphate $\xrightarrow[\text{NADP}]{\text{G-6-PDH}}$ 6-phospho-gluconolactone + NADPH

The initial rate of NADPH formation was considerably enhanced when the two enzymes were co-immobilized, as compared with the situation when they were soluble or immobilized on separate beads (27). The two-enzyme system was extended to a three-enzyme system (28, 29) and later on the enzymes of the urea cycle were co-immobilized to agarose (30). The proximity of the enzymes made the immobilized systems more efficient than the soluble ones since the out-diffusion of the intermediates was hampered due to the unstirred layer surrounding the beads.

Cross-linking of enzymes
Chemical cross-linking between sequentially operating malate dehydrogenase and citrate synthase in the citric acid cycle has been performed to analyze the kinetic behaviour of aggregated enzyme systems (31, 32). The kinetic advantages such as increased steady-state rate in the inital phase of the coupled reaction became apparent only when a crowding agent, polyethylene glycol, was included in the assay system. Improvements of the methodology by cross-linking were accomplished when the active sites of two dehydrogenases were spatially arranged face-to-face prior to cross-linking. Diffusion of the product of the first enzyme to the active site of the second enzyme was shown to be facilitated due to the proximity and proper orientation of the active sites (33).

Gene fusion
Another efficient approach to obtain proximity between enzymes is to ligate the enzymes on the DNA level. The structural genes of the enzymes of interest are fused in-frame generating an artificial bifunctional enzyme carrying both active sites when the chimeric gene is expressed in a suitable host. Fusions can be made either to the amino- or carboxy-terminal regions of the proteins depending largely on the availability of suitable restriction enzyme sites on the corresponding structural genes. If no such restriction sites are accessible at the 5'- or the 3'- ends of the genes they can be generated by site-directed mutagenesis. By using chemically synthesized DNA fragments in the cloning procedure, special properties in the linker region between the enzymes can be designed by the selection of a certain oligonucleotide sequence. In the construction of artificial fusion enzymes, the three-dimensional structure of the enzymes is most often unknown, but frequently the C- and N-terminus are surface located. A gene fusion therefore normally does not or only to a minor extent interfere with the folding of the protein. If subunit interactions are disturbed or disrupted the fusion can often simply be made at the other end of the gene. The construction prepared is then inserted into a proper expression vector and transformed into a suitable host cell. The effects caused by the bifunctional enzymes on enzyme catalysis can then be analyzed either *in vivo* or *in vitro*.

In many instances, the use of this genetic approach is advantageous over the immobilized and cross-linked enzyme systems. Large amounts of homogeneous bifunctional protein can be produced whereas the degree of crosslinking and homogeneity may vary between different preparations of chemically prepared enzyme conjugates. Additionally, much of the enzyme activity is often lost in the immobilization or cross-linking procedure which is normally not the case for gene fusion. Most often at least 50 % of the wild-type enzyme activity is retained if the entire primary structure of the native enzyme is maintained in the hybrid enzyme prepared. 2-5 amino acid residues can frequently be removed from the terminus of the enzymes without affecting their activity. However, the ratio between the enzyme activities is more or less fixed in a genetically prepared system while it is easy to change it using the other two methods.

ARTIFICIAL BIFUNCTIONAL ENZYMES

Over the years we and others have prepared a number of different artificial bi- and polyfunctional enzymes (for review see (34, 35)). In this paper I will focus on two constructions, β-galactosidase/galactokinase and β-galactosidase/galactose dehydrogenase, which both illustrate several important properties associated with such hybrid enzymes.

β-galactosidase/galactokinase
In the first attempt to construct an artificial bifunctional enzyme *in vitro* a fusion was made between β-galactosidase and galactokinase of *E. coli,* a tetrameric and monomeric enzyme, respectively (36). The 5'-end of *galK* was fused to the 3'-end of the structural gene of β-galactosidase, *lacZ*. The bifunctional gene product carried both activities although the β-galactosidase activity was reduced substantially due to 14 missing amino acids in the C-terminus. By adding those residues in a later construction the β-galactosidase activity could be restored (37). The bifunctional enzyme β-galactosidase/galactokinase had a tetrameric configuration (Figure 1) and could efficiently catalyze the reaction sequence:

$$\text{lactose} \longrightarrow \underset{\text{+ glucose}}{\text{galactose}} \xrightarrow{\quad \text{ATP} \quad} \text{galactose-1-phosphate + ADP}$$

This system was initially used as a model in studies of proximity effects between consecutive enzymes *in vitro*. By utilizing a third enzyme, galactose dehydrogenase, which is competitive to galactokinase, it was demonstrated that the galactose formed is channeled between the enzymes. The vicinity effect became more pronounced relative to a control of native enzymes when polyethylene glycol was used as a crowding agent in the reaction medium.

The linker region
In naturally occuring multifunctional enzymes no homology between the linker regions has been observed (38) and the importance of these regions is still unclear. It has been suggested that the correct folding of the protein domains in the polyfunctional *arom* enzyme (*S. cerevisiae*) depends on the linker due to pauses induced by rare combinations of codons near the domain boundaries (39). Suitable oligopeptides as candidates for general gene fusion have been presented after the examination of pronounced characteristics of linker peptides joining domains in known tertiary protein structures (40). It has been reasoned that the embodied amino acid residues should give the linker some flexibility and allow it to interact with the solvent.

In order to investigate the role of the linker to the function of an artificial bifunctional enzyme, further constructions of β-galactosidase/galactokinase fusion enzymes were made starting from the previous construction (37). Oligopeptides of different length and character were introduced between the enzymes. The choice of linker proved to be very important for both the expression of the fusion protein and its stability. Fusion proteins with polyglycine and polyproline linkers encoding polyproline and polyglycine, respectively, were not expressed to the same extent as fusion proteins with amino acids more randomly chosen.

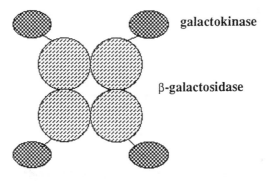

Figure 1. Schematical configuration of the β-galactosidase/galactokinase complex.

Oligonucleotide stretches of the same bases such as oligodC or oligodG were found to be difficult to express in an *E. coli* host. Proteolytic degradation took place both intracellularly as well as extracellularly during purification. This proteolysis occured mainly in the linker region between the catalytic parts. The same phenomenon has been reported for other β-galactosidase fusion proteins as well, e.g. protein A/β-galactosidase *(41)*. Linkers with multiple glycine residues in the β-galactosidase/galactokinase hybrids were shown to be the most susceptible ones. Sequences such as gly-gly-X have been shown to be proteolytic processing sites in some biological systems *(42)*. Furthermore, glycine is believed to be a flexible residue and thus might destabilize the linker. Several independent strategies to stabilize proteolytically sensitive fusion proteins have been presented *(43)*.

Artificial bifunctional enzymes *in vivo*
From all the reports dealing with enzyme interactions *in vitro* a lot of information about cellular organization has been derived. However, as the knowledge of cell metabolism becomes more detailed, the inherent complexity of living systems also becomes more apparent. To understand the importance of a certain enzyme in a metabolic pathway, further studies *in vivo* will no doubt be required. When enzymes are removed from the cells several differences arise that can change the enzyme reactions *(26)*:

- There is a potential loss of organization and compartmentation.
- Enzymes are diluted which can affect a number of interactions between macromolecules and small molecules and ions.
- The relative concentration of enzymes and substrates will change. *In vivo* the enzymes are often present in concentration comparable with or greater than their substrates.
- The kinetic parameters, K_m and v_{max}, could be significantly altered *in vivo* *(13)*.

Furthermore, the environment of the *in vitro* experiments is quite different from the *in vivo* conditions. For instance, the protein concentration is often much higher. It has been estimated to be 200-400 mg/ml *(44)*. This high intracellular protein concentration promotes protein-protein interactions that would not occur in diluted solutions. This volume exclusion effect has been mimicked by the use of polyethylene glycol *in vitro* as previously described.

Therefore, *in vitro* studies have to be extended to include studies on *in vivo* systems. Cell permeabilization is a widely used procedure where it is generally assumed that the protein organization is intact. A simple approach that allows noninvasive studies of cellular metabolism is NMR *(45, 46)*. ^{13}C-NMR studies of yeast cells have provided evidence that substrate channeling between the tricarboxylic acid cycle enzymes does occur supporting previous *in vitro* results *(47)*.

The different β-galactosidase/galactokinase fusion proteins were used as model systems to evaluate the importance of proximity between two metabolically related enzymes. β-galactosidase and galactokinase catalyze the first steps of lactose metabolism in *E. coli*. To study the function of the different hybrid enzymes *in vivo*, *E. coli* harbouring various β-galactosidase/galactokinase fusion enzymes were grown on minimal media with lactose as carbon source. Almost no differences in growth rate were visible. However, on introduction of a second plasmid encoding galactose dehydrogenase that scavenges on galactose, pronounced differences became apparent. The product of galactose dehydrogenase, galactono-lactone, is a metabolic end-product. Therefore, faster growth rates were expected for *E. coli* cells in which the intermediate galactose can be efficiently transferred or channeled to galactokinase. It was demonstrated that *E. coli* cells carrying β-galactosidase/ galactokinase fusion enzymes with short linkers (10 amino acid residues) spacing the two catalytic parts displayed faster growth rates as compared to the cells with bifunctional enzymes with longer linkers (20 residues) or two separate wild-type enzymes. The same behavior due to proximity was also observed by *in vitro* studies on the purified enzymes and crude extracts from cells producing the different β-galactosidase/galactokinase fusion proteins *(48)*.

β-galactosidase/galactose dehydrogenase
In order to further characterize artificial bifunctional enzymes a fusion between two oligomeric enzymes was carried out. In this case there is a potential risk of protein polymer formation when the assembly of subunits takes place. However, the fusion of tetrameric β-galactosidase *(E. coli)* to the C-terminus of dimeric galactose dehydrogenase *(Psedomonas fluorescens)* resulted in completely soluble protein complexes *(49)*. The oligomeric structure followed that of native β-galactosidase and consisted mainly of tetramers and hexamers. The hinge region, spacing the two enzymes, was only three amino acid residues and it is possible that a longer linker would change the quaternary structure.The galactose dehydrogenase moiety of the complex proved to be more thermostable than its native counterpart while the opposite was true for β-galactosidase.

The potential proximity effects caused by the fusion were investigated by analyzing the kinetics of the coupled enzyme reaction using purified enzymes. The fused enzyme system carried out this reaction more efficiently than a corresponding system composed of native enzymes with the same activities. The transient time of the coupled reaction was hence markedly reduced with the bifunctional enzyme. Furthermore, the overall reaction rate turned out to be higher in the fused system compared with the native system. The reason for the latter effect is not fully understood. A plausible explanation can of course be that substrate channeling is taking place between the active sites. The efficiency of the channeling was found to be dependent on the ratio of the activities between the two enzymes. When the activities of galactose dehydrogenase to β-galactosidase was equal only very small differences in catalytic behavior in comparison with the wild-type enzymes were observed. However, if the ratio was increased (8:1) the difference became pronounced resulting in a two-fold increase in the steady-state rate of the coupled reaction for the fused system compared to the native. This shift in channeling could be achieved simply by changing the pH of the reaction buffer since galactose dehydrogenase has an alkaline pH optimum while β-galactosidase has its optimum at neutral pH. In this context the kinetic parameters K_m and v_{max} must also be considered. A shift in K_m for both lactose and galactose was observed. However, these changes can contribute only partly to the observed differences in kinetic behavior between the fused and native enzyme systems. Similar changes in K_m upon complexation have been observed in natural systems as well. For instance, a decrease in K_m values has been observed when the α-ketoglutarate dehydrogenase complex and succinate thiokinase were mixed and interacted *(50)*.

In order to analyze further the subunit interactions of the β-galactosidase/ galactose dehydrogenase fusion protein we decided to express this conjugate together with native galactose dehydrogenase in *E. coli*. When crude extracts were subjected to gel filtration it was observed that galactose dehydrogenase monomers could interact with the fusion enzyme to form a predominantly tetrameric enzyme complex. This complex cannot be obtained simply by mixing native galactose dehydrogenase and β-galactosidase/galactose dehydrogenase implying that the formation of the new complex is associated with protein translation/folding *in vivo*. This suggests that a relatively well-defined enzyme complex can be formed having one subunit of galactose dehydrogenase attached to each β-galactosidase/ galactose dehydrogenase hybrid polypeptide chain. The relative galactose dehydrogenase activity of this complex was increased approximately two-fold compared to the original fusion protein. Moreover, enzyme kinetics experiments revealed that the new complex displayed further reduced transient times for the overall reaction. The thermostability of the β-galactosidase part of the fusion protein was also improved indicating that the embodied proteins behave more native-like.

DISCUSSION

The development of molecular biology has opened new possibilities to structurally link consecutive enzymes by means of in-frame gene fusion, thus creating well-defined artificial bifunctional enzymes. Initially, we fused two sequentially operating enzymes, β-galactosidase and galactokinase, with the aim of studying whether proximity between the enzymes in the system affected the overall reaction kinetics in the conversion of lactose to galactose-1-phospahte. When this fusion enzyme was employed together with a competitive enzyme, galactose dehydrogenase, it was possible to detect a small preference for the pathway utilizing galactokinase. This conclusion was drawn since the added galactose dehydrogenase could not fully compete with the galactokinase of the fusion enzyme for the galactose formed by β-galactosidase. This effect was even more pronounced when polyethylene glycol was added to the solution. Similar conclusions could be made when another bifunctional enzyme, β-galactosidase/ galactose dehydrogenase was prepared. This conjugate exhibited a markedly decreased transient time and a higher steady state rate compared to a corresponding reference system of native enzymes.

The use of hybrid bifunctional enzymes is not only useful for basic enzymatic studies but frequently also offers several practical advantages. Their purification is often simplified compared to the isolation of two wild-type proteins since most often the affinity of only one part of the protein is required during a chromatographic procedure. β-galactosidase fusion proteins can easliy be purified using either ion exchange chromatography on DEAE-agarose or affinity chromatography on p-aminobenzyl 1-thio-β-D-galactopyranoside agarose. Such ready-made enzyme conjugates are very attractive in enzymatic analysis where, for example, a dehydrogenase is often coupled to an enzymatic reaction to form an easily monitorable product, NAD(P)H. There are also several biotechnological processes which utilize consecutive enzyme reactions, for instance the enzymatic conversion of starch to high fructose syrup. The use of artificial multienzymes in these cases would be highly advantageous. The multienzyme will speed up the coupled reaction and "guide" the substrates along the enzyme sequence with little loss of intermediates by diffusion. This would be particularly valuable if the enzymes or substrates are expensive or if the intermediates are labile. A fusion protein composed of bovine P450 monooxygenase and yeast reductase was shown to have great potential for hydroxylation of progesteron (*51*).

The introduction of a fused enzyme system in a living cell would also be very valuable to regulate the production of a certain metabolite. By fusing two or more enzymes at a metabolic branch-point the intermediate substrates could be channeled efficiently to the desired pathway. This form of metabolic engineering will no doubt be a valuable tool in the utilization of transgenic microorganisms and plants in the future.

ACKNOWLEDGEMENTS

Helén Carlsson, Christer Lindbladh, Peter Ljungcrantz, Klaus Mosbach and Mats Persson are gratefully acknowledged. This project was supported by grants from the National Science Research Foundation (NFR) and the National Technical Research Foundation (TFR).

Literature Cited

1. Zubay, G.L. *Biochemistry*, MacMillan Publishing Company, New York, **1988**.
2. Srere, P.A. *Ann. Rev. Biochem.* **1988,** *56,* 89-124.
3. Srere, P.A. ; Mathews, C.K. *Methods in Enzym.* **1990,** *182,* 539-551.
4. von Döhren, H. *Trends Biochem. Sci.* **1980,** *5,* VIII.
5. Nomenclature for Multienzymes *Eur. J. Biochem.* **1989,** *185,* 485-486.
6. Keleti, T.; Ovadi, J.; Batke, *J. Prog. Biophys. Mol. Biol.* **1989,** *53,* 105-152.
7. Batke, J. *FEBS Lett.* **1989,** *251,* 13-16.
8. Batke, J. *Trends Biochem. Sci.* **1989,** *14,* 481-482.
9. Srivastava, D.K.; Bernard, S.A. *Science* **1986,** *234,* 1081-1086.
10. Srivastava, D.K.; Smolen, P.; Betts, G.F.; Fukushima, T.; Spivey, H.O.; Bernard, S.A. *Proc. Natl. Acad. Sci. U.S.A.* **1989,** *86,* 6464-6468.
11. Chock, P.B.; Gutfreund, H. *Proc. Natl. Acad. Sci. U.S.A.* **1988,** *85,* 8870-8874.
12. Wu, X.; Gutfreund, H.; Lakatos, S.; Chock, P.B. *Proc. Natl. Acad. Sci. U.S.A.* **1991,** *88,* 497-501.
13. Kvassman, J.; Pettersson, G. *Eur. J. Biochem.* **1989,** *186,* 261-264.
14. Kvassman, J.; Pettersson, G. *Eur. J. Biochem.* **1989,** *186,* 265-272.
15. Masters, C.J.; Reid, S.; Don, M. *Molec. Cell. Biochem.* **1987,** *76,* 3-14.
16. Ovadi, J. *Trends Biochem. Sci.* **1988,** *13,* 486-490.
17. Knull, H.R. (1990) in: *Structural and Organizational Aspects of Metabolic Regulation;* Srere, P.A.; Mathews, C.K., Eds.; Liss, New York, 1990, pp. 215-228.
18. Shearwin, K.; Nanhua, C.; Masters, C. *Biochem. Int.* **1989,** *19,* 723-729.
19. Srere, P.A. *Trends Biochem. Sci.* **1980,** *5,* 120-121.
20. Robinson Jr., J.B.; Inman, L.; Sumegi, B.; Srere, P.A. *J. Biol. Chem.* **1987,** *262,* 1786-1790.
21. Watford, M. *Trends Biochem. Sci.* **1989,** *14,* 313-314.
22. Friedrich, P. *Supramolecular Organization,* Pergamon Press, Oxford, U.K., 1984.
23. *Organized Multienzyme Systems;* Welch, G. R., Ed., Academic Press, New York, 1985.
24. Spivey, H.O.; Merz, J.M. *Bioessays* **1989,** *10,* 127-130.
25. Coggins, J.R.; Duncan, K.; Anton, I.A., Boocock, M.R.; Chaudhuri, S.; Lambert, J.M.; Lewendon, A.; Millar, G.; Mousdale, D.M.; Smith, D.D.S. *Biochem. Soc. Trans.* **1987,** *15,* 754-759.
26. *Fundamentals of Enzymology;* Price, N.C.; Stevens, Eds., Oxford University Press, New York, 1989.
27. Mosbach, K.; Mattiasson, B. *Acta Chem. Scand.* **1970,** *24,* 2093-2100.

28. Srere, P.A.; Mattiasson, B.; Mosbach, K. *Proc. Natl. Acad. Sci. U.S.A.* **1973,** *70,* 2534-2538.
29 Mattiasson, B.; Mosbach, K. *Biochim. Biophys. Acta* **1971,** *235,* 253-257.
30. Siegbahn, N.; Mosbach, K. *FEBS Lett.* **1982,** *137,* 6-10.
31, Mattiasson, B.; Johansson, A.-C.; Mosbach, K. *Eur. J. Biochem.* **1974,** *46,* 341-349.
32. Koch-Schmidt, A.-C.; Mattiasson, B.; Mosbach, K. *Eur. J. Biochem.* **1977,** *81,* 71-78.
33. Månsson, M.-O.; Siegbahn, N.; Mosbach, K. *Proc. Natl. Acad. Sci. U.S.A.* **1983,** *80,* 1487-1491.
34. Bülow, L.; Mosbach, K. *TIBTECH* **1991,** *9,* 226-231.
35. Bülow, L. *Biochem. Soc. Symp.* **1991,** *57,* 123-133.
36. Bülow, L.; Ljungcrantz, P.; Mosbach, K. *Bio/Technology* **1985,** *3,* 821-823.
37. Bülow, L. *Eur. J. Biochem.* **1987,** *163,* 443-448.
38. Zalkin, H.; Paluh, J.L.; van Cleemput, M.; Moye, W.; Yanofsky, C. *J. Biol. Chem.* **1984,** *259,* 3985-3992.
39. Purvis, I.J.; Bettany, A.J.E.; Santiago, T.C.; Coggins, J.R.; Duncan, K.; Eason, R.; Brown, A.J.P. *J. Mol. Biol.* **1987,** *193,* 413-417.
40. Argos, P. *J. Mol. Biol.* **1990,** *211,* 943-958.
41. Hellebust, H.; Veide, A.; Enfors, S.-O. *J. Biotechnol.* **1988,** *7,* 185-198.
42. Lopez-Otin, C.; Simon-Mateo, C.; Martinez, L.; Vinuela, E. *J. Biol. Chem.* **1989,** *264,* 9107-9110.
43. Hellebust, H.; Murby, M.; Abrahmsén, L.; Uhlén, M.; Enfors, S.-O. *Bio/Technology* **1989,** *7,* 165-168.
44. Srivastava, D.K.; Bernhard, S.A. *Curr. Top. Cell. Reg.* **1986,** *28,* 1-68.
45. Malloy, C.R. In *Structural and Organizational Aspects of Metabolic Regulation;* Srere, P.A.; Mathews, C.K. Eds.; Liss, New York, 1990, pp. 363-374.
46. Lundberg, P.; Harmsen, E.; Ho, C.; Vogel, H.J. *Anal. Biochem.* **1990,** *191,* 193-222.
47. Sümegi, B.; Sherry, A.D.; Malloy, C.R. *Biochemistry* **1990,** *29,* 9106-9110.
48. Bülow, L. *Biochem. Soc. Symp.* **1991,** *57,* 123-133
49. Ljungcrantz, P.; Carlsson, H.; Månsson, M.-O.; Buckel, P.; Mosbach, K.; Bülow, L. *Biochemistry* **1989,** *28,* 8786-8792.
50. Sümegi, B.; Gyocsi, L.; Alkonyi, I. *Biochim. Biophys. Acta* **1980,** *749,* 172-179.
51. Shibata, M.; Sakaki, T.; Yabasaki, Y.; Muramaki, H.; Ohkawa, H. *DNA* **1990,** *9,* 27-36.

RECEIVED April 9, 1992

Chapter 15

Proteins Designed for Adherence to Cellulose

Edgar Ong, Jeffrey M. Greenwood, Neil R. Gilkes, Robert C. Miller, Jr.,
R. Anthony J. Warren, and Douglas G. Kilburn

Department of Microbiology, University of British Columbia
Vancouver, British Columbia V6T 1Z3, Canada

Molecular genetic techniques have been used to produce fusion proteins containing the cellulose-binding domain (CBD) of the cellulases CenA or Cex from the bacterium *Cellulomonas fimi*. CBD_{CenA} is at the N-terminus of CenA, whereas CBD_{Cex} is at the C-terminus of Cex. Using appropriate cloning vectors, a CBD can be fused either to the N- or the C-terminus of a desired protein, an advantage if fusion at one terminus but not the other inactivates the heterologous protein. Vectors can be modified further to allow construction of fusion proteins containing sites for proteolytic removal of the cellulose-binding domain. The fusion proteins bind tightly to cellulose under normal physiological conditions but can be easily eluted with water or elevated pH, or digested with protease *in situ*, allowing purification almost to homogeneity in a single step. Under appropriate conditions, adsorption of hybrid enzymes to cellulose is effectively irreversible. CBDs thus provide a generic system for enzyme immobilization on an inexpensive, convenient matrix.

Cellulose Binding Domains

Cellulomonas fimi produces an endoglucanase (CenA, 418 amino acids) and an exoglucanase (Cex, 443 amino acids) which bind tightly to cellulose (Figure 1) (*1-3*). Each enzyme comprises a conserved sequence of about 100 amino acids separated from a non-conserved sequence of about 300 amino acids by a linker of 20 proline and threonine residues. The conserved sequence is at the amino terminus of CenA and at the carboxyl terminus of Cex. The conserved sequences are cellulose-binding domains (CBDs) (*4*) which function independently of the catalytic domains of the enzymes (*4*). Small-angle x-ray scattering analysis shows that CenA is a tadpole-shaped molecule (*5*); Cex has a similar tertiary structure (M. Schmuck and N.R. Gilkes, unpublished results). The CBD and linker form an extended tail region. The CBD forms a hair-pin loop stabilized by a disulfide bond between cysteines near each end.

0097–6156/93/0516–0185$06.00/0

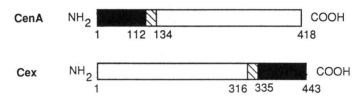

Figure 1.   Domain arrangement in CenA and Cex. The catalytic domain (unshaded area) is separated from the cellulose-binding domain (black area) by a Pro-Thr linker (striped area). The numbers refer to the amino acid residues of the mature protein.

Fusion Proteins

The purification of polypeptides produced from cloned genes is a very important aspect of biotechnology. Methods are required which yield highly purified proteins by the simplest, most direct routes. Affinity chromatography takes advantage of the interaction of a protein with a specific ligand coupled to an inert support. The affinity matrices are usually complex and expensive, requiring covalent attachment of the ligand to the support. Enzyme immobilization is another important area of biotechnology. Enzymes can be coupled covalently to inert supports, adsorbed to supports, or trapped within matrices. The preparation of the support or matrix, and the immobilization process itself may require complex and time-consuming steps and may result in a significant loss of catalytic activity. In many instances, the enzyme must be purified before immobilization. The use of CBDs to confer specific adhesive properties to proteins represents a convenient generic solution which allows purification and immobilization in a single step.

The gene fragment encoding the CBD can be fused to the gene for a protein of interest. Using this approach we have generated hybrid proteins which bind tightly to cellulose and exhibit the biological activity of the protein partner. The adsorption of such fusion proteins to cellulose through the CBD provides a simple technique for affinity purification or immobilization. A cleavage site, e.g. for a specific protease such as factor Xa, can be incorporated into the linker region to facilitate recovery of the fusion partner without the CBD. Factor Xa is a member of the blood clotting cascade. It recognizes the tetrapeptide ile, glu, gly, arg (IEGR in the single letter code) and cleaves on the carboxyl side of the arginine residue. The IEGR recognition sequence is found relatively infrequently in proteins. When this sequence is located between the CBD and the NH_2-terminus of the target polypeptide, proteolysis yields the product without extraneous amino acids from the affinity tag.

Protein Purification

A number of constructs have been made to demonstrate these applications. TnPhoA, a transposon derivative containing the alkaline phosphatase gene, was used to generate a series of gene fusions in which portions of CBD_{CenA} gene were linked to the alkaline phosphatase gene. Fusion proteins produced from constructs which contained the entire CBD_{CenA} gene could be readily adsorbed to cellulose and purified by affinity chromatography (6). Fusions containing only the N-terminal half of CBD_{CenA} did not bind to cellulose.

The CBD of CenA was fused to the N-terminus of human interleukin 2 (IL2) through a linker incorporating a factor Xa cleavage site. To facilitate cloning, a convenient restriction site within the catalytic domain of CenA was used to generate the CBD fragment. The resulting fusion protein (Figure 2a) contained a short portion of the CenA catalytic domain in addition to the factor Xa site. Cleavage of this protein with factor Xa revealed two spurious cleavage sites within the CenA catalytic domain in addition to the IEGR consensus site These extra cleavage sites were not recognized in a CenA construct containing a factor Xa cleavage site immediately after the Pro-Thr linker (CenA-IEGR). Presumably, unfolding of the CenA catalytic domain sequence as a consequence of its incomplete structure in CenA'-IL2 exposes these sites. A precise fusion of the factor Xa site to the C-terminus of the Pro-Thr linker (Figure 2b) solved this problem, highlighting the need to retain discrete, folded domain structures in hybrid proteins.

Fusion of the CBD_{Cex} to the carboxyl terminus of a ß-glucosidase from *Agrobacterium* (Abg) yielded a hybrid protein, Abg-CBD_{Cex}, with undiminished Abg activity (7). This protein was readily purified from *E. coli* lysates by adsorption

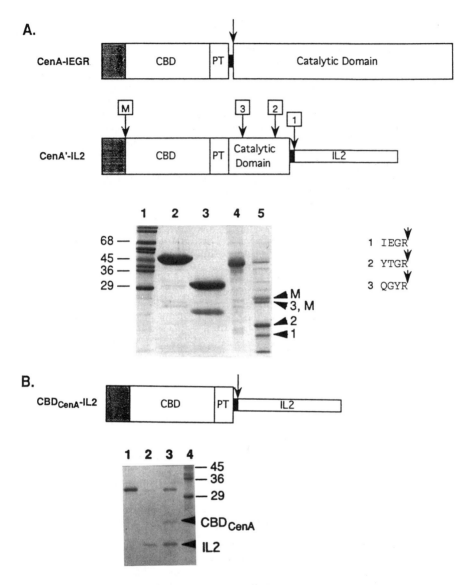

Figure 2.   Factor Xa cleavage of CenA-interleukin 2 (IL2) fusion proteins
analysed by SDS-PAGE. A: Cleavage of CenA'-IL2 with factor Xa. CenA'-
IL2 and control protein CenA-IEGR are shown with the CenA leader peptide
and factor Xa cleavage sites indicated in grey and black respectively. The SDS
gel shows factor Xa digestion of CenA-IEGR (lane 2—before digestion; lane
3—after digestion) and CenA'-IL2 (lane 4—before digestion; lane 5—after
digestion). N-terminal amino acid sequencing of marked bands in lane 5
yielded either the mature N-terminus of CenA (M) and/or three factor Xa
cleavage sites (numbered). The locations of these sites in CenA'-IL2 are
shown and they are compared with respect to factor Xa recognition sequence.
B: Factor Xa cleavage of CBD$_{CenA}$-IL2 while bound to cellulose. Lane 1—
before digestion; lane 2—after digestion, supernatant fraction; lane 3—after
digestion, cellulose-bound fraction.

to cellulose (Table I). Binding to cellulose was stable at neutral pH and at ionic strengths from 10 mM to greater than 1 M, which facilitated the removal of non-specifically bound impurities. At neutral pH, the fusion protein could be desorbed from cellulose with distilled water (Figure 3). Alternatively, Abg-CBD$_{Cex}$ could be eluted with 8M guanidinium HCl or by increasing the pH to >8.0. Binding was stable at low pH.

Binding to Cellulose

The adsorption isotherm ($[P]_{ad}$ vs. $[P]$) of CBD$_{Cex}$ to bacterial microcrystalline cellulose (BMCC) is shown in Figure 4, inset. A Scatchard plot ($[P]_{ad}/[P]$ vs. $[P]_{ad}$) of these data (Figure 4) is non-linear (concave upwards). The cellulose surface can be viewed as a two-dimensional array of overlapping sites (8). Therefore, adsorption of cellulases to cellulose cannot be modeled by a simple Langmuir isotherm. Adsorption of DNA-binding proteins on a one-dimensional array has shown that overlapping binding sites inevitably result in a non-linear Scatchard plot (9). The presence of more than one type of binding site on cellulose (e.g., amorphous and crystalline) and the negative cooperativity observed at higher concentrations of bound ligand would further increase non-linearity. Detailed modelling of the adsorption process is in progress. A Hanes plot ($[P]/[P]_{ad}$ vs. $[P]$) (10) was used to obtain an estimate of relative affinity of CBD$_{Cex}$ (Table II, legend). The relative affinities of CBD$_{Cex}$ and the fusion protein Abg-CBD$_{Cex}$ are very similar (Table II). The binding affinity of the parent exoglucanase Cex is somewhat less. Comparable values have been found for other CBD fusion proteins. These results confirm that the separate domains of these hybrid proteins function independently and are not influenced by the presence of the adjacent partner.

Adsorption isotherms describing the adsorption of CBD$_{Cex}$ to BMCC at various temperatures (4° to 50°C) and pHs (3 to 11) are shown in Figure 5. Differences in the amounts of total adsorbed protein are apparent at high protein concentrations ($[P]_0 > 40$ μM) as saturation is approached. Plots of $[P]/[P]_{ad}$ vs. $[P]$ became non-linear at high protein concentrations ($[P]_0 = 30$ to 90 μM) indicating a complex interaction of the CBD$_{Cex}$ with BMCC (data not shown). These results show that CBD$_{Cex}$ binds well to cellulose under a wide range of temperature and pH conditions which may be encountered during operation of an immobilized enzyme column.

Enzyme Immobilization

Cellulose is a convenient matrix for enzyme immobilization. It is cheap, inert and readily available in a variety of pure forms: papers, powders, cotton or membranes. CBD fusion proteins can be immobilized and purified simultaneously by adsorption to cellulose (11). Under appropriate conditions binding is virtually irreversible as shown in Figure 6. In this experiment Abg-CBD$_{Cex}$ was bound to a cellulose membrane which was then continuously perfused with a solution of p-nitrophenol-ß-D-glucoside (pNPG). Hydrolysis of this chromogenic substrate was monitored by absorbance at 405 nm. No loss in hydrolytic activity was detected over 11 days at 37°C. At 50°C the enzyme lost activity progressively over a period of three days. Examination of the cellulose at the end of the experiment indicated that, although enzyme activity was lost, the protein remained bound to the cellulose.

The thermal stability of immobilized CBD hybrid proteins was further examined using a ß-glucosidase (Cbg) from the thermophile *Caldocellum saccharolyticum* (12) linked by its C-terminus to CBD$_{Cex}$. The resulting fusion protein, Cbg-CBD$_{Cex}$, was purified from *E. coli* lysates by affinity chromatography on cellulose. The purified fusion protein was then immobilized by adsorption at

Table I. Summary of Abg-CBD$_{Cex}$ Purification by Affinity Chromatography on CF1 Cellulose

Purification step	Volume (mL)	Activity (Units.*mL^{-1})	Total activity (Units)	[Protein]** (mg.mL^{-1})	Total [protein] (mg)	Specific activity (Units.mg^{-1})	Yield (%)	Fold-purification
French press cell extract	867	21.9	18987	21.3	18467	1.02	100	1.0
Streptomycin sulfate-treated, filtered cell extract	848	17.4	14755	14.3	12126	1.22	78	1.2
CF1 column flow-through	885	0.12	106	0.78	690			
CF1 column wash	1750	0.98	1719	6.39	11179			
CF1 cellulose eluate (water elution) after Amicon ultrafiltration	22	411.1	9045	3.44	76	119.6	48	117.2

* One ß-glucosidase unit releases one µmol of p-nitrophenolate per min from 1.2 mM pNPG in phosphate buffer, pH 7.0 at 37°C.

** As determined by Coomassie blue dye-binding assay.

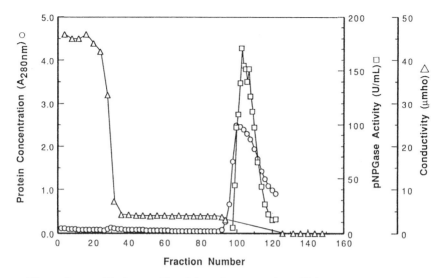

Figure 3. Elution profile of Abg-CBD$_{Cex}$ using affinity chromatography on CF1 (Whatman) cellulose. The fusion protein was eluted using distilled water and 50 mM potassium phosphate buffer, pH 7 in a concave descending gradient.

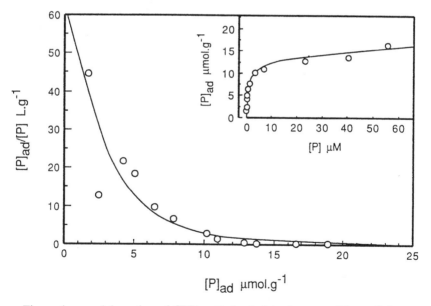

Figure 4. Adsorption of CBD$_{Cex}$ to bacterial microcrystalline cellulose (BMCC). Main panel shows a Scatchard analysis of data for CBD$_{Cex}$ ([P]$_o$ = 0.9 to 90 μM) bound to BMCC (1 mg) at 22°C. Inset shows data plotted as adsorption isotherm. [P]$_o$ refers to initial concentration of CBD$_{Cex}$. [P] refers to equilibrium concentration of CBD$_{Cex}$ free in solution after adsorption for 24 h. [P]$_{ad}$ refers to concentration of CBD$_{Cex}$ bound to BMCC and is calculated by the difference between [P]$_o$ and [P].

Table II. Relative Affinities and Saturation Levels for CBD_{Cex}, Cex and $Abg\text{-}CBD_{Cex}$ for Avicel at 4°C, pH 7*

Protein	Relative Affinity, K_r** ($L.g^{-1}$)	Saturation Level ($\mu mol.g^{-1}$ Avicel)
CBD_{Cex}	7.52	2.70
Cex	1.54	0.85
$Abg\text{-}CBD_{Cex}$	7.81	0.59

*The saturation levels were estimated from plots of $[P]_{ad}$ vs. $[P]$ at high protein concentrations ($[P]_o > 40\ \mu M$). Relative affinities were estimated from the linear plots of $[P]/[P]_{ad}$ vs. $[P]$ obtained at low protein concentrations ($[P]_o\ (CBD_{Cex}) = 0.9$ to $7\ \mu M$; $[P]_o\ (Cex) = 1$ to $3\ \mu M$; $[P]_o\ (Abg\text{-}CBD_{Cex}) = 0.15$ to $0.88\ \mu M$).
**The binding affinity is directly proportional to K_r. $K_r = K_a \cdot [N_o]$ where K_a is the equilibrium association constant and N_o is the total number of binding sites per gram of Avicel.

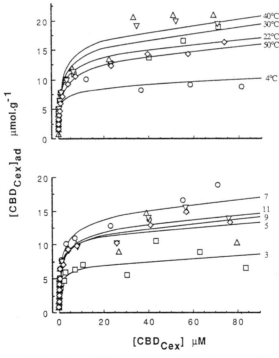

Figure 5.   Adsorption of CBD_{Cex} to bacterial microcrystalline cellulose at different temperatures (upper panel) and pHs (lower panel). Details are as in Figure 4. A constant pH of 7 and a constant temperature of 22°C were used for the temperature and pH studies, respectively. Buffers used were 25 mM citrate buffer, pH 3 and 5; 25 mM phosphate buffer, pH 7; and 25 mM carbonate buffer, pH 9 and 11.

room temperature on cellulose acetate membranes.   pNPG was perfused continuously through the membranes at 70°C.   The activity of the immobilized enzyme was monitored as for Abg-CBD$_{Cex}$.   The immobilized Cbg-CBD$_{Cex}$ was stable at 70°C for more than 70 h (Figure 7).   CBD$_{Cex}$ can thus be used for enzyme immobilization at temperature up to at least 70°C.

Our results demonstrate the utility of CBDs for the purification or immobilization of proteins.   The stable binding of CBD hybrid proteins to a readily available inexpensive cellulose support provides a convenient generic technology. The CBD can be located at either the N- or C- terminus of the hybrid protein, and, at least for the examples we have tested, can function independently without influencing the biological activity of the fusion partner.

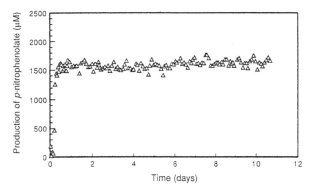

Figure 6.   Performance of an Abg-CBD$_{Cex}$ immobilized enzyme column at 37°C.   The cellulose used was dewaxed cotton (2 g).   Enzyme loading was 1.5 mg protein per g cellulose.   Flow rate was 7.8 mL per h.   Substrate used was 3 mM pNPG in 50 mM potassium phosphate buffer, pH 7.

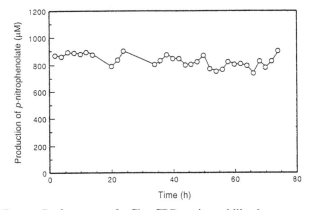

Figure 7.   Performance of a Cbg-CBD$_{Cex}$ immobilized enzyme column at 70°C.   Five stacked cellulose acetate membranes (25 mm diameter x 1 mm thick) were used at an enzyme loading of 0.25 mg total protein.   Flow rate was 9 mL per h.   Substrate used was 1.6 mM pNPG in 50 mM phosphate-citrate buffer, pH 6.2.

Acknowledgments

This work was supported by the Natural Sciences and Engineering Research Council of Canada. We thank Emily Kwan for technical help.

Literature Cited

1.   Wong, W.K.R.; Gerhard, B.; Guo, Z.M.; Kilburn, D.G.; Warren, R.A.J.;
      Miller, R.C., Jr. *Gene* **1986**, *44,* 315-324.
2.   O'Neill, G.P.; Goh, S.H.; Warren, R.A.J.; Kilburn, D.G.; Miller, R.C., Jr.
      Gene **1986**, 44, 325-330.
3.   Warren, R.A.J.; Beck, C.F.; Gilkes, N.R.; Kilburn, D.G.; Langsford,
      M.L.; Miller, R.C., Jr.; O'Neill, G.P.; Scheufens, M.; Wong, W.K.R.
      Proteins **1986**, 1, 335-341.
4.   Gilkes, N.R.; Warren, R.A.J.; Miller, R.C., Jr.; Kilburn, D.G. *J. Biol.
      Chem.* **1988**, 263, 10401-10407.
5.   Pilz, I.; Schwarz, E.; Kilburn, D.G.; Miller, R.C., Jr.; Warren, R.A.J.;
      Gilkes, N.R. *Biochem. J.* **1990**, 271, 277-280.
6.   Greenwood, J.M.; Gilkes, N.R.; Kilburn, D.G.; Miller, R.C., Jr.; Warren,
      R.A.J. *FEBS Lett.* **1989**, 244, 127-131.
7.   Ong, E.; Gilkes, N.R.; Warren, R.A.J.; Miller, R.C.; Kilburn, D.G.
      Bio/Technology **1989**, 7, 604-607.
8.   Henrissat, B.; Vigny, B.; Buleon, A.; Perez, S. *FEBS Lett.* **1988**, 231,
      177-182.
9.   McGhee, J.D., Von Hippel, P.H. *J. Mol. Biol.,* **1974**, 86, 469-89.
10.   Peitersen, N.; Medeiros, J.; Mandels, M. *Biotechnol. Bioeng.* **1977**, 19,
      1091-1094.
11.   Ong, E.; Gilkes, N.R.; Miller, R.C., Jr.; Warren, R.A.J.; Kilburn, D.G.
      Enzyme Microb. Technol., **1991**, 13, 59-65.
12.   Love, D.R.; Streiff, M.B. *Bio/Technology* **1987**, 5, 384-387.

RECEIVED March 31, 1992

Chapter 16

Modification of Regulatory Communication in Aspartate Transcarbamoylase

M. E. Wales, C. J. Strang, R. Swanson, and J. R. Wild

Department of Biochemistry and Biophysics, Texas A&M University, College Station, TX 77843-2128

The modification of the T-to-R transition of aspartate transcarbamoylase by the nucleotide end-products of de novo pyrimidine biosynthesis provides a unique opportunity to analyze the structure-function relationships involved in allostery. By combining site-directed substitutions of individual amino acids with larger structural rearrangements between functionally divergent enzymes, it is possible to ascribe functional roles to tertiary and supersecondary components of protein structure. In each of the enzymes examined to date, cytidine-5'-triphosphate (CTP) and uridine-5'-triphosphate (UTP) combine to synergistically inhibit the catalytic efficiency of the various, structurally conserved ATCases. In spite of this common allostery, CTP, UTP, and ATP (adenosine-5'-triphosphate) have different independent effects in various enzymes. The potential for independent pathways for allostery in the enzyme is being examined by protein engineering.

The formation of carbamoylaspartate from aspartic acid and carbamoyl phosphate is the first committed step of pyrimidine nucleotide biosynthesis. The biochemical organization of this step varies from the multi-enzyme complexes of eukaryotic organisms to the independent enzymes found in prokaryotic systems. The allosteric regulation of the prokaryotic enzyme is complex, since the nucleotide end-products differ in their effects on the catalytic activity of the various ATCases. Hybrid enzymes formed with native subunits from different sources demonstrate that the regulatory subunit determines the nature of the allosteric response. Protein engineering studies involving the genetic interchange of selected structural units have resulted in the formation of hybrid enzymes with altered catalytic and regulatory characteristics (1,2).

0097–6156/93/0516–0195$06.00/0

ATCases are Oligomeric Enzymes with Regulatory and Catalytic Functions Vested in Different Polypeptides or Within Multifunctional Protein Aggregates.

Aspartate transcarbamoylase (ATCase) possesses tremendous structural and regulatory variety in divergent biological systems (see Table I). For example, the *Escherichia coli* holoenzyme, which is composed of two catalytic trimers (c_3) and three regulatory dimers (r_2), is subject to allosteric regulation by the nucleotide end-products of the pathway (*3,4*). Binding of substrate, or structural analogues, promotes a structural transition (the "T-to-R" transition) in this bacterial enzyme, resulting in homotropic cooperativity. In addition, the binding of heterotropic nucleotide effectors influences the structural transitions of the bacterial dodecamer. The *Bacillus subtilis* ATCase, unlike the *E. coli* enzyme, is composed of catalytic subunits only and has no allosteric controls (*5*). The mammalian enzyme is part of a multifunctional protein aggregate encoding the preceding and subsequent enzymes in the biosynthetic pathway. The ATCase component of this multifunctional enzyme is neither influenced by allosteric responses nor does it experience a cooperative structural transition. Nonetheless, based upon the extent of functional similarities and modeling of predicted structural homologies, the various catalytic subunits of different ATCases appear to share a common ancestry with a very slow evolutionary rate (*6,7*).

Table I. Architecture and Enzymatic Characteristics of Divergent ATCases

Organism	Structure	M_r (x10^{-3})	Kinetics	Allostery
Prokaryotic				
Class A	$(c)_n(r)_n$	340-380	hyperbolic	UTP Inhibition
Class B	$2(c_3):3(r_2)$	275-315	sigmoidal	variable
Class C	(c_3)	100-140	hyperbolic	none
Eukaryotic				
S. cerevisiae	$[CA]_3$	800	hyperbolic	UTP on CPSase
Mammalian	$[CAD]_{3n}$	230-1,200	hyperbolic	UTP on CPSase

SOURCE: Adapted from ref. 2.

Biological Divergence in Regulatory Function Leads to Variation in Allosteric Controls Within the Structurally Complex Class B Oligomers.

Twelve bacterial gene systems of native ATCases have been cloned from divergent bacterial species and overproduced in *E. coli*. Studies with these enzymes have analyzed the basic kinetic and allosteric characteristics. All of the enzymes examined have the same dodecameric organization as the *E. coli* enzyme ($2c_3:3r_2$). These cloned gene systems provide a set of enzymes with functionally unique characteristics which can be used to provide insight into the mechanism of the allosteric response. Several specific differences should be emphasized:

a) Some of the *Yersinia* sp. show no heterotropic response to either CTP or ATP, *E. herbicola* has slight CTP inhibition/no activation and *Y. enterocolitica* has ATP activation/no inhibition (Table II). These enzymes all share the same subunit associations as the *E. coli* enzyme.

Table II. Enzymatic Characteristics of Divergent Class B ATCases

ATCase Type	Bacterial Species	Allosteric Characteristics
ATCase B1 (I)[a]	*E. coli* *S. typhimurium*	CTP, CTP + UTP Inhibition ATP Activation
ATCase B2 (IV)	*Y. intermedia*	CTP, UTP Inhibition ATP Activation
ATCase B3 (V)	*E. carnegiana* *E. herbicola*	sCTP[b], CTP + UTP Inhibition No Activation
ATCase B4 (IV)	*Y. enterocolitica*	No Inhibition ATP Activation
ATCase B5 (IV)	*Y. kristensenii* *Y. frederiksenii*	No Inhibition No Activation
ATCase B6 (II)	*A. hydrophila* *S. marcescens*	No Inhibition CTP, ATP Activation CTP + UTP inhibits Activation
ATCase B7 (III)	*P. vulgaris*	CTP + UTP Inhibition CTP, ATP Activation

SOURCE: Adapted from ref. 2.
[a] Tribal classifications (given in parenthesis) are according to Bergey's Manual of Determinative Bacteriology. B1-B7 indicate subgroups of the ATCase Class B enzymes.
[b] sCTP indicates only slight inhibition by CTP (<20%).

b) The report of UTP/CTP synergistic inhibition of the *E. coli* enzyme (8) has been extended to the ATCases from other sources (*P. vulgaris*, *S. marcescens*, and *E. herbicola*). In spite of different allosteric responses to the individual nucleotides, these enzymes exhibit synergistic inhibition (Table III). The ATCase from *E. herbicola* exhibits a depressed response to CTP and no response to ATP and UTP; nonetheless, CTP and UTP are strong synergistic inhibitors. The enzymes from *S. marcescens* and *P. vulgaris* have activation by both CTP and ATP but have diverged in their response to the combination of pyrimidine biosynthetic end products (CTP + UTP). With the *S. marcescens* enzyme, UTP only counteracts the CTP activation, resulting in activity levels near those without any effectors present. However, in *P. vulgaris* UTP acts as a synergistic inhibitor with CTP to give < 10% of the no effector activity level. This synergistic inhibition of the enzyme by UTP in the presence of CTP provides a regulatory logic for those enzymes which show CTP activation.

Table III. Kinetic and Allosteric Comparison of Purified Native ATCases

Enzyme[a]	$[S]_{0.5}$[b]	n_{app}	CTP[c]	ATP[c]	CTP+UTP[c]
E. coli	5	2.4	40	240	5
S. marcescens	16	2.6	150	400	130
P. vulgaris	28	3.2	150	550	10
E. herbicola	4	2.3	80	100	10

[a] The bacterial source of the ATCase enzyme is identified. In all cases, the holoenzyme (c_6r_6) was studied.
[b] The $[S]_{0.5}$ for aspartate, given in mM.
[c] Percentage relative activity in the presence of 2 mM nucleotide effector at 1/2 of the $[S]_{0.5}$ aspartate of each holoenzyme

In addition to preliminary kinetic characterization, the entire *pyrBI* gene region of four of the cloned gene systems has been sequenced: *E. coli, P. vulgaris, S. marcescens* and *E. herbicola*. Figure 1 presents an alignment of the deduced amino acid sequences of the *pyrI* genes from these strains. This type of comparative sequence analysis allows for the formulation of experimentally testable hypotheses about the function of divergent regions/residues.

In Spite of Regulatory Divergence, ATCases From Various Bacterial Sources Maintain a Highly Conserved Amino Acid Sequence.

The comparison of sequence information provides an essential element in the evaluation of the functional role of individual residues and larger structural components. The alignment of related sequences can provide predictive information that individual sequence examination can not provide. It is

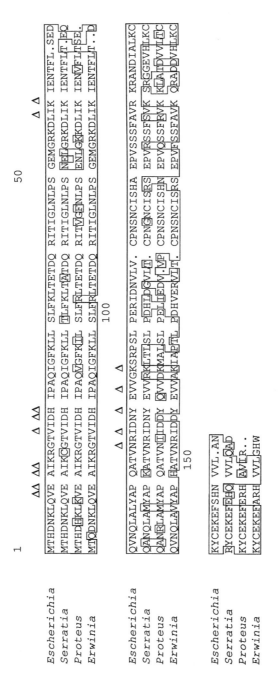

Figure 1. Comparison of the amino acid sequences of the regulatory polypeptide from select members of the *Enterobacteriaceae*. Δ indicates allosteric site residues.

possible to identify those residues which are absolutely conserved, those which appear to have constraints (such as charge or size) and to recognize regions in which there appear to be no constraints on substitution. This type of information may reflect the structure-function roles of individual residues and discrete structural regions. The inference is that those residues directly involved in catalysis, substrate binding or folding are constrained, while other residues will have more freedom for substitution during evolution. Table IV summarizes the residues of the allosteric binding site of ATCase which have been implicated in binding either ATP or CTP in the T and R conformations by X-ray crystallography (9-11).

Table IV. Residues of the Allosteric Binding Site of ATCase (9-11)

T^{ATP}	R^{ATP}	T^{CTP}	R^{CTP}	Chemistry[a]
Val 9			Val 9	ATP, CTP-ribose
Glu 10	Glu 10			ATP-base
Ala 11			Ala 11	ATP, CTP-base
Ileu 12	Ileu 12	Ileu 12	Ileu 12	ATP-base, CTP-base
		Val 17		CTP-3' OH, base
Asp 19	Asp 19	Asp 19	Asp 19	ATP, CTP-ribose
	His 20		His 20	ATP, CTP-γP
Leu 58				ATP-3' OH
Lys 60	Lys 60	Lys 60	Lys 60	ATP, CTP-base, ribose
Asn 84		Asn 84	Asn 84	ATP, CTP-αP
			Ile 86	CTP-base
Tyr 89	Tyr 89	Tyr 89	Tyr 89	ATP, CTP-base
Val 91	Val 91	Val 91	Val 91	ATP,CTP-αP,CTP-ribose
Lys 94	Lys 94	Lys 94	Lys 94	ATP,CTP-triphosphate

[a] Indicates the nucleotides and their components that interact with the amino acid.

The amino acid sequence comparisons of the enteric ATCases were remarkable for the extent of conservation observed among functionally diverged ATCases . When compared with E. coli sequences (12,13), the residues of the catalytic chain of S. marcescens (14), P. vulgaris, S. typhimurium (15), and E. herbicola have 90%, 78%, 93% and 91% absolute positional identity, respectively. [The issue of positional identity is very important relative to predictive modeling of the structural homologies.] All of the active site residues and most protein interface residues are conserved. The regulatory chains of S. marcescens, P. vulgaris and E. herbicola are slightly less conserved at 77%, 71%, and 80%, respectively, while the S. typhimurium sequence had 94% identity. Like the catalytic chain, the allosteric binding site and protein interface residues of the regulatory chain are extensively conserved (Figure 1). Although all of the directly implicated amino acids forming the structural allosteric site are conserved, there are a number of residues located in secondary positions either very near the allosteric site or very near allosteric site residues that have important consequences (Table V). Natural variation can be used to propose functional relationships within both the catalytic and regulatory polypeptides which have diverged in the ATCases from the various biological sources. For example, the site-directed change of Lys56r to Ala56r resulted in the loss of the activation by ATP and synergistic inhibition by CTP+UTP (*16*). Gly51r in the *E. coli* enzyme is substituted by glutamic acid in *P. vulgaris*, and residue Arg96r in *E. coli* has various polar amino acid substitutions in *S. marcescens*, *P. vulgaris* and *E. herbicola*.

Table V. Site-directed Mutations in the *E. coli* Enzyme Affecting Allostery

Site Substitution[a]	Allosteric Response[b]		
	CTP	ATP	CTP+UTP
Wild-type Enzyme	Inhibition	Activation	Synergism
Allosteric Binding Domain			
Lys 56r - Alanine(*16*)	Inhibition	-0-	-0-
Lys 60r - Alanine(*17*)	-0-	Activation	-0-
Lys 94r - Glutamine(*18*)	Inhibition	-0-	nd
Zinc Binding Domain			
Cys 109 - Histidine	-0-	Activation	Synergism
Asn 111 - Alanine(*19*)	-0-	-0-	-0-
Asn 113 - Alanine(*19*)	Inhibition	Activation	nd
Asn 113 - Glycine(*20*)	Inhibition	Activation	nd
Glu 119 - Aspartate	Inhibition	Activation	Synergism
Arg 130 - Glycine(*21*)	Inhibition	Activation	nd

[a] The position of the substitution is indicated, along with the naturally occurring amino acid and the site-directed alteration (e.g. Lys 56r - Alanine indicates that lysine 56 of the regulatory chain was replaced with an alanine). The reference is indicated in parenthesis after each mutation.
[b] The allosteric response is indicated as either activation, inhibition or synergistic inhibition under the respective allosteric effector. 0 indicates no effect, while nd means no data.

This type of mutational analysis can be enhanced by the use of natural variation, along with the available structural information from X-ray crystallographic refinements.

Refined Structures of Variously Liganded ATCases From *E. coli* Provide Insight into Functional Relationships.

A series of conformations of the aspartate transcarbamoylase of *E. coli* have been elucidated by W.N. Lipscomb and coworkers over the past twenty-five years. The crystal structures of the *E. coli* ATCase have been determined to 2.3 - 2.8 Å resolution in the native unliganded state (*22*), in the presence of the allosteric inhibitor CTP and the allosteric activator ATP (*9-11*), with the bisubstrate analogue N-(phosphonacetyl)-L-aspartate (PALA) (*23-25*), and related substrate analogues (*9,26,27*). The amino terminal "carbamoyl phosphate domain" (CP domain) is involved in binding carbamoylates while the carboxyl terminal "aspartate domain" (ASP domain) is involved in binding aspartate and its analogues. The active sites in each of the catalytic trimers are formed at the interfaces between adjacent catalytic polypeptides, and closure of the two domains of the catalytic polypeptide upon the substrates provides necessary tight binding for catalysis (*28,29*). The binding of purine or pyrimidine nucleotides to the allosteric binding domain (ALLO domain) of the aspartate transcarbamoylases of enteric bacteria initiates either a positive or negative heterotropic effect on the subsequent binding of substrate ligands at the active sites of the enzyme, located over 60 Å away. The coherent transmission of the allosteric signals requires faithful protein:protein communication channels within the regulatory subunit between the allosteric binding domain and the zinc binding domain (ZN domain) and from the zinc binding domain into the catalytic trimers. The nature of this transmission and the mechanism by which allosteric effectors influence the conformational transition of the holoenzyme is still unknown (*30-32*).

In spite of the presence of many, extensively refined structures of aspartate transcarbamoylase, the sheer number of residues in the dodecamer (Mr = 310,000) makes it difficult to define the detailed spatial organization of the various components and structural domains. In concert with the construction of hybrid and chimeric varieties of ATCases, a simplified structural description of the holoenzyme has been developed to make it easier to conceptualize the spatial relationships among the domains (Figure 2). This description is based on a central beta sheet structure located in each domain. The holoenzyme is represented in terms of rectangles placed in the position of each beta sheet in the holoenzyme. (The relationships were established by drawing the rectangles to enclose the entire β-sheet of each domain as represented by the molecular graphics program FRODO using the coordinates of the unliganded T-structure. In this way, the visual complexity of the structure was simplified to emphasize the tertiary structure of the domain, while still maintaining the proper spatial relationships.) The darkly shaded rectangles indicate the beta sheet structures of the upper half of the holoenzyme and lighter rectangles represent locations in the lower half. Three catalytic chains form close associations around a central three-fold axis, with the resulting trimers forming the top and bottom of the holoenzyme. The regulatory chains associate as dimers; these dimers are located around the circumference of the

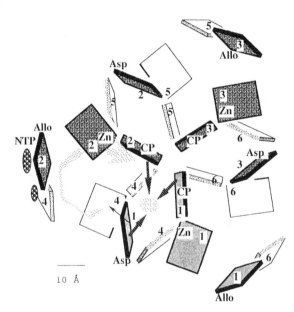

Figure 2. The holoenzyme represented in terms of rectangles in the position of the beta sheets in each domain (see text).

catalytic trimers and bridge the two trimers. In the regulatory polypeptides, the two adjacent allosteric domain beta sheets (e.g. allo 1:allo 6) dimerize into one continuous, 10-stranded sheet. This 10-stranded sheet is the locus of the nucleotide binding sites, one at each end of the sheet, on the outside surface. One pair of nucleotide binding sites is marked by textured ovals in Figure 2 ("NTP").

The beta sheets in the domains of the catalytic trimers are arranged so that they surround each active site on three sides. The wide, textured arrows schematically indicate the contributions from the three different domains to one of the active sites. This conceptualization expresses the way in which the active sites are formed "at the interfaces between adjacent catalytic polypeptides." In the nomenclature established by W.N. Lipscomb and co-workers, this active site is formed from residues contributed by catalytic chains c1 and c2. It is to be noted that each T-state active site is bridged by one regulatory dimer. For example, Zn domain 4 interacts with the 240s loop of active site 1, while Zn domain 2 interacts near the 80s loop of active site 1. These two loops, the 240s loop from c1 and the 80s loop from c2, move in to form the active site in the R state.

A zinc domain beta sheet maintains a relatively fixed relation to its associated carbamyl phosphate beta sheet between the T and R states. The two allosteric beta sheets of the dimer also move as a nearly rigid unit. However, the zinc domain and allosteric domain beta sheets of a single regulatory chain change their relative angle by about 8°, and their separation by about 0.5 Å. Thus, the molecule exhibits rigid links in the two main non-covalent associations made by the regulatory chains, but allows for movement between the covalently joined zinc and allosteric domains.

The Zinc Domains Transfer the Allosteric Signal From the Regulatory Subunits into the Catalytic Subunits.

As described in the previous section, all of the contact residues between the regulatory and catalytic chains are within the Zinc domain. Thus it is the Zinc domain which physically must transmit the regulatory signals. There are four contact regions involving the zinc domain and either the signal source (the allosteric binding domain) or the signal target (the catalytic chains). One of these regions, a "source" contact, is the large hydrophobic zinc:allo interface. This interface mediates the 8° rotation of the allosteric domain relative to the zinc domain during the T→R transition. The other three zinc contact regions involve the catalytic chains, or the "target" contacts.

The most extensive and geometrically unchanging contact with the catalytic chains involves the region of the zinc domain containing three of the four zinc-binding cysteines (residues 113-121 and 137-142). As would be expected for any essential structural feature, the amino acid sequence in this region is extensively conserved. The next most extensive interaction involves the short stretch between residues 109-114 (both of which are zinc-binding cysteines) and the C-terminal helix. This interaction is striking for two reasons:

1) the carboxy-terminus is one of the regions which exhibit maximal sequence disparity among the different ATCases, and 2) this region interacts with the catalytic chain loop (the 240s loop) that moves in to contribute to aspartate binding in the active site. This interaction exist only in the T-state of the enzyme. Finally, a sketchy interaction exists between the 130s loop of the zinc domain and helix 7 (H7) in the aspartate domain. Both of these regions exhibit high sequence variability when compared across the known sequences.

Thus, the zinc domains mediate the response of the holoenzyme to nucleotide effectors in a very interesting way. Each active site integrates input from three different nucleotide binding sites via the different zinc domains it contacts. For example, active site 1 can be influenced by 1) zinc domain 2 interactions near the 80s loop, 2) zinc domain 4 interactions with the 240s loop or 3) a long interaction between zinc domain 1 and H7 of aspartate-binding domain 1. Conversely, each nucleotide effector binding site signals three different active sites indirectly through its associated zinc domain.

Demonstrated Ability to Form Hybrid Oligomeric Enzymes From Native Regulatory and Catalytic Subunits.

An alternative to single residue mutagenesis that can provide insight into the role of protein interfaces is the use of hybrid enzymes. The first such hybrid enzyme was formed in vitro from purified catalytic subunits of *Salmonella typhimurium* and regulatory subunits from *E. coli* (*33*). These two native enzymes are very similar, and the hybrid enzyme results were somewhat inconclusive. Since that time, this approach has been extended to the in vivo construction of hybrid ATCases utilizing the cloned regulatory subunits of one bacterial enzyme and the catalytic subunits of another (*34*). The formation of over twenty hybrid holoenzymes has resulted in the following observations about the nature of the structure-function relationships of the subunits:

1. Stable hybrid enzymes can be formed both in vivo from heterologous subunits expressed from different plasmids or assembled from separated subunits in vitro (*33-36*).
2. The hybrid enzymes demonstrate a pattern of allosteric control that is determined by the nature of the regulatory subunit.
3. Most of the hybrid enzymes formed from native subunits are catalytically efficient as indicated by low $S_{0.5}$ values of 3-8 mM aspartate and the maintenance of maximal velocity.
4. The r:c protein:protein interfaces provide important molecular interactions which affect the enzymatic characteristics expected in the T-R conformational transition of the enzyme.

One of the first hybrid enzymes formed (c_3-*Serratia marcescens*::r_2-*E. coli*) was a stable oligomer of 300 kD which possessed homotropic kinetic responses and was subject to activation by ATP and inhibition by CTP (*36*). In spite of this typical allosteric response, the enzyme appeared catalytically paralyzed, requiring an increase in aspartate concentration at the $S_{0.5}$ from 5 mM to 125 mM. In most other cases, the hybrids were efficient for catalysis and, independent of the catalytic effects, the regulatory subunits always determined the nature of the allosteric response (2). This model of control extends across the widest pattern of hybrid enzyme formation (see Table VI).

Table VI. The Regulatory Chain Dictates the Allosteric Response

ATCase Organization[a]		Response to Effectors (%)[b]		
catalytic subunit	regulatory subunit	CTP	ATP	UTP
E. coli	E. coli	40	140	ne
	S. marcescens	125	135	ne
	P. vulgaris	140	170	ne
S. marcescens	E. coli	50	130	ne
	S. marcescens	135	150	ne
	P. vulgaris	145	150	ne
P. vulgaris	E. coli	25	130	ne
	S. marcescens	115	125	ne
	P. vulgaris	130	190	ne

[a] All enzymes are class B ATCases with catalytic trimers = 100,000 Da and holoenzymes = 300,000 Da.
[b] Percent relative activity in the presence of 2 mM nucleotide. Percentages below 100% represent inhibition (e.g. 5% relative activity indicates 95% inhibition), percentages above 100% are activation (e.g. 180% relative activity indicates 80% activation), ne means no effect.

Interchange of sub-domain modules of divergent ATCases to examine the structural effect of secondary and supra-secondary structures in transmitting the allosteric signals

Since the studies with hybrid enzymes demonstrated that the regulatory subunits impose their unique heterotropic responses on associated catalytic trimers in hybrid holoenzymes, the next step is to genetically reconstruct chimeric enzymes to distinguish more basic structural contributions to the catalytic and regulatory characteristics of the different enzymes. For that reason, a collection of chimeric enzymes was formed from genetically engineered subunits containing domains from the regulatory polypeptides possessing diverse allostery. The constructions currently available are derived from the ATCases of E. coli, S.marcescens and P. vulgaris. Those constructions which have been formed and the preliminary data available from these chimeric enzymes is presented in Table VII.

Table VII. Kinetic and Allosteric Responses of Chimeric Enzymes

Enzyme[a]	$[S]_{0.5}$[b]	n_{app}	Response to Effectors (%)[c]		
			ATP	CTP	C+U
$C_{ec}:R_{zn\text{-}sm::allo\text{-}ec}$	3.0	1.8	130	ne	40
$C_{ec}:R_{zn\text{-}ec::allo\text{-}sm}$	13.5	1.7	180	ne	30
$C_{ec}:R_{zn\text{-}ec::allo\text{-}pv}$	2.7	1.3	ne	ne	60
$C_{ec}:R_{zn\text{-}pv::allo\text{-}ec}$	4.0	1.2	ne	ne	88
$C_{sm}:R_{zn\text{-}sm::allo\text{-}ec}$	6.0	2.0	150	80	3
$C_{sm}:R_{zn\text{-}ec::allo\text{-}sm}$	140.0	3.3	110	ne	60
$C_{sm}:R_{zn\text{-}pv::allo\text{-}ec}$	4.0	1.3	ne	ne	65
$C_{sm}:R_{zn\text{-}ec::allo\text{-}pv}$	9.0	1.6	120	5	5
$C_{pv}:R_{zn\text{-}pv::allo\text{-}ec}$	3.7	1.0	ne	ne	ne
$C_{pv}:R_{zn\text{-}ec::allo\text{-}pv}$	4.0	1.2	ne	ne	79

[a] C, catalytic subunit; R, regulatory subunit; ec, *E. coli*; sm, *S. marcescens*; pv, *P. vulgaris*; zn, zinc domain; allo, allosteric domain; chimeric notation: $C_{ec}:R_{zn\text{-}ec::allo\text{-}sm}$, *E. coli* catalytic subunit associated with a chimeric regulatory subunit composed of the *E. coli* zinc domain and the *S. marcescens* allosteric domain.
[b] The $[S]_{0.5}$ for aspartate, given in mM.
[c] Percent relative activity in the presence of 2 mM nucleotide (see Table VI).

These studies have shown that chimeric regulatory subunits will stably associate with either *E. coli*, *S. marcescens* or *P. vulgaris* catalytic subunits. However, it appears that neither domain alone is sufficient to promote the characteristic allosteric response seen in the native enzymes and in all hybrids examined so far. In evaluating the native enzymes, the hybrid enzymes and these chimeric enzymes, the one region which is perturbed in these chimeric enzymes that is not altered in either of the other configurations, is the zinc::allosteric interface. As mentioned above, this interface undergoes significant rearrangement during the T→R transition. This is consistent with the observation that six of these enzymes have dramatically reduced Hill coefficients. What is surprising is that, in spite of this reduced cooperativity, most of the enzymes (all but one: $C_{sm}:R_{zn\text{-}ec::allo\text{-}sm}$) exhibit very low aspartate requirements. The singular exception is the $C_{sm}:R_{zn\text{-}ec::asp\text{-}sm}$ enzyme has an $[S]_{0.5}$ of 140 mM aspartate, providing further evidence that the contact between the *E. coli* zinc domain and the *S. marcescens* catalytic subunit residues results in a significantly increased substrate requirements.

Conclusion

From the viewpoint of subunit and domain exchanges of ATCases, the holoenzyme is quite resilient. Its structure-function relationships are complex yet appear to be modular and robust. The hybrid and chimeric enzymes are catalytically active and often retain consistent regulatory characteristics, although the values of various enzymatic parameters shift slightly. However, when site-directed mutations are evaluated, the enzyme appears to be more easily disrupted by a single change. The difference between these two observations is that the shuffling of evolutionarily derived units, despite their multiple amino acid differences, may be intrinsically more compatible than single site-directed alterations. In evaluating the significance of divergence between the enteric ATCases, it should be considered that the nucleotide-free ATCase is not the physiological condition. Under physiological concentrations of nucleotides, the ATCase would be liganded, so that the unliganded-catalytic response has not been tuned by selection. Perhaps this is the reason for the activation-inhibition variability seen among the native enzymes. In spite of this, all the regulated ATCases show the physiologically logical behavior of equal or higher activity with ATP than with CTP, and equal or still lower activity with both CTP and UTP.

Acknowledgments

We acknowledge the National Institute of Health, the National Science Foundation, and the Robert A. Welch Foundation for ongoing support of this research.

Literature Cited

1. Wild, J.R.; Grimsley, J.K.; Kedzie, K.M.; Wales, M.E. In *Chemical Aspects of Enzyme Biotechnology*, Baldwin, T.O., Rauschel, F.M. and Scott, A.I., Ed., Plenum Press: New York, New York, 1991, pp. 95-109.
2. Wild, J.R.; Wales, M.E. *Annu. Rev. Microbiol.* **1990**, *44*, pp. 93-118.
3. Gerhart, J.C. and Pardee, A.B. *J. Biol. Chem.* **1962**, *237*, pp. 891-896.
4. Gerhart, J.C. and Schachman, H.K. *Biochemistry* **1965**, *4*, pp. 1054-1062.
5. Brabson, J.S.; Switzer, R.L. *J. Biol. Chem.* **1975**, *250*, pp. 8664-8669.
6. Major, J.G. PhD dissertation, Texas A&M University, 1989. pp. 1-122.
7. Scully, J.L.; Evans, D.R. *Proteins* **1991**, *9*, pp. 191-206.
8. Wild, J.R.; Loughrey, S.J.; Corder, T.C. *Proc. Nat. Acad. Sci. USA* **1989**, *86*, pp. 52-56.
9. Ke, H.M.; Honzatko, R.B.; Lipscomb, W.N. *Proc. Nat. Acad. Sci. USA* **1984**, *81*, pp. 4037-4040.
10. Gouaux, J.E.; Stevens, R.C.; Lipscomb, W.N. *Biochemistry* **1990**, *29*, pp. 7702-7715.
11. Stevens, R.C.; Gouaux, J.E.; Lipscomb, W.N. *Biochemistry* **1990**, *29*, pp. 7691-7701.

12. Hoover, T.A.; Roof, W.D.; Foltermann, K.F.; O'Donovan, G.A.; Bencini, D.A.; Wild, J.R. *Proc. Nat. Acad. Sci. USA* **1983**, *80*, pp. 2462-2466.
13. Schachman, H.K.; Pauza, C.D.; Navre, M.; Karels, M.J.; Wu, L.; Yang, Y.R. *Proc. Nat. Acad. Sci. USA* **1984**, *81*, pp. 115-119.
14. Beck, D.A.; Kedzie, K.M.; Wild, J.R. *J. Biol. Chem.* **1989**, *264*, pp. 16629-16637.
15. Michaels, G.; Kelln, R.A.; Nargang, F.E. *Eur. J. Biochem.* **1987**, *166*, pp. 55-61.
16. Corder, T.S.; Wild, J.R. *J. Biol. Chem.* **1989**, *264*, pp. 7425-7430.
17. Zhang, Y.; Kantrowitz, E.R. *Biochemistry* **1989**, *28*, pp. 7313-7318.
18. Zhang, Y.; Landjimi, M.M.; Kantrowitz, E.R. *J. Biol. Chem.*, **1988**, *263*, pp. 1320-1324.
19. Eisenstein, E.; Markby, D.W.; Schachman, H.K. *Proc. Nat. Acad. Sci. USA* **1989**, *86*, pp. 3094-3098.
20. Xu, W.; Pitts, M.A.; Middleton, S.A.; Kelleher, K.S.; Kantrowitz, E.R. *Biochemistry* **1988**, *27*, pp. 5507-5515.
21. Stebbins, J.W.; Kantrowitz, E.R. *J. Biol. Chem.* **1989**, *264*, pp. 14860-14864.
22. Kim, K.H.; Pan, Z.; Honzatko, R.B; Ke, H-m; Lipscomb, W.N. *J. Mol. Biol.* **1987**, *196*, pp. 853-875.
23. Ke, H.; Lipscomb, W.N.; Cho, Y.; Honzatko, R.B. *J. Mol. Biol.* **1988**, *204*, pp. 725-747.
24. Krause, K.L.; Volz, K.W.; Lipscomb, W.N. *J. Mol. Biol.* **1987**, *193*, pp. 527-553.
25. Volz, K.W.; Krause, K.L.; Lipscomb, W.N. *Biochem. Biophys. Res. Commun.* **1986**, *136*, pp. 822-
26. Gouaux, J.E.; Lipscomb, W.N. *Proc. Nat. Acad. Sci. USA* **1988**, *85*, pp. 4205-4208.
27. Gouaux, J.E.; Lipscomb, W.N. *Biochemistry* **1990**, *29*, pp. 389-402.
28. Kantrowitz, E.R.; Lipscomb, W.N. *TIBS* **1990**, *15*, pp. 53-59.
29. Kantrowitz, E.R.; Lipscomb, W.N. *Science* **1988**, *241*, pp. 669-74.
    Wild, J.R.; Johnson, J.L.; Loughrey, S.J. *J. Bacteriol.* **1988**, *170*, pp. 446-448.
30. Hervé, G. In *Allosteric Enzymes*; Editor, G. Hervé, CRC Press: Boca Raton, Florida, 1989, pp. 61-79.
31. Stevens, R.C.; Lipscomb, W.N. *Biochem. Biophys. Res. Commun.*, **1990**, *171*, pp. 1312-1318.
32. Schachman, H.K. *J. Biol. Chem.*, **1988**, *263*, pp. 18583-19262.
33. O'Donovan, G.; Holoubek, H.; Gerhart, J.C. *Nature New Biology*, **1972**, *238*, pp. 264-266.
34. Foltermann, K.F.; Shanley, M.S.; Wild, J.R. *J. Bacteriol.*, **1983**, *157*, pp. 891-898.
35. Shanley, M.S. **1988**, PhD Dissertation, Texas A&M University, College Station, Texas.
36. Shanley, M.S.; Foltermann, K.F.; O'Donovan, G.A.; Wild, J.R. *J. Biol. Chem.* **1984**, *259*, pp. 12672-12677.

RECEIVED March 31, 1992

Chapter 17

C₁-Tetrahydrofolate Synthase
Dissection of Active Site and Domain Structure by Protein Engineering

Anice E. Thigpen[1], Charles K. Barlowe[2], and Dean R. Appling[3]

Department of Chemistry and Biochemistry, University of Texas, Austin, TX 78712

C₁-tetrahydrofolate (H₄folate) synthase is a trifunctional protein possessing the activities 10-formyl-H₄folate synthetase, 5,10-methenyl-H₄folate cyclohydrolase, and 5,10-methylene-H₄folate dehydrogenase. The current model divides the eukaryotic protein into two functionally independent domains with dehydrogenase/cyclohydrolase activities sharing an overlapping site on the N-terminal domain and synthetase activity associated with the C-terminal domain. In prokaryotes, these activities are generally catalyzed by separate monofunctional enzymes. The genes or cDNAs encoding members of this family of enzymes have been isolated from mammalian, yeast, and bacterial sources and reveal considerable conservation of amino acid sequence. In an effort to elucidate structure/function relationships in these proteins, we have utilized several recombinant DNA methodologies to dissect active site and domain structure in this family of enzymes. Site-directed and random mutagenesis has been used to identify important amino acid residues in the overlapping dehydrogenase/cyclohydrolase active site. Deletion analysis and construction and expression of chimeric forms of the trifunctional enzyme in which the two domains derive from different species have provided insights into domain structure and function.

Folate-mediated one-carbon metabolism plays an essential role in several major cellular processes including nucleic acid biosynthesis, mitochondrial and chloroplast protein biosynthesis, amino acid biosynthesis and interconversions, vitamin metabolism, and

---

[1]Current address: Department of Molecular Genetics, University of Texas Southwestern Medical Center, 5323 Harry Hines Boulevard, Dallas, TX 75235
[2]Current address: Department of Biochemistry, University of California, Berkeley, CA 94720
[3]Corresponding author

0097–6156/93/0516–0210$06.00/0

methyl group biogenesis. These pathways are summarized in Figure 1. The variety of the 3-carbon of serine, derived from glycolytic intermediates (*1*). The one-carbon unit is transferred to H_4folate in a reaction catalyzed by serine hydroxymethyltransferase (reaction 4, Figure 1), generating 5,10-methylene-H_4folate and glycine. This form of the coenzyme can be used directly in *de novo* dTMP synthesis by thymidylate synthase (reaction 6, Figure 1). 5,10-Methylene-H_4folate may also be reduced to 5-methyl-H_4folate or oxidized to 10-formyl-H_4folate depending on the needs of the cell. In rapidly growing cells, the synthesis of purines is a critical folate-dependent pathway, requiring two moles of 10-formyl-H_4folate per mole of purine ring. 5,10-Methylene-H_4folate is oxidized to 10-formyl-H_4folate via the sequential enzymes 5,10-methylene-H_4folate dehydrogenase and 5,10-methenyl-H_4folate cyclohydrolase (reactions 3 and 2, respectively). Formate represents another potential one-carbon donor (*2*) and is activated in an ATP-dependent reaction catalyzed by 10-formyl-H_4folate synthetase (reaction 1, Figure 1).

In prokaryotes, reactions 1-3 (Figure 1) are catalyzed by three separate monofunctional enzymes, with the known exceptions of *Escherichia coli* and *Clostridium thermoaceticum* in which the cyclohydrolase and dehydrogenase activities are catalyzed by bifunctional proteins. In eukaryotes, these three activities are present on one polypeptide in the form of a trifunctional enzyme. This enzyme, termed C_1-tetrahydrofolate synthase (C_1-THF synthase), is thus responsible for interconversion of the one-carbon unit between the formate and formaldehyde oxidation levels.

All of the known eukaryotic C_1-THF synthases exist as homodimers of approximately 100,000 Da. The current model divides the enzyme into two functionally independent domains with dehydrogenase/cyclohydrolase activities sharing an overlapping active site on the N-terminal domain and synthetase activity associated with the C-terminal domain. This model is supported by several lines of evidence. For example, limited proteolysis results in physical separation of activities, with the synthetase activity associated with a large proteolytic fragment (subunit M_r = 60,000-80,000) and the

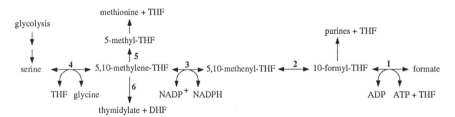

Figure 1. Tetrahydrofolate coenzymes in one-carbon metabolism. Pathways which utilize or generate one or more folate coenzymes are indicated schematically by arrows. Reactions **1**, **2** and **3**; 10-formyl-THF synthetase (EC 6.3.4.3), 5,10-methenyl-THF cyclohydrolase (EC 3.5.4.9) and 5,10-methylene-THF dehydrogenase (EC 1.5.1.5), are catalyzed by C_1-THF synthase. Other reactions shown are **4**, serine hydroxymethyltransferase (EC 2.1.2.1); **5**, 5,10-methylene-THF reductase (EC 1.5.1.20); **6**, thymidylate synthase (EC 2.1.1.45). THF, tetrahydrofolate; DHF, dihydrofolate.

dehydrogenase and cyclohydrolase activities with a small fragment (subunit $M_r = 30,000$) (3-5). Immunochemical experiments with the yeast enzyme (6) support the concept of two functionally independent domains. Villar et al. (5) used differential scanning calorimetry to demonstrate the existence of two domains in the rabbit enzyme. Schirch (7) demonstrated coordinate protection by NADP+ of the rabbit liver dehydrogenase/cyclohydrolase activities against heat inactivation. 5,10-Methenyl-H_4folate, a product of the dehydrogenase reaction, does not accumulate in the coupled dehydrogenase/cyclohydrolase reaction (7-9). Chemical modification studies with the trifunctional enzyme (6,10-12) also support the concept of an overlapping active site for the dehydrogenase/cyclohydrolase activities.

These observations raise two major questions. First, what are the spatial and functional relationships between the two structural domains of C_1-THF synthase? Second, what is the structure of the overlapping dehydrogenase/cyclohydrolase active site? A more complete understanding of the enzymology of these reactions requires new experimental approaches. The amino acid sequences of several species of C_1-THF synthase have been derived from their cloned genes or complementary DNAs (13-16). In addition, sequences are available for several monofunctional and bifunctional versions of these enzymes (17-20). In the absence of a three dimensional structure, these clones provide the opportunity for a detailed analysis of catalytic mechanisms and active site architecture of this family of enzymes. This chapter describes several approaches utilizing recombinant DNA methods to address these questions.

Site-directed mutagenesis

The structure of the dehydrogenase/cyclohydrolase active site, mechanism of the coupling of these two reactions, and the identity of catalytic residues are unknown. Chemical modification experiments with the yeast cytoplasmic C_1-THF synthase indicate the existence of at least two critical histidyl residues and at least two critical cysteinyl residues at the dehydrogenase/cyclohydrolase active site (6). The putative dehydrogenase/cyclohydrolase domain, encompassing the first 300 or so amino acids, contains 11 histidines, but only 3 cysteines (13). Oligonucleotide-mediated site-directed mutagenesis was used to individually change each cysteine contained within the dehydrogenase/cyclohydrolase domain (Cys-11,Cys-144 and Cys-257) to serine (21). The resulting proteins were over-expressed in yeast and purified for kinetic analysis. Site-specific mutations in the dehydrogenase/cyclohydrolase domain do not affect synthetase activity, consistent with the proposed domain structure. The C144S and C257S mutations result in 7-fold and 2-fold increases, respectively, in the dehydrogenase K_m for NADP+. C144S lowers the dehydrogenase maximal velocity roughly 50% while C257S has a maximal velocity similar to the wild type. Cyclohydrolase catalytic activity is reduced 20-fold by the C144S mutation but is increased 2-fold by the C257S mutation. Conversion of Cys-11 to serine has a negligible effect on dehydrogenase/cyclohydrolase activity. A double mutant, C144S/C257S, results in catalytic properties roughly multiplicative of the individual mutations. The dehydrogenase K_m for the folate substrate is not significantly changed in any of the mutants generated. These results implicate Cys-144 and Cys-257 as important active site residues for both the dehydrogenase and cyclohydrolase reactions, consistent with the overlapping active site model. Cys-144 is conserved in all five NADP$^+$-dependent 5,10-methylene-H$_4$folate dehydrogenases for which sequence information is known (Figure 2). In contrast, the two known NAD$^+$-dependent 5,10-methylene-H$_4$folate dehydrogenases, which are approximately 50% identical to their NADP$^+$-dependent counterparts, have an alanine in the equivalent position. Since the major effect of the C144S mutation is on the K$_m$ for NADP$^+$, it is tempting to speculate that Cys-144 is involved in the binding specificity of NADP$^+$ vs. NAD$^+$.

```
HBF   MLPATPWK    (166-173)
MBF   MLPATPWK    (172-179)
YM    FIPCTPYG    (173-180)
YC    FLPCTPKG    (141-148)
HC    FIPCTPKG    (144-151)
RC    FIPCTPKG    (144-151)
EC    ..PCTPRG    (140-145)
```

Figure 2. Amino acid sequence conservation surrounding active site cysteine (**bold**) in NADP- vs. NAD-dependent 5,10-methylene-H$_4$folate dehydrogenases. HBF, human bifunctional NAD-dependent dehydrogenase/cyclohydrolase (*20*); MBF, mouse bifunctional NAD-dependent dehydrogenase/cyclohydrolase (*19*); YM, yeast mitochondrial C$_1$-THF synthase (*14*); YC, yeast cytoplasmic C$_1$-THF synthase (*13*); HC, human cytoplasmic C$_1$-THF synthase (*15*); rat cytoplasmic C$_1$-THF synthase (*16*); EC, *E. coli* bifunctional NADP-dependent dehydrogenase/cyclohydrolase (*33*). All of the C$_1$-THF synthases contain the NADP-dependent dehydrogenase. Boxed residues indicate identical residues or conservative substitutions.

Random mutagenesis/functional selection

Without a crystal structure of the enzyme or additional chemical modification data that might suggest important residues, picking targets for site-directed mutagenesis becomes a guessing game. In families of related enzymes, stretches of high sequence similarity often correspond to active site regions. However, the C$_1$-THF synthases are highly conserved across their entire sequence, making it impossible to predict active site regions. We therefore developed a method in which random mutagenesis is coupled to a functional screening to identify those mutations that affect one or more of the activities of the trifunctional enzyme (*22*). The method relies on plasmid-borne expression of genes in strains of *Saccharomyces cerevisiae* that are missing one or more of the activities of C$_1$-THF synthase. These specially constructed strains allow a very simple screening procedure for the detection of mutants in any of the three reactions. Specific segments of the gene or cDNA are subjected to random mutagenesis *in vitro* before expression and screening. The chemical mutagen used, nitrous acid, deaminates deoxycytosine, deoxyadenosine, and deoxyguanosine, resulting in C to T and A to G transitions (*23*). Plasmids encoding mutant enzymes are easily recovered for sequence analysis and subsequent overexpression of the mutant protein for enzymatic or structural analysis.

The screening procedure is based on the earlier observation (*24*) that the nutritional requirement of *ser1* mutants can be met by either serine, or glycine plus formate, although growth on glycine plus formate is considerably slower. The phosphorylated pathway to serine at the phosphoserine aminotransferase reaction is blocked in *ser1* mutants. Under the glycine plus formate condition, serine is synthesized via the combined activities of C_1-THF synthase and serine hydroxymethyltransferase (reactions 1-4, Figure 1). Therefore, *ser1* mutants which are also deficient in one or more of the activities in this pathway are unable to grow on glycine plus formate.

Using this method, we have generated several mutant forms of the yeast cytoplasmic C_1-THF synthase that result in deficient synthetase and/or dehydrogenase/cyclohydrolase activities (*22,25,26*). When the synthetase domain was targeted, inactivating mutations were isolated at codons 428, 487, 492, and 565. None of these mutations affected the dehydrogenase/cyclohydrolase activities. Conversely, when the dehydrogenase/cyclohydrolase domain was targeted, inactivating mutations were isolated at codons 138, 145, 177, 188, 267, 271, and 284. The effect on cyclohydrolase activity has not been determined in these mutants. These mutations did not affect the synthetase activity. Some of the mutant enzymes harbor multiple amino acid replacements, so it will be necessary to determine which mutated residues affect activity and which are silent.

Beyond contributing information on active site residues, these redesigned enzymes have been extremely valuable in studying folate-mediated one-carbon metabolism in yeast. We have replaced the normal chromosomal gene of yeast with the mutant forms, resulting in new strains of yeast expressing full-length enzyme, but lacking one, two or all three of the C_1-THF synthase activities. These 'metabolic engineering' experiments have revealed a structural role for C_1-THF synthase in a putative multienzyme complex in *de novo* purine biosynthesis (*25*) and a new folate-dependent enzyme in yeast (*27*).

Deletion analysis

Deletion mutagenesis has been widely used to probe domain structure in multifunctional proteins. For example, many transcriptional activators have been dissected with this technique to delineate DNA binding domains, dimerization domains, and activation domains. We have used deletion mutagenesis to further define the domain structure of C_1-THF synthases from yeast and rat.

Several deletions were constructed in the yeast *ADE3* gene, encoding the cytoplasmic C_1-THF synthase, shown schematically in Figure 3 (*26*). A small internal deletion in the dehydrogenase/cyclohydrolase domain (yΔS/X; deletion of residues 114-144) resulted in a very unstable protein when expressed in yeast, with none of the three activities detectable over background. Deletion of 91 amino acids near the C-terminus of the synthetase domain (yΔCla) completely eliminated synthetase activity. Again, the protein was quite unstable and the dehydrogenase/cyclohydrolase activities were less than 10% of wild-type. Deletion of the entire synthetase domain (residues 335-946; yΔH3) results in a protein with no synthetase activity, with dehydrogenase/cyclohydrolase activity at about 10% of wild-type. Deletion of the entire dehydrogenase/cyclohydrolase domain (residues 2-328; yΔDC) resulted in a stable protein of approximately 70 kDa when expressed in yeast. This deletion completely abolished dehydrogenase/cyclohydrolase activity, as expected, but also reduced synthetase activity to less than 10% of wild-type. It is quite likely that this deletion extended through the connecting peptide into the N-

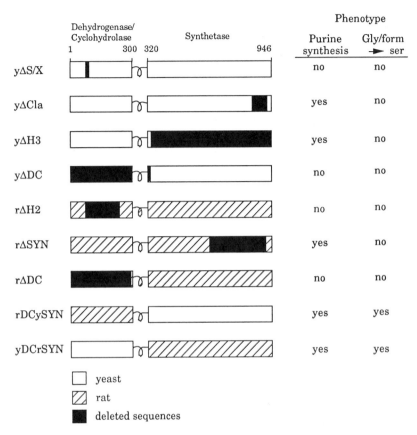

Figure 3. Growth phenotypes of *ade3⁻ ser1⁻* yeast expressing deletion mutants and domain chimeras of rat and yeast cytoplasmic C₁-THF synthases from high copy number plasmids. The two columns on the right indicate whether the construct supports the synthesis of purines or the synthesis of serine from glycine + formate. The wild-type forms of both enzymes are positive for both phenotypes. Lower case *r* and *y* refer to rat and yeast proteins, respectively. Descriptions of each construct can be found in the text.

terminus of the synthetase domain, perhaps deleting critical residues for that activity. Recently, Hum and MacKenzie (*28*) used deletion analysis to define the interdomain region of the human C₁-THF synthase to residues 292-310 (corresponding to residues 297-315 of the yeast enzyme). Furthermore, homology at the N-termini of the two bacterial monofunctional synthetases begins around position 319 of the yeast enzyme. Examination of the amino acid sequence of the yeast enzyme reveals a likely connecting region between amino acids 306-321 that contains 6 proline residues and several potential protease digestion sites.

Three deletions in the rat cytoplasmic C₁-THF synthase have recently been constructed. The first (rΔH2) deleted amino acids 133-272 from the dehydrogenase/ cyclohydrolase domain, the second (rΔSyn) deleted amino acids 563-921 from the synthetase domain, and the third (rΔDC) deleted the entire dehydrogenase/cyclohydrolase domain (amino acids 2-277) (Figure 3). None of these constructs produced stable protein that could be detected by activity or immunoblot.

Genetic complementation assays provide a sensitive measure of *in vivo* function(s) of a protein. We previously used genetic complementation of *ade3* mutants for functional selection in our random mutagenesis experiments (see above). Complementation of a yeast strain harboring an *ade3* chromosomal deletion with these deletion constructs on high-copy-number plasmids reveals some surprising results. Several of the constructs that did not exhibit enzyme activity in crude extracts nonetheless support growth of the *ade3* deletion strain in media lacking purines. In fact, all the constructs involving synthetase deletions support growth in this strain, albeit at reduced rates. On the other hand, none of the dehydrogenase/cyclohydrolase domain deletions supported growth in the absence of exogenous adenine. We have proposed that cytoplasmic C_1-THF synthase is required as a structural component of a multienzyme complex involved in *de novo* purine biosynthesis, at least in yeast (25). This putative structural function can be differentiated from the enzymatic function of C_1-THF synthase by testing for growth on glycine plus formate in place of serine. None of the deletion constructs support serine synthesis from glycine plus formate, since all three activities of C_1-THF synthase are required in this pathway (Figure 1). Thus, the structural role in purine synthesis is independent of any enzymatic function of C_1-THF synthase. The deletion results suggest that the dehydrogenase/cyclohydrolase domain is the structural portion of the protein involved in critical protein-protein interactions with other participants of the putative purine multienzyme complex. The nature and composition of this complex remains to be determined.

Domain Chimeras

One drawback to deletion analysis is that the deletions often have global effects. For example, the folding, stability, or activity of one domain may be dependent on the integrity of the deleted structure. This is apparently the case for some of the constructs described above, since many of the proteins proved to be quite unstable. A more subtle strategy is to substitute whole regions or domains of a protein with sequences from other proteins. We have used this approach to study the modular nature of the C_1-THF synthase family. These enzymes share a great deal of sequence similarity. The rat and human enzymes are greater than 90% identical; the monofunctional synthetases from *Clostridium* share as high as 46% identity with the synthetase domain of the rat enzyme (16). It is quite likely then, that these proteins are structurally related as well, and it might be possible to generate stable chimeric enzymes in which the dehydrogenase/cyclohydrolase and synthetase domains derive from different proteins. We have recently constructed two of these domain chimeras. rDCySYN is composed of the rat dehydrogenase/ cyclohydrolase domain (amino acids 1-277) fused to the yeast synthetase domain (amino acids 283-946). yDCrSYN is composed of the yeast dehydrogenase/cyclohydrolase domain (amino acids 1-334) fused to the rat synthetase domain (amino acids 331-935).

Both of these proteins have been expressed from high-copy-number plasmids in an *ade3* deletion strain. Both constructs are able to complement the purine auxotrophy of the host strain, and both support the synthesis of serine from glycine plus formate (Figure 3). The enzymatic activity of these chimeric proteins, as measured in crude extracts, is quite low, suggesting that the constructs are unstable and/or poorly expressed. Some of these extracts have been examined by immunoblotting with antisera raised against yeast or rat C_1-THF synthase and only very low levels of the full-length chimeras can be detected. Nevertheless, the *in vivo* complementation results confirm the modular nature of C_1-THF synthase and indicate that the domains derived from different sources function together efficiently enough to support growth of the yeast.

Future Directions

The work presented here represents only our initial efforts at studying the structure and functions of the multifunctional enzyme C_1-THF synthase though protein engineering. We are currently working on replacement of the $NADP^+$-dependent dehydrogenase/cyclohydrolase domain of C_1-THF synthase with a human NAD^+-dependent dehydrogenase/cyclohydrolase protein and replacement of the synthetase domain of the eukaryotic enzyme with a bacterial synthetase structure. These constructs are of interest from both the structural and metabolic points of view, and the yeast expression system provides a valuable window on *in vivo* function. However, several technical problems remain to be solved, the foremost being that of protein instability. Although most of the constructs described clearly function *in vivo*, their relative instability makes it difficult to obtain them in sufficient amounts for structural analysis. Towards this end, we are constructing a series of yeast expression vectors in which the various C_1-THF synthase sequences are fused to the C-terminus of the 76-amino acid human ubiquitin. This strategy has proven successful for the stable expression in yeast of a number of heterologous proteins (*29-32*). An improved expression system should allow the purification of enough of these proteins to carry out detailed structural studies so that we may better understand how these important multifunctional proteins function in the cell.

Acknowledgments

This work was supported by grants to D.R.A. from the National Institutes of Health (DK36913) and from the Foundation for Research.

Literature Cited

(1)   Schirch, L. In *Folates and Pterins*; R. L. Blakley and S. J. Benkovic, Ed.; Wiley: New York, 1984; Vol. 1; pp 399-431.
(2)   Barlowe, C. K.; Appling, D. R. *Biofactors* **1988**, *1*, 171-176.
(3)   Paukert, J. L.; Williams, G. R.; Rabinowitz, J. C. *Biochem. Biophys. Res. Comm.* **1977**, *77*, 147-154.
(4)   Tan, L. U. L.; Drury, E. J.; MacKenzie, R. E. *J. Biol. Chem.* **1977**, *252*, 1117-1122.
(5)   Villar, E.; Schuster, B.; Peterson, D.; Schirch, V. *J. Biol. Chem.* **1985**, *260*, 2245-2252.
(6)   Appling, D. R.; Rabinowitz, J. C. *Biochemistry* **1985**, *24*, 3540-3547.
(7)   Schirch, L. *Arch. Biochem. Biophys.* **1978**, *189*, 283-290.

(8)   Cohen, L.; MacKenzie, R. E. *Biochim. Biophys. Acta* **1978**, *522*, 311-317.
(9)   Wasserman, G. F.; Benkovic, P. A.; Young, M.; Benkovic, S. J. *Biochemistry* **1983**, *22*, 1005-1013.
(10) Schirch, L.; Mooz, E. D.; Peterson, D. In *Chemistry and Biology of Pteridines*; R. L. Kisluik and G. M. Brown, Ed.; Elsevier/North-Holland: Amsterdam, 1979; pp 495-500.
(11) Smith, D. D. S.; MacKenzie, R. E. *Can. J. Biochem. Cell Biol.* **1983**, *61*, 1166-1171.
(12) Smith, D. D. S.; MacKenzie, R. E. *Biochem. Biophys. Res. Comm.* **1985**, *128*, 148-154.
(13) Staben, C.; Rabinowitz, J. C. *J. Biol. Chem.* **1986**, *261*, 4629-4637.
(14) Shannon, K. W.; Rabinowitz, J. C. *J. Biol. Chem.* **1988**, *263*, 7717-7725.
(15) Hum, D. W.; Bell, A. W.; Rozen, R.; MacKenzie, R. E. *J. Biol. Chem.* **1988**, *263*, 15946-15950.
(16) Thigpen, A. E.; West, M. G.; Appling, D. R. *J. Biol. Chem.* **1990**, *265*, 7907-7913.
(17) Whitehead, T. R.; Rabinowitz, J. C. *J. Bacteriol.* **1988**, *170*, 3255-3261.
(18) Lovell, C. R.; Przybyla, A.; Ljungdahl, L. G. *Biochemistry* **1990**, *29*, 5687-5694.
(19) Belanger, C.; MacKenzie, R. E. *J. Biol. Chem.* **1989**, *264*, 4837-4843.
(20) Peri, K. G.; Belanger, C.; MacKenzie, R. E. *Nucleic Acids Res.* **1989**, *17*, 8853.
(21) Barlowe, C. K.; Williams, M. E.; Rabinowitz, J. C.; Appling, D. R. *Biochemistry* **1989**, *28*, 2099-2106.
(22) Barlowe, C. K.; Appling, D. R. *Biofactors* **1989**, *2*, 57-63.
(23) Myers, R. M.; Lerman, L. S.; Maniatis, T. *Science* **1985**, *229*, 242-247.
(24) McKenzie, K. Q.; Jones, E. W. *Genetics* **1977**, *86*, 85-102.
(25) Barlowe, C. K.; Appling, D. R. *Mol. Cell. Biol.* **1990**, *10*, 5679-5687.
(26) Barlowe, C. K. Ph.D. Thesis, The University of Texas at Austin, 1990.
(27) Barlowe, C. K.; Appling, D. R. *Biochemistry* **1990**, *29*, 7089-7094.
(28) Hum, D. W.; MacKenzie, R. E. *Prot. Eng.* **1991**, *4*, 493-500.
(29) Ecker, D. J.; Stadel, J. M.; Butt, T. R.; Marsh, J. A.; Monia, B. P.; Powers, D. A.; Gorman, J. A.; Clark, P. E.; Warren, F.; Shatzman, A.; Crooke, S. T. *J. Biol. Chem.* **1989**, *264*, 7715-7719.
(30) Butt, T. R.; Khan, M. I.; Marsh, J.; Ecker, D. J.; Crooke, S. T. *J. Biol. Chem.* **1988**, *263*, 16364-16371.
(31) Sone, T.; McDonnell, D. P.; O'Malley, B. W.; Pike, J. W. *J. Biol. Chem.* **1990**, *265*, 21997-22003.
(32) Baker, R. T.; Varshavsky, A. *Proc. Natl. Acad. Sci. USA* **1991**, *88*, 1090-1094.
(33) D'Ari, L.; Rabinowitz, J. C. *J. Biol. Chem.* **1991**, *266*, 23953-23958.

RECEIVED March 31, 1992

DESIGN OF CELLULASES
BY RECOMBINANT METHODS

Chapter 18

Properties of Native and Site-Mutagenized Cellobiohydrolase II

C. Barnett[1], L. Sumner[1,4], R. Berka[1,5], S. Shoemaker[1,6], H. Berg[2], M. Gritzali[3], and R. Brown[3]

[1]Genencor International, Inc., 180 Kimball Way, South San Francisco, CA 94080
[2]Biology Department, Memphis State University, Memphis, TN 38152
[3]Food Science and Human Nutrition Department, University of Florida, Gainesville, FL 32611

The cellulase system of *Trichoderma reesei* (also *T. longibrachiatum*) comprises endoglucanases, cellobiohydrolases and β-D-glucosidases which act synergistically to convert cellulose to glucose. Although cellobiohydrolase I (CBH I) is the most abundant component, cellobiohydrolase II (CBH II) is required for optimum rates of conversion of crystalline cellulose. The three dimensional structure of the catalytic core of CBH II recently reported by Swedish and Finnish investigators (*1*) has made it possible to interpret more precisely the results of experiments regarding structure-function relationships. Changes in activity and specificity due to site specific mutagenesis have been used to study the putative active site of CBH II to confirm the essentiality of specific amino acid residues and the effect on the substrate specificity and kinetics of reaction using model substrates. In this study, CBH II genes were expressed in *Aspergillus awamori* and the properties of the resulting enzymes were examined. The results indicate a multi-site enzyme with activity on polymeric and soluble substrates dependent on specific amino acid residues.

The cellulase system of *Trichoderma reesei* has been the subject of intense study over the past twenty years because of its ability to depolymerize cellulose, the most abundant component of plant derived materials and agricultural wastes. Advances in cellulase manufacturing making available lower cost commercial cellulases, as well as increased pressure to reduce the amount of solid waste have heightened interest in

[4]Current address: Tufts Medical School, Tufts University, Boston, MA 02215
[5]Current address: Novo Nordisk Biotech, Inc., Davis, CA 95616
[6]Current address: Department of Food Science and Technology, California Institute of Food and Agricultural Research, University of California, Davis, CA 95616

developing cellulase-based conversion processes. One such process is the development and commercialization of a cellulase-based simultaneous-saccharification fermentation process for the production of fuel ethanol. This process is based on mixed feedstocks, including renewable and waste materials, and is generating a clean burning transportation fuel. Ethanol is being used today as an octane enhancer and as a transportation fuel. In the future its use can significantly reduce our dependence on petroleum based fuels.

The cost and efficiency of cellulases remain major considerations in their use in commercial processes. Cellulases are about a hundred times less efficient than amylases and though much of the reason for this is due to differences in the substrates, it is felt that the cellulases can be improved to increase both the rate and extent of depolymerization. Examination of the cellulase system of *T. reesei* shows it to consist of at least five distinct enzymes that act synergistically to depolymerize crystalline forms of cellulose to give glucose and cellobiose as the major products. Among the five enzymes are three categories of hydrolytic activities. The endoglucanases, EG I and EG II are β-glucan glucanohydrolases (EC 3.2.1.4.) and randomly cleave internal β-1,4-glucosidic linkages in cellulose. The exocellobiohydrolases, CBH I and CBH II are β-1,4-glucan cellobiohydrolases (EC 3.2.1.91) and degrade cellulose from the ends of the cellulose polymer chains. CBH I, when acting upon cellulose, releases primarily cellobiose with some glucose; CBH II, however, is unique among the endoglucanases and cellobiohydrolases in that it releases almost entirely cellobiose from the hydrolysis of cellulose. The β-glucosidase or cellobiase (EC 3.2.1.21) converts cellobiose and other cellooligosaccharides to glucose.

The genes encoding the two endoglucanases, *egl1* (2) and *egl3* (3), and two cellobiohydrolases, *cbh1* (4) and *cbh2* (5-6) have been cloned and their nucleotide sequences determined. Furthermore, *cbh1* and *cbh2* have been expressed in *Saccharomyces* (7) and *cbh1* and *egl1* have been expressed in *Aspergillus nidulans* (8). Although well characterized at the genetic and biochemical level, the active site residues and their respective roles have yet to be determined for any of the cellulase enzymes. Chen et al. (5) suggested a model for CBH II based on homology to the catalytic mechanism of T4 lysozyme (9) where residues equivalent to the aspartic acid at position 175 and the glutamic acid at position 184 are involved in catalysis. At about the same time, Knowles et al. (6) suggested that the glutamic acid at position 244 is implicated in catalysis. More recently, the three-dimensional structure of the catalytic core of CBH II was reported (1). This study strongly implicated two aspartyl residues (Asp 175 and Asp 221) in the catalytic mechanism as well as several tryptophanyl residues in an extensive binding site. The structure proposed a "tunnel" into which a β-1,4-glucan chain could enter with the consequent addition of H_2O to alternate glycosidic bonds and the release of α-cellobiose as product molecules.

To test the validity of these hypotheses and to identify the active site residues in CBH II by site-directed mutagenesis, we have developed an expression system combining *Aspergillus awamori*, a fungus with a relatively low background for cellulolytic activity and no cellobiohydrolase, and the expression vector pGPT-*pyrG* (10). Using this heterologous expression system, we have identified one residue essential to the catalytic mechanism of CBH II and a second residue which seems to affect the catalytic activity of CBH II. Neither of these alterations of the CBH II protein resulted in a loss of binding to cellulose in cell walls, thus indicating the significance of the cellulose binding domain (CBD) in the substrate:enzyme association.

Materials and Methods

Fungal Strains. *Aspergillus awamori* strain (*A. niger* var. *awamori*) GC12 was derived from strain UVK143 (a glucoamylase hyper-producing mutant of strain NRRL 3112) by parasexual crossing of the following auxotrophic mutants: *A. awamori* GC5 (*pyrG5*), a uridine requiring auxotroph isolated by selection on 5-fluoro-orotic acid (*11*) following mutagenesis of UVK143f with ultraviolet light (this mutant is deficient in the enzyme orotidine 5′-monophosphate decarboxylase); *A. awamori* GC3 (*argB3*), which is an arginine requiring auxotroph isolated by filtration enrichment (*12*) following nitrosoguanidine mutagenesis of UVK143f (this mutant is specifically deficient in the enzyme ornithine carbamoyl transferase). The resultant double auxotroph (*pyrG, argB*) was designated strain GC12.

Bacterial Strains, Cloning Vectors and Plasmids. *Escherichia coli* JM101 (*13*) was used for propagation of all plasmids. The cloning vectors pUC218 and pUC219 are chimeric DNA phage-plasmid molecules derived from pUC18 and pUC19, respectively (*14*), with the insertion of the restriction sites *Xho*I, *Bgl*II, and *Cla*I in the polylinker between the *Bam*HI and the *Xba*I sites. These vectors contain the intergenic region of the bacteriophage M13 (*15*) and when used in conjunction with the helper phage M13/K07, generate single stranded DNA for use as template for site directed oligonucleotide mutagenesis (*16*) and for sequencing.

Construction of pGPT-cbh2. In order to create sites to easily remove the coding region of *cbh2*, oligonucleotide mutagenesis primers 30 base pairs in length were synthesized to insert a *Bgl*II site 24 nucleotides upstream of the methionine at the translation start site and an *Nhe*I site 21 nucleotides downstream of the stop codon in both the intronless and genomic copies of the *cbh2* gene (Figure 1).

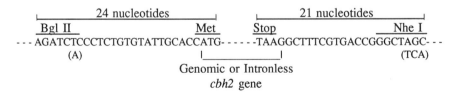

Figure 1
Nucleotide Sequence of 5′ and 3′ *cbh2* Regions

These sites were used to ligate the full length coding regions of both forms of *cbh2* into the *Bgl*II and *Xba*I sites of the expression vector pGPT-*pyrG* (*17*). This vector uses the *A. awamori* glucoamylase (*glaA*) promoter and the *A. niger glaA* terminator as transcriptional and translational controls for the expression of CBH II. Also included on the vector is the *A. nidulans pyrG*, which complements the uridine auxotrophy of our GC12 strain and serves as a selectable marker for identification of transformants on solid media containing no uridine. The entire promoter-coding region-terminator cassette can be liberated from vector sequences by restriction digestion with *Cla*I to yield a 5.0 kb fragment.

Transformation Procedure for *A. awamori*. *A. awamori* strain GC12 was protoplasted as described (*18*) and transformed by an electroporation technique described by Ward et al. (*19*). The number of transformants ranged from 5-15 per microgram of DNA.

Culture conditions. *A. awamori* CBH II transformants were grown in liquid medium containing 1 g/L Bacto Peptone (Difco), 20 g/L malt extract (Difco), 1 g/L yeast extract (Difco), 6 g/L NaNO$_3$, 0.52 g/L KCl, 34 g/L KH2PO$_4$, 1.0 g/L MgSO$_4$•7H$_2$0, 50 g/L maltose, 1 g/L trace elements (1.0 g/L, FeSO$_4$•7H$_2$0, 8.8 g/L ZnSO$_4$•7H$_2$O, 0.4 g/L CuSO$_4$•5H$_2$0 0.15 g/L MnSO$_4$•4H$_2$0, 0.1 g/L Na$_2$B$_4$0$_7$•10H$_2$0, 50 mg/L [NH$_4$]$_6$Mo$_7$0$_{24}$•4H$_2$0), 10 mL/L met-bio solution (50 g/L L-methionine, 200 mg/mL d-biotin), 0.1% Tween 80, 50 mg/mL streptomycin. All cultures were inoculated with conidia to a final concentration of 1x10^6 conidia/mL of culture medium and grown for 4 days at 37°C on a rotary shaker (New Brunswick Scientific Company, Inc.) at 200 rpm. Cultures were filtered through miracloth and filtrates collected for enzyme characterization.

Construction of CBH II Expression Vectors. Native and site-specific variants of CBH II in pJC218 were excised with *Bgl*II and *Nhe*I and ligated into *Bgl*II/*Xba*I cut pGPT-*pyrG* vector. These were used to transform *E. coli* JM101 and selected for on medium containing 50 mg/mL carbenicillin.

Isolation and Characterization of Nucleic Acids. *A. awamori* DNA and RNA were isolated as described previously (*20*). DNA samples from transformants were digested with an appropriate restriction enzyme, fractionated on 0.5% agarose gels and blotted to Nytran (Schleicher & Schuell, Keene, NH) nylon membrane. The membranes were hybridized in 50% formamide, 5X SSPE, 200 mg/mL sheared and denatured (95°C) salmon sperm DNA and with nick translated pGPT-*cbh2* plasmid (1x10^6 cpm/mL). After overnight incubation at 42°C, the membranes were washed at 55°C in 2X SSC, as described by Davis et al. (*21*) Total RNA from selected *A. awamori* transformants was fractionated electrophoretically on 1% agarose gels containing 2% formaldehyde and subsequently blotted to Nytran in 20X SSPE. The membranes were hybridized with a nick translated *cbh2* coding region fragment. Hybridization and washing conditions were the same as described above for DNA hybridization.

Site Specific Mutagenesis. Oligonucleotide-directed site specific mutagenesis was accomplished according to the method described by Carter (*16*). The precise nucleotide sequence of the genetic modifications were confirmed using the Sanger di-deoxy sequencing method (*22*).

Antibody Analysis. Screening transformants for the presence of recombinant CBH II was done using an enzyme linked immunosorbent assay. (Shoemaker and Sumner, unpublished data.) Western blot analysis was carried out as described by Towbin et al. (23).

Enzyme Purification and Analysis of rCBH II Enzymes. One liter cultures of the *A. awamori* transformants (cDNA type) which expressed CBH II enzymes were concentrated twenty fold and diafiltered into 5 mM phosphate buffer at pH = 7.8. The rCBH II protein was purified by FPLC (Pharmacia) using a Mono Q anion exchange column equilibrated in 5 mM phosphate buffer at pH = 7.8. Flow-through fractions containing rCBH II were collected and were incubated in 1% phosphoric acid-swollen cellulose (PSC) for 1 hour at 45°C. The samples were centrifuged at 2500×g to remove PSC. Production of reducing sugars, expressed as cellobiose equivalents, was determined according to the method of Nelson and Somogyi (24-25). The designation of the CBH II enzymes used in the kinetic and binding studies is given in Table I.

Table I. Recombinant CBH II (rCBH II) Enzymes[a]

Enzyme	Designation
rCBH II (from native cDNA)	rCBH II
rCBH II (Glu 184 to Gln 184)	E184Q
rCBH II (Asp 173, 175 to Asn 173, 175)	D173N/D175N
rCBH II (Asp 173 to Asn 173)	D173N
rCBH II (Asp 175 to Asn 175)	D175N
rCBH II (Glu 244 to Gln 244)	E244Q

[a]rCBH II refers to the *Aspergillus* gene product which is derived from native and genetically modified *Trichoderma* CBH II genes. CBH II purified directly from *T. reesei* cultures is designated as CBH II or native CBH II.

Reaction Product Analysis. Reaction supernatants were analyzed by HPLC using a Bio-Rad HPX65A column at 80°C. Glucose and cellobiose (Sigma) were used as standards.

Kinetic Studies. The enzymatic hydrolysis of Avicel or PSC was carried out in 50 mM pH 5.0 sodium acetate buffer at 40°C after which the reaction was stopped by exposure to boiling water for 5 minutes. Following centrifugation of the incubation mixtures, the supernatants were analyzed for reducing sugar by the Nelson-Somogyi method (24-25). The model substrate, methylumbelliferyl-β-D-cellobioside (MUC), was used in studies of specificity and kinetics of the purified native and recombinant forms of CBH II. These studies were carried out at 40°C in 50 mM pH 5.0 sodium acetate buffer and the extent of reaction determined by measuring absorbance at 346 nm (26).

Ultrastructure Analysis. The enzyme-linked colloidal gold labelling technique of Berg et al. (*27*) without poststaining was used to compare the binding affinities of native and recombinant CBH II forms (native—purified, recombinant—wild type; D173N/D175N; and E184Q) with identical sections of *Casuarina* branchlet parenchyma cell wall material. The same ratio of protein to gold was used to make each of the probes, which were then diluted similarly to give working solutions according to standard procedures (*27*).

Results and Discussion

Expression of CBH II in *A. awamori.* Intronless and genomic forms of rCBH II and the specific genetic variants D173N/D175N, E184Q, D173N, D175N, and E224Q were introduced into the expression vector pGPT-*pyrG* as outlined in the previous section. These plasmids were used to transform *A. awamori* GC12. All transformants were picked to fresh minimal medium in the absence of uridine twice successively and inoculated into the medium described in the previous section. The addition of maltose as a carbon source was necessary to induce transcription from the *glaA* promoter.   Duplicate samples of ten transformants, from both the genomic and intronless constructions were analyzed by an immunochemical method (ELISA). Approximately 70-80% of the transformants tested showed the presence of secreted CBH II. The maximum expression among the genomic transformants was determined to be 25 mg/mL and the intronless transformants reached a maximum expression level of 40-50 mg/mL (data not shown).

Total chromosomal DNA was isolated from selected high producing transformants and from selected low producing transformants. Equal amounts of DNA from each transformant were cut with the restriction endonuclease *Cla*I, fractionated on 0.5% agarose gels, blotted to Nytran and hybridized with the nick translated pGPT-CBH II. The autoradiogram given in Figure 2 shows that in each selected transformant, pGPT-*cbh2* has integrated into the host genome.   In this figure the letter C denotes intronless clones and the letter G denotes genomic clones. The end lanes (p18CB and p1G1) are purified controls cut with *Cla*I, a restriction enzyme that separates the GAM-CBH II expression unit from the vector DNA.   The lane denoted Uc is *A. awamori* untransformed DNA as a negative control. Five micrograms of genomic DNA isolated from various transformants and a negative control were run on 0.5% agarose, blotted and probed with nick translated genomic pGPT-*cbh2* plasmid.

The high producing intronless transformants, cI and cJ, contain full length tandem integrants as seen by the restriction pattern consistent with the plasmid control. They also show different copy numbers which is consistent with circular plasmid integration into the chromosome.   The intronless transformants with undetectable levels of expression of CBH II show a restriction pattern that is markedly different from the control plasmid.   This is due to an uneven recombination event resulting in the loss of either the promoter portion of the coding region and resulting in undetectable levels of CBH II expression. The high producing genomic transformants, gC and gW, do not show a restriction pattern that is consistent with a full length tandem integration as the restriction pattern does not contain the same size fragments as the control.

This is the result of uneven recombination into the chromosome while maintaining the integrity of the expression cassette.

Northern blot analysis of the high producing transformants cI, gC and gW, probed with the BglII-NheI coding region fragment is given in Figure 3. In this case, total A. awamori RNA was subjected to electrophoresis on a 3% agarose/formaldehyde gel (panel A). The gel was transferred to a nylon membrane filter (Nytran R). The membrane was probed with ^{32}P labelled intronless BglII-NheI fragment and visualized by autoradiogram (panel B). Lanes Gc, Gw and Cj are individual transformants (G is genomic and C is intronless). Lane Uc is an untransformed control and M is a Bethesda Research Labs (BRL) RNA ladder. Northern analysis shows that ample mRNA is being produced from the glaA promoter in both the intronless and the genomic CBH II producing transformants.

Analysis of rCBH II. Analysis of culture supernatants of selected transformants by SDS polyacrylamide gel electrophoresis (SDS-PAGE) with silver staining (Figure 4A) and western blot analysis (Figure 4B) show rCBH II as a broad heterogeneous band and of a lower mobility, compared to native CBH II. The lanes in both gels designated Cqf, Gqb, Cqa, Cg, Gb, Cf and Ga are individual transformants. The lane designated MW are protein molecular weight markers. The CBH II lane is purified CBH II from T. reesei and the Uc is untransformed A. awamori supernate as a negative control. This is indicative of hyperglycosylation by the host, A. awamori. The purified rCBH II gave a similar pattern upon gel analysis (data not shown). Reaction products analyzed by HPLC confirmed that the reaction product is greater than 95% cellobiose (data not shown).

The FPLC procedure allowed the concentration and purification of native and recombinant forms of CBH II. The enzymatic properties of these enzymes were compared using phosphoric acid-swollen cellulose (PSC) as substrate. The reaction products were analyzed by HPLC and confirmed as cellobiose (>95%). A comparison of specific activities using either PSC or Avicel (0.1% w/v) is shown in Table II.

Table II. Specific Activities of CBH II Enzymes

CBH II Enzyme[a]	Specific Activity (mmol glc equiv/min/mg protein)	
	PSC	Avicel
Native CBH II	4.9	0.13
Recombinant CBH II		
rCBH II-1	3.9	0.09
rCBH II-2	5.4	0.14
E184Q	5.9	0.17
D173N/D175N	0.19	<0.01
D173N	5.9	0.15
D175N	<0.05	<0.01
E244Q	8.8[b]	0.13

[a]rCBH IIs were expressed in Aspergillus and purified from culture filtrates using immunosorption columns. [b]Not yet confirmed in cultures of the same transformant.

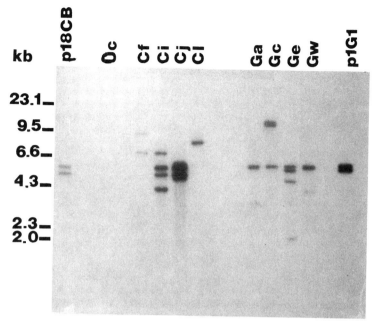

Figure 2. Southern blot analysis of selected CBH II transformants.

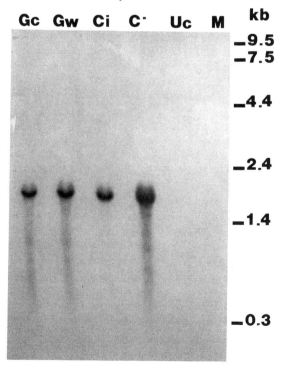

Figure 3. Northern analysis of CBH II transformants.

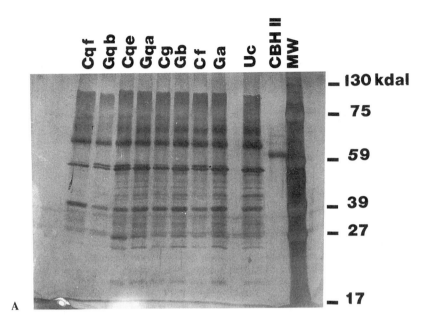

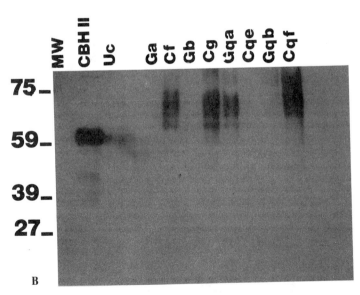

Figure 4. Polyacrylamide gel analysis of CBH II transformants. Panel A shows an SDS-PAGE with silver staining. Panel B shows western blot analysis after blotting gel onto nitrocellulose, incubating with antibody specific for CBH II, and visualizing by ^{125}I protein A.

Catalytic Specificity. Using methylumbelliferyl-β-D-cellobioside (MUC) as a model substrate the rCBH II forms were analyzed for catalytic activity. As shown in Table III all recombinant forms, except for those with the sequence for native CBH II, had the capacity to hydrolyze MUC.

Table III. Specific Activity of Purified Enzymes using 0.8 mM Methylumbelliferyl β-D-Cellobioside as Substrate

Enzyme	Specific Activity (mmol/min/mg protein)
Native	
CBH I	0.086
CBH II	<0.001
Recombinant CBH II	
rCBH II	<0.001
D173N	0.011
D175N	0.014
D173N/D175N	0.010
E184Q	<0.007

In experiments with CBH I and the double mutant D173N/D175N, the kinetic parameters for MUC hydrolysis were determined (Lineweaver-Burk data analysis) and compared. Whereas the native CBH II has no activity against MUC, the double mutant of CBH II has an enzyme-concentration-normalized V_{max} comparable to that of CBH I. (V_{max} = 0.04 µmol min^{-1} mg^{-1} for D173N/D175N, compared with V_{max} = 0.09 µmol min^{-1} mg^{-1} for CBH I). It appears that very small perturbations in the structure near the active site of CBH II permit binding and cleavage of MUC. It is noteworthy that the K_m value for the double mutant (2.27 x 10^{-3} M) is 50 times higher than that of CBH I (4.7 x 10^{-5} M); this suggests an intrinsically higher affinity for such substrates in the CBH I active site.

Ultrastructure Studies. The enzyme-gold affinity technique (27) was used with *Casuarina* branchlet parenchyma cell walls to examine specific binding of CBH II enzymes (Figure 5). The rCBH II enzymes used in this study were native (panel A), D173N/D175N (panel B), E184Q (panel C) and E244Q (panel D). The observations from many fields and several degrees of magnification, including that shown in Figure 5, reveal no significant differences in the observed density and the distribution of gold particles on the cellulose fibrils of the wall material. The evidence for this observed specificity for the cellulose component, compared to other components of the cell wall, has been described previously (27).

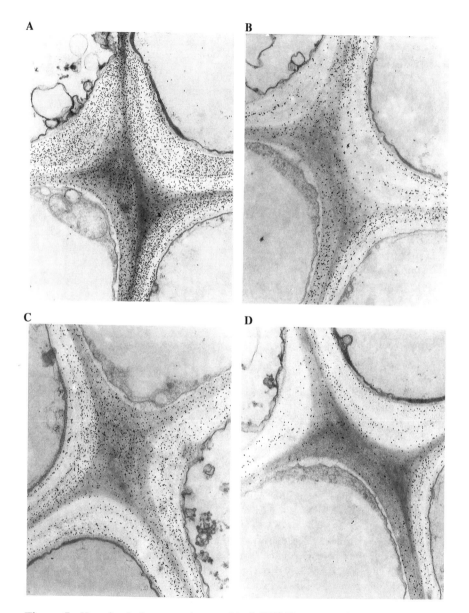

Figure 5. Unstained electron micrograph of CBH II enzyme-linked colloidal gold labeling of *Casuarina* branchlet parenchyma cell wall material. Magnification is 20,000x.

Conclusions

The different effects of the genetic modifications of CBH II enzymes on rate of PSC hydrolysis, as compared to Avicel hydrolysis, reveal that the most significant change is in the rate of Avicel hydrolysis. This seems to indicate a greater dependence on native CBH II structure for the hydrolytic cleavage of the crystalline substrate than for PSC hydrolysis.

In agreement with a previous report from other laboratories (*28*), we observe no activity of native CBH II on methylumbelliferyl-β-D-cellobioside (MUC). With respect to the present studies using MUC and rCBH II enzymes, the D173N, D175N, and D173N/D175N mutants probably allow greater accessibility and greater freedom of substrate binding, transition state formation or product release for small substrates, such as MUC. This in turn may reflect a loss of fidelity with respect to the mechanism of the native depolymerase, which is most clearly exhibited in the dramatic effect of genetic modification on the hydrolytic cleavage of Avicel. The association with the cellulose fibrils, as evidenced by the ultrastructural studies, indicate that the loss of activity is not due to an inability of the cellulose binding domain to provide proximity of enzyme and substrate.

Detailed interpretation of the structural basis for the observed changes in activity and specificity will depend on the resolution of the structure of the active site region either for intact rCBH II forms or their respective catalytic domains.

Acknowledgments

The authors would like to gratefully acknowledge support from The National Renewable Energy Laboratory (NREL; formally SERI; Subcontract HK-7-07122), Genencor International and from the GRI/IFAS co-funded research program. We also greatly appreciate the expert technical assistance of Katalin Vienne in the kinetic studies.

Literature Cited

1. Rouvinen, J.; Bergfors, T.; Teeri, T.; Knowles, J. K. C.; Jones, T. A. *Science* **1990**, *249*, 380-386.
2. Penttila, M.; Lehtovaara, P.; Nevalainen, H.; Bhikhabhai, R.; Knowles, J. *Gene* **1986**, *45*, 253-263.
3. Saloheimo, M.; Lehtovaara, P.; Penttila, M.; Teeri, T. T.; Stahlberg, J.; Johansson, G.; Pettersson, G.; Claeyssens, M.; Tomme, P.; Knowles, J. K. C. *Gene* **1988**, *63*, 11-21.
4. Shoemaker, S.; Schweickart, V.; Ladner, M.; Gelfand, D.; Kwok, S.; Myambo, K.; Innis, M. *Bio/Technol.* **1983**, *1(8)*, 687-690.
5. Chen, C. M.; Gritzali, M.; Stafford, D. W. *Bio/Technol.* **1987**, *5*, 274-278.

6. Teeri, T. T.; Lehtovaara, P.; Kauppinen, S.; Salovuori, I.; Knowles, J. *Gene* **1987,** *51,* 43-52.
7. Penttila, M. E.; Andre, L.; Lehtovaara, P.; Bailey, M.; Teeri, T. T.; Knowles, J. K. C. *Gene* **1988,** *63,* 103-112.
8. Barnett, C. C.; Berka, R. M.; Shoemaker, S. P.; Sumner, L. M.; Ward, M.; Wilson, L. J. *Abstract, 14th Fungal Biology Conference.* **1987.**
9. Paice, M. G.; Jurasek, L. *Adv. Chem. Series.* **1979,** *181,* 361-374.
10. Berka, R. M.; Barnett, C. C. *Biotech. Adv.* **1989,** *7,* 127-154.
11. van Hartingsveldt, W.; Mattern, I. K.; van Zeijl, C. M. J.; Pouwels, P. H.; van den Hondel, C. A. M. J. J. *Mol. Gen. Genet.* **1987,** *206,* 71-75.
12. Buxton, F. P.; Gwynne, D. I.; Davis, R. W. *Gene.* **1985,** *37,* 207-214.
13. Messing, J.; Crea, R.; Seeburg, P. H. *Nucleic Acids Res.* **1981,** *9,* 309-321.
14. Yanisch-Peron, C.; Viera, J.; Messing, J. *Gene.* **1985,** *33,* 103-119.
15. Mead, D. A.; Kemper, B. In *Vectors: A Survey of Molecular Cloning Vectors and Their Uses*; Rodriquez, Denhardt, D. T., Eds.; Butterworth Publishers: Stoneham, MA, 1987; pp. 85-102.
16. Carter, P. *Methods in Enzymology* **1987,** *154,* 382-403.
17. Berka, R.; Ward, M.; Thompson, S.; Fong, K.; Wilson, L.; Lamsa, M.; Gray, G. In *Advances in Gene Technology, Protein Engineering and Production*; Brew, K., Ed.; IRL Press: Washington, DC, 1988.
18. Cullen, D.; Gray, G. L.; Wilson, L. J.; Hayenga, K. J.; Lamsa, M. H.; Rey, M. W.; Norton, S.; Berka, R. M. *Bio/Technol.* **1987,** *5,* 369-376.
19. Ward, M; Wilson, L. J.; Carmona, C.; Turner, G. *Current Genetics* **1988,** *13,* 37-42.
20. Timberlake, W. E.; Barnard, E. C. *Cell* **1981,** *26,* 29-37.
21. Davis, L. G.; Dibner, M. D.; Battey, J. F. *Basic Methods in Molecular Biology;* Elsevier: New York, NY, 1986; pp. 84-87.
22. Sanger, F.; Niclen, S.; Coulson, A. R. *Proc. Nat. Acad. Sci. USA.* **1977,** *74,* 5463-5467.
23. Towbin, H.; Staehlin, T.; Gordon, J. *Proc. Nat. Acad. Sci. USA.* **1979,** *76,* 4350-4354.
24. Nelson, N. J. *J. Biol. Chem.* **1944,** *153,* 375-380.
25. Somogyi, M. J. *J. Biol. Chem.* **1952,** *195,* 19-23.
26. Rosenthal, A. L.; Saifer, A. *Anal. Biochem.* **1973,** *55,* 85-92.
27. Berg, R. H.; Erdos, G. W.; Gritzali, M.; Brown, Jr., R. D. *J. Electron Microscopy Tech.* **1988,** *8,* 371-379.
28. Claeyssens, M.; Van Tilbeurgh, H.; Tomme, P. Wood, T. M.; McRae, S. *Biochem. J.* **1989,** 261, 819-825.

RECEIVED September 16, 1992

Chapter 19

Recombinant β-Glucosidase of *Trichoderma reesei*

Tim Fowler

Genencor International, Inc., 180 Kimball Way,
South San Francisco, CA 94080

Recent advances in the genetic manipulation of *T. reesei* provide a
molecular tool with which the cellulase enzyme composition can be
altered to provide new and useful mixtures. In addition, mutagenesis
experiments can be designed to answer direct questions regarding
cellulase gene regulation and mechanism of enzyme action.
ß-glucosidase is one member of a family of cellulase enzymes that
act synergistically to hydrolyze cellulose to glucose. Studies in our
laboratory have focused on the role of extracellular ß-glucosidase in the
regulation of the other enzymes of the cellulase complex of *T. reesei* and
its function in the production of glucose from cellulose. To this end we
have cloned the gene encoding the extracellular ß-glucosidase (*bgl1*)
from *Trichoderma reesei*. (*1*). Re-introduction of the *bgl1* gene back
into the host in extra copies gives increased expression of ß-glucosidase
and results in a cellulase complex that has an increased rate of glucose
production from cellulosic substrates. Results of *bgl1* gene disruption
experiments and proposed site directed mutagenesis of the enzyme are
described.

In this chapter I will describe the cellulase complex of *Trichoderma reesei* and in
particular the genetic manipulation of this complex to produce novel strains in which the
cellulase complex profile and activity has been altered. I will focus on the extracellular
ß-glucosidase enzyme encoded by the *bgl1* gene.
    Historically, filamentous fungi have been used to produce many enzymes,
antibiotics and other biochemical products. However, methods for DNA-mediated
transformation of industrially important fungi only became generally available in the
mid 80s. This achievement provided a viable alternative to classical genetics for rapid
improvement of existing fungal strains which produce salable commodities. The
industrially important deuteromycete, *Trichoderma reesei*, is an example of such a
fungal species. *T. reesei* secretes large quantities of a hydrolytic mixture of enzymes
that act in concert to degrade crystalline cellulose to glucose. These cellulases are used
in a variety of applications; examples include the extraction of fruit and vegetable juices,
animal feed and silage processing, and malting and brewing. In addition, the

0097–6156/93/0516–0233$06.00/0

introduction of genetic engineering techniques to *Trichoderma* is leading to rapid advances in our understanding and manipulation of the cellulase complex. The cellulase enzyme complex of *T. reesei* consists of two known cellobiohydrolases, CBHI and CBHII (EC 3.2.1.91), at least two endoglucanases, EGI and EGII (EC 3.2.1.4), and at least one ß-glucosidase (EC 3.2.1.21). The endoglucanases and cellobiohydrolases are believed to act synergistically to hydrolyze crystalline cellulose to small cello-oligosaccharides (mainly cellobiose). The small oligo-dextrins are subsequently hydrolyzed to glucose by ß-glucosidase. The exact biochemistry, regulation and synergy between the different cellulases of *T. reesei* are the subject of a great deal of investigation.

Wild type strains of *T. reesei* produce extracellular cellulase at levels of a few grams per liter and in molar ratios of about CBHI (60) : CBHII (20) : EGI (10) : ß-glucosidase (1) *(5,6)*. In the biotechnology industry, selection of *T. reesei* production strains by mutagenesis and screening have resulted in strains capable of secreting in excess of 40 g/L *(38,39)*. The cellulase products from these strains can be further modified by blending with other cellulase preparations (sometimes enriched for specific components). In addition, variation in fermentation conditions enables a measure of control over the ratios of secreted enzymes. However, these methods tend to be expensive and/or labor intensive. Methods for genetic manipulation of *T. reesei* became possible with the introduction of both dominant and auxotrophic markers *(2,3,4)* and techniques such as electroporation and protoplast fusion for introducing foreign DNA into the fungal cells. These techniques are now being employed to manipulate the cellulase complex at the genetic level. Most recently, genetic engineering of *T. reesei* strains enables the complete removal or overproduction of either individual or multiple components of the cellulase complex. This means novel strains with cellulase profiles specifically tailored to defined applications can now be made (See Table I from ref. 7).

The role of the ß-glucosidase component in cellulose hydrolysis and in the regulation of the cellulase complex is currently under investigation at Genencor International. Presumably one function of ß-glucosidase is the breakdown of the cellobiose produced by the cellobiohydrolases and endoglucanases to provide glucose as a carbon source. Another function of ß-glucosidase may be to use glucose (via a transglycosylation reaction) to produce oligosaccharides that have been shown to act as potent inducers of the cellulase complex *(5,41,42)*.

Cell fractionation, immunoflourescence and electron microscopic localization indicate that the majority of ß-glucosidase is associated with the outer integuments of *T. reesei* *(37,43,44,45,46)*. It therefore makes teleological sense that for the organism to make more efficient use of available cellobiose, the major portion of the detectable ß-glucosidase activity remains associated with the cell wall *(8,9,10)*. It is believed that the association of ß-glucosidase with the cell wall is a significant factor in the reduced ability of commercial preparations of cellulase to produce glucose. Improvement of cellulase preparations by the addition of purified ß-glucosidase *(11,12,13)* or isolation of mutant strains of *T. reesei* that have increased levels of ß-glucosidase are possible solutions to this problem *(40)*.

We have begun to investigate the role of the ß-glucosidase enzyme in cellulase system at the molecular level by cloning and sequencing of the extracellular ß-glucosidase gene, *bgl1*, from *T. reesei* *(1)*. We demonstrate that transformation of the *bgl1* gene into the *T. reesei* genome in multiple copies can be used to generate strains with significant increase in extracellular ß-glucosidase activity. Finally site directed mutants of the *bgl1* gene have been created to locate residues central to catalytic activity. The long term goal of these experiments is to identify mutant forms of the ß-glucosidase enzyme that possess novel and useful enzymatic properties. The deletion of the *bgll* gene from *T. reesei* and the use of this strain as a host for the site directed mutants of ß-glucosidase are also described.

Isolation and Overexpression of the *bgll* Gene in *T. reesei.*

We have previously described the cloning and sequencing of the gene encoding the extracellular ß-glucosidase gene (*bgll*) from *T. reesei* (*1*). The primary structure of the deduced extracellular ß-glucosidase protein has several properties of note. The predicted molecular weight of the encoded ß-glucosidase protein is 74,341 daltons. The size and composition is in good agreement with the protein purified by Chirico and Brown (*14*). A 31 amino acid secretion signal peptide precedes the mature amino terminus of ß-glucosidase as deduced from the amino terminal peptide sequence and homologies to the other cellulase genes (*15, 16, 17, 18, 19*). The primary amino acid sequence of ß-glucosidase shows 7 potential N-linked glycosylation sites (*20*). The *bgll* coding region is interrupted by two putative introns of 70 and 64 base pairs that show homology to the consensus splice signals emerging for *T. reesei* and other filamentous fungi (*21*).

The following sections describe experiments in which the cellulolytic capacity of *T. reesei* strains was altered by transformation with extra copies of the *bgll* gene, resulting in the overexpression of extracellular ß-glucosidase. Alternatively, transformation with a vector designed to disrupt the *bgll* gene resulted in a strain with no apparent extracellular ß-glucosidase activity.

The ability to increase expression of interesting and/or commercially valuable proteins by genetic engineering has recently become possible in filamentous fungi. As a general rule increasing the copy number of a fungal gene through transformation usually leads to increased expression of that gene. Recent examples of this phenomenon include glucose oxidase (*goxA*, ref. *31*), glucoamylase (*glaA*, ref. *32*), and prepro-polygalacturonidase II (*pgall*, ref. *33*) expressed in *A. niger*. We have undertaken a similar approach in obtaining enhanced expression of extracellular ß-glucosidase. Extra copies of a genomic clone of *bgll* were introduced into the genome of *T. reesei* using the transformation vector called pSASß-glu (Figure 1).

Positive selection of *T. reesei* transformants containing extra copies of *bgll* was made using the *A. nidulans amdS* gene as a selectable marker (*2*). *Trichoderma* does not contain a functional equivalent of the *amdS* gene and is therefore unable to utilize acetamide as a sole nitrogen source unless the *amdS* gene is stably inherited during transformation. Several stable transformants were seen to contain multiple copies of the *bgll* gene (T. Fowler, unpublished Southern blot results). The cellulase products from these multicopy *bgll* gene transformants showed an increase in the rate of glucose release from Avicel. One transformant was chosen for a more detailed analysis and was shown to contain 5-10 additional copies of the *bgll* gene integrated into the genome, which gave rise to a 4.2 fold increase in *bgll* mRNA levels (See figure 5 from ref. *1*). In addition, data is given for the action of the cellulase preparation (named C5X) from the transformant on cellobiose, Avicel and phosphoric acid swollen cellulose (PSC). An increase in the rate of production of glucose from the cellulosic substrates was observed for each substrate (See Figure 5 from ref. *1*). These data suggest that integration of additional copies of *bgll* in the genome of *T. reesei* leads to an increase in specific message levels and corresponding extracellular protein levels. Furthermore the cellulolytic activity of *T. reesei* strains is specifically improved by transformation with the *bgll* gene.

Increased saccharification observed from relatively pure substrates were an indicator that similar results upon treatment of less well defined cellulosic materials may be obtained. The resulting increase in the rates of hydrolysis may have potential applications for biomass conversion and ethanol production.

Cytolase 123 is a Genencor cellulase preparation from a proprietary *T. reesei* strain. The same strain was used as the parent for transformation with extra copies of *bgl1* resulting in the transformant that produce C5X. A comparison of the action of Cytolase 123 and C5X was made on a cellulosic waste floc from diaper manufacturing (figure 2). The cellulase preparation containing increased levels of ß-glucosidase (C5X) released higher levels of glucose from the diaper waste over time than did an equivalent amount of Cytolase 123.

Pretreatment of a variety of biological waste materials, such as agricultural residues, forestry waste, and municipal solid waste (MSW) gives rise to crude substrates that can subsequently be used in separate hydrolysis fermentation (SHF) or simultaneous saccharification and fermentation reaction (SSF) to produce ethanol (*34*). We were interested in seeing whether the cellulase mixture, C5X, could improve the SSF process by providing more glucose as a substrate to ferment into ethanol. In the SSF process a single vessel is used to mix pretreated MSW, hydrolytic cellulase enzymes and an organism capable of fermenting the released glucose to ethanol (such as the yeast strain *Saccharomyces cerevisiae*). This simplification can be approximated in laboratory shake flask analysis using cellulase enzyme preparations, a cellulosic substrate and a yeast innoculum. Table I shows results from such an experiment on a paper fraction of municipal solid waste using Cytolase 123 and C5X as the cellulase enzyme mixtures.

From this experiment, it appears that the enhanced ß-glucosidase cellulase preparation increases the availability of glucose resulting in increased ethanol production from yeast fermentation. This result is especially pronounced at the lower dosages. One possible explanation for this observation is that higher dosages of either cellulase mixture saturates the system with glucose and the resultant high alcohol levels become rate limiting.

In conclusion, novel cellulase mixtures can be produced from genetic manipulation of a single *T. reesei* strain. In the future these designer strains will result in simplified fermentation protocols and remove the need for supplementation of additional enzymes to existing enzyme preparation. Structural cellulose found in biomass materials is a mixture of crystalline cellulose, hemicellulose and lignin. Further improvement of strains of *T. reesei* for more rapid and complete conversion of cellulosic biomass may include the cloning and overexpression of the genes encoding hemicellulases and ligninolytic enzymes.

Deletion of the *bgl1* gene from *T. reesei*.

We have described how the composition of the cellulase complex of *T. reesei* can be altered by introduction of extra copies of cellulase genes. Conversely, a targeted gene disruption can remove or interrupt cellulase gene coding sequences. Such mutations not only alter the overall composition and mode of action of the cellulase preparation but provide a host into which the disrupted gene can be reintroduced following site directed mutagenesis that is designed to modify the enzyme's activity. In addition, the manipulation of each individual component at the genetic level presents an opportunity to look in new ways at several questions central to the regulation of the cellulase complex and the hydrolysis of cellulose. For example, how is each gene is involved in the induction and regulation of the cellulase complex? What is the contribution of each component in the hydrolysis of cellulosic substrates? What is the exact composition of the *Trichoderma* cellulase complex and multiplicity of the enzyme species?

Mutants of *Trichoderma reesei* lacking the coding sequence for the extracellular ß-glucosidase gene, *bgl1*, were obtained by a targeted gene replacement event (Figure 3). A gene replacement vector was first constructed (illustrated in Figure 3). The vector

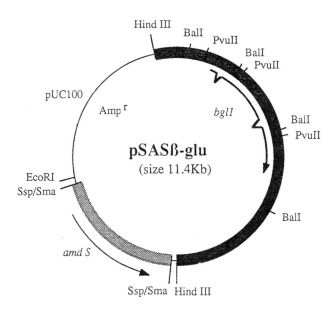

Figure 1. *Trichoderma reesei bgl1* gene overexpression vector pSASß-glu. The genomic *T. reesei bgl1* gene is contained on a 6.0 kb *Hind*III fragment. Figure source: from reference *1*.

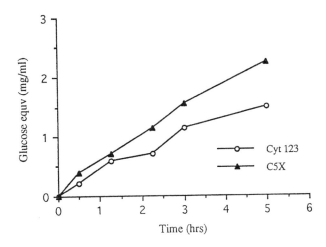

Figure 2. Comparison of Cytolase 123 and C5X action on cellulosic diaper waste. The cellulase mixtures were prepared using the same fermentation conditions. Dosage of the cellulase was 0.4mg enzyme/100mg substrate.

Table I. A Comparison of Cytolase 123 and C5X in the production of Ethanol from Cellulosic Biomass

Cellulase Activity(FPU)/ Gram Cellulose (MSW)	Comparison of Cytolase 123 and C5X [a]	
	Grams EtOH/Liter SSF RXN	
	Cytolase 123	C5X
6	1.3	3.8
12	3.3	4.5
18	4.3	5.5
24	5.0	5.8
30	5.3	5.8
36	5.3	5.8

a) The cellulase activity of a standard batch of Cytolase 123 was calculated and dosed as shown. C5X was then compared to Cytolase 123 by using an equivalent amount of protein.

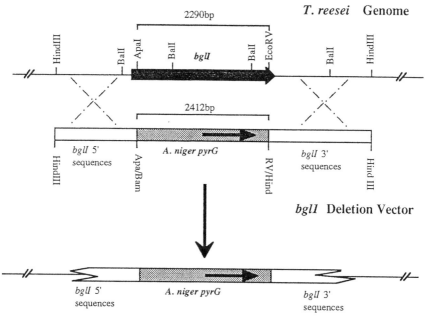

Figure 3. Schematic of the *bgl1* Gene Disruption Strategy.

was digested with *Hind*III to release a linear fragment in which the *bgl1* coding sequences were replaced with the *pyrG* gene from *Aspergillus niger* (*pyrG* encodes an enzyme required in the uridine biosynthetic pathway). Purified linear *Hind*III fragment from the disruption vector was used to transform a *T. reesei* strain P37 *pyrG69*, a uridine requiring auxotroph, to prototrophy. Transformants were screened by dot blot hybridization using *bgl1* coding sequences as a probe. The *bgl1* coding region was shown to be deleted by Southern blot analysis of transformant genomic DNA, as shown by a lack of hybridization signal when compared to the parental strain P37 *pyrG69* (data not shown). To confirm that transcription from the *bgl1* gene had also been disrupted, total RNA was isolated from the deletion transformant and P37 *pyrG69*. Northern blot analysis using the same *bgl1* probe indicated that *bgl1* specific mRNA present in P37 *pyrG69* is absent in the *bgl1* deletion strain (data not shown).

Western blot analysis established that extracellular ß-glucosidase is encoded by the *bgl1* gene. Extracellular ß-glucosidase was purified to near homogeneity by the method of Chirico and Brown (*14*) and used in the production of rabbit polyclonal antibodies. Extracellular protein from the *bgl1* deletion strain and P37, grown under inducing conditions, was separated on a 10-20% SDS polyacrylamide gel, electroblotted onto Nytran and probed using polyclonal antibodies raised against ß-glucosidase. Under conditions of induction, ß-glucosidase protein is observed in the culture broth of strain P37 but not in the *bgl1* deletion strain (data not shown). Interestingly, however, residual ß-glucosidase activity can still be detected using chromogenic substrates although the activity has been reduced by greater than an order of magnitude in comparison to P37 (data not shown). Experiments are currently in progress to determine the nature of this activity.

Other laboratories have attempted to obtain ß-glucosidase deficient strains of *T. reesei* by mutagenesis with either UV light (*35*) or gamma irradiation (*36*) Their inability to obtain non-leaky ß-glucosidase null mutations suggested to the authors that either ß-glucosidase is an essential gene (for example, involved in morphogenesis, Ref. *37*, or as an essential structural component of the cell wall) or there are at least two different ß-glucosidase genes in *T. reesei*. Evidently the extracellular ß-glucosidase encoded by the *bgl1* gene is not essential as demonstrated by the successful selection of a disruption within *bgl1*. Moreover, on the basis of DNA hybridization experiments we have not seen any evidence of sequences showing even weak homology to the *bgl1* gene within the genome of *T. reesei*. If there are other ß-glucosidase enzymes produced by *T reesei* (perhaps responsible for the residual activity on chromogenic substrates described above) they must be genetically distinct from *bgl1*. The lack of signal detection upon Western analysis of the *bgl1* disruption, using antibodies raised against the extracellular ß-glucosidase, argues against other ß-glucosidase enzyme forms arising from post-transcriptional modification of the *bgl1* mRNA or post-translational modification of the ß-glucosidase protein.

Future Directions and Conclusions.

Site Directed Mutagenesis Experiments on *bgl1*.

The deletion of the *bgl1* gene from *T. reesei* provides a host with which to study the role of extracellular ß-glucosidase in the regulation of other enzymes of the cellulase complex and its function in the hydrolysis of cellulose. The effect of the *bgl1* gene deletion on the regulation of the *T. reesei* cellulase genes and the effect on the breakdown of cellulosic materials is currently under investigation. Preliminary studies indicate that in the absence of ß-glucosidase, induction of the other cellulase genes is delayed at the level of transcription and that after a lag the *bgl1* deletion strain is able to utilize cellulose as a carbon source. It is also interesting to note that the *bgl1* deficient strain is able to utilize cellobiose as a carbon source indicating the presence of alternative uptake and utilization mechanisms.

This section describes the use of the *T. reesei* strain containing the *bgl1* disruption as a host for site directed mutants of ß-glucosidase. Significant homology was observed between the deduced ß-glucosidase protein sequence of *T. reesei* and a catalytic ß-glucosidase peptide fragment from *Aspergillus wentii* (*22*). Furthermore, this region is shared by a number of other ß-glucosidases from cellulolytic fungi, yeasts, and bacteria (Table II). A twin aspartic acid motif appears in the form of a highly conserved S/T-D-W box in the first region followed by a conserved G-L-D-M box in the second region. The twin carboxylic acid motif also appears in the catalytic site of lysozyme, giving rise to the notion that the catalytic mechanism of lysozyme and cellulases may be similar (*23*). A comparable aspartic acid/glutamic acid mechanism has been demonstrated for the ß-glucosidase from *Agrobacterium* (Withers et al, personal communication). In addition carboxyl groups have been proposed to be essential for the function of the ß-glucosidase of *Schizophyllum commune* (*24*).

To investigate further the importance of residues conserved between ß-glucosidase enzymes (See Table II) on the catalytic activity of *T. reesei* ß-glucosidase, a series of targeted changes have been introduced into the sequence of the *bgl1* gene. The long term goal of these experiments is to create ß-glucosidase enzymes with altered catalytic activities. Some useful properties that will be screened for are different pH and temperature optima, increased catalytic turnover rates and decreased product inhibition profiles. We are currently in the process of expressing these mutant enzymes (using essentially the same vector as described in Figure 1) as a component of the whole cellulase complex, or individually in a host that has been deleted for other cellulase activities.

Table II. Homology around the known active site residue of *A. wentii* ß-glucosidase with other sequenced ß-glucosidase genes

```
Butyvibrio fibrisolvens                                                    Reference
758  D E W G F E G V V V S D W W G F G E H Y K E V L A G N D I K M G C      25
Ruminococcus albus
685  K Q W G F D G F T M Y D W W A N I N D R G C A P D K N N F A A M V      26
Kluyveromyces fragalis
214  D E W K W D G M L M S D W F G T Y T T A A A I K N G L D I E F P        27
Candida pelliculosa
288  E E L G F Q G F V M T D W G A L Y S G I D A A N A G L D M D M P        28
Saccharomycopsis fibuligera 1
284  E E L G F Q G F V V S D W G A Q L S G V Y S A I S G L D M S M P        29
Saccharomycopsis fibuligera 2
288  E E L G F Q G F V V S D W A A Q M S G A Y S A I S G L D M S M P        29
Aspergillus wentii
?    A Z L G F Z G F V M S D W A A H H A G V S G A L A G L B M G S M P      22
Clostridium thermocellum
220  N E W M H D G F V V S D W G A V N D R V S G L D A G L D L E M P        30
Trichoderma reesei
225  D E L G F P G Y V M T D W N A E H T T V E S A N S G L D M S M P        1
```

The identified active site aspartic acid residue of *A. wentii* is underlined. Conserved residues are shown in bold face type.
Source: adapted from ref. *1*.

Conclusions.

The cellulolytic activity of *T. reesei* strains may be specifically improved by transformation with cloned cellulase genes. Recently transformation methods have been developed for *Trichoderma* that enable the amplification or deletion of the cellulase genes resulting in altered cellulase enzyme profiles. Similar genetic manipulations of *T. reesei* can be performed with the *bgl1* gene encoding the extracellular ß-glucosidase. The extracellular levels of ß-glucosidase can be increased by specific amplification of the *bgl1* gene in the genome of *T. reesei*. Extra copies of *bgl1* lead to increased message levels and a cellulase product that has increased cellulolytic activity. Deletion of the *bgl1* gene from the genome of *T. reesei* enables its role in cellulose hydrolysis to be determined directly. This well defined null-mutation is currently being used in our laboratory to address the questions of ß-glucosidase multiplicity, location, and role in signal transduction. In addition, the *bgl1* disruption strain will be used as a host for mutant ß-glucosidase enzyme forms whose catalytic activity has been altered by site directed mutagenesis.

Acknowledgments.

The previously unpublished data given in Table I and Figure 2 were the result of experiments performed with the help of Sharon Shoemaker, Dan Wendt and Steve Lewis of Genencor International Incorporated. The author would also like to thank Drs. Mikalina Gritzali and Ross D. Brown Jr. (University of Florida, Gainesville) for collaborative efforts with protein purification and biochemical analysis.

Literature Cited.

1. Barnett, C.B.; Berka R.; Fowler T. *Bio/technology* **1991**, *9*, 562-567.
2. Pentitila, M. ; Nevalainen, H.; Ratto, M.; Salminen, E.; Knowles, J. *Gene* **1987**, *61*, 155-164.
3. Smith, J.L.; Bayliss, F. T.; Ward, M. *Cur. Genet.* **1991**, *19*, 27-33.
4. Gruber, F.; Visser, J.; Kubicek, C.P.; de Graaff, L.H. *Curr. Genet.* **1990**, *18*, 71-76.
5. Gritzali, M.; Brown, R.D., Jr. *Advances in Chemistry series.* **1979**, *181*, 237-260.
6. Niku-Paavola, M.L. In: Proceedings of the Soviet Union - Finland seminar on bioconversion of plant raw materials by microorganisms. Tashkent, **1983**, 26-31.
7. Uusitalo, J.M.; Nevalainen, K.M.H.; Harkki, A.M.; Knowles, J.K.C.; Penttila M.E. *J. Biotechnol.* **1991**, *17*, 35-50.
8. Messner, R.; Kubicek, C. P. *Enzyme Microb. Technol.* **1990**, *12*, 685-690.
9. Kubicek, C. P. *Eur. J. Appl. Biotechnol.* **1981**, *13*, 226-231.
10. Messner, R.; Hagspiel, K.; Kubicek, C. P. *Arch. Microbiol.* **1990**, *154*, 150-155.
11. Enari, T.M.; Niku-Paavola, M.L.; Harju ,L.; Lappalainen, A.; Nummi, M. *J. Appl. Biochem.* **1981**, *3*, 157-163.
12. Sternberg, D.; Vijayakumar, P.; Reese, E. T. *Can. J. Microbiol.* **1977**, *23*, 139-147.
13. Kadam, S. K.; Demain, A. L. *Biochem. Biophys. Res. Comm.* **1989**, *161*, 706-711.
14. Chirico, W.J.; Brown, R.D. Jr. *Eur. J. Biochem.* **1987**, *165*, 333-341.
15. Shoemaker, S.; Schweickart, V.; Ladner, M.; Gelfand, D.; Kwok, S.; Myambo, K.; Innis, M. *Bio/Technology* **1983**, *1*, 691-696.

16. Chen, M.C.; Gritzali, M.; Stafford, W.D.   *Bio/Technology* **1987**, *5*, 274-278.
17. Teeri, T. T.; Lehtovaara, P.; Kauppinen, S.; Salovuori, I.; Knowles, J.K.C. *Gene* **1987**, *51*, 43-52
18. Penttila, M.; Lehtovaara, P.; Nevalainen, H.; Bhikhabhai, R.; Knowles, J.K.C.   *Gene* **1986**, *45*, 253-263.
19. Saloheimo, M.; Lehtovaara, P.; Penttila, M.; Teeri, T.T.; Stahlberg, J.; Pettersson, G.; Claeyssens, M.; Tomme, P.; Knowles J.K.C.   *Gene* **1988**, *63*, 11-21.
20. Gavel, Y.; Heijne von, G.   *Protein Engineering* **1990**, *3*, 433-442.
21. Gurr, S. J.; Unkles, S. E.; Kinghorn J. R.   In: Gene structure in eukaryotic microbes. Kinghorn J. R. (Ed.) IRL Press. **1987**, 93-139.
22. Bause, E.; Legler, G.   *Biochim. Biophys. Acta*.   **1980**, *626*, 459-465.
23. Paice, M.G.; Jurasek, L.   *Adv. Chem. Ser.* **1979**, *181*, 361-374
24. Clarke, A. J.   *Biochim. Biophys. Acta*. **1990**, *1040*, 145-152.
25. From a proprietaty Genentech database.
26. Ohmiya, K.; Takano, M.; Shimizu S.   *Nucleic Acids Research* **1990**, *18*, 671.
27. Raynal, A.; Gerbaud, C.; Francingues, M.C.; Guerineau, M.   *Curr. Genet.* **1987**, *12*, 1987.
28. Kohchi, C.; Toh-e, A.   *Nucleic Acids Research* **1985**, *13*, 6273-6282.
29. Machida, M.; Ohtsuki, I.; Fukui, S.; Yamashita, I.   *App. Env. Micro.* **1988**, *54*, 3147-3155.
30. Grabnitz, F.; Ruecknagel, K.P.; Seiss, M.; Staudenbauer, W.L.   *Mol. Gen. Genet.* **1989**, *217*, 70-76.
31. Whittington, H.; Kerry Williams, S.; Bidgood, K.; Dodsworth, N.; Peberdy, J.; Dobson, M.; Hinchliffe, E.; Ballance, D.J.   *Curr. Genet.* **1990**, *18*, 531-536.
32. Fowler, T.; Berka, R.; Ward, M.   *Curr. Genet.* **1990**, *18*, 537-545
33. Bussink, H.J.D.; Kester, H.C.M.; Visser, J.   *FEMS Lett.* **1990**, *273*, 127-130.
34. Gauss, W.F.; Suzuki, S.; Takagi, M.   U.S. Patent #3990944 **1976**.
35. Mishra, S.; Rao, S.; Deb, J.K.   *J. Gen. Micro.* **1989**, *135*, 3459-3465.
36. Strauss, J.; Kubicek, C.P.   *J. Gen. Micro.* **1990**, *136*, 1321-1326.
37. Jackson, M.A.; Talburt, D.E.   *Exp. Micol.* **1988**, *12*, 203-216.
38. Durand, H.; Baron, M.; Calmels, T.; Tiraby, G.   In : Biochemistry and Genetics of Cellulose Degradation, Aubert, J.-P.; Beguin, P. and Millet, J. (eds), New York, Academic Press. **1988a**, 135-151.
39. Durand, H.; Clanet, M.; Titalby, G.   *Enzyme Microb. Technol.* **1988b**, *10*, 341-345.
40. Kowamori, M.; Ado, Y.; Takasawa, S.   *Agr. Biol Chem.* **1986**, *50*, 2477-2482.
41. Valheri, M.P.; Leisola, M.; Kaupinnen, V.   *Biotechnol. Lett.* **1979**, *1*, 41-46.
42. Kubicek, C.K.   *J. Gen. Microbiol.* **1987**, *133*, 1481-1487.
43. Messner, R.; Hagspiel, K.; Kubicek, C.P.   *Arch. Microbiol.* **1990**, *154*, 150-155.
44. Sprey, B.   *FEMS Microbiol. Lett.* **1986**, *36*, 287-292.
45. Umile, C.; Kubicek, C.P.   *FEMS Microbiol. Lett.* **1986**, *34*, 291-295.
46. Usami, S.; Kirimura, K.; Imura, M.; Morikawa, S.   *J. Ferm. Bioeng.* **1990**, *70*, 185-187.

RECEIVED March 31, 1992

Chapter 20

Structure–Function Relationships in Cellulase Genes

David B. Wilson

Section of Biochemistry, Molecular and Cell Biology, Cornell University, Ithaca, NY 14853

Cellulases are mechanistically interesting because the hydrolysis of crystalline cellulose requires the action of a set of enzymes acting together, despite the fact that all of the enzymes catalyze the hydrolysis of a β-1,4-linkage between two glucose residues. Genetic engineering techniques are being applied to cellulase genes in order to determine the mechanism of action of cellulases and to try to engineer more active cellulases. This review describes various approaches currently used to improve cellulases and defines new directions for recombinant cellulase technology.

Cellulases are being actively studied because of the strong interest in commercializing a process for the conversion of biomass cellulose to ethanol. A major problem in such a process is the high cost of cellulase, which could be reduced from about 40% of the total cost to 2% if cellulases having a 20-fold higher specific activity could be developed (1). While it is easy to visualize how an exocellulase and an endocellulase might cooperate in cellulose hydrolysis, it is difficult to see how exocellulases could be synergistic to each other (i.e., in multi-exocellulase systems). Yet, selected exocellulases display about as much synergism as do an exocellulase and endocellulase (2).

There are several reasons for cloning cellulase genes. One is to determine the amino acid sequence of a cellulase by sequencing the DNA of the cloned cellulase gene and then translating the open reading frame. Another is to introduce a cloned gene into an organism that does not produce cellulases and that can express the gene at a high level in order to simplify the purification of the cellulase it encodes or to create useful microorganisms by adding a cellulase gene to an organism that lacks either a specific type of cellulase gene or any cellulase genes. A third is to use a cloned gene to carry out region specific mutagenesis, site directed mutagenesis, or domain shuffling experiments which can help determine the role of specific residues

0097–6156/93/0516–0243$06.00/0

or domains in the function of the cellulase encoded in the cloned gene. A fourth is to study the role of modification, such as glycosylation on enzyme activity. *Thermomonospora fusca* E_2 is an endoglucanase that is lightly glycosylated (~2% sugar). When the *T. fusca* E_2 gene is expressed in *Streptomyces lividans*, the E_2 produced is not glycosylated and yet its enzymatic activity is nearly identical to that of *T. fusca* E_2 (*3,4*).

All of these reasons apply to any gene encoding any protein; but the second and third reasons are particularly important for cellulase genes, since most cellulolytic microorganisms contain a number of cellulase genes, thus making it difficult to isolate mutations in them. Furthermore, because some cellulases display synergism (i.e., the activity of the mixture is greater than the sum of the activities of the enzymes acting alone), traces of an endocellulase in a purified exocellulase can significantly alter its apparent properties. We have seen this with *T. fusca* cellulase E_3. Our earlier preparations contained low levels of activity on carboxymethyl cellulose (CMC) which comigrated with E_3 during polyacrylamide gel electrophoresis. Recently, we found that the CMCase activity could be removed by affinity chromatography, and the new preparation had significantly less activity on filter paper than our original preparation (*2*). However, when the new E_3 preparation was assayed on filter paper with an endocellulase or with the exocellulase, cellobiohydrolase I (CBH I) from *Trichoderma reesei*, the new E_3 preparation gave a slightly higher activity than our original sample. This result shows that the change in activity of E_3 was not caused by denaturation, but probably was due to the removal of an endoglucanase that contaminated our original E_3 preparations. Similar results were reported for cellobiohydrolases I and II purified from *Penicillum pinophilum* (*5*). In this paper, it was shown that the addition of very small amounts of an endoglucanase to highly purified preparations of *P. pinophilum* CBH I and CBH II could dramatically increase the activity of mixtures of these enzymes on either cotton or Avicel. The problems caused by not removing the last traces of endoglucanases from exocellulases can be avoided if noncellulolytic host strains containing only a single cloned exocellulase gene are used as the source of the enzyme.

Certain anaerobic bacteria, such as *Clostridium thermocellum*, assemble their cellulases in large particles (called cellulosomes) on their outer surface (*6,7*). Cloning and expression of cellulase genes often provides the best way to obtain active preparations of an individual cellulase from such organisms. This is due to the difficulty in isolating individual cellulases in an active form from cellulosomes. In one case, a cloned *C. thermocellum* cellulase was not only obtained in large amounts from *E. coli* cells carrying the cloned gene, but the enzyme from the cloned strain was also crystallized (*8*).

Many different cellulase genes have been cloned from a number of species of bacteria, fungi, and plants, and these studies have been recently reviewed (*9*). Over 70 cellulase genes have been sequenced and comparisons of these sequences show that the regions coding for the catalytic domains can be grouped into seven families, with the sequences within each family showing some similarity with all the members of that family (*10*). One family contains eight xylanase genes, as well as two cellulase genes. The fact that xylanases and cellulases can have similar sequences is not surprising, because some hydrolytic enzymes have activity on both cellulose and xylan (*11,12*).

From work with other proteins, it is likely that the three-dimensional structures of all of the members of a cellulase family will be quite similar in their overall polypeptide folding pattern, although there will be significant differences that account for the specific properties of each enzyme. It is also likely that the structures of enzymes in different families will show few similarities. At this time, only two native cellulases have been crystallized and both of them were unable to bind to cellulose, thus indicating the absence of a cellulose binding domain (*8,13*). It has been possible to crystallize the catalytic domains of several cellulases and the three-dimensional structure of *T. reesei* CBH II has been determined to 2.7 Å resolution by X-ray crystallography (*13*). We have crystallized the catalytic subunit of *T. fusca* E$_2$ (*15*), which belongs to the same cellulase family as *T. reesei* CBH II, even though it is an endocellulase. We have determined the three-dimensional structure of the E$_2$ catalytic subunit and our 1.8 Å model has the same basic conformation as *T. reesei* CBH II, however, its active site is present in a cleft rather than in a tunnel as it is in CBH II. These results confirm the prediction that cellulases from the same family will have a similar overall three-dimensional structure, and a careful comparison of the two structures should provide detailed information about some of the important structural differences between exocellulases and endocellulases.

One property of cellulases and xylanases that appears to be constant among the members of a given cellulase family is the stereochemistry of cleavage. Some cellulases invert the conformation of the glycoside linkage during cleavage while others retain the β-conformation in the product. Thirteen cellulases and three xylanases have been studied at this time, including members of five different families, and all members of a given family catalyze hydrolysis with the same stereochemistry (*16,20*).

Cellulose Binding Domains

Genetic engineering techniques currently are being used to study the role of cellulose binding domains in cellulase function. These domains are present in many bacterial and fungal cellulases (*21-23*) and they can be present at either the N-terminal or C-terminal end of the catalytic domain. Since cellulases within the same gene family can differ in the location of their cellulose binding domain, the location may not be critical. Most bacterial cellulose binding domains show some homology with each other, even then the catalytic domains belong to different families (*10*). Fungal cellulase binding domains have a very different sequence from the bacterial binding domains and are much smaller (33 amino acids (aa) long rather than 100 aa)(*24*). The three dimensional structure of the *T. reesei* CBH I cellulose binding domain has been determined by two dimensional NMR, but it is not yet clear how it binds to cellulose (*25*). Studies of a *Cellulomonas fimi* cellulose binding domain, that was purified from a strain containing a modified gene that only encoded the binding domain, have shown that the binding domain disrupts the structure of cellulose fibers as seen in the electron microscope (*26*). The cellulose binding domain appears to function like the C$_1$ activity postulated many years ago (*27*); that is, it disrupts the structure of cellulose without catalyzing its hydrolysis. These results suggest that the binding domain of a cellulase not only binds the enzyme to cellulose, but also helps disrupt the interactions between cellulose molecules that make cellulose so resistant to digestion.

This probably explains why cellulases that do not have binding domains have little activity on crystalline cellulose (28).

Genetic Engineering Studies

Genetic engineering has been used to produce proteins that only contain a cellulose binding domain (26), or that only contain a catalytic domain (29), or to add a cellulose binding domain to enzymes that lack them (30). This was first done with E. coli alkaline phosphatase and the modified enzyme retained activity and could be immobilized on cellulose (30). We have attached a cellulose binding domain to the C-terminus of a Bacteroides ruminicola catalytic domain (31). The native enzyme did not bind tightly to cellulose, but the modified enzyme did (31) Furthermore, the modified enzyme had a specific activity on acid swollen cellulose that was ten times that of the original enzyme and its activity on ball milled cellulose was eight times that of the original enzyme. The modified enzyme still had little activity on Avicel, but, unlike that native enzyme, it was able to synergize with an exocellulase in Avicel digestion (31). These experiments confirm the results of previous experiments in which removal of the binding domain from active cellulases reduced their activity on insoluble substrates, but not on soluble ones and shows that at least some CMCase catalytic domains can hydrolyze insoluble cellulose when joined to a cellulose binding domain.

Cloned cellulase genes have been introduced into organisms that ferment glucose to ethanol efficiently, such as yeast or Zymomonas, to try to create organisms that can ferment cellulose to ethanol (32-34). At this time none of these modified organisms degrade cellulose fast enough to give a significant rate of ethanol production from cellulose. This is not surprising, since all known cellulolytic organisms produce several cellulases. The cen A and cex genes of Cellulomonas fimi were cloned on the same plasmid, and both were introduced into yeast (34). The yeast transformants had some activity on crystalline cellulose, but it was less than 0.1% of the activity produced by T. reesei, the most active cellulolytic organism. This low activity is probably due to low expression and the fact that the cex enzyme has a much higher activity on xylan than on cellulose. The challenge is to introduce a set of cellulase genes into the organism and get them all expressed and secreted at a high level.

Cloned cellulase genes have also been transformed back into the parent strain in order to alter the composition of the crude cellulase mixture produced by the strain so as to alter its specific activity. This has been done with T. reesei, where the gene for endoglucanase I (egl I) was introduced into both a while type strain and a strain in which the cellobiohydrolase I gene (cbh I) was inactivated (35). The egl I gene was present in an expression vector which contained both the cbh I promoter and terminator regions. Stable transformants were isolated in which the egl I gene had inserted at the chromosomal cbh I locus in both the wild type and cbh I negative strains. The transformed wild type strain made two times more endoglucanase I (EG I) than the parent strain, but the overall activity on filter paper of the crude cellulase was unchanged from that of the parent strain. The cbh I negative mutant strain carrying the egl I gene made about four times more EG I than the wild type strain, presumably because CBH I makes up 60% of the total protein produced by the wild type strain, thus its absence allowed a higher level of expression of the cloned egl I gene.

A similar experiment has been carried out in which the gene for CBH II was transformed into wild type *T. reesei* (*36*). Several stable strains were isolated that produced from two to three times more CBH II than the wild type. These trains also had more filter paper activity than the parent strain, but did not produce cellulase complex with a higher specific activity, because the amount of protein they secreted also increased several fold (*36*). In these studies, there was no correlation between the number of *cbh* II genes present in a given transformant and the amount of CBH II produced where the number of *cbh* II genes present in different strains ranged from 10 to 20 (*36*).

Site directed mutagenesis of potentially important residues in cellulases has been reported even though detailed structural information is only available for a few cellulases. Rouvinen et al. (*14*) identified two Asp residues (Asp^{175} and Asp^{221}) in the active site of *T. reesei* CBH II in their three dimensional structure that were also conserved in most related cellulases. These Asp residues were converted to Ala by site directed mutagenesis. The Asp^{175} to Ala ^{175} mutant retained 20% of the wild type activity, whereas the Asp^{221} to Ala^{221} mutant was inactive. Thus, Asp^{221} appears to be directly involved in catalysis while Asp^{175} may function to alter the pK of Asp^{221}.

Another way to identify important catalytic residues is to look for residues that are conserved in members of a given cellulase family. Baird et al. (*37*) found a sequence Asn-Glu-Pro that was present in 16 members of cellulase family A. They converted the Glu residue in this sequence in both a *Bacillus polymyxa* (Glu^{167}), and a *Bacillus subtilis* endoglucanase, to Gln. In each case, the modified cellulase had less than 5% of its original activity as tested by a CMC overlay assay of the mutant colonies. Activity was restored when the mutant genes were changed back to the original sequence, proving that it was the Glu to Gln change that inactivated the enzymes rather than secondary mutations. These workers changed two other nonconserved Glu residues in the *B. subtilis* enzyme to either Ala, Asp, or Pro, and all of the mutants retained activity. Py et al. (*38*) have studied another member of cellulase family A, *Erwinia chrysanthemi* EG2, by site directed mutagenesis. They found that conversion of either Glu^{133} or His^{98} to Ala gave proteins that did not have activity (less than 0.25%) on either CMC or p-nitrophenyl-β-D-cellobioside. Both mutants produced proteins that bound tightly to Avicel, reacted with antibodies against EG2, and had the correct molecular weight. At this time, no information is available to determine whether the mutations prevented correct folding of the protein or inactivated essential residues. Glu^{133} in EG2 is similar to Glu^{167} in the *B. polymyxa* CMCase.

Chemical Studies

Chemical modification studies also have been used to identify potential active site residues in cellulases. One such study proposed that either Glu^{126}, Asp^{130}, or Asp^{132} of *T. reesei* CBH I was an essential residue (*39*). This proposal was tested by site directed mutagenesis experiments in which Glu^{126} was changed to Gln, Asp^{130} to Asn, and Asp^{132} to Ala (*40*). Each of these mutations retained at least 30% of the wild type activity, showing that none of the residues was essential. Surprisingly, when Glu^{127} in *T. reesei* EG I, which is the equivalent of Glu^{126} in CBH I, was changed to Gln, the enzyme lost all activity. All the mutant enzymes in this study were produced in yeast which extensively glycosylates the enzymes. Mutant EG I appeared to be more extensively glycosylated than wild type EG I and overglycosylated enzyme from the wild type strain did not have activity. This result suggests that overglycosylation may have caused the loss of activity in the Glu^{127} mutant. These experiments on *T. reesei* CBH I show the danger of overinterpreting chemical modification experiments, which can give incorrect results due to secondary changes in the enzyme. Experiments using site directed mutagenesis also have to be interpreted carefully, especially when the mutations reduce activity, since the mutation can prevent the protein from folding correctly, giving the appearance of effecting an essential catalytic residue. This is probably what has occurred with the EG I Gln^{127} mutant, since it appears unlikely that the conversion of a Glu residue to a Gln residue would lead to a dramatic change in glycosylation, unless it changed the folding of the protein.

A combination of chemical mutagenesis and site directed mutagenesis was used to identify a residue that was important, but not essential, for cellulase function. Chemical modification of a single His residue resulted in a loss of 70%-80% of the activity of *Clostridium thermocellum* endoglucanase D (Cel D) as measured with 2-chloro-4-nitrophenyl-β-D-cellobioside (*41*). Attempts to identify the modified His by digestion and peptide fractionation were inconclusive because several His residues were modified at similar rates. All 12 His residues in Cel D were converted individually to Ala or to Ser by site directed mutagenesis. Six of the mutants retained 80% or more of the original activity, whereas the activity of the other six ranged from 2% to 25%. The residue that was modified in the native enzyme was determined by reacting each of the last six mutants with diethyl pyrocarbonate (DEPC), because serine does not react with DEPC. Only the mutant where His^{516} was changed to Ser was unaffected by DEPC. This result proved that His^{516} was the residue that had been modified in the wild type enzyme. Consistent with this conclusion is the fact that this mutant retained 25% of the wild type activity and His^{516} is the only His residue conserved in members of family E.

The results of these site directed mutagenesis experiments show the power of this approach in determining whether a specific residue in a cellulase is or is not essential for activity. Furthermore, they strongly support the proposal (*42*) that carboxyl side chains play an essential role in cellulase activity. However, many more experiments are needed before we have a clear understanding of the molecular mechanisms by which the different types of cellulases catalyze cellulose hydrolysis.

Literature Cited

1. Lynd, L.R.; Cushman, J.H.; Nichols, R.J.; Wyman, C.E. *Science* **1991**, *251*, 1318-1323.
2. Irwin, D.; Wilson, D.B., manuscript in preparation.
3. Ghangas, G.S.; Wilson, D.B. *Appl. Environ. Microbiol.* **1988**, *54*, 2521-2526.
4. Spezio, M. unpublished.
5. Wood, T.; McCrae, S.; Bhat, K. *Biochem J.* **1989**, *260*, 37-43.
6. Kobayashi, T.; Romaniec, M.P.M.; Fauth, U.; Demain, A.L. *Appl. Environ. Microbiol.* **1990**, *56*, 3040-3046.
7. Lamed, R.; Setter, E.; Bayer, E.A. *J. Bacteriol.* **1986**, *156*, 828-836.

8. Joliff, G.; Beguin, P.; Joy, M.; Millet, J.; Peyter, A.; Poljak, R.; Avbert, J.-P. *Bio/Technology* **1986**, *4*, 896-900.
9. Beguin, P.; Gilkes, N.R.; Kilburn, D.G.; Miller, R.C.; O'Neill, G.P.; Warren, R.A.J. *Crit. Rev. Biotechnol.* **1987**, *6*, 129-162.
10. Gilkes, N.R.; Henrissat, B.; Kilburn, D.G.; Miller, R.C. Jr.; Warren, R.A.J. *Microbiol. Reviews* **1992**, *55*, 303-315.
11. Shoemaker, S.; Watt, K.; Tsitousky, G.; Cox R. *Bio/Technology* **1983**, *1*, 687-690.
12. Woods, J.R.; Hudman, J.F.; Gregg, K.J. *Gen. Microbiol.* **1989**, *135*, 2543-2549.
13. Katsube, Y. personal communication.
14. Rouvian, J.; Bergfors, T.; Teeri, T.; Knowles, J.K.C.; Jones, T.A. *Science* **1990**, *249*, 380-386.
15. Spezio, M.; Wilson, D.B.; Karplus, A.D. manuscript in preparation.
16. Gebler, J.; Gilkes, N.; Claeyssens, M.; Wilson, D.; Beguin, P.; Wakarchuk, W.; Kilburn, D.; Miller, R.; Warren, R.A.; Withers, S. *J. Biol. Chem.* **1992** in press.
17. Withers, S.G.; Dombroski, D.; Berven, L.A.; Kilburn, D.F.; Miller, R.C. Jr.; Warren, R.A.J.; Gilkes, N.R. *Biochem. Biophys. Res. Commun.* **1986**, *139*, 487-494.
18. Meinke, A.; Braun, C.; Gilkes, N.R.; Kilburn, D.G.; Miller, R.C. Jr.; Warren, R.A.J. *J. Bacteriol* **1991**, *173*, 308-314.
19. Knowles, J.K.C.; Lehtovaara, P.; Murray, M.; Sinnott, M.L. *J. Chem. Soc. Chem. Commun.* **1988**, 1401-1402.
20. Claeyssens, M.; van Tilbeurgh, H.; Kamerling, J.P.; Berg, J.; Vrsnska, M.; Biely, P. *Biochem. J.* **1990**, *270*, 251-256.
21. van Tilbeurgh, H.; Tomme, P.; Claeyssens, M.; Bhikhabhai, R.; Pettersson, G. *FEBS Lett.* **1986**, *204*, 223-227.
22. Saloheimo, M.; Lehtovaara, P.; Penttila, M.; Teeri, T.; Stahlberg, J.; Johansson, G.; Pettersson, G.; Claeyssens, M.; Tomme, P.; Knowles, J. *Gene* **1988**, *63*, 11-21.
23. Ong, E.; Greenwood, J.M.; Gilkes, N.R.; Kilburn, D.G.; Miller, R.C. Jr.; Warren, R.A.J. *Trends Biotechnol.* **1989**, *7*, 239-243.
24. Johansson, G.; Stahlberg, J.; Lindeberg, G.; Engstrom, A.; Pettersson, G. *FEBS Lett.* **1989**, *243*, 389-393.
25. Kraulis, P.; Clore, M.; Nilges, M.; Jones, A.; Pettersson, G.; Knowles, J.; Gronenborn, A. *Biochemistry* **1989**, *28*, 7241-7257.
26. Din, N.; Gilkes, N.R.; Tekant, B.; Miller, R.C. Jr.; Anthony, R.; Warren, J.; Kilburn, D.G. *Bio/Technology* **1992**, *9*, 1096-1099.
27. Reese, E.T.; Sui, R.G.H.; Levinson, H.S.S. *Bacteriol.* **1950**, *59*, pp. 485-497.
28. Klyosov, A. *Biochemistry* **1990**, *29*, 10577-10585.
29. Irwin, D.; Wilson, D.B. manuscript in preparation.
30. Greenwood, J.M.; Gilkes, N.R.; Kilburn, D.G.; Miller, R.C. Jr.; Warren, R.A.J. *FEBS Lett.* **1989**, *244*, 127-131.
31. Maglione, G.; Russell, J.B.; Wilson, D.B. manuscript in preparation.
32. Van Arsdell, J.N.; Kwok, S.; Schweickart, V.L.; Ledner, M.B.; Gelford, D.H.; Innis, M.A. *Bio/Technology* **1987**, *5*, 60-64.
33. Brestic-Goachet, N.; Gunasekaran, P.; Cami, B.; Baratti, J.C. *J. Gen. Microbiol.* **1989**, *135*, 893-902.

34. Wong, W.K.R.; Corry, C.; Parekh, R-S.; Parekh, S.R.; Wayman, M.; Davies, R.W.; Kilburn, D.G.; Skipper, N. *Bio/Technology* **1988**, *6*, 713-719.
35. Harkki, A.; Mantyla, A.; Pentilla, M.; Muttilainen, S.; Buhler, R.; Suominen, P.; Knowles, J.; Nevalainen, H. *Enzyme Microb. Technol.* **1991**, *13*, 227-233.
36. Kubicek-Pranz, E.; Gruber, F.; Kubicek, C.J. *Biotechnol.* **1991**, *20*, 83-94.
37. Baird, S.D.; Hefford, M.A.; Johnson, D.A.; Sung, W.L.; Yaguchi, M.; Seligy, V.A. *Biotechmical and Biophys. Res. Commun.* **1990**, *169*, 1035-1039.
38. Py, B.; Bortoli-German, I.; Haiech, J.; Chippaux, M.; Barras, F. *Protein Engin.* **1991**, *4*, 325-333.
39. Tomme, P.; Claeyssens, M. *FEBS Lett.* **1989**, *243*, 239-243.
40. Mitsuishi, Y.; Nitisinprasert, S.; Saloheimo, M.; Biese, I.; Reinikainen, T.; Claeyssens, M.; Keranen, S.; Knowles, J.; Teeri, T. *FEBS Lett.* **1990**, *275*, 135-138.
41. Tomme, P.; Chauvaux, S.; Beguin, P.; Millet, J.; Aubert, J-P.; Claeyssens, M. *J. Biol. Chem.* **1991**, *266*, 10313-10318.
42. Clarke, A.J.; Yaguchi, M. *Eur. J. Biochem.* **1985**, *149*, 233-238.

RECEIVED June 12, 1992

Chapter 21

Clostridium thermocellum Cellulosome

New Mechanistic Concept for Cellulose Degradation

J. H. David Wu

Department of Chemical Engineering, University of Rochester,
Rochester, NY 14627–0166

Clostridium thermocellum is an anaerobic and thermophilic bacterium
with an optimum growth temperature of 60°C. It produces an
extracellular cellulase system shown to be highly active on crystalline
cellulose. The Avicelase activity (i.e., activity against Avicel, a
microcrystalline cellulose) of this cellulase system resides mainly in an
unusually large protein aggregate called the cellulosome. The
cellulosome is now known to contain multiple, discrete subunits and
comprise a total molecular weight of millions. An apparent ordering
to this supramolecular structure, first indicated by organization of the
genetic elements, may provide a basis for the cellulase action attributed
to *C. thermocellum* and related surface-active cellulase producers.

The *C. thermocellum* cellulosome aggregate has a very stable quaternary structure,
resistant to most detergents and other dissociating reagents (*1,2*). Although the whole
complex has been isolated and characterized, functions of individual subunits remain
unclear. Purification of individual components from the cellulosome appears to be a
prohibitive task. This issue has seriously impeded the mechanistic study of this
cellulase system.

The first insight into the mechanism of cellulose degradation by the cellulosome,
and its organization, was obtained when the two major subunits, CelL (or S_L) and
CelS (or S_S), which degrade crystalline cellulose synergistically, were identified (*3*).
An "anchor-enzyme model" was proposed to explain the synergism between these two
subunits (*4*). In this model, CelL functions as an anchor on the cellulose surface for
CelS, the catalytic subunit. This mechanism is clearly different from the
well-accepted model based on the fungal cellulase system. Its novelty has prompted
interest in cloning the *celL* and *celS* genes. Recently, the *celL* (*5,6*) and *celS* (*7,8*)
genes have been successfully cloned. Their DNA sequences reveal surprisingly
striking features which shed more light onto how the cellulosome is organized.

Furthermore, the group at Institute Pasteur, France, has independently discovered that other catalytic subunits, CelD and XynZ, also complex with the anchor CelL (9), as CelS does. The complex formation involves specific ligand-receptor interaction (10). These results confirm the original anchor-enzyme model and expand it into a more sophisticated picture, allowing initial construction of the basic structure of cellulosome. Not surprisingly, this structure depicts a novel mechanistic concept for both the supramolecular organization and enzymatic cellulose degradation.

In this article, the recent progress in cellulosome research leading to the unveiling of a proposal for its complex quaternary structure will be reviewed.

Properties of the *C. thermocellum* Cellulase System

A very important characteristic of the *C. thermocellum* cellulase system is its high specific activity toward crystalline cellulose. A comparison based on equal amounts of extracellular protein (11,12) demonstrates that the *C. thermocellum* cellulase system is much more active on cotton and Avicel than *Trichoderma reesei* cellulase. In fact, the cellulase system degrades Avicel faster than phosphoric acid-swollen Avicel (11), indicating it prefers crystalline cellulose to amorphous substrate. This is very unusual, because most cellulase systems more readily degrade amorphous substrates.

Another unusual property of the *C. thermocellum* cellulase system is its requirement for Ca^{++} for the maximum activity (12). Recent evidence indicates that Ca^{++} serves to stabilize the protein at high temperature (13,14). Ethylenediaminetetraacetate (EDTA) completely inhibits Avicelase activity (12). The cellulase system is also inhibited by certain apolar chelating agents (15). This inhibition is reversed by mixture of Fe^{++} and Fe^{+++}, suggesting that iron is involved in its catalytic action.

As expected from its anaerobic and thermophilic nature, the clostridial cellulase has a high thermostability and is sensitive to oxygen inactivation (12,15). Similar to the fungal system, it is also subject to feedback inhibition by cellobiose and, to a much lesser extent, glucose (16).

The Cellulosome: A Multicomponent and Multifunctional Protein Complex

The preference for a crystalline substrate and the requirement for Ca^{++}, and possibly iron, are unique properties among cellulases. These observations strongly suggest that the clostridial cellulase system may adopt a completely different enzymatic mechanism than those derived from the fungal system. Indeed, it did not take long for researchers to realize that this system exists as an extremely unusual multisubunit protein complex, termed cellulosome (1). Isolation and characterization of the cellulosome have been reviewed by Lamed and Bayer (17,18). Only a brief historical sketch will be provided here.

The Cellulosome as a Cellulose-Binding Factor. The cellulosome was first purified as the cellulose-binding factor from the YS strain of *C. thermocellum* based on the ability to bind to cellulose (2). Under the electron microscope, these molecules look like a group of closely related complexes with complicated quaternary structure. The complexes have diameters of about 18 nm and estimated molecular weights of about 2.1 million Daltons. At least fourteen protein subunits (S1 - S14) with molecular weights ranging from 210 to 48 KDa are associated with the isolated aggregates as revealed by SDS-PAGE. At least eight components of the cellulosome are active against CMC (i.e., determined by a CMC-overlay assay of the components separated by SDS-PAGE).

Among the subunits, S8 (M_r = 75,000) and S1 (M_r = 210,000) are the two most abundant species. The strikingly large size and abundance of S1 suggests that it probably plays an important role in the function of cellulosome. This role is suggested by studies on a mutant (AD2 [adherence-defective]) of the YS strain, which lacks the cell bound S1. The AD2 mutant fails to bind to the cellulose surface (19). Furthermore, the same mutant produces less S1 in the culture broth than the wild strain. This phenomenon is associated with an increased amount of lower molecular weight endoglucanases with decreased affinity toward cellulose (20). The studies based on the AD2 mutant, therefore, suggest that S1 is a multifunctional protein which is involved in the organization of the cellulosome, serves to anchor the cellulases to the cellulose surface, and mediates cell adhesion.

The cellulosome also occurs on the cell surface, especially during the exponential growth phase, where they form distinctive polycellulosomal protuberances with sizes ranging from 60 to 200 nm (20,21). As the culture enters the stationary phase, more cellulosomes are released into culture broth (19,22). Upon growth on cellulose, the polycellulosomal protuberances on the cell surface appear to aggregate at the contact site between the cell and the cellulose surface, forming the "contact corridor" bridging the cell and the cellulose surface (21). On the other hand, the cellulose surface, when void of cells, is coated by a layer of cellulosomes.

Cellulosome molecules of larger sizes (M_r = 100 x 10^6 and 4.5 x 10^6) have been isolated from the JW20 strain of *C. thermocellum*, which contain 20 to 35 subunits (22,23). Many of them have been demonstrated to have cellulase or xylanase activities (24). The morphology of these cellulosome molecules has been studied using electron microscopy (25). Various forms of cellulosomes, i.e. the "tight cellulosome" with tightly packed subunits and the "loose cellulosome" with loosely packed subunits, have been observed. Both forms may "decompose" into smaller structural elements containing five to eight subunits arranged equidistantly in a parallel and symmetric array along a central groove or axis. These observations indicate that the size and the morphology of cellulosomes may vary depending on the number of the structural elements in a cellulosome molecule and how these elements are arranged. [See discussions of the revised anchor-enzyme model below].

The Cellulosome as a Cellulase Complex. Attempts to purify the cellulase components from the ATCC 27405 strain of *C. thermocellum* revealed that most of the Avicelase and the majority of the CMCase activities are associated with the protein aggregates with molecular weights of a few million Daltons (3). This indicates that the major function of the cellulosome is cellulose degradation. Indeed, at least eight subunits of the YS strain cellulosome are active against CMC (2). Furthermore, isolated cellulosome from the YS strain possesses the same properties as the crude enzyme, including the requirement for a reducing agent and Ca^{++} for maximum activity, and the sensitivity to cellobiose inhibition (26).

The involvement of a protein complex with complicated quaternary structures clearly distinguishes the C. thermocellum cellulase from the fungal system. This raises questions of how many subunits are required and whether the quaternary structure they form is crucial for cellulose degradation. These questions were partially answered when a subcellulosome was isolated (27). This subcellulosome contains only six major subunits, yet displays much higher specific activity against CMC and Avicel than the crude enzyme. The subcellulosome is inactivated by sulfhydryl reagents and is inhibited by EDTA and the apolar chelating agent, o-phenanthroline. These properties are consistent with those of the crude enzyme. Therefore, at least for the standard laboratory assay, cellulose degradation by cellulosomes seems to involve only a "core unit" of the cellulosome, consisting of a small number of key subunits.

Subunits of the Cellulosome. The structure-function relationship of the cellulosome became the central theme of research since it was established that the cellulosome is the reaction center for cellulose degradation. The first step in this study is to characterize the role of the individual components. Since the cellulosome is very stable and cannot be dissociated without denaturing the protein, study in this respect has been approached mostly through the molecular cloning of cellulase (cel) genes. As a result, more than twenty cellulase, xylanase, and ß-D-glucosidase genes have been cloned into Escherichia coli (28-30). Many of those genes (including celA [31], celB [32], celC [33], celD [34], celE [35], celF [36], celH [37], xynZ [38], bglA [39], bglB [40]) have been sequenced. Table 1 lists the endoglucanase and xylanase genes that have been cloned and sequenced.

Table 1. Cloned C. thermocellum Endoglucanase and Xylanase Genes

Cloned Gene	Size (b.p.)	Predicted MW (Daltons)	Observed MW (Daltons)	ref.
CelA	1,344	52,503	56,000	(41)
CelB	1,689	63,857	66,000	(42)
CelC	1,032	40,439	38,000	(43)
CelD	1,947	72,344	65,000	(44)
CelE	2,442	90,211	------	
CelF	2,219	87,409	------	
CelH	2,702	102,301	------	
XynZ	2,511	92,159	90,000	(38)

It is clear from these cloned genes that the observed diversity in cellulase molecules produced by this bacterium is not solely due to post-translational modifications or proteolysis. The predicted sizes of most of the proteins encoded fall in the range of those of the cellulosome components (48 - 210 KDa). One striking feature of these genes is that all, except *celC*, code for a conserved, duplicated sequence of 24 amino acid residues. This duplicated sequence is located at the C-terminus of all the Cel proteins except CelE and XynZ, where the sequence is in the middle of the proteins (Figure 1).

The duplicated sequence on the CelD and XynZ has been shown to function as a binding ligand to CelL (M_r = 250,000), the largest subunit of the cellulosome of the ATCC 27405 strain (*9*). Deletion of the duplicated sequence deprive the proteins of the ability to bind to CelL. These results indicate that proteins with this conserved, duplicated sequence bind to CelL and that they are subunits of the cellulosome. In this respect, it is interesting to note that the CelCCA of *C. cellulolyticum* also contains this duplicated sequence (*45*).

CelL, with many subunits binding to it, could serve as the "scaffolding" for the cellulosome. Since many proteins contain the duplicated sequence, they could compete for the same binding site on CelL. Alternatively, a single CelL molecule could provide multiple binding sites. As will be discussed later, the DNA sequence of *cell* indicates that it indeed serves as the supporting structure of the cellulosome and provides multiple binding sites.

The Anchor-Enzyme Model

Although the crude *C. thermocellum* cellulase is very active against crystalline cellulose, none of the cloned genes code for protein with significant activity on the crystalline substrate. It is possible that the gene(s) encoding the essential subunit(s) for such activity has not been cloned. In addition, the complicated quaternary structure may be crucial for such activity. The high stability of the cellulosome and the large number of its subunits have been a serious technical impediment for attempts to unveil the mystery of how the cellulosome degrades crystalline cellulose. However, the first insight was provided when two cellulosome subunits, CelS (or S_S; M_r = 82,000) and CelL (or S_L; M_r = 250,000) were identified.

CelS was first purified by gel filtration chromatography of the cellulosome from the ATCC 27405 strain and partially dissociated with SDS (*3*). Upon dissociation, the Avicelase activity was lost. However, the activity was partially restored by combining CelS with another chromatographic fraction containing predominantly CelL. CelL was later purified by elution from an SDS-gel. The CelL thus purified retained the activity to degrade Avicel synergistically with CelS. Cellulose degradation occurred only when CelL and CelS were combined, indicating their cooperative action.

It would be tempting to explain this cooperative action by the model of synergism between endo- and exoglucanase. However, experimental evidence indicates that a unique mechanism is probably involved. The cellulose degradation probably involves the interactions between CelL, CelS and the water-insoluble cellulosic substrate. An

```
           First block                                                              
CelS    675 K L Y G D V N D D G K V N S T D A V A L K R Y V L R S G I S I N T D N A            710
CelA    413 V V Y G D V N G D G N V N S T D L T M L K R Y L L K S V T N I N R E A A             448
CelB    498 V T Y G D V N G D G R V N S S D V A L L K R Y L L G L V E N I N K E A A             533
CelD    581 V L Y G D V N D D G K V N S T D L T L L K R Y V L K A V S T L P S S K A E K N A      620
CelE    411 I L Y G D V N G D G K I N S T D C T M L K R Y I L R G I E F P S P S G I A A          450
CelF    666 I M L G G D V N F D G R I N S T D Y S R L L K R Y V I K S L E F T D P E E H Q K F I A A A  708
CelX        V K K G G D V N L D G Q V N S T D F S L L K R Y I L K Y V D I N S I N V T N A
CelH    828 I K H G D L N F D N A V N S T D L L M L K R Y I L K S L E L G T S E H E E K F K K A A  870
XynZ    426 T G L G D L N G D G N I N S S D L Q A L K R H L L G I S P L T G E A L L R A           463
CelCCA  411 I V Y G D Y N N D G N V D A L D F A G L K K Y I M A A D H A T V K N L                 445

           Second block
CelS    711 D L N E D G R V N S T D L G L K R Y I L K E I D T L P Y K N - C O O H                 741
CelA    449 D V N R D G A I N S S D M T I L K R Y L L K S I P H L P Y - C O O H                   477
CelB    534 D V N V S G T V N S T D L A M K R Y V L R S S E L P Y K - C O O H                     563
CelD    621 D V N R D G R V N S S D V T I L S R Y L I R V I E K L P I - C O O H                   649
CelE    451 D V N A D L L I N S T D L V L M K K Y I L L R S I D K F P                             480
CelF    709 D V D G N G R I N S T D L Y L V L N R Y I L K L I L E K F P A E Q - C O O H           740
CelX        D M N N D G N I N S T D I S I L K R L L R N - C O O H
CelH    871 D L N R D N K V D S T D L T I L K R Y L L Y A S E I P I - C O O H                     899
XynZ    464 D V N R S G K V D S T D Y S V L K R Y I L R I I T E F P G                             492
CelCCA  446 D V N L D N E V N A F D L A L K K Y L L G M V S K L P S N - C O O H                   475
```

Figure 1. Alignment of the conserved duplicated sequence between CelS, CelA, CelB, CelD, CelE, CelF, CelX, CelH, and XynZ of *C. thermocellum* and CelCCA of *C. cellulolyticum*. Boxed amino acids are identical or have similar chemical properties. Numbers indicate the position, within the sequence of each protein, of the first or the last amino acid shown on a line. Similar residues are: V, L, I, M, F; R, K; D, E; N, Q; Y, F, W; S, T.

anchor-enzyme model (Figure 2 [4]) has been proposed to explain this synergistic effect. In this model, CelL functions as an anchorage subunit which connects the CelS, a catalytic subunit, to the cellulose surface. This model is based on the following observations: 1) although CelS is not active on crystalline cellulose, it is active on CMC; 2) the CMCase activity of CelS is not significantly enhanced by CelL; 3) adsorption of CelS to the cellulose surface is dependent on CelL; 4) the purified CelL has no enzymatic activity.

It became apparent that CelL and CelS are the two most abundant subunits of the cellulosome. Furthermore, the reconstituted Avicelase (CelL + CelS) is capable of degrading most of the Avicel particles in the assay system (Wu and Demain, unpublished data), indicating that the crystalline portion of the cellulose is attacked. Finally, the reconstituted Avicelase has the same properties as the crude enzyme, such as requiring Ca^{++} for the maximum activity, generating predominantly cellobiose as the hydrolysis product, and the sensitivity to cellobiose inhibition (4). The reconstituted Avicelase, therefore, appears to be representative of the Avicelase activity of the crude enzyme.

The Revised Anchor-Enzyme Model

The complex of CelS and CelL represents the simplest subcellulosome active on crystalline cellulose. The anchor-enzyme model provides the first clue to the mechanism and organization of the cellulosome. The intriguing feature of the model and the technical difficulty in purifying CelL and CelS through SDS treatment have triggered interest in targeting the molecular cloning at genes for these two subunits. Recently, both celL and celS genes have been cloned. Not surprisingly, analysis of their gene structures reveals much greater details regarding how the cellulosome is organized in an anchor-enzyme configuration.

CelL gene (or *cipA* for cellulosome integrating protein) was cloned by using antibody against CelL (5). Its open-reading-frame codes for a protein of 196,800 KDa (6). An extremely striking feature of its DNA sequence is that about 75% of the gene consists of repeated sequence of about 0.5 kbp with two direct repeats in the 5' end (N-terminus of CelL) and seven direct repeats in the 3' end (C-terminus of CelL). In addition, the CelL also has the conserved, duplicated sequence at the C-terminus, which serves as a binding ligand to itself as mentioned above. The DNA sequence, therefore, suggests that CelL binds to itself. The implication of this self-binding is that CelL molecules, by binding to each other, provide a scaffolding for the quaternary structure of the cellulosome.

If CelL is the key building block for the cellulosome, how then may the various subunits interact with this hypothetical CelL scaffolding? Since all Cel proteins with the conserved, duplicated sequence would potentially bind to CelL, it is likely that each repeated domain on the CelL serves as the binding receptor for the duplicated sequence. This interesting possibility has been experimentally verified. Using ^{125}I-labeled CelD protein as a probe to screen an expression genomic library, Fujino et al. (10) obtained a truncated *cellL* (or *cipA*) gene coding for the C-terminal end of CelL. The encoded CelL fragment contains two full repeated domains (out of nine in the intact CelL). Gene deletion analysis indicated that CelD is able to bind to only one repeated domain and the same protein with the duplicated sequence deleted fails to bind.

Description of the New Model. These recent results indicate that CelL functions as an anchor not only for CelS but also for other catalytic subunits. A schematic drawing of this new model is shown in Figure 3. In this model, various catalytic subunits bind to CelL through the interaction between the duplicated sequence and the repeated domain to form a "core unit" of the cellulosome. The core units are linked to each other through the CelL's own duplicated sequence. The fact that most of the duplicated sequences lie in the C-terminus probably allows the catalytic domain to "stick out" from the core structure. Some catalytic subunits have their own cellulose binding domain (CBD) which may further enhance the binding to cellulose surface (36,46). It is interesting to note that the cellulose binding domain and the catalytic domain of CelE reside on the opposite sides of the duplicated sequence (35,46), again allowing the domains to "stick out" from the core structure. At this time, it is not clear whether there is any protein-protein interaction between the "anchored" subunits.

In a cellulosome molecule of about 2.1 million Daltons (2), two to three such core units may exist. Theoretically, larger or smaller cellulosome molecules could be formed depending on the degree of the self-association of CelL. Furthermore, the CelL scaffolding could be linear or circular and more than one of the repeated domains could be used for self-association. The geometry and the size of this self-association may depend on whether the cellulosome is in solution, on the cell surface, or on the substrate surface. This explains the observation of cellulosome molecules of different sizes and shapes (20,25) and the morphology change of cellulosome, for example, "transformation" upon binding to cellulose surface (21) or "structural decomposition" in the later stage of fermentation (25).

It is worth noting that the structure of the core unit depicted in Figure 3 is strikingly similar to the structural element revealed by electron microscopy (25). The structural element mentioned earlier is formed by "rows of equidistantly spaced polypeptides arranged parallel to the major axis" Based on the structure of this element, Mayer et al. (25) and Coughlan and Ljungdahl (47) proposed the model of "simultaneous multicutting event" leading to the cellulose degradation. If the CelL represents the major axis and the various catalytic subunits represents "the equidistantly spaced polypeptides arranged parallel to the axis", then this revised anchor-enzyme model is strikingly consistent with the structural element and the multicutting model. Mayer et al. (25) even indicated that five to eight identical subunits are present in an element, in close agreement with the number of subunits shown in Figure 3.

CelL: The Key Building Block of the Cellulosome. In the first anchor-enzyme model proposed, CelL functions only as an anchor having no catalytic activity. The lack of catalytic activity has been reported by two separate groups (2-4) both using SDS-treated CelL for assay. Contrary to this finding, a truncated, non-denatured recombinant version of CelL was shown to be active on CMC (5). This discrepancy

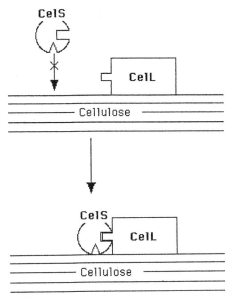

Figure 2. The anchor-enzyme model indicating that CelL functions as an anchor on the cellulose surface for CelS, the catalytic subunit.

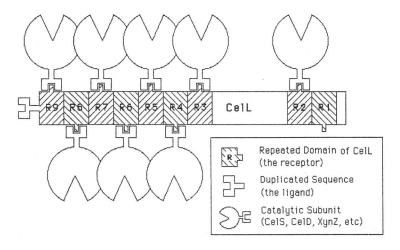

Figure 3. The revised anchor-enzyme model indicating that CelL functions as an anchor for other subunits to form a "core unit" of the cellulosome. One repeated domain (R1) on CelL is left open to indicate the potential self-association site for CelL. This site is randomly chosen in this drawing; however, this site could be specific due to the possible protein-protein interactions beyond the ligand-receptor interaction described in the model.

is likely due to the irreversible denaturation of the catalytic domain by SDS in earlier experiments. If the catalytic site lies on the repeated domain, CelL is not only an anchor, but also provides a hydrolysis site in every domain to synergize with the catalytic activities of the other subunits. As an anchor on the cellulose surface, CelL is likely to have its own cellulose binding domain. It is not clear whether the cellulose binding domain is located in the repeated domains or in the non-repeated domain. It would also be interesting to determine if CelL possesses non-hydrolytic, cellulose fiber-disrupting activity (48).

Besides its large size and repeated domains, CelL is also unique in being glycosylated. CelL contains 5-7% carbohydrate (49) and a novel carbohydrate-peptide linkage (50). The fact that the truncated recombinant CelL is active on CMC (5) and capable of binding the catalytic subunits (10) indicates that glycosylation is not essential for its catalytic activity or receptor function.

CelS: The Major Cellulosome Subunit. Although the receptor sites in CelL could be occupied by any subunits with the duplicated sequence according to the revised model, the majority of those sites will probably be occupied by CelS since it is the most abundant subunit in the cellulosome. In fact, CelS is the most abundant protein species of the total extracellular protein of the ATCC 27405 strain (Figure 4). Its equivalent in the YS strain, the S8 subunit, is also the most abundant subunit (1,2). In the structural element reported by Mayer et al. (25), the equidistantly arranged subunits have been reported to be identical; however, smaller subunits are also present in the same cellulosome molecule. Therefore, the receptor sites on CelL are probably occupied mostly by CelS with other subunits interspersed.

The S8 subunit has been shown to be active on CMC using a CMC-overlay assay (2). Its mode of action has been determined using its proteolytic fragment (S8-tr) with molecular weight of 68 KDa, which dissociates from the cellulosome after proteolysis and can be easily purified (13). It appears that the binding ligand (the duplicated sequence) is cleaved by the protease, resulting in the dissociation of S8-tr from the cellulosome (9,13). Although activity on CMC in the overlay assay suggests endoglucanase activity, S8-tr displays typical cellobiohydrolase activity (13). More importantly, its activity is stabilized by Ca^{++} and reducing agent and is strongly inhibited by cellobiose. It also produces cellobiose as the major hydrolysis product. These properties are consistent with those found in the crude enzyme, the isolated cellulosome, the subcellulosome, and the reconstituted Avicelase (CelL + CelS). Furthermore, the biosynthesis of S8 appears to be induced by growth on cellulose (20). The DNA sequence of *celS* gene shares no homology with other known *cel* genes (7,8) except the region coding for the duplicated sequence. The duplicated sequence (Figure 1) confirms its ability to bind to CelL. Finally, it is the only subunit which has been demonstrated to degrade a major portion of crystalline cellulose synergistically with CelL (3). CelS therefore plays a critical role in cellulose degradation by the cellulosome.

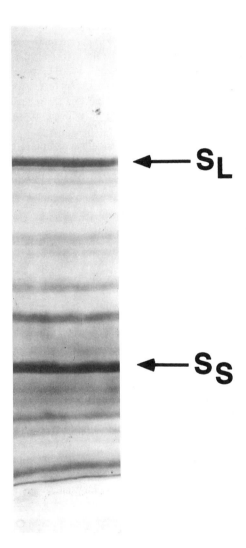

Figure 4.   SDS-PAGE pattern of the total extracellular proteins of *C. thermocellum* ATCC 27405, indicating that CelS (S_S) and CelL (S_L) are the most abundant protein species. The crude proteins were obtained by growing the bacterium on cotton.

Conclusion

In spite of the complexity of the cellulosome, it appears that its organization probably follows a very simple rule: attack of the repeated and ordered structure of the substrate with repeated and ordered domains through the quaternary structure of the enzyme molecules. An even simpler rule is used in organizing the quaternary structure by employing a universal set of ligands/receptors. Although many questions remain to be answered, the elegance and the beauty revealed by the model are fascinating. It represents a new concept not only for cellulose degradation, but also for supramolecular protein structure.

The unique properties of the *C. thermocellum* cellulase system apparently are rooted in its unique structure. As the details of this structure are elucidated at the molecular level, it may be possible to redesign the cellulosome following the same simple rules of the game.

Literature Cited

1. Lamed, R.; Setter, E.; Kenig, R.; Bayer, E.A. *Biotechnol. Bioeng. Symp.* **1983**, *13*, 163-181.
2. Lamed, R.; Setter, E.; Bayer, E.A. *J. Bacteriol.* **1983**, *156*, 828-836.
3. Wu, J.H.D.; Orme-Johnson, W.H.; Demain; A.L. *Biochemistry* **1988**, *27*, 1703-1709.
4. Wu, J.H.D.; Demain; A.L. In *Biochemistry and Genetics of Cellulose Degradation*; Aubert; J.-P.; Beguin, P.; Millet, J., Eds.; Academic Press: London, 1988; pp 117-131.
5. Romaniec, M.P.M.; Kobayashi T.; Fauth U.; Gerngross U.T.; Demain, A.L. *Appl. Biochem. Biotechnol.* **1991**, *31*, 119-134.
6. Gerngross U.T.; Romaniec, M.P.M.; Huskisson, N.S.; Demain, A.L. Personal communication.
7. Wang, W.K.; Wu, J.H.D. *Appl. Biochem. Biotechnol.* In press.
8. Wang, W.K.; Wu, J.H.D. 1992. Submitted.
9. Tokatlidis, K.; Salamitou, S.; Beguin, P.; Dhurjati, P.; Aubert, J.-P. *FEBS Lett.* **1991**, *291*, 185-188.
10. Fujino, T.; Beguin, P.; Aubert, J.-P. *FEMS Microbiol. Lett.* **1992**, *94*, 165-170.
11. Johnson, E.A. PhD Thesis, M.I.T., Cambridge, MA, 1983.
12. Johnson, E.A.; Sakajoh, M.; Halliwell, G.; Madia, A.; Demain, A.L. *Appl. Environ. Microbiol.* **1982**, *43*, 1125-1132.
13. Morag, E.; Halevy, I.; Bayer, E.A.; Lamed, R. *J. Bacteriol.* **1991**, *173*, 4155-4162.
14. Chauvaux, S., Beguin, P.; Aubert, J.-P.; Bhat, M.K.; Gow, L.A.; Wood, T.M.; Bairoch, A. *Biochem. J.* **1990**, *265*, 261-265.
15. Johnson, E.A.; Demain, A.L. *Arch. Microbiol.* **1984**, *137*, 135-138.
16. Johnson, E.A.; Reese, E.T.; Demain, A.L. *J. Appl. Biochem.* **1982**, *4*, 64-71.
17. Lamed, R; Bayer, E. A. *Adv. Appl. Microbiol.* **1988**, *33*, 1-46.

18. Lamed, R.; Bayer; E. A. In *Biochemistry and Genetics of Cellulose Degradation*; Aubert; J.-P.; Beguin, P.; Millet, J., Eds.; Academic Press: London, 1988; pp 101-116.
19. Bayer, E.A.; Kenig, R.; Lamed., R. *J. Bacteriol.* **1983**, *156*, 818-827.
20. Bayer, E.A.; Setter, E.; Lamed, R. *J. Bacteriol.* **1985**, *163*, 552-559.
21. Bayer, E.A.; Setter, E.; Lamed, R. *J. Bacteriol.* **1986**, *167*, 828-836.
22. Hon-Nami, K.; Coughlan, M.P.; Hon-nami, H.; Ljungdahl, L.G. *Arch. Microbiol.* **1986**, *145*, 13-19.
23. Coughlan, M.P.; Hon-Nami, K.; Hon-Nami, H.; Ljungdahl, L.G.; Paulin, J.J.; Rigsby, W.E. *Biochem. Biophys. Res. Commun.* **1985**, *130*, 904-909.
24. Kohring, S.; Wiegel, J.; Mayer, F. *Appl. Env. Microbiol.* **1990**, *56*, 3798-3804.
25. Mayer, F.; Coughlan, M.P.; Mori, Y.; Ljungdahl, L.G. *Appl. Env. Microbiol.* **1987**, *53*, 2785-2792.
26. Lamed, R.; Kenig, R.; Setter, E.; Bayer, E.A. *Enzyme Microb. Technol.* **1985**, *7*, 37-41.
27. Kobayashi, T.; Romaniec, M.P.M.; Fauth, U.; Demain, A.L. *Appl. Env. Microbiol.* **1990**, *56*, 3040-3046.
28. Schwarz, W.; Bronnenmeier, K.; Staudenbauer, W.L. *Biotechnol. Lett.* **1985**, *7*, 859-864.
29. Hazlewood, G.P.; Romaniec, M.P.M.; Davidson, K.; Grepinet, O.; Beguin, P.; Millet, J.; Raynaud, O.; Aubert, J.-P. *FEMS Microbiol. Lett.* **1988**, *51*, 267-282.
30. Beguin, P.; Millet, J.; Grepinet, O.; Navarro, A.; Juy, M.; Amit, A.; Poljak, R.; Aubert, J.-P. In *Biochemistry and Genetics of Cellulose Degradation*; Aubert; J.-P.; Beguin, P.; Millet, J., Eds.; Academic Press: London, 1988; pp 11-30.
31. Beguin, P.; Cornet, P.; Aubert, J-P. *J. Bacteriol.* **1985**, *162*, 102-105.
32. Grepinet, O.; Beguin, P. *Nucleic Acids Res.* **1986**, *14*, 1791-1799.
33. Schwarz, W.H.; Schimming, S.; Rucknagel, K.P.; Burgschwaiger, S.; Kreil, G.; Staudenbauer, W. *Gene* **1988**, *63*, 23-30.
34. Joliff, G.; Beguin, P.; Aubert, J.-P. *Nucleic Acids Res.* **1986**, *14*, 8605-8613.
35. Hall, J.; Hazlewood, G.P.; Barker, P.J.; Gilbert, H.J. *Gene* **1988**, *69*, 29-38.
36. Navarro, A.; Chebrou, M.-C.; Beguin, P.; Aubert, J.-P. *Res. Microbiol.* **1991**, *142*, 927-936.
37. Yague, E.; Beguin, P.; Aubert, J.-P. *Gene* **1990**, *89*, 61-67.
38. Grepinet, O.; Chebrou, M.-C.; Beguin, P. *J. Bacteriol.* **1988**, *170*, 4582-4588.
39. Grabnitz, F.; Seiss, M.; Rucknagel, K.P.; Staudenbauer, W.L. *Eur. J. Biochem.* **1991**, *200*, 301-309.
40. Grabnitz, F.; Rucknagel, K.P.; Seiss, M.; Staudenbauer, W.L. *Mol. Gen. Genet.* **1989**, *217*, 70-76.
41. Schwarz, W.; Grabnitz, F.; Staudenbauer, W.L. *Appl. Env. Microbiol.* **1986**, *51*, 1293-1299.
42. Beguin, P.; Cornet, P.; Millet, J. *Biochimie* **1983**, *65*, 495-500.
43. Petre, D.; Millet, J.; Longin, R.; Beguin, P.; Girard, H.; Aubert, J-P. *Biochimie* **1986**, *68*, 687-695.
44. Joliff, G.; Beguin, P.; Juy, M.; Millet, J.; Ryter, A.; Poljak, R.; Aubert, J.-P. *Bio/Technology* **1986**, *4*, 896-900.
45. Faure, E.; Belaich, A.; Bagnara, C.; Gaudin, C.; Belaich, J.-P. *Gene* **1989**, *84*, 39-46.

46. Durrant, A.J.; Hall, J.; Hazlewood, G.P.; Gilbert, H.J. *Biochem. J.* **1991**, *273*, 289-293.
47. Coughlan, M.P.; Ljungdahl, L.G. In *Biochemistry and Genetics of Cellulose Degradation*; Aubert; J.-P.; Beguin, P.; Millet, J., Eds.; Academic Press: London, 1988; pp 11-30.
48. Din, N.; Gilkes, N.R.; Tekant, B.; Miller, R.C.; Warren, R.A.J.; Kilburn, D. *Bio/technology* **1991**, *9*, 1096-1099.
49. Gerwig, G.J.; Kamerling, J.P.; Vliegenthart, J.F.G.; Morag, E.; Lamed, R.; Bayer, E.A. *Eur. J. Biochem.* **1991**, *196*, 115-122.
50. Gerwig, G.J.; Waard, P.; Kamerling, J.P.; Vliegenthart, J.F.G.; Morgenstern, E.; Lamed, R.; Bayer, E.A. *J. Biol. Chem.* **1989**, *264*, 1027-1035.

RECEIVED August 20, 1992

IMPROVING NATURAL ENZYMES BY CHEMICAL CROSS-LINKING

Chapter 22

Protein Chemical Cross-Linking
Implications for Protein Stabilization

Shan S. Wong[1], Michael Losiewicz[2], and Lee-Jun C. Wong[3,4]

[1]Department of Pathology and Laboratory Medicine, University of Texas Health Science Center, Houston, TX 77030
[2]Department of Chemistry, University of Massachusetts, Lowell, MA 01854
[3]Department of Biological Sciences, University of Massachusetts, Lowell, MA 01854

Chemical cross-linking of proteins is a special application of chemical modification. The cross-linkers are bifunctional compounds containing two reactive functionalities derived from group specific reagents. They may be classified into homobifunctional, heterobifunctional and zero-length cross-linkers. Different physical and chemical properties have been integrated into these cross-linking reagents, e.g., lengths and sizes, hydrophobicity and hydrophilicity, cleavability, iodinability, fluorofors, chromophores and spin labels. Examples of each class of compounds are presented. The use of the bifunctional reagents in the stabilization of proteins are discussed with regard to immobilization onto solid supports, cross-linking to other soluble proteins and intramolecular cross-linking. Examples are presented to demonstrate that the reticulation of proteins or enzymes stabilizes native molecular structures against denaturation by chemical, thermal and mechanical forces. It is suggested that the thermal stability of cross-linked proteins may be evaluated by the Arrhenius equation.

The stability of proteins and enzymes is a major concern in their industrial applications in organic synthesis, isolation and purification of chemicals, in their use as a reagent for chemical analysis, in therapeutics and diagnostics, and in the study of their structures and functions. Many methods have been evolved to preserve the integrity and activity of the native proteins. Based on thermodynamic reasoning, proteins were invariably kept at low temperatures to prolong their longevity. Although many enzymes and proteins can be stored in this manner for an extended period of time, low temperatures are not preferable in many industrial operations.

[4]Current address: Institute for Molecular Genetics, Baylor College of Medicine, Houston, TX 77030

0097–6156/93/0516–0266$06.00/0
© 1993 American Chemical Society

Furthermore, some proteins are cold sensitive and may be more stable at ambient temperatures. In an attempt to mimic the microenvironment of the proteins in the cell, various substances have been added to interact with isolated proteins. Glycerol and ethylene glycol have been used, particularly enabling the proteins to be kept at very low temperatures without being frozen. Other substances such as carbohydrates like sucrose and proteins like albumin have also been used to stabilize proteins of interest. While these methods have preserved the biological activities to various extents, the procedure introduces foreign substances which may not be desirable in many applications. A new method for protein stabilization using chemical modification has evolved. Cross-linking reagents have been used to intramolecularly cross-link and to conjugate protein or enzymes to other molecules including solid supports. This technique has been demonstrated to greatly enhance the stability of proteins. This Chapter will briefly review the characteristics of cross-linking reagents and their use in protein stabilization. Examples of proteins stabilized by chemical cross-linking will be presented.

General Characteristics of Cross-Linking Reagents

Chemical cross-linking of biological components has been applied to the study of membrane components and soluble proteins, the preparation of immunoconjugates and immunotoxins. Various reviews have appeared (*1-6*). A recent monograph covering the principle of cross-linking and its applications to various areas has also been published (*7*). Readers who are interested in detailed treatment of this area are encouraged to consult these publications. A summary review with particular reference to protein stabilization will be presented here.

Cross-linking reagents used for the stabilization of proteins are essentially chemical modification agents. These compounds contain two reactive functionalities which will react with amino acid side-chains of a protein, thus bringing two components together. A schematic presentation of these reagents is shown in Figure 1. The reactive groups are located at the two ends of the molecule connected by a backbone which may be designed to contain specific characteristics. Although any reactive functionalities may be incorporated into the head groups, the most common functional entities are acylating and alkylating agents (*8,9*). This is because the most reactive amino acid side-chains susceptible for modification are nucleophiles, such as sulfhydryl group of cysteine, amino groups of lysine and N-terminal amino acids, carboxyl groups of aspartic and glutamic acids and C-terminal amino acids, imidazolyl group of histidine, and thioether group of methionine. Thus the most common reactions with the two-headed compounds are acylation and alkylation of the protein.

Acylating agents. Acylating agents are compounds that confer acyl groups to nucleophiles. These compounds contain a good leaving group attached to the acyl group so that they are easily replaced by the reacting nucleophile. Since water is a nucleophile and is present in abundance in aqueous media, hydrolysis of the acylating agent may be an important side reaction, consuming considerable amount of the reactant. There are many acylating agents. Of particular importance are isocyanates, isothiocyanates, imidoesters, sulfonyl chlorides, N-hydroxysuccinimidyl and other activated esters, such as p-nitrophenyl ester. All of these reactive functional groups have been incorporated into cross-linkers (7). Some of these reactions are represented in Figure 2.

Alkylating agents. Among the alkylating functionalities that have been incorporated in the two-headed reagents, α-haloacetyl, N-maleimidyl, and halo-aryl derivatives are the most commom. In these reactions the nucleophile attacks the activated carbon displacing a leaving group as shown in Figure 3. When a nucleopile reacts with a halobenzene, arylation takes place.

Group specific reactions. The specificity of the cross-linking reagent for a specific amino acid side-chain depends on the relative reactivity of the nucleophile. Since the nucleophilicity of an amino acid side-chain depends on several factors, such as its electronic structure, its pK_a and its microenvironment, the reactivity of an amino acid side-chain is not specific and several side-chains may react with the same alkylating and acylating functionalities of the bifunctional reagents (7). However, the thiolate ion is the most nucleophilic (10). Thus the sulfhydryl groups of proteins will react with most of the cross-linkers at alkaline pH. For example, α-haloacetyl compounds and N-maleimido derivatives are generally considered as sulfhydryl selective. A different group of reagents that are thiol specific are disulfide and mercurial compounds. These functionalities makes the bifunctional reagents react with only thiol groups of proteins. Disulfide compounds react through a disulfide interchange reaction as shown in Figure 4 (11).

In the absence of any sulfhydryl moiety, the amino group becomes the major target of reaction. Similarly, for proteins with high content of surface amino groups, the competition for the reagent may favor such a group. In addition, thioacyl esters as a result of acylation are susceptible to hydrolysis. Thus acylating agents are in general considered amino group directing.

Other reactions. In addition to amino acids, some proteins contain prosthetic groups which may be used for cross-linking. Carbohydrates of glycoproteins are particularly useful. The sugar moieties can be oxidized with periodate to form dialdehydes which will form Schiff bases with amines. These Schiff bases may be stablized by reducing agents in a process called reductive alkylation as shown in Figure 5 (12). Instead of glycoproteins, polysaccharides may be used as cross-linkers coupling two or more proteins through their amino groups (7).

Homobifunctional cross-linkers. When two identical functional groups are incorporated at the ends of a cross-linker, a homobifunctional reagent is formed. The diacylating agents include bis-imidoesters, bis-succinimidyl derivatives, di-isocyanates, di-isothiocyantes, di-sulfonyl halides, bis-nitrophenyl esters, dialdehydes and diacylazides (7). A few of the common representative compounds are shown in Figure 6. Of the dialdehydes, glutaraldehyde has been extensively used. While it is proposed that the reaction proceeds through a Schiff base formation, the mechanism of the reaction is far from clear (13).

Among the dialkylating agents are bismaleimides, bis-haloacetyl derivatives, di-alkyl halides, and bis-oxiranes (7). Figure 7 illustrate the structure of some of these

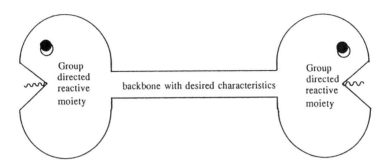

Figure 1. Schematic representation of cross-linking reagents. The reactive functional groups of these two-headed compounds are connected through a backbone. If the functional groups are identical, they are homobifunctional reagents, if different, heterobifunctional. Various structural characteristics may be incorporated into the backbone. (Reproduced with permission from ref. 7. Copyright 1991 CRC Press).

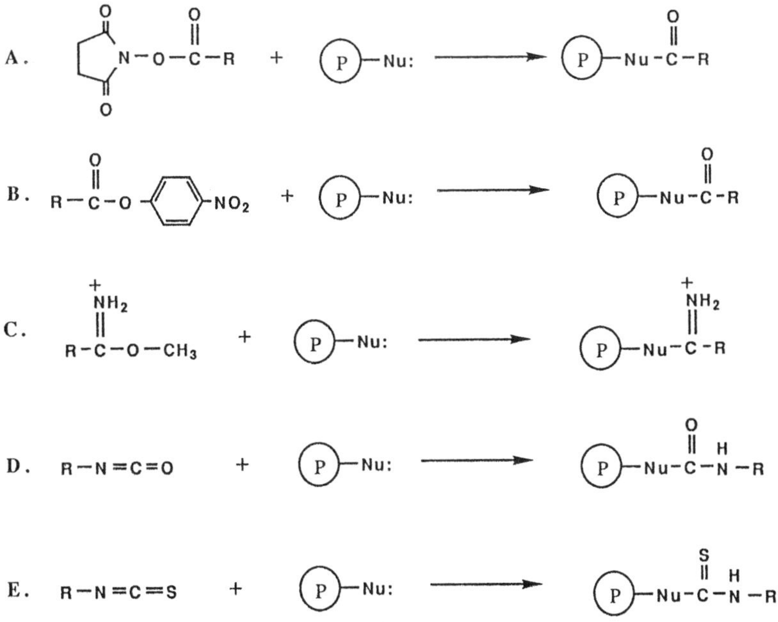

Figure 2. Commonly found acylating groups in cross-linking reagents and their reactions with nucleophiles. A. N-Hydroxysuccinimidyl ester; B. p-Nitrophenyl ester; C. Methyl imidoester; D. Isocyanate; E. Isothiocyanate.

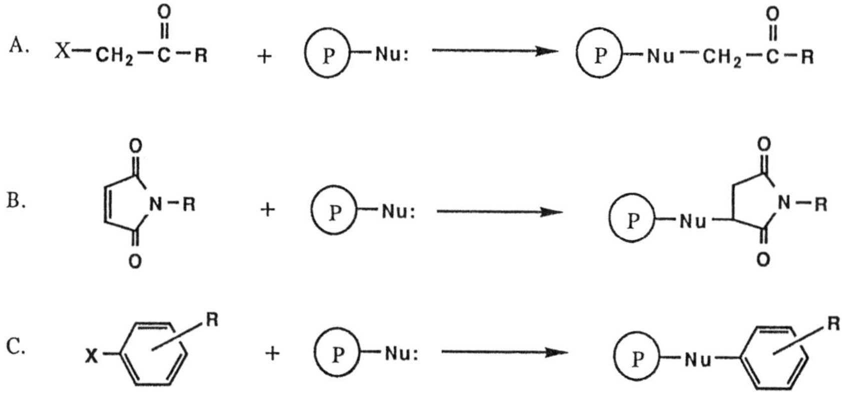

A.

B.

C.

Figure 3. Alkylating groups and their reactions with nucleophiles. A. Haloacetyl group; B. N-Maleimides; C. Aryl halides.

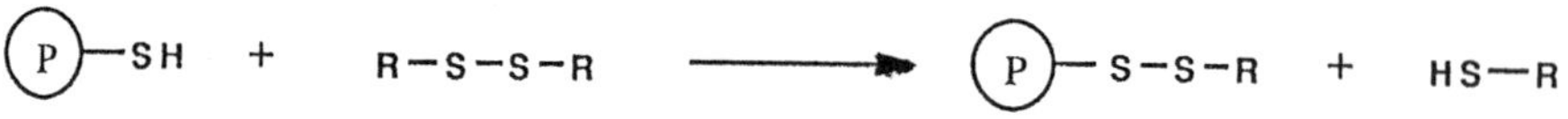

Figure 4. The disulfide interchange reaction between a thiol group of a protein and a disulfide compound.

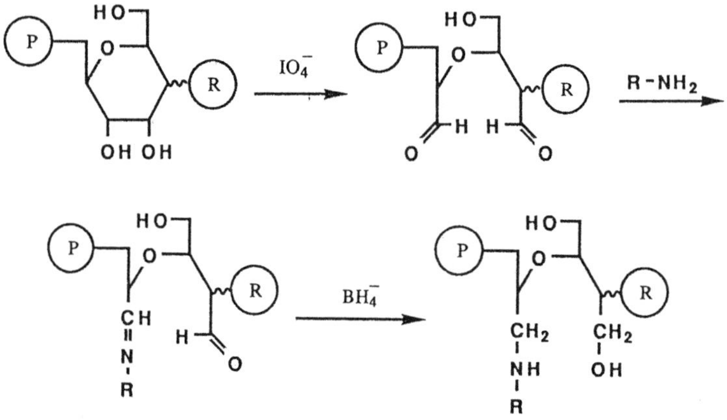

Figure 5. Reductive alkylation of an amino group with an aldehyde derived from oxidation of a sugar moiety of a glycoprotein.

compounds. As stated above, although any of the nucleophilic amino acid side-chains will react with these cross-linkers, the diacylating agents are generally thought to be amino group selective while the dialkylating agents are sulfhydryl specific. Thiol specific bis-disulfide cross-linkers have also been synthesized (*14*).

Heterobifunctional cross-linkers. Heterobifunctional cross-linkers contain two different functional groups. These two reactive functionalities can be any combination of those alkylating and acylating agents mentioned above. For example, one end of the cross-linker may be a disulfide such that it would be sulfhydryl group specific and the other end may be an acylating agent for amino group selectivity. Examples of such combinations are shown in Figure 8. Recently, the extremely reactive nitrene- and carbene-generating moieties have been incorporated to provide nondiscriminatory reactions with relatively inert proteins (*15*) (Figure 8D).

Zero-length cross-linking reagents. Zero-length cross-linkers are a special class of compounds which induce direct joining of two chemical moieties of proteins without the introduction of any extrinsic material. This is different from homo- and hetero-bifunctional reagents where a spacer is incorporated between the two cross-linked groups. Reagents that cause the formation of disulfide bonds, such as cupric di(1,10-phenanthroline), are zero-length cross-linkers. Other reagents include carbodiimides, isoxazolium derivatives, chloroformates and carbonyldiimidazole, which couple carboxyl and amino groups (*7*). These reagents react by activating the carboxyl group to form an active intermediate with which the amino group reacts as shown for carbodiimides in Figure 9.

Cleavable Reagents. In addition to the reactive head groups of the bifunctional cross-linking reagents, various functional groups have been incorporated into the backbone of these compounds to increase their versatility. For example, cleavable bonds have been incorporated to enable the cross-linked species to be separated. These include disulfide bond, vicinal glycol, azo, sulfone, ester and thioester linkages (*16-22*). Reagents including reducing and oxidizing agents, acids and bases may be used to cleave these bonds (Table I).

Hydrophobicity and Hydrophilicity. The degree of water solubility of cross-linkers may be altered by incorporating hydrophilic or hydrophobic entities into these compounds. For example, Staros (*23*) incorporated a sulfonate group onto the succinimide ring of N-hydroxysuccinimide esters to increase its hydrophilicity and decrease its membrane solubility. The inclusion of ether-oxygen, hydroxyl group, ester and amide bonds also increase the water solubility, while an increase in alkyl chain length decreases the hydrophilicity (*24*). These characteristics may be useful in certain conditions.

Size and Length. Bifunctional cross-linkers also differ in size in regard to the bulkiness of the molecule, and in length with respect to the distance between the two functional groups. The molecules can be as simple as formaldehyde (*25*) and as bulky as di[(iodoacetyl)aminomethyl]-fluorescein (*26*). The distance between the

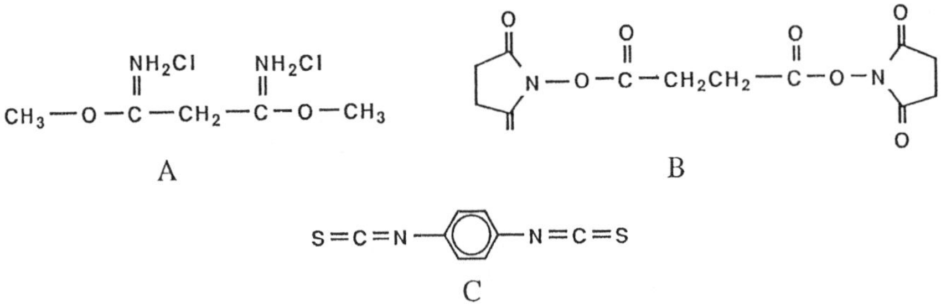

Figure 6. Examples of homobifunctional cross-linkers containing diacylating groups. A. Dimethyl malonimidate dihydrochloride; B. Bis(N-hydroxysucccinimidyl) succinate; C. 1,4-Phenylene di-isothiocyanate.

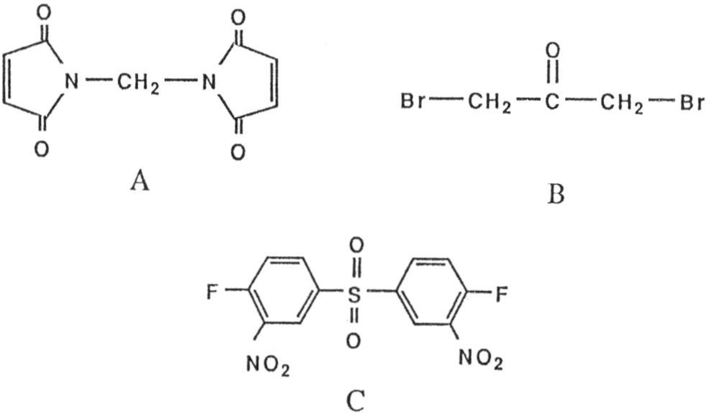

Figure 7. Examples of homobifunctional cross-linkers containing dialkylating groups. A. N, N'-Methylenebismaleimide; B. 1,3-Dibromoacetone; C. Bis(3-nitro-4-fluorophenyl)sulfone.

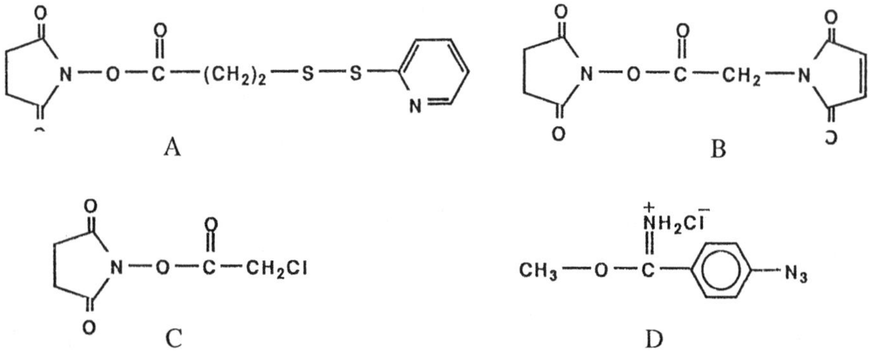

Figure 8. Examples of heterobifunctional cross-linkers. A. N-Succinimidyl 3-(2-pyridyldithio)propionate; B. N-Succinimidyl maleimidoacetate; C. N-Succinimidyliodoacetate; D. Methyl 4-azidobenzimidate.

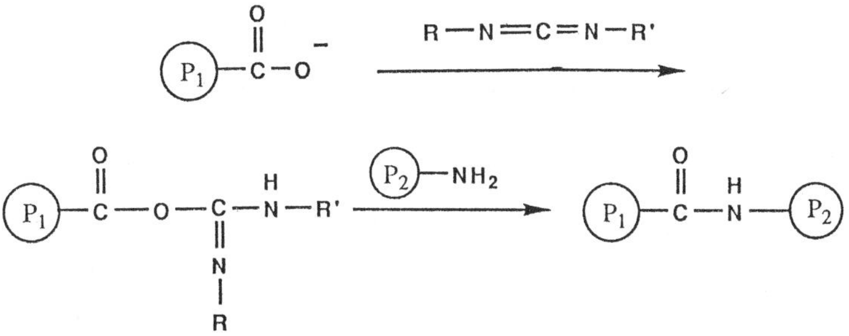

Figure 9. Cross-linking effected by a carbodiimide, a zero-length cross-linking reagent.

TABLE I

EXAMPLES OF CLEAVABLE GROUPS IN BIFUNCTIONAL REAGENTS

CLEAVABLE GROUP	CLEAVAGE CONDITION	CLEAVED PRODUCTS
$R_1-S-S-R_2$	reducing agent e.g. 2-mercaptoethanol	R_1-SH + R_2-SH
$R_1-CH-CH-R_2$ (with OH OH)	periodate	R_1-CHO + R_2-CHO
$R_1-N=N-R_2$	dithionite	R_1-NH_2 + R_2-NH_2
$R_1-\overset{O}{\underset{O}{\overset{\|}{\underset{\|}{S}}}}-R_2$	base	R_1-OH + $R_2-SO_3^-$

functional groups can be varied as well. For example, alkyl diimidoesters can be synthesized with different methylene groups giving rise to different lengths as depicted in Table II. These molecules are useful for cross-linking different groups on a protein molecule (27).

Probe labeled reagents. Various reporter groups have been incorporated into cross-linking reagents. As shown in Figure 10, these include spin labels, fluorescence and absorption probes as well as radioactive moieties (28-31). These labeled compounds have been used in the study of biological membranes and protein structures (7).

Stability of proteins by cross-linking to other components

Because the forces that contribute to the structural integrity of proteins are multi-factorial, prediction of the shelf-life of a particular protein in its native state is virtually impossible (32-35). However the stabilities of proteins and enzymes can be artificially modified. Of the many methods available, chemical cross-linking has recently been used to stabilize proteins. The rational of such an approach is based on the hypothesis that inactivation of a protein is due to unfolding of its structure and that intra- or inter-molecular cross-linking may rigidify the molecule, thus retard conformational changes towards the denatured state caused by external chemical, thermal or mechanical forces (36-37). In this context, chemical bifunctional reagents have been used to stabilize proteins by intramolecular cross-linking or by coupling the protein to other components, such as other solid supports or soluble polymers. The following sections will demonstrate some of the characteristics.

Stabilization by immobilization. Protein immobilization has received great attention because of its important applications in medical and clinical analysis, affinity chromatography, and synthetic chemistry (38-41). In addition to the characteristics of solid state chemistry, immobilization of a protein, in many circumstances, has increased the stability of the molecule (42). Virtually any cross-linking reagents may be used to couple proteins to solid supports and the various methods have been reviewed extensively (7,38-43). We have, for example, coupled galactosyltransferase to CL-Sepharose 4B with 6-aminocaproic acid through N-hydroxysuccinimidyl activation by dicyclohexyl carbodiimide (44). As shown in Figure 11, the immobilized enzyme has demonstrated increased stability towards both mechanical and thermal denaturation. The solid-bound enzyme was stable over 10 months at 4°C with the energy of inactivation raised to 30 Kcal/mol from 13 Kcal/mol for the soluble enzyme (45). Many other enzymes have demonstrated the same phenomenon of increased stability on immobilization.

Intermolecular cross-linking. Cross-linking of proteins to other soluble components may also provide the reticulating effect, strengtening the molecular structure. This is analogous to immobilization as discussed above, except that the components remain soluble in the aqueous medium. In many occassions, such arrangements also stabilize the protein. Thus, when horseradish peroxidase was cross-linked to immunoglobulin G or Jacalin, a plant lectin, with glutaraldehyde, it becomes more

TABLE II

DI-IMIDOESTERS OF DIFFERENT CHAIN LENGTHS

Cross-Linker	Maximum Distance ($\overset{o}{A}$)
$CH_3-O-\overset{\overset{NH_2Cl}{\|}}{C}-CH_2-\overset{\overset{NH_2Cl}{\|}}{C}-O-CH_3$	5
$CH_3-O-\overset{\overset{NH_2Cl}{\|}}{C}-(CH_2)_2-\overset{\overset{NH_2Cl}{\|}}{C}-O-CH_3$	6
$CH_3-O-\overset{\overset{NH_2Cl}{\|}}{C}-(CH_2)_4-\overset{\overset{NH_2Cl}{\|}}{C}-O-CH_3$	9
$CH_3-O-\overset{\overset{NH_2Cl}{\|}}{C}-(CH_2)_5-\overset{\overset{NH_2Cl}{\|}}{C}-O-CH_3$	10
$CH_3-O-\overset{\overset{NH_2Cl}{\|}}{C}-(CH_2)_6-\overset{\overset{NH_2Cl}{\|}}{C}-O-CH_3$	11
$CH_3-O-\overset{\overset{NH_2Cl}{\|}}{C}-(CH_2)_8-\overset{\overset{NH_2Cl}{\|}}{C}-O-CH_3$	14

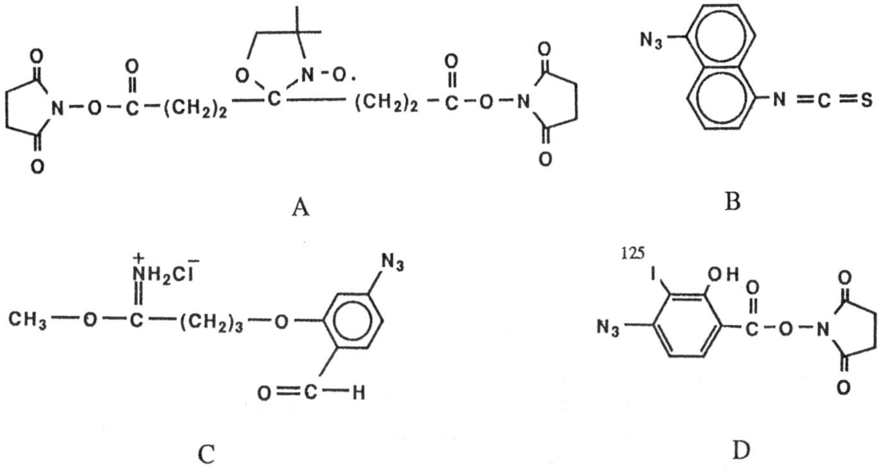

Figure 10. Examples of cross-linkers with different probes. A. Spin label; B. Fluorescence; C. Absorption; and D. Radioactive.

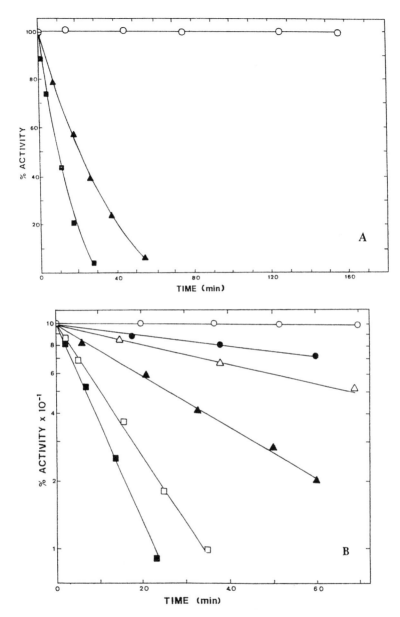

Figure 11. Increased stability of galactosyltransferase immobilized on Sepharose. A. Mechanical stability: O, immobilized enzyme; ▲, free enzyme; ■, free enzyme with Sepharose beads. B. Thermal stability: Free (closed symbols) and immobilized (open symbols) enzyme were inactivated at 75°C (■, □); 60°C, (▲, ▵); 30°C (●, O). (Reproduced with permission from ref. 45. Copyright 1985 Academic Press).

stable towards thermal denaturation with an increase in Arrhenius energy of inactivation as shown in Table III.

TABLE III

ENERGY OF INACTIVATION OF HORSERADISH PEROXIDASE CONJUGATES

Conjugates	E_a (Kcal/mol)
Peroxidase alone	35
Peroxidase-IgG	51
Peroxidase-Jacalin	43

The conjugates were prepared with glutaraldehyde. (Reproduced with permission from ref. 7. Copyright 1991 CRC Press)

Intramolecular cross-linking. Intramolecular cross-linking with bi- or polyfunctional reagents braces the molecular structure in the native state and has been shown to increase the chemical, thermal, and mechanical stability of many enzymes (*46-50*). For example, Himmel et al. (*50*) used a series of bifunctional reagents of different functional groups and lengths to intramolecularly cross-link amyloglucosidase. Although not all reagents gave the same results, some chemical cross-linkers, for example some of the diimidoesters, enhanced the thermal stability of the enzyme. As shown in Figure 12, the enzyme modified with either dimethyl succinimidate, dimethyl malonimidate, dimethyl suberimidate or dimethyl pimelimidate, retained a much higher activity after incubation for one hour at various temperatures. It was reported that in some cases the half-life of inactivation is more than doubled when incubated at 65°C (*50*).

Prediction of Protein Stability

An increase or a decrease in stability of a protein after cross-linking intramolecularly or intermolecularly to another component may be determined by studying its susceptibility to denaturation by thermal, mechanical or chemical disturbances. However, its half-life may be so prolonged that its determination may not be possible. This is particularly so for thermal denaturation at low temperatures where the half-life may be extended to months or years. In this case, the thermal stability may be inferred from the heat of denaturation obtainable by use of the Arrhenius equation:

$$\ln k = A - E_a/RT$$

When the natural logarithm of the rate constants of inactivation, k, is plotted against the reciprocal of the absolute temperatures at which the inactivation takes place, the negative slope of the line provides the value of $-E_a/R$ where R is the known gas

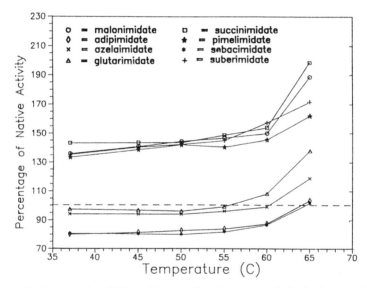

Figure 12. Increased stability of intramolecularly cross-linked glucoamylase. Glucoamylase cross-linked by various indicated reagents was preincubated at the indicated temperatures for one hour before assay. The native enzyme activity was taken as 100%. (Reproduced with permission from ref. 50. Copyright 1989 Humana Press).

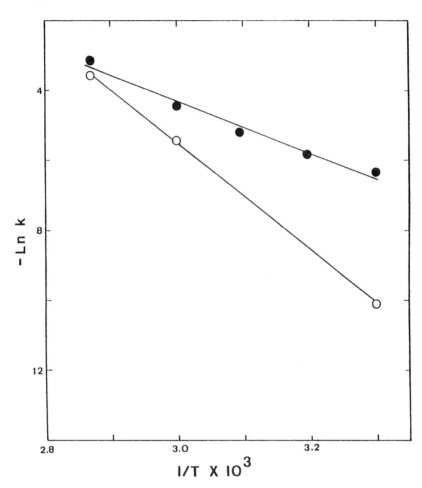

Figure 13. Arrhenius plot of inactivation of galactosyltransferase either free (closed circles) or immobilized on to Sepharose (open circles) (Reproduced with permission from ref. 45. Copyright 1985 Academic Press).

constant. The larger the value of E_a, the more energy is required for inactivation, thus the more stable is the protein. This is examplified by the denaturation of galactosyltransferase shown in Figure 13. The native enzyme has an E_a of 13 kcal/mol, whereas that of the immobilized enzyme is 30 kcal/mol.

The rate constant of inactivation of the protein at certain temperatures may be determined by measuring the rate of inactivation at that temperature. In most cases, the denaturation is a first-order process and the first order rate constant may be obtained by plotting the logarithm of the initial activity, v, against the time of incubation, t, at that particular temperature according to:

$$\ln v = C - kt$$

To evaluate the half-life of crosss-linked protein at a certain temperature, the rate constant of inactivation at that temperature is determined by extrapolation of the Arrhenius plot. The half-life can then be calculated by the following equation:

$$t_{1/2} = 0.693/k$$

Synopsis.

Although not all cross-linked proteins result in stabilization of the biological activity, it has been firmly established that both intra- and inter-molecular cross-linking can confer stability to the molecule. Where no stability or decreased stability is observed, it is possible that the reagents used may be inappropriate. A different cross-linking reagent may give a totally opposite result, as has been demonstrated by Tatsumoto et al. (*50*). Since there are so many cross-linkers available or can be synthesized, it may be safe to prostulate that there is always a cross-linking reagent that can be used to stablize a protein.

Literature Cited.

1. Ji, T. H. *Methods Enzymol.* **1983**, *91*, 508-609.
2. Han, K.-K.; Richard, C.; Delacourte, A. *Int. J. Biochem.* **1984**, *16*, 129-144.
3. Gaffney, B. J. *Biochim. Biophys. Acta* **1985**, *822*, 289-317.
4. Tamura, M.; Tamura, T.; Burnham, D. N.; Uhlinger, D. J.; Lambeth, J. D. *Arch. Biochem. Biophys.* **1989**, *275*, 23-32.
5. Wawrzynczak, E. J.; Thorpe, P. E.; in *Immunoconjugates, Antibody Conjugates in Radioimaging and Therapy of Cancer*; Vogel, E.-W.; Ed.; Oxford University Press: New York, NY, 1987, p. 28.
6. Nonisotopic Immunoassay; Ngo, T. T., Ed.; Plenum Press, New York, N.Y., 1988.
7. Wong, S.S. *Chemistry of protein conjugation and cross-linking*; CRC Press: Boca Raton, FL, 1991.
8. Means, G. E.; Feeney, R. E. *Chemical Modification of Proteins*; Holden-Day, San Francisco, CA, 1971.
9. Lundblad, R. L.; Noyes, C. M.; *Chemical Reagents for Protein Modification*; CRC Press: Boca Raton, FL, 1984; Vols. 1 and 2.

10. Edwards, J. O.; Pearson, R. G. *J. Am. Chem. Soc.* **1962**, *84*, 16-26.
11. Kimura, T.; Matsueda, R.; Nakagawa, Y.; Kaiser, E. T.; *Analyt. Biochem.* **1982**, *122*, 274-282.
12. Cabacungan, J. C.; Ahmed, A. I.; Feeney, R. E.; *Anal. Biochem.* **1982**, *124*, 272-278.
13. Hardy, P. M.; Nicholls, A. C.; Rydon, H. N.; *J. Chem. Soc. Perkin Trans.* **1976**, *1*, 958-962.
14. Bloxham, D. P.; Sharma, R. P. *Biochem. J.* **1979**, *181*, 355-366.
15. Bayley, H.; Knowles, J. R. *Methods Enzymol.* **1977**, *46*, 69-114.
16. Traut, R. R.; Bollen, A.; Sun, T. T.; Hershey, J. W. B.; Sundberg, J.; Pierce, L. R. *Biochemistry* **1973**, *12*, 3266-3273.
17. Webb, J. L. *Enzyme and Metabolic Inhibitors*; Academic Press: New York, N.Y., 1966; Vol. 2, pp. 729.
18. Smith, R. J.; Capaldi, R. A.; Muchmore, D.; Dahlquist, F. *Biochemistry* **1978**, *17*, 3719-3723.
19. Jaffe, C. L.; Lis, H.; Sharon, N. *Biochemistry* **1980**, *19*, 4423-4429.
20. Wold, F. *Methods Enzymol.* **1972**, *25*, 623-651.
21. Sato, S.; Nakao, M. *J. Biochem.* **1981**, *90*, 1177-1185.
22. Friebel, K.; Huth, H.; Jany, K. D.; Trummer, W. E. *Z. Physiol. Chem.* **1981**, *362*, 421-428.
23. Staros, J. V. *Biochemistry* **1982**, *21*, 3950-3955.
24. Fasold, H.; Bäumert, H.; Fink, G. in *Protein Cross-linking: Biochemical and Molecular Aspects*; Friedman, M., Ed.; Plenum Press: New York, NY, 1976; pp. 207.
25. Hopwood, D. *Histochemie* **1969**, *17*, 151-161.
26. Haugland, R. P. *Handbook of Fluorescent Probes and Research Chemicals*, Molecular Probes, Inc.: Eugene, Oregon, 1990, p. 22.
27. Ji, T. H. *J. Biol. Chem.* **1974**, *249*, 7841-7847.
28. Gonzalez-Ros, J. M.; Farach, M. C.; Martinez-Carrion, M. *Biochemistry* **1983**, *22*, 3807-3811.
29. Gaffney, B. J.; Willingham, G. L.; Schepp, R. S. *Biochemistry* **1983**, *22*, 881-892.
30. Ji, T. H.; Ji, I. *Analyt. Biochem.* **1982**, *121*, 286-289.
31. Sigrist, H.; Allegrini, P. R.; Kempf, C.; Schnippering, C.; Zahler, P. *Eur. J. Biochem.* **1982**, *125*, 197-201.
32. Matthew, J. B.; Gurd, F. R. N. *Methods Enzymol.* **1986**, *130*, 437-453.
33. Chothia, C. *Ann. Rev. Biochem.* **1984**, *53*, 537-572.
34. Alber, T. *Ann. Rev. Biochem.* **1989**, *58*, 765-798.
35. Dill, K. A.; Shortle, D. *Ann. Rev. Biochem.* **1991**, *60*, 795-825.
36. Martinek, K.; Klibanov, A. M.; Goldmacher, V. S., Berezin, I. V. *Biochim. Biophys. Acta* **1977**, *485*, 1-12.
37. Torchilin, V. P.; Maksimenko, A. V.; Smirnov, V. N.; Berenzin, I. V.; Klibanov, A. M.; Martinek, K. *Biochim. Biophys. Acta* **1978**, *522*, 277-283.
38. *Medical Applications of Immobilized Enzymes and Proteins*; Chang, T. M. S., Ed.; Plenum Press: New York, NY, 1977; vols. I and II.
39. *Immobilized Enzymes in Food Processing*; Pitcher, W. H., Jr., Ed.; CRC Press: Boca Raton, FL, 1979.

40. Kennedy, J. F.; Cabral, J. M. S. *Immmobilized enzymes in solid phase biochemistry*, Scouten, W. H., Ed., Wiley Interscience: New York, NY, 1983, pp 253.
41. Mosbach, K. *Ciba Found. Symp.* **1985**, *111*, 57-70.
42. Mohr, P.; Pommerening, K. *Affinity Chromatography*, Marcel Dekker: New York, NY, 1985.
43. *Affinity Chromatography*; Dean, P. D. G.; Johnson, W. S.; Middle, F. A., Eds.; IRL Press: Washington, D. C., 1985.
44. Lee, T. K.; Wong, L-J. C.; Wong, S. S. *J. Biol. Chem.* **1983**, *258*, 13166-13171.
45. Demers, A. G.; Wong, S. S. *J. Appl. Biochem.* **1985**, *7*, 122-125.
46. Torchilin, V. P.; Trubetskoy, V. S.; Omel'yanenko, V. G.; Martinek, K. *J. Mol. Catal.* **1983**, *19*, 291-303.
47. Trubetskoy, V. S.; Torchilin, V. P. *Int. J. Biochem.* **1985**, *17*, 661-663.
48. Torchilin, V. P.; Trubetskoy, V. S. *Ann. N. Y. Acad. Sci.* **1984**, *434*, 27-30.
49. Gottschalk, N.; Jaenicke, R. *Biotechnol. Appl. Biochem.* **1987**, *9*, 389-400.
50. Tatsumoto, K.; Oh, K. K.; Baker, J.O., Himmel, M. E. *Appl. Biochem. Biotechnol.* **1989**, *20*, 293-308.

RECEIVED March 31, 1992

Chapter 23

Glutaraldehyde Cross-Linking
Fast and Slow Modes

Timothy J. A. Johnson

Department of Anatomy and Neurobiology, Colorado State University,
Fort Collins, CO 80523

Intense activity in molecular cytochemistry has rekindled interest in questions regarding aldehyde chemistry in the fixation of biological specimens. The chemistry of glutaraldehyde crosslinking has been examined numerous times. The reaction of glutaraldehyde with common low molecular weight nucleophiles such as amino acids and sulfhydryl compounds, which are frequently encountered in biological systems, generates a wide range of products. The complexity of the condensation product mixture has thwarted a thorough understanding of crosslinking mechanisms. Despite this, it is useful to consider the condensation products of glutaraldehyde with itself and other low molecular weight precursors as the actual crosslinking structures. With that emphasis, this paper focuses on: 1) the molecular weight range of the condensation products as a function of available precursors, and 2) the kinetics of formation of the products.

Glutaraldehyde crosslinking has been used since the early 1960's to immobilize constituents of cells and tissues for subsequent examination by microscopy (1). Glutaraldehyde is often employed for linking affinity ligands to solid state supports for affinity chromatography (2). In industry glutaraldehyde can effectively render enzymes stable to heat or other denaturing influences (3). Stabilized enzymes are useful for repeated use in bulk processing methods.

Cells add enormous complexity because they contain a diverse biochemical milieu that is reactive with aldehydes. Aldehyde-reactive molecules in cells range from molecular masses of a few hundred daltons to greater than 10^6 daltons. The reactive molecules present themselves in states which range from individual soluble molecules to hydrated "solid state" structures. The concentrations of the reactive structures vary from cell to cell and even from one part of a cell to another.

0097−6156/93/0516−0283$06.00/0
© 1993 American Chemical Society

In the preparation of glutaraldehyde stabilized enzymes, the focus is simplified because one can purify the reactive structures (enzymes) and define their concentrations and physical state. The goal of stabilization is to immobilize denaturable structural elements. At the same time, one cannot block access to substrate binding sites by direct reaction with the sites or by burying the sites under excess crosslinking rope. The enzyme assay is an effective monitor of substrate accessibility to its binding site and product egress from the enzyme.

Two condensation polymerization schemes for glutaraldehyde crosslinking are examined in this discussion. The goal will be to give the user some practical knowledge for controlling the polymerization or crosslinking process to produce active and stable enzymes.

One of the crosslinking schemes, aldol condensation, is a slow process. The second crosslinking scheme is rapid by comparison. In the presence of primary amine, glutaraldehyde reacts to form polymers of pyridine. The size of the products of the latter chemistry, and thus the length of potential crosslinkers, can be controlled by the ratio of glutaraldehyde to amine.

Aldehyde-Amine Chemistry

Acid Producing Reactions.   Before considering aldehyde-amine crosslinking chemistry, it is useful to attend to the product often overlooked in the reaction of glutaraldehyde with amines. Acid is produced when aldehydes and amines combine rapidly to form complexes which have pK_a values that are far lower than those for the parent amines (Fig. 1) (4-7, additional references included in ref. 7). Proteins, of course, have many primary amino groups. But more important, if one chooses to use the rapid crosslinking mode by adding low molecular weight primary amines to the crosslinking mixture, as outlined below, acid production becomes significant (Fig 1). Thus, adding sufficient buffering capacity to the reaction mixture is suggested (Table 1).

The formation of acid is the primary reason for the use of buffers (7). Acid production suggests strategies for the choosing a buffer. First, buffers should not be used if they have primary amine moieties which react with aldehydes (e.g., Tris) (7). Tertiary amine based buffers (e.g., MOPS and HEPES) do not combine with aldehydes to produce acid and are excellent possibilities (7). Second, since the buffering capacity of a buffer is greatest at the pK_a, the buffer chosen should have a pK_a slightly less (0.2-0.3 pH units) than the pH needed for the experiment. Third, there should be sufficient buffering capacity to minimize the pH decrease in the reaction mixture (Table 1). Buffering equivalents can be added by increasing the concentration and/or volume of the crosslinking buffer. This consideration becomes important if one needs to use a buffer with pKa further from the experimental pH. Possible buffer choices are listed in Table 2.

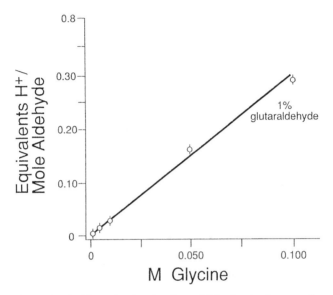

Figure 1. Acid production in glutaraldehyde-glycine reactions.

Table 1
Glutaraldehyde Induced pH Changes in Buffered Glycine[1]

Buffer	Phosphate	MOPS[2]	Cacodylate
0 M	4.50	4.50	4.50
0.05 M	6.90	6.90	6.30
0.20 M	7.20	7.25	6.90

[1]The pH was read 5 minutes after glutaraldehyde was added to buffered 0.05 M glycine. The final glutaraldehyde was 1% (0.1 M). The initial pH was adjusted to 7.40.

[2]3-N-morpholinopropane sulfonic acid.

Table 2
Alternative Buffers[1]

Buffer	pK$_a$ (37°C)
acetate	4.75
MES[2]	5.96
cacodylate	6.19
carbonate	6.37 (pK$_{a1}$)
PIPES[3]	6.66
MOPSO[2]	6.75
BES[3]	6.88
MOPS[2]	7.10
phosphate	7.21 (pK$_{a2}$)
HEPES[3]	7.31
POPSO[3]	7.63
HEPPSO[3]	7.73
HEPPS[3]	7.88
borate	9.23

[1]Alternative buffers for glutaraldehyde crosslinking. The acronyms used for buffers are described in reference 23. The zwitterionic buffers described by Good have pK$_a$ values that are much more sensitive to temperature than those of common buffers like phosphate (7, 23).

[2]Related to group B tertiary amines (6). Negligible amounts of acid expected with glutaraldehyde.

[3]Related to group A tertiary amines (6). Small amounts of acid are produced with glutaraldehyde.

Aldehyde-amine Crosslinking. Early notions about glutaraldehyde crosslinking of cells and proteins suggested that the dialdehyde formed Schiff bases with two different amino groups. The glutaraldehyde carbon chain thus bridged the amine moieties. Richards and Knowles (8) diminished the importance of the double Schiff base concept of crosslinking by pointing out that the irreversible crosslink formed with glutaraldehyde was not compatible with the reversibility of Schiff base formation. Richards and Knowles then noted that self condensation between aldehyde molecules generated α,β-unsaturated aldehydes (Fig. 2). Continued condensation yields products with two or more α,β-unsaturated aldehyde sites. These authors proposed that aldol condensation products of glutaraldehyde provided the "glue" for crosslinking in the sense that nucleophiles add to α,β-unsaturated aldehydes irreversibly (Fig. 2).

The proposal of Richards and Knowles stimulated significant efforts to determine the crosslinking chemistry (9-13). Others examined the nature of the crosslink and found that if other precursors are present, namely primary amines, a complex set of pyridine products are formed (14-17). The pyridine products provide the structural "glue" for crosslinking.

The present work investigates and discusses glutaraldehyde crosslinking in terms of the precursors and the size of the polymer products generated. The products are regarded as the actual crosslinking molecules. Glutaraldehyde based polymers assemble either by slow or by rapid kinetic processes. Examples are presented of polymer growth in the presence of other precursors in addition to glutaraldehyde.

Slow Crosslinking. The slow crosslinking process is characterized by aldol condensation reactions between glutaraldehyde molecules. The condensation products can be monitored at ~235 nm which is due to the formation of α,β-unsaturated aldol products (8, 18, 19). In neutral pH buffer glutaraldehyde condenses with itself, albeit slowly, at temperatures ranging from 0-40°C and pressures of 600-760 mm Hg. Rasmussen explored many parameters of glutaraldehyde self condensation (19). He demonstrated the increase in condensation rates with increases in the concentration of aldehyde, temperature, and pH (18, 19). Rasmussen did not report the size range of the condensation products.

In the present study, glutaraldehyde self-condensation products in a 0.2 M (2%) glutaraldehyde solution containing 0.05 M MOPS (pH 7.4) were monitored for their presence by absorption at 235 nm and for size by Sephadex G-25 gel filtration. Little change occurs at 235 nm for 60 minutes. After 20 hours at 40°C, a significant increase in adsorption at 235 nm occurs (Fig. 3). The sizes of the condensation products at 20 hours are not significantly larger than glutaraldehyde itself (Fig. 4). That is, the products do not fall within the sieving range of a Sephadex G-25 gel column. The molecular mass range of the products is estimated as between 100 and 1000 daltons.

The increase in adsorption at 235 nm suggests that glutaraldehyde molecules have condensed with each other in 20 hours at 40°C. The gel filtration profile reveals that the self-condensation crosslinking products grow slowly and remain small even after significant time periods. In terms of stabilizing protein molecules by intramolecular crosslinking with glutaraldehyde alone, only amino and sulfhydryl groups, that are proximal in space, are likely to be crosslinked by aldol condensation products.

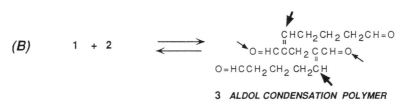

1   **2 ALDOL CONDENSATE**

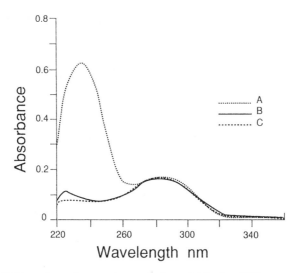

Figure 2.   Aldol condensation products of glutaraldehyde.   Bimolecular condensation yields the simple condensate 2, and further condensation yields 3 and higher order polymers. Nucleophilic groups such as primary amines react irreversibly with the α,β-unsaturated carbonyl groups forming Michael adducts (large arrowheads) (8). Reaction at the carbonyl carbon yield unsaturated Schiff bases (small arrowheads) (12). Higher order polymers provide multiple sites for crosslinking.

Figure 3. Self condensation products of glutaraldehyde. UV spectra. At 40°C for the time period 0 to 10 minutes there is virtually no change in the UV spectra of 2% glutaraldehyde in 50 mM MOPS (curves represented by A). Curves B and C represent 60 minutes and 20 hours respectively. The spectra were taken on an 8451 Hewlett Packard diode array spectrophotometer in a 1 cm path cell. Samples were diluted with 9 volumes of 50 mM MOPS prior to observing the spectra at 24°C.

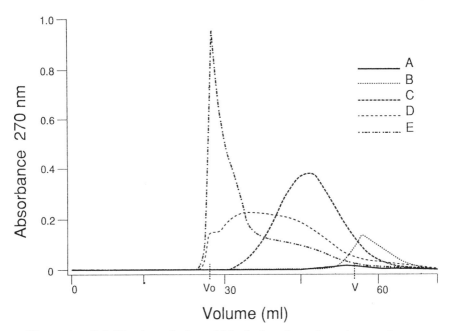

Volume (ml)

Figure 4.   Gel filtration of glutaraldehyde based condensation products on Sephadex G-25. Products of glutaraldehyde self-condensation and condensation with primary amines were chromatographed on a column of Sephadex G-25 (1.41 cm² x 48.4 cm) at 30 ml/hr. The column was equilibrated with gel buffer (0.01 M Na acetate, 0.20 M acetic acid, and 0.20 M NaCl, pH 3.4). The column effluent was monitored at 270 nm (5 mm path) with the exception noted using an ISCO V4 absorbance detector. The column liquid volume is marked with V and the excluded volume is marked with V_o. These column parameters were determined with 5' adenosine monophosphate (MW = 347) and bovine serum albumin (MW = 66,000) respectively.

At designated times the reaction products were diluted in 19 volumes of gel buffer except for the products represented by curve B which were diluted with 4 volumes of gel buffer. The experiments represented are as follows: curve A, glutaraldehyde 0 time control; curve B, 0.2 M glutaraldehyde self-condensation (20 hrs, 40°C, see Fig. 3, column effluent monitored at 240 nm); curve C, 0.20 M glutaraldehyde and 0.10 M glycine (5 min., 37°C); curve D, 0.20 M glutaraldehyde, 0.05 M glycine, and 0.025 M lysine (5 min., 37°C); and curve E, 0.20 M glutaraldehyde and 0.05 M lysine (5 min., 37°C).

Rapid Crosslinking. The rapid crosslinking process requires glutaraldehyde and other precursors, namely, low molecular weight primary amines. When the latter are added to glutaraldehyde solutions, substituted pyridine products in a range of sizes are rapidly generated. These products are the crosslinking bridges. One can control the product size by the kind of primary amine added and by the stoichiometric ratio of glutaraldehyde to primary amine (14, 17).

The addition of primary amine precursors to glutaraldehyde gives rise to pyridines and polypyridines (Fig. 5) (14-17). In a reaction of methylamine with glutaraldehyde, the intermediate cyclic iminium ion has been trapped and recovered in good yield by selective reduction (20). The polymer products are 3 dimensional networks because branching is possible at any aldehyde site. Accompanying the process is a rapid increase in absorbance at 265-270 nm (14-17). Only a short reaction time (ranging from seconds to minutes) is required to generate structures far larger than glutaraldehyde itself.

Some examples of glutaraldehyde-amine reactions demonstrate the size range of the pyridine products. Glutaraldehyde (0.20 M) and glycine (0.10 M) in 0.20 M MOPS yield products within one minute at 37°C that are large enough that they are partially excluded from the pores of G-25 (data not shown). The profile of 5 minute products is shown in Fig. 4. Products range in size from nearly excluded to smaller structures completely able to enter the gel structure. The apparent molecular masses of the products therefore range from a few hundred daltons to less than 5000. By 5 minutes, the rapid phase of growth is over. There is some growth of products in the period from 5-30 minutes according to the Sephadex G-25 chromatographic profile of the reaction products. After 30 minutes there is virtually no change after many hours at 37°C (data not shown).

Some products of the reaction of 0.20 M glutaraldehyde and 0.05 M lysine in MOPS buffer at 37°C are excluded by one minute, and by 5 minutes, excluded products predominate (Fig. 4). Again, some consolidation into larger structures occurs by 30 minutes and beyond. Most product growth takes place in the first few minutes.

Products intermediate in size range can be obtained by adding glutaraldehyde (0.20 M) to a mixture of glycine (0.05 M) and lysine (0.025 M) again in MOPS buffer. The gel filtration profile of 5 minute reaction products at 37°C shows a wide range of products from excluded products to products barely entering the gel (Fig. 3, curve C). The mixed amine products consolidated substantially between 5-30 minutes. At 30 minutes the larger products predominate.

The formation of pyridines is accompanied by a rapid uptake of oxygen as dihydropyridines are oxidized to pyridines (21).

Crosslinking, Enzyme Stabilization, and Cytochemistry. Crosslinking for the purposes of enzyme stabilization or cytochemistry requires a balance between immobilization and access to enzymes and antigens. Some immobilization is necessary for ultrastructure and enzyme stabilization. Excessive immobilization in the form of crosslinking "rope" will restrict access to epitopes by antibodies or access to enzyme catalytic sites by substrates.

The main elements of manipulative control of crosslinking with glutaraldehyde are: 1) concentration of aldehyde, 2) addition of mono- and di- primary amines, and 3) time.

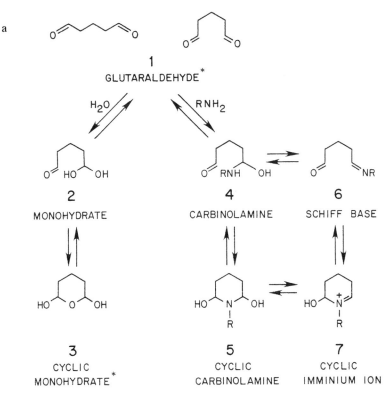

a

1
GLUTARALDEHYDE*

2
MONOHYDRATE

4
CARBINOLAMINE

6
SCHIFF BASE

3
CYCLIC
MONOHYDRATE*

5
CYCLIC
CARBINOLAMINE

7
CYCLIC
IMMINIUM ION

Figure 5.   Pathways for obtaining pyridines from glutaraldehyde-amine precursors.   (5a) Glutaraldehyde cyclization.   In water cyclic structures $\underline{3}$ represent >80% of glutaraldehyde (*20*). Glutaraldehyde cyclizes in the presence of primary amines. The cyclic iminium ion, $\underline{7}$, has been trapped in good yield (*20*, see text). (5b) Low molecular weight pyridines. Abstraction of a proton from $\underline{7}$ facilitates condensation with an additional glutaraldehyde molecule. Dihydropyridine $\underline{9}$ is obtained after another glutaraldehyde molecule condenses. Pyridine $\underline{10}$ is afforded after facile oxidation of $\underline{9}$. (5c) Pyridine polymers. If the last glutaraldehyde molecule in the scheme is replaced by a molecule with a single aldehyde function such as $\underline{8}$, polymers can be generated. This scheme suggests that the ratio of glutaraldehyde/amine is an important determinant of product size (*17*).

Continued on next page

b

7   CYCLIC IMMINIUM ION

8   ALDOL CONDENSATE

9   DIHYDROPYRIDINE

O_2

10   PYRIDINE

8 + 8   and   8 + 9

c

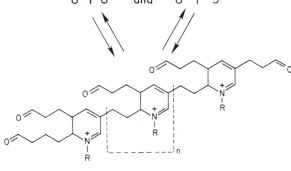

11
"DIHYDROPYRIDINE POLYMERS"

O_2

12
"PYRIDINE POLYMERS"

Figure 5. Continued

It is not likely that the largest crosslinking polymers will be helpful for maintaining enzyme activity or retaining antigenicity. Simply put, too much "rope" will sterically hinder access of substrates or antibodies. Or worse yet, excess "rope" will completely block access. It is possible to tailor the crosslink in terms of size by choice of precursors (Table 3). While some aldol condensation does occur between glutaraldehyde molecules themselves, even in the presence of primary amines, the predominant chemistry is the formation of substituted pyridine and polypyridine products (*14-17*). A large excess of glutaraldehyde causes the reaction to revert to the slow default mode of aldol crosslinking.

The time factor should be manipulated because it is easy to do. The goal is to promote the degree of crosslinking needed for stabilization but to permit subsequent biochemistry in terms of enzyme activity or epitope recognition. Product size can be controlled by quenching the polymerization reaction with acid to terminate growth. In the present work the rapid polymerization of glutaraldehyde-amine reactions was terminated by acidifying to pH < 4, i.e., by diluting into 19 volumes of acetate buffer at pH 3.4 (Fig. 4). If acidifying is not compatible with the material to be crosslinked, then rapid dilution or other means of separating small molecules must be employed.

If lysine is chosen to form the crosslinking matrix with glutaraldehyde, then addition of significant concentrations of primary amines such as glycine can be used to restrict the size of the polymer products. In practice, this means adding glycine to one-half of the glutaraldehyde concentration. For 1% glutaraldehyde (0.1 M), add 0.05 volumes of 1 M glycine ($\leq$0.05 M). This step rapidly produces short polypyridines.

In the formation of pyridine products, the ratio of glutaraldehyde to primary amine is as important as the presence of the primary amine. Pyridine polymers are favored by ratios of <2 (*17*). Pyridine monomers are favored by ratios of >3 (*17*).

It is possible to change the chemical nature of the crosslink by choosing different sidechains in the precursor amines. Thus, the negative charge carried by the carboxyl in glycine, for example, can be eliminated and a neutral hydroxyl substituted if ethanolamine is used instead. The worker can select from many amine choices according to experimental needs. Choice of the precursors allows a measure of control over the product size.

Blocking Active Aldehydes. Active aldehyde sites arising from the crosslinking structure are present and usually need to be blocked before subsequent procedures, especially those using other proteins, such as cytochemical labeling. Failure to do so will cause other proteins to accrete to the aldehyde sites generating false positives in labeling. This occurs because monoaldehydes form complexes with primary amines. While the complexes are reversible, the equilibrium lies in favor of complex (*22*). If a protein becomes a polyaldehyde after crosslinking, a polyamine antibody can form multiple aldehyde-amine complexes with the fixed protein. The probability of all complexes reversing simultaneously becomes small and the antibody is nonspecifically and, for practical purposes, irreversibly attached.

The polyaldehyde sites must be blocked with molecules which interfere least with subsequent procedures. Many large molecules have been used to accomplish the blocking. Non-specific serum or IgG are commonly used. Also, solubilized milk powder, gelatin, fish skin gelatin, and bovine serum albumin are used.

Table 3
Glutaraldehyde-based Polymers

Precursors	Product Size (daltons)	Time
Glut	>100 to <1000	5-40 hours
Glut/Glycine	>100 to <5000	5 min
Glut/Glycine/Lysine	>1000 to 5000	5 min
Glut/Lysine	>1000 to >5000	5 min

Another direction for blocking irreversible and non-specific binding is to chemically change the aldehyde sites by reduction to alcohols with NaBH$_4$ (sodium borohydride) (23). Sodium borohydride is dissolved in 0.01 M NaOH to a concentration of 100 mM. The borohydride solution is added to fixed preparations to final concentrations of 1-10 mM. After 2-5 minutes additional borohydride is added; a third addition may even be useful. The fixed preparations should be adjusted to a pH of at least ~8 because the borohydride is labile under more acidic conditions (23). Borohydride has a half-life of about 1 minute at pH 8, but only 6 sec at pH 7.

Laboratory Safety with Aldehydes. How does one handle glutaraldehyde spills and excess glutaraldehyde? The simplest and fastest method is to have a 1 M solution of glycine on hand. Glycine is a zwitterion and when the amino group reacts with glutaraldehyde, the complex (now charged via the carboxyl group of glycine) is non-volatile. As the precursors progress down the polymerization pathways, the glutaraldehyde precursor is trapped as a non-volatile and minimally reactive polymer. The investigator's eyes, lungs etc. are at little risk from the advanced polymerization products. Sufficient glycine should be added so that there is at least 0.5 moles of glycine/mole glutaraldehyde.

For small spills one should keep a wash bottle with 1 M glycine nearby and spray the spill. One volume of the glycine will react with to 10 volumes of 2% glutaraldehyde (0.2 M). Excess glutaraldehyde waste, for example, is easily detoxified by pouring the waste into a polyethylene bottle (4 liter milk container) into which 700 ml of 1 M glycine was previously added. One can fill the container with up to 4% glutaraldehyde (0.4 M) waste for rapid detoxification. Lower concentrations of glutaraldehyde need proportionately less 1 M glycine.

Acknowledgments

I thank Barbara Johnson for her suggestions and Michael Himmel for his patient efforts to see the work completed. The work was supported by the National Institutes of Health GM 39503-03 to J. Rash and T. Johnson.

Literature Cited

1. Sabatini, D. D.; Bensch, K. J.; Barnett, R. J. *J. Cell Biol.* **1963**, *17*, 19-58.
2. Molin, S.; Nygren, H.; Dolonius, L. *J. Histochem. Cytochem.* **1978**, *26*, 412-414.
3. Tatsumoto, K.; Baker, J. O.; Tucker, M. P.; Oh, K. K.; Mohagheghi, A.; Grohmann, K.; Himmel, M. E. *Appl. Biochem. Biotechnol.* **1988**, *18*, 159-174.
4. Schiff, H. *Ann. Chem.* **1901**, *319*, 59-76.
5. Levy, M. *J. Biol. Chem.* **1933**, *99*, 767-779.
6. Kallen, R. G.; Jencks, W. P. *J. Biol. Chem.* **1966**, *241*, 5864-5878.
7. Johnson, T. J. A. *J. Electron Microsc. Tech.* **1985**, *2*, 129-138.
8. Richards, F. M.; Knowles, J. R. *J. Mol. Biol.* **1968**, *37*, 231-233.
9. Whipple, E. B.; Ruta, M. *J. Org. Chem.* **1974**, *39*, 1666-1668.
10. Hardy, P. M.; Nicholls, A. C.; Rydon, H. N. *J. Chem. Soc. Chem. Comm.* **1969**, 565-566.
11. Hopwood, D. *Histochem. J.* **1972**, *4*, 267-303.
12. Monsan, P.; Puzo, G.; Mazarquil, H. *Biochemie* **1975**, *57*, 1281-1292.
13. Lubig, R.; Kusch, P.; Roper, K.; Zahn, H. *Monatschefte fur Chemie* **1981**, *112*, 1313-1323.
14. Hardy, P. M.; Nicholls, A. C.; Rydon, H. N. *J. Chem. Soc. Perkin I* **1976**, 958-962.
15. Hardy, P. M.; Hughes, G. J.; Rydon, H. N. *J. Chem. Soc. Chem. Comm.* **1976**, 157-158.
16. Hardy, P. M.; Hughes, G. J.; Rydon, H. N. *J. Chem. Soc. Perkin I* **1979**, 2282-2288.
17. Johnson, T. J. A. In The Science of Biological Specimen Preparation 1985; Mueller, M.; Becker, R. P.; Boyde, A.; Wolosewick, J. J., Eds.; SEM Inc.: AMF O'Hare, IL 60666, 1986, pp 51-62.
18. Gillet, R.; Gull, K. *Histochemie* **1972**, *30*, 162-167.
19. Rasmussen, K. E.; Albrechtsen, J. *J. Histochem.* **1974**, *38*, 19-26.
20. Borch, R. F.; Bernstein, M. D.; Durst, H. D. *J. Am. Chem. Soc.* **1971**, *93*, 2897-2904.
21. Johnson, T. J. A. *Eur. J. Cell Biol.* **1987**, *45*, 160-169.
22. Hine, J.; Yeh, C. Y.; Schmalstieg, F. C. *J. Org. Chem.* **1970**, *35*, 340-344.
23. Leppla, S. L.; Bjoraker, B. J.; Bock, R. M. *Methods Enzymol.* **1968**, *XII* Part B, 236-240.
24. Good, N. E.; Winget, G. D.; Winter, W.; Connolly, T. N.; Izawa, S.; Singh, R. M. M. *Biochem. J.* **1966**, *5*, 467-477.

RECEIVED April 29, 1992

Chapter 24

Chemical Modification

Effect on Enzyme Activities and Stabilities

A. Sadana and R. R. Raju

Department of Chemical Engineering, University of Mississippi,
University, MS 38677–9740

The chemical modification of enzymes is analyzed using a series-deactivation model. The influence of chemical modification on the specific activity of the initial enzyme state, on the stability and on the residual activity of different enzymes is presented. The chemical modification may change none, one, two, or all of the above variables for an enzyme. The analysis provides fresh physical insights into enzyme deactivation processes, and into the structure-function relationships for enzymes.

A significant amount of effort has been spent in understanding enzyme deactivation mechanisms and what affects the residual activity of enzymes. This type of effort provides significant physical insights into the enzyme structure and function, besides it helps utilize enzyme ability to its fullest extent. Basically, one would like to know how active a particular enzyme state is, and for how long can one maintain a required level of activity. Chemical modification is one means by which one can help an enzyme attain the required characteristics of enzyme activity, residual activity, and stability. Stability generally refers to an inverse measure of the rate constant for transformation of one enzyme state (in this case) to another. Residual activity refers to the activity of an enzyme form (different from the initial enzyme state), which is encountered along the inactivation pathway, and is stable enough under the stress being applied that it can accumulate and persist for a long time. This time period is a long time compared to the time required to transform the native form or some preceding non-native form almost completely into this form. This form then appears to be "permanent." The influence of modification (chemical or otherwise) on initial enzyme activity, stability, and on residual activity is important. More often than not, only one, at best two, of the above three is reported in the literature. In general, initial enzyme activity, residual activity, and stability exhibit opposing tendencies, and

0097–6156/93/0516–0296$06.00/0

thus, it is essential to report the influence of modification of enzymes on initial enzyme activity, residual activity and stability.

In this paper we will attempt to analyze enzyme deactivations based on the influence of chemical modification on the initial enzyme activity, residual activity, and on the stability. This should shed novel physical insights into enzyme deactivation mechanisms, and into the structure and function of enzymes. Surely, it is of interest to develop guiding principles in order that one may predictively attain required (and balanced) levels of initial enzyme activity, stability and residual activity for enzymes. Hopefully, this paper is one step in that direction.

Theory

Since we are interested in both the initial activity and the residual activity, enzyme deactivation data available in the literature was screened for both of these aspects. Generally, the residual activity data is available for enzyme deactivations. Since the data is reported often in terms of normalized activity (enzyme activity at any time, t divided by enzyme activity at time, t = 0), the initial specific activity is generally not available. Also, microheterogeneity of enzymes is often observed (*1*) and this factor should be considered while analyzing the influence of chemical modification on enzyme activity, stability, and residual activity.

The activity-time expression used is (*1*):

$$
\begin{aligned}
a = (1 &+ \frac{\beta_1 k_1}{k_2 - k_1} - \frac{\beta_2 k_2}{k_2 - k_1}) \exp(-k_1 t) \\
&- (\frac{k_1}{k_2 - k_1})(\beta_1 - \beta_2) \exp(-k_2 t) + \beta_2
\end{aligned}
\tag{1}
$$

This weighted-average activity expression is obtained for the series-deactivation scheme:

$$
E \xrightarrow{k_1} E_1 \xrightarrow{k_2} E_2
\tag{2}
$$

Here k_1 and k_2 are first-order deactivation rate coefficients. Let [E], [E_1], and [E_2] be the concentrations of the different enzyme states. Also, let δ, δ_1, and δ_2 be the specific activities of the E, E_1, and E_2 enzyme states, respectively. Let β_1 be the ratio of the specific activities δ_1/δ, and β_2 the ratio of the specific activities δ_2/δ. At time t equal to zero, the normalized activity, a, is equal to one. Very rarely, if at all, does one see units in the activity label in these figures. Figures 1 to 3 show curves fitted by the SAS procedure (*2*) performed on experimental data on immobilized and soluble enzymes using equation 1. The estimated values of k_1, k_2, β_1, and β_2 are given in a table that follows for the unmodified and the modified enzymes undergoing inactivation.

It may be shown that for the series deactivation scheme:

$$E \xrightarrow{k_1} E_1 \xrightarrow{k_2} E_2 \xrightarrow{k_3} E_3 \xrightarrow{k_4} E_4 \xrightarrow{k_5} \cdots \xrightarrow{k_n} E_n \xrightarrow{k_{n+1}} E_d \tag{3}$$

the weighted-average activity function is given by:

$$
\begin{aligned}
a = [1 &+ \frac{\beta_1 k_1}{k_2 - k_1} + \frac{\beta_2 k_1 k_2}{(k_2 - k_1)(k_3 - k_1)} + \frac{\beta_3 k_1 k_2 k_3}{(k_2 - k_1)(k_3 - k_1)(k_4 - k_1)} + \cdots \\
&+ \frac{\beta_n k_1 k_2 k_3 \cdots k_n}{(k_2 - k_2)(k_3 - k_1)(k_4 - k_1) \cdots (k_{n+1} - k_1)}] \exp(-k_1 t) \\
&+ [\frac{\beta_1 k_1}{k_1 - k_2} + \frac{\beta_2 k_1 k_2}{(k_1 - k_2)(k_3 - k_2)} + \frac{\beta_3 k_1 k_2 k_3}{(k_1 - k_2)(k_3 - k_2)(k_4 - k_2)} + \cdots \\
&+ \frac{\beta_n k_1 k_2 k_3 \cdots k_n}{(k_1 - k_2)(k_3 - k_2) \cdots (k_{n+1} - k_2)}] \exp(-k_2 t) + \cdots \\
&+ [\frac{\beta_n k_1 k_2 k_3 \cdots k_n}{(k_1 - k_{n+1})(k_2 - k_{n+1})(k_3 - k_{n+1}) \cdots (k_n - k_{n+1})}] \exp(k_{n+1} t)
\end{aligned}
\tag{4}
$$

Let δ_3, δ_4, δ_5, etc. be the specific activities of the E_3, E_4, E_5, enzyme states. Then β_3 = δ_3/δ, $\beta_4 = \delta_4/\delta$, $\beta_5 = \delta_5/\delta$, etc. Equations (3) and (4) involve a large number of parameters. Nevertheless, a multi-deactivation step model would be more appropriate in some cases. For example, a general equation based on this reaction scheme will be more realistic in predicting whether an enzyme is deactivated to what stage. This would be particularly useful for enzymes that can exist in different conformational states. In spite of the complexity of equation (3) it is apparently inappropriate for cross-linked enzymes, since this procedure generally produces heterogeneous molecules.

Prior to presenting some examples, it is appropriate to present certain "disclaimers" regarding the limited nature of the model that has been simplified enough to be of practical use. (a) The model describes a multi-step process that is indeed useful in describing some 'complex' enzyme inactivations. Note that a large number of inactivations can be modeled quite effectively in terms of simple first-order decays. We have simply chosen to study multi-step processes in this paper. (b) The model describes two sequential, irreversible steps. It is possible for kinetically detectable denaturation intermediates to arise from reversible steps, such as a 'pre-equilibrium' between stable and more labile forms, the latter being transformed by later steps. (c) When "activity remaining" is not measured in the "stress situation" itself, but is measured under other conditions using withdrawn aliquots, partial reversibility of the inactivation may result in "residual activities" that are not actually present in the enzyme at the point in the stress situation from which the aliquot was withdrawn.   (Dilution for assay of some samples denatured in urea is a specific example).   (d) Chemical modification of enzymes is extremely likely to introduce heterogeneity in that potential reaction sites may or may not be modified in a given enzyme molecule.   Modification at one site may interfere with subsequent modification at a neighboring site, and the effect of modification at different sites may be different even opposing.   When a hypothetical chemically modified enzyme, tested under conditions capable of completely inactivating the native enzyme (i.e., with no "residual activity"), shows a "residual activity" equivalent to half the initial activity of the native enzyme, all of the modified enzyme molecules may have been transformed by the stress into a different form that has one-half the activity per molecule.   Another possibility is that half the enzyme molecules may be stabilized to such an extent that they retain <u>all</u> of their original activity, and the other half of the enzyme molecules fall prey to competing, non-stabilizing chemical modifications, and, under the testing stress, wind up completely inactivated.   Without some means, other than activity, of measuring the state of the protein(s) we are not going to be able to distinguish between the two explanations.

Chemical modification of enzymes may lead to opposing changes in initial specific activity and residual activity.   The chemical modification may be by cross-linking agents that make the enzyme more rigid (less flexible).   The cross-links act as a clamp to "rigidify" the enzyme in its native conformation.   This leads to a decreasing initial specific activity and an increasing residual activity.   The modification may also increase the initial specific activity and decrease the residual activity of the enzyme.

Example 1. Effect of modification and presumably cross-linking of penicillinase by toluene 2,4-diisocyanate on the thermostability of the enzyme. The influence of cross-linking by toluene 2,4-diisocyanate on the initial specific activity of penicillinase (*3*) is shown in Figure 1 and in Table I. Toluene 2,4-diisocyanate binds to the ε-amino group of lysine residues in a protein and forms a stable ureido-bond (*4*). Cross-linking increases, in general, the thermostability of enzymes (*5*), including penicillinase (*6*).   The cross-linking of penicillinase by toluene 2,4-diisocyanate reduces the initial specific activity by nearly 48 percent. Cross-linking does stabilize the enzyme since the rate constant for inactivation for the first steps, k_1 decreases from 3.4 min^{-1} to 1.0 min^{-1} on modification.   The k_2 value is unchanged.   The relative residual activity is slightly more than double (β_2 equals 0.19 and 0.41 for the unmodified and modified enzyme forms, respectively). In absolute terms, the specific activities of the final enzyme state for the unmodified and the modified enzyme are 49 and 56 units/μg, respectively.   No information was given (*3*) regarding the standard deviation of enzyme activity measurements.   In many cases, it is not uncommon to obtain 20 percent variation in enzyme activity measurements.   Thus, one might reasonably argue if 49 units/μg is truly different from 56 units/μg?

Example 2. Effect of acetamidination on the thermal stability of pig heart lactate dehydrogenase. Table I also shows the influence of methylacetimidate modification on the thermal denaturation at 60°C of pig heart lactate dehydrogenase (*7*).   The figure is not given.   Lactate dehydrogenase is a tetrameric enzyme.   Out of the 24

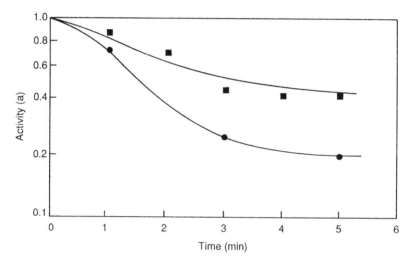

Figure 1. The effect of prior chemical modification with toluene 2,4-diisocynate on the thermal inactivation kinetics of penicillinase measured at 56°C in 0.05 M potassium phosphate buffer containing 0.25% gelatin; ● native; ■ modified by toluene 2,4-diisocyanate in the absence of substrate. (Adapted from ref. 7, Figure 1. Reproduced with permission from ref. 15. Copyright 1985 Wiley.)

Table I. Influence of Chemical Modification on Initial Specific Activity, Residual Activity, and Rate Constants for Inactivation of Enzymes

Enzyme	Chemical Modifier	Initial Specific Activity (units/μg protein)	Residual Activity (units/μg protein)	k_1 k_2 (min^{-1})	β_1	β_2	Ref.
penicillinase	None	260	49	3.4 1.1	1.3	0.19	3
penicillinase	toluene 2,4-diisocyanate (0.1 ml/mg enzyme)	136	56	1.0 1.1	1.0	0.41	3
lactate dehydrogenase	None	436	56	170 d^{-1} 180 d^{-1}	0.81	0.43	7
lactate dehydrogenase	methyl acetimidate, 2.8 mg reagent/mg protein	348	320	220 d^{-1} 250 d^{-1}	0.91	0.92	7
penicillinase in urea	None	260	185	0.071 0.094	1.1	0.71	3
penicillinase in urea	toluene 2,4-diisocyanate	136	109	0.078 0.13	1.2	0.80	3

Continued on next page

Table I. Influence of Chemical Modification on Initial Specific Activity, Residual Activity, and Rate Constants for Inactivation of Enzymes (Continued)

Enzyme	Chemical Modifier	Initial Specific Activity (units/μg protein)	Residual Activity (units/μg protein)	k_1 k_2 (min^{-1})		β_1	β_2	Ref.
mushroom tyrosinase (immobilized on collagen)	None	$\dfrac{0.2 \text{ μmol DOPA}}{\text{h-mg protein}}$	0	14 d^{-1}	19 d^{-1}	1.6	0	10
mushroom tyrosinase (immobilized on collagen)	dimethyl adipimidate	$\dfrac{0.3 \text{ μmol DOPA}}{\text{h-mg protein}}$	0	12 d^{-1}	11 d^{-1}	1.2	0	10
E. coli asparaginase	None	100% of native unmodified enzyme	0	0.23	0	0	0	11
E. coli asparaginase	succinylation: fraction of groups acylated equal to 0.26	65% of native unmodified enzyme	0	0.15	0	0	0	11

lysines per subunit, only 6.5 ± 0.5 lysines were left unmodified. On modification, the specific activity of the initial enzyme state decreases by 20 percent and the relative residual activity more than doubles. In absolute terms, the specific activities of the final enzyme state for the unmodified and modified enzyme are 188 and 320 units/µg, respectively. Note that a 20 percent decrease in the initial specific activity by chemical modification increases the specific activity of the final state by 60 percent. Since k_1 and k_2 both increase after treatment with methylacetimidate the cross links in this case destabilize the enzyme. Also, in neither case does the activity-time curve (Figures 2 a,b in reference *7*) appear to have "bottomed out" at the end of the data shown. Both enzyme preparations are losing activity 34 minutes after the start of the incubation at 60°C. Residual activity is the theoretical limiting value obtained by modeling the denaturation data using equation (1).

Chemical modification of enzymes may lead to changes in the initial specific activity and the residual activity in the same direction. These changes could be caused by both external and intrinsic (or non-external) agents. Examples of intrinsic agents could be enzyme or co-enzyme concentrations, which, for example, may convert subactive enzyme forms to more active enzyme forms. This could lead to increases in both initial specific activity and residual activity. Some alcohols stabilize proteins at low concentrations.

Example 3.   Effect of cross-linking with toluene 2,4 diisocyanate on the inactivation kinetics of penicillinase in 8 M urea. The influence of cross-linking of penicillinase in urea by toluene 2.4-diisocyanate (*3*) decreases the initial specific activity by nearly 48 percent (see Table I). The relative value of the residual activity of the final enzyme state for the modified enzyme is higher than of the unmodified enzyme (β_2 equals 0.71 and 0.80 for the unmodified and modified forms, respectively). However, in absolute terms, the specific activities of the final enzyme state for the unmodified and the modified enzyme are 185 and 108 units/µg respectively.   Since k_1 and k_2 both increase after treatment with toluene 2,4-diisocyanate, the cross links in this case destabilize the enzyme. In this case, the modification of the enzyme reduces both the specific activity of the initial enzyme state and that of the final enzyme state, and also destabilizes the enzyme. (Figure 2)

Example 4.   Effect of modification with dimethyl adipimidate on the "reaction inactivation" of mushroom tyrosinase immobilized in a collagen membrane and used in a flow reactor. Table I shows that modification by dimethyl adipimidate of mushroom tyrosinase immobilized on collagen increases the specific activity of the initial enzyme state by 50 percent (*10*). The activity-time figure is not given. The cross links provided by the dimethyl adipimidate suitably change the conformation of the active site to yield a higher catalytic activity. The estimated β_2 values for the unmodified and the modified enzymes are zero, thus, the cross-links do not provide the necessary rigidity to the enzyme for it to exhibit a residual activity. However, the cross-links do stabilize the enzyme, as they slow down the inactivation process. This is because the estimated values of k_1 and k_2 for the modified enzyme are lower than the corresponding values of the unmodified enzyme.

Example 5. Effect of succinylation on the resistance of E. coli asparaginase to inactivation by subtilisin proteolysis. The influence of succinylation on the initial specific activity and resistance of *E. coli* asparaginase to subtilisin proteolysis *(11)* is shown in Figure 3 and Table I. Succinylation was carried out to obtain the desired ratios of succinic anhydride and lysine residues. Native asparaginase is rapidly inactivated by subtilisin at a molar ratio of subtilisin to asparaginase of 1:25. A succinylation (fraction of groups acylated equal to 0.26) of *E. coli* asparaginase *(11)* leads to a decrease in the specific activity of the initial enzyme state. This extent of succinylation decreases the specific activity of the initial enzyme state to 65 percent of the unmodified enzyme value. From Figure 3 it appears that the curves for the unmodified and the 26% modified enzyme inactivation can be modelled adequately by straight lines. For these curves there would appear to be no necessity of postulating an inactivation pathway involving more than one step. The situation for these curves can be accommodated in Equation (1) by assuming $\beta_1 = 0$, and $k_2 = 0$ and/or $\beta_2 = 0$. For 26 percent modification, the observed changes in the inactivation process are changes in the initial activity (the modified enzyme exhibits a decrease compared to the unmodified enzyme) and in the (apparent first-order) rate constant (the modified enzyme exhibits a lower rate constant compared to the unmodified enzyme) for inactivation. Thus, modification in this case leads to a decrease in the specific activity of the initial state, but it also stabilizes the enzyme.

Chemical modification of enzymes may also lead to changes only in the residual activity. The specific activity of the initial enzyme state is unaltered. These types of changes may be observed when chemical modification of an enzyme molecule occurs only at positions distant from the active site. This type of modification can drastically affect residual activity, while leaving its specific activity unaltered.

Also, it is not always necessary that modification must lead to changes in initial specific activity and/or residual activity. In some cases, chemical modification of enzymes leaves both the initial specific activity and the residual activity unaltered. This type of behavior may really be split into two further types. In the first case there is no inactivation of either the unmodified or the modified enzyme. Then, the initial specific activities are equal and so are the residual activities. In the other case there is inactivation but the estimated values of β_2 are the same. Examples of the first type could include the possibility of the introduction of a "defense mechanism" against enzyme inactivation by the introduction of a chemical modifier *(13)*. It is perhaps not too unreasonable to assume that examples of the second type would be rare. This is so, since the chemical modification would have to be such that (a) it does not change either the initial specific activity or the residual activity, and (b) other deactivation characteristics such as k_1 and k_2 values may or may not change.

Conclusions

The series-deactivation model is utilized to analyze chemical modification-induced enzyme inactivations. The analysis is based on the influence of modification on the specific activity of the initial enzyme state, the residual activity, and on the inactivation rate constants. The analysis provides an appropriate framework to

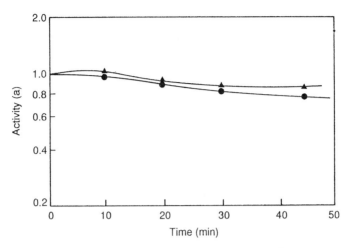

Figure 2.   The effect of cross-linking with toluene 2,4-diisocyanate on the
inactivation kinetics of penicillinase in 8 M urea,
● no additives present; ▲ toluene 2,4-diisocyanate present. (Adapted from ref. 3,
Figures 1 and 3. Reproduced with permission from ref. 15. Copyright 1985 Wiley.)

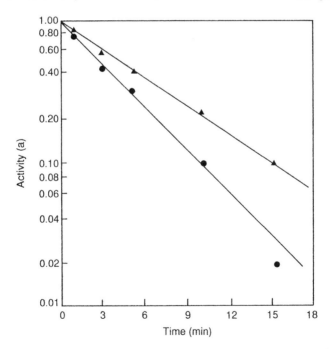

Figure 3.   Influence of succinylation on the inactivation kinetics of *E. coli*
Asparaginase,   ● no modification; ▲ fraction of groups
acylated equal to 0.26. (Adapted from ref. 11, Figure 2. Reproduced with
permission from ref. 16. Copyright 1986 C. D. Scott.)

compare enzyme deactivation data obtained by different investigators working in a wide variety of areas. By providing judicious examples wherever appropriate the analysis provides an overall perspective of the influence of chemical modification of enzymes undergoing inactivation. Finally, the analysis should provide fresh physical insights into enzyme deactivation processes and stimulate further studies to provide a better understanding of enzymes, in general.

Literature Cited

1. Sadana, A. Biocatalysis: Fundamentals Of Enzyme Deactivation Kinetics, Prentice Hall: New York, NY, 1991, p. 256.
2. SAS User's Guide, Statistics Edition, SAS Institute: Cary, NY, 1982.
3. Klemes, Y.; Citri, N. *Biochem. J.* **1980**, *187*, 529.
4. Schick, A. F.; Singer, S. J. *J. Biol. Chem.* **1961**, *236*, 2477.
5. Zaborsky, O. R., In *Enzyme Engineering*, (E. K. Pye and L. B. Wingard, Jr., eds.), Plenum Press: New York, NY, 1974, Vol. 2, pp. 115-22.
6. Klemes, Y.; Citri, N. *Biochim. Biophys. Acta* **1979**, *567*, 401.
7. Tuengler, P.; Pfleiderer, G. *Biochim. Biophys. Acta* **1977**, *484*, 1.
8. Fornaini, G.; Leoncini, G.; Segni, P.; Calabria, G.A.; Dacha, M. *Eur. J. Biochem.* **1969**, *7*, 214.
9. Yoshida, A. *J. Biol. Chem.* **1966**, *241*, 4966.
10. Letts, D.; Chase, Jr., T. *Adv. Exp. Med. Biol.* **1974**, *42*, 317.
11. Nickle, E. C.; Solomon, R. D.; Torchia, T. E.; and Wriston, Jr., J. C. *Biochim. Biophys. Acta* **1982**, *704*, 345.
12. Keradjopoulos, D.; Holdorf, A. W. *FEMS Microbiol. Lett.* **1977**, *1*, 179.
13. Eaton, J. W.; Boraas, M.; Etkins, N. L. *Adv. Exp. Med. Biol.* **1972**, *28*, 121.
14. McMahon, S.; Stern, A. *Biochim. Biophys. Acta* **1979**, *566*, 253.
15. Sadana, A. Henley, J. P. *Biotechnol. Bioeng.* **1986**, *28*, 256.
16. Sadana, A. Henley, J. P. In *Seventh Symposium on Biotechnology for Fuels and Chemicals;* Scott, C. D., Ed. Wiley: New York, 1985, p. 487.

RECEIVED April 29, 1992

Chapter 25

Cross-Linking Techniques

Applications to Enzyme and Protein Stabilization and Bioconjugate Preparation

Munishwar N. Gupta

Chemistry Department, Indian Institute of Technology, Delhi Hauz Khas, New Delhi–110 016, India

Chemical crosslinking technology was used for (a) enhancing the stability of trypsin, β-galactosidase, and concanavalin A and (b) forming protein-protein conjugates viz. trypsin–chymotrypsin, trypsin–β-galactosidase, and concanavalin A–β-galactosidase. For stabilization of the three proteins, dimethyl adipimidate was found to give the best results. The intramolecularly crosslinked trypsin, with an average of 9.5 groups modified out of 14 free amino groups present, showed a much slower rate of autolysis at 40°C compared to native trypsin. Crosslinked β-galactosidase entrapped in polyacrylamide hydrolyzed 47% of milk lactose in 6 h and at 55°C. Entrapped native enzyme hydrolyzed only 31% substrate under the same conditions. Besides preparing an insoluble aggregate of trypsin–chymotrypsin and β-galactosidase, conjugates of trypsin–chymotrypsin, trypsin–alkaline phosphatase, and Concanavalin A–β-galactosidase were also prepared and evaluated.

There is near unanimity about unfolding of the polypeptide chain as being a primary event in the denaturation of proteins (*1*). For example, in thermal denaturation, this is the initial reversible step (*2*). Thus, it follows that any approach which makes proteins rigid (reduces conformational flexibility) should impart stability. Three distinct approaches attempt to do this by creating additional linkages with parts of the polypeptide chain:

0097–6156/93/0516–0307$06.00/0

(1).   Immobilization (*2-4*)

(2).   Introduction of disulfide bridges by protein engineering (*5*)

(3).   Chemical crosslinking (*6*)

The present chapter would limit itself to the third approach. Apart from protein stabilization, another major application of crosslinking technology has been linking of different biological molecules by intermolecular crosslinking. Such bioconjugates have already found considerable applications in such diverse areas as bioconversion (*7*), medicine (*8*), and bioseparation (*9*). This chapter would also describe some work on heteroenzyme conjugates and other bioconjugate preparations using intermolecular crosslinking.

Crosslinking Methodology

When a crosslinking reagent reacts with a protein molecule, several kinds of reaction products are possible, including intramolecularly crosslinked proteins, oligomers formed due to intermolecular crosslinking, and insoluble protein aggregates. However, it is possible to design a crosslinking experiment so as to obtain the desirable product as the major reaction product.

Some general guidelines mentioned by Wold (*10*) many years ago are quite useful for this purpose:

(1).   High protein concentration would favor intermolecular crosslinking over intramolecular crosslinking.

(2).   Ph corresponding to minimum net charge on the protein would favor intermolecular crosslinking.

(3).   High reagent to protein ratio and prolonged reaction time would favor extensive crosslinking and may result in insoluble protein aggregates.

(4).   Successful formation of crosslinks depend upon the availability of suitable reactive groups within the effective range of the reagents. In the context of intramolecular crosslinking, this means that the "span" of the crosslinking reagent is a crucial parameter.

Enzyme Stabilization

Chemical Crosslinking of Trypsin. The property of trypsin to undergo autolysis in solution has resulted in this enzyme being a favorite target of various approaches of enzyme stabilization (*11-13*). Attempts at chemical crosslinking of trypsin with glutaraldehyde and two bisimidoesters [i.e., dimethyl suberimidate (DMS) and dimethyl adipimidate (DMA)] indicated that bisimidoesters are a better choice for obtaining trypsin preparations with decreased autolysis (*14*). Best results were obtained with DMA (14.3 mg/ml) using trypsin concentration of (0.25 mg/ml) in Tris-HCl buffer (0.2 M, pH 8.3) containing 25 mM Ca^{++} (*13*). Chromatography on CM-Cellulose showed that the crosslinking preparation did not contain any unmodified trypsin. Free amino group analysis showed that an average of 9.5 residues out of 14 present in trypsin were modified. SDS-PAGE analysis showed that no intermolecular crosslinking has occurred. Some characteristics of the crosslinked trypsin are summarized in Table 1 (*15*).

The crosslinked preparation showed much slower rate of autolysis at 40°C as compared to native trypsin (Figure 1). In this particular system, the formation of crosslinks was presumed and not verified. It was also not determined whether the decrease in autolysis was caused by decrease in number of bonds susceptible to tryptic cleavage or crosslinking *per se*.

Lactose Intolerance; Whey Disposal Through Chemical Crosslinking. Another enzyme chosen for chemical crosslinking was β-galactosidase. The choice of this enzyme was based upon its biotechnological usefulness (*16*). This usefulness arises because of lactose intolerance and whey as a biomass (*16*).

Lactose Intolerance. It is a metabolic disorder which is associated with the lack of adequate β-galactosidase activity. There are significant differences in the incidence of lactose intolerance among different ethnic groups. The adult intolerance has so far been observed only in northern Europeans (90%) and in the members of two nomadic pastoral tribes of Africa (80%) (*17*).

Hydrolysis of milk lactose yields low lactose milk. Such a preparation, apart from being low in lactose content, also retains most of the other nutrients present in the milk. Many commercial technologies for production of low lactose milk utilize immobilized β-galactosidase (lactase) (*18*).

Whey as a Biomass. A large amount of milk is converted into whey during the manufacture of cheese. The use of lactose present in whey in food industries has certain associated problems. Whey, as a waste product, cannot be disposed of easily as such because of its high biological oxygen demand (BOD) value. The hydrolysis of whey lactose by β-galactosidase to glucose and galactose solves these problems. These sugars have greater fermentation potentials as compared to lactose. Also, the hydrolyzed whey can also be used in food industries as such (*16*).

Crosslinking of β-Galactosidase. The above considerations prompted us to attempt crosslinking of *E. coli* β-galactosidase—a commercially available and well characterized enzyme. The crosslinking reagents employed in this work (*19*), i.e., glutaraldehyde, DMA and DMS, were specific for free amino groups in proteins. Therefore, they were a safe choice for *E. coli* β-galactosidase since it is reported that the lysine groups in the enzyme are not involved in the catalysis and the enzyme retains 80% of its activity even after all its lysine groups are modified (*20*).

Exploratory experiments indicated that the crosslinked derivative obtained with DMA was most thermostable (*19*). The free amino group analysis showed that 38% free amino groups were modified. The SDS-PAGE analysis showed that neither

Table 1. Properties of Trypsin Crosslinked with Dimethyl Adipimidate

Property	All percentage values are relative to the observed value for native trypsin taken as 100
1. Amidase activity towards benzoyl DL-arginine p-nitroanilide (BAPNA)	113%
2. Esterase activity with p-tosyl L-arginine methyl ester (TAME) as substrate	65%
3. Proteolytic activity towards: (a) Casein (b) Haemoglobin	 27% 22%
4. K_m for BAPNA at pH 8.2	1 mM, same as that for native trypsin
5. pH optimum with BAPNA as substrate	Broad range of 7-9, similar to native trypsin

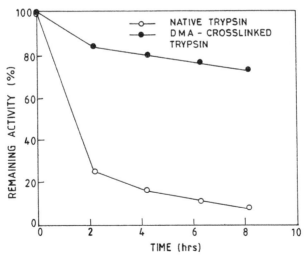

Figure 1.   Autolysis of native and DMA-crosslinked trypsin at 40°C. The protein concentration was 125 μg/ml. (Reproduced with permission from ref. 15. Copyright 1988 Butterworth–Heinemann.)

intersubunit nor intermolecular crosslinks had been formed. When the enzyme was treated with ethyl acetimidate (a monofunctional analog of DMA), although extent of free amino group modification was comparable (26%), the o-nitrophenyl β-D-galactopyranoside (ONGP) activity of the modified preparation, both before and after heat treatment (i.e., the enzyme preparations were heated at 55°C in 0.3 M sodium monophosphate buffer pH 8.0 containing 3 mM MgCl$_2$) was quite different as compared to the crosslinked enzyme (Figure 2). While this data did not completely rule out the possibility of some simple chemical modification also having taken place in case of reaction with DMA, it did confirm that the desirable change in the enzyme was the result of formation of intramolecular crosslinks (*19*).

Continuous hydrolysis of milk lactose at 50°C was monitored by using both native and the crosslinked enzyme (Figure 3). Whereas the native enzyme hydrolyzed 40% milk lactose, the crosslinked enzyme hydrolyzed 55% milk lactose in 12 h (*15*). This kind of conversion rate is considered adequate for obtaining low lactose milk based dairy products at the pilot plant level (*21*).

In order to be able to reuse crosslinked enzyme, it was entrapped in polyacrylamide (*22*). The optimization of entrapment conditions was carried out with the native enzyme, and our results show that 50% of the enzyme activity on ONGP was entrapped and the enzyme lost 20% activity during entrapment. The activity of the entrapped enzyme was considerably enhanced when a protective mixture of bovine serum albumin, cysteine, and lactose was present during entrapment. The enzyme crosslinking with DMA and entrapped was also found to be more thermostable as compared to other entrapped enzyme preparations (Figure 4).

The hydrolysis of milk lactose was carried out using native and DMA crosslinked enzymes (Figure 5). The crosslinked preparation entrapped in polyacrylamide hydrolyzed 47% of milk lactose as compared to 31% hydrolysis by entrapped native enzyme in 6 h at 55°C (*22*).

The above system illustrates the usefulness of combining crosslinking with immobilization for obtaining a reusable product with enhanced thermostability.

Insoluble β-Galactosidase Aggregate (*23*). Another way of obtaining a reusable enzyme preparation by crosslinking is to form chemical aggregates. *E. coli* β-galactosidase aggregates prepared by extensive crosslinking with glutaraldehyde retained 63% of the activity on ONGP provided bovine serum albumin and lactose were present during the crosslinking at 4°C. This activity increased to about 70% when the aggregate was homogenized for about 90 s in a mixing blender. All further work discussed below was carried out with the aggregate which had been subjected to this treatment. The K$_m$ value of the aggregate for ONGP was found to be 6 x 10^{-4} M at pH 7.5 and 25°C as compared to a value of 2.8 x 10^{-4} M for the native enzyme. The pH optimum was found to remain unchanged at 7.5. The aggregate showed considerable improvement in thermal stability at 55°C (Figure 6) which was reflected in its improved performance during continuous hydrolysis of milk lactose (Figure 7).

One reason why enzyme aggregates have not become popular is that they are difficult to handle and would give poor flow rates in columns. A solution to this

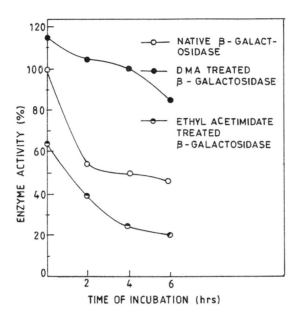

Figure 2.   Comparison of the stability of native β-galactosidase with
             β-galactosidase modified with ethyl acetimidate and DMA
             respectively.(Reproduced with permission from ref. 23. Copyright
             1988.)

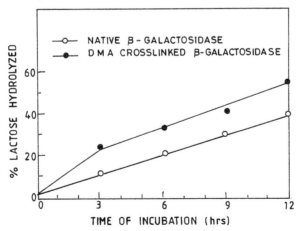

Figure 3.   Continuous lactose hydrolysis of milk by DMA modified and
             native β-galactosidase at 50°C. The enzyme concentration for
             both native as well as modified preparation was 25 μg in 2.0 ml
             reaction volume. The initial lactose concentration in the milk was
             5%. (Reproduced with permission from ref. 25. Copyright 1988.)

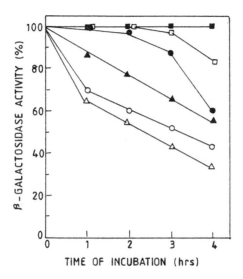

Figure 4.   Thermal stability of entrapped β-galactosidase preparations at 55°C in sodium phosphate buffer (20 mM, pH 7.5 containing 0.1 M NaCl and 3 mM MgCl$_2$).

O; Native enzyme entrapped in absence of any protective agent

△; DMS crosslinked enzyme entrapped in absence of any protective agent

□; DMA crosslinked enzyme entrapped in absence of any protective agent

●; Native enzyme entrapped in presence of bovine serum albumin (BSA) + cysteine + lactose

▲; DMS crosslinked enzyme entrapped in presence of BSA + cysteine + lactose

■; DMA crosslinked enzyme entrapped in presence of BSA + cysteine + lactose

(Reproduced with permission from ref. 32. Copyright 1988.)

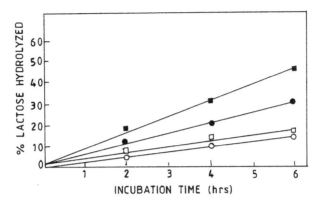

Figure 5.   Time course of hydrolysis of milk lactose at 55°C.
O; Native enzyme entrapped in absence of any protective agent
●; Native enzyme entrapped in presence of BSA + cysteine + lactose
□; DMA crosslinked enzyme entrapped in absence of any protective agent
■; DMA crosslinked enzyme entrapped in presence of BSA + cysteine + lactose
(Reproduced with permission from ref. 33. Copyright 1988.)

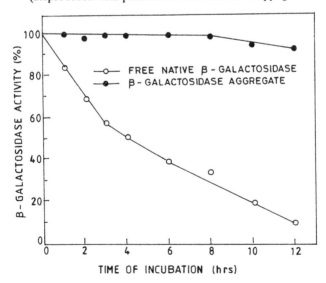

Figure 6.   Thermal stability of β-galactosidase preparation at 55°C. The enzyme activity was determined with ONGP as the substrate. (Reproduced with permission from ref. 35. Copyright 1988 Indian Academy of Sciences.)

problem may be to entrap proteins by aggregation within commercially available beads. Chemical aggregation of β-galactosidase by glutaraldehyde inside Sephadex G-200 beads showed that about 17% of the total enzyme activity added at the start was present inside beads (*24*). The K_m towards ONGP (6.3 x 10^{-4} M) in this case was nearly the same as that of the simple aggregates (*24*). There is obviously need to improve upon these results but they are encouraging.

Thermostabilization of Concanavalin A (*25*). Concanavalin A (Con A), is a lectin of considerable biological interest. Our interest in thermostabilization of Con A stems from the usefulness of this lectin in affinity separations and bioaffinity immobilization. Crosslinking of Con A (1 mg/ml) was carried out at pH 7.5 using DMA (50 mg/ml) in the presence of α-methyl mannoside—a sugar specific for Con A. The crosslinked preparation (112% activity when measured in terms of its ability to precipitate glycogen) was fractionated on Mono S column of FPLC. It resolved into three fractions. The major fraction containing 52% of the total protein was further purified on Mono Q column of FPLC. About 80% of the protein did not bind to the column. This fraction (which did not bind to Mono Q column) showed a single band on SDS-PAGE corresponding to the position of Con A monomer. This, apart from establishing homogeneity, also ruled out inter subunit and intermolecular crosslinking.

The crosslinked derivative had 98% activity as compared to native Con A and free amino group analysis showed that 17% of amino groups were modified in this derivative. This corresponded to about 2 amino residues per Con A subunit. The gel filtration of the derivative on a calibrated column of Fractogel HW-55F showed its molecular weight to be identical with native Con A.

Thermal stability of this crosslinked derivative, native Con A and ethylacetimidate reacted Con A at 70°C is shown in Figure 8. Thus, mere modification of the amino groups in Con A with monofunctional analog did not lead to thermostabilization. These results indicate the formation of one crosslink per subunit in Con A molecule as the cause for thermostabilization. Based upon earlier structural data in the literature, the position of the crosslink can be tentatively assigned between Lys-135 and Lys-138. Becker et al. (*26*) have pointed out that residues 131-168 form part of disordered structure in the molecule. Perhaps, this crosslink introduces an element of order in this region, it reduces conformational flexibility and hence leads to considerable thermostabilization.

Bioconjugate Preparation

One class of bioconjugates are the protein–protein conjugates. Enzyme linked immunoassays (*27*), immunotoxins (*28*), and enzyme targeting (*29*) are some of the important areas where protein–protein conjugates have been used. Con A–ferritin (*30*) is yet another example of a useful protein-protein conjugate. Intermolecular crosslinking has also been employed for the preparation of "neomulti-enzyme complexes" for modelling segments of metabolic pathways (*31*). It was thought that heteroenzyme conjugates combining different enzyme specificities may be useful biochemical reagents e.g. for probing complex biological structures.

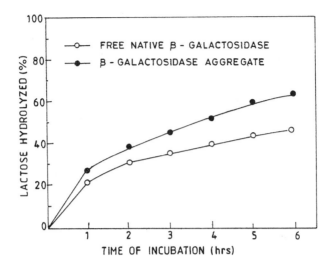

Figure 7.   Continuous lactose hydrolysis of milk by β-galactosidase
            preparation at 55°C. (Reproduced with permission from ref. 35.
            Copyright 1988 Indian Academy of Sciences.)

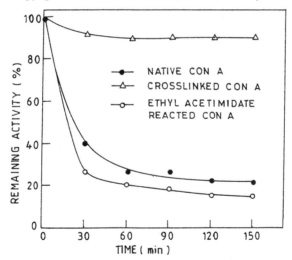

Figure 8.   Thermal denaturation of native Con A, crosslinked Con A and
            ethyl acetimidate reacted Con A at 70°C. The solutions of Con
            A and its derivatives (1 mg/ml in each case) were made in
            phosphate buffer (50 mM, pH 7.0) containing 0.5 M NaCl. The
            lectin activity was assayed by measuring the precipitation of
            glycogen. (Reproduced with permission from ref. 19. Copyright 1988
            Humana Press.)

Trypsin–Chymotrypsin Conjugate (*33*). This conjugate preparation was first attempted by glutaraldehyde. The conjugate formation could be detected by subjecting the reaction product to successive affinity chromatographies on affinity media specific for trypsin and chymotrypsin. The conjugate showed only 4% trypsin activity and 3% chymotrypsin activity assuming starting inputs of activities in each case to be 100.

The conjugate preparation was also attempted by N-succinimidyl pyridyl dithiopropionate (SPDP) (Figure 9). The main advantage of using such crosslinking reagents utilizing multi-step procedure is that undesirable side products (homoconjugates) are not formed. The use of SPDP did not result in greater yield of the desired trypsin-chymotrypsin conjugate. Trypsin component retained 56% activity and chymotrypsin component retained complete activity. The conjugate caseinolytic activity was compared with a mixture of (1:1) trypsin and chymotrypsin. If one remembers that trypsin had lost 46% activity, the conjugate seems to be an improved hybrid protease.

Trypsin–Chymotrypsin Coaggregate (*31*). Preparing insoluble heteroaggregates is yet another way of making enzyme–enzyme conjugates with twin activities and with the added advantage of easy separation and reusability. A coaggregate of trypsin–chymotrypsin prepared by extensive intermolecular crosslinking with glutaraldehyde showed significant reduction in the autolysis of the trypsin component (Figure 10). The aggregate retained 72% of the trypsin activity of native enzyme with benzoyl DL-arginine p-nitroanilide (BAPNA) as substrate, but only 4.8% of the chymotrypsin activity with benzoyl tyrosine ethyl ester BTEE as substrate. Further optimization is required so that greater retention of chymotrypsin is possible.

Trypsin–Alkaline Phosphatase Conjugate (*32*). Preparation of this conjugate was attempted by using glutaraldehyde and (DMA). The strategy for analysis and detection of the conjugate formation was similar to the one outlined above in the case of trypsin–chymotrypsin conjugate. The reaction mixture was chromatographed on benzamidine-agarose (*32*). The bound protein was eluted with benzamidine and assayed for alkaline phosphatase activity. No such activity could be detected in either of the cases. Another effort was made by oxidizing the carbohydrate moiety of alkaline phosphatase by periodate to generate aldehyde groups. This "activated" alkaline phosphatase was coupled to trypsin via Schiff base formation. In this case also, the conjugate formation was analyzed as above. Calculating on the basis of total units of alkaline phosphatase loaded on the benzamidine-agarose, only about 15% was found to bind to the affinity medium. The results did indicate that it is important to try different strategies for preparing bioconjugates. Incidentally, our failure with bifunctional reagents is understandable in view of the reported observation (*34*) that glycoenzymes are relatively "unreactive" towards chemical modification reagents since the protein surface is masked by carbohydrate moieties.

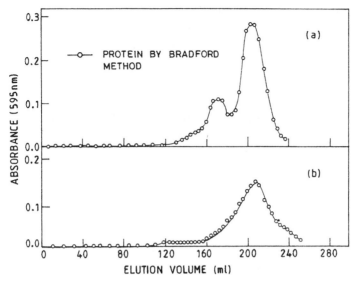

Figure 9.   (a) Gel filtration of trypsin–chymotrypsin conjugate prepared by SPDP on Sephadex G-100.
(b) Rechromatography of fractions corresponding to elution volume from 140 to 180 ml after dithiothreitol (DDT) treatment. (Reproduced with permission from ref. 19. Copyright 1988 Humana Press.)

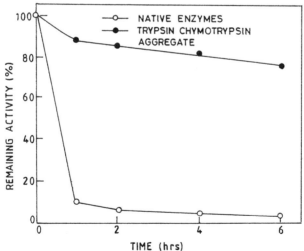

Figure 10.   Loss of tryptic activity due to autolysis. The autolysis was carried out in Tris-HCl buffer (0.05 M, pH 8.2) containing 0.025 M ethylenediamine tetraacetate (EDTA) at protein concentration of 102 mg/100 ml at 40°C. Autolysis compared with native enzymes (trypsin and chymotrypsin) mixed in 1:1 ratio on mole basis. Remaining amidase activity was measured with BAPNA as the substrate.
(Reproduced with permission from ref. 22. Copyright 1988.)

Con A–β-Galactosidase Conjugate (*35*). Bioaffinity immobilization (*36*) has lately been considered as an attractive alternate to other methods of immobilization. In view of our interest in the application of β-galactosidase in the production of low lactose milk, a conjugate of Con A with *E. coli* β-galactosidase was prepared by using glutaraldehyde as the crosslinking reagent. The conjugate was expected to bind to Sephadex columns because of the affinity of Con A towards such columns. Recovery of enzyme activity (assayed by using ONGP as substrate) is shown in Table 2. The thermal stability of the Sephadex bound conjugate, measured in terms of survival of the enzyme activity, is shown in Figure 11. The results when the Sephadex bound conjugate was used for lactose hydrolysis at 50°C are shown in Figure 12. These results show that the approach is a promising one and preparation of such lectin-enzyme conjugates may considerably enlarge the scope of affinity immobilization since a large number of lectins and the corresponding affinity media to which they bind are commercially available.

A major problem in preparing protein-protein conjugates is the low yield generally obtained in almost all the cases. Development of more efficient crosslinking techniques and use of genetic engineering to produce fusion proteins are two solutions to this problem (*37, 38*).

Also, some recent successful efforts on developing a computer modeling procedure for assessing the stereochemical suitability of pairs of residues in proteins as potential sites for introduction of cystine bridges (*39*) is a pointer towards futuristic possibilities when it should be possible to choose a proper crosslinking reagent with much less uncertainty for both enzyme stabilization and preparation of protein-protein conjugates.

Conclusion

The results described in this chapter and elsewhere (*6, 40, 41*) show that chemical crosslinking is an attractive and simple approach to enzyme stabilization. Protein engineering (*5*), while most promising, still requires greater efforts. Medium engineering (*42*) for thermostabilization is still in its infancy whereas immobilization (*3*) has an inherent problem of diffusion constraints. However, crosslinking (as well as immobilization) merely prevents unfolding of the polypeptide chain. It does not abolish irreversible covalent changes (*2*) which take place under harsh conditions such as extremes of pH or high temperatures. When end applications require the protein to function under such conditions, protein engineering is perhaps the only solution.

The advent of the protein fusion techniques (*37, 38*) may seem to render intermolecular protein crosslinking obsolete for preparation of protein–protein conjugates. However, until such a time, the fusion techniques become more economical (if ever), chemical crosslinking, as illustrated by our results, would remain a simple and viable alternate.

Table 2. Recovery of Enzyme Activity at Various Stages of
Preparation of the Conjugate

Sample	β-Galactosidase activity (%)
Con A–β-galactosidase solution	100
Con A–β-galactosidase solution, 30 min after adding glutaraldehyde	87
Effluent from Sephadex G-50 column eluted with 0.1 M NaCl	70
Effluent from Sephadex G-50 column eluted with 0.2 M glucose	10

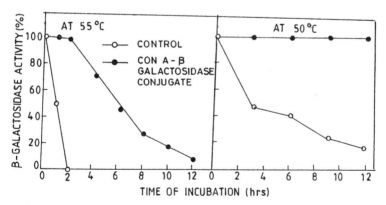

Figure 11. Thermal stability of Spehadex-bound Con A–β-galactosidase.
(Reproduced with permission from ref. 22. Copyright 1988.)

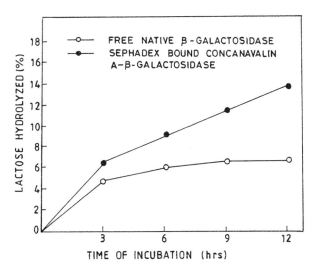

Figure 12.   Lactose hydrolysis by Sephadex-bound conjugate at 50°C. The lactose solutions (5%) were prepared in potassium phosphate buffer (0.1 M, pH 7.2, containing 3 mM Mg++). The initial activities (using ONGP) as substrate) of free native enzyme and immobilized enzyme in the samples were identical.

(Reproduced with permission from ref. 23. Copyright 1988.)

Acknowledgement
The work described here was supported by the Department of Science and Technology (Government of India) and Council of Scientific and Industrial Research, India. I wish to thank Dr. Y.S. Rajput, Dr. A. Kamra, and Dr. S.K. Khare, who carried out the work described in this chapter. I also wish to thank current members of my research group particularly Dr. S. Ahmad and Dr. R. Tyagi for their assistance in the preparation of this chapter.

Literature Cited

1. Mozhaev, V.V.; Melik-Nubarov, N.S.; Sergeeva, M.V.; Sikrnis, V.; Martineck, K. *Biocatalysis* **1990**, *3*, 179-187.

2. Gupta, M.N. *Biotechnol. Appl. Biochem.* **1991**, *14*, 1-11.

3. Gupta, M.N.; Mattiasson, B. In *Bioanalytical Applications of Enzymes* Vol. 36; Suelter, C.H., ed., John Wiley: New York, New York, 1992; pp. 1-34.

4. Cabral, J.M.S.; Kennedy, J.F. In *Protein Immobilization: Fundamentals and Applications*; Taylor, R.F., ed., Marcel Dekker: New York, New York, 1991; pp. 73-138.

5. Nosoh, Y; Sekiguchi, T. *Biocatalysis* **1988**, *1*, 257-273.

6. Martinek, K.; Torchilin, V.P. *Methods Enzymol.* **1987**, *137*, 615-624.

7. Taniguchi, M.; Kobayashi, M.; Fujii, M. *Biotechnol. Bioeng.* **1989**, *34*, 1092-1097.

8. Poznansky, M.J. *Methods Enzymol.* **1988**, *137*, 566-574.

9. Senstad, C.; Mattiasson, B. *Biotechnol. Bioeng.* **1989**, *34*, 216-220.

10. Wold, F. *Methods Enzymol.* **1975**, *25*, 623-651.

11. Telefoncu, A. *Biotechnol. Bioeng.* **1983**, *25*, 713-724.

12. Von-Specht, B.U.; Brendel, W. *Biochim. Biophys. Acta* **1977**, *484*, 109-114.

13. Abuchowski, A.; Davis, F.F. *Biochim. Biophys. Acta* **1979**, *578*, 41-46.

14. Rajput, Y.S.; Gupta, M.N. *Enzyme Microb. Technol.* **1987**, *9*, 161-163.

15. Rajput, Y.S.; Gupta, M.N. *Enzyme Microb. Technol.* **1988**, *10*, 143-150.

16. Kosaric, N.; Asher, Y.J. In *Advances in Biochemical Engineering*; Fiechter, A., Ed.; Springer-Verlag: New York, New York, 1985; *19*, pp 25-60.

17. Kretchmer, N. *Sci. Am.* **1972**, *227*, 71-78.

18. Gekas, V.; Lopez-Leiva, M. *Process Biochem.* **1985**, *20*, 2-12.

19. Khare, S.K.; Gupta, M.N. *Appl. Biochem. Biotechnol.* **1988**, *16*, 1-15.

20. Jentoft, N.; Dearborn, D.G. *J. Biol. Chem.* **1979**, *254*, 4359-4365.

21. Pastore, M.; Morisi, F. *Methods Enzymol.* **1976**, *44*, 822-830.

22. Khare, S.K.; Gupta, M.N. *Biotechnol. Bioeng.* **1988**, *31*, 829-833.

23. Khare, S.K.; Gupta, M.N. *Biotechnol. Bioeng.* **1990**, *35*, 94-98.

24. Khare, S.K.; Vaidya, S.; Gupta, M.N. *Appl. Biochem. Biotechnol.* **1991**, *27*, 205-216.

25. Kamra, A.; Gupta, M.N. *Biochim. Biophys. Acta* **1988**, *966*, 181-187.

26. Becker, J.W.; Cunningham, B.A.; Reeke, G.N., Jr.; Wang, J.L.; Edelman, G.M. In *Concanavalin A as a Tool*; Bittiger, H; Schnebli, H., Eds.; John Wiley: New York, New York, 1976; pp 33-54.

27. Walker, J.M. In *Techniques in Molecular Biology*; Walker, J.M.; Gaastra, W., Eds.; Croom Helm: London, 1987; *2*, pp 82-97.

28. Ahmad, A.; Law, K. *Trends Biotechnol.* **1988**, *6*, 246-251.

29. Shier, W.T. *Methods Enzymol.* **1985**, *112*, 248-258.

30. Nicolson, G.L.; Singer, S.J. *Proc. Natl. Acad. Sci. USA* **1971**, *68*, 942-945.

31. Ikura, K.; Okumura, K.; Sasaki, R.; Chiba, H. *Agric. Biol. Chem.* **1984**, *48*, 355-364.

32. Rajput, Y.S.; Gupta, M.N. *Biotechnol. Appl. Biochem.* **1988**, *10*, 424-250.

33. Rajput, Y.S.; Gupta, M.N. *Biotechnol. Bioeng.* **1988**, *31*, 220-223.

34. Royer, G.P. *Methods Enzymol.* **1987**, *135*, 141-146.

35. Khare, S.K.; Gupta, M.N. *J. Biosci.* **1988**, *137*, 47-54.

36. Saleemuddin, M.; Husain, Q. *Enzyme Microb. Technol.* **1991**, *13*, 290-295.

37. Sassenfeld, M.M. *Trends Biotechnol.* **1990**, *8*, 88-99.

38. Ong, E.; Gilkes, N.R.; Miller, R.C.; Warren, A.J.; Kilburn, D.C. *Enzyme Microb. Technol.* **1991**, *13*, 59-65.

39. Sowdhamini, R.; Srinivasan, N.; Shoichet, B.; Santi, D.V.; Ramakrishnan, C.; Balaram, P. *Protein Eng.* **1989**, *3*, 95-103.

40. Baker, J.O.; Oh, K.K.; Grohmann, K.; Himmel, M.E. *Biotechnol. Lett.* **1988**, *10*, 325-330.

41. Tatsumoto, K.; Oh, K.K.; Baker, J.O.; Himmel, M.E. *Appl. Biochem. Biotechnol.* **1989**, *20/21*, 293-308.

42. Gupta, M.N. *Env. J. Biochem.* **1992**, *203*, 25-32.

RECEIVED April 9, 1992

INDEXES

Author Index

Affiliation Index

Subject Index

Production: Peggy D. Smith
Indexing: Deborah H. Steiner
Acquisition: Barbara C. Tansill
Cover design: Pat Cunningham

Printed and bound by Maple Press, York, PA

Other ACS Books

Chemical Structure Software for Personal Computers
Edited by Daniel E. Meyer, Wendy A. Warr, and Richard A. Love
ACS Professional Reference Book; 107 pp;
clothbound, ISBN 0–8412–1538–3; paperback, ISBN 0–8412–1539–1

Personal Computers for Scientists: A Byte at a Time
By Glenn I. Ouchi
276 pp; clothbound, ISBN 0–8412–1000–4; paperback, ISBN 0–8412–1001–2

Biotechnology and Materials Science: Chemistry for the Future
Edited by Mary L. Good
160 pp; clothbound, ISBN 0–8412–1472–7; paperback, ISBN 0–8412–1473–5

Polymeric Materials: Chemistry for the Future
By Joseph Alper and Gordon L. Nelson
110 pp; clothbound, ISBN 0–8412–1622–3; paperback, ISBN 0–8412–1613–4

The Language of Biotechnology: A Dictionary of Terms
By John M. Walker and Michael Cox
ACS Professional Reference Book; 256 pp;
clothbound, ISBN 0–8412–1489–1; paperback, ISBN 0–8412–1490–5

Cancer: The Outlaw Cell, Second Edition
Edited by Richard E. LaFond
274 pp; clothbound, ISBN 0–8412–1419–0; paperback, ISBN 0–8412–1420–4

Practical Statistics for the Physical Sciences
By Larry L. Havlicek
ACS Professional Reference Book; 198 pp; clothbound; ISBN 0–8412–1453–0

The Basics of Technical Communicating
By B. Edward Cain
ACS Professional Reference Book; 198 pp;
clothbound, ISBN 0–8412–1451–4; paperback, ISBN 0–8412–1452–2

The ACS Style Guide: A Manual for Authors and Editors
Edited by Janet S. Dodd
264 pp; clothbound, ISBN 0–8412–0917–0; paperback, ISBN 0–8412–0943–X

Chemistry and Crime: From Sherlock Holmes to Today's Courtroom
Edited by Samuel M. Gerber
135 pp; clothbound, ISBN 0–8412–0784–4; paperback, ISBN 0–8412–0785–2

For further information and a free catalog of ACS books, contact:
American Chemical Society
Distribution Office, Department 225
1155 16th Street, NW, Washington, DC 20036
Telephone 800–227–5558